Cases

Cases Following Chapter 15

FIFTH EDITION

SERVICES MARKETING

People, Technology, Strategy

Christopher Lovelock
Yale University

Jochen Wirtz
National University of Singapore

PEARSON
Prentice Hall

Upper Saddle River, New Jersey 07458

Library of Congress Cataloging-in-Publication Data

Lovelock, Christopher H.
Services marketing: people, technology, strategy / Christopher Lovelock, Jochen Wirtz.—
5th ed.
p. cm.
Includes bibliographical references and index.
ISBN 0-13-113865-0
1. Professions—Marketing. 2. Service industries—Marketing. I. Wirtz, Jochen. II. Title.

HF5415.122.L68 2003
658.8--dc22

2003060912

Acquisitions Editor: Katie Stevens
Editor-in-Chief: Jeff Shelstad
Editorial Assistant: Rebecca Cummings
Marketing Manager: Michelle O'Brien
Marketing Assistant: Amanda Fisher
Managing Editor (Production): John Roberts
Production Editor: Maureen Wilson
Permissions Supervisor: Suzanne Grappi
Manufacturing Buyer: Michelle Klein
Cover Design: Suzanne Behnke/Studio Indigo
Cover Illustration/Photo (top to bottom): Ryan McVay/Getty Images, Inc.—Photodisc; Andersen Ross/Getty Images, Inc.—Photodisc; Ryan McVay/Getty Images, Inc.—Photodisc; C Squared Studios/Getty Images, Inc.—Photodisc
Photo Researcher: Rachel Lucas
Image Permission Coordinator: Debbie Latronica
Composition/Full-Service Project Management: Laserwords/nSight Publishing Services
Printer/Binder: Hamilton Printing Co.

Credits and acknowledgments borrowed from other sources and reproduced, with permission, in this textbook appear on appropriate page within.

Pearson Education LTD.
Pearson Education Singapore, Pte. Ltd
Pearson Education, Canada, Ltd
Pearson Education–Japan
Pearson Education Australia PTY, Limited
Pearson Education North Asia Ltd
Pearson Educación de Mexico, S.A. de C.V.
Pearson Education Malaysia, Pte. Ltd

PEARSON
Prentice Hall

10 9 8 7 6 5 4 3 2 1
ISBN 0-13-113865-0

To my brothers, Roger and Jeremy, and my sister, Rachel, with love

—CHL

To my dad, Johann Wirtz, with love

—JW

Brief Contents

Contents

Preface

The world of services has changed in dramatic ways since the first edition of *Services Marketing*. This new edition represents a significant revision, restructuring, and updating of the book to reflect the challenges facing service managers in the early 21st century. We've pooled our skills in teaching, consulting, and research to create a versatile, flexible text for instructors teaching in a variety of environments.

Services Marketing, Fifth Edition, takes a strongly managerial perspective, but the text is rooted in solid academic research, complemented by memorable concepts and frameworks. We designed the book to bridge the all-too-frequent gap between the real world and academic theory. Practical management applications are reinforced by numerous in-text boxed examples within the 15 chapters, along with 8 up-to-date readings from leading thinkers in the field and 15 superb classroom-tested cases. Additional cases, teaching materials, and instructor aids are available on the course Web site.

Preparing this new edition of *Services Marketing* has been an exciting challenge. Services marketing, once a tiny academic field championed by a handful of pioneering professors, has become a thriving area of activity. Our new edition reflects growing research efforts in both academia and business. Student interest in courses that focus on various aspects of managing service organizations, including marketing, makes a great deal of sense from a career standpoint, as most business school graduates will be going to work in service industries, and managers report that manufacturing-based models of business practice are not always useful to them.

WHAT'S NEW IN THE FIFTH EDITION?

This edition has been both streamlined and restructured to sharpen the focus on essentials and to add in-depth coverage of new concepts and ideas.

New Topics, New Structure

- The book features coverage of the latest research and developments in the service sector, ranging from customer relationship management (CRM) and Six Sigma quality to revenue (yield) management and customer feedback systems. In addition, there is substantive coverage of consumer behavior, people-management issues, branding, business-to-business services, and technology-based services.
- We emphasize that marketing strategy takes place in a highly competitive environment, reflecting our belief that service firms must be competitively positioned as well as customer focused.
- All chapters feature expanded references, with new published research findings being added to every topic.
- The text has been streamlined to avoid unnecessary repetition and restructured to ensure an enhanced sequencing of topics. Despite the addition of new material, tighter editing has resulted in a leaner and more effective set of chapters.
- We have streamlined the number of chapters to 15 (down from 18 in the previous edition). Every chapter has been revised, and some have been retitled to reflect a more focused emphasis. Material on technology and international strategy will

now be found throughout the book rather than being presented in separate chapters. Coverage of demand and capacity management, queuing, and reservations has been consolidated in a single chapter, with material on revenue management being transferred to the pricing chapter.

- Figure A presents the revised four-part structure of the book, showing how chapter topics are sequenced.

Part One
Understanding Service Products, Consumers, and Markets
• Introduction to Services Marketing
• Consumer Behavior and Service Encounters
• Positioning Services in Competitive Markets
Part Two
Key Elements of Services Marketing
• Creating the Service Product
• Designing the Service Communications Mix for Services
• Pricing and Revenue Management
• Distributing Services
Part Three
Managing the Service Delivery Process
• Designing and Managing Service Processes
• Balancing Demand and Capacity
• Planning the Service Environment
• Managing People for Service Advantage
Part Four
Implementing Services Marketing
• Managing Relationships and Building Loyalty
• Customer Feedback and Service Recovery
• Improving Service Quality and Productivity
• Organizing for Service Leadership

FIGURE A New Structure of *Services Marketing*

- Particular attention has been paid to making this new edition stimulating and highly readable. The result is a text that is clear, focused, and designed to capture student interest. Boxed inserts within each chapter feature numerous interesting examples that describe important research findings, illustrate practical applications of important service marketing concepts, and present best practices in services marketing. Many of these inserts are new to this edition.

New Readings

- Six of the eight readings are new to this edition. They are drawn from recent issues of *Business Week, Harvard Business Review, Journal of the Academy of Marketing Science, Journal of Service Research*, and *Marketing Management.*
- The readings have been selected to complement the text and explore key issues in greater depth. Selected for their readability and potential to stimulate classroom discussion, they present important insights from thoughtful practitioners and such leading service professors as Leonard Berry, Richard Chase, Raymond Fisk, Stephen Grove, Sheryl Kimes, Katherine Lemon, Roland Rust, and Valarie Zeithaml.

New Cases

The book features an exceptional selection of up-to-date, classroom-tested cases of varying lengths and levels of difficulty. We wrote a majority of the cases ourselves, and most are unavailable elsewhere. Others are drawn from the case collections of Harvard, INSEAD, and Yale.

- To offer instructors greater choice, the number of cases has been expanded from 10 to 15 (including a three-part series of short cases that can be taught in a single class or separately, as desired). The new selection provides a broader coverage of both service issues and application areas.
- Twelve of the cases are new to this edition. Most are copyrighted 2003 or 2004. All three of those cases carried over from the previous edition have been updated.

New and Improved Teaching Resources at www.prenhall.com/lovelock

- Revised and enlarged supplements include an excellent online instructor's manual.
- To further enhance the mix of teaching materials, several popular cases from previous editions of the book are being made available on the Web site for *Services Marketing*.
- Additional cases that may be downloaded from the Web site (www.prenhall.com/lovelock) include several new cases dealing primarily with nonprofit service organizations. The Web site also includes a "Note on Studying and Learning from Cases" for students.
- Detailed teaching notes are provided for all cases, including teaching objectives, suggested study questions, in-depth analysis of each question, and helpful hints on teaching strategy.
- Instructors can now select from more than 250 online PowerPoint slides, keyed to each chapter. These materials include both text slides and graphics. All slides have been designed to be clear, comprehensible, and easily readable. Visit *www.prenhall.com/lovelock* to access the PowerPoint slides. Please contact your local Prentice Hall representative if you need a faculty log-in password.

TARGET AUDIENCES AND COURSES

This text is equally suitable for courses directed at advanced undergraduates or MBA and EMBA students. *Services Marketing*, Fifth Edition, places marketing issues within a broader general management context. Whatever a manager's specific job may be, he or she has to understand and acknowledge the close ties that link the marketing, operations, and human resource functions. With that perspective in mind, this book has been designed so that instructors can make selective use of chapters, readings, and cases to teach courses of various lengths and formats in either services marketing or service management.

DISTINGUISHING FEATURES OF THE BOOK

Key features of this highly readable book include its strong managerial orientation and strategic focus, use of memorable conceptual frameworks that have been classroom tested for relevance to both undergraduate and MBA students, incorporation of key academic research findings, use of interesting examples to link theory to practice, and inclusion of carefully selected readings and cases to accompany the text chapters.

Services Marketing is designed to complement the materials found in traditional marketing principles texts. It avoids sweeping and often misleading generalizations about services, recognizing explicitly that the differences between specific categories of services (based on the nature of the underlying service process) may be as important to student understanding as the broader differences between goods marketing and services marketing. It also draws a distinction between the marketing of services and the marketing of goods *through service*.

The book shows how various technologies—and information technology in particular—are changing the nature of service delivery and can offer innovative ways for service providers and customers to relate to each other. (This is the people side of the business.)

The service sector of the economy can best be characterized by its diversity. No single conceptual model suffices to cover marketing-relevant issues among organizations ranging from huge international corporations (in such fields as airlines, banking, insurance, telecommunications, freight transportation, and professional services) to locally owned and operated small businesses, such as restaurants, laundries, taxis, optometrists, and many business-to-business services. In response, *Services Marketing* offers a carefully designed "toolbox" for service managers, teaching students how different concepts, frameworks, and analytical procedures can best be used to examine and resolve the challenges faced by managers in a variety of situations. Once introduced, many of these tools reappear in subsequent chapters.

Throughout the book, we stress the importance for service marketers of to understand the operational processes underlying service creation and delivery. These processes are grouped into four categories, each of which has distinctive implications for the nature of service encounters, the roles played by customers and service personnel, the strategic application of information technology to delivery systems, and management practice.

PEDAGOGICAL AIDS

In response to adopter requests, the following pedagogical enhancements are available for the text:

- An introduction to each chapter highlights key issues and questions to be addressed.
- Four types of boxed inserts accompany many of the chapters:
  - *Best Practice in Action* (demonstrations the application of best practices)
  - *Research Insights* (summaries of highly relevant rigorous academic research)
  - *Service Perspectives* (in-depth examples that illustrate key concepts)
  - *Management Memo* (reviews of key concepts that apply to service management)
- Interesting graphics, including reproductions of ads, are included to enhance both visual appeal and student learning.
- Review Questions and Applications Exercises are located at the end of each chapter.
- Each case includes suggested study questions.
- The *Instructor's Resource Manual for Services Marketing* includes the following:
  - Detailed course design and teaching hints, as well as two sample course outlines
  - Chapter-by-chapter teaching suggestions, along with discussion of learning objectives and sample responses to study questions and exercises
  - An overview of each reading, with suggestions on how to use it and the best chapter(s) with which to assign the reading in question
  - A description of 16 suggested student exercises and 5 comprehensive projects (designed for either individual or team use)
  - Detailed teaching notes for each of the cases, as well as suggestions for possible chapters with which they might be paired.

ACKNOWLEDGMENTS

Over the years, many colleagues in both the academic and business worlds have provided us with valuable insights into the management and marketing of services, through their writings and in conference or seminar discussions. We have also benefited enormously from in-class and after-class discussions with MBAs and executive program participants.

Although it's impossible to mention everyone who has influenced our thinking, we particularly want to express our appreciation to the following individuals: John Bateson of SHL Group; Leonard Berry of Texas A&M University; Mary Jo Bitner, Stephen Brown, and David Bowen of Arizona State University; Eileen Bridges of Kent State University; Richard Chase of the University of Southern California; Pierre Eiglier of Université d'Aix–Marseille III; Raymond Fisk of the University of New Orleans; Christian Grönroos of the Swedish School of Economics in Finland; Stephen Grove of Clemson University: Evert Gummesson of Stockholm University; John Deighton, James Heskett, Theodore Levitt, Earl Sasser, and Leonard Schlesinger, all currently or formerly of Harvard Business School; Doug Hoffman of Colorado State University; Jean-Claude Larréché of INSEAD; Robert Johnston of Warwick Business School; David Maister of Maister Associates; Anna Mattila of Pennsylvania State University; "Parsu" Parasuraman of the University of Miami; Fred Reichheld of Bain & Co.: Roland Rust and Benjamin Schneider of the University of Maryland; Charles Weinberg of the University of British Columbia; Lauren Wright of California State University, Chico; George Yip of London Business School; and Valarie Zeithaml of the University of North Carolina.

Special thanks are owed, in particular, to the insights received from the coauthors of international adaptations of *Services Marketing*: Guillermo D'Andrea of Universidad Austral, Luis Huete of IESE, Keh Hean Tat of the National University of Singapore, Denis Lapert of Reims Management School; Barbara Lewis of the Manchester School of Management; Javier Reynoso of Tec de Monterrey, Paul Patterson of the University of New South Wales; Sandra Vandermerwe of Imperial College, London; and Rhett Walker of LaTrobe University.

We thank, too, the authors (named in the section "About the Contributors") of the previously published cases and readings, as well as the copyright holders for permission to reprint these and other materials.

It takes more than authors to create a book and its supplements. Warm thanks are owed to our many research and teaching assistants who helped us with various aspects of the cases, the text, or the teaching manual: Patricia Chew, Chua Hsiao Wei, Suzy Eisinger, Tillman Fein, Cecilia C.S. Goh, Jeff Gregory, Gwee Qi Xin, Chidambara Rao Nadella, Karen Osborn, Sunil Pradhan, Sanjay Singh, Denis C.L. Tan, Kornluck Tantisaeree, Melissa Tomlinson, and Amy Whitaker. Tim Lovelock provided valued assistance on many graphics. And, of course, we're very appreciative of all the hard work put in by the editing and production staff in helping to transform our sometimes messy manuscript into a handsome published text. They include Katie Stevens, Acquisitions Editor, Michelle O'Brien, Executive Marketing Manager, and especially, Maureen Wilson, Production Editor.

CHRISTOPHER LOVELOCK

JOCHEN WIRTZ

About the Authors

As a team, Christopher Lovelock and Jochen Wirtz possess a blend of skills and experience that is ideally suited to writing an authoritative and engaging text on services marketing. Since first meeting at a service management conference in 1992, they have collaborated on a variety of projects, including cases, articles, conference papers, and the Asian adaptation of an earlier edition of *Services Marketing*.

Christopher Lovelock, one of the pioneers of services marketing, is an adjunct professor at the Yale School of Management, where he teaches an MBA services marketing course. As principal of Lovelock Associates, he consults and gives seminars and workshops for managers around the world, with a focus on managing the customer experience and planning service marketing strategy. Dr. Lovelock's distinguished academic career has included 11 years on the faculty of the Harvard Business School and two years as a visiting professor at IMD in Switzerland. He has also held appointments at Berkeley, Stanford, and the Sloan School at MIT, as well as visiting professorships at the University of Queensland in Australia and at both INSEAD and Theseus Institute in France. After obtaining a BCom and an MA in economics from the University of Edinburgh, he worked in advertising with the London office of J. Walter Thompson Co. and in corporate planning with Canadian Industries Ltd. in Montreal. Later, he obtained an MBA from Harvard and a Ph.D. from Stanford. Author or coauthor of over 60 articles, more than 100 teaching cases, and some two dozen books, Dr. Lovelock serves on the editorial review boards of the *International Journal of Service Industry Management, Journal of Service Research, Service Industries Journal, Cornell Hotel and Restaurant Administration Quarterly*, and *Marketing Management*. He is a recipient of the American Marketing Association's Award for Career Contributions to the Services Discipline and of a best article award from the *Journal of Marketing*. Recognized many times for excellence in case writing, he has twice won top honors in the *Business Week* "European Case of the Year" Award.

Jochen Wirtz is an associate professor at the National University of Singapore, where he teaches services marketing courses in executive, MBA, and undergraduate programs. He is a member of the management committee of NUS Business School, director of the Asia-Pacific Executive MBA Program, and codirector of NUS's joint EMBA program with UCLA. He received his Ph.D. in services marketing from the London Business School and holds a BA (Hons) in marketing and accounting and a professional certification in banking from Germany. Dr. Wirtz's research focuses on service management, and he has published some 40 academic articles in the *Journal of Business Research, Journal of Consumer Psychology, Journal of Retailing, Journal of Services Marketing, Journal of Service Research, Managing Service Quality*, and *Psychology and Marketing*, among others. In addition, he has also published some 70 conference papers, 5 books, and over 40 book chapters. He serves on the editorial review boards of five journals. His research awards include the Emerald Literati Club 2003 Award for Excellence for the most outstanding paper of the year in the *International Journal of Service Industry Management.* He has received several awards for outstanding teaching at NUS Business School and in 2003 won the Universitywide Outstanding Educator Award. Dr. Wirtz has also been active as a management consultant, working with both international consulting firms including Accenture, Arthur D. Little, and KPMG, and major service companies in the areas of strategy, business development, and service management. Originally from Germany, he spent seven years in London before moving to Asia.

ABOUT THE CONTRIBUTORS OF THE READINGS AND CASES

Leonard L. Berry is Distinguished Professor of Marketing at Texas A&M University, where he holds the M.B. Zale Chair of Retailing and Marketing Leadership.

Diane Brady writes for *Business Week.*

Roger Brown is cofounder and CEO of Bright Horizons Family Solutions.

Lewis P. Carbone is founder, president, and chief executive officer of Experience Engineering.

Richard B. Chase is Justin B. Dart Professor of Operations Management and director of the Center for Service Excellence at the University of Southern California.

John Deighton is Harold M. Brierley Professor of Business Administration at the Harvard Business School.

Suzy Eisinger is a member of the MBA Class of 2003 at the Yale School of Management.

Marc Epstein is a professor at Rice University.

Raymond P. Fisk is professor and chair of marketing, University of New Orleans.

Lorelle Frazer is an associate professor at Griffith University, Australia.

Frances X. Frei is an associate professor at the Harvard Business School.

Stephen J. Grove is professor of marketing at Clemson University.

Stephan H. Haeckel is founder of Adaptive Business Systems and past chairman of the Marketing Science Institute.

Sheryl E. Kimes is a professor and director of graduate studies at the School of Hotel Administration, Cornell University.

Katherine N. Lemon is an assistant professor at Boston College.

Roland T. Rust holds the David Bruce Smith Chair in Marketing at the University of Maryland, where he is director of the Center for E-Service.

Tony Simons is an associate professor at Cornell University.

Robert Westbrook is a professor at Rice University.

Valarie A. Zeithaml is Alice H. Richards Bicentennial Professor of Marketing and associate dean, MBA Programs, at the University of North Carolina.

PART ONE

Understanding Service Products, Consumers, and Markets

CHAPTER 1

Introduction to Services Marketing

Ours is a service economy and it has been for some time.
—KARL ALBRECHT AND RON ZEMKE

As consumers, we use services every day. Turning on a light, listening to the radio, talking on the telephone, taking a bus, getting a haircut, or sending clothes to the cleaners are all examples of service consumption at the individual level. The institution at which you are studying is itself a complex service organization. In addition to educational services, the facilities at today's colleges and universities usually comprise libraries, cafeterias, counseling services and placement offices, a bookstore, photocopying services, telephones and Internet connections, and maybe even a bank. Businesses and other organizations are also dependent on a wide array of services, usually purchasing on a much larger scale than individuals or households.

Unfortunately, customers are not always happy with the quality and value of the services they receive. People complain about late deliveries, incompetent personnel, inconvenient service hours, needlessly complicated procedures, long queues, and a host of other problems.

Suppliers of services, who often face stiff competition, sometimes appear to have a very different set of concerns. Many owners and managers complain about how difficult it is to make a profit, to find skilled and motivated employees, or to please customers.

Fortunately, some suppliers know how to please their customers while also running a productive, profitable operation, staffed by pleasant and competent employees. In this book, you'll be introduced to innovative service organizations, both large and small, from which you can draw important insights on how to get it right.

In this chapter, we present an overview of today's dynamic service economy and explore the following questions.

1. How important is the service sector in our economy?
2. What makes services so different from physical goods, and what are the implications for marketing services?
3. What are the important distinctions among various types of services, and how do these differences impact the way we market them?
4. What are the elements of the services marketing mix?
5. Why do service businesses need to integrate the marketing, operations, and human resource functions?
6. What are the major changes occurring in the service sector, and how are these changes affecting the nature of service competition?

SERVICES DOMINATE THE MODERN ECONOMY

The service sector is going through almost revolutionary change, which dramatically affects the way in which we live and work. New services are continually being launched to satisfy our existing needs and to meet needs that we did not even know we had. Not even 10 years ago, few people anticipated a personal need for e-mail, online banking, Web hosting, and many other new services. Today, many of us feel we can't do without them. Similar transformations are occurring in business-to-business markets.

Service organizations vary widely in size. At one end of the scale are huge international corporations operating in such industries as airlines, banking, insurance, telecommunications, and hotels. At the other end of the scale is a vast array of locally owned and operated small businesses, including restaurants, laundries, optometrists, beauty parlors, and numerous business-to-business services, to name a few.

Structure of the Service Sector

The services sector is remarkably diverse. It comprises a wide array of industries that sell to individual consumers and business customers, as well as to government agencies and nonprofit organizations. Figure 1-1 shows how the major service industries contribute to the gross domestic product (GDP) of the U.S. economy.

Services make up the bulk of today's economy and also account for most of the growth in new jobs. Unless you are already predestined for a career in a family manufacturing or agricultural business, the probability is high that you will spend your working life in service organizations. Perhaps you will even start your own service business!

The size of the service sector is increasing in almost all economies around the world. As a national economy develops, the relative share of employment among agriculture, industry (including manufacturing and mining), and services changes dramatically.[1] Even in emerging economies, service output is growing rapidly and often represents at least half of the GDP.[2] Figure 1-2 shows how the evolution to a service-dominated economy is likely to take place over time as per capita income rises. In developed countries, knowledge-based services—defined as those that are intensive users of high technology and/or have relatively highly skilled work forces—are proving the most dynamic components.[3]

To provide a better understanding of the nature of today's service-dominated economy, government statistical agencies have developed new ways to classify industries. In the United States, the 60-year-old Standard Industrial Classification (SIC) is being replaced by the new North American Industry Classification System (NAICS) (see Research Insights 1-1),[4] developed jointly with Canada and Mexico.

Why Is the Service Sector Growing?

In numerous countries, increased productivity and automation in agriculture and industry, combined with growing demand for both new and traditional services, have jointly resulted in a continuing increase over time in the percentage of the labor force that is employed in services. There's a hidden service sector within many large corporations that are classified by government statisticians as being in manufacturing, agricultural, or natural resources industries. These so-called *internal services* cover a wide range of activities, including recruitment, legal and accounting services, payroll administration, office cleaning, landscape maintenance, supply-chain management, advertising, and many other kinds of services. Organizations are increasingly choosing to outsource the internal services that can be performed more efficiently by a specialist subcontractor.

FIGURE 1-1 Contribution of Service Industries to U.S. Gross Domestic Product, 2001

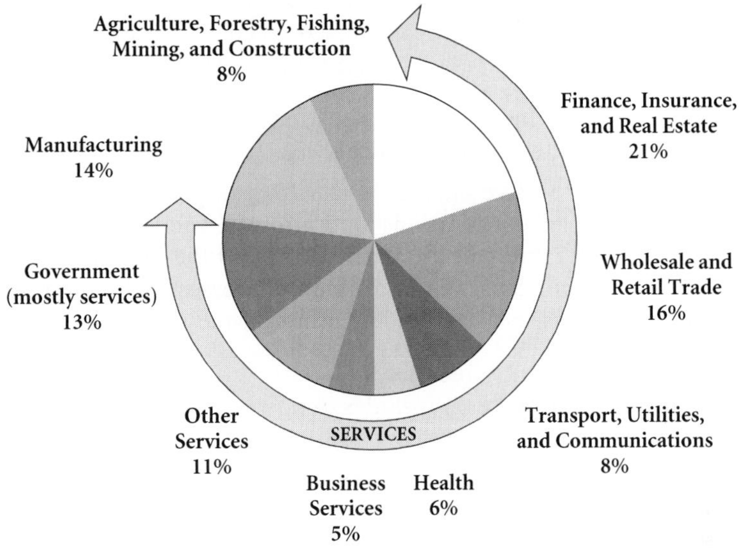

Source: U.S. Bureau of Economic Analysis, *Survey of Current Business*, November 2002, Table 2, p. 32.

FIGURE 1-2 Changing Structure of Employment as an Economy Develops

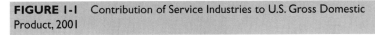

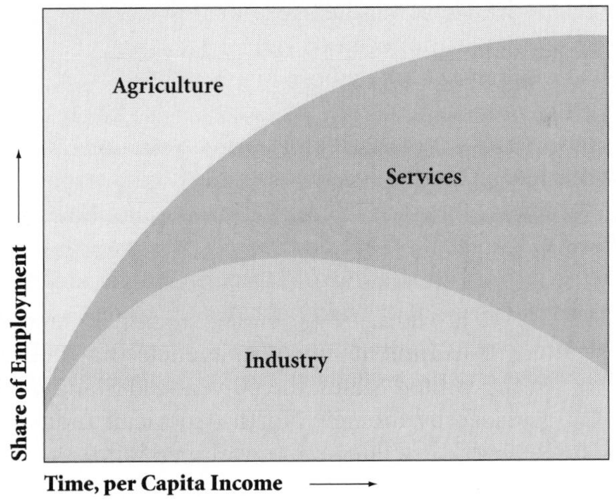

Source: International Monetary Fund, *World Economic Outlook* (Washington, D.C.: International Monetary Fund, May 1997). Reprinted with permission of International Monetary Fund. All rights reserved.

Internal services are also being spun out as separate service operations offered in the wider marketplace. When such tasks are outsourced, they become part of the competitive marketplace and are therefore more easily identifiable as contributing to the services component of the economy.

Among the forces that shape service markets are government policies, social changes, business trends, advances in information technology, and internationalization (Figure 1-3). We'll be highlighting the impact of these factors on consumption patterns and competitive strategy throughout the book.

RESEARCH INSIGHTS 1-1

INTRODUCING NAICS: A NEW WAY TO CLASSIFY THE ECONOMIES OF NORTH AMERICA

The North American Industry Classification System—developed jointly by the statistical agencies of Canada, Mexico, and the United States—offers a new approach to classifying industries in the economic statistics of the three North American Free Trade Agreement (NAFTA) countries. It replaces previous national systems, such as the 60-year-old Standard Industrial Classification formerly used in the United States.

NAICS (pronounced "nakes") includes many new service industries that have emerged in recent decades and also reclassifies as services "auxiliary" establishments that provide services, such as accounting, catering, and transportation, within manufacturing companies. Every sector of the economy has been restructured and redefined. NAICS includes 358 new industries that the SIC did not identify, 390 that are revised from their SIC counterparts, and 422 that continue substantially unchanged. These industries are grouped into 20 sectors, as opposed to only 10 SIC divisions, and reorganize data on both manufacturing and service industries.

Among the new sectors devoted to services are *Information*, which recognizes the emergence and uniqueness of businesses in the "information economy"; *Health Care and Social Assistance*; *Professional, Scientific and Professional Services*; *Arts, Entertainment and Recreation*, which includes most businesses engaged in meeting consumers' cultural, leisure, or entertainment interests; *Educational Services*; and *Accommodation and Food Services*.

Examples of new NAICS industry classifications that were not previously broken out separately are

Casino Hotels
Continuing Care Retirement Communities
Diagnostic Imaging Centers
Diet and Weight Reducing Centers
Environmental Consulting
Golf Courses and Country Clubs
Hazardous Waste Collection
HMO Medical Centers
Industrial Design Services
Investment Banking and Securities Dealing
Management Consulting Services
Satellite Telecommunications
Telemarketing Bureaus
Temporary Help Services

NAICS uses a consistent principle for classification, grouping together businesses that use similar production processes. Its goal is to make economic statistics more useful and to capture developments that encompass applications of high technology (e.g., cellular telecommunications), businesses that previously did not exist (e.g., environmental consulting), and changes in the way business is done (e.g., warehouse clubs).

Sources: Economic Classification Policy Committee, "NAICS—North American Industry Classification System: New Data for a New Economy." Washington, DC: Bureau of the Census, October 1998. See also *www.census.gov/naics*

The implications of the changes outlined earlier are several. On the positive side, there is likely to be growing demand for many services. The opening up of the service economy means that there will be greater competition.[5] In turn, more competition will stimulate innovation, not least through the application of new and improved technologies. Customer needs and behavior evolve, too, in response to changing demographics and values, as well as new options. Both individually and in combination, these developments will require managers of service organizations to focus more sharply on marketing strategy.

It has been said that the only person in the world who appreciates a change is a wet baby. However, the willingness and ability of managers in service firms to respond to the dramatic changes affecting the service economy will determine whether their own

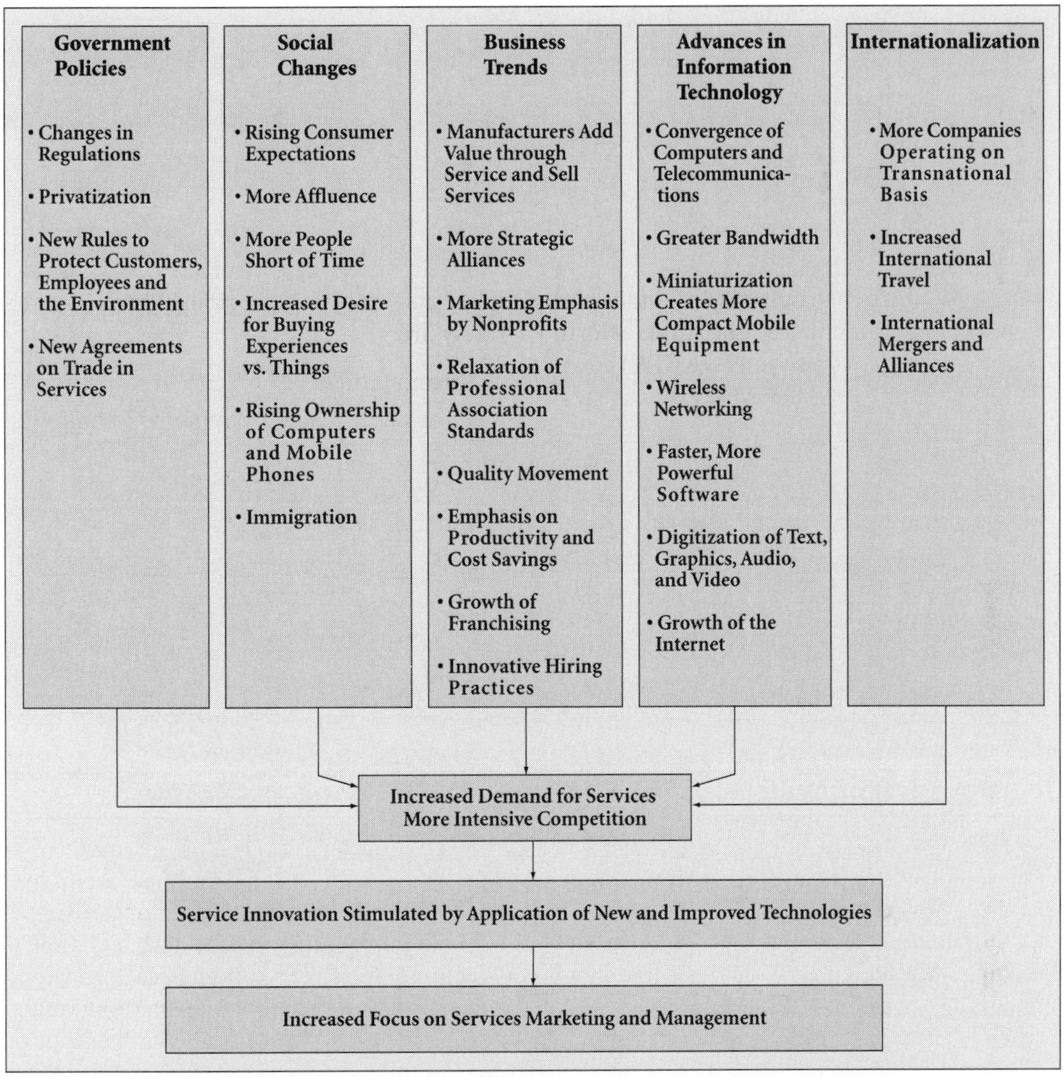

Government Policies
• Changes in Regulations
• Privatization
• New Rules to Protect Customers, Employees and the Environment
• New Agreements on Trade in Services
Social Changes
• Rising Consumer Expectations
• More Affluence
• More People Short of Time
• Increased Desire for Buying Experiences vs. Things
• Rising Ownership of Computers and Mobile Phones
• Immigration
Business Trends
• Manufacturers Add Value through Service and Sell Services
• More Strategic Alliances
• Marketing Emphasis by Nonprofits
• Relaxation of Professional Association Standards
• Quality Movement
• Emphasis on Productivity and Cost Savings
• Growth of Franchising
• Innovative Hiring Practices
Advances in Information Technology
• Convergence of Computers and Telecommunications
• Greater Bandwidth
• Miniaturization Creates More Compact Mobile Equipment
• Wireless Networking
• Faster, More Powerful Software
• Digitization of Text, Graphics, Audio, and Video
• Growth of the Internet
Internationalization
• More Companies Operating on Transnational Basis
• Increased International Travel
• International Mergers and Alliances
Increased Demand for Services
More Intensive Competition
Service Innovation Stimulated by Application of New and Improved Technologies
Increased Focus on Services Marketing and Management

FIGURE 1-3 Factors Stimulating the Transformation of the Service Economy

organizations survive and prosper or go down to defeat at the hands of more agile and adaptive competitors.

Technology Is a Key Driver of Service Innovation

The term *technology*, as commonly used, refers to the practical application of cutting-edge tools and procedures. Innovative service providers are interested in how they can use new technological developments to automate and speed up processes, reduce costs (and perhaps prices), facilitate service delivery, relate more closely to their customers and offer them more convenience, add appeal to existing products, and make it possible to develop new types of services. Throughout this book, we examine the role of technology—and especially information technology—in driving service innovation.

At least five types of technology have implications for a broad array of service industries. These are the technologies of power and energy, materials, physical design, methods of working, and information technology (IT). The application of one type of technology in any service industry often involves others in a supporting role. When people speak of "high technology," they are usually referring to modern applications derived from research and development in the physical sciences. In recent years, the focus has been on IT and, specifically, the merger of computer and telecommunications technology that facilitated the development of wireless services and the Internet, whose best-known components are e-mail and the World Wide Web.

Michael Porter, respected for his work on competitive strategy, argues persuasively that the Internet is an enabling technology that can be used in almost any industry and as part of almost any strategy.[6] Internet retailing, for instance, involves new ways of presenting merchandise, relating to customers, and taking their orders, but still requires physical channels for delivery of purchased merchandise. However, there is a group of information-based services—sometimes referred to as *e-services*—that has built strategy entirely around Internet access and delivery. eBay is perhaps the most striking example.[7] As Kenneth Boyer, Roger Hallowell, and Aleda Roth emphasize, e-services provide a unique opportunity for businesses to offer new models, but success will be dependent on careful planning and implementation.[8]

The ability of firms to generate business through technology-driven service innovations is often dependent on customers having access to the necessary equipment and infrastructure. It's predicted that the growth of broadband telecommunications, which speeds customers' interactions with Web sites, will provide a powerful stimulus for use of Internet channels.[9]

SERVICES POSE DISTINCTIVE MARKETING CHALLENGES

All *products*—a term that we use in this book to describe the core output of any type of industry—deliver benefits to the customers who purchase and use them. In the case of *goods*, the benefits come from ownership of physical objects or devices, whereas in *services*, the benefits are created by actions or performances.[10] (See Service Perspectives 1-1.) The dynamic environment of services today places a premium on effective marketing. Among the keys to competing effectively in this continually evolving and challenging environment are skills in marketing strategy and execution, areas in which many service firms have traditionally been weak.

Marketing can be viewed in several ways. It can be seen as a strategic and competitive thrust pursued by top management; as a set of functional activities, including product policy, pricing, delivery, and communications, performed by line managers; or as a customer-driven orientation for the entire organization. In this book, we seek to integrate all three perspectives. Christian Grönroos argues that the services marketing function is much broader than the activities and output of the traditional marketing department, requiring close cooperation between marketers and those managers responsible for operations and human resources.[12]

Although it's still very important to run an efficient operation, that alone is no longer enough for success. Employees must be customer service oriented in addition to being concerned about efficiency. The service product must be tailored to customer needs, priced realistically, distributed through convenient channels, and actively promoted to customers. The organization must continuously be aware of trends in the size and structure of each market in which its services compete. And, very important, the organization must monitor what its competitors are doing and have a clear strategy for achieving and maintaining competitive advantage. Today, many new market entrants are choosing to avoid head-to-head competition against established firms and are positioning their services to appeal to specific market segments.

SERVICE PERSPECTIVES 1-1

WHAT IS A SERVICE?

Reflecting the physical nature of their activities, manufacturing, mining, and agriculture are easier to describe and define than are services, which embrace a huge diversity of activities and involve many intangible inputs and outputs. Consider the following attempts to define service.

- A service is an act or performance offered by one party to another. Although the process may be tied to a physical product, the performance is transitory, often intangible in nature, and does not normally result in ownership of any of the factors of production.
- A service is an economic activity that creates value and provides benefits for customers at specific times and places by bringing about a desired change in, or on behalf of, the recipient of the service.

More amusingly services have also been described as something that can "be bought and sold, but which cannot be dropped on your foot."[11]

Are the marketing concepts and practices that have been developed in manufacturing companies directly transferable to service organizations? The answer is often no, because marketing management tasks in the service sector tend to differ from those in the manufacturing sector in several important respects.

More practical insights are provided in Table 1-1, which lists nine basic differences that can help us to distinguish the tasks associated with marketing services from those involved with marketing physical goods. Our review of these differences highlights some key managerial implications that will form the basis for much of our analysis and discussion in this and later chapters.

It's important to recognize that in identifying these differences, we are dealing with generalizations that do not apply equally to all services. Later in this chapter, we consider how different types of services present somewhat different challenges for marketers and other managers. But first, let's examine each characteristic in more detail and highlight a few fundamental marketing implications.

Customers Do Not Obtain Ownership of Services

Perhaps the key distinction between goods and services lies in the fact that customers usually derive value from services without obtaining ownership of any tangible elements; exceptions include food services and installation of spare parts during delivery of repair services. In many instances, service marketers offer customers the opportunity to rent the use of a physical object, such as a rental car or a hotel room; to hire the

TABLE 1-1 Basic Differences between Goods and Services

- Customers do not obtain ownership of services.
- Service products are ephemeral and cannot be inventoried.
- Intangible elements dominate value creation.
- Customers may be involved in the production process.
- Other people may form part of the product.
- There is greater variability in operational inputs and outputs.
- Many services are difficult for customers to evaluate.
- The time factor assumes great importance.
- Distribution channels take different forms.

labor and expertise of people; to rent, as a loan, a sum of money; to subscribe to a network; or to pay for admission to a service facility.

A key implication for marketers concerns pricing. When the firm rents out use of its physical, human, or intangible assets, time becomes an important denominator, and determining the relevant costs requires time-based calculations. Another important issue concerns what criteria drive customer-choice behavior for a rental, which tends to be short term in nature. Marketing a car-rental service to a customer, for instance, is very different from attempting to sell a car at an automobile dealership to that same person, who may intend keeping it for at least three to five years. When they are away from home, people usually rent cars for a period of 1 to 14 days. In most instances, people reserve a particular class or category of vehicle, such as compact, intermediate, or full size, rather than a specific brand and model. Instead of worrying about physical characteristics, such as color and upholstery, customers usually focus more on such elements as where pickup and delivery facilities are located and what hours they are open, extent of insurance coverage, cleanliness and maintenance of vehicles, and quality of service provided by customer-contact personnel.

Service Products Are Ephemeral and Cannot Be Inventoried

Because a service is a deed or performance, it is *ephemeral*—transitory and perishable—and so cannot usually be stocked as inventory after being produced. (Exceptions are found among those service performances that can be recorded for later use in printed or electronic form.) Although facilities, equipment, and labor can be held in readiness to create the service, these elements simply represent productive capacity, not the product itself. If there is no demand during a given time period, unused capacity is wasted. During periods when demand exceeds capacity, customers may be sent away disappointed or asked to wait until sufficient capacity is available to serve them.

A key task for service marketers, therefore, is to find ways of smoothing demand levels to match capacity through price incentives, promotions, or other means. Marketers should also be looking for opportunities to shrink a firm's productive capacity—in the form of employees, physical space, and equipment—to match predicted fluctuations in demand. If profit maximization is an important goal, then marketers should target the right segments at the right times, focusing on selling during peak periods to those segments that are willing to pay premium prices.

Intangible Elements Dominate Value Creation

Although services often include important tangible elements, such as hotel beds, restaurant meals, spare parts installed during repairs, and bank cards and checkbooks, intangible elements—including the labor and expertise of service personnel—dominate the creation of value in service performances.

A useful way to distinguish between goods and services, first suggested by Lynn Shostack, is to place them on a scale from tangible-dominant to intangible-dominant (see Figure 1-4).[13] Clearly, there are some potentially ambiguous products toward the center of this scale. One suggested economic test of whether a product should be regarded as a good or a service is whether more than half the value comes from the service elements.[14] At a full-service restaurant, for example, the cost of the food itself may account for as little as 20–30 percent of the price of the meal. Most of the value added comes from food preparation and cooking, table service, the restaurant environment, and facilities such as parking, toilets, and coatroom.

The notion of service as a performance that cannot be wrapped up and taken away afterwards leads to the use of a theatrical metaphor that likens service delivery to the staging of a play, with service personnel as the actors, the delivery system as the stage,

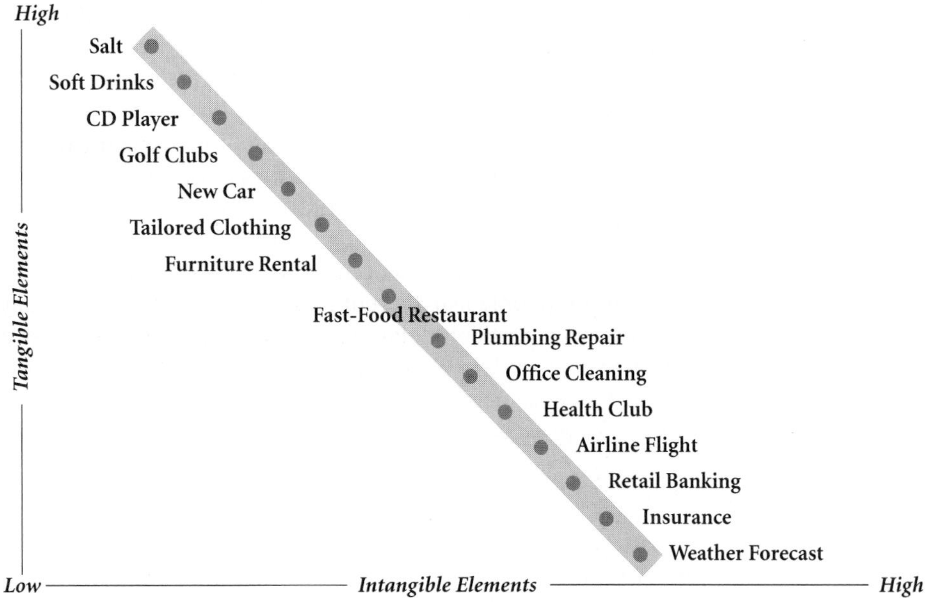

FIGURE 1-4 Value Added by Tangible versus Intangible Elements in Goods and Services

and customers as the audience.[15] In the absence of significant tangible elements, marketers may find it useful to employ physical images and metaphors to demonstrate the competencies of the service firm and to illustrate the benefits resulting from service delivery.

Customers May Be Involved in the Production Process

Many services require customers to participate in creating the service product. Customer involvement can take the form of self-service, as in using a laundromat or withdrawing money from an automated teller machine (ATM), or cooperation with service personnel in such settings as hairdressers, hotels, colleges, or hospitals. Under such circumstances, customers can be thought of as partial employees, and service firms have much to gain from trying to train their customers to make them more competent and productive.[16]

Changing the nature of the production process often affects the role that customers are asked to play in that process. In your own role as a service consumer, you know that although your main interest is in the final output, the way in which you are treated during service delivery can also have an important impact on your satisfaction. When customers are required to visit the service delivery site, that facility should be in a convenient location and open at times that suit customers' needs. Customers are more likely to return if they find that buildings and equipment are designed in ways that make them user friendly and reasonably attractive to visit.

Other People Are Often Part of the Product

The difference between one service and another often lies in the quality of employees who serve the customers. This is especially so in many high-contact services, in which customers not only come into contact with service personnel but also rub shoulders with other customers. As a result, the type of customers who patronize a particular service business can shape the nature of the service experience. If you attend a sporting event, the behavior of the fans can add to the excitement of the game if they are enthusiastic but well behaved. However, if some of them become rowdy and abusive, it can detract from the enjoyment of other spectators at the stadium.

Service firms need to devote special care to selecting, training, and motivating those employees who will be serving customers directly. In addition to possessing the technical skills required by the job, these employees also need to possess good interpersonal skills. At the same time, firms have to manage and shape customer behavior so that the misbehavior of a few will not spoil the experience for everybody else. In some instances, service marketers need to think carefully about whether it is a good idea to mix several segments together in the same service facility. Imagine a tired business traveler arriving at the hotel late at night to find it overrun by noisily partying vacationers.

There Is Greater Variability in Operational Inputs and Outputs

The presence of employees and other customers in the operational system makes it difficult to standardize and control quality in both service inputs and outputs. Manufactured goods can be produced under controlled conditions, designed to optimize both productivity and quality, and then checked for conformance with quality standards long before they reach the customer. The same is true for services performed while the customer is absent, such as processing bank checks, repairing cars, or cleaning offices at night. For those services that are consumed as they are produced, however, final "assembly" must take place under real-time conditions, which may vary from customer to customer and even from one time of day to another. As a result, mistakes are more likely to occur, and it is more difficult to shield customers from the results of such service failures. These factors make it difficult for service organizations to improve productivity, control quality, and offer a consistent product. As a former packaged-goods marketer observed some years ago after moving to a new position at Holiday Inn:

> We can't control the quality of our product as well as a Procter and Gamble control engineer on a production line can.... When you buy a box of Tide, you can reasonably be 99 and 44/100ths percent sure that this stuff will work to get your clothes clean. When you buy a Holiday Inn room, you're sure at some lesser percentage that it will work to give you a good night's sleep without any hassle, or people banging on the walls and all the bad things that can happen in a hotel.[17]

Many Services Are Difficult for Customers to Evaluate

Most physical goods tend to be relatively high in *search properties*: those characteristics of the product that a customer can evaluate prior to purchasing it, such as color, shape, price, fit, and feel. Other goods and many services, by contrast, may emphasize *experience properties*, which can be discerned only after purchase or during consumption. These properties include taste, wearability, ease of handling, quietness, and personal treatment. Finally, there are *credence properties*, which are characteristics that customers find difficult to evaluate even after consumption, because they are purchasing expertise in areas in which they are not very knowledgeable themselves. Examples are surgery; professional services, such as accountancy; and many technical repairs.[18]

Service marketers can reduce customers' perceived risk before a service purchase by helping them to match their needs to specific service features and educating them as to what to expect both during and after service delivery. A firm that develops a reputation for considerate and ethical treatment of its customers will gain the trust of its existing customers and benefit from positive word-of-mouth referrals.

The Time Factor Assumes Great Importance

Many services are delivered in real time while customers are physically present. There are limits as to how long people are willing spend at the service factory, as customers place a value on their time, and some people are willing to pay more for faster service. Increasingly, busy customers expect service to be available at times when it suits them rather than when it suits the service company. In response, more and more firms are offering extended hours, with some even staying open 24/7.

In other instances, the focus is on elapsed time. Even when customers place an order for a service to be undertaken in their absence, they have expectations about how long a particular task—whether it is repairing a machine, completing a research report, cleaning a suit, or preparing a legal document—should take to complete. In general, today's customers are increasingly time sensitive, so that speed is often seen as a key element in good service and as a way to attract new customers. Service marketers need to understand customers' time constraints and priorities, which may vary from one market segment to another, and to look for ways to compete on speed and to minimize waiting times.

Distribution Channels Take Different Forms

Manufacturers usually require physical distribution channels to move goods from factory to customers. Service businesses may choose to combine the service factory, retail outlet, and point of consumption at a single location or use electronic means to distribute their services, as in broadcasting or electronic funds transfers. Sometimes, as in banking, firms offer customers a choice of distribution channels, ranging from visiting the bank in person to conducting home banking on the Internet.

As a result of advances in computers and telecommunications, especially the growth of the Internet, electronic delivery of services is expanding rapidly. Any information-based component of a service can be delivered instantaneously to anywhere in the world. Thanks to e-mail and Web sites, even small businesses can offer their services inexpensively across vast geographic distances.

IMPORTANT DIFFERENCES EXIST AMONG SERVICES

Although it's useful to distinguish between goods and services marketing, it's also important to recognize that there are marketing-relevant differences among services themselves. The traditional way of grouping services is by industry. Service managers may say, "We're in the transportation (or hospitality, or banking, or telecommunications) business." These groupings help us to define the core products offered by the firm and to understand both customer needs and competition. However, this approach can lead to tunnel vision. One hallmark of innovative service firms is that their managers are willing to look outside their own industries for effective strategies they can adapt for use in their own organizations.

Categorizing Service Processes

Numerous proposals have been made for classifying services.[19] A particularly significant classification is based on the nature of the processes by which services are created and delivered. Marketers don't usually need to know the specifics of how physical goods are manufactured; that's the responsibility of the people who run the factory. However, the situation is different in services. Because customers are often involved in service production, marketers do need to understand the nature of the processes to which their customers may be exposed. A *process* is a particular method of operation or a series of actions, typically involving multiple steps that often need to take place in a defined sequence. Service processes range from relatively simple procedures involving only a few steps, such as filling a car's tank with fuel, to highly complex activities, such as transporting passengers on an international flight. Later, we show how these processes can be represented in *flowcharts*, diagrams that help us to understand what is going on and perhaps how a specific process might be improved.

A process implies taking an input and transforming it into output. But if that's the case, what is each service organization actually processing, and how does it perform this task? Two broad categories of things get processed in services: people and objects. In many cases, ranging from passenger transportation to education, customers themselves are the principal input to the service process. In other instances, the key input is an object, such as a malfunctioning computer that needs repair or a piece of financial data that needs to be associated with a particular account. In some services, the process is physical and something tangible takes place. In information-based services, however, the process can be intangible.

By looking at service processes from a purely operational perspective, we see that they can be categorized into four broad groups.[20] Figure 1-5 shows a four-way classification scheme based on tangible actions to either people's bodies or customers' physical possessions and intangible actions to either people's minds or their intangible assets.

Each category involves fundamentally different processes, with vital implications for marketing, operations, and human resource managers. We refer to the categories as *people processing, possession processing, mental stimulus processing*, and *information processing*. Although the industries within each category may appear to be very different, analysis will show that they do, in fact, share important process-related characteristics. As a result, managers from different industries within the same category may obtain useful insights from studying one another and then create valued innovations for their own organization.

Let's examine why these four different types of processes often have distinctive implications for marketing, operations and human resource strategies.

People Processing Since ancient times, people have sought out services directed at themselves: being transported, fed, lodged, restored to health, or made to look more beautiful. To receive these types of services, customers must physically enter the service system. Because they are an integral part of the process, they cannot obtain the benefits they desire by dealing at arm's length with service suppliers; instead, they must be prepared to spend time interacting and actively cooperating with service providers. The level of involvement required of customers may entail anything from boarding a city bus for a five-minute ride to undergoing a lengthy course of treatments at a hospital. The output from these services is a customer who has reached his or her destination or is now sporting clean and stylishly cut hair or is now in physically better health.

It's important for managers to think about process and output in terms of what happens to the customer because it helps them to identify what benefits are being created. Reflecting on the service process itself helps to identify some of the nonfinancial costs, such as time and mental and physical effort, that customers incur in obtaining these benefits.

Possession Processing Often, customers ask a service organization to provide treatment to a physical possession, which could be anything from a house to a computer or even a dog.

Customers are less physically involved with this type of service than with people-processing services. Consider the differences in your role between using passenger and

	Who or What Is the Direct Recipient of the Service?	
What Is the Nature of the Service Act?	**People**	**Possessions**
Tangible Actions	***People processing*** (services directed at people's bodies): Passenger transportation Health care Lodging Beauty salons Physical therapy Fitness centers Restaurants/bars Barbers Funeral services	***Possession processing*** (services directed at physical possessions): Freight transportation Repair and maintenance Warehousing/storage Office cleaning services Retail distribution Laundry and dry cleaning Refueling Landscaping/gardening Disposal/recycling
Intangible Actions	***Mental stimulus processing*** (services directed at people's minds): Advertising /PR Arts and entertainment Broadcasting/cable Management consulting Education Information services Music concerts Psychotherapy Religion Voice telephone	***Information processing*** (services directed at intangible assets): Accounting Banking Data processing Data transmission Insurance Legal services Programming Research Securities investment Software consulting

FIGURE 1-5 Understanding the Nature of the Service Act

freight transportation. In the first instance, you have to go along for the ride in order to obtain the benefit of getting from one location to another. With freight service, however, you can request that the firm go to your home or office to pick up the shipment and then wait for confirmation that it has been delivered.

In most possession-processing services, the customer's involvement is usually limited to dropping off the item that needs treatment, requesting the service, explaining the problem, and later returning to pick up the item and pay the bill. If the object to be processed is something that is difficult or impossible to move, such as landscaping, heavy equipment, or part of a building, the "service factory" must come to the customer, with service personnel bringing the tools and materials necessary to complete the job on site. In all instances, the output should be a satisfactory solution to a customer's problem or some tangible enhancement of the item in question.

Mental Stimulus Processing Services that interact with people's minds include education, news and information, professional advice, psychotherapy, entertainment, and certain religious practices. Anything touching people's minds has the power to shape attitudes and influence behavior. Thus, if customers are in a position of dependency or if there is potential for manipulation, strong ethical standards and careful monitoring are required. Receiving these services requires an investment of time on the customer's part. However, recipients do not necessarily have to be physically present in a service factory. They simply have to be mentally in communication with the information being presented. There is an interesting contrast here with people-processing services. Although passengers can sleep through a flight and still obtain the benefit of arriving at their desired destination a student who falls asleep in class will not be any wiser at the end than at the beginning!

Services such as entertainment and education are often created in one place and transmitted by TV or radio to individual customers in distant locations. However, these services can also be delivered "live and in person" to groups of customers from such locations as theaters or lecture halls. We need to recognize that watching a live concert on TV in one's home is not the same experience as watching the concert in a concert hall in the company of hundreds or even thousands of other people. In the latter instance, managers of concert halls find themselves facing many of the same challenges as their colleagues in people-processing services.

The core content of all services in this category is information based—whether it's music, voice, or visual images. Therefore, such services can easily be converted to digital format, recorded, and made available for subsequent replay through electronic channels or transformed into a manufactured product, such as a disk or a tape.

Information Processing Information is the most intangible form of service output, but it may be transformed into the more enduring, tangible forms, represented by letters, reports, books, tapes, or disks. Among the services that are highly dependent on effective collection and processing of information are financial and professional services, such as accounting, law, market research, management consulting, and medical diagnosis.

The extent of customer involvement in both information and mental stimulus–processing services is often determined more by tradition and a personal desire to meet the supplier face-to-face than by the needs of the operational process. Strictly speaking, personal contact is quite unnecessary in such industries as banking or insurance. Why should managers subject their firms to all the complexities of managing a people-processing service when they could deliver the same core product at arm's length? As a customer, why go to the service factory when there's no compelling need to do so?

Habit and tradition often lie at the root of existing service delivery systems and service use patterns. Professionals and their clients may say they prefer to meet face to face because they feel they learn more about each other's needs, capabilities, and personalities that way. However, experience shows that successful personal relationships, built on trust, can be created and maintained purely through telephone, Web sites, or e-mail contact. As technology improves and people continue to become more comfortable with videophones or the Internet, we can expect to see a continuing shift to arm's-length transactions.

Designing the Service Factory

The nature of customer involvement often varies sharply among the four categories of service process. Nothing can alter the fact that people-processing services require the customer to be physically present within the service factory. If you're in Pittsburgh and need to be in Paris tomorrow, you simply cannot avoid boarding an international flight and spending time in a jet high above the Atlantic. If you want your hair cut, you cannot delegate this activity to somebody else's head. You have to sit in the hairdresser's chair yourself.

When customers visit a service factory, their satisfaction will be influenced by such factors as the appearance and features of both exterior and interior service facilities,

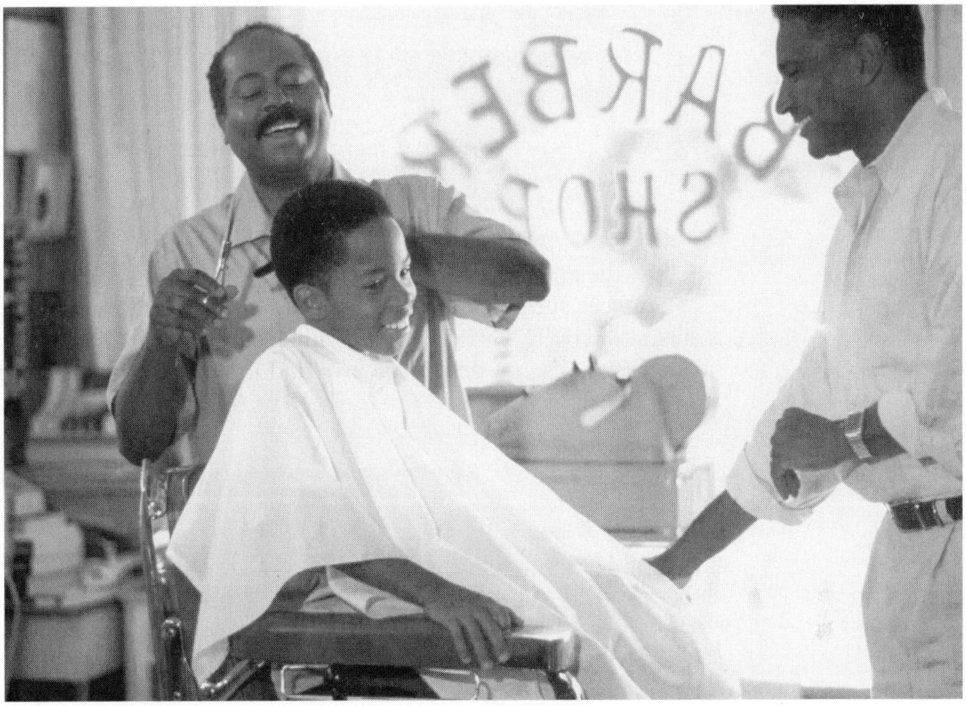

The Barbershop Is a Service Factory.

encounters with service personnel, interactions with self-service equipment, and the characteristics and behavior of other customers. When the nature of the service requires customers to be physically present throughout delivery, the process must be designed with them in mind, from the moment they arrive at the service factory. If the service factory is noisy, confusingly laid out, sited in an inconvenient location, and poorly staffed, customers are likely to be turned off.

Marketing managers need to work closely with their counterparts in operations in order to design facilities that are both pleasing to customers and efficient to operate. The exterior of a building creates important first impressions, whereas the interior can be thought of as the "stage" on which the service performance is delivered. The longer customers remain in the factory and/or the more they expect to spend on purchasing a service, the more important it is to offer facilities that are comfortable and attractive.

Using Alternative Channels for Service Delivery

Unlike the situation in people-processing services, managers responsible for possession-processing, mental stimulus–processing, and information-processing services need not require customers to visit a service factory. Instead, these managers may be able to offer a choice from one of several alternative delivery channels. Possibilities include (1) letting customers come to a user-friendly factory, (2) limiting contact to a small retail office, or "back office," that is separate from the main factory, (3) coming to the customer's home or office, and (4) conducting business at via phone, fax, e-mail or a Web site.

Let's take cleaning and pressing of clothes, a possession-processing service, as an example. One approach is to do your laundry at home. If you lack the necessary equipment, you can pay to use a laundromat, which is essentially a self-service cleaning factory. If you prefer to leave the task of laundry and dry cleaning to professionals, as many people choose to do with their best clothes, you can go to a retail store that serves as a drop-off location for dirty clothes and pickup point for newly cleaned items. Sometimes, cleaning is conducted in a space behind the store, but at other times, the clothing is transported to an

FIGURE 1-6 Two Types of Web Sites

Web sites can deliver Progressive Insurance's services directly, but …

Courtesy of Progressive Insurance.

industrial site some distance away. Home pickup and delivery are available in many cities, but this service tends to be expensive because of the extra costs involved.

Both physical and electronic channels allow customers and suppliers to conduct service transactions at arm's length. For instance, instead of shopping at a shopping center, you can study a Web site and place an order online for parcel delivery. Information-based items, such as software or research reports, can even be downloaded immediately to your computer.

Today's managers need to be creative, as the combination of information technology and modern package-transportation services, such as those of UPS, FedEx, national postal services, and other logistics firms, offers many opportunities to rethink the place and time of service delivery. Some manufacturers of small pieces of equipment allow customers to bypass retail dealers when a product needs repair. Instead, a courier will come to pick up the defective item—even supplying appropriate packaging, if necessary—ship it to a repair site, and return the item a few days later when the problem has been fixed. Electronic distribution channels offer even more convenience, as transportation time can be eliminated. For instance, using telecommunication links, engineers in a central facility, which could be located on the other side of the world, may be able to diagnose problems in defective computers and software at distant customer locations and transmit electronic signals to correct the defects.

Rethinking service-delivery procedures for all but people-processing services may allow a firm to get customers out of the factory and transform a high-contact service into a low-contact one. When the nature of the *process* makes it possible to deliver service at arm's length, the design and location of the factory can focus on purely operational priorities. The chances of success in such an endeavor depend on customer acceptance of the new approach and will be enhanced if the new procedures are user friendly, cost-effective, and offer customers greater convenience.

Land's End goods require a physical channel to reach the customer.

2003 © Land's End, Inc. Used with permission.

Making the Most of Information Technology

It's clear that *information-based services*—a term that covers both mental stimulus–processing and information-processing services—have the most to gain from advances in information technology, as telecommunications and the Internet allow the operation to be physically separated from its customers, without even the need for physical shipments. A growing number of banks are now adding Internet capabilities so that customers can access their accounts and conduct certain transactions via their mobile phones from wherever they may be.

Today, the Web is having an increasingly significant impact on distribution strategy for a broad array of industries.[21] A distinction needs to be made, however, between marketing the core product, such as insurance coverage or selling and buying shares, and the provision of supplementary services, such as ordering goods from an online retailer or making a reservation for a holiday, to enhance that core product. Much of the discussion surrounding the use of the Internet concerns supplementary services that are based on the transfer of *information relating to the product*, as opposed to downloading the core product itself. Figure 1-6 displays examples of both types of Web sites.

Balancing Supply and Demand

Sharp fluctuations in demand are a bane in the lives of many managers. As a hedge against fluctuations in demand, manufacturing firms may stock supplies of their product. This strategy enables them to enjoy the economies derived from operating factories at steady production levels. However, few service businesses can do this easily. For example, the potential income from an empty seat on an airliner is lost forever once that flight takes off. Hotel room-nights are equally "perishable." Conversely, when demand for service exceeds supply, the excess business is usually lost. If someone can't get a seat on one flight, another carrier gets the business, or the trip is canceled. In other situations, customers may be forced to wait in a queue until sufficient productive capacity is available to serve them.

In general, services that process people and physical objects are more likely to face capacity limitations than are those that are information based. Radio and television transmissions, for instance, can reach any number of homes within their receiving areas or cable distribution networks. In recent years, information processing and transmission capacity have been vastly increased by greater computing power, digital switching, and the replacement of coaxial cables with fiber-optic ones.

Technology, however, has not found similar ways to increase the capacity of those service operations that process people and their physical possessions without big jumps in costs. Thus, managing demand becomes more essential in improving productivity in those types of services that involve tangible actions. Customers must either be given incentives to use the service outside peak periods, or capacity must be allocated in advance through reservations. For example, a golf course may use both of these strategies by discounting greens fees during off-peak hours and requiring reservations for the busier tee times.

The problem for people-processing services is that there are limits to how long customers are willing to wait in line. By contrast, physical possessions, unless they are highly perishable, rarely suffer if they have to wait. What is more relevant to customers is the cost and inconvenience associated with delays in waiting to recover the item being serviced. Researchers note that there has been a continuing rise in consumer demand for convenience.[22] Customers are likely to be dissatisfied if their clean clothes or repaired cars are not ready when promised. The issue of demand and capacity management is so central to productive use of assets, and thus profitability, that we devote significant coverage to the topic in Chapter 9.

When People Become Part of the Product

In many people-processing services, customers meet a lot of employees and often interact with them for extended periods of time. These customers are also more likely to run into other customers, as many service facilities achieve their operating economies by serving large numbers of customers simultaneously. A bus, college class, restaurant meal, and hairdressing salon all tend to serve many customers at the same time. When other people become a part of the service experience, their attitudes, behavior, and appearance can enhance it or detract from it.

Direct involvement in service production means that customers evaluate the quality of employees' appearance and social skills, as well as their technical skills. And because customers also make judgments about other customers, managers find themselves trying to manage customer behavior, too. Service businesses of this type tend to be challenging to manage because of the human element.

MARKETING MUST BE INTEGRATED WITH OTHER FUNCTIONS

In this book, we don't limit our coverage to services marketing. Throughout the chapters, you'll also find continuing reference to two other important functions: service operations and human resource management. Imagine yourself as the manager of a small hotel, or, if you like, think big and picture yourself as the CEO of a major bank. In both instances, you need to be concerned about satisfying your customers on a daily basis, about operational systems running smoothly and efficiently, and about making sure that your employees are not only working productively but also delivering good service. In short, integration of activities between functions is the name of the game. Problems in any one of these three areas can negatively affect execution of tasks in the other functions and result in dissatisfied customers.

The Services Marketing Mix

When discussing strategies to market manufactured goods, marketers usually address four basic strategic elements: product, price, place (or distribution), and promotion (or communication). Collectively, these are often referred to as the *4Ps* of the marketing mix.[23] To capture the distinctive nature of service performances, we will be modifying the terminology and extending the mix by adding three elements associated with service delivery: physical environment, process, and people. Collectively, these seven elements, referred to as the *7Ps* of services marketing, represent a set of interrelated decision variables facing managers of service organizations.[24] Let's look briefly at each in turn.

Product Elements Managers must select the features of both the core product—either a good or a service—and the bundle of supplementary service elements surrounding it, with reference to the benefits desired by customers and how well competing products perform. In short, we need to be attentive to all aspects of the service performance that have the potential to create value for customers.

Place and Time Delivering product elements to customers involves decisions on the place and time of delivery, as well as on the methods and channels used. Delivery may involve physical or electronic distribution channels or both, depending on the nature of the service being provided. Use of messaging services and the Internet allows information-based services to be delivered in cyberspace for retrieval wherever and whenever it suits the customer. Firms may deliver service directly to customers or through intermediary organizations, such as retail outlets that receive a fee or a percentage of the selling price, to perform certain tasks associated with sales, service, and customer contact. Speed and convenience of place and time for the customer are becoming important determinants in service delivery strategy.

Promotion and Education No marketing program can succeed without effective communications. This component plays three vital roles: providing needed information and advice, persuading target customers of the merits of a specific product, and encouraging them to take action at specific times. In services marketing, much communication is educational in nature, especially for new customers. Companies may need to teach these customers about the benefits of the service, where and when to obtain it, and how to participate in service processes. Communications can be delivered by individuals, such as salespeople and front-line staff, or through the media, such as TV, radio, newspapers, magazines, posters, brochures, and Web sites. Promotional activities may influence brand choice, and incentives may be used to attract customers to buy.

Price and Other User Outlays This component addresses management of all the outlays incurred by customers in obtaining benefits from the service product. Consequently, services marketing strategy is not limited to the traditional pricing tasks of determining the selling price to customers, setting margins for any intermediaries, and establishing credit terms. Marketers must understand and, where feasible, seek to minimize other outlays that customers are likely to incur in purchasing and using a service. These outlays may include additional monetary costs (such as travel expenses to a service location), time expenditures, unwanted mental and physical effort, and exposure to negative sensory experiences.

Physical Environment The appearance of buildings, landscaping, vehicles, interior furnishing, equipment, staff members, signs, printed materials, and other visible cues all provide tangible evidence of a firm's service quality. Service firms need to manage physical evidence carefully, as it can have a profound impact on customers' impressions.

Process Creating and delivering product elements to customers require the design and implementation of effective processes. A *process* is the method and sequence of actions in the service performance. Badly designed processes often lead to slow, bureaucratic, and ineffective service delivery, and result in dissatisfied customers. Similarly, poor processes make it difficult for front-line staff to do their jobs well, resulting in low productivity and increased likelihood of service failure.

People Many services depend on direct interaction between customers and a firm's employees. The nature of these interactions, such as getting a haircut or talking to a call center staff, strongly influences the customer's perceptions of service quality.[25] Service quality is often assessed based on customers' interactions with front-line staff, and successful service firms devote significant effort to recruiting, training, and motivating these employees.

Linking the Marketing, Operations, and Human Resources Functions

As shown by the component elements of the 7Ps model, marketing cannot operate successfully in isolation from other functions in a service business. Three management functions play central and interrelated roles in meeting customer needs, namely, marketing, operations, and human resources. Figure 1-7 illustrates this interdependency. In later chapters, we raise the question of how marketers should relate to their colleagues from other functions in planning and implementing marketing strategies.

Service firms must understand the implications of the seven components of the services marketing mix in order to develop effective strategies. Firms whose managers succeed in developing integrated strategies will have a better chance of surviving and prospering.

Marketing Services versus Marketing Goods through Service

With the growth of the service economy and the increasing emphasis on adding value-enhancing services to manufactured goods, the line between services and manufacturing sometimes becomes blurred.[26] As Theodore Levitt, one of the world's best-known marketing experts, has observed, "There are no such things as service industries. There are only industries whose service components are greater or less than those of other industries. Everybody is in service."[27] More recently, Roland Rust, editor of the *Journal of Service Research*, suggested that manufacturing firms had got this message when he observed that "most goods businesses now view themselves primarily as services."[28]

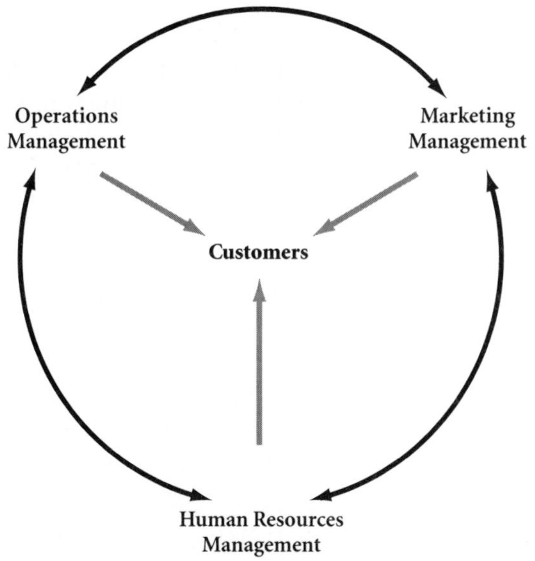

FIGURE 1-7 Interdependence of Marketing, Operations, and Human Resource Management

Nevertheless, it's important to clarify the difference between situations in which a service itself is the core product and those in which manufacturers are adopting servicelike strategies to help them market the physical goods they produce.

In this book, we draw a distinction between *marketing of services*—where a service is the core product—and *marketing through service.* In the latter case, a manufacturing firm may base its marketing strategy on a philosophy of serving customers well and adding supplementary service elements to the core product, but that core product still remains a physical good, not an intangible performance.

Many of the services that accompany physical products at the time of sale are not charged separately but are bundled in with the price of the product itself. Purchasers of a luxury car like the Lexus receive not only excellent warranty coverage but also an exceptional level of service from the dealer, based on the firm's detailed understanding of the benefits that customers seek from owning and driving a prestige brand of car. However, the Lexus is still a manufactured product, and we need to distinguish between marketing that product at the time of sale and marketing services that customers will pay for to maintain their car in good working order for several years after the sale.

Creating Value

By now it should be clear that managers need to be concerned about giving good value to customers and treating them fairly in decisions involving all elements of the 7Ps. Value can be defined as the worth of a specific action or object, relative to an individual's or organization's needs at a particular time, less the costs involved in obtaining those benefits.

Firms create value by offering the types of services that customers need, at an acceptable price. In return, firms receive value from their customers, primarily in the form of the money paid by the latter to purchase and use the services in question.[29] Such transfers of value illustrate one of the most fundamental concepts in marketing, that of *exchange*, which takes place when one party obtains value from another in return for something else of value. These exchanges aren't limited to buying and selling. An exchange of value also takes place when employees go to work for an organization. The employer gets the benefit of the worker's efforts, whereas the employee receives wages, benefits, and possibly such valued experiences as training, on-the-job experience, and working with friendly colleagues.

As a customer yourself, you regularly make decisions about whether to invest time, money, and effort to obtain a service that promises the specific benefits you seek. Perhaps the service in question solves an immediate need, such as getting a haircut or eating a pizza. Alternatively, as with getting an education, you may be prepared to take a long-term perspective before the payoff is realized. If you feel that you've had to pay more than you expected or received fewer benefits than anticipated or that you were badly treated during service delivery, the value received will be diminished. Alternatively, perhaps you or people you know have worked for a company that treated its employees poorly, even to the extent of not computing wages fairly or failing to deliver promised job-related benefits. That's not the best way for management to build employees' commitment to the firm or dedication to serving customers, is it? In fact, customers are quick to pick up on bad vibes from unhappy service workers.

No firm that seeks long-term relationships with either customers or employees can afford to mistreat them or to provide poor value on an ongoing basis. Sooner or later, shortchanging or mistreating customers and employees is likely to rebound to the firm's disadvantage. Hence, companies need a set of morally and legally defensible values to guide their actions and to shape their dealings with both employees and customers.

A useful way of thinking about "values" is as underlying beliefs about how life should be lived, how people should be treated, and how business should be conducted. To the extent possible, managers would be wise to use their firm's values as a reference point when recruiting and motivating employees. Managers should also clarify the firm's values and expectations in dealing with prospective customers, as well as make an effort to attract and retain customers who share and appreciate those same values.

More than 30 years ago, Siegmund Warburg of the investment banking house of S. G. Warburg (now SBC Warburg) remarked that

> A company's reputation for integrity, generosity, and thorough service is its most important asset, more important than any financial item. However, the reputation of a firm is like a very delicate living organism which can easily be damaged and which has to be taken care of incessantly, being mainly a matter of human behavior and human standards.[30]

Today, there is the greater scrutiny given to a firm's business ethics and the presence of tougher legislation designed to protect both customers and employees from abusive treatment. In this book, we periodically raise ethical issues as they relate to various aspects of service management.

SERVICE SUCCESS REQUIRES A FOCUS ON BOTH CUSTOMERS AND COMPETITIVE MARKETS

Recent years have seen much emphasis, especially among American corporations, on the mantra of enhancing shareholder value. However, while profits can certainly be enhanced in the short term by a vigorous effort to reduce expenses, there can be no creation of value for shareholders in the long run unless value is first created for customers. Marketing is the only management function that is dedicated to generating sales revenues for the firm. And no business can hope to sustain such a revenue stream unless it is successful in attracting and retaining customers who are willing to keep purchasing its services at prices that collectively cover all costs and leave an appropriate margin for profits and needed reinvestment. This is a challenging task in markets where many competing organizations are trying to appeal to those same customers, especially if overall market demand is either stagnant or declining.

Chapter 2 establishes a theme that will run throughout the book: being customer focused. This perspective requires understanding customer needs and behavior and how these are evolving, recognizing how customers fit within different types of service operations, and managing encounters with customers in ways that create satisfaction.

In Chapter 3, we stress a second key theme: the need to assess the strengths and weaknesses of competing organizations in what are often dynamic market environments. Marketers should select strategies that position their firms either to take advantage of evident weaknesses among competitors or to avoid head-to-head competition with stronger organizations. We emphasize the importance of being selective in targeting specific types of customers who will value what the firm has to offer relative to competing alternatives and can also be served profitably. Hence, the goal should be to develop marketing mix strategies that match targeted customers' needs and purchasing potential to the capabilities of the firm.

Retaining desirable customers in the face of active competition requires an understanding of how relationships are created and nurtured. Historically, many service

BEST PRACTICE IN ACTION 1-1

SIX CUSTOMERCENTRIC FIRMS THAT THRIVE ON INNOVATION AND GROWTH

Progressive Casualty Insurance, with eight million customers, is the fourth-largest automobile insurance company in the United States. Facing changes in both the regulatory and competitive environment, Progressive restructured its business around new ways of doing business, focusing on speed, use of technology, and outstanding customer service. To expedite claims, Progressive offers 24-hour "Immediate Response" telephone service, supplemented in many areas by representatives who, traveling in "Immediate Response" vehicles, can come quickly to the scene of accidents. Another key innovation includes offering quotes that present not only Progressive rates for the customer in question but also those offered by up to three competing companies for the same risk profile. Known for its outstanding Web service, the company has repeatedly been awarded the title "best online insurance carrier."

Southwest Airlines is the most consistently profitable airline in America. From its original base in Texas, it has successfully positioned itself as a low-cost, no-frills carrier emphasizing short- and medium-haul routes across the United States. Underlying its success are punctual, frequent flights that offer excellent value for customers, an easy-to-use online reservations service, a low-cost operations strategy that runs counter to established industry traditions, and human resource policies that have created an extraordinarily loyal and hardworking group of employees. Airlines from around the world have studied Southwest's marketing, operations, and human resource strategies, but none has yet been able to achieve its finely tuned balance.

Intrawest Corporation has spread from its Canadian base in Vancouver, to become one of the largest operators of ski resorts in North America. Its properties include Whistler, British Columbia; Mammoth, California; Copper Mountain, Colorado; and Killington, Vermont. Intrawest's expertise includes a multistep strategy of enhancing the skiing experience, building an appealing resort community that will encourage people to stay longer, and expanding into year-round activities at each resort.

Aggreko describes itself as "the world's power rental leader." Headquartered in the United Kingdom, it rents mobile electricity generators and temperature control equipment from 70 depots in 20 countries. Large companies and government agencies dominate its customer base. Much of the firm's business comes from backup operations or special events—such as the Olympics—but it is also poised to respond rapidly to emergency situations, such as natural disasters that knock out normal power supplies. Speed, flexibility, reliability, and environmental sensitivity are among Aggreko's strengths.

eBay defines its mission as "to help people trade practically anything on earth." Founded in 1995, eBay has no physical presence other than its corporate offices in California, which customers never see. Instead, it uses the power of the Web to bring buyers and sellers together, on a regional, national, or even global basis, in a cyberspace auction format. Targeting individual customers—not businesses—the company enables people to offer and bid for items in more than 4,300 categories, including cars, antiques, toys, dolls, jewelry, sports memorabilia, books, pottery, glass, coins, stamps, and much more. Part of eBay's appeal is simply that it is the world's largest person-to-person trading site, offering more new items for sale every day and more potential buyers than any other auction site.

TLContact is one of the few dot.com start-ups to have survived and prospered. It creates secure, personal home pages on the Web for hospital patients, so that their families and friends can stay in touch during medical treatment and convalescence. The young founders got the idea when their first child was born with a serious heart defect and another family member created a Web site so that information about the baby's progress through successive operations could be followed without telephoning the parents or the hospital for details. TLC now has contracts with a growing number of hospitals in the United States and Canada and offers a Spanish-language version of the service in Mexico.

firms were transaction oriented rather than relationship oriented. In operations-oriented firms, one user was seen as good as another, so long as they paid. Today, the emphasis is on developing relationship marketing strategies that will enhance satisfaction among targeted customers and build their loyalty. To achieve this loyalty, savvy service firms know that they must develop a customer-centered understanding of service quality and ensure that everyone in the organization understands his or her role in meeting customer expectations.

The winners in today's highly competitive service markets make progress by continually rethinking the way they do business, looking for innovative ways to serve customers better, and taking advantage of new developments in technology. Consider the six firms profiled in Best Practice in Action 1-1, all leaders in a diverse mix of industries. We'll be meeting each of these companies again at different points in the book.

The marketing tools and strategies that we describe in subsequent chapters emphasize a customer focus and an orientation to competitive dynamics. However, we recognize explicitly that effective integration of marketing activities with those of operations and human resources requires that marketers work closely with their colleagues to ensure that service design and delivery achieve a balance—or even better, a synergy—between quality and productivity.

CONCLUSION

Why study services? Because modern economies are driven by service businesses. Services are responsible for the creation of a substantial majority of new jobs, both skilled and unskilled, around the world. The service sector includes a tremendous variety of industries, including many activities provided by public and nonprofit organizations. It accounts for more than half the economy in most developing countries and for two-thirds or more in many highly developed economies.

As we've shown in this chapter, services differ from manufacturing organizations in many important respects and require a distinctive approach to marketing and other management functions. As a result, managers who want their enterprises to succeed cannot continue to rely solely on tools and concepts developed in the manufacturing sector. However, important differences exist between services. Rather than focusing on broad distinctions between goods and services, it's more useful to identify categories of services and to study the marketing, operations, and human resource challenges faced within each of these groups.

The four-way classification scheme discussed in this chapter focuses on the implications for customers of different types of service *processes*. Some services, such as hairdressing and passenger transport, require direct physical contact with customers, whereas other services, such as education and entertainment, center on contact with people's mind. Some services such as cleaning and freight transport, involve processing of physical objects, whereas others, such as accounting and insurance, process information. As you can now appreciate, the operational processes that underlie the creation and delivery of any service have a major impact on marketing and human resource strategies.

The array of strategic tools available to service marketers tends to be broader than commonly found in the marketing of manufacturing products. In addition to making decisions on product elements, pricing, the place and time of service delivery, and promotional strategy, service marketers find themselves involved with service delivery issues relating to people, processes, and the physical environment. Collectively, we can describe these as the 7Ps of services marketing. In using these tools, managers need to be aware that they should be selective in choosing which types of customers to serve and that success requires a continuing focus on achieving customer satisfaction and loyalty.

Review Questions

1. Is it possible for an economy to be based entirely on services? Is it good for an economy to have a large service sector? Discuss.
2. What are the main reasons for the growing share of the service sector in all major economies of the world?
3. What is so distinctive about services marketing that it requires a special approach, set of concepts, and body of knowledge?
4. To what extent do you consider the marketing mix, which has been traditionally applied to the goods sector, appropriate for the services sector?
5. Review each of the different ways in which services can be classified. How would you explain the usefulness of each framework to managers?
6. Why is time so important in services?
7. Why do marketing, operations, and human resources have to be more closely linked in services than in manufacturing? Give examples.
8. In what ways does design of the service factory affect (a) customer satisfaction with the service, and (b) employee productivity?
9. What do you see as the major ethical issues facing those responsible for creating and delivering mental stimulus–processing services?

Application Exercises

1. Visit the Web sites of the following national statistical bureaus: United States Bureau of Economic Analysis (*www.bea.gov*), Statistics Canada (*www.statcan.ca*), British Office of National Statistics (*www.statistics.gov.uk*), and Singapore (*www.singstat.gov.sg*). In each instance, obtain data on the latest trends in services as (a) a percentage of gross domestic product, (b) the percentage of employment accounted for by services, (c) breakdowns of these two statistics by type of industry, and (d) service exports and imports.
2. Give examples of how, during the past 10 years, Internet and telecommunications technologies, such as interactive voice response systems (IVRs) and mobile commerce (m-commerce) have changed some of the services that you use.
3. Choose a service company with which you are familiar and show how each of the seven elements (7 Ps) of integrated service management applies.
4. Make a list of at least 12 services that you have used during the past month.
   a. Categorize them by type of process.
   b. In which instances could you have avoided visiting the service factory and instead obtained service at arm's length? Comment.
   c. How did other customers affect your own service experiences, either positively or negatively?
5. Visit the facilities of two competing service firms in the same industry, such as two retailers, restaurants, or hotels, that you believe have different approaches to service. Compare and contrast, using one or more of the frameworks in this chapter.

Endnotes

1. Organisation for Economic Co-operation and Development, *The Service Economy*. Paris: OECD, 2000.
2. For comparative data on Latin America in the mid-1990s, see *El Mundo de Trabajo en una Economia Integrada*. Washington, DC: The World Bank, 1996. For data on Asian nations, see *Key Indicators of Developing Asian and Pacific Countries*, Manila: Asian Development Bank, 2000; Jochen Wirtz, and Christopher H. Lovelock, and Abdul Kasim Sejjadul Islam, "Service Economy Asia: Macro Trends and Their Implications," *Singapore Nanyang Business Review* 1 (July-December 2002): 5–18.
3. Michael Peneder, Serguei Kaniovsky, and Bernhard Dachs, "What Follows Tertiarisation? Structural Change and the Rise of Knowledge-Based

Industries," *The Service Industries Journal* 23 (March 2003): 47–66.

4. U.S. Department of Commerce, *North American Industry Classification System—United States*. Washington, DC: National Technical Information Service PB 2002-101430, 2002.
5. Michael D. Johnson and Anders Gustafsson, *Competing in a Service Economy* (San Franciso: Jossey-Bass, 2003).
6. Michael E. Porter, "Strategy and the Internet," *Harvard Business Review* 79 (March 2001): 62–78.
7. Robert D. Hof, "The eBay Economy," *Business Week* (August 25, 2003): 124–128.
8. Kenneth K. Boyer, Roger Hallowell, and Aleda V. Roth, "E-services: Operating Strategy—A Case Study and a Method for Analyzing Operational Benefits," *Journal of Operations Management* 20 (2002): 175–188.
9. Timothy J. Mullaney and Jay Greene, "At Last the Web Hits 100 mph," *Business Week* (June 23, 2003): 80–81.
10. Leonard L. Berry, "Services Marketing is Different," *Business* (May-June, 1980).
11. Evert Gummesson, "Lip Service: A Neglected Area in Services Marketing," *Journal of Consumer Services* 1 (Summer 1987): 19–22 (citing an unknown source). For an extended list of definitions, see Christian Grönroos, *Service Management and Marketing, 2nd ed.* (New York: John Wiley & Sons, 2001), 26–27.
12. Christian Grönroos, op. cit.
13. G. Lynn Shostack, "Breaking Free from Product Marketing," *Journal of Marketing* (April 1977).
14. W. Earl Sasser, R. Paul Olsen and D. Daryl Wyckoff, *Management of Service Operations: Text, Cases, and Readings* (Boston: Allyn & Bacon, 1978).
15. Stephen J. Grove, Raymond P. Fisk, and Joby John "Service as Theater: Guidelines and Implications" in T.A. Schwartz and D. Iacobucci, *Handbook of Services Marketing and Management* (Thousand Oaks, CA: Sage Publications, 2000), 21–36; Richard Harris, Kim Harris, and Steve Baron, "Theatrical Service Experiences: Dramatic Script Development with Employees," *International Journal of Service Industry Management* 14, no. 2 (2003): 184–199.
16. Bonnie Farber Canziani, "Leveraging Customer Competency in Service Firms," *International Journal of Service Industry Management* 8, no. 1 (1997): 5–25.
17. Gary Knisely, "Greater Marketing Emphasis by Holiday Inns Breaks Mold," *Advertising Age* (January 15, 1979).
18. This section is based on Valarie A. Zeithaml, "How Consumer Evaluation Processes Differ Between Goods and Services," in J. A. Donnelly and W.R. George, *Marketing of Services* (Chicago: American Marketing Association, 1981), 186–190.
19. See, for example, Christopher H. Lovelock, "Classifying Services to Gain Strategic Marketing Insights," *Journal of Marketing 47* (Summer 1983): 9–20; Christian Grönroos, *Service Management and Marketing* (New York: Wiley, 2000), 49–50; John Bowen, "Development of a Taxonomy of Services to Gain Strategic Marketing Insights," *Journal of the Academy of Marketing Science* 18, (Winter 1990): 43–49; Rhian Silvestro, Lyn Fitzgerald, Robert Johnston, and Christopher Voss, "Towards a Classification of Service Processes," *International Journal of Service Industry Management* 3, no. 3 (1992): 62–75, Pratibha A. Dabholkar, "Technology-Based Service Delivery," in T.A. Schwartz, D.E. Bowen, and S.W. Brown, *Advances in Services Marketing and Management, Volume 3, 1994* (Greenwich, CT: JAI Press, 1994): 241–271; and Hans Kasper, Wouter De Vries, and Piet Van Helsdingen, "Classifying Services," Chapter 2 in *Services Marketing Management: An International Perspective* (Chichester, UK: John Wiley & Sons, 1999), 43–70.
20. These classifications are derived from Lovelock (1983). For an operations based discussion of service processes, see "Dealing with Inherent Variability: The Difference between Manufacturing and Service?" *International Journal of Production Management* 7, no. 4 (1987): 13–22.
21. Leyland Pitt, Pierre Berthon, and Jean-Paul Berthon, "Changing Channels: The Impact of the Internet on Distribution Strategy," *Business Horizons* (March-April, 1999): 19–28.
22. Leonard L. Berry, Kathleen Seiders, and Dhruv Grewal, "Understanding Service Convenience," *Journal of Marketing* 66 (July 2002): 1–17.
23. The 4Ps classification of marketing decision variables was created by E. Jerome McCarthy, *Basic Marketing: A Managerial Approach,* (Homewood, IL: Richard D. Irwin, Inc., 1960).
24. Adapted from Bernard H. Booms and Mary J. Bitner, "Marketing Strategies and Organization Structures for Service Firms," in J. H. Donnelly and W.R. George, *Marketing of Services* (Chicago: American Marketing Association, 1981), 47–51.
25. For a review of the literature on this topic, see Michael D. Hartline and O. C. Ferrell, "The Management of Customer Contact Service Employees," *Journal of Marketing* 60, no. 4 (October 1996): 52–70.
26. Rogelio Oliva and Robert L. Kallenberg, "Managing the Transition from Products to Services," *International Journal of Service Industry Management* 14, no. 2 (2003): 160–172.
27. Theodore Levitt, *Marketing for Business Growth* (New York, McGraw-Hill, 1974), 5.
28. Roland Rust, "What Is the Domain of Service Research?" (Editorial), *Journal of Service Research* 1 (November 1998): 107.
29. James L. Heskett, W. Earl Sasser, and Leonard Schlesinger, *The Value Profit Chain* (New York: The Free Press, 2003).
30. Siegmund Warburg, cited in a presentation by Derek Higgs, London, September 1997.

CHAPTER 2

Consumer Behavior in Service Encounters

All the world's a stage and all the men and women merely players; They have their exits and their entrances and one man in his time plays many parts.

—William Shakespeare

As You Like It

Understanding customer behavior lies at the heart of marketing. An important theme in this chapter is that high-contact encounters between customers and service organizations differ sharply from low-contact ones. Some services, such as restaurants, hospitals, and airlines, require customers to have active contact with the organization, including visits to its facilities and face-to-face interactions with employees. By contrast, customers of service industries such as insurance and cable TV companies, rarely, if ever, visit the supplier's offices; and need to contact an employee only when something goes wrong, in which case they most likely speak to someone by telephone or send a letter or e-mail.

Customers often find it difficult to evaluate services in advance of purchase, but they do form certain expectations. Once a customer has purchased a service, marketers need to examine usage behavior. How does the customer interact with service facilities, service personnel, and even other customers, especially in the case of high-contact services? Finally, of course, marketers are interested in whether the experience of receiving the service and its benefits has met the customer's expectations.

In this chapter, we analyze the nature of service consumption and consider how firms should manage encounters to create satisfied customers and desirable outcomes for the business itself. We show how the extent of customer contact affects the nature of the service encounter, shapes customer behavior, and can impact strategies for achieving productivity and quality improvements. We explore the following questions.

1. Where does the customer fit in a service operation?
2. What perceived risks do customers face in purchasing and using services?
3. How do customers form expectations and differentiate between desired and adequate service levels?
4. Why do people often have difficulty in evaluating the services that they use?
5. How does reducing or increasing the level of customer's contact with a service supplier affect the nature of their service experiences?
6. What insights can be gained from viewing service delivery as a form of theater?

CUSTOMERS INTERACT WITH SERVICE OPERATIONS

Except with custom-designed products, customers rarely get involved in the production of manufactured goods other than removing them from packaging, perhaps doing some assembly, and getting them ready for use. However, one of the differentiating characteristics of services is the extent to which customers participate in the process of service creation and delivery. The challenge for service marketers is to understand what that experience is like for customers.

Flowcharting Customer Involvement in Service Processes

The clearest way to describe a service process is often to create a flowchart that presents the different steps visually and in sequence. Marketers find flowcharting particularly useful for defining the point(s) in the process at which the customer uses the core service and identifying the supplementary services that make up the overall service package. Using this approach enables us to see how different the customer's involvement with the service organization can be for each of the four categories of services introduced in Chapter 1: people processing, possession processing, mental stimulus processing, and information processing. Let's take one example of each category—staying in a motel, getting a DVD player repaired, obtaining a weather forecast, and purchasing health insurance. Figure 2-1 displays a simple flowchart that demonstrates what's involved in each of four scenarios. Imagine that you are the customer in each instance, and think about the extent and nature of your involvement in the service delivery process.

- *Stay at a motel (people processing).* It's late evening. You're driving on a long trip and are getting tired. You see a motel with a vacancy sign with the price displayed and decide it is time to stop for the night. You park in the lot, noting that the grounds are clean and that the buildings seem freshly painted. You enter the reception area, where a friendly clerk checks you in and gives you the key to your room. You walk with your bag across the forecourt to the room and let yourself in. After undressing and using the bathroom, you go to bed. Following a good night's sleep, you rise the next morning, shower, dress, and pack and then walk to the lobby, where you take advantage of the free coffee and donuts, return your key to a different clerk, pay, and drive away.
- *Repair a DVD player (possession processing).* When you use your DVD player, the picture quality on the TV screen is poor. Fed up with the situation, you search the Yellow Pages to find an appliance repair store in your area. At the store, the technician in the front office checks your device and declares that it needs to be adjusted and cleaned. The estimated price seems realistic, so you agree to the work and are told that the player will be ready in three days. The technician disappears into the back office with your machine, and you leave the store. On the appointed day, you return to pick up the product and pay. Back home, you plug in the machine, insert a DVD, and find that the picture is now much improved.
- *Weather forecast (mental stimulus processing).* You want to arrange a picnic trip to the lake this weekend, three days from now, but one of your friends says that she has heard that there is the possibility of a big storm. Back home that evening, you check the long-range weather forecast on TV. The meteorologist shows animated charts indicating the probable path of the storm over the next 72 hours and declares that the latest National Weather Service computer projections suggest that the storm is likely to pass well to the south of your area. Armed with this information, you call your friends to tell them that the picnic is on.

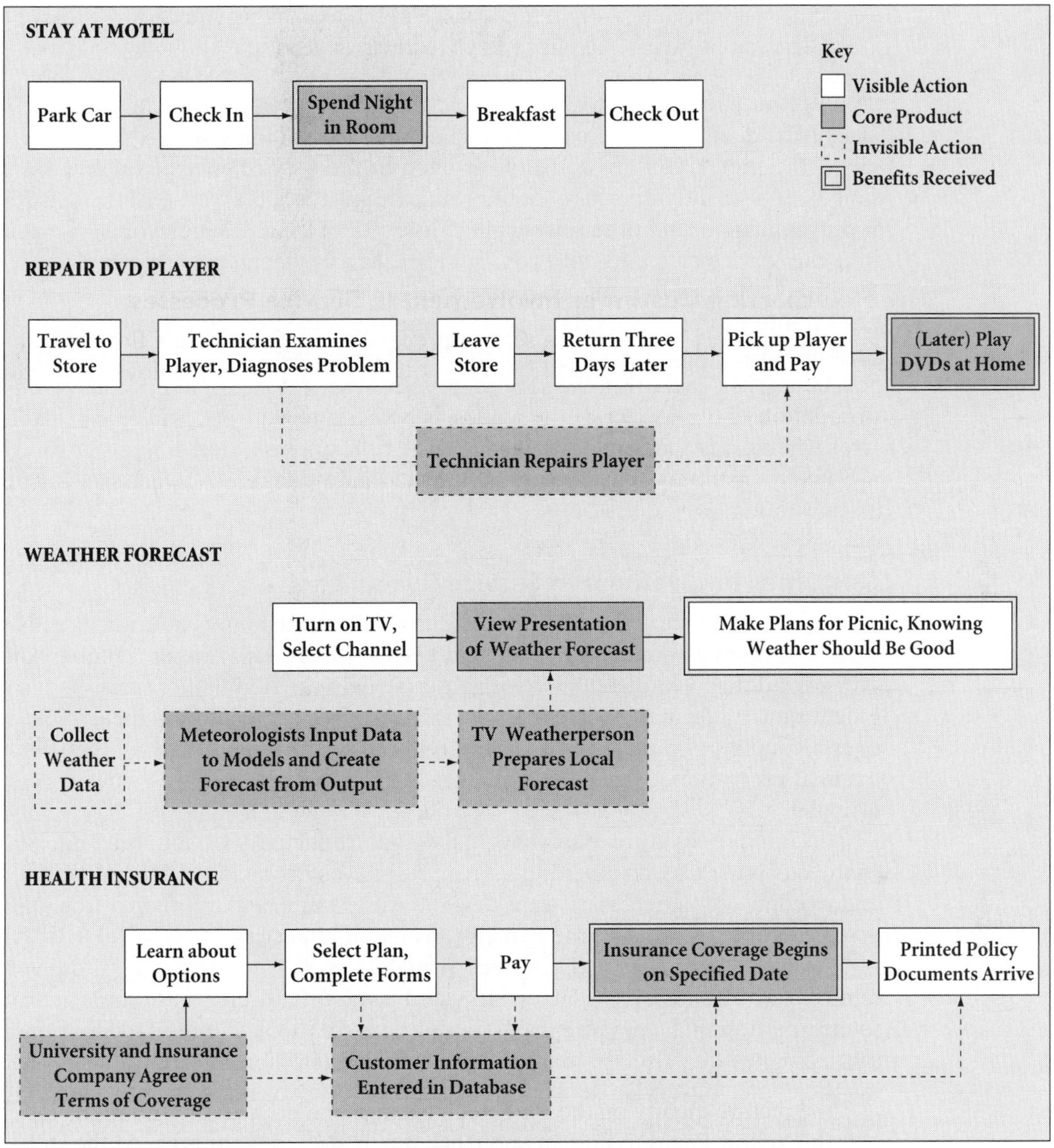

FIGURE 2-1 Simple Flowcharts for Delivery of Various Types of Services

- *Health insurance (information processing).* Your university mails you a package of information before the beginning of the new semester. This package includes a student health service brochure describing the various health insurance options available to students. Although you consider yourself very healthy except for seasonal allergies, you remember the unfortunate experience of a friend who recently incurred heavy hospital bills for treatment of a badly fractured ankle. Uninsured, he was forced to liquidate his modest savings to pay the bills. Thus, at the time of registration, you select an option that will cover the cost of hospital treatment, as well as visits to the student health center. You fill in a printed form that includes some standard questions about your medical history and then sign it. The cost of the insurance is added to your term bill. Subsequently, you receive written confirmation of your coverage in the mail. Now you no longer have to worry about the risk of unexpected medical expenses.

As you can see from these simple flowcharts, your role as a customer varies sharply from one process to another. The first two examples involve physical processes. At the motel, you are actively involved in the service, which is delivered in real time over a period of perhaps eight or nine hours. For a fee, you rent the use of a bedroom, bathroom, and other physical facilities for the night. When you leave, you can't take the service elements with you, but if the bed had been uncomfortable, you might feel tired and sore the following day. Your role at the appliance repair store, however, is limited to briefly explaining the symptoms, leaving the machine there, and returning several days later to pick it up. You have to trust the technician's competence and honesty in executing the service in your absence, as you are not involved in the production of the service. If the work has been done well, you will enjoy the benefits later when using the repaired machine. The other two services—weather forecasting and health insurance—involve intangible actions and a relatively passive role for you as a customer.

Customer Involvement in Service Encounters

A service encounter is a period of time during which customers interact directly with a service.[1] Although some service encounters—such as a taxi ride or a simple haircut—are very brief and consist of just a few discrete delivery steps, others may extend over a longer time frame and involve multiple steps. A leisurely restaurant meal might stretch over a couple of hours, whereas a visit to a theme park might last all day. If you had made a reservation, that first step might have taken place days or even weeks prior to arrival.

It's difficult to improve service quality and productivity without full understanding of the customer's involvement in a given service environment. Speeding up processes and weeding out unnecessary steps to avoid wasted time and effort are often important ways for a firm to improve the perceived value of its service.

As they interact with the service firm—its employees, impersonal delivery systems (e.g., Web sites), physical facilities, and even other users—customers are exposed to information that can influence both their expectations and their evaluations of the service. A key question for managers is whether customers' expectations change during the course of service delivery in light of the perceived quality of sequential steps in the process. Ideally, service firms should try to provide consistently high performance at each step in service delivery. But in reality, many service performances are inconsistent.

Arguing that it's more important to end on a strong note than to begin on one,[2] a principle that applies to low-contact services as well as to high-contact ones, Richard Chase and Sriram Dasu note that many commercial Web sites are designed with attractive home pages that create high expectations but become progressively less appealing and even problematic to use as customers move toward conclusion of a purchase. Research Insights 2-1 provides some additional food for thought.

Types of Service Encounters

As the level of customer contact with the service operation increases, there are likely to be more and longer service encounters. In Figure 2-2, we've grouped services into three levels of customer contact, representing the extent of interaction with service personnel, physical service elements, or both. Note that traditional retail banking, person-to-person telephone banking, and Internet banking are all in different locations on the chart.

RESEARCH INSIGHTS 2-1

LEARNING FROM LABORATORY STUDIES OF SERVICE ENCOUNTERS

A laboratory study simulates real-world events in a controlled setting. One such study explored how respondents judged hypothetical service encounters in three service categories—a weekend car rental, an international flight, and a retail purchase.[1] Within each category, one of three scenarios was presented to participants. In the first, the initial service events were performed well, the core service adequately, and the concluding steps poorly, thus creating a deteriorating trend; in the second, the situation was reversed, to create an improving trend; and in the third, a consistently adequate service was delivered from start to finish. The findings showed that a weak start that built toward a strong finish received more favorable judgments than did the other scenarios. A conclusion to be drawn from this research is that managers who are not immediately able to raise all elements of the service encounter should begin by focusing on improving the concluding events in the process rather than the opening steps.

Another laboratory study simulated a visit to a restaurant.[2] Respondents were presented with two scenarios in which they were going out to eat with a group of friends and were given information at certain key steps during the service encounter. The findings showed that respondents continuously updated their expectations during service delivery and that these evolving expectations had a larger effect on their perceptions of service quality than did perceived service performance. A key managerial insight from this study is that it's very important for managers to shape and control customers' expectations as service delivery proceeds.

[1]David E. Hansen and Peter J. Danaher, "Inconsistent Performance During the Service Encounter," *Journal of Service Research* 1 (February 1999): 227–235.

[2]Lawrence O. Hamer, Ben Shaw-Ching Liu, and D. Sudharshan, "The Effects of Intraencounter Changes in Expectations on Perceived Service Quality Models," *Journal of Service Research* 1 (February 1999): 275–289.

High-contact Services This group of services involves personal visits by customers to the service facility. Customers are actively involved with the service organization and its personnel during service delivery. All people-processing services, other than those delivered at home, are high contact. Examples include hairdressing, lodging, or medical services. Services from the other three process-based categories may also involve high levels of customer contact when, for reasons of tradition, preference, or lack of other alternatives, customers go to the service site and remain there until service delivery is completed.

Low-contact Services At the opposite end of the spectrum are services that involve little, if any, physical contact between customers and service providers. Instead, contact takes place at arm's length through the medium of physical distribution channels—such as mail or courier service or electronic channels such as telephone and Internet. Many high-contact and medium-contact services are being transformed into low-contact services as customers engage in home shopping, conduct their insurance and banking transactions by telephone, or research and purchase products through the Internet.[3]

Service Encounters as "Moments of Truth"

Richard Normann borrowed the metaphor *"moment of truth"* from bullfighting to show the importance of contact points with customers. Normann writes:

> [W]e could say that the perceived quality is realized at the moment of truth, when the service provider and the service customer confront one another in the arena. At that moment they are very much on their own. . . . It is the skill,

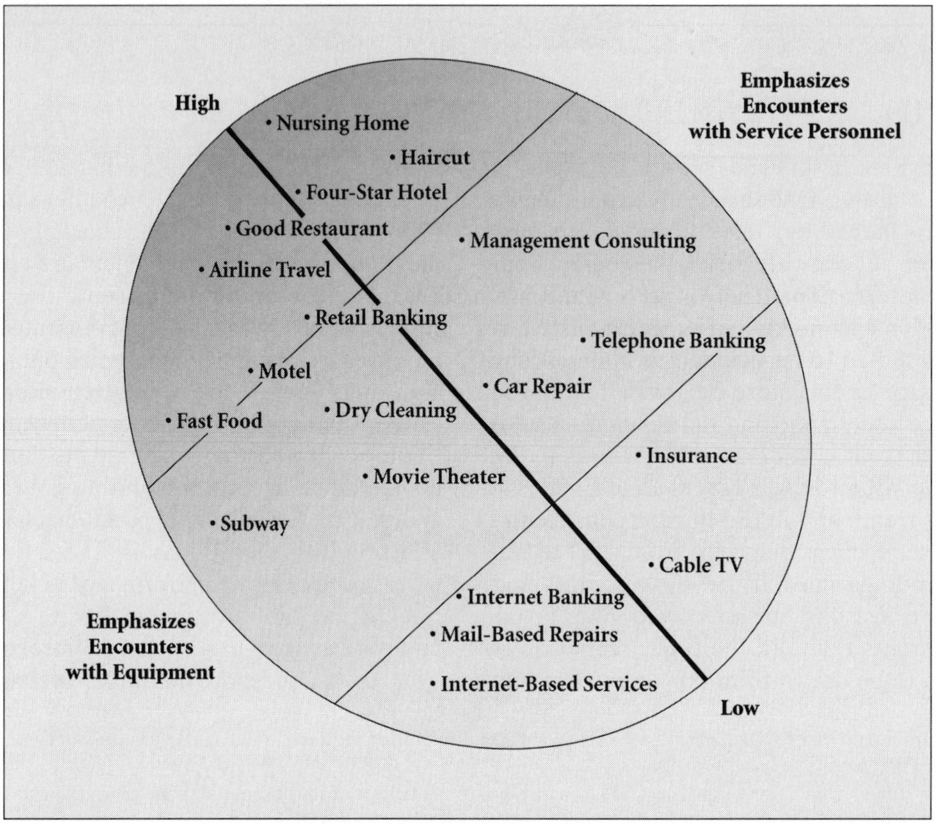

FIGURE 2-2 Levels of Customer Contact with Service Organizations

> the motivation, and the tools employed by the firm's representative and the expectations and behavior of the client which together will create the service delivery process.[4]

In bullfighting, what is at stake is the life of the bull or the matador or possibly both. The moment of truth is the instant at which the matador deftly slays the bull with his sword—hardly a very comfortable analogy for a service organization intent on building long-term relationships with its customers! Normann's point, of course, is that it's the life of the relationship that is at stake. Contrary to bullfighting, the goal of relationship marketing—which we explore in depth in Chapter 12—is to prevent one unfortunate (mis)encounter from destroying what is already, or has the potential to become, a mutually valued, long-term relationship.

Jan Carlzon, the former chief executive of Scandinavian Airlines System (SAS), used the "moment-of-truth" metaphor as a reference point for transforming SAS from an operations-driven business into a customer-driven airline. Carlzon made the following comments about his airline:

> Last year, each of our 10 million customers came into contact with approximately five SAS employees, and this contact lasted an average of 15 seconds each time. Thus, SAS is "created" 50 million times a year, 15 seconds at a time. These 50 million "moments of truth" are the moments that ultimately determine whether SAS will succeed or fail as a company. They are the moments when we must prove to our customers that SAS is their best alternative.[5]

THE PURCHASE PROCESS FOR SERVICES INVOLVES MULTIPLE STEPS

When customers decide to buy a service to meet an unfilled need, they go through what is often a complex purchase process. This process has three identifiable stages: the prepurchase stage, the service encounter stage, and the postpurchase stage. Each stage contains two or more steps (see Figure 2-3).

Prepurchase Stage

The decision to buy and use a service is made in the prepurchase stage. Individual needs and expectations are very important here because they influence what alternatives customers will consider. If the purchase is routine and relatively low risk, customers may move quickly to selecting and using a specific service provider. But when

FIGURE 2-3 The Purchase Process for Services

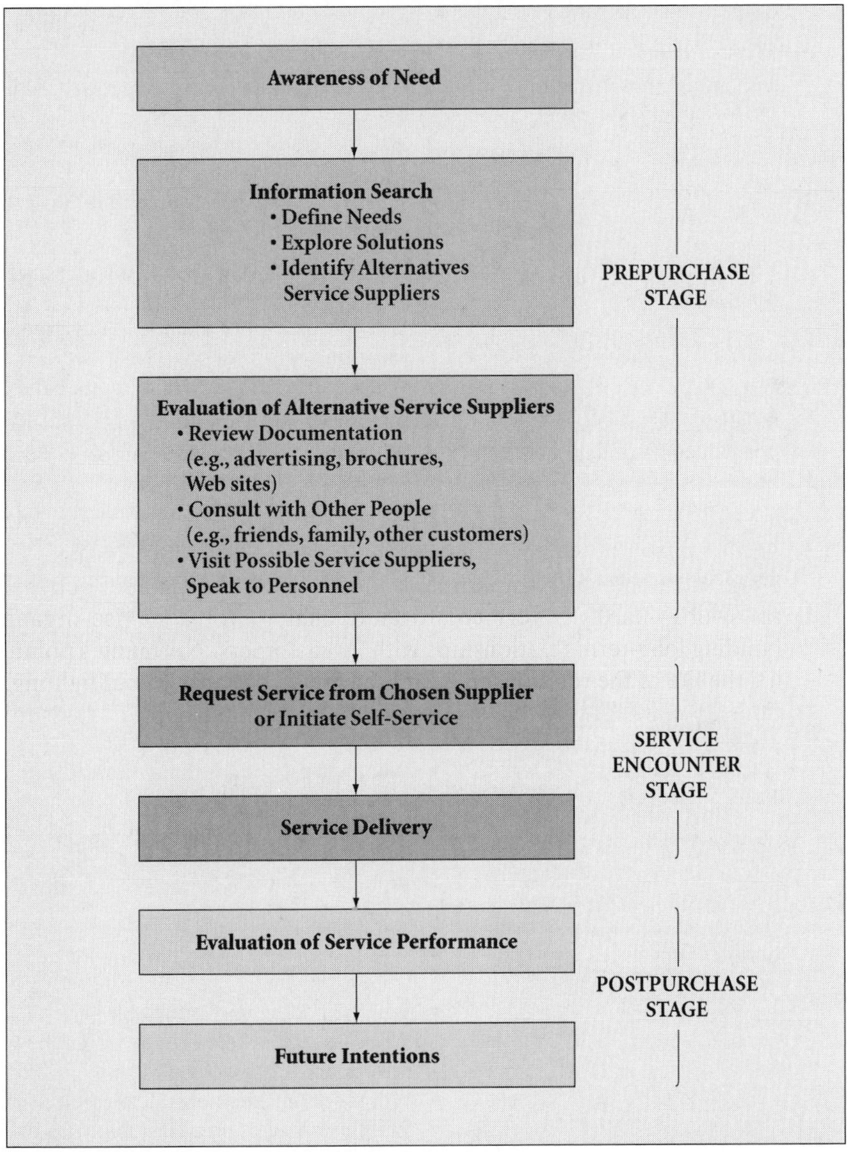

more is at stake or if a service is about to be used for the first time, customers may conduct an intensive information search. (Contrast how you approached the process of applying to college versus buying a pizza!) The next step is to identify potential suppliers and then weigh the benefits and risks of each option before making a final decision.

This element of perceived risk is especially relevant for services that are high in experience or credence attributes and thus difficult to evaluate prior to purchase and consumption. First-time users are especially likely to face greater uncertainty. Risk perceptions reflect customers' judgments of the probability of a negative outcome. The worse the possible outcome and the more likely it is to occur, the higher the perception of risk. Various types of perceived risks are outlined in Table 2-1.

When they feel uncomfortable with risks, customers can use a variety of methods to reduce them during the prepurchase stage. In fact, you've probably tried some of the following risk-reduction strategies yourself before deciding to purchase a service:

TABLE 2-1 Perceived Risks in Purchasing and Using Services

Type of Risk	*Examples of Customer Concerns*
Functional (unsatisfactory performance outcomes)	• Will this training course give me the skill I need to get a better job? • Will this credit card be accepted wherever and whenever I want to make a purchase? • Will the dry cleaner be able to remove the stains from this jacket?
Financial (monetary loss, unexpected costs)	• Will I lose money if I make the investment recommended by my stockbroker? • Will I incur a lot of unanticipated expenses if I go on this vacation? • Will repairing my car cost more than the original estimate?
Temporal (wasting time, consequences of delays)	• Will I have to wait in line before entering the exhibition? • Will service at this restaurant be so slow that I will be late for my afternoon meeting? • Will the renovations to our bathroom be completed before our friends come to stay with us?
Physical (personal injury or damage to possessions)	• Will I get hurt if I go skiing at this resort? • Will the contents of this package get damaged in the mail? • Will I fall sick if I travel abroad on vacation?
Psychological (personal fears and emotions)	• How can I be sure that this aircraft won't crash? • Will the consultant make me feel stupid? • Will the doctor's diagnosis upset me?
Social (how others think and react)	• What will my friends think of me if they learn that I stayed at this cheap motel? • Will my relatives approve of the restaurant I have chosen for the family reunion dinner? • Will my business colleagues disapprove of my selection of an unknown law firm?
Sensory (unwanted impacts on any of the five senses)	• Will I get a view of the parking lot rather than the beach from my room? • Will the bed be uncomfortable? • Will I be kept awake by noise from the guests in the room next door? • Will my room smell of stale cigarette smoke? • Will the coffee at breakfast taste disgusting?

- Seeking information from respected personal sources (family, friends, peers)
- Relying on a firm that has a good reputation
- Looking for guarantees and warranties
- Visiting service facilities or trying aspects of the service before purchasing
- Asking knowledgeable employees about competing services
- Examining tangible cues or other physical evidence
- Using the Web to compare service offerings

What can service suppliers do to reduce perceived risk among their customers? In addition to offering guarantees and encouraging prospective customers to visit their facilities, where feasible, it's important to listen to customers and determine their needs and concerns before attempting to recommend a particular solution. It's important to educate customers about the features of a particular service, describe the types of users who can most benefit from it, and offer advice on how to obtain the best results.

Service Encounter Stage

After making a purchase decision, customers experience additional contacts with their chosen service provider. The service encounter stage often begins with submitting an application, requesting a reservation, or placing an order. Contacts may take the form of personal exchanges between customers and service employees or impersonal interactions with machines or computers. In high-contact services, such as restaurants, health care, hotels, and public transportation, customers may become actively involved in one or more service processes. Often, these customers experience a variety of elements during service delivery, each of which may provide clues to service quality.

Postpurchase Stage

During the postpurchase stage, customers continue a process they began in the service encounter stage: evaluating service quality and their satisfaction/dissatisfaction with the service experience. The outcome of this process will affect their future intentions, such as whether to remain loyal to the provider that delivered service and whether to pass on positive or negative recommendations to family members and other associates.

Customers evaluate service quality by comparing what they expected with what they perceive they received from a particular supplier. If their expectations are met or exceeded, customers believe that they have received a quality service provided that the price/quality relationship is acceptable and other situational and personal factors are positive, customers are likely to be satisfied and are therefore more likely to make repeat purchases and remain loyal to that supplier. However, if the service experience does not meet their expectations, customers may complain about poor service quality, suffer in silence, or switch providers in the future.[6]

CUSTOMERS HAVE NEEDS AND EXPECTATIONS

Customers buy goods and services to meet specific needs. Needs are often deeply rooted in people's unconscious minds and may concern long-term existence and identity issues. When people feel a need, they are motivated to take action to fulfill it. In many instances, purchase of a good or service may be seen as offering the best solution to meeting a particular need. Subsequently, consumers may compare what they received against what they expected, especially if it cost them money, time, or effort that could have been devoted to obtaining an alternative solution.

In developed economies, many consumers have most of the physical goods they want and are turning to services to fill new or still unmet needs. Increased spending on more elaborate vacations, sports, entertainment, restaurant meals, and other service experiences are assuming greater priority, even at the expense of spending slightly less on physical goods.

According to Daniel Bethamy of American Express, consumers want "memorable experiences, not gadgets."[7] This shift in consumer behavior and attitudes provides opportunities for those service companies that understand and meet changing needs, continuing to adapt their offerings over time as people's needs evolve. For example, some astute service providers have capitalized on the increased interest in extreme sports by offering such services as guided mountain climbs, paragliding, white-water rafting trips, and mountain biking adventures. The notion of service experiences also extends to business and industrial situations; consider the example of modern trade shows, where exhibitors, including manufacturers, set out to engage the customer's interest through interactive presentations and even entertainment.[8]

How Expectations Are Formed

Customers' expectations about what constitutes good service vary from one business to another. For example, although accounting and veterinary surgery are both professional services, the experience of meeting an accountant to talk about your tax returns tends to be very different from visiting a vet to get treatment for your sick pet. Expectations are also likely to vary in relation to differently positioned service providers in the same industry. Travelers might expect no-frills service for a short domestic flight on a discount carrier but would undoubtedly be very dissatisfied with that same level of service, even in economy class, on a full-service airline flying from Los Angeles to Sydney or from Toronto to Paris. Consequently, it's very important for marketers to understand customer expectations of their own firm's service offerings, especially as they relate to performance on specific product elements.

When individual customers or corporate purchasing department employees evaluate the quality of a service, they may be judging it against an internal standard that existed prior to the service experience.[9] Perceived service quality results from customers' comparing the service they perceive they have received against what they expected to receive. People's expectations about services tend to be strongly influenced by their own prior experience as customers with a particular service provider, with competing services in the same industry, or with related services in different industries. If they have no relevant prior experience, customers may base their prepurchase expectations on word-of-mouth comments, news stories, or the firm's own marketing efforts.

Expectations change over time, influenced by both supplier-controlled factors, such as advertising, pricing, new technologies, and service innovation, as well as social trends, advocacy by consumer organizations, and increased access to information through the media and the Internet. For instance, health care consumers are now better informed and often seek a more participative role in decisions relating to medical treatment. Service Perspectives 2-1 describes a new assertiveness among parents of children with serious illnesses.

The Components of Customer Expectations

Customer expectations embrace several elements, including desired service, adequate service, predicted service, and a zone of tolerance that falls between the desired and

SERVICE PERSPECTIVES 2-1

PARENTS SEEK INVOLVEMENT IN MEDICAL DECISIONS AFFECTING THEIR CHILDREN

Many parents want to participate actively in decisions relating to their children's medical treatment. Thanks in part to in-depth media coverage of medical advances and health-related issues, as well as the educational efforts of consumer advocates, parents are better informed and more assertive than in previous generations, no longer willing simply to accept the recommendations of medical specialists. In particular, parents whose child has been born with congenital defects or has developed a life-threatening illness are often willing to invest immense amounts of time and energy to learn everything they can about their child's condition. Some have even founded nonprofit organizations centered on a specific disease to bring together other families facing the same problems and to help raise money for research and treatment.

The Internet has made it much easier to access health care information and research findings. A study by the Texas-based Heart Center of 160 parents who had Internet access and children with cardiac problems found that 58 percent obtained information related to their child's diagnosis. Four out of five users searching for cardiology-related information stated that locating the information was easy; of those, half could name a favorite cardiology Web site. Almost all felt that the information was helpful in further understanding their child's condition. The study reported that six parents even created interactive personal Web sites specifically related to their child's congenital heart defect.[1]

Commenting on the phenomenon of highly informed parents, Norman J. Siegel, M.D., former chair of pediatrics at Yale New Haven Children's Hospital, observed:

> It's a different practice today. The old days of "trust me, I'm going to take care of this" are completely gone. I see many patients who come in carrying a folder with printouts from the Internet and they want to know why Dr. So-and-So wrote this. They go to chat rooms, too. They want to know about the disease process if it's chronic. Some parents are almost as well informed as a young medical student or house officer.[2]

Dr. Siegel said that he welcomed the trend and enjoyed the discussions but admitted that some physicians found it difficult to adapt.

[1]C. M. Ikemba et al., "Internet Use in Families with Children Requiring Cardiac Surgery for Congenital Heart Disease," *Pediatrics* 109, no. 3 (2002): 419–422.

[2]Christopher Lovelock and Jeff Gregory, "Yale New Haven Children's Hospital," case from Yale School of Management, 2003.

adequate service levels.[10] The model shown in Figure 2-4 shows how expectations for desired service and adequate service are formed.

Desired and Adequate Service Levels The type of service customers hope to receive is termed *desired service.* It is a "wished-for" level: a combination of what customers believe can and should be delivered in the context of their personal needs. However, most customers are realistic and understand that companies can't always deliver the desired level of service; hence, they also have a threshold level of expectations, termed *adequate service*, which is defined as the minimum level of service customers will accept without being dissatisfied. Among the factors that set this expectation are situational factors affecting service performance and the level of service that might be anticipated from alternative suppliers. The levels of both desired and adequate service expectations may reflect explicit and implicit promises by the provider, word-of-mouth comments, and the customer's past experience, if any, with this organization.[11]

FIGURE 2-4 Factors Influencing Customer Expectations of Service

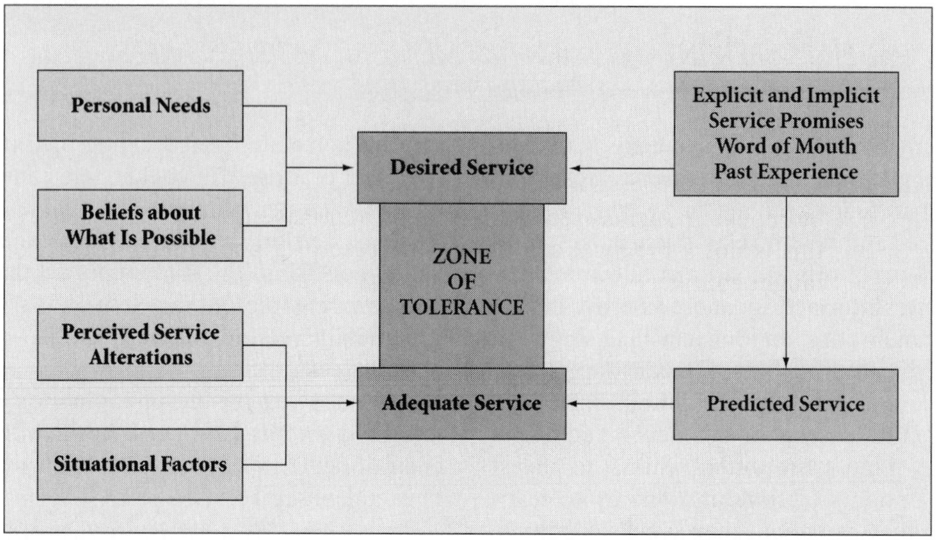

Source: Adapted from Valarie A. Zeithaml, Leonard A. Berry, and A. Parasuraman, "The Nature and Determinants of Customer Expectations of Service," *Journal of the Academy of Marketing Science* 21, no. 1 (1993): 1–12.

Predicted Service Level The level of service that customers anticipate receiving is known as *predicted service*, which directly affects how they define "adequate service" on that occasion. If good service is predicted, the adequate level will be higher than if poorer service is predicted. Customer predictions of service may be situation specific. From past experience, for example, customers visiting a museum on a summer day may expect to see larger crowds if the weather is poor than if the sun is shining. So a 10-minute wait to buy tickets on a cool, rainy day in summer might not fall below their adequate service level.

Zone of Tolerance The inherent nature of services makes consistent service delivery difficult across employees in the same company and even by the same service employee from one day to another. The extent to which customers are willing to accept this variation is called the *zone of tolerance* (refer to Figure 2-4). A performance that falls below the adequate service level will cause frustration and dissatisfaction, whereas one that exceeds the desired service level will both please and surprise customers. Another way of looking at the zone of tolerance is to think of it as the range of service within which customers don't pay explicit attention to service performance.[12] When service falls outside this range, customers will react either positively or negatively.

The zone of tolerance can increase or decrease for individual customers, depending on such factors as competition, price, or importance of specific service attributes. These factors most often affect adequate service levels, which may move up or down in response to situational factors, whereas desired service levels tend to move up very slowly in response to accumulated customer experiences. Consider a small-business owner who needs some advice from her accountant. Her ideal level of professional service may be a thoughtful response by the following day. But if she makes the request at the time of year when all accountants are busy preparing corporate and individual tax returns, she will probably know from experience not to expect a fast response. Although her ideal service level probably won't change, her zone of tolerance for response time may be much broader because she has a lower adequate service threshold.

CUSTOMERS MAY FIND IT DIFFICULT TO EVALUATE SERVICES

Service performances, especially those that contain few tangible clues, can be difficult for consumers to evaluate, both in advance of purchase and even afterward. As a result, there is a greater risk of making a purchase that proves to be disappointing. A customer who buys a physical good that proves unsatisfactory can usually return or replace it, although this action may require extra effort on the customer's part. These options are not as readily available with services. Although some services can be repeated, such as recleaning clothes that have not been satisfactorily laundered, this is not a practical solution in the case of a poorly performed play or a badly taught course.

Product Attributes Affecting Ease of Evaluation

Product attributes can be divided into search, experience, and credence properties.[13] All products can be placed on a continuum ranging from "easy to evaluate" to "difficult to evaluate," depending on whether they are high in search attributes, experience attributes, or credence attributes. As shown in Figure 2-5, most physical goods are located toward the left of the spectrum because they are high in search attributes, whereas most services tend to be located from the center to the right of the continuum.

Search Attributes Physical goods tend to emphasize those attributes that allow customers to evaluate a product before purchasing it. Style, color, texture, taste, and sound are features that allow prospective consumers to try out, taste test, or "test drive" the product prior to purchase. These tangible attributes help customers understand and evaluate what they will get in exchange for their money and reduces the sense of uncertainty or risk associated with the purchase occasion. Clothing, furniture, cars, electronic equipment, and foods are goods high in search attributes.

FIGURE 2-5 How Product Characteristics Affect Ease of Evaluation

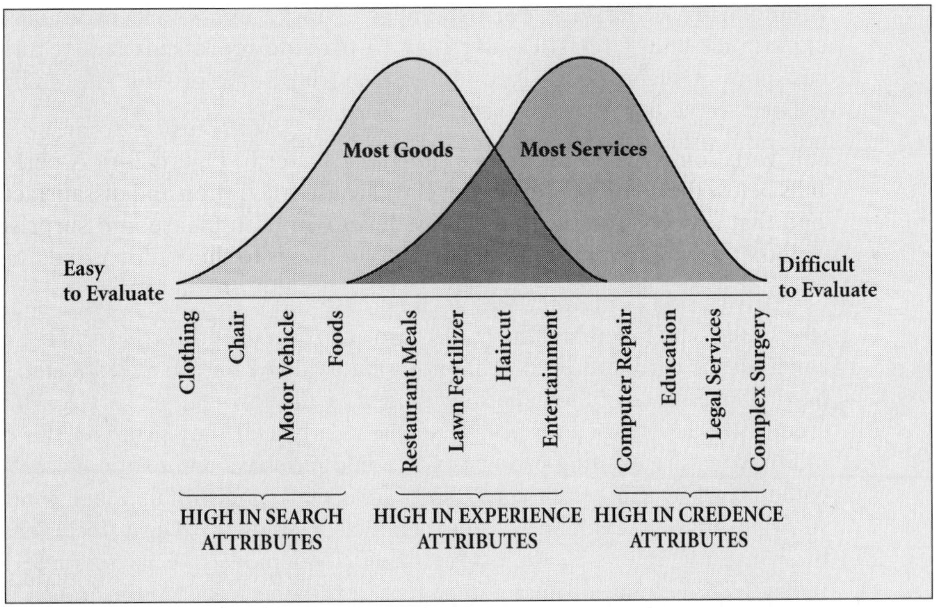

Source: Adapted from Valarie A. Zeithaml, "How Consumer Evaluation Processes Differ between Goods and Services," in J. H. Donnelly and W. R. George, *Marketing of Services* (Chicago: American Marketing Association, 1981).

Experience Attributes When attributes can't be evaluated prior to purchase, customers must experience the service to know what they are getting. Holidays, live entertainment performances, sporting events, and restaurants fall into this category. Although they can examine brochures, scroll through Web sites describing the holiday destination, view travel films, or read reviews by travel experts, people can't evaluate or feel the dramatic beauty associated with hiking in the Canadian Rockies or the magic of scuba diving in the Caribbean until they experience these activities. Nor can customers always rely on information from friends, family, or other personal sources when evaluating these and similar services, because different people may interpret or respond to the same stimuli in different ways. Think about your own experiences in following up on recommendations from friends to see a particular film. Although you probably walked into the theater with high expectations, you may have felt disappointed after viewing the film if you didn't like it as much as your friends did.

Credence Attributes Product characteristics that customers find impossible to evaluate confidently even after purchase and consumption are known as credence attributes because the customer is forced to trust that certain benefits have been delivered, even though it may be difficult to document them. For example, patients can't usually evaluate how well their dentists have performed complex dental procedures.

Strategic Responses to Difficulties in Evaluating Services

Many services tend to be high in experience and credence attributes because the performances are transitory, many intangible elements are involved, and the variability of inputs and outputs often leads to quality control problems. These characteristics present special challenges for service marketers, requiring them to find ways to reassure customers and reduce the perceived risks associated with buying and using services whose performance and value can't easily be predicted and may be difficult to ascertain even after consumption.

Intangibility of Service Performances Marketers whose products are high in experience characteristics often try to provide more search attributes for their customers. One approach is to offer a free trial. Some providers of online computer services have adopted this strategy. For example, AOL (America Online) offers potential users a free software diskette and the chance to try its services without charge for a certain number of hours. This reduces customers' concerns about entering into a paid contract without first being able to test the service. AOL hopes that consumers will be "hooked" on its Web services by the end of the free-trial period.

Advertising is another way to help customers visualize service benefits. For instance, the only tangible thing credit card customers get directly from the company is a small plastic card, followed at monthly intervals by an account statement. But that's hardly the essence of the benefits provided by this low-contact service. Think about the credit card advertisements you've seen recently. Did they promote the card itself, or did they feature exciting products you could purchase and exotic places to which you could travel by using your card? Such advertisements stimulate consumer interest by showing physical evidence of the benefits of credit card use. Insurance companies often use metaphors in their advertising. To demonstrate its size and fundamental strengths in helping protect companies from large risks, the insurance and financial firm XL Capital has portrayed its logo as a giant obelisk in Monument Valley and other dramatic settings (Figure 2-6).

FIGURE 2-6 XL Capital Promotes Its Fundamental Strengths in Insuring Large Risks

Providers of services that are high in credence characteristics have an even greater challenge. Their benefits may be so intangible that customers can't evaluate the quality of what they've received even after the service has been purchased and consumed. In this case, marketers often try to provide tangible cues to customers about their services.

Doctors, architects, lawyers, and other professionals often display their degrees and other certifications for the same reason: they want customers to "see" the credentials that qualify them to provide expert service. Many professional firms have developed Web sites to inform prospective clients about their services, highlight their expertise, and even showcase successful past engagements. Savvy organizations that have multiple points of contact with customers engage in *evidence management,* an organized and explicit approach to presenting customers with coherent evidence of their abilities in the form of clues emitted by their employees' dress and behavior, and the appearance of furnishings, equipment, and facilities.[14]

Variability and Quality Control Problems Products that are highest in search attributes are most often physical goods that are manufactured in a factory with no customer involvement and then purchased and consumed. Quality is much easier to control in this situation, as the elements of production can be more closely monitored and failures spotted before the product reaches the customer. In fact, some manufacturers, such as Motorola, claim to be able to guarantee product quality at the so-called Six Sigma level, or 99.999 percent! However, quality control for services that fall in the experience and credence ranges is complicated by customer involvement in production.

Evaluations of such services may be affected by customers' interactions with the physical setting of the business, employees, and even other customers. For example, your experience of a haircut may combine your impression of the hair salon, how well you can describe what you want to the stylist, the stylist's ability to understand and do what you've requested, and the appearance of the other customers and employees in the salon. Stylists note that it's difficult for them to do a good job if customers are uncooperative.

Many credence services have few tangible characteristics and rely on the expertise of a professional service provider to provide a quality offering. In this case, providers must be able to interact with customers effectively to produce a satisfactory product. Problems can occur when this interaction doesn't produce an outcome that meets customers' expectations, even though the service provider may not be at fault.

How Confirmation or Disconfirmation of Expectations Relate to Satisfaction

The terms *quality* and *satisfaction* are sometimes used interchangeably. However, some researchers believe that perceived service quality is but one component of customer satisfaction, which also reflects price/quality tradeoffs, as well as personal and situational factors.[15]

Satisfaction can be defined as an attitudelike judgment following a purchase act or a series of consumer product interactions.[16] Most studies are based on the theory that the confirmation/disconfirmation of preconsumption expectations is the essential determinant of satisfaction.[17] This means that customers have certain service standards in mind (their expectations) prior to consumption, observe service performance and compare it to their standards, and then form satisfaction judgments based on this comparison. The resulting judgment is labeled *negative disconfirmation* if the service is worse than expected, *positive disconfirmation* if better than expected, and simple *confirmation* if as expected.[18] When there is substantial positive disconfirmation, along with pleasure and an element of surprise, customers are likely to be delighted.

The results of a research project done by Richard Oliver, Roland Rust, and Sajeev Varki suggest that delight is a function of three components: unexpectedly high levels of performance, arousal (e.g., surprise, excitement), and positive affect (e.g., pleasure, joy, or happiness).[19] Satisfaction is a function of positively disconfirmed expectations (better than expected) and positive affect. These researchers ask: "If delight is a function of surprisingly unexpected pleasure, is it possible for delight to be manifest in truly mundane services and products, such as newspaper delivery or trash collecting?" Certainly, it is possible in such seemingly mundane fields as insurance (see Best Practice in Action 2-1). However, once customers have been delighted, their expectations are raised. Customers will be dissatisfied if service levels return to previous levels, and it will take more effort to "delight" them in the future.[20] So achieving delight requires focusing on what is currently unknown or unexpected by the customer. In short, it's more than just avoiding problems: the "zero defects" strategy.

Why is satisfaction important to service managers? There's evidence of strategic links between the level of customer satisfaction and a firm's overall performance. Researchers from the University of Michigan found that on average, every 1 percent

BEST PRACTICE IN ACTION 2-1

PROGRESSIVE INSURANCE DELIGHTS ITS CUSTOMERS

Progressive Insurance Corp. prides itself on providing extraordinary customer service, and its accomplishments in this area are impressive. Consider the following scenario. The crash site in Tampa, Florida, is chaotic and tense. Two cars are damaged, and although the passengers aren't bleeding, they are shaken up and scared. Lance Edgy, a senior claim representative for Progressive, arrives on the scene minutes after the collision. He calms the victims and advises them on medical care, repair shops, police reports, and legal procedures. Edgy invites William McAllister, Progressive's policyholder, into an air-conditioned van equipped with comfortable chairs, a desk, and two cellular phones. Even before the tow trucks have cleared away the wreckage, Edgy is able to offer his client a settlement for the market value of his totaled Mercury. McAllister, who did not appear to have been at fault in this accident, later stated in amazement: "This is great—someone coming right out here and taking charge. I didn't expect it at all."[1]

Progressive Insurance continues to find new ways to delight its customers. Its Web site, *www.progressive.com*, has been consistently rated as the top overall among a field of 16 Internet-based insurance carriers by Gomez.com (an Internet quality measurement firm), which places a priority on a site's educational, purchasing, and servicing capabilities. Progressive has also been cited for pleasantly surprising its customers with consumer-friendly innovations and extraordinary customer service.[2]

[1]Ronald Henkoff, "Service Is Everybody's Business," *Fortune* (June 27, 1994): 50.

[2]From the the Progressive Insurance Web site, *www.progressive.com*, accessed March 2003.

increase in customer satisfaction is associated with a 2.37 percent increase in a firm's return on investment (ROI).[21] And Susan Fournier and David Mick state:

> Customer satisfaction is central to the marketing concept. . . . [I]t is now common to find mission statements designed around the satisfaction notion, marketing plans and incentive programs that target satisfaction as a goal, and consumer communications that trumpet awards for satisfaction achievements in the marketplace.[22]

Determining Consumer Comfort with Service Providers

Important though satisfaction is as a performance measure, it is an evaluation that is normally made after a transaction. A methodology developed by Deborah Spake et al. for measuring a consumer's comfort level can be applied both prior to and following a given service encounter and is particularly applicable to high-contact services.[23] Prior to an interaction, the customer has only expectations concerning the transaction and so cannot easily discuss satisfaction at that point. However, the customer's comfort level with the service provider can be ascertained at every stage from prepurchase to postpurchase. In surveying consumers, Spake et al. found that respondents associated an increased comfort level with reduced perceived risk. Such words and phrases as *safety, security*, and *being worry-free* and having assurance about the quality of the service provided were mentioned, as were having peace of mind and being at ease with and trusting the service provider.

It's a mistake for service firms to rely solely on posttransaction satisfaction studies, particularly in extended high-contact encounters, because this approach inevitably misses opportunities to address problems while customers are still engaged in the process—or before they have even made a decision on use. If customers are uneasy with the prospect of using a particular service, they may decide against purchasing it. And if they feel uncomfortable with an aspect of a service encounter, they may decide to quit before completing a transaction, especially if they haven't yet had to pay for it.

Although it's not always practical to administer formal surveys in midencounter, managers can train service personnel to be more observant, so that they can identify customers who appear to be having difficulties, look frustrated, or seem otherwise ill at ease and then ask if they need assistance. If experience shows that customers are continually discomforted by a particular aspect of the service encounter, this would indicate a need for redesign and improvement.

A SERVICE BUSINESS IS A SYSTEM

The types of encounters that take place during service delivery depend to a great extent on the level of contact that customers have with the provider. A service business can be viewed as a system made up of three overlapping elements:

- *Service operations*, whereby inputs are processed and the elements of the service product are created
- *Service delivery*, during which final "assembly" of these elements takes place and the product is delivered to the customer
- *Service marketing*, which embraces all points of contact with customers, including advertising, billing, and market research

System Components

Parts of this system are visible or otherwise apparent to customers; other parts are hidden, and the customer may not even know of their existence.[24] Some writers use the terms "front office" and "back office" in referring to the visible and invisible parts of the operation. Others talk about "front stage" and "backstage," using the analogy of theater to dramatize the notion that service is a performance.[25] We like this analogy—sometimes referred to as "dramaturgy"—and will be using it throughout the book.

Service Operations Like a play in a theater, the visible components of service operations can be divided into those relating to the actors, or service personnel, and those relating to the stage set, or physical facilities, equipment, and other tangibles. What goes on backstage is of little interest to customers. Like any audience, they evaluate the production on those elements they experience during service delivery and on the perceived service outcome. Naturally, if the backstage personnel and systems (e.g., billing, ordering, account keeping) fail to perform their support tasks properly in ways that affect the quality of front-stage activities, customers will notice. For instance, restaurant patrons will be disappointed if they order fish from the menu but are told that it is unavailable or find that their food is overcooked. Other examples of backstage failures include receiving an incorrect hotel bill owing to a keying error, not receiving course grades because of a computer failure in the college registrar's office, or being delayed on a flight because the aircraft has been taken out of service for engine repairs.

The proportion of the overall service operation that is visible to customers varies according to the level of customer contact. Because high-contact services directly involve the physical person of the customer, the visible component of the service operations element tends to be substantial.

Low-contact services usually strive to minimize customer contact with the service provider, so most of the service operations element is confined to a remotely located backstage (sometimes referred to as a technical core); front-stage elements are normally limited to mail and telecommunications contacts. Think for a moment about the telephone company that you use. Do you have any idea where its exchange is located? Similarly, if you have a credit card, your transactions are likely processed far from where you live.

Service Delivery Service delivery is concerned with where, when, and how the service product is delivered to the customer. This element not only embraces the visible elements of the service operating system—buildings, equipment, and personnel—but may also involve exposure to other customers.

Using the theatrical analogy, the distinction between high-contact and low-contact services can be likened to the differences between live theater on a stage and a drama created for television. Customers of low-contact services normally never see the "factory" where the work is performed; at most, they will talk with a service provider (or problem solver) by telephone. Without buildings and furnishings or even the appearance of employees to provide tangible clues, customers must make judgments about service quality on the basis of ease of telephone access, followed by the voice and responsiveness of a telephone-based customer service representative.

When service is delivered through impersonal electronic channels, such as self-service machines, automated telephone calls to a central computer, or via the customer's own computer, there is very little traditional "theater" left to the performance. Some firms compensate for this by giving their machines names, playing recorded music, or installing moving color graphics on video screens, adding sounds, and creating computer-based interactive capabilities to give the experience a more human feeling.

Responsibility for designing and managing service delivery systems has traditionally fallen to operations managers. But marketing needs to be involved, too, to research how consumers behave during service delivery and ensure that the system is designed with their needs and concerns in mind.

Service Marketing In addition to the service delivery element, other elements contribute to the customer's overall view of a service business. These elements include communication efforts by the advertising and sales departments, telephone calls and letters from service personnel, billings from the accounting department, random exposures to service personnel and facilities, news stories and editorials in the mass media, word-of-mouth comments from current or former customers, and even participation in market research studies.

Service Marketing System

Collectively, the components just cited—along with those in the service delivery element—add up to what we call the *service marketing system*, which represents all the ways the customer may encounter or learn about the organization in question. Because services are experiential, each of these elements offers clues about the nature and quality of the service product. Inconsistency between various elements may weaken the organization's credibility in the customers' eyes. Figure 2-7 depicts the service system for a high-contact service, such as a hotel, health club, or full-service restaurant.

As you know from your own experience, the scope and the structure of the service marketing system often vary sharply from one type of organization to another. Figure 2-8

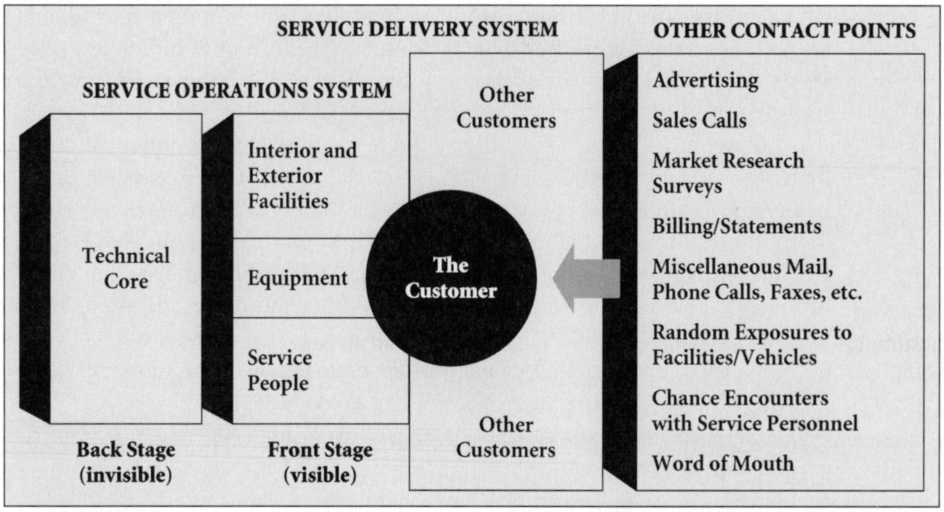

FIGURE 2-7 The Service Marketing System for a High-Contact Service

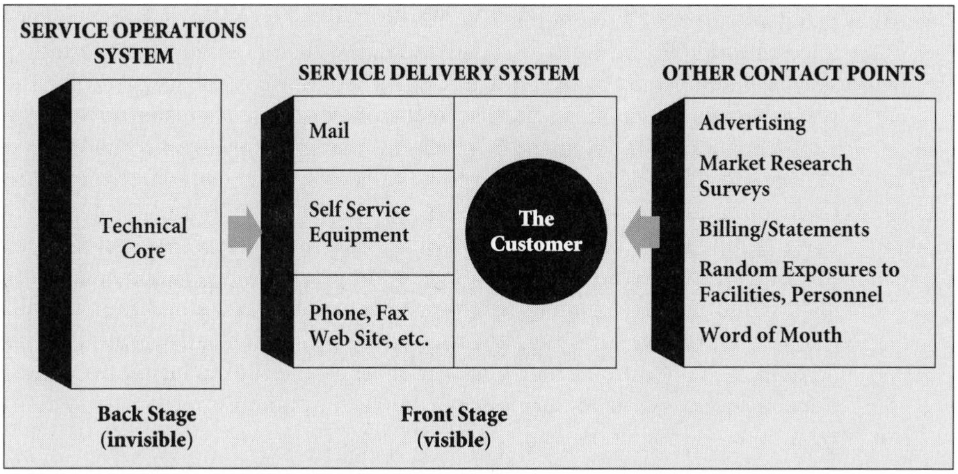

FIGURE 2-8 The Service Marketing System for a Low-Contact Service

shows how things change when we are dealing with a low-contact service, such as a credit card account or an Internet-based insurance firm. The significance of this approach to conceptualizing service creation and delivery is that it represents the customer's view, looking at the service business from the outside, as opposed to an internally focused operations perspective.

Theater as a Metaphor for Service Delivery

The theater is a good metaphor for services, as service delivery consists of a series of events that customers experience as a *performance.*[26] This approach is particularly useful for high-contact service providers, such as physicians, educators, restaurants, and hotels, and for businesses that serve many people simultaneously, such as professional sports, hospitals, and entertainment, rather than providing individualized service. In practice, the extent to which theatrical elements are present and can be used by marketers to dramatic effect depends to a large extent on the nature of the service process.

TABLE 2-2 Theatrical Considerations for Various Types of Services

Service Process Category	*Level of Contact*	*Drama Implications*
People processing	High	Because the actors and audience are in close contact, the setting and front-stage performances affect customers' perceptions of service quality. Important theater aspects include the setting design and ambience, the actors' appearance and behavior, props, costumes, and scripts. Audience members (customers) can influence one another's service experience and the perceived quality of the service performance.
Mental stimulus processing	High	If actors and audience are in close physical proximity, many of the drama implications for people-processing services may apply.
	Low	If the performance is conducted at arm's length, audience members do not typically interact. The physical appearances of the actors and setting are less important. Scripts may still be useful in ensuring that actors and audience members play their parts correctly.
Possession processing	Medium	The performance can take place at either the service firm or the audience members' home or business. Contact between actors and audience may be limited to the start and end of the service. (At these contact points, the drama elements described for people-processing services do apply but on a less substantial level.)
	Low	In some circumstances—for instance, lawn mowing and office janitorial services—the service performance may occur without the audience present. The outcomes of such services are usually tangible and may be used as a proxy for judging the quality of the service performance.
Information processing	Low	Actors and audience members have minimal contact. Both the act and the recipient (intangible assets) are intangible, and the performance usually occurs in the absence of the customer. Therefore, only the outcomes, not the process, can be assessed; however, even the outcome may be difficult for customers to evaluate.

Developed from information in Stephen J. Grove, Raymond P. Fisk, and Joby John, "Services as Theater: Guidelines and Implications," in Teresa A. Schwartz and Dawn Iacobucci, *Handbook of Service Marketing and Management* (Thousand Oaks, CA: Sage Publications, 2000), 31.

Table 2-2 provides a summary of the drama implications for the four categories of service processes identified earlier.

We can think of service facilities as containing the stage on which the drama unfolds. Sometimes the setting changes from one act to another (for example, when airline passengers move from the entrance to the terminal to the check-in stations and then on to the boarding lounge and finally step inside the aircraft). The stage may have minimal "props," as in a typical post office, or elaborate scenery, as in some modern resort hotels. Many service dramas are tightly scripted (as in the way that service is delivered in a formal restaurant setting), whereas others are improvisational (such as teaching a university class.)

Some services are more ritualized than others. In highly structured environments, such as dental services, "blocking" may define how the actors—in this case, receptionists, dental hygienists, technicians, and dentists—should move relative to the stage (the dentist's office), items of scenery (furniture and equipment), and other actors.

Not all service providers require customers to attend performances at the company's "theater," especially in a business-to-business context. In many instances, the customer's own facilities provide the stage where the service employees perform with their props. For example, outside accountants are often hired to provide specialized services at a client's site. (Although this may be convenient for customers, it isn't always very appealing for the visiting accountants, who sometimes find themselves housed in rat-infested basements or inventorying frozen food for hours in a cold-storage locker![27]) Telecommunication linkages offer an alternative performance environment, allowing customers to be involved in the drama from a remote location—a delivery option long awaited by those traveling accountants, who would probably much prefer to work for their clients from the comfort of their own offices via modems and computers.

Front-stage personnel are members of a cast, playing roles as *actors* in a drama and supported by a backstage production team. In some instances, they are expected to wear special costumes when on stage, (such as the protective clothing—traditionally white—worn by dental professionals, the fanciful uniforms often worn by hotel doormen, or the more basic brown ones worn by UPS (United Parcel Service) drivers). When service employees wear distinctive apparel, they stand out from personnel at other firms. In this respect, uniform designs can be seen as a form of packaging that provides physical evidence of brand identity.[28] In many service companies, the choice of uniform design and colors is carefully integrated with other corporate design elements. Many front-stage employees must conform to both a dress code and grooming standards, such as Disney's rule that employees can't wear beards, except as required in costumed roles.

Depending on the nature of their work, employees may be required to learn and repeat specific lines, ranging from announcements in several languages to a sales spiel (just think of the last telemarketer who called you!) to a parting salutation of "Have a nice day!" And as in the theater, companies often use scripting to define actors' behavior as well as their lines. Eye contact, smiles, and handshakes may be required in addition to a spoken greeting. Other rules of conduct may include bans on smoking, eating and drinking, or gum chewing while on duty. For more on the use of the theater metaphor as a framework for describing and analyzing service performances, see the reading by Stephen J. Grove and Raymond P. Fisk, "Service Theater: An Analytical Framework for Services Marketing," on pp. 78–87.

Role and Script Theories

Role and script theories offer some interesting insights for service providers. If we view service delivery as a theatrical experience, both employees and customers act out their parts in the performance according to predetermined *roles.* Stephen Grove and Ray Fisk define a role as "a set of behavior patterns learned through experience and communication, to be performed by an individual in a certain social interaction in order to attain maximum effectiveness in goal accomplishment.[29] Roles have also been defined as combinations of social cues, or expectations of society, that guide behavior in a specific setting or context.[30] In service encounters, employees and customers each have roles to play. The satisfaction of both parties depends on role congruence, or the extent to which each person acts out his or her prescribed role during a service encounter. Employees must perform their roles to customer expectations or risk dissatisfying or losing customers altogether. And customers, too, must "play by the rules" or risk causing problems for the firm, its employees, and even other customers.

Scripts are sequences of behavior that both employees and customers are expected to learn and follow during service delivery. Scripts are learned through experience, education, and communication with others.[31] Much like a movie script, a service script provides detailed actions that customers and employees are expected to perform. The more experience a customer has with a service company, the more familiar the script becomes. Any deviations from this known script may frustrate both customers and employees and may lead to high levels of dissatisfaction. If a company decides to change a service script (for example, by using technology to turn a high-contact service into a low-contact one), service personnel and customers should be educated about the new script and the benefits it provides.

Some scripts are highly structured and allow service employees to move through their duties quickly and efficiently, such as flight attendants' scripts for economy class. This approach helps to overcome two of the inherent challenges facing service firms: how to (1) reduce variability and (2) ensure uniform quality. The risk is that frequent repetition may lead to mindless service delivery that ignores customers' needs.

Not all services involve tightly scripted performances. For providers of highly customized services, such as doctors, educators, hair stylists, or consultants, the service script is flexible and may vary by situation and by customer. When customers are new to a service, they may not know what to expect and may be fearful of behaving incorrectly. Organizations should be ready to educate new customers about their roles in service delivery, as inappropriate behaviors can disrupt service delivery and make customers feel embarrassed and uncomfortable.

A flowchart can provide the basis for development of a well-planned script that provides a full description of what should take place during a service encounter, including the roles played by customers and service personnel at different points in the process. Figure 2-9 shows a three-player script for teeth cleaning and a simple dental examination: the patient, the receptionist, and the dental hygienist. Each has a specific role to play. In this instance, the script is driven primarily by the need to execute a technical task both proficiently and safely (note the mask and gloves). The core service of examining and cleaning teeth can be accomplished satisfactorily only if the patient cooperates in an experience that is at best neutral and at worst uncomfortable or even painful. Several elements in this script relate to information flows. Confirming and honoring appointments avoids delays for customers and ensures effective use of dental professionals' time. Obtaining patient histories and documenting analysis and treatment is vital for maintaining complete dental records and for accurate billing. Payment on receipt of treatment improves cash flow and avoids the problem of bad debts. And finally, adding greetings, statements of thanks, and good-byes displays friendly good manners and helps to humanize what most people see as a slightly unpleasant experience.

Service Firms as Teachers

Although service providers attempt to design the ideal level of customer participation into the service delivery system, it is customers' actions that in reality determine the amount of participation. Underparticipation causes customers to experience a decrease in service benefits (a student learning less or a dieter losing less weight). If customers overparticipate, they may cause the firm to spend more resources customizing a service than was originally intended (a request for customization of a hamburger at a fast-food restaurant). Service businesses must teach their customers what roles to play to optimize participation levels during service production and consumption.

The more work that customers are expected to do, the greater their need for information about how to perform for best results. The necessary education can be provided in many ways. Brochures and posted instructions are two widely used approaches.

Patient	Receptionist	Dental Hygienist
1. Phone for appointment	2. Confirm needs and set date	
3. Arrive at dental office	4. Greet patient; verify purpose; direct to waiting room; notify hygienist of arrival	5. Review notes on patient
6. Sit in waiting room		7. Greet patient and lead way to treatment room
8. Enter room; sit in dental chair		9. Verify medical and dental history; ask about any issues since previous visit
		10. Place protective covers over patient's clothes
		11. Lower dental chair; put on own protective face mask, gloves, and glasses
		12. Inspect patient's teeth (option to ask questions)
		13. Place suction device in patient's mouth
		14. Use high-speed equipment and hand tools to clean teeth in sequence
		15. Remove suction device; complete cleaning process
		16. Raise chair to sitting position; ask patient to rinse
17. Rinse mouth		18. Remove and dispose of mask and gloves; remove glasses
		19. Complete notes on treatment; return patient file to receptionist
		20. Remove covers from patient
		21. Give patient free toothbrush; offer advice on personal dental care for future
22. Rise from chair		23. Thank patient and say good-bye
24. Leave treatment room	25. Greet patient; confirm treatment received; present bill	
26. Pay bill	27. Give receipt; agree on date for next appointment; document agreed-on date	
28. Take appointment card	29. Thank patient and say good-bye	
30. Leave dental office		

FIGURE 2-9 Script for Teeth Cleaning and Simple Dental Exam

Automated machines often contain detailed operating instructions and diagrams (unfortunately, these are sometimes intelligible only to the engineers who wrote them). Thoughtful banks place a telephone beside their ATMs so that customers can call a real person for help and advice at any time if they are confused about the on-screen instructions or if the machine malfunctions. Advertising for new services often contains significant educational content.

In many businesses, customers look to employees for advice and assistance and are frustrated if they can't obtain it. Service providers, ranging from sales assistants and customer service representatives to flight attendants and nurses, must be trained to help them improve their teaching skills. As a last resort, people may turn to other customers for help.

Benjamin Schneider and David Bowen suggest giving customers a realistic service preview in advance of service delivery to provide them with a clear picture of the role they will play in service coproduction.[32] For example, a company might show a video presentation to help customers understand their role in the service encounter. This technique is used by some dentists to help patients understand the surgical processes they are about to experience and indicate how they should cooperate to help make things go as smoothly as possible.

As they explore technological alternatives to creating and delivering services, service providers are discovering that not all customers are equally receptive to new technologies. Because consumers differ in their acceptance of technology-related goods and services, marketers have become interested in segmenting customers, based on their willingness and ability to use the latest technologies.

An individual's behavior often reflects personal attitudes and beliefs. Recent research by A. Parasuraman shows that certain personal characteristics are associated with customer readiness to accept new technologies. These attributes include innovativeness, a positive view of technology, and a belief that technology offers increased control, flexibility, and efficiency in people's lives.[33] Factors that are negatively associated with the adoption of technology include distrust, a perceived lack of control, feelings of being overwhelmed by technology, and skepticism about whether the technology will perform satisfactorily. Service providers must consider these factors before implementing new technologies that may negatively affect customers' evaluations of the service experience.

CONCLUSION

Services cover a spectrum from high-contact to low-contact operations, reflecting the type of service involved and the nature of the processes used in service creation and delivery. Flowcharting helps us to understand the nature of the customer's involvement.

In all types of services, understanding and managing service encounters between customers and service personnel is central to creating satisfied customers who are willing to enter into long-term relationships with the service provider. Gaining a better understanding of how customers evaluate, select, and use services should lie at the heart of strategies for designing and delivering the service product. It also has implications for choice of service processes, presentation of physical evidence, and use of marketing communications—not least for educational purposes. Several of the distinctive characteristics of services (especially intangibility and quality control problems) result in customer evaluation procedures that differ from those involved in evaluating physical goods.

Service businesses can be divided into three overlapping systems. The operations system consists of the personnel, facilities, and equipment required to run the service operation and create the service product. Only the front-stage part of this system is visible to the customer. The delivery system incorporates the visible operations elements and customers themselves, who sometimes take an active role in helping to create the service product as opposed to being passively waited on. The higher the level of contact, the more we can apply theatrical analogies to the process of "staging" service delivery in which employees and customers play roles, often following well-defined scripts. Finally, the marketing system includes not only the delivery system, which is composed essentially of the product and distribution elements of the traditional marketing mix, but also additional components, such as billing and payment systems, exposure to advertising and salespeople, and word-of-mouth comments from other people.

Review Questions

1. Clarify the difference between high-contact and low-contact services, and explain how the nature of the customer's experience may differ between the two. Give examples.
2. Describe search, experience, and credence attributes, and give examples of each.
3. Explain why services tend to be more difficult for customers to evaluate than are goods.
4. How are customers' expectations formed? Explain the difference between desired service and adequate service with reference to a service experience you've had recently.
5. Create a simple flowchart for a service you are familiar with. Define the "front-stage" and "backstage" activities.
6. Describe the relationship between customer expectations and customer satisfaction.
7. Clarify the distinction between the service operations system, the service delivery system, and the service marketing system. Identify key distinctions in these systems between high-contact and low-contact services.

Application Exercises

1. What actions could a bank take to encourage more customers to bank by phone, mail, Internet, or through ATMs rather than visiting a branch?
2. Select three services: one high in search attributes, one high in experience attributes, and one high in credence attributes. Specify what product characteristics make those services easy or difficult for consumers to evaluate, and suggest specific strategies that marketers can adopt in each case to facilitate evaluation and reduce perceived risk.
3. What are the backstage elements of (a) a car repair facility, (b) an airline, (c) a university, and (d) a consulting firm? Under what circumstances would it be appropriate to allow customers to see some of these backstage elements, and how would you do it?
4. What roles are played by front-stage service personnel in low-contact organizations? Are these roles more or less important to customer satisfaction than in high-contact services?
5. Describe an unsatisfactory encounter that you have experienced with (a) a high-contact service and (b) a low-contact, self-service operation. In each instance, what could the service provider have done to improve the situation?
6. Develop two customer scripts: one for a standardized service and one for a customized service. What are the key differences between the two?

Endnotes

1. Richard B. Chase and Sriram Dasu, "Want to Perfect Your Company's Service? Use Behavioral Science," *Harvard Business Review* 79 (June 2001): 79–84.
2. Lynn Shostack, "Planning the Service Encounter," in *The Service Encounter*, ed. J. A. Czepiel, M. R. Solomon, and C. F. Surprenant (Lexington, MA: Lexington Books, 1985), 243–254.
3. James G. Barnes, Peter A. Dunne, and William J. Glynn, "Self-Service and Technology: Unanticipated and Unintended Effects on Customer Relationships," in Teresa A. Schwartz and Dawn Iacobucci, *Handbook of Service Marketing and Management* (Thousand Oaks, CA: Sage Publications, 2000), 89–102.
4. Normann first used the term "moments of truth" in a Swedish study in 1978; subsequently, the term appeared in English in Richard Normann, *Service Management: Strategy and Leadership in Service Businesses*, 2d ed. (Chichester, UK: John Wiley, 1991), 16–17.
5. Jan Carlzon, *Moments of Truth* (Cambridge, MA: Ballinger, 1987), 3.
6. Jaishankar Ganesh, Mark J. Arnold, and Kristy E. Reynolds, "Understanding the Customer Base of Service Providers: An Examination of the Differences between Switchers and Slayers," *Journal of Marketing* 64, no. 3 (2000): 65–87.
7. Stephanie Anderson Forest, Katie Kerwin, and Susan Jackson, "Presents That Won't Fit Under the Christmas Tree," *Business Week* (December 1, 1997): 42.

8. B. Joseph Pine and James H. Gilmore, "Welcome to the Experience Economy," *Harvard Business Review* 76 (July–August 1998): 97–108.

9. See Benjamin Schneider and David E. Bowen, *Winning the Service Game* (Boston: Harvard Business School Press, 1995); and Valarie A. Zeithaml, Leonard L. Berry, and A. Parasuraman, "The Nature and Determinants of Customer Expectations of Services," *Journal of the Academy of Marketing Science* 21 (1993): 1–12.

10. Valarie A. Zeithaml, Leonard L. Berry, and A. Parasuraman, "The Behavioral Consequences of Service Quality," *Journal of Marketing* 60 (April 1996): 31–46.

11. Cathy Johnson and Brian P. Mathews, "The Influence of Experience on Service Expectations," *International Journal of Service Industry Management* 8, no. 4 (1997): 46–61.

12. Robert Johnston, "The Zone of Tolerance: Exploring the Relationship between Service Transactions and Satisfaction with the Overall Service," *International Journal of Service Industry Management* 6, no. 5 (1995): 46–61.

13. Valarie A. Zeithaml, "How Consumer Evaluation Processes Differ between Goods and Services," in J. H. Donnelly and W. R. George, *Marketing of Services* (Chicago: American Marketing Association, 1981).

14. Leonard L. Berry and Neeli Bendapudi, "Clueing In Customers," *Harvard Business Review* 81 (February 2003): 100–107.

15. Valarie A. Zeithaml and Mary Jo Bitner, *Services Marketing: Integrating Customer Focus Across the Firm,* 3rd ed. (Burr Ridge, IL: Irwin-McGraw-Hill, 2003).

16. Youjae Yi, "A Critical Review of Customer Satisfaction," in *Review of Marketing 1990*, ed. V. A. Zeithaml, (Chicago, American Marketing Association, 1990).

17. Richard L. Oliver, "Customer Satisfaction with Service," in Teresa A. Schwartz and Dawn Iacobucci, *Handbook of Service Marketing and Management* (Thousand Oaks, CA: Sage Publications, 2000), 247–254; Jochen Wirtz and Anna S. Mattila, "Exploring the Role of Alternative Perceived Performance Measures and Needs-Congruency in the Consumer Satisfaction Process," *Journal of Consumer Psychology* 11, no. 3 (2001): 181–192.

18. Richard L. Oliver, *Satisfaction: A Behavioral Perspective on the Consumer* (New York: McGraw-Hill, 1997).

19. Richard L. Oliver, Roland T. Rust, and Sajeev Varki, "Customer Delight: Foundations, Findings, and Managerial Insight," *Journal of Retailing* 73 (Fall 1997): 311–336.

20. Roland T. Rust and Richard L. Oliver, "Should We Delight the Customer?" *Journal of the Academy of Marketing Science* 28, no. 1 (2000): 86–94.

21. Eugene W. Anderson and Vikas Mittal, "Strengthening the Satisfaction-Profit Chain," *Journal of Service Research* 3 (November 2000): 107–120.

22. Susan Fournier and David Glen Mick, "Rediscovering Satisfaction," *Journal of Marketing* 63 (October 1999): 5–23.

23. Deborah F. Spake, Sharon E. Beatty, Beverly K. Brockman, and Tammy Neal Crutchfield, "Development of the Consumer Comfort Scale: A Multi-Study Investigation of Service Relationships," *Journal of Service Research* 5, no. 4 (May 2003): 316–332.

24. Richard B. Chase, "Where Does the Customer Fit in a Service Organization?" *Harvard Business Review* 56 (November–December 1978): 137–142.

25. Stephen J. Grove, Raymond P. Fisk, and Mary Jo Bitner, "Dramatizing the Service Experience: A Managerial Approach," in T. A. Schwartz, D. E. Bowen, and S.W. Brown, *Advances in Services Marketing and Management, Vol. I* (Greenwich CT, JAI Press, 1992), 91–122. See also B. Joseph Pine II and James H. Gilmore, *The Experience Economy* (Boston: Harvard Business School Press, 1999).

26. Stephen J. Grove, Raymond P. Fisk, and Joby John, "Services as Theater: Guidelines and Implications," in Teresa A. Schwartz and Dawn Iacobucci, *Handbook of Service Marketing and Management* 21–36; Steve Baron, Kim Harris, and Richard Harris, "Retail Theater: The 'Intended Effect' of the Performance," *Journal of Service Research* 2 (November 2001): 102–117.

27. Elizabeth MacDonald, "Oh, the Horrors of Being a Visiting Accountant," *Wall Street Journal,* March 10, 1997.

28. Michael R. Solomon, "Packaging the Service Provider," *The Service Industries Journal* (July 1986).

29. Stephen J. Grove and Raymond P. Fisk, "The Dramaturgy of Services Exchange: An Analytical Framework for Services Marketing," in *Emerging Perspectives on Services Marketing,* ed. L. L. Berry, G. L. Shostack, and G.D. Upah (Chicago: American Marketing Association, 1983), 45–49.

30. Michael R. Solomon, Carol Suprenant, John A. Czepiel, and Evelyn G. Gutman, "A Role Theory Perspective on Dyadic Interactions: The Service Encounter," *Journal of Marketing* 49 (Winter 1985): 99–111.

31. See R. P. Abelson, "Script Processing in Attitude Formation and Decision-Making," in *Cognitive and Social Behavior* ed. J. S. Carrol and J. W. Payne (Hillsdale, NJ: Erlbaum, 1976), 33–45; and Ronald H. Humphrey and Blake E. Ashforth, "Cognitive

Scripts and Prototypes in Service Encounters," in *Advances in Service Marketing and Management* (Greenwich, CT: JAI Press, 1994), 175–199; Richard Harris, Kim Harris, and Steve Baron, "Theatrical Service Experiences: Dramatic Script Development with Employees," *International Journal of Service Industry Management* 14, no. 2 (2003): 184–199.

32. Benjamin Schneider and David E. Bowen, *Winning the Service Game* (Boston: Harvard Business School Press, 1995), 92.
33. A. Parasuraman, "Technology Readiness Index [TRI]: A Multiple-Item Scale to Measure Readiness to Embrace New Technologies," *Journal of Service Research* 2 (2000): 307–320.

CHAPTER 3

Positioning Services in Competitive Markets

To succeed in our overcommunicated society, a company must create a position in the prospect's mind, a position that takes into consideration not only a company's own strengths and weaknesses, but those of its competitors as well.
—AL REIS AND JACK TROUT

Ask a group of managers from various service businesses how they compete, and the chances are high that many will say simply, "on service." Press them a little further, and they may add such words and phrases *value for money, service quality, our people*, or *convenience.*

None of this is very helpful to a marketing specialist who is trying to develop strategies to help an organization compete more effectively. At issue is what makes consumers or institutional buyers select—and remain loyal to—one service supplier over another. Terms such as *service* typically subsume a variety of specific characteristics, ranging from the speed with which a service is delivered to the quality of interactions between customers and service personnel and from avoiding errors to providing desirable "extras" to supplement the core service. Likewise, *convenience* could refer to a service that's delivered at a convenient location, available at convenient times, or easy to use. Without knowing which product features are of specific interest to customers, it's difficult for managers to develop an appropriate competitive strategy.

In a highly competitive environment, there's a risk that customers will perceive little real difference between competing alternatives and so make their choices based on price. Positioning strategy is concerned with creating and maintaining distinctive differences that will be noticed and valued by those customers with whom the firm would most like to develop a long-term relationship. Successful positioning requires managers to understand both their target customers' preferences and the characteristics of their competitors' offerings.

In this chapter, we examine the need for focus in a competitive environment and review the issues involved in developing a positioning strategy. Specifically, we explore the following questions:

1. Why is it so important for service firms to adopt focused strategies in their choice of markets and products?
2. What is the distinction between important and determinant attributes in consumer choice decisions?
3. What are the key concepts underlying competitive positioning strategy in services?
4. When is it appropriate to reposition an existing service offering?
5. How can positioning maps help service marketers to better understand and respond to competitive dynamics?

FOCUS UNDERLIES THE SEARCH FOR COMPETITIVE ADVANTAGE

As competition intensifies in the service sector, it's becoming ever more important for service organizations to differentiate their products in ways that are meaningful to customers. In highly developed economies, growth is slowing in such mature consumer service industries as banking, insurance, hospitality, and education. So corporate growth will have to be based on taking share from domestic competitors or by expanding into international markets. In each instance, firms should be selective in targeting customers and seek to be distinctive in the way they present themselves. A market niche that may seem too narrow to offer sufficient sales within one country may represent a substantial market when viewed from an international or even global perspective.

Competitive strategy can take many routes. George Day observes:

> The diversity of ways a business can achieve a competitive advantage quickly defeats any generalizations or facile prescriptions .... First and foremost, a business must set itself apart from its competition. To be successful, it must identify and promote itself as the best provider of attributes that are important to target customers.[1]

What this means is that managers need to think systematically about all facets of the service package and to emphasize competitive advantage on those attributes that will be valued by customers in the target segment(s).

It is usually not realistic for a firm to try to appeal to all potential buyers in a market, because customers are varied in their needs, purchasing behavior, and consumption patterns and often also too numerous and geographically widely spread. Service firms also vary widely in their abilities to serve different types of customers. So, rather than attempting to compete in an entire market, each company needs to focus its efforts on those customers it can serve best. In marketing terms, *focus* means providing a relatively narrow product mix for a particular market segment—a group of buyers who share common characteristics, needs, purchasing behavior, or consumption patterns. This concept is at the heart of virtually all successful service firms, which have identified the strategically important elements in their service operations and have concentrated their resources on them.

The extent of a company's focus can be described on two dimensions: market focus and service focus.[2] *Market focus* is the extent to which a firm serves few or many markets, whereas *service focus* describes the extent to which a firm offers few or many services. These two dimensions define the four basic focus strategies shown in Figure 3-1.

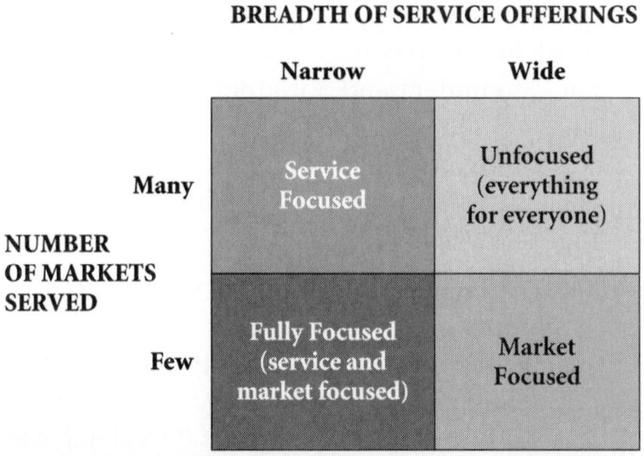

FIGURE 3-1 Basic Focus Strategies for Services

Source: Robert Johnston, "Achieving Focus in Service Organizations," *The Service Industries Journal* 16 (January 1996): 10–20.

A *fully focused* organization provides a very limited range of services (perhaps just a single core product) to a narrow and specific market segment. A *market-focused* company concentrates on a narrow market segment but has a wide range of services. *Service-focused* firms offer a narrow range of services to a fairly broad market. Finally, many service providers fall into the *unfocused* category because they try to serve broad markets and provide a wide range of services.

How should a firm select which of the three alternative "focused" strategies to pursue? Adopting a fully focused strategy presents both risks and opportunities. Developing recognized expertise in a well-defined niche may provide protection against would-be competitors and allow a firm to charge premium prices. The biggest risk is that the market may be too small to generate the volume of business needed for financial success. Other risks include the danger that demand for the service may be displaced by generic competition from alternative products or that purchasers in the chosen segment may be very susceptible to an economic downturn. One reason that firms with a narrow product line elect to serve multiple segments (a service-focused strategy) is to create a portfolio of customers that hedges against such a risk. However, as new segments are added, the firm needs to develop expertise in serving each segment, which may require a broader sales effort and greater investment in marketing communication, particularly in a b2b (business-to-business) context.

Offering a broad product line to a narrowly defined target segment often looks attractive because it offers the potential of selling multiple services to a single purchaser. But before adopting a market-focused strategy, managers need to be sure that their firms have the operational capability to do an excellent job of delivering each of the services selected. Managers also need to understand customer purchasing practices and preferences. When trying to cross-sell additional services to the same client in a business-to-business context, many firms have been disappointed to find that decisions on purchasing the new service are made by an entirely different group within the client company.

MARKET SEGMENTATION FORMS THE BASIS FOR FOCUSED STRATEGIES

Different service firms vary widely in their abilities to serve different types of customers. Hence, rather than trying to compete in an entire market, perhaps against superior competitors, each firm should adopt a strategy of market segmentation, identifying those parts, or segments, of the market that it can serve best. Firms that are in tune with customer requirements may choose to use a needs-based segmentation approach, focusing on those customers identified by research as valuing specific attributes.

Market and Microsegmentation

Because each person or corporate purchaser has distinctive (even unique) characteristics and needs, any prospective buyer is potentially a separate target segment. Traditionally, firms have sought to achieve economies of scale by marketing to all customers within a specific market segment and serving each in a similar fashion. A strategy of *mass customization*—offering a service with some individualized product elements to a large number of customers at a relatively low price—may be achieved by offering a standardized core product but tailoring supplementary service elements to fit the requirements of individual buyers.

The creation of customer databases and sophisticated analytical software makes it possible for firms to adopt *microsegmentation* strategies targeted at small groups of customers that share certain relevant characteristics at a specific point in time. (Note the strategy used by the Royal Bank of Canada, as described in Best Practice in Action 3-1).

BEST PRACTICE IN ACTION 3-1

CONTINUOUS SEGMENTATION AT THE ROYAL BANK OF CANADA

At least once a month, Toronto-based analysts at the Royal Bank of Canada (the country's largest bank) use data modeling to segment its base of ten million customers. The segmentation variables include credit risk profile, current and projected profitability, life stage, likelihood of leaving the bank, channel preference (whether customers like to use a branch, self-service machines, the call center, or the Internet), product activation (how quickly customers use a product they have bought), and propensity to purchase another product (cross-selling potential). Says a senior vice president, "Gone are the days when we had mass buckets of customers that would receive the same treatment or same offer on a monthly basis. Our marketing strategy is [now] much more personalized. Of course, it's the technology that allows us to do that."

The main source of data is the marketing information file, which records what products customers hold with the bank, the channels they use, their responses to past campaigns, transactional data, and details of any restrictions on soliciting customers. Another source is the enterprise data warehouse, which stores billing records and information from every document that a new or existing customer fills out.

Royal Bank analysts run models based on complex algorithms that can slice the bank's massive customer database into tightly profiled microsegments that are based on simultaneous use of several variables, including the probability that target customers will respond positively to a particular offer. Customized marketing programs can then be developed for each of these microsegments, giving the appearance of a highly personalized offer. The data can also be used to improve the bank's performance on unprofitable accounts by identifying these customers and offering them incentives to use lower-cost channels.

An important goal of Royal Bank's segmentation analysis is to maintain and enhance profitable relationships. The bank has found that customers who hold packages of several services are more profitable than those who don't. These customers also stay with the bank an average of three years longer. As a result of the sophisticated segmentation practices at Royal Bank, the response rates to its direct-marketing programs have jumped from an industry average of only 3 percent to as high as 30 percent.

Source: Meredith Levinson, "Slices of Lives," *CIO Magazine* (August 15, 2000).

Identifying and Selecting Target Segments

A *market segment* is composed of a group of buyers who share common characteristics, needs, purchasing behavior, or consumption patterns. Effective segmentation should group buyers into segments in ways that result in as much similarity as possible on the relevant characteristics within each segment but dissimilarity on those same characteristics between segments.

A *target segment* is one that a firm has selected from among those in the broader market and may be defined on the basis of several variables. For instance, a department store in a particular city might target residents of the metropolitan area (geographic segmentation) who have incomes within a certain range (demographic segmentation), value personal service from a knowledgeable staff, and are not highly price sensitive (both reflecting segmentation according to expressed attitudes and behavioral intentions). Because competing retailers in the city would probably be targeting the same customers, the department store would have to create a distinctive appeal (appropriate characteristics to highlight might include a wide array of merchandise categories, breadth of selection within each product category, and the availability of such supplementary services as advice and home delivery). Service firms that are developing strategies based on use of technology recognize that customers can also be segmented according to their degree of competence and comfort in using technology-based delivery systems.

An important marketing issue for any business is to accept that some market segments offer better opportunities than do others. Target segments should be selected not only on the basis of their sales and profit potential but also with reference to the firm's ability to match or exceed competing offerings directed at the same segment. Sometimes, research shows that certain market segments are "underserved," meaning that their needs are not well met by existing suppliers. Such markets are often surprisingly large.

In many emerging-market economies, huge numbers of consumers have incomes too small to attract the interest of service businesses that are accustomed to focusing on the needs of more affluent customers. Collectively, however, low-wage earners represent a very big market and may offer even greater potential for the future as many of them move upward toward middle-class status. Service Perspectives 3-1 describes an innovative approach to providing financial services to lower-income households in Mexico. Contrast this strategy with Phoenix Wealth Management's targeting of successful affluent women for its investment products (Figure 3-2).

Using Research to Develop a Service Concept for a Specific Segment

How can a firm develop the right service concept for a particular target segment? Formal research is often needed to identify what attributes of a given service are important to specific market segments and how well prospective customers perceive

SERVICE PERSPECTIVES 3-1

BANCO AZTECA CATERS TO THE LITTLE GUY

Banco Azteca, which opened in 2002, is Mexico's first new bank in nearly a decade. The bank targets the nation's sixteen million households that earn $250–$1,300 a month, working at such jobs as taxi drivers, factory hands, and teachers. Despite their combined income of $120 billion, these individuals are of little interest to most banks, which consider small accounts a nuisance. Not surprisingly, only one in twelve individuals has a savings account.

Banco Azteca was the brainchild of Ricardo Salinas Pliego, head of a retail-media-telecommunications empire that includes Grupo Elektra, Mexico's largest appliance retailer. The bank's branches, located within Elektra stores, are decorated in the green, white, and red of the Mexican flag. These branches seek to create a welcoming atmosphere and feature posters with the Azteca slogan, which translates as "A bank that's friendly and treats you well." Loans may often use customers' previously purchased possessions as collateral.

Azteca's relationship with Elektra seeks to take advantage of the retailer's fifty-year track record in consumer finance and the fact that some 70 percent of its merchandise is sold on credit. Elektra has an excellent record in credit sales, with a 97 percent repayment rate and a rich database of customers' credit histories. So top management felt it made sense to convert Elektra credit departments in each store into Azteca branches with an expanded line of services. The new bank has invested heavily in information technology, including high-tech fingerprint readers that eliminate the need for customers to present printed identification or passbooks. It also takes its services to the people through a 3,000-strong force of loan agents on motorcycles.

Source: Geri Smith, "Buy a Toaster, Open a Banking Account," *Business Week* (January 13, 2003): 54.

FIGURE 3-2 Phoenix Wealth Management Targets Successful, Affluent Women for Its Investment Products

competing organizations as performing against these attributes. But it's dangerous to overgeneralize. Strategists should recognize that the same individuals may set different priorities for attributes according to

- The purpose of using the service
- Who makes the decision

- The timing of use (time of day/week/season)
- Whether the individual is using the service alone or with a group
- The composition of that group

Consider the criteria that you might use when choosing a restaurant for lunch while on a holiday with friends or family, selecting a restaurant for an expense account business lunch at which you were meeting with a prospective client, and choosing somewhere to eat for a quick lunch with a coworker. Given a reasonable selection of alternatives, it's unlikely that you would choose the same type of restaurant in each instance, let alone the same one. It's possible, too, that if you left the decision to another person in the party, he or she would make a different choice.

Important versus Determinant Attributes

Consumers usually make their choices from alternative service offerings on the basis of perceived differences among them. But the attributes that distinguish competing services from one another are not always the most important ones. For instance, many travelers rank "safety" as their number-one consideration in air travel. They may avoid traveling by unknown carriers or on an airline that has a poor safety reputation, but after eliminating such alternatives from consideration, a traveler flying on major routes is still likely to have available several choices of carrier that are perceived as equally safe. Hence, safety is not usually an attribute that influences the customer's choice at this point.

Determinant attributes, or those that determine buyers' choices among competing alternatives, are often some way down the list of service characteristics that are important to purchasers, but they are the attributes on which customers see significant differences among competing alternatives. For example, convenience of departure and arrival times, availability of frequent flyer miles and related loyalty privileges, quality of food and drinks service on board the aircraft, or the ease of making reservations might be examples of determinant characteristics for business travelers when selecting an airline. For budget-conscious vacationers, on the other hand, price might assume primary importance.

The marketing researchers' task, of course, is to survey customers in the target segment, identify the relative importance of various attributes, and then ask which ones have been determinant during recent decisions involving a choice of service suppliers. Researchers also need to be aware of how well each competing service is perceived by customers as performing on these attributes. Findings from such research form the necessary basis for developing a positioning or repositioning campaign.[3]

One further issue in evaluating service characteristics and establishing a positioning strategy is that some attributes are easily quantified, whereas others are qualitative and highly judgmental. Price, for instance, is a straightforward quantitative measure. Punctuality of transport services can be expressed in terms of the percentage of trains, buses, or flights arriving within a specified number of minutes from the scheduled time. Both of these measures are easy to understand and therefore generalizable. But the quality of personal service or a hotel's degree of luxury are more qualitative characteristics and therefore subject to individual interpretation, although in the case of hotels, travelers may be prepared to trust the evaluations of independent rating services, such as AAA or the *Michelin Guide*.

POSITIONING DISTINGUISHES A BRAND FROM ITS COMPETITORS

Competitive positioning strategy is based on establishing and maintaining a distinctive place in the market for an organization and/or its individual product offerings. Jack Trout has distilled the essence of positioning into the following four principles:[4]

1. A company must establish a position in the minds of its targeted customers.
2. The position should be singular, providing one simple and consistent message.
3. The position must set a company apart from its competitors.
4. A company cannot be all things to all people; it must focus its efforts.

These principles apply to any type of organization that competes for customers. Understanding the principles of positioning is key to developing an effective competitive posture. The concept of positioning is certainly not limited to services—indeed, it had its origins in packaged-goods marketing—but it offers valuable insights by forcing service managers to analyze their firms' existing offerings and to provide specific answers to the following questions:

- What does our firm stand for in the minds of current and prospective customers?
- What customers do we now serve, and which ones would we like to target for the future?
- What are the characteristics of our current service offerings (core products and their accompanying supplementary service elements), and at what market segments is each one targeted?
- In each instance, how do our service offerings differ from those of the competition?
- How well do customers in the chosen target market segments perceive each of our service offerings as meeting their needs?
- What changes do we need to make to our offerings in order to strengthen our competitive position within the market segment(s) of interest to our firm?

One of the challenges in developing a viable positioning strategy is to avoid the trap of investing too heavily in points of difference that can easily be copied. As researchers Kevin Keller, Brian Sternthal, and Alice Tybout note: "Positioning needs to keep competitors out, not draw them in."[5]

When Roger and Linda Brown, founders of the Bright Horizons chain of child and care centers, were developing their business model, they took a long, hard look at the industry.[6] Discovering that for-profit child-care companies had adopted low-cost strategies and were running their centers as a commodity business, the Browns decided to differentiate their service model from the competition. The reading, "How We Built a Strong Company in a Weak Industry" by Roger Brown, reproduced on pages 88 to 92, describes the sustainable positioning strategy that Bright Horizons adopted, and the results it achieved.

Copy Positioning versus Product Positioning

Customers' brand choices reflect which brands they know and remember and how each of these brands is positioned within each customer's mind. These positions are perceptual. We need to remember that people make their decisions based on their perceptions of reality rather than on an expert's definition of that reality.

Many marketers associate positioning primarily with the communication elements of the marketing mix, notably advertising, promotions, and public relations. This view reflects the widespread use of advertising in packaged-goods marketing to create images and associations for broadly similar branded products so as to give them a special distinction in the customer's mind, an approach sometimes known as *copy positioning*. A classic example is the the rugged Western cowboy—the "Marlboro man"—created for a major cigarette brand. Note, however, that this imagery has nothing to do with the physical qualities of the tobacco; it is simply a means of differentiating and adding glamor to what is essentially a commodity. Vijay Mahajan and Yoram Wind maintain that consumers who derive emotional satisfaction from a brand are likely to be less price sensitive.[7]

Examples of how imagery may be used for positioning purposes in the service sector are found in McDonald's efforts to appear kid friendly (including its emphasis on Ronald McDonald, the clown) or Geico's humorous advertising featuring a gecko lizard. A brand may develop a reputation over time, reflecting a cumulation of associations. For instance, research has shown that Virgin, one of Britain's best-known international brand names, is associated with fun, quality, trust, and innovation.[8] Some slogans promise a specific benefit, designed to make the company stand out from its competitors: T. Rowe Price's "Invest with Confidence," Lands' End's "Shopping online beats standing in line," Stanford Executive Programs' "Powerful Ideas, Innovative Practice," or Credit Suisse First Boston's "Global Vision. Euro Knowhow." However, as Sally Dibb and Lyndon Simkin point out:

> Evidence of strong branding in the service sector does not end with such catch phrases. [The leading organizations in different fields] already have a strong brand image in the sense that customers generally know exactly what they stand for. They are, already, clearly positioned in the customers' minds.[9]

Positioning strategy is becoming more sophisticated as growing numbers of firms engage in co-branding.[10] This endeavor can take several forms, including shared facilities, joint promotions, and even co-branded products. In New England, the Stop & Shop supermarket chain has reached an agreement with Citizens Bank to install small branches of that bank inside all its stores. To obtain financial support and promotional leverage, Boston's Museum of Fine Arts seeks a prominent corporate sponsor for each of its major exhibitions. And American Airlines, Citibank, and Visa jointly offer a credit card. In each instance, the imagery associated with one brand has the potential to influence consumer perceptions of the other(s).

Our primary concern in this chapter is the role of positioning in guiding marketing strategy development for services that compete on more than imagery or vague promises. This entails decisions on substantive attributes that are important to customers, relating to product performance, price, and service availability.

To improve a product's appeal to a specific target segment, it may be necessary to change its performance on certain attributes: reduce its price, alter the times and locations when it is available, or chance the forms of delivery that are offered. In such instances, the primary task of communication—advertising, personal selling, and public relations—is to ensure that prospective customers accurately perceive the position of the service on dimensions that are important to them in making choice decisions. Additional excitement and interest may be created by evoking certain images and associations in the advertising, but these factors are likely to play only a secondary role in customer choice decisions unless competing services are perceived as virtually identical on performance, price, and availability.

Positioning's Role in Marketing Strategy

Positioning plays a pivotal role in marketing strategy because it links market analysis and competitive analysis to internal corporate analysis. From these three, a position statement can be developed that enables the service organization to answer the following questions: What is our product (or service concept)? What do we want it to become? What actions must we take to get there? Table 3-1 summarizes the principal uses of positioning analysis as a diagnostic tool, providing input to decisions relating to product development, service delivery, pricing, and communication strategy.

Developing a positioning strategy can take place at several levels, depending on the nature of the business. Among multisite, multiproduct service businesses, a position might

TABLE 3-1 Principal Uses of Positioning Analysis as a Diagnostic Tool

1. Provide a useful diagnostic tool for defining and understanding the relationships between products and markets:
   - How does the product compare with competitive offerings on specific attributes?
   - How well does product performance meet consumer needs and expectations on specific performance criteria?
   - What is the predicted consumption level for a product with a given set of performance characteristics offered at a given price?
2. Identify market opportunities for
   a. Introducing new products
      - What segments to target?
      - What attributes to offer relative to the competition?

   b. Redesigning (repositioning) existing products
      - Appeal to the same segments or to new ones?
      - What attributes to add, drop, or change?
      - What attributes to emphasize in advertising?

   c. Eliminating products that
      - Do not satisfy consumer needs
      - Face excessive competition
3. Make other marketing mix decisions to preempt or respond to competitive moves:
   a. Distribution strategies
      - Where to offer the product (locations, types of outlet)?
      - When to make the product available?

   b. Pricing strategies
      - How much to charge?
      - What billing and payment procedures to use?

   c. Communication strategies
      - What target audience(s) are most easily convinced that the product offers a competitive advantage on attributes that are important to them?
      - What message(s)? Which attributes should be emphasized and which competitors, if any, should be mentioned as the basis for comparison on those attributes?
      - Which communication channels: personal selling versus different advertising media? (Selected for their ability to not only convey the chosen message(s) to the target audience(s) but also reinforce the desired image of the product.)

be established for the entire organization, for a given service outlet, or for a specific service offered at that outlet. It is important that there be consistency in the positioning of services offered at the same location, as the image of one may spill over onto the others. For instance, if a hospital has an excellent reputation for obstetrical services, this may enhance perceptions of its services in gynecology, pediatrics, surgery, and so forth. In contrast, it would be detrimental to all services, if their positioning were conflicting.

Because of the intangible, experiential nature of many services, an explicit positioning strategy is valuable in helping prospective customers to get a mental "fix" on a product that would otherwise be rather amorphous. Failure to select a desired position in the marketplace—and to develop a marketing action plan designed to achieve and hold this position—may result in one of several possible outcomes, all undesirable:

- The organization (or one of its products) is pushed into a position where it faces head-on competition from stronger competitors.
- The organization (product) is pushed into a position that nobody else wants, because there is little customer demand.
- The organization's (product's) position is so blurred that nobody knows what its distinctive competence is.

- The organization (product) has no position at all in the marketplace because nobody has ever heard of it.

CONDUCT INTERNAL, MARKET, AND COMPETITOR ANALYSES

The research and analysis that underlie development of an effective positioning strategy are designed to highlight both opportunities and threats to the firm in the competitive marketplace, including the presence of generic competition, and competition from substituting products. Figure 3-3 identifies the basic steps involved in identifying a suitable market position and developing a strategy to reach it.

Market analysis addresses such factors as the overall level and trend of demand and the geographic location of this demand. Is demand increasing or decreasing for the benefits offered by this type of service? Are there regional or international variations in the level of demand? Alternative ways of segmenting the market should be considered and an appraisal made of the size and potential of various market segments. Research may be needed to gain a better understanding of not only customer needs and preferences within each of the different segments but also how each segment perceives the competition.

Internal corporate analysis focuses on identifying the organization's resources (financial, human labor, and know-how, and physical assets), any limitations or constraints, its goals (profitability, growth, professional preferences, and so on), and how its values shape the way it does business. Using insights from this analysis, management should be able to select a limited number of target market segments that can be served with either new or existing services.

Competitor analysis can provide a marketing strategist with a sense of competitors' strengths and weaknesses, which, in turn, may suggest opportunities for differentiation. Relating these insights back to the internal corporate analysis should suggest what might be viable opportunities for the organization to achieve differentiation and

FIGURE 3-3 Developing a Market Positioning Strategy

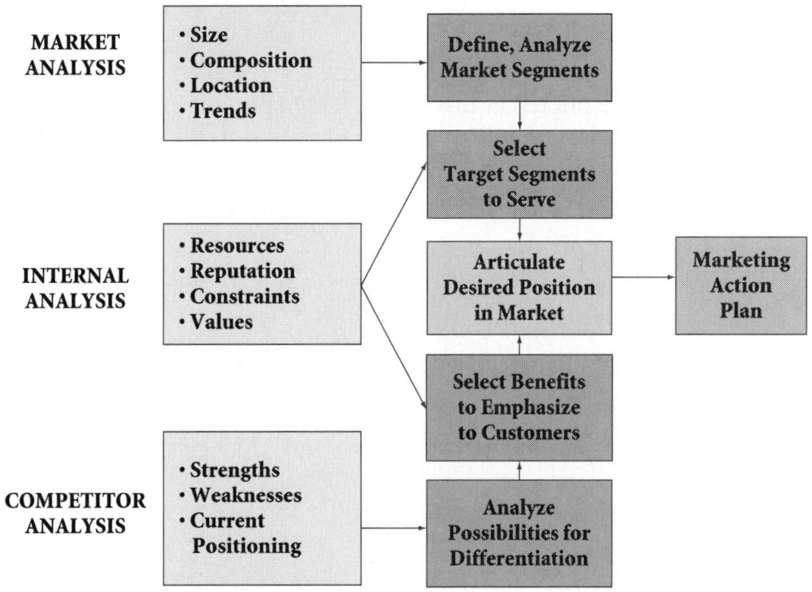

Source: Developed from an earlier schematic by Michael R. Pearce.

competitive advantage and thereby enable managers to decide which benefits should be emphasized to which target segments. This analysis should consider both direct and indirect competition.

Position statement is the outcome of integrating these three forms of analysis. This statement articulates the desired position of the organization in the marketplace and, if desired, that of each of the component services it offers. Armed with this understanding, marketers should be able to develop a specific plan of action. The cost of implementing this plan must, of course, be related to the expected payoff.

Anticipating Competitive Response

Before embarking on a specific plan of action, however, management should consider the possibility that one or more competitors might pursue the same market position. Perhaps another service organization has independently conducted the same positioning analysis and arrived at similar conclusions. Or, an existing competitor may feel threatened by the new strategy and take steps to reposition its own service so as to compete more effectively. Alternatively, a new entrant to the market may decide to play "follow the leader" yet be able to offer customers a higher service level on one or more attributes and/or a lower price.

The best way to anticipate possible competitive responses is to identify all current or potential competitors and to put oneself in their own managements' shoes by conducting an internal corporate analysis for each of these firms.[11] Coupling the insights from the analysis with data from existing market and competitive analysis (with one's own firm cast in the role of competitor) should provide a good sense of how competitors might be likely to act. If chances seem high that a stronger competitor will move to occupy the same niche with a superior service concept, it would be wise to reconsider the situation.

Some firms develop sophisticated simulation models to analyze the impact of alternative competitive moves. How would a price cut affect demand, market share, and profits? Based on past experience, how might customers in different segments respond to increases or decreases in the level of quality on specific service attributes? How long would it take before customers responded to a new advertising campaign designed to change perceptions?

Evolutionary Positioning

Positions are rarely static: They need to evolve over time in response to changing market structures, technology, competitive activity, and the evolution of the firm itself. Many types of business lend themselves to evolutionary repositioning by adding or deleting services and target segments. Some companies have shrunk their offerings and divested certain lines of business in order to be more focused. Other companies have expanded their offerings in the expectation of increasing sales to existing customers and attracting new ones. Thus, service stations have added small convenience stores offering extended hours of service, whereas supermarkets and other retailers have added banking services. New developments in technology provide many opportunities for introducing not only new services but also new delivery systems for existing products.

When a company has a trusted and successful brand, it may be possible to extend a position based on perceived quality in one type of service to a variety of related services under the same umbrella brand. Best Practice in Action 3-2 features the example of Rentokil Initial, a provider of business-to-business services that has profited from the growing trend toward outsourcing of services related to facilities maintenance.

BEST PRACTICE IN ACTION 3-2

POSITIONING A BRAND ACROSS MULTIPLE SERVICES AT RENTOKIL INITIAL

Rentokil Initial has evolved over eighty years from its origins as a manufacturer of rat poison and a pesticide for killing wood-destroying beetles. From selling poisons and pesticides, the company shifted to pest control and extermination services and then broadened its base to include many other services related to facilities maintenance.

Through organic growth and acquisition of more than 200 companies, it has grown to become the world's largest business services company, operating in more than 40 countries. Its product range is impressive and includes hygiene and cleaning, pest control, distribution and plant services, and personnel, property, and security services. Moreover, the company has been highly profitable over the years.

It sees its core competence as "the ability to carry out high quality services on other people's premises through well-recruited, well-trained, and motivated staff." Cross-selling its existing customers—that is, promoting the use of an additional service to a customer who is already using the company for one or more services—became an important aspect of its strategy.

According to its chief executive:

> We see ourselves very much as an industrial and commercial service company, with markets driven by outsourcing of blue-collar activities on the one hand, and on the other by the demand by employers for an improved and/or sustained environment for their employees.
>
> Our objective has been to create a virtuous circle. We provide a quality service in industrial and commercial activities under the same brand-name, so that a customer satisfied with one Rentokil Initial Service is potentially a satisfied customer for another.... Although it was considered somewhat odd at the time, one of the reasons we moved into [providing and maintaining] tropical plants [for building interiors] was in fact to put the brand in front of decision makers. Our service people maintaining the plants go in through the front door and are visible to the customer. This contrasts with pest control where no one really notices unless we fail.... The brand stands for honesty, reliability, consistency, integrity and technical leadership.[1]

The essence of Rentokil Initial's success lies in its ability to position each of its many business and commercial services in terms of the company's core brand values, which are highly relevant to the nature and quality of service that is delivered. In the case of acquisitions, the task of improving results often requires repositioning the attributes of the newly acquired service to reflect these brand values; related strategies include taking advantage of economies of scale, technical and people-management skills, and cross-selling possibilities. The brand image is reinforced through physical evidence in terms of distinctive uniforms, vehicle color schemes, and use of the corporate logo on all correspondence.

[1]Clive Thompson, "Rentokil Initial: Building a Strong Corporate Brand for Growth and Diversity," in *Brand Warriors,* *F. Gilmore,* ed. (London: HarperCollinsBusiness, 1997), 123–124.

USE POSITIONING MAPS TO PLOT COMPETITIVE STRATEGY

Developing a positioning "map"—a task sometimes referred to as perceptual mapping—is a useful way of representing consumers' perceptions of alternative products graphically. A map is usually confined to two attributes although three-dimensional models can be used to portray three of these attributes. When more than three dimensions are needed to describe product performance in a given market, a series of separate charts need to be drawn for visual presentation purposes. A computer model, of course, can handle as many attributes as are relevant.[12]

Information about a product (or company's position relative to any one attribute) can be inferred from market data derived from ratings by representative consumers, or both. If consumer perceptions of service characteristics differ sharply from "reality" as defined by management, marketing efforts may be needed to change these perceptions.

An Example: Applying Positioning Maps to the Hotel Industry

The hotel business is highly competitive, especially during seasons when the supply of rooms exceeds demand. Customers visiting a large city may find that they have several alternatives within each class of hotels from which to select a place to stay. The degree of luxury and comfort in physical amenities will be one choice criterion; research shows that business travelers are concerned not only with the comfort and facilities offered by their rooms, where they may wish to both work and sleep, but also with other physical spaces, ranging from the reception area, meeting rooms, and a business center to restaurants, swimming pool, and exercise facilities.

The quality and range of services offered by hotel staff is another key criterion: Can a guest get 24-hour room service? Can clothes be laundered and pressed? Is a knowledgeable concierge on duty? Are staff available to offer professional business services? Other choice criteria may relate to the ambiance of the hotel (modern architecture and decor are favored by some customers, whereas others may prefer Old World charm and antique furniture). Additional attributes include such factors as quietness, safety, cleanliness, and special rewards programs for frequent guests.

Let's look at an example, based on a real-world situation, of how developing a positioning map of its own and competing hotels helped managers of the Palace, a successful four-star hotel, develop a better understanding of future threats to its established market position in a large city we will call Belleville.

Developing the Positioning Maps Located on the edge of the booming financial district, the Palace was an elegant old hotel that had been extensively renovated and modernized a few years earlier. Its competitors included eight four-star establishments and the Grand, one of the city's oldest hotels, which had a five-star rating. The Palace had been very profitable for its owners in recent years and boasted an above-average occupancy rate. For many months of the year, it was sold out on weekdays, reflecting its strong appeal to business travelers, who were very attractive to the hotel because of their willingness to pay a higher room rate than tourists or conference delegates. But the general manager and his staff saw problems on the horizon. Planning permission had recently been granted for four large new hotels in the city, and the Grand had just started a major renovation and expansion project, which included construction of a new wing. The risk was that customers might see the Palace as falling behind.

To better understand the nature of the competitive threat, the hotel's management team worked with a consultant to prepare charts that displayed the Palace's position in the business traveler market both before and after the advent of new competition. Four attributes were selected for study: room price, level of physical luxury, level of personal service, and location. In this instance, management did not conduct new consumer research but instead inferred customer perceptions based on published information, data from past surveys, and reports from travel agents and knowledgeable hotel staff members who interacted frequently with customers. Information on competing hotels was not difficult to obtain, as the locations were known, the physical structures were relatively easy to visit and evaluate, and the sales staff kept themselves informed on pricing policies and discounts. A convenient surrogate measure for service level was the ratio of rooms per employee, easily calculated from the published number of rooms and employment data provided to the city authorities. Data from surveys of travel agents conducted by the Palace provided additional insights on the quality of personal service at each competitor.

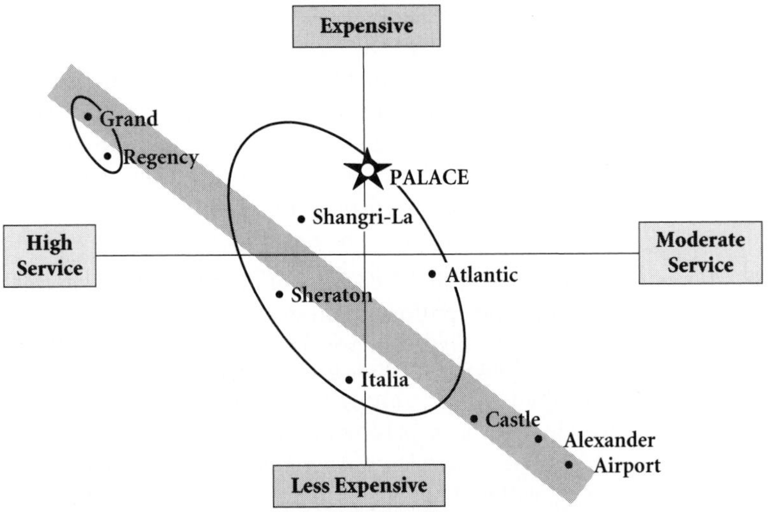

FIGURE 3-4 Positioning Map of Belleville's Principal Business Hotels: Service Level versus Price Level (Before New Competition)

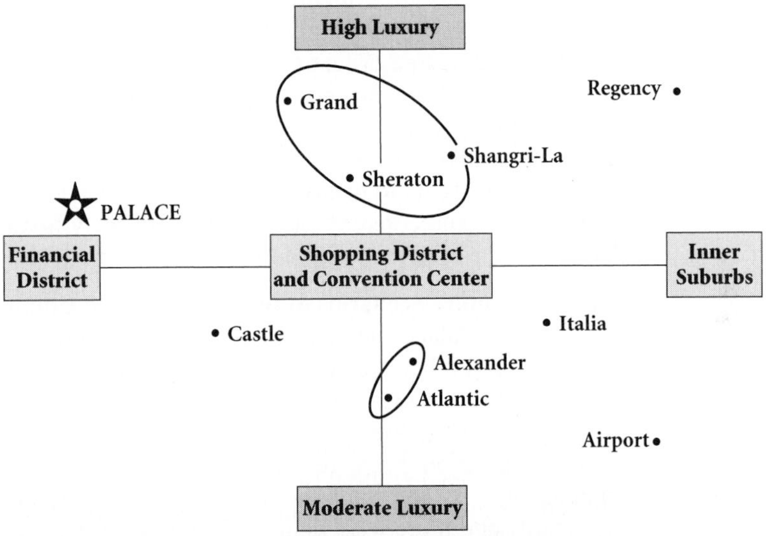

FIGURE 3-5 Positioning Map of Belleville's Principal Business Hotels: Location versus Physical Luxury (Before New Competition)

Scales were then created for each attribute. Price was simple, as the average price charged to business travelers for a standard single room at each hotel was already quantified. The ratio of rooms per employee formed the basis for a service-level scale, with low ratios being equated with high service. This scale was then modified slightly in light of what was known about the quality of service delivered by each major competitor. Level of physical luxury was more subjective. The management team identified the hotel that members agreed was the most luxurious (the Grand) and then the four-star hotel whose physical facilities they viewed as being the least luxurious (the Airport Plaza). All other four-star hotels were then rated on this attribute relative to these two benchmarks.

Location was defined with reference to the stock exchange building in the heart of the financial district, as past research had shown that a majority of the Palace's business guests were visiting destinations in this area. The location scale plotted each hotel in terms of its distance from the stock exchange. The competitive set of 10 hotels lay within a four-mile, fan-shaped radius extending from the exchange through the city's principal retail area, where the convention center was also located, to the inner suburbs and the nearby airport. Two positioning maps were created to portray the existing competitive situation. The first (Figure 3-4) showed the 10 hotels on the dimensions of price and service level; the second (Figure 3-5) displayed them on location and degree of physical luxury.

A quick glance at Figure 3-4 shows a clear correlation between the attributes of price and service: Hotels offering higher levels of service are relatively more expensive. The shaded bar running from upper left to lower right highlights this relationship, which is not a surprising one (and can be expected to continue diagonally downward for three-star and lesser-rated establishments). Further analysis shows three clusters of hotels within what is already an upscale market category. At the top end, the four-star Regency is close to the five-star Grand; in the middle, the Palace is clustered with four other hotels; and at the lower end, there is another cluster of three hotels. One surprising insight from this map is that the Palace appears to be charging significantly more (on a relative basis) than its service level would seem to justify. As its occupancy rate is very high, guests are evidently willing to pay the going rate.

In Figure 3-5 we see how the Palace is positioned relative to the competition on location and degree of luxury. We would not expect these two variables to be related, and they do not appear to be so. A key insight here is that the Palace occupies a relatively empty portion of the map. It is the only hotel in the financial district—a fact that probably explains its ability to charge more than its service level, or degree of physical luxury, would seem to justify. There are two clusters of hotels in the vicinity of the shopping district and convention center: a relatively luxurious group of three, led by the Grand, and a second group of two offering a moderate level of luxury.

Mapping Future Scenarios to Identify Potential Competitive Responses What of the future? The Palace's management team next sought to anticipate the positions of the four new hotels being constructed in Belleville, as well as the probable repositioning of the Grand (see Figures 3-6 and 3-7). The construction sites were already known; two would be in the financial district and two in the vicinity of the convention center, itself under expansion. Press releases distributed by the Grand had already declared its management's intentions: The New Grand would not only be larger but also even more luxurious, and there were plans to add new service features.

Predicting the positions of the four new hotels was not difficult for experts in the field; however, they recognized that customers might initially have more difficulty in predicting each hotel's level of performance on various attributes, especially if the customers were unfamiliar with the chain that would be operating the hotel in question. Preliminary details of the new hotels had already been released to city planners and the business community. The owners of two of the hotels had declared their intentions to seek five-star status, although this might take a few years to achieve. Three of the newcomers would be affiliated with international chains, and their strategies could be guessed by examining recent hotels opened in other cities by these same chains.

Pricing was also easy to project. New hotels use a formula for setting posted room prices (the prices typically charged to individuals staying on a weeknight in high season). This price is linked to the average construction cost per room at the rate of one dollar per night for every thousand dollars of construction costs. Thus, a 200-room hotel that costs $30 million to build (including land costs) would have an average room

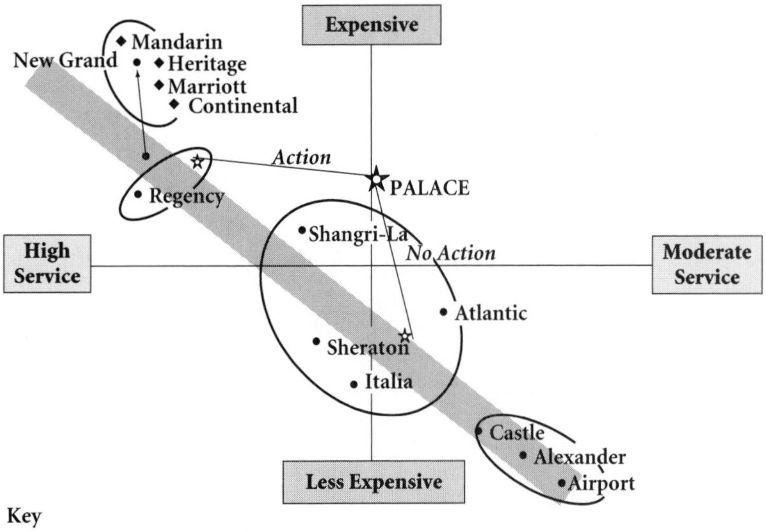

Key
◆ Denotes New Construction

FIGURE 3-6 Future Positioning Map of Belleville's Business Hotels: Service Level versus Price Level

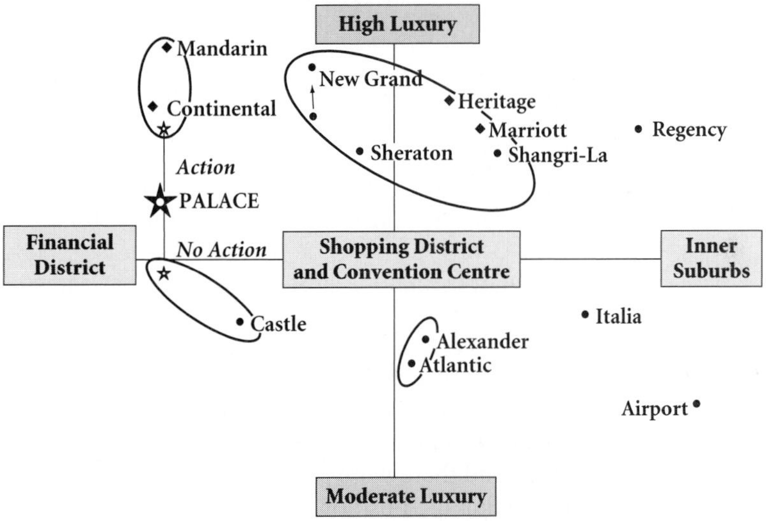

Key
◆ Denotes New Construction

FIGURE 3-7 Future Positioning Map of Belleville's Business Hotels: Location versus Physical Luxury

cost of $150,000 and would need to set a price of $150 per room night. Using this formula, Palace managers concluded that the four new hotels would have to charge significantly more than the Grand or Regency, in effect establishing what marketers call a *price umbrella* above existing price levels and thereby giving competitors the option of raising their own prices. To justify their high prices, the new hotels would have to offer customers very high standards of service and luxury. At the same time, the New Grand would need to raise its own prices to recover the costs of renovation, new construction, and enhanced service offerings (see Figure 3-6).

Assuming no changes by either the Palace or other existing hotels, the impact of the new competition in the market clearly posed a significant threat to the Palace, which would lose its unique locational advantage and in future be one of three hotels in the immediate vicinity of the financial district (Figure 3-7). The sales staff believed that many of the Palace's existing business customers would be attracted to the Continental and the Mandarin and willing to pay their higher rates in order to obtain the superior benefits offered. The other two newcomers were seen as more of a threat to the Shangri-La, Sheraton, and New Grand in the shopping district/convention center cluster. Meantime, the New Grand and the newcomers would create a high-price/high-service (and high-luxury) cluster at the top end of the market, leaving the Regency in what might prove to be a distinctive—and therefore defensible—space of its own.

Using Positioning Charts to Help Visualize Strategy

The Palace Hotel example demonstrates the insights that come from visualizing competitive situations. One of the challenges that strategic planners face is to ensure that all executives have a clear understanding of the firm's current situation before moving to discuss changes in strategy. Chan Kim and Renée Mauborgne argue that graphic representations of a firm's strategic profile and product positions are much easier to grasp than are tables of quantitative data or paragraphs of prose. Charts and maps can facilitate what they call a "visual awakening." By enabling senior managers to compare their business with that of competitors and understand the nature of competitive threats and opportunities, visual presentations can highlight gaps between how customers (or prospects) see the organization and how management sees it and thus help confirm or dispel beliefs that a service or a firm occupies a unique niche in the marketplace.[13]

By examining how anticipated changes in the competitive environment would literally redraw the current positioning map, the management team at the Palace could see that the hotel could not hope to remain in its current market position once it lost its locational advantage. Unless it moved proactively to enhance its level of service and physical luxury, raising its prices to pay for such improvements, the hotel was likely to find itself being pushed into a lower price bracket that might even make it difficult to maintain current standards of service and physical upkeep.

COMPETITIVE POSITIONING CAN BE CHANGED

Sometimes firms have to make a significant change in an existing position. Such a strategy, known as *repositioning*, could mean revising service characteristics or redefining target market segments. At the firm level, repositioning may entail abandoning certain products and withdrawing completely from some market segments. For an example of a need to reposition because of legal and ethical considerations, see Best Practice in Action 3-3.

Changing Perceptions through Advertising

Improving negative brand perceptions may require extensive redesign of the core product and/or supplementary services. However, weaknesses are sometimes perceptual rather than real. Al Ries and Jack Trout describe the case of Long Island Trust, historically the leading bank serving this large suburban area to the east of New York City.[14]

After laws were passed to permit unrestricted branch banking throughout New York State, many of the big banks from neighboring Manhattan began invading Long Island. Research showed that Long Island Trust was rated below the Chase Manhattan and Citibank banks on such key selection criteria as branch availability, full range of services offerings, service quality, and capital resources. However, Long Island Trust ranked first on helping Long Island residents and the Long Island economy.

BEST PRACTICE IN ACTION 3-3

REPOSITIONING AT DOMINO'S PIZZA

Domino's Pizza, a large multinational chain with thousands of outlets, competes in an industry in which the core product is basically a commodity. Although pizza parlors may argue that their product tastes better, competition is more likely to be based on value-added dimensions relating to service delivery. In fact, a firm that sells tough or tasteless food will probably not last long in this competitive marketplace. Some pizza parlors seek to add value by focusing on offering a pleasing restaurant environment open at convenient hours at a convenient location. Others emphasize free home delivery to meet customer needs for speedy delivery of a product that is still piping hot.

For many years, Domino's stressed speed, using the advertising slogan "30 Minutes or It's On Us" to position itself as the best performer on fast, reliable delivery. As a result, the company came to "own" the distinctive attribute of speed in the pizza delivery business. Whenever people thought of fast delivery, Domino's came to mind. According to Tom Monaghan, the company's president, the secret of the company's success and growth was: "A fanatical focus on doing one thing well."

Unfortunately, the operational pressure to maintain speedy deliveries led to a series of highly publicized traffic accidents, including deaths and injuries to teenage delivery drivers. It was even alleged that one restaurant manager, seeking to minimize the loss of income resulting from late deliveries, had instituted a "King of the Lates" award for the driver with the most late deliveries during a given week.[1]

In the face of lawsuits and mounting public outrage, Domino's withdrew its 30-minute guarantee and instituted a new slogan: "Delivering a Million Smiles a Day." To differentiate itself from the competition, the company introduced a new form of pizza bag "that thinks it's an oven." Transporting pizzas in a bag containing a state-of-the-art heating element enabled Domino's to position itself as the firm delivering the hottest and freshest pizza to the customer's door; the company then promoted its "Heatwave" pizza delivery system through a series of amusing television ads.[2]

[1]Michael Kelly, "A Deadly Delivery Problem," *Boston Globe*, July 19, 1989.

[2]Details of Domino's "Heatwave" pizza bag are taken from the company's Web site: *www.dominos.com*, October 1999.

The bank's advertising agency developed a campaign promoting the "Long Island position," playing to its perceived strengths rather than seeking to improve perceptions on attributes on which it was perceived less favorably. The tenor of the campaign can be gauged from the following extract from a bank print ad:

> Why send your money to the city if you live on the Island? It makes sense to keep your money close to home. Not at a city bank but at Long Island Trust. Where it can work for Long Island. After all, we concentrate on developing Long Island. Not Manhattan Island or some island off Kuwait.

Other advertisements in the campaign promoted similar themes, such as, "The city is a great place to visit, but would you want to bank there?"

When identical research was repeated 15 months later, Long Island Trust's position had improved on every attribute. The campaign had succeeded in reframing the bank's brand image by changing its customers' frame of reference from a global to a local perspective. Although the firm had not changed any of its core or supplementary services, the perceived strength of being a Long Island bank for Long Islanders now had a strongly positive halo effect on all other attributes.

Innovation in Positioning

Most companies focus on matching and beating their rivals, with the result that their strategies tend to emphasize the same basic dimensions of competition. However, one way to compete is to introduce new dimensions into the positioning equation that other firms cannot immediately match. James Heskett frames the issue nicely:

> The most successful service firms separate themselves from "the pack" to achieve a distinctive position in relation to their competition. They differentiate themselves . . . by altering typical characteristics of their respective industries to their competitive advantage.[15]

In Chapter 7, we look at opportunities for product innovation in services. In later chapters, we consider innovation in delivery systems.

CONCLUSION

Most service businesses face active competition. Marketers need to find ways of creating meaningful competitive advantages for their products. Ideally, a firm should target segments that it can serve better than other providers can, offering a higher level of performance than competitors on those attributes that are particularly valued by the target segment. The nature of services introduces a number of distinctive possibilities for competitive differentiation, including location, scheduling, and speed of service delivery; the caliber of service personnel; and a range of options for customer involvement in the production process.

The concept of positioning is valuable because it forces explicit recognition of the various attributes comprising the overall service concept and emphasizes the need for marketers to understand which attributes determine customer choice behavior. Positioning maps provide a visual way of summarizing research data and display how various firms are perceived as performing relative to one another on key attributes. When combined with information on the preferences of various segments, including the level of demand that might be anticipated from such segments, positioning maps may suggest opportunities for creating new services or repositioning existing ones to take advantage of unserved market needs.

Review Questions

1. Why should service firms focus their efforts? Describe the basic focus options, and illustrate them with examples.
2. What is the distinction between important and determinant attributes in consumer choice decisions? What type of research can help you to understand which is which?
3. Describe what is meant by *positioning* strategy and the marketing concepts that underlie it.
4. Identify the circumstances under which it is appropriate to reposition an existing service offering.
5. How can positioning maps help managers better understand and respond to competitive dynamics?

Application Exercises

1. Find examples of companies that illustrate each of the four focus strategies discussed in this chapter.
2. Choose an industry you are familiar with (e.g., fast-food restaurants, television networks, or grocery stores) and create a perceptual map showing the competitive positions of various

competitors in the industry, using attributes that you consider to represent key consumer choice criteria.

3. The travel agency business is losing business to online bookings offered to passengers by airline Web sites. Identify some possible focus options open to travel agencies wishing to develop new lines of business that would compensate for this loss of airline ticket sales.
4. Imagine that you are a consultant to the Palace Hotel. Consider the options facing the hotel based on the four attributes appearing in the positioning charts (Figures 3-4 and 3-5). What actions do you recommend that the Palace take in these circumstances? Justify your recommendations.

Endnotes

1. George S. Day, *Market Driven Strategy* (New York: The Free Press, 1990), 164.
2. Robert Johnston, "Achieving Focus in Service Organizations," *The Service Industries Journal* 16 (January 1996): 10–20.
3. For further insights into multiattribute modeling, see William D. Wells and David Prensky, *Consumer Behavior* (New York: John Wiley, 1996), 321–325.
4. Jack Trout, *The New Positioning: The Latest on the World's #1 Business Strategy* (New York: McGraw-Hill, 1997).
5. Kevin Lane Keller, Brian Sternthal, and Alice Tybout, "Three Questions You Need to Ask about Your Brand," *Harvard Business Review* 80 (September 2002): 84.
6. Roger Brown, "How We Built a Strong Company in a Weak Industry," *Harvard Business Review* 79 (February 2001): 51–57.
7. Vijay Mahajan and Yoram (Jerry) Wind, "Got Emotional Product Positioning?" *Marketing Management* (May-June 2002): 36–41.
8. Richard Branson, "Why We Stretch the Virgin Brand," *Evening Standard* (London), August 4, 1997.
9. Sally Dibb and Lyndon Simkin, "The Strength of Branding and Positioning in Services," *International Journal of Service Industry Management* 4, no. 1 (1993): 25–35.
10. Chris Lederer and Sam Hill, "See Your Brands through Your Customers' Eyes," *Harvard Business Review* 79 (June 2001): 125–133.
11. For a detailed approach, see Michael E. Porter, "A Framework for Competitor Analysis," chap. 3 in *Competitive Strategy* (New York: The Free Press, 1980), 47–74.
12. For examples of developing research data for perceptual mapping purposes, see Glen L. Urban and John M. Hauser, *Design and Marketing of New Products*, 2d ed. (Englewood Cliffs, NJ: Prentice-Hall, 1993).
13. W. Chan Kim and Renée Mauborgne, "Charting Your Company's Future," *Harvard Business Review* 80 (June 2002): 77–83.
14. Al Ries and Jack Trout, *Positioning: The Battle for Your Mind*, 1st edition—revised. (New York: Warner Books, 1986).
15. James L. Heskett, *Managing in the Service Economy* (Boston: Harvard Business School Press, 1984), 45.

Service Theater: An Analytical Framework for Services Marketing

STEPHEN J. GROVE
RAYMOND P. FISK

The theater metaphor is a useful framework for describing and analyzing service performances. Employees serving customers may be thought of as actors and customers as the audience that experiences the performance. The marketing implications of this metaphor are discussed for airline travel and electronic performances in cyberspace.

INTRODUCTION

The significant differences between services and physical goods have spawned numerous prescriptions for the successful design and delivery of service products. A keen understanding of the nature of services is an important first step toward achieving service excellence. Various models have been developed to help practitioners and scholars comprehend the complex character of the service experience. One early model suggests expanding the traditional marketing-mix elements of product, price, promotion, and place to include three additional Ps (i.e., participants, physical evidence, and process of service assembly) among a services marketing mix (Booms and Bitner 1981). A second model depicts the service experience as an elaborate production system of technology, management, resources, and personnel that is driven by a business mission and is responsive to customer expectations (Grönroos 1991). In a third model, services are described as a "servuction system" (a hybrid of service and production) that includes physical areas that are visible and invisible to the service customer, an inanimate environment, contact personnel, and customer interaction. (Langeard et al. 1981)

Although these models generate valuable insights regarding service experiences, none describes the complex nature of services, demonstrates their common characteristics, captures their interactive essence, and facilitates communication about their enactment in a lucid and simple fashion. Based on observations derived from the sociology and theater literatures, we propose a simple yet comprehensive framework for understanding service experiences. We contend that service experiences are theater and encompass many of the same features and principles as theatrical performances. This article explores service theater as a comprehensive framework for understanding, analyzing, and discussing service experiences. First, we examine the social and physical context of service experiences. Second, the theatrical nature of service experiences is explained. Third, airlines services are described as an example of service theater. Fourth, the service metaphor is extended to the realm of cyberspace.

THE SOCIAL AND PHYSICAL CONTEXT OF SERVICE EXPERIENCES

At any moment of any day, you may be involved in a service experience. A *service experience* occurs whenever a customer and a service organization interact. A visit to the dentist's office, a night's stay in a hotel, a session surfing the World Wide Web, or a meal in a restaurant are all examples of service experiences. Listening to a rock concert, mailing a letter, or purchasing a pair of shoes are service experiences as well. While not always the case, a service experience frequently occurs in an organization's physical environment and involves the presence of other customers. The service provided by an ocean liner, for example, encompasses the vessel and the passengers. The layout of the ship, its decor and comfort, its features and furnishings, and

Portions of this article are based on our earlier publication, "The Dramaturgy of Services Exchange: An Analytical Framework for Services Marketing" published by the American Marketing Association in 1983.

other environmental aspects affect the cruise experience. In addition, the people sharing space on the ocean liner affect one another by their number, character, and actions.

Most services are the result of one or more workers performing various tasks. To illustrate, consider the number of employees involved in making a hospital stay a success. Physicians and orderlies, nurses and their aides, porters and desk clerks, and a host of others all play a part in fashioning the patient's experience. Overall, the physical setting, the service workers and their tasks, and the other customers combine to influence the nature of the service experience.

Due to intangibility and the simultaneity of production and consumption of services, customers often have difficulty assessing the quality of the services they receive (Zeithaml 1981). Hence, the social milieu (i.e., the interaction with the workers and other customers) and the service's physical environment (i.e., the nature of the facilities and equipment) provide important cues to the excellence of the service rendered. Based on this observation, astute service organizations are wise to "tangibilize" their service offering by managing these aspects of the customers' experience (Berry 1981; Lovelock 1994; Shostack 1977). Because the staging of a theatrical performance involves many of the same considerations that are important for fashioning a successful service experience (i.e., expressive physical cues, performers and their actions, and audience participation), we suggest that it is plausible to approach services as theater.

THE THEATRICAL NATURE OF SERVICE EXPERIENCES[1]

Describing human behavior as theater is not new, but systematically applying a theater metaphor to service experiences is unique. Much of the basis for applying theater to services can be linked to observations anchored in the sociological school of thought known as *dramaturgy* as well as to an appreciation of theater as a performing art. Dramaturgy depicts social interaction in the terms and concepts of a theatrical production. The contemporary dramaturgical perspective is significantly based on the work of Erving Goffman and his book *The Presentation of Self in Everyday Life* (1959). Goffman examined the structure of social interaction when people are in the presence of others and how a definition of the behavioral situation is created and maintained, even in the face of potential disruptions. Although Goffman contends that people use theatrical devices and insights to accomplish these goals, we propose that service organizations can use similar tools to create successful service experiences for their customers. After all, just as theater is described as "an experience–a shared indivisible event that includes both those who perform and those who observe" (Wilson 1991, 3), services can be characterized in the same way. Several of the concepts that Goffman offers and others have found in the theater literature are relevant for framing services as theater. Among these are performance, performance teams, regions and region behavior, and impression management.

Performance

Performance describes an *actor*'s activity when there is continuous contact with an *audience.* By their nature, performances are designed to have same impact on an audience. Performances can be characterized as sincere or cynical. Sincere performances occur when an actor essentially becomes the role that he is playing. Cynical performances occur when an actor views a performance only as a means to an end. To create and communicate a believable performance, actors often employ various expressive devices, such as aspects of the setting, their personal appearance, and their behavioral manner.

The *setting* is comprised of the decor, furnishings, and physical layout at the performance's location, while the actor's *personal appearance* and *manner* are reflected in their dress, facial expression, gestures, demographic profile, and personality. When consistent with each other, the setting and the actor's personal profile create an important set of cues for the audience. With this in mind, it's not surprising that actors may conceal or underplay aspects of the expressive devices that may be incompatible with the desired performance. The reality portrayed in a service performance is fragile and is easily upset by even minor contradictions.

Service experiences are performances They reflect the efforts of a service organization and its workers (actors) to satisfy customer (audience) needs. Those needs might be a stylish haircut, transportation from Chicago to Toronto, care for a pet poodle, or safe

[1]Much of this discussion relies on the insight of Erving Gofman and his book, *The Presentation of Self in Everyday Life,* published by Doubleday and Company in 1959.

storage of a person's life savings. In each of these: cases, to create and sustain customer perceptions of excellence, service personnel must adhere to the principles of a successful performance. They must (1) believe in the importance of customer satisfaction (i.e., be sincere), (2) consider the communicative capability of the service setting and workers personal profiles (i.e., attend to the expressive devices), and (3) work hard to avoid contradicting the image of excellence they seek (i.e., present a consistent front). Consider the example of Ritz Carlton, where each of these performance-related directives is fastidiously followed. The result is a well-designed service delivery system that has garnered the esteemed Malcolm Baldrige Award and is a widely recognized image of excellence.

Performance Teams

Most theatrical productions require the coordinated effort of several actors to create an audience's experience. *Performance teams* are sets of actors who cooperate to create a single impression to which the audience responds. Although each member contributes in her own way, it is the combined effort of the entire team that fashions an audience's experience. In a sense, the importance of the performance is the common bond that holds a team together. Those participating in any theatrical production must respect each other's role if the performance is to be perceived as credible. When actors criticize their teammates, fail to cooperate, or neglect the effort to portray a unified front, a performance may be shattered.

Service organizations face similar consideration in the process of service delivery. Most service experiences are the result of several workers cooperating as a team. These workers may operate in full view of the customer, that is, the *cast,* or be among those who are instrumental to the service delivery yet are seldom seen. Even providing simple services such as changing automobile oil or laundering clothes requires that all employees recognize the importance of the performance promised to the customer.

A single employee can ruin the service experience for the customer by failing to enact his tasks correctly, ridiculing others' efforts, or failing to project the desired image. When the service process goes well, it is usually the result of a team effort that is unnoticed by the customer. When service fails, it is frequently because a team member did not play her assigned part. This issue takes on greater complexity as the size of the cast and support personnel increases. For instance, compare the difficulty of ensuring a successful team effort for a hotel versus a full-service car wash. The complex nature of a hotel service requires more workers, which makes creating and sustaining teamwork more difficult.

The Setting: Regions and Region Behavior

The setting where a performance occurs is an important source of information for the audience and a critical component of any theatrical production. The setting is comprised of front and back regions. The front region, or *frontstage,* is in full view of the audience and is the part of the setting that carries significant communicative capability. The frontstage and the cast members who perform there must meet the audience's approval. Attention to detail, careful planning of the physical cues, well-rehearsed scripts, and choreographed movements by the actors are all important. The back region, or *backstage,* is hidden from the audience's view and is where the preparation and support for the frontstage performance occurs. Here, actors drop their front and step out of character. In the backstage, actors may rehearse their parts, memorize their scripts, perfect their teamwork, or work through flaws in their parts. Also found backstage are various workers and equipment that contribute to the frontstage performance, but they are usually unnoticed by the audience. In a theatrical production, these include wardrobe personnel, stage crews, lighting, and sound equipment.

Normally, the two regions are kept separate owing to the risk of the audience discovering behavior and physical cues contradictory to a credible performance. Beyond observing imperfection in performances, the audience could be exposed to improper behavior and unappealing physical evidence. Cursing, slovenly demeanor, complaining, unkempt equipment, and dirty conditions might be seen. To protect against such mishaps, careful attention is often given to keeping the passageway between the two regions closed.

The typical service experience occurs in a setting marked by distinct front- and backstage areas, too. The service setting, sometimes referred to as the *servicescape* (Bitner 1992), is comprised of a front region designed to appeal to customers and to facilitate service delivery and a back region housing the operational support system of the service. The frontstage involves various props, decor, and furnishings that define the service for the customer and frame the performance. Lighting, music, air temperature, and aroma play a role here, too. For example, a restaurant can present itself as an Italian eatery, a Chinese take-out, or a French bistro by the selection of frontstage devices. However, if the backstage equipment, support staff, and management in the kitchen area go awry, all may be lost. If a diner stumbles into a food preparation area on his way to the restroom, the appearance of the chef, the backstage work conditions, the behavior of the staff, or other disruptive cues may shatter the perception of excellence. For that reason, most restaurants do not allow patrons to enter their back regions.

Actors and Impression Management

At the heart of any theatrical performance are the actors whose presence and behavior fashion the show for the audience. Some performances are better than others due to the casting and the abilities of the actors involved. The actors' task is to present or contribute to a believable performance. In general, it is the actors that the audience views as the key determinant of a show's quality. Hence, actors in a theatrical production engage in *impression management*, or the creation and maintenance of a credible show. Impression management relies on actors' abilities to convey their roles effectively. Beyond learning their parts, actors' interpretations of their roles through such things as facial expressions, gestures, and vocal inflections have much to do with a play's effect on the audience (Wilson 1991). Impression management also involves the various performers (and backstage personnel, too) adhering to defensive practices that are designed to guard against mistakes. Specifically, the actors must demonstrate loyalty, discipline, and circumspection regarding the performance.

Loyalty means that the actors must accept the importance of the performance and avoid disclosing secrets regarding its enactment to the audience or others not directly involved in the production. *Discipline* means that they are obliged to learn their parts and guard against unwittingly committing gestures or mistakes that might destroy a performance. Finally, *circumspection* means that the actors need to plan in advance how best to stage the show. If an actor reveals inside information, he is being disloyal. If he allows his personal problems to interfere with his stage responsibilities, he lacks discipline. If he fails to consider what it takes to be credible in his role, he is not circumspect. For a successful performance to occur, none of these can happen, or the impression will be damaged.

Service experiences rely on the impression-management expertise of the workers in much the same way that stage performances do. From the customers' point of view, the employees *are* the service. (Schneider and Bowen 1995; Surprenant and Solomon 1987; Tansik 1990), and their attitudes and behavior have a significant impact (Hartline and Ferrel 1996). What the workers do (their technical skills) and how they do it (their functional skills) are critical to customers' evaluations of service excellence (Grönroos 1990). The dentist, hotel clerk, and educator are assessed on how well they perform regarding the outcome of their effort (e.g., a filled cavity, properly assigned room, and information learned, respectively) and the manner in which it was done (e.g., the concern shown, the courtesy displayed, the responsiveness demonstrated).

In each service, the workers must strive to manage an impression of excellence through their adherence to defensive practices. They must (1) keep potentially destructive information undisclosed (e.g., the risk of abnormal pain from the dental drill), (2) guard against the intrusion of personal strife (e.g., resist the urge to share financial problems with the hotel guest), and (3) ensure a well-devised service delivery through forethought (e.g., anticipate students' questions regarding lecture material). These considerations can be addressed by service organizations in the hiring, training, and monitoring of their workers. The significance of impression management and the various ways an impression might be destroyed are important issues to stress in service organizations and in theatrical productions. It is not surprising that some have advocated that service training should include an acting class (Billingsley 1998; Grove, Fisk, and Knowles 1996).

Audience

Every theatrical performance is designed to appeal to a particular audience. Stated differently, if any performance is to be fully appreciated, it must conform to the audience's desires and expectations. Great performances are sometimes lost on the wrong audience. Individuals expecting to see a comedy are often disappointed with a drama. Even with the right audience, adaptations or adjustments by the actors are sometimes needed to keep the audience entertained. Hence, a successful performance requires attracting and reaching the appropriate audience. The right audience has a vested interest in seeing the show unfold smoothly. Specifically, the audience can be expected to engage in so-called protective practices which allow the show to go on when minor mishaps occur. After all, the audience attends a performance to see the entire show. If an actor misses a line or is out of place on stage or if a stage prop is missing, the audience will typically allow such miscues in the interest of enjoying the entire production. At the same time, those responsible for a stage production must ensure that some audience members do not disrupt others through their verbal or physical actions. Someone talking too loudly or crowding another's personal space can ruin the performance for other audience members.

Many services are delivered to multiple customers sharing the same servicescape, such as hotels, hospitals, schools, airlines, and restaurants. For a service experience to be successful, "recruiting the right customers is as important as recruiting the right personnel" (Gummesson 1993, 1999). Similar to the case of a stage production, the wrong customers (audience) for a service designed for others are likely to be dissatisfied (Lovelock 1994). The young couple who enter a restaurant expecting full-service, romantic dining only to find buffet-style, family dining will be disappointed. Most services are not likely to exclude paying customers simply because they do not fit the desired target audience profile. Also, antidiscrimination laws often prohibit attempts to exclude customer groups. Consequently, efforts at maintaining customer compatibility (Martin and Pranter 1989), policing the customers (Lovelock 1981), and recognizing how customers affect each other (Grove and Fisk 1997) ensure that everyone's service experience is positive.

Like theatrical productions, service providers can expect that the customers will overlook small flaws or minor problems during the process of service delivery in the interest of enjoying the service in its entirety. For that reason the dirty utensil, the hotel room that is missing a towel, or the taxi that's five minutes late are usually overlooked. Although any of these may be a failed "moment of truth" (Carlzon 1987), each is seldom significant enough by itself to destroy the overall quality of the service experience.

As a final note, successful service strategy begins with knowing the customers. Disney stresses the critical role of "guestology" (the study of the customers it services) as a key reason for its success. Disney conducts over two hundred external surveys a year; tracks demographic profiles, price sensitivity, and evaluation of attractions by guests; monitors the tens of thousands of letters and comment cards it receives; and practices management by walking around. By doing so, Disney gathers critical information that enables the design of a service experience that delights its guests (Johnson 1991).

AIRLINE SERVICE: AN APPLICATION OF SERVICE THEATER

This section develops a theatrical explanation of airline services as an illustration of the service theater concepts we have developed. Throughout the example, the service actors (airport and airline employees), service setting (airport facilities and airplane cabin), service audience (passengers), and service performance (enactment of the airline service) are interwoven to create a successful service experience. The example is developed around the theatrical device of the three-act play. Act 1 is the airport departure. Act 2 is the airline flight. Act 3 is the destination arrival.

Act 1: Airport Departure

Act 1 begins as airline passengers arrive at the front door of the airport. A porter might approach a passenger at the curb and offer to check her bags, or the passenger may decide to proceed inside the airport to the ticket counter. The ticket counter is the first frontstage area controlled by the airline. The passengers may note the cleanliness of the area and the state of the computer terminals and information displays. A performance team of ticket counter staff must work together to check in each passenger and the passenger's baggage. Every passenger's identity must be verified, his or her ticket and seating assignment must be confirmed, security questions must be asked, and any baggage must be tagged for its destination. The counter personnel are likely to exhibit efficiency, courtesy, and composure as they deal with one passenger after another. The uniforms they wear and the scripts they follow enhance their professionalism.

Once the baggage is checked, it disappears into the backstage region of the airport. The passenger is then instructed to proceed to a second frontstage area, the departure gate, where a smaller performance team of two or three airline staff prepares passengers for departure. The decor and comfort of the waiting area, the size and mix of passengers waiting to board the plane, and the efficiency with which the process unfolds will all impact passenger experiences. The staff is expected to display the same professionalism as their ticket-counter peers as they process passengers, handle ticket or seating problems, and announce airline boarding procedures and times. Like the waiting area, the staff's actions and demeanor are aspects of the unfolding service performance.

Every airline develops its own version of boarding procedures, which must be clearly conveyed to passengers to ensure efficiency. As an example, when a recent British Airways flight to London was called to board, the U.S. passengers formed a rather haphazard line of people two to three people across. One of the British Airways uniformed staff looked at the line in dismay and announced over the loudspeaker that "no one is going to go to London until you form a *proper* line." The Americans looked at each other in puzzlement and then realized that a "proper line" must be a single-file line. By contrast, Southwest Airlines has developed a nearly legendary reputation for the speed and efficiency of its boarding procedures by issuing a numbered plastic tag at check-in but no seat assignment. Based on these numbers, passengers on Southwest are boarded in groups, and they are expected to take the first seat available.

Act 2: The Airline Flight

Act 2 is the main act of the airline service and begins as passengers enter the airplane cabin. New performance teams of airline pilots and cabin personnel are the key players in act 2. The frontstage area is the cabin itself, and the backstage areas are the cockpit and the baggage compartment. A crew member, smartly attired and neatly groomed, greets the passengers as they board the plane and directs them to their seats. Once passengers have taken their seats and buckled their seat belts, the airplane will begin to pull away from the gate and taxi toward the runway. Already the passengers will be forming impressions of act 2 based on many different cues. The comfort of the seats, the amount of leg room, the air quality, the clarity of the public address system, and the colors and patterns of the cabin furnishings and carpet are consciously and unconsciously scanned. Even the number and mix of other passengers are noticed. Along the way, passengers are instructed about safety procedures. Most airlines follow a standard script to recite the safety procedures, yet others improvise. For example, it is common for a crew member on Southwest Airlines to sing the safety instructions to the passengers.

After the plane takes off, the cabin crew begins food and beverage service, and in-flight entertainment may commence. Each of these provides further cues to help passengers form impressions of the service. Meanwhile, the captain will greet the passengers over the loudspeaker and comment on flying conditions, flight time, visible landmarks along the flight, and weather at the destination. The pilot usually closes with a comment that the crew will do everything they can to make the flight pleasant and comfortable. It is noteworthy that the cabin crew usually introduces themselves to passengers, whereas the land-based crews almost never introduce themselves. The gestures and expressions of the flight attendants, the affability ascribed to the pilot by virtue of his voice, and the helpfulness of the crew in general furnish additional information that fashions the flight experience for the service's audience. Other passengers in the service audience can also strongly influence each passenger's evaluation of the flight. Babies crying, children kicking the back of seats, or drunks trying to start a conversation can play a very negative role in the evaluation of the service despite the best efforts of the airline crew.

Although standard flight procedures or scripts must be followed, flight crews must sometimes go to extra lengths to make passengers comfortable. Several years ago, one of the authors boarded a Delta Air Lines flight the morning after a major airline crash. Safety anxieties were on the minds of passengers that morning as they nervously buckled their seat belts while the plane prepared to depart. Fortunately, the pilot and crew were well aware that the passengers might be unusually tense. As the plane made its last turn onto the runway and began its acceleration for liftoff, the sounds of the *William Tell* Overture burst from the loudspeakers. The unexpected but well-known music broke the anxiety among the travelers, and the plane hurtled into the air with a cabin full of passengers laughing uproariously.

Act 3: Destination Arrival

Act 3 begins as passengers line up to exit the airplane cabin and enter the airport facilities at their destination. The airplane crew and the workers at the destination must cooperate to move the passengers out of the cabin and on their way. Attempts are made to open the cabin doors quickly and speed travelers into the terminal. The cabin crew will often take advantage of one last opportunity to demonstrate efficiency through the manner by which they dispatch this task. They also attempt to convey a personal touch by bidding the passengers farewell and thanking them for flying their airline. However, most of the activity in this act of the service performance is self-service or occurs backstage as the airline's baggage crew unloads the plane and delivers the baggage to the baggage claim area. Occasionally, passengers may catch a glimpse of baggage handlers tossing luggage onto trams to be whisked away to the terminal as they wait to deplane. This normally backstage activity then becomes a frontstage spectacle that may have significant consequences for impressions of service excellence. The horror of observing a carefully packed suitcase containing breakable souvenirs haphazardly hurled into a heap of bags has caused many travelers considerable distress.

Most airlines have at least one person directing passengers to their connecting flights, to airport exits, or to the baggage claim area once they surge into the terminal. Aided by computer devices, experience with exasperated voyagers, and a personality that can withstand the pressure akin to that faced by a traffic officer, this service performer is likely to be the final face that the passenger puts on the service personnel. The clarity of his directions, the urgency he conveys, and the courtesy he displays can confirm the excellence of the service experience. If the passenger must find her way to the baggage claim, one last scene of the airline's service performance remains to be played: the speed of baggage delivery. It is an aspect of the airline's service that often goes unappreciated when the backstage personnel and systems operate efficiently, but it is a significant source of dissatisfaction if bags are slow to arrive or are lost in transit. Once the airline passengers locate their baggage and exit the airport, the airline service experience is completed.

Throughout the three-act service experience depicted here, various actors and their roles, setting conditions and regions, audience participation and circumstances, and performance attributes play significant parts in the passengers' impression of service excellence. Conceiving the entire service as theater provides a common framework that links and organizes the many factors that contribute to a service experience. Regardless of the service considered, the metaphor of theater can be applied.

SERVICE THEATER IN CYBERSPACE

As the twentieth century drew to a close, a remarkable phenomenon occurred: the emergence and widespread adoption of electronic commerce (e-commerce). *Cyberspace* is a term used to describe the artificial reality created by computers and the Internet that makes e-commerce possible. Today, a vast array of products are bought and sold through the medium of cyberspace. Whether purchasing an automobile, financial advice, a tanning bed, or tax preparation, cyberspace brings the seller and buyer together in a manner far removed from typical retailing. Cyberspace also makes it possible for organizations to disseminate all sorts of information pertaining to their operations. Business location, availability of merchandise, hours of operation, prices, installation instructions, and more can be communicated quickly and efficiently through cyberspace. In essence, cyberspace provides a means for organizations to provide a service (whether it is the retailing of a product or provision of information). All of the service theater concepts discussed in the previous sections pertain to cyberspace just as they do for marketing services in physical space. Although the boundaries between the various components of service theater may become blurred in the seamless world of cyberspace, they are nevertheless present and pliable.

In cyberspace the service performance is electronic. Unlike most services that are delivered in physical space, a cyberspace performance can be carefully automated and tightly scripted. Like its physical-space counterpart, much of what transpires during a cyberspace performance is dictated by the stage on which it occurs. However, the setting and the service stage in cyberspace are inherently more limited in terms of physical size than those found in physical space. The user's computer screen and the narrow bandwidth feeding it constitute a cyberspace service's frontstage. These frontstage dimensions combine to create a special challenge for cyberspace service marketers, forcing them to work hard to grab their audience's attention and to provide their audience with provocative reasons to "remain seated" during the performance's enactment. After all, cyberspace customers can switch performances with the mere click of a button! Yet what a cyberspace service may lack in frontstage dimensions, it can compensate for greatly with its backstage operation. Because of the interconnected nature of the Internet, the backstage in cyberspace may be much larger than is typical in physical space. The cyberspace backstage can range from one computer server and the support staff who operate it to a large network of servers and support staff across a multisite organization that collectively sustain the service performance 24 hours a day, 7 days a week. Delivering an excellent cyberspace service experience to its audience requires an organization to choreograph and direct a performance that takes advantage of the backstage domain. Failure to do so may result in the audience's quick exit, perhaps to another service's performance. In cyberspace, there is no distance or travel time between service theaters. Further, because there are so many free services in cyberspace, there are virtually no switching costs to barricade the exit doors. Only a riveting performance will prevent switching. Obviously, the design of the frontstage, the ease of its navigation, and the story it tells must be compelling.

In cyberspace, the service actors are often masked by the performance itself. In one sense, the Web site that provides the service portrays the actors as well as the performance. Essentially, the automated nature of the Web site makes it difficult to distinguish the cyberspace performance from the actors' roles. The two are frequently seamless. Across most cyberspace services, the actions of the service actor—the behaviors that create and deliver the service—are captured by and hidden in the text and texture of the Web site itself. Although they are impossible to discern separately from the Web site, they are there nonetheless. As the technology for delivering services in cyberspace improves, it may be feasible to simulate the appearance of human actors on the Web site and produce an anthropomorphic presence that more closely reflects service interaction in physical space. For those few cyberspace services that currently provide access to a live human being via their electronic link, that is, someone who can respond to questions or inquiries, the service actor is simply a participant in a remote servicescape (Bitner 1992). In such cases, his or her performance must exhibit all of the same considerations as any service actor that is invisible yet interactive with the customer (e.g., telephone receptionists or catalogue sales personnel).

Finally, the audience that participates in cyberspace's service theater is in control of most of the action. The audience can choose the time that the "curtain will go up" and the location of the service performance itself. Hence, cyberspace organizations must design their performances so that their audience can begin the service at its convenience and depart when it wishes. The backstage support and the frontstage design must facilitate the audience's entrance into, movement about, and exit from the cyberspace setting. A further, interesting aspect is that once the audience has gained access to the service organization, it commonly chooses the story line of a service performance in cyberspace. Due to the interactive nature of an Internet Web site such as Amazon.com or Yahoo!, each customer may select a set of pages uniquely suited to his or her interests. Amazon.com tries to encourage this behavior by greeting each repeat visitor with a customized page that includes suggested books and other items based on the pattern of previous purchases. This self-directed component of the service performance ostensibly provides a greater opportunity for a satisfying outcome to the service performance, but only if care is taken to design the various theatrical dimensions of the cyberspace service with the audience in mind. The performance must be simple but provocative; the staging must be inviting yet beguiling; and the actors must be caring and creative in meeting the audience's needs. Otherwise, the cyberspace service experience bytes.

SUMMARY AND CONCLUSION

The preceding passages demonstrate the correspondence between theatrical concepts rooted in dramaturgy or stage productions and those that are important for managing the service experience. From our perspective, both theater and services are involved in a large-scale effort to manage impressions. If service organizations explore the theatrical nature of services in their industry, they are likely to discover that the concepts discussed here (and other theatrical elements) may have profound significance.

To some, viewing and framing services as theater may hint at artificiality and manipulation. In reality, when a theatrical approach to services is successfully developed, the opposite is probable. Organizations and their personnel begin to see that they are in the business of creating experiences and recognize that this effort involves all of the trappings that are commonly found in theatrical productions. Hence, there is no room for insincerity. Poor performances—ones that are not credible—are not tolerated. No one can slouch in his or her responsibility, whether it is frontstage or backstage, because everyone plays a part in the overall production. The ultimate goal is a performance that engages the customer in an experience that suspends beliefs of organizational disinterest, commercialism, impersonality, and disregard. A theatrical approach attempts this through a unified and well-executed portrayal designed to create and sustain impressions that reflect the audience's desires. This cannot happen unless the service organization accepts the premise that services are theater in their own right and works hard to ensure an excellent performance.

If customers discover that a service organization has presented a false front, they are likely to take their patronage elsewhere. Hence, service marketers must convey the significance of service theater and stress authenticity throughout the service organization. In most cases, service organizations must guard against the temptation to display canned performances. Many performances are rigidly scripted with little room for actors to improvise. Managers should learn the importance of adapting to customer needs and wants and pursuing flexible strategies in fashioning the service experience. Rather than follow a fixed script, the service worker should be empowered to tailor the performance to the audience. Service managers should also appreciate the need for appropriateness. Absurd, ludicrous, or uncaring performances are likely to yield very negative customer reviews and may result in a service performance that closes early, whereas pertinent, seemly, and caring performances are likely to be held over by popular demand. In short, service performances must respond to the desires of the service audience.

In summary, service theater provides a unifying framework for describing and communicating the service experience. To that end, we have identified the many ways service organizations share characteristics and practices that are similar to theater or a dramaturgical depiction of human behavior. Whether it is a vendor selling Lucky Dogs on Bourbon Street in New Orleans, the combined efforts of the cast members at Disney World, the telephone receptionist taking customers' orders at L.L. Bean, or the cyberspace service offered by Amazon.com, a theatrical performance is occurring. Different service experiences are likely to reflect theatrical elements to varying degrees, yet from the customer's perspective, a show is always unfolding. For example, although the appearance of L.L. Bean's setting or actors is unlikely to carry much importance for its audience's experience, the actors' demeanor and defensive practices and the service's backstage operations are sure to have a significant impact. In contrast, the Lucky Dog vendor has a different set of theatrical elements to address. The frontstage, that is, the vending cart, and the merchant's appearance are quite important to the audience's enjoyment of the service. Organizations must determine which theatrical elements are of greatest significance for forming the customers' impressions and experience.

As a conceptual tool, therefore, service theater demonstrates the implicit and explicit relationships among the service organization, its customers, its employees, and its physical or cyberspace properties. As with any metaphor, the description of services in theatrical terms facilitates communication and analysis of the phenomenon and can be used to generate researchable propositions. It is our contention that applying the theater metaphor to services provides a holistic framework and vocabulary for understanding and managing service experiences.

References

Berry, Leonard L. 1981. "Perspectives on the Retailing of Services." In *Theory in Retailing: Traditional and Non-traditional Sources,* edited by Ronald W. Stampfl and Elizabeth C. Hirschman, Chicago: American Marketing Association.

Billingsley, Kevin. 1998. "Service Providers Can Learn A Lot in Acting 101." *Marketing News* 32 (23): 13–14.

Bitner, Mary Jo. 1992. "Servicescapes: The Impact of Physical Surroundings on Customers and Employees." *Journal of Marketing* 56 (April): 57–71.

Booms, Bernard H., and Mary Jo Bitner. 1981. "Marketing Strategies and Organizational Structures for Service Firms." In *Marketing of Services,* edited by James H. Donnelly and William R. George. Chicago: American Marketing Association.

Carlzon, Jan. 1987. *Moments of Truth,* New York: Ballinger.

Goffman, Erving. 1959. *The Presentation of Self in Everyday Life.* Garden City, NY: Doubleday.

Grönroos, Christian. 1990. *Services Marketing and Management.* Lexington, MA: Lexington Books.

Grove, Stephen J., and Raymond P. Fisk. 1983. "The Dramaturgy of Services Exchange: An Analytical Framework for Services Marketing." In *Emerging Perspectives on Services Marketing,* edited by Leonard L. Berry, G. Lynn Shostack, and Gregory D. Upah. Chicago: American Marketing Association.

———. 1997. "The Impact of Other Customers on Service Experiences: A Critical Incident Examination of 'Getting Along.'" *Journal of Retailing* 73(1): 63–85.

Grove, Stephen J., Raymond P. Fisk, and Patricia A. Knowles. 1996. "Developing the Impression Management Skills of the Service Actor." Paper presented at the Frontiers in Services Marketing Conference, Nashville, Tennessee.

Gummesson, Evert. 1993. *Quality Management in Service Organizations.* St. Johns University. NY: International Service Quality Association.

Hartline, Michael D., and O. C. Ferrell. 1996. "The Management of Customer-Contact Service Employees: An Empirical Investigation." *Journal of Marketing* 60 (October): 52–70.

Johnson, Rick. 1991. "A Strategy for Service–Disney Style." *Journal of Business Strategy.* (September/October): 38–43.

Langeard, Eric, John E. G. Bateson, Christopher H. Lovelock, and Pierre Eiglier. eds. 1981. *Marketing of Services: New Insights from Consumers and Managers.* Cambridge, MA: Marketing Science Institute.

Lovelock, Christopher H. 1981. "Why Marketing Management Needs to be Different for Services." In *Marketing of Services,* edited by James H. Donnelly and William R. George. Chicago: American Marketing Association.

———. 1994. *Product Plus: How Product + Service = Competitive Advantage.* New York: McGraw-Hill.

Martin, Charles L., and Charles A. Pranter. 1989. "Compatibility Management: Customer-to-Customer Relationships in Service Environments." *Journal of Services Marketing* 3 (summer): 6–15.

Schneider, Benjamin, and David E. Bowen. 1995. *Winning the Service Game.* Boston: Harvard Business School Press.

Shostack, G. Lynn. 1977. "Breaking Free from Product Marketing." *Journal of Marketing* 41 (April): 73–80.

Surprenant, Carol F., and Michael R. Solomon. 1987. "Predictability and Personalization in Service Encounter." *Journal of Marketing* 51 (April): 86–96.

Tansik, David A. 1990. "Managing Human Resource Issues for High-Contract Service Personnel." In *Service Management Effectiveness: Balancing Strategy Organization and Human Resources, Operations, and Marketing,* edited by David Bowen, Richard B. Chase, Thomas G. Cummings, and associates. San Francisco: Jossey-Bass.

Wilson, Edwin. 1991. *The Theater Experience.* 5th ed. New York: McGraw-Hill.

Zeithaml, Valarie A. 1981. "How Consumer Evaluation Processes Differ between Goods and Services." In *Marketing of Services,* edited by James H. Donnelly and William R. George. Chicago: American Marketing Association.

How We Built a Strong Company in a Weak Industry

Roger Brown

ENTREPRENEURS WANTED: Help to grow an enterprise from scratch in industry that offers no barriers to entry, historically low margins, massive labor scarcity, no proprietary technology, few economies of scale, weak brand distinctions, and heavy regulatory oversight. Serious inquiries only.

Not many people would respond to an ad like this. But it pretty much sums up the opportunity that Linda, my wife, and I decided to pursue years ago when we founded Bright Horizons, our workplace child care and education company. And despite the challenges inherent in the industry we succeeded. We now operate more than 340 high-quality child care centers, serving 40,000 children and employing 12,000 people, and we have built a solid, profitable business.

While we're proud that our company is growing and profitable, our goal was always broader than just building a good business. Early in our careers, Linda and I had stints as management consultants, but we also had a great deal of interest and experience in human services. We both left business school, where we met, to run a CARE-sponsored effort in Cambodia to help refugee children. Later, we took leaves of absence from consulting to start a Save the Children relief program in Ethiopian refugee camps and famine-stricken Sudanese villages. When we returned after two years and launched Bright Horizons, we set out to create caring, educational environments for children that would give parents confidence in their children's well-being. After briefly examining and rejecting the idea of a nonprofit, parent cooperative model, we concluded that to realize this vision on a national scale we would need to build a strong, profitable organization that would allow us to attract large amounts of capital.

And so it was that we got into the child care field. We didn't take the plunge blindly. Before we set up shop, we took a long, hard look at the industry's weaknesses. And then we sat down and figured out a way to turn them to our advantage.

OUR STRATEGIC TWIST

When Linda and I returned from the Sudan in July 1986, child care in the United States was run more or less like a commodity business. In fact, the largest company in the industry was trying to emulate the fast-food business, claiming to be the "McDonald's of child care." That struck Linda and me as a terrible model. An environment with high turn-over and a paint-by-numbers curriculum is just the opposite of what children need and parents want. We thought we could do much better.

But we knew that in order to succeed we had to come up with a viable business model. Jack Reynolds, a friend of ours who had been a colleague of mine at the consulting firm Bain & Company, gave us an idea. He pointed out that some innovative companies, like the children's shoemaker Stride Rite, were setting up child care centers at their work sites, and that these centers tended to be of much higher quality than the ones run by the traditional chains. Why not, we thought, become an outside operator of such centers? By viewing employers rather than parents as the primary customers, we could tap into the financial and other resources of corporations and gain instant access to large pools of working parents. We could, in short, invent a whole new model for the industry.

The first thing we did was recruit three industry experts to refine our ideas. We sat down with them at our kitchen table in Cambridge, Massachusetts, to formulate a solid business plan. (Our house, incidentally,

"How We Built a Strong Company in a Weak Industry," by Roger Brown from *Harvard Business Review* (February 2001): 51–57. Reprinted by permission of Harvard Business School.

had good entrepreneurial bones. We had purchased it from Mitch Kapor, who lived in it before he achieved fame and fortune as the founder of Lotus.) We quickly saw that forming partnerships with employers offered several advantages. For one thing, we'd gain a powerful, low-cost marketing channel. We wouldn't have to sell our services to one parent at a time. More important, companies would view the centers as a way to distinguish themselves in the eyes of current and prospective employees. By giving employees access to convenient, first-rate care, they could increase the loyalty of their people and boost retention rates. Thus, our customers would have a vested interest in helping us pursue our core goal: delivering high-quality care.

And employees themselves would be attracted to our centers. By having their children next door, they could reduce their commuting times, enjoy greater peace of mind, and avoid the stress of fighting rush-hour traffic to reach a child care center in time for pickup. Parents could drop by to have lunch with their children, and nursing moms could continue to breast-feed even after they returned from maternity leave.

Our strategy, we believed, was solid. Only two things were missing: capital and customers.

We pitched our idea to Bain Capital, Bain's newly formed investment arm. Its founding partner, Mitt Romney, expressed interest, but he felt he needed a second opinion. Romney knew me quite well—I had reported to him at Bain—and he wanted reassurance from a more objective investor. That led us to the offices of the venture capital firm Bessemer Venture Partners. Bessemer's partners were intrigued by our idea, but they, too, were a little nervous. They asked us to undergo a psychiatric interview as part of the due diligence process, and despite the unusual nature of the request, we agreed. After all, Linda and I were hardly the prototypical entrepreneurial team. We'd worked together in monsoon-soaked refugee camps in Cambodia and built an emergency program that served 300,000 people in Sudan, but we didn't have much experience starting up companies. We also understood that the business world is littered with former husband-and-wife teams whose companies were torn apart as their marriages failed. Thanks to a good session on the couch and a buyer's market in the booming venture capital industry, we had our funding commitment in a matter of months.

Soon after, we signed our first customer, Prudential. The insurance company was in the process of redeveloping its Prudential Center complex in Boston, and it was looking for innovative ways to demonstrate to the city that the project would be a boon to the community. A partnership with Bright Horizons fit the bill, and in August 1987 we opened our first child care center. As a bonus, Prudential's public-relations team let the world know about the progressive model for child care that it was investing in—and that we were providing. We were on the map.

BUILDING BLOCKS FOR SUCCESS

Even with the first few breaks, the early days were difficult. I cold-called hundreds of employers, without much success, and we began to experience genuine anxiety over whether companies would see the value of a partnership with us. Many companies, we realized, were terrified of their potential liability. We solved this problem by securing insurance 50 times above the industry standard and by indemnifying our clients. Those steps proved vital. With their fears calmed, companies started to focus on the benefits of on-site child care.

Slowly, we built our customer base, and as our first centers opened their doors, the initial financial results looked encouraging. We had developed two basic models for making money. In the first, we assumed the financial risk for the operation and earned our profit margin out of the operating budget. In the second, the client simply paid us a management fee. In either case, the employers supplied the capital, investing, for example, in building and outfitting the centers. The average center broke even when it reached the 60 percent occupancy mark. When our first few centers filled up to capacity in just three months, we had proof that our vision could work.

Our commitment to quality began to pay off as well. Our competitors in the late 1980s continued to think of the industry as a commodity business. They crowed to investors about driving down labor costs, and they downplayed quality altogether, usually meeting only minimal state licensing requirements. That approach created such dissonance between what was good for shareholders and what was good for customers that it seemed destined to collapse. And just a couple of years later, it did, as the largest traditional chain filed for bankruptcy protection.

We took the opposite approach, reasoning that no *Fortune* 500 company would risk its child care center to an organization that paid its staff close to minimum wage, faced frequent violations of state licensing regulations, had high levels of parent dissatisfaction, and could not achieve national accreditation. We viewed quality as our strongest source of competitive advantage, and we knew that quality in child care begins with the employees. We surveyed the best centers we could find, and we discovered that they paid teachers 20 percent to 30 percent more than the average compensation in the field. We matched that premium and also offered comprehensive benefits, including health insurance, tuition reimbursement, 401K with a company match, and child care support.

Our emphasis on quality didn't end with employees. We committed to abiding by the strict accreditation standards set by the National Association for the Education of Young Children (NAEYC) rather than simply adhere to local licensing requirements, which vary widely from state to state. We also set out to create state-of-the-art learning environments for young children. Drawing on the capital investments from our corporate partners, we customized the centers so that their design, hours of operation, and age-group configuration matched the needs of our employer clients. And we developed a curriculum called "World at Their Fingertips," which outlined a course of study for teachers but gave them control over daily lesson plans so that the curriculum would reflect the interests of the children in the classroom. Our curriculum marked a departure from those of most traditional child care programs, which either lacked curricular guidance altogether or mandated strict, cookie-cutter lesson plans. The creative curriculum reinforced a cycle of quality. It helped our centers attract the best teachers, who in turn had the skills to fulfill and refine the curriculum.

Our commitment to quality delivers concrete benefits to our clients as well. It gives them the upper hand in the battle for talent. Merck, for instance, found that its retention rates among employees with young children—a group that had been prone to high turnover—improved dramatically. Chase Manhattan calculated that its center generated a 110 percent return on investment through reduced absenteeism. And we don't think it's any coincidence that we've retained 99 percent of our corporate partners.

OUR NEAR-DEATH EXPERIENCE

Because our early centers were so successful, we had unrealistic expectations about later centers. Replicating the success of the early programs proved more difficult than we thought, much to our investors' chagrin. For one thing, the early centers were perfectly located; they were in areas with high levels of pent-up demand. Second, they were relatively small and thus easy to fill to a profit-making capacity. When we opened our next 10 centers, they were 20 percent to 30 percent larger than the earlier ones, and none performed as well. We learned that breaking even in just three months, as the first centers had done, was unrealistic.

By 1990, some of our investors began to question whether we had enough "gray hair" and "scar tissue." We had opened approximately 30 centers and were launching several new ones each year, so the error in our center ramp-up model compounded itself. The recession in our home base of New England exacerbated our problems. One board member in particular questioned whether we knew how to eke out a profit in such a low-margin business. And several directors began to question whether high teacher salaries and low teacher-child ratios were just an artifact of our idealism and whether they were an essential element of our strategy.

A critical lesson Linda and I learned was that when the going gets tough, board members often give contradictory advice. At first, we tried to respond to all their varied points of view—"focus on profitability," "just keep growing," "hire more experienced managers," "lay off staff to reduce costs." But we soon saw that we were being pulled in too many directions and that the vision for our young company was at risk. We had to take a stand. I wrote a long memo to the board arguing that the whole enterprise was built around a quality-focused, employer-supported strategy, and that the only hope of real success was to pursue it even more deliberately. Without such a strategy, we were doomed to be a second-tier player in an unprofitable field.

After much soul-searching, the board agreed that Linda and I were still the right management team and that we had the right business model. (That decision led one of the board members to resign.) At that point, we became completely focused on managing our cash and ensuring that none of our centers lost money. We eliminated all distractions, such as several public-policy initiatives and an international joint-venture opportunity that we had been investigating. We also changed our expectations, projecting that new centers would become profitable in 9 to 12 months instead of 3 and that they would reach a mature enrollment of 80 percent to 85 percent in 18 months. But we did not reduce compensation and benefits, compromise our teacher-child ratios, or otherwise retreat from our basic strategy of high quality. The new focus paid off. We soon posted our first profitable quarter.

THRIVING IN THE BRIAR PATCH

We came out of this painful period a much stronger company. Having to defend our model gave us the opportunity to refine it. Internally, we came to refer to our plan as the "briar patch strategy." As readers of classic children's literature will remember, the legendary Br'er Rabbit managed to escape from his nemesis, Br'er Fox, by persuading the fox to throw him into a briar patch rather than cook him. The wily rabbit easily freed himself from the thickets, chiding the fox, "I was bred and born in the briar patch." We saw the child care business as our briar patch—a niche that is inhospitable to competitors but quite comfortable to those who understand its particularities. Our business model allowed us to methodically turn the following industry weaknesses into company strengths.

No Barriers to Entry

In theory, anyone can hang out a shingle and open a child care center. But our relationships with employers create formidable entry barriers for our competitors. When we operate a program at the offices of Charles Schwab or Bristol-Myers Squibb or on the campus of George Washington University, with the client's financial and marketing support, it's virtually impossible for anyone else to compete at that site. And each site provides a compelling model to demonstrate our success to potential new clients. This creates a virtuous circle: great clients build great facilities and drive innovation. We then have models that no other child care service can match. Because our competitors have no examples of operational, state-of-the-art, client-supported programs, they have trouble persuading a corporate client to take a chance on their untested program. Our current clients are also some of our best marketers. Proud CEOs often take their boards to visit their on-site child development centers, thus promoting our services to the other board members, many of whom run companies themselves.

Chronically Low Margins

The child care industry has low margins—and always will—but our model emphasizes not margins but returns to invested capital. Because corporations invest a lot of their own capital in our child care centers, minimizing our own capital investment, we can achieve high returns—on average, 50 percent per center. To date, our clients have invested a total of more than $500 million in on-site facilities, usually of our design, and they contribute about 20 percent of our revenue annually. And because each new center achieves a positive cash flow in less than a year, we are able to self-fund our growth despite after-tax margins of only 3 percent. This discipline has allowed us to produce returns of over 20 percent per year to every class of investor. Moreover, our long sales cycle, which had been so frustrating in the early years of the company, has become an asset because it allows us to predict future revenues and earnings accurately—something investors value highly.

Labor Intensity

Good child care demands well-qualified staff and high teacher-child ratios. In our view, labor is not a commodity, it is a competitive advantage—and that's exactly how we treat it. *Fortune* and *Working Mother* have named Bright Horizons one of the best places to work—an unprecedented honor for a company in the child care field. Being known as the employer of choice in our industry has set us apart from would-be competitors. Clients want to hire us because they know they can put their trust in our staff.

No Proprietary Technology

We can't rely on patents to protect us. Nevertheless, we've been aggressive in working with employers to develop innovative technologies. Indeed, serving high-tech clients such as Cisco, IBM, Motorola, and EMC forces us to stay ahead of the industry technologically. Some of our centers, for example, use Web-connected cameras that allow parents to watch streaming video of their children from their computers at work. Centers send digitally scanned or photographed artwork to parents who are away on business trips, and others post menus, calendars, and student assessments electronically. We've developed online student assessment capabilities that let teachers and parents learn more about their children's learning styles and upcoming developmental milestones. We could never have afforded to invest in these technological innovations without our clients' support and expertise.

Weak Economies of Scale

With more than 70 percent of our expenditures going to teacher compensation, we have few ways to create scale economies. Yes, we can consolidate our centers' supply purchases, but buying construction paper in bulk hardly creates significant advantages. Still, while *economies* of scale are hard to come by in our industry, we have gained many *advantages* of scale by spreading knowledge and techniques across our centers. Take our technology innovations. While we developed most of them working with a single client, we can deploy them in any center. We've also rolled out many other initiatives throughout our network, including a Get Well program in which mildly ill children receive special care and attention from licensed pediatric nurses on staff. We have also leveraged our reach by starting a program that allows a client to reserve space in any one of our centers in the United States or United Kingdom that is open to outside enrollment. This program helps address the child care needs of employees in small regional offices, employees traveling with their children, and employees working from home. Our scale advantage stems not from purchasing power but from our ability to innovate locally and deploy globally.

Weak Consumer Brands

When it comes to their children's education, parents don't look for a national brand; they want a great program and are indifferent to whether it's part of a larger network. That's why traditional childcare chains get little value from their brands, despite expensive advertising campaigns directed toward parent brand-building. But our business model enables us to focus on a set of customers—employers—who value a partnership with a strong, trusted brand. Because of Bright Horizons' reputation, customers routinely seek us out when they're considering on-site care—we do a lot less cold-calling now. Our existing clients also help strengthen our brand by recommending our organization to other companies.

Heavy Regulatory Oversight

Most child care companies take an adversarial stance toward licensing. By contrast, we see licensing as another way to gain a competitive advantage. Because of our focus on quality, we can meet the most stringent requirements. In fact, we avoid those states with the lowest standards for teacher-child ratios and other key measures, concentrating our growth in high-standards states where we can set ourselves apart. In addition, we work hard with child care advocates to promote the importance of NAEYC accreditation. We also give clients tools such as checklists and teacher-child interaction guides to assess quality when they visit centers, and we encourage them to bring in consultants. The more a client knows about quality child care, the more success we have.

LESSON PLANS FOR ANY INDUSTRY

From a business standpoint, our industry isn't the most attractive one on earth (though we believe it's one of the most important). But by taking a systematic approach to addressing its weaknesses, we've been able to grow rapidly and deliver attractive returns to investors.

We think other companies can learn from our approach. In fact, more and more industries are becoming like the child care business in their competitive characteristics. Traditional barriers to entry are weakening as capital flows to new competitors and technology upsets once-stable markets. Web-based purchasing and universal access to information are eroding economies of scale. Specialized labor is in more demand now than ever. And superbrands are giving way to microbrands targeted to the tastes of communities or even individuals. In the future, good strategy will probably have a great deal to do with making strengths out of weaknesses—and finding a good briar patch to call home.

PART TWO

Key Elements of Services Marketing

CHAPTER 4

Creating the Service Product

Each and every one of you will make or break the promise that our brand makes to customers.

—AN AMERICAN EXPRESS MANAGER SPEAKING TO HIS EMPLOYEES

All service organizations face choices about the types of products to offer and the operational procedures to use in creating them. In a customer-focused organization, these choices are often driven by market factors, with firms seeking to respond to the expressed needs of specific market segments and to differentiate the characteristics of their offerings against those of competitors. The availability of new delivery processes, such as the Internet for information-based services, allows firms to create for their existing services new methods of delivery that effectively change the nature of the service experience and create new benefits. The growth of Internet banking is a case in point. A more radical form of product innovation involves exploiting technological developments to satisfy latent needs that customers have not previously articulated or even recognized.

A service product typically consists of a core product bundled with a variety of supplementary service elements. The core elements respond to the customers' need for a basic benefit, such as transportation to a specific location, resolution of a specific health problem, a professional solution to a problem, or repair of malfunctioning equipment. Supplementary services facilitate and enhance use of the core service. They range from provision of needed information, advice, and documentation to problem solving and acts of hospitality.

Designing new services is a challenging task because it requires thinking about processes, people, and experiences, as well as outputs and benefits. Processes can be depicted through blueprints that specify employee tasks and operational sequences, as well as track the experience of the customer at each step in service delivery.

In this chapter, we consider the nature of service products, how to add value to them, and how to design them. We explore the following questions.

1. What are the key ingredients in a service product?
2. How might we categorize the supplementary services that surround core products?
3. What are some of the approaches that can be used in designing new services?
4. What is the role of branding for service products?

PLANNING AND CREATING SERVICES

What do we mean by a service "product"? In earlier chapters, we noted that a service is a "performance" rather than a "thing." When they purchase manufactured goods, customers take title to physical objects. But service performances, being intangible and ephemeral, are experienced rather than owned. Even when there are physical elements to which the customer does take title, such as a cooked meal (which is promptly consumed), a pacemaker implanted in a patient's body, a replacement part inside a car, a significant portion of the price paid by the customer is for the value added by the accompanying service elements, including labor and expertise and the use of specialized equipment.

When they are required by the nature of the service process to visit the service site—as in people-processing services—or choose to do so in other types of services—such as traditional retail bank branches—customers may be asked to participate actively in the process of service creation and delivery. If customers perform self-service, their experiences are often shaped by the nature and user friendliness (or lack thereof!) of the supporting technology. In both instances, evaluations of the service product are likely to be much more closely interwoven with the nature of the delivery process than is the case for manufactured goods.

Key Steps in Service Planning

One of the challenges in services marketing is to ensure that the task of product management maintains a strong customer focus at all times. Historically, operations management was often allowed to dominate this task, with the result that customer concerns were sometimes subjugated to operational convenience. On the other hand, marketers cannot work in isolation on new-product development, especially when its delivery entails use of new technologies; marketers need to form a partnership with operations personnel and, in the case of high-contact services, with human resource managers as well. Figure 4-1 outlines the key steps involved in planning and creating services, emphasizing the need for managers to relate market opportunities to deployment of their firms' resources: physical, technological, and human.

The task begins at the corporate level with a statement of *objectives.* This statement leads into a detailed *market and competitive analysis*, addressing each of the markets in which the firm is involved or thinking of entering. Paralleling this step is a *resource allocation analysis*, requiring definition and appraisal of the firm's resources and how they are being allocated, as well as identification of additional resources that might reasonably be obtained. This pair of steps can be thought of collectively as a form of SWOT analysis, identifying strengths, weaknesses, opportunities, and threats on both the marketing and operational/human resources fronts. Each leads to a statement of assets.

The *marketing assets statement* includes details of the firm's existing customer portfolio (including its size, profile, and value), knowledge of the market and competitors, its product line, the reputation of its brand(s), its marketing implementation skills, and its positioning strategy/ies. We saw in Chapter 3 that a positioning statement can be developed for each service that the firm offers to one or more target market segments, indicating the characteristics that distinguish that service from competitive offerings.

The marketing opportunities revealed by this analysis must now be matched against an *operating assets statement.* Can the organization afford to allocate the physical facilities, equipment, information technology, and human resources needed to market existing service products more effectively, add enhancements designed to improve competitive appeal, or create new service offerings? Conversely, does an analysis of these operating assets suggest new opportunities to improve their utilization in the marketplace? If it lacks the resources needed for a new marketing initiative, could the firm leverage its existing assets by partnering with intermediaries or even with customers

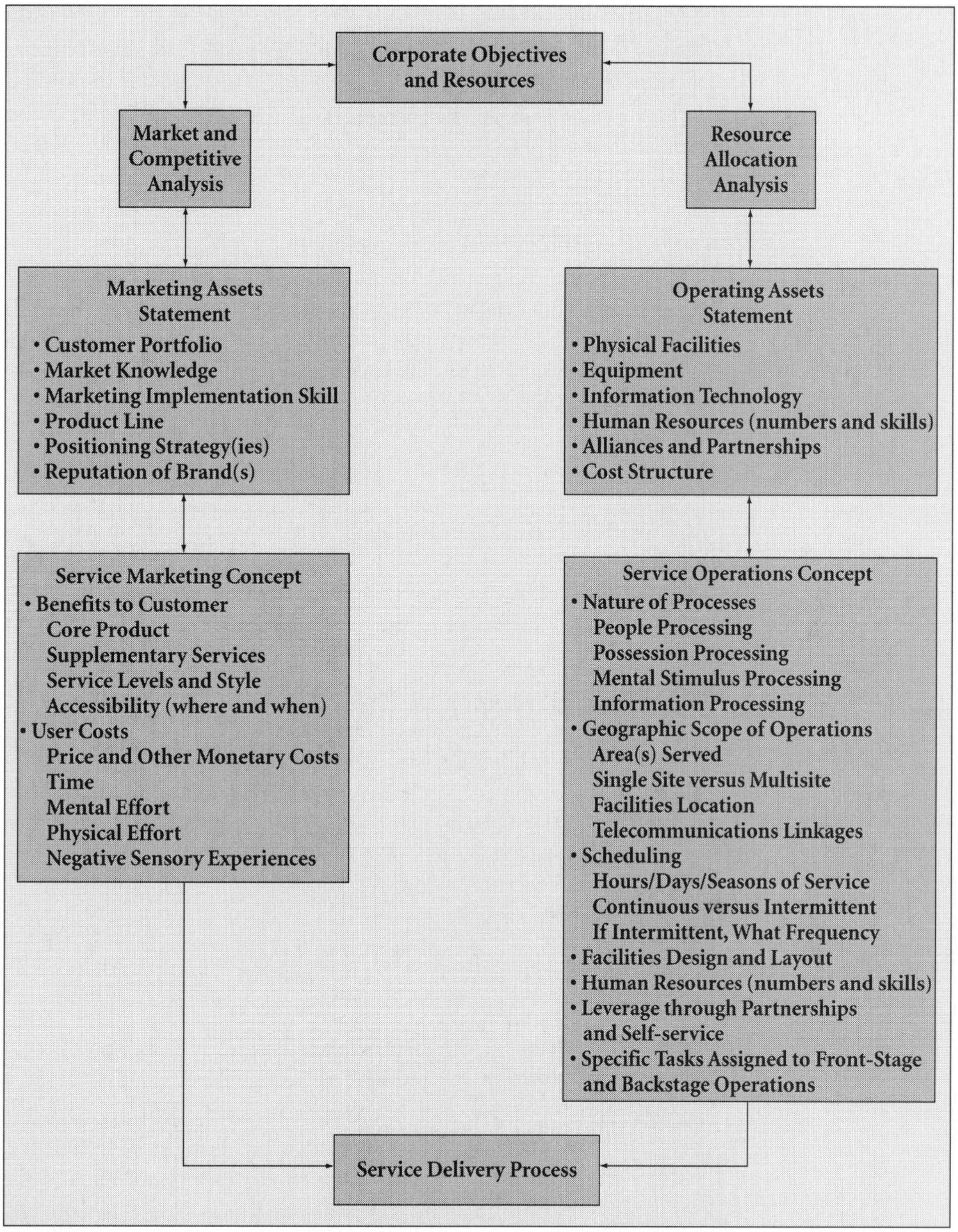

FIGURE 4-1 Planning and Creating Services

themselves? Finally, does an identified marketing opportunity promise sufficient profits to yield an acceptable return on the assets used after deducting all relevant costs?

From a marketing perspective, the next step in transforming an opportunity into reality involves creating a *service marketing concept* to clarify the benefits offered to customers and the costs they will incur in return. This marketing concept considers both core and supplementary services, their characteristics in terms of both performance level and style, and where, when, and how customers will be able to have access to them. The related costs of service include not only money but also definition of the amount of time, mental hassle, physical effort, and negative sensory experiences likely to be incurred by customers in receiving service.

A parallel step is to establish a *service operations concept*, which stipulates the nature of the processes involved (including use of information technology) and how and when the various types of operating assets should be deployed to perform specific tasks. Hence the need to define the geographic scope and scheduling of operations, describe facilities design and layout, and identify the human resources required. The operations concept also addresses opportunities for leveraging the firm's own resources through use of intermediaries or the customers themselves. Finally, the operations concept clarifies which tasks and resources will be assigned to front-stage and which to backstage operations.

Defining the marketing and operations concepts is necessarily an interactive process, as either or both may have to be modified in order to bring the two into the harmony needed to proceed with a given service offering. The planning task then moves on to a set of choices that management must make in configuring the service delivery process—the topic of Chapter 7.

The Augmented Product

Most manufacturing and service businesses offer their customers a package of benefits involving delivery of not only the core product but also a variety of service-related activities that we refer to collectively as supplementary services. Increasingly, the latter provide the differentiation that separates successful firms from the also-rans. Among both services and goods, the core product tends to become a commodity as competition increases and the industry matures. (If a firm can't do a decent job on the core elements, it's eventually going to go out of business!) Although managers continually need to consider opportunities to improve the core product, the search for competitive advantage in a mature industry often emphasizes performance on the supplementary services that are bundled with the core product.

The combination of core product and supplementary services is often referred to as the *augmented product*. Several frameworks can be used to describe augmented products in a services context. Lynn Shostack developed a molecular model (Figure 4-2), which uses a chemical analogy to help marketers visualize and manage what she terms[1] a "total market entity." Her model can be applied to either goods or services. At the center is the core benefit, addressing the basic customer need, linked to a series of other service characteristics. She argues that, as in chemical formulations, a change in one element may completely alter the nature of the entity. Surrounding the molecules are a series of bands representing price, distribution, and market positioning (communication messages).

The molecular model helps us to identify the tangible and intangible elements involved in service delivery. In an airline, for example, the intangible elements include transportation itself, service frequency, and pre-, in-, and postflight service. But the aircraft and the food and drinks that are served are all tangible. By highlighting tangible elements, marketers can determine whether their services are tangible dominant or intangible dominant. The greater the proportion of intangible elements, the more necessary it is to provide tangible clues about the features and quality of the service.

Pierre Eiglier and Eric Langeard proposed a model in which the core service is surrounded by a circle containing a series of supplementary services that are specific to that particular product.[2] Their approach, like Shostack's, emphasizes the interdependence of the various components. Those elements needed to facilitate use of the core service (such as the reception desk at a hotel) are distinguished from those that enhance the appeal of the core service (such as a fitness center and business services at a hotel).

Both models of the augmented product offer useful insights. Shostack wants us to determine which service elements are tangible and which are intangible, in order to help formulate product policy and communication programs. Eiglier and Langeard ask us to think about two issues: (1) whether supplementary services are needed to facilitate

FIGURE 4-2 Shostack's Molecular Model: Passenger Airline Service

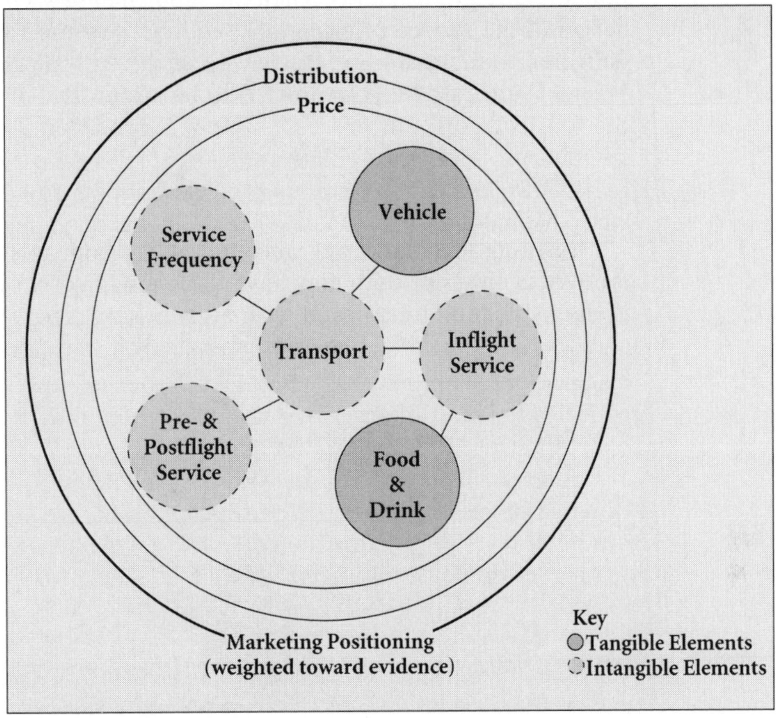

Source: G. Lynn Shostack, "Breaking Free from Product Marketing," *Journal of Marketing* 44 (April 1977): 73–80, published by the American Marketing Association. Reprinted with permission.

use of the core service or simply to add extra appeal and (2) whether customers should be charged separately for each service element or whether all elements should be bundled under a single price tag. Further insight is provided by Christian Grönroos, who clarifies the various roles played by supplementary services, describing them as either facilitating services (or goods) and supporting services (or goods).[3]

Defining the Nature of the Service Offering

When designing a service to implement a particular service marketing concept, product planners need to take a holistic view of the entire performance they want customers to experience. The design task must therefore address and integrate three key components: the core product, supplementary services, and delivery processes.

Core Product This central component addresses two questions: (1) What is the buyer really purchasing? (2) What business are we in? The core product supplies the central problem-solving benefits that customers seek. Thus, transport solves the need to move a person or a physical object from one location to another; management consulting is expected to yield expert advice on the actions that a company should take; and repair services restore a damaged or malfunctioning machine or building to good working order.

Supplementary Services These elements augment the core product, both facilitating its use and enhancing its value and appeal. The extent and level of supplementary services often play a role in differentiating and positioning the core product. Adding supplementary elements or increasing the level of performance can add value to the core product and enable the service provider to charge a higher price.

Delivery Process The third component deals with the procedures used to deliver both the core product and each of the supplementary services. In its broadest sense, the design of the service offering must address how the various service components are delivered to the customer, the nature of the customer's role in those processes, how long delivery lasts, and the prescribed level and style of service to be offered. Each of the four categories of processes—people processing, possession processing, mental stimulus processing, and information processing—has different implications for customer involvement, operational procedures, the degree of customer contact with service personnel and facilities, and requirements for supplementary services.

The integration of these three components is captured in Figure 4-3, which illustrates the service offering for an overnight stay at a hotel. The core product—overnight rental of a bedroom—is dimensioned by service level, scheduling (how long the room may be used before another payment becomes due), the nature of the process (in this instance, people processing), and the role of the customers in terms of what they are expected to do for themselves and what the hotel will do for them, such as making the bed, supplying bathroom towels, and cleaning the room.

Surrounding the core is an array of supplementary services, ranging from reservations to meals to in-room service elements. As with the core product, delivery processes must be specified for each of these elements. The more expensive the hotel, the higher the level of service on each element (for example, covered parking with

FIGURE 4-3 Depicting the Service Offering for an Overnight Hotel Stay

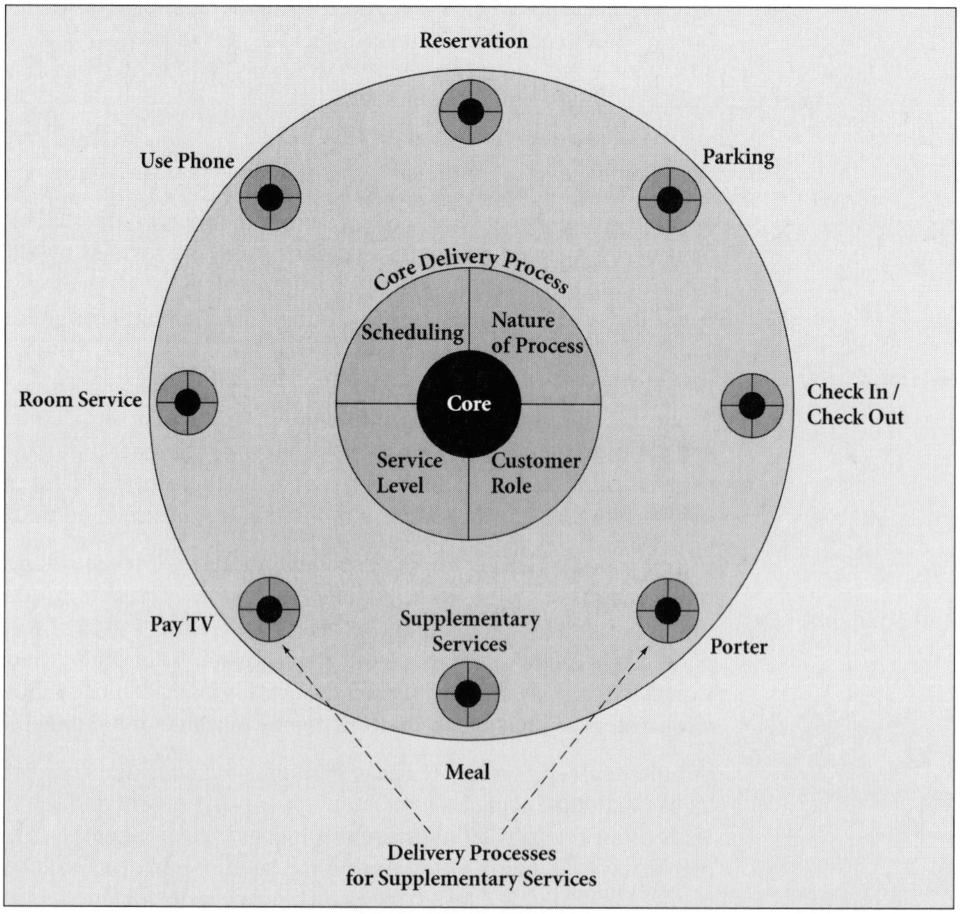

valet assistance, better food, and a broader array of movies on Pay TV). Additional services might also be offered, such as a business center, a bar, a pool, and a health club. One of the characteristics of a top-of-the line hotel is doing things for customers that they might otherwise have to do for themselves and providing an extended schedule for service delivery, including 24-hour room service.

Documenting the Delivery Sequence over Time

A fourth design component that product planners must address is the probable sequence in which customers will use each of the core and supplementary services and the approximate length of time that will be required in each instance. This information, which should reflect a good understanding of customer needs, habits, and expectations, is necessary for not only marketing purposes but also facilities planning, operations management, and personnel allocation.

It would be a mistake to assume that the customer consumes all the elements of the augmented product simultaneously. In the hotel industry, neither the core service nor its supplementary elements are all delivered continuously throughout the duration of the service performance. Certain services must necessarily be used before others. In many services, in fact, consumption of the core product is sandwiched between use of supplementary services that are needed earlier or later in the delivery sequence.

Figure 4-4 adds a temporal dimension to the various elements of the augmented hotel product, identifying when and for how long they are consumed. The example illustrated is hotel accommodation, a high-contact, people-processing service. Time plays a key role in services both from an operational standpoint as it relates to allocating and scheduling purposes and from the perspective of customers themselves.

An important aspect of service planning is determining an appropriate amount of time for the customer to spend on various service elements. In some instances, research may show that customers from a given segment expect to budget a specific amount of time for a given activity that has value for them and would not wish to be rushed (for instance, 8 hours for sleeping, an hour and a half for a business dinner, and 20 minutes for breakfast). In other instances, such as making a reservation, checking in, payment, or waiting for a car to be retrieved from valet parking, customers may wish to minimize or even eliminate time spent on what they perceive as nonproductive activities. As suggested in Service Perspectives 4-1, speedy service is often a key product attribute for customers, and implementation requires an understanding of both marketing and operational considerations.

FIGURE 4-4 Temporal Dimension to Augmented Hotel Product

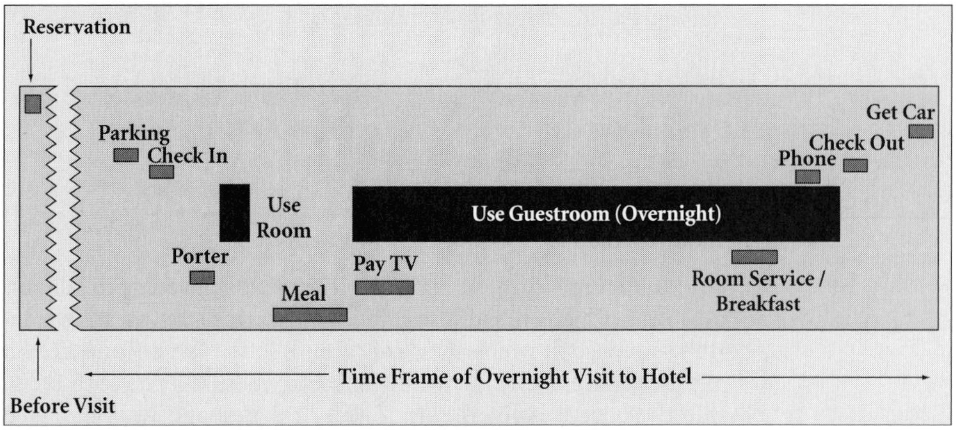

SERVICE PERSPECTIVES 4-1

PLANNING SPEEDY FOOD SERVICE

Restaurant Hospitality, a restaurant industry trade magazine, offers the following ten suggestions for serving customers quickly without making them feel as though they've been pushed out the door. Some of these tactics involve front-stage processes, whereas others take place backstage, but it is the interaction among operational strategies, marketing insights, and how staff members relate to customers that creates the desired results.

1. Distinguish between patrons in a hurry and those who are not.
2. Design specials that are quick.
3. Guide hurried customers to those specials.
4. Place the quickest, highest-margin menu items either first or last on the menu.
5. Offer dishes that can be prepared ahead of time.
6. Warn customers when they order menu items that will take a lot of time to prepare.
7. Consider short-line buffets, roving carts, and more sandwiches.
8. Offer "wrap"-style sandwiches, which are a quickly prepared, filling meal.
9. Use equipment built for speed, such as combination ovens.
10. Eliminate preparation steps that require cooks to stop cooking.

Adapted from Paul B. Hertneky, "Built for Speed," *Restaurant Hospitality* (January 1997): 58.

IDENTIFYING AND CLASSIFYING SUPPLEMENTARY SERVICES

The more we examine various types of services, the more we find that most of them have many supplementary services in common. Flowcharting, which we introduced in Chapter 2, offers an excellent way to understand the totality of the customer's service experience and identify the many types of supplementary services accompanying a core product. For instance, supplementary services at an expensive restaurant include reservations, valet parking, coatrooms, cocktails, being escorted to a table, ordering from the menu, billing, payment, and use of toilets. If you prepare flowcharts for a variety of services, you will soon notice that although core products may differ widely, common supplementary elements—from information to billing and from reservations/order taking to problem resolution—keep recurring.

Facilitating and Enhancing Supplementary Services

Of the potentially dozens of supplementary services, almost all of them can be classified into one of the following eight clusters. We list them as either *facilitating* or *enhancing* supplementary services.

FACILITATING SERVICES	ENHANCING SERVICES
• Information	• Consultation
• Order taking	• Hospitality
• Billing	• Safekeeping
• Payment	• Exceptions

In Figure 4-5, these eight clusters are displayed as petals surrounding the center of a flower, which we call the *Flower of Service*.[4] We've shown the clusters clockwise in the sequence in which they are often likely to be encountered by customers, although this sequence may vary; for instance, payment may have to be made before rather than after service is delivered. In a well-designed and well-managed service organization,

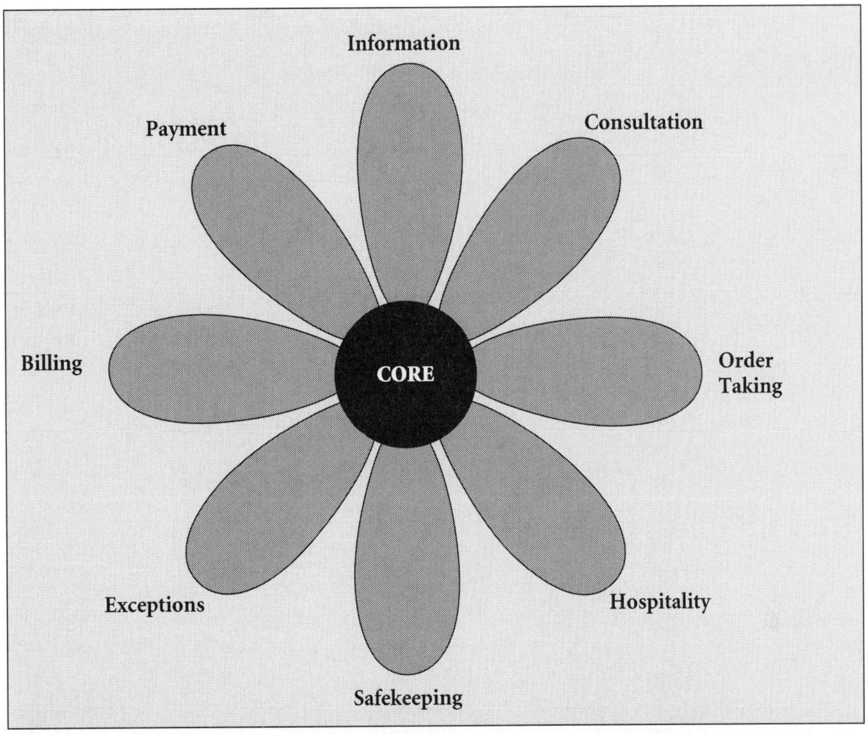

FIGURE 4-5 The Flower of Service: Core Product Surrounded by Cluster of Supplementary Services

the petals and core are fresh and well formed. A badly designed or poorly executed service is a like a flower with missing, wilted, or discolored petals. Even if the core is perfect, the overall impression of the flower is unattractive. Think about your own experiences as a customer or when purchasing on behalf of an organization. When you were dissatisfied with a particular purchase, was it the core that was at fault, or was it a problem with one or more of the petals?

Not every core product is surrounded by supplementary elements from all eight clusters. The nature of the product helps to determine which supplementary services must be offered and which might usefully be added to enhance value and make the organization easy to do business with. In general, people-processing services tend to be accompanied by more supplementary services than do the other three categories; similarly, high-contact services will have more than low-contact services.

A company's market positioning strategy helps to determine which supplementary services should be included (see Chapter 3). A strategy of adding benefits to increase customers' perceptions of quality will probably require more supplementary services (and also a higher level of performance on all such elements) than a strategy of competing on low prices. Firms that offer several grades of service—such as first class, business class, and economy class in an airline context—often differentiate them by adding extra supplementary services for each upgrade in service.

Information To obtain full value from any good or service, customers need relevant information (Table 4-1). New customers and prospects are especially information hungry. Customers' needs may include directions to the site where the product is sold (or details of how to order it), service hours, prices, and usage instructions. Further information, sometimes required by law, could include conditions of sale and use, warnings,

TABLE 4-1 Examples of Information Elements
Directions to service site
Schedules/service hours
Prices
Instructions on using core product/supplementary services
Reminders
Warnings
Conditions of sale/service
Notification of changes
Documentation
Confirmation of reservations
Summaries of account activity
Receipts and tickets

reminders, and notification of changes. Finally, customers may want documentation of what has already taken place, such as confirmation of reservations, receipts and tickets, and monthly summaries of account activity.

Companies should make sure that the information they provide is both timely and accurate, as incorrect information may annoy or inconvenience customers. Traditional ways of providing information to customers include using front-line employees (who are not always as well informed as customers might like), printed notices, brochures, and instruction books. Other information media are videotapes or software-driven tutorials, touch-screen video displays, and menu-driven recorded telephone messages. The most significant recent innovation has been corporate use of Web sites. Examples of useful applications are train and airline schedules and hotel details, assistance in locating specific retail outlets, such as restaurants and stores, and information on the services of professional firms. Many business-logistics companies offer shippers the opportunity to track the movements of their packages—each of which has been assigned a unique identification number.

Order Taking Once customers are ready to buy, a key supplementary element comes into play: accepting applications, orders, and reservations (Table 4-2). The process of order taking should be polite, fast, and accurate so that customers do not waste time and endure unnecessary mental or physical effort. Technology can be used to make order taking easier and faster for both customers and suppliers. The key lies in minimizing the time and effort required of both parties, while also ensuring completeness and accuracy.

Banks, insurance companies, and utilities require prospective customers to go through an application process designed to gather relevant information and to screen out those whose credit records or serious health problems do not meet basic enrollment criteria. Universities also require prospective students to apply for admission. Reservations, including appointments and check-in, are a special type of order taking that entitles customers to a specified unit of service, such as an airline seat, a restaurant table, a hotel room, time with a qualified professional, or admission to a theater or sports arena with designated seating. Accuracy in scheduling is vital; reserving seats for the wrong day is likely to be unpopular with customers.

Ticketless systems, based on telephone or Web site reservations, provide enormous cost savings for airlines, as there is no travel agent commission—customers book directly—and the administrative effort is drastically reduced. A paper ticket at an airline may be handled 15 times, whereas an electronic ticket requires only one step.

TABLE 4-2 Examples of Order-Taking Elements

Applications

- Membership in clubs or programs
- Subscription services (e.g., utilities)
- Prerequisite-based services (e.g., financial credit, college enrollment)

Order Entry

- On-site order fulfillment
- Mail/telephone order placement
- E-mail/Web site order placement

Reservations and Check-in

- Seats
- Tables
- Rooms
- Vehicles or equipment rental
- Professional appointments
- Admission to restricted facilities (e.g., museums, aquariums)

But some customers are disenchanted by the paperless process. Although they receive a confirmation number by phone when they make the reservations and need only to show identification at the airport to claim their seats, many people feel insecure without tangible proof that they have a seat on a particular flight.[5] And business travelers complain that needed receipts don't arrive until days or sometimes weeks after a trip, causing problems for claiming expenses from corporate accounting departments. Some airlines now offer to fax receipts and itineraries on request at the time a flight is booked.

Billing Billing is common to almost all services, unless the service is provided free of charge. Inaccurate, illegible, or incomplete bills risk disappointing customers who may, up to that point, have been quite satisfied with their experience. Such failures add insult to injury if the customer is already dissatisfied. Billing should also be timely because it serves to stimulate faster payment. Procedures range from verbal statements to a machine-displayed price and from handwritten invoices to elaborate monthly statements of account activity and fees (Table 4-3). Perhaps the simplest approach is self-billing, when the customer tallies up the amount of an order and either encloses a check or signs a credit card payment authorization. In such instances, billing and payment are combined into a single act, although the seller may still need to check for accuracy.

More and more, billing is being computerized. Despite the potential for productivity improvements, computerized billing has its dark side, as when an innocent customer tries futilely to contest an inaccurate bill and is met by an escalating sequence of ever-larger bills (compounded interest and penalty charges), accompanied by increasingly threatening, computer-generated letters.

TABLE 4-3 Examples of Billing Elements

- Periodic statements of account activity
- Invoices for individual transactions
- Verbal statements of amount due
- Machine display of amount due
- Self-billing (computed by customer)

Customers usually expect bills to be clear, informative, and itemized in ways that make it clear how the total was computed. Unexplained, arcane symbols that have all the meaning of hieroglyphics on an Egyptian monument (and are decipherable only by the high priests of accounting and data processing) do not create a favorable impression of the supplier. Nor does fuzzy printing or illegible handwriting. Laser printers, with their ability to switch fonts and typefaces and to box and to highlight, can produce statements that not only are more legible but also organize information in more useful ways. Marketing research can help here, by asking customers what information they want and how they would like it to be organized.

American Express (AmEx) built its Corporate Card business by offering companies detailed documentation of the spending patterns of individual employees and departments on travel and entertainment. Intelligent thinking about customer needs led AmEx to realize that well-organized information has value to a customer, beyond simply the basic requirement of knowing how much to pay at the end of each month.

Busy customers hate to be kept waiting for a bill to be prepared in a hotel, restaurant, or rental car lot. Many hotels and rental car firms have now created express check-out options, taking customers' credit card details in advance and documenting charges later by mail. But accuracy is essential. As customers use the express checkouts to save time, they certainly don't want to waste time later seeking corrections and refunds. An alternative express check-out procedure is used by some car rental companies. An agent meets customers as they return their cars, checks the mileage/kilometrage and fuel gauge readings, and then prints a bill on the spot, using a portable wireless terminal. Many hotels push bills showing charges to date under guestroom doors on the morning of departure; others offer customers the option of previewing their bills on the TV monitors in their rooms before checkout.

Payment In most cases, a bill requires the customer to take action on payment, and such action may be very slow in coming! One exception is bank statements that detail charges that have already been deducted from the customer's account. Increasingly, customers expect ease and convenience of payment, including credit, when they make purchases in their own countries and while traveling abroad.

A variety of options exist to facilitate customer bill paying (Table 4-4). Self-service payment systems, for instance, require customers to insert coins, banknotes, tokens, or cards in machines. But equipment breakdowns destroy the whole purpose of such a system, so good maintenance and rapid-response troubleshooting are essential. Much payment still takes place through hand-to-hand transfers of cash and checks, but credit and debit cards are growing in importance as more and more establishments accept them. Other alternatives are tokens, vouchers, coupons, or prepaid tickets. Firms benefit from prompt payment, as it reduces the amount of accounts receivable. To reinforce good behavior, NStar, a Massachusetts electrical utility, periodically sends thank-you notes to customers who have consistently paid on time.

To ensure that people pay what is due, some service businesses have instituted control systems, such as ticket checks before entering a movie theater or on board a train. However, inspectors and security officers must be trained to combine politeness with firmness in performing their jobs, so that honest customers do not feel harassed. But a visible presence often serves as a deterrent.

Consultation Now we move to enhancing supplementary services, led by consultation. In contrast to information, which suggests a simple response to customers' questions (or printed information that anticipates their needs), consultation involves a dialogue to probe customer requirements and then to develop a tailored solution. Table 4-5 provides examples of several supplementary services in the consultation category. At its simplest,

TABLE 4-4 Examples of Payment Elements

Self-Service

- Exact change in machine
- Cash in machine with change returned
- Insert prepayment card
- Insert credit/charge/debit card
- Insert token
- Electronic funds transfer
- Mail a check
- Enter credit card number online

Direct to Payee or Intermediary

- Cash handling and change giving
- Check handling
- Credit/charge/debit card handling
- Coupon redemption
- Tokens, vouchers, etc.

Automatic Deduction from Financial Deposits (e.g., bank charges)
Control and Verification

- Automated systems (e.g., machine-readable tickets that operate entry gates)
- Human systems (e.g., toll collectors, ticket inspectors)

TABLE 4-5 Examples of Consultation Elements

- Advice
- Auditing
- Personal counseling
- Tutoring/training in product use
- Management or technical consulting

consultation consists of immediate advice from a knowledgeable service person in response to the request: What do you suggest? (For example, you might ask the person who cuts your hair for advice on different hairstyles and products.) Effective consultation requires an understanding of each customer's current situation before suggesting a suitable course of action. Good customer records can be a great help in this respect, particularly if relevant data can be retrieved easily from a remote terminal.

Counseling represents a more subtle approach to consultation because it involves helping customers better understand their situations so that they can come up with their own solutions and action programs. This approach can be a particularly valuable supplement to such services as health treatment, when part of the challenge is to get customers to take a long-term view of their personal situation and to adopt more healthful behaviors, often involving some initial sacrifice. For example, diet centers, such as Weight Watchers, use counseling to help customers change behaviors so that weight loss can be sustained after the initial diet is completed.

Finally, there are more formalized efforts to provide management and technical consulting for corporate customers, such as the "solution selling" associated with marketing expensive industrial equipment and services. The sales engineer researches the customer's situation and then offers objective advice about what particular package of equipment and systems will yield the best results for the customer. Some consulting services are offered free of charge in the hope of making a sale. However, in other instances, the service is "unbundled," and customers are expected to pay for it.

TABLE 4-6 Examples of Hospitality Elements

Greeting
Food and beverages
Toilets and washrooms
Waiting facilities and amenities
• Lounges, waiting areas, seating
• Weather protection
• Magazines, entertainment, newspapers
Transport
Security

Advice can also be offered through tutorials, group training programs, and public demonstrations.

Hospitality Hospitality-related services should, ideally, reflect pleasure at meeting new customers and greeting old ones when they return. Well-managed businesses try, at least in small ways, to ensure that their employees treat customers as guests. Courtesy and consideration for customers' needs apply to both face-to-face encounters and telephone interactions (Table 4-6). Hospitality finds its full expression in face-to-face encounters. In some cases, it starts and ends with an offer of transport to and from the service site, as with courtesy shuttle buses. If customers must wait outdoors before the service can be delivered, a thoughtful service provider will offer weather protection; if indoors, a waiting area with seating and even entertainment (TV, newspapers, or magazines) to pass the time. Recruiting employees who are naturally warm, welcoming, and considerate for customer-contact jobs helps to create a hospitable atmosphere.

The quality of the hospitality services offered by a firm can increase or decrease satisfaction with the core product. This is especially true when customers cannot easily leave the people-processing service facility. Private hospitals often seek to enhance their appeals by providing the level of room service, including meals, that might be expected in a good hotel. Some airlines seek to differentiate themselves from their competitors with better meals and more attentive cabin crew; Singapore Airlines is well recognized on both counts.

Although preflight and in-flight hospitality is important, an airline journey doesn't end until passengers reach their final destination. Air travelers have come to expect departure lounges, but British Airways (BA) came up with the novel idea of an arrivals lounge for its terminals at London's Heathrow and Gatwick airports to serve passengers arriving early in the morning after a long overnight flight from the Americas, Asia, Africa, and Australia. BA offers holders of first- and business-class tickets or a BA Executive Club gold card (awarded to the airline's most frequent flyers) the opportunity to use a special lounge where they can take a shower, change, have breakfast, and make phone calls or send faxes before continuing to their final destination, feeling a lot fresher. It's a nice competitive advantage, which BA has actively promoted. Other airlines have since felt obliged to copy it.

Failures in hospitality extend to the physical design of the areas where customers wait prior to receiving service. A survey found that unappealing offices and lack of creature comforts can drive away patients of cosmetic surgeons (Research Insights 4-1).

Safekeeping While visiting a service site, customers often want assistance with their personal possessions. In fact, unless certain safekeeping services are provided, such as safe and convenient parking for their cars, some customers may not come at all. The list of potential on-site safekeeping services is long and includes provision of coatrooms; baggage transport, handling, and storage; safekeeping of valuables; and even child care

RESEARCH INSIGHT 4-1

COSMETIC SURGEONS' OFFICES TURN OFF PATIENTS

It appears that plastic surgeons could use some service marketing training along with their other courses in medical school. That's the diagnosis of two experts, Kate Altork and Douglas Dedo, who did a study of patients' reactions to doctors' offices. The researchers found that many patients will cancel a surgery, change doctors, or refuse to consider future elective surgery if they feel uneasy in the doctor's office. The study results suggested that patients don't usually "doctor-jump" because they don't like the doctor but because they don't like the context of the service experience. The list of common patient dislikes includes graphic posters of moles and skin cancers decorating office walls, uncomfortable plastic identification bracelets for patients, claustrophobic examining rooms with no windows or current reading material, bathrooms that aren't clearly marked, and not enough wastebaskets and water coolers in the waiting room.

What do patients want? Most requests are surprisingly simple and involve such creature comforts as tissues, water coolers, telephones, plants, and bowls of candy in the waiting room and live flower arrangements in the lobby. Patients also want windows in the examining rooms and gowns that wrap around the entire body. Patients would like to sit on a real chair when they talk to a doctor instead of perching on a stool or examining table. Finally, as they are disturbed by sitting next to someone in the waiting room whose head is enclosed in bandages, for example, preoperative patients prefer to be separated from postoperative patients.

These study results suggest that cosmetic surgery patients would rather visit an office that looks like a more like a health spa than a hospital ward. By thinking like service marketers, savvy surgeons could use this information to create patient-friendly environments that will complement rather than counteract their technical expertise.

Source: Lisa Bannon, "Plastic Surgeons Are Told to Pay More Attention to Appearances," *Wall Street Journal*, March 15, 1997.

and pet care (Table 4-7). Responsible businesses also worry about the safety of their customers. These days, many businesses pay close attention to safety and security issues for customers who are visiting their service facilities. When it mails out its bank statements, Wells Fargo Bank includes a brochure containing information about using its ATM machines safely. The bank seeks to educate its customers about how to protect both their ATM cards and themselves from theft and personal injury. And the bank makes sure that its machines are in brightly lit, highly visible locations to reduce any risks to its customers or their possessions.

Additional safekeeping services involve physical products that customers buy or rent: packaging, pickup and delivery, assembly, installation, cleaning, and inspection. Some of these services may be offered free; others carry a charge.

Exceptions Exceptions involve supplementary services that fall outside the routine of normal service delivery (Table 4-8). Astute businesses anticipate exceptions and develop contingency plans and guidelines in advance. That way, employees will not appear helpless and surprised when customers ask for special assistance. Well-defined procedures make it easier for employees to respond promptly and effectively.

There are several types of exceptions:

- *Special requests.* A customer may request service that requires a departure from normal operating procedures. Advance requests often relate to personal needs, including care of children, dietary requirements, medical needs, religious observance, and personal disabilities. Such special requests are common in the travel and hospitality industries.

TABLE 4-7 Examples of Safekeeping Elements

Caring for Possessions Customers Bring with Them

- Child care
- Pet care
- Parking facilities for vehicles
- Valet parking
- Coatrooms
- Luggage-handling
- Storage space
- Safe deposit boxes
- Security personnel

Caring for Goods Purchased (or Rented) by Customers

- Packaging
- Pickup
- Transportation
- Delivery
- Installation
- Inspection and diagnosis
- Cleaning
- Refueling
- Preventive maintenance
- Repairs and renovation
- Upgrade

- *Problem solving.* Situations arise when normal service delivery (or product performance) fails to run smoothly, as a result of accidents, delays, equipment failures, or customers' experiencing difficulty in using the product.
- *Handling of complaints/suggestions/compliments.* This activity requires well-defined procedures. It should be easy for customers to express dissatisfaction, offer suggestions for improvement, or pass on compliments, and service providers should be able to make an appropriate response quickly.
- *Restitution.* Many customers expect to be compensated for serious performance failures. Compensation may take the form of repairs under warranty, legal settlements, refunds, an offer of free service, or other forms of payment-in-kind.

Managers need to keep an eye on the level of exception requests. Too many requests may indicate that standard procedures need revamping. For instance, if a restaurant continually receives requests for special vegetarian meals because none are on the menu, perhaps it's time to revise the menu to include at least one such dish. A flexible approach to exceptions is generally a good idea because it reflects responsiveness to customer needs. On the other hand, having too many exceptions may compromise safety, negatively impact other customers, and overburden employees.

Managerial Implications

The eight categories of supplementary services forming the Flower of Service collectively provide many options for enhancing the core product, whether it be a good or a service. Most supplementary services do (or should) represent responses to customer needs. As noted earlier, some are facilitating services, such as information and reservations that enable customers to use the core product more effectively. Others are "extras" that enhance the core product or even reduce its nonfinancial costs (for example,

TABLE 4-8 Examples of Exceptions Elements

Special Requests in Advance of Service Delivery

- Children's needs
- Dietary requirements
- Medical or disability needs
- Religious observances
- Deviations from standard operating procedures

Handling Special Communications

- Complaints
- Compliments
- Suggestions

Problem Solving

- Warranties and guarantees against product malfunction
- Resolving difficulties that arise from using the product
- Resolving difficulties caused by accidents, service failures, and problems with staff or other customers
- Assisting customers who have suffered an accident or medical emergency

Restitution

- Refunds
- Compensation in kind for unsatisfactory goods and services
- Free repair of defective goods

meals, magazines, and entertainment are hospitality elements that help pass the time). Some elements—notably billing and payment—are, in effect, imposed by the service provider. But even if not actively desired by the customer, they still form part of the overall service experience. Any badly handled element may negatively affect customers' perceptions of service quality. The "information" and "consultation" petals illustrate the emphasis in this book on the need for education as well as promotion in communicating with service customers.

Not every core product will be surrounded by a large number of supplementary services from all eight petals. People-processing services—especially hospitality—tend to be the most demanding in terms of supplementary elements, as they involve close (and often extended) interactions with customers. When customers do not visit the service factory, the need for hospitality may be limited to simple courtesies in letters and telecommunications. Possession-processing services sometimes place heavy demands on safekeeping elements, but there may be no need for this particular petal when providing information-processing services in which customers and suppliers deal entirely at arm's length. Financial services that are provided electronically are an exception to this, however; companies must ensure that their customers' intangible financial assets are carefully safeguarded in transactions that occur via phone or the Web.

Managers face many decisions about what types of supplementary services to offer, especially in relation to product-policy and positioning issues. A study of Japanese, American, and European firms serving business-to-business markets found that most companies simply added layers of services to their core offerings without knowing what customers really valued.[6] Managers surveyed in the study indicated that they did not understand which services should be offered to customers as a standard package accompanying the core and which ones could be offered as options for an extra charge. Without this knowledge, developing effective pricing policies can be tricky. No simple rules govern pricing decisions for core products and supplementary services. But managers should continually review their own and competitors' policies to make sure that they are in line with both market practice and customer needs. We'll discuss these and other pricing issues in more detail in Chapter 9.

In summary, Tables 4-1–4-8 can serve as checklists in the continuing search for new ways to augment existing core products and to design new offerings. The lists provided in these eight tables do not claim to be all-encompassing, as some products may require specialized supplementary elements. In general, a firm that competes on a low-cost, no-frills basis will require fewer supplementary elements than one marketing an expensive, high-value-added product. Alternative levels of supplementary services around a common core may offer the basis for a product line of differentiated offerings, similar to the various classes of travel offered by airlines. Regardless of which supplementary services a firm decides to offer, all the elements in each petal should receive the care and attention needed to consistently meet defined service standards. That way, the resulting "flower" will always have a fresh and appealing appearance rather than looking wilted or disfigured by neglect.

PLANNING AND BRANDING SERVICE PRODUCTS

In recent years, more and more service businesses have started talking about their *products*—a term previously associated with manufactured goods. Some businesses even speak of their "products and services," an expression also used by service-driven manufacturing firms. What is the distinction between these two terms in today's business environment?

A *product* implies a defined and consistent "bundle of output" and also the ability to differentiate one bundle of output from another. In a manufacturing context, the concept is easy to understand and visualize. Service firms can also differentiate their products in similar fashion to the various "models" offered by manufacturers. Quick-service restaurants are sometimes described as "quasi-manufacturing" operations, as they produce a physical output combined with value-added service. At each site, they display a menu of their products, which are, of course, highly tangible: Burger connoisseurs can easily distinguish Burger King's Whopper from a Whopper with Cheese, as well as a Whopper from a Big Mac. The service comes from speedy delivery of a freshly prepared food item, the ability, in some instances, to order and pick up freshly cooked food from a drive-in location without leaving one's car, the availability within the restaurant of self-service drinks, condiments, and napkins, and the opportunity to sit down and eat one's meal at a table.

But providers of more intangible services also offer a "menu" of products, representing an assembly of carefully prescribed elements that are built around the core product and may bundle in certain value-added supplementary services. Additional supplementary services—often referred to collectively as *customer service*—may be available to facilitate delivery and use of the product, as well as billing and payment. Let's look at some examples from hotels, airlines, and computer support services.

Product Lines and Brands

Most service organizations offer a line of products rather than a single product. Some of these products are distinctly different from one another—as, for example, when a company is engaged in several areas of business. Within a specific industry, a large firm may offer several differently positioned entries, each identified by a separate brand name. The United States has more than 200 hotel brands competing for business, more than any other product category. Many hotel chains offer a family of brands; for instance, Marriott Corporation offers several brands of hotels and resorts under the Marriott umbrella brand:

- *Marriott Hotels* (big, full-service hotels in cities, offering large public areas and meeting facilities)
- *Marriott Resorts* (large, full-service hotels in resort areas, offering meeting facilities and access to extensive sporting and recreational amenities)
- *Courtyard by Marriott* (medium-sized hotels without conference facilities, targeted at business travelers who require comfortable rooms and business-related services but fewer hotel amenities)
- *Fairfield Inn* (inexpensive rooms with only limited hotel services)
- *Residence Inn* (offering a bedroom, living room, and kitchen at full-service hotel room prices, targeted at customers needing hotel amenities with more workspace and planning to stay at least several days)
- *SpringHill Suites* (moderately priced all-suites hotels, targeted at both business and pleasure travelers and offering separate working, sleeping, and eating areas, including a pantry with sink, microwave, and coffee maker)
- *TownePlace Suites* (suites with full kitchens designed for extended stays, offering residential comfort in a townhouse setting at reasonable prices)
- *Marriott Vacation Club International* (villa vacation resorts)

Each brand promises a distinct mix of benefits, targeted at a different customer segment. The offerings vary by service level (and thus price); there are also various room configurations available; certain brands are targeted at guests who will be making an extended stay; and two resort brands target primarily vacationers. In some instances, segmentation is situation based: The same individual may have different needs (and willingness to pay) under differing circumstances. The strategy of brand extension is aimed at encouraging customers to continue patronizing units within the brand family. A study of the brand-switching behavior of some 5,400 hotel customers found that brand extensions do seem to encourage customer retention but that the strategy may be less effective in discouraging switching when the number of subbrands reaches four or more.[7]

In other instances, it is unlikely that customers will choose more than a single subbrand. As an example of branding a high-tech, business-to-business product line, consider Sun Microsystems, which offers a comprehensive hardware and software support program known as SunSpectrum Support.[8] Four levels of support are available, subbranded from platinum to bronze (they are displayed in menu form in Figure 4-6). The objective is to give buyers the flexibility to choose a level of support consistent with their own organizations' needs (and willingness to pay), ranging from mission-critical support at the enterprise level to assistance with self-service support. Note the more extensive service hours available with the higher levels of support (24/7) as opposed to daytime service on weekdays at the lower levels.

Another example comes from British Airways (BA), which offers seven distinct air travel products—sometimes referred to as subbrands. There are four intercontinental offerings: First (deluxe subsonic service), Club World (business class), World Traveller Plus (premium economy class), and World Traveller (economy class); two intra-European subbrands—Club Europe (business class) and Euro-Traveller (economy class); and, within the United Kingdom, Shuttle, offering high-frequency service between London and major British cities. Each BA offering represents a specific service concept and a set of clearly stated product specifications for preflight, in-flight, and on-arrival service elements.

To provide additional focus on product, pricing, and marketing communications, responsibility for managing and developing each service is assigned to an individual management team. Through internal training and external communications, staff and

FIGURE 4-6 Four Levels of Support from Sun Microsystems

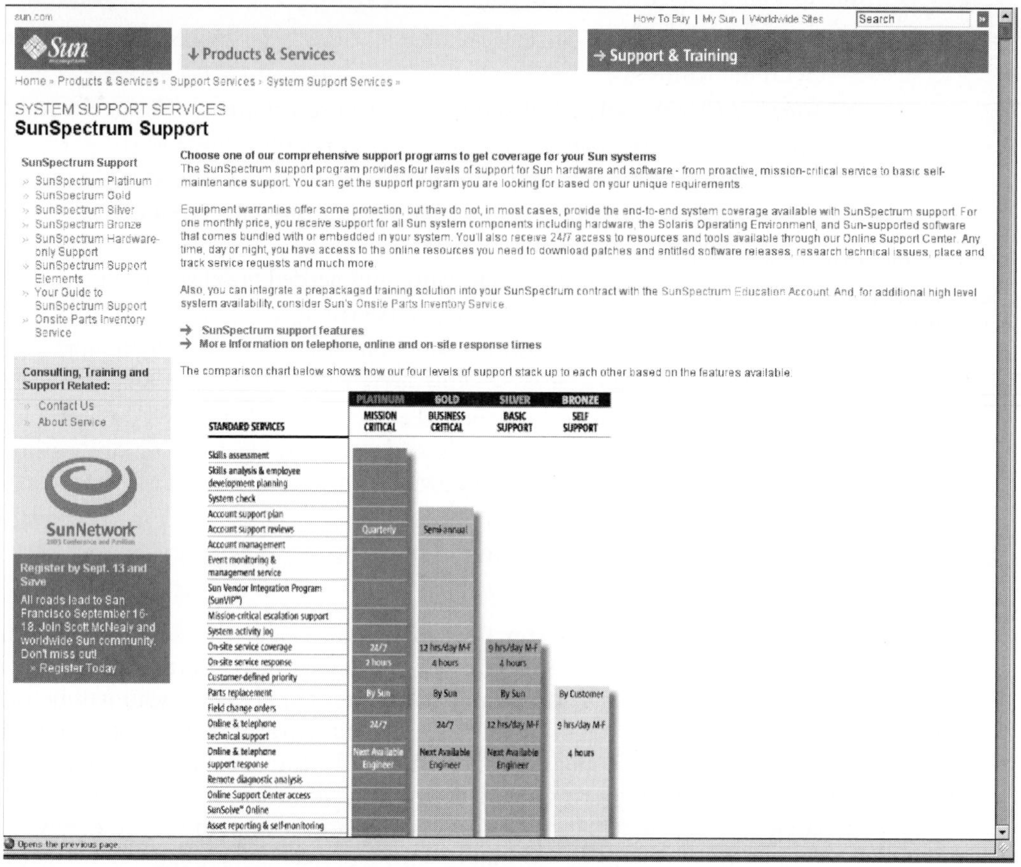

passengers alike are kept informed of the characteristics of each service. Except for Super Shuttle and nonjets, most aircraft in BA's fleet are configured in several classes. On any given route, all passengers on a particular flight receive the same core product—say, a 10-hour journey from Los Angeles to London—but the nature and extent of most of the supplementary elements differs widely, both on the ground and in the air. Passengers in Club World, for instance, not only benefit from better tangible elements, such as more comfortable seats that fold into beds, better food, and the use of an airport lounge before the flight, but also receive more personalized service from airline employees and benefit from faster service on the ground at check-in, passport control in London (special lines), and baggage retrieval (priority handling). First-class passengers are even more pampered. The higher the service level, of course, the higher the price!

Offering a Branded Experience

Branding can be used at both the corporate and product levels by almost any service business. In a well-managed firm, the corporate brand is not only easily recognized but also has meaning for customers: It stands for a particular way of doing business. Subbrands under the umbrella of a corporate brand should reflect the values of the latter. At the same time, the subbrand should communicate the particular experiences and benefits associated with a given service process.

The Forum Corporation, a consulting firm, differentiates among (1) a random customer experience with high variability; (2) a generic branded experience in which most

MANAGEMENT MEMO 4-1

MOVING TOWARD THE BRANDED CUSTOMER EXPERIENCE

Forum Corporation identifies eight basic steps to develop and deliver the Branded Customer Experience.

1. Target profitable customers, using behavior segmentation rather than demographics.
2. Achieve a superior understanding of what your targeted customers value.
3. Create a brand promise—an articulation of what target customers can expect from their experience with your organization—that is of value to customers, addresses a need and is actionable and can be incorporated into standards, and provides focus for the organization and its employees.
4. Apply that understanding to shape a truly differentiated customer experience.
5. Give employees the skills, tools, and supporting processes needed to deliver the defined customer experience.
6. Make everyone a brand manager.
7. Make promises that your processes can exceed.
8. Measure and monitor. Consistency of delivery is paramount.

Source: "Forum Issues #17" (Boston: The Forum Corporation, 1997), Joe Wheeler and Shaun Smith, "Loyalty by Design," Forum Corporation (2003), *www.forum.com/publications*, accessed March 2003.

suppliers offer a consistently similar experience, differentiated only by the presence of the brand name (ATMs are a good example); and (3) a "branded customer experience" in which the customer's experience is shaped in specific and meaningful ways.[9] (See Management Memo 4-1 for Forum's recommendations on how to achieve this.)

Around the world, many financial service firms continue to create and register brand names to distinguish the various accounts and service packages they offer. The objective of these firms is to transform a series of service elements and processes into a consistent and recognizable service experience, offering a definable and predictable output at a specified price. Unfortunately, there is often little discernible difference—other than name—between one bank's branded offering and another's, and the value proposition is unclear. As Don Shultz emphasizes: "The brand promise or value proposition is not a tag line, an icon , or a color or a graphic element, although all of these may contribute. It is, instead, the heart and soul of the brand."[10]

An important role for service marketers is to become brand champions, familiar with and responsible for shaping every aspect of the customer's experience. We can relate the notion of a branded service experience to the Flower of Service metaphor by emphasizing the need for consistency in the color and texture of each petal. Unfortunately, many service experiences remain very haphazard and create the impression of a flower stitched together with petals drawn from many different plants!

We return to a discussion of branding in the context of marketing communications strategy in Chapter 5. Additional insights can be found in the reading by Leonard L. Berry, "Cultivating Service Brand Equity," on pp. 207–216.

NEW SERVICE DEVELOPMENT

Competitive intensity and customer expectations are increasing in nearly all service industries. Thus, success lies not only in providing existing services well but also in creating new approaches to service. Because the outcome and process aspects of a service often combine to create the experience and benefits obtained by customers, both aspects must be addressed in new service development.

A Hierarchy of New Service Categories

Following are seven categories of new services, ranging from major innovations to simple style changes.

1. *Major service innovations* are new core products for markets that have not been previously defined. These products usually include both new service characteristics and radical new processes. Examples are FedEx's introduction of overnight, nationwide, express package delivery in 1971, the advent of global news service from CNN, and eBay's launch of online auction services.
2. *Major process innovations* consist of using new processes to deliver existing core products in new ways with additional benefits. For example, the University of Phoenix competes with other universities by delivering undergraduate and graduate degree programs in a nontraditional way. The university has no permanent campus but offers courses either online or at night in rented facilities. Its students get most of the benefits of a college degree in half the time and at a much lower price than they would at other universities.[11] In recent years, the growth of the Internet has led to the creation of many new start-up businesses using new retailing models that exclude use of traditional stores but save customers time and travel. Often, these models add new, information-based benefits, such as greater customization, the opportunity to visit chat rooms with fellow customers, and suggestions for additional products that match well with what has already been purchased.
3. *Product-line extensions* are additions by existing firms to their current product lines. The first company in a market to offer such a product may be seen as an innovator; the others are merely followers, often acting defensively. These new services may be targeted at existing customers to serve a broader array of needs or designed to attract new customers with different needs (or both). Delta Airlines is one of several major carriers to attempt the launch of a separate low-cost operation designed to compete with such discount carriers as JetBlue and Southwest Airlines. Telephone companies have introduced numerous value-added services, such as call waiting and call forwarding. In banking, many banks now retail insurance products in the hope of increasing the number of profitable relationships with existing customers.
4. *Process-line extensions* are less innovative than process innovations but often represent distinctive new ways of delivering existing products so as to either offer more convenience and a different experience for existing customers or to attract new customers who find the traditional approach unappealing. Most commonly, process-line extensions involve adding a lower-contact distribution channel to an existing high-contact channel, such as creating telephone- or Internet-based banking service. Barnes and Noble, the leading bookstore chain in the United States, added a new Internet subsidiary, BarnesandNoble.com, to help it compete against Amazon.com. Such dual-track approaches are sometimes referred to as "clicks and mortar." Creating self-service options to complement delivery by service employees is another form of process-line extension.
5. *Supplementary-service innovations* take the form of adding new facilitating or enhancing service elements to an existing core service or of significantly improving an existing supplementary service. Kinkos now offers customers high-speed Internet access 24/7 at most of its locations in the United States and Canada. Low-tech innovations for an existing service can be as simple as adding parking at a retail site or agreeing to accept credit cards for payment. Multiple improvements may have the effect of creating what customers perceive as an altogether new experience, even though it is built around the same core. Theme restaurants, such

as the Rainforest Café, enhance the core food service with new experiences. The cafés are designed to keep customers entertained with aquariums, live parrots, waterfalls, fiberglass monkeys, talking trees that spout environmentally related information, and regularly timed thunderstorms, complete with lightning.[12]

6. *Service improvements* are the most common type of innovation. They involve modest changes in the performance of current products, including improvements to either the core product or existing supplementary services.
7. *Style changes* represent the simplest type of innovation, typically involving no changes in either processes or performance. However, style changes are often highly visible, create excitement, and may motivate employees. Examples are repainting retail branches and vehicles in new color schemes, outfitting service employees in new uniforms, introducing a new bank check design, or making minor changes in service scripts for employees.

As the preceding typology suggests, service innovation can occur at many different levels; not every type of innovation has an impact on the characteristics of the service product or is experienced by the customer.

Physical Goods as a Source of New Service Ideas

Goods and services may be competitive substitutes when they offer the same key benefits. For example, if your lawn needs mowing, you could buy a lawn mower and do it yourself, or you could hire a lawn maintenance service to take care of the chore. Such decisions may be shaped by the customer's skills, physical capabilities, and time budget, as well as such factors as cost comparisons between purchase and use, storage space for purchased products, and anticipateed frequency of need. Many services can be built around providing an alternative to owning a physical good and doing the work oneself. Figure 4-7 shows four possible delivery alternatives each for car travel and word processing, respectively. Three of these alternatives present service opportunities. The alternatives are based on choosing between ownership and rental of the necessary physical goods, and between performing self-service or hiring another person to perform the necessary tasks.

Any new physical product has the potential to create a need for related possession-processing services, particularly if the product is a high-value, durable item. Industrial equipment may require servicing throughout its lifespan, beginning with shipping and installation and continuing with maintenance, cleaning, consulting advice, problem solving, upgrading, repair, and ultimate disposal. Historically, such after-sales services have generated important revenue streams for many years after the initial sale for such products as trucks, factory machinery, locomotives, computers, and jet engines.

FIGURE 4-7 Services as Substitutes for Owning and/or Using Goods

	OWN A PHYSICAL GOOD	RENT THE USE OF A PHYSICAL GOOD
PERFORM THE WORK ONESELF	• Drive Own Car • Type on Own Word Processor	• Rent a Car and Drive It • Rent a Word Processor and Type on It
HIRE SOMEONE TO DO THE WORK	• Hire a Chauffeur to Drive Car • Hire a Typist to Use Word Processor	• Hire a Taxi or Limousine • Send Work Out to a Secretarial Service

Reengineering Service Processes

The design of service processes has implications not only for customers but also for the cost, speed, and productivity with which the desired outcome is achieved. Improving productivity in services often requires speeding up the overall process, or cycle time, as the cost of creating a service is usually related to how long it takes to deliver each step in the process, along with any dead time between steps. Reengineering involves analyzing and redesigning processes to achieve faster and better performance.[13] To reduce overall process time, analysts must identify each step, measure how long it takes, look for opportunities to speed it up (or even eliminate it altogether), and cut out dead time. Running tasks in parallel rather than in sequence is a well-established approach to speeding up processes. (A simple household example would be to cook the vegetables for a meal while the main dish is in the oven rather than wait to cook them until after the main dish is removed.) Service companies can use blueprinting to diagram these aspects of service operations in a systematic way.

Examination of processes may also lead to creation of alternative delivery methods that are so radically different as to constitute entirely new service concepts. Options may include eliminating certain supplementary services, adding new ones, instituting self-service procedures, and rethinking where and when service is delivered.

Figure 4-8 illustrates this principle with simple flowcharts of four alternative ways to deliver meal service, as compared to a full-service restaurant. Take a look and contrast what happens front-stage at a fast-food restaurant, a drive-in restaurant, home delivery, and home catering. From the customer's perspective, what has been added to or deleted from the scenario at a full-service restaurant? And in each instance, how do these changes affect backstage activities?

Using Research to Design New Services

If it is designing a new service from scratch, how can a company figure out what features and price will create the best value for target customers? It's difficult to know without asking these customers; hence the need for research. Let's examine how the

FIGURE 4-8 Flowcharts for Meal Delivery Scenarios

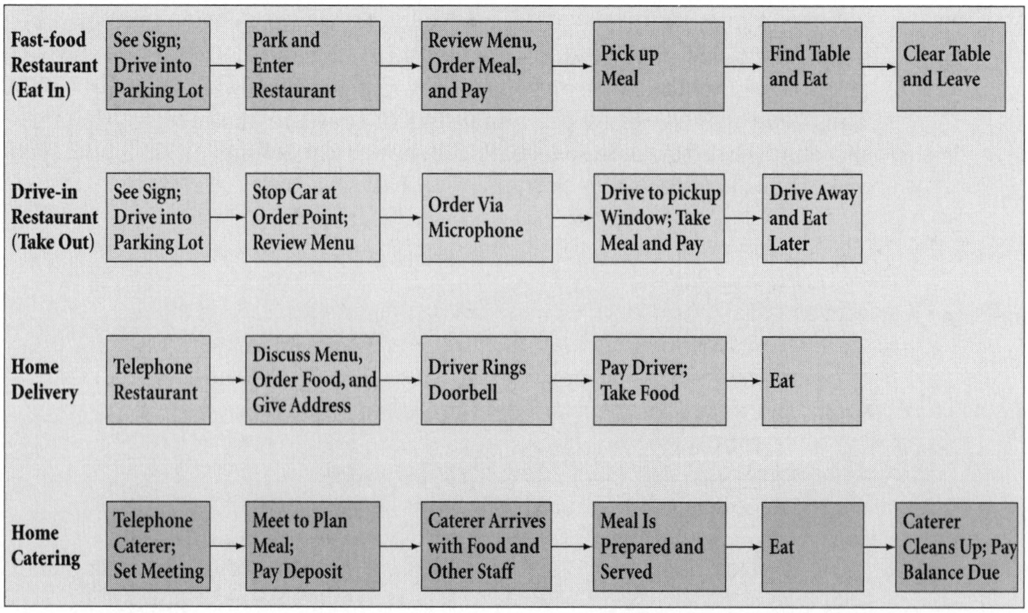

Marriott Corporation used market research experts to help with new-service development in the hotel industry.

When Marriott was designing a new chain of hotels that eventually became known as Courtyard by Marriott, it hired marketing research experts to help establish an optimal design concept.[14] As there are limits to how much service and how many amenities can be offered at any given price, Marriott needed to know how customers would make tradeoffs in order to arrive at the most satisfactory compromise in terms of value for money. The intent of the research was to get respondents to trade off various hotel service features to see which ones they valued most. Marriott's goal was to determine whether a niche existed between full-service hotels and inexpensive motels, especially in locations where demand was not high enough to justify a large full-service hotel. If such a niche existed, executives wanted to develop a product to fill that gap for business travelers.

A sample of 601 consumers from four metropolitan areas participated in the study. Researchers used a sophisticated technique known as conjoint analysis, which asks survey respondents to make tradeoffs between different groupings of attributes.[15] Another research technique, also used in the hotel industry, is discrete choice analysis.[16] The objective is to determine which mix of attributes at specific prices offers the highest degree of utility. The fifty attributes in the Marriott study were divided into the following seven factors (or sets of attributes), each containing a variety of features based on detailed studies of competing offerings:

1. *External factors*—building shape, landscaping, pool type and location, hotel size
2. *Room features*—room size and décor, climate control, location and type of bathroom, entertainment systems, other amenities
3. *Food-related services*—type and location of restaurants, menus, room service, vending machines, guest shop, in-room kitchen
4. *Lounge facilities*—location, atmosphere, type of guests
5. *Services*—reservations, registration, check-out, airport limousine, bell desk (baggage service), message center, secretarial services, car rental, laundry, valet
6. *Leisure facilities*—sauna, whirlpool, exercise room, racquetball and tennis courts, game room, children's playground
7. *Security*—guards, smoke detectors, 24/hour video camera

For each of these seven factors, respondents were presented with a series of stimulus cards displaying various levels of performance for each attribute. For instance, the "Rooms" stimulus card displayed nine attributes, each of which had three to five levels. Thus, *amenities* ranged from "small bar of soap" to "large soap, shampoo packet, shoeshine mitt" to "large soap, bath gel, shower cap, sewing kit, shampoo, special soap" and then to the highest level: "large soap, bath gel, shower cap, sewing kit, special soap, toothpaste, etc."

In the second phase of the analysis, respondents were shown a number of alternative hotel profiles, each featuring different levels of performance on the various attributes contained in the seven factors. Respondants were asked to indicate on a five-point scale how likely they would be to stay at a hotel with these features, given a specific room price per night. Figure 4-9 shows one of the 50 cards that were developed for this research. Each respondent received five cards.

The research yielded detailed guidelines for the selection of almost 200 features and service elements, representing those attributes that provided the highest utility for the customers in the target segments at prices they were willing to pay. An important aspect of the study was that it not only focused on what business travelers wanted but also identified what they liked but weren't prepared to pay for (there's a difference, after all, between wanting something and being willing to pay for it). Using these

FIGURE 4-9 Sample Description of a Hotel Offering

Room Price per Night Is $44.85

Building Size, Bar/Lounge: Large (600 rooms), 12-story hotel with:
- Quiet bar/lounge
- Enclosed central corridors and elevators
- All rooms have very large windows

Landscaping/Court: Building forms a spacious outdoor courtyard
- View from rooms of moderately landscaped courtyard with:
  many trees and shrubs
  the swimming pool plus a fountain
  terraced areas for sunning, sitting, eating

Food: Small moderately priced lounge and restaurant for hotel guests/friends
- Limited breakfast with juices, fruit, Danish, cereal, bacon, and eggs
- Lunch—soup and sandwiches only
- Evening meal—salad, soup, sandwiches, six hot entrees, including steak

Hotel/Motel Room Quality: Quality of room furnishings, carpet, etc., is similar to:
- Hyatt Regency Hotels
- Westin "Plaza" Hotels

Room Size and Function: Room one foot longer than typical hotel/motel room
- Space for comfortable sofa-bed and two chairs
- Large desk
- Coffee table
- Coffee maker and small refrigerator

Service Standards: Full service including:
- Rapid check-in/check-out systems
- Reliable message service
- Valet (laundry pick up/deliver)
- Bellman
- Someone (concierge) arranges reservations, tickets, and generally at no cost
- Cleanliness, upkeep, management similar to:
  Hyatts
  Marriotts

Leisure
- Combination indoor-outdoor pool
- Enclosed whirlpool (Jacuzzi)
- Well-equipped playroom/playground for kids

Security
- Night guard on duty 7 P.M. to 7 A.M.
- Fire/water sprinklers throughout hotel

"X" the ONE box below that best describes how likely you are to stay in this hotel/motel at this price:

Would stay there almost all the time	Would stay there on a regular basis	Would stay there now and then	Would rarely stay there	Would not stay there
☐	☐	☐	☐	☐

Source: Jerry Wind et al., "Courtyard by Marriott: Designing a Hotel Facility with Customer-Based Marketing Models," *Interfaces* (January/February; 1989): 25–47.

inputs, the design team was able to meet the specified price while retaining the features most desired by the target market.

Marriott was sufficiently encouraged by the findings to build three Courtyard by Marriott prototype hotels. After testing the concept under real-world conditions and making some refinements, the company subsequently developed a large chain whose advertising slogan became "Courtyard by Marriott—the hotel designed by business travelers." The new hotel concept filled a gap in the market with a product that represented the best balance between the price customers were prepared to pay and the physical and service features they most desired. The success of this project has led Marriott to develop additional customer-driven products—including Fairfield Inn and SpringHill Suites—using the same research methodology.

Achieving Success in New Service Development

Most of the research into new product success factors has been confined to industrial or business-to-business markets and has emphasized studies of the development process for new physical goods. Chris Storey and Christopher Easingwood argue that in developing new services, the product core is of only secondary importance. Rather, of key importance are the quality of the total service offering and of the marketing support that goes with this. Underlying success in these areas, they emphasize, is market knowledge: "Without an understanding of the marketplace, knowledge about customers, and knowledge about competitors, it is very unlikely that a new product will be a success."[17]

Stephan Tax and Ian Stuart contend that new services should be defined in terms of the extent of change required to the existing service system, relative to the interactions among participants (people), processes, and physical elements (e.g., facilities and equipment).[18] They propose a seven-step planning cycle to evaluate the feasibility and associated risks of integrating a new service development into a firm's existing service system.

Service firms are not immune to the high failure rates plaguing new manufactured products. The advent of the Internet stimulated entrepreneurs to create numerous new dot.com companies to deliver Internet-based services, but the vast majority of those start-ups failed within a few years. The reasons for failure ranged widely, including failure to meet a demonstrable consumer need, inability to cover costs from revenues, and poor execution.

To what extent can rigorously conducted and controlled development processes for new services enhance their success rate? A study by Scott Edgett and Steven Parkinson focused on discriminating between successful and unsuccessful new financial services.[19] The researchers found that the three factors contributing most to success were, in order of importance:

1. *Market synergy*. The new product fit well with the existing image of the firm, provided a superior advantage to competing products in terms of meeting customers' known needs, and received strong support during and after the launch from the firm and its branches; further, the firm had a good understanding of its customers' purchase decision behavior.
2. *Organizational factors*. There was strong interfunctional cooperation and coordination; development personnel were fully aware of why they were involved and of the importance of new products to the company.
3. *Market research factors*. Detailed and scientifically designed market research studies were conducted early in the development process with a clear idea of the type of information to be obtained; a good definition of the product concept was developed before undertaking field surveys.

Another survey of financial service firms to determine what distinguished successful from unsuccessful products yielded broadly similar findings.[20] In this instance, the key factors underlying success were determined as *synergy* (the fit between the product and the firm in terms of needed expertise and resources being present) and *internal marketing* (the support given to staff prior to launch to help them understand the new product and its underlying systems, along with details about direct competitors and support).

Courtyard by Marriott's success in a very different industry—a people-processing service with many tangible components—supports the notion that a highly structured development process will increase the chances of success for a complex service innovation. However, it's worth noting that there may be limits to the degree of structure that can and should be imposed. Bo Edvardsson, Lars Haglund, and Jan Mattsson reviewed new service development in telecommunications, transport, and financial services. The researchers concluded that

> [C]omplex processes like the development of new services cannot be formally planned altogether. Creativity and innovation cannot only rely on planning and control. There must be some elements of improvization, anarchy, and internal competition in the development of new services .... We believe that a contingency approach is needed and that creativity on the one hand and formal planning and control on the other can be balanced, with successful new services as the outcome."[21]

CONCLUSION

Designing a service product is a complex task that requires an understanding of how the core and supplementary services should be combined, sequenced, and scheduled to create an offering that meets the needs of target market segments. Many firms create an array of offerings with various performance attributes and brand each package with a distinctive name. However, unless each of these subbrands offers and fulfills a meaningful value proposition, this strategy is likely to be ineffective from a competitive standpoint. In particular, creating a distinctive branded service experience for customers requires consistency across all product elements and at all stages of the service delivery process.

Although innovation is central to effective marketing, major service innovations are relatively rare. More common is the use of new technologies to deliver existing services in new ways. In mature industries, the core service can become a commodity. The search for competitive advantage often centers on improvements to the value-creating supplementary services that surround this core. In this chapter, we grouped supplementary services into eight categories, which circle the core like the petals of a flower.

A key insight from the Flower of Service concept is that different types of core products often share use of similar supplementary elements. As a result, customers may make comparisons across industries. For instance, "If my stockbroker can give me a clear documentation of my account activity, why can't the department store where I shop?" Or "If my favorite airline can take reservations accurately, why can't the French restaurant up the street?" Such questions suggest that managers should be studying businesses outside their own industries in a search for "best-in-class" performers on specific supplementary services.

Review Questions

1. Explain the role of supplementary services. Can they be applied to goods as well as to services? If so, how might they relate to marketing strategy?
2. Explain the distinction between enhancing and facilitating supplementary services. Give several examples of each, relative to services that you have used recently
3. How is branding used in services marketing? What is the distinction between a corporate brand, such as Marriott, and the names of its various inn and hotel chains?

4. What does British Airways gain from using such subbrand names as Club World or Euro Traveller? What not simply use "business class" and "economy class"?
5. What is the purpose of such techniques as conjoint analysis in designing new services?

Application Exercises

1. Identify some real-world examples of branding from financial services, such as specific types of retail bank accounts or insurance policies, and define their characteristics. How meaningful are these brands likely to be to customers?
2. What service failures have you encountered during the past two weeks? Did they involve the core product or supplementary service elements? Identify possible causes and how such failures might be prevented in the future.

Endnotes

1. G. Lynn Shostack, "Breaking Free from Product Marketing," *Journal of Marketing* 44 (April 1977): 73–80.
2. Pierre Eiglier and Eric Langeard, "Services as Systems: Marketing Implications," in P. Eiglier, E. Langeard, C. H. Lovelock, J. E. G. Bateson, and R. F. Young, *Marketing Consumer Services: New Insights* (Cambridge, MA: Marketing Science Institute, 1977), 83–103. *Note*: An earlier version of this article was published in French in *Révue Française de Gestion* (March–April 1977): 72–84.
3. Christian Grönroos, *Service Management and Marketing,* 2d ed. (New York: Wiley, 2000), 166.
4. The Flower of Service concept presented in this section was first introduced in Christopher H. Lovelock, "Cultivating the Flower of Service: New Ways of Looking at Core and Supplementary Services," in *Marketing, Operations, and Human Resources: Insights into Services*, ed. P. Eiglier and E. Langeard (Aix-en-Provence, France: IAE, Université d'Aix-Marseille III, 1992), 296–316.
5. Calmetta Coleman, "Fliers Call Electronic Ticketing a Drag," *Wall Street Journal*, January 17, 1997.
6. James C. Anderson and James A. Narus, "Capturing the Value of Supplementary Services," *Harvard Business Review*, 73 (January–February 1995): 75–83.
7. Weizhong Jiang, Chekitan S. Dev, and Vithala R. Rao, "Brand Extension and Customer Loyalty: Evidence from the Lodging Industry," *Cornell Hotel and Restaurant Administration Quarterly* (August 2002): 5–16.
8. *www.sun.com/service/support/sunspectrum*, accessed March 2003.
9. Joe Wheeler and Shaun Smith, *Managing the Experience* (Upper Saddle River, NJ: Prentice-Hall, 2003).
10. Don E. Shultz, "Getting to the Heart of the Brand," *Marketing Management* (Sep.–Oct. 2001): 8–9.
11. See James Traub, "Drive-Thru U.," *The New Yorker* (October 20 and 27, 1997; and Joshua Macht, "Virtual You," *Inc. Magazine* (January 1998): 84–87.
12. Chad Rubel, "New Menu for Restaurants: Talking Trees and Blackjack," *Marketing News* (July 29, 1996): 1.
13. See, for example, Michael Hammer and James Champy, *Reengineering the Corporation* (New York: HarperBusiness), 1993.
14. Jerry Wind, Paul E. Green, Douglas Shifflet, and Marsha Scarbrough, "Courtyard by Marriott: Designing a Hotel Facility with Consumer-Based Marketing Models," *Interfaces* (January–February 1989): 25–47.
15. Paul E. Green, Abba M. Krieger, and Yoram (Jerry) Wind, "Thirty Years of Conjoint Analysis: Reflections and Prospects," *Interfaces* 31 (May–June 2001): S56–S73.
16. Rohit Verma, Gerhard Plashka, and Jordan J. Louviere, "Understanding Customer Choice. A Key to Successful Management of Hospitality Services," *Cornett Hotel and Restaurant Administration Quarterly* 43 (December 2002): 15–24.
17. Chris D. Storey and Christopher J. Easingwood, "The Augmented Service Offering: A Conceptualization and Study of Its Impact on New Service Success," *Journal of Product Innovation Management* 15 (1998): 335–351.
18. Stephen S. Tax and Ian Stuart, "Designing and Implementing New Services: The Challenges of Integrating Service Systems," *Journal of Retailing* 73, no. 1 (1997): 105–134.
19. Scott Edgett and Steven Parkinson, "The Development of New Financial Services: Identifying Determinants of Success and Failure," *International Journal of Service Industry Management* 5, no. 4 (1994): 24–38.
20. Christopher Storey and Christopher Easingwood, "The Impact of the New Product Development Project on the Success of Financial Services," *Service Industries Journal* 13, no. 3 (July 1993): 40–54.
21. Bo Edvardsson, Lars Haglund, and Jan Mattsson, "Analysis, Planning, Improvisation and Control in the Development of New Services," *International Journal of Service Industry Management* 6, no. 2 (1995): 24–35.

CHAPTER 5

Designing the Communications Mix for Services

Life is for one generation; a good name is forever.
—Japanese Proverb

Education costs money, but then so does ignorance.
—Sir Claus Moser

Communication is the most visible or audible—some would say intrusive—of marketing activities, but its value is limited unless it is used intelligently in conjunction with other marketing efforts. An old marketing axiom says that the fastest way to kill a poor product is to advertise it heavily. By the same token, an otherwise well-researched and well-planned marketing strategy, designed to deliver, say, new Web-based services at a reasonable price, is likely to fail if people lack knowledge of the service and how to access it.

Through communication, marketers inform existing or prospective customers about service features and benefits, price and other costs, the channels through which service is delivered, and when and where it is available. Where appropriate, persuasive arguments can be marshaled for using a particular service, and preference can be created for selecting a specific brand. And both personal instructions and impersonal communications can be used to help customers become effective participants in service delivery processes.

Much confusion surrounds the scope of marketing communication. Some people still define it narrowly as the use of paid media advertising, public relations, and professional salespeople, failing to recognize the many other ways that a modern organization can communicate with its customers. The location and atmosphere of a service delivery facility; corporate design features, such as the consistent use of colors and graphic elements; the appearance and behavior of employees; the design of a Web site—all contribute to an impression in the customer's mind that reinforces or contradicts the specific content of formal communication messages.

In this chapter, we explore the following questions.

1. What is distinctive about the nature of marketing communications for services?
2. What are the elements of the marketing communications mix, and what are the strengths and weaknesses of each major element in a services context?
3. How does the level of customer contact affect communication strategy?

4. How should marketing communication objectives be defined?
5. What is the potential value of the Internet as a communication channel?

COMMUNICATION PLAYS A KEY ROLE IN MARKETING

In a service setting, marketing communications tools are especially important because they help create powerful images and a sense of credibility, confidence, and reassurance. Marketing communications, in one form or another, are essential to a company's success. Without effective communications, prospects may never learn of a service firm's existence, what it has to offer them, or how to use its products to best advantage. Customers might be more easily lured away by competitors and competitive offerings, and there would be no proactive management and control of the firm's identity.

No longer can marketing communication be defined as narrowly as it once was. Today, marketing communications between a service firm and its customers can take many forms. Companies can inform existing or prospective customers about service features and benefits, price and other costs, and service delivery options. Marketers can also design persuasive arguments that encourage use of a particular service or reinforce customer preferences for specific brands. Both impersonal communications (e.g., direct mail and e-mail) and personal interactions (e.g., the telemarketing and sales calls Enterprise Rent-a-Car uses to establish accounts and maintain relationships) can be used effectively in developing and maintaining relationships with customers. Let's look at some specific tasks that can be performed by marketing communication.

Adding Value through Communication Content

Information and consultation are important ways to add value to a product. Prospective customers may need information and advice about what service options are available to them, where and when these services are available, how much they cost, specific features and functions, and specific service benefits. Companies also use marketing communications to persuade target customers that their service product offers the best solution to meet those customers' needs, relative to the offerings of competing firms.

Communication efforts serve to not only attract new users but also maintain contact with an organization's existing customers and build relationships with them. Nurturing customer relationships depends on a comprehensive and up-to-date customer database and the ability to use it in a personalized way.

Techniques for keeping in touch with customers and building their loyalty include direct mail and contacts by telephone or other forms of telecommunication, including faxes, e-mail, and Web sites. Doctors, dentists, and household maintenance services often send annual check-up reminders to their customers. Some businesses even send birthday and anniversary cards to valued customers. Banks and utility companies often include a brief newsletter with their account statements or print customized information on each statement in an effort to cross-sell additional services. See Best Practice in Action 5.1, which features a highly targeted campaign by an online broker.

Internal Communications

Marketing communications can be used to communicate with service employees as well as with external customers. Internal communications from senior managers to their employees play a vital role in maintaining and nurturing a corporate culture founded on specific service values. Well-planned internal marketing efforts are especially necessary in large service businesses that operate in widely dispersed sites, sometimes around the world. Even when employees are working far from the head office in

BEST PRACTICE IN ACTION 5-1

REACTIVATING IDLE ACCOUNTS VIA A TARGETED PROMOTION

Well-managed CRM (customer relationship management) systems give firms an *integrated view of the customer* that facilitates highly targeted promotions and communications strategies. Consider the following example from Accenture management consultants Kevin Quiring and Nancy Mullen:

> You glance at a message on your pager that has just come in. It is from your online broker. You almost delete it, assuming it's a pedestrian banner ad from its website that has somehow wormed its way into your pager address. Then you noticed that the message is personalized, offering you that the fees for your next trade would be waived. No way that this message was sent to their entire customer base; it would have cost them a bomb! It seems, your online broker has noticed your conspicuous lack of trading activity since your account was opened. The offer makes you want to act immediately. In retrospect, you realize it is not the eight bucks that is spurring you on, but the poignant reminder that your money has been earning zero-point-nothing percent interest for nearly a year in the brokerage account.[1]

This campaign garnered a 30 percent to 40 percent activation rate, and 20 percent to 30 percent of those customers repeated transactions after this promotional offer. Note that the majority of those accounts would have been likely candidates for closure without this reactivation campaign. The value and success in terms of increased accuracy and reduced costs are attributed to what is being commonly referred to as an *integrated view of the customer*, or IVoC in CRM language.

[1]Kevin N. Quiring and Nancy K. Mullen, "More than Data Warehousing: An Integrated View of the Customer," in *The Ultimate CRM Handbook—Strategies & Concepts for Building Enduring Customer Loyalty & Profitability,* ed. John G. Freeland (New York: McGraw-Hill, 2002), 102.

the home country, they still need to be kept informed of new policies, changes in service features, and new quality initiatives. Communications may also be needed to nurture team spirit and support common corporate goals. Consider the challenge of maintaining a unified sense of purpose at the overseas offices of such companies as Citibank, Air Canada, Marriott, or Starbucks, whose employees come from different cultures, and speak different languages but must work together to create consistent levels of service.

Effective internal communications can help ensure efficient and satisfactory service delivery, achieve productive and harmonious working relationships, and build employee trust, respect, and loyalty. Commonly used media are internal newsletters and magazines, videotapes, private corporate television networks like those owned by FedEx and Merrill Lynch, intranets (private networks of Web sites and e-mail that are inaccessible to the general public), face-to-face briefings, and promotional campaigns using displays, prizes, and recognition programs.

COMMUNICATING SERVICES PRESENTS BOTH CHALLENGES AND OPPORTUNITIES

Traditional marketing communication strategies were shaped largely by the needs and practices associated with marketing manufactured goods. But several of the differences distinguishing services from goods have a significant impact on the ways we approach the design of marketing communication programs in service businesses.[1] In particular, we need to consider the implications of intangibility in service performances, customer involvement in production, the role of customer contact personnel, the difficulty of evaluating many services, and the need to bring demand and supply into balance.

Overcome the Problems of Intangibility

Because they are performances rather than objects, the benefits of services can be difficult to communicate to customers. Banwari Mittal suggests that this intangibility creates four problems for marketers seeking to promote services' attributes or benefits: abstractness, generality, nonsearchability, and mental impalpability.[2] Emphasizing that service marketers need to create messages that clearly communicate intangible service attributes and benefits to potential consumers, he and Julie Baker discuss the implications of each of these problems and propose specific communications strategies for dealing with them (see Table 5-1).[3]

Generality refers to items that comprise a class of objects, persons, or events—for instance, airline seats, flight attendants, and cabin service. These general classes do have physical analogues, and most consumers of the service know what they are, but a key task for marketers is to communicate what makes a specific offering distinctly different from (and superior to) competing offerings.

Nonsearchability refers to the fact that intangibles cannot be searched or inspected before they are purchased. Physical service attributes, such as the appearance of a health club and the type of equipment installed, can be checked in advance, but the experience of working with the trainers can be determined only through experience. And as noted in Chapter 2, credence attributes, such as a surgeon's expertise, must be taken on faith.

TABLE 5-1 Advertising Strategies for Overcoming Intangibility

Intangibility Problem	*Advertising Strategy*	*Description*
Incorporeal Existence	**Physical Representation**	**Show Physical Components of Service**
Generality:		
• For objective claims	System documentation	Objectively document physical-system capacity
	Performance documentation	Document and cite past-performance statistics
• For subjective claims	Service-performance episode	Present an actual service-delivery incident
Nonsearchability	Consumption documentation	Obtain and present customer testimonials
	Reputation documentation	Cite independently audited performance
Abstractness	Service-consumption episode	Capture and display typical customers benefiting from the service
Impalpability	Service-process episode	Present a vivid documentary on the step-by-step service process
	Case-history episode	Present an actual case history of what the firm did for a specific client
	Service-consumption episode	An articulate narration or depiction of a customer's subjective experience

Source: Banwari Mittal and Julie Baker, "Advertising Strategies for Hospitality Services," *Cornell Hotel and Restaurant Administration Quarterly* 43 (April 2002): 53.

Abstractness refers to such concepts as financial security, expert advice, or safe transportation, which do not have one-to-one correspondence with physical objects. Therefore, it can be challenging for marketers to connect their services to those concepts.

Mental impalpability refers to the fact that many services are sufficiently complex, multidimensional, or novel that it is difficult for consumers to understand what the experience of using them will be like and what benefits will result. This factor is especially relevant for new prospects.

Commonly used strategies in advertising include the use of tangible cues whenever possible, especially for low-contact services that involve few tangible elements.[4] It's also helpful to include "vivid information" that catches the audience's attention and will produce a strong, clear impression on the senses, especially for services that are complex and highly intangible.[5] Consider the approach used by Accenture, the global management services and technology consulting company, to dramatize the abstract notion of helping clients capitalize on innovative ideas in a fast-moving world (see Figure 5-1).

In another instance, an ad by a large law firm showed a picture of empty jurors' chairs to draw attention to its trial lawyers' skills in presenting complex cases to juries, which must then withdraw from the courtroom to deliberate on the verdict. Similarly, MasterCard's television and print advertisements emphasize the tangible things that can be purchased with its credit card, complete with a listing of the price of each item. In each ad, all the items purchased with the card lead to a "priceless" experience (a clever and memorable reference to the concept of intangibility).

Some companies have created metaphors that are tangible in nature to help communicate the benefits of their service offerings. Insurance companies often use this approach to market their highly intangible products. Thus, Allstate advertises that "You're in Good Hands," and Prudential uses the Rock of Gibraltar as a symbol of corporate strength (Figure 5-2).

When possible, advertising metaphors should also include some information about *how* service benefits are provided.[6] Consider Trend Micro's problem in advertising its new antivirus monitoring service for corporate intranets at a time when many advertisements for antivirus protection were featuring devils or evil-looking insects. That approach may capture the reader's interest, but it doesn't show how virus protection works or how devastating the effects of a virus might be. In a technical context like this, explaining the problem and its solution in ways that senior management will understand is not always possible. Trend Micro's clever solution was to use the easily grasped metaphor of airport security guarding against terrorism. A picture of an aircraft was captioned "this is your company"; a briefcase containing a bomb was labeled "this is a virus," and two security officers checking that bag on an x-ray machine were captioned "This is Trend Micro." Similarly, advertising by Chubb has used the scary but humorously presented metaphor of an unsuspecting bather about to be sucked into a whirlpool to make tangible the risks that corporate directors face from personal liability suits and thereby promote the protection provided by its Personal Directors' Liability Insurance. Geico Direct uses the metaphor of making a quick stop at a fast food restaurant to emphasize how fast its insurance is (Figure 5-3).

Facilitate Customer Involvement in Production

In high-contact services, customers are often concerned about the risks associated with service delivery and consumption. These risks are sometimes financial or psychological but may also be physical, as in many outdoor sports and organized adventure activities, such as rock climbing, skiing, and white-water rafting. The providers of such services have both a legal and a moral responsibility to educate their clients. The better informed customers are of potential dangers and what to do in the event of, say, a raft

FIGURE 5-1 Accenture Promotes Its Ability to Help Clients Turn Innovative Ideas into Results

tipping its occupants into a stretch of foaming rapids, the more likely they are to remain safe and have an enjoyable experience. Basic information on signs and in instructional brochures may need to be reinforced by personal briefings from employees.

When customers are actively involved in service production, they need training to help them perform well, just as employees do. Improving productivity often involves

FIGURE 5-2 Customers Benefit from the Expertise of a Financial Professional at Prudential Financial, Inc.

Your employer provides some life insurance. But is it enough?
Find out with a free needs analysis from Prudential Financial
What are your life insurance coverage needs?
Survivor Protection
• Estimate your family's current and future cash needs
• Project Social Security and retirement income benefits
• Explore benefits of term or permanent life insurance
Education Funding
• Estimate the cost of college
• Establish a contingency funding plan
• Analyze your death benefit protection needs for college
Retirement
• Set a financial goal
• Calculate the future value of your assets
• Identify possible shortfalls in your death benefit protection
Estate Preservation
• Calculate your potential estate tax liability
• Explore strategies for reducing taxes
• Examine estate plan funding options
Avoid a common and unnecessary risk.
Today, many employee benefit plans include some form of life insurance protection. But remember, it's a benefit—not a personal life insurance plan—and in many cases, it will provide only a portion of the protection you need. Prudential Financial can review your life insurance needs and identify potential gaps in your coverage. If necessary, we can help you supplement your coverage with an individual life insurance policy.
There are no one-size-fits-all solutions.
Most employer-sponsored life insurance coverage is offered based on a simple formula—not on an analysis of your individual life insurance needs. That's why it's so important to explore supplemental coverage on your own.
Life changes can affect your needs.
A new job, a new baby or a new home can have a significant impact on your life insurance needs. You may find that your existing coverage is no longer enough. It's wise to periodically review your protection with a licensed financial professional.
Prudential's free analysis makes it easy.
There's no pressure, and no obligation. Just talk to Prudential about what matters most to you, whether it's paying for college, securing retirement, or preserving your estate. With the help of our proprietary software, we'll look for potential gaps in your existing coverage and, if necessary, we'll recommend solutions. You'll come away with a personalized report that summarizes it all.
Call today to schedule your free analysis.
Find out if your life insurance coverage is still meeting your needs. Make an appointment with one of our licensed financial professionals today.
1-800-THE-ROCK
ext. 9457
prudential.com
Prudential Financial
Growing and Protecting Your Wealth®
Life insurance policies contain exclusions, limitations, reductions of benefits and terms for keeping them in force. Your financial professional can provide you with costs and complete details. Securities products and services offered through Pruco Securities Corporation, 751 Broad St., Newark, NJ, a Prudential Financial company and member SIPC. Prudential Financial is a service mark of The Prudential Insurance Company of America, Newark, NJ and its affiliates.
IFS-A068757 Ed. 2/2002

© 2003. Prudential Financial, Inc.

innovations in service delivery. But the desired benefits won't be achieved if customers resist new, technologically based systems or avoid self-service alternatives. So, the service marketers needs to become educators. One approach recommended by advertising experts is to show service delivery in action.[7] Television is a good medium because of its ability to engage the viewer as it displays a seamless sequence of events in visual form. Some dentists show their patients videos of surgical procedures before the surgery takes place. This educational technique helps patients prepare mentally for the experience and shows them what role they should play during service delivery.

Advertising and publicity can make customers aware of changes in service features and delivery systems. Marketers often use sales promotions to motivate customers, offering them incentives to make the necessary changes in their behavior. Publicizing price discounts is one way to encourage self-service on an ongoing basis. At self-service gas pumps, for instance, the price difference from full service is often substantial. Other incentives to change include promotions that offer a chance to win a reward. And, if necessary, well-trained customer contact personnel can provide one-to-one tutoring to help customers adapt to new procedures.

Help Customers to Evaluate Service Offerings

Even if customers understand what a service is supposed to do, they may have difficulty distinguishing one firm from another and knowing what level of performance to expect from a particular supplier. Possible solutions are providing tangible clues related to service performance, highlighting the quality of equipment and facilities, and emphasizing employee characteristics, such as their qualifications, experience, commitment, and professionalism.

Some performance attributes lend themselves better to advertising than others do. When an airline wants to boast about its punctuality, reporting favorable statistics collected by a government agency offers credible support for this claim. However, airlines don't like to talk overtly about safety, because even the admission that things might go wrong makes many passengers nervous. Instead, the airlines approach this ongoing customer concern indirectly, advertising the expertise of their pilots, the newness of their aircraft, and the skills and training of their mechanics. To document the superior quality and reliability of its small-package delivery services, a FedEx advertisement showed the awards it received for being rated highest in customer satisfaction for air, ground, and international delivery from J.D. Power and Associates, widely known and respected for its customer-satisfaction research in numerous industries.

In low-contact services, in which much of the firm's expertise is hidden, firms may need to illustrate equipment, procedures, and employee activities that are taking place backstage. For instance, how do prospective buyers know whether they are getting the best value from insurance services? One approach is to show how the firm is trying to reduce losses owing to accidents or to reduce costs. Liberty Mutual has run ads using attention-getting headlines, such as "Wake up, you're dead," which shows a grim-looking auto safety expert who is researching how to prevent highway accidents caused by driver fatigue. The company's "I love dissecting humans" ad includes an amusing photo of one of the company's field investigators, who describes her work in detecting and preventing insurance fraud. The fraud-prevention ad shows just how serious the problem is for the insurance industry, with fraudulent claims amounting to an estimated $25 billion a year.

Stimulate or Dampen Demand to Match Capacity

Many live service performances, such as a seat at the theater for Friday evening's performance or a haircut at Supercuts on Tuesday morning, are time specific and can't be

other information distributed during service encounters. If it has a membership relationship with its customers and has a database containing contact information, the firm can distribute highly targeted information through direct mail, e-mail, or telephone. These channels may complement and reinforce broader communications channels or simply replace them.

Employees are a secondary audience for communication campaigns through public media. A well-designed campaign targeted at users, nonusers, or both can also be motivating for employees, especially those playing front-stage roles. In particular, it may help to shape employees' behavior if the advertising content shows them what is being promised to customers. Recent advertising by Sheraton Hotels featured uniformed employees making an explicit promise of satisfaction.

However, there's a risk of generating cynicism among employees and actively demotivating them if the communication in question promotes levels of performance that employees regard as unrealistic or even impossible to achieve. Communications directed specifically at staff are normally part of an internal marketing campaign, using company-specific channels, and so are not accessible to customers. See the discussion of internal communications earlier in this chapter.

Specifying Communication Objectives

Marketers need to be clear about their goals; otherwise, it will be difficult to formulate specific communications objectives and select the most appropriate messages and communication tools to achieve them. Table 5-2 lists common educational and promotional objectives for service businesses. Objectives may include shaping and managing customer behavior in any of the three stages of the purchase and consumption process discussed in Chapter 2: prepurchase, service encounter, and postconsumption.

To illustrate the need for specificity in developing a particular campaign, consider the case of a rental car agency that has an objective of increasing repeat-purchase rates among business travelers. To achieve this objective, the firm decides to offer an automatic upgrade for repeat users and initiate an express delivery and drop-off system in selected locations. For this program to succeed, customers must be made aware of this initiative and informed how, where, and when they can take advantage of it. A specific set of communications objectives might be: (1) to create awareness of the new offering among all existing customers; (2) to attract the attention of prospective customers in the business traveler segment, inform them of the new features, and teach them how to use the new procedures effectively; (3) to stimulate inquiries and increase prebookings; and (4) to generate a specified increase in repeat patronage of, say, 20 percent after six months.

TABLE 5-2 Common Educational and Promotional Objectives in Service Settings

- Create memorable images of specific companies and their brands.
- Build awareness of and interest in an unfamiliar service or brand.
- Build preference by communicating the strengths and benefits of a specific brand.
- Compare a service with competitors' offerings and counter competitive claims.
- Reposition a service relative to competing offerings.
- Stimulate demand in low-demand periods and discourage demand during peak periods.
- Encourage trial by offering promotional incentives.
- Reduce uncertainty and perceived risk by providing useful information and advice.
- Provide reassurance, such as by promoting service guarantees.
- Familiarize customers with service processes in advance of use.
- Teach customers how to use a service to their own best advantage.
- Recognize and reward valued customers and employees.

Key Planning Considerations

Planning a marketing communications campaign should reflect a good understanding of the service product and how well prospective buyers can evaluate its characteristics in advance of purchase. It's essential to understand target market segments and their exposure to various media, as well as consumers' awareness of the product and their attitudes toward it. Decisions include determining the content, structure, and style of the message to be communicated; its manner of presentation; and the media most suited to reaching the intended audience. Additional considerations are the budget available for execution, time frames, as defined by such factors as seasonality, market opportunities, and anticipated competitive activities; and methods of measuring and evaluating performance.

THE MARKETING COMMUNICATIONS MIX

Most service marketers have access to numerous forms of communication, referred to collectively as the *marketing communications mix*. Various communication elements have distinctive capabilities relative to the types of messages they can convey and the market segments most likely to be exposed to them. As shown in Figure 5-4, the mix includes personal contact, advertising, publicity and public relations, sales promotion, instructional materials, and corporate design.

Communication experts draw a broad division between *personal* and *impersonal* communications. Personal communications (those in the left-hand column of boxes in Figure 5-4), involve personalized messages that move in both directions between the two parties—such as personal selling, telemarketing, customer training, customer service, and word of mouth. Impersonal communications (a much larger group of possibilities depicted in all the other columns), involve messages that move in only one direction and are generally targeted at a large group of customers and prospects rather than at a single individual.

However, technology has created a gray area between personal and impersonal communications. For instance, firms often combine word processing technology with

FIGURE 5-4 The Marketing Communications Mix for Services

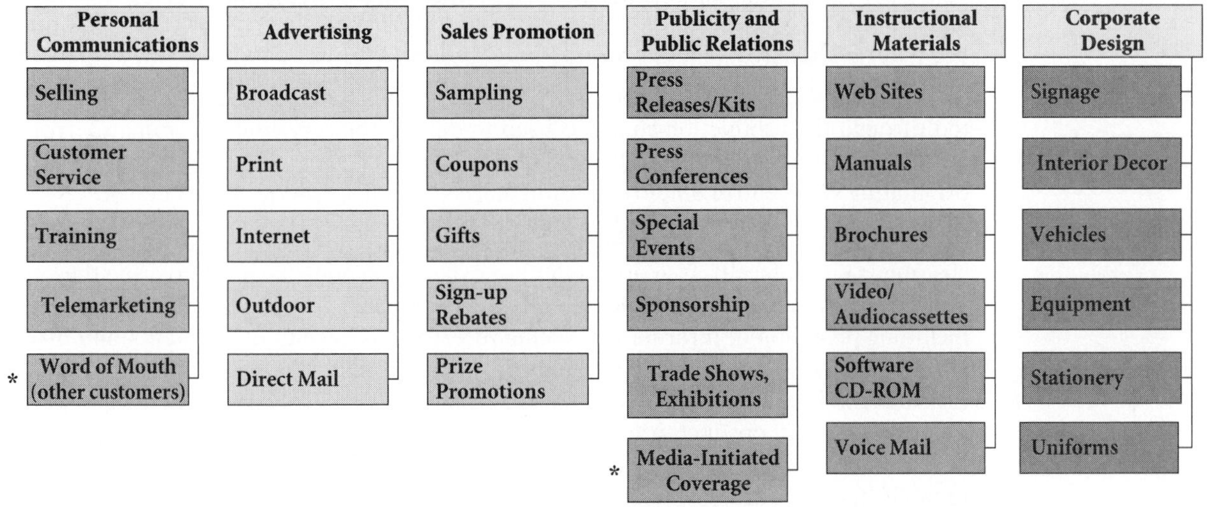

Key
*** Denotes communications originating from outside the organization**

FIGURE 5-5 Originating Sources of Messages Received by a Target Audience

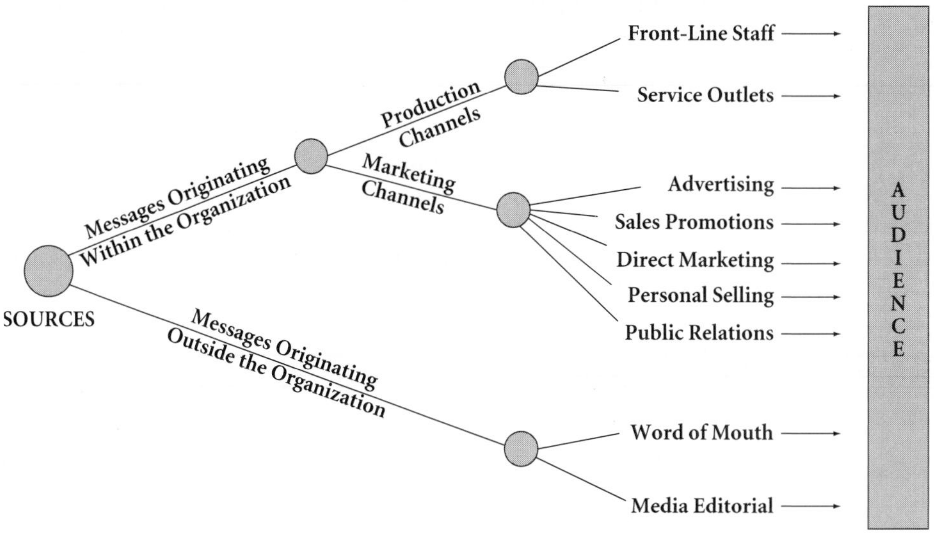

Source: Adapted from Adrian Palmer, *Principles of Services Marketing* (London: McGraw-Hill, 1994), 280.

information from a database to create an impression of personalization. Think about the direct mail and e-mail messages that you have received containing a personal salutation and perhaps some reference to your specific situation or past use of a particular product. Similarly, interactive software, voice recognition technology, and computer-generated voice prompts and responses can simulate a two-way conversation. A few firms are beginning to experiment with Web-based agents that can move on the screen, speak, and even change expressions.

It's important to clarify the source from which communications originate. As shown in Figure 5-5, not all communications messages received by the target audience originate from within the service provider's organization. Specifically, word of mouth and media stories or editorials originate from outside the organization and are not under its direct control. Messages from an internal source can be divided into those received through production channels and those transmitted through marketing channels. Let's look at the options within each of these three originating sources.

Messages Transmitted through Production Channels

In this category are communications developed within the organization and transmitted through the production channels used to deliver the service itself, primarily front-line staff and service outlets. A further subdivision is possible within this category if the originating service firm employs intermediaries to deliver service on its behalf.

Customer Service from Front-line Staff Employees in front-line positions may serve customers either face to face or by telephone. Those responsible for delivering the core service may also be responsible for delivery of a variety of supplementary services, including provision of information, taking reservations, receipt of payments, and problem solving. New customers, in particular, often rely on customer service personnel for assistance in learning how to use a service effectively and how to resolve problems.

When several products are available from the same supplier, firms encourage their customer service staff to cross-sell additional services. However, this approach is likely to fail if strategies are not properly planned and executed.[8] In the banking industry, for example, a highly competitive marketplace and new technologies have forced banks to add more services in an attempt to increase their profitability. In many banks, tellers who traditionally provided customer service are now also expected to promote new services to their customers. Despite training, many employees feel uncomfortable in this role and don't perform as effectively as salespeople.

Customer Training Some companies, especially those selling complex business-to-business services, offer formal training courses to familiarize their customers with the service product and teach them how to use it to their best advantage. Alternatively (or additionally), this task may be assigned to the same front-line personnel who handle service delivery.

Service Outlets Both planned and unintended messages reach customers through the medium of the service delivery environment itself. Impersonal messages can be distributed in the form of banners, posters, signage, brochures, video screens, and audio. As noted in other chapters, the physical design of the service outlet—what we call the *servicescape*—also sends a message to customers.[9] Corporate design consultants are sometimes asked to advise on servicescape design, to coordinate the visual elements of both interiors and exteriors—such as signage, décor, carpeting, furnishings, and uniforms—so that they complement and reinforce the positioning of the firm and shape the nature of the customers' service experiences in desired ways.

Messages Transmitted through Marketing Channels

As shown in Figure 5-4, service marketers have a wide array of communication tools at their disposal. We briefly review the principal elements.

Personal Selling Interpersonal encounters in which efforts are made to educate customers and promote preference for a particular brand or product are referred to as *personal selling.* Many firms, especially those marketing business-to-business services, maintain dedicated salesforces or employ agents and distributors to undertake personal-selling efforts on their behalf. For infrequently purchased services, such as property, insurance, and funeral services, the firm's representative may act as a consultant to help buyers make their selections.

Relationship marketing strategies are often based on account management programs, whereby customers are assigned a designated account manager who acts as an interface between the customer and the supplier. Account management is most commonly practiced in industrial and professional firms that sell relatively complex services, resulting in an ongoing need for advice, education, and consultation. Examples of account management for individual consumers can be found in insurance, investment management, and medical services.

However, face-to-face selling to new prospects is expensive. A lower-cost alternative is *telemarketing*, involving use of the telephone to reach prospective customers. It's used by about 75 percent of all industrial companies.[10] At the consumer level, there is growing frustration with the intrusive nature of telemarketing, which is often timed to reach people at home in the evening or on weekends.

Trade Shows In the business-to-business marketplace, trade shows are a popular form of publicity that also combines important personal-selling opportunities.[11] In many industries, trade shows stimulate extensive media coverage and offer business customers an opportunity to find out about the latest offerings from a wide array of suppliers in the field. Service vendors provide physical evidence in the form of exhibits, samples and demonstrations, and brochures to educate and impress these potential customers. Trade shows, one of the few instances in which large numbers of prospective buyers come to the marketer rather than the other way around, can be very productive promotional tools. A sales representative who usually reaches four to five prospective clients a day may be able to generate five qualified leads per hour at a show.

Advertising As the most dominant form of communication in consumer marketing, advertising is often the first point of contact between service marketers and their customers, serving to build awareness, inform, persuade, and remind. Advertising plays a vital role in providing factual information about services and educating customers about product features and capabilities. To demonstrate this role, Stephen Grove, Gregory Pickett, and David Laband carried out a study comparing newspaper and television advertising for goods and services.[12] Based on a review of 11,543 television advertisements over a 10-month period and of 30,940 newspaper display advertisements that appeared over a 12-month period, the researchers found that ads for services were significantly more likely than those for goods to contain factual information on price, guarantees/warranties, documentation of performance, and availability (where, when, and how to acquire products).

One of the challenges facing advertisers is how to get their messages noticed. Television and radio broadcasts are cluttered with commercials, whereas newspapers and magazines sometimes seem to contain more ads than news and features. How can a firm hope to stand out from the crowd? Longer, louder commercials and larger-format ads are not necessarily the answer. Some advertisers stand out by using striking designs or a distinctively different format. To catch readers' attention, the Humane Society used a black-and-white sketch of a winsome puppy in a magazine in which everyone else was advertising in color (Figure 5-6).

A broad array of paid advertising media is available, including broadcast (TV and radio), print (magazines and newspapers), movie theaters, and many types of outdoor media (posters, billboards, electronic message boards, and the exteriors of buses or bicycles). Some media are more focused than others, targeting specific geographic areas or audiences with a particular interest. Advertising messages delivered through mass media are often reinforced by direct-marketing tools, such as mailings, telemarketing, faxes, or e-mail.

Direct Marketing This category embraces mailings, recorded telephone messages, faxes, and e-mail. These channels offer the potential to send personalized messages to highly targeted microsegments. Direct strategies are most likely to be successful when marketers possess a detailed database of information about customers and prospects.

Sales Promotion A useful way of looking at sales promotions is as a communication attached to an incentive. Sales promotions are usually specific to a time period, price, or customer group—sometimes all three. Typically, the objective is to accelerate the purchasing decision or motivate customers to use a specific service sooner, in greater volume with each purchase, or more frequently. Sales promotions for service firms may take such forms as samples, coupons and other discounts, gifts, and competitions with prizes. Used in these forms, sales promotions add value, provide a "competitive edge," boost sales during periods when demand would otherwise be weak, speed the introduction and acceptance of new services, and generally get customers to act more quickly than they would in the absence of any promotional incentive.[13]

Some years ago, SAS International Hotels devised an interesting sales promotion targeted at older customers. If a hotel had vacant rooms, guests over 65 years of age could get a discount equivalent to their years (e.g., a 75-year-old could save 75 percent of the normal room price). All went well until a Swedish guest checked in to one of the SAS chain's hotels in Vienna, announced his age as 102, and asked to be paid 2 percent of the room rate in return for staying the night. This request was granted, whereupon the spry centenarian challenged the general manager to a game of tennis—and got that, too. (The results of the game, however, were not disclosed!) Events like these are the stuff of dreams for PR people. In this case, a clever promotion led to a humorous, widely reported story that placed the hotel chain in a favorable light.

FIGURE 5-6 Black-and-White Advertising by the Humane Society in a Color Magazine Is Designed to Catch Readers' Attention.

Public Relations PR involves efforts to stimulate positive interest in an organization and its products by sending out news releases, holding press conferences, staging special events, and sponsoring newsworthy activities put on by third parties. A basic element in public relations strategy is the preparation and distribution of press releases (including photos and/or videos) that feature stories about the company, its products, and its employees. PR executives also arrange press conferences and distribute press kits when they feel that a story is especially newsworthy. A key task performed by corporate PR specialists at many service organizations involves teaching senior managers how to present themselves well at news conferences or in radio and television interviews, especially at times of crisis or when faced with hostile questioning.

Other widely used PR techniques are recognition and reward programs, obtaining testimonials from public figures, community involvement and support, fundraising, and obtaining favorable publicity for the organization through special events and pro bono work. These tools can help a service organization build its reputation and credibility; form strong relationships with its employees, customers, and the community; and secure an image conducive to business success.

Firms can also win wide exposure through sponsorship of sporting events and other high-profile activities, where banners, decals, and other visual displays provide continuing repetition of the corporate name and symbol. For example, the United States Postal Service (USPS) has been a major sponsor of the U.S. cycling team in the annual Tour de France bicycle race. This event provides many PR and advertising opportunities for the Postal Service, including stamps, print articles, television news clips, and photos of the team members with "US Postal Service" prominently displayed on their jerseys. USPS has gained worldwide attention from the successes of team member Lance Armstrong, a cancer survivor, who won his fifth consecutive Tour de France in July 2003.

All the yachting syndicates participating in the America's Cup races have relied on corporate sponsorship to help cover the huge costs of participating in this event. Most syndicates have multiple sponsors, whose names or logos appear prominently on the

FIGURE 5-7 UBS Gained a Lot of Publicity from Its Sponsorship of the Yacht Alinghi, Winner of Both the Louis Vuitton Cup and the America's Cup in 2002–2003.

Reprinted courtesy of UBS.

yacht's sails and hulls. When the Swiss yacht *Alinghi* unexpectedly won the 2003 series in New Zealand, it was a big publicity boost for its principal sponsor, UBS, the international Swiss bank (Figure 5-7). Although sponsors of the unsuccessful contestants were less fortunate, they still received extensive media exposure for their brands over a period of several months.

Unusual activities can present an opportunity to promote a company's expertise. FedEx gained significant favorable publicity when it safely transported two giant pandas from Chengdu, China, to the National Zoo in Washington, D.C. The pandas flew in specially designed containers aboard an MD-11 aircraft renamed "FedEx PandaOne." In addition to press releases, the company also featured information about the unusual shipment on a special page in its Web site.

Messages Originating from Outside the Organization

Some of the most powerful messages about a company and its products come from outside the organization and are not controlled by the marketer.

Word of Mouth Recommendations from other customers are generally viewed as more credible than are firm-initiated promotional activities and can have a powerful influence on people's decisions to use (or avoid using) a service. In fact, the greater the risk that customers perceive in purchasing a service, the more actively they will seek and rely on word of mouth (WOM) to guide their decision making.[14] Customers who are less knowledgeable about a service rely more on WOM than do expert consumers.[15]

Because WOM can act as such a powerful and highly credible selling agent, some marketers use a variety of strategies to stimulate positive and persuasive comments from existing customers.[16] These strategies include

- Referencing other purchasers and knowledgeable individuals. For instance: "We have done a great job for ABC Corp., and if you wish, feel free to talk to Mr. Cabral, their MIS manager, who oversaw the implementation of our project."
- Creating exciting promotions that get people talking about the great service that the firm provides. Both Virgin Atlantic Airways and Southwest Airlines have run many campaigns that successfully stimulated discussions and commentary.
- Developing referral incentive schemes, such as offering an existing customer some units of free or discounted service in return for introducing new customers to the firm.
- Offering promotions that encourage customers to persuade others to join them in using the service: "Bring two friends, and the third eats for free" or "Subscribe to two mobile service plans, and we'll waive the monthly subscription fee for all subsequent family members."
- Presenting and publicizing testimonials that simulate WOM. Advertising and brochures sometimes feature comments from satisfied customers.

Research in the United States and Sweden shows that the extent and content of word of mouth is related to satisfaction levels. Customers holding strong views are likely to tell more people about their experiences than are those with milder views. And extremely dissatisfied customers tell more people than do those who are highly satisfied.[17] Noting the important role that service employees play in customer satisfaction, Dwayne Gremler, Kevin Gwinner, and Stephen Brown suggest that measures to improve the quality of customer/employee interactions may be an appropriate strategy for stimulating positive WOM.[18] Interestingly, even customers who were initially dissatisfied with a service can end up spreading positive WOM if they are delighted with the way the firm handled the service recovery.[19]

With the rapid proliferation of the Internet, the spread of personal influence has been accelerated, causing it to evolve into a "viral marketing" phenomenon that business cannot afford to ignore.[20] In fact, viral marketing has now become an industry in itself. Dot.com companies, such as Epinions.com, have built their entire businesses and Web sites around customer WOM.[21]

Editorial Coverage Although some media coverage of firms and their services is stimulated by public relations activity, broadcasters and publishers often initiate their own coverage. In addition to news stories about a company and its services, editorial coverage can take several other forms. Investigative reporters may conduct an in-depth study of a company, especially if they believe that it is putting customers at risk, cheating them, using deceptive advertising, or otherwise exploiting them. Some columnists specialize in helping customers who have been unable to get complaints resolved.

Journalists responsible for consumer affairs often contrast and compare service offerings from competing organizations, identifying their strong and weak points and offering advice on "best buys." In a more specialized context, *Consumer Reports*, the monthly publication of Consumers' Union, periodically evaluates services that are offered on a national basis, including financial services and telecommunications. The magazine recently undertook an in-depth analysis of the cellular telephone industry, commenting on the strengths and weaknesses of various service providers and seeking to determine the true cost of their often confusingly priced plans.[22]

Ethical Issues in Communication

Few aspects of marketing lend themselves so easily to misuse (and even abuse) as advertising, selling, and sales promotion. The fact that customers often find it difficult to evaluate services makes them more dependent on marketing communication for information and advice. Communication messages often include promises about the benefits that customers will receive and the quality of service delivery. When promises are made and then broken, customers are disappointed because their expectations have not been met.[23] Their disappointment and even anger will be even greater if they have wasted money, time, and effort and have no benefits to show in return or have suffered a negative impact. Employees, too, may feel disappointed and frustrated as they listen to customers' complaints about unfulfilled expectations.

Some unrealistic service promises result from poor internal communications between operations and marketing personnel about the level of service performance that customers can reasonably expect. In other instances, unethical advertisers and salespeople deliberately make exaggerated promises to secure sales. Finally, deceptive promotions lead people to think that they have a much higher chance of winning prizes or awards than is the case. Fortunately, many consumer watchdogs are on the lookout for these deceptive marketing practices. The watchdogs include consumer protection agencies, trade associations within specific industries, and journalists who investigate customer complaints and seek to expose fraud and misrepresentation.

A different type of ethical issue concerns unwanted intrusion by aggressive marketers into people's personal lives—including, perhaps, your own. You can, of course, simply turn the page if you don't want to look at an advertisement in a newspaper or magazine. Perhaps you ignore television advertising by pressing the mute button on your remote and talking to friends or family members while the commercials are on. However, the increase in telemarketing and direct mail is frustrating for those who receive unwanted sales communications. How do you feel if your evening meal at home is interrupted by a telephone call from a stranger trying to interest you in buying services in which you have no interest? Even if you are interested, you may feel, as many do, that your privacy has been violated and see the call as an unwanted intrusion.

Trade associations, such as the Direct Marketing Association, offer ways for consumers to remove their names from telemarketing and direct-mail lists in an attempt to address the growing hostility toward these types of direct-marketing techniques. In 2003, the United States Federal Trade Commission introduced the National Do Not Call registry, which allows household subscribers to avoid receiving solicitations from telemarketers. The latter face fines of up to $11,000 for calling a registered number. Within the space of a few months, tens of millions of people had signed up.[24]

BRANDING AND COMMUNICATIONS

Although brand strategy has long been associated primarily with manufactured goods, it is assuming increasing importance in services. "Branding," says Leonard Berry, "plays a special role in service companies because strong brands increase customers' trust of the invisible purchase."[25] Because branding is covered in depth in Berry's article, "Cultivating Service Brand Equity," which is reproduced as a reading on pp. 207–216, we will provide only a brief overview in this chapter.

Corporate Brands

Service branding starts with the corporate brand and is a blend of (1) *the presented brand*—how the company presents itself through its own controlled communications; (2) *external brand communications*, through nonmarketer-controlled channels, such as word of mouth and editorial coverage in broadcast and print media; and (3) *brand meaning*, which refers to the customer's dominant perceptions of the brand and the associations that come to mind, not least from personal experience.

Marketing communications plays a key role in creating *brand awareness*, which refers to a consumer's ability to recognize the brand and recall information and associations that distinguish that company from others. A strong and positive brand image is essentially a promise of future satisfaction.

Subbrands

An important trend among many service organizations is to apply branding principles to specific products or processes as a way of both distinguishing a firm's service offerings and also differentiating each of them from competing alternatives. Examples of what are sometimes referred to as subbrands—discussed in more depth in Chapter 4—include mutual funds, banking packages, classes of air travel, insurance policies, and service maintenance contracts. Typically, the corporate brand serves as an "umbrella" over all the subbrands and is explicitly associated with individual subbrands in advertising or other communications. Singapore Airlines not only brands its business class, which it calls "Raffles Class," but also trademarks as "SpaceBed" the seat that passengers in that class can transform into a bed when they want to sleep (Figure 5-8).

The Role of Corporate Design

Many service firms use a unified and distinctive visual appearance for all tangible elements to facilitate recognition and reinforce a desired brand image. Corporate design strategies are usually created by external consulting firms and include such features as stationery and promotional literature, retail signage, uniforms, and color schemes for painting vehicles, equipment, and building interiors. The objective is to provide a unifying and recognizable theme linking all the firm's operations in a branded service experience through the strategic use of physical evidence.

Corporate design is particularly important for companies operating in competitive markets, where it's necessary to stand out from the crowd and to be instantly recognizable

FIGURE 5-8 Singapore Airlines Promotes Its Raffles Class SPACEBED as "The Biggest Bed in Business Class."

Used by permission of Singapore Airlines.

in different locations. For example, gasoline retailing provides striking contrasts in corporate designs, from BP's bright green and yellow service stations to Texaco's red, black, and white and Sunoco's blue, maroon, and yellow.

Companies in the highly competitive express-delivery industry tend to use their names as a central element in their corporate designs. When Federal Express changed its trading name to the more modern FedEx, it also changed its logo to feature the new name in a distinctive logo. Consistent applications of this design were developed for use in settings ranging from business cards to boxes and from employee caps to aircraft exteriors. When FedEx Corporation decided to rebrand a ground-delivery service it had purchased, it chose the name FedEx Ground and developed an alternative color treatment of the standard logo. Its goal was to transfer the positive image of reliable, on-time service associated with its air services to its less-expensive small-package ground service. The well-known air service was then rebranded as FedEx Express. Other subbrands in what the firm refers to as "the FedEx family of companies" include FedEx Freight (regional, less-than-truckload transportation for heavyweight freight), FedEx Custom Critical (nonstop, door-to-door delivery of time-critical shipments), and FedEx Trade networks, providing customs brokerage, international freight forwarding, and trade facilitation). The company also created an internal service provider, FedEx Services, to pull together sales, marketing, and technology support for the "family" companies.

Many companies use a trademarked symbol rather than a name as their primary logo.[26] Shell makes a pun of its English name by displaying a yellow scallop shell on a red background, which has the advantage of making its vehicles and service stations instantly recognizable even in parts of the world that do not use the Roman alphabet. McDonald's "Golden Arches" is said to be the most widely recognized corporate symbol in the world. However, international companies operating in many countries need to select their designs carefully to avoid conveying a culturally inappropriate message through unfortunate choices of names, colors, or images.

At a very basic level, some companies have succeeded in creating tangible, recognizable symbols to associate with their corporate brand names. Animal motifs are common physical symbols for services. Examples include the Qantas kangaroo, the eagle of the U.S. Postal Service (also used by AeroMexico and Eagle Star Insurance), Merrill Lynch's bull, the lion of Dreyfus Funds and Royal Bank of Canada, the ram of the investment firm T. Rowe Price, and the Chinese dragon of Hong Kong's Dragonair. Merrill Lynch, the global financial services company, used its famous slogan, "We're Bullish on America," as the basis for its corporate symbol—a bull. Easily recognizable corporate symbols are especially important when services are offered in markets where the local language is not written in Roman script or where a significant proportion of the population is functionally illiterate.

MARKETING COMMUNICATIONS AND THE INTERNET

The Internet is playing an increasingly important role in marketing communication. Few companies of any size are now without a Web site, and a substantial industry has sprung up to support the design and implementation of Internet-based marketing activities. Perhaps the most remarkable aspect of the Internet is its ubiquity: A Web site hosted in one country can be accessed from almost anywhere in the world, offering the simplest form of international market entry available. In fact, as Christian Grönroos points out, "the firm cannot avoid creating interest in its offerings outside its local or national market."[27] However, creating international access and developing an international strategy are two very different things.

Internet Applications

Marketers use the Internet for a variety of communications tasks: promoting consumer awareness and interest, providing information and consultation, facilitating two-way communications with customers through e-mail and chat rooms, stimulating product trial, enabling customers to place orders, and measuring the effectiveness of specific advertising or promotional campaigns.[28] Firms can market through their own Web sites and place advertising on other sites. Advertising on the Web allows companies to supplement conventional communications channels at a reasonable cost. But as with any of the elements of the marketing communications mix, Internet advertising should be part of an integrated, well-designed communications strategy.

Many early Web sites were little more than electronic brochures, featuring attractive graphics that took too long to download. By contrast, interactive Web sites allow customers to engage in dialogue with a database and come up with customized information. Transportation firms, such as airlines and railroads, offer interactive sites that allow travelers to evaluate alternative routes and schedules for specific dates, download printed information, and make reservations online. Some sites offer discounts on hotels and airfare if reservations are made over the Internet—a tactic designed to draw customers away from intermediaries, such as travel agents.

The interactive nature of the Internet has the potential to increase customer involvement dramatically, as it is enables "self-service" marketing in which individual customers control the nature and extent of their contact with the Web sites they visit. Many banks allow customers to pay bills electronically, apply for loans over the Internet, and check their account balances online. Whistler/Blackholm ski resort in British Columbia uses its Web site to promote advance online purchase of lift tickets at a discount. The site also offers instructions on how the online ticket window works, states where to pick up the tickets, and provides responses to frequently asked questions.

Enabling marketers to communicate and establish a rapport with individual customers is one of the Web's greatest strengths. These characteristics lend themselves to a new communication strategy called *permission marketing*,[29] which is based on the idea that traditional advertising doesn't work as well any more because it fights for attention by interrupting people. For example, a 30-second television spot interrupts a viewer's favorite program, a telemarketing call interrupts a meal, and a print ad interrupts the flow of a magazine or newspaper article. In the permission-marketing model, the goal is to persuade consumers to volunteer their attention. In essence, customers are encouraged to "raise their hands" and agree to learn more about a company and its products in anticipation of receiving information or something else of value to them. This means that customers self-select into the target segment.

The Health Communication Research Institute issues prepaid phone cards to patients at doctors' offices or in hospitals as a way to measure patient satisfaction. The patient uses the phone card to call an automated service that records responses to questions about the recent medical care experience. As a reward, the caller gets 30 minutes of free long-distance calling.[30] For an illustration of how H&R Block used a promotional contest to get customers to volunteer to learn about a new tax preparation service, see Best Practice in Action 5-2.

Web Site Design Considerations

From a communication standpoint, a Web site should contain information that a company's target customers will find useful and interesting.[31] Internet users expect speedy access, easy navigation, and relevant and up-to-date content.

Service firms should set explicit communication goals for their Web sites. Is the site to be a promotional channel, a self-service option that diverts customers away from contact with service personnel, an automated news room that disseminates information about the company and its products, as well as offering an archive of past press releases, or even all of these? Some firms choose to emphasize promotional content, seeking to present the firm and its products in a favorable light and to stimulate purchase; others view their sites as educational and encourage visitors to search for needed information, even providing links to related sites.

Innovative companies are continually looking for ways to improve the appeal and usefulness of their sites. The appropriate communication content varies widely from

BEST PRACTICE IN ACTION 5-2

PERMISSION MARKETING AT H&R BLOCK

When it wanted to introduce Premium Tax, a new service, aimed at upper-income customers, H&R Block retained Seth Godin's firm, Yoyodyne, to create a contest. This promotional event was announced on selected Web sites, using banner ads that said, "H&R Block: We'll pay your taxes sweepstakes." Through the action of clicking on these banners, more than 50,000 people voluntarily provided their e-mail addresses and said "tell me more about this promotion."

In return for the chance to have their taxes paid by somebody else, these people became players in a contest. Every week for 10 weeks, they received three e-mails inviting them to answer trivia questions about taxes, H&R Block, and other relevant topics. They were given fun facts about the history of taxes or sent to H&R Block's Web site to find answers to questions. Each e-mail also included a promotional message about Premium Tax. Not everyone responded to every message—on average, about 40 percent did so. But over the life of the promotion, 97 percent of those people who entered the game stayed in.

At the end of 10 weeks, surveys were conducted of (1) those who had participated actively in the game, (2) those who had participated but less actively, and (3) a control group of nonparticipants. Among nonparticipants, knowledge of Premium Tax was essentially nonexistent. Among less-active participants, 34 percent had a good understanding of Premium Tax; for active participants, the figure was 54 percent. By creatively applying the concept of permission marketing, H&R Block acquired a database of prospects that had already received some information and education about its new service offering.

Source: William C. Taylor, "Permission Marketing" (interview with Seth Godin), *Fast Company* (April–May 1998): 198–212.

one type of service to another. A b2b site may offer visitors access to a library of technical information; by contrast, a resort hotel may include attractive photographs featuring the location, the buildings and the guest rooms, and even short videos depicting recreational options. Meantime, a radio station may display profiles and photos of key staff members, schedules of its broadcasts, background information about its programs, and access to its broadcasts via Web radio.

Marketers must also address other attributes, such as downloading speed, that affect Web site "stickiness."[32] A sticky site is one that encourages repeat visits and purchases by keeping its audience engaged with interactive communication presented in an appealing fashion. A memorable Web address helps to attract visitors to a site. Unlike phone or fax numbers, it's often possible to guess a firm's Web address, especially if it's a simple one that relates to the firm's name or business. However, firms that have come late to the Internet often find that their preferred name has already been taken. Web addresses must be actively promoted if they are to play an integral role in the firm's overall communication and service delivery strategy. This means displaying the address prominently on business cards, letterhead stationery, catalogs, advertising, promotional materials, and even vehicles.

Internet Advertising

It didn't take long for the Internet to become touted as an important new advertising medium. But after an initial burst of enthusiasm, the volume of online advertising has turned down sharply. Nevertheless, Web sites can offer advertisers some distinctive advantages.[33]

Many firms pay to place advertising banners and buttons on such portals as Yahoo or Netscape, as well as on other firms' Web sites. The usual goal is to draw online traffic to the advertiser's own site. In many instances, Web sites include advertising messages from other marketers with related but noncompeting services. Yahoo's stock quotes page, for example, features a sequence of advertisements for various financial service providers. Similarly, many Web pages devoted to a specific topic feature a small message from Amazon.com, inviting the reader to identify books on these same topics by clicking the accompanying hyperlink button to the Internet retailer's book site. In such instances, it's easy for the advertiser to measure how many visits to its own site are generated by clickthroughs.

However, the Internet has not proved to be as effective an advertising medium as many marketers originally anticipated. Experience shows that simply obtaining a large number of exposures ("eyeballs") to a banner or a skyscraper (a long, skinny ad running down one side of a Web site) or a button doesn't necessarily lead to increases in awareness, preference, or sales for the advertiser. One consequence is that the practice of paying a flat monthly rate for banner advertising is falling out of favor. Even when visitors click through to the advertiser's site, this action doesn't necessarily result in sales. Consequently, there's now more emphasis on advertising contracts that tie fees to marketing-relevant behavior by these visitors, such as providing the advertiser with some information about themselves or making a purchase.

Some companies use *reciprocal marketing*, whereby an online retailer allows its paying customers to receive promotions for another online retailer and vice versa, at no up-front cost to either party.[34] In one such promotion, RedEnvelope.com customers received an online coupon offer from Starbucks when they logged on to the RedEnvelope site. In exchange, Starbucks had a promotional link on Starbucks.com to capture a percentage of that site's customer base.

CONCLUSION

The marketing communication strategy for services requires a somewhat different emphasis from that used to market goods. The communication tasks facing service marketers include emphasizing tangible clues for services that are difficult to evaluate, clarifying the nature and sequence of the service performance, highlighting the performance of customer contact personnel, and educating the customer about how to effectively participate in service delivery.

Many communication elements are available to help companies create a distinctive position in the market and reach prospective customers. The options in the marketing communication mix include personal communications, such as personal selling and customer service, as well as impersonal communications, such as advertising, sales promotions, public relations, corporate design, and the physical evidence offered by the servicescape of the service delivery site. Instructional materials—from brochures to Web sites—often play an important role in educating customers on how to make good choices and obtain the best use from the services they have purchased. Developments in technology, especially the Internet, are changing the face of marketing communications.

Review Questions

1. In what ways do the objectives of services communications differ substantially from those of goods marketing?
2. Which elements of the marketing communications mix would you use for each of the following scenarios? Explain your answers.
   a. A newly established hair salon in a suburban shopping center
   b. An established restaurant facing declining patronage because of new competitors
   c. A large, single-office accounting firm that serves primarily business clients in a major city

3. What roles do personal selling, advertising, and public relations play in (a) attracting new customers to visit a service outlet and (b) retaining existing customers?
4. Describe the role of personal selling in service communications. Give examples of three situations in which you have encountered this approach.
5. Discuss the relative effectiveness of brochures and Web sites for promoting (a) a ski resort, (b) a business school, (c) a fitness center, and (d) a online broker.
6. Why is word of mouth considered to be so important for the marketing of services? How can a service firm that is the quality leader in its industry induce and manage WOM?

Application Exercises

1. Describe four common educational and promotional objectives in service settings, and provide a specific example for each of the objectives you list.
2. Identify one advertisement (or other means of communication) each that aims mainly at managing consumer behavior in the (a) choice, (b) consumption, and (c) postconsumption stages. Explain how they try to achieve their objectives, and discuss how effective they may be.
3. Discuss the significance of search, experience, and credence attributes for the communications strategy of a service provider. Assume that the objective of the communications strategy is to attract new customers.
4. Identify an advertisement that runs the risk of attracting mixed segments to a service business. Explain why this may happen, and state what negative consequences, if any, are likely to occur.
5. Analyze several recent public relations efforts made by service firms.
6. What tangible cues could a diving school or a dentist use for up-market positioning?
7. Explore the Web sites of a management consulting firm, an Internet retailer, and an insurance company. Critique the sites for ease of navigation, content, and visual design. What, if anything, would you change about each site?

Endnotes

1. For a useful review of research on this topic, see Kathleen Mortimer and Brian P. Mathews, "The Advertising of Services: Consumer Views v. Normative Dimensions," *The Service Industries Journal* 18 (July 1998): 14–19.
2. Banwari Mittal, "The Advertising of Services: Meeting the Challenge of Intangibility," *Journal of Service Research* 2 (August 1999): 98–116.
3. Banwari Mittal and Julie Baker, "Advertising Strategies for Hospitality Services," *Cornell Hotel and Restaurant Administration Quarterly* 43 (April 2002): 51–63.
4. William R. George and Leonard L. Berry, "Guidelines for the Advertising of Services," *Business Horizons* (July–August 1981).
5. Donna Legg and Julie Baker, "Advertising Strategies for Service Firms," in *Add Value to Your Service,* ed. C. Surprenant (Chicago: American Marketing Association, 1987), 163–168.
6. Mittal, "The Advertising of Services."
7. Legg and Baker, "Advertising Strategies"; D. J. Hill and N. Gandhi, "Services Advertising: A Framework for Effectiveness," *Journal of Services Marketing* 3 (Fall 1992): 63–76.
8. David H. Maister, "Why Cross Selling Hasn't Worked," *True Professionalism* (New York: The Free Press, 1997), 178–184.
9. Mary Jo Bitner, "Servicescapes: The Impact of Physical Surroundings on Customers and Employees," *Journal of Marketing* 56 (April 1992): 57–71.
10. Victor L. Hunter and David Tietyen, *Business to Business Marketing: Creating a Community of Customers* (Lincolnwood, IL: NTC Business Books, 1997).
11. Dana James, "Move Cautiously in Trade Show Launch," *Marketing News* (November 20, 2000): 4, 6; Elizabeth Light, "Tradeshows and Expos—Putting Your Business on Show," *Her Business* (March–April 1998): 14–18; and Susan Greco, "Trade Shows versus Face-to-Face Selling," *Inc.* (May 1992): 142.
12. Stephen J. Grove, Gregory M. Pickett, and David N. Laband, "An Empirical Examination of Factual Information Content among Service Advertisements," *The Service Industries Journal* 15 (April 1995): 216–233.
13. Ken Peattie and Sue Peattie, "Sales Promotion—A Missed Opportunity for Service Marketers," *International Journal of Service Industry Management*

5, no. 1 (1995): 6–21. See also Paul W. Farris and John A. Quelch, "In Defense of Price Promotion," *Sloan Management Review* (Fall 1987): 63–69.

14. Harvir S. Bansal and Peter A. Voyer, "Word-of-Mouth Processes within a Services Purchase Decision Context," *Journal of Service Research* 3, no. 2 (November 2000): 166–177.

15. Anna S. Mattila and Jochen Wirtz, "The Impact of Knowledge Types on the Consumer Search Process—An Investigation in the Context of Credence Services," *International Journal of Research in Service Industry Management* 13, no. 3 (2002): 214–230.

16. Jochen Wirtz and Patricia Chew, "The Effects of Incentives, Deal Proneness, Satisfaction and Tie Strength on Word-of-Mouth Behaviour," *International Journal of Service Industry Management* 13, no. 2 (2002): 141–162.

17. Eugene W. Anderson, "Customer Satisfaction and Word of Mouth," *Journal of Service Research* 1 (August 1998): 5–17; Magnus Söderlund, "Customer Satisfaction and Its Consequences on Customer Behaviour Revisited: The Impact of Different Levels of Satisfaction on Word of Mouth, Feedback to the Supplier, and Loyalty, *International Journal of Service Industry Management* 9, no. 2 (1998): 169–188; Srini S. Srinivasan, Rolph Anderson, and Kishore Ponnavolu, "Customer Loyalty in e-Commerce: An Exploration of Its Antecedents and Consequences," *Journal of Retailing* 78, no. 1 (2002): 41–50.

18. Dwayne D. Gremler, Kevin P. Gwinner, and Stephen W. Brown, "Generating Positive Word-of-Mouth Communication through Customer-Employee Relationships," *International Journal of Service Industry Management* 12, no. 1 (2000): 44–59.

19. Jeffrey G. Blodgett, Kirk L. Wakefield, and James H. Barnes, "The Effects of Customer Service on Consumers' Complaining Behavior," *Journal of Services Marketing* 9, no. 4 (1995): 31–42; Jeffrey G. Blodgett, and Ronald D. Anderson, "A Bayesian Network Model of the Consumer Complaint Process," *Journal of Service Research* 2, no. 4 (May 2000): 321–338.

20. Sandeep Krishnarmurthy, "Viral Marketing: What Is It and Why Should Every Service Marketer Care?" *Journal of Services Marketing* 15 (2001).

21. Renee Dye, "The Buzz on Buzz," *Harvard Business Review* (November–December 2000): 139–146.

22. "Three Steps to Better Cellular," *Consumer Reports* (February 2003): 15–27.

23. Louis Fabien, "Making Promises: The Power of Engagement," *Journal of Services Marketing* 11, no. 3 (1997): 206–214.

24. Federal Trade Commission, *www.ftc.gov/donotcall/*, accessed August 2003.

25. Leonard L. Berry, "Cultivating Service Brand Equity," *Journal of the Academy of Marketing Science* 28, no. 1 (2000): 128–137.

26. Abbie Griffith, "Product Decisions and Marketing's Role in New Product Development," in *Marketing Best Practices* (Orlando, FL: The Dryden Press, 2000), 253.

27. Christian Grönroos, "Internationalization Strategies for Services," *The Journal of Services Marketing* 13, no. 4/5 (1999): 290–297.

28. J. William Gurley, "How the Web Will Warp Advertising," *Fortune* (November 9, 1998): 119–120.

29. Seth Godin and Don Peppers, *Permission Marketing: Turning Strangers into Friends and Friends into Customers* (New York, Simon & Schuster, 1999).

30. Kathleen V. Schmidt, "Prepaid Phone Cards Present More Info at Much Less Cost," *Marketing News* (February 14, 2000): 4.

31. Donald Emerick, Kim Round, and Susan Joyce, *Web Marketing and Project Management* (Upper Saddle River, NJ: Prentice-Hall, 2000), 27–54.

32. Gary A. Poole, "The Riddle of the Abandoned Shopping Cart," *grok* (December 2000–January 2001): 76–82. See also Donald Emerick, Kim Round, and Susan Joyce, *Web Marketing and Project Management,* 212–213.

33. Heather Green and Ben Elgin, "Do e-Ads Have a Future?" *Business Week E.Biz* (January 22, 2001): EB44–49.

34. Dana James, "Don't Wait—Reciprocate," *Marketing News* (November 20, 2000): 13, 17.

CHAPTER 6

Pricing and Revenue Management

What is a cynic? A man who knows the price of everything and the value of nothing.
—OSCAR WILDE

Have you noticed what a wide variety of terms service organizations use to describe the *prices* they set? Universities talk about *tuition*, professional firms collect *fees*, banks charge *interest* and *service charges*, brokers take *commissions*, some expressways impose *tolls*, utilities set *tariffs*, and insurance companies determine *premiums*, and the list goes on.

A key goal of an effective pricing strategy is to manage revenues in ways that support the firm's profitability objectives. To do this, a firm has to have a good understanding of its costs, the value created for customers, and competitors' pricing. This sounds straightforward but is a real challenge for services firms, whose unit costs may be difficult to determine and fixed costs difficult to allocate appropriately across multiple service offerings. Value to customers usually varies widely between segments and even within the same segment across time. To complicate matters, demand fluctuates widely, whereas capacity tends to be relatively fixed. In addition, competitor pricing cannot be compared dollar for dollar with a firm's pricing, as services are often location and time specific.

In this chapter, we review the role of pricing in services marketing and provide some guidelines on how to develop an effective pricing strategy. Specifically, we address the following questions.

1. What are three main approaches to pricing a service?
2. Why is cost-based pricing so challenging for many service firms, and how can activity-based costing improve service costing?
3. What are the key strategies for increasing net value to customers? How are nonmonetary costs related to the net value of services?
4. Under what circumstances are service markets less price competitive?
5. How can revenue management drastically improve profitability? And how can we charge different prices to different segments without customers' feeling cheated?
6. What seven questions do marketers need to answer when designing an effective pricing schedule?

EFFECTIVE PRICING IS CENTRAL TO FINANCIAL SUCCESS

Marketing is the only function that brings revenues into the organization. All other management functions incur costs. Pricing is the mechanism by which sales are transformed into revenues. In many service industries, pricing was traditionally driven by a financial and accounting perspective, which often used cost-plus pricing. Price schedules were often tightly constrained by government regulatory agencies—and some still are. Today, however, most service businesses enjoy significant freedom in setting prices and have a good understanding of value-based and competitive pricing. These developments have led to creative pricing schedules and sophisticated yield management systems.

Pricing is typically more complex in services than in manufacturing. Because there is no ownership of services, it is usually more difficult for managers to determine the financial costs of creating a process or performance for a customer than to identify the costs associated with creating and distributing a physical good. The inability to inventory services places a premium on bringing demand and supply into balance, a task in which pricing has a key role to play. The importance of the time factor in service delivery means that speed of delivery and avoidance of waiting time often increase value. With the increase in value, customers are prepared to pay a higher price for the service.

What does a marketing perspective bring to pricing? Effective pricing strategies seek to enhance (or even maximize) the level of revenues, often by discriminating between different market segments, based on their value perceptions and ability to pay, and between different time periods, based on variations in demand levels over time.

OBJECTIVES AND FOUNDATIONS FOR SETTING PRICES

Any pricing strategy must be based on a clear understanding of a company's pricing objectives. The most common pricing objectives are related to revenue and profits, as well as to patronage, market share, and market penetration (see Table 6-1).

TABLE 6-1 Alternative Objectives for Pricing

Revenue and Profit Objectives

Seek Profit

- Make the largest possible contribution or profit.
- Achieve a specific target level, but do not seek to maximize profits.
- Maximize revenue from a fixed capacity by varying prices and target segments over time, typically using yield or revenue management systems.

Cover Costs

- Cover fully allocated costs, including institutional overhead.
- Cover costs of providing one particular service, excluding overhead.
- Cover incremental costs of selling one extra unit or to one extra customer.

Patronage and User Base–Related Objectives

Build Demand

- Maximize demand (when capacity is not a constraint), subject to achieving a certain minimum level of revenues.
- Achieve full capacity utilization, especially when high capacity utilization adds to the value created for all customers (e.g., a "full house" adds excitement to a theater play or basketball game).

Build a User Base

- Stimulate trial and adoption of a service. This is especially important for new services with high infrastructure costs and for membership-type services that generate significant revenues from their continued use after adoption (e.g., mobile phone service subscriptions, or life insurance plans).
- Build market share and/or a large user base, especially if there are significant economies of scale that can lead to a competitive cost advantage (e.g., if development or fixed costs are high).

Revenue and Profit Objectives

Within certain limits, profit-seeking firms aim to maximize long-term revenue, contribution, and profits. Perhaps top management is eager to reach a particular landmark financial target or seeks a specific percentage return on investment. Revenue targets may be broken down by division, geographic unit, type of service, and even key customer segments. This practice requires prices to be set based on a good knowledge of costing, competition, and price elasticity of the market and value perceptions, all of which we discuss later in this chapter.

In capacity-constrained organizations, financial success is often a function of ensuring optimal use of productive capacity at any given time. Hotels, for instance, seek to fill their rooms, as an empty room is an unproductive asset. Similarly, professional firms want to keep their staff members occupied. Thus, when demand is low, such organizations may offer special discounts to attract additional business. Conversely, when demand exceeds capacity, these types of businesses may increase their prices and focus on segments that are willing to pay higher amounts. We discuss these practices in detail in the section on revenue management.

Patronage and User Base–Related Objectives

In some instances, maximizing patronage, subject to achieving a certain minimum level of profits, may be more important than profit maximization. Getting a full house in a theater, sports stadium, or race track usually creates excitement that enhances the customer's experience. It also creates an image of success that serves to attract new patrons.

New services, in particular, often have trouble attracting customers. Yet in order to create the impression of a successful launch and to enhance the image of the firm, it is important that the firm is seen to be attracting a good volume of business from the right types of customers. Introductory price discounts are often used to stimulate trial and sign up customers, sometimes in combination with promotional activities, such as contests and giveaways.

In industries with membership relationships and/or in which heavy infrastructure investments have to be made (e.g., mobile phone or broadband services), it is often important to get a critical mass of users quickly. Market leadership often means low cost per user, and it generates sufficient revenue for future investments, such as upgrading technology and infrastructure. As a result, penetration pricing is often used in such industries.

Foundations for Setting Prices

The foundations underlying pricing strategy can be described as a tripod, with costs to the provider, competition, and value to the customer as the three legs (Figure 6-1). The costs that a firm needs to recover usually impose a minimum price, or floor, for a specific service offering, and the customer's perceived value of the offering sets a maximum, or ceiling. The price charged by competitors for similar or substitute services typically determines where, within the floor-to-ceiling range, the price can be set. The pricing objectives of the organization then determine where prices should be set given the feasible range provided by the pricing tripod analysis. We look at each leg of the pricing tripod in more detail in the next three sections.

COST-BASED PRICING

It's usually more difficult to establish the costs involved in producing an intangible performance than it is to identify the labor, materials, machine time, storage, and shipping costs associated with producing a physical good. Yet without a good understanding of costs, how can managers price at levels sufficient to yield a desired profit margin?

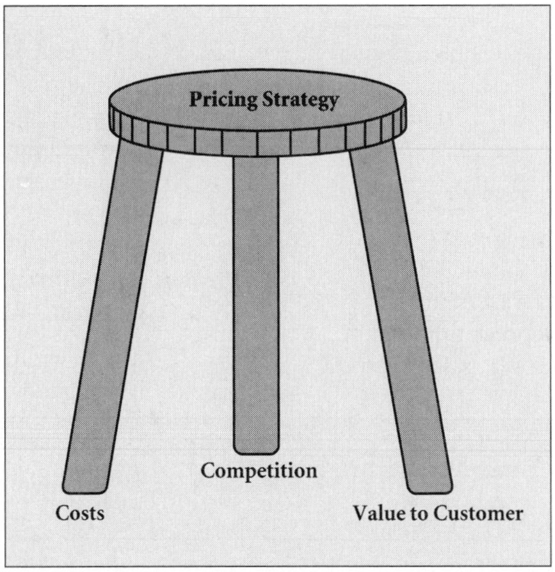

FIGURE 6-1 The Pricing Tripod

Because of the labor and infrastructure needed to create performances, many service organizations have a much higher ratio of fixed costs to variable costs than is found in manufacturing firms.

Establishing the Cost of Service

In Management Memo 6-1, we explain how service costs can be estimated, using fixed, semivariable, and variable costs, as well as how the notions of contribution and break-even analysis can help in pricing decisions. These traditional cost-accounting approaches work well for service firms with significant variable costs and/or semivariable costs (e.g., many professional services). For complex product lines with shared infrastructure (e.g., retail banking products), it may be worthwhile considering the more complex activity-based costing (ABC) approach.

A growing number of organizations have reduced their dependence on traditional cost-accounting systems and have developed activity-based cost (ABC) management systems, which recognize that virtually all activities taking place within a firm directly or indirectly support the production, marketing, and delivery of goods and services. Moreover, ABC systems link resource expenses to the variety and complexity of products produced, not only to the physical volume. An activity is a set of tasks that combine to comprise the processes needed to create and deliver the service. Each step in a flowchart constitutes an activity with which costs can be associated. This approach makes ABC ideally suited for use in a service organization.

If implemented well, the ABC approach yields reasonably accurate cost information about service business activities and processes—and about the costs of creating specific types of services, performing activities in different locations (even different countries), or serving specific customers.[1] The net result is a management tool that can help companies to pinpoint the profitability of various services, channels, market segments, and individual customers.[2]

It is essential to distinguish between those activities that are mandatory for operation within a particular service business and those that are discretionary. The traditional approach to cost control often results in a reduction of the value generated for customers, because the activity that is being pruned back is, in fact, mandatory for

MANAGEMENT MEMO 6-1

UNDERSTANDING COSTS, CONTRIBUTION, AND BREAK-EVEN ANALYSIS

Fixed costs—sometimes referred to as overheads—are those economic costs that a supplier would continue to incur (at least in the short run) even if no services were sold. These costs are likely to include rent, depreciation, utilities, taxes, insurance, salaries and wages for managers and long-term employees, security, and interest payments.

Variable costs refer to the economic costs associated with serving an additional customer, such as making an additional bank transaction or selling an additional seat on a flight. In many services, such costs are very low. For instance, very little labor or fuel cost is involved in transporting an extra passenger on a flight. In a theater, the cost of seating an extra patron is close to zero. More significant variable costs are associated with such activities as serving food and beverages or installing new parts when undertaking repairs, as they include provision of often costly physical products in addition to labor. Just because a firm has sold a service at a price that exceeds its variable cost doesn't mean that the firm is now profitable, for there are still fixed and semivariable costs to be recouped.

Semivariable costs fall in between fixed and variable costs and represent expenses that rise or fall in a stepwise fashion as the volume of business increases/decreases. Examples are adding an extra flight to meet increased demand on a specific air route or hiring a part-time employee to work in a restaurant on busy weekends.

Contribution is the difference between the variable cost of selling an extra unit of service and the money received from the buyer of that service. Contribution goes to cover fixed and semivariable costs before creating profits.

Determining and allocating economic costs can be a challenging task in some service operations because of the difficulty of deciding how to assign fixed costs in a multiservice facility, such as a hospital. For instance, certain fixed costs are associated with running the emergency unit in a hospital. But beyond that, there are fixed costs for running the hospital of which it is a part. How much of the hospital's fixed costs should be allocated to the emergency unit? A hospital manager might use one of several approaches to calculate emergency's share of overheads: (1) the percentage of total floor space that it occupies, (2) the percentage of employee hours or payroll that it accounts for, or (3) the percentage of total patient contact hours involved. Each method is likely to yield a different fixed-cost allocation: One method might show the emergency unit to be very profitable, whereas the other might make it seem like a big loss-making operation.

Managers need to know at what sales volume a service will become profitable. This is called the *break-even point*. The necessary analysis involves dividing the total fixed and semivariable costs by the contribution obtained on each unit of service. For instance, if a 100-room hotel needs to cover fixed and semivariable costs of $2 million a year, and if the average contribution per room night is $100, the hotel will need to sell 20,000 room nights per year out of a total annual capacity of 36,500. If prices are cut by an average of $20 per room night *or* if variable costs rise by $20, the contribution will drop to $80, and the hotel's break-even volume will rise to 25,000 room nights. The required sales volume needs to be related to *price sensitivity* (Will customers be willing to pay this much?), *market size* (Is the market large enough to support this level of patronage after taking competition into account?), and *maximum capacity* (the hotel in our example has a capacity of 36,500 room nights per year, assuming that no rooms are taken out of service for maintenance or renovation).

providing a certain level and quality of service. For instance, many firms have created marketing problems for themselves when they try to save money by firing large numbers of customer service employees. However, this strategy has boomeranged when it resulted in a rapid decline in service levels that spurred discontented customers to take their business elsewhere. For more details on ABC, see Management Memo 6-2.

MANAGEMENT MEMO 6-2

ACTIVITY-BASED COSTING

Traditional cost systems provide useful data for pricing purposes when a single operation creates one homogeneous product for customers who behave in broadly similar ways. However, when service businesses experience considerable variability in both inputs and outputs, it is unrealistic to assign the same proportion of indirect and support costs to each unit of output. Customers, too, often vary in the demands they place on the firm.

Costs are not intrinsically fixed or variable, argue Robin Cooper and Robert Kaplan:

> Different products, brands, customers, and distribution channels make tremendously different demands on a company's resources. . . . ABC analysis enables managers to slice into the business many different ways—by product or group of similar products, by individual customer or client group, or by distribution channel—and gives them a close up view of whatever slice they are considering. ABC analysis also illuminates exactly what activities are associated with that part of the business and how those activities are linked to the generation of revenues and the consumption of resources.[1]

Instead of focusing on expense categories, ABC analysis begins with the identification of the various activities being performed and then determines the cost of each activity as it relates to each expense category. When managers segregate activities in this way, a cost hierarchy emerges, reflecting the level at which the cost is incurred. For instance, unit-level activities need to be performed for every unit of service produced (e.g., rotating the tires on a customer's car at a service garage), whereas batch-level activities have to be performed for each batch or setup of work performed (e.g., periodically maintaining the equipment needed for tire rotation).

Other activities provide the overall capability that enables the company to produce a given type of service (e.g., establishing performance standards for tire rotation), support customers (e.g., account management) and product lines (e.g., advertising), or sustain facilities (e.g., building maintenance and insurance). Expenses are attached to each activity, based on estimates by employees of how they divide up their time among various tasks and what percentage of other resources (e.g., electricity consumption) is being consumed by each activity.

In short, the ABC hierarchy provides a structured way of thinking about the relationship between activities and the resources they consume. A key question is whether each enumerated activity adds customer value to the services that the firm is selling.

Determining customer profitability is a key issue for many businesses. Traditional cost analysis tends to result in loading the same overhead costs on all customers, leading to the assumption that larger purchasers are more profitable. By contrast, ABC analysis can pinpoint differences in the costs of serving different customers by not only identifying the types of activity associated with each customer but also determining the amount of each activity demanded. For instance, a customer who buys in large volumes but is extremely demanding in terms of the amount and level of support required may, in fact, prove to be less profitable than a small customer who requires little support.

Sources: Robert S. Kaplan, "Introduction to Activity-Based Costing," Note #9-197-076 (Boston: Harvard Business School Publishing, 1997); and Jerold L. Zimmerman, *Accounting for Decision Making and Control*, 3rd ed. (New York: McGraw-Hill, 2000).

[1]Robin Cooper and Robert S. Kaplan, "Profit Priorities from Activity-Based Costing," *Harvard Business Review* (May–June, 1991).

Pricing Implications of Cost Analysis

Companies seeking to make a profit must first set a price sufficiently high to recover the full costs of producing and marketing a service and then add a sufficient margin to yield the desired level of profit at the predicted sales volume. Service businesses with high fixed costs include those with expensive physical facilities (such as a hospital or a college), a fleet of vehicles (such as an airline or a trucking company), or a network (such as a telecommunications company, a railroad, or a gas pipeline). For such services, the variable costs of serving one extra customer may be minimal.

Under these conditions, managers may feel that they have tremendous pricing flexibility and be tempted to set a very low price for a service in order to make an extra sale. Some firms promote *loss leaders*, which are services sold at less than full cost to attract customers, who will then be tempted to buy profitable service offerings from the same organization in the future. However, there will be no profit at the end of the year unless all relevant costs have been recovered. Many service businesses have gone bankrupt because they ignored this fact. Hence, firms that compete on the basis of low prices need to have a very good understanding of their cost structure and of the sales volume needed to break even at particular prices.

Ideally, all activities and costs incurred create value for customers. Managers need to move beyond seeing costs from only an accounting perspective and instead view costs as an integral part of the company's efforts to create value for its customers. Antonella Carù and Antonella Cugini clarify the limitations of traditional cost measurement systems and recommend relating the costs of any given activity to its value generated:

> Costs have nothing to do with value, which is established by the market and, in the final analysis, by the degree of customer acceptance. The customer is not interested a priori in the cost of a product . . . but in its value and price. . . .
>
> Management control which limits itself to cost monitoring without interesting itself in value is completely one-sided. . . . The problem of businesses is not so much that of cost control as it is the separation of value activities from other activities. The market only pays for the former. Businesses which carry out unnecessary activities are destined to find themselves being overtaken by competitors which have already eliminated these.[3]

VALUE-BASED PRICING

No customer will pay more for a service than he or she thinks it is worth. So in order to set an appropriate price, marketers need to understand how customers perceive service value. As suggested by Figure 6-2, even scary experiences may have value for some customers. Gerald Smith and Thomas Nagle emphasize the importance of understanding the monetary worth of the incremental value created by a service, a task that often requires extensive marketing research, especially in business-to-business markets.[4]

Understanding Net Value

When customers purchase a service, they are weighing the perceived benefits obtained from the service against the perceived costs they will incur. Consider your own experience. As a customer, you make judgments about the benefits you expect to receive in return for your anticipated investment of money, time, and effort. Although our focus in this chapter is mainly on the monetary aspects of pricing, you have probably noticed that people often pay a premium to save time, reduce unwanted effort, and obtain greater comfort. In other words, people are willing to pay higher prices (financial costs of service) to reduce the nonmonetary costs of service.

Recognizing the various tradeoffs that customers are willing to make between these various costs, service companies sometimes create several levels of service. For example, airlines and hotel chains often provide multiple classes of service, offering customers the option of paying more in exchange for additional benefits. The essential tradeoff for people choosing to stay in a low-price motel, such as Motel 6, is that they

FIGURE 6-2 The Challenge of Value-Based Pricing: Can Sharks Create Value?

must renounce the greater physical comfort and many value-enhancing supplementary services to be found in, say, a three-star Holiday Inn that charges a higher price. Similarly, a company purchasing the "silver" level of hardware and software support from Sun Microsystems cannot count on the same speed of response, hours of service, and additional benefits offered to "platinum" customers.

Research by Valarie Zeithaml suggests that customer definitions of value may be highly personal and idiosyncratic. Four broad expressions of value emerged from her study: (1) value is low price, (2) value is whatever I want in a product, (3) value is the quality I get for the price I pay, and (4) value is what I get for what I give.[5] In this book, we base our definition of value on this fourth category and use the term *net value*, or the sum of all the perceived benefits (gross value) minus the sum of all the perceived costs of service. The greater the positive difference between the two, the greater the net value. Economists use the term *consumer surplus* to define the difference between the price customers pay and the amount they would have been willing to pay to obtain the desired benefits (or "utility") offered by a specific product.

If the perceived costs of a service are greater than the perceived benefits, the service in question will possess negative net value, and the consumer will not buy. You can think of calculations that customers make in their minds as being similar to weighing materials on a pair of scales, with product benefits in one tray and the costs associated with obtaining those benefits in the other tray (Figure 6-3). When they evaluate competing services, customers are basically comparing the relative net values.

Enhancing Gross Value

International consultant Hermann Simon argues that service pricing strategies are often unsuccessful because they lack any clear association between price and value.[6] As discussed in Chapter 4, a marketer can increase the gross value of a service by adding benefits

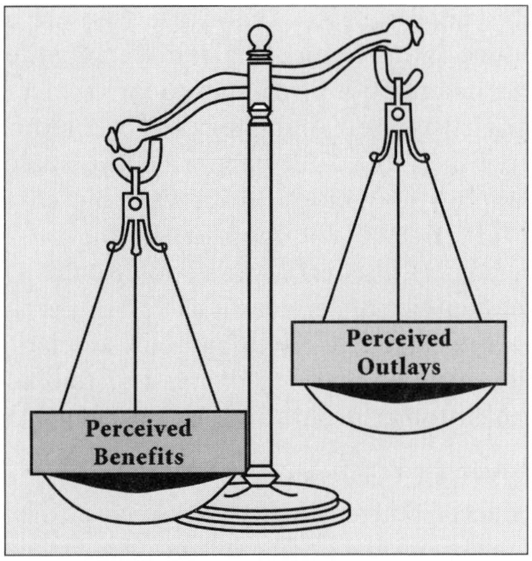

FIGURE 6-3 Net Value = Benefits − Costs

to the core product and by enhancing supplementary services. Four distinct but related strategies for capturing and communicating the value of a service are uncertainty reduction, relationship enhancement, low-cost leadership, and value perception management.[7]

Pricing Strategies to Reduce Uncertainty If customers are unsure about how much value they will receive from a particular service, they may remain with a supplier they already know or not purchase at all. Possible ways to reduce this uncertainty, individually or in combination, include benefit-driven pricing and flat-rate pricing.

Benefit-driven pricing involves pricing that aspect of the service that directly benefits customers (requiring marketers to research what aspects of the service their customers value most and what aspects they value least). For instance, prices for online information services are often based on log-on time, but what customers really value is the information that is browsed and retrieved. Customers waste time on poorly designed Web sites because they are difficult to navigate and make it difficult for users to find what they are looking for. The result is that pricing and value creation are out of sync. When ESA-IRS, a European online service provider, implemented a new pricing strategy termed "pricing for information," based on the information extracted, the company found that customers were more willing to use a time-consuming feature called ZOOM that allowed them to search several complex databases simultaneously with increased precision. Customers started staying online longer, and the use of ZOOM tripled as customers began to conduct more detailed searches. From then on, the company changed its marketing focus from selling time to selling information.

Flat-rate pricing involves quoting a fixed price in advance of service delivery in order to avoid any surprises. In essence, the risk is transferred from the customer to the supplier in the event that the service takes longer to deliver or involves more costs than anticipated. Flat-rate pricing can be effective in industries in which service prices are unpredictable and suppliers are poor at controlling their costs and the speed at which they work. Flat-rate pricing is also effective if competitors make low estimates to win business but subsequently claim that they were only giving an estimate—not making a firm pricing commitment.

Relationship Pricing How does pricing strategy relate to developing and maintaining long-term customer relationships? Discounting to win new business is not the best approach if a firm is seeking to attract customers who will remain loyal.

Research indicates that those who are attracted by cut-price offers can easily be enticed away by an offer from a competitor.[8] More creative strategies focus on giving customers both price and nonprice incentives to consolidate their business with a single supplier. A strategy of discounting prices for large purchases can often be profitable for both parties, as the customer benefits from lower prices, and the supplier may enjoy lower variable costs resulting from economies of scale. An alternative to volume discounting on a single service is for a firm to offer its customers discounts when two or more services are purchased together. The greater the number of services a customer purchases from a single supplier, the closer the relationship is likely to be. A close relationship allows the firm to learn more about the customer and improve and customize its service, and it is more inconvenient for the customer to shift its business elsewhere.

Low-Cost Leadership Low-priced services appeal to customers who are on a tight financial budget. Such services may also lead purchasers to buy in larger volumes. One challenge when pricing low is to convince customers that they should not equate price with quality. Rather, they must feel that they are getting good value. A second challenge is to ensure that economic costs are kept low enough to enable the firm to make a profit. Some service businesses have built their entire strategy around being the low-cost leader. A classic American example of a low-cost leader in the airline business is Southwest Airlines, whose low fares often compete with the price of bus, train, or car travel. Southwest's low-cost operations strategy has been studied by airlines all over the world and now has many imitators, including Ryanair and easyJet in Europe and WestJet in Canada.

Managing the Perception of Value Value is subjective, and often few customers are expert enough to truly appreciate and assess the quality and value they receive. This is especially true for credence services, whose quality customers cannot assess even after consumption (e.g.) surgery, legal advice, or management consulting services.[9] The invisibility of necessary backstage facilities and labor makes it difficult for customers to see what they are getting for their money. Consider a homeowner who calls an electrician to repair a defective circuit. The electrician arrives, carrying a small bag of tools, and then disappears into the closet where the circuit board is located, soon locates the problem, replaces a defective circuit breaker, and presto! Everything works. A mere 20 minutes have elapsed. A few days later, the homeowner is horrified to receive a bill for $90, most of it for labor charges.

Just think what the couple could have bought for that amount of money: new clothes, several compact discs, a nice dinner. What they fail to think of are all the fixed costs that the owner of the business needs to recoup: the office, telephone, insurance, vehicles, tools, fuel, and office support staff. The variable costs of the visit are also higher than they appear. To the 20 minutes spent at the house must be added 15 minutes of driving each way plus 5 minutes each to unload and reload needed tools and supplies from the van, thus effectively tripling the labor time to a total of 60 minutes devoted to this call. And the firm still has to add a margin in order to make a profit.

Not surprisingly, customers are often left feeling that they have been exploited. Hence, effective communications and even personal explanations are needed to help customers recognize and appreciate the value they receive. Similarly, marketers of high-end credence services must find ways to powerfully communicate the time, research, professional expertise, and attention to detail that go into, for example, completing a best-practice consulting project.

Reducing Related Monetary and Nonmonetary Costs

From a customer's standpoint, the price charged by a supplier is only part of the costs involved in purchasing and using a service. Other *costs of service*, are composed of both financial outlays charged by other parties and *nonmonetary* costs.

Among the financial costs of a service are not only the price paid to the supplier but also the expenses incurred by the customer in searching for, purchasing, and using the service. To give a simple example, the cost of an evening at the movies for a couple with young children usually far exceeds the price of the two tickets, because it can include such expenses as hiring a babysitter, travel, parking, food, and beverages.

The nonmonetary costs reflect the time, effort, and discomfort associated with search, purchase, and use of a service. Customers sometimes refer to these costs collectively as "effort," or "hassle." These costs tend to be higher when customers are involved in production (which is particularly important in people-processing services and in self-service), where they have to travel to the service site, wait for service, figure out queuing systems and service processes, and so on. Services that are high on experience and credence attributes may also create psychological costs, such as anxiety. Nonmonetary costs of service can be grouped into four distinct categories.

1. *Time costs* are inherent in service delivery. There is an opportunity cost to customers for the time they are involved in the service delivery process, as they could spend that time in other ways, perhaps even working to earn additional income. Internet users are often frustrated by the amount of time they waste trying to find some particular information on a Web site. Many people loath having to visit public service offices to obtain a passport, driving license, and the like not because of the fees involved but because of the time "wasted." Time spent waiting is usually seen as particularly unpleasant and carries a high perceived cost, often so high that the customer would rather not buy! In addition, time costs are often incurred when it is inconvenient; working adults, for examples, do not want to have to go to a service branch during working hours. Again, they often would rather not buy or would go to a competitor with more convenient opening hours or that offers this transaction at arm's length, such as via the Internet.
2. *Physical costs* (e.g., fatigue or discomfort) may be incurred in obtaining services, especially if customers must go to the service factory, if queuing is involved, and if delivery entails self-service.
3. *Psychological costs*, such as mental effort, perceived risk, cognitive dissonance, feelings of inadequacy, or fear, are sometimes attached to buying and using a particular service.
4. *Sensory costs* relate to unpleasant sensations affecting any of the five senses. In a service environment, these costs may include putting up with noise, unpleasant smells, drafts, excessive heat or cold, uncomfortable seating, visually unappealing environments, and even nasty tastes.

As shown in Figure 6-4, consumers can incur costs during any of the three stages of a purchase process, and therefore firms have to consider (1) *search costs*, (2) *purchase and use costs*, and (3) *postconsumption*, or *after-costs*. When you were looking at universities, how much money, time, and effort did you spend before deciding where to apply? How much time and effort would you put into selecting a new mobile phone service provider or a bank?

From a managerial perspective, it makes great sense to minimize those nonmonetary and related monetary costs to increase consumer value. Possible approaches include the following:

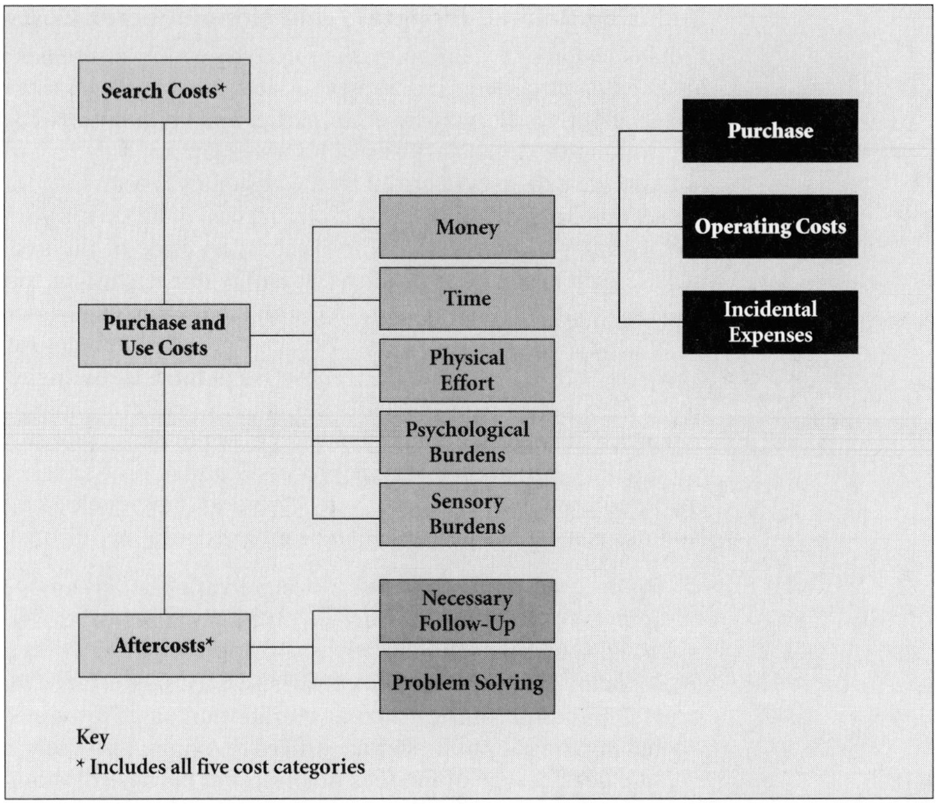

FIGURE 6-4 Defining Total User Costs

- Reducing the time costs involved in service purchase, delivery, and consumption.
- Minimizing unwanted psychological costs of service at each stage by going through the service blueprint and identifying ways to enhance the service experience by cutting or redesigning unpleasant or inconvenient steps in the process
- Eliminating unwanted physical costs of service that customers may incur, notably during the search and delivery processes.
- Decreasing unpleasant sensory costs of service by creating more attractive visual environments, reducing noise, installing more comfortable furniture and equipment, curtailing offensive smells, and the like.
- Identifying carefully what other monetary costs consumers incur and specifying ways to reduce them or offering alternatives. For example, banks often require customers to come personally to initiate telegraphic transfers or banker's checks, incurring related travel costs (e.g., gas and parking). Perhaps the process can be redesigned to be delivered online.

Perceptions of net value may vary widely among customers and from one situation to another for the same customer. One way of segmenting service markets is by sensitivity to time savings and convenience[10] versus sensitivity to price savings. Consider Figure 6-5, which identifies a choice of three clinics available to an individual who needs to obtain a routine chest x-ray. In addition to varying dollar prices for the service, there are various time and effort costs associated with using each service. Depending on the customer's priorities, nonmonetary costs may be as important as, or even more important than, the price charged by the service providers.

Which clinic would you patronize if you needed a chest x-ray (assuming all three clinics offer good technical quality)?

Clinic A	Clinic B	Clinic C
• Price $45	• Price $85	• Price $125
• Located 1 hour away by car or transit	• Located 15 minutes away by car or transit	• Located next to your office building (or college)
• Next available appointment is in 3 weeks	• Next available appointment is in 1 week	• Next available appointment is in 1 day
• Hours: Monday–Friday, 9 A.M.–5 P.M.	• Hours: Monday–Friday, 8 A.M.–10 P.M.	• Hours: Monday–Saturday, 8 A.M.–10 P.M.
• Estimated wait at clinic is about 2 hours	• Estimated wait at clinic is about 30 to 45 minutes	• By appointment; estimated wait at clinic is about 0 to 15 minutes

FIGURE 6-5 Trading Off Monetary and Nonmonetary Costs

COMPETITION-BASED PRICING

Firms with relatively undifferentiated services need to monitor what competitors are charging and should to try to price accordingly. When they see little or no difference between competing offerings, customers may choose what they perceive as the cheapest. In such a situation, the firm with the lowest cost per unit of service enjoys an enviable market advantage and often assumes *price leadership*. Here, one firm acts as the price leader, with others taking their cue from this company. You can sometimes see this phenomenon at the local level when several gas stations within a short distance of one another compete. As soon as one station raises or lowers its prices, the others follow promptly.

Price competition increases with (1) increasing number of competitors, (2) increasing number of substituting offers, (3) wider distribution of competitor and/or substitution offers, and (4) increasing surplus capacity in the industry. Although some service industries can be fiercely competitive (e.g., the airline industry or online banking), many are less so, especially when one or more of the following circumstances reduce price competition.

- *Non-price-related costs of using competing alternatives are high.* When saving time and effort are of equal or greater importance to customers than price in selecting a supplier, the intensity of price competition is reduced.
- *Personalization, customization, and switching costs matter.* In services that are highly personalized and customized, such as hair styling or family medical care, relationships with individual providers are often very important to customers, thus discouraging them from responding to competitive offers. In many other services, switching costs involve time and money, thus reducing the ability of consumers to switch easily between providers and to take advantage of lower-priced competing offers. Cellular telephone providers often require one- or two-year contracts from their subscribers, specifying significant financial penalties for early cancellation of service.

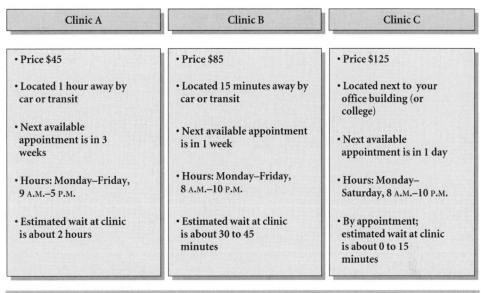

- *Time and location specificity reduce choice.* When people want to use a service at a specific location or at a particular time (or perhaps both, simultaneously), they usually find that they have fewer options. Many people choose a bank that has an ATM and/or a branch close to either the home or the office. How many brands can customers with these preferences choose from? Probably not many. If a business traveler needs to fly from San Francisco direct to Seoul, leaving next Wednesday evening after 8 p.m., the choice of airlines will be limited. And even then, not all airlines that have suitable flight connections may still have seats available.

Firms that are always reacting to competitors' pricing run the risk of setting prices lower than might be necessary. Managers should beware of falling into the trap of comparing competitors' prices dollar for dollar and then seeking to match them. Instead, managers should take into account the entire cost to customers of each competitive offering, including all related financial and nonmonetary costs and potential costs of switching. Managers should also assess the impact of distribution, time, and location factors, as well as estimating competitors' available capacity.

REVENUE MANAGEMENT

Many service businesses are now focusing on strategies to maximize the revenue, or contribution that can be derived from available capacity at any given time. Revenue management, often also called yield management, is a sophisticated form of supply-and-demand management. Airlines, hotels, and car rental firms, in particular, have become adept at varying their prices in response to the price sensitivity of various market segments at various times of the day, week, or season. The challenge is to capture sufficient customers to fill the available capacity without creating consumer surplus for customers who are willing to pay more.

How Revenue Management Works

In practice, revenue management means setting prices according to predicted demand levels among various market segments. The least-price-sensitive segment is allocated capacity first at the highest price, followed by the next segment at a lower price, and so on. As higher-paying segments often book closer to the time of consumption, firms need a disciplined approach of keeping the capacity free for them instead of simply selling on a first-come-first-serve basis. For example, business travelers often reserve airline seats, hotel rooms, and rental cars at short notice, but vacationers may book leisure travel months in advance. A good revenue management system is able to predict with reasonable accuracy how many customers will want to use a service for a given slot, flight, or day at each of several price levels and to "block" the relevant amount of capacity at each level (known as a "price bucket") in anticipation.

Reserving Capacity for High-yield Customers Advanced software has made it possible for firms to use very sophisticated mathematical models in yield management analysis. In the case of an airline, for example, these models integrate massive historical databases on past passenger travel and forecast demand of up to one year in advance for each individual departure. At fixed intervals, the revenue manager will check the actual pace of bookings (i.e., sales at a given time before departure) and compare it to the forecasted pace. Indirectly, this practice picks up competitors' pricing, too. If deviations between actual and forecasted demand are significant, adjustments to the "inventory buckets" will be made.

For example, if the booking pace for a higher-paying segment is stronger than expected, additional capacity will be allocated to this segment and taken away from the lowest-paying segment. The objective is to have the flight take off with no seat empty and each seat sold to the highest-paying segment. Ideally, no higher-paying travelers (e.g., full-fare-paying business travelers) were turned away because of "no seats available," and customers were turned away only at the lowest rate on that flight. Best Practice in Action 6-1 shows how revenue management has been implemented at American Airlines, an industry leader in this field.

Revenue management has been most effective when applied to operations that have relatively fixed capacity, a high fixed-cost structure, perishable inventory, demand that is variable and uncertain, and varying customer price sensitivity. Some industries that have successfully implemented revenue management are airlines, car rentals, hotels, and, more recently, hospitals, restaurants, golf courses, and even nonprofit organizations.[11]

Effect of Competitors' Pricing on Revenue Management Because revenue management systems monitor booking pace, competitor pricing is indirectly picked up. If a firm prices too low, it will experience a higher booking pace, and its cheaper seats will fill up quickly. That is generally not good, as it means a higher share of late booking but

BEST PRACTICE IN ACTION 6-1

PRICING SEATS ON FLIGHT AA 2015

Revenue management departments use sophisticated yield management software and powerful computers to forecast, track, and manage each flight on a given date separately. Let's look at American Airlines 2015, a popular flight from Chicago to Phoenix, Arizona, which departs daily at 5:30 P.M. on the 1,370 mile (2,200 km) journey.

The 125 seats in coach (economy class) are divided into seven fare categories, referred to by yield management specialists as "buckets." Ticket prices among these seats vary widely; round-trip fares range from $238 for a bargain excursion ticket (with various restrictions and a cancellation penalty attached) up to an unrestricted fare of $1,404. Seats are also available at an even higher price in the small first-class section. Scott McCartney tells how ongoing analysis by the computer program changes the allocation of seats within each of the seven buckets in economy class.

> In the weeks before each Chicago–Phoenix flight, American's yield management computers constantly adjust the number of seats in each bucket, taking into account tickets sold, historical ridership patterns, and connecting passengers likely to use the route as one leg of a longer trip.
>
> If advance bookings are slim, American adds seats to low-fare buckets. If business customers buy unrestricted fares earlier than expected, the yield management computer takes seats out of the discount buckets and preserves them for last-minute bookings that the database predicts will still show up.
>
> With 69 of 125 coach seats already sold four weeks before one recent departure of Flight 2015, American's computer began to limit the number of seats in lower-priced buckets. A week later, it totally shut off sales for the bottom three buckets, priced $300 or less. To a Chicago customer looking for a cheap seat, the flight was "sold out." . . .
>
> One day before departure, with 130 passengers booked for the 125-seat flight, American still offered five seats at full fare because its computer database indicated 10 passengers were likely not to show up or take other flights. Flight 2015 departed full and no one was bumped.

Although AA 2015 for that date is now history, it has not been forgotten. The booking experience for this flight was saved in the memory of the yield management program to help the airline do an even better job of forecasting in the future.

Source: Scott McCartney, "Ticket Shock: Business Fares Increase Even as Leisure Travel Keeps Getting Cheaper," *Wall Street Journal,* November 3, 1997.

high-fare-paying customers will not be able to get their seats confirmed and will therefore fly on competing airlines. If the initial pricing is too high, the firm will get too low a share of early-booking segments (which still tend to offer a reasonable yield) and may later have to sell excess capacity last minute at very low prices to still recover some contribution toward its fixed costs.

Price Elasticity

Effective revenue management requires two or more segments that attach different values to the service and have different price elasticity. To allocate and price capacity effectively, the revenue manager needs to determine how sensitive demand is to price and what net revenues will be generated at different prices for each target segment. The concept of elasticity describes how sensitive demand is to changes in price and is computed as follows:

$$\text{Price elasticity} = \frac{\text{Percentage change in demand}}{\text{Percentage change in price}}$$

When price elasticity is at "unity," sales of a service rise (or fall) by the same percentage that price falls (or rises). When a small change in price has a big impact on sales, demand for that product is said to be *price elastic*. But when a change in price has little effect on sales, demand is described as *price inelastic*. The concept is illustrated in the simple chart in Figure 6-6, which shows the price elasticity for two segments: one with a highly elastic demand (a small change in price results in a big change in the amount demanded) and the other with a highly inelastic demand (even big changes in price have little impact on the amount demanded).

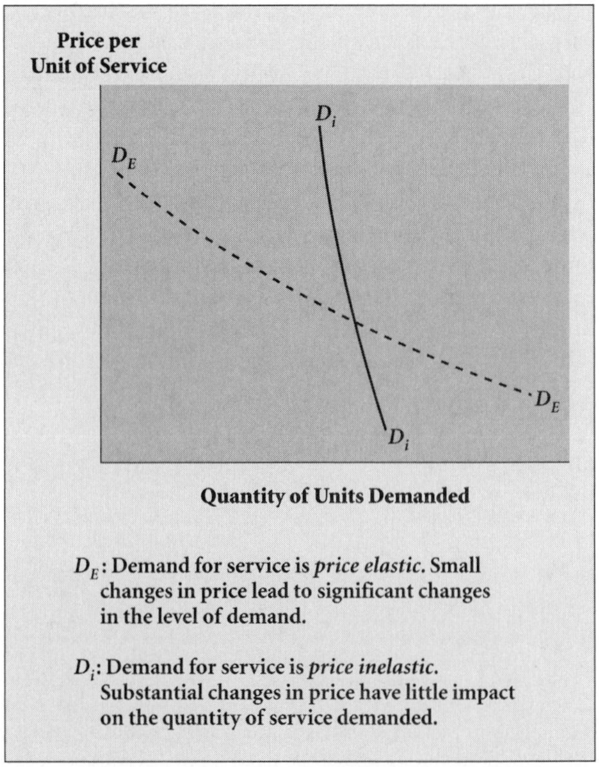
Price per Unit of Service
D_i
D_E
D_E
D_i
Quantity of Units Demanded
D_E: Demand for service is *price elastic*. Small changes in price lead to significant changes in the level of demand.
D_i: Demand for service is *price inelastic*. Substantial changes in price have little impact on the quantity of service demanded.

FIGURE 6-6 Illustrations of Price Elasticity

Designing Rate Fences

Inherent in revenue management is the concept of *price customization*—that is, charging different customers different prices for what is, in effect, the same product. As noted by Hermann Simon and Robert Dolan:

> The basic idea of price customization is simple: Have people pay prices based on the value they put on the product. Obviously you can't just hang out a sign saying "Pay me what it's worth to you" or "It's $80 if you value it that much but only $40 if you don't. You have to find a way to segment customers by their valuations. In a sense, you have to "build a fence" between high-value customers and low-value customers so the "high" buyers can't take advantage of the low price.[12] (p. 13)

How can a firm ensure that customers for whom the service offers high value are unable to take advantage of lower-price buckets? Properly designed rate fences allow customers to self-segment on the basis of service characteristics and willingness to pay and help companies to restrict lower prices to customers who are willing to accept certain restrictions on their purchase and consumption experiences.

Fences can be either *physical* or *nonphysical*. Physical fences refer to tangible product differences related to the different prices, such as the seat location in a theater or the size and furnishing of a hotel room. Nonphysical fences refer to consumption, transaction, or buyer characteristics, such as staying a certain length of time in a hotel, playing golf on a weekday afternoon, cancellation or change penalties, or booking a certain length of time ahead. Examples of common rate fences are shown in Table 6-2.

Physical fences reflect tangible differences in the service (e.g., flying first class is a different experience from flying economy class), whereas nonphysical fences refer to the same basic service (e.g., there is no difference in service whether a person bought a cheap economy class ticket over the Internet or whether someone paid full fare for it; both travelers receive the same service product).

Summary

Revenue management requires a detailed understanding of customer needs and preferences and their willingness to pay. With this information, the product and revenue manager together can design effective products that consist of the core service, physical product features (physical fences), and nonphysical product features (nonphysical fences). Next, a good understanding of the demand curve is needed so that "buckets" of inventory can be assigned to the various products and price categories. An example from the airline industry is shown in Figure 6-7. Finally, the design of revenue management systems needs to incorporate safeguards for consumers. For additional insights into revenue management strategies, see the reading by Sheryl E. Kimes and Richard B. Chase, "The Strategic Levers of Yield Management," which appears on pp. 217–227.

ETHICAL CONCERNS AND PERCEIVED FAIRNESS OF PRICING POLICIES

Customers often have difficulty understanding how much it is going to cost them to use a service. Moreover, they cannot always be sure in advance what they will receive in return for their payments. Many services are intangible, and it is often difficult to evaluate quality. Many customers implicitly assume that a higher-priced service must offer

TABLE 6-2 Key Categories of Rate Fences

Rate Fences	*Examples*
Physical (product-related) Fences	
Basic product	• Class of travel (business/economy class) • Size and furnishing of a hotel room • Seat location in a theater
Amenities	• Free breakfast at a hotel, airport pick up, etc. • Free golf cart at a golf course
Service level	• Priority wait listing, separate check-in counters with no or only short lines • Increase in baggage allowance • Dedicated service hotlines • Dedicated account management team
Nonphysical Fences	
Transaction Characteristics	
Time of booking or reservation	• Requirements for advance purchase • Must pay full fare 2 weeks before departure
Location of booking or reservation	• Passengers booking air tickets for same route in different countries charged different prices
Flexibility of ticket use	• Fees/penalties for canceling or changing a reservation (up to loss of entire ticket price) • Nonrefundable reservations fees
Consumption Characteristics	
Time or duration of use	• Early-bird special in a restaurant before 6:00 p.m. • Must stay over a Saturday night for an airline, hotel, or car rental booking. • Must stay at least for 5 nights
Location of consumption	• Price based on departure location, especially in international travel • Prices vary by location (between cities, city center versus edges of the city)
Buyer Characteristics	
Frequency or volume of consumption	• Member of certain loyalty tier with the firm (e.g., Platinum member) gets priority pricing, discounts, or loyalty benefits
Group membership	• Child, student, senior citizen discounts • Affiliation with certain groups (e.g., alumni)
Size of customer group	• Group discounts based on size of group

more benefits and greater quality than a lower-priced one. For example, a high-priced professional—say, a lawyer—is assumed to be more skilled than one who charges lower fees. Although price can serve as a surrogate for quality, it is sometimes difficult to be sure whether the extra value is there.

FIGURE 6-7 Relating Price Buckets to the Demand Curve

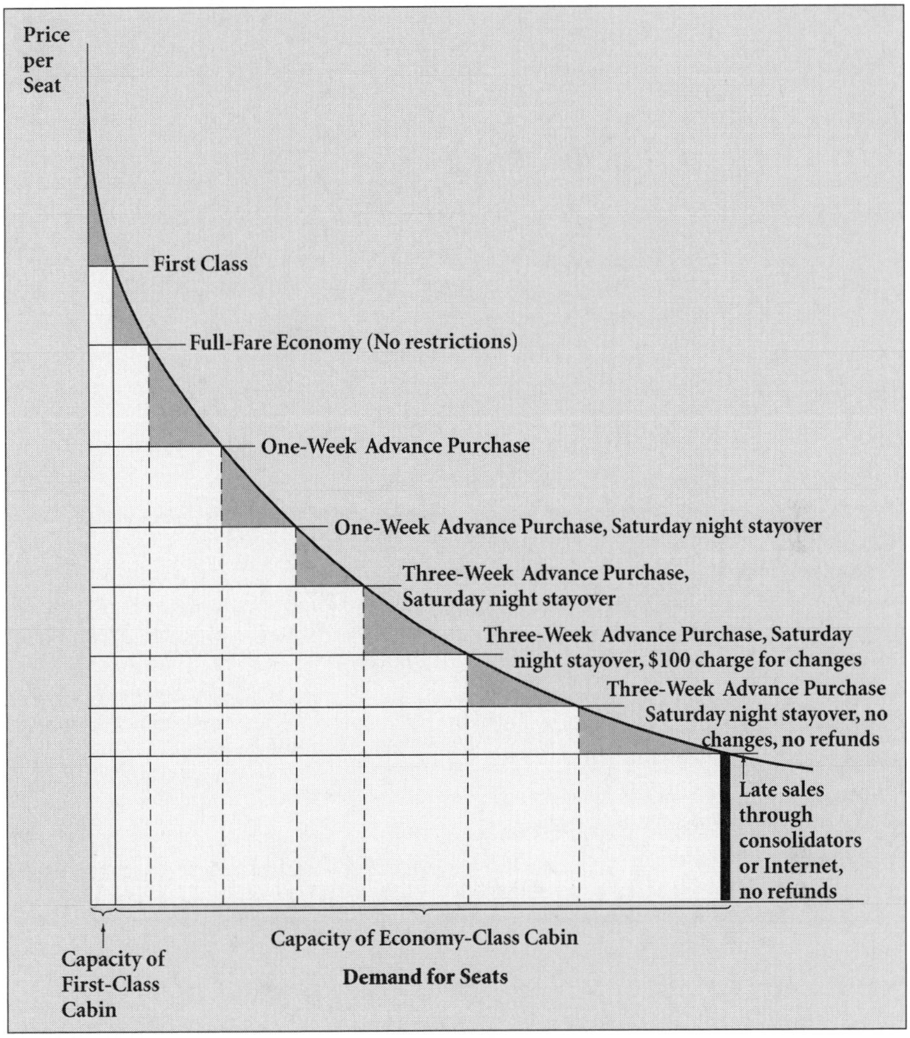

Note: Dark shaded areas denote amount of consumer surplus (goal of segmented pricing is to minimize this).

Complexity of Service-Pricing Schedules

Pricing schedules for services tend to be complex and often cannot be understood and compared across providers without complex spreadsheets or even mathematical formulas. The quoted prices typically used by consumers for price comparisons may be only the first of several expenditures they will incur. As described in Service Perspectives 6-1, cellular (mobile) phone service is particularly problematic in this respect.

Many people find it difficult to assess and forecast their own usage profiles accurately, which makes it difficult to compute comparative prices when competing suppliers base their fees on a variety of usage-related factors. It is no coincidence that the humorist Scott Adams (best known as the creator of Dilbert), used exclusively service examples when he "branded" the future of pricing as "confusiology." Noting that telecommunication companies, banks, insurance firms, and other financial service providers offer nearly identical services, he remarks:

SERVICE PERSPECTIVES 6-1

COMPLEXITY IN CELLULAR PHONE SERVICE PRICING

Recent years have seen a rapid expansion in the availability of cellular (mobile) telephone services. Significant technological improvements have expanded the capability of these services, including the ability to transmit pictures. Not surprisingly, demand has exploded, and competition has become intense in many countries. In 2002, a Roper survey found that 3 in 10 Americans aged 18 to 29 used a wireless phone as their primary phone.

In an effort to tailor their services to the widely varying needs and calling patterns of various market segments, cell phone companies have developed a bewildering array of plans that defy easy comparison across suppliers. Plans can be national, regional, or purely local in scope. Monthly fees also vary according to the number of minutes selected in advance, which typically include separate allowances for peak and off-peak minutes, reflecting the times of day and days of the week when calls are actually made. Overtime minutes and "roaming minutes" on other carriers are charged at higher rates. Some plans allow unlimited off-peak calling. Family plans let parents and children pool their monthly minutes for use on several phones as long as the total for everyone's calling doesn't exceed the monthly quota. An alternative is prepaid calling, which enables customers to buy a phone and then purchase time as needed.

Research by Consumers Union (CU) found high levels of customer dissatisfaction. One out of three subscribers to ConsumerReports.org reported seriously considering a change in wireless phone companies. Among those who had already switched, most said that they wanted better service or a better price.

In addition to poor-quality reception, dropped calls, and inaccessible service, many customer concerns related to billing and pricing, with complaints about overcharges, billing mistakes, and bills padded with extra charges. Compounding the problem was the fact that companies made it difficult to switch. Typically, subscribers sign a one- or two-year contract that imposes significant penalties, often in the range \$100–\$200, for early termination. In an editorial entitled "Cell Hell," Jim Guest, CU's president, observed:

> In the 10 years since *Consumer Reports* started rating cell phones and calling plans, we've never found an easy way to compare actual costs. From what our readers tell us, they haven't either. Each carrier presents its rates, extra charges, and calling areas differently. Deciphering one company's plan is hard enough, but comparing plans from various carriers is nearly impossible.(p. 3)[1]

CU advocates stronger regulation of the industry to protect consumers from confusing and abusive practices, including a government-mandated standard format for presenting calling plan features and charges.

Source: Guest, "Cell Hell"; and Jim Guest, "Complete Cell-Phone Guide," *Consumer Reports* (February 2003): 11–27.

[1]Jim Guest, "Cell Hell," *Consumer Reports* (February 2003): 3.

> You would think this would create a price war and drive prices down to the cost of providing it (that's what I learned between naps in my economic classes), but it isn't happening. The companies are forming efficient confusopolies so customers can't tell who has the lowest prices. Companies have learned to use the complexities of life as an economic tool.[13]

One of the roles of effective government regulation should be to discourage this tendency for certain service industries to evolve into "confusopolies."

Ethical Concerns, Perceived Fairness, and Trust

Services, especially credence services, whose quality and benefits are difficult to evaluate even after delivery, often invite performance and pricing abuses. When they don't know what they are getting from the service supplier, aren't present when the work is being performed, and lack the technical skills to know whether a good job has been done, customers are vulnerable to paying for work that wasn't done, wasn't necessary, or was not well executed.

Complexity of pricing schedules also makes it easy (and perhaps more tempting) for firms to engage in unethical behavior. In the United States, the car rental industry has attracted some notoriety for advertising bargain rental prices and then telling customers on arrival that other fees, such as collision insurance and personal insurance, are compulsory. Also, the staff sometimes fail to clarify certain "small print" contract terms, such as a high mileage charge that is added once the car exceeds a very low threshold of free miles. The "hidden extras" phenomenon for car rentals in some Florida resort towns got so bad at one point that people were joking: "The car is free, the keys are extra!" A not uncommon practice when the car is returned is to charge for refueling a partially empty tank fees that far exceed what the driver would pay at the pump.

When customers know that they are vulnerable to potential abuse, they tend to become suspicious of both the firm and its employees. This situation complicates the task of promoting and delivering service excellence.

In a revenue management context, the overdependence on the output of computer models can easily lead to pricing strategies that are full of rules and regulations, cancellation penalties, and a cynical strategy of overbooking without thought for disappointed customers who believed that they had a firm reservation. Revenue management needs to be implemented so that the firm can charge various prices without risking customer perceptions of unfairness. For example, higher prices charged during busy periods can easily be seen as price gouging, whereas the discounts during low-demand periods may reduce customer reference prices, in turn making future purchases at regular prices seem less fair. Also, it does not seem uncommon for large hotel chains to quote higher prices to non-American-sounding callers than to callers with an American accent. People who call to make a reservation for a boss are often quoted higher prices than when making reservations for their family. The ethics of those practices are questionable.[14]

Designing Fairness into Pricing Strategy

Pricing schedules have to be designed with customer perceptions of fairness in mind. Likewise, a well-implemented revenue management strategy does not mean blind pursuit of short-term yield maximization. The following specific approaches can help to reconcile pricing schedules and yield management practices with customer satisfaction, trust, and goodwill:[15]

- *Design price schedules and fences that are clear, logical, and fair.* Firms should proactively spell out all fees and expenses clearly in advance so that there are no surprises. A related approach is to develop a simple fee structure so that customers can more easily understand the financial implications of a specific usage situation. For a rate fence to be perceived as fair, customers must be able to easily understand it—the fence has to be transparent and upfront—see the logic in it, and be convinced that it is difficult to circumvent and therefore fair. Also, firms need to guard against the risk that pricing policies may become too complex. Jokes abound about travel agents having nervous breakdowns because they get a different quote every time they call the airline for a fare and because there are so many exclusions, conditions, and special offers.
- *Use high published prices and frame fences as discounts.* Rate fences framed as customer gains, or discounts, are generally perceived as fairer than those framed as customer losses, or surcharges, even if the situations are economically equivalent. For example, a customer who patronizes her hair salon on Saturdays may perceive it as profiteering if she faces a weekend surcharge. However, she is likely

to find the higher weekend price more acceptable if the hair salon advertises its peak weekend price as the published price and offers a $5 discount for weekday haircuts. Furthermore, having a high published price helps to increase the reference price and potentially quality perceptions, in addition to the feeling of being rewarded for the weekday patronage.

- *Communicate consumer benefits of revenue management.* Marketing communications should position revenue management as a win-win practice. Providing various price and value balances allows a broader spectrum of customers to self-segment and enjoy the service. It allows each customer to find the price and benefits (value) balance that best satisfies his or her needs. For example, charging a higher price for the best seats in the theater recognizes that some people are willing and able to pay more for a better location and makes it possible to sell other seats at a lower price.
- *Use bundling to "hide" discounts.* Bundling a service into a package effectively obscures the discounted price. When a cruise line includes the price of air travel or ground transportation in the cruise package, the customer knows only the total price, not the cost of the individual components. Bundling usually makes price comparisons between the bundles and its components impossible and thereby sidesteps potential unfairness perceptions and reductions in reference prices.
- *Take care of loyal customers.* To maintain goodwill and build relationships, a company should build in strategies for retaining valued customer relationships, even to the extent of not charging the maximum feasible amount on a given transaction. After all, customer perceptions of price gouging do not build trust. Also, if implemented indiscriminately, yield management systems allocate capacity during peak times to the highest-paying customers, not necessarily the most loyal customers. An intermittent availability of capacity to regular customers can cause them to become frustrated and angry and put their loyalty at risk, especially if they feel that their loyalty should be recognized and rewarded. One solution is to program yield management systems to incorporate "loyalty multipliers" for regular customers, so that reservations systems can accord preferred availability, giving them "special treatment" status, even though they may not be paying premium rates.
- *Use service recovery to compensate for overbooking.* As part of their revenue management regime, many service firms overbook to compensate for anticipated cancellations and no-shows. If a firm increases overbooking, the reduced inventory wastage will bring higher revenue. The flip side is that the incidence of not being able to honor reservations would also increase, and customers with bookings or reservations may be "bumped" by their airline or "walked" by their hotel. This can lead to a loss of customer loyalty and adversely affect a firm's reputation. Here, it is important to back up overbooking programs with well-designed service recovery procedures.

Important guidelines include: (1) giving customers a choice between retaining their reservation and being displaced with compensation for the inconvenience; (2) providing sufficient advance notice that customers are able to make alternative arrangements; (3) if possible, offering a substitute service that delights customers. A Westin beach resort that has occasional "oversales" has found that it can free up capacity by offering guests who are departing the next day the option of spending their last night in a luxury hotel near the airport or in the city at no cost. Guest feedback on the free room, upgraded service, and a night in the city after a beach holiday has been very positive. From the hotel's perspective, this practice trades the cost of securing a one-night stay in another hotel against that of turning away a multiple-night guest arriving that same day.

PUTTING SERVICE PRICING INTO PRACTICE

Although the main decision in pricing is usually seen as how much to charge, other decisions need to be made as well. Table 6-3 summarizes the questions that service marketers

TABLE 6-3 Some Pricing Issues

1. **How much should be charged for this service?**
   - What costs are the organization attempting to recover? Is the organization trying to achieve a specific profit margin or return on investment by selling this service?
   - How sensitive are customers to various prices?
   - What prices are charged by competitors?
   - What discount(s) should be offered from basic prices?
   - Are psychological pricing points (e.g., $4.95 versus $5.00) customarily used?
2. **What should be the basis of pricing?**
   - Execution of a specific task
   - Admission to a service facility
   - Units of time (hour, week, month, year)
   - Percentage commission on the value of the transaction
   - Physical resources consumed
   - Geographic distance covered
   - Weight or size of object serviced
   - Should each service element be billed independently?
   - Should a single price be charged for a bundled package?
3. **Who should collect payment?**
   - The organization that provides the service
   - A specialist intermediary (travel or ticket agent, bank, retailer, etc.)
   - How should the intermediary be compensated for this work—flat fee or percentage commission?
4. **Where should payment be made?**
   - The location at which the service is delivered
   - A convenient retail outlet or financial intermediary (e.g., bank)
   - The purchaser's home (by mail or phone)
5. **When should payment be made?**
   - Before or after delivery of the service
   - At which times of day
   - On which days of the week
6. **How should payment be made?**
   - Cash (exact change or not?)
   - Token (where can these be purchased?)
   - Stored value card
   - Check (how to verify?)
   - Electronic funds transfer
   - Charge card (credit or debit)
   - Credit account with service provider
   - Vouchers
   - Third-party payment (e.g., insurance company or government agency)?
7. **How should prices be communicated to the target market?**
   - Through what communication medium? (advertising, signage, electronic display, salespeople, customer service personnel)
   - What message content (how much emphasis should be placed on price?)

need to ask themselves as they prepare to create and implement a well-thought-out pricing strategy.

How Much to Charge?

Realistic decisions on pricing are critical for financial solvency. The pricing tripod model (Figure 6-1) provides a useful departure point. Let's revisit the three elements involved. The task begins with determining the relevant economic costs to be recovered at various sales volumes and, when appropriate, the margin, which sets the relevant floor price.

The second task is to assess market sensitivity to various prices, which includes both the overall value of the service to prospective customers and their ability to pay. This step sets a "ceiling" price for any given market segment. It is vital to make an accurate prediction of what sales volume might be obtained at various price levels.

Competitive prices provide a third input. The greater the number of similar alternatives, the more the marketing manager is pressured to keep prices on par or below those of the competition. However, do remember the many reasons why price competition is reduced in many service markets. Never simply compare competitor prices dollar for dollar!

Finally, a specific figure must be set for the price that customers will be asked to pay. Should the firm price in round numbers or try to create the impression that prices are slightly lower than they really are? If competitors promote such prices as $5.95 and $9.95, a strategy of charging $6.00 or $10.00 may convey an image of prices somewhat higher than is really the case. On the other hand, rounded prices offer convenience and simplicity—benefits that may be appreciated by both consumers and salespeople—as they help to speed up cash transactions. An ethical issue concerns the practice of promoting a price that excludes tax, service charges, and other extras. This is misleading if customers expect the quoted price to be inclusive.

What Should Be the Basis for Pricing?

It's not always easy to define a unit of service. Should price be based on completing a specific service task, such as repairing a piece of equipment, cleaning a jacket, or cutting a customer's hair? Should price be based on admission to a service performance, such as an educational program or a film, concert, or sports event? Should price be time based: for instance, using an hour of a lawyer's time, occupying a hotel room for a night, or subscribing to a satellite TV service for a month? Alternatively, should price be related to a monetary value associated with service delivery, as when an insurance company scales its premiums to reflect the amount of coverage provided or a realtor takes a commission that is a percentage of the selling price of a house?

Some service prices are tied to the consumption of physical resources, such as food, drinks, water, or natural gas. In the hospitality industry, rather than charging customers an hourly rate for occupying a table and chairs, restaurants put a sizable markup on the food and drink items consumed. Recognizing the fixed cost of table service, such as a clean tablecloth for each party, restaurants in some countries impose a fixed cover charge, which is added to the cost of the meal. Other restaurants may establish a minimum meal charge per person. Transport firms have traditionally charged by distance, with freight companies using a combination of weight or cubic volume and distance to set their rates. Such a policy has the virtue of consistency and reflects calculation of an average cost per mile (or kilometer). However, that policy ignores relative market strength on various routes, which should be included when a yield management system is used. Simplicity may suggest a flat rate, as with postal charges for domestic letters below a certain weight or a rate for packages that groups geographic distances into broad zones.

For some services, prices may include separate charges for access and for use. Recent research suggests that access or subscription fees are an important driver of adoption and customer retention, whereas use fees are much more important drivers of actual use.[16]

Price Bundling As emphasized throughout this book, many services unite a core product with a variety of supplementary services. Meals and bar service on a cruise ship offer one example; baggage service on a train or aircraft is another. Should such service packages be priced as a whole (referred to as a "bundle"), or should each element be priced separately? To the extent that people prefer to avoid making many small payments, bundled pricing may be preferable and is certainly simpler to administer. But if customers dislike feeling that they have been charged for product elements they did not use, itemized pricing may be preferable.

Bundled prices offer a service firm a certain guaranteed revenue from each customer and give the latter a clear idea in advance of how much the bill will be. Unbundled pricing provides customers with flexibility in what they choose to acquire and pay for. However, customers may be angered if they discover that the actual price of what they consume, inflated by all the "extras," is substantially higher than the advertised base price that attracted them in the first place.

Discounting As discussed in the context of yield management, selective price discounting targeted at specific market segments can offer important opportunities to attract new customers and fill capacity that would otherwise go unused. However, unless used with effective rate fences that allow a clean targeting of specific segments, a strategy of discounting should be approached cautiously. It reduces the average price and contribution received and may attract customers whose only loyalty is to the firm that can offer the lowest price on the next transaction. Volume discounts are sometimes used to cement the loyalty of large corporate customers that might otherwise spread their purchases among several suppliers.

Who Should Collect Payment?

As discussed in Chapter 4, supplementary services include information, order taking, billing, and payment. Customers appreciate a firm's making it easy to obtain price information and make reservations. Customers also expect well-presented billing and convenient procedures for making payment. Sometimes, firms delegate these tasks to intermediaries, such as travel agents, who make hotel and transport bookings and collect payment from customers; and ticket agents, who sell seats for theaters, concert halls, and sports stadiums. Although the original supplier pays a commission, the intermediary is usually able to offer customers greater convenience in terms of where, when, and how payment can be made. Using intermediaries may also result in a net savings in administrative costs. Nowadays, however, many service firms are promoting their Web sites as direct channels for customer self-service, thus by-passing traditional intermediaries and avoiding payment of commissions.

Where Should Payment Be Made?

Service delivery sites are not always conveniently located. Airports, theaters, and stadiums, for instance, are often situated some distance from where potential patrons live or work. When consumers have to purchase a service before using it, there are obvious benefits to using intermediaries that are more conveniently located or allowing payment by mail or bank transfer. A growing number of organizations now accept Internet, telephone, and fax bookings with payment by credit card.

When Should Payment Be Made?

Two basic options are to ask customers to pay in advance, as with an admission charge, airline ticket, or postage stamps or to bill them once service delivery has been completed, as with restaurant bills and repair charges. Occasionally, a service provider may ask for an initial payment in advance of service delivery, with the balance being due later. This approach is quite common with expensive repair and maintenance jobs, when the firm, often a small business with limited working capital, must buy materials up front. Indeed, as shown in Research Insights 6-1, the timing of payment may determine usage patterns.

Asking customers to pay in advance means that the buyer is paying before the benefits are received. However, prepayments may be advantageous to the customer as well as to the provider. Sometimes, it is inconvenient to pay each time a regularly patronized service, such as the post office or public transport, is used. To save time and effort, customers may prefer the convenience of buying a book of stamps or a monthly travel pass. Performing-arts organizations with heavy up-front financing requirements offer discounted subscription tickets in order to bring in money before the season begins.

How Should Payment Be Made?

Table 6-3 showed the many forms of payment. Cash may appear to be the simplest method, but it raises security problems and is inconvenient when exact change is required to operate machines. Accepting payment by check for all but the smallest purchases is now fairly widespread and offers customer benefits, although to discourage bad checks, a hefty charge may be made for returned checks ($15–20 on top of any bank charges is not uncommon at retail stores).

Credit and debit cards can be used around the world. As their acceptance has become more universal, businesses that refuse to accept them increasingly find themselves at a competitive disadvantage. Many companies also offer customers the convenience of a credit account, which generates a membership relationship between the customer and the firm. Other payment procedures include tokens or vouchers as supplements to (or instead of) cash. Tokens with a predefined value can simplify the process of paying road and bridge tolls or bus and metro fares. Vouchers are sometimes provided by social service agencies to elderly or low-income people. Such a policy achieves the same benefits as discounting but avoids the need to publicize different prices and to require cashiers to check eligibility.

Now coming into broader use are prepayment systems based on cards that store value on a magnetic strip or in a microchip embedded within the card. Service firms that want to accept payment in this form, however, must first install card readers. Service marketers should remember that the simplicity and speed with which payment is made may influence the customer's perception of overall service quality.

How Should Prices Be Communicated to the Target Markets?

Once each of the other issues has been addressed, the final task is to decide how the organization's pricing policies can best be communicated to the target market(s). People need to know the price for some product offerings well in advance of purchase and may also need to know how, where, and when that price is payable. This information must be presented in ways that are intelligible and unambiguous, so that customers will not be misled and question the ethical standards of the firm. Dismayed by the complexity of cell phone calling plans in the United States, Consumers Union has called for a simple, standardized summary of each calling plan's features that would simplify the process for consumers to compare competing offers. This would be similar

RESEARCH INSIGHT 6-1

CONSUMPTION FOLLOWS THE TIMING OF PAYMENTS

From an analysis of the payment and attendance records of a Colorado-based health club, John Gourville and Dilip Soman[1] found that members' usage patterns were closely related to their payment schedules. When members made annual, semiannual, or quarterly payments, their use of the club was highest during the months immediately following payment and then declined steadily until the next payment. In contrast, members with monthly payment plans attended the health club much more consistently and were more likely to renew, perhaps because each month's payment encouraged them to use what they were paying for. The distinctive usage patterns associated with the four alternative payment plans are schematically shown in Figure 6-A.

Gouville and Soman conclude that the timing of payment can be used more strategically than is generally done. For example, if a key objective is to encourage usage and retain members, a monthly schedule is better than annual payments.

Payment timing can also be used to manage capacity utilization. For example, a golf club that bills its annual membership fees shortly prior to the peak season will inadvertently promote demand during its busiest time. However, if the club bills its fees long before the season begins (e.g., in January rather than in May or June), a member's pain of payment will have faded by the time the peak summer months come and thereby reduce the need to get his/her money's worth. A reduction in demand during the peak period would allow the club to increase its membership.

FIGURE 6-A Usage Patterns and Payment Schedules

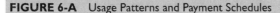

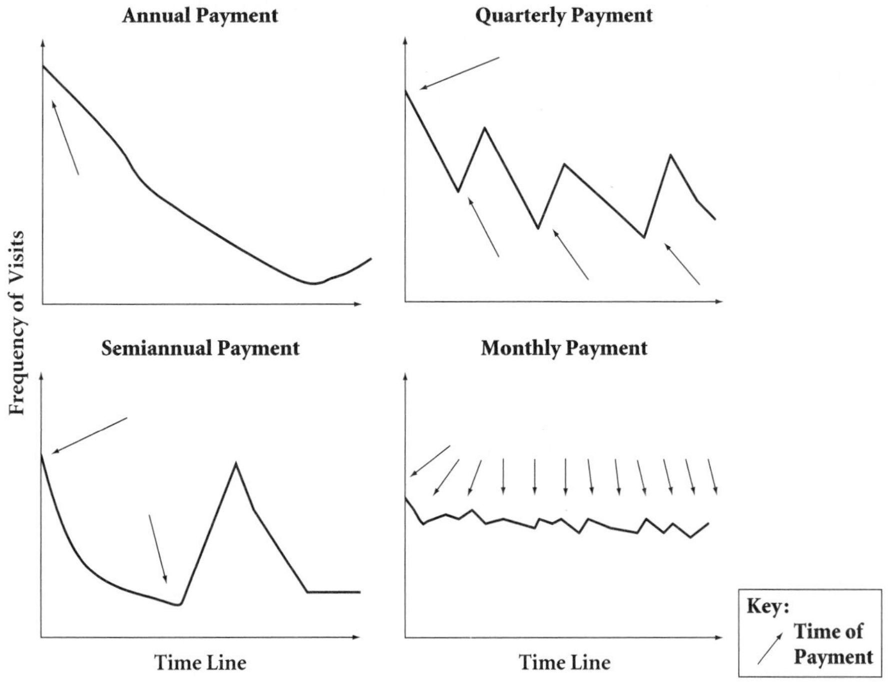

Note: Arrows denoting time of payment have been added for emphasis.

[1]John Gourville and Dilip Soman, "Pricing and the Psychology of Consumption," *Harvard Business Review* (September 2002): 90–96. Reprinted by permission of Harvard Business School Publishing.

in style to the government-mandated box printed in all credit card solicitations that lays out, in standard format and readable type, the offer's essential rates and terms.[17]

Managers must decide whether to include information on pricing in advertising for the service. It may be appropriate to relate the price to the costs of competing products. Certainly, salespeople and customer service representatives should be able to give prompt, accurate responses to customer queries about pricing, payment, and credit. Good signage at retail points of sale will save staff members from having to answer basic questions on prices.

Finally, when the price is presented in the form of an itemized bill, marketers should ensure that it is both accurate and intelligible. Hospital bills, for example, which may run to several pages and contain dozens of items, have been much criticized for inaccuracy.[18]

CONCLUSION

To determine an effective pricing strategy, a firm has to have a good understanding of its costs, the value created for customers, and competitor pricing. Defining costs tends to be more difficult in a service business than in a manufacturing operation. Without a good understanding of costs, managers cannot be sure that the prices set are, in fact, sufficient to recover all costs.

Another challenge is to relate the value that customers perceive in a service to the price they are willing to pay for it. This step requires an understanding of other costs that the customer may be incurring in purchase and use, including such nonfinancial costs as time and effort. Managers also need to recognize that the same service may not be valued in the same way by all customers, offering the potential to set different prices for different market segments.

Competitor pricing cannot be compared dollar for dollar. Services tend to be location and time specific, and competitor services have their own set of related monetary and nonmonetary costs, sometimes to the extent that the prices charged become secondary for competitive comparisons. Competitive pricing needs to take all those factors into account.

Revenue management is a powerful tool that helps to manage demand and price in different segments closer to their reservation prices. Well-designed physical and nonphysical rate fences help to define "products" for each target segment. However, great care has to be taken in the way revenue management is implemented so that customer satisfaction and perceived fairness are not compromised.

A pricing strategy must address the central issue of what price to charge for selling a given unit of service at a particular time (however that unit may be defined). Because services often combine multiple elements, pricing strategies need to be highly creative. Finally, firms need to be careful lest pricing schedules become so complex and difficult to compare that they simply confuse customers. A policy of deliberately creating confusing price schedules, including hiding certain costs that become apparent to customers only after usage, is likely to lead to accusations of unethical behavior, loss of trust, and customer dissatisfaction.

Review Questions

1. How can the three main approaches to service pricing be integrated to arrive at a good pricing point for a particular service?
2. How can a service firm compute its unit costs for pricing purposes? How do predicted and actual capacity utilization affect unit costs and profitability?
3. Why is the price charged by the firm only one, and often not the most important, component of the total cost to the consumer? When should we cut non-price-related costs to the bone, even if that incurs higher costs and a higher price to be charged?

4. Why can't we compare competitor prices dollar for dollar in a service context?
5. What types of service operations benefit most from good yield management systems, and why?
6. How can we charge different prices to different segments without customers' feeling cheated? How can we even charge the same customer different prices at different times, contexts, and/or occasions and at the same time be seen as fair?

Application Exercises

1. From a customer perspective, what serves to define value in the following services:
   a. A hairdressing salon
   b. A legal firm specializing in business and taxation law
   c. A nightclub
2. Select a service organization and find out what its pricing policies and methods are. In what respects are they similar to or different from what has been discussed in this chapter?
3. Review recent bills that you have received from service businesses, such as those for telephone, car repair, cable TV, credit card, and so on. Evaluate each one against the following criteria: (a) general appearance and clarity of presentation, (b) easily understood terms of payment, (c) avoidance of confusing terms and definitions, (d) appropriate level of detail, (e) unanticipated ("hidden") charges, (f) accuracy, (g) ease of access to customer service in case of problems or disputes.
4. How might revenue management be applied to (a) a professional firm (e.g., consulting), (b) a restaurant, and (c) a golf course? What rate fences would you use, and why?
5. Collect the pricing schedules of three leading mobile phone service providers. Identify all the pricing dimensions (e.g., air time, subscription fees, free minutes, per second/six seconds/minute billing, air time rollover, and so on) and pricing levels for each dimension—the range offered by the players in the market. Determine the usage profile for a particular target segment (e.g., a young executive who uses the phone mostly for personal calls or a full-time student). Based on the usage profile, determine the lowest-cost provider. Next, measure the pricing schedule preferences of your target segment (e.g., via conjoint analysis). Finally, advise the smallest of the three providers how to redesign its pricing schedule to make it more attractive to your target segment.
6. What are potential consumer responses to complex pricing schedules? How can we improve the perceived fairness of pricing schedules, and what are the implications of these recommendations?
7. Develop a comprehensive pricing schedule for a service of your choice. Apply the seven questions marketers need to answer for designing an effective pricing schedule.

Endnotes

1. Daniel J. Goebel, Greg W. Marshall, and William B. Locander, "Activity Based Costing: Accounting for a Marketing Orientation," *Industrial Marketing Management* 27, no. 6 (1998): 497–510; Thomas H. Stevenson and David W. E. Cabell, "Integrating Transfer Pricing Policy and Activity-Based Costing," *Journal of Internatinal Marketing* 10, no. 4 (2002): 77–88.
2. Robin Cooper and Robert S. Kaplan, "Profit Priorities from Activity-Based Costing," *Harvard Business Review* 69, no. 3 (May–June 1991): 130–135.
3. Antonella Carù and Antonella Cugini, "Profitability and Customer Satisfaction in Services: An Integrated Perspective between Marketing and Cost Management Analysis," *International Journal of Service Industry Management* 10, no. 2 (1999): 132–156.
4. Gerald E. Smith and Thomas T. Nagle, "How Much Are Customers Willing to Pay?" *Marketing Research* (Winter 2002): 20–25.
5. Valarie A. Zeithaml, "Consumer Perceptions of Price, Quality, and Value: A Means-End Model and Synthesis of Evidence," *Journal of Marketing* 52 (July 1988): 2–21.
6. Hermann Simon, "Pricing Opportunities and How to Exploit Them," *Sloan Management Review* 33 (Winter 1992): 71–84.

7. This discussion is based primarily on Leonard L. Berry and Manjit S. Yadav, "Capture and Communicate Value in the Pricing of Services," *Sloan Management Review* 37 (Summer 1996): 41–51.
8. Frederick F. Reichheld, *The Loyalty Effect* (Boston: Harvard Business School Press, 1996), 82–84.
9. Anna S. Mattila and Jochen Wirtz, "The Impact of Knowledge Types on the Consumer Search Process—An Investigation in the Context of Credence Services," *International Journal of Service Industry Management* 13, no. 3 (2002): 214–230.
10. For an excellent review and conceptual framework for understanding service convenience, refer to Leonard L. Berry, Kathleen Seiders, and Dhruv Grewal, "Understanding Service Convenience," *Journal of Marketing* 66 (July 2002): 1–17.
11. For recent work on the application of yield management to industries beyond the traditional airline, hotel, and car rental contexts, see Sheryl E. Kimes, "Revenue Management on the Links: Applying Yield Management to the Golf Industry," *Cornell Hotel and Restaurant Administration Quarterly* 41, no. 1 (2000): 120–127; Sheryl E. Kimes and Jochen Wirtz, "Perceived Fairness of Revenue Management in the U.S. Golf Industry," *Journal of Revenue and Pricing Management* 1, no. 4 (2003): 332–344; Sheryl E. Kimes and Jochen Wirtz, "Has Revenue Management Become Acceptable? Findings from an International Study and the Perceived Fairness of Rate Fences," *Journal of Service Research* 6 (November 2003): in press; Richard Metters and Vicente Vargas, "Yield Management for the Nonprofit Sector," *Journal of Service Research* 1 (February 1999): 215–226; and Anthony Ingold, Una McMahon-Beattie, and Ian Yeoman, eds., *Yield Management Strategies for the Service Industries*, 2d ed. (London: Continuum, 2000).
12. Hermann Simon and Robert J. Dolan, "Price Customization," *Marketing Management* (Fall 1998): 11–17.
13. Scott Adams, *The Dilbert^{TM} Future—Thriving on Business Stupidities in the 21st Century* (New York: HarperBusiness, 1997), 160.
14. Sheryl E. Kimes, "A Retrospective Commentary on Discounting in the Hotel Industry: A New Approach," *Cornell Hotel and Restaurant Administration Quarterly* 43 (August 2002): 92–93.
15. Parts of this section are based on Jochen Wirtz, Sheryl E. Kimes, Jeannette P. T. Ho, and Paul Patterson, "Revenue Management: Resolving Potential Customer Conflicts," *Journal of Revenue and Pricing Management* 2, no. 3 (2003).
16. Peter J. Danaher, "Optimal Pricing of New Subscription Services: An Analysis of a Market Experiment," *Marketing Science* 21 (Spring 2002): 119–129; and Gilia E. Fruchter and Ram C. Rao, "Optimal Membership Fee and Usage Price Over Time for a Network Service," *Journal of Services Research* 4 (2001): 3–15.
17. "Needed: Straight Talk about Cellphone Calling Plans," *Consumer Reports* (February 2003): 18.
18. See, for example, Anita Sharpe, "The Operation Was a Success; The Bill Was Quite a Mess," *Wall Street Journal,* September 17, 1997.

CHAPTER 7

Distributing Services

Companies best equipped for the twenty-first century will consider investment in real time systems as essential to maintaining their competitive edge and keeping their customers.

—REGIS MCKENNA

Think globally, act locally.

—JOHN NAISBITT

Delivering a service to customers involves decisions about where, when, and how. The rapid growth of the Internet and now also broadband mobile communications means that service marketing strategy must address issues of place, cyberspace, and time, paying at least as much attention to speed, scheduling, and electronic access as to the more traditional notion of physical location. Furthermore, with the heat of globalization, important questions are being raised about the design and implementation of international service marketing strategies.

In this chapter, we discuss the role that delivery plays in service marketing strategy locally and globally and explore the following questions:

1. How can services be distributed? What are the main modes of distribution?
2. What are the distinctive challenges of distributing people processing, possession processing, and information-based services?
3. What are the implications for a firm of delivering through both physical and electronic channels?
4. What roles should intermediaries play in distributing services?
5. What are the drivers of globalization of services and their distribution?

DISTRIBUTION IN A SERVICES CONTEXT

Mention distribution, and many people think of moving boxes to retailers and/or other channels for sale to end users. In a services context, we often have nothing to move, as "experiences" are not being shipped and stored, and informational transactions are increasingly conducted via electronic, not physical, channels. How, then, does distribution work in a services context? In a typical sales cycle, distribution embraces three interrelated elements:

1. *Information and promotion flow.* This element refers to the distribution of information and promotion materials relating to the service offer. The objective is to get the customer interested in buying the service.

2. *Negotiation flow*. This element focuses on reaching an agreement on the service features and configuration and the terms of the offer so that a purchase contract can be closed. The objective is to sell the right to use a service (e.g., sell a reservation or a ticket).
3. *Product flow*. Many services, especially those involving people or possession processing, require physical facilities for delivery. Here, distribution strategy requires development of a network of local sites. For information-processing services, such as weather forecasts, Internet banking transactions, distance education by satellite, broadcast news, and entertainment, the product flow can be undertaken via electronic channels, using one or more centralized sites.

Distinguishing between Distribution of Supplementary and Core Services

Distribution can relate to the core service as well to supplementary services. That is an important distinction, as many core services require a physical location, which severely restricts distribution. For instance, Club Med holidays can be consumed only at Club Med Villages, and a live performance of a Broadway show must take place at a theater in Manhattan (until it goes on tour). However, many of the supplementary services are informational in nature and can be distributed widely and cost-effectively via other means. Prospective Club Med customers can get information and consultation from a travel agent—face to face, online, by phone, or even by mail—and then make a booking through one of those channels. Similarly, tickets to the theater can be purchased through a ticketing agency, without the need for an advance trip to the physical facility.

As we look at the eight petals of the Flower of Service, we can see that no fewer than five supplementary services are information based (Figure 7-1). Information,

FIGURE 7-1 Information and Physical Processes of the Augmented Service Product

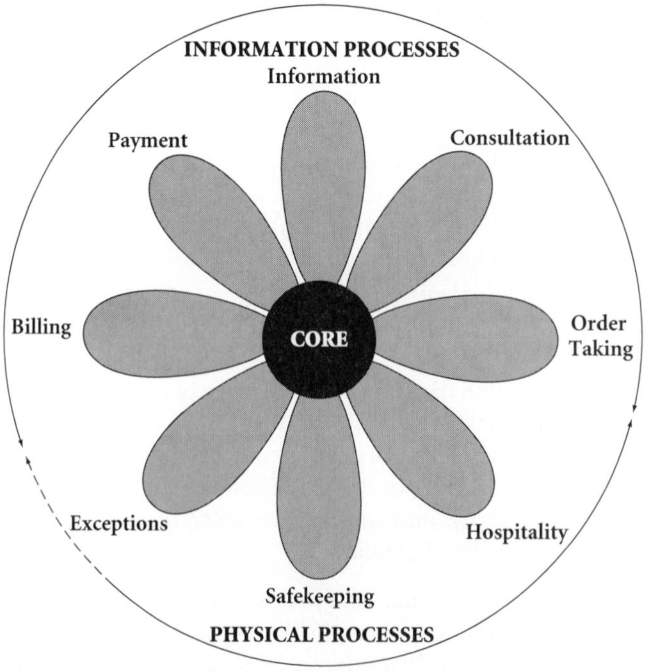

consultation, ordertaking, billing, and payment (e.g., via credit cards or electronic funds transfer) can all be transmitted by using the digital language of computers. Even service businesses that involve physical core products, such as retailing and repair, are shifting delivery of many supplementary services to the Internet, closing physical branches, and relying on speedy business logistics to enable a new strategy of arm's-length transactions with their customers.

The distribution of information, consultation, and order taking (or reservations and ticket sales) has reached extremely sophisticated levels in some global service industries, requiring a number of carefully integrated channels targeted at key customer segments. For instance, Starwood Hotels & Resorts Worldwide, whose 725 hotels include such brands as Sheraton, Westin, and St. Regis, has more than 30 global sales offices (GSOs) around the world to manage customer relationships with key global accounts, offering a one-stop solution to corporate travel planners, wholesalers, meeting planners, incentive houses, and major travel organizations.[1] The company has also set up 12 customer servicing centers (CSCs) around the world to provide one-stop customer service for its guests, covering worldwide hotel reservations, enrollment and redemption of Starwood's loyalty program, and general customer service. Guests need to call only one toll-free number to book any Starwood hotel. Reservations can also be made through electronic channels, including the Westin and Sheraton Web sites.

THE TYPE OF CONTACT: OPTIONS FOR SERVICE DELIVERY

Decisions on where, when, and how to deliver service have an important impact on the nature of customers' service experiences because they determine the types of encounters, if any, with service personnel and the price and other costs incurred to obtain the service. Several factors shape distribution and delivery strategies. A key question is: Does the nature of the service or the firm's positioning strategy require customers to be in direct physical contact with its personnel, equipment, and facilities? (As we saw in Chapter 1, this is inevitable for people-processing services but optional for other categories.) If so, do customers have to visit the facilities of the service organization, or will the latter send personnel and equipment to customers' own sites? Alternatively, can transactions between provider and customer be completed at arm's length through the use of either telecommunications or physical channels of distribution?

Another issue concerns the firm's strategy in terms of distribution sites: Should it maintain a single outlet or offer to serve customers through multiple outlets at different locations? The possible options, combining both type of contact and number of sites, can be seen in Table 7-1, which presents examples of six possibilities.

TABLE 7-1 Method of Service Delivery

	Availability of Service Outlets	
Nature of Interaction between Customer and Service Organization	***Single Site***	***Multiple Sites***
Customer goes to service organization	Theater Barbershop	Bus service Fast-food chain
Service organization comes to customer	House painting Mobile car wash	Mail delivery Auto club road service
Customer and service organization transact at arm's length (mail or electronic communications)	Credit card company Local TV station	Broadcast network Telephone company

Customers Visit the Service Site

The convenience of service factory locations and operational schedules assumes great importance when a customer has to be physically present—either throughout service delivery or even only to initiate and terminate the transaction. Elaborate statistical analysis, in the form of retail gravity models, is sometimes used to aid decisions on where to locate supermarkets relative to prospective customers' homes and workplaces. Traffic counts and pedestrian counts help to establish how many prospective customers pass by certain locations in a day. Construction of an expressway or the introduction of a new bus or rail service may have a significant effect on travel patterns and, in turn, determine which sites are now more desirable and which less so.

The tradition of having customers visit the service site for services other than in the people-processing category is now being challenged by advances in telecommunications and business logistics, which are leading to a shift to services delivered at arm's length.

Service Providers Go to Their Customers

For some types of services, the supplier visits the customer. Aramark, a firm that provides food services and facilities maintenance to schools and hospitals to sports stadiums and prisons must necessarily bring its tools and personnel to the customer's site because the need is location specific. Going to the customer's site is unavoidable whenever the object of the service is an immovable physical item, such as a tree to be pruned, installed machinery to be repaired, or a house needing pest-control treatment.

In other instances, going to the customer is optional. Because it's more expensive and time consuming for service personnel and their equipment to travel to the customer than vice versa, the trend has been toward requiring customers to come to the service provider instead (fewer doctors make house calls nowadays!). In remote areas, such as Alaska or Canada's Northwest Territory, service providers often fly to visit their customers because the latter find it so difficult to travel. Australia is famous for its Royal Flying Doctor Service, whose physicians fly to make house calls at farms and stations in the Outback.

In general, service providers are more likely to visit corporate customers at their premises than to visit individuals in their homes, reflecting the larger volume associated with business-to-business transactions. However, there may be a profitable niche in serving individuals who are willing to pay a premium for the convenience of receiving personal visits. One young veterinary doctor has built her business around house calls to sick pets. She has found that customers are glad to pay extra for a service that not only saves them time but also is less stressful for the pet than waiting in a crowded veterinary clinic full of other animals and their worried owners. Other consumer services of this nature are mobile car washing, office and in-home catering, and made-to-measure tailoring services for businesspeople.

A growing service activity involves the rental of both equipment and labor for special occasions or in response to customers wishing to increase their productive capacity during busy periods. Service Perspectives 7-1 describes the business-to-business services of Aggreko, an international company that rents generating and cooling equipment around the world.

Service Transaction Is Conducted at Arm's Length

Dealing with a service firm through arm's-length transactions may mean that a customer never sees the service facilities and never meets the service personnel face to face. An important consequence is that the number of service encounters tends to be fewer; those encounters that do take place with service personnel are more likely to be made by telephone or even more remotely, by mail, fax, or e-mail.

Repair services for small pieces of equipment sometimes require customers to ship the product to a maintenance facility, where it will be serviced and then returned again

SERVICE PERSPECTIVES 7-1

POWER AND TEMPERATURE CONTROL FOR RENT

You probably think of electricity as a power source coming from a distant power station and of air-conditioning and heating in a large structure as fixed installations. So how would you deal with the following challenges?

- Luciano Pavarotti is giving an open-air concert in Münster, Germany, and the organizers require an uninterruptible source of electrical power for the duration of the concert, independent of the local electricity supply.
- A tropical cyclone has devastated the small mining town of Pannawonica in Western Australia, destroying everything in its path, including power lines, and it's urgent that electrical power be restored as soon as possible so that the town and its infrastructure can be rebuilt.
- In Amsterdam, organizers of the World Championship Indoor Windsurfing competition need to power 27 wind turbines that will be installed along the length of a huge indoor pool to create winds with a force of 5 to 6 on the Beaufort scale (19 to 31 mph).
- A U.S. Navy submarine needs a shore-based source of power when it spends time in a remote Norwegian port.
- Sri Lanka faces an acute shortage of electricity-generating capability when water levels fall dangerously low at the country's major hydroelectric dams because of insufficient monsoon rains two years in a row.
- A large, power-generating plant in Oklahoma urgently seeks temporary capacity to replace one of its cooling towers, destroyed the previous day in a tornado.

These are all challenges faced and met by a company called Aggreko, which describes itself as "The World Leader in Temporary Utility Rental Solutions." Operating from more than 110 depots in 20 countries around the world, Aggreko rents a "fleet" of mobile electricity generators, oil-free air compressors, and temperature control devices ranging from water chillers and industrial air conditioners to giant heaters and dehumidifiers.

Aggreko's customer base is dominated by large companies and government agencies. Although a lot of its business comes from needs that are foreseen far in advance, such as backup operations during planned factory maintenance or a package of services during the filming of a James Bond movie, the firm is also poised to resolve problems arising unexpectedly from emergencies.

Much of the firm's rental equipment is contained in soundproofed, boxlike structures that can be shipped anywhere in the world and coupled to create the specific type and level of electrical power output or climate-control capability required by the client. Consultation, installation, and ongoing technical support add value to the core service. Says a company brochure: "Emphasis is placed on solving customer problems rather than just renting equipment." Some customers have a clear idea of their needs in advance, others require advice on how to develop innovative and cost-effective solutions to what may be unique problems, and still others are desperate to restore power that has been lost because of an emergency. In this last instance, speed is of the essence, as downtime can be extremely expensive, and lives may depend on the promptness of Aggreko's response.

Delivering service requires that Aggreko ship its equipment to the customer's site so that the needed power or temperature control can be available at the right place and time. Following the Pannawonica cyclone, Aggreko's West Australian team swung into action, rapidly organizing the dispatch of some 30 generators ranging in size from 60 to 750 kVA, along with cabling, refueling tankers, and other equipment. The generators were transported by means of four "road trains," each comprising a giant tractor unit hauling three 40-ft. (13 m) trailers. A full infrastructure team of technicians and additional equipment were flown in on two Hercules aircraft. The Aggreko technicians remained on site for 6 weeks, providing 24-hour service while the town was being rebuilt.

Source: Aggreko's "International Magazine," 1997; Web site *www.aggreko.com*, March 2003.

by parcel service, with the option of paying extra for express shipment. Many service providers have implemented integrated solutions with the help of courier firms, which have developed impressive solutions for their clients. The solutions range from storage and express delivery of spare parts for aircrafts as and when needed (b2b delivery), and pickup of defective mobile phones from customers' homes and delivery of the repaired phone back to the customer (b2c—business to customer—pickup and delivery).

Any information-based product can be delivered almost instantaneously through telecommunication channels to any point where a suitable reception terminal exists. As a result, physical logistics services now find themselves competing with telecommunications services. When we were writing this book, for instance, we had a choice of mail or courier services for physical shipments of the chapters in either paper or disk form. We could also fax the materials or use e-mail to send the chapters electronically. In fact, we used all three methods: Hand-drawn images were faxed, print advertisements were couriered, and the main text and chapters were sent via e-mail.

Channel Preferences Vary among Consumers

The use of various channels to deliver the same service—say, banking services delivered via the Internet, mobile phone interface, voice response system, call center, automatic teller machines, and via face to face in a branch, or visits at the customer's home—not only has various cost implications for the bank but also drastically affects the nature of the service experience for the customer. Recent research has explored consumer choice of personal, impersonal, and self-service channels and has identified the following key drivers.[2]

- The more complex and the higher the perceived risk associated with a service delivery or purchase, the higher the reliance on personal channels. For example, customers are happy to apply for credit cards using remote channels but prefer a face-to-face transaction when obtaining a mortgage.
- Consumers with higher confidence and knowledge about a service and/or the channel are more likely to use impersonal and self-service channels.
- Customers who look for the instrumental aspects of a transaction prefer more convenience, and this often means the use of impersonal and self-service channels. Customers with social motives tend to use personal channels.
- Convenience is a key driver of channel choice for the majority of consumers. Service convenience means saving consumers' time and effort rather than money. A customer's search for convenience is not confined to the purchase of core products but also includes convenient times and places. People want easy access to supplementary services, too, especially information, reservations, and problem solving. Customers are busy with their personal lives and do not have a lot of time to handle such activities as banking, insurance, and even shopping.

DECISIONS ABOUT PLACE AND TIME

How should service managers make decisions on the places where service is delivered and the times when it is available? The answer is likely to reflect customer needs and expectations, competitive activity, and the nature of the service operation. As noted earlier, the distribution strategies used for some of the supplementary service elements may differ from those used to deliver the core product. As a customer, for instance, you are probably willing to go to a particular location at a specific time to attend a sporting or entertainment event. But you probably want greater flexibility and convenience when reserving a seat in advance, so you may expect the reservations service to be open for extended hours, to offer booking and credit card payment by phone or Web, and to deliver tickets through postal or electronic channels.

Where Should Service Be Delivered in a Bricks-and-Mortar Context?

Deciding where to locate a service facility that will be visited by customers involves very different considerations from decisions related to locating the backstage elements, where cost considerations, productivity, and access to labor are often key determinants. In the former case, questions of customer convenience and preference come to the fore. Frequently purchased services that are not easily differentiated from competitors' need to be easily accessible from customers' homes or workplaces. Examples are retail banks and quick-service restaurants. However, customers may be willing to travel farther for specialty services that fit their needs well.

Locational Constraints Although customer convenience is important, operational requirements set tight constraints for some services. Airports, for instance, are often inconveniently located relative to travelers' homes, offices, or destinations. Because of noise and environmental factors, finding suitable sites for construction of new airports or expansion of existing ones is a very difficult task. (A governor of Massachusetts was once asked what would be an acceptable location for a second airport to serve Boston; he thought for a moment and then responded, "Nebraska!") As a result, airport sites are often far from the city centers, and the only way to make them less inconvenient for passengers is to install fast rail links, such as London's Heathrow Express or the futuristic 260 mph (420 km/h) service to Shanghai's new airport, the first in the world to use magnetic levitation technology. A different type of location constraint is imposed by

People Get Upset When Electronic Distribution Systems Let Them Down

other geographic factors, such as terrain and climate. By definition, ski resorts have to be in the mountains and beach resorts on the coast.

The need for economies of scale is another operational issue that may restrict choice of locations. Major hospitals offer many different health care services—even a medical school—at a single location, requiring a very large facility. Customers requiring complex, in-patient treatment must go to the service factory rather than be treated at home, although an ambulance (or even a helicopter) can be sent to pick them up. This is particularly necessary when specialized medical and nursing care is available in only a limited number of hospitals possessing the necessary equipment and skills. Medical specialists, as opposed to general practitioners, often find it convenient to locate their offices close to a hospital because it saves them time when they need to use specialized equipment or services in order to operate on their patients.

Ministores An interesting innovation among multisite service firms has been to create service factories on a very small scale in order to maximize coverage within a geographic area. Automation is one approach, as exemplified by the ATM, which offers many of the functions of a bank branch within a small self-service machine that can be located within stores, hospitals, colleges, airports, and office buildings. Another approach to smaller facilities results from rethinking the links between the front- and backstage operations. Taco Bell is often cited for its innovative K-Minus strategy, involving restaurants without kitchens.[3] The firm now confines food preparation to a central commissary from which prepared meals are shipped to restaurants and other "points of access," such as mobile food carts, where they can be reheated prior to serving.

Sometimes, firms purchase space from another provider in a complementary field. Examples include minibank branches within supermarkets and food outlets, such as Dunkin' Donuts and Subway, sharing space with a quick-service restaurant, such as Burger King.

Locating in Multipurpose Facilities The most obvious locations for consumer services are close to where customers live or work. Modern buildings are often designed to be multipurpose, featuring not only office or production space but also such services as a bank (or at least an ATM), a restaurant, a hair salon, several stores, and even a health club. Some companies even include a children's day care facility onsite to make life easier for busy working parents.

Interest is growing in siting retail and other services on transportation routes or even in bus, rail, and air terminals. Major oil companies are developing chains of retail stores to complement the fuel pumps at their service stations, thus offering customers the convenience of one-stop shopping for fuel, car supplies, food, and household products. Freeway truckstops often include laundromats, toilets, ATMs, fax machines, restaurants, and inexpensive hotels, in addition to a variety of vehicle maintenance and repair services for both trucks and cars. In one of the most interesting new retailing developments, airport terminals—designed as part of the infrastructure for air transportation services—are being transformed from nondescript areas where passengers and their bags are processed into vibrant shopping malls. (See Service Perspectives 7-2.)

When Should Service Be Delivered?

In the past, most retail and professional services in industrialized countries followed a traditional and rather restricted schedule that limited service availability to about 40 to 50 hours a week. In large measure, this routine reflected social norms (and even legal requirements or union agreements) as to what were appropriate hours for people to work and for enterprises to sell things. The situation caused a lot of inconvenience

SERVICE PERSPECTIVES 7-2

FROM AIRPORTS TO AIR MALLS

Large airports used to be places where thousands of people spent time waiting with little to keep them occupied. Airports were often bound by contract to a single food operator, which translated into expensive drinks and low-quality food at high prices. Other than visiting stores selling newspapers, magazines, and paperback books, travelers didn't have much opportunity for shopping unless they wanted to spend money on expensive (and often tawdry) souvenirs. The one exception was the tax-free shop at international airports, where opportunities to save money created a brisk trade in alcohol, perfumes, tobacco, and consumer products (e.g., cameras). Today, however, some airports have terminals that have been transformed into shopping malls. London's Heathrow Airport even has a branch of Harrods, the famous department store.

Three factors make investments in airport retailing very appealing. One is the upscale demographics of airline passengers. A second is that many passengers have plenty of time to spare while waiting for their flights. Finally, many existing terminal interiors have free space that can be put to profitable use. As terminals are expanded, new retail sites can be included as an integral part of the design.

New York's La Guardia Airport retained a Boston-based firm, MarketPlace Development, to redevelop its retailing activities in its newly renovated central terminal. At "La Guardia Marketplace," national-brand restaurants and stores, from Sbarro to Sunglass Hut, have replaced overpriced cafeteria-style food vendors and generic drugstores. Tighter security requirements mean that passengers must now check in earlier for flights and so have even more time to spend at the airport. One passenger, relaxing in La Guardia's bright, three-story atrium after making some purchases, contrasted the new facility favorably against the old, which she said "was sort of what I had expected in a New York airport: dull, kind of dirty, and not much to do."

The first (and still the most successful) custom-built airport retail complex in the United States is the Pittsburgh Air Mall, created as part of a new airport terminal and operated under a 15-year contract by BAA International, the largest global airport operator. Pittsburgh is an important hub airport serving 20 million passengers a year, most of whom are domestic travelers. Goods and services available in the Air Mall's more than 100 stores and restaurants range from tasty take-out sandwiches for passengers who don't expect a meal on their discount-priced flight, to $15 massages for tired travelers with aching backs. Perhaps the most striking statistic is that sales per square foot are four to five times those of typical U.S. regional shopping centers!

Source: Eileen Kinsella, "Noshing at New York's LaGuardia Airport," *Wall Street Journal* (January 21, 1998); BAA International *www.baa.co.uk*, accessed March 2003.

for working people who either had to shop during their lunch break (if the stores themselves didn't close for lunch) or on Saturdays (if management chose to remain open a sixth day). Historically, the idea of opening on Sunday was strongly discouraged in most Christian cultures and often prohibited by law, reflecting a long tradition based on religious practice. Among commercial services, only those devoted to entertainment and relaxation, such as cinemas, pubs, restaurants, and sporting facilities, geared their opening times toward weekends and evening hours when their customers were free. Even so, they often faced restrictions on hours of operation, especially on Sundays.

Today, the situation is different. For some highly responsive service operations, the standard has become "24/7" service: 24 hours a day, 7 days a week around the world. For an overview of the factors behind the move to more extended hours, see Management Memo 7-1. Nevertheless, some firms resist the trend to seven-day

MANAGEMENT MEMO 7-1

FACTORS THAT ENCOURAGE EXTENDED OPERATING HOURS

The move toward extended operating hours and seven-day operations has been most noticeable in the United States and Canada but is now spreading rapidly to many other countries around the world. At least five factors are driving this trend:

1. *Economic pressure from consumers.* The growing number of two-income families and single wage earners who live alone need time outside normal working hours to shop and use other services. Once one store or firm in any given area extends its hours to meet the needs of these market segments, competitors often feel obliged to follow. Retail chains have often led the way in this respect.
2. *Changes in legislation.* A second factor has been the decline, lamented by some, of support for the traditional religious view that a specific day (Sunday in predominantly Christian cultures) should be legislated as a day of rest for one and all, regardless of religious affiliation. In a multicultural society, of course, it's a moot point which day should be designated as special—for observant Jews and Seventh Day Adventists, Saturday is the Sabbath; for Muslims, Friday is the holy day; and agnostics or atheists are presumably indifferent. There has been a gradual erosion of such legislation in Western nations in recent years, although it is still firmly in place in some countries and locations. Switzerland, for example, still closes down most retail activities on Sundays—except for bread, which people like to buy freshly baked on Sunday mornings.
3. *Economic incentives to improve asset utilization.* A great deal of capital is often tied up in service facilities. The incremental cost of extending hours is often relatively modest, especially when part-time employees can be hired without paying them either overtime or benefits. If extending hours reduces crowding and increases revenues, it is economically attractive. Costs are involved in shutting down and reopening a facility like a supermarket, yet climate control and some lighting must be left running all night, and security personnel must be paid to keep an eye on the place. Even if the number of extra customers served is minimal, remaining open 24 hours has both operational and marketing advantages.
4. *Availability of employees to work during "unsocial" hours.* Changing lifestyles and a desire for part-time employment have combined to create a growing labor pool of people who are willing to work evenings and nights. Some of these workers are students looking for part-time work outside their classroom hours; some are "moonlighting," holding a full-time job by day and earning additional income by night; some are parents juggling child care responsibilities; others simply prefer to work by night and relax or sleep by day; still others are glad to obtain any paid employment, regardless of hours.
5. *Automated self-service facilities.* Self-service equipment has become increasingly reliable and user friendly. Many machines now accept card-based payments in addition to coins and banknotes. Installing unattended machines may be economically feasible in places that cannot support a staffed facility. Unless a machine requires frequent servicing or is particularly vulnerable to vandalism, the incremental cost of going from limited hours to 24-hour operation is minimal. In fact, it may be much simpler to leave machines running all the time than to turn them on and off, especially if they are placed in widely scattered locations.

operations. Atlanta-based Chick-fil-A, a highly successful restaurant chain, declares that "being closed on Sunday is part of our value proposition" and claims that giving managers and crews a day off is a factor in the firm's extremely low turnover rate.

SERVICE DELIVERY IN CYBERSPACE

Technological developments during the past 20 years have had a remarkable impact on the way in which services are produced and delivered. Developments in telecommunications and computer technology in particular continue to result in many innovations in service delivery. For example, in an effort to boost productivity and remain competitive in an increasingly competitive marketplace, banks in many countries have embarked on programs of closing bank branches and shifting customers to cheaper, electronic banking channels.

According to the American Interactive Consumer survey results conducted by the Dieringer Research Group, three of eight adults in the United States will be using online banking by 2002.[4] However, not all customers like to use self-service equipment, so migration of customers to new electronic channels may require different strategies for different segments, as well as recognition that some proportion of customers will never voluntarily shift from their preferred high-contact delivery environments. An alternative that appeals to many people, perhaps because it uses a familiar technology, is banking by voice telephone.

Service Delivery Innovations Facilitated by Technology

More recently, entrepreneurs have taken advantage of the Internet to create new services that can be delivered through electronic channels accessed by computers in customers' homes or offices. The following innovations are of particular interest:

- Development of "smart" mobile telephones and PDAs (personal digital assistants) that can link users, wherever they may be, to the Internet.
- Use of voice recognition technology, which allows customers to give information and request service simply by speaking into a phone or microphone.
- Creation of Web sites that can provide information, take orders, and even serve as a delivery channel for information-based services.
- Commercialization of smart cards containing a microchip that can store detailed information about the customer and act as an electronic purse containing digital money. The ultimate in self-service banking will be when you can not only use a smart card as an electronic wallet for a wide array of transactions but also refill it from a special card reader connected to your computer modem.

Singly or in combination, electronic channels offer a complement or alternative to traditional physical channels for delivering information-based services. Best Practice in Action 7-1 describes a multichannel application for electronic banking.

E-Commerce: The Move to Cyberspace

As a distribution channel, the Internet facilitates information flow, negotiation flow, service flow, transaction flow, and promotion flow. Compared to the traditional channels, the Net is definitely better for conducting research on consumer information-seeking and search behaviors, for getting feedback from consumers in a short period of time, and for creating communities online to market the products and services, to name a few opportunities.[5]

Among the factors luring customers into virtual stores are convenience, ease of research (obtaining information and searching for desired items or services), better prices, and broad selection. Enjoying 24-hour service with prompt delivery is particularly appealing to customers whose busy lives leave them short of time.

Many retailers, such as the giant bookstore chain Barnes and Noble, have developed a strong Internet presence to complement their physical stores in an effort to counter competition from such "cyberspace retailers" as Amazon.com, which has no stores. However, adding an Internet channel to an already established physical channel is a double-edged strategy. It requires high capital setup, and no one can be sure whether the investment will definitely lead to long-term profits and high growth potential.[6] Another major chain of booksellers, Borders, has chosen to partner with Amazon.com and has contracted with the latter to operate its Web site.

BEST PRACTICE IN ACTION 7-1

MULTI-CHANNEL BANKING WITHOUT BRANCHES AT FIRST DIRECT

First Direct, a division of HSBC, has become famous as the originator of the concept of a bank with no branches. First Direct serves more than a million customers throughout the United Kingdom (and abroad) through call centers located far from the financial powerhouses of London, a Web site, text messaging on mobile phones, and access to HSBC's large network of ATMs.

Launched in 1989 as the world's first all-telephone bank, accessible 24/7, First Direct stimulated an industrywide shift from high-contact bank branches to low-contact banking by telephone and ATMs. Responding to demands for home banking, First Direct began by introducing a PC-based home banking service that did not require customers to use an Internet provider and subsequently moved to full Internet banking in 1999.

With other financial service firms starting to offer similar services at competitive rates, the bank took another leap forward. In January 2000, First Direct—by now describing itself as "the largest virtual bank in the world"—announced that it would transform itself into an e-bank that would set the standard for e-banking. At the heart of the strategy is a multichannel approach to banking that combines the bank's experience of telephone banking with the strengths of the Internet and the versatility of the mobile phone and WAP (Wireless Application Protocol) technologies to deliver a superior service at fiercely competitive prices. As noted by chief executive Alan Hughes: "We are the first bank in the world to reengineer our entire business for the e-age. The scale of the initiative creates a new category of e-banking and sets a benchmark for the industry around the globe. More than a bank, firstdirect.com will be the first Internet banking store."[1]

A central element in this strategy is to offer Britain's most comprehensive mobile phone banking service, recognizing that more than 70 percent of all adults in the United Kingdom either own or use a mobile phone. Through SMS (Short Message Service) text messages, First Direct customers have access to ministatements on up to three accounts and can be advised when credits or debits enter or leave the account. In addition, customers are alerted automatically if their accounts go into the red. The service is complemented by WAP Internet mobile phone banking, which enables customers to carry out transactions at the push of a button on their WAP phones. By 2003, 55 percent of all customer contacts were electronic.

Although, the core person-to-person voice telephone service still remains the backbone of the bank's activities, in January 2003 the bank began testing an interactive online help agent called Cara, who moves, talks and gestures as she responds to users' questions. Jonathan Etheridge, head of E-Futures at First Direct observed: "For many years we have been leaders in customer service on the telephone, now Cara gives us the opportunity to learn how to bring some of the First Direct personality to the Web. Cara is the first step on a road which I ultimately see will bridge the gap between the relatively impersonal world of the Internet and the much richer experience of a real person on the phone."[2]

[1] *www.firstdirect.com*, accessed May 2001.

[2] *www.firstdirect.com*, accessed March 2003.

Source: Based on material in Delphine Parmenter, Jean-Claude Larréché, and Christopher Lovelock, "First Direct: Branchless Banking." Fontainebleau, France: INSEAD, 1997, and press releases distributed on *www.firstdirect.com*, accessed 2001, 2002, and March 2003.

Web sites are becoming increasingly sophisticated but also more user friendly. They often simulate the services of a well-informed sales assistant in steering customers toward items that are likely to be of interest. Some even provide the opportunity for "live" e-mail dialogue with helpful customer service personnel. Facilitating searches is another useful service on many sites, ranging from looking at what books by a particular author are available to finding schedules of flights between two cities on a specific date.

Particularly exciting are recent developments that link Web sites, customer relationship management (CRM) systems, and mobile telephony. Integrating mobile devices into the service delivery infrastructure can be used for (1) increasing the accessibility of services, (2) alerting by delivering the right information or interaction at the right time, and (3) updating to create and maintain up-to-date, real-time information.[7] For example, customers can set stock alerts on their broker's Web site and get an e-mail or SMS alert when a certain price or transaction has been conducted (alert), or they can obtain real-time information on stock prices (updating). Customers can then respond by directly trading, using their mobile phones as interface (accessing). Singapore Airlines (SIA) recently launched a departure time alert service, whereby customers can specify on their customized SIA Web site that there should be an SMS or e-mail alert if their departure time is delayed, so that they can adjust their own timing accordingly.

Almost every business process within an organization involves information in some form. Externally, the price of technology has fallen so low and access has become ever wider that service firms must take advantage of it wherever they can in developing distribution strategy. To be able to do so, argues Frances Cairncross, management editor of *The Economist,* senior managers will have to think differently about their company's structure and be prepared to modify its culture.[8]

THE ROLE OF INTERMEDIARIES

Many service organizations find it cost-effective to delegate certain tasks, usually supplementary service elements. For instance, despite their greater use of telephone call centers and the Internet, cruise lines and resort hotels still rely on travel agents to handle a significant portion of their customer interactions, such as giving out information, taking reservations, accepting payment, and ticketing. Of course, many manufacturers rely on the services of distributors or retailers to stock and sell their physical products to end users, while also taking on responsibility for such supplementary services as information, advice, order taking, delivery, installation, billing and payment, and certain types of problem solving. In some cases, manufacturers may also handle certain types of repairs and upgrades.

Delegating Specific Service Elements

How should a service provider work in partnership with one or more intermediaries to deliver a complete service package to customers? In Figure 7-2, we use the Flower of

FIGURE 7-2 Splitting Responsibilities for Supplementary Service Elements

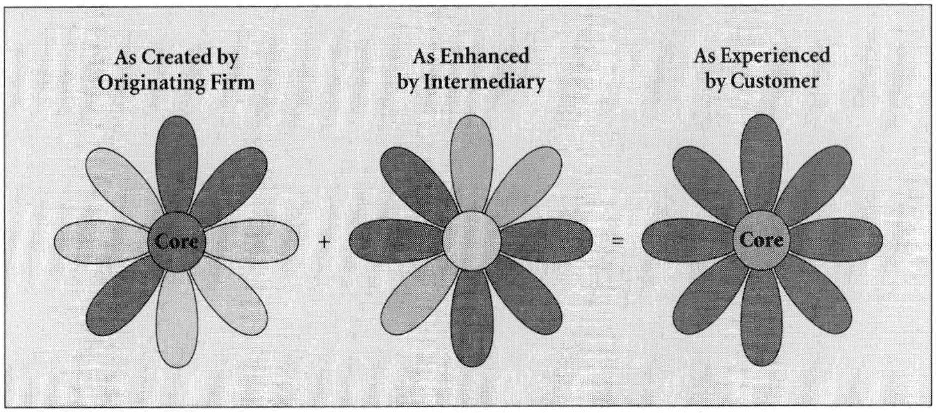

Service framework to depict an example in which the core product is delivered by the originating supplier, together with certain supplementary elements in the informational, consultation, and exceptions categories. Delivery of the remaining supplementary services packaged with this offering, however, has been delegated to an intermediary to complete the offering as experienced by the customer. In other instances, several specialist outsourcers might be involved as intermediaries for specific elements. The challenge for the original supplier is to act as guardian of the overall process, ensuring that each element offered by intermediaries fits the overall service concept to create a consistent and seamless branded service experience.

Franchising

Even delivery of the core product can be outsourced to an intermediary. This is the essence of business-format franchising. Franchising has become a popular way to expand delivery of an effective service concept embracing all 7Ps to multiple sites, without the level of investment capital that would be needed for rapid expansion of company-owned and -managed sites. It is an appealing strategy for growth-oriented service firms because franchisees are highly motivated to ensure customer orientation and high-quality service operations.[9] Although most commonly associated with fast-food outlets, franchising has been applied to a wide array of both consumer and business-to-business services, as any review of the Yellow Pages directory will show. New concepts are being created and commercialized all the time in countries around the world. Among the cases featured in this book is "Aussie Pooch Mobile," which describes a successful Australian-based franchised dog-washing service (see pp. 520–532).

Nevertheless, research by Scott Shane and Chester Spell shows that there is a significant attrition rate among franchisors in the early years of a new franchise system, with one-third of all systems failing within the first 4 years and no less than three-quarters of all franchisors ceasing to exist after 12 years.[10] The researchers found that among the factors associated with success for franchisors were being able to achieve a larger size with a more recognizable brand name, offering franchisees fewer supporting services but longer-term contracts, and having fewer headquarters staff per outlet. Because growth is very important to achieve an efficient scale, some franchisors adopt a strategy known as master franchising, which involves delegating the responsibility for recruiting, training, and supporting franchisees within a given geographic area. Master franchisees are often individuals who have already succeeded as operators of an individual franchise outlet.

A franchisor recruits entrepreneurs who are willing to invest their own time and equity in managing a previously developed service concept. In return, the franchisor provides training in how to operate and market the business, sells necessary supplies, and provides promotional support at a national or regional level to augment local marketing activities, which are paid for by the franchisee but must adhere to copy and media guidelines prescribed by the franchisor.

A disadvantage of delegating activities to franchisees is that it entails some loss of control over the delivery system and thereby over how customers experience the service. Ensuring that an intermediary adopts exactly the same priorities and procedures as prescribed by the franchisor is difficult yet vital to effective quality control. Franchisors usually seek to exercise control over all aspects of the service performance through a contract that specifies adherence to tightly defined service standards, procedures, scripts, and physical presentation. Franchisors control not only output specifications but also the appearance of the servicescape, employee performance, and such elements as service timetables.

An ongoing problem is that as franchisees gain experience, they may start to resent the various fees they pay the franchisor and believe that they can operate the business better without the constraints imposed by the agreement. The resulting disputes often lead to legal fights between the two parties.

An alternative to business-format franchising is licensing another supplier to act on the original supplier's behalf to deliver the core product. Trucking companies regularly make use of independent agents instead of locating company-owned branches in each of the cities they serve. The companies may also choose to contract with independent "owner-operators," who drive their own trucks, rather than buy their own trucks and employ full-time drivers. Similarly, universities sometimes license another educational institution to deliver courses designed by the former.

Other service distribution agreements include financial services. Banks seeking to move into investment services will often act as the distributor for mutual fund products created by an investment firm that lacks extensive distribution channels of its own. Many banks also sell insurance products underwritten by an insurance company. The banks collect a commission on the sale but are not normally involved in handling claims.

The Challenge of National Distribution in Large Markets

There are important differences between marketing services within a compact geographic area and marketing services in a federal nation covering a large geographic area, such as Canada, Australia, or the United States. Physical logistics immediately become more challenging for many types of services because of the distances involved and the existence of multiple time zones. Multiculturalism is also an issue because of the growing proportion of immigrants and the presence of indigenous peoples. In addition, firms marketing across Canada have to work in two official languages: English and French. (The latter is spoken throughout Quebec, where it is the only official language; in parts of New Brunswick, which is officially bilingual; and in northeastern Ontario). Finally, there are differences within each country between the laws and tax rates of the various states or provinces and those of the respective federal governments. The challenges in Australia and Canada, however, pale in comparison to those facing service marketers in the megaeconomy of the United States.

Overseas visitors who tour the United States are often overwhelmed by the immense size of the country, surprised by the diversity of its people, astonished by the climatic and topographic variety of the landscape, and impressed by the scale and scope of some of its business undertakings. Consider some of the statistics. Marketing at a national level in the "lower 48" states of the United States involves dealing with a population of more than 280 million people and transcontinental distances that exceed 2,500 miles (4,000 km). If Hawaii and Alaska are included, the market embraces even greater distances, covering six time zones, incredible topographic variety, and all climatic zones from Arctic to tropical. From a logistical standpoint, serving customers in all 50 states might seem at least as complex as serving customers throughout, say, Europe, North Africa and the Middle East, were it not for the fact that the United States has an exceptionally well-developed communications, transportation, and distribution infrastructure.

The United States is less homogeneous than national stereotypes might suggest. As a federal nation, the United States has a diverse patchwork of government practices. In addition to observing federal laws and paying federal taxes, service businesses operating nationwide may also need to conform to relevant state and municipal laws and plan for variations in tax policies from one state to another. Because cities, counties and special districts (such as regional transit authorities) have taxing authority in many states, there are thousands of variations in sales tax across the United States! Some states deliberately seek out new business investments by promoting their lower tax rates or offering tax incentives to encourage firms to establish or relocate factories, call centers, or back-office operations.

As the U.S. population becomes increasingly mobile and multicultural, market segmentation issues have become more complex for American service marketers operating on a national scale. In addition to the varied accents and even dialects of American English, marketers encounter growing populations of immigrants (as well as visiting tourists) who speak many other languages, headed by Spanish. American economic statistics show a wider range of household incomes and personal wealth (or lack of) than is found almost anywhere else on Earth. Corporate customers, too, often present considerable diversity, although the relevant variables may be different.

Faced with an enormous and diverse domestic marketplace, most large U.S. service companies simplify their marketing and management tasks by targeting specific market segments (refer to Chapter 3). Some firms segment on a geographic basis. Others target certain groups based on demographics, lifestyle, needs, or—in a corporate context—on industry type and company size. Smaller firms wishing to operate nationally usually choose to seek out narrow market niches, a task made easier today by the growing use of Web sites and e-mail. Yet the largest national service operations face tremendous challenges as they seek to serve multiple segments across the huge geographic area encompassed by the United States. These operations must strike a balance between standardization of strategies across all the elements embraced by the 7Ps (see Chapter 1) and adaptation to local market conditions—decisions that are especially challenging when they concern high-contact services for which customers visit the delivery site in person.

To obtain the cost efficiencies needed for competitive pricing, a growing number of service firms have elected to relocate elements of their backstage operations outside the United States.

INTERNATIONALLY DISTRIBUTED SERVICES

What are the alternative ways for a service company to tap the potential of international markets? The answer depends in part on the nature of the underlying process and the delivery system. People, possession, and information-based services have vastly different requirements on an international distribution strategy.

How Service Processes Affect International Market Entry

People-Processing Services These services require direct contact with the customer. Three options present themselves:

1. *Export the service concept.* Acting alone or in partnership with local suppliers, the firm establishes a service factory in another country. The objective may be to reach out to new customers or to follow existing corporate or individual customers to new locations (or both). This approach is commonly used by chain restaurants, hotels, car rental firms, and weight-reduction clinics, where a local presence is essential in order to be able to compete. For corporate customers, the industries are likely to be in such fields as banking, professional services, and business logistics.
2. *Import customers.*[11] Customers from other countries are invited to come to a service factory with distinctive appeal or competencies in the firm's home country. People will travel from abroad to ski at outstanding resorts, such as Whistler-Blackholm in British Columbia or Vail in Colorado. If they can afford it, people may also travel for specialist medical treatment at famous hospitals and clinics, such as Massachusetts General Hospital or the Mayo Clinic.
3. *Transport customers to new locations.* In the case of passenger transportation, embarking on international service takes the form of opening new routes to desired destinations. This strategy is generally used to attract new customers, in addition to expanding the choices for existing customers.

Service Perspectives 7-3 describes some of the ways in which a major international hotel chain has developed a global presence.

SERVICE PERSPECTIVES 7-3

GROUPE ACCOR: HOTEL INNOVATION IN A GLOBAL SETTING

Paris-based Groupe Accor is one of the world's leaders in several complementary and integrated services: hotels, travel agencies, and car rentals. According to industry experts, Accor is one of a few truly global hotel companies, with 3,800 hotels and 150,000 associates, and operations in some 140 countries. Over the years, the group has proved to be a highly innovative service provider, as reflected by its in-depth market opportunity analysis, integrated offerings, and international growth strategies.

Accor has gone from being the first truly European hotel chain to one of the largest hotel chains in the world. Accor operates several distinct categories of hotels: the four-/five-star Sofitel brand, three-/four-star Novotel, three-/four-star Mercure, and two-/three-star Ibis. Accor has also pioneered an easily prefabricated replicable budget hotel concept known as the Formula 1 chain. In the United States, Accor operates the Motel 6 chain of budget motels and Red Roof Inns and has plans for other acquisitions. Care is given to maintaining the distinctive identities of each of its hotel brands.

Accor CEO Jean-Marc Espalioux seeks to give the company the integrated structure it needs to operate and compete on a global basis. Hotel activities have been restructured into three strategic segments, reflecting their market positioning. There are also two functional divisions. The first, a global services division, is being created to spearhead the major functions common to all hotel activities: information systems, reservation systems, maintenance and technical assistance, purchasing, key accounts, and partnerships and synergy between hotel and other activities. The second, the hotel development division, is structured by brand and by region and is responsible for working with the management of each hotel brand to develop marketing, service development, and growth strategies. Says Espalioux:

> In view of the revolution in the service sector which is now taking place, I do not see any future for purely national hotel chains—except for very specific niche markets with special architecture and locations, such as Raffles in Singapore or the Ritz in Paris. National chains can't invest enough money.[1]

The group is continuing its internationalization drive, focusing on further consolidating and integrating its network, as well as building a presence in such emerging markets as Poland, Hungary, and other ex-Soviet bloc countries. Mr. Espalioux, the chief executive, is also very aware that the underlying obstacle to successful globalization in services is people:

> Globalization brings considerable challenges which are often underestimated. The principal difficulty is getting our local management to adhere to the values of the group. [They] must understand our market and culture, for example, and we have to learn about theirs.[2]

Because international cooperation, communication, and teamwork are integral to achieving global consistency, Accor has eliminated, as much as possible, hierarchy, rigid job descriptions and titles, and even organizational charts. Employees are encouraged to interact as much as possible both with their colleagues and with guests. Employees define the limits of their jobs within the context of the overall "customer experience" and are recognized and rewarded on how well they meet these definitions. In addition to these structural and organizational initiatives, video conferencing and other technologies are used extensively to create and reinforce a common, global culture among Accor employees around the world. All the group's European hotels are linked through a sophisticated IT (information technology) network, which may eventually be expanded worldwide.

Sources: Andrew Jack, "The Global Company: Why There Is No Future for National Hotel Chains," *Financial Times* (10 October, 1997); W. Chan Kim and Renee Mauborgne, "Value Innovation: The Strategic Logic of High Growth," *Harvard Business Review* (January–February 1997): 121–123; and Ken Irons, *The World of Superservice: Creating Profit through a Passion for Customer Service* (London: Addison-Wesley, 1997), 121–123; and the firm's Web site, *www.accor.fr*, accessed January 2000 and March 2003.

Possession-Processing Services This category involves services to the customer's physical possessions: repair and maintenance, freight transport, cleaning, and warehousing. Most services in this category require an ongoing local presence, regardless of whether customers drop off items at a service facility or personnel visit the customer's site. Sometimes, however, expert personnel may be flown in from a base in another country. In a few instances, a transportable item of equipment may be shipped to a foreign service center for repair, maintenance, or upgrade. Similar to passenger carriers, operators of freight transport services enter new markets by opening new routes.

Information-Based Services This group includes two categories: *mental-processing services* (services to the customer's mind, such as news and entertainment) and *information-processing services* (services to customers' intangible assets, such as banking and insurance). Information-based services can be distributed internationally in one of three ways.

1. *Export the service to a local service factory*. The service can be made available in a local facility that customers visit. For instance, a film made in Hollywood can be shown in movie theaters around the world, or a college course can be designed in one country and then be offered by approved teachers elsewhere.
2. *Import customers*. Customers may travel abroad to visit a specialist facility, in which case the service takes on the characteristics of a people-processing service. For instance, large numbers of foreign students study in U.S. and Canadian universities, and foreigners travel to Stratford-upon-Avon to see Shakespeare's plays performed in the English town where he was born.
3. *Export the information via telecommunications and transform it locally*. Rather than ship object-based services from their country of origin, the data can be downloaded from that country for physical production in local markets (even by customers themselves).

In theory, none of these information-based services requires face-to-face contact with customers, as all can potentially be delivered at arm's length through telecommunications or mail. Banking and insurance are good examples of services that can be delivered from other countries, with cash delivery available through global ATM networks. In practice, however, a local presence may be necessary to build personal relationships, conduct on-site research (as in consulting or auditing), or even to fulfill legal requirements.

Barriers to International Trade in Services

The marketing of services internationally has been the fastest-growing segment of international trade.[12] Transnational strategy involves the integration of strategy formulation and its implementation across all the countries in which the company elects to do business. Barriers to entry, historically a serious problem for foreign firms wishing to do business abroad, are slowly diminishing. The passage of free-trade legislation in recent years has been an important facilitator of transnational operations. Notable developments include NAFTA (North American Free Trade Agreement), linking Canada, Mexico, and the United States; Latin American economic blocs, such as Mercosur and Pacto Andino; and the European Union, which is expected to expand its membership in the coming years (see Management Memo 7-2).

However, operating successfully in international markets remains difficult for some services. Despite the efforts of the World Trade Organization (WTO) and its predecessor, GATT (General Agreement on Trade and Tariffs) to negotiate easier access to service markets, many hurdles remain. Airline access is a sore point. Many countries require bilateral (two-country) agreements on establishing new routes. If one country

MANAGEMENT MEMO 7-2

THE EUROPEAN UNION: MOVING TO BORDERLESS TRADE

Many of the challenging strategic decisions facing service marketers in pan-European markets are extensions of decisions already faced by firms operating on a national basis in the United States. Although geographically more compact than the United States, the 15-country European Union (EU) has an even larger population (375 million versus 285 million) and is culturally and politically more diverse, with more distinct variations in tastes and lifestyles, as well as the added complication of 11 official national languages and a variety of regional tongues, from Catalan to Welsh. As new countries join the EU, the "single market" will become even larger. The anticipated admission of several countries in Eastern Europe in the next few years and the possibility of a formal link to Turkey (whose land area straddles Europe and Asia) will add further cultural diversity and bring the EU market closer to Russia and the countries of Central Asia.

Within the EU, the European Commission has made huge progress in harmonizing standards and regulations to level the competitive playing field and discourage efforts by individual member countries to protect their own service and manufacturing industries. The results are already evident, with German companies operating mobile phone services in Britain, the British operating a Belgium-based airline, and the French operating water-related services in several European countries (as well as overseas).

Another important economic step facilitating transnational marketing on a pan-European basis is monetary union. In January 1999, the exchange values of 11 national European currencies were linked to a new currency, the euro, which completely replaced all European currencies in 2002. Now, services from Finland to Portugal are priced in euros. Other European countries, including Britain and Sweden, are predicted to switch to euros in due course.

However, although the potential for freer trade in services within the EU is increasing at a rapid rate, we need to recognize that "Greater Europe," ranging from Iceland to Russia west of the Ural Mountains, includes many countries that are likely to remain outside the Union for some years to come. Some of these countries, such as Switzerland and Norway (which both rejected membership), tend to enjoy much closer trading relations with the EU than others. Whether there will ever be full political union—a "United States of Europe"—remains a hotly debated and contested issue. However, from a services marketing standpoint, the EU is certainly moving toward the U.S. model in terms of both scale and freedom of movement.

is willing to allow entry by a new carrier but the other is not, access will be blocked. Compounding government restrictions of this nature are capacity limits at certain major airports, leading to denial of new or additional landing rights for foreign airlines. Both passenger and freight transport are affected by such restrictions.

Other constraints may include administrative delays, refusals by immigration offices to provide work-permit applications for foreign managers and workers, heavy taxes on foreign firms, domestic-preference policies designed to protect local suppliers, legal restrictions on operational and marketing procedures (including international data flows), and the lack of broadly agreed accounting standards for services. Various languages and cultural norms may require expensive changes in the nature of a service and how it is delivered and promoted. The cultural issue has been particularly significant for the entertainment industry. Many nations are wary of seeing their own culture swamped by American imports. France and Canada are among the countries that seek to protect their own artists and entertainment industries, using a variety of measures to restrict the amount of American content in local media.

As with the EU countries, NAFTA is drawing the markets of Canada, Mexico, and the United States closer together. But here, too, political and cultural factors pose barriers to closer integration in service industries ranging from airlines and banking to broadcasting and telecommunications. Nevertheless, during this decade, some major shifts will probably take place, similar to recent and proposed transborder mergers between the U.S. and Canadian railroad industries and such banking initiatives as Bank of Montreal's purchase of Harris Bank in Chicago and an equity share in Mexico's Grupo Financiero Bancomer.

Operating in multiple countries will always be more complex than operating within one, however large. However, as entry barriers decline, management decisions to expand service operations to other countries will certainly take on more of the characteristics of a firm seeking to expand across the United States. For instance, is there a tax advantage to using one country rather than another as a major base of operations? Is it necessary to have a service facility in a particular city in order to complete a network designed to serve global customers? To what extent will modifications to service features and marketing strategy have to be made in order to accommodate climatic differences or cultural preferences? Are there cost advantages to locating certain service operations in a country other than the firm's traditional home base?

Factors Favoring Adoption of Transnational Strategies

Several forces, or industry drivers, influence the trend toward globalization and the creation of transnationally integrated strategies.[13] As applied to services, these forces are market drivers, competition drivers, technology drivers, cost drivers, and government drivers. Their relative significance may vary by type of service.

Market Drivers Market factors that stimulate the move toward transnational strategies include common customer needs across many countries, global customers who demand consistent service from suppliers around the world, and the availability of international channels in the form of efficient physical supply chains or electronic networks. As large corporate customers become global, they often seek to standardize and simplify the suppliers they use in various countries for a wide array of business-to-business services. For instance, companies that operate globally often seek to minimize the number of auditors they use around the world, expressing a preference for using "Big Four" accounting firms that can apply a consistent approach (within the context of the national rules prevailing within each country of operation). A second example comes from the move to global management of telecommunications, as evidenced by the Concert service jointly offered by AT&T and BT, which enables multinational corporations to outsource management of their international telecommunications needs. Corporate banking, insurance, and management consulting are further examples. In each instance, there are real advantages in consistency, ease of access, consolidation of information, and accountability. Similarly, international business travelers and tourists often feel more comfortable with predictable international standards of performance for such travel-related services as airlines and hotels. Also, the development of international logistics capabilities among such firms as DHL, FedEx, and UPS has encouraged many manufacturers to outsource responsibility for their logistics function to a single firm, which then coordinates transportation and warehousing operations.

Competition Drivers The presence of competitors from various countries, the interdependence of countries, and the transnational policies of competitors themselves are among the key competition drivers that exercise a powerful force in many service industries. Firms may be obliged to follow their competitors into new markets in order to protect their positions elsewhere. Similarly, once a major player moves into a new foreign market, a scramble for territory among competing firms may ensue, particularly if the preferred mode of expansion involves purchasing or licensing the most successful local firms in each market.

Technology Drivers These factors tend to center on advances in information technology, such as enhanced performance and capabilities in telecommunications, computerization, and software; miniaturization of equipment; and the digitization of voice, video, and text so that all can be stored and transmitted in the digital language of computers. For information-based services, the growing availability of broadband telecommunication channels, capable of moving vast amounts of data at great speed, is playing a major role in opening up new markets. Access to the Internet, or World Wide Web, is accelerating around the world. Significant economies may be gained by centralizing "information hubs" on a continentwide or even global basis. Firms can take advantage of favorable labor costs and exchange rates by consolidating operations of supplementary services (such as reservations) or back-office functions (such as accounting) in one or a few selected countries. Moreover, advances in those technologies that lead to faster and cheaper transportation, including materials, power, and physical design, also help to shrink distance and bring countries closer together.[14]

Cost Drivers Big is sometimes beautiful from a cost standpoint. Economies of scale may be gained from operating on an international or even global basis, as well as sourcing efficiencies as a result of favorable logistics and lower costs in certain countries. Lower operating costs for telecommunications and transportation, accompanied by improved performance, facilitate entry into international markets. The effect of these drivers varies according to the level of fixed costs required to enter an industry and the potential for cost savings. Barriers to entry caused by the up-front cost of equipment and facilities may be reduced by such strategies as equipment leasing (as in airlines), seeking investor-owned facilities (such as hotels) and then obtaining management contracts, or awarding franchises to local entrepreneurs. However, cost drivers may be less applicable for primarily people-based services. When most elements of the service factory have to be replicated in multiple locations, scale economies tend to be lower and experience curves flatter.

Government Drivers Government policies can serve to encourage or discourage development of a transnationally integrated strategy. Among these drivers are favorable trade policies, compatible technical standards, and common marketing regulations. For instance, the actions taken by the European Commission to create a single market throughout the EU are a stimulus to creation of pan-European service strategies in numerous industries. Looking at a broader global picture, we can expect government drivers to be more favorable for people-processing and possession-processing services that require a significant local presence, because these services can create local employment opportunities.

Furthermore, the World Trade Organization, with its focus on the internationalization of services, has pushed governments around to world to create more favorable regulatory environments for transnational service strategies. The power of the drivers for internationalization can be seen in the case of the Qantas airliner arriving in Hong Kong, described in Service Perspectives 7-4.

Many of the factors driving internationalization and the adoption of transnational strategies also promote the trend among service industries that previously operated only at a local level to have nationwide operations. The market, cost, technological, and competitive forces that encourage creation of nationwide service businesses or franchise chains are often the same as those that subsequently drive some of the same firms to operate transnationally. Yet many types of services, from plumbers to landscaping, still remain purely local in scope, as a review of business categories in any city Yellow Pages reveals.

How the Nature of Service Processes Affects Opportunities for Internationalization

Are some types of services easier to internationalize than others? Our analysis suggests that this is indeed the case. Table 7-2 summarizes important variations in the

SERVICE PERSPECTIVES 7-4

FLIGHT TO HONG KONG: A SNAPSHOT OF GLOBALIZATION

A white and red Boeing 747, sporting the flying kangaroo of Qantas, banks low over Hong Kong's dramatic harbor, crowded with merchant vessels, as it nears the end of its 10-hour flight from Australia. Once landed, the aircraft taxis past a kaleidoscope of tail fins representing airlines from more than a dozen countries on several continents—just a sample of all the carriers that offer service to this remarkable city.

The passengers include business travelers and tourists, as well as returning residents. After passing through immigration and customs, most visitors will be heading first for their hotels, many of which belong to global chains (some of them, Hong Kong based). Some travelers will be picking up cars, reserved earlier from Hertz or one of the other well-known rental car companies with facilities at the airport. Others will take the fast train into the city. Tourists on packaged vacations are actively looking forward to enjoying Hong Kong's renowned Cantonese cuisine. Parents, however, are resigned to having their children demand to eat at the same fast-food chains that can be found back home. Many of the more affluent tourists are planning to go shopping, not only in distinctive Chinese jewelry and antiques stores but also in the internationally branded luxury stores that can be found in most world-class cities.

What brings the business travelers to this SAR (special administrative region) of China? Many are negotiating supply contracts for manufactured goods ranging from clothing to toys to computer components, whereas others have come to market their own goods and services. Some are in the shipping or construction businesses; others, in an array of service industries ranging from telecommunications to entertainment and international law. The owner of a large Australian tourism operation has come to negotiate a deal for package vacations on Queensland's famous Gold Coast. The Brussels-based Canadian senior partner of a Big Four accounting firm is half-way through a grueling round-the-world trip to persuade the offices of an international conglomerate to consolidate all its auditing business on a global basis with his firm alone. An American executive and her British colleague, both working for a large Euro-American telecom partnership, are hoping to achieve similar goals by selling a multinational corporation on the concept of employing their firm to manage all its telecommunications activities worldwide. And more than a few of the passengers either work for international banking and financial service firms or have come to Hong Kong, one of the world's most dynamic financial centers, to seek financing for their own ventures.

In the Boeing's freight hold can be found not only passengers' bags but also cargo for delivery to Hong Kong and other Chinese destinations. The freight includes mail, Australian wine, some vital spare parts for an Australian-built high-speed ferry operating out of Hong Kong, a container full of brochures and display materials about the Australian tourism industry for an upcoming trade promotion, and a variety of other high-value merchandise. Waiting at the airport for the aircraft's arrival are local Qantas personnel, baggage handlers, cleaners, mechanics and other technical staff, customs and immigration officials, and, of course, people who have come to greet individual passengers. A few are Australians, but the great majority are local Hong Kong Chinese, many of whom have never traveled very far afield. Yet in their daily lives, they patronize banks, fast-food outlets, retail stores, and insurance companies whose brand names—promoted by global advertising campaigns—may be equally familiar to their expatriate relatives living in Australia, Britain, Canada, Singapore, and the United States. They can watch CNN on cable TV, listen to the BBC World Service on the radio, make phone calls through Hong Kong Telecom (itself part of a worldwide operation), and watch movies from Hollywood either in English or dubbed into the Cantonese dialect of Chinese. Welcome to the world of global services marketing!

TABLE 7-2 Impact of Globalization Drivers on Various Service Categories

Globalization Drivers	*People Processing*	*Possession Processing*	*Information Based*
Competition	Simultaneity of production and consumption limits leverage of foreign-based competitive advantage in front-stage of service factory, but advantage in management systems can be basis for globalization.	Lead role of technology creates driver for globalization of competitors with technical edge (e.g., Singapore Airlines' technical servicing for other carriers' aircraft).	Highly vulnerable to global dominance by competitors with monopoly or competitive advantage in information (e.g., BBC, Hollywood, CNN), unless restricted by governments
Market	People differ economically and culturally, so needs for service and ability to pay may vary. Culture and education may affect willingness to do self-service.	Less variation for service to corporate possessions, but level of economic development impacts demand for services to individually owned goods.	Demand for many services is derived to a significant degree from economic and educational levels. Cultural issues may affect demand for entertainment.
Technology	Use of IT for delivery of supplementary services may be a function of ownership and familiarity with technology, including telecommunications and intelligent terminals.	Need for technology-based service delivery systems is a function of the types of possessions requiring service and the cost tradeoffs in labor substitution.	Ability to deliver core services through remote terminals may be a function of investments in computerization, quality of telecommunications infrastructure, and education levels.
Cost	Variable labor rates may impact on pricing in labor-intensive services (consider self-service in high-cost locations).	Variable labor rates may favor low-cost locations if not offset by shipment costs. Consider substituting equipment for labor.	Major cost elements can be centralized and minor cost elements localized.
Government	Social policies (e.g., health) vary widely and may affect labor costs, role of women in front-stage jobs, and hours/days on which work can be performed.	Tax laws, environmental regulations, and technical standards may decrease/increase costs and encourage/discourage certain types of activity.	Policies on education, censorship, public ownership of communications, and infrastructure standards may impact demand and supply and distort pricing.

impact of each of the five groups of drivers on three broad categories of services: people-processing services, possession-processing services, and information-based services.

People-Processing Services The service provider needs to maintain a local geographic presence, stationing the necessary personnel, buildings, equipment, vehicles, and supplies within reasonably easy reach of target customers. If the customers are themselves mobile, as are business travelers and tourists, the same customers may patronize a company's offerings in many different locations and make comparisons between them.

Possession-Processing Services These services may also be geographically constrained in many instances. A local presence is still required when the supplier must come to repair or maintain objects in a fixed location. However, smaller, transportable items can be shipped to distant service centers, although transportation costs, customs duties, and government regulations may constrain shipment across large distances or national frontiers. On the other hand, modern technology now allows certain types of service processes to be administered from a distance through electronic diagnostics and transmission of so-called remote fixes.

Information-Based Services These services, perhaps the most interesting category of services from the standpoint of global strategy development, depend on the transmission or manipulation of data in order to create value. The advent of modern global telecommunications, linking intelligent machines to powerful databases, makes it increasingly easy to deliver information-based services around the world. Local-presence requirements may be limited to a terminal, ranging from a simple telephone or fax machine to a computer or more specialized equipment, such as a bank ATM, connected to a reliable telecommunications infrastructure. If the local infrastructure is not of sufficiently high quality, the use of mobile or satellite communications may solve the problem in some instances.

CONCLUSION

Where? When? How? Responses to these three questions form the foundation of service delivery strategy. The customer's service experience is a function of both service performance and delivery characteristics.

"Where?" relates, of course, to the places where customers can obtain delivery of the core product, one or more supplementary services, or a complete package. In this chapter, we presented a categorization scheme for thinking about alternative place-related strategies, ranging from customers coming to the service site to service personnel visiting the customer, and finally a variety of options for arm's-length transactions, including delivery through both physical and electronic channels.

"When?" involves decisions on the scheduling of service delivery. Customer demands for greater convenience are leading many firms to extend their hours and days of service, with the ultimate flexibility being offered by 24/7 service every day of the year.

"How?" concerns channels and procedures for delivering the core and supplementary service elements to customers. Advances in technology are having a major impact on the alternatives available and on the economics of those alternatives. Responding to customer needs for flexibility, many firms now offer several alternatives for delivery channels.

Although service firms are much more likely than a manufacturer to control their own delivery systems, there is also a role for intermediaries to deliver either the core services, as is the case for franchisees, or supplementary services, such as travel agents.

More and more service firms are marketing across national borders. Stimulating (or constraining) the move to transnational strategies are five key industry drivers: market factors, costs, technology, government policies, and competitive forces. However, significant differences exist in the extent to which the various drivers apply to people-processing, possession-processing, and information-based services.

Review Questions

1. What is meant by "distributing services?" How can an experience or something intangible be distributed?
2. Why is it important to consider the distribution of core and supplementary services separately?
3. What risks and opportunities are entailed for a retail service firm in adding electronic channels of delivery (a) paralleling a channel involving physical stores, (b) replacing the physical stores with an all-Internet cum call center channel? Give examples.

4. Why should service marketers be concerned with new developments in mobile communications?
5. What can service marketers who are planning transnational strategies learn from studying the United States?
6. What marketing and management challenges are raised by the use of intermediaries in a service setting?
7. What are the key drivers for increasing globalization of services?
8. How does the nature of the service affect the opportunities for globalization?

Application Exercises

1. Pick a service organization and examine its use of technology in facilitating service delivery. Might there be other opportunities for technology to be used beneficially? What are these?
2. Identify three situations in which you use self-service delivery. What is your motivation for using this approach to delivery rather than having service personnel do it for you?
3. Think of three services you mostly or exclusively buy or use via the Internet. What is the value proposition of this channel to you over alternative channels (e.g., phone, mail, or branch network)?
4. Select two business-format franchises other than food service, choosing one targeted primarily at consumer markets and the other primarily at business-to-business markets. Develop a profile of each, examining strategies across each of the 7Ps and also evaluating their competitive positioning.
5. Select three service industries. In each instance, which do you see as the most significant of the five industry drivers as forces for globalization, and why?
6. Obtain recent statistics for international trade in services for the United States and another country of your choice. What are the dominant categories of service exports and imports? What factors do you think are driving trade in specific service categories? What differences do you see between the countries?

Endnotes

1. Jochen Wirtz and Jeannette P.T. Ho, "Westin in Asia: Distributing Hotel Rooms Globally," in, Christopher H. Lovelock, Jochen Wirtz, and Hean Tat Keh, *Services Marketing in Asia—Managing People, Technology and Strategy* (Singapore: Prentice-Hall, 2002), 645–651.
2. The section was based on the following research: Nancy Jo Black, Andy Lockett, Christine Ennew, Heidi Winklhofer, and Sally McKechnie, "Modelling Consumer Choice of Distribution Channels: An Illustration from Financial Services," *International Journal of Bank Marketing* 20, no. 4 (2002): 161–173; Jinkook Lee, "A Key to Marketing Financial Services: The Right Mix of Products, Services, Channels and Customers," *Journal of Services Marketing* 16, no. 3 (2002): 238–258; and Leonard L Berry, Kathleen Seiders, and Dhruv Grewal, "Understanding Service Convenience," *Journal of Marketing* 66, no. 3 (July 2002): 1–17.
3. James L. Heskett, W. Earl Sasser Jr., and Leonard A. Schlesinger, *The Service Profit Chain* (New York: The Free Press, 1997), 218–220.
4. The Dieringer Research Group, Inc., December 2002; *http://www.thedrg.com/*.
5. P. K. Kannan, "Introduction to the Special Issue: Marketing in the E-Channel," *International Journal of Electronic Commerce* 5, no. 3 (2001): 3–6.
6. Inge Geyskens, Katrijn Gielens, and Marnik G Dekimpe, "The Market Valuation of Internet Channel Additions," *Journal of Marketing* 66, no. 2 (April 2002): 102–119.
7. Katherine N. Lemon, Frederick B. Newell, and Loren J. Lemon, "The Wireless Rules for e-Service," in *New Directions in Theory and Practice*, ed. Roland T. Rust and P. K. Kannan (Armonk, NY: M. E. Sharpe, 2002), 200–232.
8. Frances Cairncross, *The Company of the Future* (Boston: Harvard Business School Press, 2002).
9. James Cross and Bruce J. Walker, "Addressing Service Marketing Challenges Through Franchising," in *Handbook of Services Marketing & Management*, eds. Teresa A. Swartz and Dawn Iacobucci (Thousand Oaks, CA: Sage Publications, 2000), 473–484.

10. Scott Shane and Chester Spell, "Factors for New Franchise Success," *Sloan Management Review* (Spring 1998), 43–50.
11. This term was coined by Curtis P. McLauglin and James A. Fitzsimmons in "e-Service: Strategies for Globalizing Service Operations," *International Journal of Service Industry Management* 7, no. 4 (1996): 43–57.
12. Rajshkhar G. Javalgi and D. Steven White, "Strategic Challenges for the Marketing of Services Internationally," *International Marketing Review* 19, no. 6 (2002): 563–581.
13. Johny K. Johansson and George S. Yip, "Exploiting Globalization Potential: U.S. and Japanese Strategies," *Strategic Management Journal* (October 1994): 579–601; Christopher H. Lovelock and George S. Yip, "Developing Global Strategies for Service Businesses," *California Management Review* 38 (Winter 1996): 64–86; Rajshkhar G. Javalgi and D. Steven White, "Strategic Challenges for the Marketing of Services Internationally," *International Marketing Review* 19, no. 6 (2002): 563–581; May Aung and Roger Heeler, "Core Competencies of Service Firms: A Framework for Strategic Decisions in International Markets," *Journal of Marketing Management* 17 (2001): 619–643.
14. Frances Cairncross, *The Death of Distance* (Boston: Harvard Business School Press, 1997).

Cultivating Service Brand Equity

LEONARD L. BERRY

In packaged goods, the product is the primary brand. However, with services, the company is the primary brand. This article, based on primary research with 14 mature, high-performance service companies, makes a case for service branding as a cornerstone of services marketing for today and tomorrow. The article presents a service-branding model that underscores the salient role of customers' service experiences in brand formation. Four primary strategies that excellent service firms use to cultivate brand equity are discussed and illustrated. Branding is not just for tangible goods; it is a principal success driver for service organizations as well.

Branding plays a special role in service companies because strong brands increase customers' trust of the invisible purchase. Strong brands enable customers to better visualize and understand intangible products. They reduce customers' perceived monetary, social, or safety risk in buying services, which are difficult to evaluate prior to purchase. Strong brands are the surrogates when the company offers no fabric to touch, no trousers to try on, no watermelons or apples to scrutinize, no automobile to test-drive.

In packaged goods, the product is the primary brand. However, with services, the company is the primary brand. The locus of brand impact differs for services because they lack the tangibility that allows packaging, labeling, and displaying. It is not possible to package and display an entertainment or transportation service in the same way as Kodak packages and displays film.

Even more significant is the source of customer value creation. Brand impact shifts from product to company as service plays a greater role in determining customer value (Berry and Parasuraman 1991). Folgers Coffee customers buy the product brand. Most are probably unaware that Folgers Coffee is a division of Procter & Gamble. It is not relevant to the purchase decision. The locus of brand impact is the product. Customers patronizing a Starbucks store, however, buy the company brand. Their service experience with Starbucks figures prominently in their perception of the brand. Starbucks founder Howard Schultz (1997) clearly understands the source of brand power in a service business:

> Our competitive advantage over the big coffee brands turned out to be our people. Supermarket sales are nonverbal and impersonal, with no personal interaction. But in a Starbucks store, you encounter real people who are informed and excited about the coffee, and enthusiastic about the brand. . . . Starbucks' success proves that a multimillion-dollar advertising program isn't a prerequisite for building a national brand—nor are the deep pockets of a big corporation. You can do it one customer at a time, one store at a time, one market at a time (p. 247)

This article presents branding as a cornerstone of services marketing for the 21st century. Our natural inclination in marketing is to associate branding with goods. Through product, package, and logo design, marketers leverage the materiality of goods in their branding efforts. They affix the brand name to the product and show the product in advertising, often associating it with distinctive symbols, signature statements, and people. Nike's swoosh logo on its products, its "Just Do It" signature statement in

"Cultivating Service Brand Equity," by Leonard L. Berry, *Journal of the Academy of Marketing Science* 28, no. 1: 128–137. Reprinted by permission of Sage Publications, Inc.

its advertising, and its subbrands linking the prowess and persona of athletic superstars to the primary brand illustrate the central role physical products play in brand development.

Branding is just as relevant to services, however. Product intangibility does not mean that brand development is less appropriate or important for services than goods, only that its application differs in certain respects. Brand development is crucial in services, given the inherent difficulty in differentiating products that lack physical differences (Zeithaml 1981) and the intense competition within service markets, many of which have been deregulated. A strong brand is "a safe place for customers" (Richards 1998). The invisibility of services makes buying them from a safe place an appealing proposition for customers. Brand cultivation was found to be a principal success driver in a study of 14 mature, high-performance service companies in a variety of industries (Berry 1999). These companies use the brand as the foundation for building trust-based relationships with customers.

The possibilities for creating a strong service brand become clearer when we examine its components. The next section discusses the principal components of a service brand, their roles, and their relationships. A discussion of strategies that service companies use to cultivate strong brands follows.

BRANDING THE COMPANY

A strong service brand is essentially a promise of future satisfaction. It is a blend of what the company says the brand is, what others say, and how the company performs the service—all from the customer's point of view. A brand is perceived. Figure 1 depicts the relationships among the principal components of a service brand: the presented brand, brand awareness, external brand communications, brand meaning, customer experience, and brand equity. The bold lines indicate primary impact and the dotted lines secondary impact.

The *presented brand* is the company's controlled communication of its identity and purpose through its advertising, service facilities, and the appearance of service providers. The company name and logo and their visual presentation, coupled with advertising theme lines and symbolic associations, are core elements of the presented brand. The presented brand is the brand message a company conceptualizes and disseminates. The company's effective presentation of its brand contributes directly to *brand awareness*, which is the customer's ability to recognize and recall the brand when provided a cue. The percentage of customers in New York City who mention Dial-A-Mattress when asked "what companies come to mind if you need to buy a mattress?" is a measure of the company's brand awareness in the market.

External brand communications refers to information customers absorb about the company and its service that essentially is uncontrolled by the company. Word-of-mouth communications and publicity are the most common forms of external brand communications. Customers may gain awareness and form impressions about a brand not only from company communications but from communications about the company offered by independent sources.

Word-of-mouth (and, increasingly word-of-keyboard) communications are common with services due to their intangible core. When the consequences of selecting the wrong service supplier are severe, service customers are especially eager for unbiased, experience-based information. Thus, word-of-mouth activity often is high preceding a customer's choice of a doctor, attorney, automobile mechanic, or college professor (Berry and Parasuraman 1991).

FIGURE 1 A Service-Branding Model

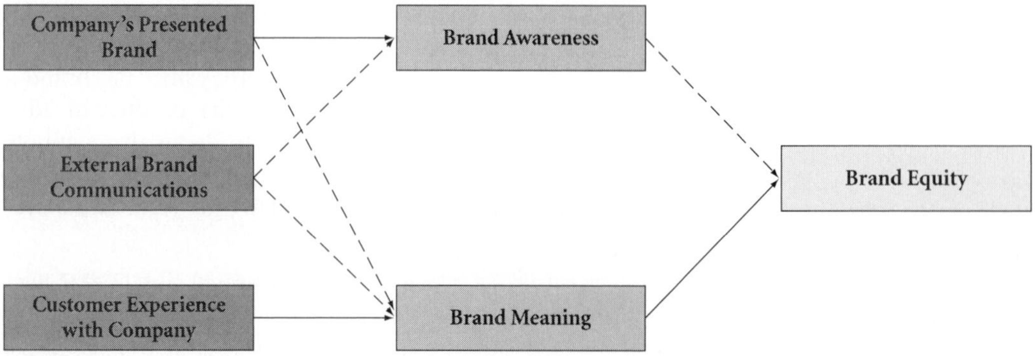

Publicity also can be influential in brand development—for better or worse. The combination of reach or coverage and authoritativeness can influence not only brand awareness but also brand meaning.

Typically, external brand communications reach fewer people than a company's own marketing communications. Moreover, the purpose of presented brand communications is to strengthen the brand; these efforts by definition are brand focused. Compared to the bold-line influence of the presented brand on brand awareness, external brand communications represent a dotted-line relationship to brand awareness and meaning. In extreme instances in which word of mouth becomes rampant or publicity wide-spread and attention getting, the dotted lines can turn to bold.

Brand meaning refers to the customer's dominant perceptions of the brand. It is the customer's snapshot impression of the brand and its associations. Brand meaning is what immediately comes to consumers' minds if you mention Wal-Mart and then Target. Most consumers have different perceptions of Wal-Mart and Target, even though both companies are general-merchandise discounters. Brand awareness is high for both companies; brand meaning is different. Target's consumer research shows that Wal-Mart's brand centers on price leadership. Low prices are Wal-Mart's main appeal. Target's appeal includes bright, comfortable stores, apparel selection, and fast checkout. As Dayton-Hudson executive Jerry Storch (1998) explains, "If we tried to go after Wal-Mart on price, we would compromise our brand. Wide aisles are critical to who we are, but they cost a lot. It is very expensive to be Target."

The fundamental difference between brand awareness and brand meaning is illustrated by Domino's Pizza versus Pizza Hut, by Charles Schwab Corporation versus Merrill Lynch, by Southwest Airlines versus Northwest Airlines. These companies all are well known by customers in their respective markets, yet their images are quite different.

What is the source of brand meaning? Although the presented brand and external communications contribute to brand meaning, the primary influence for customers who actually have experienced the service is the experience. Communications have the most influence with new customers who have had little or no direct experience with the company's service to shape their impressions. The presented brand and external communications are a new customer's only evidence of what the company stands for. However, as customers experience the company's total product, these experiences become disproportionately influential. Customers' experience-based beliefs are powerful. A presented brand can generate greater brand awareness, stimulate new customer trial, and reinforce and strengthen brand meaning with existing customers. A presented brand cannot, however, rescue a weak service. If customers' service experiences differ from the advertising message, customers will believe their experiences and not the advertising. As with goods, in services marketing customers' disappointment with the experience closes the door that traditional brand marketing helps to open.

Brand awareness and brand meaning both contribute to *brand equity* for experienced customers, but not to the same degree. Just as customer experiences disproportionately shape brand meaning, so does brand meaning disproportionately affect brand equity. Brand equity is the differential effect of brand awareness and meaning combined on customer response to the marketing of the brand (Keller 1993).

Brand equity can be positive or negative. Positive brand equity is the degree of marketing advantage a brand would hold over an unnamed or fictitiously named competitor. Negative brand equity is the degree of marketing disadvantage linked to a specific brand. Negative brand equity explains why Holiday Inn sponsored television commercials in 1997 portraying hotel housekeepers using chain-saws to destroy and then totally refurbish a Holiday Inn room. Negative brand equity also explains why Valujet assumed the name of an acquisition and renamed itself Air Tran Airlines in the year following a fatal accident, temporary grounding by the Federal Aviation Administration (FAA), and months of unfavorable publicity.

The service-branding model shown in Figure 1 differs in degree, not kind, from a packaged-goods branding model. The customer's actual experience disproportionately shapes brand meaning and equity for goods, not just for services. The principal difference in the two models is the salient role of service performance. In labor intensive service businesses, human performance rather than machine performance plays the most critical role in building the brand.

Product intangibility and the salient role of service in customer value creation focus customer attention on the company as an entity. A service company becomes its own brand, for better or for worse. The source of the experience is the locus of brand formation. With breakfast cereal, the source of the customer's experience may be Cheerios (a brand of General Mills); in snack foods it may be Ritz Crackers (a brand of Nabisco); in cooking oil it may be Mazola (a brand of the Best Foods Division of CPC International). However, with services, the company as a whole is usually viewed as the provider of the experience. Customers become aware of and develop images of American Airlines, Federal Express, Disney World, MCI, Cable News Network (CNN), and the New York Yankees. How can service companies cultivate the development of powerful brands? We now turn to a discussion of brand cultivation strategies.

BUILDING A SERVICE BRAND

Service companies build strong brands through branding distinctiveness and message consistency, by performing their core services well, from reaching customers emotionally, and by associating their brands with trust. Strong-brand companies have high "mind share" with targeted customers, which contributes to market share. Figure 2 presents four ways in which service companies build strong brands. Firms with the strongest brands typically use all four approaches.

Dare to Be Different

Service companies with the strongest brands reveal a conscious effort to be different, a conscious effort to carve out a distinct brand personality. Top brand builders almost always are mavericks that defy convention and forge new paths to reach and please customers.

The desire to create a distinct mental picture of the company for customers manifests itself in the presented brand and the customers' service experience paths in the service-branding model.

The branding strategy goal is to reinforce a demonstrably different service experience with a demonstrably different brand presentation.

Strong-brand firms never market their offer as a commodity, enacting Tom Peter's (1997) assertion that "commodization isn't inevitable" (p. 300). Invention rather than imitation rules branding efforts. Companies such as Starbucks, Target, Midwest Express Airlines, Enterprise Rent-A-Car, and Motel 6 use all of the tools at their disposal to craft a separate, integrated identity, including facilities design, service provider appearance, core service augmentation, advertising content and style, and media selection. Starbucks could squeeze more tables and chairs into their stores, but doing so would undermine what they really are selling: a respite and a social experience. Target could operate less-expensive stores with narrower aisles, but then it would look more like its competitors. Because of its two-by-two configuration of leather seats (instead of the more common three-by-three seating), Midwest Express Airline's all-coach service seems like first class. Meal service with china plates, cloth napkins, free wine or champagne, and freshly baked chocolate chip cookies reinforces the perception. The leather seats, meal service, and cookies are signature clues that augment the core service and differentiate the brand.

Enterprise Rent-A-Car customer-contact employees dress for differentiation. Men wear suits and women dresses or skirts and hose. Customers often are pleasantly surprised by the professional appearance of Enterprise employees who pick them

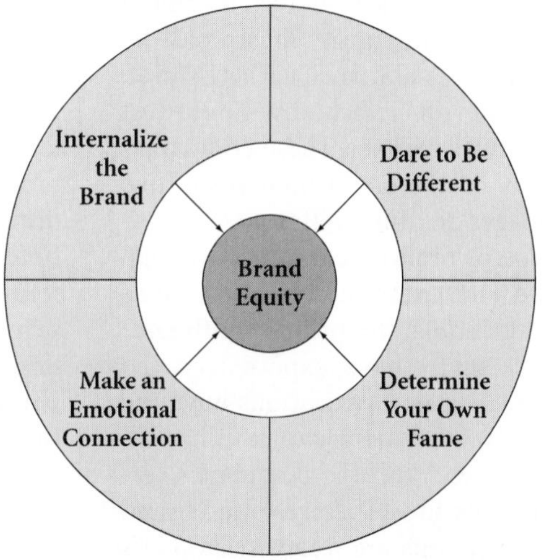

FIGURE 2 Cultivating Brand Equity

up in an auto repair garage or serve them in an Enterprise office. The least costly television commercial ever made illustrates Motel 6's efficient efforts to carve out a distinct brand personality. Mocking the higher prices of competitors, Motel 6's memorable commercial showed a totally dark screen. At the end came this line: "This is what a hotel room looks like when you are asleep."

Quick-service restaurant chain Chick-fil-A exemplifies the "dare to be different" principle. Competing against large national television advertisers such as McDonald's, Burger King, and Wendy's, Chick-fil-A has little choice but to try to establish a distinct brand personality. Any conventional branding strategy would drown from the sheer advertising weight of much bigger players.

Chick-fil-A's branding heritage is in shopping mall food courts, the company's original distribution strategy. In this environment, the company's principal marketing challenge is to offer food-court visitors a visually distinct alternative to a sea of fast-food eateries. Chick-fil-A practices inside-out marketing in its mall stores. The independent Chick-fil-A operator is the principal marketer with the mandate to bring the store to life as an advertising medium, to leverage the latent marketing power of the store front, counter area and menu boards, point-of-purchase displays, store layout, and the appearance and attitude of employees. Chick-fil-A's mall marketing strategy is to transform the store into a television screen that will command shopper attention, encourage trial, and stimulate unplanned purchases, "We pay for the customer traffic that a mall generates and have to capitalize on this opportunity," explains Steve Robinson, senior vice president, marketing, for Chick-fil-A. "We continually ask our operators: 'What are the messages you are providing from your store that are distinctive, unique, and compelling?'"

To leverage Chick-fil-A's food quality superiority that is consistently documented in blind-taste tests with competitive products, mall stores regularly invite food-court visitors to sample the product—the venerable small-piece-of-chicken-on-a-toothpick tactic. "We encourage the operators to use every possible method to get the taste of the product in people's mouths," adds Robinson.

Chick-fil-A's branding challenge both intensified and changed when the company expanded distribution beyond the mall with freestanding street stores. Now the company truly is competing against the major fast-food brands. Mall shoppers select from on-site restaurants. Consumers in their homes, workplaces, or cars have a wider choice set and creating mind share becomes an imperative for the company. McDonald's, Burger King, Wendy's, Pizza Hut, and Taco Bell have compelling reasons to spend significant dollars on advertising. Chick-fil-A, with fewer stores, regional distribution, and a network of independent store operators who fund the advertising, cannot spend nearly as much. Creating a distinct, appealing brand personality is the only way to break through the clutter of competitive advertising.

Media selection contributes to the differentiation strategy. Chick-fil-A is a committed billboard marketer because in most markets it cannot afford broadcast media alternatives. It would rather dominate one medium than spread its advertising resources thinly in multiple media. Billboards are the medium, however, not the message, and they require unique creative content to be effective. Chick-fil-A's creative breakthrough came in the form of cows who urge consumers to "Eat Mor Chikin." The Chick-fil-A cows remind consumers "that they don't have to eat a hamburger today" and present Chick-fil-A as the alternative.

What began as a billboard campaign became the center-piece of the company's presented brand. The best-brand marketing gives customers a return on their investment of time and attention; it gives customers something back (Gordon 1998). This is what the Chick-fil-A cows do. They are fun, humorous, different. They are understated, just like Chick-fil-A. They do not intrude. These animals put a smile on consumers' faces while giving a quick-service restaurant chain a more distinct and personable identity.

Determine Your Own Fame

A strong-brand service company stands for something that is important to targeted customers; the brand not only differs from competitive brands, it represents a valuable market offer. The brand conveys the company's reason for being. It captures and communicates what the company wishes to be famous for with customers.

Service companies strengthen brand equity by focusing on underserved market needs. They enhance the customers' experience by doing something that needs doing. Charles Schwab Corporation gave investors who knew what stocks they wanted to buy or sell the opportunity to do so without paying full commissions for advice they did not use. Enterprise Rent-A-Car focused on serving local people whose personal cars were temporarily unavailable to them and built a business in the replacement market. While Hertz, Avis, and National Car Rental emphasized airport locations to target travelers. Enterprise targeted people whose cars were in the shop and quietly built a rental fleet bigger than any other rental car company.

Strong-brand service companies also perform the service effectively. They not only fill a need, they fill it well. Performing a needed service and performing it better than competitors is a powerful brand-building combination. Chick-fil-A's food not only is healthier than some competitive products but also it tastes better. Ratings that are at least 1 scale point higher than that of competing entries in taste tests based on 5-point scales are typical. In Zagat's (1997) survey of 60 of the world's largest airlines on comfort, service, timeliness, and food, Midwest Express ranked 1st in the United States and was the only U.S. airline to place in the world's Top 10.

In essence, service companies with strong brand equity provide a service that customers truly value; perform it better than competitors; and effectively tell their story through communications that create awareness, stimulate trial, and reinforce customers' experiences. Over time, these companies become famous for their defining excellence, aided not only by their own controlled messages but also by customers' experiences and word-of-mouth communications.

Dial-A-Mattress is a company that has determined its own fame. Dial-A-Mattress sells bedding over the telephone 24 hours a day, 7 days a week, and delivers orders as soon as customers want them—within 2 hours if desired. The company removes the customer's old mattress at no additional cost. Explains founder, president and CEO Napoleon Barragan, "Buying a mattress is not a pleasurable experience; it's a chore. If you can make it easy for consumers, if you give them what they want, the way they want it, and when they want it, you can do business."

Thirty percent of Dial-A-Mattress's customers are referrals. The company's core service strategy makes it so simple to acquire a new mattress that many first-time customers are astonished. Instead of having to find the time and energy to visit furniture stores, to test multiple mattresses by lying or bouncing on them, to sort fact from fiction in the selling process, and to arrange for delivery in 3 or 4 days, customers can telephone Dial-A-Mattress, speak with a bedding consultant who has participated in a 6-week training regimen, receive their mattress within 2 hours if desired, and send it back with the driver if not fully satisfied. The astonishment factor stimulates customer word of mouth, which Dial-A-Mattress encourages by giving purchasers discount coupons for their friends.

Dial-A-Mattress advertises on television and radio with a consistent message: buy Sealy, Serta, or Simmons brand-name mattresses over the telephone, subject to your approval, save money, and receive your mattress when you want it, within 2 hours if you wish. The advertising often ends with the tag line: "Dial 1-800-MATTRES, and leave the last 's' off for savings."

The combination of frequent television and radio advertising, a consistent message, word-of-mouth communications, and publicity generate awareness of the Dial-A-Mattress brand. Late-night talk show host David Letterman once called Dial-A-Mattress on camera during the show, requesting that a mattress be delivered to his car in Manhattan. Dial-A-Mattress made the delivery on camera.

The company's name also contributes to brand awareness. Dial-A-Mattress is a great name because it simply, yet distinctively, conveys what and how the company sells. Because of the powerful influence of customers' actual service experiences on brand meaning and brand equity, a service company can overcome a mediocre name. However, a good one certainly helps.

The Midwest Express brand also captures and communicates a valuable market offer. Midwest Express wants to be famous for "the best care in the air," its signature statement in all advertising. The company's advertising strategy includes clearly stating, as often as possible, factual support for this assertion. Advertising consistently refers to the airline's nonstop, single class of premium service with comfortable leather seats; no middle seats; delicious food; and caring, personal attention. Advertising usually mentions the airline's top ranking by independent organizations, such as the Zagat Airline Survey or Conde Nast Traveler. The company also stresses its competitive fares that are comparable to the regular coach fares of other airlines; this message counteracts impressions that Midwest Express must be expensive because of its high-quality service.

Midwest Express likes to advertise on television in local markets. Explains Advertising Manager Jim Reichart, "Our differences translate well into television. We like to show coach—the leather seats, the smiling faces, the great food, and the glass and silverware."

Unlike Dial-A-Mattress, the Midwest Express name is not ideal. The airline flies from midwestern hubs to the Southwest, Southeast, and both coasts. Moreover, the word *Express* suggests a commuter airline, which definitely is not Midwest Express. The company's advertising typically includes pictures of one of its jets—with its signature dark-blue-on-white color motif and distinctive logo on the tail—to counteract the commuter airline impression.

Although Midwest Express is not a great name, it is a great brand. No service company better illustrates the disproportionate impact of customers' service experiences on brand meaning and equity. Among passengers who have experienced the airline's service, an ordinary corporate name evokes the image of first-class seats, good food, chocolate chip cookies, and caring personal service. The name holds rich, differentiated meaning and the company is not about to change it.

Make an Emotional Connection

In January 1998, the Harlem Globetrotters played their 20,000th basketball game in the small town of Remington, Indiana. Renowned for their ball-handling wizardry, comical routines, and old-fashioned silliness, the Globetrotters make an emotional connection to the customer. The Harlem Globetrotters is a magical brand—a brand that evokes images of fun and laughter, respect and decency, hard work, and good values. Globetrotter players are graded by the team owner on their charisma, punctuality, and ability to promote the brand. Cursing, pouting, and rudeness are forbidden. Players sign autographs after the games. "We're all aware of how precious the brand is," says Paul "Showtime" Gaffney, who performs the clown prince role once played by Meadowlark Lemon. "Each and every night, the people in the stands don't care if you just stepped off a 10-hour bus ride. They want you to be your best, and we want to be our best" (Thurow 1998:A8).

Great brands always make an emotional connection with the intended audience. They reach beyond the purely rational and purely economic level to spark feelings of closeness, affection, and trust. Consumers live in an emotional world; their emotions influence their decisions. Great brands transcend specific product features and benefits and penetrate people's emotions (Webber 1997). As Charlotte Beers (1998), chairman of J. Walter Thompson, writes: "The truth is, what makes a brand powerful is the emotional involvement of customers" (p. 39).

Brands that connect with customers' emotions are those that reflect customers' core values. In effect, the brand captures and communicates values customers hold dear. Corporate values cannot be faked in service branding. The company's true values emerge in the customer's actual experience with the service. Marketing communications cannot establish nonexistent values.

Enterprise Rent-A-Car connects emotionally with employees of local body shops, auto repair firms, and insurance companies by taking donuts to them week after week, by building personal relationships, and most of all, by keeping their service promises. Chick-fil-A's cows invite the customers' affection, but the effort is negated if customers' experiences with the service contradict the feeling. Midwest Express could portray chocolate chip cookies in its advertising, but far more powerful is actually baking them onboard for passengers and serving them with a warm smile.

Brands that connect emotionally are authentic summations of a company with a soul. As Starbucks' founder Howard Schultz (1997) writes, "The most powerful and enduring brands are built from the heart. They are real and sustainable. Their foundations are stronger because they are built with the strength of the human spirit, not an ad campaign" (p. 248).

Given the prevalence of price-oriented advertising in service markets, the minimal role of price messages in the advertising of many strong-brand service companies is notable. Companies that emphasize price in their advertising forfeit the opportunity for an emotional connection with their customers. Price-dominated marketing messages ring the emotional bell of few customers. Price advertising may be about economic value, but it is not about human values; it does not stir the soul. As Donald Hudler (1996), who helped build the Saturn automobile into an emotionally rich brand, states, "When you talk about price, you lose the opportunity to talk about yourself and build a brand" (also see Aaker 1996, chap. 2).

The St. Paul Saints, a minor-league baseball team in St. Paul, Minnesota, sells out every home game and has a long list of people on the season-ticket waiting list. The St. Paul Saints illustrate the emotional content of a strong brand. To most of its fans, the Saints are far more than just a professional baseball team. The Saints are part of the town's culture; a spirited community citizen; a maverick organization with a heart; an organization whose top management greets fans as they enter the ballpark; a team with a blind radio announcer; a team that in 1997 signed the first female pitcher, Ila Borders, ever to pitch on a regular basis for a professional men's baseball team.

The core of the Saints' presented brand is its basic value: "Fun is good." From sumo wrestling to fans racing around the bases in a contest, minievents occur during breaks in the game action. The Saints not only have a pig as the team mascot, they hold an annual contest for elementary school children to name the pig. One thousand school children participated in the 1998 name-the-pig contest; the winning entry was "The Great Hambino." The Saints hold a "Dead of Winter Tailgate Party Recipe Contest" in their parking lot to raise funds for a nonprofit community organization. An RBI (Reading Books Is Fun) Club attracted 1,000 fourth- and fifth-grade students in 1998 to participate in a reading program. Children plant flowers in the "Reading Tree" area of the stadium, and children and players paint murals on the stadium fence. The team holds a charity golf tournament.

The Saints care, and the community knows it; caring is integral to its brand. The St. Paul Saints connect emotionally with their fans and the fans with each other. "Going to a Saints game is like going to your high school reunion," explains General Manager Bill Fanning. "You may not know the people sitting next to you when the game begins, but they are old friends by the time it ends." The St. Paul Saints epitomize every branding principle discussed thus far: the company dares to be different, clearly defines its reason for being, and connects emotionally. For these and other reasons, the St. Paul Saints may be the best known minor-league baseball team in America.

Internalize the Brand

Service performers are a powerful medium for building brand meaning and equity. Their actions with customers transform brand vision to brand reality—for better or worse. Service providers make or break a brand, for the customers' actual experiences with the service always prevail in defining the brand for them. With their on-the-job performances, service providers turn a marketer-articulated brand into a customer-experienced brand.

Negative customer experiences are difficult for a company to overcome in its branding efforts, no matter how effective its marketing communications. Superior customer experiences are difficult for competitors to imitate, no matter how effective their marketing communications. As Peters (1997) writes. "It seems that you can knock off everything. . .except awesome service" (p. 457).

Services are just as intangible for employees as they are for customers. Branding is not only an opportunity to establish a mental picture of the service and its reason for being for customers; it also is an opportunity to do this for service providers. The more providers internalize the concept and values of the service, the more consistently and effectively they are likely to perform it. As David Aaker points out in an interview with *Leader to Leader* magazine ("Strategic Lessons" 1998), a common misconception about brands is that they are strictly for external purposes when, in fact, the role of a brand is to communicate inside the company also: "When a brand identity and position are clear, they help all employees—from customer service representatives to new product developers—gauge their actions in terms of a central strategy" (p. 55).

Berry and Parasuraman (1991) describe the concept of internalizing the brand:

> Internalizing the brand involves explaining and selling the brand to employees. It involves sharing with employees the research and strategy behind the presented brand. It involves creative communication of the brand to employees. It involves training employees in brand-strengthening behaviors. It involves rewarding and celebrating employees whose actions support the brand. Most of all, internalizing the brand involves *involving* employees in the care and nurturing of the brand.
>
> Employees will not feel part of nor act out the brand unless they understand it and believe in it. Marketers need to verbalize and visualize the brand for employees, so that employees will verbalize and visualize the brand for customers. Brand internalization must be an ongoing process, just as brand building is an ongoing process with customers. (p. 129)

Just as advertising is a principal brand-building tool externally, so is it a principal tool internally. Enterprise Rent-A-Car and Midwest Express are two companies that specifically consider employees to be a key audience for all of their advertising. They view advertising as a primary means for motivating and educating employees, a viewpoint supported by research that clearly shows employees are influenced by their company's advertising (Gilly and Wolfinbarger 1998).

Enterprise Rent-A-Car first advertised on national television in 1989. The company has honed a consistent presentation of its brand in television advertising: a customer in an auto repair shop phoning Enterprise for a rental car, the theme line "We'll pick you up," the signature "cloaked" car, the distinctive white-on-green *E* logo. The message is clear, and brand awareness is increasing. From 1989 to 1997, aided brand awareness for Enterprise Rent-A-Car increased fourfold according to company research. Increasing brand awareness was not the main purpose in advertising, however. The purpose was to build employee pride in the company. In 1989, company founder Jack Taylor asked his son Andy a decisive question: "You know, Andy, how would we feel if a rental car company half our size came on television and promoted the [car] replacement service?" The seed for the company's inaugural national advertising effort was planted with this simple question. "Our advertising has had a fabulous impact on our employees," comments CEO Andy Taylor. "Our existing employees are proud and prospective employees are impressed when they see that company advertising on '60 Minutes' or a National Football League game."

Midwest Express shares Enterprise Rent-A-Car's philosophy of internalizing the brand through advertising. Says Brenda Skelton, senior vice president of marketing and customer service for Midwest Express:

> Our employees are the most important audience for our marketing efforts. It is easy to market when we just have to generate customer trial. Our employees keep the customers coming back. Our national reputation has grown mainly through our reputation for service.

No company more ardently internalizes its brand than Chick-fil-A. Chick-fil-A invests significant resources to help independent store operators cultivate the Chick-fil-A brand in their local markets. The company organizes brand marketing teams to work with operators in specific markets where it is opening many freestanding stores. The teams consist of marketing, advertising, and public relations specialists from the company's headquarters staff and the marketing firms with which it works. The process begins each year with market-specific brand-equity research for Chick-fil-A and its principal competitors. The company holds operator workshops in individual markets to present the research and discuss its branding implications. The team then works with operators to develop brand-building strategies for their markets on the basis of the research.

Chick-fil-A views the local store operator as the primary brand marketer; the role of the brand marketing team and headquarters staff is to help operators become more effective. Accomplishing this role involves educating the store operators about brand marketing. The operators can withhold marketing funds or ignore the brand marketing team's advice if they so choose. Internalizing the brand through education, market-specific research, customized advising, and tracking each market's performance is critical. Chick-fil-A's Steve Robinson explains:

> Brand-building requires that we educate the operators on why—or they won't do it. This is why we have put more marketing talent in the field. We don't demand. We don't prescribe. We try to persuade by showing how they and Chick-fil-A will benefit. We have to do our homework, do the market research, show the operators why, and ultimately, show results. We cannot use marketing to drive the business unless we are willing to engage operators in the process.

Adds Kenneth Bernhardt, a longtime Chick-fil-A consultant:

> A key marketing step at Chick-fil-A has been getting the operators to take ownership of building the brand. The cows give the brand a distinct personality across markets, and the operators are strengthening the brand in their local markets. It is a powerful one-two punch.

CONCLUSION

Positive brand equity is the marketing advantage that accrues to a company from the synergy of brand awareness and brand meaning. Despite the predisposition to think of branding in the context of tangible products, brand cultivation is just as critical for services. Strong brands increase customers' trust of invisible products while helping them to better understand and visualize what they are buying. Strong-brand service companies consciously pursue distinctiveness in performing and communicating the service, use branding to define their reason for being, connect emotionally with customers, and internalize the brand for service providers so that they will build it for customers.

Dial-A-Mattress, Chick-fil-A, Midwest Express Airlines, Enterprise Rent-A-Car, and the other service companies discussed in this article are their own brands. This is the reality of creating value for customers primarily through service: the company becomes the brand. Marketing and external communications help build the brand, but nothing is more powerful than the customers' actual experiences with the service. Being served freshly haked chocolate chip cookies as you relax in a comfortable leather seat on a Midwest Express jet defines brand meaning and builds brand equity more powerfully than any advertisement.

ACKNOWLEDGMENTS

This article is based on a subset of findings from original research conducted by the author with a sample of 14 high-performance service companies. More than 250 people from the sample companies—from CEOs to frontline service providers—were interviewed. The full study is reported in Leonard L. Berry (1999), *Discovering the Soul of Service: The Nine Drivers of Sustainable Business Success* (New York: Free Press) Portions of the article are drawn or adapted from material first appearing in this book, especially from Chapter 10. Individuals quoted without citation in this article were interviewed as part of the study. The author expresses appreciation to all of the participating companies.

References

Aaker, David A. 1996. *Building Strong Brands*. New York: Free Press.

Beers, Charlotte. 1998. "Building Brands Worthy of Devotion" *Leader to Leader* 11 (Winter): 39–42.

Berry, Leonard L. 1999. *Discovering the Soul of Service: The Nine Drivers of Sustainable Business Success*. New York: Free Press.

——— and A. Parasuraman. 1991. *Marketing Services: Competing Through Quality*. New York: Free Press.

Gilly. Mary C, and Mary Wolfinbarger. 1998. "Advertising's Internal Audience." *Journal of Marketing* 62 (January): 69–88.

Gordon, Seth. 1998. "Permission Marketing." *Fast Company* 14 (April–May): 198–212.

Hudler, Donald W. 1996. "Leadership With Enthusiasm." A speech at Texas A&M University's Center for Retailing Studies Fall Symposium, Dallas, October 17.

Keller, Kevin Lane 1993. "Conceptualization, Measuring and Managing Customer-Based Brand Equity." *Journal of Marketing* 57 (January): 1–22.

Peters, Tom. 1997. *The Circle of Innovation*. New York: Knopf.

Richards, Stan. 1998. "Building a Brand." A speech at Texas A&M University's Center for Retailing Studies Fall Symposium, Dallas, October 8.

Schultz, Howard 1997. *Pour Your Heart Into It*. New York: Hyperion.

Storch, Jerry. 1998. "Building a Brand at Target Stores." A speech at Texas A&M University's Center for Retailing Studies Fall Symposium, Dallas, October 8.

"Strategic Lessons From the World's Best Brands." 1998. *Leader to Leader* 10 (Fall): 54–56.

Thurow, Roger. 1998. "A Sports Icon Regains Its Footing by Using the Moves of the Past." *Wall Street Journal*, January 21, pp. A1 and A8.

Webber, Alan M. 1997. "What Great Brands Do—An Interview of Scott Bedbury." *Fast Company* 10 (August-September): 96–100.

Zeithaml, Valarie A. 1981. "How Consumer Evaluation Processes Differ Between Goods and Services." In *Marketing of Services* Eds. James H. Donnelly and William R. George. Chicago American Marketing Association, 186–189.

The Strategic Levers of Yield Management

SHERYL E. KIMES
RICHARD B. CHASE

Yield management, controlling customer demand through the use of variable pricing and capacity management to enhance profitability, has been examined extensively in the services literature. Most of this work has been tactical and mathematical rather than managerial. In this article, the authors suggest that a broader view of yield management is valuable to both traditional and nontraditional users of the approach. Central to this broader view is the recognition of how different combinations of pricing and duration can be used as strategic levers to position service firms in their markets and the identification of tactics by which management can deploy these strategic levers. The authors also propose that further development of yield management requires that when *the service is delivered should be treated as a design variable that should be as carefully managed as the service process itself.*

Although commonly associated with marketing as a revenue management tool, yield management has significant impacts on other service business functions. It affects operations in capacity planning, human resource management in worker selection and training, and business strategy through the way the service firm positions itself in the market. Despite this widespread impact and the considerable attention it has received, formal yield management is still viewed primarily as a pricing/inventory management tool. What is lacking is a broader theory of yield management that would permit other service industries to gain the benefits of yield management-type thinking and provide insights into new areas in which experienced companies might further apply the concept. Our objective in this article is to develop the groundwork for such a theory. Our focus will be on the strategic levers available for yield management, how they have been applied in traditional yield management settings, and how they, along with some tactical tools, can be applied to other service settings.

A MODIFIED DEFINITION OF YIELD MANAGEMENT

A common definition of yield management is the application of information systems and pricing strategies to "sell the right capacity to the right customers at the right prices" (Smith, Leimkuhler, and Darrow 1992). Implicit in this definition is the notion of time-perishable capacity and, by extension, the notion of segmentation of capacity according to when it is booked, when and how long it is to be used, and according to the customer who uses it. In other words, "an hour is not an hour is not an hour" when it comes to customer preferences or capacity management. In light of this subtle point, we offer a slightly modified definition of the term. That is, yield management may be defined as managing the four Cs of perishable service: calendar (how far in advance reservations are made), clock (the time of day service is offered), capacity (the inventory of service resources), and cost (the price of the service) to manage a fifth C, customer demand, in such a way as to maximize profitability.

Strategic Levers

A successful yield management strategy is predicated on effective control of customer demand. Businesses have two interrelated strategic levers with which to accomplish this: pricing and duration of customer use. Prices can be fixed (one price for the same service for all customers for all times) or variable (different prices for different times or for different customer segments), and duration can be predictable or unpredictable.

Reprinted with permission from *Journal of Service Research* 1, no. 2 (November 1998): 156–166. Sponsored by Center for Service Marketing, Owen Graduate School of Management, Vanderbilt University.

Variable pricing to control demand is conceptually a straightforward process. It can take the form of discount prices at off-peak hours for all customers, such as low weekday rates for movies, or it can be in the form of price discounts for certain classes of customers, such as senior discounts at restaurants.

Duration control presents a more complicated decision problem but at the same time represents an area that would improve the effectiveness of yield management. By implementing duration controls, companies maximize overall revenue across all time periods rather than just during high-demand periods. If managers want to increase control over duration, they can refine their definition of duration, reduce the uncertainty of arrival, reduce the uncertainty of the duration, or reduce the amount of time between customers. We will discuss each of these tactics later.

Different industries use different combinations of variable pricing and duration control (Figure 1). Industries traditionally associated with yield management (hotel, airline, rental car, and cruise line) tend to use variable pricing and a specified or predictable duration (Quadrant 2). Movie theaters, performing arts centers, arenas, and convention centers use a fixed price for a predictable duration (Quadrant 1), whereas restaurants, golf courses, and Internet service providers use a fixed price with unpredictable customer duration (Quadrant 3). Many health care industries charge variable prices (Medicare or private pay) but do not know the duration of patient use (Quadrant 4). There is no fixed demarcation point between quadrants, so an industry may lie partially in one quadrant and partially in another. The intent of this classification method is to help industries not currently using yield management develop a strategic framework for developing yield management. More specifically, what we are trying to show is which quadrant industries are in and what they can do to move to Quadrant 2. For example, restaurant management does not have control of duration; they need to pursue some duration management approach. Or, if hotel management does not adequately control length of stay, they may want to modify their forecasting system from room nights to arrivals to enhance their reservation system.

As indicated above, successful yield management applications are generally found in Quadrant 2 industries. The reason is that a predictable duration enables clear delineation of the service portfolio, and variable pricing enables generating maximum revenue from each service offering within the portfolio. We hasten to point out that even those industries that are listed in this quadrant have structural features that inhibit them from achieving their full profit potential. A brief review of the development of yield management in the airline and hotel industries will help illustrate these points.

Airline Industry

Deregulation of the American airline industry was the major impetus for the development of yield management. Before deregulation in 1978, major carriers offered one-price service between cities. Essentially, most airlines were operating in Quadrant 1: Their

		Price	
		Fixed	**Variable**
Duration	**Predictable**	**Quadrant 1:** Movies Stadiums/Arenas Convention Centers	**Quadrant 2:** Hotels Airlines Rental Cars Cruise Lines
	Unpredictable	**Quadrant 3:** Restaurants Golf Courses Internet Service Providers	**Quadrant 4:** Continuing Care Hospitals

FIGURE 1 Typical Pricing and Duration Positioning of Selected Services Industries

		Price	
		Fixed	Variable
Duration	Predictable	Quadrant 1: Before De-regulation	Quadrant 2: Immediately after De-regulation
	Unpredictable	Quadrant 3: None Identified	Quadrant 4: Hub-and-Spoke System

FIGURE 2 The Airline Industry

flight durations were extremely predictable, and their price was fixed (Figure 2).

Immediately after deregulation, many new airlines emerged, and one airline, People's Express, developed an aggressive low-cost strategy. The People's Express story is well known: Their airfares were considerably lower than those of the major carriers, and customers were attracted to the limited service that People's Express flights offered. The major carriers such as American Airlines, United Airlines, and Delta Airlines, aided by new computerized reservation systems, employed variable pricing on a flight-by-flight basis to match or undercut fares offered by People's Express. Cost-conscious passengers then switched to the major carriers, and People's Express was eventually forced out of business. Donald Burr, the former CEO of People's Express, attributes his airline's failure to the lack of good information technology and the subsequent inability to practice yield management (Anonymous 1992; Cross 1997).

Seeing the benefits of differential pricing, most major North American carriers instituted yield management and moved into Quadrant 2. Yield management allowed airlines to determine the minimum fare (of a set mix of fares) that should be available for a specific flight. Differential pricing, in combination with the predictability of flight duration, gave them the enviable position of variable pricing with predictable duration.

Another trend that emerged after deregulation was the hub-and-spoke system. Previously, airlines operated on an origin-destination basis, and although connecting flights existed, the concept of a hub city did not. Most major airlines now operate with a hub-and-spoke system, and their forecasting and yield management systems are based around the associated flight legs (Skwarek 1996). Leg-based solutions have inherent problems and may lead to suboptimal solutions. Although the revenue on each flight leg may be optimized, revenue over the entire airline network may not. In an attempt to circumvent this problem, some airlines (notably American Airlines) developed virtual nesting systems (Smith, Leimkuhler, and Darrow 1992), in which different origin-destination pairs were classified by revenue generated. Unfortunately, current origin-destination forecasting and yield management systems have a high forecast error that results in an unreliable solution.

The lack of origin-destination forecasting may seem like a minor point, but it prevents airlines from truly managing the predictability of their duration. In a sense, the hub-and-spoke system has caused the airline industry to move into the bottom half of Quadrant 2 or the top half of Quadrant 4. The hub-and-spoke system, in combination with airline pricing systems, has created problems such as passengers attempting to obtain a lower fare by completing only one leg of their multileg flight (a "hidden city"). The empty seat on the remaining flight leg represents lost revenue to the airlines so safeguards have been instituted to avoid this problem. Only one major carrier, Southwest Airlines, has resisted the temptation of the hub-and-spoke system. This represents a competitive advantage for their yield management system because they are better able to manage the predictability of their flight durations (Anonymous 1994b).

Hotel Industry

Unlike the airline industry, traditional hotels are usually located in Quadrant 3. Although group and tour operators have multiple negotiated rates (Hoyle, Dorf, and Jones 1991; Vallen and Vallen 1991), most traditional hotels charge essentially one room rate (or perhaps a low-season and high-season rate) for transient guests. Length of stay is not explicitly considered, and forecasts are designed to predict nightly occupancy (Figure 3). Typically, the goal of the traditional hotel is to maximize occupancy for a given night, and managers seldom look at long-term revenue generation.

After the airlines started using yield management, many hotel managers were impressed with the increased revenue claimed by the airlines and applied the concept of variable pricing to the hotel industry. When hotels started using variable pricing, they did not apply the concept of qualified rates, in which customers had to meet certain requirements to obtain a lower room rate. They instead relied on top-down pricing, in which reservation agents quoted the highest rate first and, if faced with resistance, offered the next of several lower rates until the customers acquiesced or they reached a minimum level previously established by management. Many major hotel chains still use this pricing method. Although short-term revenue gains may result from top-down pricing, customers view this practice unfavorably (Kimes 1994). Most hotels using this approach forecast room nights and use the forecasted nightly occupancy rate to develop pricing recommendations (Kimes 1989). Length-of-stay issues are not considered, and occupancy and rates are managed for one night at a time.

Some hotel chains, notably Marriott and Forte Hotels, saw the benefits associated with predictable durations (Anonymous 1994a). To reap the benefits associated with duration controls, they switched from forecasting room nights to forecasting arrivals by length of stay and/or room rate. Forte charged only one rate and concentrated solely on length of stay. Guests requesting a 2-night stay might be accepted, whereas those requesting a 1-night stay might be rejected depending on the projected demand. Marriott forecasted by arrival day, length of stay, and room rate and was able to determine the best set of reservation requests to accept. Still other hotel chains tried to implement length-of-stay controls without changing their forecasting system from room nights to arrivals. Without arrival information, they had no way of knowing if their restrictions made sense or if they were unnecessarily turning away potential customers.

The focus on length of stay not only changed the forecasting systems in place at leading hotels but also changed the mathematical methods used to develop yield management recommendations. Many hotel chains (e.g., Holiday Inn, Hilton, Sheraton, and Hyatt) have instituted linear-programming-based systems in which length of stay and room rate are explicitly considered (Hensdill 1998; Vinod 1995).

FIGURE 3 The Hotel Industry

		Price	
		Fixed	Variable
Duration	Predictable	Quadrant 1: Forte	Quadrant 2: Marriott, Sheraton, Holiday Inn
	Unpredictable	Quadrant 3: Traditional Hotels	Quadrant 4: Initial Yield Management Attempts

USING THE STRATEGIC LEVERS

Industries in Quadrants 1, 3, and 4 can move into Quadrant 2 to achieve some of the revenue gains associated with yield management by manipulating duration and price. Although there are still problems facing the hotel and airline industries, their experience provides a rich context from which to understand the tactical tools needed to improve revenue generation. Specific tools associated with each strategic yield management lever can allow managers to move their company into a better revenue-generating position.

Duration Methods

If managers want to increase control over duration, they can refine their definition of duration, reduce the uncertainty of arrival, reduce the uncertainty of the duration, or reduce the amount of time between customers (Figure 4).

Refining the Definition of Duration Duration is how long customers use a service and is measured either in terms of time (i.e., the number of nights or number of hours) or by event (i.e., a meal or a round of golf). When duration is defined as an event rather than time, forecasting the length of duration generally becomes more difficult. Thus, if duration for an industry could be defined in time rather than events, better forecasting, and hence control of duration, would likely result.

Even industries that use time-based duration definitions can refine this definition and thereby enhance their operations. Most hotels sell rooms by the day, or more specifically, they sell rooms from 3 p.m. (check-in) to noon (check-out). Sheraton Hotels and The Peninsula Hotel in Beverly Hills allow customers to check in at any time of the day and check out at any time without penalty (Anonymous 1997; Barker 1998). By refining their definition of duration, they have improved customer satisfaction, made better use of capacity, and increased revenue.

Uncertainty of Arrival Because many capacity-constrained firms have perishable inventory, they must protect themselves from no-shows or late arrivals. Firms can use both internal (not involving customers) and external (involving customers) approaches to decrease uncertainty of arrival.

Internal approaches Most capacity-constrained service firms use overbooking to protect themselves against no-shows. Published overbooking models often use Markovian decision processes or simulation approaches (for example, Lieberman and Yechialli 1978; Rothstein 1971, 1985; Schlifer and Vardi 1975), but in practice many companies use service-level approaches. (Anonymous 1993; Smith, Leimkuhler, and Darrow 1992) or the critical fractile method (as suggested by Sasser, Olsen, and Wyckoff 1978). The key to a successful overbooking policy is

FIGURE 4 Methods of Managing Duration

	Possible Approaches
Refine Definition	Time Event
Uncertainty of Arrival: Internal Measures	Forecasting Overbooking
Uncertainty of Arrival: External Measures	Penalties Deposits
Uncertainty of Duration: Internal Measures	Forecasting by Time of Arrival, Length of Stay, and Customer Characteristics
Uncertainty of Duration External Measures	Penalties Restrictions Process Analysis
Reduce Time Between Customers	Process Analysis

to obtain accurate no-show and cancellation information and to develop overbooking levels that will maintain an acceptable level of customer service.

Once an overbooking policy is implemented, companies must develop good internal methods for handling displaced customers. The frontline personnel who must assist displaced customers should receive appropriate training and compensation for dealing with potentially angry consumers. Companies can choose to select which customers to displace on either a voluntary or involuntary manner. The airline industry, with its voluntary displacement system, has increased customer goodwill while increasing long-term profit (Anonymous 1993; Rothstein 1985). Other industries base their displacement decision on time of arrival (if customers are late, their reservation is no longer honored), frequency of use (regular customers are never displaced), or perceived importance (important customers are never displaced).

External approaches External approaches to reduce arrival uncertainty shift the responsibility of arriving to the customer. The deposit policies used at many capacity-constrained service firms such as cruise lines and resorts are excellent examples of external approaches. In addition, the cancellation penalties imposed by these companies represent an attempt to make customers more responsible for arriving. Restaurants are experimenting with cancellation penalties and ask customers for their credit card numbers when taking reservations (Brehaus 1998). If patrons do not arrive within 15 minutes of the reservation time, a penalty fee is charged to their credit cards. Interestingly, the car rental industry, which has considerable yield management experience, makes very limited use of external approaches. With the exception of specialty cars and vans, customers are not asked to guarantee their rental and have no responsibility for showing up. With no incentives for customers to arrive, it is not surprising that in busy tourist markets such as Florida, no-shows can account for as much as 70 percent of the reservations (Stern and Miller 1995). Besides these negative incentives, some companies use service guarantees to encourage people to show up on time. American Golf, for example, offers discounted or free play to golfers whose actual tee-off time is delayed by more than 10 minutes of their reservation time.

Uncertainty of Duration Reducing duration uncertainty enables management to better gauge capacity requirements and hence make better decisions as to which reservation requests to accept. As in the case of arrival uncertainty, both internal and external approaches can be used for this purpose.

Internal approaches Internal approaches include accurate forecasting of the length of use and the number of early and late arrivals and departures and improving the consistency of service delivery. By knowing how long customers plan to use the service, managers can make better decisions as to which reservation requests to accept. If a restaurant manager knows that parties of two take approximately 45 minutes to dine and parties of four take about 75 minutes, he or she can make better allocation decisions. Likewise, knowing how many customers will change their planned duration of use enhances capacity decisions. For example, in a hotel, accurately forecasting how many customers book for 4 nights but leave after 3, or request additional nights, facilitates room and staff allocations. Similarly, if a rental car company knows that 20 percent of its week-long rentals are returned after 5 days, the fleet supply requirement can be adjusted accordingly.

Early research and practice in yield management focused on single flight legs or room nights and did not consider duration. Expected marginal seat revenue (EMSR) based models (Belobaba 1987; Littlewood 1972) are widely used in the airline industry (Williamson 1992) and result in allocation decisions for flight legs at various days before departure. Early hotel yield management systems based minimum rate decisions on forecasted occupancy but did not consider the impact of length of stay (Kimes 1989). Some airlines have tried to compensate for the lack of duration control by using actual nesting (Smith, Leimkuhler, and Darrow 1992; Vinod 1995; Williamson 1992) but still have not achieved the goal of full origin-destination control (Vinod 1995).

Linear programming has been used to help make better duration and pricing allocation decisions (Kimes 1989; Weatherford 1995; Williamson 1992). The bid price, defined as the shadow price of the capacity constraint, can be used to determine the marginal value of an additional seat, room, or other inventory unit (Phillips 1994; Vinod 1995; Williamson 1992). This value can then be used to determine the minimum price available for different durations. Dynamic programming (Bitran and Mondschein 1995) has also been suggested as a possible method for considering hotel length of stay.

The accuracy of the forecast affects the effectiveness of the yield management system. Lee (1990), in his study of airline forecasting, found that a 10 percent improvement in forecast accuracy resulted in a 3 percent to 5 percent increase in revenue on high-demand flights.

If duration is to be explicitly addressed, forecasts of customer duration must be developed. Airlines typically forecast demand by flight leg (Lee 1990; Vinod 1995), but to truly practice duration control, airlines must forecast demand by all possible origin-destination pairs. As previously mentioned, the hub-and-spoke system has increased the number of forecasts required and the subsequent accuracy of those forecasts. Some airlines have tried to reduce the number of forecasts needed by using virtual nesting (Smith, Leimkuhler, and Darrow 1992; Vinod 1995). Preliminary research on airline-forecasting accuracy (Weatherford 1998) shows that an increase in the number of daily forecasts required increases the forecast error.

When hotels forecast customer duration, they must forecast by day of arrival, length of stay, and possible rate class (Kimes, O'Sullivan, and Scott 1998). Hotels using linear programming and bid-price approaches forecast at this level of detail, and some have developed even more detailed forecasts. The magnitude of this problem becomes apparent when you consider that for each day of arrival, a hotel might consider 10 different lengths of stay and 10 different rate classes. If room type is included, a hotel may have 200 to 300 different forecasts per day.

Consistency of duration (i.e., most customers using the service for about the same length of time) is typically achieved through internal process changes. For example, TGI Fridays redesigned their restaurant menus and service delivery systems to make dining time more consistent as well as faster. Some restaurants in the theater district of New York City have placed an hourglass on the table of each party. When the sand in the hourglass is gone, patrons have a visual cue to finish dinner and leave so they will not be late to the theater. Or, in a much different context, if a prison warden knows that 25 percent of prisoners sentenced to 10 years serve only 4, additional prisoners may be incarcerated.

External Approaches External approaches for handling uncertainty of duration generally reach the customer in the form of deposits or penalties. Some hotels have instituted early and late departure fees (Miller 1995), and airlines have penalized passengers who purchase tickets through hidden cities. Although penalties may work in the short term, they risk incurring customer wrath and hurting the company in the long run. For this reason, internal approaches are generally preferable.

Reduce Time between Customers Reducing the amount of time between customers (changeover time reduction), by definition, means that more customers can be served in the same or a shorter period of time. Although changeover time reduction is not normally considered a tool of yield management, it is a tactic that can be used to increase revenue per available inventory unit. Such tactics play an important role in the yield management strategy. Changeover time reduction has become a common strategy for airlines. Southwest Airlines and Shuttle by United both boast of 20-minute ground turnarounds of their aircraft (compared to the average of 45 minutes at most airlines) and have been able to increase the utilization of their planes (Kimes and Young 1997). Many restaurants have instituted computerized table management systems that track tables in use, the progress of the meal, and when the bill is paid. When customers leave, the table management system notifies bussers, and the table is cleared and reset (Liddle 1996). The result is an increase in table utilization and, hence, revenue per table.

Price

Industries actively practicing yield management use differential pricing–charging customers using the same service at the same time different prices, depending on customer and demand characteristics. Passengers in the economy section of a flight from New York City to Los Angeles may pay from nothing (for those using frequent-flyer vouchers) to more than $1,500. The fares vary according to the time of reservation, the restrictions imposed, or the group or company affiliation. In contrast to such Quadrant 2 pricing, Quadrant 1 and 3 industries use relatively fixed pricing and charge customers using the same service at the same time the same price.

Customers tend to develop reference prices for various transactions. If companies change price, they must do so carefully to avoid upsetting their customers (Kahneman, Knetsch, and Thaler 1986). Although it is possible to charge more solely based on high demand, customers may resent being charged different prices for essentially the same service. Two mechanisms–proper price mix and rate fences–provide opportunities to alter price while maintaining goodwill (Figure 5).

	Possible Approaches
Proper Price Mix	Price Elasticities Competitive Pricing Optimal Pricing Policies
Rate Fences: Physical	Type of Inventory Amenities
Rate Fences: Nonphysical	Restrictions Time of Usage Time of Reservation Group Membership

FIGURE 5 Methods of Managing Price

Proper Price Mix Companies must be sure that they offer a logical mix of prices from which to choose. If customers do not see much distinction between the different prices being quoted, a differential-pricing strategy may not work. Determining the best mix of prices is difficult because management often has little information on price elasticities. This, in turn, often results in pricing decisions based solely on competitive pressures. It should be noted, however, that airlines such as American Airlines have been working hard on the issues of elasticity and of multiple legs and have made some progress.

Optimal pricing policies, in which customers are asked to name the prices that they would consider to be cheap, expensive, too cheap to be of reasonable quality, and too expensive to be considered, have been developed by Taco Bell and have been tested for use with meeting planners (Lewis and Shoemaker 1997). Optimal pricing policies represent a relatively simple way of determining price sensitivity and acceptable price ranges.

Although not widely publicized, some restaurant companies are experimenting with menu pricing based on price elasticities. Large chain restaurant companies analyze the price elasticities of various menu items and make appropriate pricing changes (Kelly, Kiefer, and Burdett 1994).

Rate Fences The possession of a good pricing structure does not ensure the success of a variable pricing strategy. Companies must also have a logical rationale or, in industry terms, rate fences that can be used to justify price discrimination. (Or, as one somewhat cynical hotel executive states, "We want something we can say out loud without laughing.")

Quadrant 2 industries often use rate fences such as when the reservation is booked or when the service is consumed, to determine the price a customer will pay. Rate fences refer to qualifications that must be met to receive a discount (Hanks, Cross, and Noland 1992). Rate fences can be physical or nonphysical in nature and represent a rationale for why some customers pay different prices for the same service.

Physical rate fences include tangible features such as room type or view for hotels, seat type or location for airlines, or table location for restaurants. Other physical rate fences are the presence or absence of certain amenities (free golf cart use with a higher price, free breakfast with a higher price, or free soft drinks at a movie theater).

Nonphysical rate fences can be developed that can help shift demand to slower periods, reward regular customers, or reward reliable customers. Nonphysical rate fences include cancellation or change penalties and benefits based on when the reservation was booked, desired service duration, group membership or affiliation, and time of use.

Even today, it is common practice for companies to adopt differential pricing schemes without rate fences. Hotels use top-down pricing in which reservation agents quote the rack rate (generally the highest rate) and only quote lower rates if customers ask for them. Knowledgeable customers may know to ask for the lower rate, but inexperienced customers may not. Customers view this practice highly unfavorably (Kimes 1994).

MOVING TO A MORE PROFITABLE QUADRANT

The strategic levers described above can be used to help companies move into more profitable quadrants by making duration more predictable and/or by varying prices. Generally, companies try to manipulate one strategic lever at a time, but it is possible, although difficult, for a company to try to simultaneously adjust price and duration. The following examples of potential moves show the possibilities for various industries.

Differential Pricing

Quadrant 1 to Quadrant 2

Movie Theaters Although reservation systems and differential pricing have been used in Europe for many years. American movie theaters usually charge the same price for all seats and offer discounted seats only for matinees or for senior citizens. However, things are changing rapidly, and some new movie houses are now offering differential pricing based on seat location, time of show, and access to amenities. For example, the 70-seat Premium Cinema in Lombard, Illinois, has been booked solid since its opening April 3, 1998. Guests willing to pay $15 for access to a separate entrance with valet parking are admitted to a private lounge, where they can purchase champagne at $12 per glass and buy prime-rib sandwiches at the same price. They offer free popcorn (all you can eat) and have a full-time concierge to get it for the customers. As of yet, they have not gone to the next step of developing an overbooking strategy.

Control Duration

Quadrant 3 to Quadrant 1

Golf Courses Golf courses seem to be in the worst possible position–they charge a fixed price for an event of unknown duration. Much of the problem stems from the definition of duration as an event, typically 18 holes of golf played during daylight hours. Alternative definitions of duration abound. The golf course could sell 9-hole rounds; it could institute shotgun golf, in which different groups start simultaneously at multiple holes; or it could use express golf, in which golfers run between holes and receive two scores, elapsed time and stroke count, at the end of each round. (The latter perhaps becoming a new Olympic event.) None of these modifications reduce variability in and of themselves; however, they do provide ways of redefining duration for more creative applications of yield management.

Arrival uncertainty could be reduced by instituting deposit policies or by developing good overbooking policies. Duration uncertainty could be reduced by adding marshals to help move golfers along on the course, by provision of free golf carts to speed the time between holes, and by more accurately forecasting play length based on time of day, week, and party size. More golfers could be accommodated if tee-time intervals were reduced or if party size were better regulated.

Control Duration

Quadrant 4 to Quadrant 2

Health Care Health care organizations use differential pricing (often government mandated) but have difficulties managing duration. If hospital or nursing home managers do not know how long patients will be using beds or rooms, it is difficult to effectively plan and manage capacity. In a nursing home, the health of potential patients could be evaluated and actuarial tables used to estimate the duration of patient stay. In private and nonprofit facilities, attempts could be made to select the best mix of private-pay and Medicare patients with a bias toward private-pay patients with a long duration.

The issue of duration control of health care has caused political controversy. During the mid-1990s, insurance companies in New York reduced the maximum length of insurable hospital stay for childbirth to 1 day. After intensive lobbying pressure from hospitals and medical associations, the state legislature outlawed this practice and guaranteed all new mothers a minimum length of stay of 48 hours.

Differential Pricing

Quadrant 3 to Quadrant 4

Internet Service Providers (ISPs) ISPs offer Internet bandwidth to customers. Because not all customers use their full allotment of bandwidth at the same time, the ISP overbooks the bandwidth. If too many customers try to access the Internet at once, service deteriorates.

ISPs operate at 100 percent capacity during certain times of the day and at other times have available bandwidth. Currently, most ISPs charge a flat monthly rate for Internet access, and there is no off-peak discount. Some customers are heavy users during the day, whereas others are heavy nighttime users. ISPs must maintain a mix of these customers to operate effectively. By identifying common demographic characteristics within each segment, ISPs could target specific types of users to add to the mix (M. Freimer, personal communication, 1998).

CONCLUSION

Effective use of the strategic levers of pricing and duration control can help capacity-constrained firms make more profitable use of their resources. Real potential exists for novel use of these tools in industries not typically associated with yield management. Even companies with yield management experience can improve performance by refining their deployment of these levers. The research challenge is to help managers identify yield management opportunities and to develop appropriate pricing and duration control approaches.

Beyond where to apply yield management, there are the questions of how to develop a yield management strategy, how to train people in the tools to implement it, and how to maintain and improve customer satisfaction while applying yield management practices. In the long run, achieving the full potential from yield management lies in management's ability to market and manage every available moment as a unique product. This, in turn, requires that we treat when the service is provided as a design variable that should be as carefully managed as the service process itself. Such a reformulation presents an exciting conceptual challenge to the emerging field of service research.

References

"Adding to Forte's Fortune," (1994a), *Scorecard*, Second Quarter, 4–5.

Barker, J. (1998), "Flexible Check-in Expands," *Successful Meetings* 47 (January): 32.

Belobaba, P. P. (1987), "Air Travel Demand and Airline Seat Inventory Management," Ph.D. thesis, Massachusetts Institute of Technology.

Bitran, G. R. and S. V. Mondschein (1995), "An Application of Yield Management to the Hotel Industry Considering Multiple Day Stays," *Operations Research*, 43, 427–43.

Brehaus, B. (1998), "Handling No-Shows: Operators React to Reservation Plan," *Restaurant Business Magazine* 1 (16): 13.

"A Conversation with Don Burr," (1992), *Scorecard*, Fourth Quarter, 6–7.

Cross, R. G. (1997), *Revenue Management: Hard-Core Tactics for Market Domination*. New York: Broadway Books.

"Flying High with Herb Kelleher," (1994b), *Scorecard*, Third Quarter, 1–3.

Freimer, M. (1998), personal communication.

Hanks, R. D., R. G. Cross, and R. P. Noland. (1992), "Discounting in the Hotel Industry: A New Approach," *Cornell Hotel and Restaurant Administration Quarterly* 33 (3): 40–45.

Hensdill, C. (1998), "The Culture of Revenue Management," *Hotels* (March): 83–86.

"Hotel Adopts 24-Hour Check-in Policy," (1997), *Hospitality Law* 12 (1): 7.

Hoyle, L. H., D. C. Dorf, and T. J. A. Jones. (1991), *Managing Conventions and Group Business*, Washington, DC: The Educational Institute of the American Hotel and Motel Association.

Kahneman, D., J. Knetsch, and R. Thaler. (1986), "Fairness as a Constraint on Profit Seeking: Entitlements in the Market," *American Economic Review* 76 (4): 728–41.

Kelly, T. J., N. M. Kiefer, and K. Burdett. (1994), "A Demand-Based Approach to Menu Pricing," *Cornell Hotel and Restaurant Administration Quarterly* 34 (3): 40–45.

Kimes, S. E. (1989), "Yield Management: A Tool for Capacity-Constrained Service Firms," *Journal of Operations Management* 8 (4): 348–63.

———. (1994), "Perceived Fairness of Yield Management," *Cornell Hotel and Restaurant Administration Quarterly* 34 (1): 22–29.

Kimes, S. E. and Franklin Young. (1997), "Shuttle by United," *Interfaces* 27 (3): 1–13.

Kimes, S. E., M. O'Sullivan and D. Scott. (1998), "Hotel Forecasting Methods," working paper. Cornell University School of Hotel Administration.

Lee, A. O. (1990), "Airline Reservations Forecasting: Probabilistic and Statistical Models of the Booking Process," Ph.D. thesis, Massachusetts Institute of Technology.

Lewis, R. C and S. Shoemaker (1997), "Price Sensitivity Measurement: A Tool for the Hospitality Industry," *Cornell Hotel and Restaurant Administration Quarterly* 38 (2): 44–54.

Liddle, A. (1996), "New Computerized Table Management Reduces Guests' Waits, Empty Seats," *Nation's Restaurant News* (August 5): 22.

Lieberman, V. and U. Yechialli (1978), "On the Hotel Overlooking Problem: An Inventory Problem with Stochastic Cancellations," *Management Science* 24, 1117–26.

Littlewood, K. (1972), "Forecasting and Control of Passenger Bookings," *AGIFORS Symposium Proceedings* 12, 95–117.

Miller, L. (1995), "Check-Out Made Pricier," *Wall Street Journal*, October 20, B6.

Phillips, R. L. (1994), "A Marginal Value Approach to Airline Origin and Destination Revenue Management," in *Proceedings of the 16th Conference on System Modeling and Optimization*, J. Henry and P. Yvon, eds. New York: Springer-Verlag, 907–17.

Rothstein, M. (1971), "An Airline Overbooking Model," *Transportation Science* 5, 180–92.

———. (1985), "OR and the Airline Overbooking Problem," *Operations Research* 33 (2): 237–48.
Sasser, W. E., R. P. Olsen, and D. D. Wyckoff (1978), *Management of Service Operations*. Boston: Allyn and Bacon.
Schlifer E. and Y. Vardi. (1975), "An Airline Overbooking Policy," *Transportation Sciences* 9, 101–14.
"Simon Says," (1993), *Scorecard*, First Quarter, 10–12.
Skwarek, D. K. (1996), "Competitive Impacts of Yield Management System Components: Forecasting and Sell-Up Models," MIT Flight Transportation Lab Report No. R96–6. Cambridge, MA: Massachusetts Institute of Technology.
Smith, B. C., J. F. Leimkuhler, and R. M. Darrow. (1992), "Yield Management at American Airlines," *Interfaces* 22 (1): 8–31.
Stern, G. and L. Miller (1995), "Rental Car Companies Set to Impose Cancellation Penalties for No-Shows," *The Wall Street Journal*, December 26, A3.
Vallen, J. J. and G. K. Vallen (1991), *Check-in, Check-Out*, Dubuque, IA: William C. Brown.
Vinod, B. (1995), "Origin-and-Destination Yield Management," in *Handbook of Airline Economics*, D. Jenkins, ed. New York: McGraw-Hill, 459–68.
Weatherford, L. R. (1995), "Length of Stay Heuristics: Do They Really Make a Difference?" *Cornell Hotel and Restaurant Administration Quarterly* 36 (6): 47–56.
———(1998), "Forecasting Issues in Revenue Management," INFORMS conference presentation, Montreal, Canada, May.
Williamson, E. L. (1992), "Airline Network Seat Control," Ph.D. thesis, Massachusetts Institute of Technology.

PART THREE

Managing the Service Delivery Process

CHAPTER 8

Designing and Managing Service Processes

Ultimately, only one thing really matters in service encounters—the customer's perceptions of what occurred.

—RICHARD B. CHASE AND SRIRAM DASU

Processes are the architecture of services, describing the method and sequence in which service operating systems work and how they link together to create the service experiences and outcomes that customers will value. In high-contact services, customers themselves become an integral part of the operation. Badly designed processes, often result in slow, frustrating, and poor-quality service delivery and are likely to annoy customers. Similarly, poor processes make it difficult for frontline staff to do their jobs well, result in low productivity, and increase the risk of service failures.

One of the distinctive characteristics of many services is the way in which the customer is involved in their creation and delivery. But all too often, service design and operational execution seem to ignore the customer perspective, with each step in the process being handled as a discrete event rather than being integrated into a seamless process.

In this chapter, we emphasize the importance of service marketers' understanding how service processes work and where customers fit within the operation. Specifically, we address the following questions.

1. How can service blueprinting be used to design a service and create a satisfying experience for customers?
2. What can be done to reduce the likelihood of failures during service delivery?
3. How can service redesign improve both quality and productivity?
4. Under what circumstances should customers be viewed as coproducers of service, and what are the implications?
5. What factors lead customers to embrace or reject new self-service technologies?
6. What should managers do to control uncooperative or abusive customers?

BLUEPRINTING SERVICES TO CREATE VALUED EXPERIENCES AND PRODUCTIVE OPERATIONS

It's no easy task to design a service, especially one that must be delivered in real time with customers present in the service factory. To design services that are both satisfying for customers and operationally efficient, marketers and operations specialists need to work together. In high-contact services, in which employees interact directly with customers, it may also be appropriate to involve human resource experts in the design of service processes. A key tool in service design is blueprinting, a more sophisticated version of flowcharting (introduced in Chapter 2).

The design for a new building or a ship is usually captured on architectural drawings called blueprints, so called because reproductions have traditionally been printed on special paper on which all the drawings and annotations appear in blue. These blueprints show what the product should look like and detail the specifications to which it should conform. In contrast to the physical architecture of a building, ship, or piece of equipment, service processes have a largely intangible structure. That makes them all the more difficult to visualize. The same is true of such processes as logistics, industrial engineering, decision theory, and computer systems analysis, each of which uses techniques similar to blueprinting to describe processes involving flows, sequences, relationships, and dependencies.[1]

Developing a Blueprint

How does one get started on developing a service blueprint? First, you need to identify all the key activities involved in creating and delivering the service in question; then you must specify the linkages between these activities.[2] Initially, it is best to keep activities relatively aggregated in order to define the "big picture." Subsequently, any given activity can be refined by "drilling down" to obtain a higher level of detail. In an airline context, for instance, the passenger activity "boards aircraft" can be decomposed into steps: Wait for seat rows to be announced, give agent boarding pass for verification, walk down jetway, enter aircraft, let flight attendant verify boarding pass, find seat, stow carry-on bag, sit down.

A key characteristic of service blueprinting is that it distinguishes between what customers experience "front-stage" and the activities of employees and support processes "backstage," where customers can't see them. Between the two lies what is called the line of visibility. Operationally oriented businesses are sometimes so focused on managing backstage activities that they neglect to consider the customer's view of front-stage activities. Accounting firms, for instance, often have elaborately documented procedures and standards for how to conduct an audit properly but may lack clear standards for when and how to host a meeting with clients or how to answer the telephone when they call.

Service blueprints clarify the interactions between customers and employees and how these interactions are supported by additional activities and systems backstage. Because they show the interrelationships among employee roles, operational processes, information technology, and customer interactions, blueprints can facilitate the integration of marketing, operations, and human resource management within a firm. There is no single, required way to prepare a service blueprint, but it's recommended that a consistent approach be used within any one organization. To illustrate blueprinting later in this chapter, we adapt and simplify an approach proposed by Jane Kingman-Brundage.[3]

Blueprinting also gives managers the opportunity to identify potential process *fail points*, where there is a significant risk of things going wrong and diminishing service quality. Knowledge of such fail points enables managers to design procedures to avoid their occurrence or to prepare contingency plans (or both). Points where customers commonly have to wait can also be pinpointed. Standards can then be developed for execution of each activity, including times for completion of a task, maximum wait times between tasks, and scripts to guide interactions between staff members and customers.

Creating a Script for Employees and Customers

A well-planned script should provide a full description of the service encounter and can help identify potential or existing problems in a specific service process. Recall from Chapter 2 the discussion and script for teeth cleaning and a simple dental examination involving three players—the patient, the receptionist, and the dental hygienist (Figure 2-9). By examining existing scripts, service managers may discover ways to modify the nature of customer and employee roles to improve service delivery, increase productivity, and enhance the nature of the customer's experience. As service delivery procedures evolve in response to new technology or other factors, revised scripts may need to be developed.

Blueprinting the Restaurant Experience: A Three-Act Performance

To illustrate blueprinting of a high-contact, people-processing service, we examine the experience of dinner for two at Chez Jean, an upscale restaurant that enhances its core food service with a variety of supplementary services (Figure 8-1). A typical rule of thumb in full-service restaurants is that the cost of purchasing the food ingredients represents about 20–30 percent of the price of the meal. The balance can be seen as the "fees" that the customer is willing to pay for renting a table and chairs in a pleasant setting, hiring the services of expert food preparers and their kitchen equipment, and providing serving staff to wait on them both inside and outside the dining room.

The key components of the blueprint, reading from top to bottom, are:

1. Definition of standards for each front-stage activity (only a few examples specified in the figure)
2. Physical and other evidence for front-stage activities (specified for all steps)
3. Principal customer actions (illustrated by pictures)
4. Line of interaction
5. Front-stage actions by customer-contact personnel
6. Line of visibility
7. Backstage actions by customer contact personnel
8. Support processes involving other service personnel
9. Support processes involving information technology

From left to right, the blueprint prescribes the sequence of actions over time. In earlier chapters and the reading by Stephen Grove and Raymond Fisk (pp. 78–87), we saw that service performances can be likened to theater. To emphasize the involvement of human actors in service delivery, we have followed the practice adopted by some service organizations of using pictures to illustrate each of the 14 principal steps involving our two customers (other steps are not shown), beginning with making a reservation and concluding with departure from the restaurant after the meal. Like many high-contact services involving discrete transactions—as opposed to the continuous delivery found in, say, utility or insurance services—the "restaurant drama" can be divided into three "acts," representing activities that take place before the core product is encountered, delivery of the core product (in this case, the meal), and subsequent activities while still involved with the service provider.

The "stage," or servicescape, includes both the exterior and the interior of the restaurant. Front-stage actions take place in a very visual environment; restaurants are often quite theatrical in their use of physical evidence (such as furnishings, decor, uniforms, lighting, and table settings) and may also use background music in their efforts to create a themed environment that matches their market positioning.

Act I: Prologue and Introductory Scenes In this particular drama, Act I begins with making a reservation—an interaction conducted by telephone with an unseen employee, often hours or even days in advance of visiting the restaurant. In theatrical terms, the telephone conversation might be likened to a radio drama, with impressions being created on the evidence of the respondent's voice, speed of response, and style of the

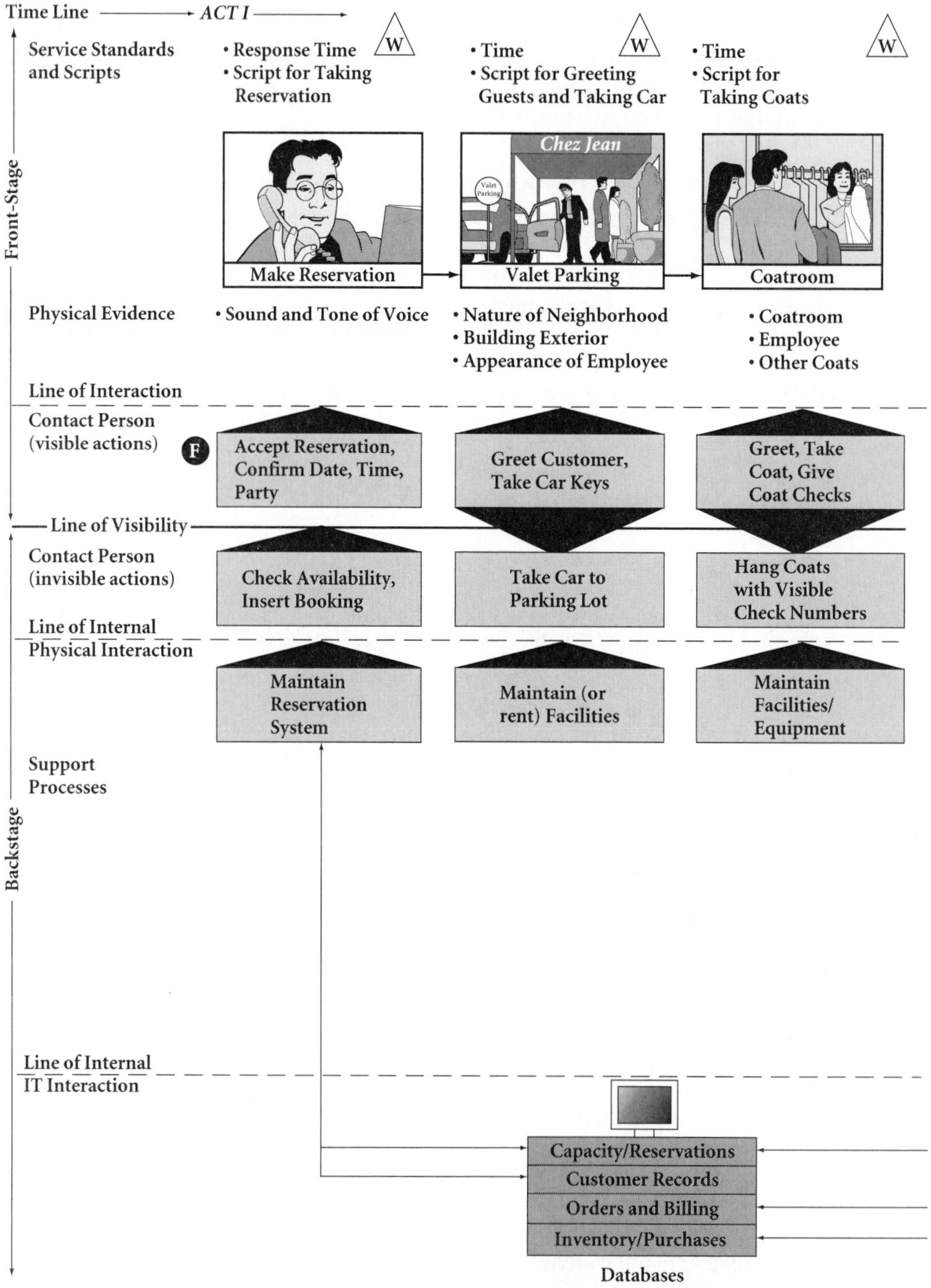

FIGURE 8-1 Blueprinting a Full-Service Restaurant Experience

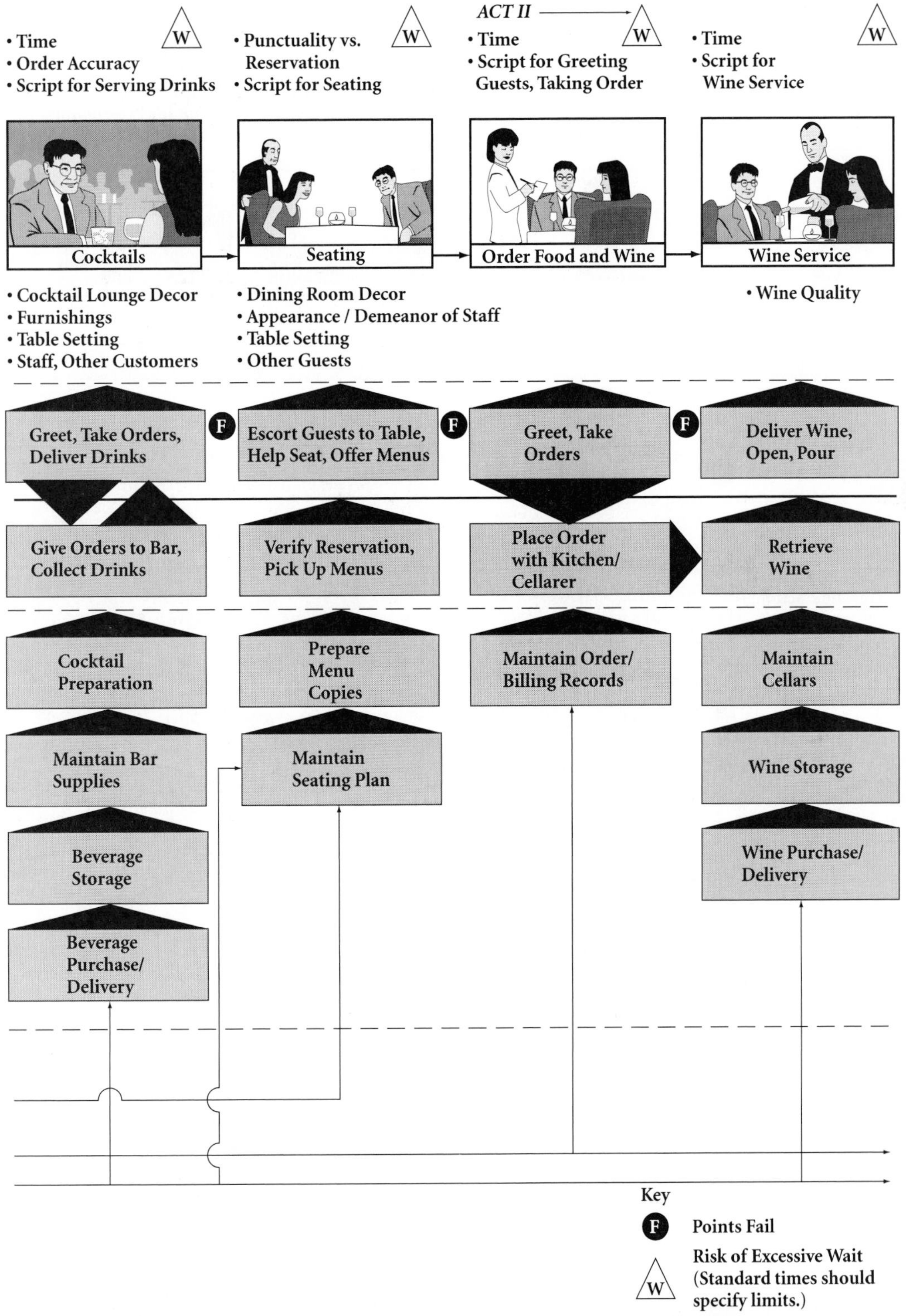

FIGURE 8-1 (Continued)

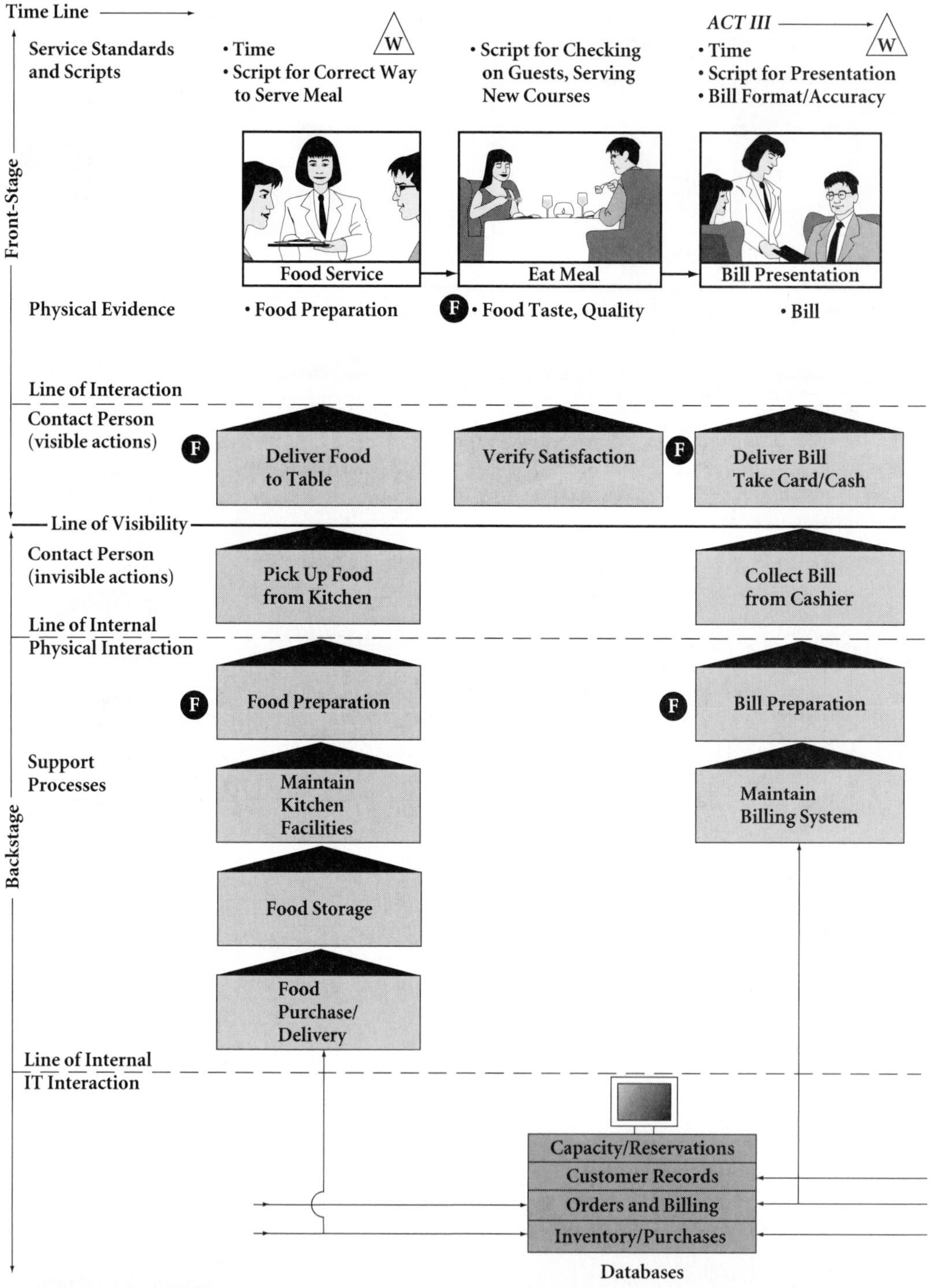

FIGURE 8-1 (Continued)

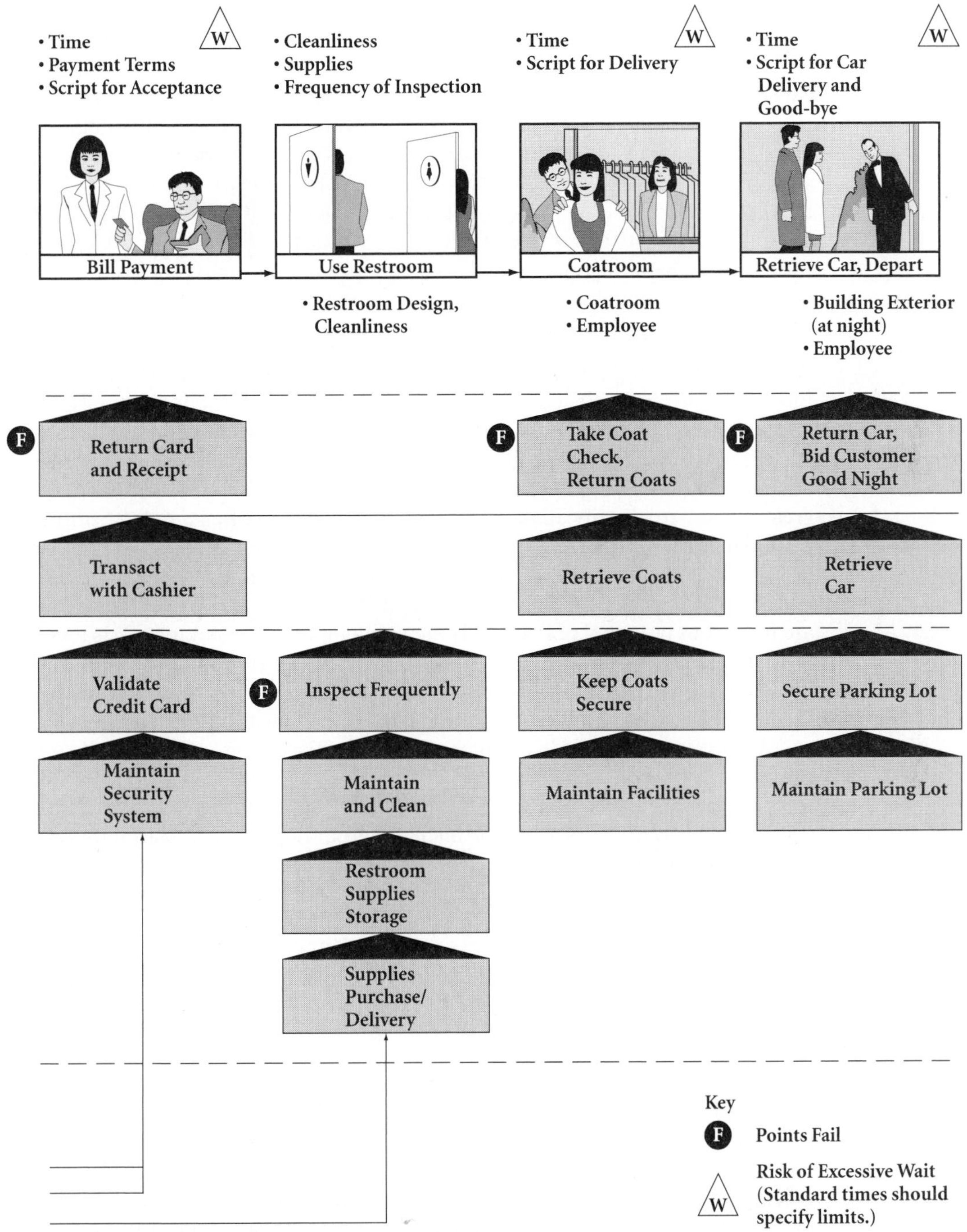

FIGURE 8-1 (Continued)

conversation. On the customers' arrival at the restaurant, a valet parks their car, and they leave their coats in the coatroom, and they enjoy a drink in the bar area while waiting for their table. The act concludes with their being escorted to a table and seated.

These five steps constitute our customers' initial experience of the restaurant performance, with each involving an interaction with an employee—by phone or face to face. By the time the customers reach their table in the dining room, they have been exposed to several supplementary services and have also encountered a sizable cast of characters, including five or more contact personnel, as well as many other customers.

Standards can be set for each service activity but should be based on a good understanding of guests' expectations. Below the line of visibility, the blueprint identifies key actions that should take place to ensure that each front-stage step is performed in a manner that meets or exceeds those expectations. These actions include recording reservations, handling customers' coats, preparing and delivering food, maintaining facilities and equipment, training and assignment of staff for each task, and using information technology to access, input, store, and transfer relevant data.

Act II: Delivery of the Core Product As the curtain rises on Act II, our customers are finally about to experience the core service they came for. For simplicity, we've condensed the meal into just four scenes. In practice, reviewing the menu and placing the order are two separate activities; meantime, meal service proceeds on a course-by-course basis. If you were running a restaurant yourself, you would need to go into greater detail to identify all the steps involved in what is often a tightly scripted drama. Assuming that all goes well, the two guests will have an excellent meal, nicely served in a pleasant atmosphere, and perhaps a fine wine to enhance it. But if the restaurant fails to satisfy customer expectations during Act II, it's going to be in serious trouble. There are numerous potential fail points. Is the menu information complete? Is it intelligible? Is everything listed on the menu available this evening? Will explanations and advice be given in a friendly and noncondescending manner for guests who have questions about specific menu items or are unsure about which wine to order?

After our guests decide on their meals, they place their order with the server, who must then pass on the details to personnel in the kitchen, bar, and billing desk. Mistakes in transmitting information are a frequent cause of quality failures in many organizations. Bad handwriting or unclear verbal requests can lead to delivery of the wrong items altogether or of the right items incorrectly prepared.

In subsequent scenes of Act II, our customers may evaluate not only the quality of food and drink—the most important dimension of all—but also how promptly it is served (not too promptly, for that would suggest frozen foods cooked by microwave) and the style of service. A technically correct performance by the server can still be spoiled by such human failures as disinterested, cold, ingratiating behavior or an overly casual manner.

Act III: The Drama Concludes The meal may be over, but much is still taking place both front-stage and backstage as the drama moves to its close. The core service has now been delivered, and we'll assume that our customers are happily digesting it. Act III should be short. The action in each of the remaining scenes should move smoothly, quickly, and pleasantly, with no shocking surprises at the end. We can hypothesize that in a North American environment, most customers' expectations would probably include the following.

- An accurate, intelligible bill is presented promptly as soon as the customer requests it.
- Payment is handled politely and expeditiously (with all major credit cards acceptable); the guests are thanked for their patronage and invited to come again.

- Customers visiting the restrooms find them clean and properly supplied.
- The right coats are promptly retrieved from the coatroom.
- The customers' car is brought to the door promptly, in the same condition as when it was left; the attendant thanks them again and bids them a good evening.

Identifying Fail Points

Running a good restaurant is a complex business, and much can go wrong. A good blueprint should draw attention to points in service delivery where things are particularly at risk of going wrong. From a customer perspective, the most serious fail points, marked in our blueprint by Ⓕ are those that will result in failure to access or enjoy the core product. They involve the reservation (Could the customer get through by phone? Was a table available at the desired time and date? Was the reservation recorded accurately?) and seating (Was a table available when promised?).

Because service delivery takes place over time, there is also the possibility of delays between specific actions, requiring the customers to wait. Common locations for such waits are identified by ⚠. Excessive waits will annoy customers. In practice, every step in the process—both front-stage and backstage—has some potential for failures and delays. In fact, failures often lead directly to delays, reflecting orders that were never passed on or time spent correcting mistakes.

David Maister coined the term OTSU (opportunity to screw up) to highlight the importance of thinking about all the things that might go wrong in delivering a particular type of service.[4] OTSUs are funny when you talk about them. John Cleese made millions laugh with his portrayal of an inept hotel manager in the television series *Fawlty Towers*. And Chevy Chase has entertained movie audiences for years by playing a customer tortured by inept, rude, or downright cruel service employees. However, customers don't always see the funny side when the joke is on them. It's only by identifying all the possible OTSUs associated with a particular task that service managers can put together a delivery system explicitly designed to avoid such problems.

Setting Service Standards

Through both formal research and on-the-job experience, service managers can learn the nature of customer expectations at each step in the process. As outlined in Chapter 2, customers' expectations range across the zone of tolerance—from desired service (an ideal) to a threshold level of merely adequate service (refer to Figure 2-4 on p. 40). For each step, service providers should design standards sufficiently high to satisfy and even delight customers; if that's not possible, service providers will need to modify customer expectations. These standards may include time parameters, the script for a technically correct performance, and prescriptions for appropriate style and demeanor. Standards must be expressed in ways that permit objective measurement.

The opening scenes of a service drama are particularly important, as customers' first impressions can affect their evaluations of quality during later stages of service delivery. Perceptions of their service experiences tend to be cumulative.[5] If a couple of things go badly wrong at the outset, customers may simply walk out. Even if they stay, they may now be looking for other things that aren't quite right. On the other hand, if the first steps go really well, customers' zones of tolerance may increase so that they are more willing to overlook minor mistakes later in the service performance. Research by Marriott Hotels indicates that four of the five top factors contributing to customer loyalty come into play during the first 10 minutes of service delivery.[6] And research into the design of doctors' offices and procedures suggests that unfavorable initial impressions can lead patients to cancel surgery or even change doctors.[7] However, performance standards should not be allowed to fall off toward the end of service delivery. Other research findings point to the importance of a strong finish and suggest that a service encounter that is perceived to start poorly but then builds in quality will be better rated than one that starts well but declines to end poorly.[8]

But how often do failures intervene to ruin the customers' experience and spoil their good humor? Can you remember situations in which the experience of a nice meal in Act II was completely spoiled by one or more failures in Act III? Our own informal research among participants in dozens of executive programs has found that the most commonly cited source of dissatisfaction with restaurants is an inability to get the bill quickly when the customers have finished their meal and are ready to leave! This seemingly minor failing, unrelated to the core product, can nevertheless leave in a customer's mouth a bad taste that taints the overall dining experience, even if everything else has gone well. When customers are on a tight time budget, making them wait unnecessarily at any point in the process is akin to stealing their time. (For some solutions to this problem, see Service Perspectives 4-1 on page 102.

Our restaurant example was deliberately chosen to illustrate a high-contact, people-processing service with which all readers are likely to be familiar. But many possession-processing services, such as repair or maintenance, and information-processing services, such as insurance or accounting, involve far less contact with customers, as much of the action takes place backstage. In these situations, a front-stage failure is likely to represent a higher proportion of the customer's service encounters with a company and may therefore be viewed even more seriously because there are fewer subsequent opportunities to create a favorable impression.

Improving Reliability of Service Processes by Failure Proofing

Careful analysis of the reasons for failure in service processes often reveals opportunities for failure proofing certain activities in order to reduce or even eliminate the risk of errors.[9] Fail-safe methods need to be designed not only for employees but also for customers, especially in services where the latter participate actively in creation and delivery processes.

Fail-Safe Methods for Service Personnel The goal of fail-safe procedures is to prevent errors, such as performing tasks incorrectly, in the wrong order, or too slowly; or doing work that wasn't requested in the first place. Solutions vary by industry but in a fast-food restaurant context may include installing strategically placed microphones to ensure that servers' and customers' voices are audible and color coding cash register keys and change trays to increase the speed and accuracy of ringing up bills, taking money from customers, and giving change. In hospitals, trays for surgical instruments have indentations for each instrument, and all the instruments used during an operation are nested in the tray. This not only ensures that a surgeon has all the tools needed for a specific operation but also highlights any missing instruments that might still be in the patient before the surgeon closes the incision.

Treatment errors occur during the contact between the server and the customer, such as lack of courteous, professional behavior. Such errors may include failure to acknowledge, listen to, or react appropriately to the customer (Figure 8-1). Among novel approaches to counter this problem are a Korean theme park's policy of sewing closed the pockets of new employees' trousers to prevent the new hires from putting their hands in their pockets and looking sloppy or disrespectful.

Tangible errors relate to failures in the physical elements of the service, and preventive measures include standards for cleaning facilities and uniforms and appropriate control and adjustment of noise, odors, light, and temperature. To simplify the task of proofreading of documents, most software programs have built-in checks for spelling and arithmetic errors.

Mirrors placed in ways that allow a worker to automatically check his or her appearance before greeting a customer foster a neat appearance. Hotels often wrap paper strips around towels to help the housekeeping staff distinguish quickly between those that are clean and those that should be replaced.

Fail-Safe Methods for the Customer Customer errors can occur in the preparation stage before a service encounter takes place. Marketing communications can help shape prior expectations and inform the customer on how to access the service correctly. For example, marketers at the service division of one computer manufacturer provide customers with a simple flowchart that clarifies the correct way to place a service call. By guiding them through three yes-or-no questions, the firm ensures that customers are ready to supply the necessary information (e.g., their equipment model and registration number) and that they contact the appropriate provider for the type of service required.

Customer errors during a service encounter can slow down service processes, waste employees' time, and even inconvenience other customers. Forgetting the steps in a service process, failing to follow steps in the correct sequence, ignoring instructions, or not specifying needs sufficiently clearly may reflect inattentiveness, misunderstanding, or simply a memory lapse. Posted instructions in highly visible locations and recorded announcements are two ways to remind customers of what they need to do.

Among the physical fail-safe devices used to control customers' behavior are chains to configure waiting lines, locks that must be turned on the inside of aircraft lavatory doors in order to switch on the interior lights (and simultaneously activate the "occupied" sign on the outside), and height bars at amusement parks to ensure that riders do not fall outside maximum and minimum size limitations. Frames and measurement scales at airports allow passengers to gauge the allowable size of their carry-on luggage. Beepers remind bank customers to remove their cards and cash from an ATM.

Customers may also make errors at the resolution stage of the service encounter. Child care centers use toy outlines on walls and floors to show where toys should be placed after use. In fast-food restaurants and school cafeterias, strategically located tray-return stands and notices on walls remind customers to return their trays. And at a growing number of hotels, the key cards that open the doors to guest rooms must be placed in a wall socket inside the room in order to activate the lights. As a result, when guests take their cards as they leave their rooms, they automatically turn out the lights.

SERVICE PROCESS REDESIGN

Service process redesign revitalizes processes that have become outdated. This does not necessarily mean that the processes were poorly designed in the first place. Rather, changes in technology, customer needs, added service features, and new offerings have made existing processes crack and creak.[10] Mitchell T. Rabkin, M.D., formerly president of Boston's Beth Israel Hospital (now Beth Israel–Deaconess Medical Center), characterized the problem as "institutional rust" and declared: "Institutions are like steel beams—they tend to rust. What was once smooth and shiny and nice tends to become rusty."[11] He suggested that there are two main reasons for this situation. The first involves external environmental changes that make existing practices obsolete and require redesign of the underlying processes—or even creation of new processes—in order for the organization to remain relevant and responsive. Environmental factors in health care include changes in competitive activity, legislation, technology, health insurance policies, and customer needs.

The second reason for institutional rusting occurs internally and often reflects a natural deterioration of internal processes, creeping bureaucracy, or the evolution of spurious, unofficial standards (see Best Practice in Action 8-1). Such symptoms as

BEST PRACTICE IN ACTION 8-1

ROOTING OUT UNOFFICIAL STANDARDS IN A HOSPITAL

One of the distinctive characteristics of Mitchell T. Rabkin's 30-year tenure as president of Boston's Beth Israel Hospital was his policy of routinely visiting all areas of the hospital. He usually did so unannounced and in a low-key fashion. No one working at the hospital was surprised to see Dr. Rabkin drop by at almost any time of the day or night. His natural curiosity gave him unparalleled insights into how effectively service procedures were working and the subtle ways in which things could go wrong. As the following story by reveals, he discovered that there is often a natural deterioration of messages over time.

> One day, I was in the EU [emergency unit], chatting with a house officer [physician] who was treating a patient with asthma. He was giving her medication through an intravenous drip. I looked at the formula for the medication and asked him, "Why are you using this particular cocktail?" "Oh," he replied, "that's hospital policy." Since I was certain that there was no such policy, I decided to investigate.
>
> What had happened went something like this. A few months earlier, Resident [physician] A says to Intern B, who is observing her treat a patient: "This is what I use for asthma." On the next month's rotation, Intern B says to new Resident C: "This is what Dr. A uses for asthma." The following month, Resident C says to Intern D, "This is what we use for asthma." And finally, within another month, Intern D is telling Resident E, "It's hospital policy to use this medication."
>
> As a result of conversations like these, well-intentioned but unofficial standards keep cropping up. It's a particular problem in a place like this, which isn't burdened by an inhuman policy manual where you must look up the policy for everything you do. We prefer to rely on people's intelligence and judgment and limit written policies to overall, more general issues. One always has to be aware of the growth of institutional rust and to be clear about what is being done and why it is being done.[1]

[1]Christopher Lovelock, *Product Plus* (New York: McGraw-Hill, 1994), 355.

extensive information exchange, data redundancy, a high ratio of checking or control activities to value-adding activities, increased exception processing, and growing numbers of customer complaints about inconvenient and unnecessary procedures often indicate that a process is not working well and requires redesign.

Examining blueprints of existing services may suggest opportunities for product improvement that might be achieved by reconfiguring delivery systems, adding or deleting specific elements, or repositioning the service to appeal to other segments. For example, Canadian Pacific Hotels (now part of Fairmont Hotels) decided to redesign its hotel services. It had already been successful with conventions, meetings, and group travel but wanted to build greater brand loyalty among business travelers. The company blueprinted the entire "guest experience" from pulling up at the hotel to getting the car keys from the valet. For each encounter, Canadian Pacific defined an expected service level based on customer feedback and created systems to monitor service performance. It also redesigned some aspects of its service processes to provide guests with more personalized service. The payoff for implementing these redesign efforts was a 16 percent increase in its share of business travelers in a single year.

Managers in charge of service process redesign projects often do not want to spend more money on better quality. Rather, they aim to achieve a quantum leap in both productivity and service quality at the same time. Restructuring or reengineering the ways in which tasks are performed has significant potential to increase output, especially in many backstage jobs.[12] Redesign efforts typically focus on achieving the following key performance measures: (1) reduced number of service failures, (2) reduced cycle time from customer initiation of a service process to its completion, (3) enhanced productivity, and (4) increased customer satisfaction. Ideally, redesign efforts should achieve all four measures simultaneously.

Service process redesign encompasses reconstitution, rearrangement, or substitution of service processes.[13] These efforts can be categorized into a number of types, including:

- *Eliminating non-value-adding steps.* Often, activities at the front- and back-end processes of services can be streamlined with the goal of focusing on the benefit-producing part of the service encounter. For example, a customer wanting to rent a car is not interested in filling out forms or processing payment and check of the returned car. Service redesign streamlines these tasks by trying to eliminate non-value-adding steps. The outcomes are typically increased productivity and customer satisfaction.
- *Shifting to self-service.* Significant productivity and sometimes even service quality gains can be achieved by increasing self-service when redesigning services. For example, FedEx succeeded in shifting more than 50 percent of its transactions from its call centers to its Web site, thus reducing the number of employees in its call centers by some 20,000 persons.
- *Delivering direct service.* This type of redesign involves bringing the service to the customer instead of bringing the customer to the service firm. This is often done to improve convenience for the customer but can also result in productivity gains if companies can do away with high-rent locations.
- *Bundling services.* Bundling services involves bundling, or grouping, multiple services into one offer, focusing on a well-defined customer group. Bundling can help increase productivity; the bundle is already tailored for a particular segment, making the transaction faster, and the marketing costs of each service are often reduced, at the same time, bundling adds value to the customer through lower transaction costs and often has a better fit to the needs of the target segment.
- *Redesigning the physical aspects of service processes.* Physical service redesign focuses on the tangible elements of a service process and includes changes to the service facilities and equipment to improve the service experience. This leads to convenience and productivity and often also enhances the satisfaction and productivity of frontline staff.

Table 8-1 summarizes the five redesign types, provides an overview of their potential benefits for the firm and its customers, and highlights potential challenges or limitations. It is important to note that these redesign types are often used in combination. For example, central to Amazon.com's success is the combined appeal of self-service, direct service, and minimization of non-value-adding steps through the effective capture of customer preferences, along with shipping and payment data.

THE CUSTOMER AS COPRODUCER

Blueprinting helps to specify the role of customers in service delivery and to identify the extent of contact between them and service providers. Blueprinting also clarifies whether the customer's role in a given service process is primarily that of passive recipient or entails active involvement in creating and producing the service.

Levels of Customer Participation

Customer participation refers to the actions and resources supplied by customers during service production and/or delivery and includes mental, physical, and even emotional inputs.[14] Some degree of customer participation in service delivery is inevitable in people-processing services and in any service involving real-time contact between customers and providers. In many instances, both the experience and the ultimate outcome reflect interactions between customers and facilities, employees, and systems.

TABLE 8-1 Five Types of Service Redesign

Approach and Concept	*Potential Company Benefits*	*Potential Customer Benefits*	*Challenges/ Limitations*
Elimination of non-value-added steps (streamlines all steps involved in a service transaction from purchase to payment)	• Improves efficiency • Increases productivity • Increases ability to customize service • Differentiates company	• Increases speed of service • Improves efficiency • Shifts tasks from customer to service firm • Separates service activation from delivery • Customizes service	• Requires extra customer education and employee training to implement smoothly and effectively
Self-service (customer assumes role of producer)	• Lowers cost • Improves productivity • Enhances technology reputation • Differentiates company	• Increases speed of service • Improves access • Saves money • Increases perception of control	• Requires customer preparation for the role • Limits face-to-face interaction • Creates difficulty in obtaining customer feedback • Creates difficulty in establishing customer loyalty/relationships
Direct service (service delivered to the customer's location)	• Eliminates store location limitations • Expands customer base • Differentiates company	• Increases convenience • Improves access	• Imposes logistical burdens • May require costly investments • Requires credibility and trust
Bundled service (combines multiple services into a package)	• Differentiates company • Aids customer retention • Increases per capita service use	• Increases convenience • Customizes service	• Requires extensive knowledge of targeted customers • May be perceived as wasteful
Physical service (manipulation of tangibles associated with the service)	• Improves employee satisfaction • Increases productivity • Differentiates company	• Increases convenience • Enhances function • Cultivates interest	• Easily imitated • Requires expense to effect and maintain • Raises customer expectations for the industry

Source: Adapted from Leonard L. Berry and Sandra K. Lampo, "Teaching an Old Service New Tricks: The Promise of Service Redesign," *Journal of Service Research* 2, no. 3 (2000): 265–275.

However, the level of this participation varies widely. Table 8-2 groups customer participation levels into three broad categories.[15]

Low Employees and systems do all the work. Products tend to be standardized, and service is provided regardless of any individual purchase. Payment may be the only required customer input. If customers come to the service factory, only their physical presence is required. Visiting a movie theater is an example. In possession-processing services, such as routine cleaning or maintenance, customers can remain entirely uninvolved with the process other than providing access to service providers and making payment.

Moderate Customer inputs are required to assist the organization in creating and delivering the service and in providing a degree of customization. These inputs may include provision of information, personal effort, or even physical possessions. When getting their hair washed and cut, customers must let the cutter know what they want and cooperate during the steps in the process. A client who wants an accountant to prepare a tax return must first pull together information and physical documentation that

TABLE 8-2 Levels of Customer Participation across Various Services

Low (Customer Presence Required During Service Delivery)	*Moderate (Customer Inputs Required for Service Creation)*	*High (Customer Coproduces the Service Product)*
Products are standardized.	Client inputs customize a standard service.	Active client participation guides the customized service.
Service is provided regardless of any individual purchase.	Provision of service requires customer purchase.	Service cannot be created apart from the customer's purchase and active participation.
Payment may be the only required customer input.	Customer inputs (information, materials) are necessary for an adequate outcome; but the service firm provides the service.	Customer inputs are mandatory and coproduce the outcome.
Examples		
Consumer Services		
Bus travel	Haircut	Marriage counseling
Motel stay	Annual physical exam	Personal training
Movie theater	Full-service restaurant	Weight-reduction program
Business-to-Business Services		
Uniform cleaning service	Agency-created advertising campaign	Management consulting
Pest control	Payroll service	Executive management seminar
Interior greenery maintenance	Independent freight transportation	Installation of wide area network (WAN)

Source: Adapted from Mary Jo Bitner, William T. Faranda, Amy R. Hubbert, and Valarie A. Zeithaml, "Customer Contributions and Roles in Service Delivery," *International Journal of Service Industry Management* 8, no. 3 (1997): 193–205.

the accountant can use to prepare the return correctly and then be prepared to respond to any questions that the latter may have.

High In these instances, customers work actively with the provider to coproduce the service. Service cannot be created apart from the customer's purchase and active participation. In fact, customers who fail to assume this role effectively and don't perform certain mandatory production tasks will jeopardize the quality of the service outcome. Some health-related services fall into this category, especially those related to improvement of the patient's physical condition, such as rehabilitation or weight loss, where customers work under professional supervision. Successful delivery of many business-to-business services requires customers and providers to work closely together as members of a team.

Self-Service Technologies

The ultimate form of involvement in service production is for customers to undertake a specific activity themselves, using facilities or systems provided by the service supplier. In effect, the customer's time and effort replace those of a service employee. In the case of telephone and Internet-based service, customers even provide their own terminals.

The concept of self-service is not new. Perhaps the most radical shift in the history of retailing occurred with the creation of supermarkets in the 1930s. For the first time, customers were required to select their own groceries from the shelves, put them in a cart, and transport them to the checkout station. Both customers and retailers saw benefits in coproduction, and the concept flourished, later spreading to other types of retail operations.

Nevertheless, early attempts to introduce self-service scanning at supermarket checkouts were unsuccessful, being resisted by consumers. It was not until the early 2000s that significant numbers of supermarkets began to give customers the option of completing their visit to the store by using a self-service checkout station, where they could scan and pay for their purchases. This development reflected not only much improved technology and reasonably foolproof processes but also an economic trade-off between the declining cost of these self-service systems and the rising cost of labor. Modern supermarket shoppers seem more willing to accept this new approach today, reflecting their greater comfort level with technology.[16]

Today's consumers are faced with an array of self-service technologies (SSTs) that allow them to produce a service independent of direct service employee involvement.[17] SSTs include automated banking terminals and self-service gasoline pumps (both introduced during the 1970s and progressively refined), automated telephone systems, (e.g., phone banking), automated hotel checkout, and numerous Internet-based services.

Information-based services lend themselves particularly well to use of SSTs and include not only such supplementary services as getting information, placing orders and reservations, and making payment but also delivery of core products in such fields as banking, research, entertainment, and self-paced education. One of the most significant innovations of the Internet era has been the development of online auctions, led by eBay. No human auctioneer is needed as an intermediary between buyers and sellers.

Many companies have developed strategies designed to encourage customers to undertake self-service through the World Wide Web. They hope to divert customers from using more expensive alternatives such as direct contact with employees, use of intermediaries such as brokers and travel agents, or voice-to-voice telephone. However, for these strategies to work well, customers need to be aware of the Web site (see Figure 8-2) and find the site easy to navigate.

FIGURE 8-2 Publicize Your Web Site

CARDWELL.
"NOW YOU TELL ME YOU HAVE A WEBSITE?!"

Source: Wall Street Journal ("Pepper & Salt"). Reprinted by permission of Cartoon Features Syndicate.

Psychological Factors in Customer Coproduction The logic of self-service has historically relied on an economic rationale, emphasizing the productivity gains and cost savings that result when customers take over work previously performed by employees. In many instances, a portion of the resulting savings is shared with customers in the form of lower prices as an inducement for them to change their behavior. However, researchers Neeli Bendapudi and Robert Leone argue that customers' psychological responses to participation in production should also be considered in self-service environments: specifically, their tendency to take credit for successful outcomes but not the blame for unsuccessful ones.[18] Their research indicated that this tendency was reduced when customers were given a choice on whether to participate in service production.

Given the significant investment in both time and money that is often required for firms to design, implement, and manage SSTs, it's critical for service marketers to understand how consumers decide between using an SST option and relying on a human provider. We need to recognize that SSTs present both advantages and disadvantages. In addition to benefiting from time and cost savings, flexibility, convenience of location, greater control over service delivery, and a higher perceived level of customization, customers may also derive fun, enjoyment, and even spontaneous delight from SST use.[19] However, there's evidence that some consumers see the introduction of SSTs into the service encounters as something of a threat, causing anxiety and stress among those who are uncomfortable with using them.[20] Some consumers view service encounters as social experiences and prefer to deal with people; others purposely try to avoid such contact especially if they have a poor perception of a firm's employees. Research by James Curran, Matthew Meuter, and Carol Surprenant found that multiple attitudes may drive customer intentions to use a specific SST, including global attitudes toward related service technologies, global attitudes toward the specific service firm, and attitudes toward its employees.[21]

SST Characteristics and Customer Attitudes Research suggests that customers both love and hate SSTs.[22] Customers love SSTs when they bail them out of difficult situations, often because SST machines are conveniently located and accessible 24/7. And, of course, a Web site is as close as the nearest computer, making this option much more accessible than the company's physical sites. Customers also love SSTs when they perform better than the alternative of being served by a service employee, enabling users to get detailed information and complete transactions more quickly than they could through face-to-face or telephone contact. Many customers are still in awe of technology and what it can do for them—when it works well.

However, customers hate SSTs when they fail. Users get angry when machines are out of service, their PIN (personal identification numbers) are not accepted, Web sites are down, tracking numbers do not work, or items are not shipped as promised. Even when SSTs do work, customers are frustrated by poorly designed technologies that make service processes difficult to understand and use. Poorly designed navigation is a common complaint about Web sites. Users also get frustrated when they themselves mess up because they have forgotten their passwords, fail to provide information as requested, or simply press the wrong buttons. Self-service logically implies that customers can cause their own dissatisfaction. However, even when it is their own fault, customers may still partially blame the service provider for not providing a simpler and more user-friendly system and then revert to the traditional human-based system on the next occasion.

Designing a virtually failure-proof Web site is no easy task and can be very expensive, but it is through such investments that companies create loyal users and positive word of mouth. Best Practice in Action 8.2 describes the emphasis on user friendliness at TLContact.com, a company profiled in depth in the case that appears on pp. 627–640.

BEST PRACTICE IN ACTION 8-2

TLCONTACT.COM CREATES AN EXCEPTIONAL USER EXPERIENCE

When his sister Sharon's five-day old baby, Matthew, underwent surgery at the University of Michigan Medical Center in early 1998 to correct a life-threatening heart defect, Mark Day was more than a thousand miles away at Stanford, studying for a Ph.D. in engineering. Feeling isolated, knowing nothing about the heart, and wanting to do something useful, Mark turned for medical information to the Internet, which was just beginning to hit its stride. Within a few weeks, he had created a simple Web site that family and friends could access. He edited the information he had gathered and loaded it on the site, together with bulletins on Matthew's condition and how the baby was responding to treatment. "It was a very simple site," Mark declared later. "If I had paid somebody else to do it for me, it probably wouldn't have cost more than a few hundred dollars." To minimize the need for e-mail, Mark added a bulletin board so that people could send messages to Sharon and her husband, Eric.

To everyone's surprise, the site proved exceptionally popular. News spread by word of mouth, and the site recorded numerous daily visitors, with more than 200 people leaving messages for the family. People who confessed that they had never before used the Internet found a way to access the site, follow baby Matthew's progress, and send messages.

Two years and three operations later, Matthew was a happy, healthy toddler. His parents, Eric and Sharon Langshur, decided to create a company, TLContact.com, to commercialize Mark's concept as a service for patients and their families. Eric and Sharon invited Mark to join the company as chief technology officer. To ensure quality control and retain intellectual capital, Mark decided to build the necessary software systems in-house rather than subcontract the task to outside vendors. He hired a skilled technical team, including programmers and graphic designers.

Recognizing that TLC's patient sites, known as CarePages, would be accessed by a wide array of individuals, many of whom would be under stress and even having their first experience using the Internet, Mark and his team placed a premium on ease of use. He commented: "It's very difficult to create a piece of software that's really user friendly. It takes an incredible amount of skill, effort, and time to develop something that's usable, functional, and scalable—meaning that it can be expanded and built upon without failing." The total cost of creating the initial functioning Web site was close to half a million dollars.

As the company grew, continued investments were made to expand the functionality of the service for patients, visitors, and sponsoring hospitals to eliminate any problems that users had reported, and to further improve user friendliness. Enhancements included an option for user feedback, addition of an e-mail notification tool to announce updated news on a CarePage, and the ability to access CarePages through a hospital's own Web site. Receiving feedback that users encountered problems when they mistyped a CarePage name and failed to gain access, TLC added software logic to fix common mistakes, thereby reducing the volume of customer service enquiries. By 2003, TLC had turned the corner financially and was growing rapidly. Heartwarming tributes from satisfied users were pouring in. But work continued to enhance the CarePage experience, with software changes and improvements being made every six to eight weeks. By this point, the firm had invested more than two million dollars in technology.

Source: Christopher Lovelock, "TLContact.com" 2003 (case reproduced on pp. 627–640).

A key problem with SSTs is that so few of them incorporate service recovery systems. In too many instances, when the process fails, there is no simple way to recover on the spot. Typically, customers are forced to telephone or make a personal visit to resolve the problem, which may be exactly what they were trying to avoid in the first place! Mary Jo Bitner suggests that managers should put their firms' SSTs to the test by asking the following basic questions:[23]

- Does the SST work reliably? Firms must ensure that SSTs work as dependably as promised and that the design is user friendly for customers. Southwest Airlines' online ticketing services have set a high standard for simplicity and reliability. The airline boasts the highest percentage of online ticket sales of any airline—clear evidence of customer acceptance.
- *Is the SST better than the interpersonal alternative?* If the SST doesn't save time or provide ease of access, cost savings, or other benefit, customers will continue to use familiar conventional processes. Amazon.com's success reflects its efforts to create a highly personalized, efficient alternative to visiting a retail store.
- *If it fails, what systems are in place to recover?* It's critical for firms to provide systems, structures, and recovery technologies that will enable prompt service recovery when things go wrong. Some banks have a phone beside each ATM, giving customers direct access to a 24-hour customer service center if they have questions or run into difficulties. Supermarkets that have installed self-service checkout lanes usually assign one employee to monitor the lanes; this practice combines security with customer assistance. In telephone-based service systems, well-designed voice-mail menus include an option for customers to reach a customer service rep.

Service Firms as Teachers

Although service providers attempt to design the ideal level of customer participation into the service delivery system, it is customers' actions that in reality determine the amount of participation. Underparticipation causes customers to experience a decrease in service benefits (for instance, a student who fails to perform the work of the course will learn less, and a dieter who doesn't follow guidelines properly will probably lose less weight). *Overparticipation* by customers may take employees away from other tasks and cause the firm to spend more resources customizing a service than was originally intended. (Consider the impact on productivity at a fast-food restaurant if all customers insisted on customization of their hamburger orders.) In order to optimize participation levels during service production and consumption, service businesses must teach their customers the roles they are expected to play.

The more work that customers are expected to do, the greater their need for information about how to perform their roles for best results. The necessary education can be provided in many ways: brochures and posted instructions, or detailed operating instructions and diagrams on automated machines. Advertising for new services often contains significant educational content. Many Web sites include a FAQ (frequently asked questions) section; eBay's Web site, for example, provides detailed instructions for getting started, including how to submit an item for auction and how to bid for items. Its Help Center features an A–Z index of topics, including advice on resolving trading concerns.

In many businesses, customers look to employees for advice and assistance and are frustrated if they can't obtain it. Service providers, ranging from sales assistants and customer service representatives to flight attendants and nurses, must be trained to help them improve their teaching skills. And people may also turn to other customers for help. The eBay Help Center includes a section titled "Ask eBay Members," which notes that eBay community members are always happy to help one an other. The Help Center includes an answer center ("get answers from community members—fast!") and a series of discussion boards ("share your interests, get help from community members, or assist others").[24]

Researchers Benjamin Schneider and David Bowen suggest giving customers a realistic service preview in advance of service delivery to provide them with a clear picture of their roles in service coproduction.[25] For example, a company might show a video presentation to help customers understand their role in a specific service encounter. This technique is used by some dentists to familiarize patients with the surgical processes they are about to experience and indicate how they should cooperate so as to help make things go as smoothly as possible.

Customers as Partial Employees

Some researchers argue that firms should view customers as "partial employees" who can influence the productivity and quality of service processes and outputs.[26] This perspective requires a change in management mindset, as Schneider and Bowen make clear:

> If you think of customers as partial employees, you begin to think very differently about what you hope customers will bring to the service encounter. Now they must bring not only expectations and needs but also relevant service production competencies that will enable them to fill the role of partial employees. The service management challenge deepens accordingly.[27]

They suggest that customers who are offered an opportunity to participate at an active level are more likely to be satisfied, regardless of whether they choose the more active role, because they like to be offered a choice.

Managing customers as partial employees requires using the same human resource strategy as managing a firm's paid employees and should follow these four steps.

1. Conduct a "job analysis" of customers' present roles in the business, and compare it against the roles that the firm would like them to play.

Self-service ticketing machines offer convenience and time savings—but only if they are easy to use and maintained in good working order.

2. Determine whether customers are aware of how they are expected to perform and have the skills needed to perform as required.
3. Motivate customers by ensuring that they will be rewarded for performing well (e.g., satisfaction from better quality and more customized output, enjoyment of participating in the *process*, a belief that their own productivity speeds the process and keeps costs down).
4. Regularly appraise customers' performance. If it is unsatisfactory, seek to change their roles and the procedures in which they are involved. Alternatively, consider "terminating" these customers (nicely, of course!) and look for new ones.

Effective human resource management starts with recruitment and selection. The same approach should hold true for "partial employees." So if coproduction requires specific skills, firms should target their marketing efforts to recruit new customers who have the competency to perform the necessary tasks.[28] After all, many colleges do just this in their student selection process!

THE PROBLEM OF CUSTOMER MISBEHAVIOR

Other customers often form an important element in service encounters. In many people-processing services, we expect to find other customers present and to share service facilities with them. The behavior of these customers can contribute positively or negatively to the functioning of specific service delivery processes and may even affect the outcome.

Customers who act in uncooperative or abusive ways are a problem for any organization. But such customers have more potential for mischief in service businesses, particularly those in which the customer comes to the service factory. As you know from your own experience, the behavior of other customers can affect your enjoyment of a service. If you like classical music and attend symphony concerts, you expect audience members to keep quiet during the performance. By contrast, a silent audience would be deadly during a rock concert or team sports event, where active audience participation adds to the excitement. There is a fine line, however, between spectator enthusiasm and abusive behavior by supporters of rival sports teams. Firms that fail to deal effectively with customer misbehaviors risk damaging their relationships with all the other customers they would like to keep.

Addressing the Challenge of Jaycustomers

Visitors to North America from other English-speaking countries are often puzzled by the term "jaywalker," that distinctively American word used to describe people who cross streets at unauthorized places or in a dangerous manner. The prefix jay comes from a 19-century slang term for a stupid person. We can create a whole vocabulary of derogatory terms by adding the prefix *jay* to existing nouns and verbs. How about *jaycustomer*, for example, to denote someone who "jayuses" a service or "jayconsumes" a physical product (and then "jaydisposes" of it afterward)?[29] We define a jaycustomer as one who acts in a thoughtless or abusive way, causing problems for the firm, its employees, and other customers.

Every service has its share of jaycustomers. But opinions on this topic seem to polarize around two opposing views of the situation. One is denial: "The customer is king" and can do no wrong. The other view sees the marketplace of customers as positively overpopulated with nasty people who cannot be trusted to behave in ways that self-respecting service providers should expect and require. The first viewpoint has received wide publicity in gung-ho management books and in motivational presentations to captive groups of employees. But the second view often appears to be dominant among cynical managers and employees who have been burned at some point by customer misbehaviors. As with so many opposing viewpoints in life, there are important grains of truth in both perspectives. What is clear, however, is that no self-respecting firm would want to have an ongoing relationship with an abusive customer.

Jaycustomers are undesirable. At worst, a firm needs to control or prevent their abusive behavior. At best, it would like to avoid attracting them in the first place. As defining the problem is the first step in resolving it, let's start by considering the various segments of jaycustomers who prey on providers of both goods and services. We've identified six broad categories and given them generic names, but many customer-contact personnel have come up with their own special terms. As you reflect on these categories, you may be tempted to add a few more of your own.

The Thief This jaycustomer has no intention of paying and sets out to steal goods and services (or to pay less than full price by switching price tickets or contesting bills on baseless grounds). Shoplifting is a major problem in retail stores. What retailers euphemistically call "shrinkage" is estimated to cost them huge sums of money in annual revenues. Many services lend themselves to clever schemes for avoiding payment. For those with technical skills, it's sometimes possible to bypass electricity meters, access telephone lines free of charge, or circumvent normal cable TV feeds. Riding free on public transportation, sneaking into movie theaters, or not paying for restaurant meals are also popular. And we mustn't forget the use of fraudulent forms of payment, such as stolen credit cards or checks drawn on accounts without any funds. Finding out how people steal a service is the first step in preventing theft or catching thieves and, where appropriate, prosecuting them. But managers should try not to alienate honest customers by degrading their service experiences. And provision must be made for honest but absent-minded customers who forget to pay.

The Rulebreaker Just as highways need safety regulations (including "Don't Jaywalk"), many service businesses need to establish rules of behavior for employees and customers to guide them safely through the various steps of the service encounter. Some of these rules are imposed by government agencies for health and safety reasons. Many restaurants have a sign that states "No shirt, no shoes—no service," demonstrating a health-related regulation. And air travel provides one of the best examples of rules designed to ensure safety; there are few other environments outside prison where healthy, mentally competent adult customers are quite so constrained (albeit with good reason).

In addition to enforcing government regulations, suppliers often impose their own rules to facilitate smooth operations, avoid unreasonable demands on employees, prevent misuse of products and facilities, protect themselves legally, and discourage individual customers from misbehaving. Ski resorts, for instance, are getting tough on careless skiers who pose risks to both themselves and others.[30] Collisions can cause serious injury and even kill. So ski patrol members must be safety oriented and sometimes take on a policing role. Just as dangerous drivers can lose their licenses, so too dangerous skiers can lose their lift tickets.

At Vail and Beaver Creek in Colorado, ski patrollers once revoked nearly 400 lift tickets in a single weekend. At Winter Park near Denver, skiers who lose their passes for dangerous behavior may have to attend a 45-minute safety class before they can get their passes back. Ski patrollers at Vermont's Okemo Mountain may issue warnings to reckless skiers by attaching a bright orange sticker to their lift tickets. If pulled over again for inappropriate behavior, such skiers may be escorted off the mountain and banned for a day or more. "We're not trying to be Gestapos on the slopes," says the resort's marketing director, "just trying to educate people."

How should a firm deal with rulebreakers? Much depends on which rules have been broken. In the case of legally enforceable ones—theft, bad debts, trying to take guns on aircraft—the courses of action need to be laid down explicitly to protect employees and to punish or discourage wrongdoing by customers. Company rules are a little more ambiguous. Are they really necessary in the first place? If not, the firm should get rid of them. Do they deal with health and safety? If so, educating customers about the rules should reduce the need for taking corrective action. The same is true for rules designed to protect the comfort and enjoyment of all customers. There are also unwritten social norms, such as "thou shalt not jump the queue," although this is a much stronger cultural expectation in the United States or Canada than in many other countries, as any visitor to Paris Disneyland can attest! Other customers can often be relied on to help service personnel enforce rules that affect everybody else; they may even take the initiative in doing so.

There are risks attached to making a lot of rules. They can make an organization appear bureaucratic and overbearing. And they can transform employees, whose orientation should be service to customers, into police officers who see (or are told to see) their most important task as enforcing all the rules. The fewer the rules, the more explicit the important ones can be.

The Belligerent You've probably seen this person in a store, at the airport, or in a hotel or restaurant: red in the face and shouting angrily or perhaps icily calm and mouthing off insults, threats, and obscenities.[31] Things don't always work as they should: Machines break down, service is clumsy, customers are ignored, a flight is delayed, an order is delivered incorrectly, staff are unhelpful, a promise is broken. Or perhaps the customer in question is expressing resentment at being told to abide by the rules. Service personnel are often abused, even when they are not to blame. If an employee lacks authority to resolve the problem, the belligerent may become madder still, even to the point of physical attack. Drunkenness and drug abuse add extra layers of complication. Organizations that care about their employees go to great efforts to develop skills in dealing with these difficult situations. Role-playing training exercises help employees develop the self-confidence and assertiveness they need to deal with upset, belligerent customers (sometimes referred to as "irates"). Employees also need to learn how to defuse anger, calm anxiety, and comfort distress, particularly when there is good reason for the customer to be upset with the organization's performance.

The problem of "air rage" has attracted particular attention in recent years because of the risks that it poses to innocent people (see Service Perspectives 8-1). Blair Berkley and Mohammad Ala note that even before the events of September 11, 2001, violent passengers were considered to be the number-one security concern in the airline industry.[32]

What should an employee do when an aggressive customer brushes off attempts to defuse the situation? In a public environment, one priority should be to move the person away from other customers. Sometimes, supervisors may have to arbitrate disputes between customers and staff members; at other times, supervisors need to stand behind the employee's actions. If a customer has physically assaulted an employee, it may be necessary to summon security officers or the police. Some firms try to conceal such events, fearing bad publicity. But others feel obliged to make a public stand on behalf of their employees, such as the Body Shop manager who ordered an ill-tempered customer out of the store, telling her: "I won't stand for your rudeness to my staff."

Telephone rudeness poses a different challenge. Service personnel have been known to hang up on angry customers, but that action doesn't resolve the problem. Bank customers, for instance, tend to get upset when learning that checks have been returned because they are overdrawn (which means they've broken the rules) or that a request for a loan has been denied. One approach for handling customers who continue to berate a telephone-based employee is for the latter to say firmly:

SERVICE PERSPECTIVES 8-1

AIR RAGE: UNRULY PASSENGERS POSE A GROWING PROBLEM

Joining the term *road rage*—coined in 1988 to describe angry, aggressive drivers who threaten other road users—is the newer term, *air rage*. Perpetrators of air rage are violent, unruly passengers who endanger flight attendants, pilots, and other passengers. Incidents of air rage are perpetrated by only a tiny fraction of all airline passengers—reportedly about 5,000 times a year—but each incident in the air may affect the comfort and safety of hundreds of other people.

Although terrorism is an ongoing concern, out-of-control passengers too pose a serious threat to safety. On a flight from Orlando, Florida, to London, a drunken passenger smashed a video screen and began ramming a window, telling fellow passengers that they were about to "get sucked out and die." The crew strapped him down, and the aircraft made an unscheduled landing in Bangor, Maine, where U.S. marshals arrested him. Another unscheduled stop in Bangor involved a drug smuggler flying from Jamaica to the Netherlands. When a balloon filled with cocaine ruptured in his stomach, he went berserk, pounding a bathroom door to pieces and grabbing a female passenger by the throat.

On a flight from London to Spain, a passenger who was already drunk at the time of boarding became angry when a flight attendant told him not to smoke in the lavatory and then refused to serve him another drink. Later, he smashed her over the head with a duty-free vodka bottle before being restrained by other passengers (she required 18 stitches to close the wound). Other dangerous incidents have included throwing hot coffee at flight attendants, head butting a copilot, trying to break into the cockpit, throwing a flight attendant across three rows of seats, and attempting to open an emergency door in flight. In an incident with a tragic outcome, a violent passenger was restrained and ultimately suffocated by other passengers after he kicked through the cockpit door of an airliner 20 minutes before it was scheduled to land in Salt Lake City.

A growing number of carriers are taking air rage perpetrators to court. Northwest Airlines permanently blacklisted three violent travelers from flying on its aircraft. British Airways gives out "warning cards" to any passenger getting dangerously out of control. Celebrities are not immune to air rage. Rock star Courtney Love blamed her "potty mouth" after being arrested on arrival in London for disruptive behavior on board a flight from Los Angeles. Some airlines carry physical restraints to subdue out-of-control passengers until they can be handed over to airport authorities.

In April 2000, the U.S. Congress increased the civil penalty for air rage from $1,100 to $25,000 in an attempt to discourage passengers from misbehaving. Criminal penalties—a $10,000 fine and up to 20 years in jail—can also be imposed for the most serious incidents. Some airlines have been reluctant to publicize this information for fear of appearing confrontational or intimidating. However, the visible implementation of antiterrorist security precautions has made it more acceptable to tighten enforcement of procedures designed to control and punish air rage.

What causes air rage? Researchers suggest that air travel has become increasingly stressful as a result of crowding and longer flights; the airlines themselves may have contributed to the problem by squeezing rows of seats more tightly together and failing to explain delays. Findings suggest that risk factors for air travel stress include anxiety and an anger-prone personality; they also show that traveling on unfamiliar routes is more stressful than on a familiar one. Another factor may be restrictions on smoking. But alcohol abuse underlies a majority of incidents.

Airlines are training their employees to handle violent individuals and to spot problem passengers before they start causing serious problems. Some carriers offer travelers specific suggestions on how to relax during long flights. And some airlines have considered offering nicotine patches to passengers who are desperate for a smoke but are no longer allowed to light up.

Source: Daniel Eisenberg, "Acting Up in the Air," *Time*, December 21, 1998; "Air Rage Capital: Bangor Becomes Nation's Flight Problem Drop Point," *Baltimore Sun*, September, 1999; Melanie Trottman and Chip Cummins, "Passenger's Death Prompts Calls for Improved 'Air Rage' Procedures," *Wall Street Journal*, September 26, 2000; Blair J. Berkley and Mohammad Ala, "Identifying and Controlling Threatening Airline Passengers," *Cornell Hotel and Restaurant Administration Quarterly* 42 (August–September 2001): 6–24.

"This conversation isn't getting us anywhere. Why don't I call you back in a few minutes when you've had time to digest the information?" In many cases, a break for reflection is exactly what's needed.

The Family Feuders People who get into arguments (or worse) with other customers—often members of their own family—make up a subcategory of belligerents we call family feuders. Employee intervention may calm the situation or make it worse. Some situations require detailed analysis and a carefully measured response. Others, such as customers starting a food fight in a nice restaurant, require almost instantaneous response. Service managers in these situations need to be prepared to think on their feet and act quickly.

The Vandal The level of physical abuse to which service facilities and equipment can be subjected is truly astonishing. Soft drinks are poured into bank cash machines; graffiti is scrawled on both interior and exterior surfaces; burn holes from cigarettes scar carpets, tablecloths, and bedcovers; bus seats are slashed and hotel furniture broken; telephone handsets are torn off; customers' cars are vandalized; glass is smashed and fabrics torn. The list is endless. Customers don't cause all the damage, of course. Bored or drunk young people are the source of much exterior vandalism. And disgruntled employees have been known to commit sabotage. But much of the problem does originate with paying customers who choose to misbehave. Alcohol and drugs are sometimes the cause, psychological problems may contribute, and carelessness can play a role. There are also occasions when unhappy customers, feeling mistreated by the service provider, try to take revenge in some way.

The best cure for vandalism is prevention. Improved security discourages some vandals. Good lighting helps, as does open design of public areas. Companies can choose pleasing yet vandal-resistant surfaces, protective coverings for equipment, and rugged furnishings. Educating customers on how to use equipment properly (rather than fighting with it) and providing warnings about fragile objects can reduce the likelihood of abuse or careless handling. And there are economic sanctions: security deposits or signed agreements in which customers agree to pay for any damage they cause.

What should managers do if prevention fails and damage is done? If the perpetrator is caught, they should first clarify whether there are any extenuating circumstances (because accidents do happen). Sanctions for deliberate damage can range from a warning to prosecution. As for the physical damage, it's best to fix it quickly (within any constraints imposed by legal or insurance considerations). The general manager of a bus company had the right idea when he said: "If one of our buses is vandalized, whether it's a broken window, a slashed seat, or graffiti on the ceiling, we take it out of service immediately, so nobody sees it. Otherwise you just give the same idea to five other characters who were too dumb to think of it in the first place!"[33]

The Deadbeat Leaving aside the thief, customers have many reasons for failing to pay for services they have received. Once again, preventive action is better than a cure. A growing number of firms insist on prepayment. Any form of ticket sale is a good example of this. Direct-marketing organizations ask for your credit card number as they take your order, as do most hotels when you make a reservation. The next best thing is to present the customer with a bill immediately on completion of service. If the bill is to be sent by mail, the firm should send it promptly, while the service is still fresh in the customer's mind.

Not every apparent delinquent is a hopeless deadbeat. Perhaps there's good reason for the delay and acceptable payment arrangements can be worked out. A key question is whether such a personalized approach can be cost justified, relative to the results obtained by purchasing the services of a collection agency. There may be other considerations, too. If the client's problems are only temporary, what is the long-term value of maintaining the relationship? Will it create positive goodwill and word of mouth to help the customer work things out? These decisions are judgment calls, but if creating and maintaining long-term relationships is the firm's ultimate goal, they bear exploration.

CONCLUSION

This chapter emphasized the importance of designing and managing service processes, which are the heart of the service product and significantly shape the customer experience. We covered in-depth blueprinting as a powerful tool to understand, make tangible, analyze, and improve service processes. Blueprinting helps to identify and reduce service fail points and provides important insights for service process redesign.

An important part of process design is to define the roles customers should play in the production of services. Their level of desired participation needs to be determined, and customers need to be motivated and taught to play their part in the service delivery.

Review Questions

1. What is the role of blueprinting in designing, managing, and redesigning service processes?
2. How can fail-safe procedures be used to reduce service failures?
3. Explain how blueprinting helps to identify the relationship between core and supplementary services.
4. How do creation and evaluation of a service blueprint help managers understand the role of time in service delivery?
5. Why is periodic process redesign necessary, and what are the main types of service process redesign?
6. Why does the customer's role as a coproducer need to be designed into service processes? What are the implications of considering customers as partial employees?
7. Explain what factors make customers like and dislike self-service technologies.
8. What are the various types of jaycustomers, and how can a service firm deal with their behavior?

Application Exercises

1. Prepare a script for a basic physical examination at a doctor's office. How much participation is required of the customer for the process to work smoothly? In what ways can insufficient cooperation by the customer derail the process? What can the doctor's office do in advance to achieve the necessary cooperation?
2. Review the blueprint of the restaurant visit in Figure 8-1. Identify several possible OTSUs for each step in the front-stage process. Consider possible causes underlying each potential failure, and suggest ways to eliminate or minimize these problems.
3. Prepare a flowchart of a service with which you are familiar.
   a. What are the tangible cues or indicators of quality from the customer's perspective, considering the line of visibility.
   b. Are all steps in the process necessary?
   c. To what extent is standardization possible and advisable throughout the process?
   d. Where are potential fail points located, and how they could be designed out of the process, or what service recovery procedures could be introduced?
   e. What are potential measures of process performance?
4. Observe supermarket shoppers who use self-service checkout lanes and compare those shoppers to ones who use the services of a checker. What differences do you observe? How many of those conducting self-service scanning appear to run into difficulties, and how do they resolve their problems?

5. Identify one Web site that is exceptionally user friendly and another that is not. What factors make for a satisfying user experience in the first instance and a frustrating one in the second? Specify recommendations for improvements in the second Web site.
6. Identify the potential behavior of jaycustomers for a service of your choice. How can the service process be designed to minimize or control their behavior?

Endnotes

1. See G. Lynn Shostack, "Understanding Services through Blueprinting" in T. Schwartz et al., *Advances in Services Marketing and Management, 1992* (Greenwich, CT: JAI Press, 1992), 75–90.
2. G. Lynn Shostack, "Designing Services That Deliver," *Harvard Business Review* (January–February 1984): 133–39.
3. Jane Kingman-Brundage, "The ABCs of Service System Blueprinting," in *Designing a Winning Service Strategy*, ed. M. J. Bitner and L. A. Crosby (Chicago: American Marketing Association, 1989).
4. David Maister, now president of Maister Associates, coined the term OTSU while teaching at Harvard Business School in the 1980s.
5. See, for example, Eric J. Arnould and Linda L. Price, "River Magic: Extraordinary Experience and the Extended Service Encounter," *Journal of Consumer Research* 20 (June 1993): 24–25; Eric J. Arnould and Linda L. Price, "Collaring the Cheshire Cat: Studying Customers' Services Experience through Metaphors," *The Service Industries Journal* 16 (October 1996): 421–442; and Nick Johns and Phil Tyas, "Customer Perceptions of Service Operations: Gestalt, Incident or Mythology?" *The Service Industries Journal* 17 (July 1997): 474–488.
6. "How Marriott Makes a Great First Impression," *The Service Edge* 6 (May 1993): 5.
7. Lisa Bannon, "Plastic Surgeons Are Told to Pay More Attention to Appearances," *Wall Street Journal*, March 15, 1997.
8. David E. Hansen and Peter J. Danaher, "Inconsistent Performance During the Service Encounter: What's a Good Start Worth?" *Journal of Service Research* 1 (February 1999): 227–235; Richard B. Chase and Sriram Dasu, "Want to Perfect Your Company's Service? Use Behavioral Science." *Harvard Business Review* 79 (June 2001): 78–85.
9. This section is based in part on Richard B. Chase and Douglas M. Stewart, "Make Your Service Fail-Safe," *Sloan Management Review* (Spring 1994): 35–44.
10. Jochen Wirtz and Monica Tomlin, "Institutionalizing Customer-Driven Learning through Fully Integrated Customer Feedback Systems," *Managing Service Quality* 10, no. 4 (2000): 205–215.
11. Mitchell T. Rabkin, M.D., cited in Christopher H. Lovelock, *Product Plus* (New York: McGraw-Hill, 1994), 354–55.
12. See, for example, Michael Hammer and James Champy, *Reeingineering the Corporation* (New York: Harper Business, 1993).
13. This material is based partially on Leonard L. Berry and Sandra K. Lampo, "Teaching an Old Service New Tricks—The Promise of Service Redesign," *Journal of Service Research* 2, no. 3 (February 2000): 265–275. Berry and Lampo identified the following five service redesign concepts: self-service, direct service, preservice, bundled service, and physical service. We have expanded some of these concepts to embrace more of the productivity-enhancing aspects of process redesign, such as eliminating non-value-adding work steps in all stages of service delivery.
14. Amy Risch Rodie and Susan Schultz Klein, "Customer Participation in Services Production and Delivery," in *Handbook of Service Marketing and Management*, ed. T. A. Schwartz and D. Iacobucci (Thousand Oaks, CA: Sage Publications, 2000), 111–125.
15. Mary Jo Bitner, William T. Faranda, Amy R. Hubbert, and Valarie A. Zeitham, "Customer Contributions and Roles in Service Delivery," *International Journal of Service Industry Management* 8, no. 3 (1997): 193–205.
16. Pratibha A. Dabholkar, L. Michelle Bobbitt, and Eun-Ju Lee, "Understanding Consumer Motivation and Behavior Related to Self-Scanning in Retailing," *International Journal of Service Industry Management* 14, no. 1 (2003): 59–95.
17. Matthew L. Meuter, Amy L. Ostrom, Robert I. Roundtree, and Mary Jo Bitner, "Self-Service Technologies: Understanding Customer Satisfaction with Technology-Based Service Encounters," *Journal of Marketing* 64 (July 2000): 50–64.
18. Neeli Bendapudi and Robert P. Leone, "Psychological Implications of Customer Participation in Co-Production," *Journal of Marketing* 67 (January 2003): 14–28.
19. Pratibha A. Dabholkar, "Consumer Evaluations of New Technology-Based Self-Service Options: An Investigation of Alternative Models of Service Quality," *International Journal of Research in Marketing* 13 (1996): 29–51; Mary Jo Bitner, Stephen W. Brown, and Matthew L. Meuter, "Technology Infusion in Service Encounters," *Journal of the Academy of Marketing Science* 28, no. 1 (2000): 138–149; Dabholkar et al., 2003 op. cit.
20. David G. Mick and Susan Fournier, "Paradoxes of Technology: Consumer Cognizance, Emotions, and

Coping Strategies," *Journal of Consumer Research* 25 (September 1998): 123–43.

21. James M. Curran, Matthew L. Meuter, and Carol G. Surprenant, "Intentions to Use Self-Service Technologies: A Confluence of Multiple Attitudes," *Journal of Service Research* 5 (February 2003): 209–224.

22. Meuter et al., 2000; Mary Jo Bitner, "Self-Service Technologies: What Do Customers Expect?" *Marketing Management* (Spring 2001): 10–11.

23. Bitner, 2001, op. cit.

24. *www.ebay.com*, accessed April 2003.

25. Benjamin Schneider and David E. Bowen, *Winning the Service Game* (Boston: Harvard Business School Press, 1995), 92.

26. David E. Bowen, "Managing Customers as Human Resources in Service Organizations," *Human Resources Management* 25, no. 3 (1986): 371–383.

27. Benjamin Schneider and David E. Bowen, op. cit. p. 85.

28. Bonnie Farber Canziani, "Leveraging Customer Competency in Service Firms," *International Journal of Service Industry Management* 8, no. 1 (1997): 5–25.

29. This section is adapted from Christopher Lovelock, *Product Plus* (New York: McGraw-Hill, 1994): chapter 15.

30. Based on Rob Ortega and Emily Nelson, "Skiing Deaths May Fuel Calls for Helmets," *Wall Street Journal*, January 7, 1998.

31. For an amusing and explicit depiction of various types of belligerent customers, see Ron Zemke and Kristin Anderson, "The Customers from Hell," *Training* 26 (February 1990): 25–31 [reprinted in John E. G. Bateson and K. Douglas Hoffman, *Managing Services Marketing, 4/E* (Fort Worth, TX: The Dryden Press, 1999), 61–62].

32. Blair J. Berkley and Mohammad Ala, "Identifying and Controlling Threatening Airline Passengers," *Cornell Hotel and Restaurant Administration Quarterly* 42 (August–September 2001): 6–24.

33. Christopher Lovelock, *Product Plus* (New York: McGraw-Hill, 1994), 236.

CHAPTER 9

Balancing Demand and Capacity

Balancing the supply and demand sides of a service industry is not easy, and whether a manager does it well or not makes all the difference

—W. EARL SASSER, JR.

They also serve who only stand and wait.

—JOHN MILTON

Fluctuating demand is a major challenge for many types of service organizations, including restaurants, vacation resorts, courier services, consulting firms, tax authorities, and call centers. These demand fluctuations, which may range in frequency from hourly to seasonal, play havoc with efficient use of productive assets. By working collaboratively with managers in operations and human resources, service marketers may be able to develop strategies to bring demand and capacity into balance in ways that generate benefits for customers as well as for service suppliers.

In this chapter, we consider the nature of demand and supply in services and explore the following questions.

1. In a service context, what is meant by "capacity," and how is it measured?
2. Can variations in demand be predicted and their causes identified?
3. How can capacity management techniques be used to match variations in demand?
4. What marketing strategies are available to service firms to smooth out fluctuations in demand?
5. If customers must wait for service, how can this activity be made less burdensome for them?
6. What is involved in designing an effective reservations system?

FLUCTUATIONS IN DEMAND THREATEN SERVICE PRODUCTIVITY

Unlike manufactured goods, services are perishable and normally cannot be stockpiled for sale at a later date. This is a problem for any capacity-constrained service that faces wide swings in demand. The problem is most commonly found among services that process people or physical possessions: transportation, lodging, food service, repair and maintenance, entertainment, and health care. This problem also affects labor-intensive, information-processing services, such as accounting and tax preparation, that face cyclical shifts in demand.

Effective use of productive capacity is one of the secrets of success in such businesses. The goal should not be to use staff, labor, equipment, and facilities as much as possible but rather to use them as *productively* as possible. At the same time, the search for productivity must not be allowed to undermine service quality and degrade the customer experience.

From Excess Demand to Excess Capacity

The problem is a familiar one. "It's either feast or famine for us!" sighs the manager. "In peak periods, we're disappointing prospective customers by turning them away. And in low periods, our facilities are idle, our employees are standing around looking bored, and we're losing money."

At any given moment, a fixed-capacity service may face one of four conditions (see Figure 9-1):

1. *Excess demand*. The level of demand exceeds maximum available capacity, with the result that some customers are denied service and business is lost.
2. *Demand exceeds optimum capacity*. No one is turned away, but conditions are crowded, and customers are likely to perceive a deterioration in quality of service and to feel dissatisfied.
3. *Demand and supply are well balanced*. This is the level of optimum capacity. Staff and facilities are busy without being overworked, and customers receive good service without delays.
4. *Excess capacity*. Demand is below optimum capacity, and productive resources are underutilized, resulting in low productivity. Low use also poses a risk that customers may find the experience disappointing or have doubts about the viability of the service.

Sometimes, optimum and maximum capacities are one and the same. At a live theater or sports performance, a full house is grand, as it stimulates the players and creates a sense of excitement and audience participation. The net result? A more satisfying experience for all. But with most other services, you probably feel that you get better service if the facility is not operating at full capacity. The quality of restaurant service, for instance, often deteriorates when every table is occupied, because the staff members are rushed and there is a greater likelihood of errors or delays. If you are traveling alone in an aircraft with high-density seating, you tend to feel more comfortable if the seat next to you is

FIGURE 9-1 Implications of Variations in Demand Relative to Capacity

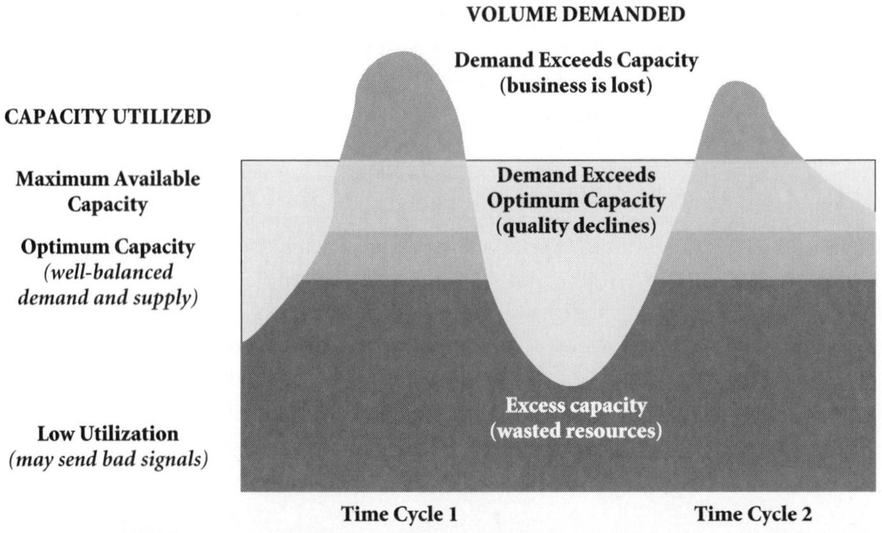

empty. When repair and maintenance shops are fully scheduled, delays may result if there is no slack in the system to allow for unexpected problems in completing particular jobs.

There are two basic approaches to the problem of fluctuating demand. One is to adjust the level of capacity to meet variations in demand. This approach requires an understanding of what constitutes productive capacity and how it may be increased or decreased on an incremental basis. The second approach is to manage the level of demand, using marketing strategies to smooth out the peaks and fill in the valleys so as to generate a more consistent flow of requests for service. Many firms use a mix of both approaches.[1]

MANY SERVICE ORGANIZATIONS ARE CAPACITY-CONSTRAINED

A firm's capacity to serve additional customers at a particular time are often limited. Service firms may also be constrained in terms of being unable to reduce their productive capacity during periods of low demand. In general, organizations that engage in physical processes, such as people or possession processing, are more likely to face capacity constraints than are those that engage in information-based processes. A radio station, for instance, may be constrained in its geographic reach by the strength of its signal, but within that radius, any number of listeners can tune in to a broadcast.

Defining Productive Capacity

The term *productive capacity* refers to the resources or assets that a firm can use to create goods and services. In a service context, productive capacity can take several forms:

- *Physical facilities designed to contain customers* and used for delivering people-processing services or mental stimulus processing services. Examples are medical clinics, hotels, passenger aircrafts, and college classrooms. The primary capacity constraint is likely to be defined in terms of such furnishings as beds, rooms, or seats. In some cases, local regulations may set an upper limit to the number of people allowed in for health or safety reasons.
- *Physical facilities designed for storing or processing goods* that either belong to customers or are being offered to them for sale. Examples are pipelines, warehouses, parking lots, or railroad freight cars.
- *Physical equipment used to process people, possessions, or information*, which may embrace a huge range of items and be very situation specific. Diagnostic equipment, airport security detectors, toll gates, bank ATMs, and "seats" in a call center are among the many items whose absence in sufficient numbers for a given level of demand can bring service to a crawl (or a complete stop).
- *Labor*, a key element of productive capacity in all high-contact services and many low-contact ones. Staffing levels—whether for restaurant servers, nurses, or call center staff—need to be sufficient to meet anticipated demand; otherwise, customers are kept waiting or service is rushed. Professional services are especially dependent on highly skilled staff to create high-value-added, information-based output. Abraham Lincoln captured it well when he remarked: that "A lawyer's time and expertise are his stock in trade."
- *Infrastructure* Many organizations are dependent on access to sufficient capacity in the public or private infrastructure to be able to deliver quality service to their own customers. Capacity problems of this nature may include congested airways that lead to air traffic restrictions on flights, traffic jams on major highways, and power failures or brownouts caused by reduced voltage.

Measures of capacity utilization include the number of hours (or percentage of total available time) that facilities, labor, and equipment are productively engaged in revenue operation and the units or percentage of available space (e.g., seats, cubic freight capacity, telecommunications bandwidth) that is used in revenue operations. Human beings tend to be far more variable than equipment in their ability to sustain consistent levels of output over time. One tired or poorly trained employee staffing a single station in an assembly-line service operation, such as a cafeteria restaurant or a motor vehicle license bureau, can slow the entire service to a crawl.

Many services, such as health care or repair and maintenance, involve multiple actions delivered sequentially. This means that a service organization's capacity to satisfy demand is constrained by one or more of its physical facilities, equipment, personnel, and the number and sequence of services provided. In a well-planned, well-managed service operation, the capacity of the facility, supporting equipment, and service personnel will be in balance. Similarly, sequential operations will be designed to minimize the likelihood of bottlenecks at any point in the process. Best Practice in Action 9-1 describes how one airline sought to improve its capacity to serve at the check-in stage.

Financial success in capacity-constrained businesses is, in large measure, a function of management's ability to use productive capacity—staff, labor, equipment, and facilities—as efficiently and as profitably as possible. In practice, however, it is difficult to achieve this ideal all the time. The level of demand varies over time, often randomly, and the time and effort required to process each person or thing may vary widely at any point in the process. In general, processing times for people are more variable than for objects or things, reflecting varying levels of preparedness ("I've lost my credit card"), argumentative versus cooperative personalities ("If you won't give me a table with a view, I'll have to ask for your supervisor"), and so forth. But service tasks are not necessarily homogeneous. In both professional services and repair jobs, diagnosis and treatment times vary according to the nature of the customers' problems.

Capacity Levels Can Sometimes Be Stretched or Shrunk

Some capacity is elastic in its ability to absorb extra demand. A subway car, for instance, may offer 40 seats and allow standing room for another 60 passengers with adequate handrail and floor space for all. Yet at rush hours, perhaps up to 200 standees can be accommodated under sardinelike conditions. Similarly, the capacity of service personnel can be stretched and may be able to work at high levels of efficiency for short periods of time. However, staff would quickly tire and begin providing inferior service if they had to work at that pace all day long.

Even where capacity appears fixed, as when it is based on the number of seats, there may still be opportunities to accept extra business at busy times. Some airlines, for instance, increase the capacity of their aircraft by switching to a higher-capacity aircraft to a certain route on a busy day. Similarly, a restaurant may add extra tables and chairs. Upper limits to such practices are often set by safety standards or by the capacity of supporting services, such as the kitchen.

Another strategy for stretching capacity within a given time frame is to use the facilities for longer periods. Restaurants may open for early dinners and late suppers, and universities may offer evening classes and summer-semester programs. Alternatively, the average amount of time that customers (or their possessions) spend in process may be reduced. Sometimes, this is achieved by minimizing slack time, as when the bill is presented promptly to a group of diners relaxing at the table after a meal. In other instances, it may be achieved by cutting back the level of service, as when restaurants offer a simpler menu at busy times of the day.

Adjusting Capacity to Match Demand

Another set of options involves tailoring the overall level of capacity to match variations in demand, a strategy also known as *chasing demand.* Managers can take several actions to adjust capacity as needed:[2]

- *Schedule downtime during periods of low demand.* To ensure that 100 percent of capacity is available during peak periods, repairs and renovations should be conducted when demand is expected to be low. Employee holidays should also be taken during such periods.
- *Use part-time employees.* Many organizations hire extra workers during their busiest periods. Examples include postal workers and retail shop assistants at Christmas time, extra staff in tax preparation service firms at the end of the financial year, and additional hotel employees during holiday periods and major conventions.
- *Rent or share extra facilities and equipment.* To limit investment in fixed assets, a service business may be able to rent extra space or machines at peak times. Firms with complementary demand patterns may enter into formal sharing agreements.
- *Cross-train employees.* Even when the service delivery system appears to be operating at full capacity, certain physical elements and their attendant employees may be underutilized. Employees who can be cross-trained to perform a variety of tasks can be shifted to bottleneck points as needed, thereby increasing total system capacity. In supermarkets, for instance, the manager may call on stockers to operate cash registers when checkout lines start to get too long. Likewise, during slow periods, the cashiers may be asked to help stock shelves.

Sometimes, the problem lies not in the overall capacity but in the mix that's available to serve the needs of various market segments. For instance, on a given flight, an airline may have too few seats in economy class even though seats in the business-class cabin are empty; or, a hotel may find itself short of suites one day when standard rooms are still available. One solution lies in designing physical facilities to be flexible. Some hotels build rooms with connecting doors. With the door between two rooms locked, the hotel can sell two bedrooms; with the door unlocked and one of the bedrooms converted into a sitting room, the hotel can now offer a suite.

Facing stiff competition from Airbus Industrie, the Boeing Co. received what were described, tongue-in-cheek, as "outrageous demands" from prospective customers when it was designing its B-777 airliner. The airlines wanted an aircraft in which galleys and lavatories could be relocated, plumbing and all, almost anywhere in the cabin within a matter of hours. Boeing gulped but solved this challenging problem. Airlines can

BEST PRACTICE IN ACTION 9-1

IMPROVING CHECK-IN SERVICE AT LOGAN AIRPORT

To streamline its check-in service at Boston's Logan International Airport, a major airline turned to MIT Professor Richard Larson, who heads a consulting firm called QED. Technicians from QED installed pressure-sensitive rubber mats on the floor in front of the ticket counters. Pressure from each customer's foot on approaching or leaving the counter recorded the exact time on an electronic device embedded in the mats. From the resulting data, Larson was able to profile the waiting situation at the airline's counters, including average waiting times, how long each transaction took, how many customers waited longer than a given length of time (and at what hours on what days), and even how many bailed out of a long line. Analysis of these data, collected over a long time period, yielded information that helped the airline plan its staffing levels to match more closely the demand levels projected at different times.

Source: Richard Saltus, "Lines, Lines, Lines, Lines . . . The Experts Are Trying to Ease the Wait," *Boston Globe,* October 5, 1992.

rearrange the passenger cabin of the "Triple Seven" within hours, reconfiguring it with varying numbers of seats allocated among one, two, or three classes.

Not all unsold productive capacity is wasted. Many firms take a strategic approach to disposition of anticipated surplus capacity, allocating it in advance to build relationships with customers, suppliers, employees, and intermediaries.[3] Possible applications include free trials for prospective customers and for intermediaries who sell to end customers, employee rewards, and bartering with the firm's own suppliers. Among the most widely bartered services are advertising space or airtime, airline seats, and hotel rooms.

PATTERNS AND DETERMINANTS OF DEMAND

Now let's look at the other side of the equation. To control variations in demand for a particular service, managers need to determine what factors govern that demand.

Understanding Patterns of Demand

Research should begin by getting some answers to a series of important questions about the patterns of demand and their underlying causes (Table 9-1).

As you think about some of the seemingly "random" causes, consider how rain and cold affect the use of indoor and outdoor recreational or entertainment services. Then reflect on how heart attacks and births affect the demand for hospital services. Imagine

TABLE 9-1 Questions about the Patterns of Demand and Their Underlying Causes[4]

1. *Do demand levels follow a predictable cycle?*

If so, is the duration of the **demand cycle**

- One *day* (varies by hour)
- One *week* (varies by day)
- One *month* (varies by day or by week)
- One *year* (varies by month or by season or reflects annual public holidays)
- Another period

2. *What are the underlying causes of these cyclical variations?*

- Employment schedules
- Billing and tax payment/refund cycles
- Wage and salary payment dates
- School hours and vacations
- Seasonal changes in climate
- Occurrence of public or religious holidays
- Natural cycles, such as coastal tides

3. *Do demand levels seem to change randomly?*

If so, could the underlying causes be

- Day-to-day changes in the weather
- Health events whose occurrence cannot be pinpointed exactly
- Accidents, fires, and certain criminal activities
- Natural disasters (e.g., earthquakes, storms, mudslides, and volcanic eruptions)

4. *Can demand for a particular service over time be disaggregated by market segment* to reflect such components as

- Use patterns by a particular type of customer or for a particular purpose
- Variations in the net profitability of each completed transaction

what it is like to be a police officer, firefighter, or ambulance driver: You never know exactly where your next call will come from or what the nature of the emergency will be. Finally, consider the impact of natural disasters, such as earthquakes, tornadoes, and hurricanes, on not only emergency services but also disaster-recovery specialists and insurance firms.

Most periodic cycles influencing demand for a particular service vary in length from 1 day to 12 months. The impact of seasonal cycles is well known and affects demand for a broad array of services. Low demand in the off-season poses significant problems for tourism promoters.

In many instances, multiple cycles may operate simultaneously. For example, demand levels for public transport may vary by time of day (highest during commute hours), day of week (less travel to work on weekends but more leisure travel), and season of year (more travel by tourists in summer). The demand for service during the peak period on a Monday in summer is likely to be very different from the level during the peak period on a Saturday in winter, reflecting day-of-week and seasonal variations jointly.

Analyzing Drivers of Demand

No strategy for smoothing demand is likely to succeed unless it is based on an understanding of why customers from a specific market segment choose to use the service when they do. It's difficult for hotels to convince business travelers to remain on Saturday nights, as few executives do business over the weekend. Instead, hotel managers may do better to promote weekend use of their facilities for conferences or pleasure travel. Attempts to get commuters to shift their travel to off-peak periods will probably fail, as such travel is determined by people's employment hours. Instead, efforts should be directed at employers to persuade them to adopt flextime or staggered working hours. These firms recognize that no amount of price discounting is likely to develop business out of season. However, summer resort areas, such as Cape Cod, may have good opportunities to build business during the "shoulder seasons" of spring and fall (which some consider the most attractive times to visit the Cape) by promoting different attractions—such as hiking, birdwatching, visiting museums, and looking for bargains in antique stores—and altering the mix and focus of services to target a different type of clientele.

Keeping good records of each transaction helps enormously when it comes to analyzing demand patterns based on past experience. Best-practice queuing systems supported by sophisticated software can track customer consumption patterns by date and time of day automatically. Where relevant, it's also useful to record weather conditions and other special factors (e.g., a strike, an accident, a big convention in town, a price change, or a launch of a competing service) that might have influenced demand.

Dividing Demand by Market Segment

Random fluctuations are usually caused by factors beyond management's control. But analysis will sometimes reveal that a predictable demand cycle for one segment is concealed within a broader, seemingly random pattern. This fact illustrates the importance of breaking down demand on a segment-by-segment basis. For instance, a repair and maintenance shop that services industrial electrical equipment may already know that a certain proportion of its work consists of regularly scheduled contracts to perform preventive maintenance. The balance may come from walk-in business and emergency repairs. Although it might seem difficult to predict or control the timing and volume of such work, further analysis could show that walk-in business was more prevalent on some days of the week than on others and that emergency repairs were frequently requested following damage sustained during thunderstorms (which tend to be seasonal in nature and can often be forecast a day or two in advance).

Not all demand is desirable. In fact, some requests for service are inappropriate and make it difficult for the organization to respond to the legitimate needs of its target customers. As discussed in Best Practice in Action 9-2, many 911 calls are not really problems that fire, police, or ambulance services should be dispatched to solve. Discouraging undesirable demand such as this through marketing campaigns or screening procedures will not, of course, eliminate random fluctuations in the remaining demand. But it may help to keep peak demand levels within the service capacity of the organization.

Can marketing efforts smooth out random fluctuations in demand? The answer is generally no. For example, a retail store might experience wide swings in daily patronage but note that a core group of customers visited every weekday to buy staple items, such as newspapers and candy.

The ease with which total demand can be broken down into smaller components depends on the nature of the records kept by management. If each customer transaction is recorded separately and backed up by detailed notes (as in a medical or dental visit or an accountant's audit), the task of understanding demand is greatly simplified. In subscription and charge account services, when each customer's identity is known and itemized monthly bills are sent, managers can gain some immediate insights into use patterns. Telephone and electrical services, for example can even track subscriber consumption patterns by time of day. Although these data may not always yield specific information on the purpose for which the service is being used, it is often possible to make informed judgments about the volume of sales generated by various user groups.

DEMAND LEVELS CAN BE MANAGED

There are five basic approaches to managing demand. The first, which has the virtue of simplicity but little else, involves *taking no action and leaving demand to find its own levels.* Eventually, customers learn from experience or word of mouth when they can expect to stand in line to use the service and when it will be available without delay. The trouble is, they may also learn to find a more responsive competitor, and low off-peak utilization cannot be improved unless action is taken. More interventionist approaches involve influencing the level of demand at any given time by taking active steps to *reduce demand in peak periods* and to *increase demand in periods of excess capacity.*

Two more approaches involve *inventorying demand until capacity becomes available.* A firm can accomplish this either by introducing a booking, or *reservations,* system that promises customers access to capacity at specified times or by *creating formalized queuing systems* (or by a combination of the two).

Table 9-2 links these five approaches to the two problem situations of excess demand and excess capacity and provides a brief strategic commentary on each. Many service businesses face both situations at different points in the cycle of demand and should consider use of the interventionist strategies described.

Marketing Strategies to Reshape Demand

Several marketing-mix variables have roles to play in stimulating demand during periods of excess capacity and in decreasing or shifting demand during periods of insufficient capacity. Price is often the first variable to be proposed for bringing demand and supply into balance, but changes in product, distribution strategy, and communication efforts can also play an important role. Although each element is discussed separately, effective demand-management efforts often require changes in two or more elements jointly.

TABLE 9-2 Alternative Demand-Management Strategies for Various Capacity Situations

	Capacity Situation Relative to Demand	
Approach Used to Manage Demand	***Insufficient Capacity (excess demand)***	***Excess Capacity (insufficient demand)***
Take no action	Unorganized queuing results (may irritate customers and discourage future use)	Capacity is wasted (customers may have a disappointing experience for services like theater)
Reduce demand	Higher prices will increase profits; communication can encourage use in other time slots (can this effort be focused on less profitable and desirable segments?)	Take no action (but see preceding)
Increase demand	Take no action unless opportunities exist to stimulate (and give priority to) more profitable segments	Lower prices selectively (try to avoid cannibalizing existing business; ensure that all relevant costs are covered); use communications and variation in products and distribution (but recognize extra costs, if any, and make sure that appropriate tradeoffs are made between profitability and use levels)
Inventory demand by reservation system	Consider priority system for most desirable segments; make other customers shift to off-peak period or to future peak	Clarify that space is available and that no reservations are needed
Inventory demand by formalized queuing	Consider override for most desirable segments; try to keep waiting customers occupied and comfortable; try to predict wait period accurately	Not applicable

Use Price and Other Costs to Manage Demand One of the most direct ways of reducing excess demand at peak periods is to charge customers more money to use the service during those periods. Other costs, too, may have a similar effect. For instance, if customers learn that they are likely to face increased costs of time and effort during peak periods, this information may lead those who dislike spending time waiting in crowded and unpleasant conditions to try later. Similarly, the lure of cheaper prices and an expectation of no waiting may encourage at least some people to change the timing of their behavior, whether it be shopping, travel, or visiting a museum.

Some firms use pricing strategy in sophisticated ways in order to balance supply and demand. For the monetary price of a service to be effective as a demand-management tool, managers must have some sense of the shape and slope of a product's demand curve—that is, how the quantity of service demanded responds to increases or decreases in the price per unit at a particular point in time. (Figure 9-2 shows a sample demand curve.) It's important to determine whether the demand curve for a specific service varies sharply from one time period to another. (Will the same person be willing to pay more for a weekend stay in a hotel on Cape Cod in summer than in winter? The answer is probably yes.) If so, significantly different pricing schemes may be needed to fill capacity in each time period. To complicate matters further, there may be separate demand curves for different segments within each time period (business travelers are usually less price sensitive than vacationers).

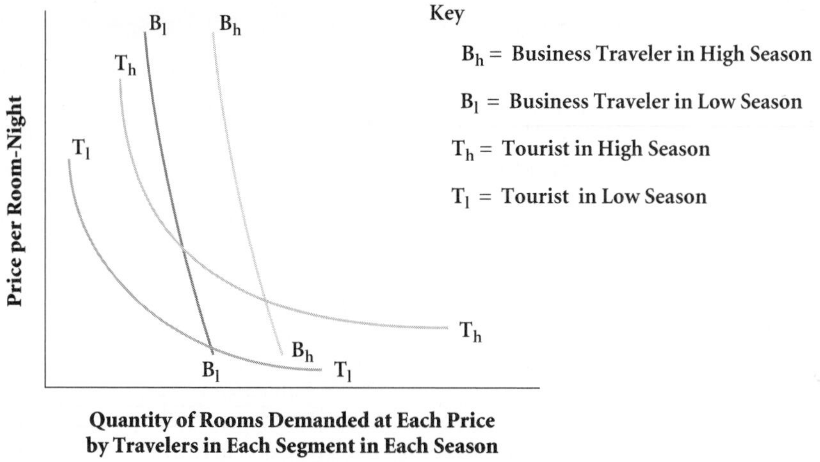

FIGURE 9-2 Hotel Demand Curves by Segment and by Season

One of the most difficult tasks facing service marketers is to determine the nature of all these various demand curves. Research, trial and error, and analysis of parallel situations in other locations or in comparable services are all ways of obtaining an understanding of the situation. Many service businesses explicitly recognize the existence of various demand curves by establishing distinct classes of service, each priced at levels appropriate to the demand curve of a particular segment. In essence, each segment receives a variation of the basic product, with value being added to the core service through supplementary services to appeal to higher-paying segments. For instance, in computer and printing service firms, product enhancement takes the form of faster turnaround and more specialized services; in hotels, a distinction is made between rooms of different sizes and amenities and with different views.

In each case, the objective is to maximize the revenues received from each segment. When capacity is constrained, however, the goal in a profit-seeking business should be to ensure that as much capacity as possible is used by the most profitable segments available at any given time. Airlines, for instance, hold a certain number of seats for business passengers paying full fare and place restrictive conditions on excursion fares for tourists (such as requiring advance purchase and a Saturday night stay) in order to prevent business travelers from taking advantage of cheap fares designed to attract tourists who can help fill the aircraft. Pricing strategies of this nature are known as *yield management* (see Chapter 6).

Change Product Elements Although pricing is often a commonly advocated method of balancing supply and demand, it is not quite as universally feasible for services as for goods. A rather obvious example is provided by the respective problems of a ski manufacturer and a ski slope operator during the summer (see Best Practice in Action 9-3). The former can either produce for inventory or try to sell skis in the summer at a discount. If the skis are sufficiently discounted, some customers will buy before the ski season in order to save money. However, in the absence of skiing opportunities, no skiers would buy lift tickets for use on a midsummer day at any price. So, to encourage summer use of the lifts, the operator has to change the service product offering.

Similar thinking prevails at a variety of other seasonal businesses. Thus, tax preparation firms offer bookkeeping and consulting services to small businesses in slack months, educational institutions offer weekend and summer programs for adults and senior citizens, and small pleasure boats offer cruises in the summer and a dockside venue for private functions in winter months. These firms recognize that no amount of

BEST PRACTICE IN ACTION 9-2

DISCOURAGING DEMAND FOR NONEMERGENCY CALLS

Have you ever wondered what it's like to be a dispatcher for an emergency telephone service, such as 911? People differ widely in what they consider to be an emergency.

Imagine yourself in the huge communications room at Police Headquarters in New York. A gray-haired sergeant is talking patiently by phone to a woman who has dialed 911 because she's afraid that her cat is stuck in a tree. "Ma'am, have you ever seen a cat skeleton in a tree?" the sergeant asks her. "All those cats get down somehow, don't they?" After the woman has hung up, the sergeant turns to a visitor and shrugs. "These kinds of calls keep pouring in," he says. "What can you do?" The trouble is, when they call the emergency number with complaints about noisy parties next door, pleas to rescue cats, or requests to turn off leaking fire hydrants, people may be slowing response times to fires, heart attacks, or violent crimes.

At one point, the situation in New York City got so bad that officials were forced to develop a marketing campaign to discourage people from making inappropriate requests for emergency assistance through the 911 number. The problem was that what might seem like an emergency to the caller—a beloved cat stuck up a tree, a noisy party that was preventing someone from getting needed sleep—was not a life- (or property-) threatening situation of the type that the city's emergency services were poised to resolve. So a communications campaign, using a variety of media, was developed to urge people not to call 911 unless they were reporting a *dangerous emergency.* For help in resolving other problems, people were asked to call their local police station or other city agencies. The ad shown in Figure 9-A appeared on New York buses and subways.

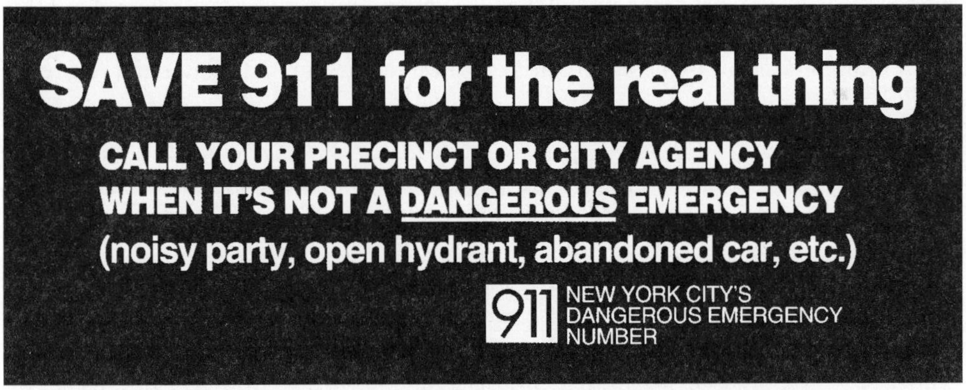

SAVE 911 for the real thing
CALL YOUR PRECINCT OR CITY AGENCY
WHEN IT'S NOT A DANGEROUS EMERGENCY
(noisy party, open hydrant, abandoned car, etc.)
911
NEW YORK CITY'S
DANGEROUS EMERGENCY
NUMBER

FIGURE 9-A Ad Discouraging Nonemergency Calls to 911

price discounting is likely to develop business out of season and that new value propositions targeted at different segments are needed.

Many service offerings remain unchanged throughout the year, but others undergo significant modifications according to the season. Hospitals, for example, usually offer the same array of services throughout the year. By contrast, resort hotels sharply alter the mix and focus of their peripheral services, such as dining, entertainment, and sports, to reflect customers' seasonal preferences.

There can be variations in the product offering even during the course of a 24-hour period. Some restaurants provide a good example of this, marking the passage of the hours with changing menus and levels of service, variations in lighting and decor, opening and closing of the bar, and the presence or absence of entertainment. The goal is to appeal to different needs within the same group of customers, to reach out to different customer segments, or to do both, according to the time of day.

BEST PRACTICE IN ACTION 9-3

SUMMER ON THE SKI SLOPES

It used to be that ski resorts shut down once the snow melted and the slopes became unskiable. The chairlifts stopped operating, the restaurants closed, and the lodges were locked and shuttered until winter approached and the snows fell again. In time, however, some ski operators recognized that a mountain offers summer pleasures, too, and kept lodging and restaurants open for hikers and picnickers. Some operators even built Alpine Slides—curving tracks in which wheeled toboggans could run from the summit to the base—and thus created demand for tickets on the ski lifts. With the construction of condominiums for sale, demand increased for warm-weather activities as the owners flocked to the mountains in summer and early fall.

The arrival of the mountain biking craze created opportunities for equipment rentals as well as chairlift rides. Killington Resort in Vermont has long encouraged summer visitors to ride to the summit, see the view, and eat at the mountaintop restaurant. But now it also enjoys a booking business in renting mountain bikes and related equipment (such as helmets). Beside the base lodge, where skiers would find rack after rack of skis for rent in winter, the summer visitor can now choose from rows of mountain bikes. Bikers transport their vehicles up to the summit on specially equipped chair lifts and then ride them down designated trails. Serious hikers reverse the process, climbing to the summit via trails that seek to avoid descending bikes—getting refreshments at the restaurant, and then taking the chairlift back down to the base. Once in a while, a biker will actually choose to ride up the mountain, but such gluttons for punishment are few and far between.

Most large ski resorts look for a variety of additional ways to attract guests to their hotels and rental homes during the summer. Mont Tremblant, Quebec, for instance, is located beside an attractive lake. In addition to swimming and other water sports on the lake, the resort offers visitors such activities as a championship golf course, tennis, roller blading, and a children's daycamp. And hikers and mountain bikers come to ride the lifts up the mountain (Figure 9-B).

FIGURE 9-B Riding the Chairlift up Mont Tremblant to Hike and Bike Rather Than Ski

Modify the Place and Time of Delivery Rather than seeking to modify demand for a service that continues to be offered at the same time in the same place, some firms respond to market needs by modifying the time and place of delivery. Three basic options are available.

The first represents a strategy of *no change*: Regardless of the level of demand, the service continues to be offered in the same location at the same times. By contrast, the second strategy involves *varying the times when the service is available,* reflecting changes in customer preference by day of week, by season, and so forth. Theaters and cinema complexes often offer matinees on weekends, when people have more leisure time throughout the day; during the summer, cafes and restaurants may stay open later because of the general inclination of people to enjoy the longer, balmier evenings outdoors; and shops may extend their hours in the lead-up to Christmas or during school holiday periods.

A third strategy involves *offering the service to customers at a new location.* One approach is to operate mobile units that take the service to customers rather than requiring them to visit fixed-site service locations. Traveling libraries, mobile car wash services, in-office tailoring services, home-delivered meals and catering services, and vans equipped with primary care medical facilities are examples of this. A cleaning and repair firm that wishes to generate business during low-demand periods might offer free pick-up and delivery of portable items that need servicing. Alternatively, service firms whose productive assets are mobile may choose to follow the market when that, too, is mobile. For instance, some car rental firms establish seasonal branch offices in resort communities. In these new locations, the firms often change the schedule of service hours (as well as certain product features) to conform to local needs and preferences.

Promotion and Education Even if the other variables of the marketing mix remain unchanged, communication efforts alone may be able to help smooth demand. Signage, advertising, publicity, and sales messages can be used to educate customers about the timing of peak periods and encourage customers to avail themselves of the service at off-peak times when there will be fewer delays. Examples include post office requests to "Mail Early for Christmas," public transport messages urging noncommuters—such as shoppers or tourists—to avoid the crush conditions of the commute hours, and communications from sales reps for industrial maintenance firms advising customers of periods when preventive maintenance work can be done quickly. In addition, management can ask service personnel (or intermediaries, such as travel agents) to encourage customers with discretionary schedules to favor off-peak periods.

Changes in pricing, product characteristics, and distribution must be communicated clearly. If a firm wants to obtain a specific response to variations in marketing-mix elements, it must, of course, inform customers fully about their options. As discussed in Chapter 5, short-term promotions, combining both pricing and communication elements, as well as other incentives, may provide customers with attractive incentives to shift the timing of service use.

INVENTORY DEMAND THROUGH WAITING LINES AND RESERVATIONS

One of the challenges of services is that, being performances, they cannot normally be stored for later use. A haircutter cannot prepackage a haircut for the following day; the haircut must be done in real time. In an ideal world, nobody would ever have to wait to conduct a service transaction. But firms cannot afford to provide extensive extra capacity that would go unused most of the time. As we have seen, a variety of procedures can bring demand and supply into balance. But what's a manager to do when the possibilities for shaping demand and adjusting capacity have been exhausted and yet supply and demand are still out of balance? Not taking any action and leaving customers to sort things out is no recipe for customer satisfaction. Rather than allowing matters to degenerate into a random free-for-all, customer-oriented firms try to develop strategies for ensuring order, predictability, and fairness.

In businesses whose demand regularly exceeds supply, managers can often take steps to inventory demand. This task can be achieved in one of two ways: (1) by asking customers to wait in line (queuing), usually on a first-come first-served basis, or (2) by offering them the opportunity of reserving, or booking space in advance (see Best Practice in Action 9-4).

Waiting: A Universal Phenomenon

It's estimated that Americans spend 37 billion hours a year (an average of almost 150 hours per person) waiting in lines, "during which time they fret, fidget, and scowl," according to *Washington Post.*[5] Similar (or worse) situations seem to prevail

BEST PRACTICE IN ACTION 9-4

CUTTING THE WAIT FOR RETAIL BANKING CUSTOMERS

How should a big retail bank respond to increased competition from new financial service providers? A large bank in Chicago decided that enhancing service to its customers would be an important element in its strategy. One opportunity for improvement was to reduce the amount of time that customers spent waiting in line for service in the bank's retail branches—a frequent source of complaints. Recognizing that no single action could resolve the problem satisfactorily, the bank adopted a three-pronged approach.

First, technological improvements were made to the service operation, starting with the introduction of an electronic queuing system that not only routed customers to the next available teller station but also provided supervisors with online information to help match staffing to customer demand. Meantime, computer enhancements provided tellers with more information about their customers, enabling the tellers to handle more requests without leaving their stations. And new cash machines for tellers saved them from selecting bills and counting them twice (yielding a time savings of 30 seconds for each cash-withdrawal transaction).

Second, changes were made to human resource strategies. The bank adopted a new job description for teller managers that made them responsible for customer queuing times and for expediting transactions. The bank also created an officer-of-the-day program, under which a designated officer was equipped with a beeper and assigned to help staff with complicated transactions that might otherwise slow them down. A new job category of peak-time teller was introduced, paying premium wages for 12 to 18 hours of work a week. Existing full-time tellers were given cash incentives and recognition in reward for improved productivity on predicted high-volume days. Finally, management reorganized meal arrangements. On busy days, lunch breaks were reduced to half-hour periods and staff received catered meals; meantime, the bank cafeteria was opened earlier to serve peak-time tellers.

A third set of changes centered on customer-oriented improvements to the delivery system. Quick-drop desks were established on busy days to handle deposits and simple requests, whereas newly created express-teller stations were reserved for deposits and check cashing. Lobby hours were expanded from 38 to 56 hours a week, including Sundays. A customer brochure, *How to Lose Wait*, alerted customers to busy periods and suggested ways of avoiding delays.

Subsequently, internal measures and customer surveys showed that the improvements had not only reduced customer wait times but also increased customer perceptions that this bank was "the best" bank in the region for minimal waits in teller lines. The bank also found that adoption of extended hours had deflected some of the "noon rush" to before-work and after-work periods.

Source: Based on an example in Leonard L. Berry and Linda R. Cooper, "Competing with Time-Saving Service," *Business* 40, no. 2 (1990): 3–7.

around the world. Richard Larson suggests that, when everything is added up, the average person may spend as much as 30 minutes a day waiting in line, which translates to 20 months of waiting in an 80-year lifetime![6]

Nobody likes to be kept waiting (Figure 9-3). It's boring, time wasting, and sometimes physically uncomfortable, especially if there is nowhere to sit or you are outdoors.

FIGURE 9-3 Hertz Helps Its Customers to Avoid the Time and Hassle of Waiting in Line

And yet waiting for a service process is an almost universal phenomenon: Almost every organization faces the problem of waiting lines somewhere in its operation. People are kept waiting on the phone, they line up with their supermarket carts to check out their grocery purchases, they wait for their bills after a restaurant meal, and they sit in their cars, waiting to enter drive-in car washes and to pay at tollbooths.

Physical and inanimate objects wait for processing, too. Customers' e-mails sit in customer service staff members' in-boxes, appliances wait to be repaired, checks wait to be cleared at a bank, an incoming phone call waits to be switched to a customer service rep. In each instance, a customer may be waiting for the outcome of that work: an answer to an e-mail, an appliance that is working again, a check credited to the customer's balance, or useful contact with the service rep (instead of being kept on hold, listening to a recorded message that keeps repeating, "your call is important to us").

Why Waiting Lines Occur

Waiting lines—known to operations researchers and the British as "queues"—occur whenever the number of arrivals at a facility exceeds the capacity of the system to process them. In a very real sense, queues are a symptom of unresolved capacity management problems. Analysis and modeling of queues is a well-established branch of operations management. Queuing theory has been traced back to 1917, when a Danish telephone engineer was charged with determining how large the switching unit in a telephone system had to be to keep the number of busy signals within reason.[7]

As the telephone example suggests, not all queues take the form of a physical waiting line in a single location. When they deal with a service supplier at arm's length, as in information-processing services, customers call from home, office, or college, using such telecommunication channels as voice telephone or the Internet. Typically, calls are answered in the order received, often requiring customers to wait their turn in a virtual line. Some physical queues are geographically dispersed. Travelers wait at many different locations for the taxis they have ordered by phone to arrive and pick them up.

Many Web sites now allow people to do things for themselves, such as obtaining information or making reservations, that formerly required making telephone calls or visiting a service facility in person. Companies often promote the time savings that can be obtained. Although accessing the Web can be slow sometimes, at least the wait is conducted while the customer is comfortably seated and able to attend to other matters while waiting.

Increasing capacity by adding more tellers was only one of several actions taken to reduce wait times in our Best Practice in Action 9-4 example on the Chicago bank. But adding extra servers is not always the optimal solution when customer satisfaction must be balanced against cost considerations. Like that bank, managers should consider a variety of alternatives, such as

- Rethinking the design of the queuing system
- Redesigning processes to shorten the time of each transaction
- Managing customers' behavior and their perceptions of the wait
- Installing a reservations system

Queue Configurations

A variety of queue types exist, and the challenge for managers is to select the most appropriate procedure. Figure 9-4 shows several types that you have probably experienced yourself. In *single line sequential stages*, customers proceed through several serving operations, as in a cafeteria. Bottlenecks may occur at any stage where the process takes longer to execute than at previous stages. Many cafeterias have lines at

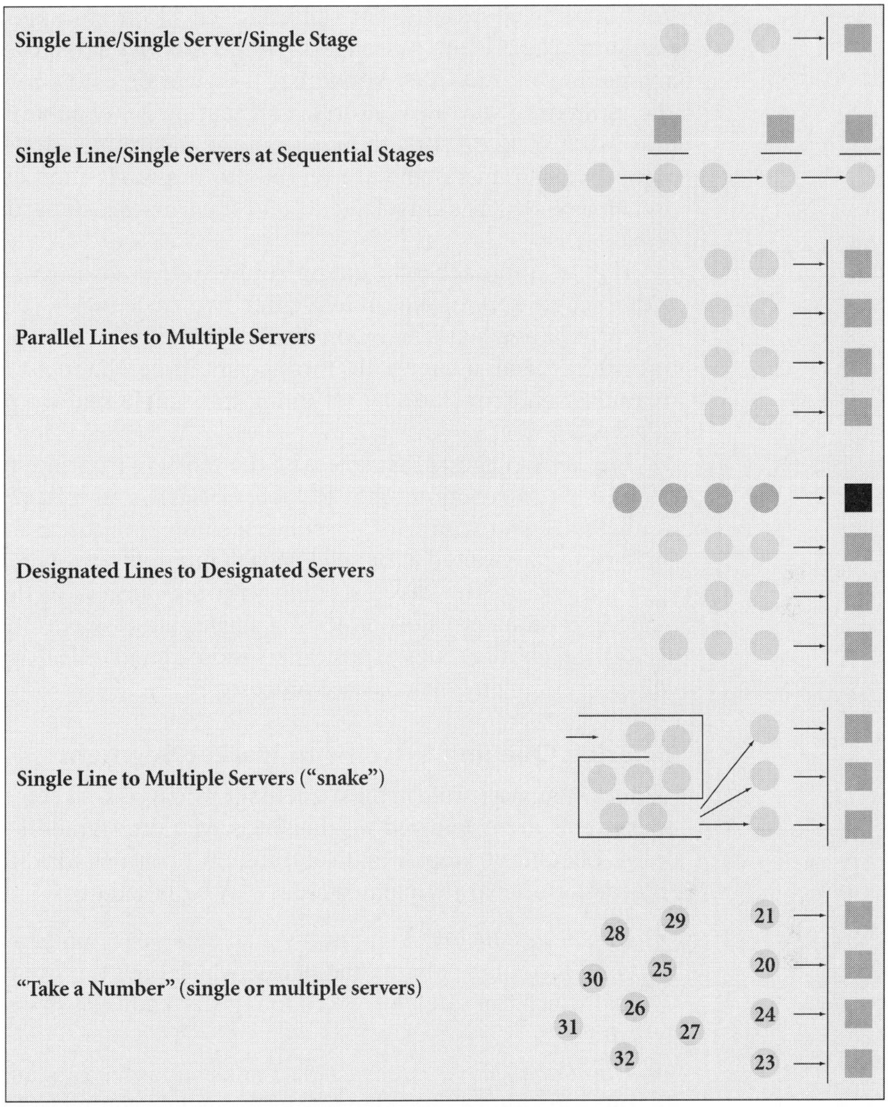

FIGURE 9-4 Alternative Queue Configurations

the cash register because the cashier takes longer to calculate how much you owe and to make change than the servers take to slap food on your plate.

Parallel lines to multiple servers offer more than one serving station, allowing customers to select one of several lines in which to wait. Banks and ticket windows are common examples. Fast-food restaurants usually have several serving lines in operation at busy times of day, with each offering the full menu. A parallel system can have either a single stage or multiple stages. The disadvantage of this design is that lines may not move at equal speed. How many times have you chosen what looked like the shortest line only to watch in frustration as the lines on either side of you move at twice the speed because someone in your line had a complicated transaction? A common solution here is to create a *single line to multiple servers* (commonly known as a "snake"). This approach is encountered frequently at post offices and airport check-in counters.

Designated lines involve assigning different lines to specific categories of customer. Examples include express lines (e.g., 12 or fewer items) and regular lines at supermarket checkouts, and different check-in stations for first-, business-, and economy-class airline passengers. *Take a number* saves customers the need to stand in a queue, because they know that they will be called in sequence. This procedure allows them to sit down and relax (if seating is available) or to guess how long the wait will be and do something else in the meantime—but at the risk of losing their place if earlier customers are served more quickly than expected. Users of this approach include large travel agents and supermarket departments, such as the butcher or baker.

Hybrid approaches to queue configuration also exist. For instance, a cafeteria with a single serving line might offer two cash register stations at the final stage. Similarly, patients at a small medical clinic might visit a single receptionist for registration; proceed sequentially through multiple channels for testing, diagnosis, and treatment; and conclude by returning to a single line for payment at the receptionist's desk.

Research suggests that selecting the most appropriate type of queue is important to customer satisfaction. Anat Rafaeli, G. Barron, and K. Haber found that the way a waiting area is structured can produce feelings of injustice and unfairness in customers. Customers who waited in parallel lines to multiple servers reported significantly higher agitation and greater dissatisfaction with the fairness of the service delivery process than did customers who waited in a single line ("snake") to access multiple servers, even though both groups of customers waited an identical amount of time and were involved in completely fair service processes.[8]

Tailoring Queuing Systems to Market Segments

Although the basic rule in most queuing systems is first come first served, not all queuing systems are organized on this basis. Market segmentation is sometimes used to design queuing strategies that set different priorities for different types of customers. Allocation to separate queuing areas may be based on

- *Urgency of the job.* At many hospital emergency units, a triage nurse is assigned to greet incoming patients and decide which ones require priority medical treatment and which can safely be asked to register and then sit down while they wait their turn.
- *Duration of service transaction.* Banks, supermarkets, and other retail services often institute express lanes for shorter, less complicated tasks.
- *Payment of a premium price.* Airlines usually offer separate check-in lines for first-class and economy-class passengers, with a higher ratio of personnel to passengers in the first-class line, resulting in reduced waits for those who have paid more for their tickets.
- *Importance of the customer.* A special area may be reserved for members of frequent user clubs. Airlines often provide lounges, offering newspapers and free refreshments, where frequent flyers can wait for their flights in greater comfort.

MINIMIZING PERCEPTIONS OF WAITING TIME

Research shows that people often think they have waited longer for a service than they in fact did. Studies of public transportation use, for instance, have shown that travelers perceive time spent waiting for a bus or train as passing one and a half to seven times more slowly than the time spent traveling in the vehicle.[9] People don't like wasting their time on unproductive activities any more than they like wasting money. Customer dissatisfaction with delays in receiving service can often stimulate strong emotions, including anger.[10]

The Psychology of Waiting Time

The noted philosopher William James observed: "Boredom results from being attentive to the passage of time itself." Savvy service marketers recognize that customers experience waiting time in differing ways, depending on the circumstances. Table 9-3 highlights 10 propositions on the psychology of waiting lines.

When increasing capacity is simply not feasible, service providers should try to be creative and look for ways to make waiting more palatable for customers. Doctors and

TABLE 9-3 Ten Propositions on the Psychology of Waiting Lines[11]

1. *Unoccupied time feels longer than occupied time.* When you're sitting around with nothing to do, time seems to crawl. The challenge for service organizations is to give customers something to do or to distract them while waiting.
2. *Pre- and postprocess waits feel longer than in-process waits.* Waiting to buy a ticket to enter a theme park is different from waiting to ride on a roller coaster once you're in the park. There's also a difference between waiting for coffee to arrive near the end of a restaurant meal and waiting for the server to bring you the check once you're ready to leave.
3. *Anxiety makes waits seem longer.* Can you remember waiting for someone to show at a rendezvous and worrying about whether you had got the time or the location correct? While waiting in unfamiliar locations, especially outdoors and after dark, people often worry about their personal safety.
4. *Uncertain waits are longer than known, finite waits.* Although any wait may be frustrating, we can usually adjust mentally to a wait of known length. It's the unknown that keeps us on edge. Imagine waiting for a delayed flight and not being told how long the delay is going to be. You don't know whether you have the time to get up and walk around the terminal or whether to stay at the gate in case the flight is called any minute.
5. *Unexplained waits are longer than explained waits.* Have you ever been in a subway or an elevator that has stopped for no apparent reason, without anyone telling you why? In addition to uncertainty about the length of the wait, there's added worry about what is going to happen. Has there been an accident on the line? Will you have to leave the train in the tunnel? Is the elevator broken? Will you be stuck for hours in close proximity with strangers?
6. *Unfair waits are longer than equitable waits.* Expectations about what is fair or unfair sometimes vary from one culture or country to another. In the United States, Canada, or Britain, for example, people expect everybody to wait their turn in line and are likely to get irritated if they see others jumping ahead or being given priority for no apparent good reason.
7. *The more valuable the service, the longer people will wait.* People will queue overnight under uncomfortable conditions to get good seats at a major concert or sports event that is expected to sell out.
8. *Solo waits feel longer than group waits.* Waiting with one or more people you know is reassuring. Conversation with friends can help to pass the time, but not everyone is comfortable talking to a stranger.
9. *Physically uncomfortable waits feel longer than comfortable waits.* "My feet are killing me!" is one of the most frequently heard comments when people are forced to stand in line for a long time. And whether seated or unseated, waiting seems more burdensome if the temperature is too hot or too cold, if it's drafty or windy, and if there is no protection from rain or snow.
10. *Unfamiliar waits seem longer than familiar ones.* Frequent users of a service know what to expect and are less likely to worry while waiting. New or occasional users of a service, by contrast, are often nervous, wondering not only about the probable length of the wait but also about what happens next.

dentists stock their waiting rooms with piles of magazines for people to read while waiting. Car repair facilities may have a television for customers to watch. One tire dealer even provides customers with free popcorn, soft drinks, coffee, and ice cream while they wait for their cars to be returned.

An experiment at a large bank in Boston found that installing an electronic news display in the lobby led to greater customer satisfaction but didn't reduce the perceived time spent waiting for teller service.[12] In some locations, transit operators erect heated shelters equipped with seats make it pleasanter for travelers to wait for a bus or train in cold weather. Restaurants solve the waiting problem by inviting dinner guests to have a drink in the bar until their table is ready, which not only makes money for the house but also keeps the customers occupied. In similar fashion, guests waiting in line for a show at a casino may find themselves queuing in a corridor lined with slot machines.

The doorman at one Marriott Hotel has taken it upon himself to bring a combination barometer/thermometer to work each day, hanging it on a pillar at the hotel entrance where guests waiting can spend a moment or two examining it while they wait for a taxi or for their car to be delivered from the valet parking.[13] Theme park operators cleverly design their waiting areas to make the wait look shorter than it really is, finding ways to give customers in line the impression of constant progress and make time seem to pass more quickly by keeping customers amused or diverted while they wait. Recognizing that customers don't want to waste time on either preprocess or postprocess waits, rental car firms try to minimize customer waiting when the car is returned, having agents with wireless, handheld terminals meet customers in the parking area, enter fuel and mileage, and then compute and print bills on the spot.

Giving Customers Information on Waits

Does it help to tell people how long they are likely to have to wait for service? Common sense would suggest that this is useful information for customers, as it allows them to make decisions about whether they can afford to take the time to wait now or should come back later. It also enables them to plan the use of their time while waiting.

An experimental study in Canada looked at how students responded to waits while conducting transactions by computer—a situation similar to waiting on the telephone in that there are no visual clues as to the probable wait time.[14] The study examined dissatisfaction with waits of 5, 10, or 15 minutes under three conditions: (1) the student subjects were told nothing, (2) they were told how long the wait was likely to be, or (3) they were told what their place in line was. The results suggested that for five-minute waits, it was not necessary to provide information to improve satisfaction. For waits of 10 or 15 minutes, offering information appeared to improve customers' evaluations of service. However, for longer waits, the researchers suggest that it may be more positive to let people know how their place in line is changing than to let them know how much time remains before they will be served. One conclusion we might draw is that people prefer to see (or sense) that the line is moving rather than to watch the clock.

CREATING AN EFFECTIVE RESERVATIONS SYSTEM

Ask someone what services come to mind when you talk about reservations, and most likely will cite airlines, hotels, restaurants, car rentals, and theater seats. Suggest synonyms (e.g.) bookings or appointments, and they may add haircuts, visits to doctors and consultants, vacation rentals, and service calls to fix anything from a broken refrigerator to a neurotic computer.

Reservations are supposed to guarantee that service will be available when the customer wants it. Systems vary from a simple appointments book for a doctor's office, using handwritten entries, to a central, computerized data bank for an airline's worldwide operations. When goods require servicing, their owners may not wish to be parted from them for long. Households with only one car, for example, or factories with a vital piece of equipment often cannot afford to be without such items for more than a day or two. So a reservations system may be necessary for service businesses in such fields as repair and maintenance. By requiring reservations for routine maintenance, management can ensure that some time will be kept free for handling emergency jobs, which, because they carry a premium price, generate a much higher margin.

Reservations systems are commonly used by many people-processing services, such as restaurants, hotels, airlines, hairdressing salons, doctors, and dentists. The presence of such systems enables demand to be controlled and smoothed out in a more manageable way. By capturing data, reservations systems also help organizations to prepare financial projections.

Taking bookings also serves to presell a service, to inform customers, and to educate them about what to expect. Customers who hold reservations should be able to count on avoiding a queue, as they have been guaranteed service at a specific time. A well-organized reservations system allows the organization to deflect demand for service from a first-choice time to earlier or later times, from one class of service to another ("upgrades" and "downgrades"), and even from first-choice locations to alternative ones. However, problems arise when customers fail to show or when service firms overbook. Marketing strategies for dealing with these operational problems include requiring a deposit, canceling nonpaid bookings after a certain time, and providing compensation to victims of overbooking.

The challenge in designing reservations systems is to make them fast and user friendly for both staff and customers. Many firms now allow customers to make their own reservations on a Web site—a trend that seems certain to grow. Whether they talk with a reservations agent or make their own bookings, customers want quick answers to queries about service availability at a preferred time. Customers also appreciate further system-provided information about the type of service they are reserving. For instance, can a hotel assign a specific room on request? Or, at least, can it assign a room with a view of the lake rather than one with a view of the parking lot and the nearby power station?

Yield-Focused Reservations Strategies

Service organizations often use percentage of capacity sold as a measure of operational efficiency. Transport services talk of the "load factor" achieved, hotels of their "occupancy rate," and hospitals of their "census." Similarly, professional firms can calculate what proportion of a partner's or an employee's time is classified as billable hours, and repair shops can look at utilization of both equipment and labor. By themselves, however, these percentage figures tell us little of the relative profitability of the business attracted, as high utilization rates may be obtained at the expense of heavy discounting or even outright giveaways.

More and more, service firms are looking at their "yield"—that is, the average revenue received per unit of capacity. The aim is to maximize this yield in order to improve profitability. As noted in Chapter 6, pricing strategies designed to achieve this goal are widely used in such capacity-constrained industries as passenger airlines, hotels, and car rentals. Formalized yield management systems, based on mathematical modeling, are of greatest value for service firms that find it expensive to modify their capacity but incur relatively low costs when they sell another unit of available capacity.[15] Other characteristics encouraging use of such programs include fluctuating demand levels, ability to segment markets by extent of price sensitivity, and sale of services well in advance of use.

Yield analysis forces managers to recognize the opportunity cost of allocating capacity to one customer or market segment when another might subsequently yield a higher rate. Consider the following problems facing sales managers for various types of capacity-constrained service organizations.

- Should a hotel accept an advance booking from a tour group of 200 room nights at $80 each when these same room nights might possibly be sold later at short notice to business travelers at the full posted rate of $140?
- Should a railroad with 30 empty freight cars at its disposal accept an immediate request for a shipment worth $900 per car or hold the cars idle for a few more days in the hope of getting a priority shipment that would be twice as valuable?
- How many seats on a particular flight should an airline sell in advance to tour groups and passengers traveling at special excursion rates?
- Should an industrial repair and maintenance shop reserve a certain proportion of productive capacity each day for emergency repair jobs that offer a high contribution margin and the potential to build long-term customer loyalty, or should the shop simply follow a strategy of making sure that there are sufficient jobs, mostly involving routine maintenance, to keep its employees fully occupied?
- Should a print shop process all jobs on a first-come first-served basis, with a guaranteed delivery time for each job, or should it charge a premium rate for "rush" work and tell customers with "standard" jobs to expect some variability in completion dates?

Decisions on such problems deserve to be handled with a little more sophistication than resorting to the "bird-in-the-hand-is-worth-two-in-the-bush" formula. So managers need a way of figuring out the chances of getting more profitable business if they wait. Good information, based on detailed record keeping of past use and supported by current market intelligence and good marketing sense, is the key. The decision to accept or reject business should be based on a realistic estimate of the probabilities of obtaining higher-rated business and awareness of the need to maintain established (and desirable) customer relationships. Managers who decide on the basis of guesswork and "gut feel" are little better than gamblers who bet on rolls of the dice.

A clear plan is needed, based on analysis of past performance and current market data, that indicates how much capacity should be allocated on specific dates to various types of customers at certain prices. Based on this plan, "selective sell" targets can be assigned to advertising and sales personnel, reflecting allocation of available capacity among various market segments on specific future dates. The last thing a firm wants its sales force to do is to encourage price-sensitive market segments to buy capacity on dates when sales projections predict that there will be strong demand from customers willing to pay full price. Unfortunately, in some industries, the lowest-rated business often books the farthest ahead: tour groups, which pay much lower room rates than individual travelers, often ask airlines and hotels to block space more than a year in advance.

Figure 9-5 illustrates capacity allocation in a hotel setting, where demand from various types of customers varies not only by day of the week but also by season. These allocation decisions by segment, captured in reservations databases that are accessible worldwide, tell reservations personnel when to stop accepting reservations at certain prices, even though many rooms may still remain unbooked. Loyalty program members, who are primarily business travelers, are obviously a particularly desirable segment.

Similar charts can be constructed for most capacity-constrained businesses. In some instances, capacity is measured in terms of seats for a given performance, seat miles, or room nights; in others, it may be in terms of machine time, labor time, billable professional hours, vehicle miles, or storage volume, whichever is the scarce resource.

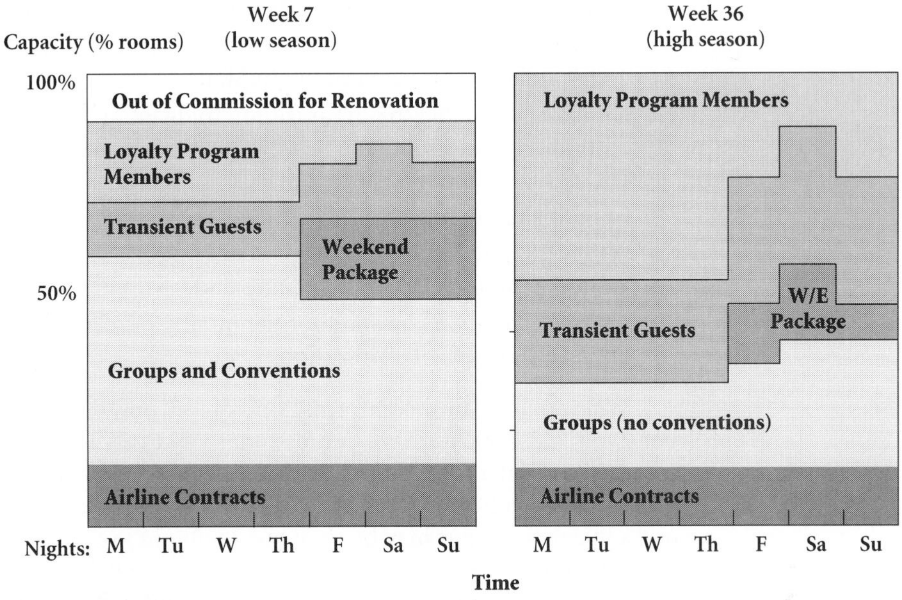

FIGURE 9-5 Setting Capacity Allocation Targets by Segment for a Hotel

Unless it's easy to divert business from one facility to a similar alternative, allocation-planning decisions will have to be made at the level of geographic operating units. So each hotel, repair and maintenance center, or computer service bureau may need its own plan. On the other hand, transport vehicles are a mobile capacity that can be allocated across any geographic area the vehicles are able to serve.

In large organizations, such as major airlines or hotel chains, the market is very dynamic, as the situation is changing all the time. For instance, the demand for both business and pleasure travel reflects current or anticipated economic conditions. Although many business travelers are not price sensitive, some companies insist that employees shop for the best travel bargains they can find within the constraints of their business travel needs. Pleasure travelers are often very price sensitive; a special promotion, involving discounted fares and room rates, may encourage people to undertake a trip that they would not otherwise have made.

Viewed from the perspective of the individual hotel or airline, competitive activity has the potential to play havoc with patronage forecasts. Imagine that you are a hotel owner and a new hotel opens across the street with a special discount offer. How will it affect you? Alternatively, consider the impact if an existing competitor burns down! The airline business is notoriously changeable. Fares can be slashed overnight. A competitor may introduce a new nonstop service between two cities or cut back its existing schedule on another route. Travel agents and savvy customers watch these movements like hawks and may be quick to cancel one reservation (even if it involves paying a penalty) in order to take advantage of a better price or a more convenient schedule that can be obtained elsewhere.

Effective Demand and Capacity Management Requires Information

Managers require substantial information to help them develop effective strategies to manage demand and capacity and then monitor subsequent performance in the marketplace. Following are some important categories of information for this purpose.

- *Historical data* on the level and composition of demand over time, including responses to changes in price or other marketing variables

- *Forecasts* of the level of demand for each major segment under specified conditions
- *Segment-by-segment data* to help management evaluate the impact of periodic cycles and random demand fluctuations
- *Cost data* to enable the organization to distinguish between fixed and variable costs and to determine the relative profitability of incremental unit sales to different segments and at different prices
- In multisite organizations, *identification of meaningful variations in the levels and composition of demand* on a site-by-site basis
- *Customer attitudes* toward queuing under varying conditions
- *Customer opinions* on whether the quality of service delivered varies with different levels of capacity utilization

Where might all this information come from? Most large organizations with expensive fixed capacity have professional yield or revenue management systems (see Chapter 6). For organizations without such systems, the needed data are probably already being collected within the organization, although not necessarily by marketers, and some new studies may be required to obtain the necessary data. A stream of information comes into most service businesses, especially from distilling the multitude of individual transactions conducted. Sales receipts alone often contain vast amounts of detail. Most service businesses collect detailed information for operational and accounting purposes. Although some do not record details of individual transactions, a majority have the potential to associate specific customers with specific transactions. Unfortunately, the marketing value of these data is often overlooked and the data are not always stored in ways that permit easy retrieval and analysis for marketing purposes. Nevertheless, collection and storage of customer transaction data can often be reformatted to provide marketers with some of the information they require, including how existing segments have responded to past changes in marketing variables.

Other information may have to be collected through special studies, such as customer surveys or reviews of analogous situations. It may also be necessary to collect information on competitive performance, because changes in the capacity or strategy of competitors may require corrective action.

When new strategies are under consideration, operations researchers can often contribute useful insights by developing simulation models of the impact of changes in various variables. Such an approach is particularly useful in service "network" environments, such as theme parks and ski resorts, where customers can choose among multiple activities at the same site. Madeleine Pullman and Gary Thompson modeled customer behavior at a ski resort, where skiers can choose among various lifts and ski runs of varying lengths and levels of difficulty. Through analysis, the researchers were able to determine the potential future impact of lift capacity upgrades (bigger or faster chairlifts), capacity expansion in the form of extended skiing terrain, industry growth, day-to-day price variations, customer response to information about wait times at various lifts, and changes in the customer mix.[16]

CONCLUSION

Because many capacity-constrained service organizations have heavy fixed costs, even modest improvements in capacity utilization can have a significant effect on the bottom line. In this chapter, we have also shown how managers can transform fixed costs into variable costs through such strategies as using rented facilities or part-time labor. Creating a more flexible approach to productive capacity allows a firm to adopt strategy to match capacity to demand, (a "chase demand" strategy), thereby improving productivity.

Decisions on *place and time* are closely associated with balancing demand and capacity. Demand is often a function of where the service is located and when it is offered. As we saw with the example of the mountain resorts, the appeal of many destinations varies with the seasons. Marketing strategies involving use of *product elements, price,* and *promotion and education* are often useful in managing the level of demand for a service at a particular place and time.

The time-bound nature of services is a critical management issue today, especially with customers becoming more time sensitive and more conscious of their personal time constraints and availability. People-processing services are particularly likely to impose the burden of unwanted waiting on their customers, who cannot avoid coming to the "factory" for service. Reservations can shape the timing of arrivals, but sometimes queuing is inevitable. Managers who can act to save customers more time (or at least make time pass more pleasantly) than the competition can are often able to create a competitive advantage for their organizations.

Review Questions

1. Why is capacity management particularly significant for service firms?
2. What is meant by "chasing demand"?
3. What does "inventory" mean for service firms, and why is it perishable?
4. How does optimum capacity utilization differ from maximum capacity utilization? Give examples of situations in which the two may be the same and of ones in which they differ.
5. For a service organization of your choice, identify its particular patterns of demand with reference to the checklist provided in Table 9-1.
   a. What is the nature of this service organization's approach to capacity and demand management?
   b. What changes would you recommend in relation to its management of capacity and demand? Why?
6. What do you see as the advantages and disadvantages of the various types of queues for an organization serving large numbers of customers?

Application Exercises

1. Identify some specific examples of companies in your community (or region) that significantly change their product and/or marketing-mix variables in order to encourage patronage during periods of low demand.
2. Give examples, based on your own experience, of a reservations system that worked well and of one that worked badly. Identify and evaluate the reasons for the success and failure of these two systems. What recommendations would you make to both firms to improve (or further improve in case of the good example) their reservations systems.
3. Review the 10 propositions on the psychology of waiting lines. Which are the most relevant in (a) a city bus stop on a cold, dark evening, (b) check-in for a flight at the airport, (c) a doctor's office where patients are seated, and (d) a ticket line for a football game that is expected to be a sellout.

Endnotes

1. Kenneth J. Klassen and Thomas R. Rohleder, "Combining Operations and Marketing to Manage Capacity and Demand in Services," *The Service Industries Journal* 21 (April 2001): 1–30.
2. Based on material in James A. Fitzsimmons and M. J. Fitzsimmons, *Service Management: Operations, Strategy, and Information Technology,* 3d ed. (New York: Irwin McGraw-Hill, 2000), and W. Earl Sasser, Jr., "Match Supply and Demand in Service Industries," *Harvard Business Review* (November–December 1976).
3. Irene C.L. Ng, Jochen Wirtz, and Khai Sheang Lee, "The Strategic Role of Unused Service Capacity," *International Journal of Service Industry Management* 10, no. 2 (1999): 211–238.

4. Christopher H. Lovelock "Strategies for Managing Capacity-Constrained Service Organisations," *The Service Industries Journal* (November 1984): 12–30.
5. Malcolm Galdwell, "The Bottom Line for Lots of Time Spent in America," *Washington Post* syndicated article (February 1993).
6. Dave Wielenga, "Not So Fine Lines," *Los Angeles Times* (November 28, 1997).
7. Richard Saltus, "Lines, Lines, Lines, Lines... The Experts Are Trying to Ease the Wait," *Boston Globe* (October 5, 1992).
8. Anat Rafaeli, G. Barron, and K. Haber, "The Effects of Queue Structure on Attitudes," *Journal of Service Research* 5 (November 2002): 125–139.
9. Jay R. Chernow, "Measuring the Values of Travel Time Savings, *Journal of Consumer Research* 7 (March 1981): 360–371. [*Note:* this entire issue was devoted to the consumption of time.]
10. Ana B. Casado Diaz, and Francisco J. Más Ruiz, "The Consumer's Reaction to Delays in Service," *International Journal of Service Industry Management* 13, no. 2 (2002): 118–140.
11. Based on David H. Maister, "The Psychology of Waiting Lines," In J. A. Czepiel, M. R. Solomon, and C. F. Surprenant, *The Service Encounter* (Lexington, MA: Lexington Books/D.C. Heath, 1986), 113–123; M. M. Davis and J. Heineke, "Understanding the Roles of the Customer and the Operation for Better Queue Management," *International Journal of Service Industry Management* 7, no. 5 (1994): 21–34; and Peter Jones and Emma Peppiat, "Managing Perceptions of Waiting Times in Service Queues," *International Journal of Service Industry Management* 7, no. 5 (1996): 47–61.
12. Karen L. Katz, Blaire M. Larson, and Richard C. Larson, "Prescription for the Waiting-in-Line Blues: Entertain, Enlighten, and Engage," *Sloan Management Review* (Winter 1991): 44–53.
13. Bill Fromm and Len Schlesinger, *The Real Heroes of Business and Not a CEO Among Them* (New York: Currency Doubleday, 1994), 7.
14. Michael K. Hui and David K. Tse, "What to Tell Customers in Waits of Different Lengths: An Integrative Model of Service Evaluation," *Journal of Marketing* 80, no. 2 (April 1996): 81–90.
15. Sheryl E. Kimes and Richard B. Chase, "The Strategic Levers of Yield Management," *Journal of Service Research* 1 (November 1998): 156–166; Anthony Ingold, Una McMahon-Beattie, and Ian Yeoman, eds., *Yield Management Strategies for the Service Industries,* 2d ed. (London: Continuum, 2000).
16. Madeleine E. Pullman and Gary M. Thompson, "Evaluating Capacity- and Demand-Management Decisions at a Ski Resort," *Cornell Hotel and Restaurant Administration Quarterly* 43 (December 2002): 25–36; and Madeleine E. Pullman and Gary Thompson, "Strategies for Integrating Capacity with Demand in Service Networks," *Journal of Service Research* 5 (February 2003): 169–183.

CHAPTER 10

Planning the Service Environment

Managers . . . need to develop a better understanding of the interface between the resources they manipulate in atmospherics and the experience they want to create for the customer.

—JEAN-CHARLES CHEBAT AND LAURETTE DUBÉ

Restaurant design has become as compelling an element as menu, food and wine . . . in determining a restaurant's success.

—DANNY MEYER

The physical service environment plays an important role in shaping the service experience and delivering customer satisfaction. Disney theme parks, often cited as vivid examples of service environments that make every customer feel comfortable and highly satisfied, leave a long-lasting impression. But in fact, organizations of all types—from hospitals to hotels to restaurants to offices of professional firms—have come to recognize that the service environment is an important component of their overall value proposition.

In this chapter, which relates back to our discussion in Chapter 2 of the notion of service as a form of theater, we look at the importance of carefully designing service environments that help to engineer customer experiences, convey the target image of the firm, solicit the desired responses from customers and employees, and support service operations and productivity. Specifically, we explore the following questions.

1. What is the purpose of the service environment?
2. What are the various effects that the service environment can have on people?
3. What are the theories behind people's responses?
4. What are the dimensions of the service environment?
5. How can we design a servicescape to achieve the desired effects?

THE PURPOSE OF SERVICE ENVIRONMENTS

Service environments, also called servicescapes,[1] relate to the style and appearance of the physical surroundings and other experiential elements encountered by customers at service delivery sites. Designing the service environment is an art that takes considerable time and effort and can be expensive to implement. Once designed and built, service environments are not always easy to change. Let's examine why many service firms take so much trouble to shape the environment in which their customers and service personnel will interact.

Image, Positioning, and Differentiation

For organizations delivering high-contact services, the design of the physical environment and the way in which tasks are performed by customer-contact personnel jointly play a vital role in creating a particular corporate identity and shaping the nature of the customer's experience. The service environment and its accompanying atmosphere impact buyer behavior in three important ways:

1. *As a message-creating medium*, using symbolic cues to communicate to the intended audience about the distinctive nature and quality of the service experience
2. *As an attention-creating medium*, to make the servicescape stand out from those of competing establishments and to attract customers from target segments
3. *As an effect-creating medium*, using colors, textures, sounds, scents, and spatial design to enhance the desired service experience and/or to heighten an appetite for certain goods, services, or experiences

Part of the Service Experience Services are often intangible, and customers cannot assess quality well. Here, customers frequently use the service environment as an important quality proxy, and firms take great pains to signal quality and to portray the desired image. Think about the reception area of successful professional firms, such as investment banks or management consulting firms, where the decor and furnishings tend to be elegant and designed to impress.

Figure 10-1 shows two lobbies—the Orbit Hotel and Hostel in Los Angeles and the Four Seasons Hotel in New York City—which cater to two very different target segments. One caters to younger guests who love fun and have low budgets; the other, to a more mature, affluent, and more prestigious clientele that includes upscale business travelers. Each servicescape clearly communicates and reinforces its hotel's respective positioning and is particularly important in setting service expectations as guests arrive. In retailing, the store environment affects the perceived quality of the merchandise. Consumers infer higher merchandise quality if the goods are displayed in an ambient environment conveying a prestige image than in one that creates a discount image.[2]

Many servicescapes are purely functional. Firms trying to convey the impression of low-price service do so by locating in inexpensive neighborhoods, occupying buildings with a simple appearance, minimizing wasteful use of space, and dressing their employees in practical, inexpensive uniforms. However, servicescapes do not always shape customer perceptions and behavior in ways intended by their creators. Veronique Aubert-Gamet notes that customers often make creative use of physical spaces and objects for different purposes. For instance, businesspeople may set aside a restaurant table for use as a temporary office desk, with papers spread around and a laptop computer and mobile phone positioned on its surface, competing for space with the food and beverages.[3] Smart designers keep an eye open for such trends, which may even lead to the creation of a new service concept!

Part of the Value Proposition Physical surroundings help to shape appropriate feelings and reactions in customers and employees. Consider how effectively many amusement parks use the servicescape concept to enhance their service offerings. The clean environment of Disneyland or Denmark's Legoland, along with employees in colorful costumes, all contribute to the sense of fun and excitement that visitors encounter on

FIGURE 10-1 Comparison of Hotel Lobbies

Lobby of Orbit Hotel and Hostel, Los Angeles
Source: www.hostelworld.com, accessed January 20, 2003

Lobby of Four Seasons Hotel, New York

arrival and throughout their visit. By contrast, leading hospitals such as the Mayo Clinic seek to relieve stress, convey caring and respect, and symbolize confidence through their architecture, interior design, and employee dress codes.[4]

An illustration of servicescapes as a core part of the value proposition through engineering service experiences are resort hotels. Club Med's villages, designed to create a totally carefree atmosphere, may have provided the original inspiration for "get-away" holiday environments. New destination resorts are not only far more luxurious than Club Med but also draw inspiration from theme parks to create fantasy environments, both inside and outside.

Perhaps the most extreme examples come from Las Vegas. Facing competition from numerous casinos in other locations, Las Vegas has been trying to reposition itself away from being an adult destination once described in a London newspaper as "the electric Sodom and Gomorrah," to a somewhat more wholesome family fun resort. The gambling is still there, of course, but many of the huge hotels recently built (or rebuilt) have been transformed into visually striking entertainment centers that feature such attractions as erupting "volcanoes," mock sea battles, and even reproductions of Venice and its canals.

Facilitating the Service Encounter and Enhancing Productivity

Service environments are often designed to facilitate the service encounter and to increase productivity. Richard Chase and Douglas Stewart have highlighted ways in which fail-safe methods embodied in the service environment can help reduce service failures and support a fast and smooth service delivery process.[5] For example, color-coded keys on cash registers allow cashiers to identify the numerical figures and product codes that each button stands for. To foster a neat appearance of frontline staff, mirrors can be placed where staff can automatically check their appearance before going "on stage" to meet customers. Child-care centers use toy outlines on walls and floors to show where toys should be placed after use. In fast-food restaurants and school cafeterias, strategically located tray-return stands and notices on walls remind customers to return their trays.

CONSUMER RESPONSES TO SERVICE ENVIRONMENTS

The field of environmental psychology studies how people respond to environments. Services marketing academics have applied the theories from this field to better understand and manage customer responses to service environments.

Feelings as a Key Driver of Customer Responses to Service Environments

The Mehrabian-Russell Stimulus-Response Model Figure 10-2 shows a simple yet fundamental model of how people respond to environments. The model, adopted from environmental psychology, holds that the environment and its conscious and unconscious perception and interpretation influence how people feel in that environment.[6] People's feelings, in turn, drive their responses to that environment. Feelings are central to the model, which posits that feelings, rather than perceptions or thoughts, drive behavior. For example, we don't avoid an environment simply because there are a lot of people around us; rather, we are deterred by the unpleasant feeling of crowding, of people being in our way, of lacking perceived control, and of not being able to get what we want as quickly as we wish to. If we had all the time in the world and felt excited about being part of the crowd during seasonal festivities, exposure to the same number

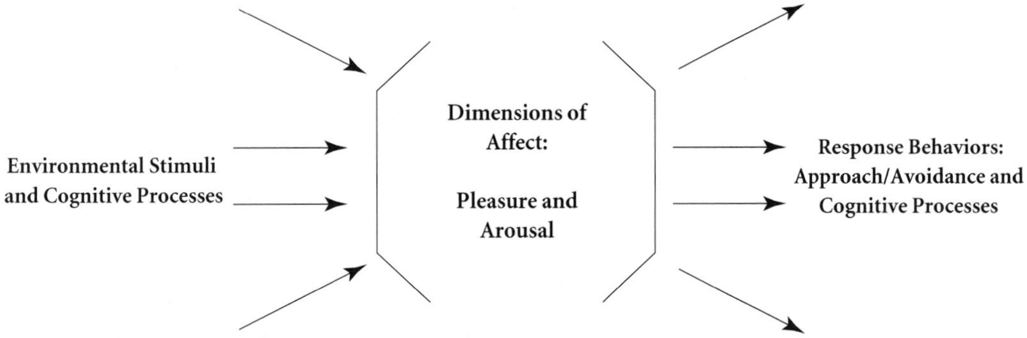

FIGURE 10-2 The Mehrabian-Russell Stimulus-Response Model

of people might lead to feelings of pleasure and excitement that would lead us to want to stay and explore that environment.

In environmental psychology, the typical outcome variable is *approach* or *avoidance* of an environment. Of course, in services marketing, we can add a long list of additional outcomes that a firm might want to manage, including how much money people spend while on the firm's premises and how satisfied people are with the service experience after they have left the environment.

The Russell Model of Affect Given that affect, or feeling, is central to how people respond to an environment, we need to understand those feelings better. Russell's model of affect is widely used to help in understanding feelings in service environments.[7] As shown in Figure 10-3, emotional responses to environments can be described along two main dimensions: pleasure and arousal. Pleasure is a direct, subjective response to the environment, depending on how much the individual likes or dislikes the environment. Arousal refers to how stimulated the individual feels, ranging from deep sleep (lowest level of internal activity) to highest levels of adrenaline in the bloodstream, for example, when bungee-jumping (highest level of internal activity). The arousal quality is much less subjective than the pleasure quality. Arousal quality depends largely on the information rate, or load, of an environment. For example, environments are stimulating (have a high information rate) when they are complex, have motion or change in it, and have novel and surprising elements. A relaxing environment (with a low information rate) has the opposite characteristics.

How can all our feelings and emotions be explained by only two dimensions? Russell separated the cognitive, or thinking, part of emotions from these two basic underlying emotional dimensions. Thus, the emotion of anger about a service failure

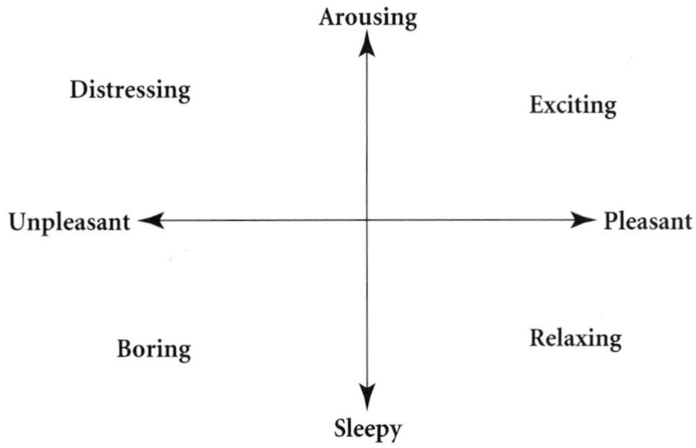

FIGURE 10-3 The Russell Model of Affect

could be modeled as high arousal and high displeasure, which would locate it in the Distressing region in our model, combined with a cognitive attribution process. When a customer attributes a service failure to the firm—blames the firm for something under the firm's control and the firm is not doing much to avoid its happening again—this powerful cognitive attribution process feeds directly into high arousal and displeasure. Similarly, most other emotions can be dissected into their cognitive and affective components.

The advantage of Russell's model of affect is its simplicity, as it allows a direct assessment of how customers feel while they are in the service environment. Firms can set targets for affective states. For example, a bungee-jumping business or roller-coaster operator might want its customers to feel aroused (assuming that there is little pleasure when having to gather all one's courage before jumping); a disco or theme park operator may want customers to feel excited (which is a relatively high arousal environment combined with pleasure); a bank may want its customers to feel confident; a spa may want customers to feel relaxed; and an airline operating a long-haul overnight flight may want its passengers to feel sleepy after dinner. Later in this chapter, we discuss how service environments can be designed to deliver the types of service experiences desired by customers.

Drivers of Affect Affect can be caused by perceptions and cognitive processes of any degree of complexity. However, the more complex a cognitive process becomes, the more powerful its potential impact on affect. For example, a customer's disappointment with service level and food quality in a restaurant (a complex cognitive process, with perceived quality compared to previously held service expectations) cannot be compensated by a simple cognitive process, such as the subconscious perception of pleasant background music. Yet this does not mean that such simple processes are unimportant.

In practice, the large majority of service encounters are routine, with little high-level cognitive processing. We tend to be on "autopilot" and follow our service scripts when doing routine transactions, such as using the subway, entering a fast-food restaurant, or conducting business at a bank. Here, which is most of the time, it is the simple cognitive processes—the conscious and even unconscious perceptions of space, colors, scents, and so on—that determine how people feel in the service setting. However, should higher levels of cognitive processes be triggered—for instance, through something surprising in the service environment, it is the interpretation of this surprise that determine people's feelings.[8]

Behavioral Consequences of Affect At the most basic level, pleasant environments result in approach; unpleasant ones, in avoidance behaviors. Arousal acts as an amplifier of the basic effect of pleasure on behavior. If the environment is pleasant, increasing arousal can lead to excitement, leading to a stronger positive consumer response. Conversely, if a service environment is inherently unpleasant, one should avoid increasing arousal levels, as this would move customers into the Distressing region. For example, loud fast-beat music would increase the stress levels of shoppers trying to make their way through crowded aisles on a pre-Christmas Friday evening. In such situations, the information load of the environment should be lowered.

For some services, customers have strong affective expectations. Think of a romantic candlelight dinner in a restaurant, a relaxing spa visit, or an exciting time at the stadium or the disco. When customers have strong affective expectations, it is important to design the environment to match those expectations.[9]

Finally, how people feel during the service encounter is an important driver of customer loyalty. For example, positive affect has been shown to drive hedonic shopping value, which in turn increases repeat purchasing behavior, whereas negative affect mostly reduces utilitarian shopping value and thereby lowers customer share.[10]

Linking Theory to Servicescapes

Building on the basic models in environmental psychology, Mary Jo Bitner has developed a comprehensive model that she named the servicescape.[11] Figure 10-4 shows the main dimensions that she identified in service environments, which include ambient conditions, space/functionality, and signs, symbols, and artifacts. Because individuals tend to perceive these dimensions holistically, the key to effective design is how well each individual dimension fits together with everything else.

Next, the model shows that there are customer and employee-response moderators. This means that the same service environment can have different effects on different customers, depending on what they like: Beauty lies in the eyes of the beholder and is subjective. Rap music may be sheer pleasure to some customer segments and sheer torture to others.

One important contribution of Bitner's model was that she included employee responses in the service environment. After all, employees spend much more time there than do customers, and it's crucially important that designers become aware of how a particular environment enhances (or at least does not reduce) the productivity of frontline personnel and the quality of service they deliver.

Internal customer and employee responses can be categorized into cognitive responses (e.g., quality perceptions and beliefs), emotional responses (e.g., feelings and moods), and psychological responses (e.g., pain and comfort). These internal responses

FIGURE 10-4 The Servicescapes Model

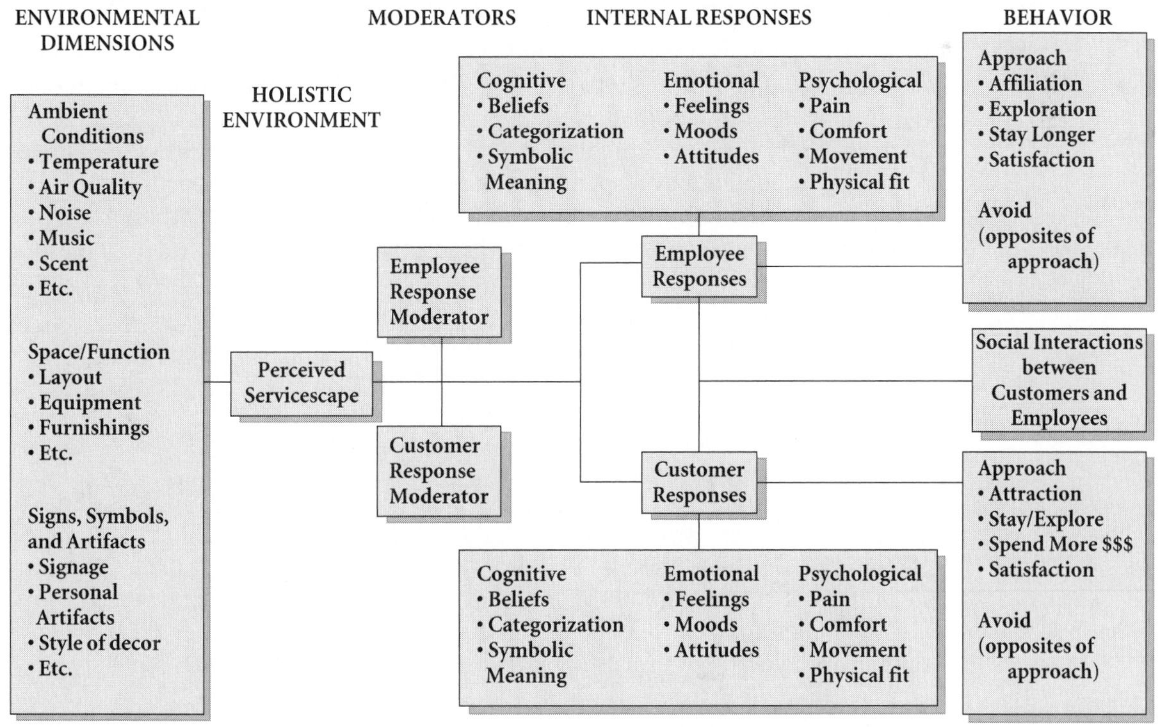

Source: Mary Jo Bitner, "Servicescapes: The Impact of Physical Surroundings on Customers and Employees," *Journal of Marketing* 56 (April 1992): 57–71. American Marketing Association.

lead to overt behavioral responses, such as avoiding a crowded department store or responding positively to a relaxing environment by remaining there longer and spending extra money on impulse purchases. It's important to understand that the behavioral responses of customers and employees must be shaped in ways that facilitate production and purchase of high-quality services. Consider how the outcomes of service transactions may differ when both customers and frontline staff feel agitated and stressed rather than relaxed and happy.

DIMENSIONS OF THE SERVICE ENVIRONMENT

Service environments are complex and have many design elements. Table 10-1, for example, presents an overview of all the design elements that might be encountered in a retail outlet. In this section, we focus on the main dimensions of the service environment in the servicescape model: the ambient conditions, space and functionality, and signs, symbols, and artifacts.[12]

The Impact of Ambient Conditions

Ambient conditions are those characteristics of the environment pertaining to our five senses. Even when not consciously noted, they may still affect people's emotional well-being, perceptions, and even attitudes and behaviors. The ambient environment, or atmosphere, is a gestalt concept, composed of literally hundreds of design elements and details that have to work together to create the desired service environment.[13] The resulting atmosphere creates a mood that is perceived and interpreted by the customer.[14] Ambient conditions are perceived both separately and holistically and include lighting and color schemes, size and shape perceptions, sounds, temperature, and scents. Clever design of these conditions can elicit desired behavioral responses among consumers. Consider the innovative thinking underlying the new trend to transform dental clinics into relaxing dental spas, as described in Best Practice in Action 10-1.

Music Even if played at barely audible volumes, music can have a powerful effect on perceptions and behaviors in service settings. As shown in the servicescape model in Figure 10-4, the various structural characteristics of music, such as tempo, volume, and harmony, are perceived holistically, and their effect on internal and behavioral responses is moderated by respondent characteristics (e.g., younger people tend to like different music and therefore respond differently from older people to the same piece of music).[15] Numerous research studies have found that fast-tempo music and high-volume music increase arousal levels,[16] which can then lead people to walk faster and to talk and eat more quickly in restaurants.[17] People tend to adjust their pace, either voluntarily or involuntarily, to match the tempo of music. This means that restaurants can speed up table turnover by increasing the tempo and volume of the music and serve more diners or slow diners down with slow-beat music and lower volume to keep them longer in the restaurant and increase beverage revenues.

A restaurant study conducted over eight weeks showed that beverage revenue increased by 41 percent and the total gross margin by 15 percent when slow-beat rather than fast-beat music was played (see Table 10-2 for details). Customers dining in a slow-music environment spent an average of 15 minutes longer in the restaurant than did individuals in a fast-music condition.[18] Likewise, shoppers walked less rapidly when slow music was played and increased their level of impulse purchases.[19] Playing familiar music in a store was shown to stimulate shoppers and thereby reduce their browsing time, whereas playing unfamiliar music induced shoppers to spend more time there.[20] In consumer wait situations, music can be used effectively to shorten the perceived waiting time and increase customer satisfaction.[21] Relaxing music proved

TABLE 10-1 Design Elements of a Retail Store Environment

Dimensions	*Design Elements*	
Exterior facilities	• Architectural style • Height of building • Size of building • Color of building • Exterior walls and exterior signs • Storefront • Marquee • Lawns and gardens	• Window displays • Entrances • Visibility • Uniqueness • Surrounding stores • Surrounding areas • Parking and accessibility • Congestion
General interior	• Flooring and carpeting • Color schemes • Lighting • Scents • Odors (e.g., tobacco smoke) • Sounds and music • Fixtures • Wall composition • Wall textures (paint, wallpaper) • Ceiling composition	• Temperature • Cleanliness • Width of aisles • Dressing facilities • Vertical transportation • Dead areas • Merchandise layout and displays • Price levels and displays • Cash register placement • Technology/modernization
Store layout	• Allocation of floor space for selling, merchandise, personnel, and customers • Placement of merchandise • Grouping of merchandise • Workstation placement • Placement of equipment • Placement of cash register	• Waiting areas • Traffic flow • Waiting queues • Furniture • Dead areas • Department locations • Arrangements within departments
Interior displays	• Point-of-purchase displays • Posters, signs, and cards • Pictures and artwork • Wall decorations • Themesetting • Ensemble	• Racks and cases • Product display • Price display • Cut cases and dump bins • Mobiles
Social dimensions	• Personnel characteristics • Employee uniforms • Crowding	• Customer characteristics • Privacy • Self-service

Source: Adapted from Barry Berman and Joel R. Evans, Retail *Management—A Strategic Approach*, 8th ed. (Upper Saddle River, NJ: Prentice-Hall 2001), 604; L. W. Turley and Ronald E. Milliman, "Atmospheric Effects on Shopping Behavior: A Review of the Experimental Literature," *Journal of Business Research* 49 (2000): 193–211.

effective in lowering stress levels in a hospital's surgery waiting room.[22] And pleasant music has even been shown to enhance customers' perception of and attitude toward service personnel.[23]

Scent An ambient smell is one that pervades an environment, may or may not be consciously perceived by customers, and is not related to any particular product. We are experiencing the power of smell when we are hungry and get a whiff of freshly baked croissants long before we pass a Delifrance Café. This smell makes us aware of our hunger and suggests a solution (e.g., walk into Delifrance and get some food). The

BEST PRACTICE IN ACTION 10-1

CUTTING THE FEAR FACTOR AT THE DENTIST

Dentistry is not a service that most people look forward to. Some patients simply find it uncomfortable, especially if they have to remain in a dental chair for an extended period. Many are afraid of the pain associated with certain procedures. And others risk their health by avoiding going to the dentist altogether. But now some practitioners are embracing "spa dentistry," featuring juice bars, neck rubs, foot massages, and even scented candles and the sound of wind chimes to pamper patients and distract them from necessarily invasive treatments inside their mouths.

"It's not about gimmicks," says Timothy Dotson, owner of the Perfect Teeth Dental Spa in Chicago, as a patient breathed strawberry-scented nitrous oxide. "It's treating people the way they want to be treated. It helps a lot of people overcome fear." His patients seem to agree. "Nobody likes coming to the dentist, but this makes it so much easier," remarked one woman as she waited for a crown while a heated massage pad was kneading her back.

Hot towels, massages, aromatherapy, coffee, fresh cranberry-orange bread, and white wine spritzers reflect dentists' efforts to meet changing consumer expectations, especially at a time when there is growing consumer demand for aesthetic care to whiten and reshape teeth to create a perfect smile. The goal is to entice patients who might otherwise find visiting the dentist a stressful situation. Many dentists who offer spa services do not charge extra for them, arguing that their cost is more than covered by repeat business and increased patient referrals.

In Houston, Max Greenfield has embellished his Image Max Dental Spa with fountains and modern art. Patients can change into a robe, sample eight aromas of oxygen, and meditate in a relaxation room decorated like a Japanese garden. The dental area features lambskin leather chairs, hot aromatherapy towels, and a procedure known as "bubble gum jet massage" that uses air and water to clean teeth.

Although dental offices from Los Angeles to New York are adopting spa techniques, some question whether this touchy-feely approach is good dentistry or simply a passing fad. "I just can't see mingling the two businesses together," remarked the dean of one university dental school.

Source: "Dentists Offer New Services to Cut the Fear Factor," *Chicago Tribune*, syndicated article, February 2003.

TABLE 10-2 Impact of Music on Restaurant Diners

Restaurant Patron Behaviors	*Fast-beat Music Environment*	*Slow-beat Music Environment*	*Difference between Slow and Fast-Beat Environments*	
			Absolute Difference	*Percentage Difference*
Customer time spent at the table	45 min	56 min	+ 11 min	+ 24%
Spending on food	$55.12	$55.81	+ $0.69	+ 1%
Spending on beverages	$21.62	$30.47	+ $8.85	+ 41%
Total spending	$76.74	$86.28	+ $9.54	+ 12%
Estimated gross margin	$48.62	$55.82	+ $7.20	+ 15%

Source: Ronald E. Milliman, "Using Background Music to Affect the Behavior of Supermarket Shoppers," *Journal of Marketing* 56, no. 3 (1982): 86–91.

TABLE 10-3 The Effects of Scents on the Perceptions of Store Environments

Evaluation	*Unscented Environment: Mean Ratings*	*Scented Environment: Mean Ratings*	*Difference between Unscented and Scented Environments*
Store evaluation			
• Negative/positive	4.65	5.24	+ 0.59
• Outdated/modern image	3.76	4.72	+ 0.96
Store environment			
• Unattractive/attractive	4.12	4.98	+ 0.86
• Drab/colorful	3.63	4.72	+ 1.09
• Boring/stimulating	3.75	4.40	+ 0.65
Merchandise			
• Outdated/up-to-date style	4.71	5.43	+ 0.72
• Inadequate/adequate range	3.80	4.65	+ 0.85
• Low/high quality	4.81	5.48	+ 0.67
• Low/high price	5.20	4.93	− 0.27

Note: The mean ratings are based on a scale from 1 to 7.
Source: Eric R. Spangenberg, Ayn E. Crowley, and Pamela W. Henderson, "Improving the Store Environment: Do Olfactory Cues Affect Evaluations and Behaviors?" *Journal of Marketing* 60 (April 1996): 67–80.

same works for bakeries, cafes, pizzerias, and the like. Other examples include the smell of freshly baked cookies on Main Street in Disney's Magic Kingdom to relax customers and provide a feeling of warmth or the smell of potpourri in Victoria's Secret stores to create the ambiance of a lingerie closet.[24] The presence of scent can have a strong impact on mood, affective and evaluative responses, and even purchase intentions and in-store behaviors.[25] Table 10-3 shows the effects scent had in a retail environment on the perception of the store, store environment, and merchandise.

Olfaction researcher Alan R. Hirsch, M.D., of the Smell & Taste Treatment and Research Foundation based in Chicago, is convinced that in some 10 years, we will understand scents so well that we will be able to use them to effectively manage people's behaviors.[26] Service marketers will be interested in how to make you hungry and thirsty in the restaurant, relax you in a dentist's waiting room, and energize you to work out harder in a gym. Scent researcher Bryan Raudenbush has found that sniffing peppermint while exercising will not increase a person's vim and vigor but that the oil from the aromatic plant makes exercising more pleasurable, thus encouraging people to exercise longer.[27] In aromatherapy, it is generally accepted that scents have distinct characteristics and can be used to solicit certain emotional, physiological, and behavioral responses. Table 10-4 shows the generally assumed effects of specific scents on people as prescribed by aromatherapy. In service settings, research has shown that scents can have significant impact on customer perceptions, attitudes, and behaviors.

- Gamblers plunked 45 percent more quarters into slot machines when a Las Vegas casino was scented with a pleasant artificial smell. When the intensity of the scent was increased, spending jumped by 53 percent.[28] Think of the impact this revenue increase can have on a casino, which has largely fixed costs!
- People were more willing to buy Nike sneakers and pay more for them—an average of US$10.33 more per pair—when they tried on the shoes in a floral-scented

TABLE 10-4 Aromatherapy: The Effects of Fragrances on People

Fragrance	*Aroma Type*	*Aroma-therapy Class*	*Traditional Use*	*Potential Psychological Impact on People*
Orange	Citrus	Calming	Soothing agent, astringent	Soothes nerves and has a calming and relaxing effect, especially for nervous or jittery people
Bergamot	Citrus	Calming, balancing	Calming, balancing, antiseptic, deodorant, soothing agent	Has a soothing and calming effect, helps to make people feel comfortable
Mimosa	Floral	Calming, balancing	Muscle relaxant, soothing agent	Helps relaxation and makes people feel comfortable and calm; creates a harmonious and balanced feel
Black pepper	Spicy	Balancing, soothing	Muscle relaxant, aphrodisiac	Helps to balance people's emotions and enables people to feel sexually aroused
Lavender	Herbaceous	Calming, balancing, soothing	Muscle relaxant, soothing agent, astringent, skin conditioner	Relaxing and calming; helps to create a homey and comfortable feel
Jasmine	Floral	Uplifting, balancing	Emollient, soothing agent, aphrodisiac, antiseptic	Helps to make people feel refreshed, joyful, comfortable, and sexually aroused
Grapefruit	Citrus	Energizing	Astringent, soothing agent, skin conditioner; help in keeping skin smooth and supple	Stimulating, refreshing, reviving, and improves mental clarity and alertness; can even enhance physical strength and energy
Lemon	Citrus	Energizing, uplifting	Antiseptic, soothing agent	Boosts energy levels and helps to make people feel happy and rejuvenated
Peppermint	Minty	Energizing, stimulating	Insect repellent, antiseptic, help in cleansing skin	Increases attention level; boosts energy
Eucalyptus	Camphoraceous	Toning, stimulating	Deodorant, antiseptic, soothing agent; helps remove odor and can be used to cleanse skin	Stimulating and energizing; helps to create balance and the feeling of cleanliness and hygiene

Source: http://www.fragrant.demon.co.uk and *http://www.naha.org/WhatisAromatherapy*; Dana Butcher, "Aromatherapy—Its Past and Future," *Drug and Cosmetic Industry* 16, no. 3 (1998): 22–24; Shirley Price and Len Price, *Aromatherapy for Health Professionals*, 2d ed. (New York: Churchill Livingstone, 1999), 145–160; Anna S. Mattila and Jochen Wirtz, "Congruency of Scent and Music as a Driver of In-Store Evaluations and Behavior," *Journal of Retailing* 77 (2001): 273–289.

room. The same effect was found even when the scent was so faint that people could not detect it (the scent was unconsciously perceived).[29]

- Many restaurants like to serve garlic bread as an appetizer, and research shows why. A recent study found that smelling and eating garlic bread during dinner reduced the number of negative interactions by an average of 0.17 incidents, or by 23 percent per family member per minute, while at the same time increasing pleasant interactions by 0.25 incidents per family member per minute.[30] This promotes and maintains shared family experiences and, in a restaurant context, makes it a more satisfying dining experience.

Color Color "is stimulating, calming, expressive, disturbing, impressional, cultural, exuberant, symbolic. It pervades every aspect of our lives, embellishes the ordinary, and gives beauty and drama to everyday objects."[31] Researchers have found that colors have a strong impact on people's feelings.[32] The de facto system used in psychological research is the Munsell System, which defines colors in the three dimensions of hue, value, and chroma.[33] *Hue* is the pigment of the color (red, orange, yellow, green, blue, or violet). *Value* is the degree of lightness or darkness of the color relative to a scale that extends from pure black to pure white. *Chroma* refers to hue intensity, saturation, or brilliance; high-chroma colors have a high intensity of pigmentation in them and are perceived as rich and vivid, whereas low-chroma colors are perceived as dull.

Hues are classified as *warm* colors (red, orange, and yellow hues) and *cold* colors (blue and green), with orange (a mix of red and yellow) being the warmest and blue being the coldest of the colors. These colors can be used to manage the warmth of an environment. For example, if a violet is too warm, you can cool it off by reducing red. Or if a red is too cold, warm it up by giving it a shot of orange.[34] Warm colors are associated with elated mood states and arousal but also heightened anxiety, whereas cool colors reduce arousal levels and can elicit such emotions as peacefulness, calmness, love, and happiness.[35] Table 10-5 summarizes common associations and responses to colors.

Research in a service environment context has shown that despite differing color preferences, people are generally drawn to warm-color environments. Paradoxically, however, findings show that red-hued retail environments are perceived as negative, tense, and less attractive than are cool-color environments.[36] Warm colors encourage

TABLE 10-5 Common Associations and Human Responses to Colors

Color	*Degree of Warmth*	*Nature Symbol*	*Common Associations and Human Responses to Colors*
Red	Warm	Earth	High energy and passion; can excite, stimulate, and increase arousal levels and blood pressure
Orange	Warmest	Sunset	Emotions, expression, and warmth; noted for its ability to encourage verbal expression of emotions
Yellow	Warm	Sun	Optimism, clarity, and intellect; bright yellow often noted for its mood-enhancing ability
Green	Cool	Growth, grass, and trees	Nurturing, healing, and unconditional love
Blue	Coolest	Sky and ocean	Relaxation, serenity, and loyalty; lowers blood pressure; is a healing color for nervous disorders and for relieving headaches, because of its cooling and calming nature
Indigo	Cool	Sunset	Meditation and spirituality
Violet	Cool	Violet flower	Spirituality; reduces stress and can create an inner feeling of calm

Source: Sara O. Marberry and Laurie Zagon, *The Power of Color—Creating Healthy Interior Spaces* (New York: John Wiley, 1995), 18; and Sarah Lynch, *Bold Colors for Modern Rooms: Bright Ideas for People Who Love Color* (Gloucester, MA: Rockport Publishers, 2001), 24–29.

fast decision making and in service situations are best suited for low-involvement decisions or impulse purchases. Cool colors are favored when consumers need time to make high-involvement purchases.[37]

Although we have an understanding of the general impact of colors, their use in any specific context needs to be approached with caution. For example, a transportation company in Israel decided to paint its buses green as part of an environmentalism public relations campaign. Reactions from multiple groups of people to this seemingly simple act were unexpectedly negative. Some customers found the green color as hampering service performance (because the green buses blended in with the environment and were more difficult to see) or as representing undesirable notions such as terrorism or enemy sports teams, and as aesthetically unappealing and inappropriate.[38]

A good example of using color schemes to enhance the service experience is provided by the HealthPark Medical Center in Fort Meyers, Florida, which has combined full-spectrum color in its lobby with unusual lighting to achieve a dreamlike setting. The lobby walls are washed with rainbow colors by an arrangement of high-intensity blue, green, violet, red, orange, and yellow lamps. Craig Roeder, the lighting designer for the hospital, explained, "It's a hospital. People walk into it worried and sick. I tried to design an entrance space that provides them with light and energy—to 'beam them up' a little bit before they get to the patient rooms."[39]

Spatial Layout and Functionality

As service environments generally have to fulfill specific purposes and customer needs, spatial layout and functionality are particularly important. *Spatial layout* refers to the size and shape of furnishings, counters, and potential machinery and equipment and the ways in which they are arranged. *Functionality* refers to the ability of those items to facilitate the performance of service transactions. Spatial layout and functionality affect buying behavior, customer satisfaction, and, consequently, the business performance of the service facility.

Signs, Symbols, and Artifacts

Many things in the service environment act as explicit or implicit signals to communicate the firm's image, help customers find their way (e.g., to certain service counters, departments, or the exit), and convey the rules of behavior (e.g., smoking/no-smoking areas or queuing systems). In particular, first-time customers will automatically try to draw meaning from the signs, symbols, and artifacts and will want to draw cues from the environment to help them form expectations about the type and level of service that is being offered and to guide them through the service environment and service process.

Customers become disoriented when they cannot derive clear signals from a servicescape, resulting in anxiety and uncertainty about how to proceed and how to obtain the desired service. Inexperienced customers and newcomers can easily feel lost in a confusing environment and experience anger and frustration as a result. Think about the last time you were in a hurry and tried to find your way through an unfamiliar hospital, shopping center, or airport where the signs and other directional cues were not intuitive to you.

The challenge for servicescape designers is to use signs, symbols, and artifacts to guide customers clearly through the process of service delivery. This task assumes particular importance in situations characterized by a high proportion of new or infrequent customers and/or a high degree of self-service, especially when few service staff are available to help guide customers through the process. In such situations, signs, symbols, and artifacts have to communicate clearly and teach the service process in as intuitive a manner as possible.

BEST PRACTICE IN ACTION 10-2

GUIDELINES FOR PARKING DESIGN

Parking lots play an important role at many service facilities. Effective use of signs, symbols, and artifacts in a parking lot or garage helps customers find their way, manages their behavior, and portrays a positive image for the sponsoring organization.

- *Friendly warnings.* All warning signs should communicate a customer benefit: for instance, "Fire lane: For everyone's safety, we ask you not to park in the fire lane."
- *Fresh paint.* Curbs, crosswalks, and lot lines should be repainted regularly before any cracking, peeling, or disrepair becomes evident. Proactive and frequent repainting give positive cleanliness cues and projects a positive image.
- *Safety lighting.* Good lighting that penetrates all areas makes life easier for customers and enhances safety. Firms may want to draw attention to this feature with notices stating: "Parking lots have been specially lit for your safety."
- *Maternity parking.* Handicapped spaces are often required by law but require special stickers on the vehicle. A few thoughtful organizations have designated expectant-mother parking spaces, painted with a blue/pink stork. This strategy demonstrates a sense of caring and understanding of customer needs.[1]
- *Helpful parking aids.* Forgetting where one left the family car in a huge lot or parking garage can be a nightmare. Many parking garages have adopted color-coded floors to help customers remember which level they parked on. But Boston's Logan Airport goes beyond that. Each level has a theme associated with Massachusetts, such as Paul Revere's Ride, Cape Cod, or the Boston Marathon. An image is attached to each theme: a man on horseback, a lighthouse, or a runner. While waiting for the elevator, travelers hear a few bars of music tied to the theme for that level; in the case of the Boston Marathon floor, it's the theme music from *Chariots of Fire,* an Oscar-winning movie about an Olympic runner.

[1]Lewis P. Carbone and Stephen H. Haeckel, "Engineering Customer Experiences," *Marketing Management* 3, no. 3 (Winter 1994): 9–18.

At many service facilities, customers' first point of contact is likely to be the parking lot. As emphasized in Best Practice in Action 10-2, the principles of effective environment design apply even in this most mundane environment.

People as Part of the Service Environment

The appearance and behavior of both service personnel and customers can reinforce or detract from the impression created by a service environment. Within the constraints imposed by legal obligations and skill requirements, service firms may seek to recruit staff to fill specific roles, costume them in uniforms consistent with the servicescape in which they will be working, and script their speech and movements. Likewise, marketing communications may seek to attract customers who will not only appreciate the ambience created by the service provider but also actively enhance it by their appearance and behavior. In hospitality and retail settings, newcomers often survey the array of existing customers before deciding whether to patronize the establishment.

Figure 10-5 shows the interior of two restaurants. Imagine that you have just entered each of these two dining rooms. How is each positioning itself within the restaurant industry? What sort of meal experience can you expect? And what are the clues that you use to make your judgments? In particular, what inferences do you draw from looking at the customers who are already seated in each restaurant?

FIGURE 10-5 Distinctive servicescapes—from table settings to furniture and room design—create different customer expectations of these two restaurants.

PUTTING IT ALL TOGETHER

Although individuals often perceive particular aspects or individual design features of an environment, it is the total configuration of all those design features that determines consumer responses. Consumers perceive service environments holistically, and consumer responses to a physical environment depend on ensemble effects or configurations.[40]

In the reading "How to Lead the Customer Experience" (reproduced on pages 341 to 345), Stephan Haeckel, Lewis Carbone, and Leonard Berry declare that: "No single clue provides the magic for a distinctive preferred experience. The benefit comes in the integrated design and layering of clues."[41]

Design with a Holistic View

Whether a dark, glossy wooden floor is the perfect flooring depends on everything else in that service environment, including the type, color scheme, and materials of the furniture; the lighting; and the promotional materials, to the overall brand perception and positioning of the firm. Servicescapes have to be seen holistically, which means that no dimension of the design can be optimized in isolation, because everything depends on everything else. Research Insight 10-1 shows that even the arousal elements of scent and music interact and need to be considered in conjunction to elicit the desired consumer responses.

The holistic characteristic of environments makes designing service environments an art, so much so that professional designers tend to focus on specific types of servicescapes. For example, a handful of famous interior designers do nothing but create hotel lobbies around the world. Similarly, some design experts focus exclusively on restaurants, bars, clubs, cafes and bistros, retail outlets, or health care facilities, and so forth.[42]

Design from a Customer's Perspective

Many service environments are built with an emphasis on aesthetic values, and designers sometimes forget the most important factor to consider when designing service environments: the customers who will be using them. Ron Kaufman, a consultant and trainer on service excellence, experienced the following design flaws in two new high-profile service environments.

- "A new Sheraton Hotel just had opened in Jordan without clear signage that would guide guests from the ballrooms to the restrooms. The signs that did exist were etched in muted gold on dark marble pillars. More 'obvious' signs were apparently inappropriate amidst such elegant décor. Very swish, very chic, but who were they designing it for?"
- "At the Dragon Air lounge in Hong Kong's new airport, a partition of colorful glass hung from the ceiling. My luggage lightly brushed against it as I walked inside. The entire partition shook and several panels came undone. A staff member hurried over and began carefully reassembling the panels. (Thank goodness nothing broke.) I apologized profusely. 'Don't worry,' she replied, This happens all the time."

An airport lounge is a heavy-traffic area. People are always moving in and out. Ron Kaufman keeps asking: "What were the interior designers thinking? Who were they designing it for?"

"I am regularly amazed," declared Kaufman, "by brand new facilities that are obviously user 'unfriendly'! Huge investments of time and money ... but who are they designing it for? What were the architects thinking about? Size? Grandeur? Physical exercise? Who were they designing it for?" He draws the following key learning point: "It's easy to get caught up in designing new things that are 'cool' or 'elegant' or 'hot.' But if you don't keep your customer in mind throughout, you could end up with an investment that's not."[43]

RESEARCH INSIGHT 10-1

MATCH AND MISMATCH OF SCENT AND MUSIC IN THE SERVICESCAPE

Whether a certain type of background enhances consumer responses depends on the ambient scent of the service environment. Using a field experiment in a gift store. Anna Mattila and Jochen Wirtz manipulated two types of pleasant music and pleasant scent that differed in their arousing qualities. Consumer impulse purchasing and satisfaction were measured for the various music and scent conditions.

The experiment used two compact discs from the Tune Your Brain series by Elizabeth Miles, an ethnomusicologist. The low-arousal music was the *Relaxing Collection*, featuring slow-tempo music; the high-arousal music consisted of the *Energizing* Collection, featuring fast-tempo music. Similarly, scent was manipulated to have high- or low-arousal quality. Lavender was used for the low-arousal scent because of its relaxing and calming properties. Grapefruit was used for the high-arousal scent because of its stimulating properties, which can refresh, revive, and improve mental clarity and alertness and can even enhance physical strength and energy.

The results of this experiment show that when the arousal qualities of music and ambient scent were matched, consumers responded more favorably. Figures 10-A and B show these effects clearly. For instance, scenting the store with low-arousal scent, (lavender) combined with slow-tempo music, led to higher satisfaction and impulse purchases than did using that scent with high-arousal music. Playing fast-tempo music had a more positive effect when the store was scented with grapefruit (high-arousal scent) rather than with lavender. This study showed that when environmental stimuli act together to provide a coherent atmosphere, consumers in that environment will respond more positively.

These findings suggest that bookstores might induce people to linger longer and buy more by playing slow-tempo music combined with a relaxing scent, or event managers might consider using arousing scents aromas to enhance excitement.

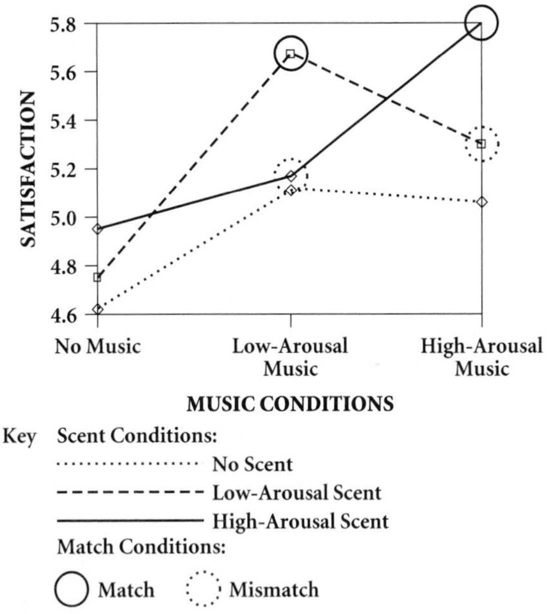

FIGURE 10-A The Impact of Scent and Music on Satisfaction

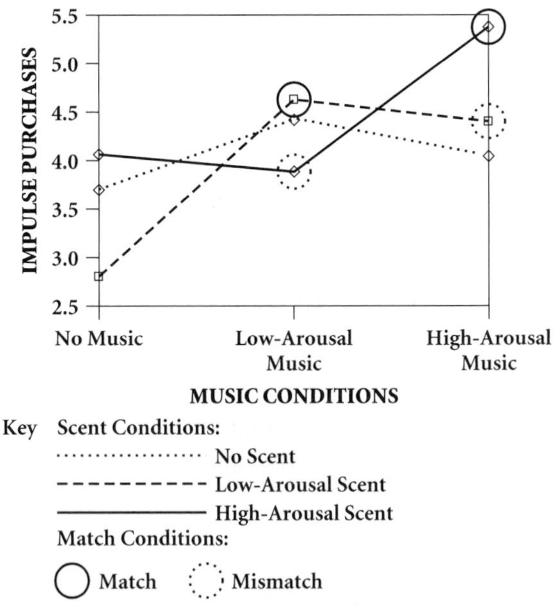

FIGURE 10-B The Impact of Scent and Music on Impulse Purchases

Note: Both charts are on a scale from 1 to 7, with 7 being the extreme positive response. The solid-line circles show the match conditions, where both music and scent are either stimulating or relaxing, and the intermitted-line circles show the mismatch conditions, where one stimulus is relaxing and the other stimulating (relaxing music and stimulating scent, or stimulating music and relaxing scent).

Source: Anna S. Mattila and Jochen Wirtz, "Congruency of Scent and Music as a Driver of In-Store Evaluations and Behavior," *Journal of Retailing* 77 (2001): 273–289. Reprinted by permission.

In a recent study, Alain d'Astous explored environmental aspects that irritate shoppers. His findings highlighted the following two categories of problems:

1. Ambient conditions (ordered by severity of irritation):
   - Store not clean
   - Too hot inside the store or the shopping center
   - Music too loud inside the store
   - Bad smell in the store
2. Environmental design variables:
   - No mirror in the dressing room
   - Unable to find what one needs
   - Inadequate directions within the store
   - Arrangement of store items changed
   - Store too small
   - Finding the way in a large shopping center.[44]

Contrast Kaufman's experiences and d'Astou's findings with the Disney example in Best Practice in Action 10-3.

Use Tools That Can Guide the Servicescape Design

How do we find out what irritates our customers, and how can we potentially further enhance the good aspects of our servicescape? Among the tools that can be used to better understand the customers' view of and responses to service environments are the following:

- *Keen observation* of customers' behavior and responses to the service environment by management, supervisors, branch managers, and frontline staff.

BEST PRACTICE IN ACTION 10-3

DESIGN OF DISNEY'S MAGIC KINGDOM

Walt Disney was one of the undisputed champions of designing service environments. His tradition of amazingly careful and detailed planning has become one of his company's hallmarks and is visible everywhere in its theme parks. For example, Main Street is angled to make it seem longer on entry into the Magic Kingdom than it actually is. With myriad facilities and attractions strategically inclined and located at each side of the street, people look forward to the relatively long journey to the Castle. However, looking down the slope from the Castle back toward the entrance makes Main Street appear shorter than it really is, relieving exhaustion and rejuvenating guests. It encourages strolling, which minimizes the number of people who take buses and so eliminates the threatening problem of traffic congestion.

Meandering sidewalks with multiple attractions keep guests feeling entertained both by the planned activities and by watching other guests; rubbish bins are plentiful and always in sight to convey the message that littering is prohibited. Repainting of facilities is a routine procedure that signals a high level of maintenance and cleanliness.

Disney's servicescape design and upkeep help to script customer experiences. They also create pleasure and satisfaction for guests not only in its theme parks but also in its cruise ships and hotels.

Source: Lewis P. Carbone and Stephen H. Haeckel, "Engineering Customer Experiences," *Marketing Management* 3, no. 3 (Winter 1994): 10–11; Kathy Merlock Jackson, *Walt Disney, A Bio-Bibliography.* (Westport, CT: Greenwood Press, 1993), 36–39; Andrew Lainsbury, *Once Upon an American Dream: The Story of Euro Disneyland* (Lawrence, KS: University Press of Kansas, 2000), 64–72.

- *Feedback and ideas from frontline staff and customers*, using a broad array of research tools, ranging from suggestion boxes to focus groups and surveys. (The latter are often called environmental surveys if they focus on the design of the service environment.)
- *Field experiments* to manipulate specific dimensions in an environment and the effects observed. For instance, one can experiment with the use of various types of music and scents and then measure the time and money customers spend in the environment and their level of satisfaction. Laboratory experiments, using slides or videos or other ways to simulate real-world service environments (such as computer-simulated virtual tours), can be used effectively to examine the impact of changes in design elements that cannot easily be manipulated in a field experiment. Examples are testing of alternative color schemes, spatial layouts, or styles of furnishing.
- *Blueprinting*, or service mapping, described in Chapter 8, can be extended to include the physical evidence in the environment. Design elements and tangible cues can be documented as the customer moves through each step of the service delivery process. Photos and videos can supplement the map to make it more vivid.

Table 10-6 shows an analysis of a customer's visit to a movie theater, identifying how various environmental elements at each step exceeded or failed to meet them. The service process was broken up into increments, steps, decisions, duties, and activities—all designed to take the customer through the entire service encounter. The more a service company can see, understand, and experience the same things as its customers, the better equipped it will be to realize errors in the design of its environment and to further improve on what is already functioning well.

CONCLUSION

The service environment plays a major part in shaping customers' perception of a firm's image and positioning. As service quality is often difficult to assess objectively, customers frequently use the service environment as an important quality signal. A well-designed service environment makes customers feel good and boosts their satisfaction and at the same time enhances the productivity of the service operation.

The theoretical underpinnings for understanding the effects of service environments on customers come from the environmental psychology literature. The Mehrabian-Russell Stimulus-Response model holds that environments influence people's affective state (or feelings), which in turn drives their behavior in that environment. Affect can be modeled with the two key dimensions of pleasure and arousal, which together determine whether people approach and spend time and money in an environment or whether they avoid it. The servicescape model built on these theories and developed a comprehensive framework that explains how customers and service staff respond to service environments.

The main dimensions of service environments are ambient conditions (including music, scents, and colors), spatial layout and functionality, and signs, symbols, and artifacts. Each dimension can have important effects on customer responses. For example, the presence or absence of background music—and even type of music, including its tempo and volume—can make significant differences in customer satisfaction, quality perceptions, and such behaviors as time and money spent in the environment. The other design variables can have similar effects.

TABLE 10-6 A Visit to the Movies: The Service Environment as Perceived by the Customer

Steps in the Service Encounter	*Design of the Service Environment*	
	Exceeds Expectations	***Fails Expectations***
Locate a parking lot	Ample room in a bright place near to the entrance, with a security officer protecting your valuables	Insufficient parking spaces, so patrons have to park in another lot
Queuing up to obtain tickets	Strategic placement of mirrors posters of upcoming movies, and entertainment news to ease perception of long wait, if any; movies and time slots easily seen; ticket availability clearly communicated	A long queue and having to wait for a long while; difficult to see quickly what movies are being shown at what time slots and whether tickets still available
Checking of tickets to enter the theater	A very well maintained lobby with clear directions to the theater and posters of the movie to enhance patrons' experience	A dirty lobby with rubbish strewn and unclear or misleading directions to the movie theater
Go to the washroom before the movie starts	Sparkling clean, spacious, brightly lit, dry floors, well stocked, nice decor, clear mirrors wiped regularly	Dirty, with an unbearable odor; broken toilets; no hand towels, soap, or toilet paper; overcrowded; dusty and dirty mirrors
Enter the theater and locate your seat	Spotless theater; well designed with no bad seats; sufficient lighting to locate your seat; spacious, comfortable chairs, with drink and popcorn holders on each seat; and a suitable temperature	Rubbish on the floor, broken seats, sticky floors, gloomy and insufficient lighting, burnt-out exit signs
Watch the movie	Excellent sound system and film quality, nice audience, an enjoyable and memorable entertainment experience overall	Substandard sound and movie equipment, uncooperative audience that talks and smokes because of lack of "No Smoking" and other signs; a disturbing and unenjoyable entertainment experience overall
Leave the theater and return to the car	Friendly service staff greet patrons as they leave; an easy exit through a brightly lit and safe parking area back to the car with the help of clear lot signs	A difficult trip, as patrons squeeze through a narrow exit, unable to find the car because of no or insufficient lighting

Source: Adapted from Steven Albrecht, "See Things from the Customer's Point of View—How to Use the 'Cycles of Service' to Understand What the Customer Goes through to Do Business with You," *World's Executive Digest* (December 1996): 53–58.

Putting it all together is difficult, as environments are perceived holistically. That means that no individual aspect of the environment can be optimized without considering everything else in that environment. This makes designing service environments an art, and professional designers focus on the design of specific service environments, such as hotel lobbies, restaurants, clubs, cafes and bistros, retail outlets, health care facilities, and so on. Furthermore, apart from an aesthetical perspective, the best service environments are designed with the customer's perspective in mind. The environment needs to facilitate smooth movement through the service process.

Review Questions

1. Compare and contrast the strategic and functional roles of service environments within a service organization.
2. What are affective expectations? What is their role in driving customer satisfaction with service encounters?
3. What is the relationship, or link, between the Russell Model of Affect and Bitner's servicescape model?
4. Why is it likely that various customers and service staff respond differently to the same service environment?
5. Select a bad and a good waiting experience and contrast the situations with respect to the aesthetics of the surrounding, diversions, people waiting, and attitude of servers.
6. Explain the dimensions of ambient conditions and how each can influence customer responses to the service environment.
7. What are the roles of signs, symbols, and artifacts?
8. What are the implications of the fact that environments are perceived holistically?
9. What tools are available for aiding our understanding of customer responses and for guiding the design and improvements of service environments?

Application Exercises

1. Identify firms from three different service sectors in which the service environment is a crucial part of the overall value proposition. Analyze and explain in detail the value that is being delivered by the service environment.
2. Visit a service environment and have a detailed look around. Experience the environment and try and feel how the various design parameters shape what you feel and how you behave in that setting.
3. Visit a self-service environment and analyze how the design dimensions guide you through the service process. What do you find most effective for you, and what seems least effective? How could that environment be improved to further ease the "way finding" for self-service customers?

Endnotes

1. The term was coined by Mary Jo Bitner in her paper "Servicescapes: The Impact of Physical Surroundings on Customers and Employees," *Journal of Marketing* 56 (1992): 57–71.
2. Julie Baker, Dhruv Grewal, and A. Parasuraman, "The Influence of Store Environment on Quality Inferences and Store Image," *Journal of the Academy of Marketing Science* 22, no. 4 (1994): 328–339.
3. Véronique Aubert-Gamet, "Twisting Servicescapes: Diversion of the Physical Environment in a Reappropriation Process," *International Journal of Service Industry Management* 8, no. 1 (1997): 26–41.
4. Leonard L. Berry and Neeli Bendapudi, "Clueing in Customers," *Harvard Business Review* 81 (February 2003): 100–107.
5. Richard B. Chase and Douglas M. Stewart, "Making Your Service Fail-Safe," *Sloan Management Review* 35 (1994): 35–44.
6. Robert J. Donovan and John R. Rossiter, "Store Atmosphere: An Environmental Psychology

Approach," *Journal of Retailing* 58, no. 1 (1982): 34–57.

7. James A. Russell, "A Circumplex Model of Affect," *Journal of Personality and Social Psychology* 39, no. 6 (1980): 1161–1178.
8. Jochen Wirtz and John E. G. Bateson, "Consumer Satisfaction with Services: Integrating the Environmental Perspective in Services Marketing into the Traditional Disconfirmation Paradigm," *Journal of Business Research* 44, no. 1 (1999): 55–66.
9. Jochen Wirtz, Anna S. Mattila, and Rachel L. P. Tan, "The Moderating Role of Target-Arousal on the Impact of Affect on Satisfaction—An Examination in the Context of Service Experiences," *Journal of Retailing* 76, no. 3 (2000): 347–365.
10. Barry J. Babin and Jill S. Attaway, "Atmospheric Affect as a Tool for Creating Value and Gaining Share of Customer," *Journal of Business Research* 49 (2000): 91–99.
11. Mary Jo Bitner, "Service Environments: The Impact of Physical Surroundings on Customers and Employees," *Journal of Marketing* 56 (April 1992): 57–71.
12. For a comprehensive review of experimental studies on the atmospheric effects, refer to L.W. Turley and Ronald E. Milliman, "Atmospheric Effects on Shopping Behavior: A Review of the Experimental Literature," *Journal of Business Research* 49 (2000): 193–211.
13. Patrick M. Dunne, Robert F. Lusch, and David A. Griffith, *Retailing*, 4th ed. (Orlando, FL: Hartcourt, 2002), 518.
14. Barry Davies and Philippa Ward, *Managing Retail Consumption* (West Sussex, England: John Wiley, 2002), 179.
15. Steve Oakes, "The Influence of the Musicscape within Service Environments," *Journal of Services Marketing* 14, no. 7 (2000): 539–556.
16. Morris B. Holbrook and Punam Anand, "Effects of Tempo and Situational Arousal on the Listener's Perceptual and Affective Responses to Music," *Psychology of Music* 18 (1990): 150–162; and S. J. Rohner and R. Miller, "Degrees of Familiar and Affective Music and Their Effects on State Anxiety," *Journal of Music Therapy* 17, no. 1 (1980): 2–15.
17. Ronald E. Milliman, "The Influence of Background Music on the Behavior of Restaurant Patrons," *Journal of Consumer Research* 13 (1986): 286–289.
18. Clare Caldwell and Sally A. Hibbert, "The Influence of Music Tempo and Musical Preference on Restaurant Patrons' Behavior," *Psychology and Marketing* 19, no. 11 (2002): 895–917.
19. Ronald E. Milliman, "Using Background Music to Affect the Behavior of Supermarket Shoppers," *Journal of Marketing* 56, no. 3 (1982): 86–91.
20. Richard F. Yalch and Eric R. Spangenberg, "The Effects of Music in a Retail Setting on Real and Perceived Shopping Times," *Journal of Business Research* 49 (2000): 139–147.
21. Michael K. Hui, Laurette Dubé, and Jean-Charles Chebat, "The Impact of Music on Consumers Reactions to Waiting for Services," *Journal of Retailing* 73, no. 1 (1997): 87–104.
22. David A. Tansik and Robert Routhieaux, "Customer Stress-Relaxation: The Impact of Music in a Hospital Waiting Room," *International Journal of Service Industry Management* 10, no. 1 (1999): 68–81.
23. Laurette Dubé and Sylvie Morin, "Background Music Pleasure and Store Evaluation Intensity Effects and Psychological Mechanisms," *Journal of Business Research* 54 (2001): 107–113.
24. Dunne, Lusch, and Griffith, *Retailing,* 520.
25. Paula Fitzerald Bone and Pam Scholder Ellen, "Scents in the Marketplace: Explaining a Fraction of Olfaction," *Journal of Retailing* 75, no. 2 (1999): 243–262.
26. Alan R. Hirsch, *Dr. Hirsch's Guide to Scentsational Weight Loss* (London, HarperCollins, UK: January 1997), 12–15.
27. Mike Fillon, "No Added Pep in Peppermint," *WebMD Feature*, September 22, 2000, *http://mywebmd.com/health* and *wellness/living-better/default.htm* (February 17, 2003).
28. Alan R. Hirsch, "Effects of Ambient Odors on Slot Machine Usage in a Las Vegas Casino," *Psychology and Marketing* 12, no. 7 (1995): 585–594.
29. Alan R. Hirsch and S. E. Gay, "Effect on Ambient Olfactory Stimuli on the Evaluation of a Common Consumer Product," *Chemical Senses* 16 (1991): 535.
30. Alan R. Hirsch, "Effects of Garlic Bread on Family Interactions," *Journal of American Psychosomatic Society* 62, no. 1 (2000): 1434.
31. Linda Holtzschuhe, *Understanding Color—An Introduction for Designers*, 2d ed. (New York: John Wiley, 2002), 1.
32. Gerald J. Gorn, Chattopadhyay Amitava, Tracey Yi, and Darren Dahl, "Effects of Color as an Executional Cue in Advertising: They're in the Shade," *Management Science* 43, no. 10 (1997): 1387–1400; Ayn E. Crowley, "The Two-Dimensional Impact of Color on Shopping," *Marketing Letters* 4, no. 1 (1993): 59–69.
33. Albert Henry Munsell, *A Munsell Color Product* (New York: Kollmorgen Corporation 1996).
34. Holtzschuhe, *Understanding Color*, 51.
35. Heinrich Zollinger, *Color: A Multidisciplinary Approach* (Zurich: Verlag Helvetica Chimica Acta (VHCA) Weinheim, Wiley-VCH, 1999), 71–79.
36. Joseph A. Bellizzi, Ayn E. Crowley, and Ronald W. Hasty, "The Effects of Color in Store Design," *Journal of Retailing* 59, no. 1 (1983): 21–45.
37. John E. G. Bateson and K. Douglas Hoffman, *Managing Services Marketing*, 4th ed. (Orlando, FL: Dryden Press, 1999), 143.

38. Anat Rafaeli and Iris Vilnai-Yavetz, "Discerning Organizational Boundaries through Physical Artifacts," in *Managing Boundaries in Organizations: Multiple Perspectives*, ed. N. Paulsen and T. Hernes (Basingstoke, UK: Hampshire, Macmillan, 2003).

39. Sara O. Marberry and Laurie Zagon, *The Power of Color—Creating Healthy Interior Spaces* (New York: John Wiley, 1995), 38.

40. Anna S. Mattila and Jochen Wirtz, "Congruency of Scent and Music as a Driver of In-Store Evaluations and Behavior," *Journal of Retailing* 77 (2001): 273–289.

41. Stephan H. Haeckel, Lewis P. Carbone, and Leonard L. Berry, "How to Lead the Customer Experience," *Marketing Management* (January/February 2003): 19–23.

42. Christine M. Piotrowski and Elizabeth A. Rogers, *Designing Commercial Interiors* (New York: John Wiley, 1999); Martin M. Pegler, *Cafes & Bistros* (New York: Retail Reporting Corporation, 1998); Paco Asensio, *Bars & Restaurants* (New York: HarperCollins International, 2002); and Bethan Ryder, *Bar and Club Design* (London: Laurence King Publishing, 2002).

43. Ron Kaufman, "Service Power: Who Were They Designing It For?" Newsletter (May 2001), *http://RonKaufman.com*.

44. Alain d'Astous, "Irritating Aspects of the Shopping Environment," *Journal of Business Research* 49 (2000): 149–156.

CHAPTER 11

Managing People for Service Advantage

The old adage "People are your most important asset" is wrong. The right *people are your most important asset.*

—JIM COLLINS

Among the most demanding jobs in service businesses are the so-called frontline jobs. Employees are expected to be fast and efficient at executing operational tasks, as well as courteous and helpful in dealing with customers. In fact, frontline employees are a key input for delivering service excellence and competitive advantage. Behind most of today's successful service organizations stands a firm commitment to effective management of human resources (HR), including recruitment, selection, training, motivation, and retention of employees. Organizations that display this commitment are also characterized by a distinctive culture of service leadership and role modeling by top management. It is probably more difficult for competitors to duplicate high-performance human assets than any other corporate resource.

In this chapter, we focus on the people side of service management and explore the following questions.

1. Why is the front line so crucially important to the success of a service firm?
2. Why is the work of service staff so demanding, challenging, and often difficult?
3. What are the cycles of failure, mediocrity, and success in HR for service firms?
4. How do we get it right? How are we to attract, select, train, motivate, and retain outstanding frontline staff?
5. What is the role of a service culture and service leadership in sustainable service excellence?

SERVICE STAFF ARE CRUCIALLY IMPORTANT

Almost everybody can recount a horror story about a dreadful experience with a service business. If pressed, many of these same people can also recount a really good service experience. Service personnel usually feature prominently in such dramas and are in roles as either uncaring, incompetent, mean-spirited villains or heroes who went out of their way to help customers by anticipating their needs and resolving problems in a helpful and empathetic manner. From the firm's perspective, service staff are crucially important, as they can be a key determinant of customer loyalty (or defections) and therefore play an important role in the service-profit chain.

Service Personnel as a Source of Customer Loyalty and Competitive Advantage

From a customer's perspective, the encounter with service staff is probably the most important aspect of a service. From the firm's perspective, the service levels and the way service is delivered by the front line can be an important source of differentiation as well as competitive advantage. In addition, the strength of the customer/frontline staff relationship is often an important driver of customer loyalty.[1] Service staff is so important to customers and the firm's competitive positioning because the front line

- *Is a core part of the product.* Often, the service staff is the most visible element of the service, delivers the service, and significantly determines service quality.
- *Is the service firm.* Frontline staff represent the service firm; from a customer's perspective, the front line is the firm.
- *Is the brand.* Frontline staff and service are often a core part of the brand. It is the staff that determines whether the brand promise gets delivered.

Furthermore, frontline staff play a key role in anticipating customers' needs, customizing the service delivery, and building personalized relationships with customers, which ultimately lead to customer loyalty. How attentive staff can be in anticipating customers' needs is shown in the following example. Steve Posner, a veteran room waiter at Ritz-Carlton, says that he continually tries to anticipate what guests might want. He puts extra silverware on the table: "This may be for a child, so I also bring a small spoon for the soup." He includes Al steak sauce with hamburger orders: "They may not even have thought they wanted it, but they're happy to find it there." He puts a plate of lemon wedges next to a Coke: "Always bring more than you think people need." The aim isn't to lay out a table in some fussily proper way but to make sure that guests' "unexpressed wishes and needs" are met. "As a waiter, you're the pre-guest. You have to try to think the way a guest would."[2]

This and many other success stories of employees' showing discretionary effort that made a difference have reinforced the truism that highly motivated people are at the core of service excellence. They are increasingly a key variable for creating and maintaining competitive positioning and advantage.

The important impact of service staff on customer loyalty was integrated and formalized by James Heskett and his colleagues in their research on the service-profit chain.[3] The authors demonstrate the chain of relationships between (1) satisfaction, retention, and productivity; (2) service value; (3) customer satisfaction and loyalty; and (4) revenue growth and profitability. Unlike in manufacturing, our frontline staff are in continual contact with customers, and we have solid evidence showing that employee satisfaction and customer satisfaction are highly correlated.[4] This chapter focuses on how to get satisfied, loyal, and productive service staff; the chapters in Part Four of this book focus on how to manage customer loyalty.

The Front Line in Low-Contact Services

Most of the published research in service management and many of the best-practice examples featured in this chapter relate to high-contact services. This is not entirely surprising, as the people in these jobs are so visible. They are the actors who appear front-stage in the service drama when they serve the customer. Here, it is obvious why the front line is crucially important to customers and therefore to the competitive positioning of the firm as well. However, there is an increasing trend across virtually all types of services toward low-contact delivery channels, such as call centers. Many routine transactions are now being conducted without even involving the frontline staff at all. Some examples are the many types of services that are provided via Web sites, automatic teller machines (ATMs), and interactive voice response (IVR) systems. In light of these trends, is the front line really that important, especially when more and more routine transactions are being shifted to low- or no-contact channels?

Although the quality of the technology and self-service interface (e.g., the Web site, the ATM network, and the IVRs) is becoming the core engine for service delivery and its importance has been elevated drastically, the quality of frontline staff still remains crucially important. Most people have not called the service hotline or visited a service center or shop of their mobile operator or their credit card company more than once or twice in the past 12 months and interacted with frontline staff there. However, it is these one or two service encounters that are critical. These are the "moments of truth" that drive a customer's perceptions of the service firm. Also, it is likely that these interactions are not about routine transactions but about service problems and special requests. These very few contacts determine whether a customer thinks, "Customer service is excellent, and this is one important reason why I bank with you," or "Your service stinks. I don't like interacting with you, and I am going to spread the word about how bad your service is!"

A service firm's differentiation rests on these few moments of truth. Therefore, the service delivered by the front line, whether it is "ear to ear" or via e-mail rather than face to face, is still highly visible and important to the customer and therefore a critical component of the strategy and marketing mix of service firms.

FRONTLINE WORK IS DIFFICULT AND STRESSFUL

The service-profit chain has high-performing, satisfied employees as a key requirement for achieving service excellence and customer loyalty. However, these employees work in some of the most demanding jobs in service firms.

Boundary Spanning

The literature on organizational behavior refers to service staff as boundary spanners, linking the inside of an organization to the outside world, operating at the boundary of the company, and transferring information between the inside and the outside world. Because of the position they occupy, boundary spanners often have conflicting roles. Customer-contact personnel must attend to both operational and marketing goals. To illustrate, service staff are expected to delight customers and at the same time be fast and efficient at executing operational tasks. On top of that, they are often expected to do selling and cross-selling as well. For instance, "We've got some nice desserts to follow your main course" or "Now would be a good time to open a separate account to save for your children's education."

In short, frontline staff may perform triple roles: producing service quality, productivity, and sales. The multiplicity of roles in service jobs often leads to role conflict and role stress among employees.[5]

Sources of Conflict

Three main causes of role stress in frontline positions are person/role, organization/client, and interclient conflicts.

Person/Role Conflict Service staff feel conflicts between what their jobs require and their own personalities, self-perceptions, and beliefs. For example, the job may require staff to smile and be friendly even to rude customers. Providing quality service requires an independent, warm, and friendly personality. These traits are more likely to be found in people with higher self-esteem. However, many frontline jobs are often perceived as low-level jobs requiring little education, offering low pay, and often lacking future prospects. If an organization is not able to "professionalize" its frontline jobs and move away from such an image, these jobs may be inconsistent with staff members' self-perceptions and lead to person/role conflicts.

Organization/Client Conflict Service employees frequently face the dilemma of whether they should follow the company's rules or satisfy customer demands. This conflict, also called the two-bosses dilemma, arises when customers request services, extras, or exceptions that violate organizational rules. This conflict is especially acute in non-customer-oriented organizations. Here, staff members frequently have to deal with conflicting customer needs and requests, as well as organizational rules, procedures, and productivity requirements. Research Insight 11-1 shows how call center staff cope with the tension between productivity and quality.

Interclient Conflict Conflicts between customers are not uncommon (e.g., smoking in nonsmoking sections, jumping queues, speaking on a mobile phone in a cinema, and noisy guests in a restaurant), and it usually falls to the service staff to call the other customer to order. This is a stressful and unpleasant task, as it is difficult and often impossible to satisfy both sides.

Emotional Labor

The term *emotional labor* was coined by Arlie Hochschild in her book *The Managed Heart*.[6] Emotional labor arises from the discrepancy between the way frontline staff feel inside and the emotions they are expected to portray in front of customers. Frontline staff are expected to be cheerful, genial, compassionate, sincere, or even self-effacing: emotions that can be conveyed through facial expressions, gestures, and words. In the event that they do not feel such emotions, employees are required to quell their true feelings in order to conform to customer expectations.

The stress of emotional labor is nicely illustrated in the following, probably apocryphal, story. A flight attendant was approached by a passenger with "Let's have a smile." She replied with "Okay. I'll tell you what, first you smile and then I'll smile, okay?" He smiled. "Good," she said. "Now hold that for 15 hours," and walked away.[7]

Emotional labor is a very real problem faced by frontline staff, and companies are now taking steps to help staff to deal with the problem. For example, because of Singapore Airlines' reputation for service excellence, its customers tend to have very high expectations and can be very demanding. This puts considerable pressure on its frontline staff. The Commercial Training Manager of Singapore Airlines (SIA) explained:

> We have recently undertaken an external survey and it appears that more of the "demanding customers" choose to fly with SIA. So the staff are really under a lot of pressure. We have a motto: "If SIA can't do it for you, no other airline can." So we encourage staff to try to sort things out, and to do as much as they can for the customer. Although they are very proud, and indeed protective of the company, we need to help them deal with the emotional turmoil of having to handle their customers well, and at the same time, feel they're not being taking advantage of. The challenge is to help our staff deal with difficult situations and take the brickbats. This will be the next thrust of our training programs.[8]

Firms need to be aware of ongoing emotional stress among their employees and to devise ways of alleviating it, including training on how to deal with emotional stress and how to cope with pressure from customers. Figure 11-1 captures emotional labor with humor.

RESEARCH INSIGHT 11-1

PRODUCTIVITY AND SERVICE QUALITY OF FRONTLINE STAFF

What mechanisms govern productivity and quality for frontline service employees? Does the tension of competing demands from customers and management have dysfunctional consequences? What resources help counter these dysfunctional effects? Seeking answers, Professor Jagdip Singh of Case Western Reserve University conducted a survey of full-time employees working in customer-contact jobs at a financial service company's telephone center.

The nature of the job required these frontline employees to coordinate tasks with their coworkers and to receive regular directions and guidelines from supervisors. The employees were expected to meet daily quotas for call volumes and were randomly monitored against service quality standards. Their work setting contained many characteristics of a burnout environment: long hours, lack of autonomy, insufficient resources, and ongoing demands to meet quotas and goals.

All employees received a survey packet at home, containing a questionnaire, a cover letter from the researchers, a letter of endorsement from the company president, and a postage-paid return envelope addressed to the researchers. Participants were assured of anonymity and asked to complete the survey at home. Usable responses were received from 306 frontline employees, a response rate of 30 percent.

The questionnaire included scales designed to measure a variety of constructs:

- *Role stressors* measured the ambiguity perceived by frontline staff about both the company (in terms of such dimensions as task flexibility, priorities, workload, and getting promoted) and customers (nature of interactions, amount of service offered, handling objections and criticism, and presenting company strengths). Stressors also measured the role conflict inherent in trying to meet conflicting demands from various departments, although staff members lacked the training and resources needed to get the required volume of work done well.
- *Burnout tendencies* measured emotional feelings about top management (dismay, alienation, and emotional exhaustion from trying to meet expectations) and about customers (strain, indifference toward and depersonalization of customers, and overwork).
- *Task control and boss support* measured frontline employees' perceived ability to influence the tasks and decisions affecting their jobs, as well as their perceptions of the boss's fairness, supportiveness, and competence.
- *Job outcomes* measured employees' level of commitment and likelihood of quitting.
- *Performance productivity* addressed both contact output (customer contact time, measured automatically, meeting quotas and targets, following procedures), and backroom work (accurate completion of paperwork and adherence to company policies and procedures).
- *Performance* included building customers' trust and confidence, giving prompt and individualized attention, going beyond defined responsibilities to help customers even at the expense of not meeting productivity goals, consistently resolving customer concerns the first time, and providing accurate information.

The findings showed that frontline employees' productivity was unaffected by burnout tendencies but negatively impacted by conflict between resources and demands and by role ambiguity relative to customers. Singh believes that employees seek to maintain their productivity, even in the face of burnout, because the relevant indicators are visible and relate to pay and job retention. By contrast, the quality of service, which is less quantifiable and less visible, is likely to be damaged directly as employees burn out on customers. An unexpected finding was the negative correlation between organizational commitment and service quality, indicating that frontline employees who are more committed to the organization may be less committed to customers, and vice versa. Providing greater task control and boss support helps to shield employees from role stress, burnout, and thoughts of quitting, while also enhancing positive attitudes.

Source: Jagdip Singh, "Performance Productivity and Quality of Frontline Employees in Service Organizations," *Journal of Marketing* 64 (April 2000): 15–34.

FIGURE 11-1 Dilbert Encounters Emotional Labor at the Bank

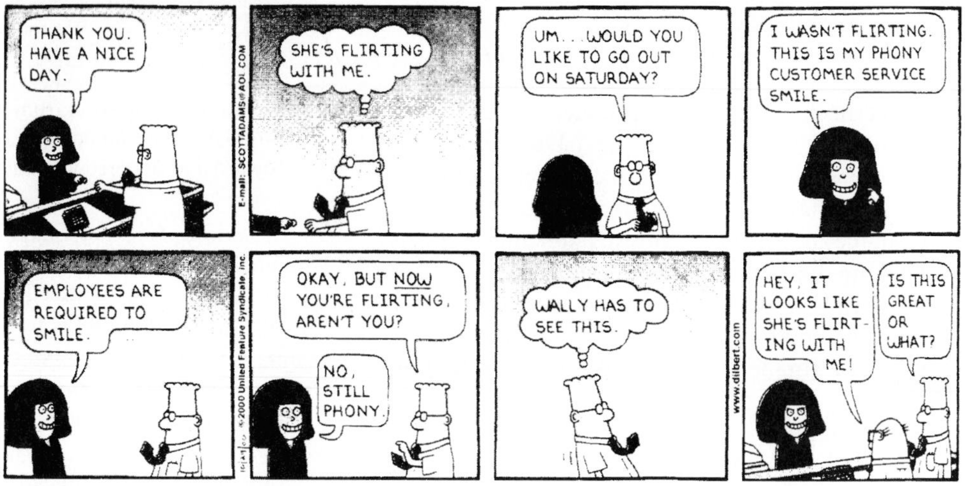

DILBERT reprinted by permission of United Syndicate, Inc.

Service Sweatshops?

Rapid developments in information technology are permitting service businesses to make radical improvements in business processes and even completely reengineer their operations. These developments sometimes result in wrenching changes in the nature of work for existing employees. Where face-to-face contact has been replaced by use of the Internet or telephone-based services, firms have redefined and relocated jobs, created new employee profiles for recruiting purposes, and sought to hire employees with a different set of qualifications.

As a result of the growing shift from high-contact to low-contact services, a large and increasing number of customer-contact employees work by telephone or e-mail, never meeting customers face to face. For example, more than 3 percent of the total U.S. workforce is now employed in call centers as so-called customer service representatives (CSRs).[9]

When well designed, such jobs can be rewarding and often offer mothers and students flexible working hours and part-time jobs (some 50 percent of call center workers are single mothers or students).[10] In fact, recent research has shown that part-time workers are more satisfied with their work as CSRs than are full-time staff and performed just as well.[11] At worst, CSR jobs place employees in an electronic equivalent of the old-fashioned sweatshop. Even in the best "managed contact centers," as call centers are often called, the work is intense, with CSRs expected to deal with up to two calls a minute under a high level of monitoring (including trips to the toilet and breaks). There's a famous (and true) story about a supervisor who offered his staff diapers so that they spent less time in toilets, away from their phones.[12]

Success in this area involves a number of measures. Among them are screening applicants to make sure that they already know how to present themselves well on the telephone and have the potential to learn additional skills, training them carefully, and giving them a well-designed working environment.

CYCLES OF FAILURE, MEDIOCRITY, AND SUCCESS

All too often, bad working environments translate into dreadful service, with employees treating customers the way their managers treat them. Businesses with high employee turnover are frequently stuck in what has been termed the "*cycle of failure*." Businesses that offer job security but little scope for personal initiative may suffer from an equally undesirable "*cycle of mediocrity*." However, if managed well, there is potential for a virtuous cycle in service employment, termed the "*cycle of success*."[13]

The Cycle of Failure

In many service industries, the search for productivity is on with a vengeance. One solution takes the form of simplifying work routines and hiring workers as cheaply as possible to perform repetitive work tasks that require little or no training. Among consumer services, departmental stores, fast-food restaurants, and call center operations are often cited as examples where this problem abounds, although there are notable exceptions. The cycle of failure captures the implications of such a strategy, with its two concentric but interactive cycles: one involving failures with employees; the second, with customers (Figure 11-2).

The *employee cycle of failure* begins with a narrow design of jobs to accommodate low skill levels, an emphasis on rules rather than service, and the use of technology to control quality. A strategy of low wages is accompanied by minimal effort on selection or training. Consequences include bored employees who lack the ability to respond to customer problems, become dissatisfied, and develop a poor service attitude. Outcomes

FIGURE 11-2 The Cycle of Failure

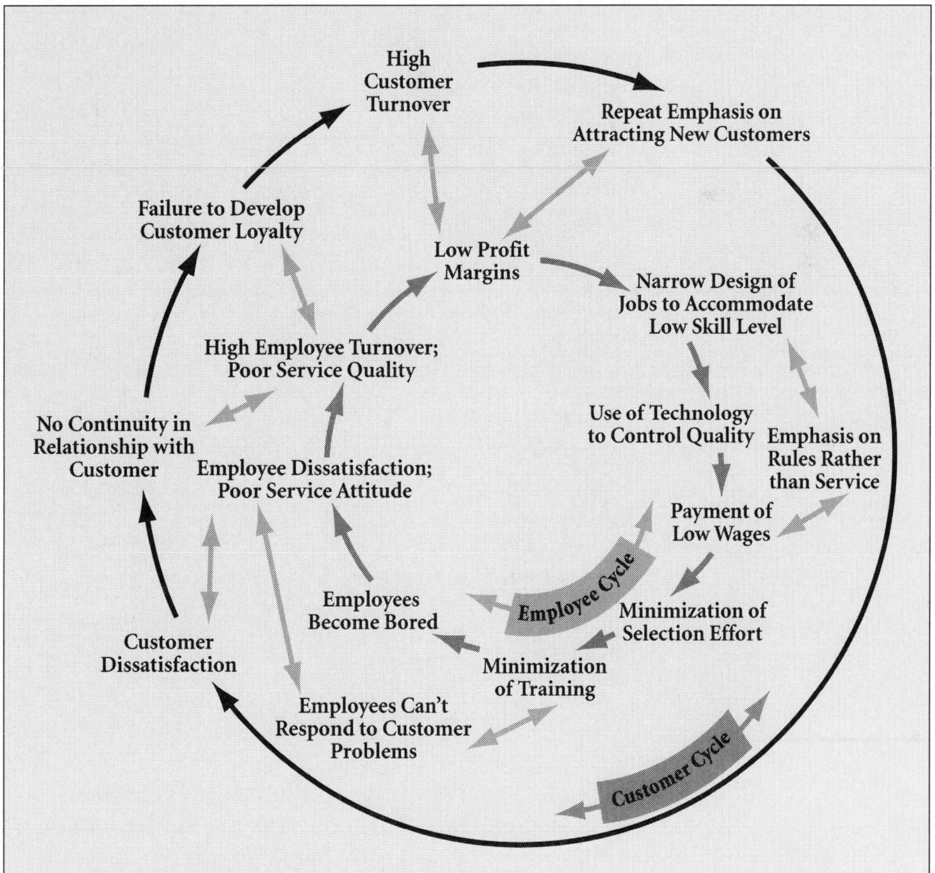

Source: Leonard L. Schlesinger and James L. Heskett, "Breaking the Cycle of Failure in Services," *Sloan Management Review* 31 (Spring 1991): 17–28. Reprinted by permission of publisher. Copyright © 2003 by Massachusetts Institute of Technology. All rights reserved.

for the firm are low service quality and high employee turnover. Because of weak profit margins, the cycle repeats itself with the hiring of more low-paid employees to work in this unrewarding atmosphere. Some service firms can reach such low levels of employee morale that frontline staff engage in "service sabotage," as featured in Research Insight 11-2 rather than deliver service excellence.[14]

The *customer cycle of failure* begins with repeated emphasis on attracting new customers, who become dissatisfied with employee performance and the lack of continuity implicit in continually changing faces. These customers fail to develop any loyalty to the supplier and turn over as rapidly as the staff. This requires an ongoing search for new customers to maintain sales volume. The departure of discontented customers is especially worrying in light of what we now know about the greater profitability of a loyal customer base.

Managers have offered excuses and justifications for perpetuating this cycle.

- "You just can't get good people nowadays."
- "People just don't want to work today."
- "To get good people would cost too much, and you can't pass on these cost increases to customers."
- "It's not worth training our frontline people when they leave you so quickly."
- "High turnover is simply an inevitable part of our business. You've got to learn to live with it."[15]

Too many managers make shortsighted assumptions about the financial implications of low-pay/high-turnover human resource strategies. Part of the problem is the failure to measure all relevant costs. Often omitted are three key cost variables: the cost of continual recruiting, hiring, and training (which is as much a time cost for managers as a financial cost); the lower productivity of inexperienced new workers; and the costs of continually attracting new customers (requiring extensive advertising and promotional discounts). Also ignored are two revenue variables: future revenue streams that might have continued for years but are lost when unhappy customers take their business elsewhere, and potential income from prospective customers who are turned off by negative word of mouth. Finally, there are less easily quantifiable costs, such as disruptions to service while a job remains unfilled and loss of the departing employee's knowledge of the business (and its customers).

The Cycle of Mediocrity Another vicious employment cycle is the "cycle of mediocrity" (Figure 11-3). It is most likely to be found in large, bureaucratic organizations, often typified by state monopolies, industrial cartels, or regulated oligopolies, where there is little incentive to improve performance and where fear of entrenched unions may discourage management from adopting more innovative labor practices.

In such environments, service delivery standards tend to be prescribed by rigid rulebooks, oriented toward standardized service, operational efficiencies, and prevention of both employee fraud and favoritism toward specific customers. Employees are often expected to spend their entire working lives with the organization. Job responsibilities tend to be narrowly and unimaginatively defined, tightly categorized by grade and scope of responsibilities, and further rigidified by union work rules. Salary increases and promotions are based on longevity. Successful performance in a job is often measured by absence of mistakes rather than by high productivity or outstanding customer service. Training focuses on learning the rules and the technical aspects of the job, not on improving human interactions with customers and coworkers. As allowances for flexibility or employee initiative are minimal, jobs tend to be boring and repetitive. However, in contrast to the cycle of failure, most positions provide adequate pay and often good benefits, combined with high security. Thus,

RESEARCH INSIGHTS 11-2

SERVICE SABOTAGE BY THE FRONT LINE

The next time we are dissatisfied with the service provided by service employees—in a restaurant, for example—it's worth pausing for a moment to think about the consequences of complaining about the service. One might become the unknowing victim of a malicious case of service sabotage, such as having something unhygienic added to one's food.

Interestingly, there is a relatively high incidence of service sabotage by frontline employees. In their study of 182 frontline staff, Lloyd Harris and Emmanuel Ogbonna found that 90 percent of them accepted that frontline behavior with malicious intent to reduce or spoil the service—service sabotage—is an everyday occurrence in their organizations.

The researchers classify service sabotage along two dimensions: covert/overt, and routinized intermittent behaviors. Covert behaviors are concealed from customers, whereas overt actions are purposefully displayed, often to coworkers and also customers. Routinized behaviors are ingrained into the culture, whereas intermittent actions are sporadic and less common. Some true examples of service sabotage classified along the two dimensions are shown in Figure 11-A.

FIGURE 11-A Examples of Services Sabotage

Openness of Service Sabotage Behaviors

Covert ⟷ Overt

Normality of Service Sabotage Behaviors

Routinized ⟷ Intermittent

Customary/Private Service Sabotage

"Many customers are rude or difficult, not even polite like you or I. Getting your own back evens the score. There are lots of things that you do that no one but you will ever know —smaller portions, dodgy wine, a bad beer—all that and you serve with a smile! Sweet revenge!"

—Waiter

"It's perfectly normal to file against some of the s**t that happens. Managers have always asked for more than's fair and customers have always wanted something for nothing. Getting back at them is natural—it's always happened, nothing new in that."

—Front-of-House Operative

Customer/Public Service Sabotage

"You can put on a real old show. You know—if the guest is in a hurry, you slow it right down and drag it right out and if they want to chat, you can do the monosyllabic stuff. And all the time you know that your mates are round the corner laughing their heads off!"

—Front-of-House Operative

"The trick is to do it in a way that they can't complain about. I mean, you can't push it too far but some of them are so stupid that you can talk to them like a four year old and they would not notice. I mean, really putting them down is really patronizing. It's great fun to watch!"

—Waiter

Sporadic/Private Service Sabotage

"I don't often work with them but the night shift here really gets to me. They are always complaining. So to get back at them, just occasionally, I put a spanner in the works—accidentally-on-purpose misread their food orders, slow the service down, stop the glass washer so that they run out—nothing heavy."

—Senior Chef

"I don't know why I do it. Sometimes it's simply a bad day, a lousy week, I dunno—but kicking someone's bags down the back stairs is not that unusual—not every day—I guess a couple of times a month."

—Front-of-House Supervisor

Sporadic/Public Service Sabotage

"The trick is to get them and then straight away launch into the apologies. I've seen it done thousands of times—burning hot plates into someone's hands, gravy dripped on sleeves, drink spilt on backs, wigs knocked off—that was funny—soups split in laps, you get the idea!"

—Long-Serving General Attendant

"Listen, there's this rule that we are supposed to greet all customers and smile at them if they pass within 5 meters. Well, this ain't done 'cos we think it's silly but this guy we decided to do it to. It started off with the waiters—we'd all go up to him and grin at him and say 'hello.' But it spread. Before you know it, managers and all have cottoned on and this poor chap is being met and greeted every two steps! He doesn't know what the hell is going on! It was so funny—the guy spent the last three nights in his room—he didn't dare go in the restaurant."

—Housekeeping Supervisor

Source: Adapted from Lloyd C. Harris and Emmanuel Ogbonna, "Exploring Service Sabotage: The Antecedents, Types, and Consequences of Frontline, Deviant, Antiservice Behaviors," *Journal of Service Research* 4, no. 3 (2002): 163–183.

FIGURE 11-3 The Cycle of Mediocrity

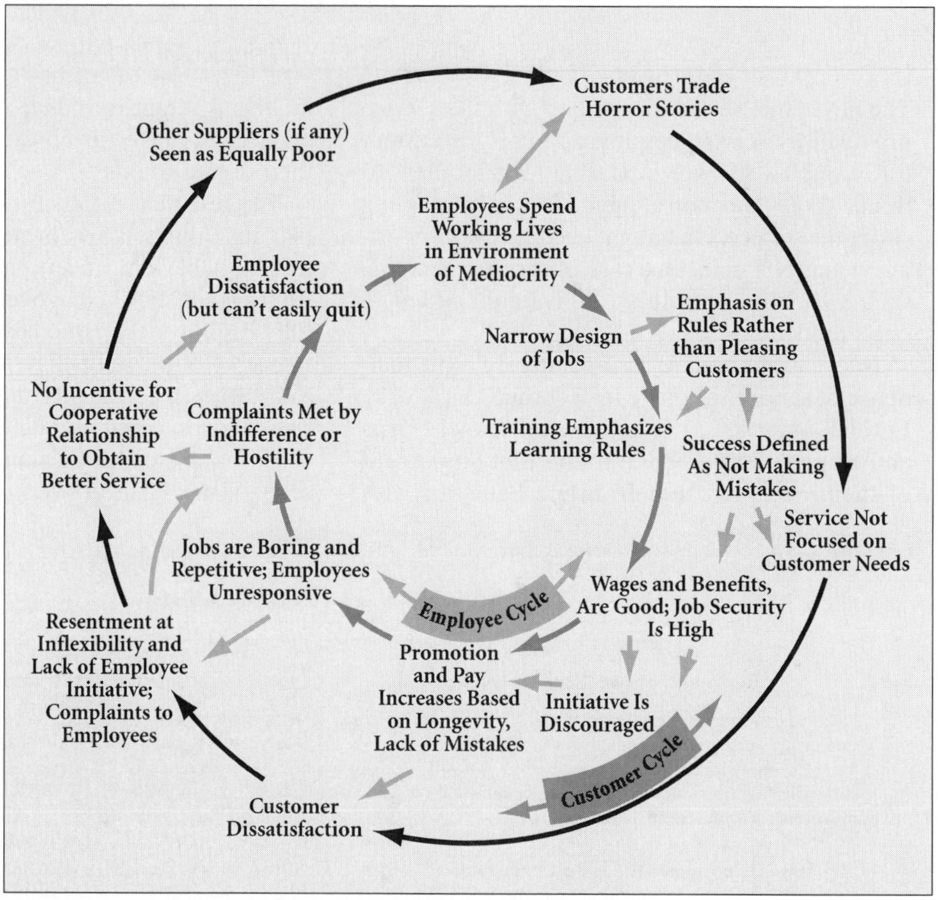

Source: Christopher Lovelock, "Managing Services: The Human Factor" in *Understanding Service Management*, ed. W. J. Glynn and J. G. Barnes (Chichester, UK John Wiley, 1995), 228.

employees are reluctant to leave. This lack of mobility is compounded by an absence of marketable skills that would be valued by organizations in other fields of endeavor.

Customers find such organizations frustrating to deal with. Faced with bureaucratic hassles, lack of service flexibility, and unwillingness of employees to make an effort to serve them well, users of the service may become resentful. What happens when there is nowhere else for customers to go, either because the service provider holds a monopoly or because all other available players are perceived as being equally bad or worse?

We should not be surprised if dissatisfied customers display hostility toward service employees who feel trapped in their jobs and are powerless to improve the situation. Employees may then protect themselves through such mechanisms as withdrawing into indifference, playing overtly by the rulebook, or countering rudeness with rudeness. The net result would be a vicious cycle of mediocrity in which unhappy customers continually complain to sullen employees (and also to other customers) about poor service and bad attitudes, generating greater defensiveness and lack of caring on the part of the staff. Under such circumstances, customers have little incentive to cooperate with the organization to achieve better service.

The Cycle of Success Some firms reject the assumptions underlying the cycles of failure or mediocrity. Instead, these firms take a long-term view of financial performance, seeking to prosper by investing in their people in order to create a "Cycle of Success" (Figure 11-4).

As with failure or mediocrity, success applies to both employees and customers. Attractive compensation packages are used to attract good-quality staff. Broadened job designs are accompanied by training and empowerment practices that allow frontline staff to control quality. With more focused recruitment, more intensive training, and better wages, employees are likely to be happier in their work and to provide higher-quality, customer-pleasing service. Regular customers also appreciate the continuity in service relationships resulting from lower turnover and so are more likely to remain loyal. Profit margins tend to be higher, and the organization is free to focus its marketing efforts on reinforcing customer loyalty through customer-retention strategies. These strategies are usually much more profitable than are those for attracting new customers. Even public service organizations are increasingly working toward cycles of success and offer their users good-quality service at a lower cost to the public.[16]

A powerful demonstration of a frontline staff member working in the cycle of success is waitress Cora Griffin (featured in Best Practice in Action 11-1). Many of the themes in her nine rules of success are the result of good HR strategies for service firms.

FIGURE 11-4 The Cycle of Success

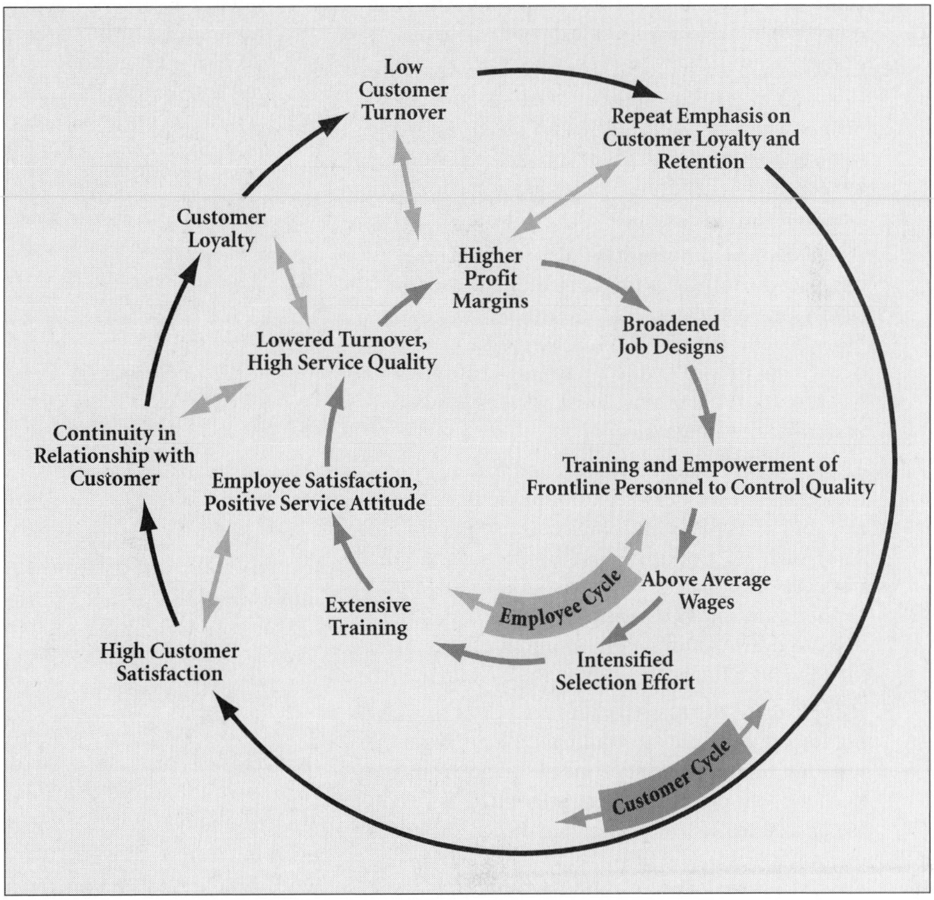

Source: Leonard L. Schlesinger and James L. Heskett, "Breaking the Cycle of Failure in Services," *Sloan Management Review* 31 (Spring 1991): 17–28. Reprinted by permission of publisher. Copyright © 2003 by Massachusetts Institute of Technology. All rights reserved.

BEST PRACTICE IN ACTION 11-1

CORA GRIFFITH: THE OUTSTANDING WAITRESS

Cora Griffith, a waitress for the Orchard Café at the Paper Valley Hotel in Appleton, Wisconsin, is superb in her role, appreciated by first-time customers, famous with her regular customers, and revered by her coworkers. Cora loves her work, and it shows. Comfortable in a role that she believes is the right one for her, she implements the following nine rules of success.

1. *Treat customers like family.* First-time customers are not allowed to feel like strangers. Cheerful and proactive, Cora smiles, chats, and includes everyone at the table in the conversation. She is as respectful to children as she is to adults and makes it a point to learn and use everyone's name. "I want people to feel like they're sitting down to dinner right at my house. I want them to feel they're welcome, that they can get comfortable, that they can relax. I don't just serve people, I pamper them."
2. *Listen first.* Cora has developed her listening skills to the point that she rarely writes down customers' orders. She listens carefully and provides a customized service: "Are they in a hurry? Or do they have a special diet or like their selection cooked in a certain way?"
3. *Anticipate customers' wants.* She replenishes beverages and brings extra bread and butter in a timely manner. One regular customer, for example, who likes honey with her coffee, gets it without having to ask. "I don't want my customers to have to ask for anything, so I always try to anticipate what they might need."
4. *Simple things make the difference.* She manages the details of her service, monitoring the cleanliness of the utensils and their correct placement. The fold for napkins must be just right. She inspects each plate in the kitchen before taking it to the table. She provides crayons for small children to draw pictures while waiting for the meal. "It's the little things that please the customer."
5. *Work smart.* Cora scans all her tables at once, looking for opportunities to combine tasks. "Never do just one thing at a time. And never go from the kitchen to the dining room empty-handed. Take coffee or iced tea or water with you." When she refills one water glass, she refills others. When clearing one plate, she clears others. "You have to be organized, and you have to keep in touch with the big picture."
6. *Keep learning.* Cora makes it an ongoing effort to improve her existing skills and to learn new ones.
7. *Success is where you find it.* Cora is contented with her work. She finds satisfaction in pleasing her customers, and she enjoys helping other people enjoy. Her positive attitude is a positive force in the restaurant. She is difficult to ignore. "If customers come to the restaurant in a bad mood, I'll try to cheer them up before they leave." Her definition of success: "To be happy in life."
8. *All for one, and one for all.* She has been working with many of the same coworkers for more than eight years. The team members support one another on the crazy days when 300 conventioneers come to the restaurant for breakfast at the same time. Everyone pitches in and helps. The waitstaff cover for one another, the managers bus the tables, and the chefs garnish the plates. "We are like a little family. We know each other very well and we help each other out. If we have a crazy day, I'll go in the kitchen towards the end of the shift and say, 'Man, I'm just proud of us. We really worked hard today.'"
9. *Take pride in your work.* Cora believes in the importance of her work and in the need to do it well. "I don't think of myself as 'just a waitress'. . . . I've chosen to be a waitress. I'm doing this to my full potential, and I give it my best. I tell anyone who's starting out: take pride in what you do. You're never just an anything, no matter what you do. You give it your all . . . and you do it with pride."

Cora Griffith is a success story. She is loyal to her employer and dedicated to her customers and coworkers. A perfectionist who seeks continuous improvement, Cora's enthusiasm for her work and unflagging spirit create an energy that radiates through the restaurant. She is proud of being a waitress, proud of "touching lives." Says Cora: "I have always wanted to do my best. However, the owners really are the ones who taught me how important it is to take care of the customer and who gave me the freedom to do it. The company always has listened to my concerns and followed up. Had I not worked for the Orchard Café, I would have been a good waitress, but I would not have been the same waitress."

Source: Leonard L. Berry, *Discovering the Soul of Service—The Nine Drivers of Sustainable Business Success* (New York: Tree Press), 156–159.

HUMAN RESOURCES MANAGEMENT: HOW TO GET IT RIGHT

Any rational manager would like to operate in the cycle of success. HR strategies can help service firms to move in that direction. Specifically, we discuss how firms can hire, motivate, and retain engaged service employees who are willing and able to perform along the three common dimensions of their jobs: delivering service excellence/customer satisfaction, productivity, and often sales as well.

Also, it is naïve to think that it is sufficient to satisfy employees and that then they will perform. Employee satisfaction should be seen as necessary but not sufficient for having high-performing staff. For instance, a recent study showed that employee effort was a strong driver of customer satisfaction over and above employee satisfaction.[17] As Jim Collins said, "The old adage 'People are the most important asset' is wrong. The right people are your most important asset."[18] We would like to add to this: ". . . and the wrong people are a liability." Getting it right starts with hiring the right people.

Hire the Right People

Hiring the right people includes competing for receiving applications from the best employees in the labor market and then selecting from this wide pool the best candidates for the given jobs to be filled.

Be the Preferred Employer To be able to select and hire the best people, they first have to apply for a job with you and then accept your job offer over other potential offers (the best people tend to be selected by several firms). Thus, a firm has to first compete for talent market share,[19] or as McKinsey & Company called it, "the war for talent."[20] Competing in the labor market means having an attractive value proposition for prospective employees and includes such factors having a good image as an employer in the community and delivering high-quality products and services that make employees feel proud to be part of the team.

Furthermore, the compensation package cannot be below average: Top people expect above-average packages. In our experience, it takes a salary in the range of the 65th to 80th percentile of the market to attract top performers to top companies. One does not have to be a top paymaster if other important aspects of the value proposition are attractive. In short, understand the needs of your target employees, and get your value proposition right.

Select the Right People There's no such thing as the perfect employee. Different positions are often best filled by people with different skill sets, styles, and personalities. For example, the Walt Disney Company assesses prospective employees in terms of their potential for on-stage or backstage work. On-stage workers, known as cast members, are assigned to those roles for which their appearance, personalities, and skills provide the best match. Also, as Robert Levering and Milton Moskowitz stress:

> No company is perfect for everyone. This may be especially true in good places to work since these firms tend to have real character . . . their own culture. Companies with distinctive personalities tend to attract—and repel—certain types of individuals.[21]

What makes outstanding service performers so special? Often it is things that *cannot* be taught. It is the qualities that are intrinsic to the people and qualities they would bring with them to any employer. As one study of high performers observed:

> Energy . . . cannot be taught, it has to be hired. The same is true for charm, for detail orientation, for work ethic, for neatness. Some of these things can be enhanced with on-the-job training . . . or incentives. . . . But by and large, such qualities are instilled early on.[22]

Also, HR managers have discovered that although good manners and the need to smile and make eye contact can be taught, warmth itself cannot. The only realistic solution is to change the organization's recruitment criteria to favor candidates with naturally warm personalities. According to Jim Collins: "The right people are those who would exhibit the desired behaviors anyway, as a natural extension of their character and attitude, regardless of any control and incentive system."[23]

The logical conclusion is that service firms should devote great care to attracting and hiring the right candidates. Best Practice in Action 11-2 shows how Southwest Airlines takes great care in hiring staff with the right attitude and with a personality that fits the Southwest culture.

Identify the Best Candidates

Excellent service firms use a number of ways to identify the best candidates in their applicant pool. They observe behavior, conduct personality tests, interview applicants, and provide applicants with a realistic job preview.[24]

Observe Behavior Make a decision to hire based on behavior you observe, not words you hear. As John Wooden said: "Show me what you can do, don't tell me what you can do. Too often, the big talkers are the little doers."[25] Behavior can be observed directly or indirectly by using behavioral simulations or assessment center tests that use standardized situations in which applicants can be observed to see whether they display the kind of behaviors the firm's clients would expect. As described in Best Practice in Action 11-2, Southwest Airlines observes applicants closely during a day of interviews. Also, past behavior is the best predictor of future behavior: Hire the person who has won awards for excellent service, received many complimentary letters, and has great references from past employers.

Conduct Personality Tests Use personality tests that are relevant for a particular job. For example, willingness to treat customers and colleagues with courtesy, consideration and tact, perceptiveness of customer needs, and ability to communicate accurately and pleasantly are traits that can be measured. Hiring decisions based on such tests tend to be accurate.

For example, the Ritz-Carlton Hotels Group has been using personality profiles on all job applicants for the past 10 years. Staff members are selected for their natural predisposition for working in a service context. Inherent traits, such as a ready smile, a willingness to help others, and an affinity for multitasking, enable people to go beyond learned skills. An applicant to Ritz-Carlton shared about her experience of going through the personality test for a job as a junior-level concierge at the Ritz-Carlton Millenia Singapore. Her best advice: Tell the truth. These are experts; they will know if you are lying. "On the big day, they asked if I liked helping people, if I was an organized person and if I liked to smile a lot. Yes, yes and yes, I said. But I had to support it with real life examples. This, at times, felt rather intrusive. To answer the first question for instance, I had to say a bit about the person I had helped—why she needed help, for example. The test forced me to recall even insignificant things I had done, like learning how to say hello in different languages, which helped to get a fix on my character."[26]

Apart from intensive interview-based psychological tests, cost-effective Internet-based testing kits are available. Here, applicants enter their test responses to a Web-based questionnaire, and the prospective employer receives the analysis, the suitability of the candidate, and a hiring recommendation. (For a leading global supplier of such

BEST PRACTICE IN ACTION 11-2

HIRING AT SOUTHWEST AIRLINES

Southwest hires people with the right attitude and with personality that matches its corporate personality. Humor is the key. Herb Kelleher, Southwest's legendary former CEO and now Chairman of the Board of Southwest Airlines, said, "I want flying to be a helluva lot of fun! We look for attitudes; people with a sense of humor who don't take themselves too seriously. We'll train you on whatever it is you have to do, but the one thing Southwest cannot change in people is inherent attitudes." Southwest has one fundamental, consistent principle: Hire people with the right spirit. Southwest looks for people with other-oriented, outgoing personalities: individuals who become part of an extended family of people who work hard and have fun at the same time.

Southwest's painstaking approach to interviewing continues to evolve in light of experience. It is perhaps at its most innovative in the selection of flight attendants. A daylong visit to the company usually begins with applicants gathered in a group. Recruiters watch how well they interact with one another (another chance for such observation will come at lunchtime).

Then comes a series of personal interviews. Each candidate has three one-on-one "behavioral-type" interviews during the course of the day. Based on input from supervisors and peers in a given job category, interviewers target 8 to 10 dimensions for each position. For a flight attendant, these dimensions might include a willingness to take initiative, compassion, flexibility, sensitivity to people, sincerity, a customer service orientation, and a predisposition to be a team player. Even humor is being "tested." Prospective employees are typically asked, "Tell me how you recently used your sense of humor in a work environment. Tell me how you have used humor to defuse a difficult situation."

Southwest describes the ideal interview as "a conversation," in which the goal is to make candidates comfortable. "The first interview of the day tends to be a bit stiff, the second is more comfortable, and by the third they tell us a whole lot more. It's really hard to fake it under those circumstances." The three interviewers don't discuss candidates during the day but compare notes afterward, to reduce the risk of bias.

To help select people with the right attitude, Southwest invites supervisors and peers (with whom future candidates will be working) to participate in the in-depth interviewing and selection process. In this way, existing employees buy into the recruitment process and feel a sense of responsibility for mentoring new recruits and helping them to become successful in the job (rather than wondering, as an interviewer put it, "who hired this turkey?"). More unusually, Southwest invites its own frequent flyers to participate in the initial interviews for flight attendants and to tell the candidates what they, the passengers, value.

The interviewing team asks a group of potential employees to prepare a five-minute presentation about themselves and gives them plenty of time to prepare. As the presentations are delivered, the interviewers watch not only the speakers but also the audience to see which applicants are using their time to work on their own presentations and which are enthusiastically cheering on and supporting their potential coworkers. Unselfish people who will support their teammates are the ones who catch Southwest's eyes, not the applicants who are tempted to polish their own presentations while others are speaking.

By hiring the right attitude, the company is able to foster the so-called Southwest spirit—an intangible quality in people that causes them to want to do whatever it takes and to want to go that extra mile whenever they need to.

Source: Kevin and Jackie Freiberg, *Nuts! Southwest Airlines' Crazy Recipe for Business and Personal Success* (New York: Broadway Books, 1997), 64–69, and Christopher Lovelock, *Product Plus* (New York: McGraw-Hill 1994), 323–326.

tests, see the SHL Group at *www.shlgroup.com.*) Also, people differ in their disposition to be generally positive and happy versus generally negative and unhappy.[27] It is better to hire upbeat and happy people, because customers report higher satisfaction when being served by more satisfied staff.[28]

Conduct Multiple, Structured Interviews To improve hiring decisions, successful recruiters like to conduct structured interviews built around job requirements and to use more than one interviewer. People tend to be more careful in their judgments when they know that another individual is also evaluating the same applicant. Another advantage of using two or more interviewers is that it reduces the risk of "similar to me" biases (we all like people who are similar to ourselves).

Give Applicants a Realistic Preview of the Job[29] During the recruitment process, service companies should let the candidates know the reality of the job. This gives candidates a chance to "try on the job" and assess whether it's a fit. At the same time, recruiters can observe how candidates respond to the job's realities. This is a way for the company to let some candidates self-select themselves out if they find the job unsuitable. At the same time, the company can manage the new employee's expectations of their job. Many service companies adopt this approach. For example, a chain of French bakery cafes, Au Bon Pain, lets applicants work for two paid days in a café prior to the final selection interview. Here, managers can observe candidates in action, and candidates can assess whether they like the job and the work environment.[30]

Train Service Employees Actively

When a firm has good people, investments in training can yield outstanding results. Service champions show a strong commitment in words, dollars, and action to training. As Benjamin Schneider and David Bowen put it: "The combination of attracting a diverse and competent applicant pool, utilizing effective techniques for hiring the most appropriate people from that pool, and then training the heck out of them would be gangbusters in any market."[31] Service employees need to learn the following:

- *The organizational culture, purpose and strategy.* Start strong with new hires, focus on getting emotional commitment to the firm's core strategy, and promote core values, such as commitment to service excellence, responsiveness, team spirit, and mutual respect, honesty, and integrity. Use managers to teach and focus on "what," "why," and "how" rather than on the specifics of the job.[32] For example, new recruits at Disneyland attend the "Disney University Orientation." It starts with a detailed discussion of the company history and philosophy, the service standards expected of cast members, and a comprehensive tour of Disneyland's operations.[33]
- *Interpersonal and technical skills.* Interpersonal skills tend to be generic across service jobs and include visual communications skills, such as making eye contact, attentive listening, body language, and even facial expressions. Technical skills encompass all the required knowledge related to processes (e.g., how to handle a merchandized return), machines (e.g., how to operate the terminal or cash machine), and rules and regulations related to customer service processes. Both technical and interpersonal skills are *necessary*, but neither alone is *sufficient* for optimal job performance.[34]
- *Product/service knowledge.* Product knowledge is a key aspect of service quality. Staff members must be able to explain product features effectively and also position the product correctly. For instance, in Best Practice in Action 11-3, Jennifer

BEST PRACTICE IN ACTION 11-3

COACHING AT DIAL-A-MATTRESS

Coaching is a common method services leaders use to train and develop staff. Dial-A-Mattress's Jennifer Grassano is a bedding consultant (BC) for three days a week and a coach to other BCs for one day a week. She focuses on staff members whose productivity and sales performance are slumping.

Her first step is to listen in on the BCs' telephone calls with customers. She will listen for about an hour and take detailed notes on each call. The BCs understand that their calls may be monitored, but they receive no advance notice, as that would defeat the purpose.

Next, she conducts a coaching session with that staff member, reviewing the person's strengths and areas for improvements. Grassano knows how difficult it is to maintain a high energy level and convey enthusiasm when handling some 60 calls per shift. She likes to suggest new tactics and phrasings "to spark up their presentation." One BC was not responding effectively when customers asked why one mattress was more expensive than another. Here, she stressed the need to paint pictures in the customer's mind:

Customers are at our mercy when buying bedding. They don't know the difference between one coil system and another. It is just like buying a carburetor for my car. I don't even know what a carburetor looks like. We have to use very descriptive words to help bedding customers make the decision that is right for them. Tell the customer that the more costly mattress has richer, finer padding with a blend of silk and wool. Don't just say the mattress has more layers of padding.

About two months after the initial coaching session, Grassano conducts a follow-up monitoring session with that BC. She then compares the BC's performance before and after the coaching session to assess the effectiveness of the training.

Grassano's experience and productivity as a BC give her the credibility as a coach. "If I am not doing well as a BC, then who am I to be a coach? I have to lead by example. I would be much less effective if I was a full-time trainer." She clearly relishes the opportunity to share her knowledge and pass on her craft.

Source: Leonard L. Berry, *Discovering the Soul of Service—The Nine Drivers of Sustainable Business Success* (New York: The Free Press, 1999), 171–172.

Grassano of Dial-A-Mattress coaches individual staff members on how to paint pictures in the customer's mind.

Of course, training has to result in tangible changes in behavior. If staff members do not apply what they have learned, the investment is wasted. Learning is not only about becoming smarter but also about changing behaviors and improving decision making. To achieve this, practice and reinforcement are needed. The role of supervisors in following up on learning objectives is crucial for achieving learning.

Training and learning professionalize the frontline staff and moves them away from the common (self)-image of being in low-end jobs. Well-trained employees are and feel like professionals. A waiter, who knows about food, cooking, wines, dining etiquette, and how to effectively interact with customers (even complaining ones), feels professional, has higher self-esteem, and is respected by his customers. Training is therefore extremely effective in reducing person/role stress.

Empower the Front Line

Virtually all breakthrough service firms have legendary stories of employees who recovered failed service transactions or walked the extra mile to make a customer's day or avoid some kind of disaster for that client (as an example, see Best Practice in Action 11-4).[35] To allow this to happen, employees have to be empowered. Nordstrom trains and trusts its employees to do the right thing and empowers them to do so. Its

BEST PRACTICE IN ACTION 11-4

EMPOWERMENT AT NORDSTROM

Van Mensah, a men's apparel sales associate at Nordstrom, received a disturbing letter from one of his loyal customers. The gentleman had purchased some $2,000 worth of shirts and ties from Mensah and mistakenly washed the shirts in hot water. They all shrank. He was writing to ask Mensah's professional advice on how he should deal with his predicament. (The gentleman did not complain and readily conceded his mistake.)

Mensah immediately called the customer and offered to replace those shirts with new ones at no charge. He asked the customer to mail the other shirts back to Nordstrom at Nordstrom's expense. "I didn't have to ask for anyone's permission to do what I did for that customer," said Mensah. "Nordstrom would rather leave it up to me to decide what's best."

Middlemas, a Nordstrom's veteran, said to employees, "You will never be criticized for doing too much for a customer, you will only be criticized for doing too little. If you're ever in doubt as to what to do in a situation, always make a decision that favors the customer before the company." Nordtrom's Employee Handbook confirms this:

Welcome to Nordstrom

We're glad to have you with our Company.
Our number one goal is to provide outstanding customer service.
Set both your personal and professional goals high.
We have great confidence in your ability to achieve them.
Nordstrom Rules:
Rule #1: Use your good judgment in all situations.
There will be no additional rules.
Please feel free to ask your department manager, store manager, or division general manager any question at any time.

Source: Robert Spector and Patrick D. McCarthy, *The Nordstrom Way* (New York: John Wiley, 2000), 15–16, 95.

employee handbook has only one rule: "Use good judgment in all situations." Employee self-direction has become increasingly important, especially in service firms, because frontline staff frequently operate on their own, face to face with their customers, and it tends to be difficult for managers to closely monitor their behavior.[36] Research also linked that high empowerment to higher customer satisfaction.[37]

For many services, providing employees with greater discretion (and training in how to use their judgment) can enable them to provide superior service on the spot. They do not have to take time to seek permission from supervisors. Empowerment looks to frontline staff to find solutions to service problems and to make appropriate decisions about customizing service delivery. Success is dependent on what is sometimes called *enablement*: giving service workers the training, tools, and resources they need to take on these new responsibilities.

Is Empowerment Always Appropriate? Advocates claim that the empowerment approach is more likely to yield motivated employees and satisfied customers than is the "production-line" alternative, in which management designs a relatively standardized system and expects workers to execute tasks within narrow guidelines.

However, David Bowen and Edward Lawler suggest that different situations may require different solutions, declaring that "both the empowerment and production-line approaches have their advantages . . . and . . . each fits certain situations. The key is to choose the management approach that best meets the needs of both employees and customers."[38] Not all employees are necessarily eager to be empowered, and many employees do not seek personal growth within their jobs and would prefer to work to specific directions than to use their own initiative. Research has shown that a strategy of empowerment is most likely to be appropriate when most of the following factors are present within the organization and its environment:

- The firm's business strategy is based on competitive differentiation and on offering personalized, customized service.
- The approach to customers is based on extended relationships rather than on short-term transactions.
- The organization uses technologies that are complex and nonroutine.
- The business environment is unpredictable, and surprises are to be expected.
- Existing managers are comfortable with letting employees work independently for the benefit of both the organization and its customers.
- Employees have a strong need to grow and deepen their skills in the work environment, are interested in working with others, and have good interpersonal and group process skills.

Bowen and Lawler also warn against being seduced into too great a focus on service recovery—systematic efforts to correct a problem and retain a customer's goodwill—if it is at the expense of service delivery reliability, noting: "It is possible to confuse good service with inspiring stories about empowered employees excelling at the art of recovery."[39] Moreover, Chris Argyris warns that many employees have become cynical about the gap between the myth and reality of empowerment. Many of them feel that most corporate talk about empowerment is lip service. Many executives claim to be empowering their employees, but the latter find that they are either second-guessed or left out in the cold on big decisions.[40]

Control versus Involvement The production-line approach to managing people is based on the well-established "control" model of organization design and management. There are clearly defined roles, top-down control systems, hierarchical pyramid structures, and an assumption that the management knows best. Empowerment, by contrast, is based on the "involvement," or "commitment," model, which assumes that most employees can make good decisions and produce good ideas for operating the business if they are properly socialized, trained, and informed. This model also assumes that employees can be internally motivated to perform effectively and that they are capable of self-control and self-direction. Information technology allows employees to telecommute, working from their homes while linked to a corporate network. New approaches to management and team building are needed for such approaches to succeed.

Schneider and Bowen emphasize that "empowerment isn't just the act of 'setting the frontline free' or 'throwing away the policy manuals.' It requires systematically redistributing four key ingredients throughout the organization, from the top downwards."[41] The four features are

1. *Power* to make decisions that influence work procedures and organizational direction (e.g., through quality circles and self-managing teams)
2. *Information* about organizational performance (e.g., operating results and measures of competitive performance)
3. *Rewards* based on organizational performance (e.g., bonuses, profit sharing, and stock options)
4. *Knowledge* that enables employees to understand and contribute to organizational performance (e.g., problem-solving skills)

In the control model, these four features are concentrated at the top of the organization; in the involvement model, these features are pushed down through the organization.

Levels of Employee Involvement The empowerment and production-line approaches are at opposite ends of a spectrum that reflects increasing levels of employee involvement as additional knowledge, information, power, and rewards are pushed down to the front line. Empowerment can take place at several levels:

- *Suggestion involvement* empowers employees to make recommendations through formalized programs. McDonald's, often portrayed as an archetype of the production-line approach, listens closely to its front line. Innovations, ranging from Egg McMuffin to methods of wrapping burgers without leaving a thumbprint on the bun, were invented by employees.
- *Job involvement* represents a dramatic opening up of job content. Jobs are redesigned to allow employees to use a wider array of skills. In complex service organizations, such as airlines and hospitals, where individual employees cannot offer all facets of a service, job involvement is often accomplished through use of teams. To cope with the added demands accompanying this form of empowerment, employees require training, and supervisors need to be reoriented from directing the group to facilitating its performance in supportive ways.
- *High involvement* gives even the lowest-level employees a sense of involvement in the company's overall performance. Information is shared. Employees develop skills in teamwork, problem solving, and business operations and participate in work-unit management decisions. There is profit sharing and often employee ownership of stock or options in the business.

Southwest Airlines is an example of a high-involvement company, promoting common sense and flexibility. The company trusts its employees and gives them the latitude, discretion, and authority they need to do their jobs. Southwest has eliminated inflexible work rules and rigid job descriptions so its people can assume ownership for getting the job done and getting the planes out on time, regardless of whose "official" responsibility it is. This gives employees the flexibility to help one another when needed. Employees adopt a "whatever it takes" mentality.

Southwest mechanics and pilots have the freedom and latitude to help ramp agents load bags. When a flight is running late because of weather, it's not uncommon to see pilots helping customers in wheelchairs board the plane, helping the operations agents take boarding passes, or helping the flight attendants clean up the cabin between flights. All these actions are their way of adapting to the situation and taking ownership for getting customers on board more quickly. In addition, Southwest employees apply common sense, not rules, when it's in the best interests of the customer.

Rod Jones, assistant chief pilot, recalls a captain who left the gate with a senior citizen who had boarded the wrong plane. The customer was confused and very upset. Southwest asks pilots not to go back to the gate with an incorrectly boarded customer. In this case, the captain was concerned about this individual's well-being. "So, he adapted to the situation." says Jones. "He came back in to the gate, deplaned the customer, pushed back out, and gave us an irregularity report. Even though he broke the rules, he used his judgment and did what he thought was best. And we said, 'Attaboy!' "[42]

Build High-Performance Service Delivery Teams

The nature of many services requires people to work in teams, often across functions, if they want to offer seamless customer service processes. Traditionally, many firms were organized by functional structures, with one department in charge of consulting and selling (e.g., selling a mobile phone with a subscription contract), for example, and another in charge of customer service (e.g., activation of value-added services, changes of subscription plans), and a third, for billing. This type of structure prevents internal service teams from viewing end customers as their own and can also mean poorer teamwork across functions, slower service, and more errors between functions. When customers have service problems, they easily fall between the cracks.

Empirical research has confirmed that frontline staff themselves regard a lack of interdepartmental support as an important factor in hindering them from satisfying their customers.[43] Because of these problems, we increasingly need cross-functional teams that serve customers from start to finish.

The Power of Teamwork in Services Jon Katzenbach and Douglas Smith define a team as "a small number of people with complementary skills who are committed to a common purpose, set of performance goals, and approach for which they hold themselves mutually accountable."[44] Teams, training, and empowerment go hand in hand. Teams facilitate communication between team members and the sharing of knowledge. By operating like a small, independent unit, service teams take on more responsibility and require less supervision than do more traditional, functionally organized customer service units. Furthermore, teams often set higher performance targets for themselves than supervisors would set. Pressure to perform is high within a good team.[45]

Best Practice in Action 11-5 shows how Singapore Airlines not only uses teams to provide emotional support and to mentor its cabin crew but also how the company effectively assesses, rewards, and promotes staff.

Some academics even feel that there is too much emphasis on hiring "individual stars," particularly in the United States, which places high importance on the ability and motivation of the individual as contrasted with organizational or team ability and motivation. Charles O'Reilly and Jeffrey Pfeffer, two Stanford professors, emphasize

BEST PRACTICE IN ACTION 11-5

SINGAPORE AIRLINE'S TEAM CONCEPT

SIA works hard to create esprit de corps among its cabin crew. This is made more difficult by the fact that many crew members are scattered around the world. SIA's answer is the "team concept."

Choo Poh Leong, Senior Manager Cabin Crew Performance, explained:

> In order to effectively manage our 6,600 crew, we divide them into teams, small units, with a team leader in charge of about 13 people. We will roster them to fly together as much as we can. Flying together, as a unit, allows them to build up camaraderie, and crew members feel like they are part of a team, not just a member. The team leader will get to know them well, their strengths and weaknesses, and will become their mentor and their counsel, and someone to whom they can turn if they need help or advice. The "check trainers" oversee 12 or 13 teams and fly with them whenever possible, not only to inspect their performance, but also to help their team develop.
>
> The interaction within each of the teams is very strong. As a result, when a team leader does a staff appraisal they really know the staff. You would be amazed how meticulous and detailed each staff record is. So, in this way, we have good control, and through the control, we can ensure that the crew delivers the promise. They know that they're being constantly monitored and so they deliver. If there are problems, we will know about them and we can send them for re-training. Those who are good will be selected for promotion.

Source: Jochen Wirtz and Robert Johnston, "Singapore Airlines: What It Takes to Sustain Service Excellence—A Senior Management Perspective," *Managing Service Quality* 13, no. 1 (2003): 10–19.

that how people work in teams is often as important as how good people are and that stars can be outperformed by others through superior teamwork.[46]

Team members take great pride at Custom Research Inc. (CRI), a highly progressive and successful marketing research firm. How true team members feel about working in CRI teams is illustrated in the following quotes:[47]

- "I like being on the team. You feel like you belong. Everyone knows what's going on."
- "We take ownership. Everyone accepts responsibility and jumps in to help."
- "When a client needs something in an hour, we work together to solve the problem."
- "There are no slugs. Everyone pulls their weight."

Creating Successful Service Delivery Teams[48] It's not easy to make teams function well. If people are not prepared for teamwork and if the team structure is not set up right, a firm risks having initially enthusiastic volunteers who lack the competencies that teamwork requires. The skills needed include not only cooperation, listening to others, coaching, and encouraging one another but also an understanding of how to air differences, tell one another hard truths, and ask tough questions. All these require training.

Management also needs to set up a structure that will steer the teams toward success. A good example is American Express Latin America, which developed the following rules for making its teams work.

- Each team has an "owner": a person who owns the team's problems.
- Each team has a leader who monitors team progress and team process. Team leaders are selected for their strong business knowledge and people skills.
- Each team has a quality facilitator: someone who knows how to make teams work and who can remove barriers to progress and train others to work together effectively.[49]

Motivate and Energize People

Once a firm has hired the right people, trained them well, empowered them, and organized them in effective service delivery teams, how can it ensure that they will deliver service excellence?[50] Staff performance is a function of ability and motivation. Hiring, training, empowerment, and teams give you able people, and reward systems are the key to motivation. Service staff must get the message that providing quality service holds the key for being rewarded. Motivating and rewarding strong service performers are two of the most effective ways of retaining them. Staff pick up quickly whether those who get promoted are the truly outstanding service providers and whether those who get fired are those who do not deliver at the customer level.

A major way service businesses fail is that they do not use the full range of available rewards effectively. Many firms think in terms of money as reward, but it does not pass the test of an effective reward. Receiving a fair salary is a hygiene factor rather than a motivating factor. Paying more than what is seen as fair has only short-term motivating effects and wears off quickly. Bonuses, which are contingent on performance, on the other hand, have to be earned again and again and therefore tend to be more lasting in their effectiveness. Other, more lasting rewards are the job content itself, recognition and feedback, and goal accomplishment.

Job Content People are motivated and satisfied simply by knowing that they are doing a good job. They feel good about themselves and like to reinforce that feeling. This is true especially if the job also offers a variety of activities, requires the completion of "whole" and identifiable pieces of work, is seen as significant in the sense that it has an impact on the lives of others, comes with autonomy, and has a source of direct and clear feedback about how well employees did their work (e.g., grateful customers or sales).

Feedback and Recognition Humans are social beings and derive a sense of identity and belonging to an organization from the recognition and feedback they receive from the people around them: their customers, colleagues, and bosses. If employees are being recognized and thanked for service excellence, they will desire to deliver it. (We discuss how to measure and use customer feedback in detail in Chapter 13.)

Goal Accomplishment Goals focus people's energy. Goals that are specific, difficult but attainable, and accepted by the staff are strong motivators and yield higher performance than do no goals or vague goals (e.g., "do your best") or goals that are impossible to achieve.[51] In short, goals are effective motivators.

The following are important points to note for effective goal setting.[52]

- Achieving goals is a reward in itself when those goals are seen as important.
- Goal accomplishment can be used as a basis for giving rewards, including pay, feedback, and recognition. Feedback and recognition from peers can be given sooner, more cheaply, and more effectively than pay and have the additional benefit of gratifying an employee's self-esteem.
- Service employee goals that are specific and difficult must be set publicly to be accepted. Although goals must be specific, they can be something intangible, such as improved employee courtesy ratings.
- Progress reports about goal accomplishment (feedback) and goal accomplishment itself must be public events (recognition) if they are to gratify employees' esteem need.
- It is mostly unnecessary to specify the means to achieve goals. Feedback on progress while pursuing the goal serves as a corrective function. As long as the goal is specific, difficult but achievable, and accepted, goal pursuit will result in goal accomplishment, even in the absence of other rewards.

Successful firms recognize that people issues are complex (Figure 11-5). Charles O'Reilly and Jeffrey Pfeffer conducted in-depth research on why some companies can succeed over long periods of time in highly competitive industries without having the usual sources of competitive advantage, such as barriers of entry or proprietary technology. They concluded that these firms did not succeed by winning the war for talent (although these firms were hiring extremely carefully for fit) "but by fully using the talent and unlocking the motivation of the people" they already had in their organizations.[53]

The Role of Unions

Unions and service excellence do not seem to gel. The power of organized labor is widely cited as an excuse for not adopting new approaches in both service and manufacturing businesses. "We'd never get it past the unions," managers say, wringing their hands and muttering darkly about restrictive work practices. Unions are often portrayed as villains in the press, especially when high-profile strikes inconvenience millions. Many managers seem to be rather antagonistic toward unions.

FIGURE 11-5 "People issues are complex. Managing them doesn't have to be." Hewitt Associates, a professional firm delivering human capital management services, captures employees' complexity in its advertising

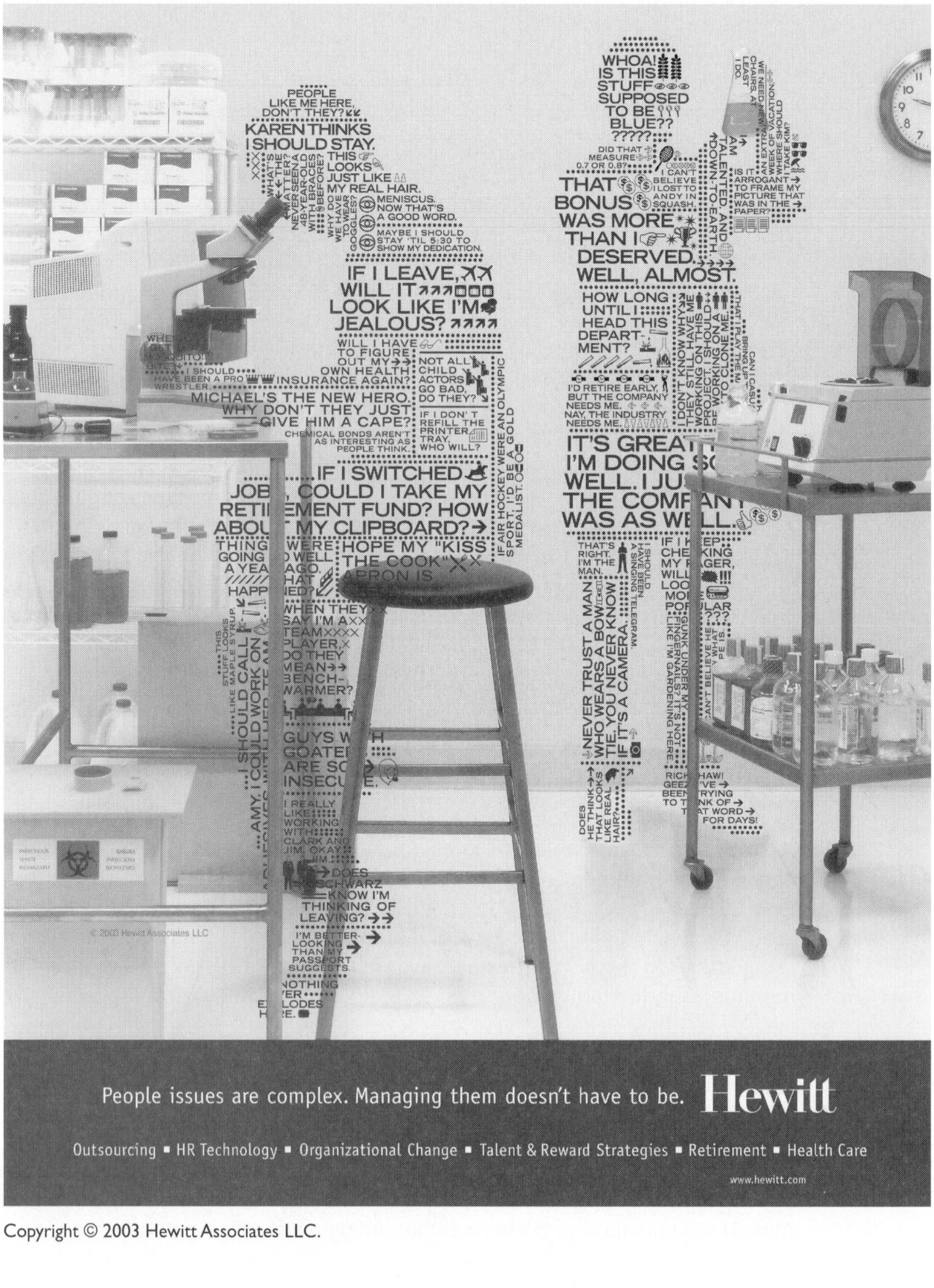

Jeffrey Pfeffer has observed wryly that "the subject of unions and collective bargaining is . . . one that causes otherwise sensible people to lose their objectivity."[54] He urges a pragmatic approach to this issue, emphasizing that "the effects of unions depend very much on what *management* does." The higher wages, lower turnover, clearly established grievance procedures and improved working conditions often found in highly unionized organizations will yield positive benefits in a well-managed service organization.

Contrary to this negative view, many of the world's most successful service businesses are, in fact, highly unionized. The presence of unions in a service company is not an automatic barrier to high performance and innovation unless there is a long history of mistrust, acrimonious relationships, and confrontation. However, management consultation and negotiation with union representatives are essential if employees are to accept new ideas (conditions that are equally valid in nonunionized firms). The challenge is to work jointly with unions to create a climate for service.

SERVICE LEADERSHIP AND CULTURE

So far, we have discussed the key strategies that help to move an organization toward service excellence. However, to truly get there, we need a strong culture that is continuously reinforced and developed by the firm's management. A "charismatic leadership," also called transformational leadership, fundamentally changes the values, goals, and aspirations of the front line to be consistent with the firm's. Here, staff are more likely to perform their best and show performance "above and beyond the call of duty," because it is consistent with their own values, beliefs, and attitudes.[55]

Similarly, Leonard Berry advocates a value-driven leadership that inspires and guides service providers. Leadership should bring out the passion for serving and tap the creativity of service providers, nourish their energy and commitment, and give them a fulfilled working life. Among the core values Berry found in excellent service firms were excellence, innovation, joy, teamwork, respect, integrity, and social profit.[56] These values are part of the firm's culture. A service culture can be defined as

- Shared perceptions of *what* is important in an organization
- Shared values and beliefs about *why* those things are important[57]

Employees rely heavily on their perceptions of what is important by their perceptions of what the company and their leaders do, not so much what they say. Employees gain their understanding of what is important through the daily experiences they have with the firm's human resource, operations, and marketing practices and procedures.

In strong service culture, the entire organization focuses on the front line and understands that it is the lifeline of the business. The organization understands that the revenues for today and tomorrow are driven largely by what happens at the service encounter. Figure 11-6 shows the inverted pyramid, which highlights the importance of the front line and shows that the role of top management and middle management is to support the frontline staff in their task of delivering service excellence to their customers.

In firms with a passion for service, top management shows by its actions that what happens at the front line is crucially important, by being informed and actively involved. Top managers achieve this by regularly talking to and working with frontline staff and customers. Many spend significant amounts of time at the front line, serving customers. For example, Disney World's management spends two weeks every year in frontline staff jobs, such as sweeping streets, selling ice cream, or being

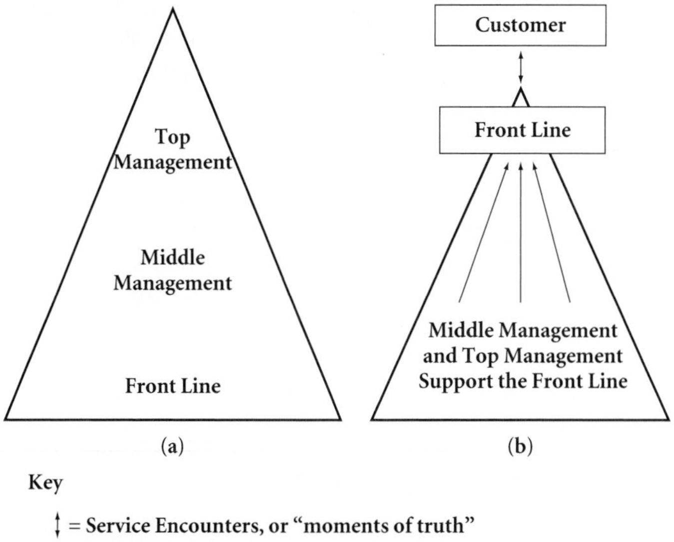

FIGURE 11-6 (a) The Traditional Organizational Pyramid; (b) The Inverted Pyramid with a Customer and Frontline Focus

ride attendants, to gain a better appreciation and understanding of what happens on the ground.[58]

Service leaders are interested not only in the big picture but also on the details of service; they see opportunities in nuances that competitors might consider trivial, and they believe that the way the firm handles little things sets the tone for how it handles everything else.

Apart from a strong leadership that focuses on the front line, it takes a strong communications effort to shape the culture and get the message to the troops. Service leaders use multiple tools to build their service culture, ranging from training to core principles to company events and celebrations.

For example, Ritz-Carlton translated the key product and service requirements of its customers into the Ritz-Carlton Gold Standards, which include a credo, motto, three steps of service, and 20 "Ritz-Carlton Basics" (see Best Practice in Action 11-6). Tim Kirkpatrick, Director of Training and Development of Ritz-Carlton's Boston Common Hotel said, "The Gold Standards are part of our uniform, just like your name tag. But remember, it's just a laminated card until you put it into action."[59] To reinforce these standards, every morning briefing includes a discussion of one of the standards. The aim of rotating these discussions is to keep the Ritz-Carlton philosophy at the center of its employees' minds.

Another great example of a firm with a strong culture is Southwest Airlines, which uses continuously new and creative ways to strengthen its culture. Southwest's Culture Committee members are zealots when it comes to the continuation of Southwest's family feel. The committee represents everyone from flight attendants and reservationists to top executives. "The Culture Committee is not made up of Big Shots; it is a committee of Big Hearts."[60] Culture Committee members are not out to gain power. They use the power of the Southwest spirit to better connect people to the cultural foundations of the company. The committee works behind the scenes to

BEST PRACTICE IN ACTION 11-6

RITZ-CARLTON'S GOLD STANDARDS

THREE STEPS OF SERVICE

1

A warm and sincere greeting. Use the guest name, if and when possible.

2

Anticipation and compliance with guest needs.

3

Fond farewell. Give them a warm good-bye and use their names, if and when possible.

"We Are Ladies and Gentlemen Serving Ladies and Gentlemen"

THE EMPLOYEE PROMISE

At The Ritz-Carlton, our Ladies and Gentlemen are the most important resource in our service commitment to our guests.

By applying the principles of trust, honesty, respect, integrity and commitment, we nurture and maximize talent to the benefit of each individual and the company.

The Ritz-Carlton fosters a work environment where diversity is valued, quality of life is enhanced, individual aspirations are fulfilled, and The Ritz-Carlton mystique is strengthened.

THE RITZ-CARLTON®

CREDO

The Ritz-Carlton Hotel is a place where the genuine care and comfort of our guests is our highest mission.

We pledge to provide the finest personal service and facilities for our guests who will always enjoy a warm, relaxed yet refined ambience.

The Ritz-Carlton experience enlivens the senses, instills well-being, and fulfills even the unexpressed wishes and needs of our guests.

THE RITZ-CARLTON® BASICS

1. The Credo is the principal belief of our Company. It must be known, owned and energized by all.
2. Our Motto is: "We Are Ladies and Gentlemen serving Ladies and Gentlemen." As service professionals, we treat our guests and each other with respect and dignity.
3. The Three Steps of Service are the foundation of Ritz-Carlton hospitality. These steps must be used in every interaction to ensure satisfaction, retention and loyalty.
4. The Employee Promise is the basis for our Ritz-Carlton work environment. It will be honored by all employees.
5. All employees will successfully complete annual Training Certification for their position.
6. Company objectives are communicated to all employees. It is everyone's responsibility to support them.
7. To create pride and joy in the workplace, all employees have the right to be involved in the planning of the work that affects them.
8. Each employee will continuously identify defects (M.R. B.I.V.) throughout the Hotel.
9. It is the responsibility of each employee to create a work environment of teamwork and lateral service so that the needs of our guests and each other are met.
10. Each employee is empowered. For example, when a guest has a problem or needs something special, you should break away from your regular duties to address and resolve the issue.
11. Uncompromising levels of cleanliness are the responsibility of every employee.
12. To provide the finest personal service for our guests, each employee is responsible for identifying and recording individual guest preferences.
13. Never lose a guest. Instant guest pacification is the responsibility of each employee. Whoever receives a complaint will own it, resolve it to the guest's satisfaction and record it.
14. "Smile – We are on stage." Always maintain positive eye contact. Use the proper vocabulary with our guests and each other. (Use words like – "Good Morning," "Certainly," "I'll be happy to" and "My pleasure.")
15. Be an ambassador of your Hotel in and outside of the workplace. Always speak positively. Communicate any concerns to the appropriate person.
16. Escort guests rather than pointing out directions to another area of the Hotel.
17. Use Ritz-Carlton telephone etiquette. Answer within three rings with a "smile." Use the guest's name when possible. When necessary, ask the caller "May I place you on hold?" Do not screen calls. Eliminate call transfers whenever possible. Adhere to voice mail standards.
18. Take pride in and care of your personal appearance. Everyone is responsible for conveying a professional image by adhering to Ritz-Carlton clothing and grooming standards.
19. Think safety first. Each employee is responsible for creating a safe, secure and accident free environment for all guests and each other. Be aware of all fire and safety emergency procedures and report any security risks immediately.
20. Protecting the assets of a Ritz-Carlton hotel is the responsibility of every employee. Conserve energy, properly maintain our Hotels and protect the environment.

Source: The Ritz-Carlton Hotel Company, LLC. Reprinted with permission.

foster Southwest's commitment to its core values. Following are examples of events held to reinforce Southwest's culture:

- *Walk a Mile in My Shoes.* This program helped Southwest employees gain an appreciation for other people's jobs. Employees were asked to visit a different department on their days off and to spend a minimum of six hours on the "walk." These participants were rewarded with not only transferable round-trip passes but also goodwill and increased morale.
- *A Day in the Field.* This activity is practiced throughout the company all year long. Barri Tucker, then a senior communications representative in the executive office, for example, once joined three flight attendants working a three-day trip. Tucker gained by experiencing the company from a new angle and hearing directly from customers. She was able to see how important it was for corporate headquarters to support Southwest's frontline employees.
- *Helping Hands.* Southwest sent out volunteers from around the system to lighten the load of employees in the cities where Southwest was in direct competition with United's Shuttle. This not only built momentum and strengthened the troops for the battle with United but also helped rekindle the fighting spirit of Southwest employees.[61]

Empirical research in the hotel industry shows that Southwest's management is right to walk the talk. In their study of 6,500 employees at 76 Holiday Inn hotels, Judi McLean Park and Tony Simons measured whether the hotel managers showed behavioral integrity, using measures such as "My manager delivers on promises" and "My manager practices what he preached." These statements were first correlated with employee responses to such questions as "I am proud to tell others I am part of this hotel" and "My coworkers go out of the way to accommodate guests' special requests" and then to revenues and profitability.

The results were stunning. They showed that behavioral integrity of a hotel's manager was highly correlated with employees' trust, commitment, and willingness to go the extra mile. Furthermore, of all manager behaviors measured, it was the single most important factor driving profitability. In fact, an increase of a mere 1.8 in a hotel's overall behavioral integrity score on a 5-point scale was associated with a 2.5 percent increase in revenue and a $250,000 increase in profits per year per hotel.[62]

A further discussion of this research and the factors that can undermine a manager's behavioral integrity can be found in the reading by Tony Simons, "The High Cost of Lost Trust," which appears on pages 346 to 347.

CONCLUSION

Successful service organizations are committed to effective management of human resources (HR). Figure 11-7 summarizes our main recommendations for successful HR strategies in service firms.

Successful HR strategies in services start with competing for talent by being the preferred employer, followed by careful hiring, painstaking training, empowering staff who then have the authority and self-confidence to use their own initiative in delivering service excellence. Successful HR strategies also involve effective use of service delivery teams, as well as energizing and motivating the front line with a full set of rewards: pay, satisfying job content, recognition and feedback, and goal accomplishment. Top

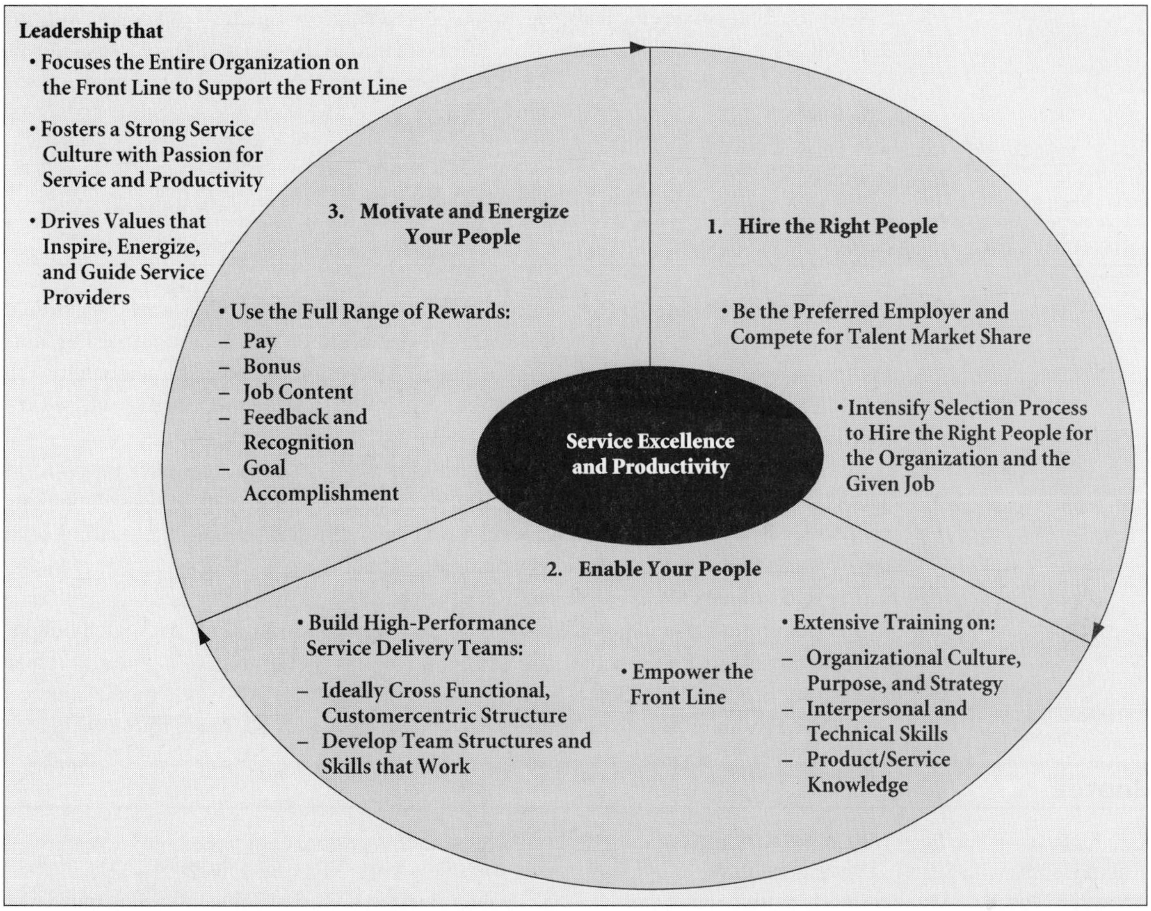

FIGURE 11-7 Wheel of Successful HR in Service Firms

and middle management continuously reinforce a strong culture that emphasizes service excellence and productivity. Employees understand and support the goals of an organization, and a value-driven leadership inspires and guides service providers and brings their passion for serving to the full and gives them a fulfilled working life.

The market and financial results can be phenomenal and often lead to a sustainable competitive advantage. It is probably more difficult to duplicate high-performance human assets than any other corporate resource.

Review Questions

1. Discuss the role service personnel play in creating or destroying customer loyalty.
2. What is emotional labor? Explain the ways in which it may cause stress for employees in specific jobs. Illustrate with suitable examples.
3. What are the key barriers for firms to break the cycle of failure and move into the cycle of success?
4. List five ways in which investment in hiring and selection, training, and ongoing motivation of employees will pay dividends in customer satisfaction for (a) a restaurant, (b) an airline, (c) a hospital, and (d) a consulting firm.

5. Identify the factors favoring a strategy of employee empowerment.
6. Define what is meant by the control and involvement models of management.
7. Identify the factors needed to make service teams successful in (a) an airline and (b) a restaurant.
8. How can a service firm build a strong service culture that emphasizes service excellence and productivity?

Application Exercises

1. A recruiting advertisement for airline cabin crew shows a picture of a small boy sitting in an airline seat and clutching a teddy bear. The headline reads: "His mom told him not to talk to strangers. So what's he having for lunch?" Describe the types of personalities that you think would be (a) attracted to apply for the job by that ad and (b) discouraged from applying.
2. Consider the following jobs: emergency ward nurse, bill collector, computer repair technician, supermarket cashier, dentist, flight attendant, kindergarten teacher, prosecuting attorney, server in a family restaurant, server in an expensive French restaurant, stockbroker, and undertaker. What types of emotions would you expect the people in each of those jobs to display to customers? What drives your expectations?
3. As a human resources manager, which issues do you see as most likely to create boundary-spanning problems for customer-contact employees in a customer call center at a major Internet service provider? Select four issues, and indicate how you would mediate between operations and marketing to create a satisfactory outcome for all three groups.

Endnotes

1. Liliana L. Bove and Lester W. Johnson, "Customer Relationships with Service Personnel: Do We Measure Closeness, Quality or Strength?" *Journal of Business Research* 54 (2001): 189–197.
2. Paul Hemp, "My Week as a Room-Service Waiter at the Ritz," *Harvard Business Review* (June 2002): 8–11.
3. James L. Heskett, Thomas O. Jones, Gary W. Loveman, W. Earl Sasser, Jr., and Leonard A. Schlesinger, "Putting the Service-Profit Chain to Work," *Harvard Business Review* (March–April 1994).
4. Benjamin Schneider and David E. Bowen, "The Service Organization: Human Resources Management Is Crucial," *Organizational Dynamics* 21, no. 4 (Spring 1993): 39–52.
5. David E. Bowen and Benjamin Schneider, "Boundary-Spanning Role Employees and the Service Encounter: Some Guidelines for Management and Research," in J. A. Czepiel, M. R. Solomon, and C. F. Surprenant, *The Service Encounter* (Lexington, MA: Lexington Books, 1985), 127–148.
6. Arlie R. Hochschild, *The Managed Heart: Commercialization of Human Feeling* (Berkeley: University of California Press, 1983).
7. Arlie Hochschild, "Emotional Labor in the Friendly Skies," *Psychology Today* (June 1982): 13–15. Cited in Valarie A. Zeithaml and Mary Jo Bitner, *Services Marketing: Integrating Customer Focus across the Firm* (New York: McGraw-Hill, 2003), 322.
8. Jochen Wirtz and Robert Johnston, "Singapore Airlines: What It Takes to Sustain Service Excellence—A Senior Management Perspective," *Managing Service Quality* 13, no. 1 (2003).
9. Call Centre News, "Call Centre Statistics," *www.callcenternews.com*, January 23, 2003.
10. "Call Centres—The Asians are Coming, Again," *The Economist* (April 28, 2001): 55.
11. Dan Moshavi and James R. Terbord, "The Job Satisfaction and Performance of Contingent and Regular Customer Service Representatives—A Human Capital Perspective," *International Journal of Service Industry Management* 13, no. 4 (2002): 333–347.
12. Knowsley, "Call Centres."
13. The terms "cycle of failure" and "cycle of success" were coined by Leonard L. Schlesinger and James L. Heskett, "Breaking the Cycle of Failure in Services," *Sloan Management Review* (Spring 1991): 17–28. The term "cycle of mediocrity" comes from Christopher H. Lovelock, "Managing Services: The Human Factor," in *Understanding Services Management*, ed. W. J. Glynn and J. G. Barnes (Chichester, UK: John Wiley, 1995), 228.

14. Lloyd C. Harris and Emmanuel Ogbonna, "Exploring Service Sabotage: The Antecedents, Types, and Consequences of Frontline, Deviant, Antiservice Behaviors," *Journal of Service Research* 4, no. 3 (2002): 163–183.
15. Leonard Schlesinger and James L. Heskett, "Breaking the Cycle of Failure," *Sloan Management Review* (Spring 1991): 17–28.
16. Reg Price and Roderick J. Brodie, "Transforming a Public Service Organization from Inside Out to Outside In," *Journal of Service Research* 4, no. 1 (2001): 50–59.
17. Mahn Hee Yoon, "The Effect of Work Climate on Critical Employee and Customer Outcomes," *International Journal of Service Industry Management* 12, no. 5 (2001): 500–521.
18. Jim Collins, "Turning Goals into Results: The Power of Catalytic Mechanisms," *Harvard Business Review* 77 (July–August 1999): 77.
19. Leonard L. Berry and A. Parasuraman, *Marketing Services—Competing Through Quality* (New York: The Free Press, 1991), 151–152.
20. Charles A. O'Reilly III and Jeffrey Pfeffer, *Hidden Value—How Great Companies Achieve Extraordinary Results with Ordinary People* (Boston: Harvard Business School Press, 2000), 1.
21. Robert Levering and Milton Moskowitz, *The 100 Best Companies to Work for in America* (New York: Currency/Doubleday, 1993), xvii.
22. Bill Fromm and Len Schlesinger, *The Real Heroes of Business* (New York: Currency Doubleday, 1994), 315–316.
23. Jim Collins, "Turning Goals into Results: The Power of Catalytic Mechanisms," *Harvard Business Review* (July–August 1999): 77.
24. This section was adapted from Benjamin Schneider and David E. Bowen, *Winning the Service Game* (Boston: Harvard Business School Press, 1995), 115–126.
25. John Wooden, *A Lifetime of Observations and Reflections On and Off the Court* (Chicago: Lincolnwood, 1997), 66.
26. Serene Goh, "All the Right Staff," and Arlina Arshad, "Putting Your Personality to the Test," *The Straits Times,* 5 September 2001.
27. Timothy A. Judge, "The Dispositional Perspective in Human Resources Research," in *Research in Personnel and Human Resources Management*, 10th ed., Ken Rowland and Gerald Ferris (Greenwich, CT: JAI Press, 1992), 31–72.
28. For a review of this literature, see Benjamin Schneider, "Service Quality and Profits: Can You Have Your Cake and Eat It, Too?" *Human Resource Planning* 14, no. 2 (1991): 151–157.
29. This section was adapted from Leonard L. Berry, *On Great Service—A Framework for Action* (New York: The Free Press, 1995), 181–182.
30. Schlesinger and Heskett, "Breaking the Cycle of Failure," 26.
31. Schneider and Bowen, *Winning the Service Game*, 131.
32. Leonard L. Berry, *Discovering the Soul of Service—The Nine Drivers of Sustainable Business Success* (New York: The Free Press, 1999), 161.
33. Schneider and Bowen, *Winning the Service Game,* 138–139.
34. David A. Tansik, "Managing Human Resource Issues for High Contact Service Personnel," in *Service Management Effectiveness*, ed. D. E. Bowen, R. B. Chase, T. G. Cummings, and Associates (San Francisco: Jossey-Bass, 1990), 152–176.
35. Parts of this section are based on David E. Bowen, and Edward E. Lawler, III, "The Empowerment of Service Workers: What, Why, How and When," *Sloan Management Review* (Spring 1992): 32–39.
36. Dana Yagil, "The Relationship of Customer Satisfaction and Service Workers' Perceived Control—Examination of Three Models," *International Journal of Service Industry Management* 13, no. 4 (2002): 382–398.
37. Graham L. Bradley and Beverley A. Sparks, "Customer Reactions to Staff Empowerment: Mediators and Moderators," *Journal of Applied Social Psychology* 30, no. 5 (2000): 991–1012.
38. Bowen and Lawler, "The Empowerment of Service Workers," 31–39.
39. Ibid.
40. Chris Argyris, "Empowerment: The Emperor's New Clothes," *Harvard Business Review* (May–June, 1998): 98–106.
41. Schneider and Bowen, *Winning the Service Game,* 250.
42. This paragraph is based on Kevin Freiberg and Jackie Freiberg, *Nuts! Southwest Airlines' Crazy Recipe for Business and Personal Success* (New York: Broadway Books, 1997), 87–88.
43. Andrew Sergeant and Stephen Frenkel, "When Do Customer Contact Employees Satisfy Customers?" *Journal of Service Research* 3, no. 1 (August 2000): 18–34.
44. Jon R. Katzenbach and Douglas K. Smith, "The Discipline of Teams," *Harvard Business Review* (March–April, 1993): 112.
45. Leonard L. Berry, *On Great Service*, 131.
46. Charles A. O'Reilly III and Jeffrey Pfeffer, *Hidden Value*, 9.
47. Leonard L. Berry, *Discovering the Soul of Service*, 189.
48. This section is based on Schneider and Bowen, *Winning the Service Game*, 141; and Leonard L. Berry, *On Great Service*, 225.

49. Ron Zemke, "Experience Shows Intuition Isn't the Best Guide to Teamwork," *The Service Edge* 7, no. 1 (January 1994): 5.

50. This section is based on Schneider and Bowen, *Winning the Service Game*, 145–173.

51. A good summary of goal setting and motivation at work can be found in Edwin A. Locke and Gary Latham, *A Theory of Goal Setting and Task Performance* (Englewood Cliffs, NJ: Prentice-Hall, 1990).

52. Schneider and Bowen, *Winning the Service Game*, 165.

53. Charles A. O'Reilly III and Jeffrey Pfeffer, *Hidden Value*, 232.

54. Jeffrey Pfeffer, *Competitive Advantage through People* (Boston: Harvard Business School Press, 1994), 160–163.

55. Scott B. MacKenzie, Philip M. Podsakoff, and Gregory A. Rich, "Transformational and Transactional Leadership and Salesperson Performance," *Journal of the Academy of Marketing Science* 29, no. 2 (2001): 115–134.

56. Leonard L. Berry, *On Great Service*, 236–237.

57. Schneider and Bowen, *Winning the Service Game*, 240.

58. Catherine DeVrye, *Good Service Is Good Business* (Upper Saddle River, NJ: Prentice-Hall, 2000), 11.

59. Paul Hemp, "My Week as a Room-Service Waiter at the Ritz," *Harvard Business Review* 80 (June 2002): 52.

60. Freiberg and Freibergs, *Nuts!*

61. Adapted from ibid., 165–168.

62. Tony Simons, "The High Cost of Lost Trust," *Harvard Business Review* (September 2002): 2–3.

The High Cost of Lost Trust

Tony Simons

When employees doubt a manager's integrity, the problem can show up on the bottom line. This article reports striking findings from a survey of more than 6,500 employees at 76 Holiday Inns in the U.S. and Canada.

Everyone knows that leaders have to "walk the talk," right? Think of the manager who hangs "Customers Come First" placards in every department and a month later cuts the customer service staff. He may have a good reason for the layoffs—indeed, he may have had no choice—but he has undermined his staff's trust, and there will be a price to pay.

But what's the real cost? Clearly it will be extracted in hard-to-measure ways: Staffers may be less engaged in their work, less receptive to new ideas, less willing to follow the leader on the next offensive. Surprisingly, though, no one has directly measured the impact of walking the talk on the bottom line. A colleague, Judi McLean Parks, and I set out to do just that.

We hypothesized that when employees sense an inconsistency between what their bosses say and do, it triggers a cascade of effects, depressing employees' trust, commitment, and willingness to go the extra mile. These effects, we reasoned, would reduce customer satisfaction and increase employee turnover, harming profitability.

To measure this expected chain reaction in a competitive service market, we surveyed more than 6,500 employees at 76 U.S. and Canadian Holiday Inn hotels. We provided questionnaires in English, Spanish, Chinese, Creole French, and Vietnamese and administered oral surveys to roughly 500 illiterate employees. We asked workers to rank, on a five-point scale, how closely their managers' words and actions were aligned—what we call the managers' *behavioral integrity*—by evaluating statements such as "My manager delivers on promises" and "My manager practices what he preaches." We queried the employees about their commitment and the service environment at their hotels with statements such as "I am proud to tell others I am part of this hotel" and "My coworkers go out of their way to accommodate guests' special requests." Finally, we correlated the responses with the hotels' customer satisfaction surveys, personnel records, and financial records.

The ripple effect we saw was stunning. Hotels where employees strongly believed their managers followed through on promises and demonstrated the values they preached were substantially more profitable than those whose managers scored average or lower. So strong was the link, in fact, that a one-eighth point improvement in a hotel's score on the five-point scale could be expected to increase the hotel's profitability by 2.5 percent of revenues—in this study, that translates to a profit increase of more than $250,000 per year per hotel. No other single aspect of manager behavior that we measured had as large an impact on profits.

THE INTEGRITY TEST

The notion that behavioral integrity is important should be common sense: Align your words and actions in a way employees see. Keep your promises. Don't "spin." It seems simple. But if it's so simple, why is it so rarely observed? Management theorists and other social scientists have identified several reasons why maintaining integrity is hard:

Sticky Labels The label of "hypocrite" is stickier than its opposite. It takes evidence of only a single lie for a manager to be branded a "liar." In contrast, a person has to tell a whole lot of truth to qualify as a "straight shooter." Credibility, as we have all seen, is slow to build and quick to dissipate. A generally

Tony Simons, "The High Cost of Lost Trust," *Harvard Business Review* (September 2002): 2–3. Reprinted by permission of Harvard Business School.

straightforward manager who is caught breaking an important promise will likely have trouble recovering.

Competing Stakeholders Managers, like politicians, juggle diverse stakeholder groups, each with its preferred language and distinct interests. Because managers have such an array of constituents and roles, a clash of words and actions is almost inevitable, especially when people in one group receive a message intended for another. Recall the executive who cut his customer service staff: While he was rallying the team with "customers first" pronouncements, he was also promising shareholders that he'd cut department budgets by 15 percent. The priorities he expressed to the two groups differed, but they're not necessarily incompatible. Is this hypocrisy or astute management of different stakeholders? It depends on whom you ask.

Shifting Policies Periods of organizational change are particularly threatening to behavioral integrity. Departments change at different speeds, managers can become confused or ambivalent about a new approach, policies may seem inconsistent. In an executive reshuffling, experienced managers might understand that Jack does things differently from the way Jim used to and might excuse Jack from Jim's promises—but the line employees are likely to hear only an inconsistent management voice and will blame the inconsistency on their manager's character.

Changing Fashions The world is awash in management ideas, and new ones appear with ever-increasing frequency. A 1994 study revealed that the average U.S. company had committed itself to 11.8 of 25 currently popular management tools and techniques. That's partly because managers use new techniques to show that they're on the cutting edge. But often such ideas fail, are phased out, or, worse, are quickly replaced with new ones. Consider "quality circles," a tool adopted by 90 percent of *Fortune* 500 companies between 1980 and 1982 and abandoned by 80 percent of them within five years. This rapid cycling through management fads creates cynical employees who have learned to be skeptical of managers touting new techniques. It is good for managers to explore and experiment, but there is a cost to dabbling.

Unclear Priorities Most managers have some level of confusion about company and work priorities, and a manager who is confused about priorities is more likely to shift to a new management approach with each persuasive speaker or magazine article. Employees will interpret this well-meaning inconsistency as a lack of behavioral integrity.

Blind Spots Of all the factors that can undermine behavioral integrity, among the most dangerous is managers' inability to see an integrity problem in themselves. The issue often arises because of our natural desire to see ourselves as consistent. In many companies, a manager's path to success seems to lie in verbal endorsements of espoused values, while his actual behavior is expected to align with certain implicit norms and standards that may be more widely accepted. For example, managers often talk about empowerment without actually yielding any power. When this happens, psychological defense mechanisms activate to divert the manager's attention from the contradiction so he can feel better about himself. The self-deception tends to perpetuate the problem.

It isn't easy to identify behavioral integrity problems or to manage them, but these tasks are pivotal for good leadership. We used surveys to examine the issue at a large hotel company. Other companies might start their own self-examinations with frank employee surveys to see just how well their managers are walking the talk. Given the likelihood—and high cost—of missteps, it's simply good business to make behavioral integrity a continuing focus.

How to Lead the Customer Experience

Stephan H. Haeckel, Lewis P. Carbone, and Leonard L. Berry

Customers always have an experience when they interact with a firm. The question for managers is whether the firm is prepared to systematically manage the customers' experience or simply hope for the best. The customers' overall experience—influenced by sensory and emotional clues—evokes a value perception that determines brand preference. Through experience management principles, a firm can design a composite of clues that resonate with customers and earn their loyalty.

Business strategies centered on the holistic design and delivery of total customer experiences consistently create superior customer value. Holistic experiences begin and end long before and after actual transactions. They incorporate functional and affective attributes. They are orchestrated to deliver both intrinsic and extrinsic values. And they result in stronger, more sustainable customer preference than do independently managed communication, process, and service-centric strategies.

By "total experience" we mean the feelings customers take away from their interaction with a firm's goods, services, and "atmospheric" stimuli. Companies that interact with customers can't avoid giving them a total experience. They can, however, avoid managing it in a systematic way, and almost all do. Organizations that simply tweak design elements or focus on the customer experience in isolated pockets of their business will be disappointed in the results.

A number of organizations are starting to systematically apply customer experience management principles to strengthen customer preference and improve business outcomes. Unlike many goods or service enhancements, the holistic nature of these experiential designs makes it very difficult for competitors to copy them. Customer value creation is moving into a new arena—one that encompasses goods and service quality, but is a broader concept.

The customer's total experience directly affects perceptions of value, word-of-mouth endorsement, and repatronage intentions. A well-prepared, well-served meal consumed in a noisy restaurant with uncomfortable chairs is one experience for customers. The same food served the same way in a comfortable and relaxing environment is a completely different experience. The meal and the atmosphere are inextricably linked; both are part of the customer's overall restaurant experience. The facility design; servers' skills, attitudes, body language, choice of words, tone, inflection, and dress; pace of service; presentation and taste of the food; noise level; smell; texture of tableware; spacing, height, and shape of tables; and a multitude of other stimuli all coalesce into a positive, neutral, or negative experience.

The problem-solving properties of goods and services provide functional benefits. Managers must recognize two realities, however. First, competing goods and services often are quite similar in functionality. Second, customers desire more than functionality. They are emotional beings who also want intangible values such as a sense of control, fun, aesthetic pleasure, and enhanced self-esteem.

Companies compete best when they combine functional and emotional benefits in their market offer. Firms that make customers feel good are formidable competitors because customers like to feel good and few companies make them feel that way. Emotional bonds between firms and customers are difficult for competitors to penetrate.

CREATING CLUES

Customers always have an experience when they interact with an organization. They consciously and unconsciously filter a barrage of "clues" and organize

Stephan H. Haeckel, Lewis P. Carbone, and Leonard L. Berry, "How to Lead the Customer Experience," *Marketing Management* (January–February 2003): 18, 19–23.

them into a set of impressions, both rational and emotional. Anything perceived or sensed (or recognized by its absence) is an experience clue. If you can see, smell, taste, or hear it, it's a clue. Goods and services emit clues, as does the physical environment in which they're offered. The employees are another source of experience clues. Each clue carries a message; the composite of clues creates the total experience.

Effectively managing the customers' experience involves presenting an integrated series of clues that collectively meet or exceed customers' expectations. One category of clues concerns the actual functioning of the good or service. Did the key issued at the front desk open the hotel room door? Did the room's television set work? Was the wake-up call made as promised? These goods and service clues strictly concern functionality and are interpreted primarily by the conscious and logical circuitry of the brain.

A second category of clues stimulates the brain's emotional circuitry and evokes affective responses. The smell and feel of leather upholstery, the sound and smell of a steak on the grill, and the laugh, phrasing, and tone of voice of the person answering the customer service call line are clues that envelop the functionality of a good or service. Two types of clues affect customers' emotional perceptions: mechanics (clues emitted by things) and humanics (clues emitted by people).

The distinction between functional service clues and humanics clues is subtle. A retail salesperson who answers a customer's question about what other stores might carry an out-of-stock item is producing a functional service clue. The salesperson's choice of words, tone, and body language produce humanics clues. One salesperson may offer the information grudgingly or disinterestedly. Another may offer the information enthusiastically. The information is accurate in both cases, but the customer's emotional response to the two salespeople is quite different.

In the August 2000 issue of *Travel & Leisure*, Peter John Lindberg reported on Singapore Airlines, which is consistently rated by travelers as one of the world's best airlines. It invests heavily to orchestrate in-flight service mechanics and humanics clues, including fresh orchids in first- and business-class bathrooms, galley carts scrubbed before every flight, and female flight attendants who wear designer dresses and receive intensive training in body posture, grooming, and voice tone. One veteran flight attendant believes the dresses reduce air-rage incidents: "It's hard to be nasty to a girl in a sarong kebaya. Put them in pants, and passengers think they can take more abuse."

Functional, mechanics, and humanics clues are synergistic rather than additive; they must be melded from creation to execution. To fully leverage experience as a customer value proposition, organizations must understand and manage the emotional component of experiences with the same rigor they bring to managing manufactured product and service functionality.

THE CUSTOMER EXPERIENCE

Customer experience management focuses different parts of an organization on the common goal of creating an integrated, aligned customer feeling. It provides a means for breaking down organizational barriers. We have identified three fundamental principles that provide a foundation for creating distinctive customer value through experiences. Each requires a cross-functional organizational perspective.

Principle 1: Fuse experiential breadth and depth. Experiential breadth refers to the sequence of experience customers have in interacting with an organization. These experiences may begin well before customers pass through the firm's doors. For example, hotel guests' experiences begin before they walk into the lobby. Was the reservations agent competent and courteous? Was the hotel easy to find and access? And, even further back in the experience journey, was the promotional packet the hotel sent about its loyalty program well-designed and informative? Imagine the opportunity for a hotel company in defining the full breadth of the customers' experience, becoming attuned to the hundreds of clues along the way and seeking to manage these clues to evoke positive perceptions.

Whereas breadth refers to identifiable stages customers undergo in the experience, depth refers to the number and diversity of sensory clues at each stage. The more layers of multi-sensory clues that reinforce the targeted impression, the more successful an organization will be in anchoring and sustaining that impression in the customer's perception. Consider the depth of reinforcing clues embedded in the room experience at a Ritz-Carlton hotel. They typically include plush carpet, distinctive furniture and rich fabrics; the smell of fresh flowers; a complimentary refreshment stocked in the room; a welcome call from the concierge offering assistance; an iron and ironing board; a robe, thick towels, and distinctively scented "Ritz-Carlton" shampoos; a leather-bound television viewing guide with a bookmark on the current day; room service 24 hours a day; turn-down service; and *The New York Times* and *Wall Street Journal* delivered outside one's door in the morning.

Congruence or fusion of clues within and among experience stages is critical. Incongruent clues convey an incongruent message with customers likely to recall facets of the experience most salient to their needs. This is why a spacious, well-furnished hotel lobby can't make up for a cramped, poorly furnished hotel room. Guests don't live in the lobby. However, if lobby clues fuse with guest room clues, then one part of the experience reinforces another.

Principle 2: Use mechanics and humanics to improve function. In some cases, humanics and mechanics clues can be introduced to enhance goods or service functionality. Customers process these different types of clues holistically, so firms should manage them as such. Stimuli that envelop goods or services can affect customers' perceptions of functional quality. Mechanics and humanics must be simultaneously addressed and blended with the functional clues of the offering into reciprocally supported experience clues.

Roger Ulrich, a landscape architect with Texas A&M University, has done considerable research documenting how environmental factors in a hospital can affect patients' medical outcomes. For example, Ulrich has found that surgery patients with a bedside window overlooking trees had more favorable recovery courses than patients overlooking a brick wall. Based on accumulating research in environmental psychophysiology, Ulrich recommends designing hospital environments that foster patient control (including their privacy), encourage social support from family and friends, and provide access to nature and other positive distractions. The field of environmental psychophysiology has developed from the fundamental idea that environment affects function.

Principle 3: Connect emotionally. Organizations with effective experience management systems understand and respond to the emotional needs of their customers. They orchestrate a series of clues designed to provoke positive emotional reactions, such as joy, awe, interest, affection, and trust. They integrate emotional value into the total experience because consumers are not Spock-like Vulcans who make purchases on the basis of cold logic.

Managing customers' experiences requires awareness of all of their senses throughout the experience. Sight, motion, sound, smell, taste, and touch are direct pathways to customers' emotions. Connecting with customers in a sensory way is crucial to managing positive emotional elements of the experience.

The sensory-loaded experience of buying and consuming Krispy Kreme doughnuts illustrates the power of emotional connections with customers. At a time when consumers are inundated with information on healthy eating, Krispy Kreme's fried doughnut oozing with glaze enticed more than 3,000 people to wait in a Denver line extending for three city blocks on opening day. Even the name connects on a sensory level. Everything conspires to evoke a feeling of "delicious decadence."

No logical reason compels a person to stand in a long line for hours to buy a doughnut. But an experience so effectively choreographed and integrated with the product is hard to resist. The performance includes the counter person going into the production area, which is in full view, to box up the customer's dozen "original glazed" doughnuts hot off the line. A neon sign in the window lights up only when "HOT Donuts" are actually coming off the line, further heightening the anticipation. The light almost creates a Pavlovian response that, combined with the tempting smell that's pumped outside, brings customers in off the street like cartoon characters hypnotized by a pleasurable wafting scent. The customer walks out with a warm box, still another sensory clue. With its multi-sensory managed experience, Krispy Kreme makes customers feel good about indulging and forgetting their diets. And yes, the doughnuts taste very good.

MANAGEMENT TOOLS

More than anything else, customer experience management requires customer empathy—seeing what the customer sees, feeling what the customer feels. Organizations don't develop experience management competency overnight. They need to apply specialized tools in the context of a systematic methodology.

An experience audit is used to thoroughly analyze the current customer experience and to illuminate customers' emotional responses to specific clues. Videotape and digital photographs document actual customer experiences and provide the raw data for comprehensive study and categorization of clues. Hours of video are generated—some (with appropriate notification and approval) from pinhole cameras imbedded in wrist-watches, handbags, coats, or hats. Additionally, in-depth interviews with customers and employees reveal their feelings about different aspects of an experience and the emotional associations it generates.

Emotional strands are defined during an experience audit. An emotional strand is a charting of the emotional highs and lows customers commonly experience in a specific setting or situation. For example, female apparel customers commonly move from an emotional high when spotting a great-looking dress in a store to the emotional low if the dress doesn't fit. A goal of experience management is anticipating customers' emotional highs and lows and designing clues to support customers in their emotional strand.

An experience motif is developed based on findings from the experience audit and the organization's core values and branding strategy. Captured in a few words, the motif becomes the North Star—the foundation and filter for integrating and reconciling all elements of the experience. The motif is the unifying element for every clue in the experience design. One financial institution wanted its customers to feel "recognized, reassured, and engaged," terminology formalized into a motif. Subsequently, only clues that reinforced these three motif watchwords were incorporated into the experience design.

Based on the experience motif and other experience design criteria, clues are developed and translated into a blueprint. Mechanics clues are represented graphically in drawings on the blueprint, and humanics clues are described in employee role performance narratives. These narratives, which capture the tone and texture of desired performance, augment existing job descriptions that typically concern job functions rather than performance of a role. The blueprint and narratives become a critical part of an organization's roadmap for communicating, implementing, monitoring, and measuring the outcomes of an experience management system.

CASE STUDY

The Health and Wellness Center by Doylestown Hospital (Doylestown, Penn.) is a one-of-a-kind healthcare model: a combination clinic, health club, and spa with interactive health design services. Patrons just as frequently visit the center for their daily workout or to browse the bookstore as they do for outpatient surgery, a diabetes check, or their annual mammogram.

Construction of the Health and Wellness Center was completed in spring 2001 and expanded the hospital's market into a nearby, rapidly growing community. Beyond the business motivation was management's deepseated determination to make a positive difference in serving the community's modern healthcare needs. This legacy of community service dates from the turn of the century when an inspired women's group, the Village Improvement Association (VIA), founded Doylestown Hospital, which it still owns and oversees. It remains the only women's club in the United States to own and operate a community hospital.

The mandate for the new Center was to create a distinctive healthcare experience integrating traditional medical services with specialized retail, wellness, and fitness services. This means incorporating medical specialties like cardiology, orthopedics, dentistry, day surgery, and women's diagnostics with a full spa and fitness center, an interactive learning center, a restaurant, and a bookstore.

During the construction phase, senior hospital staff began applying experience management techniques. The resulting experience design became central to the planning and development of the facility. The services provided are related through a distinctive architectural and landscape design.

Connecting Emotionally An experience audit provided deep insights into the basic emotions that surface in patients while on their health and wellness experience journey. Patients shared their feeling that medical process generally predominates over staff empathy for their personal situation. The experience audit, along with internal strategy sessions, produced an experience motif centered on patrons feeling understood, strengthened, and renewed through every interaction with the Health and Wellness Center.

The Center included only clues that reinforce understanding, strengthening, and renewal in the experience design. For example, in addition to standard amenities, the spa and fitness center are capable of downloading patient profiles sent from physicians and health design services—a clue that signals a unique understanding of that person's needs. Spa personnel will have information that an MS patient's whirlpool cannot exceed a certain temperature. In the fitness center, they will be aware of certain parameters for someone just coming out of cardiac rehab. In women's diagnostics, completion of a mammogram is rewarded with a coupon for the restaurant or bookstore—a strengthening and renewing clue. The meticulous building design adheres to the principles of Feng Shui that focus on energy and revitalization.

Integrating Clues The center's experience management design specified more than 200 clues derived from the experience motif:

- Seasonal healing gardens surrounding the building, complete with meditation benches, music, and a labyrinth walk
- A 25-foot interior waterfall and pond
- A unique stone and wood atrium surrounding the waterfall that serves as a central and communal gathering point
- Internet hookups, overstuffed chairs, and library-style newspaper and magazine racks throughout the atrium
- A fitness center and spa that provide support to cardiac and orthopedic rehab patients as well as the public
- Health design nurses whose sole role is to help consumers create a customized health plan and then mentor and monitor their journey
- Numerous seminars and community events built around health and wellness
- Mammograms and blood pressure checks available without an appointment
- Beepers allowing clients to wait for appointments or test results in any area of the facility
- A bookstore and lending library centered on wellness and linked to the leading recommended Web sites on disease management and wellness strategies
- Distinguishing staff behaviors ranging from voice inflection to gestures to reinforce the motif

Customizing Healthcare A key element of the differentiated experience is the Health Design Center, which provides customized, coordinated health and wellness plans. Studies show people place great value in coordinated healthcare and the perceived benefit expands dramatically when a person must deal with multiple conditions. The Health Design Center, available to anyone who desires the experience, provides an effective way of delivering a sense of unity and completeness.

The Health Design Center opened with one nurse and has expanded to three in a year's time. While most of the health design services are on a fee basis and not covered by insurance, customized health designs have become a popular service, with more than 200 generated per month.

No single clue at the Health and Wellness Center provides the magic for a distinctive, preferred experience. The benefit comes in the integrated design and layering of clues that support the Center's experience motif. It's the cumulative effect of the customer's take-away feeling from the experience.

The Center is making a difference. Benchmarked against other high-performing health facilities in the nation, it ranked third out of 357 facilities in its first participation in the national Press Ganey patient satisfaction survey. The Center scored in the 98th percentile in overall satisfaction and in the 99th percentile for "sensitivity to patient needs" and "explanations given by staff."

DELIVERING THE BRAND

An increasing number of experience-oriented executives will soon be changing their understanding of what their brand should be in the future. In fact, they will be changing their very understanding of what "brand" means. Rather than creating a set of messages and images that associate a company and its products with emotional values, experience pioneers will be focused on creating a business that delivers the brand as an experience incorporating these values. And this, we assert, is the real transformation, the real meaning, and the real potential of becoming a customer-centric business.[1]

[1] *Authors' note:* The authors acknowledge the contribution of Suzie Goan, experience director of Experience Engineering Inc. in Minneapolis.

PART FOUR

Implementing Services Marketing

CHAPTER 12

Managing Relationships and Building Loyalty

The first step in managing a loyalty-based business system is finding and acquiring the right customers.

—FREDERICK F. REICHHELD

Strategy first, then CRM.

—STEVEN S. RAMSEY

Targeting, acquiring, and retaining the "right" customers is at the core of many successful service firms. In this chapter, we emphasize the importance of carefully choosing target segments and taking pains to build and maintain their loyalty through well-conceived relationship marketing strategies.[1] Underlying this strategy is the notion of market segmentation, introduced in Chapter 3. More and more firms are trying to decide which types of customers they can serve well rather than trying to be all things to all people. Once a firm has won customers it sees as desirable, the challenge shifts to building relationships and turning them into loyal customers who will generate a growing revenue stream for the firm in the future.

Building relationships is a challenge, especially when a firm has many, often millions, of customers who interact with the firm in many ways (from e-mail to call centers to face-to-face interactions). When implemented well, customer relationship management (CRM) systems provide managers with the tools to understand their customers and tailor their service, cross-selling, and retention efforts, often on a one-on-one basis.

In this chapter, we explore the following questions.

1. Why is customer loyalty an important driver of profitability for service firms?
2. How can a firm calculate the lifetime value of its customers?
3. What strategies are associated with the concept of relationship marketing?
4. Why is it especially important for service firms to target the "right" customers?
5. How can tiering of service, loyalty bonds, and membership programs help in building customer loyalty?
6. What is the role of CRM systems in delivering customized services and building loyalty?

THE SEARCH FOR CUSTOMER LOYALTY

Loyalty is an old-fashioned word that has traditionally been used to describe fidelity and enthusiastic devotion to a country, cause, or individual. More recently, it has been used in a business context to describe a customer's willingness to continue patronizing a firm over the long term, purchasing and using its goods and services on a repeated and preferably exclusive basis, and recommending the firm's products to friends and associates. However, brand loyalty extends beyond behavior to include preference, liking, and future intentions. Richard Oliver has argued that consumers first become loyal in a cognitive sense, perceiving from brand attribute information that one brand is preferable to its alternatives.[2] At the second stage is affective loyalty, whereby a consumer develops a liking for the brand, based on cumulatively satisfying usage occasions. Such attitudes are not easily dislodged by counterarguments from competitors. At the third stage is conative loyalty, whereby the consumer is committed to rebuying the same brand. This should lead to the fourth stage, which is action loyalty, whereby the consumer exhibits consistent repurchase behavior.

"Few companies think of customers as annuities," says Frederick Reichheld, coauthor of *The Loyalty Effect* and a major researcher in this field.[3] And yet that is precisely what a loyal customer can mean to a firm: a consistent source of revenue over a period of many years. However, this loyalty cannot be taken for granted. It will continue only as long as the customer feels that he or she is receiving better value (including superior quality relative to price) than could be obtained by switching to another supplier. If the original firm does something to disappoint the customer or if a competitor starts to offer significantly better value, there is a risk that the customer will defect.

During the cold war, "defector" was a nasty word, describing disloyal people who sold out their own side and went over to the enemy. Even when they defected toward "our" side rather than away from it, they were still suspect. Today, in a marketing context, *defection* is used to describe customers who drop off a company's radar screen and transfer their brand loyalty to another supplier. Frederick Reichheld and Earl Sasser popularized the term *zero defections*, which they describe as keeping every customer the company can profitably serve.[4] Not only does a rising defection rate indicate that something is wrong with quality (or that competitors offer better value), it may also signal a coming fall in profits. Large customers don't necessarily disappear overnight. They may signal their mounting dissatisfaction by steadily reducing their purchases and shifting part of their business elsewhere.

Why Is Customer Loyalty Important to a Firm's Profitability?

How much is a loyal customer worth in terms of profits? In a classic study, Reichheld and Sasser analyzed the profit per customer in various service businesses, categorized by the number of years that a customer had been with the firm.[5] The researchers found that the longer customers remained with a firm in each of these industries, the more profitable they became to serve. Annual profits per customer, which have been indexed over a five-year period for easier comparison, are summarized in Figure 12-1. The industries studied (with average profits from a first-year customer shown in parentheses) were credit cards ($30), industrial laundry ($144), industrial distribution ($45), and automobile servicing ($25). Similar loyalty effects were also uncovered in the Internet context, where it typically took more than a year to recoup acquisition costs, and profits increased as customers stayed longer with the firm.[6]

Underlying this profit growth, say Reichheld and Sasser, are four factors working to the supplier's advantage to create incremental profits. In order of magnitude at the end of seven years, these factors are

FIGURE 12-1 How Much Profit a Customer Generates over Time

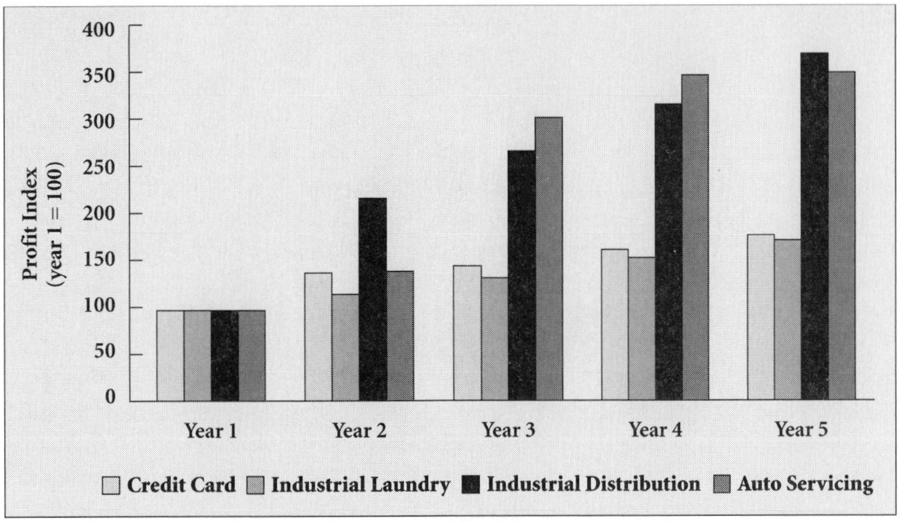

Source: Based on data in Frederick F. Reichheld and W. Earl Sasser Jr., "Zero Defections: Quality Comes to Services," *Harvard Business Review* 68 (September–October 1990): 105–111. Reprinted by permission of Harvard Business School.

1. *Profit derived from increased purchases* (or, in a credit card or banking environment, higher account balances). Over time, business customers often grow larger and so need to purchase in greater quantities. Individuals may also purchase more as their families grow or as they become more affluent. Both types of customers may decide to consolidate their purchases with a single supplier that provides high-quality service.
2. *Profit from reduced operating costs.* As customers become more experienced, they make fewer demands on the supplier (for instance, less need for information and assistance). They may also make fewer mistakes in operational processes, thus contributing to greater productivity.
3. *Profit from referrals to other customers.* Positive word-of-mouth recommendations are like free sales and advertising, saving the firm from having to invest as much money in these activities.
4. *Profit from price premium.* New customers often benefit from introductory promotional discounts, whereas long-term customers are more likely to pay regular prices. Moreover, when customers trust a supplier, they may be more willing to pay higher prices at peak periods or for express work.

Figure 12-2 shows the relative contribution of each of these factors over a seven-year period, based on an analysis of 19 product categories (both goods and services). Reichheld argues that the economic benefits of customer loyalty noted earlier often explain why one firm is more profitable than a competitor. Furthermore, the up-front costs of attracting these buyers can be amortized over many years.

However, it would be a mistake to assume that loyal customers are always more profitable than those making one-time transactions.[7] On the cost side, not all types of services incur heavy promotional expenditures to attract a new customer. Sometimes, it is more important to invest in a good retail location that will attract walk-in traffic. Unlike banks, insurance companies, and other "membership" organizations that require an application process and specific procedures to establish a new account, many service firms face no set-up costs when a new customer first seeks to make a purchase.

FIGURE 12-2 Why Customers Are More Profitable over Time

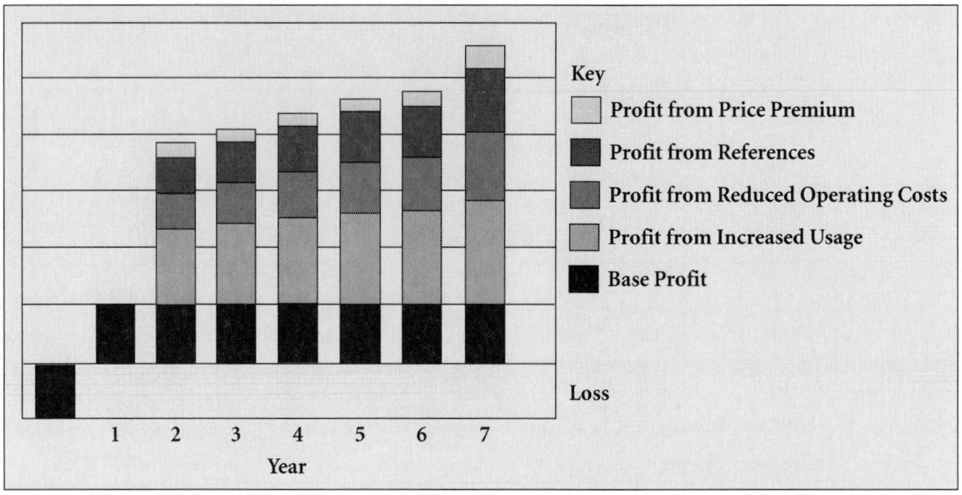

Source: Frederick F. Reichheld and W. Earl Sasser Jr., "Zero Defections: Quality Comes to Services," *Harvard Business Review* (September–October 1990): 105–111. Reprinted by permission of Harvard Business School.

On the revenue side, loyal customers may not necessarily spend more than one-time buyers and in some instances may even expect price discounts. Finally, revenue does not necessarily increase with time for all types of customers.[8]

Recent work has also shown that the profit impact of a customer can vary dramatically, depending on the stage of the product life cycle the service is in. For instance, referrals of satisfied customers and negative word of mouth of defected customers have a much higher profit impact in the early stages of the product life cycle than in later stages.[9]

Customer Lifetime Value and Customer Equity

Once we recognize that relationships with loyal customers have the potential to generate an ongoing stream of profits, it becomes clear that those customers are an important financial asset for the firm. As such, they increase the value of the firm in the event of a sale. Viewed from this financial perspective, marketing programs designed to attract new customers, build relationships, increase sales from existing customers, and maintain relationships into the future should rightly be seen as investments rather than just operating expenses.[10]

Customer equity management is a new approach to marketing and corporate strategy that finally puts customers, and more important, strategies designed to grow the value of each customer, at the heart of the organization.[11] *Customer equity* refers to the total sum of the discounted lifetime values of all the firm's current customers. Roland Rust, Valarie Zeithaml, and Katharine Lemon argue that "In fast-moving and dynamic industries that involve customer relationships, products come and go, but customers remain."[12] The implication is that customers and customer equity may be more central to corporate strategy than brands and *brand equity* (which we define as the incremental value that customers add subjectively to a product in excess of its objective value without the brand name).

So, how can a firm calculate its customer equity? The task requires a procedure for calculating the discounted value of each individual customer throughout his or her expected lifetime as a customer of the firm to determine the *customer lifetime value* (CLV). The sum of the CLVs for all customers equates to the firm's customer equity. As shown in Management Memo 12-1, calculating CLV requires an understanding of the costs and revenues associated with a customer on a year-by-year basis. Undertaking these calculations can be simplified by developing a segment-by-segment assessment, instead of studying each customer individually.[13]

Enhancing customer equity should be a key driver of marketing strategy. As Alan Grant and Leonard Schlesinger declare: "Achieving the full profit potential of each customer relationship should be the fundamental goal of every business.... Even using conservative estimates, the gap between most companies' current and full potential performance is enormous."[14] They urge managers to document the current purchasing behavior of customers in each target segment and then ask the following questions: What would be the impact on sales and profits if each customer exhibited the ideal behavior profile of (1) buying all services offered by the firm, (2) using these to the exclusion of any purchases from competitors, and (3) paying full price? How long, on average, do customers remain with the firm? What impact would it have if they remained customers for life?

In many instances, firms need to examine opportunities to cross-sell new services to existing customers. They should be considering how frequent-user programs that are designed to reward loyalty can help to cement relationships more tightly and increase the firm's share of wallet when customers are buying from several suppliers. Getting customers to pay higher prices than they have been used to, however, may be more difficult unless competitors are also trying to reduce the availability of discount promotions.

MANAGEMENT MEMO 12-1

WORKSHEET FOR CALCULATING CUSTOMER LIFETIME VALUE

Calculating customer value is an inexact science that is subject to a variety of assumptions. You may want to try varying these assumptions to see how it affects the final figures. Generally speaking, revenues per customer are easier to track on an individualized basis than are the associated costs of serving a customer, unless (1) no individual records are kept and/or (2) the accounts served are very large and all account-related costs are individually documented and assigned.

ACQUISITION REVENUES LESS COSTS

If individual account records are kept, the initial application fee paid and initial purchase (if relevant) should be found in these records. Costs, by contrast, may have to be based on average data. For instance, the marketing cost of acquiring a new client can be calculated by dividing the total marketing costs (advertising, promotions, selling, etc.) devoted toward acquiring new customers by the total number of new customers acquired during the same period. If each acquisition takes place over an extended period of time, you may want to build in a lagged effect between when marketing expenditures are incurred and when new customers come on board. The cost of credit checks—where relevant—must be divided by the number of new customers, not the total number of applicants, because some applicants will probably fail this hurdle. Account set-up costs will also be an average figure in most organizations.

ANNUAL REVENUES AND COSTS

If annual sales, account fees, and service fees are documented on an individual-account basis, account revenue streams (except referrals) can be easily identified. The first priority is to segment your customer base by the length of its relationship with your firm. Depending on the sophistication and precision of your firm's records, annual costs in each category may be directly assigned to an individual account holder or averaged for all account holders in that age category.

VALUE OF REFERRALS

Computing the value of referrals requires a variety of assumptions. To get started, you may need to conduct surveys to determine (1) what percentage of new customers claim that they were influenced by a recommendation from another customer and (2) what other marketing activities also drew the firm to that individual's attention. From these two items, estimates can be made of what percentage of the credit for all new customers should be assigned to referrals. Additional research may be needed to clarify whether "older" customers are more likely to be effective recommenders than "younger" ones.

NET PRESENT VALUE

Calculating net present value (NPV) from a future profit stream will require choice of an appropriate annual discount figure. (This could reflect estimates of future inflation rates.) It also requires assessment of how long the average relationship lasts. The NPV of a customer, then, is the sum of the anticipated annual profit on each customer for the projected relationship lifetime, suitably discounted each year into the future.

Acquisition			*Year 1*	*Year 2*	*Year 3*	*Year n*
Initial Revenue		*Annual Revenues*				
Application fee[a]	____	Annual account fee[a]	____	____	____	____
Initial purchase[a]	____	Sales	____	____	____	____
		Service fees[a]	____	____	____	____
		Value of referrals[b]	____	____	____	____
Total Revenues	____					
Initial Costs		*Annual Costs*				
Marketing	____	Account management	____	____	____	____
Credit check[a]	____	Cost of sales	____	____	____	____
Account setup[a]	____	Write-offs (e.g., bad debts)	____	____	____	____
Less total costs	____		____	____	____	____
Net Profit (Loss)	____		____	____	____	____

[a]If applicable.

[b]Anticipated profits from each new customer referred (could be limited to the first year or expressed as the net present value of the estimated future stream of profits through year n); this value could be negative if an unhappy customer starts to spread negative word of mouth that causes existing customers to defect.

UNDERSTANDING THE CUSTOMER/FIRM RELATIONSHIP

A fundamental distinction exists between strategies intended to bring about a single transaction and those designed to create extended relationships with customers. The term *relationship marketing* has been widely used to describe the latter type of activity, but until recently it was defined only loosely. Research by Nicole Coviello, Roderick Brodie, and Hugh Munro suggests that there are, in fact, four distinct types of marketing—transactional marketing and three categories of what they call relational marketing: database marketing, interaction marketing, and network marketing.[15]

Transactional Marketing

A transaction is an event during which an exchange of value takes place between two parties. But even a series of transactions doesn't necessarily constitute a relationship, which requires mutual recognition and knowledge between the parties. When each transaction between a customer and a supplier is essentially discrete and anonymous, with no long-term record kept of a customer's purchasing history and little or no mutual recognition between the customer and employees, no meaningful marketing relationship can be said to exist.

With very few exceptions, consumers buying manufactured goods for household use do so at discrete intervals, paying for each purchase separately and rarely entering into a formal relationship with the original manufacturer. Nevertheless, these customers may have a relationship with the dealer or retail intermediary that sells the goods. The same is true for many services, ranging from passenger transport to food service or visits to a cinema, where each purchase and use is a discrete event.

Database Marketing

In database marketing, the focus is still on the market transaction but now includes information exchange. Marketers rely on information technology, usually in the form of a database, to form a relationship with targeted customers and to retain their patronage over time. However, the nature of these relationships is often not a close one, with communication being driven and managed by the seller. Technology is used to (1) identify and build a database of current and potential customers, (2) deliver differentiated messages based on consumers' characteristics and preferences, and (3) track each relationship to monitor the cost of acquiring the consumer and the lifetime value of the resulting purchases.[16] Although technology can be used to personalize the relationship (as in word-processed letters that insert the customer's name), relations remain somewhat distant. Utility services, such as electricity, gas, and cable TV, are good examples.

Interaction Marketing

A closer relationship exists when there is face-to-face interaction between customers and representatives of the supplier (or "ear-to-ear" interaction by phone). Although the service itself remains important, value is added by people and social processes. Interactions may include negotiations and sharing of insights in both directions. This type of relationship has long existed in many local environments, ranging from community banks to dentistry, where buyer and seller know and trust each other. It is also commonly found in many business-to-business services. Both the firm and the customer are prepared to invest resources (including time) to develop a mutually beneficial relationship. This investment may include time spent sharing and recording information. Consider the following observation of a large telecommunications operator seeking to enter into a dialogue with its small-business customers:

> [C]ustomers demanded a continuing dialog focused on an understanding of their needs, as opposed to a tactical contact aiming to sell them the "flavor of the month." Customers were also motivated by continuity of contact, wanting to deal with a specific person on a regular basis. They would spend up to 20 minutes disclosing information about their business and needs, but having invested that amount of time, they expect the relationship to be perpetuated.[17]

As service companies grow larger and make increasing use of such technologies as interactive Web sites and self-service equipment, maintaining meaningful relationships with customers becomes a significant marketing challenge. The most sophisticated service organizations effectively combine database and interaction marketing.

Network Marketing

We often say that someone is a "good networker" because he or she is able to put individuals in touch with others who have a mutual interest. This type of marketing occurs primarily in a business-to-business context, where firms commit resources to develop positions in a network of relationships with customers, distributors, suppliers, the media, consultants, trade associations, government agencies, competitors, and even the customers of their customers. Often, a team of individuals within the supplier's firm must collaborate to provide effective service to a parallel team within the customer's organization. However, the concept of networking is also relevant in consumer marketing environments, where customers are encouraged to refer friends and acquaintances to the service provider. Individual customers may have relationships with different individuals or departments within a supplier firm, depending on the situation. These relationships may range from discussions with sales and marketing personnel, to service encounters in the field to membership in a loyalty program, to the pursuit of complaints.

The four types of marketing we have described are not necessarily mutually exclusive. A firm may have transactions with some customers who have neither the desire nor the need to make future purchases, while working hard to serve others whom it is encouraging to climb the loyalty ladder. Evert Gummesson advocates *total relationship marketing,* described as

> [M]arketing based on relationships, networks, and interaction, recognizing that marketing is embedded in the total management of the networks of the selling organization, the market, and society. It is directed to long-term, win-win relationships with individual customers, and value is jointly created between the parties involved.[18]

He identifies no fewer than 30 types of relationships within the broader context of total relationship marketing.

Creating "Membership" Relationships

Although some services involve discrete transactions, others involve purchasers' receiving service on a continuing basis. Even where the transactions are themselves discrete, there may still be an opportunity to create an ongoing relationship. The differing natures of the following situations offer an opportunity for categorizing services. First, we can ask: Does the supplier enter into a formal "membership" relationship with customers, as with telephone subscriptions, banking, and the family doctor? Or is there no defined relationship? The second question is: Is the service delivered on a continuous basis, as in insurance, broadcasting, and police protection? Or is each transaction recorded and charged separately? Table 12-1 shows the matrix resulting from this categorization, with examples in each category.

A *membership relationship*, a formalized relationship between the firm and an identifiable customer, may offer special benefits to both parties. Services involving discrete transactions can be transformed into membership relationships either by selling the service in bulk (for instance, a theater series subscription or a commuter ticket on public transport) or by offering extra benefits to customers who choose to register with the firm (loyalty programs for hotels, airlines, and car rental firms fall into this category). The advantage to the service organization of having membership relationships is that it knows who its current customers are and, usually, what use they make of the services offered. This information can be valuable for segmentation purposes if good records are kept and the data are readily accessible for analysis. Knowing the identities and addresses of current customers enables the organization to make effective use of direct mail (including e-mail), telephone selling, and personal sales calls—all highly targeted methods of marketing communication. In turn, members can be given access to special numbers or even designated account managers to facilitate their communications with the firm.

TABLE 12-1 Relationships with Customers

	Type of Relationship between the Service Organization and Its Customers	
Nature of Service Delivery	*Membership Relationship*	*No Formal Relationship*
Continuous delivery of service	Insurance	Radio station
	Cable TV subscription	Police protection
	College enrollment	Lighthouse
	Banking	Public highway
Discrete transactions	Long-distance calls from subscriber phone	Car rental Mail service
	Theater series subscription	Toll highway
	Travel on commuter ticket	Pay phone
	Repair under warranty	Movie theater
	Health treatment for	Public transportation
	HMO member	Restaurant

TARGETING THE RIGHT CUSTOMERS

Many elements are involved in creating long-term customer relationships and loyalty. The process starts by identifying and targeting the right customers. Whom should we be serving? is a question that every service business needs to raise periodically. Customers often differ widely in terms of needs and the value they can contribute to a company. Not all customers offer a good fit with the organization's capabilities, delivery technologies, and strategic direction.

Good Relationships Start with a Good Fit

If they want to build successful customer relationships, companies need to be selective about the segments they target. In this section, we emphasize the importance of choosing to serve a portfolio of several carefully chosen target segments and taking pains to build and maintain their loyalty. (If you have not previously taken a marketing course, you will find it useful to review Management Memo 12-2.)

Matching customers to the firm's capabilities is vital. Managers must think carefully about how customer needs relate to such operational elements as speed and quality, the times when service is available, the firm's capacity to serve many customers simultaneously, and the physical features and appearance of service facilities. Managers also need to consider how well their service personnel can meet the expectations of specific types of customers, in terms of both personal style and technical competence. Finally, managers need to ask themselves whether their company can match or exceed competing services that are directed at the same types of customers.

The result of carefully targeting customers by matching the company's capabilities and strengths with customer needs should be a superior service offering in the eyes of those customers who value what the firm has to offer. Frederick Reichheld said that "the result should be a win-win situation, where profits are earned through the success and satisfaction of customers, and not at their expense."[19]

Searching for Value, Not Just Numbers

Too many service firms still focus on the *number* of customers they serve—an important issue for operations and human resource planning—without giving sufficient attention to the *value* of each customer. Generally speaking, heavy users buy more frequently and in larger volumes and are more profitable than are occasional users.

MANAGEMENT MEMO 12-2

IDENTIFYING AND SELECTING TARGET SEGMENTS

Market segmentation is central to almost any professionally planned and executed marketing program. The concept of segmentation recognizes that customers and prospects within a market vary across a variety of dimensions and that not every segment constitutes a desirable target for the firm's marketing efforts.

A market segment consists of a group of current and potential customers who share common characteristics, needs, purchasing behavior, or consumption patterns. Effective segmentation should group buyers into segments in ways that result in as much similarity as possible on the relevant characteristics *within* each segment but dissimilarity on those same characteristics *between* each segment. Two broad categories of variables useful in describing the differences between segments are user characteristics and usage behavior.

User characteristics may vary from one person to another, reflecting *demographic* characteristics (for instance, age, income, and education), *geographic* location, and *psychographics* (the attitudes, values, lifestyles, and opinions of decision makers and users). *Technographics*—a term recently trademarked by Forrester Research—describes the extent to which customers are willing and able to use the latest technology. Another important segmentation variable is user needs and the specific benefits that individuals and corporate purchasers seek from consuming a particular good or service.

Usage behavior relates to how a product is purchased, delivered, and used. Among such variables are when and where purchase and consumption take place, the quantities consumed ("heavy users" are always of particular interest to marketers), the frequency and purpose of use, the occasions when consumption takes place (sometimes referred to as "occasion segmentation"), and sensitivity to marketing variables (e.g., advertising, pricing, speed, and other service features), and availability of alternative delivery systems.

After evaluating different segments in the market, a firm should focus its marketing efforts by *targeting one or more segments* that fit well with the firm's capabilities and goals. Target segments are often defined on the basis of several variables. For instance, a hotel in a particular city might target prospective guests who share certain user characteristics, such as (1) traveling on business (demographic segmentation), (2) visiting clients within a defined area around the hotel (geographic segmentation), and (3) willingness to pay a certain daily room rate (user response).

When researching the marketplace, service marketers should be looking for answers to the following questions.

- In what useful ways can the market for our firm's service be segmented?
- What are the needs of the specific segments we have identified?
- Which of these segments best fits our institution's mission and our current operational capabilities?
- What do customers in each segment see as our firm's competitive advantages and disadvantages? Are the latter correctable?
- In the light of this analysis, which specific segment(s) should we target?
- How should we differentiate our marketing efforts from those of the competition to attract and retain the types of customers we want?
- What is the long-term financial value of a loyal customer in each segment we currently serve (and those we would like to serve)?
- How should our firm build long-term relationships with customers from the target segments?
- What strategies are needed to create long-term loyalty?

Think about the activities you do on a regular basis. Do you have a favorite restaurant or pizza parlor where you often eat with friends or family? Is there a movie theater that you patronize regularly? Do you use your mobile phone all the time and for a lot of different services, from SMS to international roaming?

If you answered yes to any of these questions, you are potentially a lot more interesting to the management of the organizations in question than is a one-time visitor who is simply passing through town. The revenue stream from your purchases, and those of others like you, may amount to quite a considerable sum over the course of the year. Sometimes, your value as a frequent user is openly recognized and appreciated. You sense that the business is tailoring its service features, including service hours and prices, to attract people like you and doing its best to make you loyal. In other instances, however, you may feel that nobody knows or cares who you are. Your purchases may make you a valuable customer, but you certainly do not feel valued.

We also note that not all segments are worth serving, and it may not be realistic to try to retain them. Roger Hallowell, a Harvard Business School professor, makes this point nicely in a discussion of banking:

> A bank's population of customers undoubtedly contains individuals who either cannot be satisfied, given the service levels and pricing the bank is capable of offering, or will never be profitable, given their banking activity (their use of resources relative to the revenue they supply). Any bank would be wise to target and serve only those customers whose needs it can meet better than its competitors in a profitable manner. These are the customers who are most likely to remain with that bank for long periods, who will purchase multiple products and services, who will recommend that bank to their friends and relations, and who may be the source of superior returns to the bank's shareholders.[20]

Relationship customers are by definition not buying commodity services. Service customers who buy based strictly on lowest price (a minority in most markets) are not good target customers for relationship marketing in the first place. These deal-prone customers continually seek the lowest price on offer.[21]

Acquiring the right customers can bring in long-term revenues, continued growth from referrals, and enhanced satisfaction from employees whose daily jobs are improved when they can deal with appreciative customers. Attracting the wrong customers typically results in costly churn, a diminished company reputation, and disillusioned employees. Ironically, it is often the firms that are highly focused and selective in their acquisition rather than those that focus on unbridled acquisition that are growing quickly over long periods.[22] Best Practice in Action 12-1 shows how Vanguard designed its products and pricing to attract and retain the right customers for its business model.

Marketers shouldn't assume that the "right customers" are always high spenders. Depending on the service business model, the right customers can come from a large group of people that no other supplier is doing a good job of serving. Many firms have successfully built strategies serving customer segments that were neglected by established players that didn't perceive them as sufficiently "valuable." Examples are Enterprise Rent-A-Car, which targeted customers who need a temporary replacement car and avoided the more traditional segment of business travelers pursued by its principal competitors; Charles Schwab, which focused on retail stock buyers; and Paychex, which provides small businesses with payroll and HR services.[23]

But marketers also need to recognize that some customers simply are not worth serving, because they are too difficult to please or unable to decide on what they want. Figure 12-3 provides an illustration.

Selecting an Appropriate Customer Portfolio

Artists and writers often prepare portfolios of their work to show to prospective purchasers or employers. The term *portfolio* also describes the collection of financial

BEST PRACTICE IN ACTION 12-1

VANGUARD DISCOURAGES THE ACQUISITION OF "WRONG" CUSTOMERS

The Vanguard Group is a growth leader in the mutual fund industry and built its $550 billion in managed assets by painstakingly targeting the right customers for its business model. Its share of new sales, which was around 25 percent, reflected its share of assets, or market share. However, it had a far lower share of redemptions, which gave it a market share of net cash flows of 55 percent (new sales minus redemptions) and made it the fastest-growing mutual fund in its industry.

How did Vanguard achieve such low redemption rates? The secret was in its careful acquisition and its product and pricing strategies, which encouraged the acquisition of the "right" customers.

John Bogle, Vanguard's founder, believed in the superiority of index funds and that their lower management fees would lead to higher returns over the long run. He offered Vanguard's clients unparalleled low management fees through a policy of not trading (its index funds hold the market they are designed to track), not having a sales force, and spending only a fraction of what its competitors did on advertising. Another important part of keeping the costs low has been to discourage the acquisition of customers who are not long-term index holders.

John Bogle attributes the high level of customer loyalty Vanguard achieved to a great deal of focus on customer defections, which in the fund context are redemption rates. "I watched them like a hawk," he explained, and analyzed them more carefully than new sales to ensure that Vanguard's customer acquisition strategy was on course. Low redemption rates meant that the firm was attracting the right kind of loyal, long-term investors. The inherent stability of its loyal customer base has been key to Vanguard's cost advantage. Bogle's pickiness became legendary. He scrutinized individual redemptions with a fine-tooth comb to see who let the wrong kind of customers on board. When an institutional investor redeemed $25 million from an index fund bought only nine months earlier, he regarded the acquisition of this customer a failure of the system. He explained, "We don't want short-term investors. They muck up the game at the expense of the long-term investor." At the end of his chairman's letter to the Vanguard Index Trust, Bogle reiterated: "We urge them [short-term investors] to look elsewhere for their investment opportunities."

This care and attention to acquiring the right customers became legendary. For example, Vanguard turned away an institutional investor that wanted to invest $40 million, because Vanguard suspected that the customer would churn the investment within the next few weeks, creating extra costs for existing customers. The potential customer complained to Vanguard's CEO, who not only supported the decision but also used it as an opportunity to reinforce to his teams why they needed to be selective about the customers they accept.

Vanguard also introduced a number of industry-practice changes that discouraged active traders from buying its funds. For example, Vanguard did not allow telephone transfers for index funds, redemption fees were added to some funds, and the standard practice subsidizing new accounts at the expense of existing customers was rejected as being disloyal to its core investor base. These product and pricing policies in effect turned away heavy traders but made the fund uniquely attractive for the long-term investor.

Finally, Vanguard's pricing was set up to reward loyal customers. For many of its funds, investors pay a one-time up-front fee, that goes into the funds themselves to compensate all current investors for the administrative costs of selling new shares. In essence, this fee subsidizes long-term investors and penalizes short-term investors. Another novel pricing approach was the creation of its Admiral shares for loyal investors, which carried an expense fee one-third below ordinary shares (0.12 percent per year instead of 0.18 percent).

Source: Frederick F. Reichheld, *Loyalty Rules! How Today's Leaders Build Lasting Relationships* (Boston: Harvard Business School Press, 2001): 24–29, 84–87, 144–145.

FIGURE 12-3 Avoiding the "Wrong" Type of Customer

instruments held by an investor or the array of loans advanced by a bank. In financial services, the goal of portfolio analysis is to determine the mix of investments (or loans) that is appropriate to one's needs, resources, and risk preference. In an investment portfolio, the contents should change over time in response to the performance of individual portfolio elements, as well as reflect changes in the customer's situation or preferences.

We can apply the concept of portfolio to service businesses with an established base of customers. Different segments offer different value for a service firm. Like investments, some types of customers may be more profitable than others in the short term, but others may have greater potential for long-term growth. Similarly, the spending patterns of some customers may be stable over time, whereas others may be more volatile; companies in cyclical industries tend to spend heavily in boom times but cut back sharply in recessions. A wise firm may seek a mix of such segments in order to reduce the risks that various types of customers might be affected by market or macroeconomic forces.[24]

As David Maister emphasizes, marketing is about getting *better* business, not simply *more* business.[25] The caliber of a professional firm is measured by the type of clients it serves and the nature of the tasks on which it works. Volume alone is no measure of excellence, sustainability, or profitability. In professional services, such as consulting firms or legal partnerships, the mix of business attracted may play an important role in both defining the firm and providing a suitable mix of assignments for staff members at different levels in the organization.

ANALYZING AND MANAGING THE CUSTOMER BASE

Marketers should adopt a strategic approach to retaining, upgrading, and even terminating customers. Customer retention involves developing long-term, cost-effective links with customers for the mutual benefit of both parties, but these efforts need not necessarily target all a firm's customers with the same level of intensity. Recent research has confirmed that most firms have several tiers of customers in terms of profitability and that these tiers often have quite different service expectations and needs. According to Valarie Zeithaml, Roland Rust, and Katharine Lemon, it's critical that service firms understand the needs of customers within different profitability tiers and adjust their service levels accordingly.[26]

Tiering the Customer Base

Customer tiers can be developed around various levels of profit contribution, different needs (including sensitivities to such variables as price, comfort, and speed), and identifiable personal profiles, such as demographics. (Service Perspective 12-1 describes the various customer tiers from the perspective of a market research agency.) Zeithaml, Rust, and Lemon illustrated this principle through a four-level pyramid, as shown in Figure 12-4.

Platinum These customers, who constitute a very small percentage of a firm's customer base, are heavy users and contribute a large share of the profits generated. Typically, this segment is less price sensitive but expects highest service levels in return and is likely to be willing to invest in and try new services.

Gold The gold tier forms a larger percentage of customers than the platinum, but individual customers contribute less profit than do platinum customers. Gold-tier customers tend to be slightly more price sensitive and less committed to the firm.

Iron These customers provide the bulk of customer base. Because their numbers give the firm economies of scale, they are often important so that a firm can build and maintain a certain capacity level and infrastructure, which is often needed for serving gold and platinum customers. However, iron customers in themselves are often only marginally profitable. Their level of business is not sufficiently substantial for special treatment.

FIGURE 12-4 The Customer Pyramid

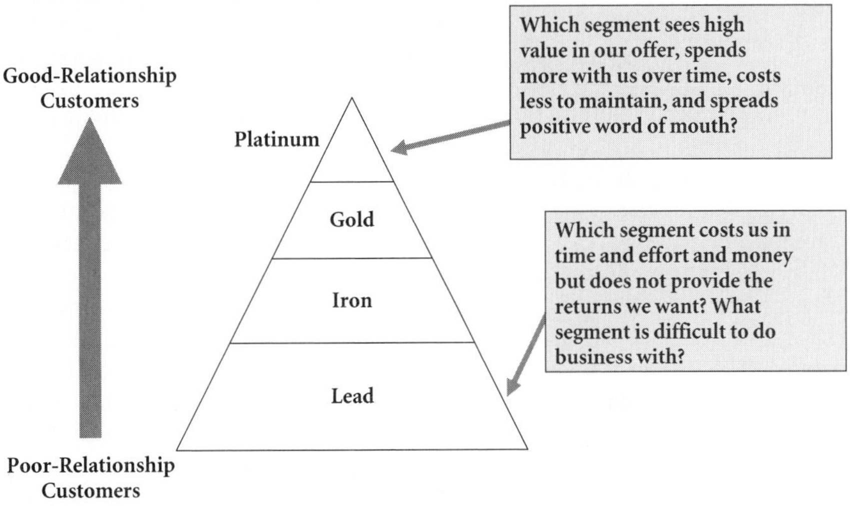
Good-Relationship Customers
Poor-Relationship Customers
Platinum
Gold
Iron
Lead
Which segment sees high value in our offer, spends more with us over time, costs less to maintain, and spreads positive word of mouth?
Which segment costs us in time and effort and money but does not provide the returns we want? What segment is difficult to do business with?

Source: Valarie A Zeithaml, Roland T. Rust, and Katharine N. Lemon, "The Customer Pyramid: Creating and Serving Profitable Customers," *California Management Review* 43, no. 4 (Summer 2001): 118. Copyright © 2001 by The Regents of the University of California. Reprinted by permission of The Regents.

Lead Lead-tier customers tend to generate low revenues for a firm but often still require the same level of service as iron customers, which turns them into a loss-making segment from a firm's perspective.

Retaining, Upgrading, and Terminating Customers

Generally, customer tiers are based on not only profitability but also other identifiable characteristics common among these different segments. Instead of providing the same level of service to all customers, each segment receives a customized service level, based on its requirements and value to the firm. For example, the platinum tier will receive some exclusive benefits not available to other segments. The benefit levels for platinum and gold customers are often designed with retention in mind, because these customers are the ones that competitors would like to entice to switch.

Marketing efforts can be used to encourage an increased volume of purchases, upgrading the type of service used, or cross-selling additional services to any of the four tiers. However, these efforts have a different thrust for each of the tiers, reflecting their differing needs, usage behaviors, and spending patterns. Among segments for which the firm already has a high share of wallet, the focus should be on nurturing, defending, and retaining these customers, potentially via loyalty programs.[27]

For lead-tier customers, the options are to either migrate them to the iron segment or terminate them. Migration can be achieved via a combination of strategies, including base fees and price increases. Imposing a minimum fee that is waived when a certain level of revenue is generated may encourage customers who use several suppliers to consolidate their transactions with a single provider. There may be opportunities to shape customer behavior in ways that will reduce the cost of serving them; for instance, transaction charges for electronic channels may be priced lower than for people-intensive channels. Another option is to create an attractively priced low-cost platform. In the cellular telephone industry, for example, low-use mobile users are directed to prepaid packages that do not require the firm to send out bills and collect payments, thus eliminating the risk of bad debts on such accounts.

Terminating customers comes as a logical consequence of the realization that not all existing customer relationships are worth keeping. Many relationships are no longer

SERVICE PERSPECTIVE 12-1

TIERING THE CUSTOMERS OF A MARKET RESEARCH AGENCY

Tiering its clients helped a leading U.S. market research agency to better understand its customers. The agency defined *platinum clients* as large accounts that were not only willing to plan a certain amount of research work during the year but also able to commit to the timing, scope, and nature of their projects, which made capacity management and project planning much easier for the research firm. The acquisition costs for projects sold to these clients were only between 2 and 5 percent of project values (as compared to as much as 25 percent for clients that required extensive proposal work and project-by-project bidding). Platinum accounts were also more willing to try new services and to buy a wider range of services from their preferred provider. These customers were generally very satisfied with the research agency's work and were willing to act as references to potential new clients.

Gold accounts had a similar profile to platinum clients but were more price sensitive and more inclined to spread their budgets across several firms. Although these accounts had been clients for many years, they were not willing to commit their research work for a year in advance, even though the research firm would have been able to offer them better quality and priority in capacity allocation.

Iron accounts spent moderate amounts on research and commissioned work on a project basis. Selling costs were high, as these firms tended to send out requests for proposals (RFPs) to a number of firms for all their projects. These firms sought the lowest price and often did not give the research firm sufficient time for to perform a good-quality job.

Lead accounts conducted only isolated, low-cost, "quick-and-dirty" in projects, with little opportunity for the research firm to add value or to apply its skill sets appropriately. Sales costs were high, as the client typically invited several firms to quote. Furthermore, because these firms were inexperienced in conducting research and in working with research agencies, selling a project often took several meetings and required multiple revisions to the proposal. Lead accounts also tended to be high maintenance, as they did not understand research work well; they often changed project parameters, scope, and deliverables midstream and then expected the research agency to absorb the cost of any rework, thus further reducing the profitability of the engagement.

Source: Valarie A Zeithaml, Roland T. Rust, and Katharine N. Lemon, "The Customer Pyramid: Creating and Serving Profitable Customers," *California Management Review* 43, no. 4 (Summer 2001): 127–128

profitable for the firm, as they may cost more to maintain than the revenues they generate. Some customers no longer fit the firm's strategy, either because it has changed or because the customers' behavior and needs have changed. Just as investors need to dispose of poor investments and banks may have to write off bad loans, each service firm needs to regularly evaluate its customer portfolio and consider terminating unsuccessful relationships. Legal and ethical considerations, of course, will determine whether it is proper to take such actions.

Occasionally, customers are fired outright, although concern for due process is still important. Certain relationships involve adherence to mutually agreed rules. Bank customers who bounce too many checks, students who are caught cheating in examinations, or country club members who consistently abuse the facilities or other people may be asked to leave or face expulsion. In other instances, termination may be somewhat less confrontational. Banks wishing to divest themselves of certain types of accounts that no longer fit with corporate priorities have been known to sell them to other banks. (One example is credit card holders who receive a letter in the mail, telling them that their accounts have been transferred to another card issuer.) Alternatively, a doctor or lawyer may suggest to unprofitable, difficult and/or dissatisfied clients that they should consider switching to another provider whose expertise or style is more suited to their needs and expectations.

BUILDING CUSTOMER LOYALTY

What makes customers loyal to a firm, and how can marketers increase their loyalty? In this section, we first review the common loyalty drivers for customers and then explore the foundations of loyalty and how firms can build or enhance such loyalty drivers further.

Customers' View of Relational Benefits

Research by Kevin Gwinner, Dwayne Gremler, and Mary Jo Bitner suggests that relationships create value for individual consumers through such factors as inspiring greater confidence, offering social benefits, and providing special treatment (see Research Insights 12-1). Piyush Kumar emphasizes that relationships in a business-to-business service are dependent largely on the quality of the interactions between individuals at each of the partnering firms.[28] "As relationships strengthen over a period of time," he observes, "the service provider's personnel often assume the role of outsourced departments and make critical decisions on behalf of their clients."

The Foundations of Customer Loyalty

The foundation for true loyalty lies in customer satisfaction. Highly satisfied or even delighted customers are more likely to become loyal apostles of a firm, consolidate their buying with one suppler, and spread positive word of mouth. In contrast, dissatisfaction drives customers away and is a key factor in switching behavior.

Figure 12-5 divides the satisfaction/loyalty relationship into three main zones. The *zone of defection* is at low satisfaction levels. Customers will switch unless switching costs are high or there are no viable or convenient alternatives. Extremely dissatisfied

FIGURE 12-5 The Customer Satisfaction/Loyalty Relationship

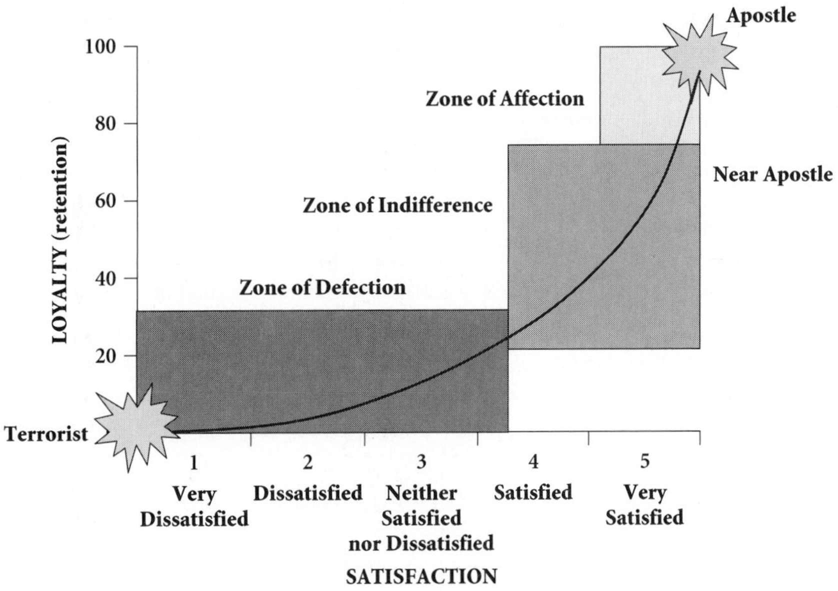

Source: Adapted from Thomas O. Jones and W. Earl Sasser, Jr., "Why Satisfied Customers Defect," *Harvard Business Review* (November–December 1995): 91. Reprinted by permission of Harvard Business School.

RESEARCH INSIGHTS 12-1

HOW CUSTOMERS SEE RELATIONAL BENEFITS IN SERVICE INDUSTRIES

What benefits do customers see themselves receiving from an extended relationship with a service firm? Researchers seeking answers to this question conducted two studies. The first consisted of in-depth interviews with 21 respondents, in their own homes, from a broad cross-section of backgrounds. These interviews averaged 48 minutes in length. Respondents were asked to identify service providers they used on a regular basis and were invited to identify and discuss any benefits they received as a result of being a regular customer. Following are some of the comments.

- "I like him [hair stylist]. . . . He's really funny and always has lots of good jokes. He's kind of like a friend now."
- "I know what I'm getting—I know that if I go to a restaurant that I regularly go to, rather than taking a chance on all of the new restaurants, the food will be good."
- "I often get price breaks. The little bakery that I go to in the morning, every once in a while, they'll give me a free muffin and say, 'You're a good customer, it's on us today.'"
- "You can get better service than drop-in customers . . . . We continue to go to the same automobile repair shop because we have gotten to know the owner on a kind of personal basis, and he . . . can always work us in."
- "Once people feel comfortable, they don't want to switch to another dentist. They don't want to train or break a new dentist in."

After evaluating and categorizing the comments, the researchers designed a second study in which some survey questionnaires were distributed to a convenience sample of about 400 people. The subjects were told to select a specific service provider with which they had a strong, established relationship. Then the questionnaire asked them to assess the extent to which they received each of 21 benefits (derived from analysis of the first study) as a result of their relationship with the specific provider they had identified. Finally, they were asked to assess the importance of these benefits for them.

A total of 299 usable surveys were returned. A factor analysis of the results showed that most of the benefits that customers derived from relationships could be grouped into three clusters. The first, and most important, group concerned what the researchers labeled confidence benefits, followed by social benefits and special treatment.

- *Confidence benefits* included feelings by customers that in an established relationship, there was less risk of something going wrong, confidence in correct performance, ability to trust the provider, lowered anxiety when purchasing, knowing what to expect, and receipt of the firm's highest level of service.
- *Social benefits* embraced mutual recognition between customers and employees, being known by name, friendship with the service provider, and enjoyment of certain social aspects of the relationship.
- *Special-treatment benefits* included better prices, discounts on special deals that were unavailable to most other customers, extra services, higher priority when there was a wait, and faster service than most other customers received.

Source: Kevin P. Gwinner, Dwayne D. Gremler, and Mary Jo Bitner, "Relational Benefits in Services Industries: The Customer's Perspective," *Journal of the Academy of Marketing Science* 26, no. 2 (1998): 101–114.

customers can turn into "terrorists," providing an abundance of negative word of mouth for the service provider. The *zone of indifference* is at intermediate satisfaction levels. Here, customers are willing to switch if they find a better alternative. The *zone of affection* is at very high satisfaction levels, and customers here can have such high attitudinal loyalty that they do not look for alternative service providers. Customers who praise the firm in public and refer others to the firm are described as "apostles."

Creating Bonds with Customers

Having the right portfolio of customer segments, attracting the right customers, tiering the service, and delivering high levels of satisfaction are a solid foundation for creating customer loyalty, as shown in Figure 12-6. However, there is more that firms can do to "bond" more closely with their customers; specific strategies for loyalty bonds are summarized in item 2 in the figure.[29] At the same time, service marketers should be working to identify and eliminate the factors that result in "churn," or the loss of existing customers and the need to replace them with new ones.

Deepening the Relationship To tie customers more closely to the firm, deepening the relationship via bundling and/or cross-selling services is an effective strategy. For example, banks like to sell as many financial products into an account or household as possible. Once a family has its current account, credit card, savings account, safe-deposit box, car loan, mortgage, and so on, with the same bank, the relationship is so deep that switching becomes a major exercise and is unlikely unless, of course, the customer is extremely dissatisfied with the bank.

Reward-Based Bonds Within any competitive product category, managers recognize that few customers consistently buy only one brand, especially if service delivery involves a discrete transaction (such as a car rental) rather than being continuous, (as

FIGURE 12-6 The Wheel of Loyalty

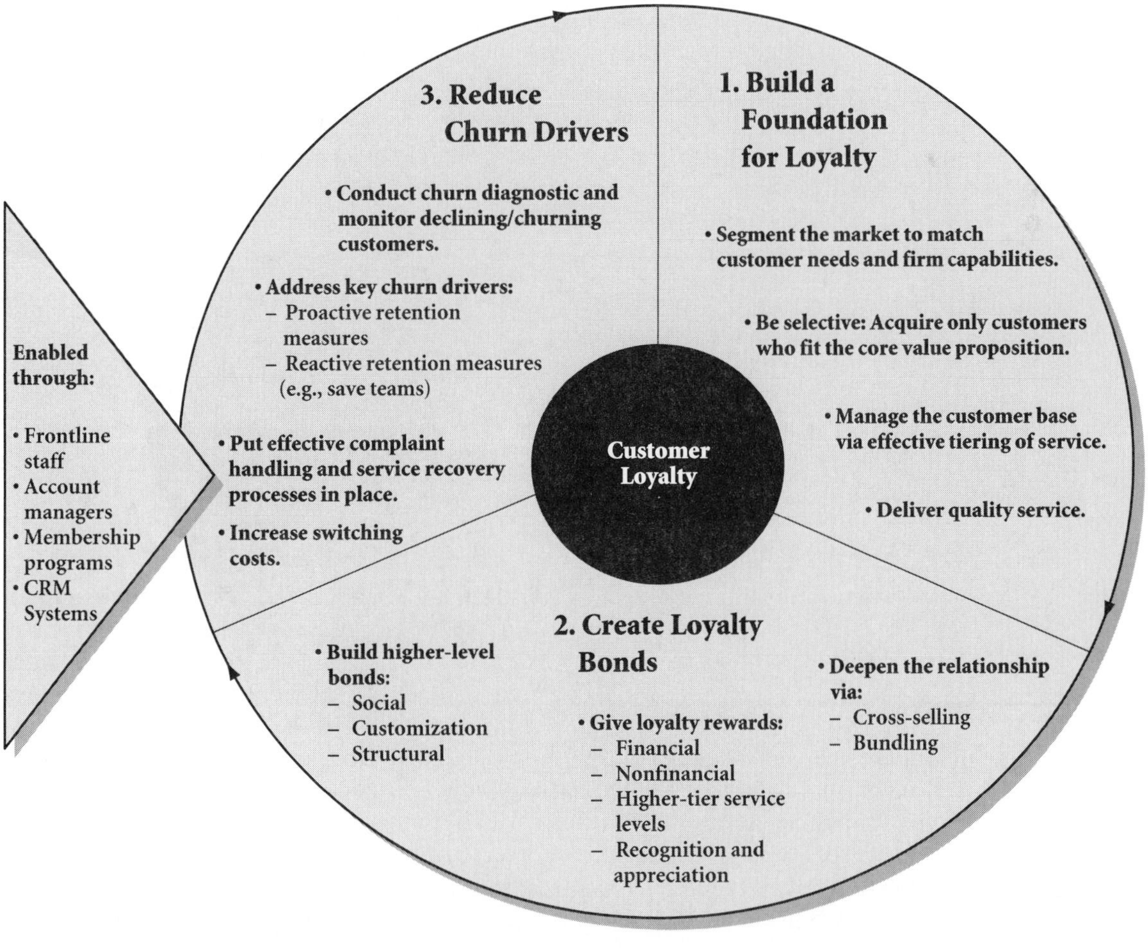

with insurance coverage). In many instances, consumers are loyal to several brands while spurning others—sometimes described as "polygamous loyalty" (not to be confused with variety seeking, which results in consumers' flitting butterflylike from brand to brand, without any fixed allegiance at all). In such instances, the marketing goal becomes one of strengthening the customer's preference for one brand over the others.

Incentives that offer rewards based on the frequency or value of purchase combination of both represent a basic level of customer bonds. Reward-based bonds can be financial or nonfinancial. Financial bonds are built when loyal customers are rewarded with incentives that have a financial value, such as discounts on purchases and loyalty-program rewards, such as frequent flier miles or the cash-back programs provided by some credit card issuers, based on the level of spending charged by card members.

Nonfinancial rewards provide customers with benefits or value that cannot be translated directly into monetary terms. Examples are giving priority to loyalty-program members for waitlists and access to call centers and operators. Some airlines provide such benefits as higher baggage allowances, priority upgrading, and access to airport lounges to its frequent flyers, even when they are flying in economy class. In the b2b context, offering service extras often plays a key role in building and sustaining relationships between vendors and purchasers of industrial goods.[30] Informal loyalty rewards, sometimes found in small businesses, may take the form of periodically giving regular customers a small treat as a way of thanking them.

Important intangible rewards may take the form of special recognition and appreciation. Customers tend to value the extra attention given to their needs, as well as the implicit service guarantee offered by higher-tier memberships, including efforts to meet special requests. One objective of reward-based bonds is to motivate customers to consolidate their purchases with one provider or at least make it the preferred provider. Tiered loyalty programs often provide direct incentives for customers to achieve the next higher level of membership. However, regard-based loyalty programs are relatively easy for other suppliers to copy and rarely provide a sustained competitive advantage. By contrast, the higher-level bonds that we discuss next tend to be more sustainable.

Social Bonds Have you ever noticed how your favorite hairdresser addresses you by name when you go for a haircut or asks why you haven't been in for a long time and hopes everything went well when you were away on a long business trip? Social bonds are typically based on personal relationships between providers and customers. Alternatively, they may reflect pride or satisfaction in holding membership in an organization. Although social bonds are more difficult to build than financial bonds and may require considerable time to achieve, they are, for that same reason, also more difficult for other suppliers to replicate for that same customer. A firm that has created social bonds with its customers has a better chance of retaining them for the long term.

Customization Bonds These bonds are built when the service provider succeeds in providing customized service to its loyal customers. One-to-one marketing is a more specialized form of customization whereby each individual is treated as a segment.[31] Many large hotel chains capture their customers' preferences through their loyalty-program databases; when those customers arrive at the hotel, they find that their individual needs have already been anticipated, from preferred drinks and snacks in the room refrigerator to the kind of pillow they like and the newspaper they want to receive in the morning. A customer who becomes used to this special service may find it difficult to adjust to another service provider that is not able to customize the service (at least immediately, as it takes time for the new provider to learn about someone's needs).

Structural Bonds Structural bonds are seen mostly in b2b settings and aim to stimulate loyalty through structural relationships between the provider and the customer. Examples are joint investments in projects and sharing of information, processes, and equipment. Structural bonds can be created in a b2c environment, too. For instance, some airlines have introduced SMS and e-mail alerts for flight arrival and departure times so that travelers do not have to waste time waiting at the airport in the case of delays. Some car rental companies offer travelers the opportunity to create customized pages on the firm's Web site, where they can retrieve details of past trips, including the types of cars, insurance coverage, and so forth. This simplifies and speeds the task of making new bookings. Once customers have integrated their way of doing things with the firm's processes, structural bonds are created that link those customers to the firm and make it more difficult for competition to draw them away (see Figure 12-7).

Creation of Customer Bonds through Membership Relationships and Loyalty Programs

As a marketing strategy, many service businesses seek ways to develop formal, ongoing "membership" relations with customers. Hotels, for instance, have developed "frequent-guest programs" offering priority reservations, upgraded rooms, and other rewards for frequent guests. Many nonprofit organizations, such as museums, create membership programs in order to reinforce the links with their most active supporters, offering them such extra benefits as private showings and meetings with curators or artists as a reward for annual donations. The marketing task here is to determine how to build sales and revenues (or, in the case of nonprofits, donations) through such "memberships," while avoiding the risk of freezing out a large volume of desirable casual business. The case study "Massachusetts Audubon Society" (see pp. 588–603) addresses the challenge for a nonprofit organization of deepening member involvement with the institution.

Transforming Discrete Transactions to Membership Relationships Discrete transactions, when each use involves a payment to the service supplier by an essentially "anonymous" consumer, are typical of such services as transport, restaurants, cinemas, and shoe repairs. The problem for marketers of such services is that they tend to be less informed about who their customers are and what use each customer makes of the service than are their counterparts in membership-type organizations. Managers in businesses that sell discrete transactions have to work a little harder to establish relationships. In small businesses, such as hairdressers, frequent customers are (or should be) welcomed as "regulars" whose needs and preferences are remembered. Keeping formal records of customers' needs, preferences, and purchasing behavior is useful even in small firms, as it helps employees avoid having to ask repetitive questions on each service occasion, allows them to personalize the service given to each customer, and also enables the firm to anticipate future needs.

In large companies with substantial customer bases, transactions can still be transformed into relationships by implementing loyalty-reward programs, which require customers to apply for membership cards with which transactions can be captured and customers' preferences communicated to the front line. Account management programs may be added to the loyalty program by offering a special telephone number to call for assistance or even naming a designated account representative. Long-term contracts between suppliers and their customers take the nature of relationships to a higher level, transforming them into partnerships and strategic alliances.

A number of other service businesses have sought to copy the airline industry with loyalty programs of their own. Hotels, car rental firms, telephone companies, retailers, and even credit card issuers have been among those that seek to identify and reward

Get 1,000 HHonors bonus points
for booking online from the
comfort of your home.
(No matter what your definition of comfort is.)

Book online and stay by February 28, 2003, to earn 1,000 Hilton HHonors® bonus points.

Just cozy up to hiltonhhonors.com to make your next reservation using your

Hilton HHonors account number. Book online and stay between January 1 and

February 28, 2003, and you'll earn an extra 1,000 HHonors bonus points. It's yet

another simple, convenient and comfortable way to get even more with Hilton HHonors.

hiltonhhonors.com

You must be a member of Hilton HHonors to earn HHonors points. Please allow three weeks after you complete your stay for the online reservation bonus to appear in your Hilton HHonors® account. This offer applies to reservations made on the Hilton®, Conrad®, Doubletree®, Embassy Suites Hotels®, Hampton Inn®, Hampton Inn & Suites®, Hilton Garden Inn® and Homewood Suites® by Hilton Web sites. The 1,000 HHonors bonus points cannot be earned in addition to any other HHonors points or airline miles online reservations bonus. Hilton HHonors membership, earning of Points & Miles® and redemption of points are subject to HHonors Terms and Conditions. ©2003 Hilton HHonors Worldwide.

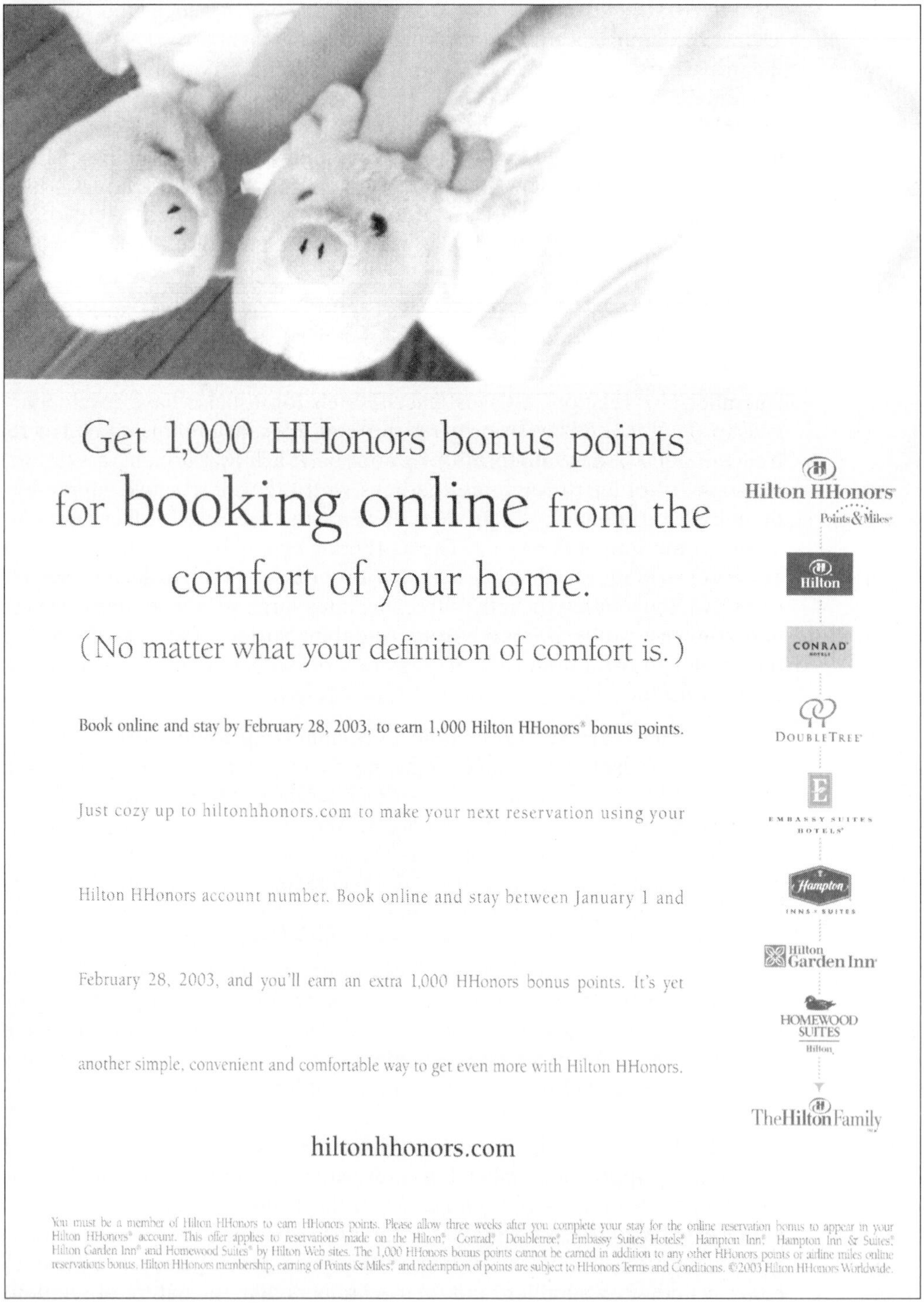

Reprinted courtesy of Hilton Hotel Corporation.

their best customers. Although some provide their own rewards—such as free merchandise, class of vehicle upgrades, or free hotel rooms in vacation resorts—many firms denominate their awards in miles that can be credited to a selected frequent flyer program. In short, air miles have become a form of promotional currency in the service sector. Best Practice in Action 12-2 describes how British Airways (BA) has designed its Executive Club.

Of course, rewards alone will not suffice to retain a firm's most desirable customers. If customers are dissatisfied with the quality of service they receive or believe that they can obtain better value from a less expensive service, they may quickly become disloyal. No service company that has instituted an awards program for frequent users can ever afford to lose sight of its broader goals of offering high service quality and good value relative to the price and other costs incurred by customers.

One of the risks associated with emphasizing relationships with high-value customers is that a firm may allow service to other customers to deteriorate. In the reading, "Why Service Stinks" (pages 466 to 473), Diane Brady explores the negative aspects of customer stratification.

Customer Perceptions of Loyalty-Reward Programs Recent research in the credit card industry suggests that loyalty programs strengthen the customers' perception of the value proposition and lead to increased revenues, owing to fewer defections and higher use levels.[32] To assess the potential of a loyalty program to alter normal patterns of behavior, Dowling and Uncles argue that marketers need to examine three psychological effects.[33]

- *Brand loyalty versus deal loyalty*. To what extent are customers loyal to the core service (or brand) rather than to the loyalty program itself? Marketers should focus on loyalty programs that directly support the value proposition and positioning of the product in question.
- *How buyers value rewards*. Several elements determine a loyalty program's value to customers: (1) the cash value of the redemption rewards (if customers had to purchase them); (2) the range of choice among rewards—for instance a selection of gifts rather than a single gift); (3) the aspirational value of the rewards (something exotic that the consumer would not normally purchase may have greater appeal than a cash-back offer); (4) whether the amount of use required to obtain an award places it within the realm of possibility for any given consumer; (5) the ease of using the program and making claims for redemption; and (6) the psychological benefits of belonging to the program and accumulating points.
- *Timing*. How soon can customers obtain benefits from participating in the rewards program? Deferred gratification tends to weaken the appeal of a loyalty program. One solution is to send customers periodic statements of their account status, indicating progress toward reaching a particular milestone and promoting the rewards that might be forthcoming when that point is reached.

Managing and Curtailing Drivers of Customer Defections

So far, we have discussed drivers of loyalty and strategies to tie customers more closely to the firm. An alternative approach is to understand drivers of customer defections, or churn, and work on eliminating or reducing those drivers. For example, in the mobile phone industry, players regularly conduct "churn diagnostics": the analysis of data warehouse information on churned and declining customers, exit interviews (call center staff often have a short set of questions they ask when a customer cancels an account, to gain a better understanding of why customers defect), and in-depth interviews of former customers by a third-party research agency, which typically yield a more detailed understanding of churn drivers.

BEST PRACTICE IN ACTION 12-2

REWARDING VALUE OF USE, NOT ONLY FREQUENCY, AT BRITISH AIRWAYS

Many international carriers initially resisted creating frequent flyer programs of their own. They were concerned not only about the expense but also that these programs required the airline to give award claimants free seats that could have been sold, during periods of high demand, to paying passengers. British Airways (BA) created its own program, known as Executive Club, in 1992. Until that point, its response to the competitive pressure of these programs had been limited to giving its passengers miles in an American carrier's awards program. However, senior BA management wanted to capture the competitive leverage inherent in learning more about its best customers and building their loyalty to the brand.

Unlike some programs, in which customer usage is measured simply in miles, Executive Club members receive both *air miles* toward redemption of air travel awards and *points* toward silver- or gold-tier status for travel on BA. However, no points are offered for flights ticketed in certain discount-fare categories. Certain flights on BA's subsidiary airlines also qualify for points and miles. With the creation of the OneWorld airline alliance with American Airlines, Cathay Pacific, Qantas, and other carriers, Executive Club members have been able to earn miles and points by flying these partner airlines, too.

As shown in Table 12-A, silver- and gold-tier members are entitled to special benefits, such as priority reservations and a superior level of on-the-ground service, while they are traveling. For instance, even if a gold-tier member is traveling in economy class, he or she will be entitled to first-class standards of treatment at check-in and in the airport lounges. However, although miles can be accumulated indefinitely, as long as a member flies at least once every three years (if not, they expire),

TABLE 12-A Benefits Offered by British Airways to Its Most Valued Passengers

Benefit	*Silver Tier Members*	*Gold Tier Members*
Reservations	Dedicated silver phone line	Dedicated gold phone line
Reservation assurance	If flight is full, guaranteed seat in economy when booking full fare ticket at least 24 hours in advance	If flight is full, guaranteed seat in economy when booking full fare ticket at least 24 hours in advance
Priority waitlist and standby	Higher priority	Highest priority
Advance notification of delays over 4 hours from U.S. or Canada	Yes	Yes
Check-in desk	Club (when traveling economy class)	First (when traveling Club or economy class)
Lounge access	Club departure lounges	First-class departure lounges and use of arrivals lounges in London if traveling economy class on intercontinental flights
Preferred boarding	Board aircraft at leisure	Board aircraft at leisure
Special services assistance		Problem solving beyond that accorded to other BA travelers
Bonus air miles	+25%	+50%
Upgrade for two		Free upgrade to next cabin for member and companion after earning 2,500 tier points in one year; another upgrade for two after 3,500 points in same year

Source: British Airways Executive Club, *www.britishairways.com/execclub*, accessed September 2003.

tier status is valid for only 15 months beyond the calendar year in which it was earned. In short, the right to special privileges must be re-earned every year. The objective of awarding tier status (which is not unique to BA) is to encourage passengers who have a choice of airlines to concentrate their travel on British Airways rather than to join several frequent flyer programs and collect mileage awards from all of them. Few passengers travel with such frequency that they will be able to obtain the benefits of gold-tier status (or its equivalent) on more than one airline. However, one of the rewards of that status may be the ability to use lounges and other amenities in airlines that belong to the same international alliance (such as OneWorld or Star Alliance; the latter alliance includes United, Air Canada, and Lufthansa).

The assignment of points also varies according to the class of service. BA seeks to recognize higher ticket expenditures with proportionately higher awards. Longer trips earn more points than shorter ones (a domestic or short-haul European trip in economy class generates 20 points, a transatlantic trip 60 points, and a trip from the U.K. to Australia, 110 points).

To reward purchase of higher-priced tickets, members earn points at double the economy rate if they travel in Club (business class) and at triple the rate in First. Likewise, passengers get class-of-service mileage bonuses for both Club (+25 percent) and First (+50 percent). In contrast, certain deeply discounted fares do not qualify for points at all.

To encourage gold- and silver-tier members to remain loyal, BA offers them incentives to retain their current tier status (or to move up from silver to gold). Silver-tier members receive a 25 percent bonus on all air miles, regardless of class of service, whereas gold-tier members receive a 50 percent bonus. In other words, it doesn't pay to spread the miles among several frequent flyer programs!

Although the airline makes no promises on complimentary upgrades, members of BA's Executive Club are more likely to receive such an invitation than are other passengers, with tier status being an important consideration. For obvious reasons, however, BA does not wish its most frequent travelers to feel that they can plan on buying a less expensive ticket and then automatically receiving an upgrade.

Common Churn Drivers Susan Keveaney conducted a large-scale study across a range of services and found several key reasons why customers switch to another provider[34] (Figure 12-8). Core service failures were mentioned by 44 percent of respondents as a reason for switching; unsatisfactory service encounters by 34 percent; high, deceptive, or unfair pricing by 30 percent; inconvenience in terms of time, location, or delays by 21 percent, and poor response to service failure by 17 percent. Many respondents described a decision to switch as resulting from interrelated incidents, such as a service failure followed by an unsatisfactory service recovery.

Strategies to Reduce Churn Keveaney's findings underscore the importance of delivering service quality (discussed in Chapter 14), effective complaint handling and service recovery (Chapter 13), minimizing inconvenience and other nonmonetary costs, and fair and transparent pricing (Chapter 6). In addition to these generic churn drivers, firms may encounter churn drivers that are specific to their own industries. For example, in cellular phone services, handset replacement needs are a common reason for subscribers to discontinue an existing subscription plan and subscribe to a new plan that typically comes with a heavily subsidized new handset. Mobile phone service providers typically provide handset subsidies ranging from $50 to $200 per unit, depending on the value of the subscription fee and the length of the contract.

To prevent handset-related churn, many providers offer proactive handset replacement programs, whereby current subscribers can buy subsidized handsets from their providers at regular intervals or even receive them for free when redeeming loyalty points earned on their mobile usage. Reactive retention measures include specially trained call center staff: so-called save teams, which deal with customers who intend to cancel their

FIGURE 12-8 Causes Behind Customer Service Switching

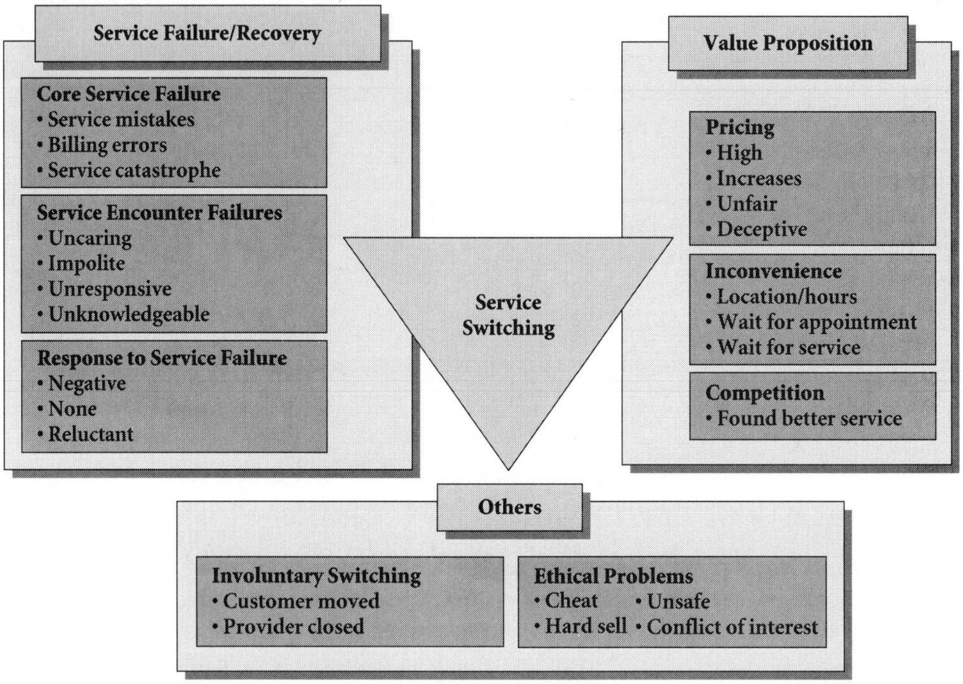

Source: Adapted from Susan M. Keaveney, "Customer Switching Behavior in Service Industries: An Exploratory Study," *Journal of Marketing* 59 (April 1995): 71–82.

accounts. Their main job is to listen to customer needs and issues and try to address them, with the key focus of retaining the customer. So-called churn-alert systems monitor the use patterns of individual customers and flag and trigger proactive retention efforts, such as sending a voucher and/or having a customer service representative call the customer to check on the health of the customer relationship and initiate corrective action if needed.

Another way to reduce churn is to increase switching barriers.[35] Many services have natural switching costs (e.g., it is a lot of work for customers to change their primary banking account, especially when many direct debits, credits, and other related banking services are tied to that account).[36] However, some switching costs can be created by instituting contractual penalties for switching, such as the transfer fees levied by some brokerage firms for moving shares and bonds to another financial institution. However, firms need to be cautious about being perceived as holding their customers hostage. A firm with high switching barriers and poor service quality is likely to generate negative attitudes and bad word of mouth.

CUSTOMER RELATIONSHIP MANAGEMENT SYSTEMS

Service marketers have understood for some time the power of relationship management, and certain industries have applied it for decades. Examples include the corner grocery store, the neighborhood car repair shop, and providers of banking services to high-net-worth clients.

Mention customer relationship management (CRM), and costly and complex information technology (IT) systems and infrastructure, and CRM vendors such as SAP, Siebel Systems, PeopleSoft, and Oracle, immediately come to mind. However, CRM in fact, signifies the whole process by which relationships with the customers are built and maintained.

Objectives of CRM Systems

Many firms have large numbers (often millions) of customers, many different touch points (for instance, tellers, call center staff, self-service machines, and Web sites), at multiple geographic locations. At a single large facility, it's unlikely that a customer will be served by the same frontline staff on two consecutive visits. In such situations, managers historically lacked the tools to practice relationship marketing. But today, CRM systems act as an enabler, capturing customer information and delivering it to the various touch points.

From a customer perspective, well-implemented CRM systems can offer a "unified customer interface," which means that at each transaction, the relevant account details, knowledge of customer preferences and past transactions, or history of a service problem are at the fingertips of the person serving the customer. This can result in a vast service improvement.

From a company perspective, CRM systems allow the company to better understand, segment, and tier its customer base; better target promotions and cross-selling; and even implement churn-alert systems that signal whether a customer is in danger of defecting.[37]

Management Memo 12-2 highlights some common CRM applications.

Designing a CRM Strategy

Unfortunately, the majority of CRM implementations fail. According to the Gartner Group, the implementation failure rate is 55 percent; and Accenture claims it to be around 60 percent. A key reason for this high failure rate is that firms often equate installing CRM systems with having a customer relationship strategy. They forget that the system is merely a tool to enhance the firm's customer servicing capabilities and is not the strategy itself. Seasoned McKinsey consultants believe that even CRM systems that have been implemented and have not yet been showing results can be well positioned for future success. They recommend taking a step back and focusing on how to build customer loyalty rather than focusing on the technology itself.[38] Similarly,

MANAGEMENT MEMO 12-2

COMMON CRM APPLICATIONS

- *Data collection.* The system captures customer data, such as contact details, demographics, purchasing history, service preferences, and the like.
- *Data analysis.* The captured data are analyzed and categorized by the system according to criteria set by firm. This information is used to tier the customer base and tailor service delivery accordingly.
- *Sales force automation.* Sales leads, cross-sell, and up-sell opportunities can be effectively identified and processed, and the entire sales cycle from lead generation to close of sales and after-sales service can be tracked and facilitated through the CRM system.
- *Marketing automation.* Mining of customer data enables the firm to target its market. A good CRM system enables the firm to achieve one-to-one marketing and cost savings. This results in increasing the return on investment (ROI) on its marketing expenditure. CRM systems also enable the assessment of the effectiveness of marketing campaigns through the analysis of responses.
- *Call center automation.* Call center staff have customer information at their fingertips and can improve their service levels to all customers. Furthermore, caller ID and account numbers allow call centers to identify the customer tier the caller belongs to and to tailor the service accordingly. For example, platinum callers get priority in waiting loops.

Darrell Rigby, Frederick Reichheld, and Phil Schefter recommend focusing on the customer strategy and not the technology, posing the question:

> If your best customers knew that you planned to invest $130 million to increase their loyalty..., how would they tell you to spend it? Would they want you to create a loyalty card or would they ask you to open more cash registers and keep enough milk in stock. The answer depends on the kind of company you are and the kinds of relationships you and your customers want to have with one another.[39]

Among the key questions managers should debate when defining their customer relationship strategy for a potential CRM system implementation are the following.

- How should our value proposition change to increase customer loyalty?
- How much customization or one-to-one marketing and service delivery are appropriate and profitable?
- What is the incremental profit potential of increasing the share of wallet with our current customers? How much does this vary by customer tier and/or segment?
- How much time and resources can we allocate to CRM right now?
- If we believe in customer relationship management, why haven't we taken more steps in that direction in the past? What can we do today to develop customer relationships without spending on technology?[40]

Answering these questions may lead to the conclusion that a CRM system may currently not be the best investment or highest priority or that a scaled-down version may suffice to deliver the intended customer strategy. In any case, we emphasize that the system is merely a tool to drive the strategy and must thus be tailored to deliver that strategy.

CONCLUSION

Many elements are involved in gaining market share and increasing share of wallet (the proportion of a customer's spending on a specific service category obtained by a particular supplier), cross-selling other products and services to existing customers, and creating long-term loyalty. The process starts by identifying and targeting the right customers, then learning about their needs, including their preferences for various forms of service delivery. Translating this knowledge into service delivery, tiered service levels, and customer relationship strategies are the key steps toward achieving customer loyalty.

Marketers need to pay special attention to those customers who offer the firm the greatest value, as they purchase its products with the greatest frequency and spend the most on premium services. Programs to reward frequent users—of which the most highly developed are the frequent flyer clubs created by the airlines—identify and provide rewards for high-value customers and facilitate tiered service delivery. These programs also enable marketers to track the behavior of high-value customers in terms of where and when they use the service, what service classes or types of product they buy, and how much they spend.

Review Questions

1. How can you estimate a customer's lifetime value (CLV)?
2. Why is targeting the "right customers" so important for successful customer relationship management?
3. What is meant by a customer portfolio? How should a firm determine the most appropriate mix of customers to have?

4. What criteria should a marketing manager use to decide which of several possible segments should be targeted by the firm?
5. What is tiering of services?
6. What are some key measures that can be used to create customer bonds and encourage long-term relationships with customers?
7. What are the arguments for spending money to keep existing customers loyal?
8. What is the role of CRM in delivering a customer relationship strategy?
9. Review the Reading "Why Service Stinks" (pages 466 to 473). Do you agree with the author's view that loyalty programs result in poor service for less-valuable customers? If so, what do you recommend should be done about this situation?

Application Exercises

1. For each of three service businesses that you patronize on a regular basis, complete the following sentence: "I am loyal to this business because ______________________________."
2. What conclusions do you draw about (a) yourself as a consumer and (b) the performance of each of the businesses? Assess whether any of these businesses managed to develop a sustainable competitive advantage through the way it won your loyalty.
3. For two service businesses that you used several times but have now ceased to patronize (or plan to stop patronizing soon) because you were dissatisfied, complete the sentence: "I stopped using (or will soon stop using) this organization as a customer because __________."
4. Again, what conclusions do you draw about yourself and the firms in question? How could each of these firms potentially avoid your defection? What could each of these firms do to avoid defections in the future of customers with a similar profile to yours?
5. Evaluate the strengths and weaknesses of frequent-user programs in various service industries.
6. Design a questionnaire and conduct a survey asking about two loyalty programs. The first is about a membership/loyalty program your classmates or their families like best and that makes them loyal to that firm. The second is about a loyalty program that is not well perceived and does not seem to add value to the customer. Use open-ended questions, such as "What motivated you to sign up in the first place?" "Why are you using this program?" "Has participating in the program changed your purchasing/usage behavior in any way?" "Has it made you less likely to use competing suppliers?" "What do you think of the rewards available?" "Did membership in the program lead to any immediate benefits in the use of the service?" "What role does the loyalty program play in making you loyal?" "What three things do you like best/like least/need improvements about this loyalty/membership program?" Analyze what features make loyalty/membership programs successful and what features do not achieve the desired results. Use frameworks, such as the wheel of loyalty, to guide your analysis and presentation.

Endnotes

1. Steven S. Ramsey, "Introduction: Strategy First, then CRM," in *The Ultimate CRM Handbook—Strategies & Concepts for Building Enduring Customer Loyalty & Profitability*, ed. John G. Freeland (New York: McGraw-Hill, 2002), 13.
2. Richard L. Oliver, "Whence Consumer Loyalty?" *Journal of Marketing* 63 (Special issue, 1999): 33–44.
3. Frederick F. Reichheld and Thomas Teal, *The Loyalty Effect* (Boston: Harvard Business School Press, 1996).
4. Frederick F. Reichheld and W. Earl Sasser, Jr., "Zero Defections: Quality Comes to Services," *Harvard Business Review* 68 (October 1990): 105–111.
5. Ibid.
6. Frederick F. Reichheld and Phil Schefter, "E-Loyalty—Your Secret Weapon on the Web," *Harvard Business Review* 80 (July–August, 2002): 105–113.
7. Grahame R. Dowling and Mark Uncles, "Do Customer Loyalty Programs Really Work?" *Sloan Management Review* (Summer 1997): 71–81; and Werner Reinartz and V. Kumar, "The Mismanagement of Customer Loyalty," *Harvard Business Review* (July 2002): 86–94.
8. Werner J. Reinartz and V. Kumar, "On the Profitability of Long-Life Customers in a Noncontractual Setting: An Empirical Investigation and Implications for Marketing," *Journal of Marketing* 64 (October 2000): 17–35.

9. John E. Hogan, Katherine N. Lemon, and Barak Libai, "What Is the True Cost of a Lost Customer?" *Journal of Services Research* 5, no. 3 (2003): 196–208.
10. David Bell, John Deighton, Werner J. Reinartz, Roland T. Rust, and Gordon Swartz, "Seven Barriers to Customer Equity Management," *Journal of Service Research* 5 (August 2002): 77–85.
11. Katherine N. Lemon, Roland T. Rust, and Valarie A. Zeithaml, "What Drives Customer Equity?" *Marketing Management* (Spring 2001): 20–25.
12. Roland T. Rust, Valarie A. Zeithaml, and Katherine N. Lemon, *Driving Customer Equity* (New York: The Free Press, 2000), 3.
13. Barak Libai, Das Narandayas, and Clive Humby, "Toward an Individual Customer Profitability Model: A Segment-Based Approach," *Journal of Service Research* 5 (August 2002): 69–76.
14. Alan W. H. Grant and Leonard H. Schlesinger, "Realize Your Customer's Full Profit Potential," *Harvard Business Review* (September–October, 1995): 59–75.
15. Nicole E. Coviello, Roderick J. Brodie, and Hugh J. Munro, "Understanding Contemporary Marketing: Development of a Classification Scheme," *Journal of Marketing Management* 13, no. 6 (1995): 501–522.
16. J. R. Copulsky and M. J. Wolf, "Relationship Marketing: Positioning for the Future," *Journal of Business Strategy,"* 11, no. 4 (1990): 16–20.
17. Christopher Lovelock and Martin Bless, taken from the case "BT: Telephone Account Management," Lausanne, Switzerland: International Institute for Management Development, 1992.
18. Evert Gummesson, *Total Relationship Marketing* (Oxford, England: Butterworth-Heinemann, 1999), 24.
19. Frederick F. Reichheld, *Loyalty Rules—How Today's Leaders Build Lasting Relationships* (Boston: Harvard Business School Press, 2001), 45.
20. Roger Hallowell, "The Relationships of Customer Satisfaction, Customer Loyalty, and Profitability: An Empirical Study," *International Journal of Service Industry Management* 7, no. 4 (1996): 38.
21. Leonard L. Berry, *Discovering the Soul of Service—The Nine Drivers of Sustainable Success* (New York: The Free Press, 1999), 148–149.
22. Frederick F. Reichheld, *Loyalty Rules—How Today's Leaders Build Lasting Relationships* (Boston: Harvard Business School Press, 2001), 43, 84–85.
23. David Rosenblum, Doug Tomlinson, and Larry Scott, "Bottom-Feeding for Blockbuster Business," *Harvard Business Review* (March 2003): 52–59.
24. Ravi Dahr and Rashi Glazer, "Hedging Customers," *Harvard Business Review* 81 (May 2003): 86–92.
25. (See especially Chapter 20) of David H. Maister, *True Professionalism* (New York: The Free Press, 1997).
26. Valarie A. Zeithaml, Roland T. Rust, and Katharine N. Lemon, "The Customer Pyramid: Creating and Serving Profitable Customers," *California Management Review* 43, no. 4 (Summer 2001): 118–142.
27. Werner J. Reinartz and V. Kumar, "The Impact of Customer Relationship Characteristics on Profitable Lifetime Duration," *Journal of Marketing* 67, no. 1 (2003): 77–99.
28. Piyush Kumar, "The Impact of Long-Term Client Relationships on the Performance of Business Service Firms," *Journal of Service Research* 2 (August 1999): 4–18.
29. Valarie A. Zeithaml and Mary Jo Bitner, *Services Marketing*, 3d ed. (New York: McGraw-Hill, 2003), 175; and Leonard L. Berry and A. Parasuraman, "Three Levels of Relationship Marketing," in *Marketing Services—Competing through Quality* (New York: The Free Press, 1991), 136–142.
30. Barbara Bund Jackson, "Build Relationships that Last," *Harvard Business Review* (November–December 1985): 120–128.
31. Don Peppers and Martha Rogers, *The One-to-One Manager* (New York: Currency/Doubleday, 1999).
32. Ruth N. Bolton, P. K. Kannan, and Matthew D. Bramlett, "Implications of Loyalty Program Membership and Service Experience for Customer Retention and Value," *Journal of the Academy of Marketing Science* 28, no. 1 (2000): 95–108.
33. Dowling and Uncles, "Do Customer Loyalty Programs Really Work?" 1997, 74.
34. Susan M. Keaveney, "Customer Switching Behavior in Service Industries: An Exploratory Study," *Journal of Marketing* 59 (April 1995): 71–82.
35. Jonathan Lee, Janghyuk Lee, and Lawrence Feick, "The Impact of Switching Costs on the Consumer Satisfaction-Loyalty Link: Mobile Phone Service in France," *Journal of Services Marketing* 15, no. 1 (2001): 35–48.
36. Moonkyu Lee and Lawrence F. Cunningham, "A Cost/Benefit Approach to Understanding Loyalty," *Journal of Services Marketing* 15, no. 2 (2001): 113–130.
37. Kevin N. Quiring and Nancy K. Mullen, "More than Data Warehousing: An Integrated View of the Customer," in *The Ultimate CRM Handbook—Strategies & Concepts for Building Enduring Customer Loyalty & Profitability*, ed. John G. Freeland (New York: McGraw-Hill, 2002), 102–108.
38. Manuel Ebner, Arthur Hu, Daniel Levitt, and Jim McCrory, "How to Rescue CRM?" *The McKinsey Quarterly* 4 (Technology, 2002).
39. Darrell K. Rigby, Frederick F. Reichheld, and Phil Schefter, "Avoid the Four Perils of CRM," *Harvard Business Review* (February 2002): 108.
40. Ibid., 103.

CHAPTER 13

Customer Feedback and Service Recovery

One of the surest signs of a bad or declining relationship is the absence of complaints from the customer. Nobody is ever that satisfied, especially not over an extended period of time.

—THEODORE LEVITT

To err is human; to recover, divine.

—CHRISTOPHER W. L. HART, JAMES L. HESKETT, AND W. EARL SASSER JR.

The first law of service productivity and quality might be: Do it right the first time. But we cannot ignore the fact that failures continue to occur, sometimes for reasons outside the organization's control. You have probably noticed from your own experience that the various "moments of truth" in service encounters are especially vulnerable to breakdowns. Such distinctive service characteristics as real-time performance, customer involvement, and people as part of the product greatly increase the chance of service failures. How well a firm handles complaints and resolves problems may determine whether it builds customer loyalty or watches former customers take their business elsewhere.

In this chapter, we explore the following questions.

1. Why do customers complain, and what do they expect from the firm?
2. How should an effective service recovery strategy be designed?
3. Under what circumstances should firms offer service guarantees, and is it wise to make them unconditional?
4. How should firms and their frontline staff respond to abusive and/or opportunistic customers?
5. How can organizations institutionalize systematic and continuous learning from customer feedback?

CUSTOMER COMPLAINING BEHAVIOR

Chances are that you will not be satisfied with at least some of the services you receive. How do you respond to your dissatisfaction with this service? Do you complain informally to an employee, ask to speak to the manager, or file a complaint? If not, perhaps you just mutter darkly to yourself, grumble to your friends and family, and choose an alternative supplier the next time you need a similar type of service.

If you are among those who do not complain about poor service, you are not alone. Research around the globe has shown that most people will not complain, especially if they think it will do no good.

Customer Response Options to Service Failures

Figure 13-1 depicts the courses of action a customer may take in response to a service failure. This model suggests at least three major courses of action.

1. Take some form of public action (including complaining to the firm or to a third party, such as a customer advocacy group, customer affairs or regulatory agency, or even civil or criminal courts).
2. Take some form of private action (including abandoning the supplier).
3. Take no action.

It is important to remember that the customer may pursue any one or a combination of the alternatives. Managers need to be aware that the impact of a defection can go far beyond the loss of that person's future revenue stream. Angry customers often tell many other people about their problems. The Internet allows unhappy customers to reach thousands of people by posting complaints on bulletin boards or setting up Web sites to publicize their bad experiences with specific organizations.[1]

Understanding Customer Responses to Service Failures

To be able to deal effectively with dissatisfied and complaining customers, managers need to understand key aspects of complaining behavior, starting with several questions.

FIGURE 13-1 Customer Response Categories to Service Failures

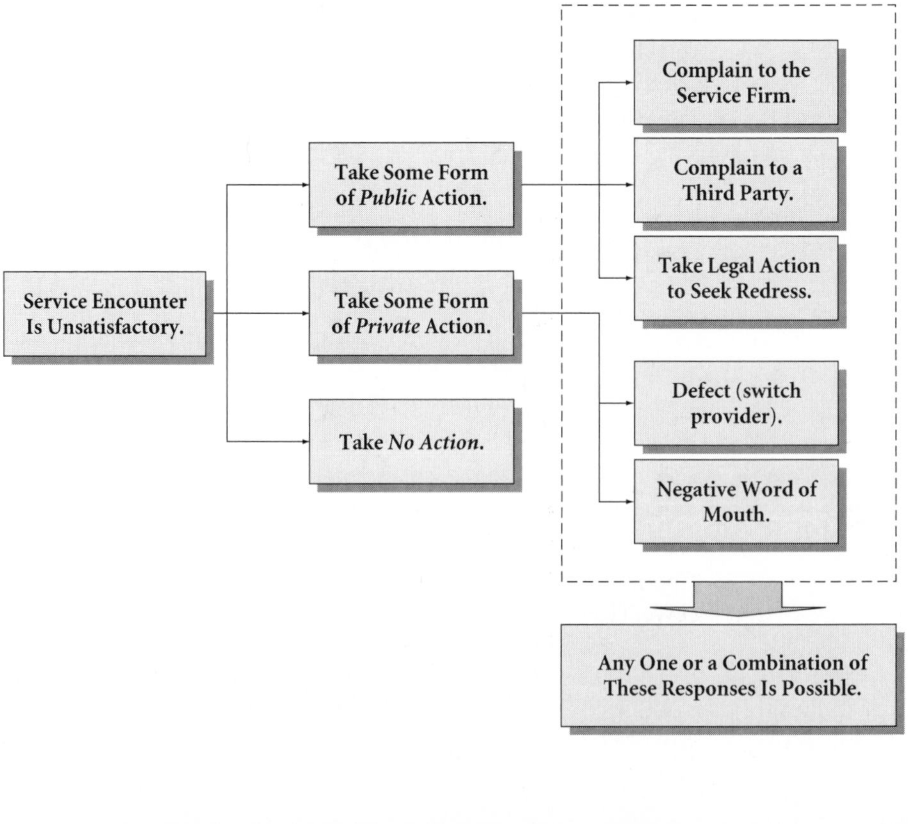

Why Do Customers Complain? In general, studies of consumer complaining behavior have identified four main purposes for complaining:

1. *Obtain restitution or compensation.* Often, consumers complain to recover some economic loss by seeking a refund, compensation, and/or have the service performed again.
2. *Vent their anger.* Some customers complain to rebuild self-esteem and/or to vent their anger and frustration. When service processes are bureaucratic and unreasonable or when employees are rude, deliberately intimidating, or apparently uncaring, the customers' self-esteem, self-worth, or sense of fairness can be negatively affected. They may become angry and emotional.
3. *Help to improve the service.* When customers are highly involved with a service (e.g., at a college, an alumni association, or their main banking connection), they give feedback to try and contribute toward service improvements. These customers are motivated by the prospect of getting better service in the future.
4. *For altruistic reasons.* Finally, some customers are motivated by altruistic reasons. They want to spare other customers from experiencing the same problems, and they might feel bad if a problem is not highlighted.

What Proportion of Unhappy Customers Complain? Research shows that on average, only 5 to 10 percent of customers who have been unhappy with a service actually complain.[2] Sometimes, the percentage is far lower. One of the authors of this book analyzed the complaints a public bus company received, which occurred at the rate of about three complaints for every million passenger trips. Assuming two trips a day, a person would need 1,370 years (roughly 27 lifetimes) to make a million trips. In other words, the rate of complaints was incredibly low, given that public bus companies are usually not known for good service. However, although generally only a minority of dissatisfied customers complain, there is evidence that consumers across the world are becoming better informed, more self-confident, and more assertive about seeking satisfactory outcomes for their complaints.

Why Don't Unhappy Customers Complain? TARP, a customer satisfaction and measurement firm, has identified a number of reasons why customers don't complain.[3] Some don't wish to take the time to write a letter, fill out a form, or make a phone call, especially if they don't see the service as sufficiently important to merit the effort. Many customers see the payoff as uncertain and believe that no one would be concerned about their problem or willing to resolve it. In some situations, people simply do not know where to go or what to do.

Additionally, many people feel that complaining is unpleasant. They may be afraid of confrontation, especially if the complaint involves someone whom the customer knows and may have to deal with again. Complaining behavior can be influenced by role perceptions and social norms. In services in which customers have "low power" (defined as the perceived ability to influence or control the transaction), they are less likely to voice complaints.[4] This is particularly true when the problem involves professional service providers, such as doctors, lawyers, or architects. Social norms tend to discourage customer criticism of such individuals, because of their perceived expertise.

In theory, firms should be able to minimize some of these barriers by offering customers the opportunity to complain through easy-to-use impersonal channels such as the Internet. However, Kaisa Snellman and Tiina Vihtkari argue that use of electronic channels is not likely to change complaining behavior if customers continue to believe that the service provider will not attempt to solve their problems.[5]

Who Is Most Likely to Complain? Research findings consistently show that people in higher socioeconomic levels are more likely to complain than those in lower levels. Their better education, higher income, and greater social involvement give them the confidence, knowledge, and motivation to speak up when they encounter problems.[6] Further, those who complain also tend to be more knowledgeable about the products in question.

Where Do Customers Complain? Studies show that the majority of complaints are made at the place where the service was received. One of the authors of this book recently completed a consulting project developing and implementing a customer feedback system and found an astounding 99+ percent of customer feedback was given face to face or over the phone to customer service representatives. Only less than 1 percent of all complaints were submitted via e-mail, letters, faxes, or customer feedback cards. A survey of airline passengers found that only 3 percent of respondents who were unhappy with their meal actually complained about it, and they all complained to the flight attendant! None complained to the company's headquarters or to a consumer affairs office.[7]

In practice, even when customers do complain, managers often do not hear about the complaints made to frontline staff. Less than 5 percent of the complaints reach corporate headquarters.[8]

Customer Expectations about Their Complaints

Whenever a service failure occurs, people expect to be adequately compensated in a fair manner. However, recent studies have shown that many customers feel that they were not treated fairly and did not receive adequate justice. When this happens, customer reactions tend to be immediate, emotional, and enduring.[9]

Stephen Tax and Stephen Brown found that as much as 85 percent of the variation in the satisfaction with a service recovery was determined by the three dimensions of fairness shown in Figure 13-2.[10]

FIGURE 13-2 Three Dimensions of Perceived Fairness in Service Recovery Processes

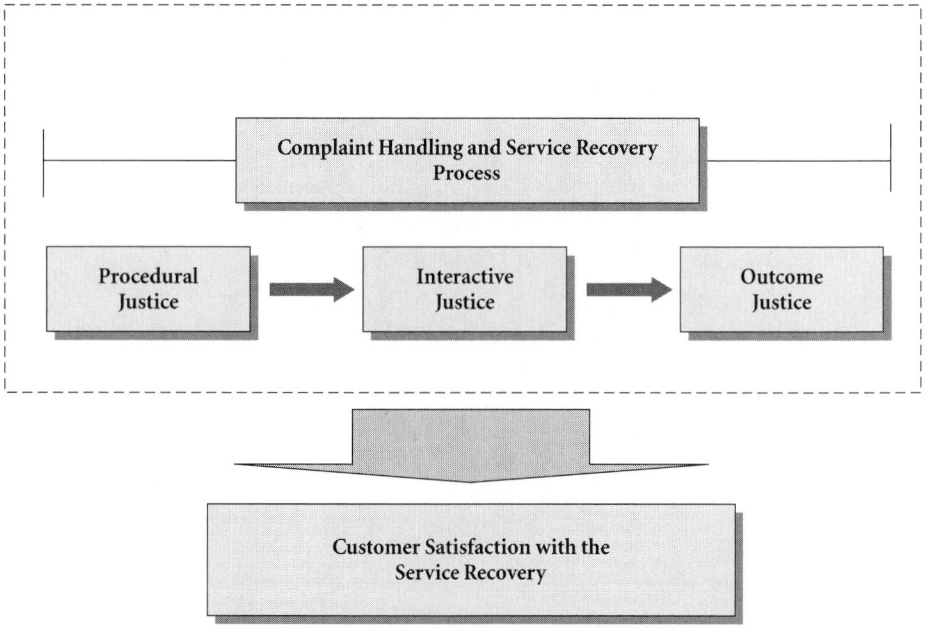

Source: Stephen S. Tax and Stephen W. Brown, "Recovering and Learning from Service Failure," *Sloan Management Review* 49, no. 1 (Fall 1998): 75–88. Reprinted by permission of publisher.

1. *Procedural justice* has to do with the policies and rules that any customer will have to go through in order to seek fairness. Here, customers expect the firm to assume responsibility, which is the key to the start of a fair procedure, followed by a convenient and responsive recovery process. That includes flexibility of the system and consideration of customer inputs into the recovery process.
2. *Interactional justice* involves the firm's employees who provide the service recovery and their behavior toward the customer. Giving an explanation for the failure and making an effort to resolve the problem are very important. However, the recovery effort must be perceived as genuine, honest, and polite.
3. *Outcome justice* pertains to the compensation that a customer receives as a result of the losses and inconveniences incurred because of the service failure. This includes compensation for not only the failure but also the time, effort, and energy spent during the process of service recovery.[11]

CUSTOMER RESPONSES TO EFFECTIVE SERVICE RECOVERY

"Thank Heavens for Complainers" was the provocative title of an article about customer complaining behavior, which also featured a successful manager exclaiming, "Thank goodness I've got a dissatisfied customer on the phone! The ones I worry about are the ones I never hear from."[12] Customers who do complain give a firm the chance to correct problems (including some the firm may not even know it has), restore relationships with the complainer, and improve future satisfaction for all.

Service recovery is an umbrella term for systematic efforts by a firm to correct a problem following a service failure and retain a customer's goodwill. Service recovery efforts play a crucial role in achieving (or restoring) customer satisfaction. In every organization, things may occur that have a negative impact on its relationships with customers. The true test of a firm's commitment to satisfaction and service *quality* isn't in the advertising promises but in the way it responds when things go wrong for the customer.

Effective service recovery requires thoughtful procedures for resolving problems and handling disgruntled customers. It is critical for firms to have effective recovery strategies, because under the following conditions, even a single service problem can destroy a customer's confidence in a firm.

- The failure is totally outrageous (for instance, blatant dishonesty on the part of the supplier).
- The problem fits a pattern of failure rather than being an isolated incident.
- The recovery efforts are weak, serving to compound the original problem rather than correct it.[13]

The risk of defection is high, especially when a variety of competing alternatives are available. One study of customer switching behavior in service industries found that close to 60 percent of all respondents who reported changing suppliers did so because of a service failure: 25 percent cited failures in the core service, 19 percent reported an unsatisfactory encounter with an employee, 10 percent reported an unsatisfactory response to a prior service failure, and 4 percent described unethical behavior on the part of the provider.[14]

Impact of Effective Service Recovery on Customer Loyalty

When complaints are satisfactorily resolved, the customers involved are much more likely to remain loyal. TARP research found that intentions to repurchase for different types of products ranged from 9 to 37 percent when customers were dissatisfied but did not complain. For a major complaint, the retention rate increased from 9 to 19 percent if customers complained and the company offered a sympathetic ear but was unable to resolve the complaint to the satisfaction of the customer. If the complaint could be resolved to the satisfaction of the customer, retention rate jumped to 54 percent. The highest retention rate was achieved when problems were fixed quickly, typically on the spot, whereupon it jumped to 82 percent.[15]

The conclusion to be drawn is that complaint handling should be seen as a profit center and not a cost center. When a dissatisfied customer defects, the firm loses more than the value of the next transaction. It may also lose a long-term stream of profits from that customer and from anyone else who switches suppliers or is deterred from doing business with that firm because of negative comments from an unhappy friend. Thus, it pays to invest in service recovery designed to protect those long-term profits.

The Service Recovery Paradox

The service recovery paradox refers to the sometimes observed effect that customers who experience a service failure and then have it resolved to their full satisfaction are more likely to make future purchases than are customers who have no problem in the first place.[16] A study of repeated service failures in a retail banking context showed that the service recovery paradox held for the first service failure that was recovered to customers' full satisfaction.[17] However, when a second service failure occurred, the paradox disappeared. It seems that customers may forgive a firm once but get disillusioned if failures recur. Furthermore, the study also showed that customers' expectations were raised after they experienced a very good recovery; thus, excellent recovery becomes the standard they expect for dealing with future failures.

Some recent studies have challenged the existence of the service recovery paradox. For example, Tor Andreassen conducted a major study with some 8,600 telephone interviews across a wide range of consumer services. The findings showed that after a service recovery, customers' intention to repurchase, and their perceptions of and attitudes toward the company, never surpassed the ratings of satisfied customers who did not experience a service problem in the first place. This was true even when the service recovery had gone very well and the customer expressed full satisfaction with the recovery.[18]

"Please listen carefully as some of our menu options have changed. For customer service, go fly a kite. For technical support, whistle in the wind until the cows come home. For repair service, wait for you-know-what to freeze over...."

"Thank you for calling Customer Service. If you're calm and rational, press 1. If you're a whiner, press 2. If you're a hot head, press 3...."

Whether a customer comes out delighted from a service recovery probably also depends on the severity and "recoverability" of the failure. No one can replace spoilt wedding photos, a ruined holiday, or an injury caused by some service equipment. In such situations, it's difficult to imagine anyone being truly delighted even when a most professional service recovery is conducted. Contrast these examples with a lost hotel reservation, for which the recovery is an upgrade to a suite. When the service is recovered in a way that allows the delivery of a superior product, the customer is, of course, delighted and probably hopes for another lost reservation in the future.

The best strategy is to do it right the first time. As Michael Hargrove puts it: "Service recovery is turning a service failure into an opportunity you wish you never had."[19] It is critical that service recovery be well executed, but failures cannot be tolerated. Unfortunately, empirical evidence shows that a large proportion of customers are dissatisfied with the outcome of their complaints. In recent studies, some 40 to 60 percent of customers reported dissatisfaction with the service recovery process.[20]

PRINCIPLES OF EFFECTIVE SERVICE RECOVERY SYSTEMS

Recognizing that current customers are a valuable asset base, managers need to develop effective procedures for service recovery following unsatisfactory experiences. We discuss three guiding principles for how to do this well: Make it easy for customers to give feedback, enable effective service recovery, and establish appropriate compensation levels. The components of an effective service recovery system are shown in Figure 13-3.

Make It Easy for Customers to Give Feedback

How can managers overcome unhappy customers' reluctance to complain about service failures? The best way is to address the reasons for their reluctance directly. Table 13-1

FIGURE 13-3 Components of an Effective Service Recovery System

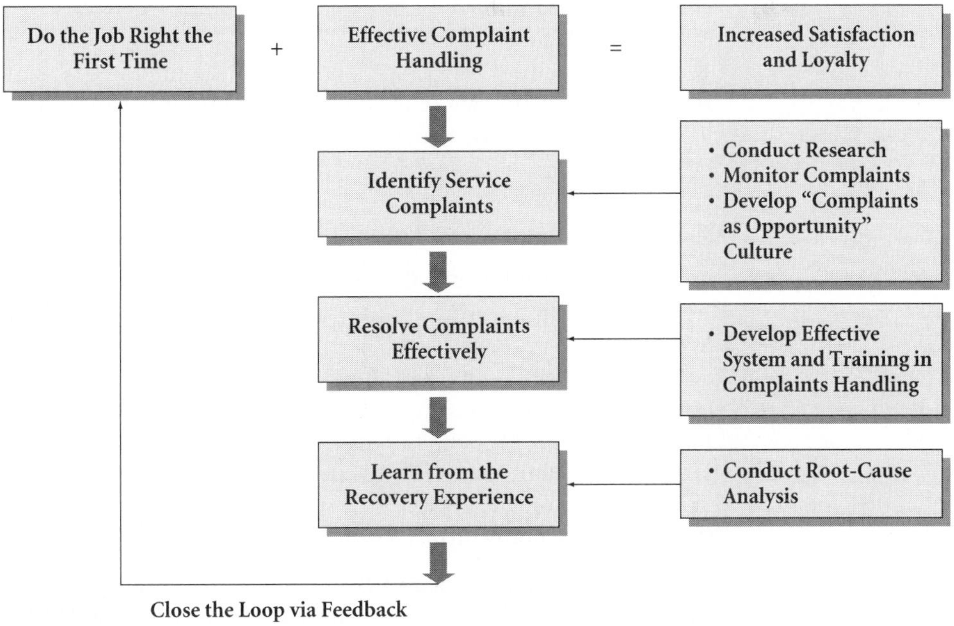

Source: Adapted from Christopher H. Lovelock, Paul G. Patterson, and Rhett Walker, *Services Marketing: Australia and New Zealand* (Sydney: Prentice-Hall Australia, 1998), 455.

TABLE 13-1 Strategies to Reduce Customer Complaint Barriers

Complaint Barriers for Dissatisfied Customers	*Strategies to Reduce These Barriers*
Inconvenience	Make feedback easy and convenient:
• Difficult to find the right complaint procedure • Effort, e.g., writing and mailing a letter	• Print customer service hotline numbers and e-mail and postal addresses on all customer communications materials (letters, faxes, bills, brochures, phone book listing, yellow pages, etc.)
Doubtful payoff	Reassure customers that their feedback will be taken seriously and will pay off:
• Uncertain whether any or what action will be taken by the firm to address the issue the customer is unhappy with	• Have service recovery procedures in place and communicate this to customers, e.g., in customer newsletter and Web site. • Feature service improvements that resulted from customer feedback.
Unpleasantness	Make providing feedback a positive experience:
• Fear of being treated rudely	• Thank customers for their feedback (can be done publicly and in general by addressing the entire customer base).
• Fear of being hassled • Feeling embarrassed	• Train the front line not to hassle and to make customers feel comfortable. • Allow for anonymous feedback.

gives an overview of potential measures that can be taken to overcome those reasons. Many companies have improved their complaint-collection procedures by adding special toll-free phone lines, links on their Web sites, prominently displayed customer comment cards in their branches, or even providing video terminals for recording complaints. In their customer newsletter, some companies feature service improvements that were the direct result of customer feedback under the motto "you told us, and we responded."

Enable Effective Service Recovery

Recovering from service failures takes more than pious expressions of determination to resolve any problems that may occur. It requires commitment, planning, and clear guidelines. Specifically, effective service recovery procedures should be (1) proactive, (2) planned, (3) trained, and (4) empowered. By having such procedures in place, the frontline staff will be able to take charge if a service failure occurs and be more likely to deliver a satisfactory resolution to the problem.

Service Recovery Should Be Proactive Service recovery needs to be initiated on the spot, ideally before customers have a chance to complain (see Best Practice in Action 13-1). Service personnel should be sensitized to signs of dissatisfaction and ask whether customers might be experiencing a problem. For example, the waiter may ask a guest who has eaten only half of his dinner "Is everything all right, sir?" The guest may say, "Yes, thank you, I am not very hungry" or "The steak is well done, but I had asked for medium-rare, plus it is very salty." The latter response then gives the waiter a chance to recover the service rather than have an unhappy diner leave the restaurant and potentially not return.

Recovery Procedures Need to Be Planned Contingency plans have to be developed for service failures, especially for those that can occur regularly and cannot be designed out of the system. Revenue management practices in the travel and hospitality industries often result in overbooking. To simplify the task of frontline staff, firms

BEST PRACTICE IN ACTION 13-1

EFFECTIVE SERVICE RECOVERY IN ACTION

The lobby is deserted. It is not difficult to overhear the conversation between the night manager at the Marriott Long Wharf Hotel in Boston and the late-arriving guest.

"Yes, Dr. Jones, we've been expecting you. I know you are scheduled to be here three nights. I'm sorry to tell you, sir, but we are booked solid tonight. A large number of guests we assumed were checking out did not. Where is your meeting tomorrow, sir?"

The doctor told the clerk where it was.

"That's near the Omni Parker House! That's not very far from here. Let me call them and get you a room for the evening. I'll be right back."

A few minutes later, the desk clerk returned with the good news.

"They're holding a room for you at the Omni Parker House, sir. And, of course, we'll pick up the tab. I'll forward any phone calls that come here for you. Here's a letter that will explain the situation and expedite your check-in, along with my business card so you can call me directly here at the front desk if you have any problems."

The doctor's mood was moving from exasperation toward calm. But the desk clerk was not finished with the encounter. He reached into the cash drawer. "Here are two $5 bills. That should more than cover your cab fare from here to the Parker House and back again in the morning. We don't have a problem tomorrow night, just tonight. And here's a coupon that will get you complimentary continental breakfast on our concierge level on the fifth floor tomorrow morning . . . and again, I am so sorry this happened."

As the doctor walks away, the night manager turns to the desk clerk, "Give him about 15 minutes and then call to make sure everything went okay."

A week later when it was still a peak period for hotels in that city, the same guest who had overheard the exchange is in a taxi, en route to the same hotel. Along the way, he tells about the great service recovery episode he had witnessed the week before. The pair arrived at the hotel and made their way to the front desk, ready to check in.

They are greeted with unexpected news: "I am so sorry, gentlemen. I know you were scheduled here for two nights. But we are booked solid tonight. Where is your meeting scheduled tomorrow?"

The would-be guests exchange a rueful glance as they give the desk clerk their future plans. "That's near the Meridien. Let me call over there and see if I can get you a room. It won't but take a minute." As the clerk walks away, the tale teller says, "I'll bet he comes back with a letter and a business card."

Sure enough, the desk clerk returns to deliver the solution; not a robotic script but all the elements from the previous week's show were on display. What the tale teller thought he witnessed the previous week as pure desk-clerk initiative, he now realized, was planned, a spontaneous-feeling yet predetermined response to a specific category of customer problem.

Source: Ron Zemke and Chip R. Bell, *Knock Your Socks Off Service Recovery* (New York: AMACOM, 2000), 59–60.

should identify the most common service problems and develop predetermined solution sets for employees to follow.

Recovery Skills Must Be Taught Customers easily feel insecure at the point of service failure because things are not turning out as anticipated. Effective training arms frontline staff with the confidence and competence to turn distress into delight.[21]

Recovery Requires Empowered Employees Service recovery efforts should be flexible, and employees should be empowered to use their judgment and communication skills to develop solutions that will satisfy complaining customers.[22] This is especially true for out-of-the-ordinary failures for which a firm may not have developed and trained potential solution sets. Employees need to have the authority to make decisions and spend money in order to resolve service problems promptly and recover customer goodwill.

How Generous Should Compensation Be?

Clearly, vastly different costs are associated with possible recovery strategies. How much compensation should a firm offer when there has been a service failure? Or would an apology be sufficient instead? The following rules of thumb can help to answer these questions:

- *What is the firm's market positioning?* If a firm is known for service excellence and charges a high premium for quality, customers will expect service failures to be rare, so the firm should make a demonstrable effort to recover the few failures that do occur and be prepared to offer something of significant value. But in a more downscale, mass-market business, customers are likely to consider something quite modest, such as a free coffee or dessert, as fair compensation.
- *How severe was the service failure?* The general guideline is "let the punishment fit the crime." Customers expect less for minor inconveniences and a much more significant compensation if major damage in terms of time, effort, annoyance, anxiety, and so on, was caused on the customer's side.
- *Who is the affected customer?* Long-term customers and those who spend heavily at a service provider expect more, and it is worth making an effort to save their business. Once-off customers tend to be less demanding and have less economic importance to the firm. Hence, compensation can be less but should still be fair. There is always the possibility that a first-time user will become a repeat customer if treated fairly. The overall rule of thumb for compensation at service failures should be "well-dosed generosity." Being perceived as stingy adds insult to injury, and the firm would probably be better off apologizing rather than offering a minimal compensation.

Overly generous compensation is not only expensive but may even be negatively interpreted by customers.[23] It may raise questions about the soundness of the business and lead customers to become suspicious about the underlying motives. Customers may worry about the implications for the employee as well as for the business. Also, overgenerosity does not seem to result in higher repeat purchase rates than simply offering a fair compensation.[24] There is also the risk that a reputation for overgenerosity might encourage dishonest customers to "seek" service failures.

Dealing with Complaining Customers

Both managers and frontline employees must be prepared to deal with angry customers who are confrontational and sometimes behave in insulting ways toward service personnel who aren't at fault in any way. Management Memo 13-1 provides specific guidelines for effective problem resolution, designed to help calm upset customers and to deliver a resolution they will see as fair and satisfying.

SERVICE GUARANTEES

A growing number of companies offer customers a satisfaction guarantee, promising that if service delivery fails to meet predefined standards, the customer is entitled to one or more forms of compensation, such as an easy-to-claim replacement, refund, or credit. Some firms place conditions on these guarantees; others offer them unconditionally.

MANAGEMENT MEMO 13-1

HANDLING CUSTOMER COMPLAINTS

1. *Act quickly.* If the complaint is made during service delivery, time is of the essence to achieve a full recovery. When complaints are made after the fact, many companies have established policies of responding within 24 hours or sooner. Even when full resolution is likely to take longer, fast acknowledgment remains very important.
2. *Admit mistakes, but don't be defensive.* Acting defensively may suggest that the organization has something to hide or is reluctant to fully explore the situation.
3. *Show that you understand the problem from each customer's point of view.* Seeing situations through the customers' eyes is the only way to understand what they think has gone wrong and why they are upset. Service personnel should avoid jumping to conclusions with their own interpretations.
4. *Don't argue with customers.* The goal should be to gather facts to reach a mutually acceptable solution, not to win a debate or prove that the customer is an idiot. Arguing gets in the way of listening and seldom diffuses anger.
5. *Acknowledge the customer's feelings,* either tacitly or explicitly (for example, "I can understand why you're upset"). This action helps to build rapport, the first step in rebuilding a bruised relationship.
6. *Give customers the benefit of the doubt.* Not all customers are truthful, and not all complaints are justified. But customers should be treated as though they have a valid complaint until clear evidence to the contrary emerges. If a lot of money is at stake (as in insurance claims or potential lawsuits), careful investigation is warranted. If the amount involved is small, it may not be worth haggling over a refund or other compensation. However, it's still a good idea to check records to see whether there is a past history of dubious complaints by the same customer.
7. *Clarify the steps needed to solve the problem.* When instant solutions aren't possible, telling customers how the organization plans to proceed shows that corrective action is being taken. It also sets expectations about the time involved, so firms should be careful not to overpromise!
8. *Keep customers informed of progress.* Nobody likes being left in the dark. Uncertainty breeds anxiety and stress. People tend to be more accepting of disruptions if they know what is going on and receive periodic progress reports.
9. *Consider compensation.* When customers do not receive the service outcomes they have paid for or have suffered serious inconvenience and/or loss of time and money because the service failed, either a monetary payment or an offer of equivalent service in kind is appropriate. This type of recovery strategy may also reduce the risk of legal action by an angry customer. Service guarantees often lay out in advance what such compensation will be, and the firm should ensure that all guarantees are met.
10. *Persevere to regain customer goodwill.* When customers have been disappointed, one of the biggest challenges is to restore their confidence and preserve the relationship for the future. Perseverance may be required to defuse customers' anger and to convince them that actions are being taken to avoid a recurrence of the problem. Truly exceptional recovery efforts can be extremely effective in building loyalty and referrals.

The Power of Service Guarantees

Christopher Hart declares that service guarantees are powerful tools for both promoting and achieving service quality, for the following reasons:[25]

- Guarantees force firms to focus on what their customers want and expect in each element of the service.
- Guarantees set clear standards, telling customers and employees alike what the company stands for. Payouts to compensate customers for poor service cause managers to take guarantees seriously, because they highlight the financial costs of quality failures.
- Guarantees require the development of systems for generating meaningful customer feedback and acting on it.
- Guarantees force service organizations to understand why they fail and encourage them to identify and overcome potential fail points.

- Guarantees build "marketing muscle" by reducing the risk of the purchase decision and building long-term loyalty.

From the customer's perspective, the primary function of service guarantees is to lower the perceived risks associated with purchase.[26] The presence of a guarantee may also make it easier for customers to complain and more likely that they will do so, since they will anticipate that frontline employees will be prepared to resolve the problem and provide appropriate compensation. Sara Björlin Lidén and Per Skålén found that even when dissatisfied customers were unaware that a service guarantee existed before making their complaints, they were positively impressed to learn that the company has a pre-planned procedure for handling failures and to find that their complaints were taken seriously.[27]

The benefits of service guarantees can be seen clearly in the case of Hampton Inn's 100% Satisfaction Guarantee (see Figure 13-4), which has now been extended to Embassy Suites and Homewood Suites.[28] As a business-building program, Hampton's strategy of offering to refund the cost of the room to a guest who expresses dissatisfaction has attracted new customers and also served as a powerful retention device. People choose to stay at a Hampton Inn because they are confident that they will be satisfied. At least as important, the guarantee has become a vital tool to help managers identify new opportunities for quality improvement.

Discussing the impact on staff and managers, the marketing vice president of Hampton Inn stated, "Designing the guarantee made us understand what made guests satisfied, rather than what *we thought* made them satisfied." It became imperative that everyone from reservationists and frontline employees to general managers and personnel at corporate headquarters listen carefully to guests, anticipate their needs to the greatest extent possible, and remedy problems quickly so that guests were satisfied with the solution. Viewing a hotel's function in this customercentric way had a profound impact on the way the firm conducted business.

FIGURE 13-4 The Hampton Inn 100% Satisfaction Guarantee

Source: "Hampton Inn 100% Satisfaction Guarantee, Research Justifying the Guarantee." Used with permission of the Hilton Family. All rights reserved.

The guarantee "turned up the pressure in the hose," as one manager put it, showing where "leaks" existed and providing the financial incentive to plug them. As a result, the guarantee has had an important impact on product consistency and service delivery across the Hampton Inn chain. Finally, studies of the 100% Satisfaction Guarantee's impact have shown a dramatically positive effect on financial performance.

How to Design Service Guarantees

Some guarantees are simple and unconditional. Others appear to have been written by lawyers and contain many restrictions. Compare the examples in Service Perspectives 13-1

SERVICE PERSPECTIVES 13-1

EXAMPLES OF SERVICE GUARANTEES

U.S. POSTAL SERVICE EXPRESS MAIL GUARANTEE

Service Guarantee: Express Mail international mailings are not covered by this service agreement. Military shipments delayed due to Customs inspections are also excluded. If the shipment is mailed at a designated USPS Express Mail facility on or before the specified time for overnight delivery to the addressee, delivery to the addressee or agent will be attempted before the guaranteed time the next delivery day. Signature of the addressee, addressee's agent, or delivery employee is required upon delivery. If a delivery attempt is not made by the guaranteed time and the mailer makes a claim for refund, the USPS will refund the postage unless: 1) delivery was attempted but could not be made or the article was available for pickup at destination, 2) this shipment was delayed by strike or work stoppage, or 3) detention was made for a law enforcement purpose.

Source: Printed on back of Express Mail receipt.

EXCERPT FROM THE "QUALITY STANDARD GUARANTEES" FROM AN OFFICE SERVICES COMPANY

- We guarantee 6-hour turnaround on documents of two pages or less . . . (does not include client subsequent changes or equipment failures).
- We guarantee that there will be a receptionist to greet you and your visitors during normal business hours . . . (short breaks of less than five minutes are not subject to this guarantee).
- You will not be obligated to pay rent for any day on which there is not a manager on site to assist you (lunch and reasonable breaks are expected and not subject to this guarantee).

Source: Reproduced in Eileen C. Shapiro, *Fad Surfing in the Boardroom* (Reading, MA: Addison-Wesley, 1995), 180.

THE BUGS BURGER BUG KILLER GUARANTEE (A PEST CONTROL COMPANY)

- You don't owe us a penny until all the pests on your premises have been eradicated.
- If you're ever dissatisfied with the BBBK's service you will receive a refund for as much as 12 months of service—plus fees for another exterminator of your choice for the next year.
- If a guest spots a pest on your premises, the exterminator will pay for the guest's meal or room, send a letter of apology and pay for a future meal or stay.
- If your premises are closed down because of the presence of roaches or rodents, BBBK will pay any fines, as well as all lost profit, plus $5000.

Source: Reproduced in Christopher W. Hart, "The Power of Unconditional Service Guarantees," *Harvard Business Review* (July–August 1990).

L.L. BEAN'S GUARANTEE

Our Guarantee. Our products are guaranteed to give you 100% satisfaction in every way. Return anything purchased from us at any time if it proves otherwise. We will replace it, refund your purchase price or credit your credit card. We do not want you to have anything from L.L. Bean that is not completely satisfactory.

Source: Printed in all L.L. Bean catalogs and on the company's Web site, *www.llbean.com/customerService/aboutLLBean/guarantee.html*, April 2003.

and ask yourself which guarantees instill trust and confidence in you and would make you like to do business with that supplier.

Both the L.L. Bean and BBBK guarantees are powerful, unconditional, and instill trust. The others are weakened by the many conditions, Hart argues that service guarantees should be designed to meet the following criteria:[29]

- *Unconditional.* Whatever is promised in the guarantee must be totally unconditional, and there should not be any element of surprise for customers.
- *Easy to understand and communicate* to customers so they are clearly aware of the benefits that can be gained from the guarantee.
- *Meaningful to customers* in terms of what they would find important in a guarantee with compensation that should be more than adequate to cover the service failure.
- *Easy to invoke.* Less of the guarantee should be dependent on the customer and more on the service provider.
- *Easy to collect.* If a service failure occurs, customers should be able to collect on the guarantee without any problems.
- *Credible.* The guarantee should be believable.

Is Full Satisfaction the Best You Can Guarantee?

Full-satisfaction guarantees have generally been considered the best possible design. Recently, however, it has been suggested that the ambiguity often associated with such guarantees can lead to discounting of their perceived value. Customers may ask: "What does full satisfaction mean?" or "Can I invoke a guarantee when I am dissatisfied, although the fault does not lie with the service firm?"[30]

In a recent study, Jochen Wirtz and Doreen Kum introduced a new guarantee: the "combined guarantee."[31] This guarantee combines the wide scope of a full-satisfaction guarantee with the low uncertainty of specific performance standards. The combined guarantee was shown to be superior to the pure full-satisfaction or attribute-specific guarantee designs. Should the consumer be dissatisfied with any element of the service, the full-satisfaction coverage of the combined guarantee applies. Table 13-2 shows examples of the various types of guarantees.

Is It Always Appropriate to Introduce a Service Guarantee?

Managers should think carefully about their firm's strengths and weaknesses before deciding to introduce a service guarantee. In many instances, it may be inappropriate to do so.[32]

Companies that already have a strong reputation for high-quality service may not need a guarantee. In fact, it might even be incongruent with their image to offer one. A guarantee may add no value for a service company whose name alone ensures very high quality and may even confuse the market.[33] By contrast a firm whose service is currently poor must first work to improve quality to a level above that at which the guarantee might be invoked on a regular basis by most of its customers.

Service firms whose quality is truly uncontrollable because of external forces would be foolish to consider a guarantee. When it realized that it was paying out substantial refunds because it had insufficient control over its railroad infrastructure, Amtrak was forced to drop a service guarantee that included reimbursement of fares in the event of unpunctual train service.

In a market where consumers see little financial, personal, or physiological risk associated with purchasing and using a service, a guarantee adds little value but still costs money to design, implement, and manage. Where little perceived difference in service quality among competing firms exists, the first-company to institute a guarantee may be able to obtain a first-mover advantage and create a valued differentiation for its services. If more than one competitor already has a guarantee in place, offering a guarantee

TABLE 13-2 Types of Service Guarantees

Term	*Guarantee Scope*	*Examples*
Single attribute-specific guarantee	One key attribute of the service is covered by the guarantee.	"Any of three specified popular pizzas is guaranteed to be served within 10 minutes of ordering on working days between 12 A.M. and 2 P.M. If the pizza is late, the customer's next order is free."
Multiattribute-specific guarantee	A few important attributes of the service are covered by the guarantee.	Minneapolis Marriott's Guarantee: "Our quality commitment to you is to provide: • A friendly, efficient check-in • A clean, comfortable room, where everything works • A friendly efficient check-out If we, in your opinion, do not deliver on this commitment, we will give you $20 in cash. No questions asked. It is your interpretation."
Full-satisfaction guarantee	All aspects of the service are covered by the guarantee. There are no exceptions.	Lands' End's Guarantee: "If you are not completely satisfied with any item you buy from us, at any time during your use of it, return it and we will refund your full purchase price. We mean every word of it. Whatever. Whenever. Always. But to make sure this is perfectly clear, we've decided to simplify it further. GUARANTEED. Period."
Combined guarantee	All aspects of the service are covered by the full-satisfaction promise of the guarantee. Explicit minimum-performance standards on important attributes are included in the guarantee to reduce uncertainty.	Datapro Information Services guarantees "to deliver the report on time, to high quality standards, and to the contents outlined in this proposal. Should we fail to deliver according to this guarantee, *or should you be dissatisfied with any aspect of our work,* you can deduct any amount from the final payment which is deemed as fair."

Adapted from Jochen Wirtz and Doreen Kum, "Designing Service Guarantees—Is Full Satisfaction the Best You Can Guarantee?" *Journal of Services Marketing* 15, no. 4 (2001): 282–299.

may become a qualifier for the industry, and the only real way to make an impact is to launch a highly distinctive guarantee beyond that already offered by competitors.

DISCOURAGING ABUSE AND OPPORTUNISTIC BEHAVIOR

Throughout this chapter, we advocate that firms should welcome complaints and invocations of service guarantees and even encourage them. But how can this be done without inviting potential abuse by that undesirable group of people whom we call jay customers? (See Chapter 8.)

Dishonest customers can take advantage of generous service recovery strategies, service guarantees, or simply a strong customer orientation in a number of ways. For example, they may steal from the firm, refuse to pay for the service, fake dissatisfaction, purposefully cause service failures to occur, or overstate losses at the time of genuine service failures. What steps can a firm take to protect itself against opportunistic customer behavior?

Treating customers with suspicion is likely to alienate them, especially in situations of service failure. The president of TARP (the company that undertook the studies of complaining behavior described earlier) notes:

> Our research has found that premeditated rip-offs represent 1 to 2 percent of the customer base in most organizations. However, most organizations

defend themselves against unscrupulous customers by ... treating the 98 percent of honest customers like crooks to catch the 2 percent who *are* crooks.[34]

Using this knowledge, the working assumptions should be: If in doubt, believe the customer. However, as Service Perspectives 13-2 shows, it is crucial to monitor the invocations of service guarantees or payments compensating for service failure, maintaining databases of all such cases and monitoring repeated service payouts to the same customer. For example, one airline found that the same customer lost his suitcase on three consecutive flights. The chances of this truly happening are probably lower than winning in the national lottery, so frontline staff were made aware of this individual. The next time he checked in his suitcase, the check-in staff videotaped the suitcase almost from check-in to pickup in the baggage claim at the destination. It turned out that a companion collected the suitcase and took it through while the traveler again made his way to the lost-baggage counter to report his missing suitcase. This time, the police were waiting for him and his friend.

LEARNING FROM CUSTOMER FEEDBACK

There are two ways of looking at complaints: first, as individual customer problems, each of which requires a resolution; second, as a stream of information that can be used to measure quality and suggest improvements.[35] So far in this chapter, we have taken the former perspective; the individual customer. In this section, we discuss how customer feedback can be systematically collected, analyzed, and disseminated via an institutionalized customer feedback system (CFS) to achieve customer-driven learning.

Key Objectives of Effective Customer Feedback Systems

"It is not the strongest species that survive, nor the most intelligent, but the ones most responsive to change" wrote Charles Darwin. Similarly, many strategists have concluded

SERVICE PERSPECTIVE 13-2

TRACKING DOWN GUESTS WHO CHEAT

As part of its guarantee tracking system, Hampton Inn has developed ways to identify guests who appeared to be cheating—using aliases or different satisfaction problems to invoke the guarantee repeatedly in order to get the cost of their room refunded. Guests showing high invocation trends receive personalized attention and follow-up from the company's guest assistance team. Wherever possible, senior managers telephone these guests to ask about their recent stays. The conversation might go as follows: "Hello, Mr. Jones. I'm the director of guest assistance at Hampton Inn, and I see that you've had some difficulty with the last four properties you've visited. Since we take our guarantee very seriously, I thought I'd give you a call and find out what the problems were."

The typical response is dead silence! Sometimes, the silence is followed by questions of how headquarters could possibly know about the problems. These calls have their humorous moments as well. One individual, who had invoked the guarantee 17 times in what appeared to be a trip that took him across the United States and back, was asked, innocuously, "Where do you like to stay when you travel?" "Hampton Inn," came the enthusiastic response. "But," said the executive making the call, "our records show that the last 17 times you have stayed at a Hampton Inn, you have invoked the 100% Satisfaction Guarantee." "That's why I like them!" proclaimed the guest (who turned out to be a long-distance truckdriver).

Source: Christopher W. Hart and Elizabeth Long, *Extraordinary Guarantees* (New York: AMACOM, 1997).

that in increasingly competitive markets, the ultimate competitive advantage for a firm is to learn and change more rapidly than the competition.[36] Specific objectives of effective customer feedback systems typically fall into three main categories.

Assessment and Benchmarking of Service Quality and Performance The objective is to answer the question, How satisfied are our customers? This objective includes learning about how well a firm performed in comparison to its main competitor(s), how it performed in comparison to the previous year, whether investments in certain service aspects have paid off in terms of customer satisfaction, and where the firm wants to be the following year. Often, a key objective of comparison against other units (branches, teams, competitors) is to motivate managers and service staff to improve performance, especially when the results are linked to compensation.

Customer-Driven Learning and Improvements Here, the objective is to answer the questions, Why our customers are unhappy? and Where and how can we improve? For this, more specific or detailed information on processes and products is required to guide a firm's service improvement efforts and to pinpoint areas with potentially high returns for quality investment. This objective is also about gaining an understanding of the things that other suppliers do well and those that make customers happy.

Creating a Customer-Oriented Service Culture This objective is concerned with focusing the organization on customer needs and customer satisfaction and rallying the entire organization toward a culture of service quality.

The Case for Using a Mix of Customer Feedback Collection Tools

Table 13-3 gives an overview of typically used feedback tools and their ability to meet various requirements. Recognizing that different tools have different strengths and weaknesses, service marketers should select a mix of customer feedback collection tools that jointly deliver the needed information. As Leonard Berry and A. Parasuraman observe, "Combining approaches enables a firm to tap the strengths of each and compensate for weaknesses."[37]

TABLE 13-3 Strengths and Weaknesses of Key Customer Feedback Collection Tools (meets requirements fully, ●; moderately, ◑; hardly/not at all, ○)

	Level of Measurement							
Collection Tools	*Firm*	*Process*	*Transaction specific*	*Actionable*	*Representative, Reliable*	*Potential for Service Recovery*	*First-Hand Learning*	*Cost-Effectiveness*
Total market survey (including competitors)	●	○	○	○	●	○	○	○
Annual survey on overall satisfaction	●	◑	○	○	●	○	○	○
Transactional survey	●	●	◑	◑	●	○	○	○
Service feedback cards	◑	●	●	◑	◑	●	◑	●
Mystery shopping	○	◑	●	●	○	○	◑	○
Unsolicited feedback (e.g., complaints)	○	◑	●	●	○	●	◑	●
Focus group discussions	○	◑	●	●	○	◑	●	◑
Service reviews	○	◑	●	●	○	●	●	◑

Source: Adapted from Jochen Wirtz and Monica Tomlin, "Institutionalizing Customer-Driven Learning through Fully Integrated Customer Feedback Systems," *Managing Service Quality* 10, no. 4 (2000): 210.

Total Market Surveys, Annual Surveys, and Transactional Surveys Total market surveys and *annual surveys* typically measure satisfaction with all major customer service processes and products. The level of measurement is usually at a high level, with the objective of obtaining a global index or indicator of overall service satisfaction for the entire firm. This could be based on indexed (e.g., using various attribute ratings) and/or weighted data (e.g., weighted by core segments and/or products).

Overall indices such as these tell how satisfied customers are but not why they are happy or unhappy. There are limits to the number of questions that can be asked about each individual process or product. For example, a typical retail bank has some 30 to 50 key customer service processes (e.g., from car loan applications to cash deposits at the teller). Because of the sheer number of processes, many surveys have room for only one or two questions per process (e.g., How satisfied are you with our ATM services?) and cannot address issues in greater detail.

In contrast, *transactional surveys* are typically conducted after customers have completed a specific transaction and query them about this process in some depth. At this point, all key attributes and aspects of ATM services could be included in the survey, including some open-ended questions, such as "liked best," "liked least," and "suggested improvements." Such feedback is more actionable, can tell the firm why customers are happy or unhappy with the process, and may yield specific insights on how to improve customer satisfaction.

All three survey types are representative and reliable when designed properly. Representativeness and reliability are required for (1) accurate assessments of where the company, a process, branch, or individual stands relative to quality goals (changes in quality are not the result of sample biases and/or random errors); and (2) evaluations of individuals, staff, teams, branches, and/or processes, especially when incentive schemes are linked to such measures. The methodology has to be watertight if staff are to trust and buy into the results, especially when surveys deliver bad news.

The potential for service recovery is important and should, if possible, be designed into feedback collection tools. However, many surveys promise anonymity, making it impossible to identify and respond to dissatisfied respondents. In personal encounters or telephone surveys, interviewers can be instructed to ask customers whether they would like the firm to get back to them on dissatisfying issues.

Service Feedback Cards This powerful and inexpensive tool involves giving customers a feedback card following completion of each major service process and inviting them to return it by mail or other means to a central customer feedback unit. For example, a feedback card can be attached to each housing loan approval letter or to each hospital invoice. Although these cards are a good indicator of process quality and yield specific feedback on what works well and what doesn't, the respondents tend not to be representative, being biased toward customers who are either very satisfied or very dissatisfied.

Mystery Shopping Service businesses often use this method to determine whether frontline staff are displaying desired behaviors. Banks, retailers, car rental firms, and hotels are among the industries making active use of mystery shoppers. For example, the central reservation offices of a global hotel chain contracts for a large-scale monthly mystery caller survey to assess the skills of individual associates related to the phone sales process. Such actions as correct positioning of the various products, up-selling and cross-selling, and closing the deal are measured. On top of that, the survey also assesses the quality of the phone conversation on such dimensions as "a warm and friendly greeting" and "establishing rapport with the caller." Mystery shopping gives highly actionable and in-depth insights for coaching, training, and performance evaluation.

Because the number of mystery calls or visits is typically small, no individual survey is reliable or representative. However, if a particular staff member performs well (or poorly) month after month, managers can infer with reasonable confidence that this person's performance is good (or poor).

Unsolicited Customer Feedback Customer complaints, compliments, and suggestions can be transformed into a stream of information that can be used to help monitor quality and highlight improvements needed to the service design and delivery. Complaints and compliments are rich sources of detailed feedback on what drives customers nuts and what delights them.

Similar to feedback cards, unsolicited feedback is not a reliable measure of overall customer satisfaction, but it is a good source of improvement ideas. If the objective of collecting feedback is mainly to get feedback on what to improve (rather than for benchmarking and/or assessing staff), reliability and representativeness are not needed, and more qualitative tools, such as complaints/compliments or focus groups, generally suffice.

Detailed customer complaint and compliment letters, recorded telephone conversations, and direct feedback from employees can serve as an excellent tool for communicating internally what customers want and enable employees and managers at all levels to "listen" to customers first-hand. This first-hand learning is much more powerful for shaping the thinking and customer orientation of service staff than is using statistics and reports.

For example, Singapore Airlines prints complaint and compliment letters in its monthly employee magazine, *Outlook*. Southwest Airlines shows staff videotapes containing footage of customers providing feedback. Seeing customers giving comments about their service leaves a much deeper and lasting impression on staff and motivates them toward further improvement.

Focus Group Discussions and Service Reviews Both tools give great specific insights on potential service improvements and ideas. Typically, focus groups are organized by key customer segments or user groups to drill down on the needs of these users.

Service reviews are in-depth one-on-one interviews, usually conducted once a year with a firm's most valuable customers. Usually, a senior executive of the firm visits the customers and discusses such issues as how well the firm performed the previous year and what should be maintained or changed. Subsequently, that individual discusses the feedback from these customers with each of their account managers. The senior executive and the relevant account manager then send a follow-up letter to each customer, detailing how the firm will respond to that customer's service needs and how the account will be managed the following year. Apart from providing an excellent learning opportunity (especially when the reviews across all customers are compiled and analyzed), service reviews focus on retention of the most valuable customers and get high marks for service recovery potential.

As we noted earlier, there are advantages to using a mix of feedback tools. Best Practice in Action 13-2 features FedEx's excellent customer feedback system, which combines various customer feedback collection tools with a detailed process performance measurement system.

Capturing Unsolicited Customer Feedback

For complaints, suggestions, and inquiries to be useful as research input, they have to be funneled into a central collection point, logged, categorized, and analyzed.[38] That requires a system for capturing customer feedback where it is made and then reporting it to a central unit. Some firms use a simple intranet site to record all feedback received by any staff member. Coordinating such activities is not a simple matter, because of the many entry points, including the following:

BEST PRACTICE IN ACTION 13-2

THE FEDEX CORPORATION'S APPROACH TO LISTENING TO THE VOICE OF THE CUSTOMER

"We believe that service quality must be mathematically measured," declares Frederick W. Smith, Chairman, President, and CEO of FedEx Corporation. The company has a commitment to clear, frequently repeated quality goals, followed up with continuous measurement of progress against those goals. This practice forms the foundation for its approach to quality.

FedEx initially set two ambitious quality goals: (1) 100 percent customer satisfaction for every interaction and transaction and (2) 100 percent service performance on every package handled. Customer satisfaction was measured by the percentage of on-time deliveries, which referred to the number of packages delivered on time as a percentage of total package volume. However, as things turned out, percentage of on-time delivery was an internal standard that was not synonymous with customer satisfaction.

- *Service Quality Index.* FedEx had systematically cataloged customer complaints, so it was able to develop what CEO Smith calls the "Hierarchy of Horrors": the eight most common complaints by customers. This list became the foundation on which FedEx built its customer feedback system. FedEx refined the list and developed the Service Quality Index (SQI—pronounced "sky"), a 12-item measure of satisfaction and service quality from the customer's viewpoint. Weights have been assigned to each item, based on its relative importance in determining overall customer satisfaction. All items are tracked daily, in order to compute a continuous index. In addition to the SQI, which has been modified over time to reflect changes in procedures, services, and customer priorities, FedEx uses a variety of other ways to capture feedback.
- *Customer Satisfaction Survey.* This is a telephone survey conducted on a quarterly basis with several thousand randomly selected customers, stratified by its key segments. The results are relayed to senior management on a quarterly basis.
- *Targeted Customer Satisfaction Survey.* This survey covers specific customer service processes and is conducted on a semiannual basis with clients who have experienced one of the specific FedEx processes within the past three months.
- *FedEx Center Comment Cards.* Comment cards are collected from each FedEx storefront business center. The results are tabulated twice a year and relayed to managers in charge of the centers.
- *Online Customer Feedback Surveys.* FedEx has commissioned regular studies to get feedback for its online services (e.g., such package tracking) as well as ad hoc studies on new products.

The information from these various customer feedback measures has helped FedEx to maintain a leadership role in its industry and has played an important role in enabling the firm to receive the prestigious Malcolm Baldridge National Quality Award.

Source: "Blueprints for Service Quality: The Federal Express Approach," *AMA Management Briefing*, New York: American Management Association, 1991, 51–64; and Linda Rosencrance, "BetaSphere Delivers FedEx Some Customer Feedback," *Computerworld* 14, no.14 (2000): 36.

- The firm's own frontline employees, who may be in contact with customers face to face, by telephone, or via mail, fax, or e-mail
- Intermediary organizations acting on behalf of the original supplier
- Managers who normally work backstage but who are contacted by a customer seeking higher authority
- Suggestion or complaint cards mailed, e-mailed, posted on the firm's Web site, or placed in a special box
- Complaints to third parties: consumer advocate groups, legislative agencies, trade organizations, and other customers.

Analysis, Reporting, and Dissemination of Customer Feedback

Choosing the relevant feedback tools and collecting customer feedback is meaningless if the company is unable to disseminate the information to the relevant parties to take action. Hence, to drive continuous improvement and learning, a reporting system needs to deliver feedback and its analysis to frontline staff, process owners, branch or department managers, and top management.

The feedback loop to the front line should be immediate for complaints and compliments, as is practiced in a number of service businesses where complaints, compliments, and suggestions are discussed with staff during a daily morning briefing. In addition, we recommend three types of service performance reports to provide the information necessary for service management and team learning.

1. A monthly Service Performance Update provides process owners with timely feedback on customer comments and operational process performance. Here, the verbatim feedback is provided to the process manager, who can, in turn, discuss them with his or her service staff.
2. A quarterly Service Performance Review provides process owners and branch or department managers with trends in process performance and service quality.
3. An annual Service Performance Report gives top management a representative assessment of the status and long-term trends relating to customer satisfaction with the firm's services.

The reports should be short and reader friendly, focusing on key indicators and providing an easily understood commentary.

CONCLUSION

Collecting customer feedback via complaints, suggestions, and compliments provides a means of increasing customer satisfaction. It is an opportunity to get into the hearts and minds of the customer. In all but the worst instances, complaining customers are indicating that they want to continue their relationship with the firm, but they are also indicating that all is not well and that they expect the company to make things right.

Service firms need to develop effective strategies to recover from service failures so that they can maintain customer goodwill. That is vital for the long-term success of the company. Even the best recovery strategy is not as good as being treated right the first time. Well-designed unconditional service guarantees have proved to be a powerful vehicle for identifying and justifying needed improvements, as well as creating a culture in which staff members take proactive steps to ensure that the customers will be satisfied.

Finally, a service firm and its staff must also learn from their mistakes and try to ensure that problems are being eliminated. Customer feedback systems should ensure that information originating from complaints, compliments, and other feedback tools is systematically collected, analyzed, and disseminated to drive service improvements. The ultimate objective of an effective customer feedback system is to institutionalize systematic and continuous customer-driven learning.

Review Questions

1. Why don't unhappy customers complain? What do customers expect the firm to do once they have filed a complaint?
2. Why would a firm prefer its unhappy customers to come forward and complain?

3. What is the service recovery paradox? Under what conditions is this paradox most likely to hold? Why is it best to deliver the service as planned, even should the paradox hold in a specific context?
4. What could a firm do to make it easy for dissatisfied customers to complain?
5. Why should a service recovery strategy be proactive and planned and require trained and empowered staff?
6. How generous should compensations related to service recovery be? What are the economic costs to the firm of the typical types of compensation firms offer?
7. How should service guarantees be designed? What are the benefits of service guarantees over and above a good complaint-handling and service recovery system?
8. What are the main objectives of customer feedback systems?
9. What customer feedback collection tools do you know, and what are the strengths and weaknesses of each of these tools?

Application Exercises

1. Think about the last time you experienced a less than satisfactory service experience. Did you complain? Why? If you did not complain, explain why not.
2. When was the last time you were truly satisfied with an organization's response to your complaint? Describe in detail what happened and what made you satisfied.
3. What would be an appropriate service recovery policy for a wrongly bounced check for (a) your local savings bank, (b) a major national bank, and (c) a high-end private bank for high-net-worth individuals. Explain your rationale, and also compute the economic costs of the alternative service recovery policies.
4. Design a highly effective service guarantee for a service with high perceived risk. Explain why and how your guarantee would reduce perceived risk of potential customers and why current customers would appreciate being offered this guarantee, although they are already a customer of that firm and therefore are likely to perceive lower levels of risk.
5. Collect a few customer feedback forms and tools (e.g., customer feedback cards, questionnaires, and online forms) and assess how the information gathered in those tools can be used to achieve the three main objectives of effective customer feedback systems.
6. How generous should compensation be? Review the following incident and comment. Then evaluate the available options, comment on each, select the one you recommend, and defend your decision.

   "The shrimp cocktail was half frozen. The waitress apologized, and didn't charge me for any of my dinner," was the response of a very satisfied customer about the service recovery he received. Consider the following range of service recovery policies a restaurant chain could set.

   - *Option 1:* Smile and apologize, defrost the prawn cocktail, return it, and smile and apologize again.
   - *Option 2:* Smile and apologize, replace the prawn cocktail with a new one, and smile and apologize again.
   - *Option 3:* Smile, apologize, replace the prawn cocktail, and offer a free coffee or dessert.
   - *Option 4:* Smile, apologize, replace the prawn cocktail, and waive the bill of $80 for the entire dinner.
   - *Option 5:* Smile, apologize, replace the prawn cocktail, waive the bill for the entire dinner, and offer a free bottle of champagne.
   - *Option 6:* Smile, apologize, waive the bill for the entire dinner, offer a free bottle of champagne, and give a voucher valid for another dinner (to be redeemed within three months).

   Try to establish the costs for each policy. Some answers are providedin Endnote 39. But before peeking, try first to think about the costs yourself.

Endnotes

1. Bernd Stauss, "Global Word of Mouth," *Marketing Management* (Fall 1997): 28–30.
2. Stephen S. Tax and Stephen W. Brown, "Recovering and Learning from Service Failure," *Sloan Management Review* 49, no. 1 (Fall 1998): 75–88.
3. Technical Assistance Research Programs Institute (TARP), *Consumer Complaint Handling in America; An Update Study, Part II* (Washington D.C.: TARP and U.S. Office of Consumer Affairs), April 1986; and Nancy Stephens and Kevin P. Gwinner, "Why Don't Some People Complain? A Cognitive-Emotive Process Model of Consumer Complaining Behavior," *Journal of the Academy of Marketing Science* 26, no. 3 (1998): 172–189.
4. Cathy Goodwin and B. J. Verhage, "Role Perceptions of Services: A Cross-Cultural Comparison with Behavioral Implications," *Journal of Economic Psychology* 10 (1990): 543–558.
5. Kaisa Snellman and Tiina Vihtkari, "Customer Complaining Behavior in Technology-based Service Encounters," *International Journal of Service Industry Management* 14, no. 2 (2003): 217–231.
6. Nancy Stephens, "Complaining," in *Handbook of Services Marketing and Management*, ed. Teresa A. Swartz and Dawn Iacobucci (Thousand Oaks, CA: Sage Publications, 2000), 291.
7. John Goodman, "Basic Facts on Customer Complaint Behavior and the Impact of Service on the Bottom Line," *Competitive Advantage* (June 1999): 1–5.
8. Technical Assistance Research Programs Institute (TARP), *Consumer Complaint Handling*.
9. Kathleen Seiders and Leonard L. Berry, "Service Fairness: What It Is and Why It Matters," *Academy of Management Executive* 12, no. 2 (1990): 8–20.
10. Tax and Brown "Recovering and Learning from Service Failure."
11. See the following papers on the role of perceived fairness in customer responses to service recovery efforts: Stephen S. Tax and Stephen W. Brown, "Service Recovery: Research, Insight and Practice," in *Handbook of Services Marketing and Management*, ed. Teresa A. Swartz and Dawn Iacobucci (Thousand Oaks, CA: Sage Publications, 2000), 277; Tor Wallin Andreassen, "Antecedents of Service Recovery," *European Journal of Marketing* 34, no. 1 and 2 (2000): 156–175; Ko de Ruyter and Martin Wetzel, "Customer Equity Considerations in Service Recovery," *International Journal of Service Industry Management* 11, no. 1 (2002): 91–108; and Janet R. McColl-Kennedy and Beverley A. Sparks, "Application of Fairness Theory to Service Failures and Service Recovery," *Journal of Service Research* 5, no. 3 (2003): 251–266.
12. Oren Harari, "Thank Heavens for Complainers," *Management Review* (March 1997): 25–29.
13. Leonard L. Berry, *On Great Service: A Framework for Action* (New York: The Free Press, 1995), 94.
14. Susan M. Keveaney, "Customer Switching Behavior in Service Industries: An Exploratory Study," *Journal of Marketing* 59 (April 1995): 71–82.
15. TARP, *Consumer Complaint Handling*.
16. Stefan Michel, "Analyzing Service Failures and Recoveries: A Process Approach," *International Journal of Service Industry Management* 12, no. 1 (2001): 20–33.
17. James G. Maxham III and Richard G. Netemeyer, "A Longitudinal Study of Complaining Customers Evaluations of Multiple Service Failures and Recovery Efforts," *Journal of Marketing* 66, no. 4 (2002): 57–72.
18. Tor Wallin Andreassen, "From Disgust to Delight: Do Customers Hold a Grudge?" *Journal of Service Research* 4, no. 1 (2001): 39–49. Other recent studies also confirmed that the service recovery paradox does not hold universally: Michael A. McCollough, Leonard L. Berry, and Manjit S. Yadav, "An Empirical Investigation of Customer Satisfaction after Service Failure and Recovery," *Journal of Service Research* 3, no. 2 (2000): 121–137; and James G. Maxhamm III, "Service Recovery's Influence on Consumer Satisfaction, Positive Word-of-Mouth, and Purchase Intentions," *Journal of Business Research* 54 (2001): 11–24.
19. Michael Hargrove, reported in Ron Kaufman, *UP Your Service!* (Singapore: Ron Kaufman Plc. Ltd., 2000), 225.
20. Steven S. Tax and Steven W. Brown, "Recovering and Learning from Service Failure"; and Stephen S. Tax, Stephen W. Brown, and Murali Chandrashekaran, "Customer Evaluation of Service Complaint Experiences: Implications for Relationship Marketing," *Journal of Marketing* 62, no. 2 (Spring 1998): 60–76.
21. Ron Zemke and Chip R. Bell, *Knock Your Socks Off Service Recovery* (New York: AMACOM, 2000), 60.
22. Barbara R. Lewis, "Customer Care in Services," in *Understanding Services Management,* ed. W. J. Glynn and J. G. Barnes (Chichester, UK: John Wiley, 1995), 57–89.
23. Hooman Estelami and Peter De Maeyer, "Customer Reactions to Service Provider Overgenerosity," *Journal of Service Research* 4, no. 3 (2002): 205–217.
24. Rhonda Mack, Rene Mueller, John Crotts, and Amanda Broderick, "Perceptions, Corrections and Defections: Implications for Service Recovery in the Restaurant Industry," *Managing Service Quality* 10, no. 6 (2000): 339–346.

25. Christopher W. L. Hart, "The Power of Unconditional Service Guarantees," *Harvard Business Review* (July–August 1990): 54–62.
26. L. A. Tucci and J. Talaga, "Service Guarantees and Consumers' Evaluation of Services," *Journal of Services Marketing* 11, no. 1 (1997): 10–18; Amy Ostrom and Dawn Iacobucci, "The Effect of Guarantees on Consumers' Evaluation of Services," *Journal of Services Marketing* 12, no. 5 (1998): 362–78.
27. Sara Björlin Lidén and Per Skålén, "The Effect of Service Guarantees on Service Recovery," *International Journal of Service Industry Management* 14, no. 1 (2003): 36–58.
28. Christopher W. Hart and Elizabeth Long, *Extraordinary Guarantees* (New York: AMACOM, 1997).
29. Christopher W. Hart, "The Power of Unconditional Service Guarantees."
30. Gordon H. McDougall, Terence Levesque, and Peter VanderPlaat, "Designing the Service Guarantee: Unconditional or Specific?" *Journal of Services Marketing* 12, no. 4 (1998): 278–293; and Jochen Wirtz, "Development of a Service Guarantee Model," *Asia Pacific Journal of Management* 15, no. 1 (1998): 51–75.
31. Jochen Wirtz and Doreen Kum, "Designing Service Guarantees—Is Full Satisfaction the Best You Can Guarantee?" *Journal of Services Marketing* 15, no. 4 (2001): 282–299.
32. Amy L. Ostrom and Christopher Hart, "Service Guarantee: Research and Practice," in *Handbook of Services Marketing and Management*, ed. T. Schwartz and D. Iacobucci (Thousand Oaks, CA: Sage Publications, 2000), 299–316.
33. Jochen Wirtz, Doreen Kum, and Khai Sheang Lee, "Should a Firm with a Reputation for Outstanding Service Quality Offer a Service Guarantee?" *Journal of Services Marketing* 14, no. 6 (2000): 502–512.
34. John Goodman, quoted in "Improving Service Doesn't Always Require Big Investment," *The Service Edge* (July–August, 1990): 3.
35. This section is based partially on Jochen Wirtz and Monica Tomlin, "Institutionalizing Customer-Driven Learning through Fully Integrated Customer Feedback Systems," *Managing Service Quality* 10, no. 4 (2000): 205–215.
36. W. E. Baker and J. M. Sinkula, "The Synergistic Effect of Market Orientation and Learning Orientation on Organizational Performance," *Journal of the Academy of Marketing Science* 27, no. 4 (1999): 411–427.
37. Leonard L. Berry and A. Parasuraman provide an excellent overview of all key research approaches discussed in this section, as well as several other tools in "Listening to the Customer—The Concept of a Service Quality Information System," *Sloan Management Review* (Spring 1997): 65–76.
38. Robert Johnston and Sandy Mehra, "Best-Practice Complaint Management," *Academy of Management Executive* 16, no. 4 (2002): 145–154.
39. Data for calculation of recovery costs in Application Exercise 6

- *Option 1.* This recovery strategy has no direct costs beyond the time needed for the additional workstep.
- *Option 2.* Costs are as for option 1, plus the material costs of the shrimp cocktail, which typically would be at around $\frac{1}{3}$ of the price charged in a restaurant, or around \$3 to \$6.
- *Option 3.* Costs are as for option 2, plus the extra costs incurred by the free coffee or dessert. These extra costs are dependent on whether they constitute incremental consumption (the diner would not have had a coffee or a dessert) or whether they substitute consumption. In the former case, the costs are only the material costs; in the latter, this recovery strategy replaces revenue, and the cost is the replaced revenue (e.g., \$4 for the revenue forgone owing to one cup of coffee sold less). The costs of the recovery policy of a free coffee could be computed as follows: Probability of incremental consumption × costs of incremental consumption, plus probability of substitution consumption × menu price for that item.
- *Option 4.* Costs are as for option 1, plus the full \$80, as this is the revenue that is forgone. It is irrelevant here that the food costs may have been only one-third of the revenue lost.
- *Option 5.* As for option 4, plus the costs for the bottle of champagne, which needs to be computed using the probabilities of incremental and substitution consumption and their respective costs.
- *Option 6.* As for option 5, plus the costs of the voucher. The voucher costs depend on whether it substitutes consumption or whether it is incremental.

CHAPTER 14

Improving Service Quality and Productivity

Not everything that counts can be counted, and not everything that can be counted, counts.
—ALBERT EINSTEIN

Our mission remains inviolable: Offer the customer the best service we can provide; cut our costs to the bone; and generate a surplus to continue the unending process of renewal.
—JOSEPH PILLAY
Chairman, Singapore Airlines

Productivity—working faster and more efficiently in order to reduce costs—has been a managerial imperative since the 1970s. During the 1980s and early 1990s, improving quality became a major priority. In a service context, this strategy entails creating better service processes and outcomes to improve customer satisfaction. At the beginning of the 21st century, we're seeing growing emphasis on linking these two strategies in order to create better value for both customers and the firm.

Both quality and productivity have historically been seen as issues for operations managers. When improvements in these areas required better employee selection, training, and supervision—or renegotiation of labor agreements relating to job assignments and work rules—human resource managers were expected to get involved too. It was not until service quality was explicitly linked to customer satisfaction that marketers, too, were seen as having an important role to play.

Broadly defined, the task of value enhancement requires quality-improvement programs to deliver and continuously enhance the benefits desired by customers. At the same time, productivity-improvement efforts must seek to reduce the associated costs. The challenge is to ensure that these two programs are mutually reinforcing in achieving common goals rather than operating at loggerheads with each other in pursuit of conflicting goals.

In this chapter, we review the challenges involved in improving both productivity and quality in service organizations and explore the following questions.

1. What is meant by *quality* and *productivity* in a service context, and why should they be linked when formulating marketing strategy?
2. How can we diagnose and address service quality problems?
3. What are the key tools for improving service productivity?
4. How do such concepts as TQM, ISO 9000, Malcom-Baldrige Approach, and Six Sigma relate to managing and improving productivity and service quality?

INTEGRATING SERVICE QUALITY AND PRODUCTIVITY STRATEGIES

A key theme running through this book is that, where services are concerned, marketing cannot operate in isolation from other functional areas. Tasks that might be considered the sole preserve of operations in a manufacturing environment need to involve marketers because customers are often exposed to—even actively involved in—service processes. Making service processes more efficient does not necessarily result in a better-quality experience for customers; nor does it always lead to improved benefits for them. Likewise, getting service employees to work faster may sometimes be welcomed by customers but at other times may make customers feel rushed and unwanted. Thus, marketing, operations, and human resource managers need to communicate with one another to ensure that they can deliver quality experiences more efficiently.

Similarly, implementing marketing strategies to improve customer satisfaction with services can prove costly and disruptive for an organization if the implications for operations and human resources have not been carefully thought through. Hence, quality- and productivity-improvement strategies need to be considered jointly rather than in isolation.

Writing in the early 1990s, Swedish professor Evert Gummesson observed that, although service quality must be viewed in conjunction with service productivity and profitability, service quality had been widely researched but not service productivity.[1] Today, the situation is changing, and in the course of this chapter, we present insights from several recent research studies on service productivity.

Marketing's interest in service quality is obvious when one thinks about it: Poor quality places a firm at a competitive disadvantage. If customers perceive quality as unsatisfactory, they may be quick to take their business elsewhere. Recent years have witnessed a veritable explosion of discontent with service quality at a time when the quality of many manufactured goods seems to have improved significantly.

From a marketing standpoint, a key issue is whether customers notice competing suppliers' differences in quality. Consultant Brad Gale puts it succinctly when he says that "value is simply quality, however the *customer* defines it, offered at the right price."[2] Improving quality in the eyes of the customer pays off for the companies that provide it. Data from the PIMS (Profit Impact of Market Strategy) show that a perceived quality advantage leads to higher profits.[3]

Similarly, improving productivity is important to marketers for several reasons. First, it helps to keep costs down. Lower costs either mean higher profits or the ability to hold down prices. The company with the lowest costs in an industry has the option to position itself as the low-price leader—usually a significant advantage among price-sensitive market segments. Second, firms with lower costs also generate higher margins, giving those firms the option of spending more than the competition in marketing activities, improved customer service, and supplementary services. Such firms may also be able to offer higher margins to attract and reward the best distributors and intermediaries. Third is the opportunity to secure the firm's long-term future through investments in new service technologies and in research to create superior new services, improved features, and innovative delivery systems. Finally, efforts to improve productivity often have an impact on customers. Marketers are responsible for ensuring that negative impacts are avoided or minimized and that new procedures are carefully presented to customers. Positive impacts can be promoted as a new advantage.

Quality and productivity are twin paths to creating value for both customers and companies. In broad terms, quality focuses on the benefits created for the customer's side of the equation, and productivity is the financial costs incurred by the firm, which may subsequently be passed on to customers, primarily in the form of price. Carefully integrating quality- and productivity-improvement programs will improve the long-term profitability of the firm.

WHAT IS SERVICE QUALITY?

What do we mean when we speak of service quality? Company personnel need a common understanding in order to be able to address such issues as the measurement of service quality, the identification of causes of service quality shortfalls, and the design and implementation of corrective actions.

Perspectives on Service Quality

The word *quality* means different things to people according to the context. David Garvin identifies five perspectives on quality.[4]

1. The transcendent view of quality is synonymous with innate excellence: a mark of uncompromising standards and high achievement. This viewpoint is often applied to the performing and visual arts. It argues that people learn to recognize quality only through the experience gained from repeated exposure. From a practical standpoint, however, suggesting that managers or customers will know quality when they see it is not very helpful.
2. The product-based approach sees quality as a precise and measurable variable. Differences in quality, it argues, reflect differences in the amount of an ingredient or attribute possessed by the product. Because this view is totally objective, it fails to account for differences in the tastes, needs, and preferences of individual customers (or even entire market segments).
3. User-based definitions start with the premise that quality lies in the eyes of the beholder. These definitions equate quality with maximum satisfaction. This subjective, demand-oriented perspective recognizes that different customers have different wants and needs.
4. The manufacturing-based approach is supply based and is concerned primarily with engineering and manufacturing practices. (In services, we would say that quality is operations driven.) It focuses on conformance to internally developed specifications, which are often driven by productivity and cost-containment goals.
5. Value-based definitions define quality in terms of value and price. By considering the tradeoff between performance (or conformance) and price, quality comes to be defined as "affordable excellence."

Garvin suggests that these alternative views of quality help to explain the conflicts that sometimes arise between managers in different functional departments. However, he goes on to argue:

> Despite the potential for conflict, companies can benefit from such multiple perspectives. Reliance on a single definition of quality is a frequent source of problems. . . . Because each approach has its predictable blind spots, companies are likely to suffer fewer problems if they employ multiple perspectives on quality, actively shifting the approach they take as products move from

design to market. . . . Success normally requires close coordination of the activities of each function.[5]

Contrasting Quality Components in Manufacturing and Services

Manufacturing-Based Components of Quality To incorporate the various perspectives, Garvin developed the following components of quality that could be useful as a framework for analysis and strategic planning: (1) performance (primary operating characteristics), (2) features (bells and whistles), (3) reliability (probability of malfunction or failure), (4) conformance (ability to meet specifications), (5) durability (how long the product continues to provide value to the customer), (6) serviceability (speed, courtesy, competence, and ease of having problems fixed), (8) aesthetics (how the product appeals to any or all of the user's five senses), and (9) perceived quality (associations, such as the reputation of the company or brand name). Although these categories were developed from a manufacturing perspective, they also address the notion of "serviceability" of a physical good.

Service-Based Components Researchers argue that the distinctive nature of services requires a distinctive approach to defining and measuring service quality. As a result of the intangible, multifaceted nature of many services, it may be harder to evaluate the quality of a service than of a good. Because customers are often involved in service production—particularly in people-processing services—a distinction needs to be drawn between the *process* of service delivery (what Christian Grönroos calls functional quality) and the actual *output* of the service (what he calls technical quality).[6] Grönroos and others also suggest that the perceived quality of a service is the result of an evaluation process in which customers compare their perceptions of service delivery and its outcome against what they expect.

The most extensive research into service quality is strongly user oriented. From focus group research, Valarie Zeithaml, A. Parasuraman, and Leonard Berry, identified 10 criteria consumers use in evaluating service quality (Table 14-1). In subsequent research, they found a high degree of correlation among several of these variables and so consolidated them into five broad dimensions:

1. Tangibles (appearance of physical elements)
2. Reliability (dependable, accurate performance)
3. Responsiveness (promptness and helpfulness)
4. Assurance (competence, courtesy, credibility, and security)
5. Empathy (easy access, good communications, and customer understanding)[7]

Only one of these five dimensions, reliability, has a direct parallel to findings from Garvin's research on manufacturing quality.

Capturing the Customer's Perspective of Service Quality

To measure customer satisfaction with different aspects of service quality, Valarie Zeithaml and her colleagues developed a survey research instrument called SERVQUAL.[8] It's based on the premise that customers can evaluate a firm's service quality by comparing their perceptions of its service with their own expectations. SERVQUAL is seen as a generic measurement tool that can be applied across a broad spectrum of service industries. In its basic form, the scale contains 21 perception items and a series of expectation items, reflecting the five dimensions of service quality (see Table 14-2). Respondents complete a series of scales that measure their expectations of companies in a particular industry on a wide array of specific service characteristics. Using those same characteristics, respondents are subsequently asked to record their perceptions of a specific company whose services they have used. When perceived performance ratings are lower than expectations, this is a sign of poor quality. The reverse indicates good quality.

TABLE 14-1 Generic Dimensions Customers Use to Evaluate Service Quality

Dimension	*Definition*	*Examples of Customers' Questions*
Credibility	Trustworthiness, believability, honesty of the service provider	Does the hospital have a good reputation? Does my stockbroker refrain from pressuring me to buy? Does the repair firm guarantee its work?
Security	Freedom from danger, risk, or doubt	Is it safe for me to use the bank's ATMs at night? Is my credit card protected against unauthorized use? Can I be sure that my insurance policy provides complete coverage?
Access	Approachability and ease of contact	How easy is it for me to talk to a supervisor when I have a problem? Does the airline have a 24-hour toll-free phone number? Is the hotel conveniently located?
Communication	Listening to customers and keeping them informed in language they can understand	When I have a complaint, is the manager willing to listen to me? Does my doctor avoid using technical jargon? Does the electrician call when unable to keep a scheduled appointment?
Understanding the customer	Making the effort to know customers and their needs	Does someone in the hotel recognize me as a regular customer? Does my stockbroker try to determine my specific financial objectives? Is the moving company willing to accommodate my schedule?
Tangibles	Appearance of physical facilities, equipment, personnel, and communication materials	Are the hotel's facilities attractive? Is my accountant dressed appropriately? Is my bank statement easy to understand?
Reliability	Ability to perform the promised service dependably and accurately	Does my lawyer call me back when promised? Is my telephone bill free of errors? Is my television repaired right the first time?
Responsiveness	Willingness to help customers and provide prompt service	When there's a problem, does the firm resolve it quickly? Is my stockbroker willing to answer my questions? Is the cable TV company willing to give me a specific time when the installer will show up?
Competence	Possession of the skills and knowledge required to perform the service	Can the bank teller process my transaction without fumbling around? Is my travel agent able to obtain the information I need when I call? Does the dentist appear competent?
Courtesy	Politeness, respect, consideration, and friendliness of contact personnel	Does the flight attendant have a pleasant demeanor? Are the telephone operators consistently polite when answering my calls? Does the plumber take off muddy shoes before stepping on my carpet?

Source: Adapted from Valarie A. Zeithaml, A. Parasuraman, and Leonard L. Berry, *Delivering Quality Service: Balancing Customer Perceptions and Expectations* (New York: The Free Press, 1990).

Although SERVQUAL has been widely used by service companies, doubts have been expressed about both its conceptual foundation and methodological limitations.[9] To evaluate the stability of the five underlying dimensions when applied to a variety of service industries, Gerhard Mels, Christo Boshoff, and Denon Nel analyzed data sets from banks, insurance brokers, vehicle repair firms, electrical repair companies, and life

TABLE 14-2 The SERVQUAL Scale

The SERVQUAL scale includes five dimensions: tangibles, reliability, responsiveness, assurance, and empathy. Within each dimension are several items measured on a seven-point scale from *strongly agree* to *strongly disagree*, for a total of 21 items.

SERVQUAL Questions

Note: For actual survey respondents, instructions are also included, and each statement is accompanied by a seven-point scale ranging from "strongly agree = 7" to "strongly disagree = 1." Only the end points of the scale are labeled; there are no words above the numbers 2 through 6.

Tangibles

- Excellent banks (refer to cable TV companies, hospitals, or the appropriate service business throughout the questionnaire) will have modern-looking equipment.
- The physical facilities at excellent banks will be visually appealing.
- Employees at excellent banks will be neat in appearance.
- Materials (e.g., brochures or statements) associated with the service will be visually appealing in an excellent bank.

Reliability

- When excellent banks promise to do something by a certain time, they will do so.
- When customers have a problem, excellent banks will show a sincere interest in solving it.
- Excellent banks will perform the service right the first time.
- Excellent banks will provide their services at the time they promise to do so.
- Excellent banks will insist on error-free records.

Responsiveness

- Employees of excellent banks will tell customers exactly when service will be performed.
- Employees of excellent banks will give prompt service to customers.
- Employees of excellent banks will always be willing to help customers.
- Employees of excellent banks will never be too busy to respond to customer requests.

Assurance

- The behavior of employees of excellent banks will instill confidence in customers.
- Customers of excellent banks will feel safe in their transactions.
- Employees of excellent banks will be consistently courteous with customers.
- Employees of excellent banks will have the knowledge to answer customer questions.

Empathy

- Excellent banks will give customers individual attention.
- Excellent banks will have operating hours convenient to all their customers.
- Excellent banks will have employees who give customers personal attention.
- The employees of excellent banks will understand the specific needs of their customers.

Source: Adapted from A. Parasuraman, Valarie A. Zeithaml, and Leonard Berry, "SERVQUAL: A Multiple Item Scale for Measuring Consumer Perceptions of Service Quality," *Journal of Retailing* 64 (1988): 12–40.

insurance firms.[10] Their findings suggest that, in reality, SERVQUAL scores measure only two factors: intrinsic service quality (resembling what Grönroos termed functional quality) and extrinsic service quality (which refers to the tangible aspects of service delivery and "*resembles to some extent* what Grönroos refers to as technical quality"[11]).

These findings do not undermine the value of Zeithaml, Parasuraman, and Berry's achievement in identifying some of the key underlying constructs in service quality, but they do highlight the difficulty of measuring customer perceptions of quality. Anne Smith notes that the majority of researchers using SERVQUAL have omitted from, added to, or altered the list of statements purporting to measure service quality.[12]

Comparing performance to expectations works well in reasonably competitive markets in which customers have sufficient knowledge to purposefully choose a service that meets their needs and wants. However, in uncompetitive markets or if customers do not have free choice (e.g., because switching costs would be prohibitive or because of time or location constraints), there are risks to defining service quality primarily in terms of customers' satisfaction with outcomes relative to their prior expectations. If customers' expectations are low and service delivery proves to be marginally better than the dismal level that had been expected, we can hardly claim that customers are receiving good-quality service! In such situations, it is better to use needs or wants as comparison standards and to define good service quality as meeting or exceeding customer wants and needs rather than expectations.[13]

Satisfaction-based research into quality assumes that customers are dealing with services that are high in search or experience characteristics (see Chapter 2). A problem arises when they are asked to evaluate the quality of those services that are high in *credence* characteristics, such as complex legal cases or medical treatments, which they find difficult to evaluate even after delivery is completed. In short, the customers may not be sure what to expect in advance and may not know for years—if ever—how good a job the professional did. A natural tendency in such situations is for clients or patients to use process factors and tangible cues as proxies to evaluate quality.

Process factors include customers' feelings about the providers' personal style and satisfaction levels with those supplementary elements that they are competent to evaluate (for example, the tastiness of hospital meals or the clarity of bills for legal services). As a result, customers' perceptions of core service quality may be strongly influenced by their evaluation of process attributes and tangible elements of the service—a halo effect.[14] In order to obtain credible measures of professional performance quality, it may be necessary to include peer reviews of both process and outcomes as these relate to service execution on the core product.

Susan Devlin and H. K. Dong offer guidelines on how to measure service quality across every aspect of the business in a real-world setting.[15] To help customers recall and evaluate their service experiences, these authors suggest taking customers through each step of their service encounters (this approach is sometimes referred to as a walk-through audit).

THE GAP MODEL: A CONCEPTUAL TOOL TO IDENTIFY AND CORRECT SERVICE QUALITY PROBLEMS

If one accepts the view that quality entails consistently meeting or exceeding customers' expectations, the manager's task is to balance customer expectations and perceptions and to close any gaps between the two.

Gaps in Service Design and Delivery

Zeithaml, Berry, and Parasuraman identify four potential gaps within the service organization that may lead to a final and most serious gap: the difference between what customers expected and what they perceived was delivered.[16] Figure 14-1 extends and refines their framework to identify a total of seven types of gaps that can occur at various points during the design and delivery of a service performance.

FIGURE 14-1 Seven Service Quality Gaps

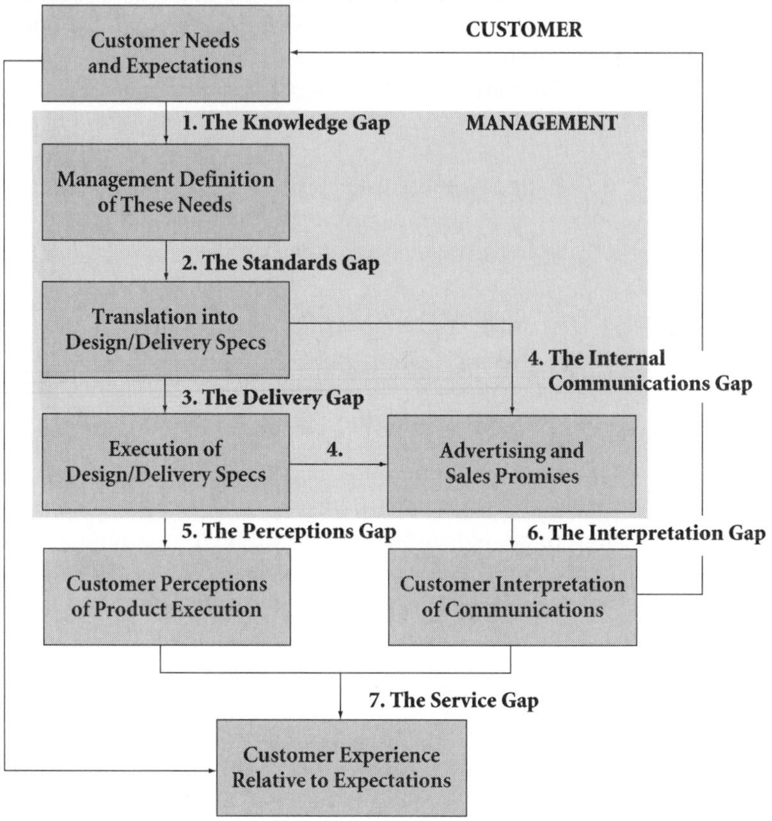

Source: Adapted from Christopher Lovelock, *Product Plus* (New York: McGraw-Hill, 1994), 112.

1. *The knowledge gap* is the difference between what service providers believe customers expect and customers' actual needs and expectations.
2. *The standards gap* is the difference between management's perceptions of customer expectations and the quality standards established for service delivery.
3. *The delivery gap* is the difference between specified delivery standards and the service provider's actual performance on these standards.
4. *The internal communications gap* is the difference between what the company's advertising and sales personnel think are the product's features, performance, and service quality level and what the company is actually able to deliver.
5. *The perceptions gap* is the difference between what is, in fact, delivered and what customers perceive they have received (because they are unable to accurately evaluate service quality).
6. *The interpretation gap* is the difference between what a service provider's communication efforts (in advance of service delivery) promise and what a customer thinks was promised by these communications.
7. *The service gap* is the difference between what customers expect to receive and their perceptions of the service that is delivered.

Gaps 1, 5, 6, and 7 represent external gaps between the customer and the organization. Gaps 2, 3, and 4 are internal gaps occurring between different functions and departments within the organization.

Gaps at any point in service design and delivery can damage relationships with customers. The service gap is the most critical; hence, the ultimate goal in improving service quality is to close or narrow this gap as much as possible. To achieve this, however, service organizations may need to work on one or more of the other six gaps depicted in Figure 14-1. Improving service quality requires identifying the specific causes of each gap and then developing strategies to close them.

Core Strategies to Address Service Quality Gaps

Zeithaml, Parasuraman, and Berry propose a series of generic steps for closing gaps 1 to 4.[17] Their prescriptions (relabeled to conform to the terminology of Figure 14-1), are summarized in Table 14-3.

What about gaps 5 and 6? Gap 5—the perceptions gap—recognizes that customers do not always correctly understand what the service has done for them. This situation is particularly likely to occur with credence services, for which it is difficult to judge performance even after delivery. Some service personnel make it a point to not only keep customers informed during service delivery but also debrief them at the end and, sometimes, offer tangible evidence. For instance, a doctor may explain to a patient what took place during a medical procedure, such as surgery, what was found—if anything—that differed from what was expected, and what the patient can expect for the future. To explain the nature of a complex repair, a technician may give a similar debriefing to the customer who commissioned it and provide physical evidence in the form of showing the damaged components that had to be replaced.

To reduce gap 6—the interpretation gap—communication specialists in the firm need to pretest all advertising, brochures, telephone scripts, and Web site content *before* they are published. Pretesting, widely used by advertising agencies, involves presenting communication materials to a sample of customers in advance of publication. Those participating in the pretest can be asked their opinion of the communications in question and what they interpret the specific or implied promises to mean. If their interpretation is not what the firm intended, changes to text copy or images will be needed. Service personnel who communicate with customers directly—including, but not limited to, sales and customer service—should ensure through questioning that customers understand their presentations correctly.

The strength of the gap methodology is that it offers generic insights and solutions that can be applied across different industries. What it doesn't attempt, of course, is to identify specific quality failures that may occur in particular service businesses. Each firm must develop its own customized approach to ensure that service quality becomes and remains a key objective.

MEASURING AND IMPROVING SERVICE QUALITY

It is commonly said that what is not measured is not managed. Without measurement, managers can't be sure whether service quality gaps exist, let alone what types of gaps, where they exist, and what potential corrective actions should be taken. And, of course, measurement is needed to determine whether goals for improvement are being met after changes have been implemented.

Soft and Hard Service Quality Measures

Customer-defined standards and measures of service quality can be grouped into two broad categories: soft and hard. Soft measures are those that cannot easily be observed and must be collected by talking to customers, employees, or others. As noted by Valarie Zeithaml and Mary Jo Bitner, "Soft standards provide direction, guidance and

TABLE 14-3 Prescriptions for Closing Service Gaps

Gap 1	***Prescription: Learn What Customers Expect***
	Understand customer expectations through research, complaint analysis,customer panels, etc.
	Increase direct interactions between managers and customers to improve understanding.
	Improve upward communication from contact personnel to management.
	Turn information and insights into action.
Gap 2	***Prescription: Establish the Right Service Quality Standards***
	Ensure that top management displays ongoing commitment to quality as defined by customers.
	Set, communicate, and reinforce customer-oriented service standards for all work units.
	Train managers in the skills needed to lead employees to deliver quality service.
	Become receptive to new ways of doing business that overcome barriers to delivering quality service.
	Standardize repetitive work tasks to ensure consistency and reliability by substituting hard technology for human contact and improving work methods (soft technology).
	Establish clear service quality goals that are challenging, realistic, and explicitly designed to meet customer expectations.
	Clarify which job tasks have the biggest impact on quality and should receive the highest priority.
	Ensure that employees understand and accept goals and priorities.
	Measure performance and provide regular feedback.
	Reward managers and employees for attaining quality goals.
Gap 3	***Prescription: Ensure That Service Performance Meets Standards***
	Clarify employee roles.
	Ensure that all employees understand how their jobs contribute to customer satisfaction.
	Match employees to jobs by selecting for the abilities and skills needed to perform each job well.
	Provide employees with the technical training needed to perform their assigned tasks effectively.
	Develop innovative recruitment and retention methods to attract the best people and build loyalty.
	Enhance performance by selecting the most appropriate and reliable technology and equipment.
	Teach employees about customer expectations, perceptions, and problems.
	Train employees in interpersonal skills, especially for dealing with customers under stressful conditions.
	Eliminate role conflict among employees by involving them in the process of setting standards.
	Train employees in priority setting and time management.
	Measure employee performance and tie compensation and recognition to delivery of quality service.
	Develop reward systems that are meaningful, timely, simple, accurate, and fair.
	Empower managers and employees in the field by pushing decision-making power down the organization; allow them greater discretion in the methods they use to reach goals.
	Ensure that employees working at internal support jobs provide good service to customer-contact personnel.
	Build teamwork so that employees work well together, and use team rewards as incentives.
	Treat customers as partial employees; clarify their roles in service delivery; and train and motivate them to perform well in their roles as coproducers.
Gap 4	***Prescription: Ensure That Communication Promises Are Realistic***
	Seek inputs from operations personnel when new advertising programs are being created.
	Develop advertising that features real employees performing their jobs.
	Allow service providers to preview advertisements before customers are exposed to them.
	Get sales staff to involve operations staff in face-to-face meetings with customers.
	Develop internal educational, motivational, and advertising campaigns to strengthen links among marketing, operations, and human resource departments.
	Ensure that consistent standards of service are delivered across multiple locations.
	Ensure that advertising content accurately reflects those service characteristics that are most important to customers in their encounters with the organization.
	Manage customers' expectations by letting them know what is and is not possible—and the reasons why.
	Identify and explain uncontrollable reasons for shortcomings in service performance.
	Offer customers different levels of service at different prices, explaining the distinctions.

Source: Distilled from chapters 4, 5, 6, and 7 of Valarie A. Zeithaml, A. Parasuraman, and Leonard L. Berry, *Delivering Quality Service: Balancing Customer Perceptions and Expectations* (New York: The Free Press, 1990).

feedback to employees on ways to achieve customer satisfaction and can be quantified by measuring customer perceptions and beliefs."[18] SERVQUAL is an example of a sophisticated soft measurement system.

By contrast, hard standards and measures relate to those characteristics and activities that can be counted, timed, or measured through audits. Such measures may include how many telephone calls were abandoned while the customer was on hold, how many minutes customers had to wait in line at a particular stage in the service delivery, the time required to complete a specific task, the temperature of a particular food item, how many trains arrived late, how many bags were lost, how many patients made a complete recovery following a specific type of operation, and how many orders were filled correctly. Standards are often set with reference to the percentage of occasions on which a particular measure is achieved. The challenge for service marketers is to ensure that operational measures of service quality reflect customer input.

Organizations that are known for excellent service make use of both soft and hard measures. These organizations are good at listening to both their customers and their customer-contact employees. The larger the organization, the more important it is to create formalized feedback programs using a variety of professionally designed and implemented research procedures.

Soft Measures of Service Quality How can companies measure their performance against soft standards of service quality? according to Leonard Berry and A. Parasuraman:

> [C]ompanies need to establish ongoing listening systems using multiple methods among different customer groups. A single service quality study is a snapshot taken at a point in time and from a particular angle. Deeper insight and more informed decision making come from a continuing series of snapshots taken from various angles and through different lenses, which form the essence of systematic listening.[19]

They recommend that ongoing research be conducted through a portfolio of research approaches. Key customercentric service quality measures (which we review in Chapter 12) include total market surveys, annual surveys, transactional surveys, service feedback cards, mystery shopping, analysis of unsolicited feedback, focus group discussions, and service reviews. Among other soft measures are the following:

- *Ongoing surveys of account holders* by telephone or mail, using scientific sampling procedures to determine customers' satisfaction in terms of broader relationship issues
- *Customer advisory panels* to offer feedback and advice on service performance
- *Employee surveys and panels* to determine perceptions of the quality of service delivered to customers on specific dimensions, barriers to better service, and suggestions for improvement

Designing and implementing a large-scale customer survey to measure service across a wide array of attributes is no simple task. Line managers sometimes view the findings as threatening when direct comparisons are made of the performance of different departments or branches.

Hard Measures of Service Quality Hard measures typically refer to operational processes or outcomes and include such data as uptime, service response times, failure rates, and delivery costs. In a complex service operation, multiple measures of service quality will be recorded at many different points. In low-contact services, in which customers are not deeply involved in the service delivery process, many operational measures apply to backstage activities that have only a second-order effect on customers.

FedEx was one of the first service companies to understand the need for a firmwide index of service quality that embraced all the key activities that had an impact on customers. By publishing a single, composite index on a frequent basis, senior managers hoped that all FedEx employees would work toward improving quality. The firm recognized the danger of using as targets percentages, because they might lead to complacency. In an organization as large as FedEx, which ships millions of packages a day, delivering even 99 percent of packages on time or having 99.9 percent of flights arrive safely would lead to horrendous problems. Instead, top management decided to approach quality measurement from the baseline of zero failures. As noted by one senior executive:

> It's only when you examine the types of failures, the number that occur of each type, and the reasons why, that you begin to improve the quality of your service. For us the trick was to express quality failures in absolute numbers. That led us to develop the Service Quality Index or SQI [pronounced "sky"], which takes each of 12 different events that occur every day, takes the numbers of those events and multiplies them by a weight . . . based on the amount of aggravation caused to customers—as evidenced by their tendency to write to Federal Express and complain about them.[20]

The design of this "hard" index reflected the findings of extensive "soft" customer research and has been periodically modified in light of new research insights. Looking at service failures from the customer's perspective, the SQI measures daily the occurrence of 12 activities that are likely to lead to customer dissatisfaction. Each activity is assigned a weighting that reflects the seriousness of that event for customers. The index is composed by taking the raw number of daily occurrences for each event day and multiplying it by the relevant weighting to create a point score. The points are then totaled across all 12 activities to generate that day's index (Table 14-4). As with a golf score, the lower the index, the better the performance. However, unlike golf, the SQI involves substantial numbers—typically six figures—reflecting the huge number of

TABLE 14-4 Composition of FedEx's Service Quality Index (SQI)

Failure Type	*Weighting Factor × No. of Incidents = Daily Points*	
Late delivery—right day	1	
Late delivery—wrong day	5	
Tracing requests unanswered	1	
Complaints reopened	5	
Missing proofs of delivery	1	
Invoice adjustments	1	
Missed pickups	10	
Lost packages	10	
Damaged packages	10	
Aircraft delays (minutes)	5	
Overgoods (packages missing labels)	5	
Abandoned calls	1	
Total Failure Points (SQI)		XXX,XXX

Source: Christopher Lovelock, *Product Plus* (New York: McGraw-Hill, 1994), 131.

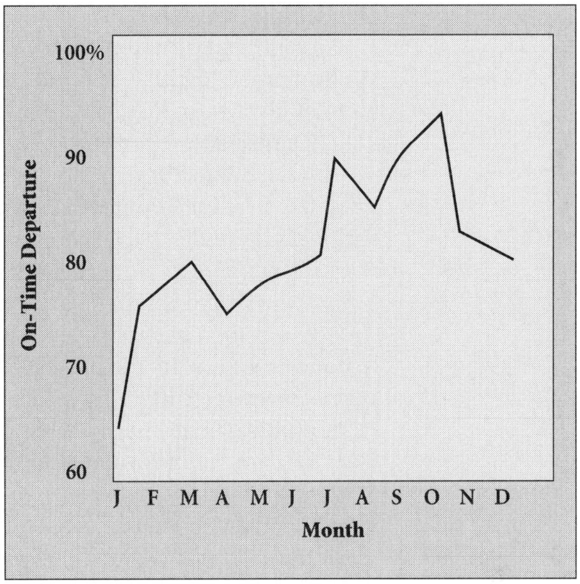

FIGURE 14-2 Control Chart for Departure Delays, Showing Percentage of Flights Departing within 15 Minutes of Schedule

packages shipped daily. An annual goal is set for the average daily SQI, based on reducing the occurrence of failures over the previous year's total.

To ensure a continuing focus on each separate component of the SQI, FedEx established 12 Quality Action Teams, one for each component. The teams were charged with understanding and correcting the root causes underlying the observed problems.

Control charts offer a simple method of displaying performance over time against specific quality standards. The charts can be used to monitor and communicate individual variables or an overall index. Because the charts are visual, trends are easily identified. Figure 14-2 shows an airline's performance on the important hard standard of on-time departures. The trends displayed suggest that this issue needs to be addressed by management, as performance is erratic and not very satisfactory. Of course, control charts are only as good as the data on which they are based.

Tools for Analyzing and Addressing Service Quality Problems

When a problem is caused by controllable, internal forces, there's no excuse for allowing it to recur. In fact, maintaining customers' goodwill after a service failure depends on keeping promises made to the effect that "we're taking steps to ensure that it doesn't happen again!" With prevention in mind, let's look briefly at some tools for determining the root causes of specific service quality problems.

Root-Cause Analysis: The Fishbone Diagram Cause-and-effect analysis uses a technique first developed by Japanese quality expert Kaoru Ishikawa. Groups of managers and staff brainstorm all the possible reasons that might cause a specific problem. The resulting factors are then categorized into one of five groupings—equipment, manpower (or people), material, procedures, and other—on a cause-and-effect chart, popularly known as a fishbone diagram because of its shape. This technique has been used for many years in manufacturing and, more recently, also in services.

To sharpen the value of the analysis for use in service organizations, we show an extended framework that comprises eight rather than five groupings.[21] "People" has been divided into "front-stage personnel" and "backstage personnel" to highlight the fact that front-stage service problems are often experienced directly by customers, whereas backstage failures tend to show up more obliquely through a ripple effect. "Information" has been split out from "procedures," recognizing that many service problems result from information failures, especially failures by front-stage personnel to tell customers what to do and when. In an airline context, for instance, poor announcement of departures may lead passengers to arrive late at the gate. Finally, there is a new category: "customers."

In manufacturing, customers have little impact on day-to-day operational processes, but in a high-contact services, they are involved in front-stage operations. If they don't play their own roles correctly, customers may reduce service productivity and cause quality problems for themselves and other customers. For instance, an aircraft can be delayed if a passenger tries to board at the last minute with an oversized suitcase that then has to be loaded into the cargo hold. An example of the extended fishbone is shown in Figure 14-3, displaying 27 possible reasons for late departures of passenger aircraft.[22] Once all the main potential causes for flight delays have been identified, it's necessary to assess how much impact each cause has on actual delays.

Pareto analysis (named after the Italian economist who first developed it) seeks to identify the principal causes of observed outcomes. This type of analysis underlies the so-called 80/20 rule, because it often reveals that around 80 percent of the value of one variable (in this instance, number of service failures) is accounted for by only 20 percent of the causal variable (number of possible causes).

In the airline example, findings showed that 88 percent of the company's late-departing flights from the airports it served were caused by only four (15 percent) of all the possible factors. In fact, more than half the delays were caused by a single factor: acceptance of late passengers (situations when the staff held a flight for one more passenger who was checking in after the official cutoff time). On such occasions, the airline made a friend of that late passenger—possibly encouraging a repeat of this undesirable

FIGURE 14-3 Cause-and-Effect Chart for Flight Departure Delays

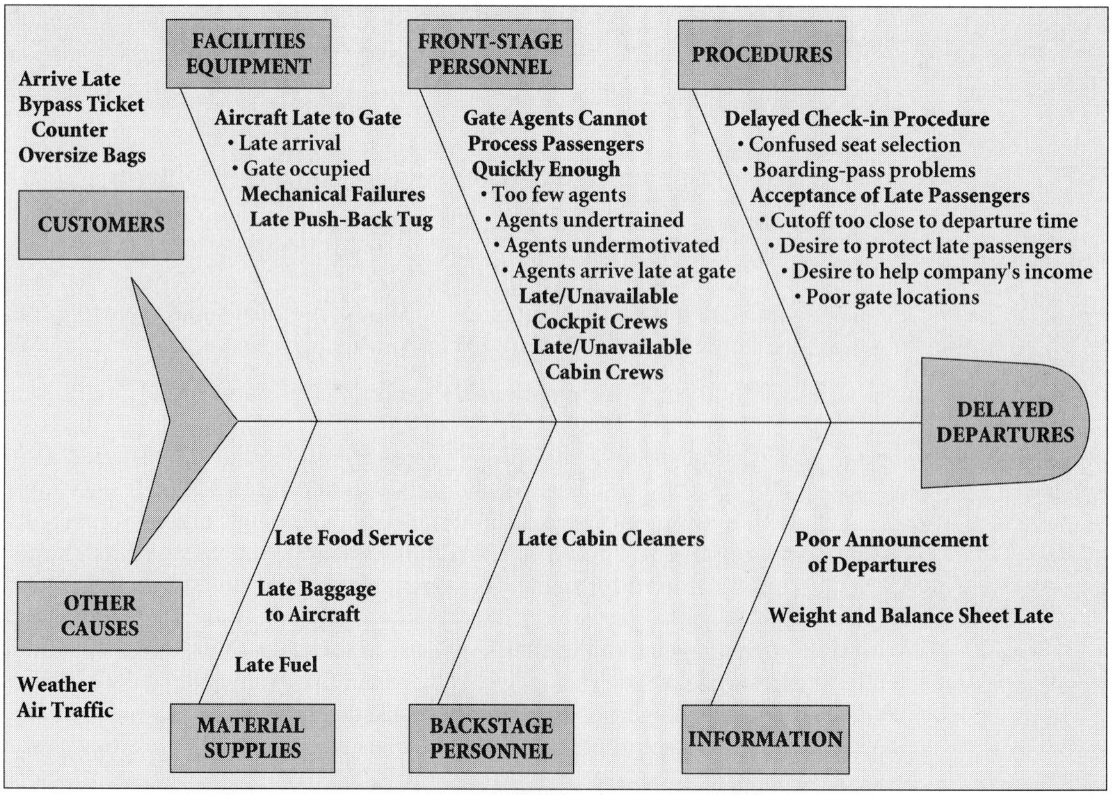

on a future occasion—but risked alienating all the other passengers who were already on board, waiting for the aircraft to depart. Other major delays included waiting for pushback (a vehicle must arrive to pull the aircraft away from the gate), waiting for fueling, and delays in signing the weight and balance sheet (a safety requirement relating to the distribution of the aircraft's load that the captain must observe on each flight). Further analysis, however, showed some significant variations in reasons from one airport to another (see Figure 14-4). Combining the fishbone diagram and Pareto analysis serves to highlight the main causes of service failure.

Blueprinting As described in Chapter 8, a well-constructed blueprint is a powerful tool for identifying fail points. It enables us to visualize the process of service delivery by depicting the sequence of front-stage interactions that customers experience as they encounter service providers, facilities, and equipment, together with supporting backstage activities, which are hidden from the customers and are not part of their service experience.

Blueprints can be used to identify potential *fail points* where failures are most likely to occur. Blueprints help us to understand how failures at one point (such as incorrect entry of an appointment date) may have a ripple effect later in the process (the customer arrives at the doctor's office and is told that the doctor is unavailable). Using frequency counts, managers can identify the specific types of failures that occur most frequently and thus need urgent attention. One desirable solution is to design fail points out of the system. (Management Memo 14-1 describes one such technique poka yokes.) In the case of failures that cannot easily be designed out of a process or are not easily prevented (such

FIGURE 14-4 Analysis of Causes of Flight Departure Delays

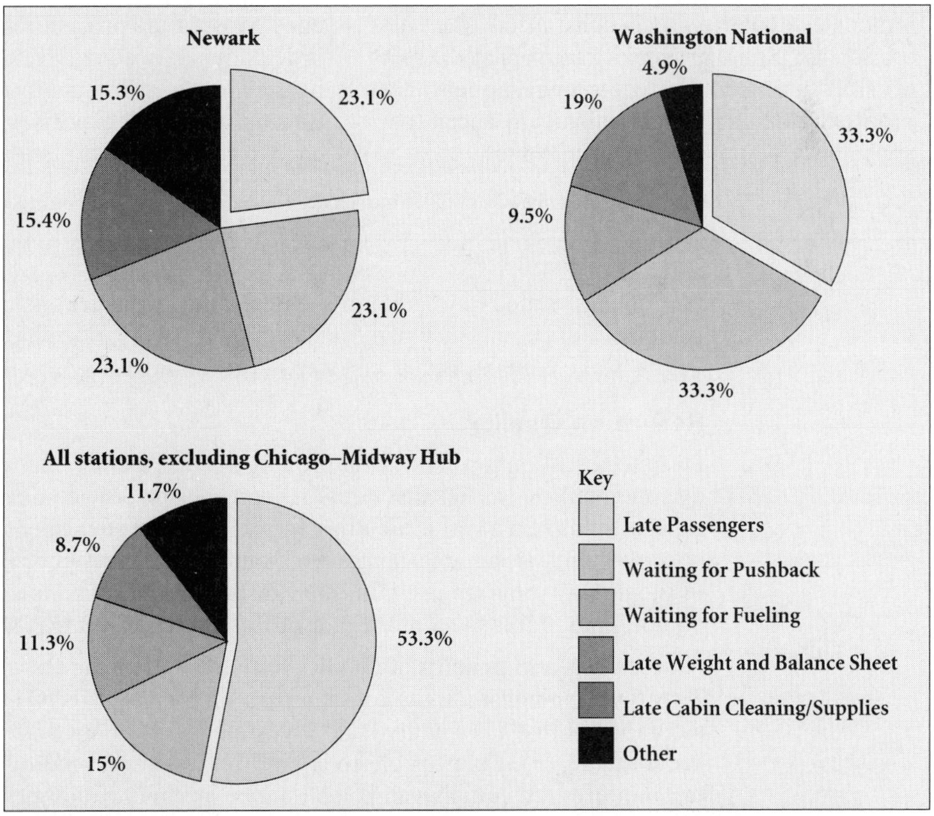

Source: Based on D. Daryl Wyckoff, "New Tools for Achieving Service Quality," *Cornell Hotel and Restaurant Administration Quarterly* (November 1984).

MANAGEMENT MEMO 14-1

POKA-YOKES: AN EFFECTIVE TOOL TO DESIGN FAIL POINTS OUT OF SERVICE PROCESSES

One of the most useful TQM (Total Quality Management) methods in manufacturing is the application of poka-yoke, or fail-safe methods to prevent errors in manufacturing processes. Richard Chase and Douglas Stewart introduced this concept to fail-safe service processes.

Part of the challenge of implementing poka-yokes in a service context is the need to address not only server errors but also customer errors. Server poka-yokes ensure that service staff do things correctly, as requested, in the right order, and at the right speed. For instance, surgical instrument trays have indentations for each instrument required for a given operation, so it is clear if the surgeon has not removed all instruments from the patient before closing the incision.

Some service firms use poka-yokes to ensure that certain steps or standards in the customer staff interaction are adhered to. A bank ensures eye contact by requiring tellers to record the customer's eye color on a checklist at the start of a transaction. Some firms place mirrors at the exits of staff areas to foster a neat appearance. Frontline staff can then automatically check their appearance before greeting a customer.

Customer poka-yokes usually focus on preparing the customer for the encounter (including getting them to bring the right materials for the transaction and to arrive on time, if applicable), understanding and anticipating their role in the service transaction, and selecting the correct service or transaction. For example, dress-code requests may be printed on invitations, reminders of dental appointments may be sent, and instructions may be displayed on customers' bank cards and statements to ("Please have your account and PIN number ready before calling our service reps"). A poka-yoke that addresses customer errors during the encounter is beepers at ATMs so that customers do not forget to take their cards. At one restaurant, servers place round coasters in front of those diners who have ordered a decaffeinated coffee and square coasters in front of the others.

Designing poka-yokes is part art and part science. Most of the procedures seem trivial, but this is actually a key advantage of this method. It can be used to design frequently occurring service failures out of service processes and to ensure adherence to certain service standards or service steps.

Source: Richard B. Chase and Douglas M. Stewart, "Make Your Service Fail-Safe," *Sloan Management Review* (Spring 1994): 35–44.

as problems related to weather or the public infrastructure), solutions may center on development of contingency plans and service recovery guidelines. Knowing what can go wrong where is an important first step in preventing service quality problems.

Return on Quality

Despite the attention paid to improving service quality, many companies have been disappointed by the results. Firms recognized for service quality efforts have sometimes run into financial difficulties, in part because they spent too lavishly on quality improvements. In some instances, such outcomes reflect poor or incomplete execution of the quality program itself. In other instances, improved measures of service quality do not seem to translate into bigger profits, increased market share, or higher sales.

Assess Costs and Benefits of Quality Initiatives Roland Rust, Anthony Zahonik, and Timothy Keiningham argue for a "return on quality" (ROQ) approach, based on the assumptions that (1) quality is an investment, (2) quality efforts must be financially accountable, (3) it is possible to spend too much on quality, and (4) not all quality expenditures are equally valid.[23] An important implication of the ROQ perspective is that quality-improvement efforts may benefit from being related to productivity-improvement programs.

Should firms employ quality improvement programs to achieve simultaneously both revenue expansion through enhanced customer satisfaction and cost reduction through greater efficiency? In a study of managers seeking to obtain a financial return from quality improvements, it was found that firms whose strategies emphasized revenue expansion outperformed firms that focused on cost reduction or tried to emphasize both revenue expansion and cost reduction simultaneously.[24]

To determine the feasibility of new quality-improvement efforts, they must be carefully costed in advance and then related to anticipated customer response. Will the program enable the firm to increase customer loyalty (reduce defections), increase share of wallet, and/or attract more customers (e.g., through word of mouth of current customers), and if so, how much additional net income will be generated? With good documentation, it is sometimes possible for a firm that operates in multiple locations to examine past experience and determine whether a relationship exists between service quality and revenues. (See Research Insights 14-1).

RESEARCH INSIGHTS 14-1

QUALITY OF FACILITIES AND ROOM REVENUES AT HOLIDAY INN

To determine the relationship between product quality and financial performance in a hotel context, Sheryl Kimes analyzed three years of quality and operational performance data from 1,135 franchised Holiday Inn hotels in the United States and Canada. Indicators of product quality came from the franchisor's quality assurance reports. These reports were based on unannounced, semiannual inspections by trained quality auditors who were rotated among different regions and who spent most of a day inspecting and rating 19 areas of each hotel. Twelve of these areas were included in the study: two relating to the guest rooms (bedroom and bathroom) and ten relating to so-called commercial areas (e.g., exterior, lobby, public restrooms, dining facilities, lounge facilities, corridors, meeting area, recreation area, kitchen, back of house). Each area typically included 10 to 12 individual items that could be passed or failed. The inspector noted the number of defects for each area and the total number for the entire hotel.

Holiday Inn Worldwide also provided data on revenue per available room (RevPAR) at each hotel. To adjust for differences in local conditions, Kimes analyzed sales and revenue statistics obtained from thousands of U.S. and Canadian hotels and reported in the monthly Smith Travel Accommodation Reports (a widely used service in the travel industry). This data enabled Kimes to calculate the RevPAR for the immediate midscale competitors of each Holiday Inn hotel. The resulting information was then used to normalize the RevPARs for all Holiday Inns in the sample so that they were now truly comparable. The average daily room rate at the time was about $50.

The analysis was conducted using six-month intervals over a three-year period. For the purposes of the research, a hotel that had failed at least one item in an area was considered "defective" in that area. A comparison was then made, on an area-by-area basis, of the average normalized RevPAR for hotels that were defective in an area against those that were "nondefective."

The findings showed that as the number of defects in a hotel increased, the RevPAR decreased. Hotel areas that showed a particularly strong impact on RevPAR were the exterior, the guest room, and the guest bathroom. Even a single deficiency resulted in a statistically significant reduction in RevPAR, but the combination of deficiencies in all three areas showed an even larger effect on RevPAR over time. Kimes calculated that the average annual revenue impact on a defective hotel was $204,400.

Using a ROQ perspective, the implication was that the primary focus of increased expenditures on housekeeping and preventive maintenance should be the hotel exterior, the guest rooms, and bathrooms.

Source: Sheryl E. Kimes, "The Relationship between Product Quality and Revenue per Available Room at Holiday Inn," *Journal of Service Research* 2 (November 1999): 138–144.

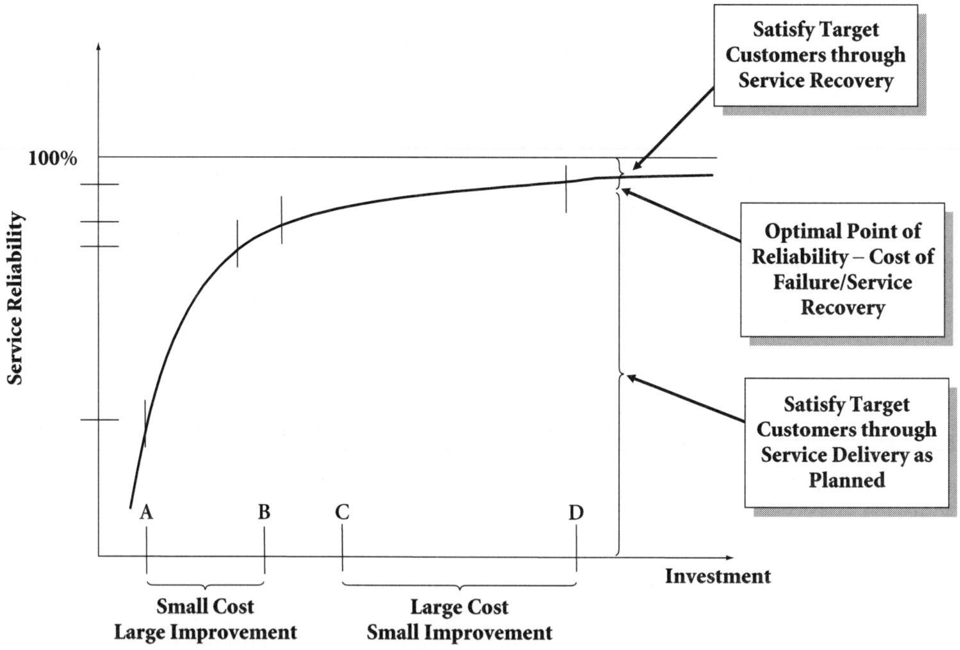

FIGURE 14-5 When Does Improving Service Reliability Become Unprofitable?

Determine the Optimal Level of Reliability A company with poor service quality can often achieve big jumps in reliability with relatively modest investments in improvements. As illustrated in Figure 14.5, initial investments in reducing service failure often bring dramatic results, but at some point diminishing returns set in, as further improvements require increasing levels of investment, even becoming prohibitively expensive. What level of reliability should we target?

Typically, the cost of service recovery is lower than the cost of an unhappy customer. This suggests a strategy of increasing reliability up to the point that the incremental improvement equals the cost of service recovery or the cost of failure. Although this strategy results in a service that is less than 100 percent failure free, the firm can still aim to satisfy 100 percent of its target customers by ensuring that either they receive the service as planned or, if a failure occurs, they obtain a satisfying service recovery (see Chapter 13).

DEFINING AND MEASURING PRODUCTIVITY

Simply defined, productivity measures the amount of output produced relative to the amount of inputs used. Hence, improvements in productivity require an increase in the ratio of outputs to inputs. An improvement in this ratio might be achieved by cutting the resources required to create a given volume of output or by increasing the output obtained from a given level of inputs.

Defining Productivity in a Service Context

What do we mean by "input" in a service context? Input varies according to the nature of the business but may include labor (both physical and intellectual), materials, energy, and capital (consisting of land, buildings, equipment, information systems, and financial assets). The intangible nature of service performances makes it more difficult to measure the productivity of service industries than that of manufacturing. The problem is especially acute for information-based services. A manufacturer's output consists of products, such as cars, packages of soap powder, transformers, or drill bits, that can all be counted and readily sorted into models or categories. Because production and consumption are separated in time, defective items that are caught by quality control inspectors will either be recycled or reworked, thus adding to their respective input costs.

Measuring productivity is difficult in services when the output is hard to define. In a people-processing service, such as a hospital, we can look at the number of patients treated in the course of a year and at the hospital's "census," or average bed occupancy. But how do we account for the different types of interventions performed, such as removal of cancerous tumors, treatment of diabetes, or setting of broken bones? What about differences between patients? How do we evaluate the inevitable difference in outcomes? Some patients get better, some develop complications, and sadly, some even die. Relatively few standardized medical procedures offer highly predictable outcomes.

The measurement task is perhaps simpler in possession-processing services, as many are quasi-manufacturing organizations, performing routine tasks with easily measurable inputs and outputs. Examples are garages that change a car's oil and rotate its tires or fast-food restaurants that offer limited and simple menus. However, the task gets more complicated when the garage mechanic has to find and repair a water leak or when we are dealing with a French restaurant known for its varied and exceptional cuisine. What about information-based services? How should we define the output of a bank or a consulting firm? And how does the latter's output compare to a law firm's?

Service Efficiency, Productivity, and Effectiveness

We need to distinguish among efficiency, productivity, and effectiveness.[25] *Efficiency* involves comparison to a standard that is usually time based, such as how long it takes for an employee to perform a particular task relative to a predefined standard. *Productivity*, however, involves financial valuation of outputs to inputs. *Effectiveness*, by contrast, can be defined as the degree to which an organization is meeting its goals.

A major problem in measuring service productivity concerns variability. As James Heskett points out, traditional measures of service output tend to ignore variations in the quality or value of service. In freight transport, for instance, a ton-mile of output for freight that is delivered late is treated the same for productivity purposes as a similar shipment delivered on time.[26]

Another approach—counting the number of customers served per unit of time—suffers from the same shortcoming. What happens when an increase in customer throughput is achieved at the expense of perceived service quality? Suppose that a hairdresser who serves three customers per hour that increases output to one every fifteen minutes—giving what is technically just as good a haircut—by using a faster but noisier hairdryer, eliminating all conversation, and generally rushing. Even if the haircut itself is just as good, the delivery process may be perceived as functionally inferior, leading customers to rate the overall service experience less positively. The Dilbert cartoon in Figure 14-6 captures the absurdity of a single-minded focus on speed to the exclusion of developing good customer rapport.

The problem is that classical techniques of productivity measurement focus on outputs rather than *outcomes*, stressing efficiency but neglecting *effectiveness*. In the long run, organizations that are more effective in consistently delivering outcomes desired by customers should be able to command higher prices for their output. The need to emphasize effectiveness and outcomes suggests that issues of productivity cannot be divorced from those of quality and value. Loyal customers who remain with a firm tend to become more profitable over time, an indication of the payback to be obtained from providing quality service. In this vein, John Shaw suggests that measures of productivity growth in services should focus on customers as the denominator.[27] He proposes the following units of analysis and comparison:

FIGURE 14-6 Insights from Dilbert, by Scott Adams: Overemphasis on speed may result in curt and unfriendly service for customers.

DILBERT reprinted by permission of United Syndicate, Inc.

- Profitability by customer
- Capital used per customer
- Shareholder equity used per customer

These measures tell the firm how it is doing. But what managers and employees also need are insights as to how better results may be achieved. One insight in this respect comes from Frances Frei and Patrick Harker, who focus on the underlying processes in retail banking and developed a methodology to help managers understand how much inefficiency in a business process stems from the process design selected and how much from process execution.[28]

IMPROVING SERVICE PRODUCTIVITY

Intensive competition in many service sectors pushes firms to continually seek ways to improve their productivity. This section discusses various potential approaches to and sources of productivity gains.

Generic Productivity-Improvement Strategies

The task of improving service productivity has traditionally been assigned to operations managers, whose approach has typically centered on such actions as

- Careful control of costs at every step in the process
- Efforts to reduce wasteful use of materials or labor
- Matching productive capacity to average levels of demand rather than peak levels, so that workers and equipment are not underemployed for extended periods
- Replacement of workers by automated machines
- Providing employees with equipment and databases that enable them to work faster or to a higher level of quality
- Teaching employees how to work more productively (faster is not necessarily better if it leads to mistakes or unsatisfactory work that has to be redone)
- Broadening the array of tasks that a service worker can perform (which may require revised labor agreements) so as to eliminate bottlenecks and wasteful downtime by allowing managers to deploy workers wherever they are most needed
- Installing expert systems that allow paraprofessionals to take on work previously performed by more experienced individuals earning higher salaries

Although improving productivity can be approached in an incremental way, major gains often require reengineering of customer service processes, also known as service process redesign, as discussed in Chapter 8.

Customer-Driven Approaches to Improve Productivity

If customers are deeply involved in the service production process (typically, people-processing services), operations managers should be examining how customers' inputs can be made more productive. Marketing managers should be thinking about what marketing strategies should be used to influence customers to behave in more productive ways. Three such strategies are changing the timing of customer demand, involving customers more actively in the production process, and asking customers to use third parties.

Changing the Timing of Customer Demand Managing demand in capacity-constrained service businesses has been a recurring theme in this book (see especially Chapters 6 and 9). Customers often complain that the services they use are crowded and congested, reflecting time-of-day, seasonal, or other cyclical peaks in demand. During the off-peak periods in those same cycles, managers often worry that there are too few customers and that their facilities and staff are not fully productive. By shifting demand away from peaks, managers can make better use of their productive assets and provide better service. Post office advertising campaigns to encourage people to "mail early for Christmas" have had some success in getting people to plan ahead rather than leave it until a few days before the holiday to send their cards and packages.

However, some demand cannot easily be shifted without the cooperation of third parties, such as employers and schools, which control working hours and holiday schedules. To fill idle capacity during off-peak hours, marketers may need to target new market segments with different needs and schedules rather than focus exclusively on current segments. If the peaks and valleys of demand can be smoothed and capacity utilization improved, productivity will increase as output increases with constant inputs (assuming negligible variable costs).

Involve Customers More in Production Customers who assume a more active role in the service production and delivery process can take over some labor tasks from the service organization (Figure 14-7). Benefits for both parties may result when customers perform self-service.

Many technological innovations are designed to get customers to perform tasks previously undertaken by service employees. Today, many companies are trying to encourage customers who have access to the Internet to obtain information from the firm's corporate Web sites and even to place orders through the Web rather than telephone employees at the company's offices. For such changes to succeed, Web sites must be made user friendly and easy to navigate, and customers must be convinced that it is safe to provide credit card information over the Web. Some companies have been offering promotional incentives (such as a credit of 10,000 air miles to a frequent flyer program) to encourage customers to make an initial order on the Web.

Even five-star hotels with traditionally high levels of personal service have been asking their guests to do more of the work. For example, in-room safe-deposit boxes and voice mail attached to telephones have been implemented in most hotel rooms. In the past, these services were provided by a service counter or concierge. However, despite the reduction in personal service, this innovation has been positioned as a benefit that is more convenient for customers. They can have fast and easy access to their in-room safe-deposit boxes and can easily see from a blinking light on the phone whether there is a voice mail waiting for them rather than having to contact the concierge.

- Define the opportunities
- Measure key steps/inputs
- Analyze to identify root causes
- Improve performance
- Control to maintain performance

Choosing a Methodology

As there are various approaches to systematically improving a service firm's service quality and productivity, the question arises which approach should be adopted: TQM, ISO 9000, the Malcolm-Baldrige model, or Six Sigma? Some firms have even implemented more than one program. In terms of complexity, it seems that TQM can be applied at differing levels of sophistication, and basic tools, such as flowcharting, frequency charts, and fishbone diagrams, probably should be adopted by any type of service firm. ISO 9000 seems the next level of commitment and complexity, followed by the Malcolm-Baldrige Model and, finally, Six Sigma.

By reviewing the various approaches, it becomes clear that, in fact, any one of them can be a useful framework for understanding customer needs, analyzing processes, and improving service quality and productivity. Firms can choose a particular program, depending on their own needs and desired level of sophistication. Each program has its own merits, and firms can adopt more than one program to supplement each other. For example, the ISO 9000 program can be used for standardizing the procedures and process documentation, which can lead to reduction in variability. Six Sigma and Malcolm-Baldrige programs can be used to improve processes and to focus on performance improvement across the organization.

A key success factor of any of these programs depends on how well the particular quality-improvement program is integrated with the overall business strategy. Firms that adopt one of these programs because of peer pressure or as a marketing tool will be less likely to succeed than firms that view these programs as useful development tools.[40] Rather, service champions make best practices in service quality management a core part of their organizational culture.[41]

The National Institute of Standards and Technology (NIST), which organizes the Malcolm-Baldrige Award program, tracked a hypothetical stock index called the "Baldrige-Index" of Malcolm-Baldrige Award winners and observed that winners consistently outperformed the S&P 500 index.[42] Ironically, the two-time winner of the award and Six Sigma pioneer, Motorola, has been suffering recently financially and losing market share to its main rivals, in part through failure to keep up with new technology. Success cannot be taken for granted, and implementation, commitment, and continual adaptation to changing markets, technologies, and environments are keys for sustained success.

Endnotes

1. Evert Gummesson, "Service Management: An Evaluation and the Future," *International Journal of Service Industry Management* 5, no. 1 (1994): 77–96.
2. Bradley T. Gale, *Managing Customer Value* (New York: The Free Press, 1994).
3. Robert D. Buzzell and Bradley T. Gale, *The PIMS Principles—Linking Strategy to Performance* (New York: The Free Press, 1987).
4. David A. Garvin, *Managing Quality* (New York: The Free Press, 1988), especially Chapter 3.
5. Ibid., 48–49.
6. Christian Grönroos, *Service Management and Marketing* (Lexington, MA: Lexington Books, 1990), Chapter 2.
7. Valarie A. Zeithaml, A. Parasuraman, and Leonard L. Berry, *Delivering Quality Service* (New York: The Free Press, 1990).
8. A. Parasuraman, Valarie A. Zeithaml, and Leonard Berry, "SERVQUAL: A Multiple Item Scale for Measuring Consumer Perceptions of Service Quality," *Journal of Retailing* 64 (1988): 12–40.

9. See, for instance, Francis Buttle, "SERVQUAL: Review, Critique, Research Agenda," *European Journal of Marketing* 30, no. 1 (1996): 8–32; Simon S. K. Lam and Ka Shing Woo, "Measuring Service Quality: A Test-Retest Reliability Investigation of SERVQUAL," *Journal of the Market Research Society* 39 (April 1997): 381–393; Terrence H. Witkowski, and Mary F. Wolfinbarger, "Comparative Service Quality: German and American Ratings Across Service Settings," *Journal of Business Research* 55 (2002): 875–881.
10. Gerhard Mels, Christo Boshoff, and Denon Nel, "The Dimensions of Service Quality: The Original European Perspective Revisited," *The Service Industries Journal* 17 (January 1997): 173–189.
11. Grönroos, *Service Management and Marketing.*
12. Anne M. Smith, "Measuring Service Quality: Is SERVQUAL Now Redundant?" *Journal of Marketing Management* 11 (Jan/Feb/April 1995): 257–276.
13. Jochen Wirtz and Anna S. Mattila, "Exploring the Role of Alternative Perceived Performance Measures and Needs-Congruency in the Consumer Satisfaction Process," *Journal of Consumer Psychology* 11, no. 3 (2001): 181–192.
14. Jochen Wirtz, "Halo in Customer Satisfaction Measures—The Role of Purpose of Rating, Number of Attributes, and Customer Involvement," *International Journal of Service Industry Management* 14, no. 1 (2003): 96–119.
15. Susan J. Devlin and H. K. Dong, "Service Quality from the Customers' Perspective," *Marketing Research* 6, no. 1 (1994): 5–13.
16. Valarie A. Zeithaml, Leonard L. Berry, and A. Parasuraman, "Communication and Control Processes in the Delivery of Services," *Journal of Marketing* 52 (April 1988): 36–58.
17. Zeithaml et al., *Delivering Quality Service.*
18. Valarie A. Zeithaml and Mary Jo Bitner, *Services Marketing 3/E*, (New York: McGraw-Hill, 2003), 261.
19. Leonard L. Berry and A. Parasuraman, "Listening to the Customer—The Concept of a Service Quality Information System," *Sloan Management Review* (Spring 1997): 65–76.
20. Comments by Thomas R. Oliver, then senior vice president, sales and customer service, Federal Express; reported in Christopher H. Lovelock, *Federal Express: Quality Improvement Program, Lausanne: International Institute for Management Development* (1990).
21. Christopher Lovelock, *Product Plus: How Product + Service = Competitive Advantage* (New York: McGraw-Hill, 1994), 218.
22. These categories and the research data that follow have been adapted from information in D. Daryl Wyckoff, "New Tools for Achieving Service Quality," *Cornell Hotel and Restaurant Administration Quarterly* (August–September 2001): 25–38.
23. Roland T. Rust, Anthony J. Zahonik, and Timothy L. Keiningham, "Return on Quality (ROQ): Making Service Quality Financially Accountable," *Journal of Marketing* 59 (April 1995): 58–70.
24. Roland T. Rust, Christine Moorman, and Peter R. Dickson, "Getting Return on Quality: Revenue Expansion, Cost Reduction, or Both?" *Journal of Marketing* 66 (October 2002), 7–24.
25. Kenneth J. Klassen, Randolph M. Russell, and James J. Chrisman, "Efficiency and Productivity Measures for High Contact Services," *The Service Industries Journal* 18 (October 1998): 1–18.
26. James L. Heskett, *Managing in the Service Economy* (New York: The Free Press, 1986).
27. John C. Shaw, *The Service Focus* (Homewood, IL: Dow Jones-Irwin, 1990), 152–3.
28. Frances X. Frei and Patrick T. Harker, "Measuring the Efficiency of Service Delivery Processes: An Application to Retail Banking," *Journal of Service Research* 1 (May 1999): 300–312.
29. Eric Langeard, John E. G. Bateson, Christopher H. Lovelock, and Pierre Eiglier, *Services Marketing: New Insights from Consumers and Managers* (Cambridge, MA: Marketing Science Institute, 1981), especially Chapter 2. A good summary of this research is provided in J. E. G. Bateson, "Self-Service Consumer: An Exploratory Study," *Journal of Retailing* 51 (Fall 1985): 49–76.
30. Cathy Goodwin, "I Can Do It Myself: Training the Service Consumer to Contribute to Service Productivity," *Journal of Services Marketing* 2 (Fall 1988): 71–78.
31. Colin Armistead and Simon Machin, "Business Process Management: Implications for Productivity in Multi-stage Service Networks," *International Journal of Service Industry Management* 9, no. 4 (1998): 323–336.
32. Wickham Skinner, "The Productivity Paradox," *McKinsey Quarterly* (Winter 1987): 36–45.
33. G.S. Sureshchandar, Chandrasekharan Rajendran and R.N. Anantharaman, "A Holistic Model for Total Service Quality," *International Journal of Service Industry Management* 12, no. 4 (2001): 378–412.
34. ISO (2001), The ISO survey of ISO 9000 and ISO14000 certificates (Eleventh cycle), International Organization for Standards, Geneva, 2001.
35. Susan Meyer Goldstein and Sharon B. Schweikhart, "Empirical Support for the Baldrige Award Framework in U.S. Hospitals," *Health Care Management Review* 27, no. 1 (2002): 62–75.
36. Allan Shirks, William B. Weeks and Annie Stein, "Baldrige-Based Quality Awards: Veterans Health Administration's 3-Year Experience," *Quality Management in Health Care* 10, no. 3 (2002): 47–54; and National Institute of Standards and Technology, "Baldrige FAQs,"

http:www.nist.gov./public_affairs/factsheet/baldfaqs.htm. Accessed April 2003.

37. Jim Biolos, "Six Sigma Meets the Service Economy," *Harvard Business Review* (November 2002): 3–5.

38. Mikel Harry and Richard Schroeder, *Six Sigma—The Breakthrough Management Strategy Revolutionizing the World's Top Corporations*. (New York: Currency. 2000): 232.

39. Peter S. Pande, Robert P. Neuman and Ronald R. Cavanagh, *The Six Sigma Way: How GE, Motorola, and Other Top Companies Are Honing Their Performance* (New York: McGraw-Hill 2000).

40. Gavin Dick, Kevin Gallimore and Jane C. Brown, "ISO9000 and Quality Emphasis: An Empirical study of Front-Room and Back Room Dominated Service Industries," *International Journal of Service Industry Management* 12, no. 2 (2001): 114–136; and Adrian Hughes and David N. Halsall, "Comparison of the 14 Deadly Diseases and the Business Excellence Model," *Total Quality Management* 13, no. 2 (2002): 255–263.

41. Cathy A. Enz and Judy A. Siguaw, "Best Practices in Service Quality," *Cornell Hotel and Restaurant Administration Quarterly* (October 2000): 20–29.

42. Eight NIST Stock Investment Study (Gaithersburg, MD: National Institute of Standards and Technology March 2002).

CHAPTER 15

Organizing for Service Leadership

Marketing is so basic that it cannot be considered a separate function.... It is the whole business seen from the point of view of its final result, that is, from the customer's point of view. Concern and responsibility for marketing must, therefore, permeate all areas of the enterprise.

—PETER DRUCKER

The increasingly fast-moving and competitive environment we will face in the twenty-first century demands more leadership from more people to make enterprises prosper.

—JOHN P. KOTTER

What comes to mind when you hear the term "service leadership"? Do you think in terms of market leadership, focusing on those companies that are viewed as leaders in a particular service industry? Alternatively, do you associate leadership with individuals, thinking of the role of the chief executive in leading the organization or of leadership positions at different levels in a service business? In practice, service leadership embraces all these perspectives.

Realistically, it is very difficult for a firm to achieve and maintain leadership in an industry if it lacks human leaders who can articulate a vision and help to bring it about. The emphasis could be setting the standards for service quality, initiating important innovations, using new technologies for competitive advantage, defining the terms on which the company seeks to compete, and creating an outstanding place to work.

This chapter recognizes that marketing activities in service organizations extend beyond the responsibilities assigned to a traditional marketing department. We examine the challenging task of leading a market-oriented service business and explore the following questions.

1. What are the implications of the service-profit chain for service management?
2. Why do the marketing, operations, and human resource management functions need to be closely coordinated and integrated in service businesses?
3. What are the causes of interfunctional tensions, and how can they be avoided?
4. What actions are required to move a service firm from a reactive position of merely being available for service toward the status of world-class service delivery?
5. What role do service leaders play in fostering success within their organizations?

THE SEARCH FOR SYNERGY IN SERVICE MANAGEMENT

A service leader offers services that are known for superior value and quality and has marketing strategies that beat the competition yet is viewed as a trustworthy organization that does business in ethical ways. The company should be seen as a leader in operations, too—respected for its superior operational processes and innovative use of technology. Finally, it should be recognized as an outstanding place to work, leading its industry in human resource management practices and creating loyal, productive, and customer-oriented employees. Southwest Airlines has achieved all these criteria (Best Practice in Action 15-1).

Attaining service leadership requires a coherent vision of what it takes to succeed, defined and driven by a strong, effective leadership team. And implementation involves careful coordination of marketing (which includes customer service), operations (which includes management of technology), and human resources. As emphasized throughout this book, the marketing function in service businesses cannot easily be separated from other management activities.

Although there's a long tradition of functional specialization in business, such a narrow perspective tends to get in the way of effective service management. One of the challenges facing senior managers in any type of organization is to avoid creating what are sometimes referred to as "functional silos" in which each function exists in isolation

FIGURE 15-1 The Service Profit Chain

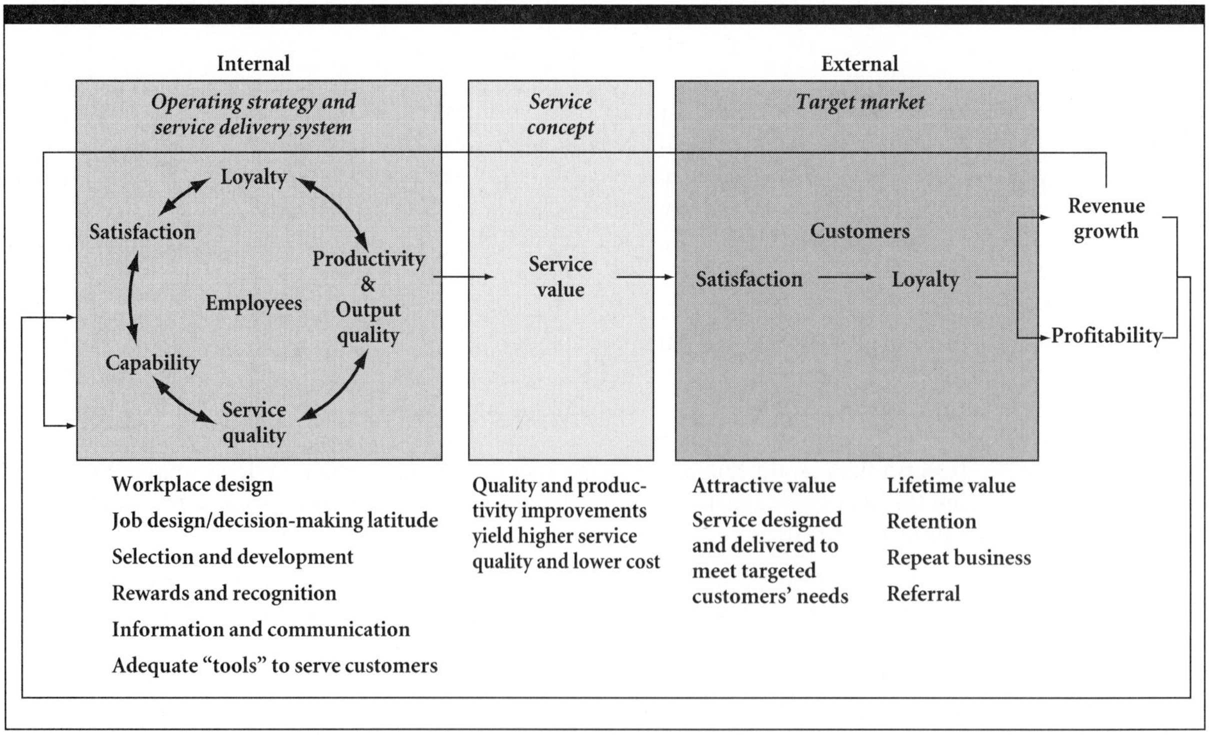

Source: Adapted and reprinted by permission of *Harvard Business Review*. An exhibit from "Putting the Service Profit Chain to Work," by James L. Heskett, Thomas O. Jones, Gary W. Loveman, W. Earl Sasser Jr., and Leonard A. Schlesinger (March-April 1994): 166.

from the others, jealously guarding its independence. Ideally, service firms should be organized in ways that enable the three functions of marketing, operations, and human resources to work closely together if a service organization is to be responsive to its various stakeholders.

Integrating Marketing, Operations, and Human Resources

Using the concept of what they call the *service-profit chain*, Heskett et al. lay out a series of hypothesized links in achieving success in service businesses (see Figure 15-1).[1] The themes and relationships underlying the service-profit chain illustrate the mutual dependency among marketing, operations, and human resources. Although managers within each function may have specific responsibilities, effective coordination is the name of the game. They all must participate in strategic planning, and the execution of specific tasks must be well coordinated. Responsibility for the tasks assigned to each function may be present entirely within one firm or distributed between the originating service organization and its subcontractors, which must work in close partnership if the desired results are to be achieved. Other functions, such as accounting or finance, present less need for close integration because they're less involved in the ongoing processes of service creation and delivery.

The service-profit chain highlights the behaviors required of service leaders in order to manage their organizations effectively (see Table 15-1). Links 1 and 2 focus on customers and include an emphasis on identifying and understanding customer needs, investments to ensure customer retention, and a commitment to adopting new performance measures that track such variables as satisfaction and loyalty among both customers and employees.[2] Link 3 focuses on the value for customers created by the service concept and highlights the need for investments to create higher service quality and productivity improvements to reduce costs.

Another set of service leadership behaviors (links 4–7) relate to employees and include spending time on the front line, investing in the development of promising managers, and supporting the design of jobs that offer greater latitude for employees. Also included in this category is the concept that paying higher wages decreases labor costs after reduced turnover, higher productivity, and higher quality are taken into account. Underlying the chain's success (link 8) is top-management leadership. Clearly, implementation of the service-profit chain requires a thorough understanding of how marketing, operations, and human resources each relate to a company's broader strategic concerns.

TABLE 15-1 Links in the Service-Profit Chain

1. Customer loyalty drives profitability and growth.
2. Customer satisfaction drives customer loyalty.
3. Value drives customer satisfaction.
4. Employee productivity drives value.
5. Employee loyalty drives productivity.
6. Employee satisfaction drives loyalty.
7. Internal quality drives employee satisfaction.
8. Top-management leadership underlies the chain's success.

Source: James L. Heskett et al., "Putting the Service-Profit Chain to Work," *Harvard Business Review* (March–April 1994); and James L. Heskett, W. Earl Sasser, and Leonard L. Schlesinger, *The Service Profit Chain* (Boston: Harvard Business School Press, 1997).

BEST PRACTICE IN ACTION 15-1

SOUTHWEST AIRLINES: A SERVICE LEADER WITH A COMMON TOUCH

In 30 years, Southwest Airlines has gone from a feisty start-up to an industry leader whose performance is closely studied by other airlines from around the world. The company has always been a maverick in the airline industry. At the outset, what turned heads was Southwest's unconventional marketing strategies, with their zany promotions, outrageous stewardess uniforms, off-peak discount prices, creative advertising, and attention-getting public relations activities. But communications, however clever, only make promises. The airline owes its long-term success to its continuing efforts to provide customers with better value than its competitors. It has been cited by *Fortune* as one of the most admired companies in the United States and consistently ranks near the top in the magazine's annual list of the 100 best companies to work for. Herbert D. Kelleher, Southwest's chairman, and former longtime CEO and president, has been recognized many times as one of the country's best managers, and Colleen Barrett, Southwest's current president and COO, is keeping up the tradition.

Southwest launched its first flights in June 1971 amid a blaze of clever publicity. The airline featured numerous service innovations, a tiny fleet of four new Boeing 737s (later reduced to three), frequent and punctual service, easy check-in, friendly and highly motivated staff, and lower fares. Its cheeky slogan was "The somebody else up there who loves you." From that small beginning, Southwest has become one of the largest domestic air operations in the United States, serving almost 60 cities located from coast to coast and carrying more than five million passengers a month. In 2002, Southwest generated revenues of $5.5 billion. Despite a down economy. Southwest's recent advertising highlights its phenomenal growth with the phrase "You are now free to move about the country."

Southwest has moved relentlessly into one new market after another, winning and keeping new customers and gaining a significant share of all passengers on the routes that it serves. (On any given day, about 80 percent of Southwest's passengers are repeat customers.) It has greatly expanded the market for air travel by bringing frequent, inexpensive airline service to communities and people for whom air travel was previously inaccessible. Attempts by competitors to counter its expansion have failed conspicuously.

Southwest's simple, coherent philosophy has been a major factor in its continuing success. The company has consistently adhered to its low-cost priorities and low-fare market niche. At the heart of its approach to operations is a search for simplicity that minimizes wasted time, lowers expenses, and creates the inexpensive, reliable service that its passengers desire. Lower costs allow Southwest to charge lower fares, making it the price leader in most of its markets. Lower fares attract more passengers. More passengers mean more frequent flights, which in turn attract

more customers—especially business travelers, who appreciate the convenience. More flights, more passengers, and lower costs have meant profits for Southwest even during recessions.

From an operational perspective, Southwest refuses to play by the rules of conventional airline wisdom (except, of course, those relating to safety, where it has an exceptional record). The company offers no assigned seating, so it has no need to store seat assignments in its reservations database, no need for equipment to print paper boarding passes, and no need to verify seating arrangements at check-in. The net result is more cost savings, simpler procedures for employees, faster service at the check-in desk, and faster boarding. Southwest was also the first airline to offer a Web site and has actively encouraged customers to make their bookings on the Internet—the lowest-cost approach—instead of telephoning the airline or using travel agents. By mid-2003, 53 percent of passenger revenues were generated by online bookings.

Additional savings result from the airline's decision to provide only the most basic food service. Storing, heating, and serving traditional in-flight meals require galley space, heavy food carts, and sometimes more cabin crew to serve it than the minimum number established by safety regulations. Provisioning at the start of the flight takes time, and there's more to unload at the destination. As all these factors raise costs, Southwest serves only light snacks and encourages customers to bring their own food on board.

Southwest won't interline with other carriers (which means that it will not transfer passenger baggage to or from flights on other airlines), because its passengers would then be dependent on the on-time performance of another airline. Not having to transfer bags between its own flights and those of other airlines speeds up the turnaround time between arrival and departure—often as little as 15 minutes—and reduces the risk of lost bags. In addition, Southwest won't accept another carrier's ticket for a trip on the same route—a practice that greatly simplifies its accounting procedures.

There's more. Southwest's operations are not built around the large-scale hub-and-spoke systems that enable competing airlines to offer passengers a large number of city-pair destinations, with an intervening change at the hub. Aircraft descend in droves on a hub airport during a relatively brief period, passengers change flights, and then all the aircraft depart again in quick succession. The downside is that the amount of required ground-service capacity—airport gates, ground personnel, and ramp equipment—is determined by these peak periods of intense activity. The net result is that both equipment and personnel spend less time in productive activity. Moreover, one late-arriving flight can delay all departures.

The great majority of Southwest's routes are designed around short-haul point-to-point services, with an average aircraft trip length in 2003 of 537 miles (865 km). Passengers can change flights at intermediate points, but the schedules aren't necessarily designed to facilitate tight connections. The advantage to Southwest is that its point-to-point flights can be spaced more evenly over the day (as long as departure times are convenient for passengers), and no one aircraft needs to be held for another. Southwest's fleet of some 380 aircraft consists only of Boeing 737s. Standardizing on one aircraft type simplifies maintenance, spares, flight operations, and training. Any pilot can fly any aircraft, any flight attendant is familiar with it, and any mechanic can maintain it. Overseas services would involve flying new types of aircraft with which Southwest has no experience.

In addition to its finely tuned operations strategy, Southwest also pays close attention to human resource issues. The company is known for its dedicated employees, who remain loyal because they like their jobs and enjoy the working environment. In part, Southwest's positive work environment can be attributed to very selective recruitment. Another factor is stock ownership. Collectively, employees own 13 percent of the company's outstanding shares. Equally important is that management spends at least as much time courting its employees as it does the passengers the airline serves. As Kelleher says, "If you don't treat your employees right, they won't treat other people well."

Source: Christopher Lovelock, *Product Plus* (New York: McGraw-Hill, 1994), Chapters 1 and 6; *Southwest Airlines Co. Annual Report*, 1999–2002 (Dallas: Southwest Airlines, 2000–2003), Southwest Airlines Web site, *www.southwest.com*, accessed February 2001 and August 2003; "The Top 25 Managers of the Year," *Business Week* (January 8, 2001): 73; Robert Levering and Milton Moskowitz, "The 100 Best Companies to Work For," *Fortune* (January 8, 2001): 148–168; and Wendg Zellner and Michael Arndt, "Holding Steady," *Business Week* (February 3, 2003): 66–68.

The Marketing Function

As we've noted before, production and consumption are usually clearly separated in manufacturing firms. It's not normally necessary for production personnel to have direct involvement with customers where consumer goods are concerned. In such firms, marketing acts as a link between producers and consumers, providing the manufacturing division with guidelines for product specifications that reflect consumer needs, as well as projections of market demand, information on competitive activity, and feedback on performance in the marketplace. Marketing personnel also work with logistics and transportation specialists to develop distribution strategies.

In service firms, things are different. Many service operations—especially those involving people-processing services—are literally "factories in the field" that customers enter whenever they need the service in question. In a large chain (such as hotels, fast-food restaurants, or car rental agencies), the company's service delivery sites may be located across a country, a continent, or even the entire world. When customers are actively involved in production and the service output is consumed as it is produced, direct contact between production (operations) and consumers is mandatory. Even in such services as repair and maintenance, where customers don't get actively involved in production, they may still have contact with service employees at the beginning and end of the service delivery process. In some cases, of course, there's no contact with personnel, as customers are expected to serve themselves independently or communicate through more impersonal media, such as mail, e-mail, or Web sites.

In manufacturing firms, marketers assume full responsibility for the product once it leaves the production line, often working closely with channel intermediaries, such as retailers. In many services, by contrast, operations management is responsible for running service distribution systems, including retail outlets. Moreover, contact between operations personnel and customers is the rule rather than the exception, although the extent of this contact varies according to the nature of the service. Yet, as we have seen in the course of this book, there remains a need in service businesses for a strong, efficient marketing organization to perform the following tasks.

- Evaluate and select the market segments to serve.
- Research customer needs and preferences within each segment.
- Monitor competitive offerings, identifying their principal characteristics, quality levels, and the strategies used to bring them to market.
- Design the core product to meet the needs of the chosen market segments and ensure that they match or exceed those of competitive offerings.
- Select and establish service levels for supplementary elements needed to enhance the value and appeal of the core product or to facilitate its purchase and use.
- Collaborate with operations personnel in designing the entire service process to ensure that it is "user friendly" and reflects customer needs and preferences.
- Set prices that reflect costs, competitive strategies, and consumer sensitivity to different price levels.
- Tailor location and scheduling of service availability to customers' needs and preferences.
- Develop appropriate communications strategies to transmit messages informing prospective customers about the service and promoting its advantages, without overpromising.
- Develop performance standards, based on customer needs and expectations, for establishing and measuring service quality levels.
- Ensure that all customer-contact personnel—whether they work for operations, marketing, or an intermediary—understand the firm's desired market position and customer expectations of their own performance.

- Create programs for rewarding and reinforcing customer loyalty.
- Conduct research to evaluate customer satisfaction following service delivery and identify any aspects requiring changes or improvements.

The net result of these requirements is that the services marketing function is closely interrelated with—and dependent on—the procedures, personnel, and facilities managed by the operations function, as well as on the quality of the service personnel recruited and trained by the human resources function. Although initially seen as a poor relation by many operations managers, marketing now possesses significant management clout in many service businesses, with important implications for strategy, organizational design, and assignment of responsibilities.

The Operations Function

Although marketing's importance has increased, the operations function still dominates line management in most service businesses. This is hardly surprising, because operations—typically the largest functional group—remains responsible for most of the processes involved in creating and delivering the service product. Operations must obtain the necessary resources, maintain operating equipment and facilities, manage the level of capacity over time, and transform inputs into outputs efficiently. When service delivery is halted for any reason, it is up to operations to restore service as quickly as possible.

Unlike marketing, the operations function is responsible for activities taking place both backstage and front-stage. Operations managers—who may be divided among several subgroups—are usually responsible for maintaining buildings and equipment, including company-owned retail outlets and other customer facilities. In high-contact, labor-intensive services, operations managers may direct the work of large numbers of employees, including many who serve customers directly in widely dispersed locations. The ongoing push for cost savings and higher productivity in the service sector requires a continuing effort by all operations personnel to achieve greater efficiency in service delivery.

An increasingly important role—often assigned to a separate department—is management of the firm's information technology infrastructure. In technology-driven firms, operations managers with the appropriate technical skills work with research and development specialists to design and introduce innovative delivery systems, including use of the Internet. But it's essential to understand the implications of such innovations for both employees and customers.

The Human Resources Function

Few service organizations are so technologically advanced that they can be operated without frontline staff. Indeed, many service industries remain highly labor intensive, although the need for technical skills is increasing. People are required to perform operational tasks (either front-stage or backstage), to execute a wide array of marketing tasks, and to provide administrative support.

Historically, responsibility for matters relating to employees was often divided among a number of departments, such as personnel, compensation, industrial relations, and organization development (or training). But during the 1980s, human resources emerged as a separate management function. As defined by academic specialists, "Human resource management (HRM) involves all managerial decisions and actions that affect the nature of the relationship between the organization and its employees—its human resources."[3]

Just as some forward-looking service businesses have developed an expanded vision of marketing, viewing it from a strategic perspective rather than a narrow functional and tactical one, so is HRM coming to be seen as a key element in business strategy. People-related activities in a modern service corporation can be subsumed under four broad policy areas.[4]

1. *Human resource flow* is concerned with ensuring that the right number of people and mix of competencies are available to meet the firm's long-term strategic requirements. Issues include recruitment, training, career development, and promotions.
2. *Work systems* involve all tasks associated with arranging people, information, facilities, and technology to create (or support) the services produced by the organization.
3. *Reward systems* send powerful messages to all employees about what kind of organization management seeks to create and maintain, especially regarding desired attitudes and behavior. Not all rewards are financial in nature; recognition can be a powerful motivator.
4. *Employee influence* relates to employee inputs concerning business goals, pay, working conditions, career progression, employment security, and the design and implementation of work tasks. The movement toward greater empowerment of employees represents a shift in the nature and extent of employee influence.[5]

In many service businesses, the caliber and commitment of the labor force have become a major source of competitive advantage. This is especially true in high-contact services, in which customers can discern differences between competing firms' employees.[6] A strong commitment by top management to human resources (like that exhibited by Southwest Airlines' Chairman Herb Kelleher and President and COO Colleen Barrett) is a feature of many successful service firms.[7] To the extent that employees understand and support the goals of their organization, have the skills and training needed to succeed in their jobs, and recognize the importance of creating and maintaining customer satisfaction, both marketing and operations activities should be easier to manage.

To adopt an increasingly strategic role, HR needs to shift its emphasis away from many of the routine, bureaucratic tasks such as payroll and benefits administration that previously consumed much of management's time. Investments in technology can reduce some of the burden, but progressive firms are going even further, outsourcing many noncore administrative tasks (Figure 15-2).

For HRM to succeed, argues Terri Kabachnick, "it must be a business-driven function with a thorough understanding of the organization's big picture. It must be viewed as a strategic consulting partner, providing innovative solutions and influencing key decisions and policies."[8] Among the tasks that she believes that HRM should perform are:

- Installing systems that measure an applicant's beliefs and values for comparison to the company's beliefs and values, in order to replace "gut instinct" hiring decisions that often result in rapid turnover
- Studying similar industries and identifying what lessons can be learned from their HRM policies
- Challenging corporate personnel policies if they no longer make sense in today's environment and describing how proposed changes (e.g., job sharing) will affect the bottom line
- Demonstrating that HRM is in the business of developing and retaining productive workers rather than simply being a training department.

Reducing Interfunctional Conflict

As service firms place more emphasis on developing a strong market orientation and serving customers well, there's increased potential for conflict among the three functions, especially between marketing and operations. How comfortably can the three

FIGURE 15-2 "So why would you do HR Administration in-house?" ADP makes the case for outsourcing repetitive HR tasks to a specialist provider.

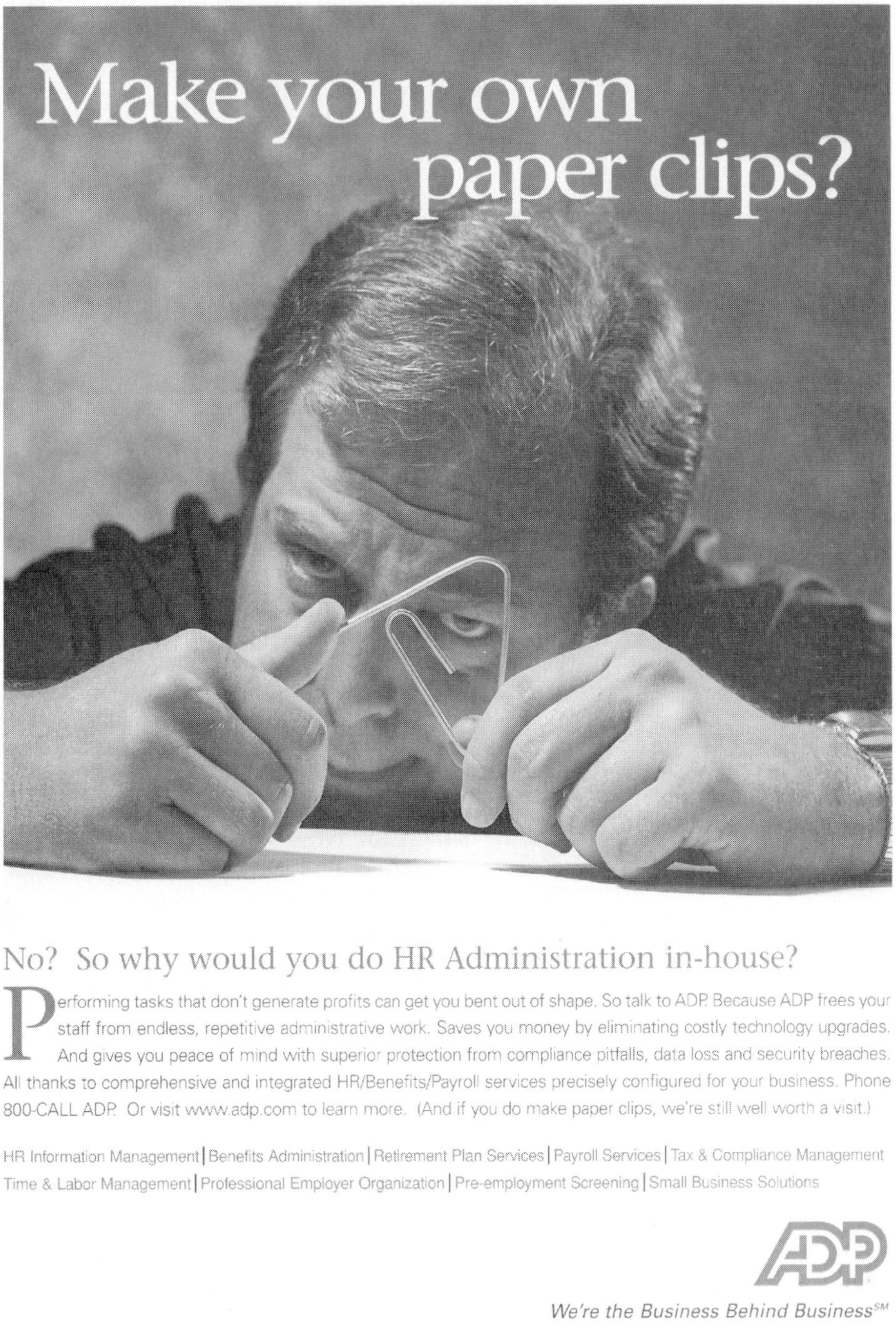

Make your own paper clips?
No? So why would you do HR Administration in-house?
Performing tasks that don't generate profits can get you bent out of shape. So talk to ADP. Because ADP frees your staff from endless, repetitive administrative work. Saves you money by eliminating costly technology upgrades. And gives you peace of mind with superior protection from compliance pitfalls, data loss and security breaches. All thanks to comprehensive and integrated HR/Benefits/Payroll services precisely configured for your business. Phone 800-CALL ADP. Or visit www.adp.com to learn more. (And if you do make paper clips, we're still well worth a visit.)
HR Information Management | Benefits Administration | Retirement Plan Services | Payroll Services | Tax & Compliance Management
Time & Labor Management | Professional Employer Organization | Pre-employment Screening | Small Business Solutions
ADP
We're the Business Behind Business℠

Used with permission of ADP ® Automatic Data Processing, Inc.

functions coexist in a service business, and how are their relative roles perceived? Sandra Vandermerwe makes the point that high-value-creating enterprises should be thinking in term of *activities*, not functions.[9] Yet in many firms, we still find individuals from marketing and operations backgrounds at odds with each other. For instance, marketers may see their role as one of continually adding value to the product offering in order to enhance its appeal to customers and thereby increase sales. Operations managers, by contrast, often take the view that their job is to pare back these elements to reflect the reality of service constraints—such as staff and equipment—and the accompanying need for cost containment. Conflicts may also occur between human resources and the other two functions, especially where employees are in boundary-spanning roles that require them to balance the seemingly conflicting goals imposed by marketing and operations.

Marketers who want to avoid conflicts with operations should familiarize themselves with the issues that typically provide the foundation for operations strategy. Changing traditional organizational perspectives doesn't come readily to managers who have been comfortable with established approaches. It's easy for them to become obsessed with their own functional tasks, forgetting that all areas of the company must pull together to create a customer-driven organization. As long as a service business continues to be organized along functional lines (and many are), achieving the necessary coordination and strategic synergy requires that top management establish clear imperatives for each function.

Each imperative should relate to customers and define how a specific function contributes to the overall mission. Part of the challenge of service management is to ensure that each of these three functional imperatives is compatible with the others and that all are mutually reinforcing. Although a firm will need to phrase each imperative in ways that are specific to its own business, we can express them generically as follows:

- *The marketing imperative:* To target specific types of customers whom the firm is well equipped to serve and create ongoing relationships with them by delivering a carefully defined service product package in return for a price that offers value to customers and the potential for profits to the firm. Customers will recognize this package as being one of consistent quality that delivers solutions to their needs and is superior to competing alternatives.
- *The operations imperative:* To create and deliver the specified service package to targeted customers by selecting those operational techniques that allow the firm to consistently meet customer-driven cost, schedule, and quality goals and also enable the business to reduce its costs through continuing improvements in productivity. The chosen operational methods will match skills that employees and intermediaries or contractors currently possess or can be trained to develop. The firm will have the resources to support these operations with the necessary facilities, equipment, and technology while avoiding negative impacts on employees and the broader community.
- *The human resources imperative:* To recruit, train, and motivate managers, supervisors, and employees who can work well together for a realistic compensation package to balance the twin goals of customer satisfaction and operational effectiveness. Employees will want to stay with the firm and to enhance their own skills because they value the working environment, appreciate the opportunities that it presents, and take pride in the services they help to create and deliver.

CREATING A LEADING SERVICE ORGANIZATION

In your own life as a consumer, you have probably encountered an assortment of service performances ranging from extremely satisfying to infuriatingly bad. You may know some organizations that you can always trust to deliver good service, whereas others are rather unpredictable, offering good service one day and indifferent service the next. Perhaps you even know of a few businesses that consistently deliver bad service and mistreat their customers.

From Losers to Leaders: Four Levels of Service Performance

Service leadership is not based on outstanding performance within a single dimension. Rather, it reflects excellence across multiple dimensions. In an effort to capture this performance spectrum, we need to evaluate the organization within each of the three functional areas: marketing, operations, and human resources. Table 15-2 modifies and extends an operations-oriented framework proposed by Richard Chase and Robert Hayes.[10] It categorizes service performers into four levels: loser, nonentity, professional, and leader. At each level, there is a brief description of a typical organization across 12 dimensions.

Under the marketing function, we look at the role of marketing, competitive appeal, customer profile, and service quality. Under the operations function, we consider the role of operations, service delivery (front-stage), backstage operations, productivity, and introduction of new technology. Finally, under the human resources function, we consider the role of HRM, the workforce, and frontline management. Obviously, there are overlaps between these dimensions and across functions. Additionally, there may be variations in the relative importance of some dimensions between industries. However, the goal is to obtain some insights into what needs to be changed in organizations that are not performing as well as they might.

Service Losers These organizations are at the bottom of the barrel from both customer and managerial perspectives, getting failing grades in marketing, operations, and human resource management alike. Customers patronize them for reasons other than performance; typically, because there is no viable alternative—which is one reason why service losers continue to survive. Such organizations see service delivery as a necessary evil. New technology is introduced only under duress, and the uncaring workforce is a negative constraint on performance. The cycles of failure and mediocrity presented in Figures 11-1 and 11-2 (pp. 315 and 317) describe how such organizations behave and what the consequences are.

Service Nonentities Although their performance still leaves much to be desired, nonentities have eliminated the worst features of losers. As shown in Table 15-2, nonentities are dominated by a traditional operations mindset, typically based on achieving cost savings through standardization. Their marketing strategies are unsophisticated, and the roles of human resources and operations might be summed up, respectively, by the philosophies "adequate is good enough" and "if it ain't broke, don't fix it." Consumers neither seek out nor avoid such organizations. Often, several such firms can be found competing in lackluster fashion within a given marketplace, and each one may be almost indistinguishable from the others. Periodic price discounts tend to be the primary means of trying to attract new customers.

Service Professionals These organizations are in a different league from nonentities and have a clear market-positioning strategy. Customers within the target segments seek out these firms based on their sustained reputation for meeting expectations. Marketing is more sophisticated, using targeted communications and pricing based on value to the customer. Research is used to measure customer satisfaction and obtain ideas for service enhancement. Operations and marketing work together to introduce new delivery systems and recognize the tradeoff between productivity and customer-defined quality. There are explicit links between backstage and front-stage activities and a much more proactive, investment-oriented approach to human resource management than is found among nonentities.

Service Leaders These organizations are the *crème de la crème* of their respective industries. Whereas service professionals are good, service leaders are outstanding. Their company names are synonymous with service excellence and an ability to delight

TABLE 15-2 Four Levels of Service Performance

Level	*1. Loser*	*2. Nonentity*
	Marketing Function	
Role of marketing	Tactical role only; advertising and promotions lack focus; no involvement in product or pricing decision	Uses mix of selling and mass communication, using simple segmentation strategy; makes selective use of price discounts and promotions; conducts and tabulates basic satisfaction surveys
Competitive appeal	Customers patronize firm for reasons other than performance	Customers neither seek out nor avoid the firm
Customer profile	Unspecified; a mass market to be served at a minimum cost	One or more segments whose basic needs are understood
Service quality	Highly variable, usually unsatisfactory Subservient to operations priorities	Meets some customer expectations; consistent on one or two key dimensions, but not all
	Operations Function	
Role of operations	Reactive; cost oriented	The principal line management function: Creates and delivers product, focuses on standardization as key to productivity, defines quality from internal perspective
Service delivery (front-stage)	A necessary evil. Locations and schedules are unrelated to preferences of customers, who are routinely ignored	Sticklers for tradition; "If it ain't broke, don't fix it;" tight rules for customers; each step in delivery run independently
Backstage operations	Divorced from front-stage; cogs in a machine	Contributes to individual front-stage delivery steps but organized separately; unfamiliar with customers
Productivity	Undefined; managers are punished for failing to stick within budget	Based on standardization; rewarded for keeping costs below budget
Introduction of new technology	Late adopter, under duress, when necessary for survival	Follows the crowd when justified by cost savings
	Human Resources Function	
Role of human resources	Supplies low-cost employees who meet minimum skill requirements for the job	Recruits and trains employees who can perform competently
Workforce	Negative constraint: poor performers, don't care, disloyal	Adequate resource, follows procedures but uninspired; turnover often high
Frontline management	Controls workers	Controls the process

Note: This framework was inspired by–and expands upon–work in service operations management by Richard Chase and Robert Hayes.

3. Professional	*4. Leader*
Marketing Function	
Has clear positioning strategy against competition; uses focused communications with distinctive appeals to clarify promises and educate customers; pricing is based on value; monitors customer usage and operates loyalty programs; uses a variety of research techniques to measure customer satisfaction and obtain ideas for service enhancements; works with operations to introduce new delivery systems	Innovative leader in chosen segments, known for marketing skills; brands at product/process level; conducts sophisticated analysis of relational databases as inputs to one-to-one marketing and proactive account management; uses state-of-the art research techniques; uses concept testing, observation, and use of lead customers as inputs to new-product development; close to operations/HR
Customers seek out the firm, based on its sustained reputation for meeting customer expectations	Company name is synonymous with service excellence; its ability to delight customers raises expectations to levels that competitors can't meet
Groups of individuals whose variation in needs and value to the firm are clearly understood	Individuals are selected and retained based on their future value to the firm, including their potential for new service opportunities and their ability to stimulate innovation.
Consistently meets or exceeds customer expectations across multiple dimensions	Raises customer expectations to new levels; improves continuously
Operations Function	
Plays a strategic role in competitive strategy; recognizes tradeoff between productivity and customer-defined quality; willing to outsource; monitors competing operations for ideas, threats	Recognized for innovation, focus, and excellence; an equal partner with marketing and HR management; has in-house research capability and academic contacts; continually experimenting
Driven by customer satisfaction, not tradition; willing to customize, embrace new approaches; emphasis on speed, convenience, and comfort	Delivery is a seamless process organized around the customer; employees know whom they are serving; focuses on continuous improvement
Process is explicitly linked to front-stage activities; sees role as serving "internal customers," who in turn serve external customers	Closely integrated with front-stage delivery, even when geographically far apart; understands how own role relates to overall process of serving external customers; continuing dialogue
Focuses on reengineering backstage processes; avoids productivity improvements that will degrade customers' service experience; continually refining processes for efficiency	Understands concept of return on quality; actively seeks customer involvement in productivity improvement; ongoing testing of new processes and technologies
An early adopter when IT promises to enhance service for customers and provide a competitive edge	Works with technology leaders to develop new applications that create first-mover advantage; seeks to perform at levels competitors can't match
Human Resources Function	
Invests in selective recruiting, ongoing training; keeps close to employees, promotes upward mobility; strives to enhance quality of working life	Sees quality of employees as strategic advantage; firm is recognized as outstanding place to work; HR helps top management to nurture culture
Motivated, hard working, allowed some discretion in choice of procedures, offers suggestions	Innovative and empowered; very loyal, committed to firm's values and goals; creates procedures
Listens to customers; coaches and facilitates workers	Source of new ideas for top management; mentors workers to enhance career growth, value to firm

Service losers often treat their customers as though the latter are the losers.

customers. Service leaders are recognized for their innovation in each functional area of management, as well as for their excellent internal communications and coordination among these three functions—often the result of a relatively flat organizational structure and extensive use of teams. As a result, service delivery is a seamless process organized around the customer.

Marketing efforts by service leaders make extensive use of relational databases that offer strategic insights about customers, who are often addressed on a one-to-one basis. Concept testing, observation, and contacts with lead customers are used in the development of new, breakthrough services that respond to previously unrecognized needs. Operations specialists work with technology leaders around the world to develop new applications that will create a first-mover advantage and enable the firm to perform at levels that competitors cannot hope to reach for a long period of time. Senior executives see quality of employees as a strategic advantage. HRM works with them to develop and maintain a service-oriented culture and to create an outstanding working environment that simplifies the task of attracting and retaining the best people.[11] The employees themselves are committed to the firm's values and goals. Because they are empowered and quick to embrace change, they are an ongoing source of new ideas.

Moving to a Higher Level of Performance

Firms can move either up or down the performance ladder. Once-stellar performers can become complacent and sluggish. Organizations that are devoted to satisfying their current customers may miss important shifts in the marketplace and find themselves turning into has-beens. These businesses may continue to serve a loyal but dwindling band of conservative customers but are unable to attract demanding new consumers with different expectations. Companies whose original success was based on mastery of a specific technological process may find that, in defending their control of that process, they have encouraged competitors to find higher-performing alternatives. And organizations whose management has worked for years to build up a loyal workforce with a strong service ethic may find that such a culture can be quickly destroyed as a result of a merger or acquisition that brings in new leaders who emphasize short-term profits. Unfortunately, senior managers sometimes delude themselves into thinking that their company has achieved a superior level of performance when, in fact, the foundations of that success are crumbling.

In most markets, we can also find companies that are moving up the performance ladder through conscious efforts to coordinate their marketing, operations, and human resource management functions in order to establish more favorable competitive positions and better satisfy their customers. Best Practice in Action 15-2 describes how a Scandinavian ferry company successfully enhanced the performance level of a newly acquired subsidiary.

BEST PRACTICE IN ACTION 15-2

BUILDING MARKETING COMPETENCE IN A FERRY COMPANY

When Stena Line purchased Sealink British Ferries (whose routes linked Britain to Ireland, France, Belgium, and Norway), the Scandinavian company more than doubled in size to become one of the world's largest car-ferry operators. Stena was known for its commitment to service quality and boasted a whole department dedicated to monitoring quality improvements. By contrast, this philosophy was described as "alien" to Sealink's culture, which reflected a top-down, military-style structure that focused on the operational aspects of ship movements. The quality of customers' experiences received only secondary consideration.

Sealink's managerial weaknesses included a lack of attention to strategic developments in a rapidly evolving industry. There was growing competition from other companies that were purchasing new, high-speed ferries that offered customers a faster and more comfortable ride than traditional ships. At Sealink, top management exercised tight control, issuing directives to middle managers in each division. The general approach had been to create companywide standards that could be applied across all divisions rather than customizing policies to the needs of individual routes. All decisions at the divisional level were subject to head-office review. Divisional managers themselves were separated by two levels of management from the functional teams engaged in the actual operation. This organizational structure led to conflicts, slow decision making, and inability to respond quickly to market changes.

Stena's philosophy was very different. The parent company operated a decentralized structure, believing that it was important for each management function to be responsible for its own activities and accountable for the results. Stena wanted management decisions in the new subsidiary to be taken by people who were close to the market and who understood the local variations in competition and demand. Some central functions were moved out to the divisions, including much of the responsibility for marketing activities. New skills and perspectives came from a combination of retraining, transfers, and outside hiring.

Prior to the merger, no priority had been given to punctual or reliable operations. Ferries were often late, but standard excuses were used on the weekly reports, customer complaints were ignored, and there was little pressure from customer service managers to improve the situation. After the takeover, however, the situation started to change. The operational problem of late departures and arrivals was resolved through concentration on individual problem areas. On one route, for instance, the port manager involved all operational staff and gave each person "ownership" of a specific aspect of the improvement process. They kept detailed records of each sailing, together with reasons for late departures, as well as monitoring competitors to see how their ferries were performing. Apart from helping to solve problems, this participative approach created close liaison between staff members in different job positions; it also helped members of the customer service staff to learn from experience. Within two years, the Stena ferries on this route were operating at close to 100 percent punctuality.

On-board service was another area singled out for improvement. Historically, customer service managers did what was convenient for staff rather than for customers. For instance, staff members would take their meal breaks at times when customer demand for the service was greatest. As one observer noted, "customers were ignored during the first and last half hour on board, when facilities were closed.... Customers were left to find their own way around [the ship].... Staff only responded to customers when [they] initiated a direct request and made some effort to attract their attention." So personnel from each on-board functional area chose a specific area for improvement and worked in small groups to achieve this. In the short run, some teams were more successful than others, resulting in inconsistent levels of service and customer orientation from one ship to another. In time, customer service managers shared ideas and reviewed their experiences, making adaptations where needed for individual ships. Table 15-A highlights key changes during the first two years. In combination, these changes contributed to eventual success in achieving consistent service levels on all sailings and all ferries.

TABLE 15-A Changing Contexts, Competencies, and Performance Following the Takeover

	Inherited Situation	*Situation after Two Years*
External Context	Inactive competition—"share" market with one competitor	Aggressive competitive activity (two competitors, one operating new, high-speed ferries)
	Static market demand	Growing market
Internal Context	Centralized organization	Decentralized organization
	Centralized decision making	Delegation to specialized decision-making units
	Top-management directives	Key manager responsible for each unit team
Managerial Competencies		
Knowledge	General to industry rather than to local market	Understand both industry and local market
Experience	Operational and tactical	Operational and decision making
	General, industry based	Functional management responsibility
	Noncompetitive environment	Exposed to competitive environment
Expertise	Vague approach to judging situations	Diagnostic judgmental capabilities
	Short-term focus	Longer-term focus
	Generalist competencies	Specific skills for functional tasks
Marketing Decision Making		
Planning	React to internal circumstances and external threats	Proactive identification of problems
	Minimal information search or evaluation of alternatives	Collect information, consider options
	Focus on tactical issues	Choose among several options
	Inconsistent with other marketing activities	Consistent with other marketing activities
Actions	Follow top-management directives	Delegation of responsibility
	Look to next in line for responsibility	Responsibility and ownership for activity
	Minimal or intermittent communication between functions	Liaison between functions
Marketing Efforts		
Prepurchase	Mostly media advertising	Advertising plus promotions and informational materials
Service delivery	Slow, manual booking system	New, computerized reservation system
	Focus on tangible aspects of on-board customer service (e.g., seating, cabins, food, bar)	Better tangibles, sharply improved staff/customer interactions
	Little pressure on operations to improve poor punctuality	Highly reliable, punctual service
	Poor communications at ports and on board ships	Much improved signage, printed guides, electronic message boards, public announcements
	Reactive approach to problem solving	Proactive approach to welcoming customers and solving their problems

Source: Adapted from Audrey Gilmore, "Services Marketing Management Competencies: A Ferry Company Example," *International Journal of Service Industry Management* 9, no. 1 (1998): 74–92; and Web site: *www7.stenaline.co.uk*, accessed April 2003.

IN SEARCH OF LEADERSHIP

Service leaders are those firms that stand out in their respective markets and industries. But it still requires human leaders to take them in the right direction, set the right strategic priorities, and ensure that the relevant strategies are implemented throughout the organization. Much of the literature on leadership is concerned with turnarounds and transformation. It is easy to see why poorly performing organizations may require a major transformation of their cultures and operating procedures in order to make them more competitive. But in times of rapid change, even high-performing firms need to evolve on a continuing basis, transforming themselves in evolutionary fashion.

Leading a Service Organization

John Kotter, perhaps the best-known authority on leadership, argues that in most successful change-management processes, people need to move through eight complicated and often time-consuming stages:[12]

1. Creating a sense of urgency to develop the impetus for change
2. Putting together a strong enough team to direct the process
3. Creating an appropriate vision of where the organization needs to go
4. Communicating that new vision broadly
5. Empowering employees to act on that vision
6. Producing sufficient short-term results to create credibility and counter cynicism
7. Building momentum and using that to tackle the tougher change problems
8. Anchoring the new behaviors in the organizational culture

Leadership versus Management The primary force behind successful change is *leadership*, which is concerned with the development of vision and strategies and the empowerment of people to overcome obstacles and make the vision happen. *Management*, by contrast, involves keeping the current situation operating through planning, budgeting, organizing, staffing, controlling, and problem solving. Warren Bennis and Burt Nanus distinguish between leaders who emphasize the emotional and even spiritual resources of an organization and managers who stress its physical resources, such as raw materials, technology, and capital.[13] Says Kotter:

> Leadership works through people and culture. It's soft and hot. Management works through hierarchy and systems. It's harder and cooler.... The fundamental purpose of management is to keep the current system functioning. The fundamental purpose of leadership is to produce useful change, especially nonincremental change. It's possible to have too much or too little of either. Strong leadership with no management risks chaos; the organization might walk right off a cliff. Strong management with no leadership tends to entrench an organization in deadly bureaucracy.[14]

However, leadership is an essential and growing aspect of managerial work because the rate of change has been increasing. Reflecting the stimulus of both intense competition and technological advances, new services or service features are being introduced at a faster rate and tend to have shorter life cycles (if, indeed, they even survive the introductory phase). Meantime, the competitive environment shifts continually as a result of international firms' entering new geographic markets, mergers and acquisitions, and the exit of former competitors. The process of service delivery itself has speeded up, with customers demanding faster service and faster responses when things go wrong. As a result, declares Kotter, effective top executives may now spend up to 80 percent of their time leading, double the figure required not that long ago. Even those at the bottom of the management hierarchy may spend at least 20 percent of their time on leadership.

Setting Direction versus Planning People often confuse these two activities. Planning, according to Kotter, is a management process, designed to produce orderly results, not change. Setting a direction, by contrast, is more inductive than deductive. Leaders look for patterns, relationships, and linkages that help to explain things and suggest future trends. Direction setting creates visions and strategies that describe a business, technology, or corporate culture in terms of what it should become over the long term and that articulate a feasible way of achieving this goal. Effective leaders have a talent for simplicity in communicating with others who may not share their background or knowledge; they know their audiences and are able to distill their messages, conveying even complicated concepts in just a few phrases.[15]

Many of the best visions and strategies are not brilliantly innovative; rather, they combine some basic insights and translate them into a realistic competitive strategy that serves the interests of customers, employees, and stockholders. Some visions, however, fall into the category that Gary Hamel and C. K. Pralahad describe as "stretch"—a challenge to attain new levels of performance and competitive advantage that might, at first sight, seem to be beyond the organization's reach.[16] Stretching to achieve such bold goals requires creative reappraisal of traditional ways of doing business and leverage of existing resources through partnerships. It also requires creating the energy and the will among managers and employees alike to perform at higher levels than they believe themselves able to do.

Planning follows and complements direction setting, serving as a useful reality check and a road map for strategic execution. A good plan provides an action agenda for accomplishing the mission, using existing resources or identifying potential new sources.

Leadership Qualities

Many commentators have written on the topic of leadership. It has even been described as a service in its own right.[17] The qualities often ascribed to leaders include vision, charisma, persistence, high expectations, expertise, empathy, persuasiveness, and integrity. Typical prescriptions for leader behavior stress the importance of establishing (or preserving) a culture that is relevant to corporate success, putting in place an effective strategic-planning process, instilling a sense of cohesion in the organization, and providing continuing examples of desired behaviors. For instance, the late Sam Walton, the legendary founder of the Wal-Mart retail chain, highlighted the role of managers as "servant leaders."[18] Jim Collins also concluded that a leader does not require a larger-than-life personality. Rather, he considers it important for a leader to be able to take a company to greatness to have personal humility blended with intensive professional will, ferocious resolve, and the tendency to give credit to others while taking the blame to themselves.[19]

Leonard Berry argues that service leadership requires a special perspective. "Regardless of the target markets, the specific services, or the pricing strategy, service leaders visualize quality of service as the foundation for competing."[20] Recognizing the key role of employees in delivering service, he emphasizes that service leaders need to believe in the people who work for them and make communicating with employees a priority. Love of the business is another service leadership characteristic he highlights, to the extent that it combines natural enthusiasm with the right setting in which to express it. Such enthusiasm motivates individuals to teach the business to others and to pass on to them the nuances, secrets, and craft of operating it. Berry also stresses the importance for leaders to be driven by a set of core values they infuse into the organization, arguing: "A critical role of values-driven leaders is cultivating the leadership qualities of others in the organization." And he notes that "values-driven leaders rely on their values to navigate their companies through difficult periods."[21]

Recent research suggests that a transformational leadership is the preferred style in achieving work outcomes. Transformational leaders operate on the basis of deeply held personal values, change their followers' goals and beliefs, and develop their followers' capacity to look beyond their self-interests by using

- *Charisma*, providing vision and a sense of mission, instilling pride in employees, and gaining respect and trust
- *Inspirational motivation*, communicating high expectations and expressing important purposes in simple ways
- *Intellectual stimulation*, promoting rationality, logic, and careful problem solving
- *Individual consideration*, paying close attention to individual differences among employees and coaching and advising staff through personal attention[22]

However, Rakesh Kharana warns against excessive emphasis on charisma in selecting CEOs, arguing that it leads to unrealistic expectations.[23] He also highlights the unethical behavior that may occur when charismatic but unprincipled leaders induce blind obedience in their followers, citing the illegal behavior stimulated by the leadership of Enron, which eventually led to the company's financial collapse.

In hierarchical organizations, structured on a military model, it's often assumed that leadership at the top is sufficient. But as Sandra Vandermerwe points out, forward-looking service businesses need to be more flexible. Today's greater emphasis on using teams within service businesses means, she argues, that

> [L]eaders are everywhere, disseminated throughout the teams. They are found especially in the customer facing and interfacing jobs in order that decision-making will lead to long-lasting relationships with customers . . . leaders are customer and project champions who energize the group by virtue of their enthusiasm, interest, and know-how.[24]

Transformational Leadership: Evolution versus Turnaround

There are important distinctions between enabling a successful organization to evolve in a dynamic market place, and trying to turn around a dysfunctional organization. In the case of Wal-Mart, Sam Walton created both the company and the culture, so his task was to preserve that culture as the company grew and to select a successor who would maintain an appropriate culture as the company continued to grow. Herb Kelleher was one of the founders of Southwest Airlines, using his legal skills in his initial role as the company's general counsel; later, he came to deploy his considerable human-relations skills as CEO. Meg Whitman was recruited as CEO of eBay when it became clear to the founders that the fledgling Internet start-up needed leadership from someone possessing the insights and discipline of an experienced marketer. (For her view of leadership, see Best Practice in Action 15-3.)

BEST PRACTICE IN ACTION 15-3

HOW EBAY CEO MEG WHITMAN SEES THE ROLE OF LEADER

A business leader has to keep her organization focused on the mission. That sounds easy but it can be tremendously challenging in today's competitive and ever-changing business environment. A leader also has to motivate potential partners to join the cause. eBay is successful because we have consistently remained focused on our mission, our customers, and a few key business fundamentals. As a company, we believe that the price of inaction is far greater than the cost of making a mistake.

Source: Deborah Blagg and Susan Young, "What Makes a Good Leader?" *Harvard Business School Bulletin* (February 2001): 32.

J. W. (Bill) Marriott, Jr., inherited from his father the position of chief executive of the company that bears the family name. Although it was the son who transformed the company from its emphasis on restaurant and food service into a global hotel corporation, he strove to maintain the corporate culture that flowed from the founder's philosophy and values:

> "Take care of the employees and customers," my father emphasized.... My father knew that if he had happy employees, he would have happy customers, and then that would result in a good bottom line.[25]

Transformation can take place in two distinct ways. One involves Darwinian-style evolution—continual mutations designed to ensure the survival of the fittest. *Evolution* means that top management evolves the focus and strategy of the firm to take advantage of changing conditions and the advent of new technologies. Without a continuing series of mutations, it is unlikely that a firm can remain successful in a dynamic marketplace.

A different type of transformation occurs in turnaround situations. American Express, long an icon in the travel and financial services arena, stumbled in the early 1990s when its attempts to diversify proved unsuccessful. Observers claimed that its elitist culture had insulated it from the changing market environment, in which the Amex charge card business faced intense competition from banks that issued Visa and MasterCard credit and debit cards.[26] In 1993, the board forced out Amex CEO James Robinson III, the scion of an old Atlanta banking family, and replaced him with the much more down-to-earth Harvey Golub, who immediately insisted that the company start using objective, quantitative measures to gauge performance.

Working closely with Kenneth Chenault, who headed the Amex card business, Golub attacked the company's bloated costs, eliminated lavish perks, and restructured the organization, achieving more than $3 billion in savings. Chenault, who was later named president and chief operating officer, broadened the appeal of Amex cards by offering new features, creating new types of cards, and signing up mass-market retailers, including Wal-Mart. In 2001, Golub retired, handing the baton to Chenault, his chosen successor, who faced the challenge of maintaining the company's global momentum in a continuously evolving marketplace.

According to Harvard professor and noted author Rosabeth Moss Kanter, it can be advantageous in turnaround situations to bring in a new CEO from outside the organization.[27] Such individuals, she argues, are better able to disentangle system dynamics because they were not previously caught up in them, and to voice problems and change habits. New CEOs may also have more credibility in representing and respecting customers. Exemplary turnaround leaders, she says, understand the powerful, unifying effect of focusing on customers. This focus can facilitate the difficult task of obtaining collaboration across departments and divisions. In addition to breaking down barriers between marketing, operations, and human resources, or between various product or geographic divisions, turnaround CEOs may also need to reorient financial priorities to enable collaborative groups to tackle new business opportunities.

Professors Chan Kim and Renée Mauborgne of INSEAD have identified four hurdles that leaders face in reorienting and formulating strategy.[28] *Cognitive hurdles* are present when people cannot agree on the causes of current problems and the need for change. *Resource hurdles* exist when the organization is constrained by limited funds. *Motivational hurdles* prevent a strategy's rapid execution when employees are reluctant to make needed changes. And *political hurdles* take the form of organized resistance from powerful vested interests seeking to protect their positions.

Turning around an organization that has limited resources requires concentrating those resources where the need and the likely payoffs are greatest. As an example of effective leadership under such conditions, Kim and Mauborgne highlight the work of William Bratton, who achieved fame during a 20-year police career in Boston and New York. Bratton believed in putting his key managers face-to-face with the problems that were of greatest concern to the public. When he became chief of the New York Transit Police, Bratton found that none of the senior staff officers rode the subway. So he required all transit police officials, including himself, to ride the subway to work and to meetings, even at night, instead of traveling in cars provided by the city. In that way, senior officials were exposed to the reality of the problems faced by millions of ordinary citizens and by police officers who strove to keep order.

Bratton's predecessors had lobbied for money to increase the number of subway cops, believing that the only way to stop muggers was to have officers ride every subway line and patrol each of the system's 700 exits and entrances. By contrast, Bratton had his staff analyze where subway crimes were being committed. Finding that the vast majority occurred at only a few stations and on a couple of lines, the chief redeployed his officers to focus on the problem areas and shifted a number of uniformed officers into plain clothes. Coupled with time-saving innovations in arrest processing procedures, this dramatic reallocation of resources resulted in a significant reduction in subway crime without new investment in resources.

One of the traits of successful leaders is their ability to role model the behavior they expect of managers and other employees. Often, this requires the approach known as "management by wandering around," popularized by Thomas Peters and Robert Waterman in their book *In Search of Excellence.*[29] Wandering around involves regular visits, sometimes unannounced, to different areas of the company's operation. This approach provides insights into both backstage and front-stage operations, the ability to observe and meet both employees and customers, and an opportunity to see how corporate strategy is implemented on the front line. Periodically, this approach may lead to a recognition that changes are needed in that strategy. Encountering the CEO on such a visit can also be motivating for service personnel. When Herb Kelleher was CEO of Southwest Airlines, no one was surprised to see him turn up at a Southwest maintenance hanger at two o'clock in the morning or even to encounter him working an occasional stint as a flight attendant.

In addition to internal leadership, chief executives such as Walton, Kelleher, Whitman, Marriott, Carlzon, and Schwab have assumed external leadership roles, serving as ambassadors for their companies in the public arena and promoting the quality and value of their firms' services. Marriott and Schwab have often appeared in their companies' advertising and Kelleher did so occasionally. There is a risk, of course, that prominent leaders may become too externally focused at the risk of their internal effectiveness. A CEO who enjoys an enormous income (often through exercise of huge stock options), maintains a princely lifestyle, and basks in widespread publicity may even turn off low-paid service workers at the bottom of the organization. Another risk is that a leadership style and focus that has served the company well in the past may become inappropriate for a changing environment.

Evaluating Leadership Potential

The need for leadership is not confined to chief executives or other top managers. Leadership traits are needed of everyone in a supervisory or managerial position, including those heading teams. FedEx believes this so strongly that it requires all employees interested in entering the ranks of first-line management to participate in its Leadership Evaluation and Awareness Process (LEAP).[30]

LEAP's first step involves participation in an introductory, one-day class that familiarizes candidates with managerial responsibilities. About one candidate in five concludes at this point that "management is not for me." The next step is a three- to six-month period during which the candidate's manager coaches him or her, based on a series of leadership attributes identified by the company. A third step involves peer assessment by a number of the candidate's coworkers (selected by the manager). Finally, the candidate must present written and oral arguments regarding specific leadership scenarios to a group of managers trained in LEAP assessment; this panel compares its findings to those from the other sources.

FedEx emphasizes leadership at every level through its "Survey Feedback Action" surveys, including the Leadership Index, in which subordinates rate their managers along 10 dimensions. Unfortunately, not every company is equally thorough in addressing the role of leadership at all levels in the organization. In many firms, promotional decisions often appear haphazard or based on such criteria as duration of tenure in a previous position.

Leadership, Culture, and Climate

To close this chapter, we take a brief look at a theme that runs throughout this chapter and, indeed, the book: the leader's role in nurturing an effective culture within the firm.[31] *Organizational culture* can be defined as including

- Shared perceptions or themes regarding what is important in the organization
- Shared values about what is right and wrong
- Shared understanding about what works and what doesn't work
- Shared beliefs and assumptions about *why* these things are important
- Shared styles of working and relating to others

Organizational climate represents the tangible surface layer on top of the organization's underlying culture. Among six key factors that influence an organization's working environment are its *flexibility* (how free employees feel to innovate); their sense of *responsibility* to the organization; the level of *standards* that people set; the perceived aptness of *rewards*; the *clarity* people have about mission and values; and the level of *commitment* to a common purpose.[32] From an employee perspective, this climate is directly related to managerial policies and procedures, especially those associated with human resource management. In short, climate represents the shared perceptions of employees about the practices, procedures, and types of behaviors that get rewarded and supported in a particular setting.

Because multiple climates often exist simultaneously within a single organization, a climate must relate to something specific—for instance, service, support, innovation, or safety. A climate for service refers to employee perceptions of those practices, procedures, and behaviors that are expected with regard to customer service and service quality and that get rewarded when performed well. Essential features of a service-oriented culture include clear marketing goals and a strong drive to be the best in delivering superior value or service quality.[33]

Leaders are responsible for creating cultures and the service climates that go along with them. Transformational leadership may require changing a culture that has become dysfunctional in the context of what it takes to be successful. Why are some leaders more effective than others in bringing about a desired change in climate? As presented in Research Insights 15-1, research suggests that it may be a matter of style.

Creating a new climate for service, based on an understanding of what is needed for market success, may require a radical rethinking of human resource management activities, operational procedures, and the firm's reward and recognition policies.

RESEARCH INSIGHT 15-1

THE IMPACT OF LEADERSHIP STYLES ON CLIMATE

Daniel Goleman, an applied psychologist at Rutgers University, is known for his work on emotional intelligence—the ability to manage ourselves and our relationships effectively. Having earlier identified six styles of leadership, he investigated how successful each style has proved to be in affecting climate or working atmosphere, based on a major study of the behavior and impact on their organizations of thousands of executives.

Coercive leaders demand immediate compliance ("Do what I tell you") and were found to have a negative impact on climate. Goleman comments that this controlling style, often highly confrontational, has value only in a crisis or in dealing with problem employees. *Pace-setting leaders* set high standards for performance and exemplify these through their own energetic behavior; this style can be summarized as "Do as I do, now." Somewhat surprisingly, it, too, was found to have a negative impact on climate. In practice, the pace-setting leader may destroy morale by assuming too much, too soon, of subordinates—expecting them to already know what to do and how to do it. Finding others to be less capable than expected, the leader may lapse into obsessing over details and micromanaging. This style is likely to work only when seeking to get quick results from a highly motivated and competent team.

The research found that the most effective style for achieving a positive change in climate came from *authoritative leaders* who have the skills and personality to mobilize people toward a vision, building confidence and using a "Come with me" approach. The research also found that three other styles had quite positive impacts on climate: *affiliative leaders*, who believe that "People come first," seeking to create harmony and build emotional bonds; *democratic leaders*, who forge consensus through participation ("What do you think?"); and *coaching leaders*, who work to develop people for the future and whose style might be summarized as "Try this."

Source: Daniel Goleman, "Leadership that Gets Results," *Harvard Business Review* 78 (March–April 2000): 78–93.

Newcomers to an organization must quickly familiarize themselves with the existing culture; otherwise, they will find themselves being led by it rather than leading through it and, if necessary, changing it.

CONCLUSION

No organization can hope to achieve and maintain market leadership without human leaders who articulate and communicate a vision and are backed by individuals with the management skills to make it happen. Service leadership in an industry requires high performance across a number of dimensions that fall within the scope of the marketing, operations, and HRM functions.

Within any given service organization, marketing has to coexist with operations—traditionally the dominant function—whose concerns are centered on cost and efficiency rather than on customers. Marketing must also coexist with human resource management, which usually recruits and trains service personnel, including those who have direct contact with the customers. An ongoing challenge is to balance the concerns of each function not only at the head office but also in the field. Ultimately, a company's ability to effectively integrate marketing, operations, and human resources management will determine whether it is classified as a service loser, a service nonentity, a service professional, or a service leader.

Review Questions

1. What kinds of tasks are traditionally assigned to (a) marketing, (b) operations, and (c) human resource management?
2. What are the causes of tension among the marketing, operations, and human resource functions? Provide specific examples of how these tensions might vary from one service industry to another.
3. How are the four levels of service performance defined? Based on your own service experiences, provide an example of a company for each category.
4. Which level of service performance do you think best describes Southwest Airlines? Explain your answer, using specific examples from Best Practice in Action 15-1.
5. What is the difference between leadership and management? Illustrate with examples.
6. What is meant by transformational leadership? Explain how the challenges in services marketing and management differ between an organization that is undergoing evolutionary change and one that requires a turnaround.
7. "Exemplary turnaround leaders understand the powerful, unifying effect of focusing on customers." Comment on this statement. Is a focus on customers by the CEO more likely to have a unifying effect within a company under turnaround conditions than at other times?
8. What is the relationship among leadership, climate, and culture?

Application Exercises

1. Contrast the roles of marketing, operations, and human resources in (1) a gas station chain, (2) a Web-based brokerage firm, and (3) an insurance company.
2. Select a company that you know well and obtain additional information from a literature review, Web site, company publications, and so on. Evaluate the company on as many dimensions of service performance as you can, identifying where you believe it fits on the service performance spectrum shown in Table 15-2.
3. Profile an individual whose leadership skills have played a significant role in the success of a service organization, identifying personal characteristics that you consider important.

Endnotes

1. James L. Heskett, Thomas O. Jones, Gary W. Loveman, W. Earl Sasser, Jr., and Leonard A. Schlesinger, "Putting the Service-Profit Chain to Work," *Harvard Business Review* (March–April 1994); and James L. Heskett, W. Earl Sasser, Jr., and Leonard A. Schlesinger, *The Service Profit Chain* (New York: The Free Press, 1997).
2. Note that a relationship between employee satisfaction and customer satisfaction may be more likely in high-contact situations in which employee behavior is an important aspect of the customers' experience. See Rhian Silvestro and Stuart Cross, "Applying the Service Profit Chain in a Retail Environment: Challenging the "Satisfaction Mirror," *International Journal of Service Industry Management* 11, no. 3 (2000): 244–268.
3. M. Beer, B. Spector, P. R. Lawrence, D. Q. Mills, and R. E. Walton, *Human Resource Management: A General Manager's Perspective* (New York: The Free Press, 1985).
4. Ibid.
5. David E. Bowen and Edward T. Lawler, III, "The Empowerment of Service Workers: What, Why, How and When," *Sloan Management Review* (Spring 1992): 31–39.
6. See, for example, Jeffrey Pfeffer, *Competitive Advantage through People* (Boston: Harvard Business School Press, 1994).
7. See, for example, Benjamin Schneider and David E. Bowen, *Winning the Service Game* (Boston: Harvard Business School Press, 1995); and Leonard L. Berry, *On Great Service: A Framework for Action* (New York: The Free Press, 1995), Chapters 8–10.
8. Terri Kabachnick, "The Strategic Role of Human Resources," *Arthur Andersen Retailing Issues Letter* 11, no. 1 (January 1999): 3.
9. Sandra Vandermerwe, *From Tin Soldiers to Russian Dolls* (Oxford, England: Butterworth-Heinemann, 1993), 82.
10. Richard B. Chase and Robert H. Hayes, "Beefing Up Operations in Service Firms," *Sloan Management Review* (Fall 1991): 15–26.

11. Claudia H. Deutsch, "Management: Companies Scramble to Fill Shoes at the Top," *nytimes.com*, November 1, 2000.
12. John P. Kotter, *What Leaders Really Do* (Boston: Harvard Business School Press, 1999), 10–11.
13. Warren Bennis and Burt Nanus, *Leaders: The Strategies for Taking Charge* (New York: Harper and Row, 1985), 92.
14. Kotter, *What Leaders Really Do*, 10–11.
15. Deborah Blagg and Susan Young, "What Makes a Leader?" *Harvard Business School Bulletin* (February 2001): 31–36.
16. Gary Hamel and C. K. Prahlahad, *Competing for the Future* (Boston: Harvard Business School Press, 1994).
17. See, for instance, the special issue "Leadership as a Service" (Celeste Wilderom, guest editor), *International Journal of Service Industry Management* 3, no. 2, 1992.
18. Heskett, Sasser, and Schlesinger, *The Service Profit Chain*, 236.
19. Jim Collins, "Level 5 Leadership: The Triumph of Humility and Fierce Resolve," *Harvard Business Review* (January 2001): 66–76.
20. Berry, *On Great Service*, 9.
21. Leonard L. Berry, *Discovering the Soul of Service* (New York,: The Free Press, 1999), 44, 47. See also D. Micheal Abrashoff, "Retention through Redemption," *Harvard Business Review* (February 2001): 136–141, which provides a fascinating example on successful leadership in the U.S. Navy.
22. John H. Humphreys, "Transformational Leader Behavior, Proximity and Successful Services Marketing," *Journal of Services Marketing* 16, no. 6 (2002): 487–502.
23. Rakesh Khurana, "The Curse of the Superstar CEO," *Harvard Business Review* 80 (September 2002): 60–66.
24. Sandra Vandermerwe, *From Tin Soldiers to Russian Dolls*, 129.
25. M. Sheridan, "J. W. Marriott, Jr., Chairman and President, Marriott Corporation," *Sky Magazine* (March 1987): 46–53.
26. Nelson D. Schwartz, "What's in the Cards for Amex?" *Fortune* (January 22, 2001): 58–70.
27. Rosabeth Moss Kanter, "Leadership and the Psychology of Turnaround," *Harvard Business Review* 81 (June 2003): 58–67.
28. W. Chan Kim and Renée Mauborgne, "Tipping Point Leadership," *Harvard Business Review* 81 (April 2003): 61–69.
29. Thomas J. Peters and Robert H. Waterman, *In Search of Excellence* (New York: Harper and Row, 1982), 122.
30. Christopher Lovelock, "Federal Express: Quality Improvement Program," IMD case (Cranfield, UK: European Case Clearing House, 1990).
31. This section is based, in part, on Benjamin Schneider and David E. Bowen, *Winning the Service Game* (Boston: Harvard Business School Press, 1995); and David E. Bowen, Benjamin Schneider, and Sandra S. Kim, "Shaping Service Cultures through Strategic Human Resource Management," in *Handbook of Services Marketing and Management*, ed. T. Schwartz and D. Iacobucci (Thousand Oaks, CA: Sage Publications, 2000), 439–454.
32. Daniel Goleman, "Leadership that Gets Results," *Harvard Business Review* 78 (March–April 2000): 78–93.
33. Hans Kasper, "Culture and Leadership in Market-Oriented Service Organisations," *European Journal of Marketing* 36, no. 9/10 (2002): 1047–1057.

Where Should the Next Marketing Dollar Go?

Roland T. Rust, Katherine N. Lemon, and Valarie A. Zeithaml

Where should the next marketing dollar go? Marketing executives should spend it where it will have the greatest impact on the lifetime values of the business' customers. In short, it should help build customer equity. Value equity, brand equity, and relationship equity all drive customer equity, and these drivers include every possible marketing expenditure. By focusing on the drivers that have the greatest impact on customer equity, a firm can focus its efforts most efficiently to grow its customer equity and add to the firm's value.

The marketing vice president of a B2B company needs to revive company sales, which have slipped recently. Should she invest in a new ad campaign to boost brand equity? Should she invest in a new customer information system to strengthen customer relationships? Should she invest in improvements in service quality? Or reduce prices by cutting costs?

Few firms can do more than guess at the answers to these questions. In many firms, the marketing function is inefficient, unaccountable, and imprecise. Too often there are no solid numbers to show which marketing initiatives will be successful and which will fail. When return on investment cannot be calculated, all investments look the same. To be safe, firms too often cover all of their bases equally—increasing the value customers perceive, building brands, and trying to retain customers through loyalty programs. Some of those expenditures turn out to be poor investments because they miss their targets.

The era of the inefficient, unaccountable marketing function must end. Marketing research information and databases that gather and store information about customer choice and customer profitability are paving the way for a new, focused marketing function. In this new environment, expenditures can finally be concentrated where they will have the greatest impact.

We need to cut back on ineffective marketing expenditures while boosting the performance of our most effective marketing strategies. The key to this powerful combination is having a valid measure to evaluate all marketing expenditures on the same basis. Customer lifetime value offers such a metric at the individual customer level. Customer equity—the combined lifetime values of the collective customer base—provides the basis for comparing strategic marketing alternatives. Evaluating how much the return from an investment exceeds the cost of capital can make marketing more exacting because it helps firms choose intelligently among options, cutting out the alternatives that yield an unacceptable return. Quantifying the projected financial return for each marketing expenditure makes marketing more accountable. The result is a new, surgically precise approach that identifies strategic initiatives with the greatest impact on the long-term profitability of the firm's customer base, thereby escalating the firm's value.

MARKET SHARE IS A REARVIEW MIRROR

Market share is a systematically inadequate measure of a firm's performance because it tells us about the recent past but ignores the future. What good is current market share if business is going to decline in the future?

To see this, consider Cadillac in the '70s and '80s. Cadillac had some of the most loyal customers in the industry. An entire generation of car buyers considered the name "Cadillac" to be synonymous with American luxury. Cadillac's market share in the U.S.

Roland T. Rust, Katherine N. Lemon, and Valarie A. Zeithaml, "Where Should the Next Marketing Dollar Go?" *Marketing Management* (September/October 2001): 25–28.

luxury car segment was high (51 percent in 1976). What could be wrong?

Unfortunately, the average customer lifetime value among Cadillac's customers was not particularly high because Cadillac's buyer population tended to be older (i.e., averaging age 60). Many of the older Cadillac buyers were on their last car. Cadillac's market share was good, but its customer equity share was bad.

Now compare BMW. Its youthful and vigorous image could not immediately win the market share war, but it ensured a younger customer base with a higher customer lifetime value. Ultimately BMW surpassed Cadillac even in current market share. Cadillac's share now is about 15 percent, down from 51 percent! And BMW's customer equity is now much higher than Cadillac's because it has more customers, and the average customer lifetime value is higher.

If market share is not the answer, then how can we measure whether a marketing expenditure is effective? The answer is clear—what matters is the effect on the firm's customer equity. In other words, not only do we care about how a marketing expenditure affects current sales, we also care about future sales. Customer lifetime value and customer equity are the name of the game.

DRIVERS OF CUSTOMER EQUITY

As we discussed in a previous article ("What Drives Customer Equity?" *Marketing Management*, Spring 2001), building up a firm's customer equity requires building up the three drivers of customer equity: value equity, brand equity, and relationship equity (also known as retention equity). Value equity represents the objective appraisal of the brand (things like perceptions of quality, price, and convenience); brand equity is the subjective appraisal of the brand (things like brand awareness and attitude toward the brand); and relationship equity involves the special relationship elements that link the customer with the brand (e.g., frequent buyer programs). We can think of customer equity as having a tree structure, as depicted in Exhibit 1.

SHARPENING THE FOUR "P"S

Marketing's usual four "P"s fit into the customer equity drivers. In fact, the customer equity drivers supply new insight with respect to the purpose of marketing expenditures. For example, the first "P," promotion, can have as its goal increasing value equity (communicating messages about quality, price, or convenience), expanding brand equity (perhaps through increasing awareness or brand attitudes), or increasing relationship equity (communicating messages about loyalty programs). The second "P," price, is clearly part of value equity. The third "P," product, is present both in value equity (objective elements, such as product specifications) and in brand equity (subjective elements, such as brand image). The fourth "P," place, is present in value equity (through convenience) and relationship equity (through channel relationships).

A fifth "P," people, has become more relevant as relationships become more important than transactions. It is well-represented in the customer equity framework through relationship equity. The customer equity framework includes all of the usual marketing expenditure categories and can help evaluate any marketing expenditure according to how it influences customer equity and its drivers.

CUSTOMER SATISFACTION MEASUREMENT

Current best practice in customer satisfaction measurement provides guidelines for managing customer equity. Customer satisfaction measurement routinely involves tree structures such as in Exhibit 1, showing how customer retention is driven by overall customer satisfaction, which is driven by the key drivers of satisfaction (e.g., satisfaction with service). These may be driven by sub-drivers (e.g., satisfaction with responsiveness or billing). From there, companies may drill down, creating as extensive a tree as necessary to produce actionable information.

Typically firms use cross-sectional customer surveys, with statistical models used to quantify the relationships between a variable (e.g., overall satisfaction) and its drivers (e.g., service) for any level of the tree. A similar tree structure and similar cross-sectional surveys may be used to model customer equity. The only difference is that the customer equity drivers are used to predict brand switching at the level of the individual customer. The customer's estimated brand-switching tendencies, along with knowledge of the customer's typical purchase frequency and purchase volume, make it easier to calculate the customer's estimated lifetime value.

From a practical standpoint, the surveys necessary for a customer equity analysis are essentially straightforward extensions of the customer satisfaction

EXHIBIT 1 Pathways to Customer Equity

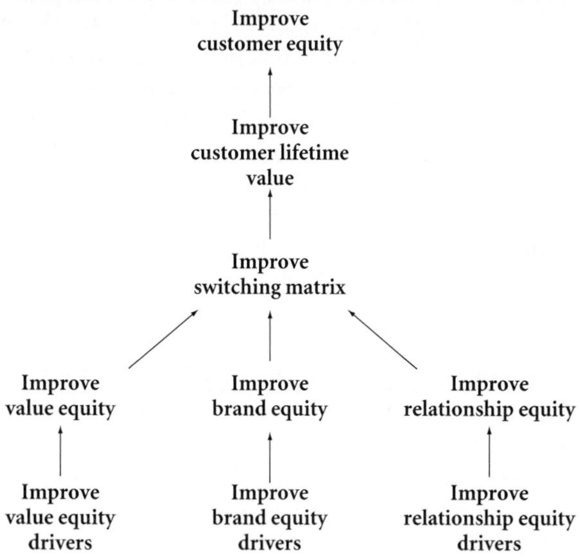

surveys the firm probably already does on a regular basis. The population sampled includes customers in the market (both our firm's customers and other customers). The items on the survey correspond to the branches on the tree in **Exhibit 1**. The survey obtains perceptions not only about our firm, but about the competing firms as well. This information is essential to understanding brand switching. In addition, we collect data on other variables affecting customer lifetime value, such as average frequency and volume of purchase.

The complete measurement framework and statistical details are beyond the scope of this article, but are covered more fully in our book, *Driving Customer Equity: How Customer Lifetime Value is Reshaping Corporate Strategy* (Free Press, 2000), and working paper, "Modeling Customer Equity" (University of Maryland, 2001). The main point to remember is that now any improvement in one of the drivers (or sub-drivers) of customer equity will result in a projected improvement in the firm's customer equity.

IMPORTANCE-PERFORMANCE MAPS

The concept of the importance-performance map, which has proven so useful in customer satisfaction measurement and customer value analysis, also applies to the drivers and sub-drivers of customer equity. The idea is very simple. As demonstrated in **Exhibit 2**, a graph can plot importance (high to low) against performance (high to low). Prime targets for marketing effort are those drivers (or sub-drivers) with high importance and low performance. To guide interpretation, the graph sometimes includes a diagonal line. Then drivers below the line are good targets for improvement.

A firm can derive importance measures for customer equity analysis in a wide variety of ways, including the dollar opportunity (shift in customer equity) of matching the best firm in the market on a driver or a driver's regression weight. In our experience, these types of derived importance weights are superior to self-stated importance weights. To derive performance measures for customer equity, marketers may examine the mean performance score given by the customers on a driver, or the percentage of "top box" or "bottom box" scores. For strategic purposes, we find it useful to scale the performance axis from worst in market ("low") to best in market ("high").

To see how importance-performance charts can be used to focus marketing strategy, consider the case of Alamo Rent A Car. (See Exhibits 2 and 3.) Data for this analysis were obtained in a pilot study conducted in two northeastern communities and are not intended to be projectable to a national population. However a national sample could easily be drawn, as could segment-specific samples intended to study customer equity in particular market segments.

Exhibit 2 shows that value equity is important in the rental car industry, with brand equity and relationship equity being less important. It also shows that Alamo performs relatively well on relationship equity, but worse on value equity and brand equity. The obvious strategic target is value equity, a very important area where Alamo fares poorly.

Exhibit 3 shows how we can drill down to the sub-driver level. Within value equity the key sub-drivers are quality, price, and convenience. Convenience is the most important, followed by quality and price. Alamo's performance is very good on the price dimension, but poor on quality and convenience. Given the importance of convenience and Alamo's poor performance on that sub-driver, it seems clear that the appropriate strategic target for Alamo is to improve value equity by providing more convenience to its customers.

The statistical details are beyond the scope of this article, but it is possible to address the projected financial impact of changes in the drivers and/or sub-drivers of customer equity. This enables firms to project return on investment from marketing expenditures, based on the effect on customer equity.

In their recent book, *Counterintuitive Marketing* (Free Press, 2000), Kevin Clancy and Peter Krieg note

EXHIBIT 2 Importance-Performance Map (Drivers): Alamo Rent A Car

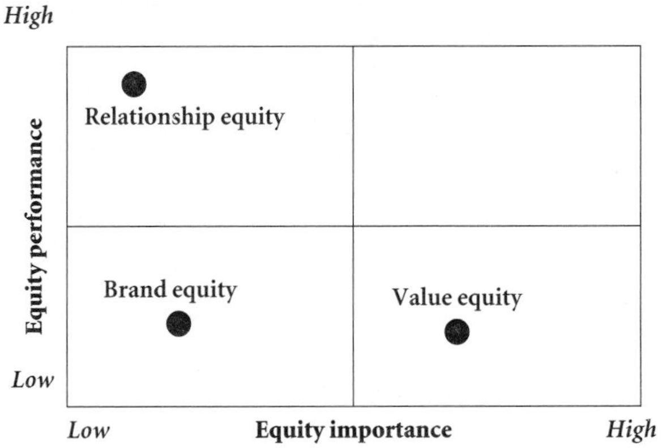

EXHIBIT 3 Importance-Performance Map (Sub-Drivers): Alamo Rent A Car

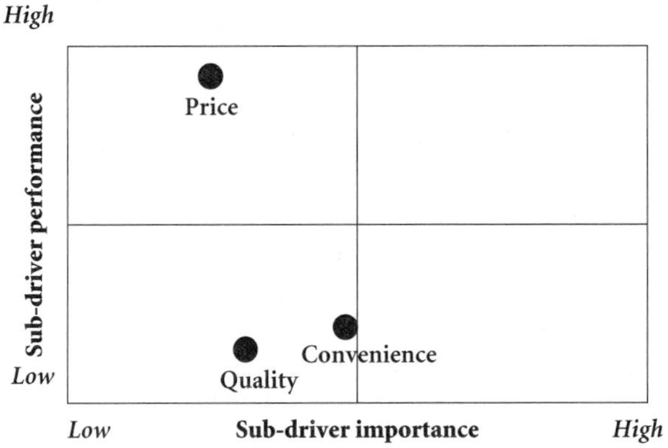

that too much of modern marketing is done by gut feel, often with disastrous results. The customer equity approach, by contrast, is an objective approach to strategy. Decisions are based on solid research and analysis, and the results provide clear strategic directions. Our method permits management to trade off one kind of expenditure (e.g., advertising) against another (e.g., service quality improvement or loyalty programs). By considering all expenditures on the common basis of customer equity, it's easier to recognize priorities. And because only cross-sectional data collection is required, it is possible to implement the customer equity framework very quickly.

To do this, first determine the relevant set of competitors and the relevant market segments. Often this will already be known within the firm. Then determine the key sub-drivers of value equity, brand equity, and relationship equity in the industry. Most firms have already done much of this background work. Next, redesign the customer satisfaction survey to address the customer equity drivers and sub-drivers and to collect necessary usage information.

It's also important to survey the customers, conduct statistical analysis, and build importance-performance maps. Based on the analysis and maps, a firm can identify the key strategic targets (customer equity driver and sub-driver(s)) and then shift resources to the strategic targets. Finally, in the next period (perhaps next year) a firm can survey again, monitor progress, and note competitive changes in customer perceptions. This becomes a regular strategic planning cycle within the firm and helps managers make smart decisions about where the next marketing dollar should go.

Why Service Stinks

DIANE BRADY

Companies know just how good a customer you are — and unless you are a high roller, they would rather lose you than take the time to fix your problem.

When Tom Unger of New Haven started banking at First Union Corp. several years ago, he knew he wasn't top of the heap. But Unger didn't realize just how dispensable he was until mysterious service charges started showing up on his account. He called the bank's toll-free number, only to reach a bored service representative who brushed him off. Then he wrote two letters, neither of which received a response. A First Union spokeswoman, Mary Eshet, says the bank doesn't discuss individual accounts but notes that customer service has been steadily improving. Not for Unger. He left. "They wouldn't even give me the courtesy of listening to my complaint," he says.

And Unger ought to know bad service when he sees it. He works as a customer-service representative at an electric utility where the top 350 business clients are served by six people. The next tier of 700 are handled by six more, and 30,000 others get Unger and one other rep to serve their needs. Meanwhile, the 300,000 residential customers at the lowest end are left with an 800 number. As Unger explains: "We don't ignore anyone, but our biggest customers certainly get more attention than the rest."

As time goes on, that service gap is only growing wider. Studies by groups ranging from the Council of Better Business Bureaus Inc. to the University of Michigan vividly detail what consumers already know: Good service is increasingly rare (see Figures A and B). From passengers languishing in airport queues to bank clients caught in voice-mail hell, most consumers feel they're getting squeezed by Corporate

FIGURE A

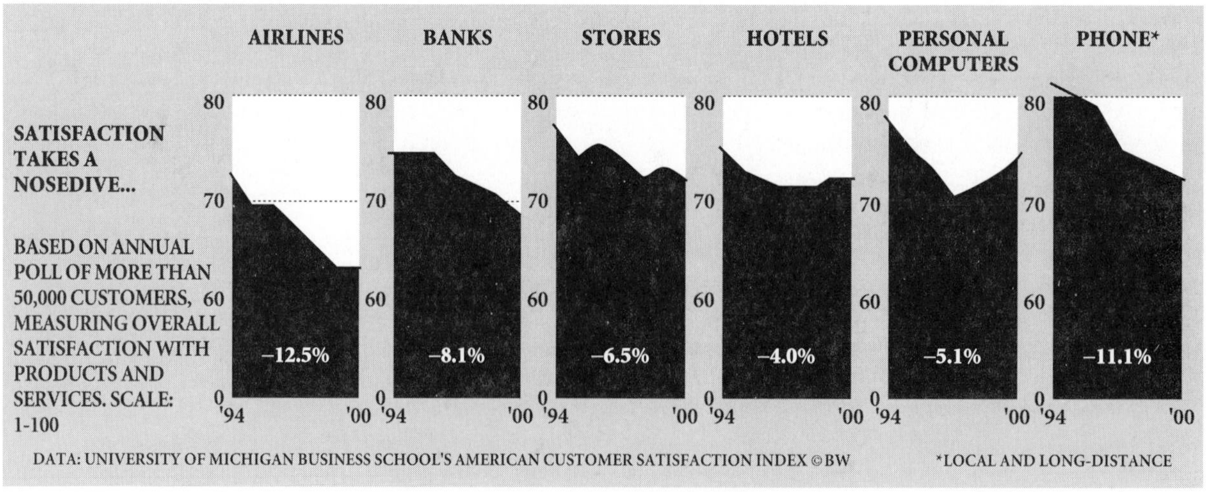

Diane Brady, "Why Service Stinks," *Business Week*, October 23, 2000. Reprinted by permission.

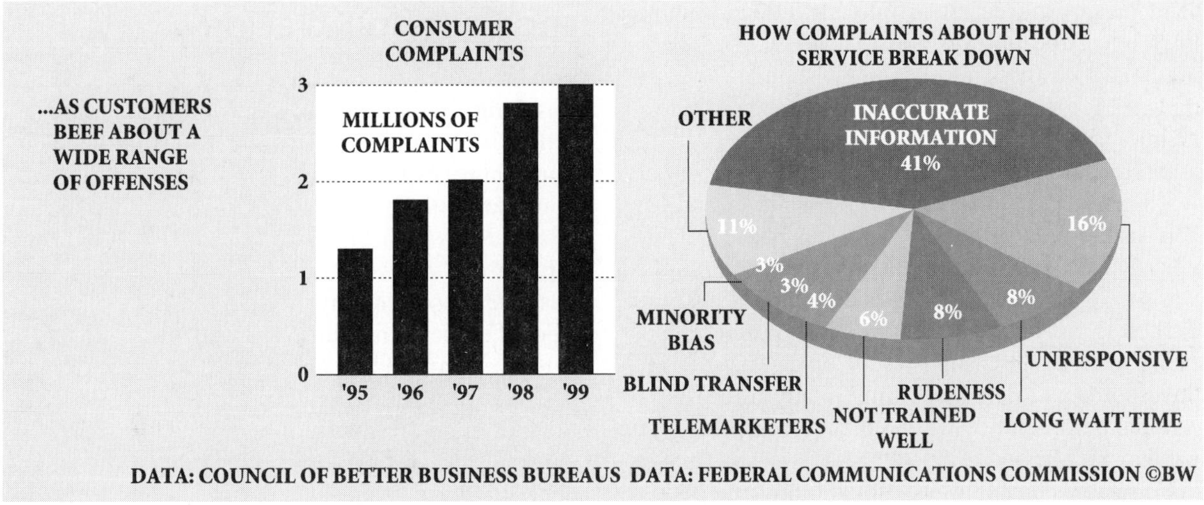

FIGURE B

America's push for profits and productivity. The result is more efficiencies for companies—and more frustration for their less valuable customers. "Time saved for them is not time saved for us," says Claes Fornell, a University of Michigan professor who created the school's consumer satisfaction index, which shows broad declines across an array of industries. Fornell points to slight improvements in areas like autos and computers.

Andrew Chan's experience with Ikea is typical. The Manhattan artist recently hauled a table home from an Ikea store in New Jersey only to discover that all the screws and brackets were missing. When he called to complain, the giant furniture retailer refused to send out the missing items and insisted he come back to pick them up himself, even though he doesn't own a car. Maybe he just reached the wrong guy, says Tom Cox, customer-service manager for Ikea North America, noting that the usual procedure is to mail small items out within a couple of days.

NO ELEPHANT?

Life isn't so tough for everyone, though. Roy Sharda, a Chicago Internet executive and road warrior is a "platinum" customer of Starwood Hotels & Resorts Worldwide. When he wanted to propose to his girlfriend, Starwood's Sheraton Agra in India arranged entry to the Taj Mahal after hours so he could pop the question in private. Starwood also threw in a horse-drawn carriage, flowers, a personalized meal, upgrades to the presidential suite, and a cheering reception line led by the general manager. It's no wonder Sharda feels he was "treated like true royalty."

Welcome to the new consumer apartheid. Those long lines and frustrating telephone trees aren't always the result of companies simply not caring about pleasing the customer anymore. Increasingly, companies have made a deliberate decision to give some people skimpy service because that's all their business is worth. Call it the dark side of the technology boom, where marketers can amass a mountain of data that gives them an almost Orwellian view of each buyer. Consumers have become commodities to pamper, squeeze, or toss away, according to Leonard L. Berry, marketing professor at Texas A&M University. He sees "a decline in the level of respect given to customers and their experiences."

More important, technology is creating a radical new business model that alters the whole dynamic of customer service. For the first time, companies can truly measure exactly what such service costs on an individual level and assess the return on each dollar. They can know exactly how much business someone generates, what he is likely to buy, and how much it costs to answer the phone. That allows them to deliver a level of service based on each person's potential to produce a profit—and not a single phone call more.

The result could be a whole new stratification of consumer society. The top tier may enjoy an unprecedented level of personal attention. But those who fall below a certain level of profitability for too long may find themselves bounced from the customer rolls altogether or facing fees that all but usher them out the door. A few years ago, GE Capital decided to charge $25 a year to GE Rewards MasterCard holders who didn't rack up at least that much in annual interest charges. The message was clear: Those who pay their bills in full each month don't boost the bottom line. GE has since sold its credit-card business to First USA. Others are charging extra for things like deliveries and repairs or reducing service staff in stores and call centers.

Instead of providing premium service across the board, companies may offer to move people to the front of the line for a fee. "There has been a fundamental shift in how companies assess customer value and apply their resources," says Cincinnati marketing consultant Richard G. Barlow. He argues that managers increasingly treat top clients with kid gloves and cast the masses "into a labyrinth of low-cost customer service where, if they complain, you just live with it."

Companies have always known that some people don't pay their way. Ravi Dhar, an associate professor at Yale University, cites the old rule that 80 percent of profits come from 20 percent of customers. "The rest nag you, call you, and don't add much revenue," he says. But technology changed everything. To start, it has become much easier to track and measure individual transactions across businesses. Second, the Web has also opened up options. People can now serve themselves at their convenience at a negligible cost, but they have to accept little or no human contact in return. Such huge savings in service costs have proven irresistible to marketers, who are doing everything possible to push their customers—especially low-margin ones—toward self-service.

FRONT-LOADING ELITE

That's a far cry from the days when the customer was king. In the data-rich new millennium, sales staff no longer let you return goods without question while rushing to shake your hand. And they don't particularly want to hear from you again unless you're worth the effort. How they define that top tier can vary a lot by industry. Airlines and hotels love those who buy premier offerings again and again. Financial institutions, on the other hand, salivate over day traders and the plastic-addicted who pay heavy interest charges because they cover only the minimum on their monthly credit-card bills.

Almost everyone is doing it (see Table A). Charles Schwab Corp.'s top-rated Signature clients—who start with at least $100,000 in assets or trade 12 times a year—never wait longer than 15 seconds to get a call answered, while other customers can wait 10 minutes or more. At Sears, Roebuck & Co., big spenders on the company's credit card get to choose a preferred two-hour time slot for repair calls while regular patrons are given a four-hour slot. Maytag Corp. provides premium service to people who buy pricey products such as its front-loading Neptune washing machines, which sell for about $1,000, twice the cost of a top-loading washer. This group gets a dedicated staff of "product experts," an exclusive toll-free number, and speedy service on repairs. When people are paying this much, "they not only want more service;

TABLE A How You Can Get Stiffed

Flying

Canceled flight? No problem. With top status, you're whisked past the queue, handed a ticket for the next flight, and driven to the first-class lounge.

Billing

Big spenders can expect special discounts, promotional offers, and other goodies when they open their bills. The rest might get higher fees, stripped-down service, and a machine to answer their questions.

Banking

There's nothing like a big bank account to get those complaints answered and service charges waived every time. Get pegged as a money-loser, and your negotiating clout vanishes.

Lodging

Another day, another upgrade for frequent guests. Sip champagne before the chef prepares your meal. First-time guest? So sorry. Your room is up three flights and to the left.

Retailing

Welcome to an after-hours preview for key customers where great sales abound and staff await your every need. Out in the aisles, it's back to self-service.

they deserve it," says Dale Reeder, Maytag's general manager of customer service.

Of course, while some companies gloat about the growing attention to their top tier, most hate to admit that the bottom rungs are getting less. GE Capital would not talk. Sprint Corp. and WorldCom Inc. declined repeated requests to speak about service divisions. Off the record, one company official explains that customers don't like to know they're being treated differently.

Obviously, taking service away from the low spenders doesn't generate much positive press for companies. Look at AT&T, which recently agreed to remove its minimum usage charges on the 28 million residential customers in its lowest-level basic plan, many of whom don't make enough calls to turn a profit. "To a lot of people, it's not important that a company make money," says AT&T Senior Vice-President Howard E. McNally, who argues that AT&T is still treated by regulators and the public as a carrier of last resort. Now, it's trying to push up profits by giving top callers everything from better rates to free premium cable channels.

SERIAL CALLERS

Is this service divide fair? That depends on your perspective. In an era when labor costs are rising while prices have come under pressure, U.S. companies insist they simply can't afford to spend big bucks giving every customer the hands-on service of yesteryear (see Table B). Adrian J. Slywotzky, a partner with Mercer Management Consulting Inc., estimates that gross margins in many industries have shrunk an average of 5 to 10 percentage points over the past decade because of competition. "Customers used to be more profitable 10 years ago, and they're becoming more different than similar" in how they want to be served, he says.

The new ability to segment customers into ever finer categories doesn't have to be bad news for consumers. In many cases, the trade-off in service means lower prices. Susanne D. Lyons, chief marketing officer at Charles Schwab, points out that the commission charged on Schwab stock trades has dropped by two-thirds over the past five years. Costs to Schwab, meanwhile, vary from a few cents for Web deals to several dollars per live interaction. And companies note that they're delivering a much wider range of products and services than ever before—as well as more ways to handle transactions. Thanks to the Internet, for example, consumers have far better tools to conveniently serve themselves.

Look at a company like Fidelity Investments, which not only has a mind-boggling menu of fund options but now lets people do research and manipulate their accounts without an intermediary. Ten years ago, the company got 97,000 calls a day, of which half were automated. It now gets about 550,000 Web site visits a day and more than 700,000

TABLE B "We're Sorry, All of Our Agents Are Busy with More Valuable Customers"

Companies have become sophisticated about figuring out if you're worth pampering—or whether to just let the phone keep ringing. Here are some of their techniques:

Coding

Some companies grade customers based on how profitable their business is. They give each account a code with instructions to service staff on how to handle each category.

Routing

Based on the customer's code, call centers route customers to different queues. Big spenders are whisked to high-level problem solvers. Others may never speak to a live person at all.

Targeting

Choice customers have fees waived and get other hidden discounts based on the value of their business. Less valuable customers may never even know the promotions exist.

Sharing

Companies sell data about your transaction history to outsiders. You can be slotted before you even walk in the door, since your buying potential has already been measured.

TABLE C Making the Grade: How to Get Better Service

Consolidate Your Activities
Few things elevate status and trim costs like spending big in one place. Be on the lookout for packages or programs that reward loyal behavior.
Protect Your Privacy
Avoid surveys and be frugal with releasing credit-card or Social Security information. The less companies know, the less they can slot you.
Jump the Phone Queue
If you want to reach a live human, don't admit to having a touch-tone phone at the prompt. Or listen for options that are less likely to be handled automatically.
Fight Back
If you feel badly treated, complain. Make sure management knows just how much business you represent and that you're willing to take it elsewhere.

daily calls, about three-quarters of which go to automated systems that cost the company less than a buck each, including development and research costs. The rest are handled by human beings, which costs about $13 per call. No wonder Fidelity last year contacted 25,000 high-cost "serial" callers and told them they must use the Web or automated calls for simple account and price information. Each name was flagged and routed to a special representative who would direct callers back to automated services—and tell them how to use it. "If all our customers chose to go through live reps, it would be cost-prohibitive," says a Fidelity spokeswoman.

ENTITLED?

Segmenting is one way to manage those costs efficiently. Bass Hotels & Resorts, owners of such brands as Holiday Inn and Inter-Continental Hotels, knows so much about individual response rates to its promotions that it no longer bothers sending deals to those who did not bite in the past. The result: 50 percent slashed off mailing costs but a 20 percent jump in response rates. "As information becomes more sophisticated, the whole area of customer service is becoming much more complex," says Chief Marketing Officer Ravi Saligram.

Consumers themselves have cast a vote against high-quality service by increasingly choosing price, choice, and convenience over all else. Not that convenience always takes the sting out of rotten service—witness Priceline.com Inc., the ultimate self-service site that lets customers name their own price for plane tickets, hotels, and other goods. Many consumers didn't fully understand the trade-offs, such as being forced to stop over on flights, take whatever brand was handed to them, and forgo the right to any refund. And when things went wrong, critics say, no one was around to help. The result: a slew of complaints that has prompted at least one state investigation. Priceline.com responds that it's revamping the Web site and intensifying efforts to improve customer service. While many consumers refuse to pay more for service, they're clearly dismayed when service is taken away. "People have higher expectations now than two or three years ago because we have all this information at our fingertips," says Jupiter Communications Inc. analyst David Daniels.

Indeed, marketers point to what they call a growing culture of entitlement, where consumers are much more demanding about getting what they want. One reason is the explosion of choices, with everything from hundreds of cable channels to new players emerging from deregulated industries like airlines and telecom companies. Meanwhile, years of rewards programs such as frequent-flier miles have contributed to the new mind-set. Those who know their worth expect special privileges that reflect it. Says Bonnie S. Reitz, senior vice-president for marketing, sales, and distribution at Continental Airlines Inc.: "We've got a hugely educated, informed, and more experienced consumer out there now."

For top-dollar clients, all this technology allows corporations to feign an almost small-town intimacy. Marketers can know your name, your spending habits, and even details of your personal life. Centura Banks Inc. of Raleigh, N.C., now rates its 2 million customers on a profitability scale from 1 to 5.

The real moneymakers get calls from service reps several times a year for what Controller Terry Earley calls "a friendly chat" and even an annual call from the CEO to wish them happy holidays. No wonder attrition in this group is down by 50 percent since 1996, while the percentage of unprofitable customers has slipped to 21 percent from 27 percent.

Even for the lower tier, companies insist that this intense focus on data is leading to service that's better than ever. To start with, it's more customized. And while executives admit to pushing self-help instead of staff, they contend that such service is often preferable. After all, many banking customers prefer using automated teller machines to standing in line at their local branch. American Airlines Inc., the pioneer of customer segmentation with its two-decade-old loyalty program, says it's not ignoring those in the cheap seats, pointing to the airline's recent move to add more legroom in economy class. Says Elizabeth S. Crandall, managing director of personalized marketing: "We're just putting more of our energies into rewarding our best customers."

MARKED MAN

This segmentation of sales, marketing, and service, based on a wealth of personal information, raises some troubling questions about privacy. It threatens to become an intensely personal form of "redlining"—the controversial practice of identifying and avoiding unprofitable neighborhoods or types of people. Unlike traditional loyalty programs, the new tiers are not only highly individualized but they are often invisible. You don't know when you're being directed to a different telephone queue or sales promotion. You don't hear about the benefits you're missing. You don't realize your power to negotiate with everyone from gate agents to bank employees is predetermined by the code that pops up next to your name on a computer screen.

When the curtain is pulled back on such sophisticated tiering, it can reveal some uses of customer information that are downright disturbing. Steve Reed, a West Coast sales executive, was shocked when a United Airlines Inc. ticketing agent told him: "Wow, somebody doesn't like you." Not only did she have access to his Premier Executive account information but there was a nasty note about an argument he had had with a gate agent in San Francisco several months earlier. In retrospect, he feels that explained why staff seemed less accommodating following the incident. Now, Reed refuses to give more than his name for fear "of being coded and marked for repercussions." United spokesman Joe Hopkins says such notes give agents a more complete picture of passengers. "It's not always negative information," says Hopkins, adding that the practice is common throughout the industry.

Those who don't make the top tier have no idea how good things can be for the free-spending few. American Express Co. has a new Centurion concierge service that promises to get members almost anything from anywhere in the world. The program, with an annual fee of $1,000, is open by invitation only. "We're seeing a lot of people who value service more than price," says Alfred F. Kelly Jr., AmEx group president for consumer and small-business services. Dean Burri, a Rock Hill (S.C.) insurance executive, found out how the other half lives when he joined their ranks. Once he became a platinum customer of Starwood Hotels, it seemed there was nothing the hotel operator wouldn't do for him. When the Four Points Hotel in Lubbock, Tex., was completely booked for Texas Tech freshman orientation in August, it bumped a lower-status guest to get Burri a last-minute room. Starwood says that's part of the platinum policy, noting that ejected customers are put elsewhere and compensated for inconvenience. With the right status, says Burri, "you get completely different treatment."

The distinctions in customer status are getting sliced ever finer. Continental Airlines Inc. has started rolling out a Customer Information System where every one of its 43,000 gate, reservation, and service agents will immediately know the history and value of each customer. A so-called intelligent engine not only mines data on status but also suggests remedies and perks, from automatic coupons for service delays to priority for upgrades, giving the carrier more consistency in staff behavior and service delivery. The technology will even allow Continental staff to note details about the preferences of top customers so the airline can offer them extra services. As Vice-President Reitz puts it: "We even know if they put their eyeshades on and go to sleep." Such tiering pays off. Thanks to its heavy emphasis on top-tier clients, about 47 percent of Continental's customers now pay higher-cost, unrestricted fares, up from 38 percent in 1995.

Elsewhere, the selectivity is more subtle. At All First Bank in Baltimore, only those slotted as top customers get the option to click on a Web icon that directs them to a live service agent for a phone conversation. The rest never see it. First Union meanwhile, codes its credit-card customers with tiny colored squares that flash when service reps call up an account on their computer screens. Green means the person is a profitable customer and should be granted waivers or otherwise given white-glove treatment. Reds are the money losers who have almost no negotiating power, and yellow is a more discretionary category in between. "The information helps our people make decisions on fees and rates," explains First Union spokeswoman Mary Eshet.

Banks are especially motivated to take such steps because they have one of the widest gaps in profitability. Market Line Associates, an Atlanta financial consultancy, estimates that the top 20 percent of customers at a typical commercial bank generate up to six times as much revenue as they cost, while the bottom fifth cost three to four times more than they make for the company. Gartner Group Inc. recently found that, among banks with deposits of more than $4 billion, 68 percent are segmenting customers into profitability tranches while many more have plans to do so.

Tiering, however, poses some drawbacks for marketers. For one thing, most programs fail to measure the potential value of a customer. Most companies can still measure only past transactions—and some find it tough to combine information from different business units. The problem, of course, is that what someone spends today is not always a good predictor of what they'll spend tomorrow. Life situations and spending habits can change. In some cases, low activity may be a direct result of the consumer's dissatisfaction with current offerings. "We have to be careful not to make judgments based on a person's interaction with us," cautions Steven P. Young, vice-president for worldwide customer care at Compaq Computer Corp.'s consumer-products group. "It may not reflect their intentions or future behavior."

PAY NOT TO WAIT?

Already, innovative players are striving to use their treasure trove of information to move customers up the value chain instead of letting them walk out the door. Capital One Financial Corp. of Falls Church, Va., is an acknowledged master of tiering, offering more than 6,000 credit cards and up to 20,000 permutations of other products, from phone cards to insurance. That range lets the company match clients with someone who has appropriate expertise. "We look at every single customer contact as an opportunity to make an unprofitable customer profitable or make a profitable customer more profitable," says Marge Connelly, senior vice-president for domestic card operations.

HOW TO IMPROVE YOUR PROFILE

Even if you're not a big spender, there are ways to improve your standing with companies in order to command better service. The key is to recognize that your spending habits, payment history, and any information you volunteer can be used for or against you. What's more, if you do think you're being pegged at a low tier, there are ways to get the recognition you feel you deserve.

The first step in fighting segmentation is to be stingy with the information you give out–especially if it's unlikely to help your status. Don't fill out surveys, sweepstakes forms, or applications if you're not comfortable with how the information might be used. Be wary when a company asks if it can alert you to other products and services. A yes may permit them to sell data that you don't want distributed.

Pigeonholing The Consumers Union (CU) points out that it's unnecessary to fill out surveys with warranty cards. Just send in a proof of purchase with your name and address. "Protecting your privacy is a significant tool to prevent yourself from being pigeonholed as undesirable," says Gene Kimmelman, Washington co-director for the CU. It's equally important to recognize what kind of information companies are looking for. If you don't live in an upmarket Zip Code, consider using your work address for correspondence. Be optimistic when estimating your income or spending: The better the numbers look, the better you'll be treated.

Still, it's tough to keep personal information to yourself, especially when companies are compiling data on the business they do with you. A critical concern for all consumers is their actual payment record. Donna Fluss, a vice-president at the technology consultants Gartner Group Inc., advises pulling your credit history at least once a year to check if there are any liens or mistakes. "You may discover that you're listed as having missed a payment that you thought you made on time," she says. The three main reporting bureaus–Experian, Trans Union, and Equifax–charge a small fee for a copy of your credit history. If, however you have recently been denied credit, employment, or insurance, such a report is free from all three companies. The largest bureau is Equifax, which has data on 190 million Americans, but all three may have slightly different records based on who reports to them.

Multiple credit cards can be a mistake, especially if they're the no-frills variety that are frequently offered to less desirable candidates. Not only can they drain the credit you might need for other activities, but they're also unlikely to propel you into a higher category. Using a spouse's card or account is also to be avoided, because it robs you of a chance to build your own credit history. If a mistake is made on your account, fight it.

Pros disagree on tactics for bypassing the service maze. One customer representative argues that when calling a service center it's better to punch in no account number if you're a low-value customer. The reason? Without proper identification, he says, a live person has to get on the line. "Pretend you're calling from a rotary phone," he advises. But another tactic may be to punch zero or choose an option that's likely to get immediate attention.

In the end, resistance may be futile, and the best strategy for beating the system may be to join it. Shop around for the best company, and try to consolidate your business there. These days, the best way to ensure good service is to make yourself look like a high-value, free-spending customer.

In the future, therefore, the service divide may become much more transparent. The trade-off between price and service could be explicit, and customers will be able to choose where they want to fall on that continuum. In essence, customer service will become just another product for sale. Walker Digital, the research lab run by priceline.com founder Jay S. Walker, has patented a "value-based queuing" of phone calls that allows companies to prioritize calls according to what each person will pay. As Walker Digital CEO Vikas Kapoor argues, customers can say: "I don't want to wait in line—I'll pay to reduce my wait time."

For consumers, though, the reality is that service as we've known it has changed forever. As Roger S. Siboni, chief executive of customer-service software provider E. piphany Inc., points out, not all customers are the same. "Some you want to absolutely retain and throw rose petals at their feet," Siboni says. "Others will never be profitable." Armed with detailed data on who's who, companies are learning that it makes financial sense to serve people based on what they're worth. The rest can serve themselves or simply go away.

Linking Actions to Profits in Strategic Decision Making

MARC J. EPSTEIN AND ROBERT A. WESTBROOK

The action-profit linkage model helps managers to identify and measure key drivers of business success and profit, develop causal links among them, and estimate the impact of actions to bring them about. This process leads to a focus on those strategies with the highest payoff. Example are provided from banking and waste disposal.

Many companies find that it's not enough to "increase customer satisfaction" or "raise product quality." They must know conclusively how such departmental pursuits affect the profitability of the company as a whole.

Between 1990 and 1993, customers of the commercial waste-collection services of Browning-Ferris Industries (BFI) defected to competitors at a rate of 11% to 13% per year. Senior managers focused on raising customer satisfaction, but between 1995 and 1997, the defection rate increased to 13% to 15%. BFI's original growth strategy of acquiring similar businesses that would provide new customers had become too expensive. The only alternative appeared to be customer retention, so managers began exploring what effect it could have on profit. When they discovered that a mere 1% decline in customer defection would yield a pretax profit increase of $41 million, customer retention took on heightened importance. Managers learned to follow a chain of links from poor customer satisfaction back to a specific problem action and then invest in correcting it.

The result was dramatic. Falling customer-satisfaction scores leveled off and then began to climb rapidly. Customer-defection rates dropped to below 10%. BFI was able to sustain profitability in the face of losses from its other business operations. Managers learned about the links from the customer-service-dependability rating to overall customer satisfaction to the customer-defection rate. They could see which specific actions would have the best payoff, and they invested in those.

BFI is one of a growing number of companies that are moving beyond a vague desire for "shareholder value" and "customer focus" and asking the questions that can get them there. How does a company identify and measure causal relationships between parts of its organization? What really drives profit and creates value? How does an operating or capital-investment decision affect profit?

That type of probing goes beyond individual departmental goals to a cross-functional view of the company's objectives and relationships. Human-resource departments strive to improve employee satisfaction. Marketing departments focus on achieving higher levels of customer satisfaction and loyalty. Operations functions attempt to raise product quality. Those goals differ, but each department ultimately shares a larger goal: Make the company more profitable.

Companies may have success meeting departmental goals, but they often stop analyzing cause and effect once the goal is met. Later they wonder why a string of individual successes hasn't led to an increase in corporate profit or shareholder value. They don't see that because their analysis fails to bridge functions and actions, they can't hope to reap the highest corporate profit.

When forced by competition and the failure of other alternatives, some companies *have* attempted to make the cross-functional link between their actions and profit, but their approach is usually piecemeal. Lacking a general framework to start with, they waste time and money establishing links through trial and error.

A way to eliminate some of the uncertainty in defining links can be found in the action-profit linkage

Acknowledgments: The authors wish to express their appreciation to two anonymous reviewers who offered thoughtful suggestions.
Reprinted from "Linking Actions to Profits in Stragic Decision Making," by Mark J. Epstein and Robert A. Westbrook, *MIT Sloan Management Review* 42, no. 3 (Spring 2001): 39-49 by permission of publisher.

(APL) model, which lets managers see just how any action within any corporate function affects overall profitability.[1] Managers can identify and measure key drivers of business success and profit, develop causal links among them and estimate the impact of actions taken to bring them about. They can narrow their strategies to the areas with the highest payoff. Thus attention shifts from a preoccupation with individual performance metrics to an awareness of how those metrics work as a system and how they can increase profit and shareholder value.

Where the Payoff Comes From

At certain points in their history, companies that have linked actions to profit have had dramatic results: Sears, Roebuck and Co., for example, was able to see that a 5.0-point improvement in employee attitudes would drive a 1.3-point improvement in customer satisfaction, which would drive a 0.5 percent improvement in revenue growth. Sears went from a loss of nearly $4 billion in 1992 to a profit of $1.5 billion five years later.[2] Although there are many possible explanations for that turnaround, Sears managers believed it was largely due to a culture change; an abbreviated APL model played a role in that change.

Managers at the Canadian Imperial Bank of Commerce (CIBC) and BFI also saw the payoff from carefully identifying, articulating and measuring the causal relationships between actions and profit.

THE ACTION-PROFIT LINKAGE MODEL

The APL model begins with corporate strategy and moves to four main components: company actions, delivered product/service, customer actions and economic impact. Connecting those components are many intervening variables. Managers can evaluate the profitability of any action the company takes by examining the links between the action, intervening variables and the resulting changes to customer revenue—minus the costs of the action. They can customize the model to a particular industry or business context by substituting actual performance metrics for the more-general variables.

Corporate strategy is the collection of activities or actions a company chooses to perform or not to perform.* The term "company actions" refers to management decisions that alter the company's activities. The model allows for six broad domains of company action, corresponding to the organization's functional areas: operations, information technology (IT), human resources, marketing and sales, finance and accounting, and external relations. Companies can add domains as appropriate when they customize the general model.

Each domain has many possible activities. The ones below are merely representative; each enterprise will have its own set.

- *Operations*—create and maintain technology, design jobs and processes, create supply chains, establish maintenance programs, design facilities.
- *IT*—manage information systems, develop system architecture, acquire hardware and software.
- *Human resources*—hire and train staff, manage labor relations, devise company safety and health programs, evaluate employees, communicate internally, restructure organizations.
- *Marketing and sales*—conceptualize new products and services, set pricing, advertise, self, establish distribution, bill customers.
- *Finance and accounting*—devise financial structure, do capital budgeting, establish dividend policy, manage foreign exchange, do financial reporting, manage cash.
- *External relations*—communicate with external stakeholders, lobby, maintain media relations, establish community relations.

Each activity comprises many specific possible actions. The pricing activity in marketing and sales might include raising or lowering the price or offering introductory discounts. Each action will affect the delivered product or service, the costs—or both.

A business can trace its actions through the various components all the way to corporate profitability. (See "Tracing the Links.") Managers establish links by analyzing the relationships between specific metrics. To customize the general model, they use existing metrics and devise new ones to complete the path of links from an action to corporate profit. A diagram of

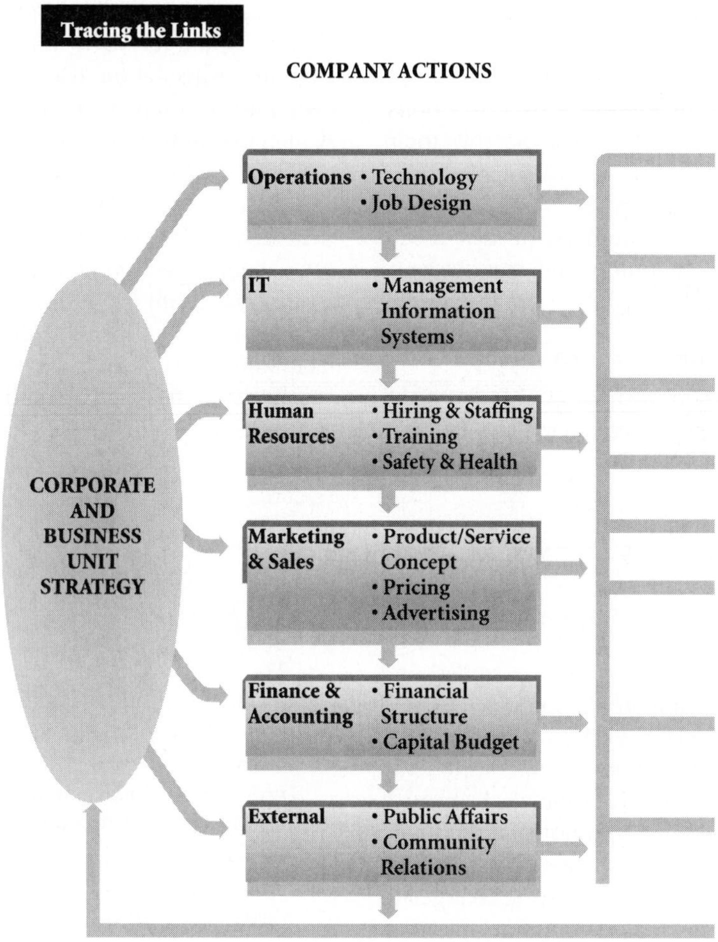

the general model must limit itself to links between the large components. The meaningful links, however, are between specific metrics and variables. For example, for an auto manufacturer, the link from product or service characteristics to product or service perceptions might be a link from "build quality measured by defects per 100 cars" to "customer ratings of vehicle reliability."

The links between components may be simple and direct, but the model allows any variable to be linked to any other variable. Such flexibility is APL's main difference from other profitability models.

*M.E. Porter, "What is Strategy?" *Harvard Business Review* 77 (November–December 1999): 61–78.

Canadian Imperial Bank of Commerce In 1996, CIBC, a national bank with 6 million customers and $250 billion in assets, was facing increased competition from deregulation. Its customer defection rate was approaching 10 percent, with another 15 percent of its customers estimated to be on the fence or close to defection. Seriously concerned, senior managers pondered how to reestablish the bank's market position. A first step would be to articulate the drivers of business success.[3] Hoping to learn how their own behavior was affecting customer retention, they decided to develop a model to link action to profit. (See "How Does Management Behavior Affect Customer Loyalty?")

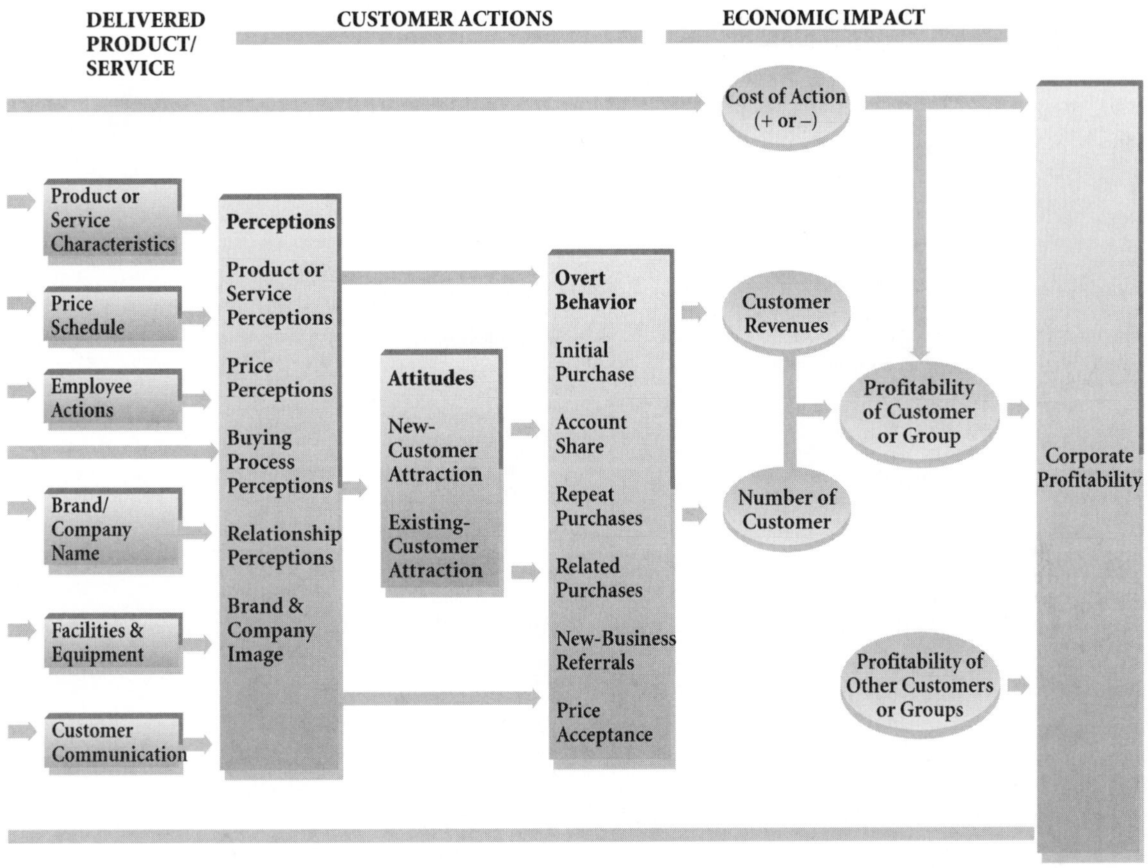

HOW DOES MANAGEMENT BEHAVIOR AFFECT CUSTOMER LOYALTY?

In seeking to understand how actions affect customer loyalty, the Canadian Imperial Bank of Commerce (CIBC) developed a model to explore links among management behavior, employee commitment, customer loyalty—and ultimately profit. (See "Canadian Imperial Bank of Commerce Creates a Model.")

Working backward, CIBC linked shareholder value (profit) to customer actions (customer loyalty behavior). The model then traced the drivers of customer loyalty, which CIBC was able to identify after analyzing volumes of customer data. The model went on to link customer loyalty behavior with employee commitment. Employee commitment behaviors, which demonstrated employees' satisfaction with and loyalty to the company, included responding efficiently to requests, meeting commitments, recommending the company at a place to work and staying with the organization. Then CIBC identified employee-commitment drivers: company culture, degree of customer orientation reward and recognition, workload, learning (ability to improve skills) and leadership (management leadership behavior).

By analyzing the links in the model, CIBC managers learned that a 5% increase in employee commitment yields in 2% increase in customer loyalty—which increases profitability by $72 million annually.

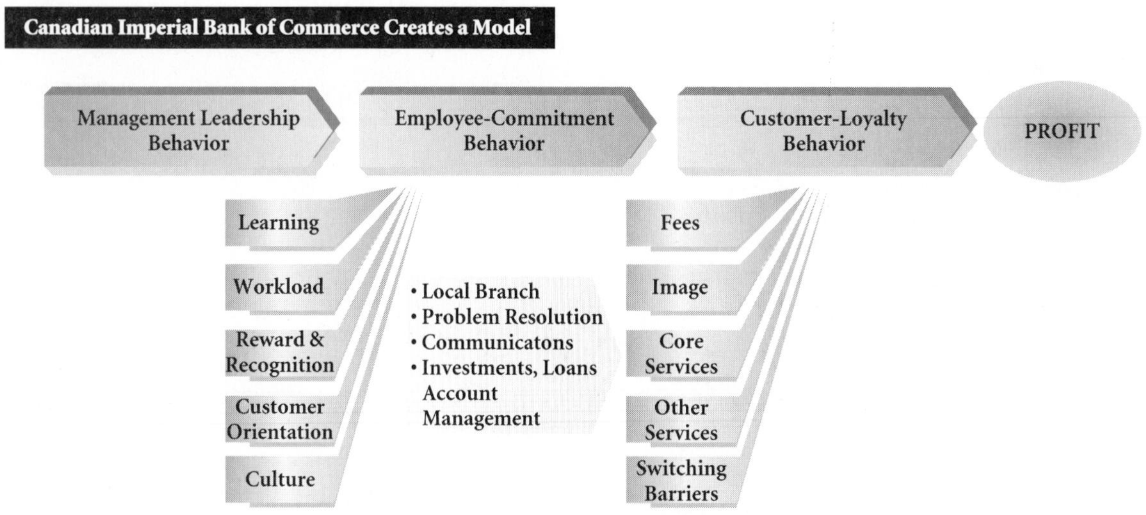

CIBC's model asserts that profit is driven by customer behavior, which is driven by employee commitment, which is influenced by leadership from management. CIBC created parallel models for four customer groups: personal groups (consumers), small businesses, large businesses and insurance groups. The bank used surveys to gather the considerable information required for analyzing the links. It also invested in a customer-information warehouse, with more than 1,000 data attributes per customer and 25 rolling months of data.

From that information, CIBC, with the help of consultants, was able to define customer-loyalty variables. Variables included customers' intentions—to continue using the banking services purchased, to recommend the bank to other customers, to purchase more of the bank's services, and to use the bank's services exclusively. CIBC then linked those loyalty variables to their drivers: what customers thought about core services, noncore services, banking fees, the bank's image and barriers to switching banks. Finally, it elaborated each loyalty driver for its own drivers. For example, it found that core-services loyalty is linked to such factors as customers' evaluation of the local branch and the bank's efficiency in resolving problems.

The model helped CIBC managers identify key relationships. For example, they found that a 1-point increase in any of the loyalty-behavior elements increases profits by $0.60 per month per customer. They also found that a 5 percent increase in employee commitment yields a 2 percent increase in customer loyalty, which increases profitability by $72 million annually.

The BFI Story In 1998, BFI (now part of Arizona-based Allied Waste) was the second-largest waste-disposal company in North America, serving both business and household customers throughout the United States, Canada, Europe, the Middle East and the Pacific Rim. It had revenues of $4.7 billion and profits of $338 million.

But BFI wasn't always so profitable.[4] From 1990 to 1993, its customer defection rate was 11 percent to 13 percent per year. The company tried rigorous contract enforcement, price reductions, customer newsletters and other relationship-marketing activities. Nothing helped. Managers developed a comprehensive customer-satisfaction management and tracking program, surveying customers in each locale quarterly and reporting results to each collection district for action. It tried incentive compensation, recognition programs and more internal communications. Still customer satisfaction declined, and customer defection increased.

But once BFI senior executives determined that cutting customer turnover by 1 percent would yield nearly $41 million in pretax profit, they began to focus on customer-satisfaction drivers. With the aid of a consultant, BFI developed a complete set of links between actions and profits.

The model helped BFI managers look at the specific drivers of customer satisfaction. They were able to see that customers' perceptions of BFI's dependability were key. That led them to look at breaches in service and determine that missed pickups had the largest effect on how customers perceived service dependability. As BFI managers studied the causes of missed pickups, they were able to identify measures to reduce them, such as training drivers better, standardizing procedures, offering incentive compensation, improving driver communication with central dispatch and capturing customer information. They prioritized the measures and directed all 180 collection districts to implement them.

Defection dropped to less than 10 percent, and profits increased. BFI was able to see a path from perceived service dependability to customer satisfaction to reduced defection—to profit. A 2-point gain in service dependability led to a 1-point gain in overall customer satisfaction, which led to a 1 percent decline in customer defection, which produced a pretax increase in profits of $41 million. (See "How Missed Trash Pickups Affect Profits.")

A Decision-Making Tool

To improve decision making, managers must trace how company actions affect profitability overall and across the entire enterprise. As its name implies, the action-profit linkage model helps managers investigate the relationships between action and profit. (See "The Action-Profit Linkage Model.") It lets them make informed decisions that enable actions to achieve the highest possible profit.

HOW MISSED TRASH PICKUPS AFFECT PROFITS

BFI, a waste-disposal company, wanted to know why its customer-defection rate was so high. It developed a model to learn what drove customer satisfaction and to examine how an action—for example, missed pickups—affected profitability. (See "Tracing the Sources of Profit".)

BFI managers began with customer satisfaction and worked backward. Their measurement program indicated that customer satisfaction was tied to customer perceptions of a variety of factors, including billing, customer service, waste bins, sales representatives, etc. The most powerful perception was service dependability, and the company focused its efforts here. A root-cause analysis revealed that perceived dependability was directly related to the number of scheduled pickups that truck drivers missed.

A second root-cause analysis led to the main causes for the missed pickups, such as inadequate training, confusing procedures, incorrect route addresses, etc. Managers were then able to identify the most cost-effective corrective actions, and invest in programs to implement them. The model thus forced managers to find the best ways of reducing customer losses.

Tracing the Sources of Profit

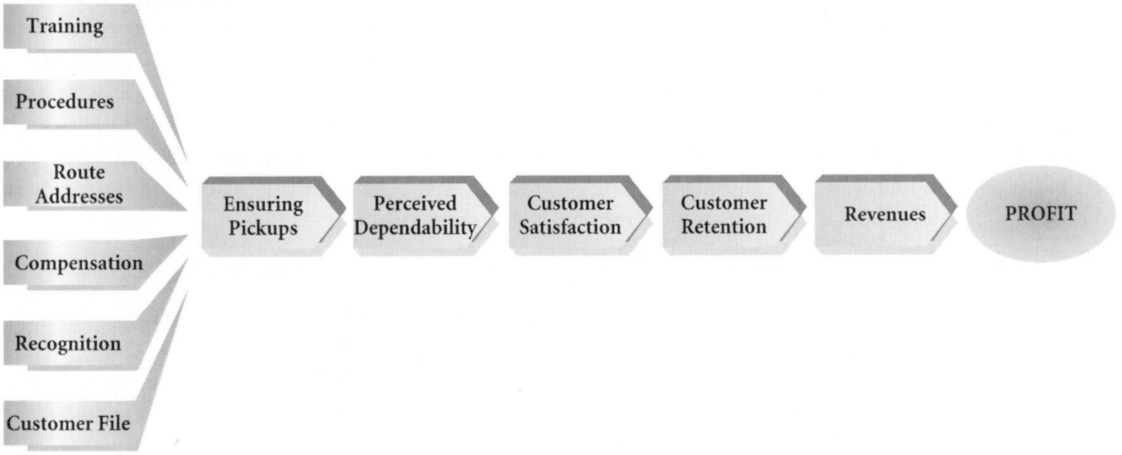

Linking action and profit isn't a new idea, but the other models are generally implemented on a limited scale or within specific functions. (See "How Other Models Compare With the APL Model.")

The APL model has several advantages over other models. First, it focuses attention on the company's specific actions and their effects on employees, customers and, ultimately, corporate profitability. The focus is not limited to the pursuit of intermediate goals such as customer satisfaction, loyalty or quality. That distinction is important because actions, unlike customer satisfaction and loyalty, are directly related to revenues and costs and are therefore accountable—also because the relationship between customer satisfaction and profitability is neither simple nor consistent across all companies.

HOW OTHER MODELS COMPARE WITH THE APL MODEL

Service-Profit Chain (SPC) The SPC which asserts that employee satisfaction is related to customer satisfaction and that the latter benefits profitability, is a special case of the action-profit linkage models. However, it omits drivers other than those of employee satisfaction. Moreover, it only *assumes* the link between customer satisfaction and company profitability. It does not specifically analyze or confirm it. The APL model, in contrast, considers the actions needed to set the full chain of effects in motion and evaluates links from an action all the way to corporate profitability.

Return on Quality (ROQ) The ROQ framework, which says that you can trace improved company profitability to its drivers through a chain of variables, is also a special case of the APL model.[2] However, the ROQ concerns itself only with improving product quality. Although quality is without question an important potential profit driver, it is not the only one. The APL allows for possible parallel chains of effects.

Balanced Scorecard The balanced scorecard concept focuses on the drivers of corporate performance.[3] The idea is to use those drivers in a management system to implement strategy. Like the APL model, the balanced scorecard emphasizes establishing links among key performance metrics. It relies on increased use of both leading and lagging performance indicators—and both financial and nonfinancial performance metrics linked to strategy. However, the APL model focuses more on the company's actions. It also directs management to establish the actual observed relationships between the organization's measures and to identify the links that lead to the most profitable actions. Hence the balanced scorecard and the APL model work together: The APL model helps make the drivers and links more explicit and so supports the strategy implementation that the balanced scorecard offers.

Customer Profitability Analysis The goal of this approach is to assess what drives customer revenues and costs using activity based costing—and thereby to determine the profitability of individual customers. Activity based costing focuses on determining the company activities that cause costs to occur, rather than on merely allocating what has been spent. The idea is to understand cost drivers better and then relate costs to products, services and customers.[4]

However, unlike the APL model, customer profitability analysis does not allow for *network effects*—how the behavior of one customer or a customer segment affects other customers or segments. Thus companies cannot assess the total profitability of serving customers, which might be greater or less than the profitability that results from deducting allocated costs from direct revenues.

[1] J.L. Heskett, W.E. Sasser, Jr., and L.A. Schlesinger, *The Service Profit Chain: How Leading Companies Link Profit and Growth to Loyalty, Satisfaction, and Value* (New York: The Free Press, 1997).
[2] R.T. Rust, A.J. Zahorik, and T.L. Keiningham, "Return on Quality (ROQ) Making Service Quality Financially Accountable," *Journal of Marketing* 59, no. 2 (April 1995): 58–70.
[3] R.S. Kaplan and D.P. Norton, *The Balanced Scorecard: Translating Strategy into Action* (Boston: Harvard Business School Press, 1996); and R.S. Kaplan and D.P. Norton, *The Strategy-Focused Organization* (Boston: Harvard Business School Press, 2001).
[4] R.S. Kaplan and R. Cooper, *Cost and Effect: Using Integrated Cost Systems to Drive Profitability and Performance* (Boston: Harvard Business School Press, 1998).

Second, APL fosters an investment-based approach to managing the trade-offs in decision making because managers link their actions to overall corporate profitability, not to local consequences. Defining the links between investment choices and corporate profitability will help improve decisions made to implement strategy.

Third, companies can adapt the APL model to many business situations. Links that drive profit differ across actions, customer segments, industries and company size, and APL's flexibility lets managers explore multiple routes to long-term profitability.

Finally, the APL model is not tied to any specific data-collection or estimation procedure. It uses an iterative process that starts with estimating links. As companies accumulate data and learning, the process becomes more data-driven and the estimates more comprehensive. Developing and testing their customized models, companies begin to limit their investments to those that improve profitability; the model's output discourages investment in unprofitable areas.

From Action to Profitability

A company using the APL model begins with corporate strategy and moves from there to component one, company actions. Once the enterprise has decided which actions it wants to explore, it can begin defining the path from the action to corporate profitability. The corporate-profitability segment of the model then feeds back into the corporate strategy. In other words, as managers articulate the links from an action to profitability, they get valuable insight into improving the business strategy.

Component two is delivered product/service—everything the business makes available to customers for purchase. It comprises product attributes, brand, customer-service activities and more.

The elements of component two link to several forms of component three, customer actions. The first subgroup is perceptions—what customers think about the delivered product or service. Customer perceptions, which are based on direct experience with the product or on the company's communications, are indispensable for linking actions to profit, since they represent the first step in the buying process.[5]

Perceptions can determine whether existing and new customers feel inclined to buy or rebuy the product. Thus, perceptions drive the second customer-actions subgroup, attitudes, including customer satisfaction and new-customer attraction.[6] Attitudes, in turn, drive the third customer-actions subgroup, overt behavior—customers' purchasing responses.

Major component four, economic impact, takes the cost of the company action and the revenue resulting from customers' overt behavior—and arrives at the action's contribution to profit. Some aspects of customers' overt behavior (say, new-business referral) determine the number of customers the company will receive. Other aspects (say, repeat buying) determine the revenue each customer will generate per year. The number of customers times the average customer revenue will yield the total revenue all customers generate.

Companies can attribute the cost of an action either directly to individual customers (as in the case of improving the quality of airline meals) or indirectly (for example, in adding financial-planning staff). After managers deduct the cost from customer revenue, they arrive at the profitability of each customer group. The last step is to roll up all customer-group profitability results into corporate profitability. Managers of companies with few customers do not need to establish customer groups or segments, but can do the analysis on individual customers.

Frequently, an action intended for a specific customer group can change the profitability of other groups. When Microsoft launched its Windows 2000 Professional Edition to its business customers, some of its introductory advertising also induced individuals to buy the consumer version. Both the intended effect of its business-to-business advertising, as well as its unintended effect on consumers influenced Microsoft's total profitability. The APL model accounts for such network effects by incorporating and measuring links between products or business units.

Developing a Customized Model

The general APL model is just a starting point for exploring relationships among key performance metrics. The process of customizing the general APL model is just as valuable as the final model with defined links because it gets managers to focus on relationships. For that reason, customization should involve a wide cross section of the senior management team.

Establish Links The first phase in customizing the APL model involves laying out the links hypothesized from reviewing the business situation. The links are based on managers' experience and intuition. Employees and customers also may be a helpful source of hypotheses about links involving their own behavior. CIBC, for example, defined the link from its service process to customer loyalty by surveying employees.

Define Metrics and Collect Data In the second phase, the company defines metrics for each variable in the model and collects data to test the validity of the customized model it has hypothesized. (See "Guidelines for Measurement and Data Collection.")

A company will seldom have all the necessary metrics. Even a business with abundant data in their information systems may, like CIBC, decide to make additional investments in IT or in data warehousing to compile all the information.

To develop metrics for the model, a company can:

- extract metrics (for example, average customer revenue) from its information system;

GUIDELINES FOR MEASUREMENT AND DATA COLLECTION

It is helpful to consider sample measures for variables in each component of the APL model. For example, the variables for component one; company actions, can be measured either with a simple yes or no as to whether the company has taken the action—or with some numeric value. (See "Sample Measures for Variables in the APL Model's Main Components.") The approach helps managers analyze the effect of the action as they progressively link it to other variables in the model. Once they have finished analyzing the links, they can determine the effect of the action on profit.

Sample Measures for Variables in the APL Model's Main Components

Model Component	*Variables*	*Sample Metrics*	*Data Source*
Company Actions	Operations	Use of a particular process-design alternative	All from company records
	Information technology	Use of enterprise-resource-planning software	
	Human resources	Number and type of training programs	
	Marketing & sales	Local vs. centralized customer service	
	Finance & accounting	Debt-to-equity ratio	
	External	Number of lobbyists, public-relations budget	
Delivered Product or Service	Product/service characteristics	Failure rate, performance specifications	Company testing records
	Employee actions	Response time to fulfill customer orders	Mystery shopper study
	Price schedule	Ratio of price to average price of competitors	
	Customer communications	Number of ad exposures per month	Reader/viewer survey
Customer Actions	Perceptions*	(All based on 7- or 10-point rating scales)	All from syndicated survey research on a representative cross section of existing and prospective customers
	Product/service	Service dependability	
	Price	Reasonableness of price, frequency of discount	
	Buying process	Ease of ordering, on-time delivery	
	Relationship	Ability to rely on sales rep expertise	
	Brand/company image	Industry leader, Innovativeness	
	Attitudes*		
	New-customer attraction	Purchase-Intention rating scale (5- or 11-point)	All from syndicated customer surveys
	Customer satisfaction	Overall-satisfaction rating scale (5-, 7-, 10- or 11-point)	

	Overt behavior		
	Initial purchase	Percentage of customers who have purchased at least once	All obtained from customers or syndicated tracking survey of all customers in market
	Account share	Percentage of all purchases of product/service per period	
	Repurchase	Percentage of customers making repeat purchases	
	New-business referrals	Percentage of customers making a referral, average number of referrals each	
	Price acceptance	Average price paid by customers	
Economic Impact	Cost of action	Expense of action or investment cost (dollars)	General ledger
	Customer revenues	Sales to specific customers per period (dollars)	Historical account records

*Metrics for the perceptions and attitudes variables in the customer actions component are especially important because the success of efforts to link actions to profits depends on them. Although some managers may have reservations about the accuracy of measures for such variables, our tools and procedures have been affective in establishing links.

- develop metrics (for example, customer-defection rates or activity-based cost of company actions) from data in its information system;
- develop metrics (for example, sales-call frequency) from data to be captured by its information system;
- purchase metrics (for example, the buying patterns of prospective customers or objective service-quality indicators) from research companies, syndicated data sources, and the like; or
- generate metrics (for example, customer-satisfaction and perceptions measures) from its own or commissioned surveys.

There is also the question of the appropriate unit of analysis for the metrics. For example, should a bank gather customer-survey data on individual customers, branch offices, trading areas, regions or across the company as a whole? Should it gather the data once or repeatedly? For some links, such as the link from customer-perception metrics to attitude metrics, the unit of analysis should be the individual customer. For others, such as the link between the delivered product or service and customer perceptions, the unit of analysis should be the operating unit. If the company is a bank, the operating unit might be the branch office, and the metric could be a mystery-shopper study of service quality. The bank would then aggregate its individual-customer-perception ratings into an average for the branch and relate that to the service-quality metric for that branch.

Sometimes the only unit of analysis available is the company as a whole. For example, IT limitations may force a bank to measure customer defection for all its customers rather than for each branch individually. In that case, the bank would gather the measures over several succeeding time periods.

Analyze Links In the third phase, the company assesses the strength of the links through a statistical analysis of the collected data. Multiple-regression analysis works best because it provides numerical estimates of the strength of relationships between predictor (or cause) variables and a single dependent (or effect) variable.

Assessing the proposed model's fit is important. If the fit is poor, the company must return to the first phase to identify missing elements or variables—or to the second phase to get better metrics. If the fit is adequate, the company retains the strongest links for interpretation and application.

As the company evaluates the initial model, it will inevitably add links and drop any that lack enough evidence of a strong relationship. Phase three is critical because it is here that a final model emerges. The focus then shifts to applying the model to support decision making.

Updating the Customized Model

Companies should monitor the customized APL model for any changes in the links among metrics. External factors can change. For example, customer expectations might increase; a new competitor might emerge. Internal factors also could change—for example, if the company undergoes a reorganization. Even the passage of time may alter the relationships among model elements.

Updating requires reassessing metrics and links. Companies with a relatively unstable operating environment may have to update more often than those with stable environments, but the benefits of maintaining the model—continued insight into actions that are profitable—make the frequent adjustment worth the trouble.

To see how a model can expand, consider a hotel with this chain of links: incentive compensation to the cleaning staff → cleanliness of guest rooms → customer satisfaction → customer retention → customer revenues. Over time, the higher levels of customer satisfaction lead to better interaction between customers and customer-contact employees, which increases the number of compliments about the staff. Employee job satisfaction increases because of expressions of customer support, employee turnover is reduced, and personnel hiring and training costs go down. Thus the model gains several links, and the original action "incentive compensation to cleaning staff" has an increased impact on profitability. That increase would be lost on managers who did not conduct such an analysis, limiting their ability to identify the actions and investments that would lead to the most profit.

Some Implementation Advice

Managers who develop and implement sound APL models will be the first to agree that measurement is difficult and evaluating causal relationships between metrics even more so. Often a company cannot develop model elements in rapid succession. For example, it cannot measure the impact of a new advertising campaign on customer perceptions without a sufficient waiting period. Not allowing for the appropriate leading or lagging indicators can nullify or distort relationships.

Sometimes metrics may interact to affect the resulting variable more severely than they do individually, which makes it harder to analyze links. Organizational changes, new products, new technologies and new sales channels—all require that a company rethink its APL model.

Such challenges to accurately estimating links do not prevent a company from building an APL model. Rather, they point to the need for the right model-development environment:

- *Managers must be committed to the effort.* Senior managers must consistently support the process of identifying and measuring causal relationships. They could demonstrate importance by asking about the effort in monthly operating reviews, for example.
- *Approximations are better than nothing.* Managers must be willing to accept approximations and predictions that point in the right direction, rather than insist on perfect estimation and wind up with no way to trace the impact of an action on profit.
- *Keep it simple.* The model should have an intuitive or common-sense basis so that the rest of the organization can readily understand it.
- *Carefully articulate and communicate the model.* Managers should communicate the model throughout management ranks and actively encourage its use to support decision making. The simpler the model, the easier that will be. The model's introduction should be treated like any other organizational change.
- *Consider a partial model.* Customizing a complete APL model involves significant management time, data costs, analytical effort and internal communication. It may not be worth it, depending on how much the model improves decision making and resource allocation. A partial model, one that features only certain actions or potential actions, may be a more cost-effective approach.
- *Don't minimize the process benefit.* Companies can benefit by using the model to guide their thinking about the links among their own metrics, even if they do not gather data to test the model fully.

The APL model helps managers understand how they can create superior value and competitive advantage for their company. By identifying the most useful linkages between actions and profit, the model fosters a common management focus on the variables that matter most. (See "Why Use the Action-Profit Linkage Model?") Even more important, the model helps develop disciplined thinking about profit drivers by tracing them back through the customer, the product offering and ultimately the

WHY USE THE ACTION-PROFIT LINKAGE MODEL?

The APL model provides a management tool that:

- focuses on the drivers of value and how managers can create value;
- aids in identifying and measuring causal relationships;
- refines the balanced scorecard and shareholder-value models, making them more specific;
- leads managers to be more cross-functional and focus on profitability rather than on a single goal such as customer satisfaction;
- narrows attention to specific actions and their payoffs;
- encourages managers to link all actions to overall corporate profitability; and
- is easily adapted to all organization types.

company's actions. Getting the management team focused on a common thought process is among the most important things a CEO can do to improve managers' decision making in both strategy and strategy implementation.

Additional Resources

Much of what has been written about profitability modeling does not take a cross-functional approach. Author Marc Epstein's "Customer Profitability Analysis," published last year by the Society of Management Accountants of Canada, integrates material on activity-based costing, marketing considerations and performance drivers.

Epstein and Bill Birchard's *Counting What Counts: Turning Corporate Accountability to Competitive Advantage*, published in 1999 by Perseus Books, presents a broad model that demonstrates the importance of identifying and the measuring performance drivers and the causal relationships between them.

The balanced scorecard is another valuable approach that works well with the action-profit linkage model. Robert Kapian and David Norton offer a complete balanced-scorecard discussion, including an extensive treatment of strategy maps, in "The Strategy-Focused Organization: How Balanced Scorecard Companies Thrive in the New Business Environment."

Analyzing links is perhaps the hardest part of profitability modeling. In their 1997 Free Press book, "The Service Profit Chain," James L. Heskett and colleagues provide many examples of how companies linked employee satisfaction, customer satisfaction and corporate profits. Anthony Rucci, Steven Kim and Richard Quinn look at how to identify and measure links among employee behavior, customer satisfaction and profitability in a January-February 1998 Harvard Business Review article.

Customer satisfaction is at the heart of many profit relationships. Michael Johnson and Anders Gustafeson offer a comprehensive discussion in "Improving Customer Satisfaction, Loyalty, and Profit: An Integrated Measurement and Management System" (San Francisco: Jossey-Bass, 2000). And in a Fall 1999 Marketing Management article, Timothy Keiningham and colleagues look at how one company used customer-satisfaction information to improve market share and profitability.

References

1. M.J. Epstein, P. Kumar and R.A. Westbrook, "The Drivers of Customer and Corporate Profitability: Modeling, Measuring and Managing the Causal Relationships," *Advances in Management Accounting* 9 (2000): 43–72.
2. A.J. Rucci, S.P. Kim and R.T. Quinn, "The Employes-Customer-Profit Chain at Sears," *Harvard Business Review* 76 (January-February 1998): 83–97.
3. J. Tofani, "The People Connection: Changing Stakeholder Behavior To Improve Performance at CIBC" (presentation at the 12th Annual Customer Satisfaction & Quality Conference of the American Marketing Association and American Society for Quality, San Antonio, Texas, February 22, 2000).
4. R.A. Westbrook, *BFI: Customer Satisfaction Program* (Houston: Rice University, 2000).
5. Our categorization reflects an elaboration of the useful taxonomy proposed by R. Kaplan and D. Norton in *The Balanced Scorecard: Translating Strategy into Action* (Boston: Harvard Business School Press, 1996).
6. Customer perceptions were first identified as the drivers of customer satisfaction in R.A. Westbrook, "Sources of Satisfaction with Retail Outlets," *Journal of Retailing* 57 (Fall 1981): 68–85.

Case 1 Sullivan Ford Auto World

CHRISTOPHER LOVELOCK

A young health care manager unexpectedly finds herself running a family-owned car dealership that is in trouble. She is very concerned about the poor performance of the service department and wonders whether a turnaround is possible.

Viewed from Wilson Avenue, the dealership presented a festive sight. Strings of triangular pennants in red, white, and blue fluttered gaily in the late afternoon breeze. Rows of new-model cars gleamed and winked in the sunlight. Geraniums graced the flowerbeds outside the showroom entrance. A huge rotating sign at the corner of Wilson Avenue and Route 78 sported the Ford logo and identified the business as Sullivan Ford Auto World. Banners below urged "Let's Make a Deal!"

Inside the handsome, high-ceilinged showroom, three of the new-model Fords were on display: a dark-green Explorer SUV, a red Mustang convertible, and a white Taurus sedan. Each vehicle was polished to a high sheen. Two groups of customers were chatting with salespeople, and a middle-aged man sat in the driver's seat of the Mustang, studying the controls.

Upstairs in the comfortably furnished general manager's office, Carol Sullivan-Diaz finished running another spreadsheet analysis on her laptop. She felt tired and depressed. Her father, Walter Sullivan, had died four weeks earlier at age 56 of a sudden heart attack. As executor of his estate, the bank had asked her to temporarily assume the position of general manager of the dealership. The only visible changes she had made to her father's office were installing a fax machine and laser printer, but she had been very busy analyzing the current position of the business.

Sullivan-Diaz did not like the look of the numbers on the printout. Auto World's financial situation had been deteriorating for 18 months, and it had been running in the red for the first half of the current year. Despite low interest rates, new-car sales had declined, reflecting a turndown in the regional economy. Margins had been squeezed by promotions and other efforts to move new cars off the lot. Industry forecasts of future sales were discouraging, and so were her own financial projections for Auto World's sales department. Service revenues, which were below average for a dealership of this size, had also declined, although the service department still made a small surplus.

Had she had made a mistake last week, Carol wondered, in turning down Bill Froelich's offer to buy the business? It was true that the price offered had been substantially below the offer from Froelich that her father had rejected two years earlier, but the business had been more profitable then.

THE SULLIVAN FAMILY

Walter Sullivan had purchased a small Ford dealership in 1981, renaming it Sullivan's Auto World, and had built it up to become one of the best known in the metropolitan area. In 1996, he had borrowed heavily to purchase the current site at a major suburban highway intersection, in an area of town with many new housing developments.

There had been a dealership on the site, but the buildings were 30 years old. Sullivan had retained the service and repair bays but had torn down the showroom in front of them and replaced it with an attractive modern facility. On moving to the new location, which was substantially larger than the old one, he had renamed his business Sullivan Ford Auto World.

Everybody had seemed to know Walt Sullivan. He had been a consummate showman and entrepreneur, appearing in his own radio and television commercials and active in community affairs. His approach to car sales had emphasized promotions, discounts, and deals in order to maintain volume. He was never happier than when making a sale.

Carol Sullivan-Diaz, aged 28, was the eldest of Walter and Carmen Sullivan's three daughters. After obtaining a bachelor's degree in economics, she had gone on to take an MBA degree and had then embarked on a career in health care management. She was married to Dr. Roberto Diaz, a surgeon at St. Luke's Hospital. Her 20-year-old twin sisters, Gail and Joanne, who were students at the nearby university, lived with their mother.

In her own student days, Sullivan-Diaz had worked part time in her father's business on secretarial and bookkeeping tasks and also as a service writer in the service department, so she was quite familiar with the operations of the dealership. At business school, she had decided on a career in health care management. After graduation, she had worked as an executive assistant to the president of St. Luke's, a large teaching hospital. Two years later, she joined Metropolitan Health Plan as assistant director of marketing, a position she had now held for almost three years. Her responsibilities included attracting new members, complaint handling, market research, and member retention programs.

Carol's employer had given her a six-week leave of absence to put her father's affairs in order. She doubted that she could extend that leave much beyond the two weeks still remaining. Neither she nor other family members were interested in making a career of running the dealership. However, she was prepared to take time out from her health care career to work on a turnaround if that seemed a viable proposition. She had been successful in her present job and believed it would not be difficult to find another health management position in the future.

THE DEALERSHIP

Like other car dealerships, Sullivan Ford Auto World operated both sales and service departments, often referred to in the trade as "front end" and "back end," respectively. Both new and used vehicles were sold, as a high proportion of new car and van purchases involved trading in the purchaser's existing vehicle. Auto World would also buy well-maintained used cars at auction for resale. Purchasers who decided that they could not afford a new car would often buy a "preowned" vehicle instead, whereas shoppers who came in looking for a used car could sometimes be persuaded to buy a new one. Before being put on sale, used vehicles were carefully serviced, with parts being replaced as needed, and were then thoroughly cleaned by a detailer whose services were hired as needed. Dents and other blemishes were removed at a nearby body shop, and occasionally the vehicle's paintwork was resprayed.

The front end of the dealership employed a sales manager, seven salespeople, an office manager, and a secretary. One of the salespeople had given notice and would be leaving at the end of the following week. The service department, when fully staffed, consisted of a service manager, a parts supervisor, nine mechanics, and two service writers. The Sullivan twins often worked part time as service writers, filling in at busy periods, when one of the other writers was sick or on vacation, or when—as currently—there was an unfilled vacancy. The job entailed scheduling appointments for repairs and maintenance, writing up each work order, calling customers with repair estimates, and assisting customers when they returned to pick up the cars and pay for the work that had been done.

Sullivan-Diaz knew from her own experience as a service writer that it could be a stressful job. Few people liked to be without their car, even for a day. When a car broke down or was having problems, the owner was often nervous about how long it would take to get it fixed and, if the warranty had expired, how much the labor and parts would cost. Customers were quite unforgiving when a problem was not fixed completely on the first attempt and they had to return their vehicle for further work.

Major mechanical failures were not usually difficult to repair, although the parts-replacement costs might be expensive. It was often the "little" things, such as water leaks and wiring problems, that were the most difficult to diagnose and correct, and it might be necessary for the customer to return two or three times before such a problem was resolved. In these situations, parts and materials costs were relatively low, but labor costs mounted up quickly, being charged out at $45 an hour. Customers could sometimes be quite abusive, yelling at service writers over the phone or arguing with service writers, mechanics, and the service manager in person.

Turnover in the service writer job was high, which was one reason why Carol—and more recently her sisters—had often been pressed into service by their father to "hold the fort," as he described it. More than once, she had seen an exasperated service writer respond sharply to a complaining customer or hang up on one who was being abusive over the telephone. Gail and Joanne were currently taking turns to cover the vacant position, but there were times when both of them had classes and the dealership had only one service writer on duty.

By national standards, Sullivan Ford Auto World stood toward the lower end of medium-sized dealerships, selling around 1,100 cars a year, equally divided between new and used vehicles. In the most recent year, its revenues totaled $26.6 million from new- and used-car sales and $2.9 million from service and parts, down from $30.5 million and $3.6 million, respectively, in the previous year. Although the unit value of car sales was high, the margins were quite low, with margins for new cars being substantially lower than for used ones. Industry guidelines suggested that the contribution margin, known as the departmental selling gross, from car sales should be about 5.5 percent of sales revenues and around 25 percent of revenues from service. In a typical dealership, 60 percent of the selling gross had traditionally come from sales and 40 percent from service, but the balance was shifting from sales to service. The selling gross was then applied to fixed expenses, such as administrative salaries, rent or mortgage payments, and utilities.

For the most recent 12 months at Auto World, Sullivan-Diaz had determined that the selling gross figures were 4.6 percent and 24 percent, respectively, both of them lower than in the previous year and insufficient to cover the dealership's fixed expenses. Her father had made no mention of financial difficulties, and she had been shocked to learn from the bank after his death that Auto World had been two months behind in mortgage payments on the property. Further analysis also showed that accounts payable had also risen sharply in the previous six months. Fortunately, the dealership held a large insurance policy on Sullivan's life, and the proceeds from this had been more than sufficient to bring mortgage payments up to date, pay down all overdue accounts, and leave some funds for future contingencies.

OUTLOOK

The opportunities for expanding new-car sales did not appear promising, given declining consumer confidence and recent layoffs at several local plants that were expected to hurt the local economy. However, promotional incentives had reduced the inventory to manageable levels. From discussions with Larry Winters, Auto World's sales manager, Sullivan-Diaz had concluded that costs could be cut by not replacing the departing sales rep, maintaining inventory at its current reduced level, and trying to make more efficient use of advertising and promotion. Although he did not have Walter's exuberant personality, Winters had been Auto World's leading sales rep before being promoted and had shown strong managerial capabilities in his current position.

As she reviewed the figures for the service department, Sullivan-Diaz wondered what potential might exist for improving its sales volume and selling gross. Her father had never been very interested in the parts and service business, seeing it simply as a necessary adjunct of the dealership. "Customers always seem to be miserable back there," he had once remarked to her. "But here in the front end, everybody's happy when someone buys a new car." The service facility was not easily visible from the main highway, being hidden behind the showroom. Although the building looked old and greasy, the equipment itself was modern and well maintained. There was sufficient capacity to handle more repair work, but a higher volume would require hiring one or more new mechanics.

Customers were required to bring cars in for servicing before 8:30 A.M. After parking their cars, customers entered the service building by a side door and waited their turn to see the service writers, who occupied a cramped room with peeling paint and an interior window overlooking the service bays. Customers stood while work orders for their cars were prepared. Ringing telephones frequently interrupted the process. Filing cabinets containing customer records and other documents lined the far wall of the room.

If the work were of a routine nature, such as an oil change or tuneup, the customer was given an estimate immediately. For more complex jobs, the customer would be called with an estimate later in the morning once the car had been examined. Customers were required to pick up their cars by 6:00 P.M. on the day the work was completed. On several occasions, Carol had urged her father to computerize the service work-order process, but he had never acted on her suggestions, so all orders continued to be handwritten on large yellow sheets, with carbon copies below.

The service manager, Rick Obert, who was in his late forties, had held the position since Auto World opened at its current location. The Sullivan family considered him to be technically skilled, and he managed the mechanics effectively. However, his manner with customers could be gruff and argumentative.

CUSTOMER SURVEY RESULTS

Another set of data that Sullivan-Diaz had studied carefully were the results of the customer satisfaction surveys that were mailed to the dealership monthly by a research firm retained by the Ford Motor Company. Purchasers of all new Ford cars were sent a questionnaire by mail within 30 days of making the purchase and asked to use a five-point scale to rate their satisfaction with the dealership sales department, vehicle preparation, and the characteristics of the vehicle itself. The questionnaire asked how likely the purchaser would be to recommend the dealership, the salesperson, and the manufacturer to someone else. Other questions asked whether the customers had been introduced to the dealer's service department and been given explanations on what to do if their cars needed service. Finally, there were some classification questions relating to customer demographics.

A second survey was sent to new-car purchasers nine months after they had bought their cars. This questionnaire began by asking about satisfaction with the vehicle and then asked customers whether they had taken their vehicles to the selling dealer for service of any kind. If so, respondents were then asked to rate the service department on 14 attributes—ranging from the attitudes of service personnel to the quality of the work performed—and then to rate their overall satisfaction with service from the dealer.

Customers were also asked about where they would go in the future for maintenance service, minor mechanical and electrical repairs, major repairs in those same categories, and body work. The options listed for service were selling dealer, another Ford dealer, "some other place," or "do-it-yourself." Finally, there were questions about overall satisfaction with the dealer sales department and the dea lership in general, as well as the likelihood of their purchasing another Ford Motor Company product and buying it from the same dealership.

Dealers received monthly reports summarizing customer ratings of their dealership for the most recent month and for several previous months. To provide a comparison to how other Ford dealerships performed, the reports also included regional and national rating averages. After analysis, completed questionnaires were returned to the dealership; because these included each customer's name, a dealer could see which customers were satisfied and which were not.

In the 30-day survey of new purchasers, Auto World achieved better than average ratings on most dimensions. One finding that puzzled Carol was that almost 90 percent of respondents answered "yes" when asked whether someone from Auto World had explained what to do if they needed service, but less than a third said that they had been introduced to someone in the service department. She resolved to ask Larry Winters about this discrepancy.

The nine-month survey findings disturbed her. Although vehicle ratings were in line with national averages, the overall level of satisfaction with service at Auto World was consistently low, placing it in the bottom 25 percent of all Ford dealerships.

The worst ratings for service concerned promptness of writing up orders, convenience of scheduling the work, convenience of service hours, and appearance of the service department. On length of time to complete the work, availability of needed parts, and quality of work done ("Was it fixed right?"), Auto World's rating was close to the average. For interpersonal variables, such as attitude of service department personnel, politeness, understanding of customer problems, and explanation of work performed, its ratings were relatively poor.

When Sullivan-Diaz reviewed the individual questionnaires, she found that there was a wide degree of variation between customers' responses on these interpersonal variables, ranging all the way across a 5-point scale from "completely satisfied" to "very dissatisfied." Curious, she had gone to the service files and examined the records for several dozen customers who had recently completed the nine-month surveys. At least part of the ratings could be explained by which service writers the customer had dealt with. Those who had been served two or more times by her sisters, for instance, gave much better ratings than those who had dealt primarily with Jim Fiskell, the service writer who had recently quit.

Perhaps the most worrying responses were those relating to customers' likely use of Auto World's service department in the future. More than half indicated that they would use another Ford dealer or "some other place" for maintenance service, such as oil change, lubrication, or tuneup, or for minor mechanical and electrical repairs. About 30 percent would use another source for major repairs. The rating for overall satisfaction with the selling dealer after nine months was below average, and the customer's likelihood of purchasing from the same dealership again was a full point below that of buying another Ford product.

OPTIONS

Sullivan-Diaz pushed aside the spreadsheets she had printed out and shut down her laptop. It was time to go home for dinner. She saw the options for the dealership as basically twofold: Either prepare the business for an early sale at what would amount to a distress price, or take a year or two to try to turn it around financially. In the latter instance, if the turnaround succeeded, the business could subsequently be sold at a higher price than it presently commanded, or the family could install a general manager to run the dealership for them.

Bill Froelich, owner of another nearby dealership and three more in nearby cities, had offered to buy Auto World for a price that represented a fair valuation of the net assets, according to Auto World's accountants, plus $250,000 in goodwill. However, the rule of thumb when the auto industry was enjoying good times was that goodwill should be valued at $1,200 per vehicle sold each year. Carol knew that Froelich was eager to develop a network of dealerships in order to achieve economies of scale. His prices on new cars were very competitive, and his nearest dealership clustered several franchises—Ford, Lincoln-Mercury, Volvo, and Jaguar—on a single large property.

AN UNWELCOME DISTURBANCE

As Carol left her office, she spotted the sales manager coming up the stairs leading from the showroom floor. "Larry," she said, "I've got a question for you."

"Fire away!" replied the sales manager.

"I've been looking at the customer satisfaction surveys. Why aren't our sales reps introducing new customers to the folks in the Service Department? It's supposedly part of our sales protocol, but it seems to be happening only about one-third of the time!"

Larry Winters shuffled his feet. "Well, Carol, basically I leave it to their discretion. We tell them about service, of course, but some of the guys on the floor feel a bit uncomfortable taking folks over to the service bays after they've been in here. It's quite a contrast, if you know what I mean."

Suddenly, the sound of shouting arose from the floor below. A man of about 40, wearing a windbreaker and jeans, was standing in the doorway, yelling at one of the salespeople. The two managers could catch snatches of what he was saying, in between various obscenities:

". . . three visits . . . still not fixed right . . . service stinks . . . who's in charge here?" Everybody else in the showroom had stopped what they were doing and had turned to look at the newcomer.

Winters looked at his young employer and rolled his eyes. "If there was something your dad couldn't stand, it was guys like that, yelling and screaming in the showroom and asking for the boss. Walt would go hide out in his office! Don't worry, Tom'll take care of that fellow and get him out of here. What a jerk!"

"No," said Sullivan-Diaz, "I'll deal with him! One thing I learned when I worked at St. Luke's was that you don't let people yell about their problems in front of everybody else. You take them off somewhere, calm them down, and find out what's bugging them."

She stepped quickly down the stairs, wondering to herself, "What else have I learned in health care that I can apply to this business?"

Study Questions

1. *How does marketing cars differ from marketing service for those same vehicles?*
2. *Compare and contrast the sales and service departments at Auto World.*
3. *Prepare a flow chart of the servicing of a car that requires repair or maintenance*
4. *What useful parallels do you see between running an automobile sales and service dealership and running health care services?*
5. *What advice would you give to Carol Sullivan-Diaz?*

Case 2 Four Customers in Search of Solutions

CHRISTOPHER LOVELOCK

Four telephone subscribers from suburban Toronto call to complain about a variety of problems. How should the telephone company respond to each?

Among the many customers of Bell Canada in Toronto, Ontario, are four individuals living on Willow Street in a middle-class suburb of the city. Each of them has a telephone-related problem and decides to call the company about it.

Winston Chen

Winston Chen grumbles continually about the amount of his home telephone bill (which is, in fact, in the top 2 percent of all household phone bills in Ontario). There are many calls to countries in Southeast Asia on weekday evenings, almost daily calls to Kingston (a smaller city not far from Toronto) around midday, and calls to Vancouver, British Columbia, most weekends. One day, Mr. Chen receives a telephone bill that is even larger than usual. On reviewing the bill, he is convinced that he has been overcharged, so he calls Bell's customer service department to complain and request an adjustment.

Marie Portillo

Marie Portillo has missed several important calls recently because the caller received a busy signal. She phones the telephone company to determine possible solutions to this problem. Ms. Portillo's telephone bill is at the median level for a household subscriber. Most of the calls from her house are local, but there are occasional international calls to Mexico or to countries in South America. She does not subscribe to any value-added services.

Eleanor Vanderbilt

During the past several weeks, Mrs. Vanderbilt has been distressed to receive a series of obscene telephone calls. It sounds like the same person each time. She calls to see whether the telephone company can put a stop to this harassment. Her phone bill is in the bottom 10 percent of all household subscriber bills, and almost all calls are local.

Richard Robbins

For more than a week, the phone line at Rich Robbins's house has been making strange humming and crackling noises, making it difficult to hear what the other person is saying. After two of his friends comment on these distracting noises, Mr. Robbins's calls Bell and reports the problem. His guess is that it is being caused by the answering machine, which is getting old and sometimes loses messages. Mr. Robbins's phone bill is at the 75th percentile for a household subscriber. Most of the calls are made to locations within Canada, usually in the evenings and on weekends, although a few calls are to the United States, too.

Study Questions

1. *Based strictly on the information in the case, how many possibilities do you see to segment the telecommunications market?*
2. *As a customer service rep at the telephone company, how would you address each of the problems and complaints reported?*
3. *Do you see any marketing opportunities for Bell in any of these complaints?*

Case 3 Commerce Bank

FRANCES X. FREI

The hardest thing about becoming a big bank is not becoming a big bank.

—DOUGLAS PAULS, CHIEF FINANCIAL OFFICER

Commerce Bank competes on high cost and high service, offering an appealing branch environment and extended hours of service but paying lower interest rates on deposits than competitors. Should management go ahead with a new concept for attracting customers to the branches called "Retailtainment"?

Deborah Jacovelli looked up from her desk as a big pumpkin, a Dalmation, and a masked crusader ran by her office. It was business as usual at Commerce University, Commerce Bank's Cherry Hill, New Jersey, training center, but it was also Halloween on a rainy day in 2002 and the employees were getting into it with their usual enthusiasm. As dean of Commerce University, Jacovelli had witnessed the development of many innovative methods for energizing the company's employees. Halloween costumes and people decorating their cubicles, hardly typical bank behavior, were not at all strange at Commerce. Jacovelli noticed that someone had adorned the giant "C" character outside her office with a cape.

It took a special kind of person to deliver the high-quality customer service Commerce Bank promised. Happy customers were the bank's top priority. An internal system of incentives and cultural training implemented by Jacovelli and her coworkers to reinforce a deep commitment to "*WOW!*ing" customers included awards, commendations, and compensation, as well as intense training and education. "We want to exceed customers' expectations every time they visit our bank," insisted Commerce Chairman and CEO Vernon W. Hill II. Commerce referred to its branches as "stores" and looked for operational comparisons to retailers such as Starbucks and Home Depot rather than the bank next door. How does Starbucks get you to pay $6 for a cup of coffee?" mused Hill. "It's the retail experience. That's what we care about and it's paying off. Some critics say our stock price is high for the banking sector, but if you look at other power retailers and compare our multiples, we are undervalued." Since 1990, Commerce's stock price had increased twentyfold (**Exhibits 1** and **2** present company financials and branch data.)

Because Commerce encouraged customers to visit its branches, or stores, it wanted the experience to be positive even when the branch was busy. A handful of competitors were beginning to copy some of Commerce's extra service features, such as weekend and evening hours, prompting the bank to be mindful of staying one step ahead. With coffee and newspapers already available to waiting customers, the bank considered adding entertainment to the lobbies of its stores. "Retailtainment," proposed in 2002, was Commerce's latest idea for "*WOW!*ing" customers. Among the ideas piloted as part of this "atmosphere enhancement" concept were free hot dogs, a guitar player and juggler, and an employee on roller blades dressed as a big "C" character. While not completely off the map for a bank that encouraged its employees to dress up in costume, this latest program concerned Jacovelli. She wondered whether customers really wanted to be entertained when they visited a bank branch. Even with a program limited to Fridays, if execution at different branches varied, would the consistency of great service be put at risk? Had the bank, Jacovelli worried, finally taken the retail experience a step too far?

Professor Frances X. Frei and Research Associate Corey Hajim prepared this case. HBS cases are developed solely as the basis for class discussion. Cases are not intended to serve as endorsements, sources of primary data, or illustrations of effective or ineffective management.

EXHIBIT 1a Commerce Bank Income Statement (year ending December 31; $ in thousands)

	12/31/2001	*12/31/2000*	*12/31/1999*	*12/31/1998*
Total interest income	624,986	522,941	392,980	296,765
Total interest expense	218,754	219,976	141,855	116,711
Net interest income	406,232	302,965	251,125	180,054
Provision for loan and lease losses	26,384	13,931	9,175	5,865
Total non-interest income	197,894	155,527	96,831	73,837
Salaries and employee benefits	*197,658*	*145,557*	*110,136*	*80,592*
Premises and equipment	*89,747*	*71,313*	*52,433*	*39,110*
Additional non-interest expense	*137,069*	*107,600*	*74,582*	*51,718*
Total non-interest expense	424,474	324,470	237,151	171,420
Pre-tax net operating income	153,268	120,091	101,630	76,606
Securities gains (losses)	1,439	3,213	1,943	2,934
Applicable income taxes	49,695	40,084	34,127	27,308
Income before extra-ordinary items	105,012	83,240	69,446	52,232
Extraordinary gains—net	0	0	0	0
Net Income	*105,012*	*83,240*	*69,446*	*52,232*

Source: FDIC Web site, *http://www.fdic.gov/*, accessed February 23, 2003.

EXHIBIT 1b Commerce Bank Employees and Branches

	2001	*2000*	*1999*	*1998*
Employees	5,329	4,228	3,407	2,424
Branches	185	150	120	88

Source: FDIC Web site, *http://www.fdic.gov/*, accessed February 23, 2003.

EXHIBIT 2a Commerce Bank Balance Sheet (year ending December 31; $ in thousands)

	2001	*2000*	*1999*	*1998*
Cash and due from depository institutions	584,850	486,994	431,173	313,919
Securities	5,212,214	3,497,522	2,828,777	2,394,476
Net loans and leases	4,652,015	3,712,051	2,978,017	1,943,052
Bank premises and fixed assets	410,451	321,261	229,917	151,677
All other assets	1,411,636	843,176	263,444	175,826
Total assets	12,271,166	8,861,004	6,731,328	4,979,150
Total deposits	10,228,810	7,437,279	5,674,837	4,601,544
Other borrowed funds	90	9,638	205,483	26,004
Equity capital	700,747	537,343	385,404	321,434
All other liabilities	1,341,719	876,753	465,534	130,168
Total liabilities and capital	12,271,166	8,861,004	6,731,328	4,979,150

Source: FDIC Web site, *http://www.fdic.gov/*, accessed February 23, 2003.

EXHIBIT 2b Commerce Bank Deposit and Loan Information (year ending December 31; $ in thousands)

	2001	*2000*	*1999*	*1998*
Interest-bearing deposits	9,221,383	6,753,279	4,652,945	3,578,041
Loan loss allowance	66,981	48,680	38,381	26,409
Non-current loans and leases	17,616	14,749	9,921	7,749

Source: FDIC Web site, *http://www.fdic.gov/*, accessed February 23, 2003.

THE BANKING INDUSTRY

Products

Retail banks offered deposit and loan products, which were widely considered to be commodity products. Deposit products were a way for customers to store their money with the institution in exchange for access to the payment system (through electronic transfers and checks), interest on their money, and contact with the bank service infrastructure (branches, ATMs, call center, and Internet). Deposit products tended to be more transaction oriented than loan products, although not every deposit product was associated with ongoing transactions. For example, in the case of certificates of deposit, a customer agreed to store money with the bank for a set amount of time at a higher interest rate than a typical, "demand" deposit account.

Banks typically had a dozen or more types of checking accounts distinguished by a variety of characteristics including minimum balance required to avoid fees, channel access, checks that could be written free of charge, and overdraft protection.[1]

In 2001, the banking industry loaned almost 90% of its deposit base. In addition, growth in both deposits and loans was about 20% over the period of 1998 to 2001. (See **Exhibits 3a** and **3b** for the consolidated balance sheet and deposit and loan information for the banking industry.) Large institutions that experienced larger than average growth typically accomplished this through mergers and acquisitions.

Two important trends in the industry evolved. The first was a push to increase the "cross-sell" of products—the number of products each customer used. Although the industry did not formally track this number, on average, customers tended to hold 1.5–2.5 products at an institution. Most companies had cross-sell goals that were significantly higher than this level. The second trend was towards growing

EXHIBIT 3a Industry Statistics: Consolidated Commercial Banking Industry Balance Sheet (year ending December 31; $ in millions)

	2001	*2000*	*1999*	*1998*
Cash and due from depository institutions	390,965	369,919	368,456	356,704
Securities	1,179,694	1,078,983	1,046,530	979,855
Net loans and leases	3,823,167	3,755,371	3,432,892	3,181,025
Bank premises and fixed assets	76,757	75,795	73,749	71,308
All other assets	1,098,491	964,543	815,639	853,640
Total assets	**6,569,074**	**6,244,810**	**5,736,160**	**5,442,531**
Total deposits	4,391,610	4,179,634	3,831,104	3,681,428
Other borrowed funds	567,743	570,657	555,316	416,696
Equity capital	597,137	530,721	479,731	462,142
All other liabilities	1,012,584	963,598	869,006	882,264
Total liabilities and capital	**6,569,074**	**6,244,610**	**5,735,180**	**5,442,531**

Source: FDIC Web site, *http://www.fdic.gov/*, accessed February 23, 2003.

[1]Overdraft protection allowed customers to write a check over their current account balance, whereby the bank then made a short-term loan to cover the difference.

EXHIBIT 3b Industry Statistics: Consolidated Commercial Banking Industry Deposit and Loan Information (year ending December 31; $ in millions)

	2001	*2000*	*1999*	*1998*
Interest-bearing deposits	3,505,277	3,423,073	3,127,704	2,961,347
Loan loss allowance	72,314	64,145	58,767	57,261
Non-current loans and leases	54,906	42,942	33,002	31,253

Source: FDIC Web site, *http://www.fdic.gov/*, accessed February 23, 2003.

EXHIBIT 3c Consolidated Commercial Banking Industry Income Statement (year ending December 31; $ in millions)

	12/31/2001	*12/31/2000*	*12/31/1999*	*12/31/1998*
Total interest income	402,853	428,448	367,291	362,016
Total interest expense	187,696	224,488	175,149	179,265
Net interest income	215,157	203,960	192,141	182,752
Provision for loan and lease losses	43,420	30,013	21,817	22,215
Total non-interest income	157,049	153,370	144,373	123,642
Salaries and employee benefits	*92,630*	*88,567*	*85,451*	*79,101*
Premises and equipment	*27,570*	*26,781*	*25,795*	*24,155*
Additional non-interest expense	*102,097*	*100,763*	*92,967*	*90,877*
Total non-interest expense	222,297	216,111	204,213	194,133
Pre-tax net operating income	106,488	111,206	110,485	90,046
Securities gains (losses)	4,478	(2,283)	180	3,131
Applicable income taxes	36,741	37,946	39,343	31,931
Income before extraordinary items	74,226	70,977	71,322	61,245
Extraordinary gains—net	(248)	(32)	169	507
Net Income	**73,976**	**70,945**	**71,491**	**61,752**

Source: FDIC Web site, *http://www.fdic.gov/*, accessed February 23, 2003.

revenues from fees customers paid for certain transactions and functionality. From 1998 to 2001, fee revenue, also known as non-interest income, had increased at 27%, a much higher rate than interest revenue, or interest income, which grew at 11% (**Exhibit 3c**).

Service

Banks typically used demographics such as age, income, and geographic location to help segment customers. More recently, many banks had been calculating individual customer profitability, used in part to help determine how to differentiate service amongst customers. Customer satisfaction with the banking industry had historically been quite low, with satisfaction being significantly higher for the smaller credit unions (**Exhibit 4**).

A retail bank could lose up to a third of its customer base each year to attrition. Even the best performers lost 15%. By far the largest attrition occurred in the first year of a banking relationship. A study of the banking industry found that 34% of customers that leave a bank indicated that they did so out of dissatisfaction with steep fees and fee surprises, poor service, and errors. Thirty-four percent left as a result of a geographic move, primarily because they were outside the reach of current bank branch locations. Fifteen percent of customers left because of availability of more convenience elsewhere such as longer hours.[2]

Distribution

Customers selected their bank for a variety of reasons. The decision was often heavily influenced by

[2]David Dove and Chuck Robinson, "Mind the Back Door While you Greet New Customers," *American Banker*, August 22, 2002.

EXHIBIT 4 Customer Satisfaction Comparisons

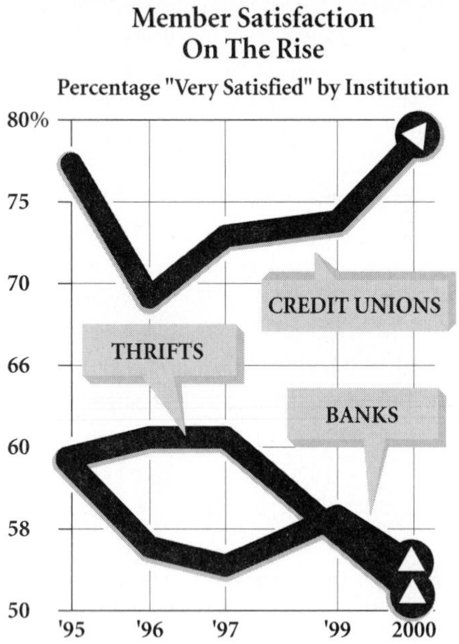

Source: Adapted from *American Banker*/2000 Gallup Consumer Survey.

proximity of a local branch. In response, banks created enormous branch networks, with the number of branches increasing even as the number of banks decreased (see **Exhibit 5**). Many branches changed hands as banks merged, either becoming part of the merged entity, or sold off to another bank after a merger due to redundancy.

Banks also created large ATM networks. Customers could access their bank's ATM for free and other bank's ATMs for a fee or sometimes for two fees—one by the owner of the ATM and one by the customer's bank for processing the out-of-network transaction. Originally ATMs had been considered cost centers, but due to the ability to generate fee income, ATMs were increasingly viewed as profit centers.

In addition, virtually every bank had a call center open 24 hours a day, 7 days a week, as well as a voice response unit (VRU) whereby customers could execute an increasing number of transactions via the telephone without having to talk to a live agent. By 2002, Internet banking was commonplace, providing customers the ability to view balances, move money between accounts, and pay bills electronically, which often incurred a $5 monthly fee.

As a result of the lower marginal cost associated with the electronic channels, most banks actively encouraged customers to move their transactions from full-service channels to self-service channels. Banks strongly advertised the availability and convenience of the electronic channels, offered monetary incentives for using the channels, and occasionally monetary penalties for using the more expensive channels (e.g., charging $3 to visit the teller).

Employees

Front-line employees in retail banks were often selected for their ability to perform repeated tasks, interact with customers, and their willingness to accept relatively low wages. Training primarily consisted of learning about bank-specific policies and procedures as well as the various features amongst the dozens of deposit and loan products available at any point in time. The latter became especially important after mergers, when customers from one institution where often forced into new products with unfamiliar attributes. Compliance with processes and understanding of specific product attributes was paramount in the industry. Key measures of performance were volume of calls handled and number of transactions processed.

THE COMMERCE STORY

When Hill founded Commerce Bank in 1973, he was determined to be different. "The world," he reasoned, "did not need another 'me-too' bank. I had no capital, no brand name, and I had to search for a way

EXHIBIT 5 Employees and Branches

	2001	*2000*	*1999*	*1998*
Number of employees (full-time equivalent)	1,701,721	1,670,861	1,657,602	1,626,978
Branches	65,654	64,079	63,684	61,957
Number of Institutions	6,080	8,315	8,579	8,773

Source: FDIC Web site, *http://www.fdic.gov/*, accessed February 23, 2003.

to differentiate from the other players." With $1.5 million he started a community bank in southern New Jersey and since had grown it, without acquisitions, into Pennsylvania, Delaware, and New York.

Hill created a retail franchise with branches typically open from 7:30AM–8:00PM during the week and modified hours on Saturday and Sunday. If the branch was in a busy location, its drive-through window might be open as late as midnight. Or, more precisely, ten minutes after midnight, as stated in the company's 10-minute rule, which asserted that branches should open 10 minutes early and stay open 10 minutes late.

When customers came into branches to open a checking account, they were treated with outgoing, friendly service. After the customer selected from the four different checking accounts (**Exhibit 6**), Commerce routinely gave a free gift for opening the account.

Deposit growth had averaged over 30% per year since 1996. In 2001 alone Commerce deposits grew by almost 40% (Exhibit 2a and 2b) while its households grew by 20%. By comparison, cumulative deposit growth in the United States was 5% in 2001 (Exhibit 3a). Hill reflected on the Commerce approach:

Other banks decided to push consumers out of the branch because it is the high-cost delivery channel. They wanted to push them online. We totally reject that. You can't name me one retailer in this country that has pushed people where they don't want to go and succeeded. But the banks decided to push to electronic delivery, and they have totally failed. Our model is, we are going to give you the best of every channel knowing you are going to use all of them. The result is not only do we have the highest deposit-rate growth in this country by a long factor, but our online usage is 34%, which is higher than Wells Fargo.

I don't have to make a sale to you every day. Once you open your account I am making money on your balances. The big-bank attitude sees a customer as a cost, not a revenue generator. I don't see it that way.

You cannot find me any retailer who has driven store count down and has survived, and yet banks think they can drive customers out of their branches and still keep their business. I find that very hard to understand. We have some branches that get 100,000 customer visits a month; the

EXHIBIT 6 Commerce Checking Product Descriptions

Commerce offered checking accounts with the first year free of monthly service fees regardless of balance.* This included free first order of checks.

ATM withdrawals were available at any ATM and purchases anywhere Visa® was accepted. Transactions were immediately deducted from checking account and detailed in monthly statements.

Any Commerce Bank checking account could be combined with a cash reserve line for protection from overdrafts. Commerce had four types of checking accounts:

Standard Checking

- A $100 minimum balance resulted in no monthly service fees.

Interest Checking

- No monthly service fees with a $1,000 balance. Unlimited check writing and interest.

50 Plus Club

- Customers over 50 who maintained a $100 minimum balance incurred no account maintenance charge for a checking account with interest, free checks, money orders, notary service, and travelers' checks.

Consumer Checking

- No minimum balance requirement and no per check charge for the first eight checks each month for a $3 monthly fee.

Source: Company Web site.

*Online banking—checking balances and account details—was free. A $5 fee was charged per month for electronic bill paying in which customers could pay their bills through the Commerce Web site.

average branch gets 40,000. As a comparison, an average McDonald's gets 25,000 per month.

GROWTH

To Commerce, New York City represented an enormous opportunity. "Everyone will tell you that New York is the most over-banked market in the country," Hill said. "I think it is the most under-banked market in the country. There are $500 billion in deposits in New York." Commerce did not enter its newest market quietly. Commerce spent $500,000 per branch on promotion, five times its usual spend, which included direct mailings, ads on subway and phone kiosks, and with the help of street vendors, 10,000 hot dogs given away wrapped in Commerce napkins.[3] Success was immediate. Commerce broke even in half the time it usually did, even with four times higher costs than any other region.

Hill maintained that the business should continue to grow organically. "No one has built a power retailer in this country through mergers and acquisitions," he emphasized. "You can only build a delivery model like this from scratch. Mergers and acquisitions are cost-cutting devices at their heart, and the merger of cultures and the dilution of brand is a formula for failure. Every big bank merger in this country has failed." In Hill's view, "it's easier to build a bank than to fix one."

It had taken 18 years for Commerce to grow to $1 billion in deposits, but it now surpassed this amount in individual quarters. Commerce expected to ultimately reach $100 billion in deposits and total 1,000 locations, from Washington, D.C., to Boston. Commerce's success was not limited to deposit growth. The bank's net income doubled from 1998–2001, compared with 20% for the industry as a whole. Doug Pauls, Commerce's chief financial officer, recalled the projections he saw when he came on board: "I am an accountant by trade and therefore a little conservative by nature, so when I looked at the projections in 1994 after I arrived here I thought they were pretty aggressive. But I wish I had that original plan, because we have completely blown that away."

DEBITS AND CREDITS

Deposits

"We believe the value of a bank is not its loan base," Hill explained, "but rather the deposit base, what we call core deposits. Those are deposits that come to you for non-rate reasons. We are generally the lowest ratepayers in every market." Commerce's deposit rates were often half a percent lower than those of competitors.

Commerce's focus on its consumer business was unusual for the banking industry. Commerce generated more than half its deposits from its consumer business, compared with most banks whose consumer business was closer to a third of overall business. Hill observed:

> Banks had given up on growing altogether because they thought you had to pay the highest deposit rate to get growth. The big players decided in the late '80s, early '90s that it was too much trouble gathering and growing deposits on the consumer side. On the one hand, they began to fund themselves in the wholesale market; on the other hand, they began to cut costs in the retail network.

Pauls added: "When people ask Vernon if he is concerned about competition, he says not really, because they are fighting an air war while we are winning the ground war at the store level. We can't lose sight of that. Deposit growth at the store level is the basis of everything we do."

A branch network with longer hours inevitably has higher costs, which readily showed up in the expense ratio of a bank.[4] "A low expense ratio is a minus, not a plus," Hill emphasized. "The guys with a low expense ratio are every day disinvesting in their business." Hill had committed to investing in providing service in his branches after asking customers what they wanted. "We asked people, 'Why do you open a new account?' " Hill recalled. "Three percent of people said they wanted the highest rate; 62% said they picked a bank for service, convenience, and those kinds of things. Well, the competition is competing on the 3%; we decided to compete on the 62%."

Commerce looked for ways to save money, but not by counting savings on the income statement; instead it gave back to customers. Hill described this strategy:

> Every time Wal-Mart beats a supplier down to get a better deal they don't take that extra and add it to the bottom line; they improve the value proposition to the customer. This year we saved millions in expenses by switching ATM contracts, which we invested back to our customers.

[3]Chuck Salter, "Lessons from the Best Bank in America," *Fast Company*, May 2002, p. 91.

[4]Expense ratio in the percentage of income spent on operating expenses; it is a common measure of a bank's cost structure.

We could have taken that right to the bottom line, but what we decided to do is eliminate our fees to our ATM and check cards for the entire company. We don't charge for our cards, we don't charge for transactions, and in New York City if you use someone else's machine and they charge you a dollar and a half, we give you that dollar and a half back.[5] That is what a power retailer does. You use your competitive advantage to get stronger, not to make more money.

Loans

Loans made by Commerce were assigned to the branches that serviced the customers. The branches also received credit for the deposits. This was not the case across the industry. Falese described the more typical structure:

> At Fleet if the health-care lending group produces deposits they keep the credit in their group, and yet the branch has to service the account. The Fleet branch manager hates the health-care manager because the branch has to service the account and gets no credit. At Commerce the branch managers love the health-care bankers because the branch gets the account credit. That little adjustment entirely changes the dynamics.

Commerce's loan-to-deposit ratio was significantly below the industry average, and loans were considered carefully. "We don't make enough money in terms of the spread to justify taking credit risk," Falese explained. "The customer's ability to repay is the most important thing. Some of our best loans are the ones, we did not make." Added Pauls: "The way we look at credit and credit quality is a lot tougher [than our competition]. Deals that would get approved elsewhere might not get approved here." Commerce focused most of its lending on commercial real estate projects, home mortgages, and consumer loans.[6]

Loan customers were encouraged to open deposit accounts with Commerce. For Falese, it was policy. He explained:

> Most other banks are driven by loans. My attitude is no deposit, no loan. We decentralize the delivery of the loan so that at some point you have to come in to the branch and sign the papers. The loan officer is also the branch manager. And that is when we encourage you to let us manage your deposits as well. My job is to make sure we make sound loans that get repaid and at the same time that we generate core deposits.

NOT CUSTOMERS, FANS

"We're not here to satisfy customers, we're here to blow them away," remarked John Manning, one of Commerce's most well-known employee trainers. "If you talk to our customers, they don't like us, they love us." Hill corroborated: "People buy our products because they trust our brand." Added Pauls:

> I'll go out to lunch around here and be in line at a Wendy's and someone in front of me will see my Commerce pin and start talking about how great Commerce Bank is. They love the fact that people know them when they walk in, that they are treated well; they are so happy with us they can't believe it. For one of our advertisements we used real customers, and the people who were directing the commercials marveled at how much these customers wanted to tell our story and how they felt about the institution.

Commerce branches were built to be inviting, with floor to ceiling windows and ample parking (**Exhibit 7**). Commerce branches were replicated with remarkable consistency. "We know every screw in the model," Hill said. Most branches were built from scratch for about $1 million. With few exceptions, they had the same white-brick exterior capped with a black metal roof, the same black-and-white marble, the same no-frills checking and savings accounts, and the same lollipops and dog biscuits. "It makes life easier for customers," says chief marketing officer John Cunningham. "They know what the deal is wherever they visit one of our banks."[7]

For Commerce, deciding where to put a branch was just as important as what the building looked like. Hill sought a corner that was busy, but not too busy, with a good residential and commercial mix. Ultimately, Hill, who was also part owner of 45 Burger Kings in the Philadelphia suburbs, made the call himself, a decision that he insisted has more to do with gut feel than with demographic research. Usually, though, it's in the competition's backyard. If a competitor closed, the staff at the nearby Commerce branch was

---

[5] Reimbursement of ATM charges up to $5 per month.

[6] Jay Palmer, "Service Master," *Barron's*, January 28, 2002.

[7] Salter, Lessons from the Best Bank in America," *Fast Company*, May 2002.

EXHIBIT 7

awarded $5,000.[8] Commerce's branches broke even within a year to 18 months. The average bank took three years.

Commerce had several customer-centric programs instilled in its branch culture. "I think extended hours started down the [Jersey] Shore, to be able to service people who were down there for the weekend," Pauls recalled. "Then we realized that it would make sense at all our branches." Hill explained. "My competitors think we did it so that people could bank with us on Sunday. If no one ever banked with us on Sunday the initiative would still be successful, because it sent a message to the customer: I am always there for you." When it rained, bank employees often escorted customers to their cars under Commerce umbrellas. The company gave out 300,000 pens a month as well as dog biscuits and red Commerce lollipops at drive-through banking windows. Hill made no apologies for spending money on these sorts of things:

> If you think like a retailer, then you're constantly coming up with ways to enhance the customer experience. Like the phones we added to Commerce ATM machines in case customers need to reach the call center. Or the 'check view' feature on the bank's Web site that allows customers to see an image of the front and back of a check a day after it has been deposited. Or the bright-red Penny Arcades in the lobby.

When Hill learned that other banks had started refusing to accept large numbers of coins or were charging customers to do so, he saw an opportunity.

> We said, 'We're going to spend $10 million to take your coins.' The Penny Arcade is more than a mere convenience. The real appeal—and the payoff—is that it's fun. Kids want to use it. Pack rats need to use it. People waiting in line at the teller counter can't help but watch when someone steps up to the machine lugging a coffee can filled with coins. In its own small way, the Penny Arcade transforms the bank into a more interesting and appealing place. And that is how you create traffic.

In 2001, Commerce's Penny Arcades handled 750,000 transactions, which totaled $71.7 million. The machines accepted coins and returned a receipt that could be handed to any teller in exchange for bills. There was no charge for the program, for customers or non-customers. Falese called it "Marketing 101": "If customers come, keep doing it."

Up until 2001, Carole Robbins, a new Commerce customer and a conference planner in Manhattan, was perfectly happy with her bank, but that was before it was acquired by Citibank. "Why am I switching from the meanies over there?" asks Robbins, as she glances over at the Citibank across the street from the new Commerce branch at 55th Street and Sixth Avenue. It was 8:15AM and Robbins had already taken care of her banking for the day. "If I treated my customers the way they treated me, I'd be out of business." In fact, mergers have been an enormous source of deposit growth for Commerce—when other bank's merge, Commerce's deposits tend to increase dramatically (**Exhibit 8**).[9]

"[Commerce] is a blast from the past: a bank with an old-fashioned approach to service," continued Robbins. "There's a different attitude here like

---

[8]Salter, Lessons from the Best Bank in America," *Fast Company*, May 2002.
[9]Salter, "Lessons from the Best Bank in America," *Fast Company*, May 2002.

EXHIBIT 8 Effect of Mergers on Deposit Growth

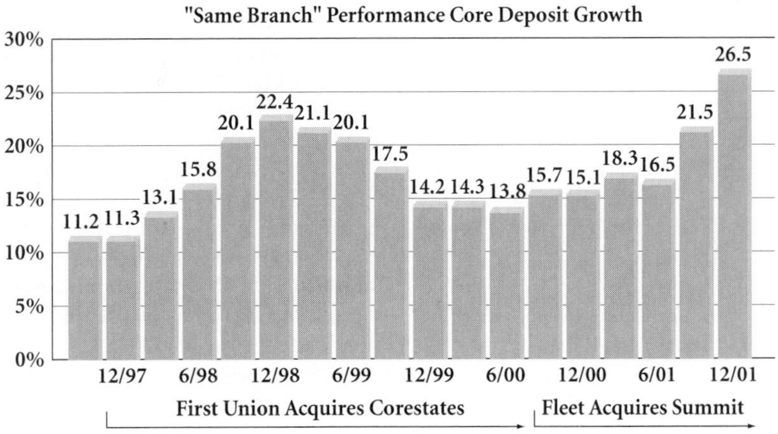

Source: Company documents.

we're all in this together. But time will tell. All restaurants are good in the beginning too."[10]

WOW!

We're asking you to forget the way you delivered your skills at other banks.

—VERNON HILL, CHIEF EXECUTIVE OFFICER[11]

Good service had a name at Commerce Bank; it was *"WOW!"* Nine people had gotten together in 1994 and developed the program Jacovelli explained:

> We needed a framework for teaching folks service, so we came up with the SMART principles [**Exhibit 9**]. Then we decided we needed to be able to measure the impact of that service on both external and internal customers. Now the program is called "managing for *WOW!*"—our terminology for process improvement. All offices have quality-assurance results that they have to live by. As people meet their goals or exceed them there are celebrations.

EXHIBIT 9 SMART Principles

Say "Yes" to Customers!

- Don't hide behind bank policy. Refer situations which conflict with policy to your supervisor.
- Void forbidden phrases:
  "No . . ."
  "We can't do that."
  "I don't know."
  "Sorry you'll have to . . ."

Make each customer feel special!

- Be personable, pleasant, and positive!
- Politely address customers by their surname.
- SMILE!

Always keep customer promises!

- Take ownership of a customer's problem—solve it for them. Don't play corporate "Ping-Pong."
- If you can't correct the basic problem, take care of the mess it caused.

Recover

- To err is human! To recover, divine!

Think like the customer!

- Always exceed the customer's expectations!

WOW! stickers, little red Cs that were awarded to employees who *WOW*!ed customers either internally or externally, could be redeemed for merchandise such as Commerce sweatshirts, T-shirts, mugs, and radios. Every year since 1997 Commerce held its *WOW!* Awards to honor outstanding service performers for the year in a variety of categories (**Exhibit 10**). The first year the ceremony had taken the form of a small luncheon at a local country club. In 2003, the bank's 30th anniversary, all Commerce employees were scheduled to gather at Radio City Music Hall in Manhattan. Commerce employees were

[10]Salter, "Lessons from the Best Bank in America," *Fast Company*, May 2002.
[11]Salter, "Lessons from the Best Bank in America," *Fast Company*, May 2002.

EXHIBIT 10 WOW! Awards 2001

Award	Nominee Criteria
Retailer of the Year	Core Deposit Growth, Total Deposit Growth, Consumer Loan Growth, WOW Shops, Total Losses, Employee Turnover
Rookie of the Year	Core Deposit Growth, Total Deposit Growth, Consumer Loan Growth, WOW Shops, Total Losses, Employee Turnover
Best Assistant Manager of the Year	Cash Items, Employee Turnover, WOW Shops
Best Head Teller of the Year	Cash Average vs. Cash Master, Teller Differences, WOW Shops/Drive-thru Competition, Check Cashing Violations, ATM Up Time
Best Full-time Teller of the Year	Teller Differences, WOW Shops
Best Part-time Teller of the Year	Teller Differences, WOW Shops
Best Customer Service Rep of the Year	Procedure Violations, WOW Shops

Other awards included: Best Supporting Role By An Officer, Best Supporting Role By A Non-Officer, Best Regional Lender, Best Middle-Market Lender, Best Consumer Lender, Best Specialized Lender, Best Sales Representative, Best Customer Service Representative, Best Supporting Role, Outstanding Institutional Performance, Outstanding Retail Sales Performance, and the Instructor of the Year

Source: Company documents

actors, the *WOW!* Awards their Academy Awards; employees peppered the ceremony with musical performances. The most glamorous prize, for retailer of the year, was the use of a Porsche Boxster for one year and was awarded to a branch manager.

More than parties and awards, *WOW!* was an integral part of the training process at Commerce University, a full-time education and training facility staffed by 41 employees. All new employees underwent an intense introduction to Commerce culture during a class called "Traditions," characterized as "part game show, part training session, part common sense." Employees were taught how to smile, shake hands, and greet customers. "Smiles have teeth," insisted Manning, adding, "voice mail is not *WOW!*" Employees were told by executive vice president of retail banking Dennis DiFlorio: "Don't come here for a job, come to be a leader, be passionate." Hill added his vision to the employees: "In many ways, you have joined a service cult. Nordstrom's has its Nordies, Commerce has its WOW! team. "We can't call ours Commies," DiFlorio explained.[12]

Commerce wanted raving enthusiasts, people who would get a kick out of providing great service. It did not hurt to be a little crazy. "We hire wack jobs," Manning explained to a room full of bank officers. "You're all wack jobs. And it is your responsibility to go out there and find more wack jobs." Recruiting was emphasized repeatedly to new employees, who were given stacks of cards to hand out to people who provided excellent service, whether in another bank, a restaurant, a retail store, or a gas station.

Weekly events like Red Fridays kept the bank playful. That's when the *WOW!* Patrol would visit branches and take photographs of staffers who were wearing red. Even customers would get in on the act. "It sounds juvenile," says Manning, "but people like getting their picture taken with Mr. C [the Commerce mascot]."

Commerce had two mascots. Mr. C, was a jolly, oversized red letter with white gloves. He was a walking logo, Commerce's version of the Golden Arches. Buzz, Commerce's second mascot, was an overjoyed, human-sized bee who ensured that the staff was creating buzz within the branches. In addition, internally, Dr. Wow, the ultra-mysterious character that no employee had ever met, responded to letters and gives out awards.[13]

Commerce University was the in-house training *WOW!* program generator. In addition to indoctrinating new employees, the university offered courses for existing employees, from part-time tellers to senior executives. An award of stock options often accompanied course completion. The university also acted as a training ground for future employees. In cooperation with Drexel University, high school students were invited to attend Camp Business, a free

[12]Salter, "Lessons from the Best Bank in America," *Fast Company*, May 2002.
[13]Salter, "Lessons from the Best Bank in America," *Fast Company*, May 2002.

10-day program that covered general business topics as well as the Commerce strategy.

Mystery shopping, also referred to as *WOW!* shops, was a significant component of performance measurement.[14] A staff of five Commerce University employees managed a team of 100 mystery shoppers, who collectively performed over 14,000 mystery shops annually. Each shopper was given a card with questions and considerations to rate during a visit to a branch. In addition to evaluating the overall condition of the branch, shoppers looked for a handshake followed by the standard Commerce greeting "Hi! My name is _____. How may I help you today?" If the employee said "can" instead of "may," if the customer-service rep did not walk the shopper to a desk or give her the appropriate brochure, if the attitude wasn't perceived as genuine, the branch received a lower rating.[15]

Because salary increases were based on shopping results, the information from the shops was posted on an internal database for all branch managers to see. Leagues were organized whereby branches in different regions might compete against one another for the most impeccable service report. Mystery shopping also went beyond Commerce, with shoppers being sent to competitors' branches to open new accounts and test service.

WOW! was interwoven with the organization in many ways. One infamous aspect was the "kill the stupid rule" program, whereby employees who suggested an alternative to a stupid rule were paid $50.

Commerce made it easy for customers who wanted to talk to a person on the phone to opt out of the automated voice-response unit. Moreover, the live agents with whom they were connected adhered to a dress code far stricter than was typical of a call center setting. "We expect *WOW!* service to extend into everything we do," explained vice president of training and development Thomas DiSabatina. "You never know who will walk through our call center—stockholders, the press, Mr. Hill—and we want our reps to represent the *WOW!*. It also reinforces their role of responsibility and accountability to bring the best to our fans."

Commerce vans, each painted blue and red and emblazoned with a logo, were considered free advertising by the bank. "If you ask the competition," Hill explained, "they will tell you that they do not paint their vans because they are afraid of getting robbed. Well, it is just ridiculous because the vans drive around with checks, not money, and besides, there hasn't been a robbery since 1945." In New York some vans drove around empty. *WOW!* was everywhere.

STAFFING

With rapid growth, staffing was a perennial challenge. Continued success relied on getting the right people, integrating them into the Commerce culture, and training them. In Manhattan, for example, Commerce conducted 2,000 interviews for 40 positions. "This is not the job for someone who's interested in being cool or indifferent," Manning said.[16]

Falese characterized his hiring philosophy as emphasizing engagement both internally among employees and externally among employees and customers:

> We're pretty good at getting people in here and getting them to stay. I've had only one senior manager in the last 10 years who did not fit, and we knew it four months into it. I check in at three months, six months, and a year and ask what is working, what isn't, how is volume, what do you like? Many bankers outside of Commerce delegate so much of their work they lose touch with their customers, their skills, and their contacts. They rarely visit customers and think that business development is playing golf. They are not engaged.

Falese actively monitored the labor market, sniffing around for talent. He considered experienced people who might be available only part time. "It's okay to hire someone part time, someone who has retired and has 30 years of experience," he insisted. "There is no substitute for experience in a local market. Experience lets you know who the local entrepreneurs are, those who have been able to manage their business through the cycles." Falese used prospective employee interviews to learn about competitors' organizations and kept tabs on who worked where. He observed: "Mergers have created a pool of talent. We are engaged in markets, and we know who the better performers are in each market. I have organizational charts of all of my competitors. I know who their lending officers are; I know who their secretaries are, administrative assistants, clerking officers, operations people, and branch managers."

---

[14]Mystery shopping involved anonymous visits by evaluators hired part time solely for the purpose of rating service.
[15]Salter, "Lessons from the Best Bank in America," *Fast Company*, May 2002.
[16]Salter, "Lessons from the Best Bank in America," *Fast Company*, May 2002.

RETAILTAINMENT

Proposed in 2002 to improve the service experience for customers waiting in branches, Retailtainment encouraged branch managers to suggest ideas, even wacky ones, for entertaining branch customers on Friday afternoons. "We wanted customers to expect the unexpected and leave with a smile," explained Jacovelli. New ideas were needed to keep Commerce ahead of the competition. "We need the next penny arcade," remarked Pauls.

Competitors were beginning to adopt some of Commerce's basic service offerings and to emphasize the human side of service with advertising and marketing campaigns. Seattle-based Washington Mutual, a recent entrant in the New York market, had launched its own retail-experience bank, termed an "un-bank," which included roaming tellers, a children's play area, and no desks. ING, a Dutch bank with little branch presence in the United States, opened a café-style location in mid-town Manhattan that served espresso and savings accounts to customers seated at tables provided with free Internet terminals. Even Bank of America was experimenting with televisions to entertain customers waiting in lines.[17]

With some of its competitors offering better rates, Commerce, if it was to stay ahead, had to ensure that its value proposition was clear in customers' minds. Commerce deliberately competed on service, not price. It paid lower rates on deposits in order to pay for enhanced service. The question was, how far should it take differentiating on service? Jacovelli recalled a phone conversation she had with a friend who complained that although it was nice to be greeted by an employee and given a promotional pen, she would prefer that employee get behind the counter and help speed the line through a busy branch. Complained another customer: "There are too many greeters standing around not doing anything."[18] Jacovelli wondered if people really wanted entertainment while they banked.

Some branches had other problems with Retailtainment. Jacovelli related a call she received while away on a business trip about a recent mishap: "The branch manager had arranged for a hot dog cart and a juggler in the branch, all approved by marketing. The hot dog vendor had to use the restroom, and while he was gone his cart caught on fire. When the juggler tried to help, he also caught on fire. That evening it was all over the local news. It was a disaster."

As with any program implemented in a decentralized context, Jacovelli was concerned about branding implications. The bank had worked hard to ensure that its branches all had the same look and feel, embracing the philosophy of building from scratch wherever possible to control the branch environment. Retailtainment encouraged branch managers to be creative. Described Jacovelli:

> The branch managers know their customers better than anyone and should be encouraged to do whatever's necessary to satisfy their needs. However, as we've seen from experience, it is dangerous to leave people completely to their own devices. Some in the organization feel that with proper training and guidelines we can make Retailtainment a success. Others think that it is not the best use of our attention or resources and that we should stick to executing our existing service model. This is important for us because it centers on service and our entire success is dependent upon service. At the end of the day Commerce is one bank, one brand, and our success will be on delivering better service than the competition. The question is what role Retailtainment will have in our delivering on our mission.

Nearly 79% of consumers surveyed who used a credit union as their primary financial institution in 2000 said they were "very satisfied," with their financial institution as compared with 53% of consumers who use a retail bank. Savings and loans and other thrifts scored 51% in this area.[19]

Study Questions

1. *What do you see as the key elements in Commerce Bank's current service model?*
2. *In terms of market targeting, what types of customers are an ideal fit for Commerce Bank?*
3. *How is Commerce positioned against other retail banks? Is this position sustainable?*
4. *How well does "Retailtainment" fit with Commerce's service model? What action do you recommend on this proposal?*

---

[17]Wasserman, "Welcome to the Un-Bank," *Brandweek*, November 4, 2002.

[18]Salter, "Lessons from the Best Bank in America," *Fast Company*, May 2002, p. 58.

[19]Questions were asked on a 5-point scale, with "very satisfied," "satisfied," "neither satisfied nor dissatisfied," "dissatisfied," and "very dissatisfied" as the alternatives.

Case 4 Giordano: International Expansion

JOCHEN WIRTZ

. . . We are committed to provide our customers with value-for-money merchandise, professional customer service and comfortable shopping experience at convenient locations.

—GIORDANO'S CORPORATE MISSION

As it looks to the future, a successful Asian retailer of casual apparel abstract must decide whether to maintain its existing positioning strategy. Management wonders what factors will be critical to success and whether the firm's competitive strengths are readily transferable to new international markets.

Giordano, a retailer of casual clothes in East Asia, Southeast Asia, and the Middle East, was operating in more than 20 territories by 2002. It had outlets in China, Dubai, Hong Kong, Macao, Philippines, Saudi Arabia, Singapore, South Korea, and Taiwan. Sales had grown from HK$712 million in 1989 to HK$3,479 million in 2001 (**Exhibit 1**). The company's board and top-management team sought to maintain its success in existing markets and to enter new markets in Asia and beyond. Several issues were under discussion. The first concerned Giordano's positioning. In what ways, if at all, should Giordano change its current positioning? The second concerned the critical factors that had contributed to Giordano's success. Would these factors remain critical over the coming years? Finally, as Giordano seeks to enter new markets around the world, there was debate over whether its competitive strengths were readily transferable to other markets.

COMPANY BACKGROUND

Giordano was founded in Hong Kong by Jimmy Lai in 1980. To give his venture a more sophisticated image, Lai picked an Italian name for his retail chain. In 1981, Giordano started selling casual clothes manufactured predominantly for the U.S. market by a Hong Kong–based manufacturer, the Comitex Group. In 1983, Giordano scaled back on its wholesale operation and started to set up its own retail shops in Hong Kong. It also began to expand its market by distributing Giordano merchandise in Taiwan through a joint venture. In 1985, it opened its first retail outlet in Singapore.

However, in 1987, sales were low, and Lai realized that the pricey retail chain concept was unprofitable. Under a new management team, Giordano changed its strategy. Until 1987, it had sold exclusively men's casual apparel. When it realized that an increasing number of female customers were attracted to its stores, Giordano repositioned itself as a retailer of value-for-money merchandise, selling discounted casual unisex apparel, with the goal of maximizing unit sales instead of margins. Its shift in strategy was successful (Exhibit 1). Jimmy Lai left the company in 1991 to pursue other interests. In 2002, Giordano was headed by Peter Lau Kwok Kuen, who held the titles of chairman and chief executive. A typical Giordano store is shown in **Exhibit 2**.

MANAGEMENT VALUES AND STYLE

The willingness to try new ways of doing things and learning from past errors was an integral part of Lai's management philosophy. He saw the occasional failure as a current limitation that indirectly pointed management to the right decision in the future. To demonstrate his commitment to this philosophy, Lai took the lead by being a role model for his employees ". . . Like in a meeting, I say, 'look, I have made this mistake. I'm sorry for that. I hope everybody learns from this. If I can make mistakes, who the hell do you think you are that you can't make mistakes?'" He also believed

Notes: This case is based on information and quotes in a wide array of published sources. All Financial data are in Hong Kong dollars. Exchange rates in early 2003 were: HK$1.00 = US$0.128.

EXHIBIT 1 Giordano Financial Highlights, 1994–2002 (in millions of HK$)

(Consolidated)	*2002**	*2001*	*2000*	*1999*	*1998*	*1997*	*1996*	*1995*	*1994*
Turnover	1,760	3,479	3,431	3,092.2	2,609.2	3,014.4	3,522.0	3,482.0	2,863.7
Turnover increase (percentage)	NA	1.4%	11.0%	18.5%	(13.4%)	(14.4%)	1.2%	21.6%	22.7%
Profit after tax and minority interests	194.0	377.0	416	360.0	76.1	68.0	261.2	250.2	195.3
Profit after tax and minority interests increase (percentage)	NA	(9.4%)	15.6%	375.0%	11.9%	(74.0%)	4.4%	28.1%	41.9%
Shareholders' fund	NA	1,695	1,558	1,449	1,135	1,069	1,220	976	593
Working capital	NA	798	1014	960	725	655	752	560	410
Total debt to equity ratio	NA	0.4	0.3	0.3	0.3	0.3	0.4	0.7	0.9
Bank borrowings to equity ratio	NA	NA	NA	0	0	0	0	0	0.1
Inventory turnover on sales (days)	NA	30	32	28	44	48	58	55	53
Return on total assets (percentage)	NA	15.9%	19.7%	18.8%	5.3%	4.8%	16.5%	16.4%	18.8%
Return on average equity (percentage)	NA	23.2%	27.7%	27.9%	6.9%	5.9%	23.8%	31.8%	35.8%
Return on sales	NA	10.8	12.1	11.6	2.9	2.3	7.4	7.2	6.8
Earning per share (cents)	NA	26.3	29.3	25.65	5.40	4.80	18.45	19.40	15.45
Cash dividend per share (cents)	NA	14.00	15.25	17.25	2.25	2.50	8.00	6.75	5.50

Note: NA indicates that data were not available.

*Figures are for the first six months of Giordano's 2002 financial year, ended 30 June 2002. Percentages for 2002 were calculated over the figures for same period in the previous year.

strongly in empowerment—if everyone was allowed to contribute and participate, mistakes could be minimized.

Another factor that contributed to the firm's success was its dedicated, ever-smiling sales force. Giordano considered front-line workers to be its customer service heroes. Charles Fung, chief operations officer and executive director (Southeast Asia) remarked:

> Even the most sophisticated training program won't guarantee the best customer service. People are the key. They make exceptional service possible. Training is merely a skeleton of a customer service programme. It's the people who deliver that give it form and meaning.

Giordano had stringent selection procedures to make sure that only those candidates who matched the desired employee profile were selected. Selection continued into its training workshops. Fung called the workshops "attitude training." The service orientation and character of a new employee was tested in these workshops. These situations, he added, were an

EXHIBIT 2 Typical Giordano Storefront

appropriate screening tool for "weeding out those made of grit and mettle."

Giordano's philosophy of quality service could be observed in its overseas outlets as well. Its Singapore operations, for example, achieved ISO 9002 certification. Its obsession with providing excellent customer service was described by Fung:

> The only way to keep abreast with stiff competition in the retail market is to know the customers' needs and serve them well. Customers pay our paycheques: they are our bosses.... Giordano considers service to be a very important element [in trying to draw customers] . . . service is in the blood of every member of our staff.

According to Fung, everyone who joined Giordano, even office employees, had to work in a store for at least one week as part of his or her training. "They must understand and appreciate every detail of the operations," he declared. "How can they offer proper customer assistance—internal and external—if they don't know what goes on in operations?"

Giordano invested heavily in training its employees. In Singapore, for instance, it spent 3.9 percent of its overall payroll in 1998 on training, with each employee receiving an average of 224 hours of training per year. It had a training room complete with one-way mirrors, video cameras, and other electronic paraphernalia. A training consultant and seven full-time line trainers conducted training sessions for every new sales staff, and existing staff members were required to take refresher courses. The company's commitment to training and developing its staff was recognized when it was awarded the People Developer Award in 1998. Giordano also received the Hong Kong Management Association Certificate of Merit for Excellence in Training in 2001. Fung explained:

> Training is important. Every organization is providing its employees training. However, what is more important is the transfer of learning to the store. When there is a transfer of learning, each dollar invested in training yields a high return. We try to encourage this [transfer of learning]

by cultivating a culture and by providing positive reinforcement, rewarding those who practice what they learned.

Giordano offered what Fung claimed was "one of the most attractive packages in an industry where employee turnover is high. We generally pay more than what the market pays." By 2002, Giordano was trying to motivate its people mainly through a base salary that matched market rate plus additional, performance-related bonuses. These initiatives and Giordano's emphasis on training had resulted in a lower staff turnover rate.

Managing its vital human resources (HR) became a challenge to Giordano when it decided to expand into global markets. To replicate its high service-quality positioning, Giordano needed to consider the HR issues involved in setting up retail outlets on unfamiliar ground. For example, the recruitment, selection, and training of local employees could require modifications to its formula for success in its current markets, owing to differences in the culture, education, and technology of the new countries. Labor regulations could also affect HR policies, such as compensation and providing welfare. Finally, expatriate policies for staff seconded to help run Giordano outside their home country and management practices needed to be considered.

FOCUSING GIORDANO'S ORGANIZATIONAL STRUCTURE ON SIMPLICITY AND SPEED

Giordano maintained a flat organizational structure. Fung believed that "this gives us the intensity to react to market changes on a day-to-day basis." The company had a relaxed management style, in which managers worked closely with line staff members There were no separate offices for higher and top management; instead, their desks were located next to their staff's, separated only by shoulder-high panels. This closeness allowed easy communication, efficient project management, and speedy decision making, which were all seen as critical ingredients to success amid fast-changing consumer tastes and fashion trends. Speed allowed Giordano to keep its product-development cycle short, and the firm made similar demands on its suppliers.

COMPETITION

Giordano's home base, Hong Kong, was flooded with retailers, both large and small. To beat what was often described as the dog-eat-dog competition prevalent in Asia—especially in Hong Kong—founder Jimmy Lai believed that Giordano must develop a distinctive competitive advantage. Although many retail outlets in Hong Kong competed almost exclusively on price, Lai felt differently about Giordano. Citing successful Western retailers, Lai astutely observed that there were other key factors for success. He started to benchmark Giordano against best-practice organizations in four key areas: (1) computerization (from The Limited), (2) a tightly controlled menu (from McDonald's), (3) frugality (from Wal-Mart), and (4) value pricing (as implemented at the British retail chain Marks & Spencer).

The emphasis on service and the value-for-money concept had proved to be successful. Lai was convinced that service was the best way to make customers return to Giordano again and again. Lai declared: "We are not just a shirt retailer, we are not just an apparel retailer. We are also a service retailer because we sell feeling. Let's make the guy feel good about coming into here [our stores]."

SERVICE

Giordano's commitment to service began with the Customer Service Campaign in 1989. In that campaign, yellow badges bearing the words "Giordano Means Service" were worn by every Giordano employee. This philosophy had three tenets: "We welcome unlimited try-ons; we exchange—no questions asked, and we serve with a smile." The yellow badges reminded employees that they were there to deliver excellent customer service. The firm had received numerous service-related awards over the years (**Exhibit 3**). It had also been ranked number one for eight consecutive years by the *Far Eastern Economic Review* for being innovative in responding to customers' needs.

Management had launched several creative, customer-focused campaigns and promotions to extend its service orientation. For instance, in Singapore, Giordano asked its customers what they thought would be the fairest price to charge for a pair of jeans and charged the price each customer was willing to pay. This one-month campaign was immensely successful, with some 3,000 pairs of jeans sold every day during the promotion. In another service-related campaign, customers were given a free T-shirt for criticizing Giordano's service. More than 10,000 T-shirts were given away. Far from being only another brand-building campaign, Giordano responded seriously to

EXHIBIT 3 Recent Giordano Company Awards

Award	*Awarding organisation*	*Category*	*Year(s)*
ISO 9002*	SISIR		1994
American Service Excellence Award	American Express	Fashion/Apparel	1995
Ear Award	Radio Corporation of Singapore	Listeners' Choice and Creative Merits	1996
Excellent Service Award**	Singapore Productivity and Standards Board		1996, 1997, 1998
People Developer Award	Singapore Productivity and Standards Board		1998
HKRMA Customer Service Award	Hong Kong Retail Management Association		1999
The Fourth Hong Kong Awards for Services	Hong Kong Trade Development Council	Export Marketing & Customer Service	2000
Grand Award (Giordano International)	Hong Kong Trade Development Council	Export Marketing	2002
Grand Award (Giordano Ladies)	Hong Kong Retail Management Association		2002

Note: Awards given to the Giordano Originals Singapore.

*ISO 9002 refers to the guidelines from the Geneva-based International Organisation for Standardisation for companies that produce and install products.

** To be nominated for the Excellent Service Award, a company must have had, among other things, significant training and other programs that ensured quality service. These include systems for recognizing employees and for customer feedback.

the feedback collected. For example, the Giordano logo was removed from some of its merchandise, as some customers liked the quality but not the "value-for-money" image of the Giordano brand.

Against advice that it would be abused, Lai also introduced a no-questions-asked and no-time-limit worldwide exchange policy, which made it one of the few retailers in Asia outside Japan with such a generous exchange policy. Giordano claimed that returns were less than 0.1 percent of sales.

To ensure that every store and individual employee provided excellent customer service, performance evaluations were conducted frequently at the store level, as well as for individual employees. The service standard of each store was evaluated twice every month, whereas individual employees were evaluated once every two months. Internal competitions were designed to motivate employees and store teams to do their best in serving customers. Every month, Giordano awarded the "Service Star" to individual employees, based on nominations provided by shoppers. In addition, every Giordano store was evaluated every month by mystery shoppers. Based on the combined results of these evaluations, the "Best Service Shop" award was given to the top store. Customer feedback cards were available at all stores and were collected and posted at the office for further action.

VALUE FOR MONEY

Lai explained the rationale for Giordano's value for money policy:

> Consumers are learning a lot better about what value is. Out of ignorance, people chose the brand. But the label does not matter, so the business has become value driven, because when people recognise value, that is the only game in town. So we always ask ourselves how can we sell it cheaper, make it more convenient for the consumer to buy and deliver faster today than yesterday. That is all value, because convenience is value for the consumer. Time is value for the customer.

Giordano was able to consistently sell value-for-money merchandise through careful selection of suppliers, strict cost control, and by resisting the temptation to increase retail prices unnecessarily. For instance, to provide greater shopping convenience to customers, Giordano in Singapore located its operations in densely populated housing complexes in addition to its outlets in the traditional downtown retail areas.

INVENTORY CONTROL

In markets with expensive retail space, most retailers tried to maximize use of every square foot of the store for sales opportunities. Giordano was no different. Its strategy involved not having a back storeroom in each store. Instead, a central distribution center replaced the function of a back storeroom. Information technology facilitated inventory management and demand forecasting. When an item was sold, the barcode information, identifying size, color, style, and price, was recorded by the point-of-sale cash register and transmitted to the company's main computer. At the end of each day, the information was compiled at the store level and sent to the sales department and the distribution center. The compiled sales information became the store's order for the following day. Orders were filled during the night and were ready for delivery by early morning, ensuring that before a Giordano store opened for business, new inventory was already on the shelves.

Another advantage of its IT system was that information was disseminated to production facilities in real time. Such information allowed customers' purchase patterns to be understood, and this provided valuable input to its manufacturing operations, resulting in fewer problems and costs related to slow-moving inventory. As one manager noted, "If there is a slow-selling item, we will decide immediately how to sell it as quickly as possible. When the sales of an item hits a minimum momentum, we pull it out, instead of thinking of how to revitalize its [slow-selling] sales." As a result, Giordano stores were seldom out of stock of any item of merchandise.

The use of technology also afforded more efficient inventory holding. Giordano's inventory turnover on sales was reduced from 58 days in 1996 to 28 days in 1999 and to 30 days in 2001, allowing it to thrive on lower gross margins. Savings were passed to customers, thus reinforcing its value-for-money philosophy. All in all, despite the relatively higher margins as compared to their peers, Giordano was still able to post healthy profits. Such efficiency became a crucial factor when periodic price wars were encountered. In 2002, the company was targeting more on gross profit and gross margin growth than on top-line growth and had managed to grow its gross margin amid a subdued retail market.

Besides the use of IT and real-time information generated from the information system, Giordano owed its success in inventory control to close integration of the purchasing and selling functions. As Fung elaborated:

> "There are two very common scenarios that many retailers encounter: slow-selling items stuck in the warehouse and fast-selling popular items that are out of stock. Giordano tries to minimise the probability of the occurrence of these two scenarios, which requires close integration between the purchasing and selling departments.
>
> In the 1980s and early 1990s, when few retailers would use IT to manage their inventory, the use of IT gave Giordano a leading edge. However, today, when many retailers are using such technology, it is no longer our real distinctive competitive strength. In a time when there is information overload, it is the organizational culture in Giordano to intelligently use the information that sets us apart from the rest." And this was further explained by Lai: "None of this is novel. Marks and Spencer in Britain, The Gap and Wal-Mart in America and Seven-Eleven in Japan have used similar systems for years. Nowadays, information flows so fast that anybody can acquire or imitate ideas. What matters is how well the ideas are executed."

Thanks to rapid development in Internet and intranet technologies, packaged solutions, such as MS Office, point of sale (POS) and enterprise resource planning (ERP) software, and supporting telecommunications services (e.g., broadband Internet access), retailers could acquire integrated IT and logistics technology more easily and more cost-effectively than ever before.

PRODUCT POSITIONING

Fung recognized the importance of limiting the firm's expansion and focusing on one specific area. Simplicity and focus were reflected in the way Giordano merchandised its goods. Its stores featured no more than 100 variants of 17 core items, whereas competing retailers might feature 200 to 300 items. He believed that merchandising a wide range of products made it difficult to react quickly to market changes.

Giordano's willingness to experiment with new ideas and its perseverance despite past failures could also be seen in its introduction of new product lines. Its venture into midpriced women's fashion,

Giordano Ladies, featured a line of smart blouses, dress pants, and skirts and targeted executive women. The company hoped to benefit from the fatter profit margins enjoyed in more upscale niches of women's clothing—about 50 to 60 percent compared to 40 percent for casual wear.

Here, however, Giordano ran into some difficulties as it found itself competing in a market crowded with seasoned players. Although there were no complaints about the look or quality of the new line, it had to compete with more than a dozen established brands already on the racks, including Theme and Esprit. Initially, the firm failed to differentiate its new clothing line from its mainstream product line and even tried to sell both through the same outlets. In 1999, however, it took advantage of the financial troubles facing such rivals as Theme, as well as the post-Asian currency crisis boom in many parts of Asia, to aggressively relaunch its Giordano Ladies' line, which met with great success. As of February 28, 2002, the reinforced Giordano Ladies' focuses on a select segment, with 33 Gio Ladies shops in Hong Kong, Taiwan, China, Indonesia, and the Middle East, offering personalized service (e.g., staff are trained to memorize names of regular customers and recall past purchases).

During the late 1990s, Giordano began to reposition its brand by emphasizing differentiated, functionally value-added products and broadening its appeal by improving on visual merchandising and apparel. For instance, a large portion of its capital expenditure (totaling HK$112 million for the year ended 2001) went to renovating its stores to enhance leasehold improvements, furniture, fixtures, and office equipment. Typical store interiors are shown in **Exhibits 4** and **5**. Giordano's relatively midpriced positioning worked well: inexpensive yet contemporary-looking outfits appealed to Asia's frugal customers, especially during the Asian economic crisis. However, over time, this positioning became inconsistent with the brand image that Giordano tried hard to build over the years. As one senior executive remarked, "The feeling went from 'this is nice and good value' to 'this is cheap.' When you try to live off selling 100 Hong Kong-dollar shirts, it catches up with you."

EXHIBIT 4 A Typical Store Layout

EXHIBIT 7 Competitive Financial Data for Giordano, Esprit, The Gap, Theme, and Bossini (1999 data expressed in millions of HK$)

	Giordano	*Esprit*	*The Gap*	*Theme*	*Bossini*
Turnover	3,092	5,994	90,756	319	1,109
Profit after tax and minority interests	360	430	8,791	(218)	18
Working capital	762	478	3,470	(243.0)	182
Return on total assets (percentage)	18.8%	NA	24.6%	NA	NA
Return on average equity (percentage)	30.5%	33.1%	59.2%	NA	6.5%
Return on sales (percentage)	11.6%	7.2%	9.7%	(68.3%)	1.6%
Price/Sales ratio	2.07	1.33	1.97	0.82	0.23
Sales growth	18.5%	17.8%	28.5%	(69.8%)	(22.4%)
No. of employees	6,237	4,471	NA	NA	869
Sales per employee	495,779	1,340,599	NA	NA	1,276,254

Note: Esprit reports its earnings in euro; The Gap, in US$. All reported figures have been converted into HK$ at the following exchange rate (as of Feb. 2001): US$1 = euro $1.09 = HK$7.8.

Source: Annual report 1999, Giordano International; *Financial Highlights 1999*, Esprit International; *Annual report 1999*, The Gap Financial Report 1999, Bossini International Holdings Limited.

EXHIBIT 8 Geographical Presence of Giordano and Principal Competitors, February 2001

Country	*Giordano*	*Hang Ten*	*Bossini*	*Baleno*	*Esprit*	*Theme*
Asia						
HK/Macao	X	X	X	X	X	X
Singapore	X	X	X	—	X	X
South Korea	X	X	—	—	X	X
Taiwan	X	X	X	X	X	X
China	X	X	X	X	X	X
Malaysia	X	X	—	—	X	X
Indonesia	X	X	—	—	X	X
Philippines	X	X	—	—	X	X
Thailand	X	X	—	—	X	X
World						
U.S. and Canada	—	X	X	—	X	X
Europe	—	X	X	—	X	X
Japan	X	X	—	—	X	X
Australia	X	X	—	—	X	X
Total	**750**	**NA**	**173**	**125**	**8,470**	**200**

Note: X indicates presence in the country/region;—indicates no presence; NA indicates data not available.

hand, Bossini was very strong in Hong Kong and relatively strong in Singapore but had little presence in Taiwan and China.

Esprit was an international fashion lifestyle brand, engaged principally in the image and product design, sourcing, manufacturing, and retail and wholesale distribution of a wide range of women's, men's, and children's apparel: foot wear: and accessories and other products under the Esprit brand name. Esprit promoted a "lifestyle" image, and its products were strategically positioned as good quality and value for money—a position that Giordano was occupying. By the turn of the century, Esprit had a distribution network of more than 8,000 stores and outlets in 40 countries in Europe, Asia, Canada, and Australia. The main markets were in Europe, which accounted for approximately 65 percent sales, and in Asia, which accounted for approximately 34 percent of 2000 sales. The Esprit brand products were sold principally via directly managed retail outlets, wholesale customers (including department stores, specialty stores, and franchisees), and by licensees for products manufactured under license, principally through the licensees' own distribution networks.

Theme International Holdings Limited was founded in Hong Kong in 1986 by Chairman and Chief Executive Officer Kenneth Lai. He identified a niche in the local market for high-quality, fashionable ladies' business wear, although the firm subsequently expanded into casual wear. The Theme label and chain was in direct competition with Giordano Ladies'. From the first store in 1986 to a chain comprising more than 200 outlets in Hong Kong, China, Korea, Macao, Taiwan, Singapore, Malaysia, Indonesia, the Philippines, Japan, Thailand, Canada, and Holland, the phenomenal growth of Theme was built on a vertically integrated corporate structure and advanced management system. However, its ambitious expansion proved to be costly in view of the crisis, with interest soaring on high levels of debt. In 1999, the company announced a HK$106.1 million net loss for the six months up to September 30, 1998, and it closed 23 retail outlets in Hong Kong, which traded under its subsidiary, The Clothing Shop. Theme International was subsequently acquired by High Fashion International, a Hong Kong–based fashion retailer specializing in up-market, trendy apparel.

Although each of these firms had slightly different positioning strategies and targeted dissimilar but overlapping segments, they all competed in a number of similar areas. For example, all firms heavily emphasised advertising and sales promotion: selling fashionable clothes at attractive prices. Almost all stores were also situated primarily in good ground-floor areas, drawing high-volume traffic and facilitating shopping, browsing, and impulse buying. However, none had been able to match the great customer value offered by Giordano.

A study by *Interbrand* of top Asian marquee brands ranked Giordano number 20, making it Asia's highest-ranking general apparel retailer. The clothing names next in line were Australia's Quicksilver at number 45 and Country Road at number 47. However, a spokesman for advertising agency McCann-Erickson remarked, "It's a good brand, but not a great one. Compared to other international brands, it doesn't shape opinion."

A threat from U.S.–based The Gap was also looming. Giordano was aware that the American retailer was invading Asia. The Gap was already in Japan. After 2005, when garment quotas were likely to be abolished, imports into the region were expected to become more cost-effective. With this in mind, the Giordano Unisex line had upgraded its market position since the Asian crisis and launched the BSE brand in 1999 to cater to the value-for-money segment.

GIORDANO'S GROWTH STRATEGY

Early in its existence, Giordano management had realized that it was difficult to achieve substantial growth and economies of scale as long as the firm operated only in Hong Kong and saw the answer as lying in regional expansion. By 2002, Giordano had 1,259 stores in 25 markets (**Exhibits 9** and **10**).

Driven in part by its desire for growth and in part by the need to reduce its dependence on Asia in the wake of the 1998 economic meltdown, Giordano eventually set its sights on markets outside Asia. Australia was an early target, and the number of retail outlets increased from 4 in 1999 to 31 in 2001, with sales turnover reaching HK$29 million by the end of that year, by which point it boasted retail outlets in Brisbane, Melbourne, and Sydney. As part of Giordano's globalization process, it planned to open up its first shops in Germany and Japan during the first half of 2001.

Although the Asian financial crisis had caused Giordano to rethink its regional strategy, it was still determined to enter and further penetrate new Asian markets. This determination led to the successful expansion in mainland China, where retail outlets grew from 253 stores in 1999 to 532 stores by late September 2002. Giordano's management foresaw both challenges and opportunities arising from the People's Republic's new acceptance as a member of the World Trade Organization.

Giordano opened 12 more stores in Indonesia during 2001, bringing its total in that country to 22 stores, located in Jakarta, Surabaya, and Bali. In Malaysia, Giordano planned to refurnish its Malaysian outlets and intensify its local promotional campaigns to consolidate its leadership position in the Malaysia market. To improve store profitability, Giordano had already converted some of its franchised Malaysian stores into company-owned stores.

The senior management team knew that Giordano's future success in such markets would depend on a detailed understanding of consumer tastes and preferences for fabrics, colors, and advertising. In the past, the firm had relied on maintaining

EXHIBIT 9 Operational Highlights for Retail and Distribution Division (figures as at year end unless specified otherwise)

	*30 Sept. 2002**	*2001*	*2000*	*1999*	*1998*	*1997*	*1996*	*1995*	*1994*	*1993*
Number of retail outlets:										
• Directly managed by the Group	NA	456	367	317	308	324	294	280	283	257
• Franchised	NA	703	553	423	370	316	221	171	77	481
Total number of retail outlets	1,259	1,159	920	740	678	640	515	451	360	738
Retail floor area directly managed by the Group (sq. ft.)	NA	597,800	465,800	301,100	358,500	313,800	295,500	286,200	282,700	209,500
Sales per square foot (HK$)	NA	5,100	7,400	8,400	6,800	8,000	9,900	10,500	10,600	12,600
Number of employees	8,600**	8,287	7,166	6,237	6,319	8,175	10,004	10,348	6,863	2,330
Comparable store sales Increase/(decrease) (percentage)	(2.5%)**	(4%)	4%	21%	(13)%	(11)%	(6)%	8%	(9)%	15%
Number of sales associates	NA	2,603	2,417	2,026	1,681	1,929	1,958	2,069	1,928	1,502

Notes: *Figures as compared to same period in the previous year.

**Data as of June 30, 2002.

EXHIBIT 10 Key Regional Statistics for Giordano, 30 June 2002

	Taiwan	*Hong Kong*	*China*	*Singapore*	*Malaysia*
Net sales (HK$ millions)	359	390	408	177	NA
Retail sales					
Sales per sq. ft (HK$)	NA	NA	NA	NA	NA
Percentage change in retail sales (comparing with same period in 2001)	(11.4%)	2.1%	9.1%	4.7%	NA
Retail floor area (sq. ft.)	230,200	115,100	408,700	39,800	NA
Number of sales associates	NA	NA	NA	NA	NA
Total Number of outlets (30 Sept. 2002)	182	71	532	47	38

a consistent strategy across countries, including such elements as positioning, service levels, information systems, logistics, and human resource policies. However, implementation of such tactical elements as promotional campaigns was usually left mostly to local managers. A country's overall performance in terms of sales, contribution, service levels, and customer feedback was monitored by regional headquarters (for instance, Singapore for Southeast Asia) and the head office in Hong Kong. Weekly performance reports were distributed to all managers.

As the organization expanded beyond Asia, it was becoming clear that different strategies had to be developed for different regions or countries. For instance, to enhance profitability in Mainland China, the company recognized that better sourcing was needed to enhance price competitiveness. Turning around the Taiwan operation required refocusing on basic designs, streamlining product portfolio, and implementing the company's micromarketing strategy more aggressively. The company was continuing to explore the market in Japan and planned to open a few more stores in the second half of the year. And in Europe, it was investigating a variety of distribution channels.

THE FUTURE

Although Giordano had been extremely successful, the challenge facing top management was how it could maintain this success in the years ahead. A key issue on the agenda was how the Giordano brand should be positioned against the competition in both new and existing markets. Was a repositioning required in existing markets, and would it be necessary to follow different positioning strategies for different markets (e.g., Hong Kong versus Southeast Asia)?

A second issue was the sustainability of Giordano's key success factors. It clearly understood its core competencies and the pillars of its success, but it had to carefully explore how they were likely to develop over the coming years. Which of its competitive advantages were likely to be sustainable, and which ones were likely to be eroded?

A third issue was Giordano's growth strategy in Asia as well as across continents. Would Giordano's competitive strengths be readily transferable to other markets? Would strategic adaptations to IT strategy and marketing mix be required, or would tactical moves suffice?

Study Questions

1. *How would you describe and evaluate Giordano's product, business, and corporate strategies?*
2. *How would you describe and evaluate Giordano's current positioning strategy. Should Giordano reposition itself against its competitors in its current and new markets, and should it have different positioning strategies for different geographic markets?*
3. *What are Giordano's key success factors and sources of competitive advantage? Are its competitive advantages sustainable, and how would they develop in the future?*
4. *Could Giordano transfer its key success factors to new markets as it expanded in both Asia and other parts of the world?*
5. *How do you think Giordano had/would have to adapt its marketing and operations strategies and tactics when entering and penetrating your country?*
6. *What general lessons can be learned from Giordano for other major clothing retailers in your country?*

References

"Aiming High: Asia's 50 Most Competitive Companies," *Asia Inc.* (June 6, 1997): 34–7.

"An All-New Dress for Success," *Asia Week* 25, no. 41 (Oct. 5, 1999).

"And the Winning Store Is, Again . . ." *Straits Times (Singapore)*, 2 Dec. 1995.

Ang, Swee Hoon, "Giordano Holdings Limited," in *Cases in Marketing Management and Strategy: An Asian-Pacific Perspective*, ed. John A. Quelch, Siew Meng Leong, Swee Hoon Ang, and Chin Tiong Tan, (Singapore: Prentice-Hall, 1996), 182–190.

"Asia: Giordano Plans Expansion," *Sing Tao Daily*, 29 June 1999.

"Asian IPO Focus: Analysts See Little to Like in HK's Veeko," *Dow Jones International News*, 12 April 1999.

Austria, Cecille, "The Bottom Line," *World Executive's Digest* (19 Dec. 1994): 17–20.

"Casual-Wear Chain Prospers on Cost-Cutting Regime," *South China Morning Post*, 15 Oct. 1999.

"China: HK Companies Commended by Forbes for Best Practices," *China Business Information Network*, 12 Nov. 1999.

"China, Korea to Become Main Markets for Giordano," *Dow Jones Asian Equities Report*, 21 May 2001.

Clifford, Mark, "Extra Large," *Far Eastern Economic Review* (2 Dec. 1993): 72–76.

"Company Looks Outside Asia," *Dow Jones International News*, 12 Aug 1998.

"Creditors Push Struggling Theme Fashion Outlet into Liquidation," *South China Morning Post*, 11 March 1999.

Esprit International, *Financial Highlights 1999.*

"Fashion Free-Fall," *Asian Wall Street Journal*, 9 Nov 1998.

The Gap, *Annual Report 1999.*

"Giordano's After-Tax Earnings Soared in First Half," *Asian Wall Street Journal*, 27 July 1999.

"Giordano All Dressed up to Enter India Chaitali Chakravarty," *Economic Times*, 15 Oct. 2001.

"Giordano Comes out of the Cold," *Business Week*, 31 May 1999.

"Giordano to Concentrate on Retail and Distribution of Value for Money Clothing and Accessories," *South China Morning Post*, 2 June 2002.

"Giordano Details $700 Million Expansion," *South China Morning Post*, 4 Dec. 1999.

"Giordano Dreams up Sale for Insomniacs," *Business Times (Singapore)*, 6 May 1994.

"Giordano Employs New Approach to Team Building and Staff Training," *Middle East Company News*, 7 Aug. 2002.

"Giordano Expects to Set up Ops in Europe October," *AFX (AP)*, 19 June 2000.

"Giordano Has Little Esprit de Corps with Rival," *Asian Wall Street Journal*, 13 Dec. 2002.

Giordano Holdings Limited, *Annual Reports for 1993, 1997.*

Giordano International Limited, *Announcement of Results Dec. 31, 2000.*

Giordano International Limited, *Annual Reports for 1998–2002.*

"Giordano Increases Net Profit on Sales in Mainland China," *Asian Wall Street Journal*, 9 Aug. 2002.

"Giordano Intl 1998 Net Profit," *AFX (AP)*, 25 March 1999 (from Dow Jones Interactive).

"Giordano to Invest HK$1000M for Japan expansion," *Dow Jones Asian Equities Report*, 1 Nov 2001.

"Giordano Launches Staff Training Programme," *Al-Bawaba News*, 8 Aug. 2002.

"Giordano to Leave Germany," *The Standard*, 3 Oct. 2002.

"Giordano May Open 100 Stores on Mainland in 2003," *Business Daily Update*, 8 Nov. 2002.

"Giordano to Open Causeway Bay Megastore by 2002," *Dow Jones Asian Equities Report*, 3 Dec. 2001.

"Giordano to Open 50–100 Mega Stores in Mainland China," *Asian Wall Street Journal*, 26 Apr. 2002.

"Giordano to Open 60 New Stores in the Delta," *Standard*, 22 Jan. 2003.

"Giordano Out of the Running to Buy Theme: High Fashion International Emerges as Favourite in Race for Control," *South China Morning Post*, 25 Nov. 1999.

"Giordano Predicts Further Growth as Net Profit Reaches $46.3 Million," *Asian Wall Street Journal*, 3 March 2000.

"Giordano Scores with Smart Moves," *Straits Times (Singapore)*, 11 Sept. 1993.

"Giordano Seeks to Acquire Chain Stores in Australia," *AFX (AP)*, 8 February 2000.

"Giordano to Slow Down Expansion in China," *Business Daily Update*, 22 Jan. 2003.

"Giordano Spreads Its Wings," *Straits Times (Singapore)*, 13 March 1994.

"Giordano 12-mth Target Price Raised to 16.00 HKD," *AFX (AP)*, 16 May 2000.

"Good Service Has Brought Giordano Soaring Sales," *Business Times (Singapore)*, 6 Aug. 1993.

"High-End Training to Get More Funding," *Straits Times*, 1 Oct. 1998.

"HK Bossini International Fiscal Year Net Profit HK$17.6 Million vs. HK$45.5 Million Loss," *Dow Jones Business News*, 16 July 1999.

"HK Giordano Gets Green Light to Reopen in Shanghai," *Dow Jones International News*, 9 June 1999.

"Hong Kong: High Fashion to Takeover Theme." *Sing Tao Daily*, 26 Nov. 1999.

"Hong Kong Retailer Raced to New Markets, Spurring Everbright Loan," *Asian Wall Street Journal*, 7 April 1998.

"Hubris Catches up to Theme," *Globe and Mail*, 7 April 1998.

"In HK: Retail Shares Win Praise Amid Companies' Losses," *Asian Wall Street Journal*, 25 June 1999.

"Interview," by Frances Huang, *AFX (AP)*, 16 Sept. 1998 (from Dow Jones Interactive).

Mills, D. Quinn, and Richard C. Wei, "Giordano Holdings Ltd.," Harvard Business School, N9-495-002.

"Old Loss Masks Giordano Growth," *South China Morning Post*, 5 March 1999.

"Service Means Training," *Straits Times*, 7 Oct. 1998.

"Simple Winning Formula," *Business Times*, 6 Aug. 1993.

"The Outlook for Asian Retailing," *Discount Merchandiser*, May 1999.

"Theme International Unit to Close 23 Stores," *Asian Wall Street Journal*, 4 Aug. 1998.

"U.S. News Brief: Benetton Group," *Wall Street Journal Europe*, Dec. 17 1998.

"What Is the People Developer," *Straits Times*, 30 Sept. 1998.

Case 5 Aussie Pooch Mobile

CHRISTOPHER LOVELOCK AND LORELLE FRAZER

After creating a mobile service that washes dogs outside their owners' homes, a young entrepreneur has successfully franchised the concept. Her firm now has more than 100 franchisees in many parts of Australia, as well as a few in other countries. She and her management team are debating how best to plan future expansion.

Elaine and Paul Beal drew up in their 4 × 4 outside 22 Ferndale Avenue, towing a bright blue trailer with red and white lettering. As Aussie Pooch Mobile franchisees whose territory covered four suburbs of Brisbane, Australia, they were having a busy day. It was only 1:00 P.M. and they had already washed and groomed 16 dogs at 12 houses. Now they were at their last appointment: a "pooch party" of 10 dogs at number 22, where five other residents of the street had arranged to have their dogs washed twice a month.

Prior to their arrival outside the house, there had been ferocious growling and snarling from a fierce-looking Rottweiler. But when the animal caught sight of the brightly colored trailer, he and two other dogs in the yard bounded forward eagerly to the chain link fence, in a flurry of barking and wagging tails.

Throughout residential areas of Brisbane and in a number of other Australian cities, dogs of all shapes and sizes were being washed and groomed by Aussie Pooch Mobile franchisees. By early 2002, the company had grown to more than 100 franchisees and claimed to be "Australia's largest mobile dog wash and care company." A key issue facing its managing director, Christine Taylor, and members of the management team was how to plan and shape future expansion.

COMPANY BACKGROUND

Located in Burpengary, Queensland, just north of Brisbane, Aussie Pooch Mobile Pty. Ltd. (APM) was founded in 1991 by Christine Taylor, then aged 22. Taylor had learned customer service early, working in her parents' bait and tackle shop from the age of 8. Growing up in an environment with dogs and horses as pets, she knew she wanted to work with animals and learned dog-grooming skills from working in a local salon. At 16, Chris left school and began her own grooming business on a part-time basis, using a bathtub in the family garage. Because she was still too young to drive, her parents took her to pick up the dogs from their owners. She washed and groomed the animals at home and then returned them.

Once Taylor had learned to drive and bought her own car, she decided to take her service to the customers. So she went mobile, creating a trailer in which the dogs could be washed outside their owners' homes, and naming the fledgling venture The Aussie Pooch Mobile. Soon, it became a full-time job. Eventually, she found she had more business than she could handle alone, so she hired assistants. The next step was to add a second trailer. Newly married, she and her husband, David McNamara, ploughed their profits into the purchase of additional trailers and gradually expanded until they had six mobile units.

Development of a Franchise

The idea of franchising came to Taylor when she found herself physically constrained by a difficult pregnancy:

> David would go bike riding or head to the coast and have fun with the jet ski and I was stuck at home and felt like I was going nuts, because I'm a really active person. I was hungry for information on how to expand the business, so I started researching other companies and reading heaps of books and came up with franchising as the best way to go, since it would provide capital and also allow a dedicated group of small business people to help expand the business further.

As existing units were converted from employees to franchisee operations, Taylor noticed that they quickly became about 20 percent more profitable. Initially, APM focused on Brisbane and the surrounding region of southeast Queensland. Subsequently, it expanded into New South Wales and South Australia in 1995; into Canberra, Australian Capital Territory (ACT), in 1999; and into Victoria in 2000 (**Exhibit 1**). Expansion into Western Australia was expected in mid-2002. In 1996, a New Zealand division of the firm was launched in Tauranga, a small city some 200 km (125 miles) southeast of Auckland, under the name Kiwi Pooch Mobile. In 2001 Aussie Pooch Mobile launched into the United Kingdom, beginning with a town in eastern England. Soon, there were four operators under a master franchisee. Early 2002 saw the official launch of The Pooch Mobile Malaysia, also under a master franchisee.

By early 2002, the company had 125 mobile units in Australia, of which 55 were located in Queensland, 42 in New South Wales, 8 in ACT, 12 in South Australia, and 8 in Victoria. In addition, representatives operated another six company-owned units. The company bathed more than 20,000 dogs each month and had an annual turnover of some $3 million.[1] APM was a member of the Franchise Council of Australia and complied with the Franchising Code of Conduct. The management team consisted of Chris Taylor as managing director and David McNamara as director responsible for overseeing trailer design and systems support. Each state had its own manager and training team. The central support office also housed staff who provided further assistance to managers and franchisees.

Expansion had benefited from the leverage provided by several master franchisees, who had obtained the rights to work a large territory and sell franchises within it. Said Taylor:

EXHIBIT 1 Map of Australia

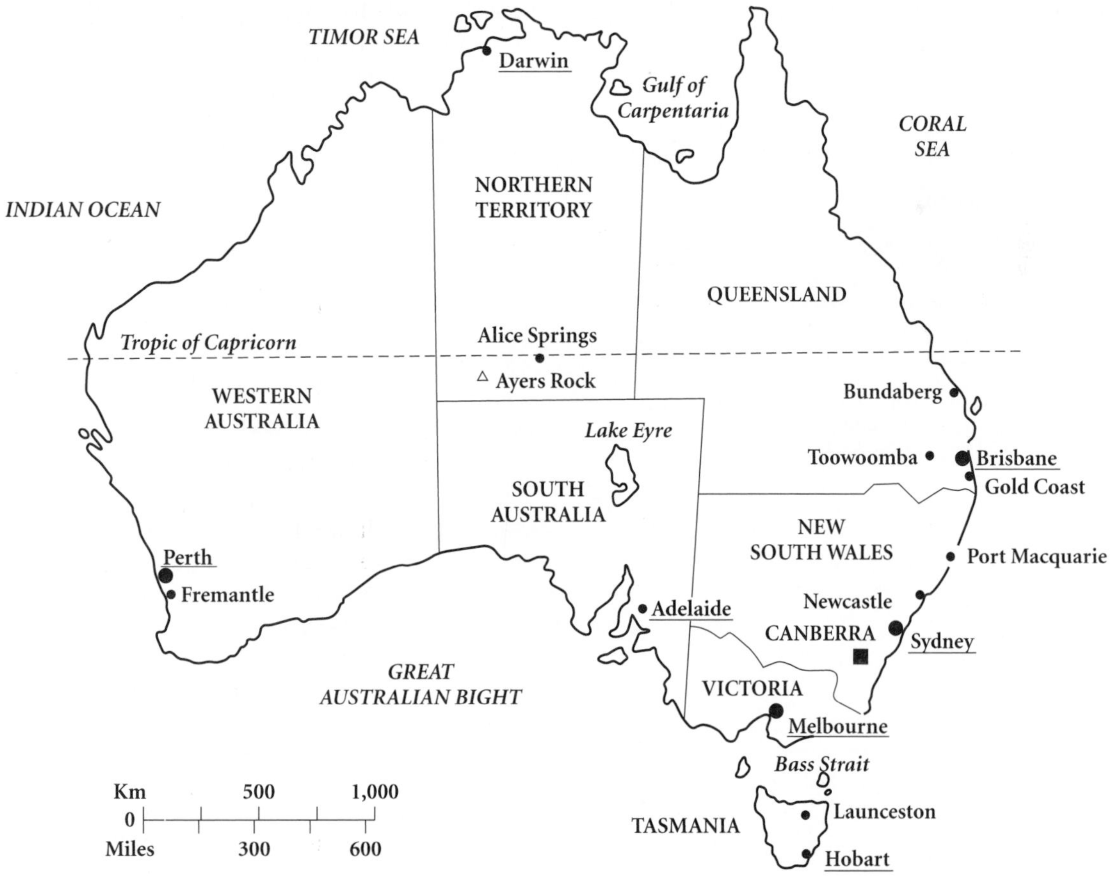

[1]Financial data are in Australian dollars (exchange rates in early 2002 were: A$1.00 = US$0.57 =€0.58).

I look at the business as if it's my first child. I see it now starting to get into those early teens where it wants to go alone, but it still needs me to hold its hand a little bit, whereas initially it needed me there the whole time. With the support staff we have in place, the business is now gaining the support structure it needs to work without me; this is what I am aiming towards. I appreciate that a team of people can achieve much more than one person alone.

The Service Concept

Aussie Pooch Mobile specialized in bringing its dog-washing services to customers' homes. Dogs were washed in a hydrobath installed in a specially designed trailer, which was parked in the street. The trailer had partly open sides and a roof to provide protection from sun and rain (**Exhibit 2**). Apart from flea-control products and a few grooming aids, APM did not attempt to sell dog food and other pet supplies. The company had resisted the temptation to diversify into other fields. "Our niche is in the dog bathing industry," declared Chris Taylor:

I don't want us to be a jack of all trades because you'll never be good at anything. We now have an exclusive range of products that customer demand has driven us to providing, but we still work closely with vets and pet shops and are by no means a pet shop on wheels.

In contrast to retail pet service stores, where customers brought their animals to the store or kennel, APM brought the service to customers' homes, with the trailer being parked outside on the street. The use of hydrobath equipment, in which warm, pressurized water was pumped through a showerhead, enabled operators to clean dogs more thoroughly than would be possible with a garden hose. The bath was designed to rid the dog of fleas and ticks and improve its skin condition as well as to clean its coat and eliminate smells. Customers supplied water and electrical power.

The fee paid by customers varied from $15–$30 per dog, depending on breed and size, condition of coat and skin, behavior, and geographic location, with discounts for multiple animals at the same address. On average, regular customers paid a fee of $25 for one dog, $47 for two, and $66 for three. At

EXHIBIT 2 The Aussie Pooch Mobile Trailer

The rear door of the trailer has been swung open, and the franchisee is washing a dog inside.

"pooch parties," a concept developed at APM, the homeowner acting as host typically received one complimentary dogwash at the discretion of the operator. Additional services, for which an extra fee was charged, included the recently introduced aromatherapy bath ($2.50) and blow-drying of the animal's coat for $5–$10 (on average, $8). Blow drying was especially recommended in cool weather to prevent the animal from getting cold.

Operators also offered free advice to customers about their dogs' diet and health care, including such issues as ticks and skin problems. Operators encouraged customers to have their dogs bathed on a regular basis. The most commonly scheduled frequencies were once every two or four weeks.

A Satisfied User

The process of bathing a dog involved a sequence of carefully coordinated actions, as exemplified by Elaine Beal's treatment of Zak, the Rottweiler. "Hello, my darling, who's a good boy?" crooned Elaine as she patted the enthusiastic dog, placed him on a leash, and led him out through the gate to the footpath on this warm, sunny day. Paul busied himself connecting hoses and electrical cords to the house, while Elaine began back-combing Zak's coat in order to set it up for the water to get underneath. She then led the now placid dog to the hydrobath inside the trailer, where he sat patiently while she removed his leash and clipped him to a special collar in the bath for security. Meanwhile, the water had been heating to the desired temperature.

Over the next few minutes Elaine bathed the dog, applied a medicated herbal shampoo to his coat, and rinsed him thoroughly with the pressure-driven hose (**Exhibit 3**). After releasing Zak from the special collar and reattaching his leash, she led him out of the hydrobath and onto the footpath, where she wrapped him in a chamois cloth and dried him. Next, she cleaned the dog's ears and eyes

EXHIBIT 3 Elaine Beal Bathes Zak the Rottweiler in an Aussie Pooch Mobile Hydrobath

with disposable baby wipes, all the time continuing to talk soothingly to him. She checked his coat and skin to ensure that there were no ticks or skin problems, gave his nails a quick clip, and sprayed an herbal conditioner and deodorizer onto Zak's now gleaming coat and brushed it in. Returning Zak to the yard and removing the leash, Elaine patted him and gave him a large biscuit, specially formulated to protect the animal's teeth.

THE AUSTRALIAN MARKET

Australia's population of 19.3 million in 2001 was small in relation to the country's vast land area of 7.7 million km^2 (almost 3 million square miles). By contrast, the United States had a population of 285 million people on a land area, including Alaska and Hawaii, of 9.2 million km^2. A federal nation, Australia was divided into six states—New South Wales (NSW), Victoria, Queensland, South Australia, Western Australia, and the island of Tasmania—plus two territories: the large but thinly populated Northern Territory and the small Australian Capital Territory (ACT), which contained the federal capital, Canberra, and its suburbs and was an enclave within NSW. The average annual earnings for employed persons were $35,000.

With much of the interior of the continent uninhabitable and many other areas inhospitable to permanent settlement, most of the Australian population was concentrated in a narrow coastal band running clockwise from Brisbane on the southeast coast through Sydney and Melbourne to Adelaide, the capital of South Australia. Some 2,700 km (1,600 miles) to the west lay Perth, known as the most isolated city in the world. A breakdown of the population by state and territory is shown in **Exhibit 4**. The northern half of the country was in the tropics, Brisbane and Perth enjoyed a subtropical climate, and the remaining major cities had a temperate climate (**Exhibit 5**). Melbourne was known for its sharp fluctuations in temperature.

There were about four million domestic dogs in the country, and approximately 42 percent of the nation's 7.4 million households owned at least one. Ownership rates were slightly above average in Tasmania, the Northern Territory, and Queensland and somewhat below average in Victoria and the ACT. In 1995, it was estimated that Australians spent an estimated $1.3 billion on dog-related goods and services, of which 46 percent went to dog food, 22 percent to veterinary services, 12 percent to dog products and equipment, and 11 percent to other services, including washing and grooming (**Exhibit 6**).

EXHIBIT 4 Population of Australia by State and Territory, June 2001

State/Territory	*Population (000)*
New South Wales	6,533
Victoria	4,829
Queensland	3,628
South Australia	1,502
Western Australia	1,910
Tasmania	470
Australian Capital Territory	314
Northern Territory	198
Australia Total	**19,387**

Source: Australian Bureau of Statistics 2001

EXHIBIT 5 Average Temperatures for Principal Australian Cities (in degrees Celsius)*

	July (winter)		*January (summer)*	
	High	*Low*	*High*	*Low*
Adelaide, SA	14.9	6.9	27.9	15.7
Brisbane, Qld	20.6	9.5	29.1	20.9
Canberra, ACT	11.5	0.0	28.5	13.6
Darwin, NT	30.7	19.7	32.4	25.2
Hobart, Tas	12.3	4.0	22.3	11.9
Melbourne, Vic	12.9	5.2	26.0	13.5
Perth, WA	17.7	8.1	31.5	16.9
Sydney, NSW	16.9	6.9	26.3	18.6

Source: Australian Bureau of Meteorology: *http://www.bom.gov.au*

*Celsius to Fahrenheit conversion: 0°C = 32°F, 10°C = 50°F, 20°C = 68°F, 30°C = 86°F.

EXHIBIT 6 Distribution of Consumer Expenditures on Dog-Related Goods and Services, 1995

Product/service	*Allocation (%)*
Dog food	46
Vet charges	21
Dog products	10
Dog equipment	2
Dog services	11
Pet purchases	5
Other expenses	4
Total dog-related expenditures	*$1.3 billion*

Source: BIS Shrapnell Survey 1995.

Franchising in Australia

By the beginning of the 21st century, the Australian franchising sector had reached a stage of early maturity. McDonald's, KFC, and Pizza Hut opened their first outlets in Australia in the 1970s. These imported systems were followed by many home-grown business-format franchises, such as Just Cuts (hairdressing), Snap Printing, Eagle Boys Pizza, and VIP Home Services, all of which grew into large domestic systems and then expanded internationally, principally to New Zealand and Southeast Asia.

In 2002, Australia boasted approximately 700 business-format franchise systems holding more than 50,000 outlets. Although the United States had many more systems and outlets, Australia had more franchisors per capita, reflecting the relative ease of entry into franchising in this country. Most of the growth in franchising had occurred in business-format franchising as opposed to product franchising.

Business-format franchises provided franchisees with a full business system and the rights to operate under the franchisor's brand name, whereas product franchises merely allowed independent operators to supply a manufacturer's product, such as car dealerships or soft-drink bottlers. Typically, franchisees were required to pay an up-front franchise fee (averaging $30,000 in service industries and $40,000 in retailing) for the right to operate under the franchise system within a defined geographic area. This initial fee was included in the total start-up cost of the business (ranging from around $60,000 in the service sector to more than $200,000 in the retail industry). In addition, franchisees paid a royalty on all sales and an ongoing contribution toward advertising and promotional activities that were designed to build brand awareness and preference. Would-be franchisees who lacked sufficient capital might be able to obtain bank financing against personal assets, such as property or an acceptable guarantor.

Franchising Trends

The rapid growth of franchising had been stimulated in part by demographic trends, including the increase in dual-income families, which had led to greater demand for outsourcing of such household services as lawn mowing, house cleaning, and pet grooming. Some franchise systems offered multiple concepts under a single corporate brand name. For instance, VIP Home Services had separate franchises available in lawn mowing, cleaning, car washing, and rubbish removal. Additional growth came from conversion of existing individual businesses to a franchise format. For instance, Eagle Boys Pizza had often approached local pizza operators and offered them the opportunity to join this franchise.

Almost half the franchise systems in Australia were in retail trade (32 percent nonfood and 14 percent food). Another large and growing industry was the property and business services sector (20 percent), as shown in **Exhibit 7**. Most franchisees were former white-collar workers or blue-collar supervisors who craved independence and a lifestyle change.

Over the years, Australia's franchising sector had experienced a myriad of regulatory regimes. Finally in 1998, in response to perceived problems in many franchising systems, the federal government introduced a mandatory Franchising Code of Conduct,

EXHIBIT 7 Distribution of Franchise Systems in Australia by Industry, 1999

Industry	*Percentage*
Retail trade (nonfood)	31
Property and business services	20
Retail trade (food)	14
Personal and other services	7
Construction and trade services	6
Accommodation, cafes, and restaurants	4
Education	4
Cultural and recreation services	4
Unclassified	3
Manufacturing and printing	3
Finance and insurance	2
Transport and storage	1
Communication services	1
Total (all industries)	***100***

Source: Lorelle Frazer and Colin McCosker, *Franchising Australia 1999* (Franchise Council of Australia/University of Southern Queensland, Toowoomba, 1999), 39.

administered under the Trade Practices Act. Among other things, the Code required that potential franchisees be given full disclosure about the franchisor's background and operations prior to signing a franchise agreement. In contrast, the franchising sector in the United States faced a patchwork of regulations that varied from one state to another. Yet in the United Kingdom, there were no specific franchising regulations beyond those applying to all corporations operating in designated industries.

Master franchising arrangements had become common in Australian franchise systems. Under master franchising, a local entrepreneur was awarded the rights to subfranchise the system within a specific geographic area, such as an entire state. Because of Australia's vast geographic size, it was difficult for a franchisor to monitor franchisees who were located far from the head office. The solution was to delegate to master franchisees many of the tasks normally handled by the franchisor itself, making them responsible for recruiting, selecting, training, and monitoring franchisees in their territories, as well as overseeing marketing and operations.

Not all franchisees proved successful, and individual outlets periodically failed. The main reasons for failure appeared to be poor choice of location or territory and a franchisee's own shortcomings. In addition to the obvious technical skills required in a given field, success often hinged on possession of sales and communication abilities. Disputes in franchising were not uncommon but could usually be resolved internally without recourse to legal action. The causes of conflict most frequently cited by franchisees related to franchise fees and alleged misrepresentations made by the franchisor. By contrast, franchisors cited conflicts based on lack of adherence to the system by franchisees.

Australia was home to a number of internationally known franchise operators, including Hertz Rent-a-Car, Avis, McDonald's, KFC, Pizza Hut, Subway, Kwik Kopy, and Snap-on Tools. By contrast, most Burger King outlets operated under the name Hungry Jack's, an acquired Australian chain with significant brand equity.

Jim's Group

One of Australia's best-known locally developed franchisors was Melbourne-based Jim's Group, which described itself as one of the world's largest home service franchise organizations. The company had originated with a mowing service started by Jim Penman in Melbourne in 1982, when he abandoned ideas of an academic career after his Ph.D. thesis was rejected. In 1989, Penman began franchising the service, now known as Jim's Mowing, as a way to facilitate expansion. The business grew rapidly, using master franchisees in various regions to recruit and manage individual franchisees. The company's dark green trucks, displaying a larger-than-life logo of Penman himself, bearded and wearing a hat, soon became a familiar sight on suburban streets around Melbourne. Before long, the franchise expanded to other parts of Victoria and then to other states.

Over the following years, an array of other home-related services were launched under the Jim's brand, including Jim's Trees, Jim's Paving, Jim's Cleaning, Jim's Appliance Repair, and Jim's Floors. Each service division featured the well-recognized logo of Jim Penman's face on a different colored background. Jim's Dogwash made its debut in 1996, employing a bright red, fully enclosed trailer, emblazoned by a logo that had been amended to show Jim with a dog. By early 2002, Jim's Group comprised more than two dozen different service divisions, more than 90 master franchisees, and some 1,900 individual franchisees. In many instances, master franchisees were responsible for two or more service divisions within their regions. Jim's Group's philosophy was to price franchises according to local market conditions. If work in a prospective territory was easy to find but franchisees difficult to attract, the price might be lowered somewhat, but not too much; otherwise, the company felt that there would be insufficient commitment.

In recent years, Jim's Group had expanded overseas. In New Zealand, it had six master franchisees and 232 franchisees and offered mowing, tree work, cleaning, and dogwashing services. It had also established a significant presence for Jim's Mowing in the Canadian province of British Columbia. But attempts to launch Jim's Mowing in the United States had failed, owing to difficulty in finding good operators.

Jim's Dogwash had more than 60 franchises operating in Australia (primarily in Victoria) and New Zealand. This firm's experience had shown that growth was hampered by the shortage of suitable franchisees, as operators needed to be dog lovers with a background in dog care.

FRANCHISING STRATEGY AT AUSSIE POOCH MOBILE

New APM franchisees were recruited through newspaper advertisements and "advertorials" (**Exhibit 8**),

EXHIBIT 8 Examples of Franchisee Recruitment Advertisements and Promotional Materials

Turn your passion for Dogs into cash... If you have a passion for dogs and enjoy the outside you will love being part of our proven business system. It's fun and easy to manage. The Aussie PoochMobile Franchise provides you with...*Specialised training in all aspects of running your business. *Ongoing support. * All your equipment. * An exclusive territory. * Proven marketing campaigns. * Guaranteed income of $600 per week and/or established regular income.
Aussie Pooch Mobile
MOBILE HYDROBATH
1300 369 369
Full Time and Part Time areas available
So to find out more call Call 1300 369 369
and ask for our free information pack
www.aussiepm.com.au
© This publication is the intellectual property of CREATIVE PARTNERS PTY. LTD. Holding Company for Aussie Pooch (The Gap) Any non-aithorised use will contravene the Copyright Act and will result in legal action

Aussie Pooch Mobile provides you with a package of everything you need to start your business. This includes...
Full training in all aspects of the business
Exclusive Territory
Advertising Campaign
Insurance cover (6mths for New areas)
Guaranteed income: $600per week for the first ten weeks. (New areas)
Centralised booking office
Brand New Trailer (New areas)
Grooming Equipment
Uniforms
Advertising Material
Stationery
Customers from Day 1
Plus...
Ongoing Training
Ongoing Support
Monthly Newsletter
Regular fun days and training events
Franchise Advisory Council
New & Established Areas Available

as well as by word of mouth. The concept appealed to individuals who sought to become self-employed but wanted the security of a proven business system rather than striking out entirely on their own. Interested individuals were invited to meet with a representative of the company to learn more. If they wished to proceed further, they had to complete an application form and submit a deposit of $250 to hold a particular area for a maximum of four weeks, during which the applicant could further investigate the characteristics and prospects of the designated territory. This fee was credited to the purchase cost of the franchise if the applicant decided to proceed or returned if the applicant withdrew. A new franchise cost $24,000 (up from $19,500 in 1999). An additional 10 percent had to be added to this fee to pay the recently introduced federal goods and services tax (GST). **Exhibit 9** identifies how APM costed out the various elements.

Selection Requirements for Prospective Franchisees

The company had set a minimum educational requirement of passing year 10 of high school (or equivalent). Taylor noted that successful applicants tended to be outdoor people who shared four characteristics:

> They are self motivated and outgoing. They love dogs and they want to work for themselves. Obviously, being great with dogs is one part of the business—our franchisees understand that the dog's even an extended member of the customer's

EXHIBIT 9 Aussie Pooch Mobile: Breakdown of Franchise Purchase Cost, 2002 vs. 1999

Item	*1999*		*2002*	
	$	*$*	*$*	*$*
Initial training		2,200.00		2,200.00
Initial franchise fee		4,021.50		6,173.00
Guaranteed income		5,000.00		N/A
Exclusive territory plus trailer registration		N/A		6,600.00
Fixtures, fittings, stock, insurance, etc.:				
• Aussie Pooch Mobile trailer and hydrobath	4,860.00		5,340.00	
• Consumables (shampoo, conditioner, etc.)	160.00		230.00	
• Trade equipment and uniforms	920.00		881.65	
• Insurances	338.50	6,278.50	575.35	7,027.00
Initial advertising		2,000.00		2,000.00
Total franchise cost*		**$19,500.00**		**$24,000.00**

*Total franchise costs excludes 10% GST, introduced in July 2000.

family—but it's really important that they can handle the bookwork side of the business as well, because that's basically where your bread and butter is made.

Other desirable characteristics included people skills and patience, as well as a good telephone manner. Would-be franchisees also had to have a valid driver's license, access to a vehicle that was capable of towing a trailer, and the ability to do this type of driving in an urban setting. Originally, Taylor had expected that most franchisees would be relatively young, with parents being willing to buy their children a franchise and set them up with a job, but in fact only about half of all franchisees were aged 21–30; 40 percent were aged 31–40 and 10 percent were in their 40s or 50s. About 60 percent were female. Potential franchisees were offered a trial work period with an operator to see whether they liked the job and were suited to the business, including not only skills with both animals and people but also sufficient physical fitness.

In return for the franchise fee, successful applicants received the rights to a geographically defined franchise, typically comprising about 12,000 homes. Franchisees also obtained an APM trailer with all necessary products and solutions to service the first 100 dogs, as well as red uniform shirts and cap, advertising material, and stationery. The trailer was built to industrial-grade standards, and its design included many refinements developed by APM in consultation with franchisees to simplify the process of dog washing and enhance the experience for the animal. Operators were required to travel with a mobile phone, which they had to pay for themselves.

In addition to franchised territories, APM had six company-owned outlets. These were operated by representatives, who leased the territory and equipment and in return paid APM 25 percent of the gross weekly revenues (including GST). Taylor had no plans to increase the number of representatives. The reps were generally individuals who either could not currently afford the start-up cost or who were being evaluated by the company for their suitability as franchisees. Typically, reps either became franchisees within about six months or left the company.

Assisting New Franchisees

The franchisor provided two weeks' preopening training for all new franchisees, and representatives also spent about 10 hours with each one to help them open their new territories. Training topics included operational and business procedures, effective use of the telephone, hydrobathing techniques, dog-grooming techniques, and information on dog health and behavior. Franchisees were given a detailed operations manual containing 104 pages of instructions on running the business in accordance with company standards.

To help new franchisees get started, APM placed advertisements in local newspapers for a period of 20 weeks. It also prepared human-interest stories for distribution to these newspapers. Other promotional activities at the time of launch included distributing pamphlets in the territory and writing to local vets and pet shops to inform them of the business. APM guaranteed new franchisees a weekly income of $600 for the first ten weeks and paid for a package of insurance policies for six months, after which the franchisee became responsible for the coverage.

Fees and Services

Ongoing support by the franchisor included marketing efforts, monthly newsletters, a telephone hotline service for advice, an insurance package, regular (but brief) field visits, and additional training. If a franchisee fell sick or wished to take a vacation, APM would offer advice on how to best deal with this situation, in many cases being able to organize a trained person to help out. It also organized for franchisees in the major metropolitan areas periodic meetings at which guest presenters spoke on topics relating to franchise operations. Previous guest speakers had included veterinarians, natural therapists, pharmacists, and accountants. More recently, APM had offered one-day seminars, providing more team support and generating greater motivation than the traditional meeting style.

In return for these services, franchisees paid a royalty fee of 10 percent of their gross weekly income, plus an advertising levy of an additional 2.5 percent. Income was reported on a weekly basis, and fees had to be paid weekly. In addition to these fees, operating costs for a franchisee included car-related expenses and purchase of consumable products, such as shampoo, insurance, telephone, and stationery. **Exhibit 10** shows the average weekly costs that a typical franchisee might expect to incur.

Franchisees included several couples, like the Beals, but Taylor believed that having two operators work together was not really efficient, although it could be companionable. Paul Beal, a retired advertising executive, had other interests and did not always accompany Elaine. Some couples split the work, with one operating three days a week and the other three or even four days. All franchisees were required to be substantially involved in the hands-on running of the business; some had more than one territory and employed additional operators to help them.

EXHIBIT 10 Average Annual Operating Expenses for an Aussie Pooch Mobile Franchisee, 2002 vs. 1999

Expense	*1999* *$*	*2002* *$*
Consumable products	3,552	2,880
Car registration	430	430
Car insurance	500	500
Petrol	2,400	3,360
Insurances	642	1,151
Repairs and maintenance	1,104	1,104
Phones, stationery, etc.	1,440	1,920
Communication levy	624	624
Franchise royalties	4,416	5,583
Advertising levy	1,104	1,395
Total	**$16,212**	**$18,947**

To further support individual franchisees, APM had formed a Franchise Advisory Council, composed of a group of experienced franchisees who had volunteered their time to help other franchisees and the system as a whole. Each franchisee was assigned to a team leader, who was a member of the FAC. The Council facilitated communications between franchisees and the support office, meeting with the managers every three months to discuss various issues within the company.

MARKETING AND COMPETITION

The company advertised Aussie Pooch Mobile service in the yellow pages and paid for listings in the white pages of local phone directories. It promoted a single telephone number nationwide in Australia, staffed by an answering service 24 hours a day, seven days a week. Customers paid only a local call charge of 25 cents to access this number. They could leave their name and telephone number, which would then be electronically sorted and forwarded via alphanumeric pagers to the appropriate franchisee, who would then return the call to arrange a convenient appointment time. APM also offered expert advice on local advertising and promotions and made promotional products and advertising templates available to franchisees. Other corporate communications activities included maintaining the Web site (*www.hydrobath.com*), distributing public relations releases to the media, and controlling all aspects of corporate identity, such as trailer design, business cards, and uniforms.

"I try to hold the reins pretty tightly on advertising matters," said Taylor, noting that the franchise agreement required individual franchisees to submit their plans for promotional activities for corporate approval. She shook her head as she remembered an early disaster, involving an unauthorized campaign by a franchisee who had placed an offer of a free dog wash in a widely distributed coupon book. Unfortunately, this promotion had set no expiration date or geographic restriction, with the result that customers were still presenting the coupon more than a year later across several franchise territories.

With APM's approval, some franchisees had developed additional promotional ideas. For example, Elaine and Paul Beal wrote informative articles and human-interest stories about dogs for their local newspaper. When a client's dog died, Elaine sent a sympathy card and presented the owner with a small tree to plant in memory of the pet.

Developing a Territory

Obtaining new customers and retaining existing ones was an important aspect of each franchisee's work. The brightly colored trailer often attracted questions from passers-by and presented a useful opportunity to promote the service. Operators could ask satisfied customers to recommend the service to their friends and neighbors. Encouraging owners to increase the frequency of washing their dogs was another way to build business. Knowing that a dog might become lonely when its owner was absent and was likely to develop behavior problems, Elaine Beal sometimes recommended the acquisition of a "companion pet." As Paul remarked, "Having two dogs is not twice the trouble; it halves the problem!"

However, to maximize profitability, franchisees also had to operate as efficiently as possible, minimizing time spent in non-revenue-producing activities, such as travel, setup, and socializing. As business grew, some franchisees employed additional operators to handle the excess workload, so that the trailer might be in service extended hours, seven days a week. Eventually, a busy territory might be split, with a portion being sold off to a new franchisee.

APM encouraged this practice. The company had found that franchisees reached a comfort zone at about 80 dogs a week, and then their business stopped growing because they could not physically wash any more dogs. Franchisees could set their own price when selling all or part of a territory, and APM helped them to coordinate the sale. When a territory was split, a franchisee was usually motivated to rebuild the remaining half to its maximum potential.

Competition

Although many dog owners had traditionally washed their animals themselves (or had not even bothered), there was a growing trend toward paying a third party to handle this task. Dog-washing services fell into two broad groups. One consisted of fixed-site operations to which dog owners brought their animals for bathing. The location of these businesses included retail sites in suburban shopping areas, kennels, and service providers' own homes or garages. The second type of competition, which had grown in popularity in recent years, consisted of mobile operations that traveled to customers' homes.

With few barriers to entry, there were numerous dog-washing services in most major metropolitan areas; many of these services included the word "hydrobath" in their names. In Brisbane, for example, the yellow pages listed 16 mobile suppliers in addition to APM and 29 fixed-site suppliers, a few of which also washed other types of animals (**Exhibit 11**). The majority of dog-washing services in Australia were believed to be stand-alone operations, but there were other franchisors in addition to Aussie Pooch Mobile. Of these, the most significant appeared to be Jim's Dogwash and Hydrodog.

Jim's Dogwash (part of Melbourne-based Jim's Group) had nine master franchisees and 52 franchises in Australia and four masters and nine franchisees in New Zealand (**Exhibit 12**). Jim's expansion strategy had been achieved in part by creating smaller territories than APM and pricing them relatively inexpensively, in order to stimulate recruitment of new franchisees. A territory, typically encompassing about 2,000 homes, currently sold for $10,000 (comprising an initial franchise fee of $6,000: $3,000 for the trailer, and $1,000 for other equipment) plus 10 percent GST. Jim's fee for washing a dog, including blow drying, ranged from $28 to $38. However, the firm did not offer aromatherapy or anything similar.

Another franchised dog-washing operation was Hydrodog, based on the Gold Coast in Queensland, with 49 units in Queensland, 9 in New South Wales, 8 in Western Australia, and one each in Victoria, South Australia, and the Northern Territory. Hydrodog began franchising in 1994. By 2002, a new franchise unit cost $24,950 (including GST), of which $10,800 was accounted for by the initial franchise fee for a 10,000-home territory. In addition to their dog-grooming services, which included blow-drying and ranged in price from $15 to $40, Hydrodog franchisees sold dog food products, including dry biscuits and cooked or raw meats (chicken, beef, or kangaroo). They did not offer aromatherapy.

DEVELOPING A STRATEGY FOR THE FUTURE

Managing continued expansion presented an ongoing challenge to the directors of Aussie Pooch Mobile.

EXHIBIT 11 Competing Dog-Washing Services in the Greater Brisbane Area, 2002

(A) Services including the word "mobile" in their names

A & Jane's Mobile Dog Wash
A Spotless Dog Mobile Hydrobath
Alan's Mobile Dog and Cat Wash
Fancy Tails Mobile Hydrobath
Fido's Mobile Dog Wash and Clipping
Go-Go's Mobile Pet Parlour
Happy Pets Mobile Hydrobath
Itch-Eeze Mobile Dog Grooming and Hydrobath Service
James' Mobile Pet Grooming and Hydrobath
My Pets Mobile Hydrobath
Paw Prints Mobile Dog Grooming
Preen A Pooch-Mobile
Sallie's Mobile Dogwash
Scrappy Doo's Mobile Hydrobath
Superdog Mobile Hydrobath
Western Suburbs Mobile Dog Bath

(B) Other listings containing the words "bath," "wash," hydro," or similar allusions

Akleena K9 Mobile Hydrobath
Aussie Dog Hydrobath
Budget K9 Baths
Conmurra Hydrobaths
Dandy Dog Hydrobath
Dial A Dogwash
Doggy Dunk
Flush-Puppy
Heavenly Hydropet
Helen's Hydrobath
Herbal Dog Wash
Home Hydrobath Service
Hydro-Hound
Jo's Hydrowash
K9 Aquatics
K9 Kleeners
Keep Em Kleen
Maggie's Shampooch
Nome's Turbo Pet Wash
P.R. Turbo Pet Wash
Paws n More Hydrobath and Pet Care Services
Puppy Paws Dog Wash
Rainbow Mobile Dog Wash
Redlands Mobile Pet Grooming and Hydrobath
Splish Splash Hydrobath
Scrubba Dub Dog
Soapy Dog
Super Clean Professional Dog Wash
Tidy Tim's Hydrobath

Source: Yellow Pages Online, March 2002 under "Dog & Cat Clipping & Grooming" (excludes services delivered only to cats).

EXHIBIT 12 Profile of Jim's Group Franchisees

Location	*All Master Franchisees*[a]	*Master Dogwash Franchisees*	*Individual Dogwash Franchisees*
Victoria	41	6	36
New South Wales + ACT	8	1	7
Queensland	13	—	—
South Australia	6	1	4
Western Australia	13	—	3
Tasmania	1	—	—
Northern Territory	1	1	2
Australia	83	9	52
New Zealand	6	4	9
Canada	1	—	—
Grand Total	**90**	**13**	**61**

[a]All Service divisions
Source: Jim's Group Web site: *www.jims.net*, January 2002.

However, as Chris Taylor pointed out, "You can be the largest but you may not be the best. Our focus is on doing a good job and making our franchisees successful."

To facilitate expansion outside its original base of southeast Queensland, APM had appointed a franchise sales manager in Sydney for the New South Wales market and another in Melbourne for both Victoria and South Australia. One question was whether to adopt a formal strategy of appointing master franchisees. Currently, master franchises were on the Gold Coast (a fast-growing resort and residential area southeast of Brisbane), in the ACT, and in the regional cities of Toowoomba and Bundaberg in Queensland and in Newcastle and Port Macquarie in New South Wales.

For some years, Taylor had been attracted by the idea of expanding internationally. In 1996, the company had licensed a franchisee in New Zealand to operate a subsidiary named Kiwi Pooch Mobile. However, only one unit was operating by early 2002, and she wondered how best to increase this number. Another subsidiary had been established as a master franchise in the French province of New Caledonia, a large island northeast of Australia. Launched in late 2000 under the name of La Pooch Mobile, it had one unit. Another master franchise territory had been established in Malaysia in late 2001, and two units were operating in 2002.

In 2001, APM had granted exclusive rights for operation in the United Kingdom to a British entrepreneur, who operated under the name The Pooch Mobile. Thus far, four units were operating in the English county of Lincolnshire, some 200 km (125 miles) north of London. This individual noted that English people traditionally washed their dogs very infrequently, often as little as once every two to three years, but once they had tried The Pooch Mobile, they quickly converted to becoming monthly clients, primarily for the hygiene benefits.

As the company grew, the directors knew it was likely to face increased competition from other providers of dog-washing services. But as one successful franchisee remarked: "Competition keeps us on our toes. It's hard being in the lead and maintaining the lead if you haven't got anybody on your tail."

Study Questions

1. *What factors drive demand for APM's services?*
2. *What are relevant ways of segmenting the market within a new geographic area?*
3. *Compare and contrast the tasks involved in recruiting new customers and recruiting new franchisees.*
4. *From a franchisee's perspective, what is the advantage offered by belonging to the Aussie Pooch Mobile franchise rather than going it alone? How does the value of the relationship change as the franchisee's business matures in a particular territory?*
5. *In planning for future expansion, how should Christine Taylor evaluate the market potential in Australia versus that of overseas? What strategy do you recommend and why?*

Case 6 Visiting Nurse Associations of America

CHRISTOPHER LOVELOCK AND SUZY EISINGER

Senior managers at VNAA, the national organization representing community-based visiting nurse associations, are concerned at the inaccurate public image of these agencies at a time of strong competition from for-profit home-health services. They wonder how to strengthen the organization and best assist their members.

"The current perception of VNAs," remarked Pamela Sawyer, "is that everybody has heard of visiting nurse agencies but they are not quite sure what they do." As vice president of partnerships and education for the Visiting Nurse Associations of America (VNAA), the national organization for these agencies, Sawyer was considering what marketing approaches might be appropriate to clarify the role of VNAs in delivering home health care to communities across the United States. She continued:

> Many people think that VNAs are a nice group of women who come to your home and provide basic nursing services. They don't associate them with having the expertise and sophistication to satisfy today's complex home healthcare needs. We want VNAs to be perceived as providing state-of-the-art services, with a level of attention and personal care that no other group can match, plus a recognition that they are in the local community and that there's no better organization for delivering home healthcare. Also, we want the public to be aware that the VNAA is the organization that supports, promotes and advances the local VNAs in their mission.

HOME HEALTH CARE IN THE UNITED STATES

Although small as a proportion of the total health care system in the United States, home health care had become one of its most rapidly growing elements. In 2002, the value of this market (excluding drugs) was estimated at \$46.5 billion and expenditures by freestanding agencies were projected to grow at an annual rate of 8.1% through 2010.[1]

Home care was increasingly seen as a desirable and cost-effective alternative to institutional care. Driving forces included an aging population, technological advances in equipment design and treatment protocols, patient preferences, and efforts to reduce the cost of health care. In particular, patients were being sent home from the hospital after shorter stays than previously, while certain procedures that formerly would have required inpatient stays were now being handled on an out-patient or day-surgery basis.

The AARP (a national membership organization for people aged 50 and older) reported that 85% of older men and women preferred to remain in their own homes when they needed health care. Providing care in the home kept costs down by eliminating the resources required for overnight stays at the hospital. Although the average cost to Medicare for one day at a hospital was \$2,753, the average cost per visit from a visiting nurse agency was only \$103.

Background

Home health care services could be divided into two broad categories: short-term care and long-term care. Patients recovering from an injury, surgery, or temporary illness only required assistance for a short period of time until they were able to return to their previous routine. But patients with chronic conditions required ongoing home care for an extended period. In some instances, hospice care for the terminally ill could be provided at home until the patient died or was moved to a residential facility.

The objective of home health care was to allow patients of all ages to live in the familiar surroundings

This case was prepared solely for use as a learning tool. It is not intended to serve as an endorsement, source of primary data, or illustration of effective or ineffective management.

[1]Includes home nursing, respiratory, durable equipment, and home infusion, but excludes drugs. *Source:* Center for Medicare and Medicaid Services (1998 data, 2002 projection).

of their homes while still receiving essential medical treatments and monitoring of their welfare. To achieve this result, home care agencies also delivered physical, occupational and speech therapy, and provided medically-related social work services. Many agencies offered homemaker and "chore" services designed to help patients live independent lives. These non-medical services might include shopping, cooking, housekeeping, transportation, and other forms of personal care.

The top five conditions among home health patients were: diabetes, osteo-arthritis, congestive heart failure, chronic obstructive pulmonary disease, and hip and knee replacements.

Service Providers

Providers of home health care included both for-profit companies and not-for-profit agencies. On the for-profit side, large health care networks and chains had gained market share by developing economies of scale and wide geographic coverage. This made their services attractive to third-party payors, including health maintenance organizations (HMOs) and managed-care plans that sought to control the level and intensity of care.

The largest provider, Gentiva Health Services, had 12,000 active caregivers and 350 service delivery units. In 2002, it served half a million clients and had annual revenues of some $760 million. Another large chain was Bayada Nurses, with 5,000 caregivers and 80 offices in 13 states. In addition, specialized staffing agencies offered home health providers access to freelance health care workers possessing a wide variety of skills.

Non-profit providers included the community-based visiting nurse associations (VNAs), hospital-based services, and independent agencies. A home health service operated by (or affiliated with) a hospital had an advantage, because in-patients often learned about it while at the hospital and chose to use it after being discharged, even when they had used another provider beforehand.

Revenue Sources

There were several ways for providers to cover the cost of their services. They included federal funds, mostly through Medicare and Medicaid; private third-party payers such as HMOs, managed care organizations, and private insurance; and some disease-specific nonprofit organizations such as the American Cancer Society and the Multiple Sclerosis Society. If a service was not covered by a third-party payor, the patient would have to cover the expenses personally.

In 2003, some 7,800 home health providers were Medicare and/or Medicaid certified. Medicare was the national health insurance program for Americans aged 65 and over while Medicaid was a federally funded and state administered program that paid certain health care expenses for low-income consumers with no significant assets. To become certified, agencies had to meet federal standards for patient care and management.

Non-certified agencies focused their attention on patients with private health insurance or on affluent individuals who could pay the fees themselves. However, there was some speculation as to the quality of care provided. During the late 1990s, reports of scandal among some of these agencies had demonstrated the potential for abuse and fraud.

National Organizations for Home Health Care

Three national organizations promoted the concept of home health care and represented the interests of providers. All were active in lobbying for favorable federal regulations for the industry and improved reimbursement rates.

The National Association for Home Care and Hospice (NAHC), located in Washington, DC, described itself as "the nation's largest trade association representing the interests and concerns of home care agencies, hospices, home care aide organizations, and medical equipment suppliers." Founded in 1982 it represented both for-profit and non-profit organizations. Annual dues for provider members (which included a number of visiting nurse agencies) ranged from $500 to $7,400, based on agency revenues. Corporate members with multiple branches paid $10,000 plus $1,000 per branch. Businesses that provided products or services to home care agencies could join as associate members for $1,000 plus $500 per branch. NAHC held an annual conference with educational workshops and a "HOMECAREXPO." It also developed and published manuals.

The second largest organization was the American Association for Home Care (AAHomecare), which asserted that it represented "all the elements of home-care under one roof." Membership included home-care providers of all types, including nonprofit agencies. AAHomecare represented many of the healthcare chains, including home medical equipment providers and rehabilitation technology services. Located in the suburbs of Washington, DC, it had over 3,000 members.

The Visiting Nurse Associations of America (VNAA) was the only national organization that restricted its primary class of membership to nonprofit, community-based, visiting nurse agencies (VNAs). As such, it represented a much narrower interest within home care than the other two organizations. However, other organizations serving the industry could join as associates. In 2003, VNAA had 155 members.

In addition to the national associations, each state had its own state association in which membership was open to any provider. The three national organizations all encouraged their members to join their local state associations as well, because each state had its own legislative initiatives affecting the home health care industry.

VISITING NURSE ASSOCIATIONS

The visiting nurse movement dated back to the mid-19th century. It was conceived in Great Britain by Florence Nightingale—usually recognized as the founder of the modern nursing profession—and William Rathbone, who promoted home delivery of basic health care by compassionate professionals traveling to visit the sick, disabled, and elderly. The idea of "healing in the home" was later advanced in the United States by Lillian Wald, who invented the term "public health nurse" to describe the basis for the modern practice of visiting nurses. The first official Visiting Nurse Association was founded in Albany, New York in 1880. Visiting nurse agencies soon began spreading to major metropolitan areas, suburban neighborhoods and rural communities.[2]

Early priorities were ensuring the survival of infants by providing mothers with nutrition supplies and other health care, and fighting contagious diseases by cleaning the home environment. As health conditions improved in the United States, the mission of VNAs expanded to providing health care to anyone beset by an illness, injury or disability that left them homebound. By the end of the 20th century, the VNAs were especially well known for their care of the elderly and the terminally ill.

In 2003, there were 501 VNAs in 40 states, located in settings from small towns to major cities. Each was an autonomous, community-based nonprofit organization. Because their business involved traveling to patients' homes, each VNA focused on the specific needs of people in its surrounding community. Together, the VNAs served over four million individuals each year and had annual operating revenues of approximately $4 billion. A typical mid-sized VNA served some 5,000 patients annually and made 150,000 patient visits, seeing some patients as frequently as 3–5 times a week.

VNA Services

The VNAs cared for patients in their homes, provided an array of public services, and also worked as health educators. They were best known for their skilled nursing services in a variety of fields, including pediatrics and mental health. Many VNAs had expertise in such specialized areas as hospice care for the terminally ill, preventive health care, pain management, and use of assisted breathing devices such as home ventilators. They offered special programs for the elderly, the chronically sick, and for both adults and children living with HIV/AIDS.

"We do it all, we see it all," remarked one visiting nurse, describing the remarkable variety of her work, which typically involved five to seven visits each day to patients of all ages and an array of medical needs, living in homes that ranged from spacious and clean to cluttered and highly unsanitary. Visiting nurses, about 97% of whom were female, were registered nurses (RNs) who had previously gained significant clinical experience in institutional settings. Part of a nurse's work involved monitoring patients' progress in between hospital- or clinic-based medical interventions; she often used sophisticated portable equipment that she could transport in her car. Many nurses were equipped with laptop computers, enabling them to access and update detailed patient records, complete documentation required for reimbursement or regulatory purposes, and share files with VNA offices, physicians, and other caregivers serving the same patients.

Looking ahead, progressive VNAs were eager to explore new applications of technology, especially telemedicine, which involved using telephone or

[2]Not all nonprofit, community-based, visiting nurse agencies included the term "Visiting Nurse Association" in their names, but collectively they are referred to here as VNAs.

cable services to transmit real-time data about patients' conditions. For instance, patients could be taught to hook themselves up to a monitor that could be accessed by a nurse from a remote location. Installing a small camera in a patient's house would allow the individual (or another caregiver) to film and transmit images relevant to that person's medical situation. Such innovations might enable a nurse to make as many as 20 patient contacts from an office cubicle in the time required for only a handful of house visits. However, the lack of funds for equipment, training, and operating costs was a barrier to implementation.

Health experts recognized the role played by VNAs in promoting disease prevention. Doctors and government agencies often relied on them to handle such basic tasks as publicizing and delivering immunizations. A VNA was often the only local agency with the resources, expertise, and community knowledge to provide this help. Each year, the VNAs gave some two million influenza immunizations between October and January.

Not all VNA services involved medical care and not all employees had professional nursing qualifications. VNAs also delivered physical, occupational and speech therapy in the home, provided medically-related social work services, and often ran adult day care centers. As part of their commitment to holistic health care, many VNAs offered homemaker and "chore" services designed to help patients remain in their homes and live independent lives. Most agencies also administered Meals-on-Wheels programs, sponsored a variety of wellness clinics, and facilitated support groups for patients with cancer, Alzheimer's, and Parkinson's, as well as organizing groups for family caregivers.

As community-based agencies, VNAs developed programs and competencies to fit local needs. Operating as nonprofit organizations, they were governed by boards of directors that typically included a number of community leaders. Leveraging their nonprofit status, VNAs sought to keep costs down by using volunteers for such tasks as raising funds, visiting hospice patients in their homes, delivering meals, and assisting in wellness clinics. They solicited donations to help purchase equipment and cover operating costs. Lacking retained earnings, they depended on grants and donations to provide seed money for service innovations. Success in fundraising varied widely, ranging from $9,000 to $3.1 million per year, and averaging around $300,000. Development department budgets ranged from zero to $1.1 million, averaging about $200,000.

Financial and Regulatory Environment

Only a few patients paid directly for the services they received. Instead, VNAs looked to third-party payors, primarily the federal Medicare program, state Medicaid programs, and medical insurance companies. Recent federal legislation had resulted in significant reductions in Medicare reimbursements from previous levels. People were concerned that budgetary deficits at both the federal and state levels might result in future funding cuts.

The VNAs were committed to providing care for anyone, without regard to their ability to pay. About 50% of home health care recipients received Medicaid benefits and of these individuals, half were served by VNAs. In 2002, 60% of the VNAs' revenue came from Medicare, 15% from Medicaid, 23% from third-party payors, 1% from donations, and 1% from private payors. In large cities, Medicaid assumed greater significance. By contrast, the payor mix at the for-profit Gentiva chain was 21% Medicare, 22% Medicaid/other state, 54% private insurance, and 2% private pay.

EVOLUTION OF THE VNAA

Until the early 1980s, visiting nurse agencies dominated the delivery of home health care. Only nonprofit and public providers were licensed to receive Medicare reimbursement for their services. But the environment of home health care changed dramatically in 1983 following passage of federal legislation that allowed for-profit providers to bill their services to Medicare. These new regulations resulted in a huge increase in the number of for-profit home care operators, most of which promoted their services aggressively. The VNAs were unprepared for this vigorous new competition and their market share began to decline steeply. Unable to cover costs, many VNAs closed.

Responding to this threat, a group of VNAs across the nation collaborated to create the Visiting Nurse Associations of America (VNAA) as a national not-for-profit membership organization to represent their interests. The objective of the new organization was to "support, promote and advance VNAs in their mission to serve their communities." From 1983–97, the VNAA's offices were located in Denver, Colorado.

Some agency leaders argued that the VNA movement needed to take advantage of its coast-to-coast presence and should operate like a form of national franchise, especially in negotiating price, delivery protocols, and other issues with large managed care organizations. But most agencies saw their strengths as lying within their communities; they preferred to negotiate individually, and were unwilling to give up their autonomy.

The 1997 Balanced Budget Act included a moratorium through 2000 on Medicare reimbursements for home health care. This freeze set reimbursements at each provider's historic cost per patient, in contrast to the previous practice of reimbursing for costs up to a cap. This moratorium was particularly damaging for the VNAs, who were the low-cost providers in the field. Twenty-two agencies closed during this period and others merged or joined other health care systems in order to reduce costs further. In Massachusetts, for example, three small VNAs on Cape Cod merged into a single agency which then affiliated with Cape Cod Healthcare, a regional nonprofit organization comprising two hospitals and other providers of health-related services.

In response to this latest crisis, the VNAA board moved to restructure the organization and develop a higher profile. It decided to relocate the headquarters on the East Coast, which not only had the highest concentration of visiting nurse agencies but would also be closer to the nation's leading medical institutions and policymakers. The search began for a new CEO, with the choice of a specific city to be determined by the appointee.

The successful candidate, Carolyn Markey, selected Boston as the new VNAA headquarters. Her clinical training as a registered nurse and 21 years of experience in home health care administration was a good match for the VNAA position. Markey had previously served as CEO for Special Care Home Health Services/AdvantageHEALTH Corporation, which was merging with another company. With her, she brought several members of her former management team, including Pamela Sawyer and Jean Ellis, who became VP-partnerships and education and VP-member services and business development, respectively. Both Sawyer and Ellis had prior nursing experience.

In 1999, the VNAA opened a second office in Washington, DC, with the objective of building stronger relationships with lawmakers in Congress. Kathy Thompson relocated to Washington to open this office as VP-legislative and public affairs. Thompson was already familiar with Capitol Hill, as she had spent eight years as both a legislative assistant and lobbyist for the American Speech-Language-Hearing Association before joining the VNAA in Denver in 1993. She worked with legislators, helping them to draft new bills with provisions favorable to home health care and reimbursement. Bob Wardwell, VP-regulatory and public affairs, educated members of Congress about the implications of existing legislation, seeking to get regulations amended if necessary.

Structure and Activities

The VNAA had 10 staff members in its Boston office, working to facilitate information sharing and promote best practices among the membership. It was governed by a 15-member board composed of ten directors representing VNAs from different parts of the country, four directors at large, and the CEO of the VNAA itself. Board members were nominated and voted by the membership. The board, in conjunction with VNAA senior management, developed the organization's strategic management plan.

Services to members included assistance and advice on cost control, meeting government requirements, and processing complex paperwork. Activities included an annual conference and exhibition, workshops, and teleconferences. An important initiative concerned the use of technology in the field—including telemedicine procedures and laptops—to enable VNAs to deliver quality care in a more efficient manner. **Exhibit 1** shows an organization chart.

Operating revenues in 2002 amounted to \$2,057,226, some 23% above budget, reflecting higher revenues than projected in all categories, especially group purchasing. Income from member dues accounted for 42% of operating revenues, with most of the balance coming from group purchasing (32%), conference fees (10%), sponsorships (7%), and product sales (7%). An income statement is shown in **Exhibit 2**. In addition, the organization received \$801,284 in grants and donations, including a \$444,000 grant from the Langeloth Foundation. Although membership had remained flat during 2002, the strong financial performance reflected active member participation in events, success in obtaining sponsorship of programs, and management's ability to keep costs down.

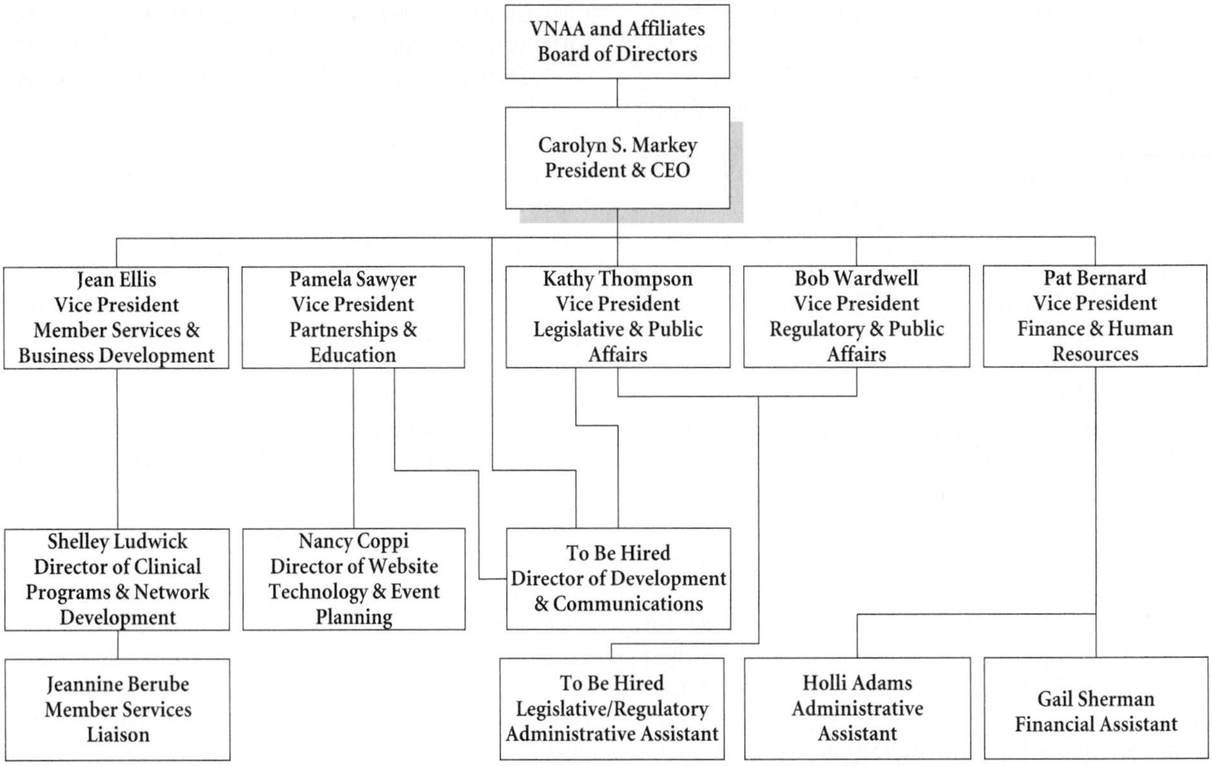

EXHIBIT 1 Visiting Nurse Associations of America Organizational Chart

EXHIBIT 2 VNAA: Statement of Revenues and Expenses, 2002

	YTD Actual	*YTD Budget*	*YTD Variance*
Revenues			
Member Dues	857,175	825,085	32,090
Conference Fees	201,861	166,618	35,243
Sponsorships	139,000	112,000	27,000
Group Purchasing	668,052	431,880	236,172
Administrative Fees	22,486	0	22,486
Product Sales	142,308	112,008	30,300
Interest and Other	26,344	22,806	3,538
Sub-total—Operating Revenue	2,057,226	1,670,397	386,829
Contributions	33,123	25,685	7,438
Grant Revenue	801,284	457,800	343,484
Total Revenues	2,891,633	2,153,882	737,751
Expenses			
Personnel costs	1,051,621	1,024,066	27,555
Printing	84,312	55,740	8,572
Travel and Meetings	144,031	133,938	10,093
Rent	103,987	104,661	(874)
Telephone	40,152	35,585	4,567

EXHIBIT 2 (Continued)

	YTD Actual	*YTD Budget*	*YTD Variance*
Expenses			
Bad Debts	33,140	39,769	(6,629)
Legal, Accounting and Consultants	164,931	152,093	12,838
Postage	36,110	34,509	1,601
Office Supplies	9,702	8,258	1,444
Contracted Services—Educational Outreach	533,284	359,250	174,034
Other	310,441	191,297	119,144
Total Expenses	2,491,711	2,139,166	352,545
Net Income (loss)	399,922	14,716	385,206

Membership

Membership in VNAA was divided into affiliates and associates. Affiliate membership was restricted to VNAs and to other nonprofits that provided similar health services in areas not served by a current VNAA member. Key reasons for belonging to VNAA were to leverage its role in influencing legislation and regulatory changes, engage in educational activities, participate in group purchasing, and take advantage of networking opportunities. Associate membership was open to health care organizations that promoted home care services and represented interests conducive to the VNAA, as well as to organizations that supplied goods and services to the industry.

In early 2003, there were 151 affiliate members and 4 associate members. Annual dues for affiliates were based on a sliding scale, ranging from $570 for organizations with revenues under $300,000 up to $7,420 for those with revenues of $6 million and higher. Associate members paid $2,500.

VNAA was currently engaged in a membership drive to encourage more VNAs to join the organization and to attract more associate members. Most VNAs belonged to their local state associations, which were inexpensive to join, but some were financially hard pressed and felt they could not afford VNAA fees. Many agencies belonged to The National Association for Home Care and Hospice (NAHC), viewing it as the largest and therefore most influential organization in home health care. Some belonged to both NAHC and VNAA. However, others perceived NAHC as trying to be "all things to all people" in home health and preferred the clear focus of VNAA.

Affiliate members came from 40 states and varied widely in size. Some 12% had annual revenues in the range $20–$50 million, 20% were in the $10–$20 million range, 25% had revenues between $5–$10 million, and the balance had revenues ranging from less than $1 million up to $5 million. Some commanded a significant share of their local home health care markets, whereas others were only small players, so the size of an agency was not necessarily a reflection of local market size. In total, VNAA members accounted for annual revenues of around $2 billion and had some 90,000 employees.

A typical VNAA member with $10 million in revenues had some 200 FTE employees, of whom about half were RNs, 15% were other professionals (including physical, occupational, and speech/language therapists), and 15% were administrative support staff in the back office. The remainder comprised home health aides, homemakers, and child care attendants. Agencies in areas with significant minority populations often employed interpreters. Not all employees worked full-time and some positions were filled on a per diem basis as needed. On average, a VNA served around 5,000 patients a year, but might visit some of these as frequently as 3–5 times a week.

The VNAA's most untypical member, the Visiting Nurse Service of New York, was by far the largest VNA in the country. Founded in 1893, it had annual revenues of $668 million in 2001 and received $6.4 million in gifts. It had branch offices in all five boroughs of New York City and its 7,750 caregivers—including nurses, home health aides, social workers, and therapists—made over two million patient visits a year. VNS of New York was also unusual in having a substantial endowment. "It's the 800-pound gorilla of our business, "declared Pamela Sawyer.

Resource Constraints

Several trends in the health care industry were limiting the resources available to VNAs. In addition to the constraints on Medicare reimbursement, many managed care organizations were reducing reimbursement for home health services. Funding from local United Way organizations was crucial to many VNAs but had been falling steadily, reflecting a decline in individual contributions to the United Way.

Additionally, few VNAs had been successful in raising funds for themselves, either through annual appeals or bequests. Many people didn't even realize that the VNAs needed donations. The recently hired director of philanthropy for one of the larger agencies identified a variety of misconceptions among prospective donors, who thought the organization was fully funded by reimbursements or by the local hospitals. People in the local community, she observed, also perceived the VNA as a very small entity.

> When I told them our budget was over $30 million, they simply couldn't believe it! Also there was a misunderstanding of why the VNA was seeking money. "What do you need it for?" they would ask, because they would see one nurse walk through the door but not the great financial needs that lay behind this simple action. It was much easier for them to understand the needs of their local hospital—when it wanted to build a new wing, of course it needed money.

An additional problem was the shortage of registered nurses (RNs) and home health aides (HHAs). Fewer nurses were entering the workforce and some were even leaving the profession. As a result, the average age of RNs in the United States continued to rise, with only 31.7% under the age of 40. Although demographic trends continued to increase the demand for home health aides, recruitment and retention were widely reported to be problems. There was concern that high turnover rates among HHAs might result in higher provider costs and lower quality of care.

To address these needs, the VNAA needed a cost-effective method of providing members with education and information. In 2002, it began to develop an enhanced website, with the help of a grant from the Langeloth Foundation in New York. The goal was to use this site, *www.vnaa.org*, as a channel for delivering web-based courses for RNs and HHAs, as well as information about home healthcare for patients and caregivers.

VNAA VENTURES: THE FOUR AREAS OF FOCUS

In 1997, the board had developed four areas of focus through which the VNAA planned to carry out its mission to support local VNAs. These areas were National Imaging, Member Services, Business Development, and Legislative Issues.

National Imaging

By 2003, only 9% of the home care providers that billed to Medicare were VNAs. With so many competing providers, national imaging strategy sought to differentiate the VNAs as the home health care experts. Carolyn Markey observed: "I knew from my days at Advantage that the VNA name was powerful, but it surprised me to discover that the name is even stronger than I had realized."

However, although the name was recognizable, respected by elected officials, and carried positive associations, there was widespread ignorance at the consumer level about the actual scope of VNA activities. Pamela Sawyer described her recent experience when staffing a booth at a "campaign fair" featuring nonprofit organizations that received funds from planned giving campaigns:

> It was amazing to me. Unless someone had a family member who received home health care through a VNA, nobody had a clue who we were. People thought, "you're the visitors, you're the volunteers, you're the people who come and sit with sick people." There was no concept of the VNA's technical capabilities.

As community-based agencies offering a wide range of services, the VNAs had been unable to develop a consistent national image for themselves. Only 70% of the member organizations actually employed the name Visiting Nurse Association; 8% called themselves Visiting Nurse Service and another 9% had a name that included the words Visiting Nurse. The remaining 13% styled themselves differently. For example, the visiting nurse agency in Columbus, Ohio, had adopted the name "LifeCare Alliance." Remarked Sawyer:

> Many VNAs thought that it wasn't sexy enough to be a VNA and they changed their names. They became Genesis, they became United, they became this, they became that. And then they realized that, wait a second, maybe we should have kept our name as "VNA."

This situation complicated the task of identifying an agency as a VNA. In fact, the name "Visiting Nurse Association" had never even been trademarked, so that in theory, anyone could use it. To address this issue, the VNAA registered its own name and created a distinctive heart-shaped logo and slogan, "At the Heart of home health care." (See **Exhibit 3**.) Members were permitted to use this image on any material, but only a few had taken advantage of this opportunity.

Member Services

Discounts on Purchases of Supplies VNAA offered members the opportunity to save money on

EXHIBIT 3 VNAA Logos

For use by VNAA

VNAA Visiting Nurse Associations of America®

At the Heart of home health care™

At the Heart of home health care™

Available for use by affiliate members of VNAA

MEMBER VNAA Visiting Nurse Associations of America™

purchases of costly equipment and supplies. As VP of member services and business development, Jean Ellis contracted with vendors and suppliers to provide discounts ranging from 10–40% on some high-ticket items. The VNAA itself received a commission of 3% on the value of these group purchases. By 2003, there were 26 contracts in place, covering such categories as telemedicine products, vaccines, medical/surgical supplies, documentation forms, home care consulting services, and personal response monitors for patients. Ellis estimated that a VNA with revenues of $10 million might be able to save as much as $30,000 to $100,000 a year by taking advantage of these discounts, instead of purchasing from local suppliers.

However, encouraging members to take advantage of these opportunities had sometimes proved a difficult task. As an integral part of their communities, VNAs favored local suppliers over national ones. If the CEO of a local agency suggested buying through the VNAA group purchase program, she might find a board member arguing in favor of continuing to support local suppliers. The VNAA could only recommend the national contracts to their members, citing the difference in savings as an incentive. As a result, it could not offer a guaranteed volume as a bargaining chip in negotiations with suppliers.

On-Line Services The VNAA Institute offered members the opportunity to enroll employees in a large number of web-based courses created by leading medical institutions and to participate in live web-events sponsored by Healthstream, a for-profit company active in healthcare education. Affiliate members of the VNAA obtained a password, which allowed them to view these courses, as well as other information posted by the VNAA offices in Boston and Washington.

Business Development

The business development area of focus concentrated on finding and promoting ventures that could generate revenues in excess of costs for member VNAs as well as for the VNAA itself. "We'd like to help the VNAs become less dependent on their traditional revenue sources of Medicare and Medicaid," declared Ellis. "While we don't want our members to walk away from those sources, we want to create new opportunities for them." She noted that initiatives fell into several categories:

1. Contracts with managed care organizations for reimbursement of services
2. Corporate partnerships focusing on public education
3. Partnerships with public and private organizations to supply services
4. Facilitating the sharing of local business development plans between VNAs

Contracts with Managed Care Organizations Like HMOs, MCOs enrolled members for different levels of health care benefits and provided them with a selection of specific health care providers they could use. Endeavoring to take advantage of their scale, MCOs sought to deal with one centralized location when negotiating contracts for reimbursement of home health services. In 2003, the VNAA had 20 contracts covering services in more than 400 locations in 40 states. It had recently obtained substantial increases in reimbursement rates for its members on several contracts. However, not all VNAs were eager to participate, because individual agencies sometimes preferred to contract with a hospital system that gave a more favorable rate.

Corporate Educational Partnerships A typical corporate partnership involved teaming up with a pharmaceutical or medical supplies company to conduct health-related educational programs in local communities. The VNAA had partnered with GlaxoSmithKline and Endo Pharmaceuticals, among other industry leaders. Opportunities for the local VNAs to get involved were posted on the VNAA website and the staff then selected specific partners for the corporation. Sawyer declared that the VNAA was eager to undertake more disease-specific educational programs in conjunction with a corporate partner.

> This is a huge, huge area that we'd really like to focus on more. It gives us recognition, it gives the members recognition and speaks to their mission of disease prevention and health promotion, and it generates income for all of us. The value of the awareness is incredible.

Important factors in selection of a VNA for one of these partnerships might include proven strengths in a relevant activity (e.g., as an immunizer), an entrepreneurial orientation, and location in a good market for publicity. One such partnership was the Tetanus awareness program, sponsored by Aventis Pasteur, a large pharmaceutical company that produced the only vaccine for this disease. In 2002, the VNAA secured a $244,000 grant from the company to promote awareness of the risks of tetanus and diphtheria and application of the preventive "Td" vaccination. This project complemented a national education program by the National Foundation for Infectious Diseases (NFID). "Td" booster clinics were piloted during February–March, 2003 in Warwick, RI; Tulsa, OK; and San Leandro, CA. If successful, seven more locations would be added between April and July.

Each participating VNA would receive $3,000 to compensate them for its costs, which included staffing (two nurses and a secretary/volunteer) and supplies for a 4-hour clinic (excluding the vaccine). It would also receive a separate reimbursement for ordering the "Td" vaccine (200 doses/event) from the VNAA. In addition, each VNA received assistance from two staff consultants to handle on-site media relations and event coordination, develop and plan promotional activities, and secure paid promotional spots on a local radio station. Local media were contacted in advance and local celebrities secured to attend and sign autographs. Pamphlets from the NFID and the VNAA would be distributed and Carolyn Markey would attend each event to make a presentation on behalf of VNAA. Aventis received no publicity but benefited from the communications through such a credible channel.

Ellis cautioned that the VNAA needed to be careful about entering into corporate partnerships. As opportunities presented themselves, she observed:

> We have to go back and ask, "Is this consistent with our four areas of focus?" I think we know the membership well enough and their missions well enough now to know what is an absolute turn-off and what will work. If it's education in their community or if it's preventive medicine, that's a seller, but don't ask them to get involved in anything proprietary, like handing out product samples or coupons.

Partnerships to Provide Services The third area of business development was partnerships with corporations and government agencies to provide services. For example, VNAA had enjoyed a working partnership since 1998 with Aetna, a large insurance company, to provide immunizations and flu shots to the firm's employees in some 53 locations across the United States. The VNAA provided central billing for the Aetna Corporate Flu Program and each participating VNA received a pre-negotiated reimbursement sufficient to cover its costs and result in a modest surplus.

Another example was the VNAA's partnership with Logistics Health, Inc (LHI), an occupational health company that already had a partnership with the federal government for immunization and screening services, including military anthrax vaccine programs. In 2002, the Center for Disease Control (CDC) entered into a contract with LHI to provide CDC lab workers with anthrax immunizations on a voluntary basis. LHI subcontracted with the VNAA to provide these services to CDC lab workers throughout the country. The VNAA then advertised this opportunity to its members, announcing that they had negotiated "very competitive rates for nursing time" and would assist the members in coordinating the logistics.

Sharing between Members The VNAA also facilitated sharing of business development ventures among members. For example, if one VNA created a successful adult day health program, it was encouraged to share this information with the VNAA, which planned to set up bulletin boards on a members-only section of the website. Then, if another member subsequently enquired about such programs, the VNAA could refer this inquiry to an agency that had already had experience in this area. "I get calls all the time," remarked Sawyer, "wanting to know who's got a program in such and such?"

Going a step further, Ellis noted that the business development committee of the board had plans to develop new private-pay turnkey programs:

> We're looking at creating some niche programs. One idea that has come up is a program that individual VNAs in resort areas could market to local hotels, so that when a hotel has a guest coming in who needs medical care, it will contact its local VNA to provide the required services. We hope to put together a couple of programs like that this year and to create a turnkey kit, including everything from identifying your audience and developing marketing activities to policies and procedures and staffing protocols. The idea is that any member would be able to access that kit on our website and duplicate it in their community.

Legislative Issues

As the demonstrably lowest-cost providers of home health care, the visiting nurse agencies had emerged as industry leaders. Lawmakers began turning to the VNAA for advice and accurate information about the needs of home care providers. Since the opening of the Washington office, home care advocates—including the VNAA—had successfully obtained higher reimbursement rates for home-based services for three years in a row. But, given the ballooning federal deficit, the future outlook was seen as bleak.

Kathy Thompson, VP-legislative and public affairs, met with congressmen and their staff to raise concerns about those aspects of Medicare and Medicaid that hurt the VNAs. She helped draft legislation, attended hearings, testified, and wrote reports. She also acted as a spokesperson for home health care and talked to reporters. In March 2003, the U.S. House of Representatives unanimously passed a resolution to establish an Annual National Visiting Nurse Association Week, to be celebrated May 6–12 each year. If also passed by the Senate, the legislation would be sent to the President to be signed into law.

The VNAA was known on Capitol Hill for helping lawmakers to understand the most important issues at hand in home health care. There was wide respect, too, for the charitable role played by member agencies. Commenting on how the VNAA differed from NAHC and AAHomecare on legislative issues, Thompson observed:

> Our interests overlap with the other associations, particularly on the big Medicare issues. We've been fighting a 15 percent cut in reimbursement for about five years now since the Balanced Budget Act of 1997 was passed.
>
> But we may take slightly different approaches on some of those issues, particularly when it comes to payment methodology. For instance, the Act set up a payment methodology that reimbursed agencies according to their historical costs. So if agencies had high Medicare costs, they were going to get more reimbursement per patient than the low-cost provider. That was inherently unfair, because it turns out, at least through a number of different studies, including one from the General Accounting Office, that VNAs didn't have less costly patients, we just provided more efficient care. So we have to take a different position from those associations on reimbursement. We advocated for a national reimbursement rate based not on historical costs, but on averages.

Priorities for 2003 focused on increasing both Medicare and Medicaid reimbursement rates; obtaining appropriations to help fund VNA-specific programs such as maternal and child health, prevention of diabetes, asthma and obesity, and health promotion; and exemption of mass vaccination from regulations that required extensive paperwork.

The Washington office disseminated information to all members about legislation and policy issues and, when necessary, urged them to contact their representatives and senators. Examples of these website postings are shown in **Exhibit 4**. Thompson believed that individual VNAs, because of their strong standing in local communities, had significant credibility and influence with elected officials.

THE WAY AHEAD

At a meeting of the senior management team, Pamela Sawyer argued that the VNAA should set some specific marketing goals for the organization. But she expressed concern that the existing brand name, VNAA, lacked a clear identify, often being

EXHIBIT 4 Example of Legislative Alert Posted on VNAA Website

PHONE CALLS TO HOUSE OF REPRESENTATIVES ARE CRITICAL TO KEEPING 5% RURAL ADD-ON AND NURSE REINVESTMENT ACT FUNDING:

Your help is essential to keeping the Senata-passed 5% rural add-on in the FY 2003 Omnibus Appropriations Bill (H.J. Res. 2) and the $20 million Nurse Reinvestment Act funding (also in H.J. Res. 2).

ALSO URGE YOUR U.S. REPRESENTATIVES TO COSPONSOR "NATIONAL VNAs WEEK" LEGISLATION

Congressman Ed Markey (D-MA) is preparing to re-introduce legislation next week commemorating "National VNAs Week."

confused with a local VNA or even an unrelated organization. "We need to determine what to call ourselves," agreed Carolyn Markey, "then communicate that throughout the membership and incorporate it into all marketing initiatives." One option that appealed to the team was to rebrand the VNAA as the "VNAs of America."

"One problem," interjected Jean Ellis, "is that we don't really have a marketing line item in the budget, except for the website, which is funded by the Langeloth Foundation. We need to establish some marketing priorities, consider possible strategies for achieving them, and then decide how we're going to finance these efforts."

Study Questions

1. *In what ways is the VNAA similar to, and different from, a for-profit franchise chain?*
2. *How is the VNAA positioned against other associations representing the interests of home-health care providers? What do you see as the VNAA's relative strengths and weaknesses?*
3. *What do you think that VNAs who join the association expect from their membership? How might VNAA enlarge the number of members?*
4. *Recommend a set of marketing objectives for the VNAA and propose specific strategies to achieve these goals.*

Case 7 The Accra Beach Hotel

Block Booking of Capacity during a Peak Period

SHERYL KIMES, JOCHEN WIRTZ, AND CHRISTOPHER LOVELOCK

The sales manager for a Caribbean hotel wonders whether to accept a large block booking at a discount rate from a group participating in an international sporting event. Do the promised publicity benefits justify the risk of turning away guests from higher-paying segments?

Cherita Howard, sales manager for the Accra Beach Hotel, a 141-room hotel on the Caribbean island of Barbados, was debating what to do about a request from the West Indies Cricket Board. More than six months ahead, the Board wanted to book a large block of rooms during several of the hotel's busiest times and was asking for a discount. In return, the Board promised to promote the Accra Beach in all advertising materials and television broadcasts as the host hotel for the upcoming West Indies Cricket Series, an important international sporting event.

THE HOTEL

The Accra Beach Hotel and Resort had a prime beach front location on the south coast of Barbados, just a short distance from the airport and the capital city of Bridgetown. Located on $3\frac{1}{2}$ acres of tropical landscape and fronting one of the best beaches on Barbados, the hotel featured rooms offering panoramic views of the ocean, pool, or island.

Note: Certain data have been disguised.

The centerpiece of its lush gardens was the large swimming pool, which had a shallow bank for lounging and a swim-up bar. In addition, there was a squash court and a fully equipped gym. Golf was available only 15 minutes away at the Barbados Golf Club, with which the hotel was affiliated.

The Accra Beach had two restaurants and two bars, as well as extensive banquet and conference facilities. It offered state-of-the-art conference facilities to local, regional, and international corporate clients and had hosted a number of large summits in recent years. Three conference rooms, which could be configured in a number of ways, served as the setting for corporate meetings, training seminars, product displays, dinners, and wedding receptions. A business center provided guests with Internet access, faxing capabilities, and photocopying services.

The hotel's 122 standard rooms were categorized into three groups—(island view, pool view, and ocean view)—and there were also 13 island-view junior suites and six penthouse suites, each decorated in tropical pastel prints and handcrafted furniture. All rooms were equipped with cable/satellite TV, air-conditioning, ceiling fans, hair dryer, coffee percolator, direct-dial telephone, bathtub/shower, and a balcony.

Standard rooms were configured with either a king-size bed or two twin beds in the Island and Ocean View categories; the Pool View rooms had two double beds. The six Penthouse Suites, which all offered ocean views, contained all the features listed for the standard rooms, as well as added comforts. They were built on two levels, featuring a living room with a bar area on the third floor of the hotel and a bedroom accessed by an internal stairway on the fourth floor. These suites also had a bathroom containing a Jacuzzi, shower stall, double vanity basin, and a skylight. The thirteen Junior Suites were fitted with either a double bed or two twin beds, as well as a living room area with a sofa that converted to another bed.

HOTEL PERFORMANCE

The Accra Beach enjoyed a relatively high occupancy rate, with the highest occupancy being achieved from January through March and the lowest during the summer (**Exhibit 1**). Pricing followed a similar pattern, with the highest room rates (US$150–$170) being achieved from December through March but relatively low rates ($120) during the summer months (**Exhibit 2**). The hotel's RevPAR (revenue

EXHIBIT 1 Accra Beach Hotel Monthly Occupancy Rate

Year	*Month*	*Occupancy (%)*
2 years ago	January	87.7
2 years ago	February	94.1
2 years ago	March	91.9
2 years ago	April	78.7
2 years ago	May	76.7
2 years ago	June	70.7
2 years ago	July	82.0
2 years ago	August	84.9
2 years ago	September	64.7
2 years ago	October	82.0
2 years ago	November	83.8
2 years ago	December	66.1
Last year	January	87.6
Last year	February	88.8
Last year	March	90.3
Last year	April	82.0
Last year	May	74.7
Last year	June	69.1
Last year	July	76.7
Last year	August	70.5
Last year	September	64.7
Last year	October	71.3
Last year	November	81.7
Last year	December	72.1

EXHIBIT 2 Accra Beach Hotel Average Daily Room Rate

Year	*Month*	*Average Room Rate (in US$)*
2 years ago	January	$159.05
2 years ago	February	$153.73
2 years ago	March	$157.00
2 years ago	April	$153.70
2 years ago	May	$144.00
2 years ago	June	$136.69
2 years ago	July	$122.13
2 years ago	August	$121.03
2 years ago	September	$123.45
2 years ago	October	$129.03
2 years ago	November	$141.03
2 years ago	December	$152.87
Last year	January	$162.04
Last year	February	$167.50
Last year	March	$158.44
Last year	April	$150.15
Last year	May	$141.79
Last year	June	$136.46
Last year	July	$128.49
Last year	August	$128.49
Last year	September	$127.11
Last year	October	$132.76
Last year	November	$141.86
Last year	December	$151.59

per available room—a product of the occupancy rate times the average room rate) showed even more variation, with RevPARs exceeding $140 from January through March but falling to less than $100 from June through October (**Exhibit 3**). Rates on the Penthouse suites ranged from $310 to $395, whereas Junior Suites ranged from $195 to $235. Guests had to pay Barbados value-added tax (VAT) of 7.5 percent on room charges and 15 percent on meals.

The hotel's annual operating budget was approximately $7 million, with sales and marketing costs (excluding salaries and other overheads) amounting to about 1 percent of the budget. The Accra Beach had traditionally promoted itself as a resort destination, but in recent years had been promoting its convenient location and had succeeded in attracting many business customers. Cherita worked extensively with tour operators and corporate travel managers.

A majority of hotel guests were corporate clients from such companies as Barbados Cable & Wireless and the Caribbean International Banking Corporation (**Exhibit 4**). The composition of the hotel's clientele had changed significantly over the past few years. Traditionally, the hotel's guests had been dominated by tourists from Britain and Canada. But the percentage of corporate customers had increased dramatically, attracted by the hotel's convenient access to both the airport and Bridgetown. Most of these guests came from the Caribbean and North America and were in Barbados for business meetings with local companies. Some guests visited frequently.

Sometimes, guests who were on vacation (particularly during the winter months) felt uncomfortable finding themselves surrounded by businesspeople. As one vacationer put it, "There's just something weird about being on vacation and going to the beach and then seeing suit-clad businesspeople chatting on their cell phones." However, the hotel achieved a higher average room rate from business guests than from vacationers and had found the volume of corporate business to be much more stable than that from tour operators and individual guests.

EXHIBIT 3 Accra Beach Hotel Revenue per Available Room (RevPAR)

Year	*Month*	*Revenue per Available Room (in US$)*
2 years ago	January	$139.49
2 years ago	February	$144.66
2 years ago	March	$144.28
2 years ago	April	$120.96
2 years ago	May	$110.45
2 years ago	June	$96.64
2 years ago	July	$100.15
2 years ago	August	$102.75
2 years ago	September	$79.87
2 years ago	October	$105.80
2 years ago	November	$118.18
2 years ago	December	$101.05
Last year	January	$141.90
Last year	February	$148.67
Last year	March	$143.02
Last year	April	$123.12
Last year	May	$105.87
Last year	June	$94.23
Last year	July	$98.55
Last year	August	$90.59
Last year	September	$82.24
Last year	October	$94.62
Last year	November	$115.89
Last year	December	$109.24

Note: RevPAR refers to revenue per available room and is computed by multiplying the room occupancy rate (see Exhibit 1) by the average room rate (Exhibit 2).

THE WEST INDIES CRICKET BOARD

Cherita Howard, the hotel's sales manager, had been approached by the West Indies Cricket Board (WICB) about the possibility of the Accra Beach Hotel's serving as the host hotel for the following spring's West Indies Cricket Home Series, an important international sporting event among cricket-loving nations. The location of this event rotated among several Caribbean nations, and Barbados would be hosting the next one, which would feature visiting teams from India and New Zealand.

Cherita and Jon Martineau, general manager of the hotel, both thought that the marketing exposure associated with hosting the teams would be very beneficial for the hotel but were concerned about accepting the business because they knew from past experience that many of the desired dates were usually very busy days for the hotel. The two were sure that the rate that the WICB was willing to pay would be lower than the average rate of US$140–$150 they normally achieved during these times. In contrast to regular guests, who could usually be counted on to have a number of meals at the hotel, team members and officials would probably be less likely to dine at the hotel, because they would be on a per diem budget.

On average, both corporate customers and vacationers spent about $13 per person for breakfast and about $25 per person for dinner. The margin on food and beverage was approximately 30 percent. About

EXHIBIT 4 Accra Beach Hotel: Market Segments 2002

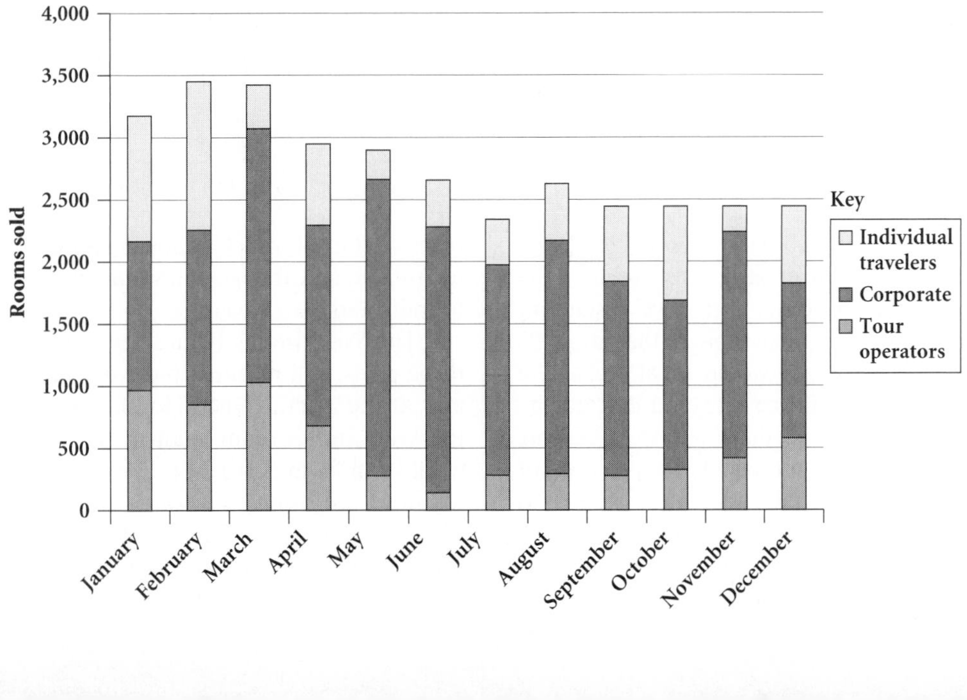

EXHIBIT 5 Room Sales and Average Daily Room Rates for Same Periods in Previous Year (excludes suites)

Date of WICB Home Series	*Rooms Sold Last Year During the Same Period*	*Average Daily Room Rate (ADR) in US$*
Part 1		
4/24	141	$129
4/25	138	$120
4/26	131	$128
4/27	132	$135
4/28	120	$133
4/29	125	$124
4/30	141	$119
5/1	141	$124
5/2	141	$121
Part 1		
5/3	139	$122
5/4	102	$118
5/5	78	$126
5/6	85	$130
5/7	110	$138
Part II		
5/27	96	$131
5/28	111	$132
5/29	111	$136
5/30	122	$136
Part III		
6/17	121	$125
6/18	115	$122
6/19	109	$126
6/20	115	$111
6/21	122	$110
6/22	113	$105
6/23	127	$106
6/24	141	$101
6/25	141	$110
6/26	120	$115

80 percent of all guests had breakfast at the hotel, and approximately 30 percent of all guests dined at the hotel (there were many other attractive restaurant options nearby). Jon Martineau thought that about 95 percent of the cricket group would breakfast at the hotel (as it was included in the rate) but that maybe only 10 percent would dine there. He worried, too, about how other guests might react to the presence of the cricket teams. Still, the publicity benefits appeared substantial. The WICB had promised to list the Accra Beach as the host hotel in all promotional materials and during the televised matches. Broadcasts would reach cricket-playing Caribbean nations from Jamaica to Trinidad and Tobago and would also be transmitted to India and New Zealand.

The West Indies Home Series was divided into three parts, and all three parts would require bookings at the Accra Beach Hotel. The first part pitted the West Indies team against the Indian team and would run from April 24 to May 7. The second part featured the same two teams and would run from May 27 to May 30. The final part showcased the West Indies team against the New Zealand team and would run from June 17 to 26.

The WICB wanted 50 rooms (including two suites at no additional cost) throughout each part of the series and was willing to pay US$130 per night per room, inclusive of both breakfast and VAT. Each team had to be housed on a single floor of the hotel. In addition, the WICB insisted that laundry service for team uniforms (cricket teams typically wear all-white clothing) and practice gear be provided at no additional charge for all team members. Cherita estimated that it would cost the hotel about $20 per day if they could do the laundry in-house but about $200 per day if they had to send it to an outside source.

Cherita called Ferne Armstrong, the hotel's reservations manager, and asked her what she thought. Like Cherita, Ferne was concerned about the possible displacement of higher-paying customers but offered to do further investigation into the expected room sales and associated room rates for the desired dates. As the dates were more than six months in the future, Ferne had not yet developed forecasts. But she was able to provide data on room sales and average room rates from most of the same days of the previous year (**Exhibit 5**).

Soon after Cherita returned to her office to analyze the data, she was interrupted by a phone call from the head of the WICB, wanting to know the status of his request. She promised to have an answer for him before the end of the day. As soon as she hung up, Jon Martineau called and chatted about the huge marketing potential of being the host hotel.

Cherita shook her head and wondered, "What should I do?"

Study Questions

1. *What factors lead to variations in demand for rooms at a hotel such as the Accra Beach?*
2. *Identify the various market segments currently served by the hotel. What are the pros and cons for the hotel of seeking to serve customers from several segments?*
3. *What are the key considerations facing the hotel as it reviews the booking requests from the West Indies Cricket Board?*
4. *What are the financial implications of accepting or not accepting the WICB request? What action should Cherita Howard take, and why?*

Case 8 Coyote Loco

Evaluating Opportunities for Revenue Management

Sheryl Kimes, Jochen Wirtz, and Christopher Lovelock

The owners of a popular restaurant have conducted a detailed study of its operations, including variations in demand by day of the week and time of day. They wonder how to use the resulting insights to improve profitability.

"We're turning customers away during peak hours and operating half empty at other times," declared Elaine Alexander. "As a result, our margins are slim." She and her husband, John, were co-owners of Coyote Loco, a 99-seat restaurant in Ithaca, a college town of 70,000 inhabitants located on one of the scenic Finger Lakes in upstate New York.

Rather than simply accepting these demand swings as a fact of life in the food service business, the Alexanders were eager to pursue ways of resolving the financial problems that the situation presented. Through the nearby School of Hotel and Restaurant Administration at Cornell University, they had learned that a few restaurants were exploring the possibility of adopting revenue management strategies similar to those used in the airline and hotel industries and wondered whether such an approach might work in their own establishment. (See **Appendix A** for an overview of revenue management.)

THE RESTAURANT

Located on the outskirts of Ithaca, about a mile from the Cornell University campus, Coyote Loco offered moderately priced California-style Mexican food. Lunch was served from 11:00 A.M. to 2:30 P.M., then snacks until 6:00 P.M., after which dinner was served through 11:00 P.M. To encourage bar sales during the slow period between lunch and dinner, there was a "happy hour" from 4:00 P.M. to 6:00 P.M. on weekdays, during which drinks were offered for half price.

Staffing levels varied, ranging from three to ten in the front of the house and three to six in the kitchen, depending on anticipated demand levels. There was always a manager on duty. About 60 percent of the employees were full time and included a mix of local residents and students. Front-of-the-house employees were mostly in their twenties, and there was a fairly high turnover rate among the student employees (particularly at the end of the school year). The restaurant also employed two full-time managers. Elaine Alexander worked in a management capacity on a regular basis, but John Alexander was not involved in day-to-day operations.

The Alexanders had operated the restaurant since 1991. The building was originally a train station and had subsequently housed several restaurants. Working with two other partners, John and Elaine purchased the building, remodeled it, and opened Coyote Loco. It quickly proved successful and attracted a good mix of local people and students. Although the bar was popular, the Alexanders had tried to ensure that the restaurant did not become a "bar" destination, because they did not want to have the associated liability problems. They had a large group of loyal customers who dined at the restaurant at least once a week. Reflecting the extensive university community, Ithaca boasted more than 150 restaurants offering a wide array of cuisines, dining styles, and price levels. Coyote Loco was less than a mile from an area known as "Collegetown," which had a wide variety of restaurants.

The building housing Coyote Loco ("Crazy Coyote") was a long wooden structure, painted blue on the outside with aqua window frames and decorated with several large yellow stars. The interior was divided into a main restaurant and a bar area, which was reached by stairs, as it was several feet higher than the main floor. The restaurant area featured four-foot-high wooden paneling and cream-colored walls, on which hung reproductions of artwork from galleries in Santa Fe, New Mexico, including fantasy paintings of coyotes. The bar area featured lighter-colored woodwork, and

The authors acknowledge the assistance of Michael Wat-lon Ma. Certain confidential data have been disguised.

its blue ceiling with yellow stars reprised the exterior design.

There were 68 seats in the restaurant area: two 6-tops (tables with seats for six) and fourteen 4-tops. The bar, which was used for dining on busy nights and also served as the de facto waiting area for not-yet-seated diners, had 31 seats (eleven 2-tops and nine bar stools). During Ithaca's warm-weather summer months, an outdoor patio provided seating for an additional 66 customers. **Exhibit 1a** shows the floor plan, **1b** the restaurant, and **1c** the bar.

The menu comprised approximately eleven appetizers, thirty to forty entrées, and about half a dozen desserts. Individual appetizers ranged in price from $2.99 to $6.99, and entrées accompanied by a salad ranged from $11.99 to $14.99, but there was also a wide array of inexpensive dishes, such as enchiladas and pollo verde, priced between $6.99 and $8.99 (see **Appendix B**). All items were also available for takeout. Coyote Loco had a full bar, offering a wide range of alcoholic beverages. Its signature margaritas were very popular and sold for $5. Beers ranged in price from $2 to $4, and the restaurant offered an array of wines by the glass or the bottle.

ESTABLISHING THE BASELINE

Because Coyote Loco had a fixed seating capacity, revenue management analysis recognized that its financial performance was a function of not only how many seats were occupied from one hour to another but also how much revenue was earned per available seat hour, a measure referred to as RevPASH. To create a profile of their current operations, the Alexanders collected information on guest-arrival patterns over time, the mix of party sizes patronizing the restaurant, how long they remained at the restaurant, and the amount of each party's check.

Guest-Arrival and Spending Patterns

Data on arrival patterns at Coyote Loco were captured on an hourly basis, using the restaurant's Micros 2700 POS system. There were significant

EXHIBIT 1a Coyote Loco Floor Plan

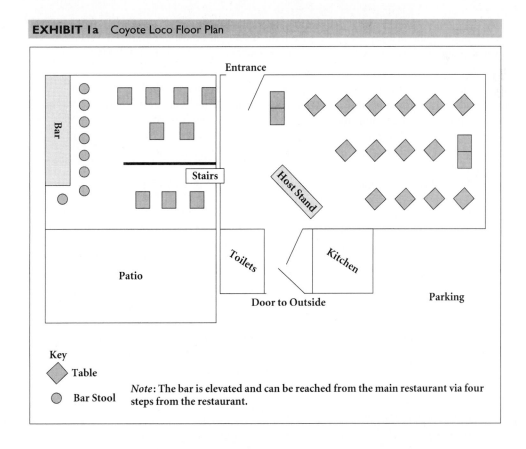

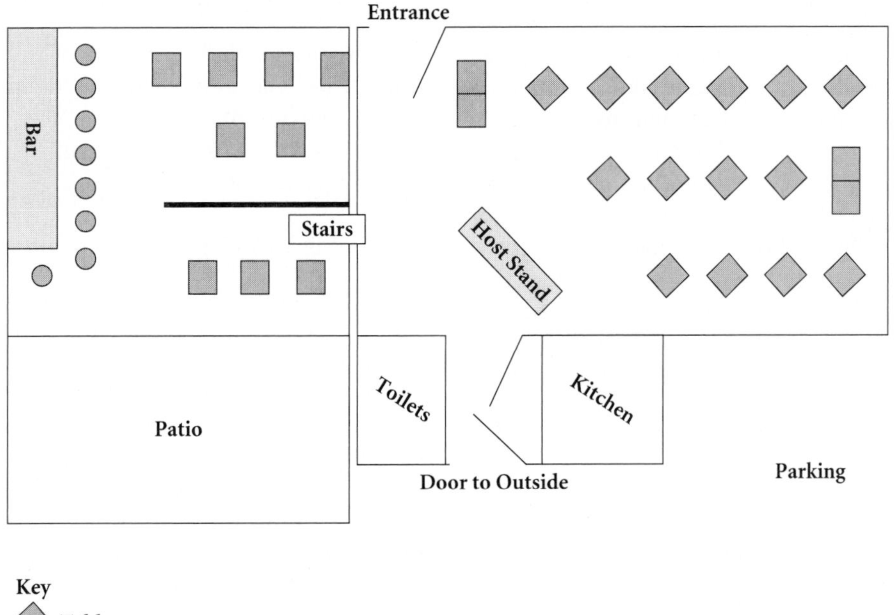

Note: The bar is elevated and can be reached from the main restaurant via four steps from the restaurant.

EXHIBIT 1b Interior of Coyote Loco Restaurant

The restaurant layout in this photo differs from the floor plan shown in Exhibit 1a, which shows the usual layout. The layout shown in the photo was arranged for the Valentine's Day period.

variations over one-hour intervals during peak periods. Although POS (point-of-sale) data contained detailed information on all transactions, including guests' spending, it had some limitations.

For example, the opening time of a check might not reflect the arrival time of guests who had waited to be seated. Similarly, if the cashier had not promptly rung up the check once the table was vacated, the closing time of the check might not indicate exactly when the guests left the dining room. However, as more than 95 percent of the checks were opened within five minutes of true arrival, the system was considered accurate in estimating meal timing.

Coyote Loco was busiest on Friday and Saturday nights between 6:00 P.M. and 8:00 P.M. Sunday was the next-busiest night, with the other nights of the week being much slower. The lunchtime business was relatively slow every day (**Exhibits 2** and **3**).

Party Size Mix

The Alexanders also collected information on the party size mix (**Exhibit 4**). They had thought that the restaurant appealed to parties of four or more customers, but the data surprised them, showing that over 60 percent of customers came in parties of only one or two. Less than 5 percent of dinner patrons came in parties of six or more.

Estimating Unconstrained Demand

One limitation of the actual-arrivals data was that the number of arrivals did not represent the true, *unconstrained demand* (defined as the number of customers a restaurant could handle if its capacity were unlimited). For instance, at busy times, some customers who wanted to dine at the restaurant might be turned away, leave after waiting for a while, or simply observe from the doorway that the restaurant was busy and never even enter.

Observation showed that on Fridays and Saturdays, approximately 20 customers each night were turned away or walked out before being seated. However, diners seeking reservations were rarely disappointed, as nearly all reservations were accepted and honored.

EXHIBIT 1c Coyote Loco Bar

EXHIBIT 2 Guest Arrival Patterns at Coyote Loco

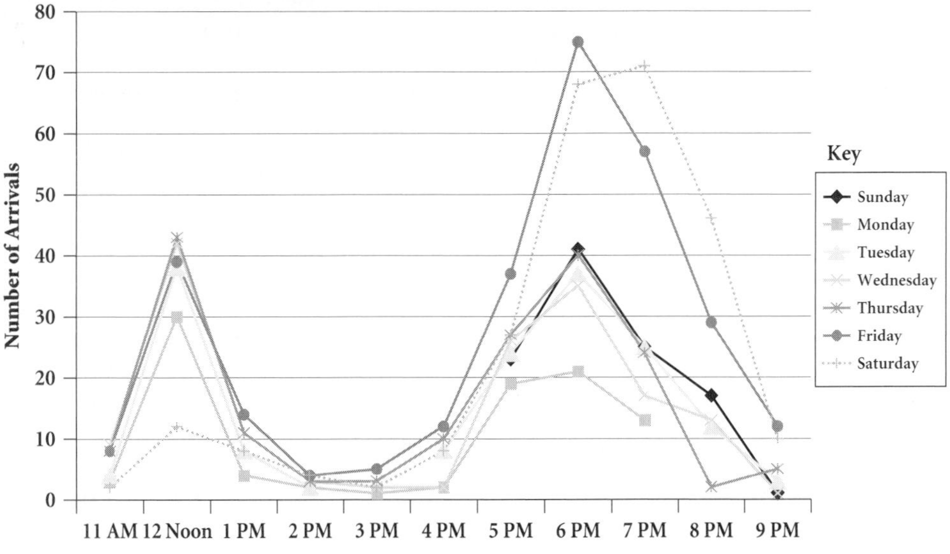

EXHIBIT 3 Number of Guests Arriving for a Meal by Time of Day and Day of Week (37 guests arrived for a meal e.g., between 6:00 P.M. 6:59 P.M. on Tuesday)

	11 AM	*12 PM*	*1 PM*	*2 PM*	*3 PM*	*4 PM*	*5 PM*	*6 PM*	*7 PM*	*8 PM*	*9 PM*
Sunday							23	41	25	17	1
Monday	3	30	4	2	1	2	19	21	13		
Tuesday	4	38	8	2		8	24	37	25	12	3
Wednesday	9	42	11	3	2	2	26	35	17	13	1
Thursday	8	43	11	3	3	10	27	40	24	2	5
Friday	8	39	14	4	5	12	37	75	57	29	12

EXHIBIT 4 Distribution of Number of Persons in Each Guest Party

	Lunch	*Dinner*
1	10.6%	8.6%
2	57.5	51.5
3	15.5	13.9
4	7.9	12.7
5	5.2	4.1
6	1.1	4.6
7	0.5	2.0
8+	1.6	2.5

Meal Duration

Analysis of the POS data showed that the average dining time was approximately one hour, with a standard deviation of about thirty minutes. However, the Alexanders believed that there were significant variations in these averages from one time of day to another and even between different days of the week. So a time study was conducted, and its findings confirmed this belief. **Exhibit 5** shows the means and standard deviations of dining times by hourly period and by day of week.

Course Timing

To understand how long guests spent on the different elements of the meal, a detailed timing study was conducted during dinner hours for 12 nights during February 2003, regarded as a representative period. Student observers sat in an unobtrusive spot and recorded the times of the various transactions. The findings from this study (**Exhibit 6**) helped to verify the results from the POS data.

Approximately 21 minutes after the server first approached the table, appetizers were delivered.

EXHIBIT 5 Meal Duration by Day of Week and Time of Day: Mean and *(standard deviation)* in Hours and Minutes

	11 AM	*12 PM*	*1 PM*	*2 PM*	*3 PM*	*4 PM*	*5 PM*	*6 PM*	*7 PM*	*8 PM*	*9 PM*
Sunday						n.a.	1:23 *(0:50)*	1:15 *(0:26)*	1:16 *(0:30)*	1:18 *(0:40)*	n.a.
Monday	1:04 *(0:20)*	1:04 *(0:31)*	1:18 *(0:40)*	1:05 *(0:11)*	n.a.	1:04 *(0:01)*	1:14 *(0:29)*	1:09 *(0:26)*	0:57 *(0:16)*	n.a.	n.a.
Tuesday	0:58 *(0:37)*	1:08 *(0:29)*	1:00 *(0:17)*	2:02 *(0:12)*	n.a.	1:40 *(0:53)*	1:18 *(0:31)*	1:24 *(0:39)*	1:19 *(0:37)*	1:21 *(0:24)*	1:05 *(0:14)*
Wednesday	1:11 *(0:37)*	1:20 *(0:29)*	0:58 *(0:29)*	1:14 *(0:42)*	0:38 *(0:34)*	1:14 *(0:11)*	1:12 *(0:32)*	0:59 *(0:24)*	1:16 *(0:28)*	0:57 *(0:22)*	0:00 *(0:00)*
Thursday	1:15 *(0:16)*	1:19 *(0:40)*	0:56 *(0:30)*	1:01 *(0:05)*	2:03 *(0:48)*	1:28 *(0:39)*	1:30 *(0:43)*	1:11 *(0:31)*	1:18 *(0:24)*	1:26 *(0:21)*	0:54 *(0:25)*
Friday	0:44 *(0:12)*	1:21 *(0:43)*	1:20 *(0:34)*	0:47 *(0:11)*	1:01 *(0:29)*	1:36 *(0:29)*	1:03 *(0:26)*	1:10 *(0:22)*	1:03 *(0:26)*	1:08 *(0:23)*	1:02 *(0:13)*
Saturday	1:08 *(0:31)*	1:10 *(0:43)*	1:20 *(0:25)*	1:21 *(0:23)*	0:48 *(0:17)*	1:07 *(0:17)*	1:17 *(0:38)*	1:15 *(0:35)*	1:12 *(0:34)*	1:11 *(0:27)*	0:55 *(0:12)*

Example: Guests arriving for a meal between 5:00 P.M.–5:59 P.M. on Tuesday spent an average 1 hour 18 minutes at their table (with a standard deviation of 31 minutes.

n.a. refers to times when the restaurant was open but there was no business activity.

EXHIBIT 6 Course Timing: Mean and (Standard Deviation) in Hours, Minutes, and Seconds

	Mean	*Standard Deviation*
Seat to Greet	2:12	2:17
Greet to Drinks	7:01	5:31
Drinks to Order	2:52	2:57
Order to Appetizer	8:35	5:06
Order to Entrée	18:01	7:49
Entrée to Check Request	28:24	15:42
Check Request to Check Delivered	3:21	2:28
Check Delivered to Check Picked Up	4:31	5:35
Check Picked Up to Change	1:59	1:54
Change to Departure	5:25	6:47
Departure to Bussed	18:12	16:38
Bussed to Reseated	5:41	6:21
Total Time (Seated to Departure)	**1:09:07**	**23:23**

Note: The sum of the meal segment times does not add to the total dining time (seated to departure), because of rounding difference.

Entrées were delivered a little more than eighteen minutes after the appetizer was delivered. The payment process took about twelve minutes. On average, the total dining time (from arrival at the table to departure) was one hour and nine minutes, with a standard deviation of about 23 minutes.

Average Check and Revenue per Available Seat Hour (RevPASH)

By looking at the average check and the revenue per available seat hour, it was possible to calculate seat occupancy. The average check per person varied by time of day and day of week and averaged $14.55 (**Exhibit 7**). As expected, the RevPASH also varied widely, ranging from zero to a high of $10.80 on Saturdays at 7:00 P.M. (**Exhibit 8**). The highest RevPASH figures were achieved on Fridays and Saturdays between 6:00 P.M. and 8:00 P.M, times when all tables were often occupied.

Interactions with Customers

Less than 10 percent of Coyote Loco's customers made reservations. Experience showed that customers holding reservations sometimes arrived late (and occasionally not at all) or showed up with more or fewer people in their party than originally indicated. When an appropriately sized table became available near the reserved time, the manager held that table. It was not unusual to see reserved tables remain empty for over half an hour, even when other guests were waiting.

The host was responsible for greeting guests, handling takeout orders, answering the phone, and helping with service. The waiting space at Coyote Loco was somewhat inadequate during busy periods; when the waiting-time estimates communicated

EXHIBIT 7 Average Check by Day of Week and Hour of Day

	11 AM	*12 Noon*	*1 PM*	*2 PM*	*3 PM*	*4 PM*	*5 PM*	*6 PM*	*7 PM*	*8 PM*	*9 PM*
Sunday							$15.36	$16.66	$17.19	$15.17	$12.29
Monday	$8.27	$11.60	$17.74	$10.67	$7.00	$14.44	$17.39	$19.66	$16.38		
Tuesday	$10.78	$10.93	$12.04	$12.33		$14.67	$16.77	$18.34	$18.84	$16.68	$17.03
Wednesday	$12.15	$9.69	$8.54	$11.23	$3.50	$21.28	$17.43	$17.11	$19.02	$15.57	$11.47
Thursday	$12.36	$10.98	$9.78	$15.27	$14.41	$16.29	$15.62	$18.97	$19.04	$20.94	$11.88
Friday	$11.50	$11.30	$10.70	$11.38	$8.58	$14.18	$18.67	$16.85	$17.58	$16.35	$16.77
Saturday	$14.33	$11.46	$10.00	$15.54	$13.41	$21.48	$16.76	$17.31	$17.79	$16.95	$19.73

EXHIBIT 8 RevPASH (revenue per available seat hour) Patterns by Day of Week and Hour

	11 AM	*12 Noon*	*1 PM*	*2 PM*	*3 PM*	*4 PM*	*5 PM*	*6 PM*	*7 PM*	*8 PM*	*9 PM*
Sunday	$0.00	$0.00	$0.00	$0.00	$0.00	$0.00	$2.08	$5.43	$3.00	$1.59	$0.03
Monday	$0.18	$2.13	$0.36	$0.11	$0.02	$0.27	$1.66	$2.44	$1.15	$0.00	$0.00
Tuesday	$0.17	$2.12	$0.51	$0.13	$0.00	$0.66	$1.84	$3.59	$2.43	$0.98	$0.35
Wednesday	$0.46	$2.06	$0.36	$0.13	$0.01	$0.14	$2.39	$2.90	$1.56	$0.87	$0.05
Thursday	$0.74	$2.36	$0.56	$0.22	$0.23	$0.99	$2.22	$4.26	$2.42	$0.37	$0.83
Friday	$0.67	$2.72	$0.88	$0.25	$0.35	$1.20	$4.30	$9.08	$7.78	$3.95	$1.43
Saturday	$0.18	$0.91	$0.61	$0.42	$0.14	$0.91	$4.03	$9.24	$10.80	$5.28	$0.96

to guests by the host proved overly optimistic, which happened quite frequently, customers sometimes became frustrated, and some even left before being seated.

Once a table became available, the host was notified and tried to find the next party on the waiting list. There were often lags between when the table became ready, the host was notified, and the party was identified and informed. After the party had been seated, the server responsible for that table was expected to greet the customers and offer to take drink orders. But if he or she was unaware of the new party, already busy, or simply inattentive, the customers might be kept waiting.

At Coyote Loco, servers had to walk up several stairs to the bar to pick up drink orders. On busy nights when the bar area was full, the servers often had difficulty navigating their way through the throng of customers. The bartender was, of course, busy at such times, and so servers might have to wait before their customers' drink orders could be filled. If the bartender appeared to be exceptionally busy, the server might even leave to attend to other duties. As a result, the party at the table might be kept waiting some time before receiving its drinks.

Having delivered drinks, the server offered to take the party's meal orders. Servers were trained to suggest possible appetizers, but the large number of unfamiliar Mexican-style entrées on the menu often confused diners, in which case they might ask their server to explain the courses. If servers were also unfamiliar with how the various menu items were prepared, this could delay things further. Not all customers ordered both appetizers and entrées, especially as every table was supplied with ample servings of chips and salsa. Potential problems included long waits and poor timing of the appetizer and entrée delivery. In addition, food runners sometimes delivered the wrong order to a table.

After clearing away the entrée dishes, servers approached the table to offer dessert and coffee. On average, about 31 percent of customers ordered a

EXHIBIT 9 Monthly Profit and Loss Statement at Coyote Loco

Revenue				
Food	$49,721			71%
Beverage	$20,696			29%
Total	$70,417			
Expenses				
Cost of food and beverage		$20,687		29%
Labor expenses		$26,083		37%
Controllable expenses		$7,707		11%
Cleaning			$401	
Laundry			$844	
Paper goods			$739	
R & M			$1,424	
Rentals			$329	
Small wares			$848	
Expenses				
Supplies			$219	
Miscellaneous			$316	
Utilities			$2,587	
Marketing		$1,359		2%
Uncontrollable expenses		$11,268		16%
Credit card			$1,461	
Taxes			$1,059	
Rent			$8,748	
Total expenses		$67,104		
Net Income	**$3,313**			**5%**

dessert (ranging in price from $3.50 to $5.00), and 25 percent requested coffee or tea, which cost $1.25. Some customers concluded their meals quickly, but others took their time. Once the customers were ready to leave, they requested the check. But this process might be delayed if they had problems finding their server, if the latter were slow in arranging for payment, or if the payment-processing systems were operating sluggishly.

Once they had paid, most customers left the restaurant, but some chose to linger. If the host forgot to offer a farewell to departing guests and record that their table had been vacated, the server and busser might not notice that this table was now ready for bussing and resetting.

DEVELOPING A REVENUE MANAGEMENT STRATEGY

John and Elaine Alexander knew that their profit margin at Coyote Loco was relatively small. In a representative month, they had a net income of $3,313 on revenues of $70,417 (**Exhibit 9**). Labor was their highest expense, followed by food and beverage purchases. They were very interested in examining how the data from their study might be used to develop a revenue management strategy that would improve the restaurant's profitability. However, they recognized that changes in existing procedures could affect both customers and staff members and wanted to minimize any negative impact.

APPENDIX A

Restaurant Revenue Management

Revenue (or yield) management was first developed in the mid-1980s and has been successfully used by the airline and hotel industries for many years. However, it has only recently been applied to the restaurant industry.

Revenue management is a sophisticated form of supply-and-demand management. Its primary focus is managing customer demand through the use of variable pricing and capacity management to maximize profitability. The four strategic levers for revenue management are calendar (reservations, bookings), clock (duration controls, turnover rates), capacity (demand smoothing and capacity adjustment), and pricing (price fences,[1] discounts). Through the application of information technology, pricing strategy, and service product/process design, revenue management helps companies to sell the right product at the right time to the right customer for the right price.

A variety of methods, both mathematical and managerial, are available to capacity-constrained service businesses to estimate unconstrained demand (the number of customers a business could handle if its capacity were unlimited). Restaurants, for example, can have someone count the number of guests who walk out before being served and can also track the number of requests for reservations that must be declined during busy periods.

Experts believe that revenue management is particularly suited for the restaurant industry, reflecting its relatively finite capacity of available tables, perishable inventory, microsegmented markets of restaurant guests, fluctuating demand, low ratios of variable to fixed costs, and services that can be reserved in advance or delivered after a queuing delay.

Success in revenue management is typically measured in revenue per available time-based inventory unit. In the airline industry, this becomes revenue per available seat mile; in the hotel industry, revenue per available room night; and in the restaurant industry, revenue per available seat hour (RevPASH). The revenue per available time-based inventory unit can be calculated by multiplying the capacity utilization by the average price.

To be able to apply revenue management, a restaurant should (1) document its baseline performance, (2) understand the determinants of that performance, (3) develop a revenue management strategy, (4) implement the strategy, and (5) monitor performance.

[1]Fences are rules or procedures that prevent or discourage customers willing to pay a higher price from trading down into a lower-price category. Physical fences include observable customer characteristics (e.g., age, disability) and service characteristics, such as travel class, room size, or package category. Nonphysical fences include advance purchase requirements, cancellation or rebooking penalties, requirements for Saturday-night stayovers, time of day/week/season, and group membership or affiliation (e.g., AAA, AARP, alumni).

APPENDIX B

Selected Pages from Coyote Loco's Menu

ANTOJITOS

CALAMARE CON CHIPOTLE Deep-fried squid served with an earthy, spicy dipping sauce made with chipotle chilies 5.99

NACHO GRANDES A generous portion of crisp, fresh-made corn tortilla chips, melted jack cheese, sour cream, Loco Beans, guacamole, grilled chicken, and choice of salsa. 6.99

FLAUTAS CON PAPAS Y QUESO Three crisp corn tortillas filled with jack cheese, potatoes, and roasted peppers. Served with guacamole and choice of salsa. 5.99

PIZZA CON QUESO DE CABRA An open-faced crisp flour tortilla, topped with goat cheese, roasted red peppers, and herbs. 6.99

ANTOJITOS COMBO Need appetizers for your entire table? Can't make a decision? Try our combo platter that is built to suit your crowd. The combination of jalapeño rellenos, Loco onion rings, flautas, nachos, and buffalo chicken fingers gives you something for everyone. 9.99 (serves 4) 17.99 (serves 8)

JALAPEÑOS RELLENOS Jalapeño chile halves filled with rich cream cheese, then breaded and deep-fried. Served with an orange and cilantro dipping sauce. 5.99

SOPA TARASCA A black bean and roasted tomato soup with anaheim chilies and fresh herbs. 2.99

QUESADILLA CON POLLO Folded, toasted flour tortillas filled with grilled chicken, jack cheese, and topped with choice of salsa 6.99

PLATOS UNUSUALES

(Our house specialties - each served with a salad)

POLLO COLORADO CON CREMA Tender chicken breast in a crisp seasoned buttermilk coating, finished with our Salsa Colorado made with ancho chilies, topped with sour cream. Served with Loco Rice and Beans. 12.99

POLLO EN MOLE POBLANO Mexico's most complex and intriguing sauce, that must be tasted to be believed. Made with ancho and pasilla chilies, almonds, sesame seeds, coriander, cloves, cinnamon, anise, and a touch of chocolate served over a sauteed chicken breast. Served with Loco Rice and Beans on the side. 12.99

CAMARONES EN CHILI PASILLA Jumbo shrimp sauteed in butter-flavored pasilla chilies, citrus zest, nd a touch of garlic. Served with Loco Rice and Beans. 14.99

CAMARONES CON PESTO Grilled shrimp in a roasted tomato sauce topped with our goat cheese cilantro pesto. Served with Loco Rice and Beans. 14.99

BISTEC A LA PARILLA Tender steak grilled to order and served with pasilla chili butter (on the side if you like). Topped with Loco onion rings and a side of Loco Beans. 14.99

VERDURAS CON PASTA PENNE Grilled zucchini, bell peppers, eggplant, and onions tossed with olive oil seasoned with a light touch of chipotle chilies and lime zest served on a bed of pasta and garnished with cilantro. 11.99

TAMALES CON FRIJOLES Mexican corn meal with corn, green chilies, and jack cheese spread on a corn husk and topped with black bean chili. Rolled and cooked in a steamer. Served with Loco Rice and salsa. 12.99

A 15% gratuity may be added to parties of eight or more.

PLATOS USUALES

(Have it your way - as a burrito or as a taco!)

BURRITOS A large flour tortilla stuffed to the legal limit with Loco Beans, jack cheese, and choice of filling. Served with Loco Rice and choice of salsa.

TACOS Corn tortillas served either soft or fried with shredded lettuce, cheese, and choice of filling. Both are served with Loco Rice and Beans.

SIX PACK RACK Sample one of each filling in either corn shells (tacos) or flour tortillas (burritos). pollo verde, verduras, calabacitas, puerco pibil, chili colorado, and frijoles. 10.99

POLLO VERDE Our first and forever favorite, served at our booth at the Farmer's Market since 1989. Chicken simmered in a tomatillo sauce. 8.99

VERDURAS Potatoes, carrots, onions and chipotles chilies. 7.99

CALABACITAS Fresh seasoned mushrooms, zucchini, and corn. 7.99

PUERCO PIBIL Shredded braised pork in a Yucatecan sauce of orange and achiote. 8.99

CHILI COLORADO Shredded beef in an ancho chili sauce. 8.99

FRIJOLES Homemade black bean chili. 7.99

Study Questions

1. *What do you see as the key differences between hotels, airlines, and restaurants in relation to possibilities for implementing revenue management strategies?*
2. *Review the study findings presented in Exhibits 2 through 8. In each instance, what are the key insights?*
3. *What specific actions might be taken to improve profitability at Coyote Loco? Discuss the pros and cons of each.*
4. *Propose a revenue management strategy for Coyote Loco and estimate its financial impact. How might the Alexanders minimize any potential negative impacts on customers and staff?*

Case 9 Menton Bank

Christopher Lovelock

Problems arise when a large bank, attempting to develop a stronger customer service orientation, enlarges the tellers' responsibilities to include selling activities.

"I'm concerned about Karen," said Margaret Costanzo to David Reeves. The two bank officers were seated in the former's office at Menton Bank. Costanzo was a vice president of the bank and manager of the Victory Square branch, the third largest in Menton's large branch network. She and Reeves, the branch's customer service director, were having an employee appraisal meeting. Reeves was responsible for the customer service department, which coordinated the activities of the customer service representatives (CSRs, formerly known as tellers) and the customer assistance representatives (CARs, formerly known as new-accounts assistants).

Costanzo and Reeves were discussing Karen Mitchell, a 24-year-old customer service rep who had applied for the soon-to-be-vacant position of head CSR. Mitchell had been with the bank for three and a half years. She had applied for the position of what had then been called head teller a year earlier, but the job had gone to a candidate with more seniority. Now that individual was leaving—his wife had been transferred to a new job in another city—and the position was once again open. Two other candidates had also applied for the job.

Both Costanzo and Reeves were agreed that, against all criteria used in the past, Karen Mitchell would have been the obvious choice for head teller. She was both fast and accurate in her work, presented a smart and professional appearance, and was well liked by customers and her fellow CSRs. However, the nature of the teller's job had been significantly revised nine months earlier to add a stronger marketing component. CSRs were now expected to offer polite suggestions that customers use automated teller machines (ATMs) for simple transactions. They were also required to stimulate customer interest in the broadening array of financial services offered by the bank. "The problem with Karen," as Reeves put it, "is that she simply refuses to sell."

THE NEW FOCUS ON CUSTOMER SERVICE AT MENTON BANK

Although it was the largest bank in the region, Menton had historically focused on corporate business, and its share of the retail consumer banking business had declined in the face of aggressive competition from other financial institutions. Three years earlier, the Board of Directors had appointed a new chief executive officer (CEO) and given him the mandate of developing a stronger consumer orientation at the retail level. The goal was to seize the initiative in marketing the ever-increasing array of financial services now available to retail customers. The CEO's strategy, after putting in a new management team, was to begin by ordering an expansion and speed-up of Menton's investment in electronic delivery systems, which fallen behind the competition. To achieve this strategy, a new banking technology team had been created.

During the past 18 months, the bank had tripled the number of automated teller machines (ATMs) located inside its branches, replacing older ATMs with new models featuring color touch screens and capable of a broader array of transactions. Menton was already a member of several ATM networks, giving its customers access to freestanding 24-hour booths in shopping centers, airports, and other high-traffic locations. The installation of new ATMs was coupled with a renovation program designed to improve the physical appearance of the branches. A pilot program to test the impact of these "new-look" branches was already under way. Longer term, top management intended to redesign the interior of each branch. As more customers switched to electronic banking from remote locations, the bank planned to close a number of its smaller branches.

Another important move had been to introduce automated telephone banking, which allowed customers to check account balances and to move funds from one account to another by touching specific keys on their phone in response to the instructions of a computerized voice. This service was available 24/7, and utilization was rising steadily. Customers could also call a central customer service office to speak with a bank representative concerning service questions or problems with their accounts, as well as to request new-account applications or new checkbooks, which would be sent by mail. This office currently operated on weekdays from 8:00 A.M. to 8:00 P.M. and on Saturdays from 8:00 A.M. to 2:00 P.M., but Menton was evaluating the possibility of expanding the operation to include a broad array of retail bank services offered on a 24-hour basis.

Finally, the technology team had completely redesigned the bank's Web site to make it possible to offer Internet banking services. Customers now had on-line access to their accounts and could also obtain information about bank services, branch locations and service hours, location of ATMs, as well as answers to commonly asked questions. All these actions seemed to be bearing fruit. In the most recent six months, Menton had seen a significant increase in the number of new accounts opened, as compared to the same period the previous year. And quarterly survey data showed that Menton Bank was steadily increasing its share of new deposits in the region.

CUSTOMER SERVICE ISSUES

New financial products had been introduced at a rapid rate. But the bank found that many existing "platform" staff—known as new accounts assistants—were ill equipped to sell these services, because of lack of product knowledge and inadequate training in selling skills. As Costanzo recalled:

> The problem was that they were so used to sitting at their desks waiting for a customer to approach them with a specific request, such as a mortgage or car loan, that it was hard to get them to take a more positive approach that involved actively probing for customer needs. Their whole job seemed to revolve around filling out forms. We were way behind most other banks in this respect.

As the automation program proceeded, the mix of activities performed by the tellers started to change. A growing number of customers were using the ATMs and automated telephone banking for a broad array of transactions, including cash withdrawals and deposits (from the ATMs), transfers of funds between accounts, and requesting account balances. The ATMs at the Victory Square branch had the highest utilization of any of Menton's branches, reflecting the large number of students and young professionals served at that location. Costanzo noted that customers who were older or less well educated seemed to prefer being served by "a real person, rather than a machine."

A year earlier, the head office had selected three branches, including Victory Square, as test sites for a new customer service program that included a radical redesign of the branch interior. The Victory Square branch was in a busy urban location, about one mile from the central business district and less than a 10-minute walk from the campus of a large university. The branch was surrounded by retail stores and close to commercial and professional offices. The other test branches were among the bank's larger suburban offices in two metropolitan areas and were located in a shopping mall and next to a big hospital, respectively.

As part of the branch renovation program, each of these three branches had previously been remodeled to include no fewer than four ATMs (Victory Square had six), which could be closed off from the rest of the branch so that they would remain accessible to customers 24 hours a day. Further remodeling was then undertaken to locate a customer service desk near the entrance; close to each desk were two electronic information terminals, featuring color touch screens that customers could activate to obtain information on a variety of bank services. The teller stations were redesigned to provide two levels of service: an express station for simple deposits and for cashing of approved checks and regular stations for the full array of services provided by tellers. The number of stations open at a given time was varied to reflect the volume of anticipated business, and staffing arrangements were changed to ensure that more tellers were on hand to serve customers during the busiest periods. Finally, the platform area in each branch was reconstructed to create what the architect described as "a friendly, yet professional appearance," and attractively furnished.

HUMAN RESOURCES

With the new environment came new training programs for the staff of these three branches and new job descriptions and job titles: customer assistance representatives (for the platform staff), customer service representatives (for the tellers), and customer service director (instead of assistant branch manager). The head teller position was renamed head CSR. Details of the new job descriptions are shown in the **appendix**. The training programs for each group included sessions designed to develop improved knowledge of both new and existing retail products. (CARs received more extensive training in this area than did CSRs.) The CARs also attended a 15-hour course, offered in three separate sessions, on basic selling skills. This program covered key steps in the sales process, including building a relationship, exploring customer needs, determining a solution, and overcoming objections.

The sales training program for CSRs, by contrast, consisted of just two two-hour sessions designed to develop skills in recognizing and probing customer needs, presenting product features and benefits, overcoming objections, and referring customers to CARs. All staff members in customer service positions participated in sessions designed to improve their communication skills and professional image: clothing and personal grooming and interactions with customers were all discussed. Said the trainer, "Remember, people's money is too important to entrust to someone who doesn't look and act the part!"

CARs were instructed to rise from their seats and shake hands with customers. Both CARs and CSRs were given exercises designed to improve their listening skills and their powers of observation. All employees working where they could be seen by customers were ordered to refrain from drinking soda and chewing gum on the job. (Smoking by both employees and customers had been banned some years earlier under the bank's smoke-free office policy.)

Although they anticipated that most of the increased emphasis on selling would fall to the CARs, Menton Bank's management also foresaw a limited selling role for the customer service reps, who would be expected to mention various products and facilities offered by the bank as they served customers at the teller windows. For instance, if a customer happened to say something about an upcoming vacation, the CSR was supposed to mention traveler's checks; if the customer complained about bounced checks, the CSR should suggest speaking to a CAR about opening a personal line of credit that would provide an automatic overdraft protection; if the customer mentioned investments, the CSR was expected to refer him or her to a CAR, who could provide information on money market accounts, certificates of deposit, or Menton's discount brokerage service. All CSRs were supplied with their own business cards. When making a referral, CSRs were expected to write the customer's name and the product of interest on the back of a card, give it to the customer, and send that individual to the customer assistance desks.

In an effort to motivate CSRs at the three branches to sell specific financial products, the bank experimented with various incentive programs. The first involved cash bonuses for referrals to CARs that resulted in sale of specific products. During a one-month period, CSRs were offered a $50 bonus for each referral leading to a customer's opening a personal line of credit account; the CARs received a $20 bonus for each account they opened, regardless whether it came as a referral or simply a walk-in. Eight such bonuses were paid to CSRs at Victory Square, with three each going to two of the full-time CSRs: Jean Warshawski and Bruce Greenfield. Karen Mitchell was not among the recipients. However, this program was not renewed, as it was felt that there were other, more cost-effective means of marketing this product. In addition, Reeves, the customer service director, had reason to believe that Bruce Greenfield had colluded with one of the CARs, his girlfriend, to claim referrals that he had not, in fact, made. Another test branch reported similar suspicions of two of its CSRs.

A second promotion followed and was based on allocating credits to the CSRs for successful referrals. The value of the credit varied according to the nature of the product—for instance, a debit card was worth 500 credits—and accumulated credits could be exchanged for merchandise gifts. This program was deemed ineffective and was discontinued after three months. The basic problem seemed to be that the value of the gifts was seen as too low in relation to the amount of effort required. Other problems with these promotional schemes included lack of product knowledge on the part of the CSRs and time pressures when many customers were waiting in line to be served.

The bank had next turned to an approach that, in David Reeves' words, "used the stick rather than the carrot." All CSRs had traditionally been evaluated twice yearly on a variety of criteria, including accuracy, speed, quality of interactions with customers, punctuality of arrival for work, job attitudes, cooperation with other employees, and professional image. The evaluation process assigned a number of points to each criterion, with accuracy and speed being the most heavily weighted. In addition to appraisals by the customer service director and the branch manager, with input from the head CSR, Menton had recently instituted a program of anonymous visits by what was popularly known as the "mystery client." Each CSR was visited at least once a quarter by a professional evaluator posing as a customer. This individual's appraisal of the CSR's appearance, performance, and attitude was included in the overall evaluation. The number of points scored by each CSR had a direct impact on merit pay raises and on selection for promotion to the head CSR position or to platform jobs.

To encourage improved product knowledge and "consultative selling" by CSRs, the evaluation process was revised to include points assigned for each individual's success in sales referrals. Under the new evaluation scheme, the maximum number of points assignable for effectiveness in making sales—directly or through referrals to CARs—amounted to 30 percent of the potential total score. Although CSR-initiated sales had risen significantly in the most recent half-year, Reeves sensed that morale had dropped among this group; in contrast, the CARs' enthusiasm and commitment had risen significantly. He had also noticed an increase in CSR errors. One CSR had quit, complaining about too much pressure.

Karen Mitchell

Under the old scoring system, Karen Mitchell had been the highest-scoring teller/CSR for four consecutive half-years. But after two half-years under the new system, her ranking had dropped to fourth out of the seven full-time tellers. The top-ranking CSR, Mary Bell, had been with Menton Bank for sixteen years but had declined repeated invitations to apply for a head teller position, saying that she was happy where she was, earning at the top of the CSR scale, and did not want "the extra worry and responsibility." Mitchell ranked first on all but one of the operationally related criteria (interactions with customers, where she ranked second) but sixth on selling effectiveness (**Exhibit 1**).

Costanzo and Reeves had spoken to Mitchell about her performance and expressed disappointment. Mitchell had informed them, respectfully but firmly, that she saw the most important aspect of her job as giving customers fast, accurate, and courteous service, telling the two bank officers:

> I did try this selling thing but it just seemed to annoy people. Some said they were in a hurry and couldn't talk now, others looked at me as if I were slightly crazy to bring up the subject of a different bank service than the one they were currently transacting. And then, when you got

EXHIBIT 1 Menton Bank: Summary of Performance Evaluation Scores for CSRs at Victory Square Branch During Latest Two Half-Year Periods

		Operational Criteria[1] *(max.: 70 points)*		*Selling Effectiveness*[2] *(max.: 30 points)*		*Total Score*	
CSR name[3]	*Length of Full-Time Bank Service*	*1st Half*	*2nd Half*	*1st Half*	*2nd Half*	*1st Half*	*2nd Half*
Mary Bell	16 years, 10 months	65	64	16	20	81	84
Scott Dubois	2 years, 3 months	63	61	15	19	78	80
Bruce Greenfield	12 months	48	42	20	26	68	68
Karen Mitchell	3 years, 7 months	67	67	13	12	80	79
Sharon Rubin	1 year, 4 months	53	55	8	9	61	64
Swee Hoon Chen	7 months	—	50	—	22	—	72
Jean Warshawski	2 years, 1 month	57	55	21	28	79	83

[1]Totals based on sum of ratings points against various criteria, including accuracy, work production, attendance and punctuality, personal appearance, organization of work, initiative, cooperation with others, problem-solving ability, and quality of interaction with customers.

[2]Points awarded for both direct sales by CSR (e.g., traveler's checks) and referral selling by CSR to CAR (e.g., debit card, certificates of deposit, personal line of credit).

[3]Full-time CSRs only (part-time CSRs were evaluated separately).

the odd person who seemed interested, you could hear the other customers in the line grumbling about the slow service.

Really, the last straw was when I noticed on the computer screen that this woman had several thousand in her savings account so I suggested to her, just as the trainer had told us, that she could earn more interest if she opened a money market account. Well, she told me it was none of my business what she did with her money, and stomped off. Don't get me wrong, I love being able to help customers, and if they ask for my advice, I'll gladly tell them about what the bank has to offer.

Selecting a New Head CSR

Two weeks after this meeting, it was announced that the head CSR was leaving. The job entailed some supervision of the work of the other CSRs (including allocation of work assignments and scheduling part-time CSRs at busy periods or during employee vacations), consultation on—and, where possible, resolution of—any problems occurring at the teller stations, and handling of large cash deposits and withdrawals by local retailers (see position description in the appendix). When not engaged in such tasks, the head CSR was expected to operate a regular teller window.

The pay scale for a head CSR ranged from \$8.00 to \$13.50 per hour, depending on qualifications, seniority, and branch size, as compared to a range \$6.20 to \$10.30 per hour for CSRs. The pay scale for CARs ranged from \$7.10 to \$12.00. Full-time employees (who were not unionized) worked a 40-hour week, including some evenings until 6:00 P.M. and certain Saturday mornings. Costanzo indicated that the pay scales were typical for banks in the region, although the average CSR at Menton was better qualified than those at smaller banks and therefore higher on the scale. Karen Mitchell was currently earning \$9.10 per hour, reflecting her education, which included a diploma in business administration, three-and-a-half years' experience, and significant past merit increases. If promoted to head CSR, she would qualify for an initial rate of \$11.00 an hour. When applications for the positions closed, Mitchell was one of three candidates. The other two candidates were Jean Warshawski, 42, another CSR at the Victory Square branch; and Curtis Richter, 24, the head CSR at one of Menton Bank's small suburban branches, who was seeking more responsibility.

Warshawski was married with two sons in school. She had started working as a part-time teller at Victory Square some three years previously, switching to full-time work a year later in order, as she said, to put away some money for her boys' college education. Warshawski was a cheerful woman with a jolly laugh. She had a wonderful memory for people's names, and Reeves had often seen her greeting customers on the street or in a restaurant during her lunch hour. Reviewing her evaluations over the previous three years, Reeves noted that she had initially performed poorly on accuracy and at one point, when she was still a part-timer, had been put on probation because of frequent inaccuracies in the balance in her cash drawer at the end of the day. Although Reeves considered her much improved on this score, he still saw room for improvement. The customer service director had also had occasion to reprimand her for tardiness during the past year. Warshawski attributed this to health problems with her elder son, who, she said, was now responding to treatment.

Both Reeves and Costanzo had observed Warshawski at work and agreed that her interactions with customers were exceptionally good, although she tended to be overly chatty and was not as fast as Karen Mitchell. She seemed to have a natural ability to size up customers and to decide which ones were good prospects for a quick sales pitch on a specific financial product. Although slightly untidy in her personal appearance, she was very well organized in her work and was quick to help her fellow CSRs, especially new hires. She was currently earning \$8.20 per hour as a CSR and would qualify for a rate of \$10.40 as head CSR. In the most recent six months, Warshawski had ranked ahead of Mitchell as a result of being very successful in consultative selling (**Exhibit 1**).

Richter, the third candidate, was not working in one of the three test branches and so had not been exposed to the consultative selling program and its corresponding evaluation scheme. However, he had received excellent evaluations for his work in Menton's small Longmeadow branch, where he had been employed for three years. A move to Victory Square would increase his earnings from \$9.40 to \$10.40 per hour. Reeves and Costanzo had interviewed Richter and considered him intelligent and personable. He had joined the bank after dropping out of college midway through his third year but had recently started taking evening courses in order to complete his degree. The Longmeadow branch was located in an older part of town, where commercial and retail activity were rather stagnant. This branch (which was rumored to be under consideration for closure) had not yet been renovated and had no ATMs, although there was an ATM accessible to Menton customers one block away. Richter supervised three CSRs and reported directly to the branch manager, who spoke very highly of him. As there were no CARs in this branch, Richter and another experienced CSR took turns handling new accounts and loan or mortgage applications.

Costanzo and Reeves were troubled by the decision that faced them. Prior to the bank's shift in focus, Mitchell would have been the natural choice for the head CSR job, which, in turn, could be a stepping stone to further promotions, including customer assistance representative, customer service director, and, eventually, manager of a small branch or a management position in the head office. Mitchell had told her superiors that she was interested in making a career in banking and that she was eager to take on further responsibilities.

Compounding the problem was the fact that the three branches testing the improved branch design and new customer service program had just completed a full year of the test. Costanzo knew that sales and profits were up significantly at all three branches, relative to the bank's performance as a whole. She anticipated that top management would want to extend the program systemwide after making any modifications that seemed desirable.

Study Questions

1. *Identify and evaluate the steps taken by Menton Bank to develop a stronger customer orientation in its retail branches?*
2. *How would you compare and contrast the jobs of CAR and CSR? How important is each (a) to bank operations and (b) to customer satisfaction?*
3. *What are the strengths and weaknesses of Karen Mitchell and other candidates for head CSR?*
4. *What action do you recommend for filling the head CSR position?*

APPENDIX

Menton Bank: Job Descriptions for Customer Service Staff in Branches

Previous Job Description for Teller

FUNCTION: Provides customer services by receiving, paying out, and keeping accurate records of all moneys involved in paying and receiving transactions. Promotes the bank's services.

Responsibilities

1. Serves customers
   —Accepts deposits, verifies cash and endorsements, and gives customers their receipts
   —Cashes checks within the limits assigned or refers customers to supervisor for authorization
   —Accepts savings deposits and withdrawals, verifies signatures, and posts interest and balances as necessary
   —Accepts loan, credit card, utility, and other payments
   —Issues money orders, cashier's checks, traveler's checks, and foreign currency
   —Reconciles customer statements and confers with bookkeeping personnel regarding discrepancies in balances or other problems
   —Issues credit card advances
2. Prepares individual daily settlement of teller cash and proof transactions
3. Prepares branch daily journal and general ledger
4. Promotes the bank's services
   —Cross-sells other bank services appropriate to customer's needs
   —Answers inquiries regarding bank matters
   —Directs customers to other departments for specialized services
5. Assists with other branch duties
   —Receipts night and mail deposits
   —Reconciles ATM transactions
   —Provides safe-deposit services
   —Performs secretarial duties

New Job Description for Customer Service Representative

FUNCTION: Provides customers with the highest-quality services, with special emphasis on recognizing customer need and cross-selling appropriate bank services. Plays an active role in developing and maintaining good relations.

Responsibilities

1. Presents and communicates the best-possible customer service
   —Greets all customers with a courteous, friendly attitude
   —Provides fast, accurate, friendly service
   —Uses customer's name whenever possible
2. Sells bank services and maintains customer relations
   —Cross-sells retail services by identifying and referring valid prospects to a customer assistance representative or customer service director. When time permits (no other customers waiting in line), should actively cross-sell retail services.
   —Develops new business by acquainting noncustomers with bank services and existing customers with additional services that they are not currently using.
3. Provides a prompt and efficient operation on a professional level
   —Receives cash and/or checks for checking accounts, savings accounts, taxes withheld, loan payments, MasterCard Visa, mortgage payments, money orders, traveler's checks, cashier's checks.
   —Verifies amount of cash and/or checks received, being alert to counterfeit or fraudulent items.
   —Cashes checks in accordance with bank policy. Watches for stop payments and holds funds per bank policy.
   —Receives payment of collection items, safe-deposit rentals, and other miscellaneous items.
   —Confers with head CSR or customer service director on nonroutine situations.
   —Sells traveler's checks, money orders, monthly transit passes, and cashier's checks and may redeem coupons and sell or redeem foreign currency.
   —Prepares coin and currency orders as necessary.
   —Services, maintains, and settles ATMs as required.
   —Ensures that only minimum cash exposure necessary for efficient operation is kept in cash drawer; removes excess cash immediately to secured location.
   —Prepares accurate and timely daily settlement of work.
   —Performs bookkeeping and operational functions as assigned by customer service director.

New Job Description for Head Customer Service Representative

FUNCTION: Supervises all customer service representatives in the designated branch office, ensuring efficient operation and the highest-quality service to customers. Plays an active role in developing and maintaining good customer relations. Assists other branch personnel on request.

Responsibilities

1. Supervises the CSRs in the branch
   —Allocates work, coordinates work flow, reviews and revises work procedures.
   —Ensures that teller area is adequately and efficiently staffed with well-trained, qualified personnel. Assists CSRs with more complex transactions.
   —Resolves routine personnel problems, referring more complex situations to customer service director.
   —Participates in decisions concerning performance appraisal, promotions, wage changes, transfers, and termination of subordinate CSR staff.
2. Assumes responsibility for CSRs' money
   —Buys and sells money in the vault, ensuring adequacy of branch currency and coin supply.
   —Ensures that CSRs and cash sheets are in balance.
   —Maintains necessary records, including daily branch journal and general ledger.
3. Accepts deposits and withdrawals by business customers at the commercial window
4. Operates teller window to provide services to retail customers (see Responsibilities for CSRs)

New Job Description for Customer Assistance Representative

FUNCTION: Provides services and guidance to customers/prospects seeking banking relationships or related information. Promotes and sells needed products and responds to special requests by existing customers.

Responsibilities

1. Provides prompt, efficient, and friendly service to all customers and prospective customers
   —Describes and sells bank services to customers/prospects who approach them directly or via referral from customer service reps or other bank personnel.
   —Answers customers' questions regarding bank services, hours, etc.
2. Identifies and responds to customers' needs
   —Promotes and sells retail services and identifies any existing cross-sell opportunities.
   —Opens new accounts for individuals, businesses, and private organizations.
   —Prepares temporary checks and deposit slips for new checking/NOW accounts.
   —Sells checks and deposit slips.
   —Interviews and takes applications for and pays out on installment/charge card accounts and other credit-related products.
   —Certifies checks.
   —Handles stop payment requests.
   —Responds to telephone mail inquiries from customers or bank personnel.
   —Receives notification of name or address changes and takes necessary action.
   —Takes action on notification of lost passbooks, credit cards, ATM cards, collateral, and other lost or stolen items.
   —Demonstrates ATMs to customers and assists with problems.
   —Coordinates closing of accounts and ascertains reasons.
3. Sells and services all retail products
   —Advises customers and processes applications for all products covered in CAR training programs (and updates).
   —Initiates referrals to the appropriate department when a trust or corporate business need is identified.

New Job Description for Customer Service Director

FUNCTION: Supervises customer service representatives, customer assistance representatives, and other staff as assigned to provide the most effective and profitable retail banking delivery system in the local marketplace. Supervises sales efforts and provides feedback to management concerning response to products and services by current and prospective banking customers. Communicates goals and results to those supervised and ensures that operational standards are met in order to achieve outstanding customer service.

Responsibilities

1. Supervises effective delivery of retail products
   —Selects, trains, and manages CSRs and CARs
   —Assigns duties and work schedules
   —Completes performance reviews
2. Personally, and through those supervised, renders the highest level of professional and efficient customer service available in the local marketplace
   —Provides high level of service while implementing most efficient and customer-sensitive staffing schedules
   —Supervises all on-the-job programs within office

—Ensures that outstanding customer service standards are achieved
—Directs remedial programs for CSRs and CARs as necessary

3. Develops retail sales effectiveness to the degree necessary to achieve market share objectives
—Ensures that all CSRs and CARs possess comprehensive product knowledge
—Directs coordinated cross-sell program within office at all times
—Reports staff training needs to branch manager and/or regional training director

4. Ensures adherence to operational standards
—Oversees preparation of daily and monthly operational and sales reports
—Estimates, approves, and coordinates branch cash needs in advance
—Oversees ATM processing function
—Handles or consults with CSRs/CARs on more complex transactions
—Ensures clean and businesslike appearance of the branch facility

5. Informs branch manager of customer response to products
—Reports customer complaints and types of sales resistance encountered
—Describes and summarizes reasons for account closings

6. Communicates effectively the goals and results of the bank to those under supervision
—Reduces office goals into format that translates to goals for each CSR or CAR
—Reports sales and cross-sell results to all CSRs and CARs
—Conducts sales- and service-oriented staff meetings with CSRs/CARs on a regular basis
—Attends all scheduled customer service management meetings organized by regional office

Case 10 Vick's Pizza Corporation

Christopher Lovelock

A national chain of pizza restaurants promotes speed as a major competitive advantage for its home delivery services. But it suddenly finds itself facing legal challenges and bad publicity as a result of fatal accidents involving the teenagers who drive its delivery trucks.

Victor Firenze, chief executive of Vick's Pizza Corporation, looked somber as he addressed senior executives of the national pizza restaurant chain that bore his nickname. "We're facing yet another lawsuit for injuries due to alleged dangerous driving by one of our delivery drivers," he announced at the company's head office in Illinois. "It comes on top of some very bad publicity about accidents involving our drivers in recent years."

BACKGROUND

Speed had always been a key strategic thrust for Vick's Pizza, which used the slogan, "It's quick at Vick's." The company's restaurants not only prepared pizza rapidly but also delivered it quickly. The company's promise to home deliver a pizza within 30 minutes of a phone order or to cut $3 off the price had boosted it from a single pizzeria 20 years earlier to the status of a national chain with thousands of outlets and over $3 billion in sales. But now a growing number of critics were saying that, in Vick's case, at least, speed was a killer.

Vick's executives argued that the system did not promote fast or reckless driving. "The speed takes place in the store—not on the road," declared a spokesperson. "We can custom-make a pizza within 10 to 12 minutes. Our average delivery area is only 1 to 2 miles, so there's enough time to deliver."

THE SAFETY PROBLEM

The company's own records indicated that during the previous year, accidents involving Vick's drivers had cost 20 lives, 18 of them during pizza runs. But it had declined to specify how many of the victims were employees. Randell Meins, Vick's vice president for corporate communications, stated in a television interview that the company had always encouraged drivers to take care, had never penalized late drivers, was urging franchise owners and store managers to promote safe driving, and would soon implement a new safety course for all Vick's drivers.

Meins cited the owner of several franchises in Ohio, who had declared: "We never ask a driver to break the speed limit. We never want them to do anything unsafe on the road. And we always tell them to fasten their seat belts." Although acknowledging that "even one death is too many," Meins noted that with 230 million pizzas delivered last year, this works out to only one death per 11.5 million pies. "We're not minimizing the deaths by any means," Meins said. "But that's what the mathematics show."

Martina Gomes, director of a nonprofit safety research and advocacy group, expressed outrage over the Vick's statistic. "Great!" she said. "Now we know the value of the life of a 17-year-old—11.5 million pizzas." Gomes offered her own statistical analysis. Vick's, she said, employed some 75,000 part-time drivers. Assuming that this amounted to the equivalent of 20,000 full-time drivers—four for each of the 5,000 Vick's outlets—she claimed that 20 deaths in one year meant that the company's drivers faced a death rate between three and six times higher than that in the construction industry and twice as high as that of miners.

"The point is this," said Gomes. "Would parents let their kids drive for Vick's if they knew they were three times more likely to die doing that job than if they were working in construction?"

Scott and Linda Hurding's 17-year-old son had been the latest Vick's driver to die, the only Vick's employee so far during the current year. Hustling to deliver pizzas in a semirural area near Dallas, Texas,

Mike Hurding often covered 100 miles a night. His parents and classmates said that he was proud that he almost always made the delivery within the 30-minute limit and was determined never to get the "King of the Lates" badge allegedly given every week by his franchisor to the driver most often late on deliveries.

Mike died when the company-owned pickup he was driving in a delivery run skidded off a wet road and hit a utility pole as he tried to avoid another car that was braking to make a left-hand turn. A police reconstruction of the accident concluded that Mike had been driving at 45 mph on a road with a 30 mph speed limit and was not wearing a seat belt. The other driver was not charged. Vick's subsequently offered the Hurding family about $5,000 in worker's compensation to cover funeral costs. Gomes estimated that the 20 deaths during the previous year had cost Vick's some $90,000 in death benefits. Like many other critics of the company, she argued that Vick's was unconcerned because the cost was so low. Accordingly, she had written to Victor Firenze, asking that Vick's pay $500,000 to each accident victim, abandon the 30-minute rule, and hire only drivers aged 18 or older.

Linda Hurding, Mike's mother, told a TV reporter that Vick's guarantee to deliver each pizza within 30 minutes or knock $3 off the price was just "a license to speed." Blaming this policy for their son's death, the Hurding parents and a group of family friends had started a petition drive asking for federal restrictions on the policy. Within a month of beginning their drive, the petitioners had delivered the first batch of more than 1,500 signatures to the offices of their U.S. senator. "We're angry and we're fighting," the Hurdings said. Meantime, a state agency in Texas was looking into the case to determine whether Vick's policy violated the Occupational Safety and Health Act under its jurisdiction.

Vick's faced criticism and legal action on other fronts as well. In Eugene, Oregon, the widow of a motorcyclist allegedly struck and killed by a Vick's driver nine months earlier had sued the company for damages. In Atlanta, attorney Anders Mundel had just filed suit on behalf of Wilson and Jennifer Groncki, who suffered neck, back, and arm injuries when their car was broadsided by a Vick's delivery truck whose driver had run a stop sign as she left a Vick's store with four pizzas for home delivery.

The Gronckis alleged that the store manager had rushed to the scene of the wreck and yelled, "Let's get this pizza on the road!" In addition to unspecified monetary damages, the suit sought to force Vick's to abandon the 30-minute rule, which the attorney called "a grossly negligent corporate policy."

Attorney Mundel was also helping other lawyers around the country to press cases against the company and had organized an information network, including a Web site, to coordinate the filing of cases in different jurisdictions. "Even if Vick's franchisees, managers, and executives do not actively encourage reckless driving," he argued, "the 30-minute rule acts as an inherent encouragement, putting great pressure on the drivers."

As part of her research, safety advocate Gomes had interviewed a number of current and former Vick's employees, several of whom preferred to remain anonymous for fear of reprisals from the managers at the stores where they worked. Gomes claimed that her research showed that "the vast majority" of the company's drivers were under 18.

Nelson Chen, a 20-year-old college student and former part-time Vick's employee who had worked in several Vick's outlets in southern California over a three-year period, told Gomes that he and other drivers "speeded all the time. I would even run stop signs—anything to make those deliveries." Declining to give her last name, Sue, a 19-year-old Vick's driver in Kansas, said that managers "get uptight when pizzas are running late and start yelling at everyone to hurry up, hurry up!"

A consultant familiar with the industry agreed: "There's a lot of pressure to speed. It's not written in the manuals, but it's there. If a driver goes out with four deliveries and ends up with only a minute to make that last one but figures he's two minutes away, he's going to speed, he's going to cut corners."

RESPONDING TO THE PROBLEM

Two weeks after Mike Hurding's death, Vick's sent a letter to its corporate-owned stores and its franchisees, stating that it was company policy to hire drivers 18 or older. This directive, however, was not binding on the franchisees, who operated some 65 percent of all Vick's restaurants.

The newly filed Atlanta lawsuit, together with continuing criticism of the company, had been widely reported in the media. Firenze and his colleagues were worried. Historically, the company had enjoyed a positive public image and a reputation as a generous donor to local community activities. "We definitely have a perception problem," said Meins. "We're taking a lot of heat right now." But Harry Carpaccio, the senior vice president of marketing, warned against taking precipitous action. "The last thing we need to do is to panic," he declared. "The 30-minute guarantee is very, very important to our customers. Sales could be hard hit if we drop it."

Study Questions

1. *Flowchart Vicks' service delivery system from receipt of the order to delivery of the pizza to the customer. Why are pizzas sometimes delivered late?*
2. *How important is the thirty-minute guarantee?*
3. *How serious is the present situation for Vick's Pizza Corporation? How well has it handled the situation so far?*
4. *If you were a senior manager of Vick's Pizza Corporation, what do you think the company should do now? Why?*

Case 11 Hilton HHonors Worldwide: Loyalty Wars

JOHN DEIGHTON AND STOWE SHOEMAKER

Hilton Hotels regards frequent guest programs as the industry's most important marketing tool, directing promotional and customer service efforts at the heavy user. How should management of Hilton's international guest rewards program respond when a competitor ups the ante in the loyalty stakes?

Jeff Diskin, head of Hilton HHonors® (Hilton's guest reward program), opened the *Wall Street Journal* on February 2, 1999, and read the headline, "Hotels Raise the Ante in Business-Travel Game." The story read, "Starwood Hotels and Resorts Worldwide Inc. is expected to unveil tomorrow an aggressive frequent-guest program that it hopes will help lure more business travelers to its Sheraton, Westin and other hotels. Accompanied by a $50 million ad campaign, the program ratchets up the stakes in the loyalty-program game that big corporate hotel companies, including Starwood and its rivals at Marriott, Hilton and Hyatt are playing."[1]

Diskin did not hide his concern. "These guys are raising their costs, and they're probably raising mine too. They are reducing the cost-effectiveness of the industry's most important marketing tool by deficit spending against their program. Loyalty programs have been at the core of how we attract and retain our best customers for over a decade. But they are only as cost-effective as our competitors let them be."

Loyalty Marketing Programs

The idea of rewarding loyalty had its origins in coupons and trading stamps. First in the 1900s and again in the 1950s, America experienced episodes of trading stamp frenzy that became so intense that Congressional investigations were mounted. Retailers would give customers small adhesive stamps in proportion to the amount of their purchases, to be pasted into books and eventually redeemed for merchandise. The best-known operator had been the S&H Green Stamp Company. Both episodes had lasted about 20 years, declining as the consumer passion for collecting abated and vendors came to the conclusion that any advantage they might once have held had been competed away by emulators.

Loyalty marketing in its modern form was born in 1981 when American Airlines introduced the Advantage frequent flyer program, giving "miles" in proportion to the miles traveled, redeemable for free travel. It did so in response to the competitive pressure that followed airline deregulation. The American Airlines program had no need of stamps, because it took advantage of the data-warehousing capabilities of computers. Soon program administrators realized that they had a tool that did not merely reward loyalty, but identified by name and address the people who accounted for most of aviation's revenues, and made a one-to-one relationship possible.

Competing airlines launched their own programs, but, unlike stamps programs, frequent flyer programs seemed to survive emulation. By 1990, almost all airlines offered them. In the late 1990s, Delta Air Lines and United Airlines linked their programs together, as did American and US Airways in the United States. Internationally, United Airlines and Lufthansa combined with eleven other airlines to form Star Alliance, and American, British, and four others formed an alliance called Oneworld. In these alliances, qualifying flights on any of the member airlines could be credited to the frequent flyer club of the flyer's choice.

As the decade ended, computer-based frequency programs were common in many service industries, including car rental, department stores, video and book retailing, credit cards, movie theaters, and the hotel industry.

[1]*Wall Street Journal*, February 2, 1999, page B1.

Business School Case 9-501-010. Professor John Deighton of Harvard Business School and Professor Stowe Shoemaker of the William F. Harrah College of Hotel Administration, University of Nevada, Las Vegas, prepared this case as the basis for class discussion. The case reflects the status of Hilton Hotels Corporation and Hilton HHonors Worldwide as of January 1999. Hilton has made numerous changes since that time, including Hilton Hotels Corporation's acquisition of Promus Hotel Corporation. March 18, 2002.

EXHIBIT 1 The United States Lodging Industry

	Countries	*Properties*	*Rooms*	*Owned Properties*	*Franchised Properties*	*Management Contracts*
Marriott International[1]	53	1,764	339,200	49	936	776
Bass Hotels and Resorts[2]	90	2,700	447,967	76	2439	185
Hilton Hotels Corp.[3]	11	272	91,060	39	207	16
Starwood Hotels and Resorts Worldwide, Inc.[4]	72	695	212,950	171	291	233
Hyatt[5]	45	246	93,729	NA	NA	NA
Carlson[6]	50	581	112,089	1	542	38
Hilton International[7]	50	224	62,941	154	0	70
Promus[8]	11	1,398	198,526	160	1,059	179

Source: World Trade Organization and Company Information.

[1]Includes Marriott Hotels, Resorts and Suites; Courtyard, Residence Inn, TownePlace Suites, Fairfield Inn, SpringHill Suites, Marriott Vacation Club International; Conference Centers, Marriott Executive Residences, Ritz-Carlton, Renaissance, Ramada International.

[2]Includes Inter-continental, Forum, Crowne Plaza, Holiday Inn, Holiday Inn Express, Staybridge.

[3]Includes Hilton Hotels, Hilton Garden Inns, Hilton Suites, Hilton Grand Vacation Clubs, and Conrad International.

[4]Includes St. Regis, Westin Hotels and Resorts, Sheraton Hotels and Resorts, Four Points, Sheraton Inns, The W Hotels. Does not include other Starwood owned hotels, flagged under other brands (93 properties for 29,322 rooms).

[5] Includes Hyatt Hotels, Hyatt International, and Southern Pacific Hotel Corporation (SPHC). Because it is a privately held corporation, it will not divulge the breakdown of rooms between ownership, franchise, and management contract.

[6]Includes Radisson Hotels Worldwide, Regent International Hotels, Country Inns and Suites.

[7]A wholly owned subsidiary of what was once known as the Ladbroke Group. In Spring 1999, Ladbroke changed their name to Hilton Group PLC to reflect the emphasis on hotels.

[8]Includes such brands as Doubletree, Red Lion, Hampton Inn, Hampton Inn & Suites, Embassy Suites, and Homewood Suites.

THE HOTEL INDUSTRY

Chain brands were a major factor in the global hotel market of 13.6 million rooms.[2] The chains supplied reservation services, field sales operations, loyalty program administration and the management of hotel properties, under well-recognized names like Hilton and Marriott. See **Exhibit 1** for details of the seven largest U.S. hotel chains competing in the business class hotel segment.

While the brands stood for quality, there was less standardization of operations in hotel chains than in many other services. The reason was that behind a consumer's experience of a hotel brand might lie any of many methods of control. A branded hotel might be owned and managed by the chain, but it might be owned by a third party and managed by the chain, or owned by the chain and managed by a franchisee, or, in some cases, owned and managed by the franchisee. Occasionally chains managed each other's brands, because one chain could be another's franchisee. Starwood, for example, ran hotels under the Hilton brand as Hilton's franchisee. Information about competitors' operating procedures therefore circulated quite freely in the industry.

Consumers

For most Americans, a stay in a hotel was a relatively rare event. Of the 74% of Americans who traveled overnight in a year, only 41% used a hotel, motel or resort. The market in which Hilton competed was smaller still, defined by price point and trip purpose, and divided among business, convention and leisure segments.

The business segment accounted for one-third of all room-nights in the market that Hilton served. About two-thirds of these stays were at rates negotiated between the guest's employer and the chain, but

[2]World Trade Organization.

since most corporations negotiated rates with two and sometimes three hotel chains, business travelers had some discretion to choose where they would stay. About one-third of business travelers did not have access to negotiated corporate rates and had full discretion to choose their hotel.

The convention segment, comprising convention, conference and other meeting-related travel, accounted for another third of room-nights in Hilton's competitive set. The choice of hotel in this instance was in the hands of a small number of professional conference organizers, typically employees of professional associations and major corporations.

The leisure segment accounted for the final third. Leisure guests were price sensitive, often making their selections from among packages of airline, car, tours and hotels assembled by a small group of wholesalers and tour organizers at rates discounted below business rates.

Although the chains as a whole experienced demand from all segments, individual properties tended to draw disproportionately from one segment or another. Resort hotels served leisure travelers and some conventioneers, convention hotels depended on group and business travel, and hotels near airports were patronized by guests on business, for example. These segmentation schemes, however, obscured the fact that the individuals in segments differentiated by trip purpose and price point were often the same people. Frequent travelers patronized hotels of various kinds and price segments, depending for example, on whether a stay was a reimbursable business expense, a vacation, or a personal expense.

Competition

Four large global brands dominated the business class hotel market (**Table A**). Each competed at more than one price point. **Exhibit 2** shows the price

TABLE A

Marriott International	339,200 rooms
Starwood Hotels and Resorts	212,900 rooms
Hyatt Hotels	93,700 rooms
Hilton Hotels	91,100 rooms
Hilton International	62,900 rooms

EXHIBIT 2 Price Segments in the Lodging Industry

- Luxury: average rack rate over $125, full-service hotels with deluxe amenities for leisure travelers and special amenities for business and meeting markets. Chains in this segment include Four Seasons, Hilton, Hyatt, Inter-Continental (a Bass Hotels and Resort Brand), Marriott Hotels and Resorts, Renaissance (a Marriott International brand), Ritz Carlton (also a Marriott International brand), Sheraton (a Starwood Hotels and Resorts Brand) and Westin (also a Starwood Hotels and Resorts Brand).
- Upscale: average rack rate between $100 and $125, full service hotels with standard amenities. Includes most all-suite, non-extended-stay brands. Crowne Plaza (a Bass Hotels and Resort Brand), Doubletree Guest Suites (a Promus Hotel Corp. brand), Embassy Suites (also a Promus Hotel Corp. brand), Radisson (a Carlson Worldwide Hospitality brand), Hilton Inn, and Clarion (a Choice Hotels Brand) are all examples of chains in this segment.
- Mid-market with food and beverage (F&B): Average rack rate between $60-$90, full-service hotels with lower service levels and amenities than the Upscale segment. Examples include Best Western, Courtyard (a Marriott International brand), Garden Inn (a Hilton brand), Holiday Inn (a Bass Hotels and Resorts brand), and Howard Johnson (a Cendant brand).
- Mid-market without F&B: Average rack rate between $45–$70, with limited-service and comparable amenities to the Mid-market with F&B segment. Examples of chains in this segment include Hampton Inns (a Promus brand), Holiday Inn Express (a Bass Hotels and Resorts brand), and Comfort Inn (a Choice Hotels brand).
- Economy: Average rack rate between $40 and $65, with limited service and few amenities. Fairfield Inn (a Marriott International brand), Red Roof Inn, Travelodge, and Days Inn of America (a Cendant brand) are examples of economy chains.
- Budget: Average rack rate between $30–$60, with limited service and basic amenities. Motel 6, Super 8, and Econo Lodge are the best known chains in this segment.
- Extended Stay: Average rack rate between $60–$90, targeted to extended stay market and designed for extended length of stay. Marriott International has the following two brands in this market: Residence Inn by Marriott and Towneplace Suites. Other chains include Homewood Suites (a Bass Hotels and Resort), Summerfield Suites, and Extended Stay America.

Source: U.S. lodging chains segmented by RealTime Hotel Reports Inc., authors of the 1998 Lodging Survey.

EXHIBIT 3 Segments Served by the Major Chains

	Luxury	*Upscale*	*Mid-Market with Food and Beverage*	*Mid-Market without Food and Beverage*	*Economy*	*Budget*	*Extended Stay*
Hilton	X	X	X	X			
Hyatt	X						
Marriott	X	X	X		X		X
Starwood	X	X	X				X

Source: Company records.

points in the industry, and **Exhibit 3** shows the distribution of brands across price points.

Starwood: Beginning in 1991, Barry Sternlicht built Starwood Hotels and Resorts Worldwide from a base in a real estate investment trust. In January 1998, Starwood bought Westin Hotels and Resorts and a month later it bought ITT Corporation, which included Sheraton Hotels and Resorts, after a well-publicized battle with Hilton Hotels Corporation. By the year-end, Starwood had under unified management the Westin, Sheraton, St. Regis, Four Points and Caesar's Palace brands. Starwood had recently announced plans to create a new brand, W, aimed at younger professionals.

Marriott: Marriott International operated and franchised hotels under the Marriott, Ritz-Carlton, Renaissance, Residence Inn, Courtyard, Towneplace Suites, Fairfield Inn, Springhill Suites, and Ramada International brands. It also operated conference centers, and provided furnished corporate housing. A real estate investment trust, Host Marriott, owned some of the properties operated by Marriott International, as well as some Hyatt, Four Season and Swissotel properties.

Hyatt: The Pritzker family of Chicago owned Hyatt Corporation, the only privately owned major hotel chain. Hyatt comprised Hyatt Hotels, operating hotels and resorts in the United States, Canada, and the Caribbean; and Hyatt International, operating overseas. Hyatt also owned Southern Pacific Hotel Group, a three- and four-star hotel chain based primarily in Australia. Although the companies operated independently, they ran joint marketing programs.

The 1990s had been a time of consolidation and rationalization in the lodging industry, partly due to application of information technologies to reservation systems and control of operations. Jeff Diskin reflected on the trend: "Historically, bigger has been better because it has led to economies of scale, and bigger and better brands to leverage. Historically, big players could win even if they did not do a particularly good job on service, performance or programs. Now (after the Starwood deal) there's another big player. It would have been nice if it had been Hilton that was the largest hotel chain in the world, but biggest is not the only way to be best."

MARKETING THE HILTON BRAND

The Hilton brand was controlled by two entirely unrelated corporations, Hilton Hotels Corporation (HHC) based in Beverley Hills, CA and Hilton International (HIC) headquartered near London, England. In 1997, however, HHC and HIC reached an agreement to reunify the Hilton brand worldwide. They agreed to cooperate on sales and marketing, standardize operations, and run the Hilton HHonors loyalty program across all HHC and HIC hotels. At the end of 1998, HHC divested itself of casino interests, and announced, "a new era as a dedicated hotel company."

The exit from gaming, the reunification of Hilton's worldwide marketing, and the extension of the brand into the middle market under the Hilton Garden Inn name, were initiatives that followed the appointment in 1997 of Stephen F. Bollenbach as president and chief executive officer of Hilton. Bollenbach had served as chief financial officer of Marriott and most recently as chief financial officer of Disney, and he brought to Hilton a passion for branding. To some members of the Hilton management team, the focus on brand development was a welcome one. "Hilton's advantage has been a well-recognized name, but a potentially limiting factor has been a widely varying product, and the challenge of managing customer expectation with such a variety of product offerings. Since Hilton includes everything from world-renowned properties like The Waldorf-Astoria and Hilton Hawaiian Village to the smaller middle-market Hilton Garden Inns, it's important to give consumers a clear sense of what to expect from the various types of hotels," observed one manager.

In mid-1999, the properties branded as Hilton hotels comprised:

- 39 Owned or partly owned by HHC in the United States
- 207 Franchised by HHC to third-party managers in the United States
- 16 Managed by HHC in the United States on behalf of third-party owners
- 10 Managed internationally under HHC's Conrad International brand
- 220 Managed by HIC in over 50 countries excluding the USA

The executives at Hilton HHonors worked for these 492 hotels and their 154,000 rooms. The previous year had been successful. Revenues had been in the region of $158 per night per guest, and occupancy had exceeded break-even. Hotels like Hilton's tended to cover fixed costs at about 68% occupancy and 80% of all revenue at higher occupancy levels flowed to the bottom line. Advertising, selling and other marketing costs (a component of fixed costs) for this group of hotels were not published, but industry norms ran at about $750 per room per year.[3]

Hilton HHonors® Program

Hilton HHonors was the name Hilton gave to its program designed to build loyalty to the Hilton brand worldwide. Hilton HHonors Worldwide (HHW) operated the program, not as a profit center but as a service to its two parents, HHC and HIC. It was required to break even each year and to measure its effectiveness through a complex set of program metrics. Jeff Diskin ran the limited liability corporation with a staff of 30, with one VP overseeing the program's marketing efforts, and one VP with operational and customer service oversight. **Exhibit 4** shows the Income Statement for HHW.

EXHIBIT 4 Hilton HHonors Worldwide: 1998 Income Statement

(While these data are broadly reflective of the economic situation, certain competitively sensitive information has been masked.)

	$ (thousands)	
Revenue		
Contribution from hotels		
Domestic	$39,755	
International	$10,100	
Strategic partner contributions	$18,841	
Membership fees[1]	$1,141	
Total		**$69,837**
Expense		
Redemptions		
Cash payments to hotels	$12,654	
Deferred liability[2]	$9,436	
Airline miles purchases	$17,851	
Member acquisition expenses	$7,273	
Member communication expenses	4,236	
Program administration expenses	$17,988	
Total		**$69,438**
Net Income		**$399**

Source: Company records (masked).

Note from casewriter: For purposes of consistency in calculation among class members, assume an average nightly revenue of $158 per room. Assume that airline miles are purchased from the airline by Hilton at 1 cent per mile.

[1] From members of the Hilton Senior HHonors program only. The Senior HHonors program invited people over 60 to receive discounted stays in exchange for a membership fee. Regular HHonors members do not pay a membership fee.

[2] More points were issued than redeemed. From the outstanding balance a deferred liability was charged to HHW's income statement, based on estimating the proportion of points that would ultimately be redeemed.

[3]For the purpose of consistency in calculation among class members, assume an occupancy of 70%. The information in this paragraph has been masked. No data of this kind are publicly available and these data are not to be interpreted as indicative of information private to either HHC or HIC.

Membership in the Hilton HHonors program was open to anyone who applied, at no charge. Members earned points toward their Hilton HHonors account whenever they stayed at HHC or HIC hotels. When Hilton HHonors members accumulated enough points in the program, they could redeem them for stays at HHonors hotels, or use them to buy products and services from partner companies, or convert them to miles in airline frequent flyer programs. **Exhibit 5** shows how points in the program flowed among participants in the program, as detailed in the text that follows.

There were four tiers of membership—Blue, Silver, Gold and Diamond. The program worked as follows at the Blue level in 1998.

- When a member stayed at a Hilton hotel and paid a so-called business rate,[4] the hotel typically paid HHW 4.5 cents per dollar of the guest's folio (folio is the total charge by the guest before taxes). HHW credited the guest's Hilton HHonors account with 10 points per eligible dollar of folio.
- Hilton guests could earn mileage in partner airline frequent flyer programs for the same stay that earned them HHonors points, a practice known as Double Dipping.® (Hilton was the only hotel chain to offer Double Dipping: other chains with frequency programs required guests to choose between points in the hotel program or miles in the airline program.) If the member chose to Double Dip, HHW bought miles from the relevant airline and credited the guest's airline frequent flyer account at 500 miles per stay.
- If the guest used points to pay for a stay, HHW reimbursed the hosting hotel at more than the costs incremental to the cost of leaving the room empty, but less than the revenue from a paying guest. The points needed to earn a stay depended on the class of hotel, and fell when occupancy was low. As illustration, redemption rates ranged from 5,000 points to get 50% off the $128 cost of a weekend at the Hilton Albuquerque, to 25,000 points for a free weekend night at the $239 per night Hilton Boston Back Bay. A number of exotic rewards were offered, such as a two-person, seven-night diving adventure in the Red Sea for 350,000 points, including hotel and airfare.

EXHIBIT 5 How the Hilton HHonors Program Works

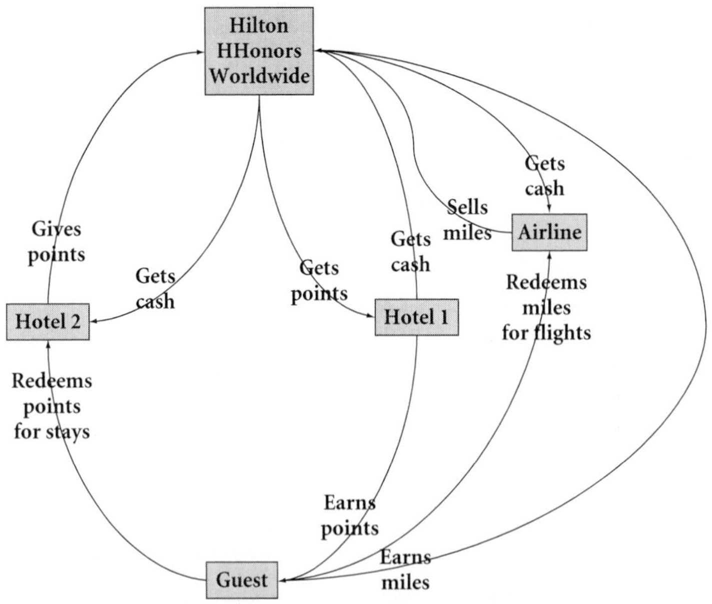

[4]Hilton distinguished three kinds of rate. "Business rates" were higher than "leisure rates," which in turn were higher than "ineligible rates," which referred to group tour wholesale rates, airline crew rates, and other deeply discounted rates.

- Members earned points by renting a car, flying with a partner airline, using the Hilton Credit Card from American Express or buying products promoted in mailings by partners such as FTD Florists and Mrs. Field's Cookies. Members could buy points at $10 per thousand for up to 20% of the points needed for a reward.
- Members had other benefits besides free stays. They had a priority reservation telephone number. Check-in went faster because information on preferences was on file. Members were favored over non-members when they asked for late checkout. If members were dissatisfied, they were guaranteed a room upgrade certificate in exchange for a letter explaining their dissatisfaction. Points could be exchanged for airline miles, and viceversa, and to buy partner products such as airline tickets, flowers, Mrs. Field's Cookies, Cannordale bicycles, AAA membership, Princess Cruises and car rentals.

Members were awarded Silver VIP status if they stayed at HHonors hotels four times in a year. They earned a 15% bonus on Base points, received a 5,000-point bonus after seven stays in a quarter, and a 10,000-point discount when they claimed a reward costing 100,000 points. They were given a certificate for an upgrade to the best room in the hotel after every fifth stay.

Members were awarded Gold VIP status if they stayed at HHonors hotels 16 times or for 36 nights in a year. They earned a 25% bonus on Base points, received a 5,000-point bonus after seven stays in a quarter, and a 20,000-point discount when they claimed a reward costing 100,000 points. They were given a certificate for an upgrade to the best room in the hotel after every fifth stay, and were upgraded to best available room at time of check-in.

The top 1% of members were given Diamond VIP status. This level was not mentioned in promotional material, and no benefits were promised. Diskin explained, "Our goal at the time was to under-promise and over-deliver. If you stay a lot, we say thank you, and as a reward we want to give you Diamond VIP status. We get a lot more bang, more affinity, more vesting from the customer if we do something unexpected. As an industry, we should never overpromise. It leads the public to decide that this is all smoke and mirrors, and it makes it harder for us to deliver genuine value." **Table B** shows HHW's member activity in 1998.

A further 712,000 stays averaging 2.4 nights were recorded in 1998 for which no Hilton HHonors membership card was presented but instead airline miles were claimed and airline membership numbers were captured, so that the guest could be given a unique identifier in the Hilton database. Spending on these stays totaled $327 million.

Guests identified by their HHonors or airline membership numbers occupied 22.5% of all the rooms occupied in the Hilton Hotels and Hilton International network in a year. They were a much smaller proportion of all the guests who stayed with Hilton in a year, because they tended to be frequent travelers. Hilton's research found that Hilton HHonors members spent about $4.6 billion on accommodation per year, not all of which was with Hilton. The industry estimated that members of the frequent stayer programs of all the major hotel chains represented a market worth $11.1 billion, and that the average member belonged to 3.5 programs.

Table B Members' Paid Activity in 1998

	Members (000)	*Members Active in 1998 (000)*	*Stays for Which Members Paid (000)*	*Nights for Which They Paid (000)*	*Spending on Which They Earned Points ($000)*	*Stays per Active Member in 1998*	*Nights per Active Member in 1998*	*Reward Nights Claimed by Members*
Diamond	24	20	310	521	$62,000	15.5	26.1	27,000
Gold	220	84	1,110	1,916	$266,000	13.2	22.8	34,200
Silver	694	324	1,023	1,999	$341,000	3.2	6.2	70,200
Blue	1,712	992	1,121	2,579	$439,000	1.1	2.6	48,600
Total	**2,650**	**1,420**	**3,564**	**7,015**	**$1,108,000**	**2.5**	**4.9**	**180,000**

Source: Company records. (Certain competitively sensitive information has been masked.)

Rationales for the Program

1. Revenue and yield management

Hotel profitability was acutely sensitive to revenue. A trend in the industry was to appoint a "revenue manager" to each property to oversee the day-to-day decisions that affected hotel revenue. Yield management models were probabilistic algorithms that helped this manager set reservations policy. They used past history and other statistical data to make continuously updated recommendations regarding hotel booking patterns and what price to offer a particular guest. Simulation studies had shown that when booking was guided by a good yield management model, a company's revenue increased by 20% over a simple "first come, first served, fixed price" policy.

In the hotel industry, effectively managing yield meant utilizing a model to predict that a room was highly likely to come available due to cancellation or no-show, as well as driving business to higher-paying or longer-staying guests. Variable pricing meant that the rate charged for a room depended not only on its size and fittings, but also on the day of booking, the day of occupation, length of stay, and customer characteristics. Of these factors, customer characteristics were the most problematic.

Customer characteristics were needed by the model to estimate "walking cost," the cost of turning a customer away. That cost in turn depended on the customer's future lifetime value to the chain, a function of their willingness to pay and past loyalty to the chain. These were considered "soft" variables, notoriously difficult to estimate. The better the historical information on a customer, however, the better the estimate. As Adam Burke, HHonors' Senior Director of Marketing for North America put it, "Who gets the room—the person paying $20 more that you may never see again, or the guy spending thousands of dollars in the system? If we have the right data, the model can be smart enough to know the difference." Some in the hotel industry argued that a benefit of a frequent guest program was to let the reservations system make those distinctions.

2. Collaborating with partners

HHW partnered with 25 airlines, 3 car rental firms and a number of other firms. Burke explained, "Why is Mrs. Field's Cookies in the program? We have several objectives—regional relevance to consumers, access to partners' customers, making it easier for members to attain rewards. A franchisee may say, 'Why are we doing something with FTD Florists?' We point out that their investment keeps costs down and gives a broader range of rewards to our members."

Adam explained why Hilton offered Double Dipping. "We have 2.5 million members. The airline frequent flyer programs have 20, 30, 40 million members who aren't HHonors members and do travel a lot. Airlines don't mind us talking to their members because—through Double Dipping—we don't compete with their programs. In fact, we complement them by allowing our joint customers to earn both currencies."

3. Working with franchisees

The Hilton HHonors program was a strong factor in persuading hotel owners to become Hilton franchisees or give Hilton a management contract to run their property. Franchisees tended to be smaller hotels, more dependent on "road warrior" business than many of Hilton's convention hotels, resort hotels and flagship properties. They saw value in a frequent guest program to attract business, and HHW's program cost was comparable to or lower than its competitors. The program's ability to drive business, however, remained its biggest selling point. Diskin elaborated, "Seven or eight years ago some operators were concerned about the cost of the program. We took a bunch of the most vocal, critical guys and we put them in a room for two days with us to discuss the importance of building long-term customer loyalty, and they came out saying 'We need to spend more money on the program!' "

4. Relations with guests

The program let the most valuable guests be recognized on-property. Diskin explained, "In a sense, the loyalty program is a safe haven for the guest. If there is a problem and it is not taken care of at the property level, the guest can contact our customer service team. It's a mechanism to make sure we hear about those problems. We also do outbound after-visit calling, and we call HHonors members because they're the best database, and the most critical guests we have. They have the most experience; and the highest expectations. "We do feedback groups with members in addition to focus groups and quantitative research. We invite a bunch of members in the hotel down for dinner, and we say we want to talk about a subject. I get calls from people that are lifelong loyalists, not because of any changes we've made, but because once we invited them and asked them their opinion. People care about organizations that care about them."

Hilton customized a guest's hotel experience. Diskin explained, "We build guest profiles that keep track of preferences, enabling the hotel to provide customized services. For instance, consider the guest that always wants a room that is for non-smokers and has a double bed. This information can be stored as part of the member's record so that when she or he makes a reservation, the guest will receive this type of room without having to ask, no matter where the guest is staying."

HHW used direct mail to cultivate the relationship between members and the Hilton brand. Diskin explained, "Certainly you want to focus much of your effort on your highest revenue guests, but there are also opportunities to reach out and try to target other customer segments. For example, we worked with a non-travel partner to overlay data from their customer files onto our total membership base, and identified segments that might like vacation ownership, others who would be great for the casinos, and some that might like the business and teleconferencing services we offer."

Jeff Diskin was concerned that some travelers spread their hotel patronage among several chains and did not receive the service to which their total expenditure entitled them. He noted, "Our research suggests that a quarter of the frequent travelers are members of loyalty programs but don't have true loyalty to any one brand. They never get to enjoy the benefits of elite program status because they don't consolidate their business with one chain. They typically don't see the value in any of the loyalty schemes because they haven't changed their stay behavior to see the benefits."

5. Helping travel managers gain compliance

A significant proportion of Hilton's business came from contracts with large corporate clients. Hilton offered discounted rates if the corporation delivered enough stays.

"If you are a corporate travel manager," Adam Burke explained, "you want employees to comply with the corporate travel policy. You negotiated a rate by promising a volume of stays. While some travel managers can tell employees that they have to follow the company policy if they want to get reimbursed, many others can only recommend. What if someone is a very loyal Marriott customer, yet Marriott is not one of that company's preferred vendors? A travel office is going to have a real hard time getting that guy to stay at Hilton if they can't mandate it."

"We respond with a roster of offerings to give that Marriott traveler a personal incentive to use us, the preferred vendor. Our overall objective is to use the program as a tool that can help the travel manager with compliance to their overall travel policy."

Member Attitudes

HHW made extensive use of conjoint analysis to measure what members wanted from the Hilton HHonors program. Adam Burke explained, "Members come in for an hour-and-a-half interview. They're asked to trade off program elements, including services and amenities in the hotel, based on the value they place on those attributes relative to their cost. The results help us determine the appropriate priorities for modifying the program. We find that different people have different needs. Some people are service-oriented. No amount of miles or points is ever going to replace a warm welcome and being recognized by the hotel as a loyal customer. Other people are games-players. They go after free stays, and they know the rules as well as we do. We've been in feedback groups where these people will educate us on how our program works! And, of course, many people are a combination of both."

Using a sample that was broadly representative of the program's upper tier membership categories, program research found that Hilton HHonors members had an average of over 30 stays in all hotel chains per year, staying 4.2 nights per stay. Between 1997 and 1998, Hilton experienced a 17.5% increase in member utilization of HHonors hotels globally. Despite this improvement, more than half of HHonors member stays went to competing chains annually—this was primarily attributable to Hilton's relatively limited network size and distribution. The conjoint analysis suggested that roughly one in five HHonors member stays were solely attributable to their membership in the program—making these stays purely incremental.

The study found that the most important features of a hotel program were room upgrades and airline miles, followed by free hotel stays, and a variety of on-property benefits and services. Members wanted a streamlined reward redemption process, and points that did not expire. These findings led to refinements in the terms of membership for 1999, but Diskin was exploring more innovative approaches to the rewards program.

Diskin recognized that in their market research studies, consumers tended to describe an ideal program that was simply a version of the programs with which they were familiar. He was looking for more radical innovation.

> Hilton and Marriott tend to attract "games players." We want to compete effectively on the reward elements, but also introduce them to the more high touch, high feel kind of guest experience as well. The customer base that we have accumulated comprises games-players primarily. So we've got to deliver that benefit, but still go further.
>
> We've been on a mission to dramatically improve the stay experience for members of the upper tier ranks of the program. That is the key to competitive distinctiveness. That's not something that anybody can imitate. We want our best customers to feel that when they go to Hilton, they know Hilton knows they're the best customer and they're treated special. We want them to think, "I'm going to have the kind of room I want, I'm going to have the kind of stay I like, and if I have a problem, they're going to take care of it." We want the staff to know who's coming in each day, and make sure that these guests get a personal welcome. Our new customer reservation system will get more information down to the hotel. We'll know a lot more about our incoming guests. We will have a guest manager in the hotel whose job it is to make you feel special and to address any concerns you may have.

THE STARWOOD ANNOUNCEMENT

The *Wall Street Journal* of February 2, 1999, announced the birth of the Starwood Preferred Guest Program, covering Westin Hotels Resorts, Sheraton Hotels Resorts, The Luxury Collection, Four Points, Caesar's and Starwood's new W brand hotels, representing more than 550 participating properties worldwide. It became clear that Starwood was adding program features that might be expensive to match. Four features in particular were of concern.

No blackout dates	All frequent guest and airline programs until now had ruled that members could not claim free travel during the very height of seasonal demand and when local events guaranteed a hotel full occupancy. Starwood was saying that if there was a room to rent, points were as good as money.
No capacity control	Programs until now had let hotel properties limit the number of rooms for free stays. Starwood was telling hotels that all unreserved rooms should be available to guests paying with points.
Paperless rewards	Guests had had previously to exchange points for a certificate, and then use the certificate to pay for an authorized stay. Under Starwood's system, individual properties would be able to accept points to pay for a stay.
Hotel reimbursement	Now that blackout dates were abolished, a property, particularly an attractive vacation destination, might have to contend with many more points-paying guests than before. Starwood therefore raised the rate at which it reimbursed hotels for these stays. To meet the cost, it charged participating hotels 20–100% more than its competitors on paid stays.

Starwood was pledging to invest $50 million in advertising to publicize the program—significantly more than HHW had historically spent on program communications. **Exhibit 6** compares the loyalty programs of the four major business class hotel chains after the Starwood announcement.

Diskin's Dilemma

Without any doubt Starwood had raised the ante in the competition for customer loyalty. Jeff Diskin had to decide whether to match or pass. He mused:

> Do we have to compete point for point? Or do we want to take a different positioning and hold on to our loyal members and differentiate HHonors from Starwood and other competitors? We're in a cycle where for ten years the cost to our hotels of our frequent guest program as a percent of the folio has been cycling down. Yet activation,

EXHIBIT 6 Membership Offerings of the Four Major Business Class Hotel Chains in 1998

Chain	*Membership Restrictions*[1]	*Point Value*	*Eligible Charges*	*New Member Bonus*	*Airline Mileage Accrual*
Starwood	One stay per year to remain active - basic; 10 stays or 25 room nights per year—medium; 25 stays or 50 room nights	2 Starpoints = $1 basic; 3 Starpoints = $1 medium or premium	Room rate, F&B, laundry/ valet, phone, in-room movies	Periodically	Starpoints earned can be converted to miles 1:1; cannot earn both points and miles for the same stay
Hilton	One stay per year to remain active—Blue; 4 stays per year or 10 nights—medium; 16 stays per year or 36 nights—premium; 28 stays or 60 nights—top	10pts = $1—Blue; +15% bonus on points earned medium; +25% bonus on points earned premium; +50% bonus on points earned top	Room rate, F&B, laundry, phone	Periodically	500 miles per qualifying stay in addition to point earnings
Hyatt	One stay per year to remain active—basic; 5 stays or 15 nights per year—medium; 25 stays or 50 nights per year—premium	5pts = $1; +15% bonus on points earned medium; + 30% bonus premium on points earned	Room rate, F&B, laundry, phone	Periodically	500 miles per stay; not available if earning points
Marriott	No requirements for basic; 15 nights per year—medium; 50 nights per year—premium	10pts = $1; + 20% bonus on points earned medium; + 25% bonus on points earned premium	Room rate, F&B, laundry, phone	Double points first 120 days	3 miles per dollar spent at full service hotels; 1 mile per dollar spent at other hotels; not available if earning points

[1]Most programs run three tiers. For ease of comparison, the three levels are named basic, medium, and premium. HHonors has four tiers.

EXHIBIT 6 (Continued)

Chain	*Affinity Credit Card Point Accrual*	*Point Purchase*	*Bonus Threshold Reward*	*Exchange Hotel Points for Airline Miles*	*Hotel Rewards*
Starwood	1,000 hotel pts first card use; 1 hotel pt = $1 spent; 4 hotel points = $1 spent at Starwood hotels	NA	NA	1 to 1 conversion except JAL, KLM, Ansett, Qantas, Air New Zealand; 5,000 bonus miles when you convert 20,000 hotel points; minimum 2,000 Starpoints-basic; minimum 15,000 medium; no minimum for premium	5 categories; 1 free night category 1 is 3,000 Starpoints; 1 free night category 5 is 12,000 Starpoints
Hilton	5,000 hotel pts for application; 2,500 hotel points first card use; 2 hotel pts = $1 spent; 3 hotel pts = $1 spent at HHonors Hotels.	$10 = 1,000 pts up to 20% of the total points of the reward	2,000 pts = 4 stays per quarter;	10,000 pts = 1,500 miles; 20,000 pts = 3,500 miles; 50,000 pts = 10,000 miles; minimum 10,000 hotel points exchange, can also exchange airline miles for hotel points	5 categories: free weekend night 10,000 lowest; 35,000 highest
Hyatt	None	$10 = 500 pts up to 10% of the total points of the reward	None basic;	3 pts = 1 mile; minimum 9,000 point exchange	Weekend night no category: 8,000 pts; if premium time there is an additional 5,000 pts; come with partner awards
Marriott	5,000 hotel pts first card use; 1 hotel pt = $1 spent; 3 hotel points = $1 spent at Marriott Rewards hotels	$10 = 1,000 pts up to 10% of the total points of the reward	None basic;	10,000 pts = 2,000 miles; 20,000 pts = 5,000 miles; 30,000 pts = 10,000 miles; minimum = 10,000 hotel point exchange	2 categories: 20,000 free weekend low category; and 30,000 high category

retention, and member spend per visit, all have improved. If we can deliver the same amount of business to the Hilton brand and it costs less, Hilton makes more margin. That attracts investors, franchise ownership, new builders. That's another reason why they buy the Hilton flag.

As Diskin saw it, Starwood's Preferred Guest announcement was a solution to a problem Hilton did not have, arising from its recent purchases of the Sheraton and Westin chains:

> They are trying to develop the Starwood brand with the Starwood Preferred Guest program. They are targeting the most lucrative part of the business, the individual business traveler, where Sheraton and Westin independently have never been as effective as Marriott, Hyatt and Hilton. Sheraton's frequent guest program wasn't very effective. They changed it every few years; they used to have members pay for it. Westin never had enough critical mass of properties for it to be important for enough people. So now, together they can address Westin's critical mass problem and Sheraton's relevance.

But if frequent guest programs were a good idea, perhaps bigger programs were an even better idea. Diskin reflected,

> Hotel properties routinely pay 10% commission to a travel agent to bring them a guest. Yet they continually scrutinize the cost of these programs. Of course, they're justified in doing so, but the return on investment clearly justifies the expenditure. And our competitors certainly seem to see a value in increasing their investment in their programs.

Diskin tried to predict Hyatt and Marriott's response to the Starwood announcement. The industry was quite competitive enough. He thought back to his early years at United Airlines and recalled the damage that price wars had done to that industry.

Study Questions

1. *What are the strengths and weaknesses of the Hilton HHonors program from the standpoints of:*
   a. *Hilton Hotels Corp and Hilton International*
   b. *member properties (franchised hotels)*
   c. *guests*
   d. *corporate travel departments*
2. *How does the value generated to Hilton by the program compare to its cost?*
3. *What is Starwood attempting to do and how should Jeff Diskin respond?*

Case 12 Massachusetts Audubon Society

CHRISTOPHER LOVELOCK

We embrace a vision of Massachusetts in which people appreciate and understand native plants and animals and their habitats and work together to ensure that they are truly protected.

From the barrier beaches, heathlands, and salt marshes of the coast; to the vernal pools, red maple swamps, and forests of the interior; all the way to the fens and mountaintops of the Berkshire highlands, the Commonwealth's natural splendor encompasses an abundance of scenic and ecological treasures. But unless and until the public develops a conservation ethic that incorporates a love and respect for nature with a willingness to act on its behalf, we are in danger of losing this natural wealth forever.

—FROM THE STRATEGIC PLAN 2000–2010

A nonprofit environmental organization that operates more than forty wildlife sanctuaries seeks to develop a strategy to increase the loyalty and involvement of its current members. Findings from a survey of its membership may offer some insights.

Several pairs of cardinals were fluttering around the bird feeder outside the Audubon Shop at Drumlin Farm Wildlife Sanctuary; the scarlet and crimson plumage of the males stood out vividly against the bare trees. Nearby, under the watchful eyes of their teachers and a sanctuary naturalist, a group of schoolchildren were chattering excitedly as they walked down the path toward the enclosure where the farm animals were located.

Despite the chill in the air on this November day, several people were lined up in the reception area to gain admission to the sanctuary. The staff member on duty was explaining sympathetically to two visitors from New York that their membership in the National Audubon Society did not, unfortunately, entitle them to free admission at Massachusetts Audubon Society sanctuaries, as the two organizations had no formal relationship.

Steven Solomon and Susannah Caffry watched the bright red birds from the warm interior of the shop as they put on their jackets. Solomon was vice president of Mass Audubon's resources division, and Caffry was director of marketing and communication. They had been meeting with the store manager and were now about to return to the nearby mansion that served as the Society's headquarters. Both were scheduled to participate in a task force discussion of how to develop a new communications strategy targeted at existing members. "The key to success," Solomon told Caffry as they stepped outside, "lies in finding ways to engage our members more actively in Mass Audubon."

HISTORY OF THE AUDUBON MOVEMENT

In the late 19th century, there were no laws in the United States to control the hunting of birds and animals. Entire species went into decline, and two birds—the great auk and the Carolina parakeet—were exterminated. Migratory fowl were killed in immense numbers, with hunters traveling to the coastal marshes of Massachusetts from as far away as Ohio.

Among those who spoke up against this slaughter was George Bird Grinnell, editor of the magazine *Forest and Stream*. In 1886, he created the nation's first bird preservation organization, which

Note: Certain data in this case have been disguised.

he named the Audubon Society after John James Audubon (1785–1851), the great American naturalist and wildlife painter. Within three months, more than 38,000 people had joined the society. But Grinnell was unable to cater to such a large, geographically dispersed group and had to disband the society after a couple of years.

The Audubon Societies

In 1896, two socially prominent cousins from Boston's Back Bay—Harriet Hemenway and Minna Hall—galvanized public support and formed the Massachusetts Audubon Society, which soon had 900 members. Refusing to wear hats and clothing decorated with plumes or other bird parts, they lobbied politicians and newspaper editors for protection of birds. Several months later, the Pennsylvania Audubon Society was founded, and by 1899 another 15 states had established Audubon societies.

In 1901, several local Audubon Societies formed the National Association of Audubon Societies for the Protection of Wild Birds and Animals. Both this association and local societies worked for passage of bird protection laws. An early priority included state bans on selling the plumes of native birds. National legislation included the Federal Migratory Bird Treaty Act of 1918 and creation of a National Wildlife Refuge system where birds would be safe from hunters. Over the years, additional state societies affiliated or merged with the National Association (later renamed the National Audubon Society). By 2001, the Massachusetts Audubon Society was one of only a handful of state societies remaining unaffiliated with the national society.

Other Players in the Environmental Movement

There were literally hundreds of environmental organizations in the United States, with most being local or regional. Some pursued a broad agenda; others focused on a specific goal, such as the Rails-to-Trails Conservancy, which sought to convert thousands of miles of unused railroad corridors into trails for recreation and nature appreciation.

National players included Friends of the Earth, National Audubon Society, Sierra Club, The Nature Conservancy, and the Wilderness Society. Several of these organizations had chapters or offices in Massachusetts. The Appalachian Mountain Club was regional, with chapters throughout the northeast United States. By contrast, Mass Audubon, the Trustees of Reservations, and MASSPIRG confined their activities to Massachusetts. (See the **Appendix** for brief profiles.)

Although organizations sometimes worked in coalitions to advocate specific political agenda, they also competed for funding and, to some extent, for members. On occasion, some of them had even competed for the same piece of environmentally sensitive property. The Nature Conservancy protected 17,000 acres (70 km^2) in the state, Mass Audubon held 29,000 acres (120 km^2), and The Trustees of Reservations had more than 45,000 acres (180 km^2). Many other nonprofit organizations operated individual sanctuaries and nature centers or preserved land from development through land trusts.

In the public sector, preservation and conservation agencies included the National Park Service, which was best known in Massachusetts for the 43,600-acre (176 km^2) Cape Cod National Seashore. The Commonwealth of Massachusetts preserved land for recreational purposes through a number of state parks, and many towns and cities had parks and conservation land trusts of their own. The motivations ranged from keeping attractive vistas and recreational areas out of the hands of developers to preserving habitats for threatened animal and plant species and protecting local water supplies.

EVOLUTION OF MASS AUDUBON

From its initial focus on bird protection, the Massachusetts Audubon Society (MAS) embraced a variety of conservation issues, including the protection of land and habitat, especially wetlands. In 1916, it created America's first private wildlife sanctuary at Moose Hill, 20 miles (32 km) southwest of Boston, later adding many other sanctuaries. It became known for its lectures, guided nature walks, and educational programs for children. MAS created the first environmental summer camp for children and one of the first natural history travel programs to offer guided nature tours and birding trips overseas. It also opened one of the first stores to focus on natural history merchandise.

In 1952, Louise Ayer Hathaway bequeathed to MAS her Drumlin Farm estate in Lincoln, 15 miles north of Boston. Her will stipulated that this working New England farm was to serve as a sanctuary for wildlife and as a model farm to show young city dwellers how food was grown. The accompanying mansion became the Society's new headquarters.

Under the presidency of Gerard Bertrand (1980–1998), MAS acquired many threatened locations through gift or purchase. It also helped landowners to obtain conservation restrictions that offered tax benefits and then assumed management of their properties. These strategies were made possible by active fundraising and a growing membership.

Bertrand also reemphasized the Society's historical commitment to the study, observation, and protection of birds. Like the renowned ornithologist Roger Tory Peterson, he recognized that birds were an "ecological litmus paper." Because of their rapid metabolism and wide geographic range, bird populations were quick to reflect changes in the environment. Hence a documented decline in bird numbers provided an early warning of environmental deterioration. Key initiatives during this period included plans for two urban sanctuaries to better serve the needs of city dwellers, especially urban children. Completion of the new Boston Nature Center, constructed on the 67-acre grounds of a former state mental hospital, was scheduled for fall 2002.

Membership grew from 26,600 in 1980 to 67,000 in 1998; the area of land protected by the Society rose from 11,600 to 28,000 acres (**Exhibit 1**). The number of research studies and educational programs also increased substantially. Following the Centennial celebrations of 1996 and completion of a $34 million capital campaign, Bertrand left to chair Bird Life International; later he was also named vice chairman of the National Audubon Society's board of directors.

New Leadership

Although proud of the amount of wildlife habitat now protected by the Society, some board members and staff were concerned by the absence of a comprehensive plan to guide future direction. They worried that years of rapid growth were affecting Mass Audubon's ability to do the best possible job of managing the many properties it had acquired. As Bancroft Poor, VP–Operations, recalled: "The Society was really stretched by the years of expansion and some of the infrastructure was near the breaking point."

In January 1999, the board appointed Laura Johnson as the Society's new president. Johnson came to MAS from a 16-year career with The Nature Conservancy (TNC), an international environmental organization that maintained the largest private system of nature sanctuaries in the world. A native of Massachusetts and a lawyer by training, Johnson had initially worked on legal issues for TNC but soon switched over to management, eventually being placed in charge of 12 states as eastern regional director. Reflecting on her time with TNC, she noted that it was a very focused organization with a culture of measurement. In particular, she said, the Conservancy offered a clear and compelling message about its goal of identifying important landscapes for protection, purchasing them, and protecting them. People could readily understand that their donations made a difference and thus feel a part of the enterprise.

A key motivation for Johnson was to be involved in creating an overall conservation ethic in Massachusetts, a task that she believed MAS performed better than any other organization. She was very concerned that modern lifestyles tended to separate people, especially children, from the natural environment. "Kids today are not outside, they're indoors playing on their computers," she said. "Or if they are outside, it's to play in a soccer game. Parents are afraid to let them wander." In Johnson's view, simply protecting land would be insufficient if

EXHIBIT 1 Massachusetts Audubon Society: Key Statistics, 1980–2001

Year	*# Members (000)*	*# Acres Protected*[1] *(000)*	*Operating Revenue ($000)*	*Operating Gifts/Grants ($000)*	*Endowment*[2] *($ million)*
1980	26.6	11.6	2,529	362	10.9
1985	31.0	12.4	4,180	490	22.8
1990	48.0	18.1	6,955	1,017	35.2
1995	55.1	23.9	9,042	1,486	57.1
2000	67.6	28.6	13,791	2,584	92.3
2001	65.4	29.1	14,113	2,863	89.2

Source: MAS records

[1]1,000 acres = approximately 400 hectares (ha) or 4 square kilometers (km^2)

[2]Endowment is shown at market value except for land, which is valued at either its original purchase price or at $1 if donated as a gift (based on the Society's intention never to sell).

in the future, people forgot why the land in question was important, did not feel connected to it, and had no stake in it.

Johnson soon articulated a need to sharpen the Society's focus and develop a clear sense of direction. Despite a strong "feel-good" sentiment toward the organization, relatively few members, she discovered, had a sense of the array of activities in which it was engaged and made assumptions that tended to mirror how they had come to join the organization. For instance, birders thought MAS was about birds, young families from the Boston area thought in terms of Drumlin Farm, and individuals who cared about public policy perceived the Society in terms of lobbying activities on Beacon Hill, site of the Massachusetts state government. So the first question Johnson asked was: "What are we and what do we want to be?"

Developing a Strategic Plan for 2000–2010

Over a six-month period in 1999, Johnson led and guided a comprehensive strategic planning effort. Its goals were to assess MAS strengths and resources, to evaluate the status of the Massachusetts environment and the impact of widespread changes, and to clearly define critical conservation issues. This assessment would enable MAS to define its own specific role relative to other conservation organizations. McKinsey & Co., the international consulting firm, gave pro bono support to the project.

A strong consensus emerged that biological conservation—that is, maintaining sustainable populations of the state's native biological diversity—lay at the heart of the Society's work. In looking toward the future, staff, the board, volunteers, and members reaffirmed their belief, passionately in many cases, that all the Society's efforts should be directed toward protecting the nature of Massachusetts. From this belief emerged a common vision (reproduced at the beginning of this case) and a specific role for the Society:

> The Massachusetts Audubon Society serves both as a leader and as a catalyst for conservation, by acting directly to protect the nature of Massachusetts and by stimulating individual and institutional action through education, advocacy, and habitat protection.

The phrase "Protecting the Nature of Massachusetts," which had been used sporadically up to this point, was adopted as the organization's signature and appeared beneath the Society's name on publications and stationery.

The strategic plan identified five major threats to biodiversity: loss of habitat to development, fragmentation of wildlife habitat, disruption of natural ecological cycles and processes through human alterations, the crowding out of native plants and animals by invasive species, and incompatible land use, such as using open space for recreational activities that damaged plants and threatened wildlife.

Following board approval of the plan, Johnson launched an in-depth examination of educational activities at MAS. In addition, the board directed a science review committee, composed of distinguished educators and scientists, to examine scientific activities at Mass Audubon. It also commissioned a study of information technology needs.

Education Plan

Discussions with staff members revealed that existing education programs, although high quality and well respected, lacked a common focus and connection to Mass Audubon themes and mission. Johnson acknowledged that the biggest challenge was to identify the most effective ways to use education to stimulate conservation action:

> We needed to find the best way to leverage our unique strengths—our sanctuary system, our scientific expertise, our advocacy capability, and our tremendously passionate staff—so that Mass Audubon could be a catalyst for conservation. We do thousands of programs, so there's plenty of activity to measure and we could say great things in terms of the number of programs held and the number of schoolchildren involved. But none of those measures would identify what the activities accomplished in terms of making a difference.
>
> Our teacher naturalists do a wonderful job with our programs, but it's a very expensive business model. And not every visitor to our sanctuaries wants to enroll in a program for a day or even a couple of hours. So we decided to explore an array of activities to get the message across. Our education director said at one point that we have this cultural bias at Mass Audubon that if we can just open up people's heads and dump into their heads what we know, they'll become just like us! But it doesn't work that way. We now have this paradigm from "caring to knowledge to action." When people act, that's the impact.

The education master plan emphasized the importance of creating significant outdoor experiences that might bring about transformations in people's environmental attitudes and values. Research showed that among children, shared family experiences in nature had the greatest influence in forming their attitudes as adults. To meet varied learning styles, the plan called for a mix of live programs, nature center exhibits, and self-guided trails at sanctuaries, along with opportunities for learning through publications, audiovisual media, interactive pages on the MAS Web site, and articles in local newspapers.

ORGANIZATION AND RESTRUCTURING

By 2001, MAS operated 58 wildlife sanctuaries across the Commonwealth, of which 41 were open to the public and 23 were staffed (**Exhibit 2**). They ranged in size from 4-acre (1.5 ha) Nahant Thicket, a magnet for migrating songbirds on an otherwise rocky peninsula, to Ipswich River, which comprised 2,265 acres (917 ha) of forests, meadows, and wetlands. There were 511,000 visits to the sanctuaries in 2001, including some 145,000 schoolchildren. The five most popular sanctuaries—Blue Hills Trailside Museum on the western edge of greater Boston, Daniel Webster and North River on the South Shore, Wellfleet Bay on Cape Cod, and Drumlin Farm in Lincoln—jointly accounted for 70 percent of all visitation.

Historically, some sanctuaries had operated with a high degree of independence from MAS headquarters, targeting local residents, schools, and vacationers. Their directors were often well known in the communities they served. Sanctuaries were under considerable pressure to increase program revenues each year to help balance the budget. However, the result was often what one director described as "a hodgepodge of programs, many of which have little to do with the society's mission."

MAS was one of only two environmental organizations that monitored the Massachusetts state government and promoted a specific environmental agenda. Although some members were invested in these statewide advocacy efforts, others saw Mass Audubon simply in terms of their local sanctuary. Declared one staff member, "In our members' eyes, we can be as big as a major advocacy issue or as small as a favorite trail."

For the fiscal year ending June 30, 2001, MAS had an operating income of $14.6 million and generated a small surplus, as it had done for the past three years. Gifts, grants, and unrestricted bequests totaled $3.3 million and membership dues, $2.7 million; income from programs and investments each amounted to $4.2 million; and revenues from all other sources, including profits from the Audubon shop, a Mass Audubon credit card, and the Society's Natural History Travel program came to $0.2 million (**Exhibit 3**). Salaries and benefits accounted for more than 70 percent of all expenses.

MAS was governed by a 27-member board of directors, who elected from among their number a chair, three vice-chairs, and a treasurer. Providing

EXHIBIT 2 Map of Massachusetts, Showing Location of Sanctuaries

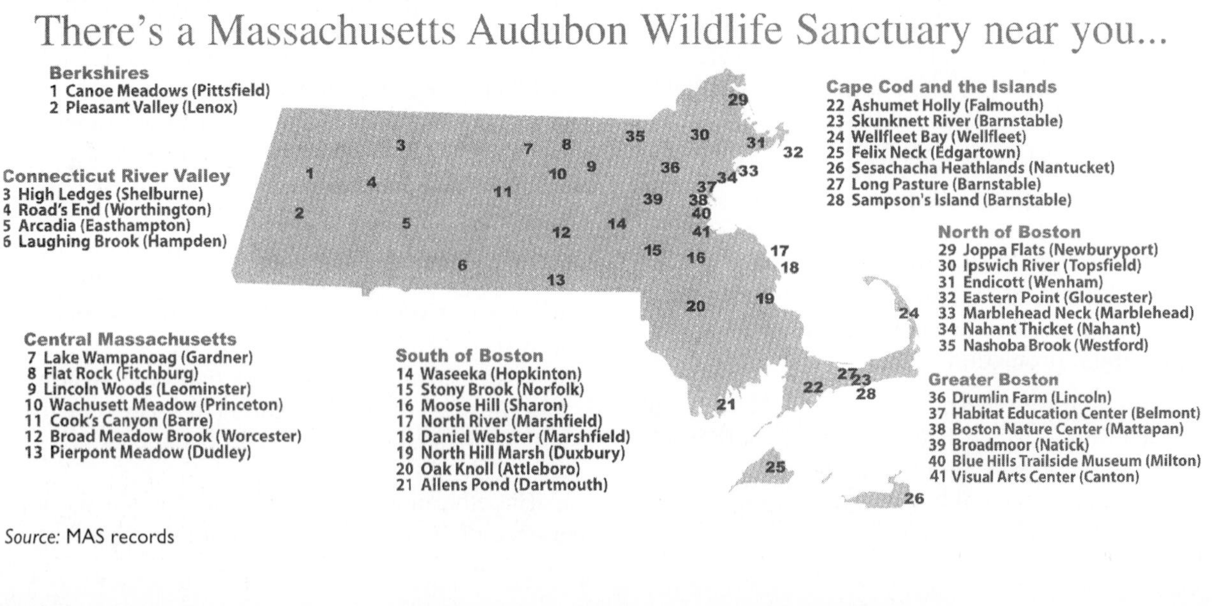

Source: MAS records

EXHIBIT 3 Massachusetts Audubon Society: Income and Expenditures for Year Ending June 30, 2001

General Operating Fund Results

Income	FY2001	FY2000	FY1999
Gifts, Grants, and Unrestricted Bequests	$3,316,026	$2,828,367	$2,715,680
Membership Dues	2,674,903	2,970,806	2,989,157
Program Income	4,204,456	4,279,522	4,025,015
Investment Income	4,203,946	3,695,367	3,402,787
Other Income	248,471	270,035	63,757
	$14,647,802	**$14,044,097**	**$13,196,396**
Expenses			
Salary and Benefits	$10,340,546	$9,773,809	$8,957,708
Nonsalary Program Expenses	2,739,611	2,751,009	2,756,377
Other Expenses	1,447,333	1,369,989	1,168,420
	$14,527,490	**$13,894,807**	**$12,882,505**
Surplus/(Deficit)	**$120,312**	**$149,290**	**$313,891**

A complete copy of the audited financial statements is available upon request from Mass Audubon Vice President for Operations Bancroft Poor at 781-259-9506 x7150. Members should feel free to call with any questions about the organization's finances.

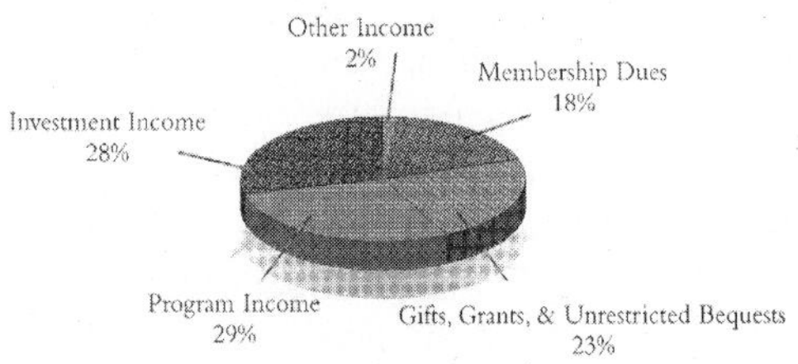

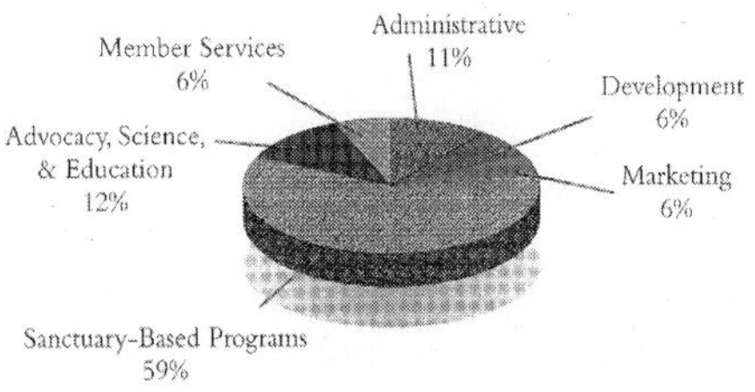

Source: MAS records

additional expertise and support was a board-appointed council, whose 75 members were drawn from across the state, often being recommended by staff members at HQ or the sanctuaries. This governance structure, adopted in 1999, replaced an unwieldy 80-member board, which lacked clear roles and expectations for its members and had no term limits for the various categories of directors.

One outcome of the strategic planning process was changes to the design of the MAS organization. The revised structure in place in 2001 consisted of four divisions, each of which was each headed by a vice president reporting to Laura Johnson (**Exhibit 4**).

Conservation Science and Ecological Management was formerly within Programs but in response to the findings of the Science Review Committee was established as a separate division in order to sharpen its focus and raise its stature. It included a bird conservation department, GIS/data management, and five scientists with responsibilities for each of the three regions, the education department, and advocacy.

Operations was headed by Bancroft Poor, the CFO, whose responsibilities included administrative and financial operations, capital assets and planning, human resources, and information technology. The *Programs* division incorporated advocacy, education, land protection, the sanctuaries, and the Society's overnight summer camp. Finally, the *Resources* division was created to integrate fundraising, membership, and marketing activities and to raise their visibility.

The Resources Division

To head the new Resources Division, Johnson hired Steven L. Solomon, previously vice president of resources at the Museum of Science in Boston. Earlier, he had also worked for the Boston Symphony Orchestra and the Museum of Fine Arts, as well as Harvard's Graduate School of Design. Solomon was attracted by the changes that were taking place at MAS and shared Johnson's belief that development and marketing should be linked. He declared:

> There are a lot of organizations that have separate marketing and development divisions, but in fact they have so many interlocking elements that they

EXHIBIT 4 Organization Chart

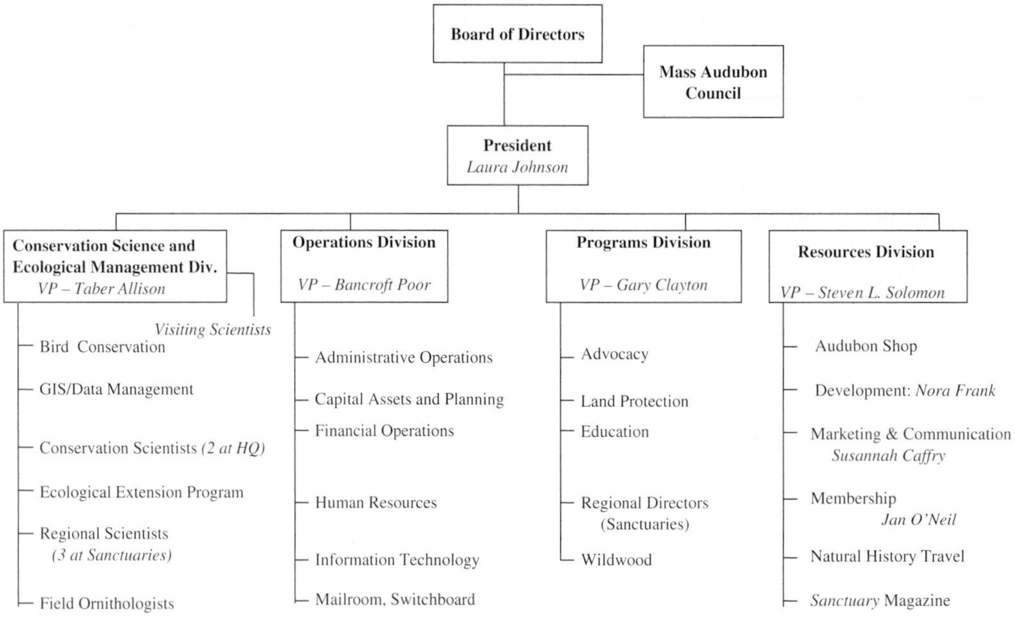

Source: MAS records

need to work closely together. When you're working in development at the level we are, it's based almost entirely on relationships. We want to be like Britain's RSBP [Royal Society for the Protection of Birds], which has a very clearly defined philosophy: "Membership is everybody's job."

The new division included the directors of development, marketing and communication, and membership; the editor of *Sanctuary*, the Society's bimonthly magazine; the manager of Natural History Travel, which organized naturalist-led tours (particularly for birders) to destinations around the world; and the manager of the Audubon Shop.

Development

Development activities embraced an annual fund to raise unrestricted gifts and capital campaigns to fund specific projects. All members were urged to contribute to the annual appeal; most were contacted by mail, although major donors might be solicited personally. Capital campaigns ran several years and usually involved intensive advance planning and early solicitation of major gifts. Several campaigns were currently in progress: $4 million for new facilities at the Wellfleet sanctuary, $2 million for new information technology, $6 million for Drumlin Farm, and $1.2 million for Wildwood, the new residential summer camp.

Nora Frank, director of development, had joined Mass Audubon in 1998 as manager of major gifts after working in admissions, development, and marketing for a residential school. She believed strongly in the need to keep donors and members involved and informed:

> One way to engage people is to let them know what we are doing and what their money is supporting. Right now, we don't have any common vehicle outside of solicitation that tells people what we are doing with their money, applauds them for helping to make a difference, and tells them how they can get further involved. Money comes in every time we use *Sanctuary* to highlight a specific need, even when we don't specifically ask for it. People do want to get involved but we haven't been letting them know what's happening.

Membership

Jan O'Neil had joined Mass Audubon as director of membership in February 2001. "Coming to Mass Audubon was a great opportunity to transition from dealing with many different organizations to focusing on one that I'd been a member of almost my whole life," remarked O'Neil. Her prior experience included 12 years with the New Boston Group, a telemarketing firm that made fundraising calls for nonprofits, many of them in the environmental area. She then spent two years working for Target Analysis Group, which performed detailed analytical studies for nonprofit clients.

O'Neil was a strong proponent of using reliable data as the basis for planning and evaluating membership and fundraising strategies. As she examined Mass Audubon's membership program, she found that there was insufficient information in the database to enable her to create detailed profiles of the membership. The lack of reliable benchmark data meant that it was difficult to document what was going on. One of her initial tasks was to find ways to validate which membership strategies worked and which didn't, rather than simply continuing past practices or relying on conjecture. At her previous job, she remarked with a smile, they had a saying: "The plural of anecdote is not data."

As part of the $2 million technology initiative, some $400,000 was being invested in new membership and development software, together with associated installation and training. The new software would have extremely robust data storage and reporting capabilities, greatly enhancing the membership department's ability to profile and track members.

Between 1997 and 1999, MAS membership had surged from 54,400 to 67,400 households, spurred by the $34 million Centennial fundraising campaign, which included a $400,000 advertising campaign involving radio, billboards, and press. Membership had since fallen back to around 65,000 household members. Like many nonprofits, MAS experienced churn in its membership, with about 20 percent turning over each year. Although that was less than in most organizations, there was still a continuing need to recruit new members. Regular household membership cost $47 ($37 for individuals), but new members could join initially for only $25. Forty-five percent of new members were recruited at the sanctuaries and 42 percent through direct-mail solicitation. The balance joined as a result of visiting Mass Audubon's Web site, word-of-mouth recommendations, or other encounters.

Admission charges to the sanctuaries for nonmembers ranged from $3 for adults and $2 for children up to $6/$4 at Drumlin Farm. As one aspect of their pitch, admissions staff were trained to point out the savings associated with joining immediately and then being able to make this and future visits for the next year free of charge. It had proved a particularly compelling sell for families.

Direct-mail solicitation involved purchase of mailing lists from brokers or swapping of membership lists with other nonprofits. Some 500,000–700,000 letters were mailed each year, at an average cost of $0.39 each, and typically yielded a response rate of around 1 percent. A recent mailing came in a colorful envelope bearing the slogan "Coming soon to a neighborhood near you" and a picture of a bird standing on a for-sale sign in open countryside. The letter inside was headed "Massachusetts Is Disappearing!" and warned that every day, the state lost 44 acres of land to development. The letter then described Mass Audubon's conservation, education, and advocacy efforts and promoted the benefits of membership. New members received a welcome package of materials. The unit cost to MAS was about $3.25, exclusive of any premiums offered as inducements.

O'Neil noted that only 55 percent of first-year members would renew their membership, but this figure compared favorably to those of comparable national organizations, for which renewal rates were typically only 30–35 percent. The estimated annual printing and mailing costs for renewals was $195,000. Although some members remained loyal for life, a board member with expertise in marketing estimated that the average duration of a member relationship that was renewed after the first year was eight years. In general, said O'Neil, "The longer someone has been a member, the more likely they are to stay a member." Added Solomon: "Members who are happily engaged are much more likely to renew."

At renewal time, members were encouraged to migrate to higher levels of membership: Supporting ($60), Defender ($75), Donor ($100), Protector ($150), Sponsor ($250), Patron ($500), and Leadership Friend ($1,250). Dues for the last-named category had been raised from $1,000 the previous year. Members of this group received a number of benefits, including invitations to exclusive events, meetings with Mass Audubon scientists and sanctuary directors, and special outings, such as naturalist-led hikes or canoe trips. A small fee was sometimes charged for outings in order to preserve the full tax deductibility of the membership contribution. O'Neil and her colleagues in the Resources Division had been discussing the possibility of developing supplementary benefits for members enrolled in some of the other levels.

In addition to free admission to the sanctuaries, all members received six issues of *Sanctuary* magazine each year; discounts on MAS courses, lectures, programs, and day camps; and savings on purchases from the sanctuary shops. Depending on location, they might also receive newsletters from their nearest sanctuary. O'Neil estimated the annual printing and

EXHIBIT 5 MAS Membership by Contribution Level, June 30, 2001

Level	*Dues*	*Number*
Introductory	$25	12,093
Student	$20	460
Individual	$37	9,224
Family	$47	28,908
Supporting	$60	6,366
Defender	$75	2,152
Donor	$100	3,335
Protector	$150	1,092
Sponsor	$250	433
Patron	$500	205
Leadership Friend	$1,000	584
Complimentary		520
TOTAL		**65,372**

Source: MAS Membership Department

mailing costs associated with serving members at $330,000. This did not include the cost of staff time.

Premiums, such as day packs or tote bags bearing the Mass Audubon logo, were often used as inducements to renew at a higher level. The unit cost of purchasing and mailing such a premium was about $5. Former members were contacted for up to ten years in an effort to get them to rejoin. **Exhibit 5** shows the division of membership among the different levels at the end of the 2000–2001 fiscal year. About 70 percent of members renewed at the same rate, 20 percent upgraded, and 10 percent downgraded.

Marketing and Communication

Susannah Caffry had joined Mass Audubon in October 2000. After leaving college, she entered the telecommunications industry but found the work increasingly unrewarding. A keen outdoorswoman, she took a three-month sabbatical during which she went on an intensive canoeing trip with Outward Bound. Her experience convinced her that she wanted to work in the nonprofit sector, and she accepted an offer from Outward Bound to join its Boston operation as director of admissions, later being promoted to vice president of marketing and public relations. In addition to communications, her work included recommendations on design, scheduling, and pricing of courses and programs.

MAS had earlier employed a director of marketing to manage communication activities associated with the Society's Centennial. As these activities wound down, the position was expanded to include development activities, but the attention given to marketing dwindled due to the more pressing needs of fundraising. The incumbent left at the same time the Resources Division was created, and Caffry was recruited by Steve Solomon for the newly defined position of director of marketing and communication.

Caffry said she was attracted to Mass Audubon by the commitment to marketing among the leadership but had found that not everyone in the organization understood or appreciated the value of a marketing perspective. More than once, she admitted, somebody had told her, "We don't like the M-word!" An important task involved marketing Wildwood, the Society's new summer camp for children. Because some staff members assumed that marketing activities involved only communication tasks, such as signage and development of brochures, it took her some time, she admitted, to become involved in decisions on scheduling, pricing, and service features at the camp, all of which she saw as critical to success.

Caffry spent her first few months gathering information and learning how people on the staff, board, and council felt about marketing-related issues at Mass Audubon. She encountered passionately held views that were often widely divergent. There were, for instance, those who loved *Sanctuary* magazine because they saw it as "pure" and free from overt marketing and promotion of Mass Audubon's programs and agenda. Others, by contrast, regarded it as "elitist" and "arrogant," noting that the stories presupposed a level of technical understanding of the environment beyond that held by nonspecialists. Similar variations in viewpoint surrounded the newsletters published by the individual sanctuaries and also the Web site. Summarizing the situation, Caffry remarked:

> There was no holistic approach as to how we were communicating. We had many different vehicles but they weren't held to any consistent message. I found a lot of conflicting opinions concerning the objectives of Mass Audubon's different communications activities. For instance there was no consensus at all as to what the purpose of *Sanctuary* magazine was. I also discovered that our annual report was not meeting the needs of our development office. This is a fundamental, critical communication effort for nonprofits.
>
> I see our overall objective as bringing together the communications activities without undermining the strengths of the organization—an important one being the commitment and feeling of ownership demonstrated by the sanctuary directors and other program staff.

Communication Strategy Task Force

Prior to Solomon's arrival, there had been no explicit strategy for coordinating all the Society's communications efforts. As a board member, Alfred (Appy) Chandler had long been concerned about the fragmentation of communication efforts, with each group, such as advocacy, attending to its own portfolio and operating relatively independently of the others. *Sanctuary* magazine, the Society's primary periodical for members, was started, he declared, "not as a mouthpiece of Mass Audubon but almost as an independent journal that would carry articles about the Society's mission as opposed to stories about Mass Audubon itself."

There had been an in-house publishing effort that produced books and field guides, a variety of organization staff who wrote press releases, and public relations efforts by the development office, such as staffing a booth at a flower show or other event. Meantime, many of the individual sanctuaries were publishing their own newsletters, but they lacked a coordinated formatting and often failed to convey any real sense of being part of a larger, statewide organization. Chandler promoted the need for an integrated communication strategy to pull all the pieces together, so that the Society could speak with a single voice.

In June 2001, Laura Johnson facilitated a meeting of MAS Council members to define the challenges that the Society faced with regard to its communications strategy. Among the key themes that emerged from the break-out groups at this meeting were a need for greater clarity in terms of "what, why, when, and to whom?" and a sense that the Society was not doing a good enough job of telling the MAS story to either its members or the general public. Break-out reports emphasized the need to find ways to strengthen the "brand" and to better understand members and their preferences. Finally, a range of opinions was expressed about *Sanctuary;* although most agreed that it was a high-quality magazine, many argued that it needed to clarify its purpose.

The following month, the board approved creation of a communication strategy task force to work with a consulting firm and MAS staff. Its purpose was to "oversee a review and analysis of current external communication activities and preparation of a communication plan for the Society, including recommendations for long-term strategy." Its scope extended to membership, education, public relations, advocacy, marketing, sanctuary activities, and publications. The task force was composed of board and council members who either had marketing and communications expertise or represented a consumer point of view. Chandler was named as chair. Commenting on the role of the consultant, EMI Strategic Marketing, Caffry observed:

> The consultant was very useful. There were so many sacred cows at Mass Audubon, so many personal feelings, and so many emotions that the consultant could ask questions that I, frankly, could not. There's a certain amount of skepticism in some quarters about the work related to communications and marketing. Not everybody is eager to see change and we have joked that there's a great deal of "anticipointment" related to the communication plan.

Focus and Objectives

After some debate, the task force decided to focus on developing a communications strategy for the existing membership, with the primary objective being to increase member value. This would be achieved through better education of members about Mass Audubon's mission, by engaging them actively in "protecting the nature of Massachusetts, increasing their support for MAS programs, and growing their financial contributions."

Additional objectives were (1) to reinforce MAS's role and positioning as the leader in conservation, environmental education, and advocacy within Massachusetts, thus differentiating it from other environmental organizations; (2) to establish a clear, distinctive, contemporary image for the Society, portraying it as dynamic, current, and important; and (3) to communicate more cost-effectively through better use of all available media and channels. The work of the task force included reviewing Mass Audubon's existing communications, undertaking a competitive audit of those organizations whose activities and appeal overlapped MAS in some measure (see the Appendix), and conducting a detailed survey.

Member Survey

Recognizing that existing knowledge of members' interests and perceptions was largely anecdotal, the task force decided to conduct a large-scale survey of members. It sought to identify channels for future communications, understand how members perceived MAS, and determine the relative importance they placed on its mission and programs. Additional goals included gauging the degree of membership overlap between MAS and other organizations and determining whether there were meaningful differences between demographic groups in their reactions to MAS communications and content.

Working with the consultant, the task force developed a mail questionnaire that was bound around the cover of the Sept./Oct. 2001 issue of *Sanctuary* magazine and mailed to 62,000 members. More than 8,000 completed questionnaires were returned and promptly reviewed to gather any handwritten comments. Work on manually keying, coding, and cleaning the quantitative data concluded after 4,448 questionnaires, which was viewed as more than enough responses for the proposed statistical analysis.

Following a review of the preliminary tabulations (**Exhibit 6**), cross-tabs were run to determine how member views and priorities related to member characteristics on a wide array of segmentation variables. One aspect of this analysis involved segmenting members according to their most important reason for joining Mass Audubon. The top three reasons, accounting for 90 percent of respondents, were "believe in the organization and mission" (34 percent), "to protect the environment" (30 percent), and "to visit the sanctuaries" (26 percent).

Analysis showed that, compared to the first two groups, those who joined primarily to visit the sanctuaries tended to be younger and were more likely to have children under 18 in their households. Over 90 percent had visited a sanctuary within the past year, compared to about three-fourths of those in the other segments. They were somewhat less likely to have made a gift to the Society, and a higher proportion of them belonged at the $47 (or lower) membership levels. Although they were less likely to read *Sanctuary* magazine in depth, they expressed more interest than the other groups in receiving a newsletter that listed MAS programs, classes, and events.

EVALUATION

After returning to the headquarters building from their visit to the Audubon Shop, Solomon and Caffry joined other members of the task force in the boardroom. The topic for discussion involved drawing some preliminary conclusions from the survey results and the competitive audit and relating these insights to current communication efforts. Within the next few weeks, the task force was expected to present the board with recommendations for a new communications program.

EXHIBIT 6 Responses to Selected Questions on Member Survey, September 2001 (*N* = 4,448)

Why did you become a member of Mass Audubon? Please rank importance:

	# 1	*# 2*	*# 3*
Believe in organization and mission	34%	35%	12%
Protect the environment	30	29	15
Visit the sanctuaries	26	21	25
Participate in programs, classes, events	6	8	10
Participate in birding related events, seminars	3	3	5
Get *Sanctuary* magazine	1	4	9

How important are the following aspects of Mass Audubon's mission to you?
(5-point scale: 5 = extremely important, 4 = very important)

	5	*4*
Protecting the environment for wildlife	81%	14%
Saving land from development	75	15
Providing nature preserves to walk/hike, enjoy birds/wildlife	60	29
Educating kids about the natural world/environment	60	27
Being an advocate for legal actions to protect environment	55	24

How often have you visited a Mass Audubon sanctuary or site in the past year?

Not visited	21%
1 visit	17
2–3 visits	24
< visits	38

What do you know about the relationship between National Audubon and Mass Audubon?

Same group	1%
MA is local branch	21
Separate organizations	48
Don't know	30

EXHIBIT 6 (Continued)

Do you read Sanctuary magazine?
Yes: 96% No: 4%

If yes, how frequently?
Always: 43% Frequently: 27% Sometimes: 18% Skim: 12%

Do you read the newsletter from your local sanctuary?
Yes: 78% No: 16% No response: 6%

If yes, how frequently?
Always: 50% Frequently: 26% Sometimes: 14% Skim: 10%

How interested would you be in a newsletter that listed MA programs, classes, and events across the state?
Extremely: 9% Very: 20% Somewhat: 51% Not at all: 20%

If interested, how often would you want to receive this listing?
Bimonthly: 15% Quarterly: 56% Two times per year: 29%

Do you have an e-mail address for personal mail?
Yes: 74% No: 26%

If yes, would you be interested in learning about MA events by e-mail?
Yes: 46% No: 54%

If yes, how often would you like to receive e-mails?
Weekly: 12% Monthly: 61% Quarterly: 27%

What types of things would you like to be informed about via e-mail?

Calendars of events at sanctuaries	72%
News about important public legislation/policy in Mass.	58
Mass Audubon activities to protect the nature of Mass.	57
Environment-related events in Mass.	55
News about the sanctuaries	48
News about your local sanctuary only	24

Have you ever visited our Web site?
Yes: 18% No: 82%

Have you ever visited other environmental Web sites?
Yes: 38% No: 62%

If yes, how often do you visit environmental Web sites in a month?
Once: 53% 2–3 times: 29% 4–10 times: 13% 11 or more: 5% (Mean = 2.8)

Would you come to the Mass Audubon Web site to sign up for events?
Yes: 63% No: 37%

Would you go to interesting Mass Audubon events more than 20 miles from home?
Yes: 63% No: 37%

If yes, how many miles would you travel?
20 miles: 5% 30 miles: 28% 50 miles: 49% 100+ miles: 18%

To which environmental organizations do you belong? Are you a member of any of these?

Mass Audubon	100%	PBS/WGBH	83%
The Nature Conservancy	38	Museum of Fine Arts	42
Trustees of Reservations	27	WBUR	36
Appalachian Mountain Club	18	Museum of Science	25
World Wildlife	15	New England Aquarium	15
National Audubon	15	Franklin Park Zoo	8
Other	27		

Source: MAS records. Certain data have been disguised

Study questions

1. *How is MAS currently positioned against other environmental organizations in Massachusetts?*
2. *What is a new member potentially worth to MAS? (hint: use customer lifetime value analysis). Beyond the financial issue, why is membership important to MAS?*
3. *What approaches should MAS use to retain members and to persuade them to upgrade their membership levels?*
4. *As a participant in the Task Force on Member Communications Strategy, what actions would you recommend to the board?*

APPENDIX A

Profiles of Selected Environmental Organizations

Appalachian Mountain Club (*www.outdoors.org*) Founded in 1876 and headquartered in Boston, the AMC had some 94,000 members and described itself as "America's oldest conservation and recreation organization." Membership cost $40 for an individual and $65 for a family. AMC's mission statement emphasized "protection, enjoyment, and wise use of the mountains, rivers, and trails of the Northeast." Its 125th Anniversary Capital Campaign had a target of $30 million. AMC had 12 chapters extending from Maine to Washington D.C., including four in Massachusetts that collectively accounted for some 32,000 members. The Club's active publication program included *AMC Outdoors*, an award-winning monthly member magazine dedicated to recreation and conservation in the Northeast; *Appalachia*, described as "America's longest-running journal of mountaineering and conservation"; many trail and field guides; and a variety of recreation-oriented "how-to" books. AMC offered environmental education programs and sought to develop the skills and understanding needed to enjoy, protect, and advocate for the backcountry. Outdoor recreation services included group trips, trail maintenance, and provision of a network of camps, campgrounds, lodges, and cabins, as well as a chain of high-mountain huts for hikers and climbers along the New Hampshire segments of the Appalachian Mountain Trail.

Friends of the Earth (*www.foe.org*) FoE was founded in 1972 by a former Sierra Club president who felt that the latter organization was insufficiently vigorous in its defense of the environment. Based in Washington, D.C., it was a national nonprofit advocacy organization with affiliates in 66 countries, "dedicated to protecting the planet from environmental degradation; preserving biological, cultural, and ethnic diversity; and empowering citizens to have an influential voice in decisions affecting the quality of the environment—and their lives." In the United States, FoE worked to preserve clean air and water, advocate public health protection, and examine the root causes of environmental degradation. It researched government policies and tax programs and engaged in lobbying and legal action. FoE's Economics for the Earth program focused on the economics of protecting the environment and included the "Green Scissors" campaign—an alliance of environmentalists and conservative taxpayer organizations dedicated to cutting government subsidies that resulted in environmental damage. Its legal program to ensure enforcement of, and compliance with, U.S. environmental laws was located in FoE's Northeast office in Burlington, Vermont. Membership could be obtained for a donation of $25 or more. Members received a quarterly newsletter, *EarthFocus*, and the biweekly *EarthFocus Online*. They were also entitled to discounts on FoE publications and merchandise.

National Audubon Society (*www.audubon.org*) Based in New York, NAS boasted 550,000 members, 508 chapters, and 100 sanctuaries and nature centers from coast to coast, including eight in Connecticut and two in Maine but none in Massachusetts. Dedicated to the preservation of birds, other wildlife, and habitat, it employed more than 300 staff members and had assets of some $170 million. Expenses in 2000 totaled $58 million, of which $8.7 million was devoted to marketing and communications and $23 million to field operations. Membership cost $35, but new members could enroll for only $20. Benefits included membership in the local chapter (which usually organized a variety of activities) and receipt of the widely praised bimonthly magazine *Audubon*, which had won many awards in such fields as nature photography, essays, and design. NAS's 1995 strategic plan committed it to decentralize activities, with a goal of moving from nine regional offices to, ultimately, 50 state programs. In pursuit of this goal, the president had actively encouraged independent state Audubon societies to join or affiliate themselves with NAS. By 2001, the only states in which NAS lacked offices or chapters were Massachusetts, New Hampshire, and Rhode Island, each of which had its own state society. NAS lobbied actively in Washington on issues that were central to its mission, including improved funding of the National Wildlife Refuge system. Chapters worked at the state and local levels. Seeking to protect migratory birds, NAS was also active in Bermuda, the U.S. Virgin Islands, many Central American countries, and parts of South America. The Society was actively engaged in a major rebranding program, including a revised logo, and was now promoting itself simply as "Audubon."

Sierra Club (*www.sierraclub.org*) Based in San Francisco, the Sierra Club took its name from California's Sierra Nevada range and was founded in 1892 by the famous naturalist, writer, and conservationist John Muir. From its early days, it combined organization of group excursions in the mountains with political activity to create national parks and forest reserves. Over subsequent decades, it was often successful in fighting proposals for damming of wild and scenic rivers across large areas of the western United States. It gradually evolved into a national organization, with a strong presence in Washington, using education, lobbying, and litigation to achieve its environmental goals. From the 1970s onward, it broadened its emphasis to fight for clean air and water and extended its antidam crusade to other countries, including Canada and Brazil. Its mission emphasized enjoyment, exploration, and preservation of the "wild places of the earth," promoting responsible use of resources and education to protect and restore the quality of both the natural and human environment. By 2001, it had some 700,000 members and chapters in many states, including Massachusetts. The club organized more than 300 national and international outings in addition to the numerous outings organized by local chapters. Members received a monthly environmental newsletter, *The Planet*, and an attractive glossy bimonthly magazine, *Sierra*.

The Trustees of Reservations (*www.thetrustees.org*) Founded in 1891, this Massachusetts organization maintained 91 reservations representing many of the state's most scenic, ecologically rich, and historically important landscapes. Its landholdings, which also included several historic buildings, protected some 45,000 acres (180 km^2) through ownership or conservation restrictions. Collectively, the reservations provided a wide range of recreational opportunities. The organization also offered function rentals at the large Crane Estate in Ipswich and bed-and-breakfast accommodation at this and one other property. Basic membership cost $40 for individuals or $60 for couples and families. Benefits included a free guidebook, a 50 percent discount off admission charges at TTOR reservations, discounts in its shops, and receipt of a quarterly newsletter.

Masspirg (*www.masspirg.org*) The Massachusetts Public Interest Research Group was one of 26 independent, state-based research groups advocating for the public interest in their home states. In 1983, an alliance of state-based PIRGs created US PIRG (*www.uspirg.org*) to share ideas and resources and, where appropriate, coordinate regional or national efforts. MASSPIRG sought to uncover threats to public health or well-being and fight to end them, using investigative research, media exposés, grassroots organizing, advocacy, and litigation. Its stated goal was to deliver persistent, results-oriented, public-interest activism that protected the environment, encouraged a fair and sustainable economy, and fostered responsive, democratic government. Among the six programs it was pursuing in Massachusetts were the environment (open space, recycling, clean water, and toxics), energy (efficiency and clean, renewable power), and transportation (efficient and environmentally sound). Each program director worked with many different constituencies in support of specific goals. Located in Boston close to the Massachusetts State House, the organization had a full-time attorney on its staff. Members received *MASSPIRG MASSCITIZEN*, a quarterly report of activities.

The Nature Conservancy (*www.nature.org*) Founded in 1951, TNC defined its mission as preserving "the plants, animals, and natural communities that represent the diversity of life on Earth by protecting the lands and waters they need to survive." Its approach was to protect carefully chosen portfolios of land and water within scientifically defined ecoregions, in order to ensure the survival of each region's biological diversity. TNC had a reputation as a very focused organization that used a nonconfrontational approach to achieve its goals. By 2002, it had successfully protected 12.6 million acres (50,000 km^2) in the United States and an additional 80.2 million acres (325,000 km^2) across Canada, the Asia-Pacific Region, the Caribbean, and Latin America. It had 1,400 preserves, one million members, and had launched a $1 billion campaign—the largest private conservation campaign ever undertaken—to save 200 of the world's "Last Great Places." TNC's approaches used outright purchase and management of land under partnerships or conservation easements. A few of its properties, principally in the western United States, offered accommodation and excursions, but none of those in Massachusetts did. TNC was based in Arlington,

Virginia, and published *Nature News*, an interactive newsletter for members sent once or twice monthly by e-mail, as well as *Nature Conservancy* magazine, which had recently been revamped and was offered free of charge to members enrolled at the $50 or higher level. Basic membership was $25 a year.

The Wilderness Society (*www.wilderness.org*) Founded in 1935, TWS worked to develop a nationwide network of wildlands through public education, scientific analysis, and advocacy. Its goal was "to ensure that future generations will enjoy the clean air and water, wildlife, beauty, and opportunities for recreation, and renewal that pristine forests, rivers, deserts, and mountains provide." Headquartered in Washington, TWS had eight regional offices across the country, including one in Boston. The activities of the northeast region focused on the Great Northern Forest—"the largest and last continuous wild forest east of the Mississippi River"—which stretched from northern New York state, across the northern Green and White Mountains, to the remote wetlands of eastern Maine. In return for a contribution of $30 or more, members received the Society's annual full-color publication *Wilderness Year*, a quarterly color newsletter, and member alerts.

Case 13 The Accellion Service Guarantee

JOCHEN WIRTZ AND JILL KLEIN

A high-tech company introduces what it considers to be a bold service quality guarantee to communicate its commitment to service excellence to customers, prospects, and its own employees.

Accellion was a young high-tech firm with leading-edge technology in the distributed file storage, management, and delivery market space. Still new to the industry, the firm aimed to become the global backbone for the next generation of Internet-based applications.

Its main value proposition to the world's largest enterprises ("the Global 2000"), as well as to Internet-based providers of premium content, was to allow them to serve their users faster, increase operational efficiencies, and lower total costs. Specifically, Accellion customers could improve the access time for downloading and uploading files by more than 200%. This performance improvement was achieved by locating an intelligent storage and file management system at the "edges of the Internet" and thereby delivering content from regions located closer to the end user. The typical time-consuming routing through many servers and hubs could be avoided using Accellion's infrastructure.

The need for an Internet infrastructure to deliver high bandwidth content to end-users had never been greater. There was a trend towards multimedia and personalized Web content, all of which could not be delivered efficiently by existing infrastructure, which routed data through the congested network of servers that form the backbone of the Internet. This prompted Accellion to develop and launch a new service: distributed file storage, management and delivery. Accellion provided an applications platform that resided on independent servers, which were directly connected to the users' Internet Service Providers (ISPs), thereby avoided the congested "centres" of the Internet. This decreased access time and allowed Accellion to distribute specialized content and applications more efficiently. For more information on Accellion's value proposition, visit its website at: *http://www.accellion.com*.

To market Accellion's value proposition, the CEO, Warren J. Kaplan, and the firm's chief strategist, S. Mohan, felt that key success factors for Accellion's aggressive growth strategy were its leading-edge technology, excellence in service delivery, and high customer satisfaction. They envisioned that customers would prefer to leverage Accellion's technology and partnerships instead of managing the details of deploying, maintaining and upgrading their own storage infrastructure for distributed Internet applications. To build a customer-driven culture and credibly communicate service excellence to the market, Accellion aimed to harness the power of service guarantees.

Cost effective services for improving performance and reliability were becoming critical, as the widespread use of multimedia and other large files increased exponentially. The value proposition was clearly attractive, but how could Accellion convince prospective clients that its technology and service actually could deliver what they promised?

Mohan felt that a Quality of Service (QoS) Guarantee would be a powerful tool to make its promises credible and at the same time push his team to deliver what had been promised. Mark Ranford, Accellion's Director for Product Management, and Mohan spearheaded the development of the QoS Guarantee. They finally launched the QoS Guarantee (shown in **Exhibit 1**) stating that "it is a revolutionary statement of our commitment to the customer to do whatever it takes to ensure satisfaction." The official launch of the guarantee was announced to all staff by email (**Exhibit 2**).

Their QoS Guarantee, however, was just part of Accellion's push for operational excellence. Many factors worked together to keep the company focused on its clients and providing the best possible service, so that it could create a large and loyal customer base for its innovative product. Thus, it was

EXHIBIT 1 Accellion's Service Guarantee

Quality Of Service Guarantee

The Accellion Quality of Service Guarantee defines Accellion's assurance and commitment to providing the Customer with value-added Service and is incorporated into Accellion's Customer Contract. The definition of terms used herein is the same as those found in the Customer Contract.

1. **Performance Guarantee**

   Accellion guarantees that the performance of the Network in uploading and downloading content, as a result of using the Accellion Service, will be no less than 200% of that which is achieved by a benchmark origin site being accessed from the edges of the Internet. For all purposes herein, performance measurement tests will be conducted by Accellion.

2. **Availability Guarantee**

   Accellion guarantees 100% Service availability, excluding Force Majuere and Scheduled Maintenance for Customers who have opted for our replication services.

3. **Customer Service Guarantee**

   Should Accellion fail to meet the service levels set out in Sections 1 and 2 above, Accellion will credit the Customer's account with one (1) month's service fee for the month affected when the failure(s) occurred, provided the Customer gives written notice to Accellion of such failure within five (5) days from the date such failure occurred. The Customer's failure to comply with this requirement will forfeit the Customer's right to receive such credit.

   Accellion will notify the Customer no less than 48 hours (2 days) in advance of Scheduled Maintenance. If the Service becomes unavailable for any other reason, Accellion will promptly notify the Customer and take all necessary action to restore the Service.

   Accellion maintains a 24-hour support center and will provide the Customer with a response to any inquiry in relation to the Service no more than 2 hours from the time of receipt of such query by customer service.

4. **Security and Privacy Policy**

   Accellion has complete respect for the Customer's privacy and that of any Customer data stored in Accellion servers. The Accellion Service does not require Customers to provide any end-user private details for the data being stored on the servers. All information provided to Accellion by the Customer is stored for the Customer's sole benefit. Accellion will not share, disclose or sell any personally identifiable information to which it may have access and will ensure that the Customer's information and data is kept secure.

   Disclosure of Customer's information or data in Accellion's possession shall only be made where such disclosure is necessary for compliance with a court order, to protect the rights or property of Accellion and to enforce the terms of use of the Service as provided in the Contract.

   Accellion will ensure that the Customer's information and data is kept secure and protected from unauthorized access or improper use, which includes taking all reasonable steps to verify the Customer's identity before granting access.

EXHIBIT 2 Email to all Accellion Staff, Announcing the Launch of the QoS Guarantee

Dear Team,

I am pleased to forward to everyone our industry's leading Quality of Service guarantee (QoS). Please read it over very carefully. You will find it to be very aggressive, and it puts the ownership on everyone in this company to deliver. Customers don't want a Service Level Agreement (SLA), they just want their network up and running all the time. That is why we have created this no questions asked guarantee. This type of guarantee has proven successful in other industries where service is key to success (e.g., Industry Leaders such as Gartner Group, LL Bean, Nordstrom, etc.).

As a member of the Accellion team, you are key to our client's satisfaction.

Thanks in advance for your support in making our clients and ourselves successful.

very important to raise awareness for Accellion's unique value proposition and convince the early adopters of the advantages.

Accellion's customers reacted positively. One customer stated, "Hey, look at this. I haven't seen anything like it. No one offers 100% availability. That's tremendous." Another customer exclaimed, "You must really be confident in your service. This really is risk free now, isn't it?" Accellion was committed to its guarantee and strongly believed that having the best network and technology partners would enable it to deliver on its promise.

Study Questions

1. *Evaluate the design of Accellion's guarantee shown in Exhibit 1. How effective will it be in communicating service excellence to potential and current customers? Would you recommend any changes to its design or implementation?*
2. *Will the guarantee be successful in creating a culture for service excellence within Accellion? What else may be needed for achieving such a culture?*
3. *Do you think customers might take advantage of this guarantee and "stage" service failures to invoke the guarantee? If yes, how could Accellion minimize potential cheating on its guarantee?*

Case 14a Innovation at Progressive (A): Pay-As-You-Go Insurance

Frances X. Frei

Our motive . . . was to delight the customer, maybe even shock the consumer a little for competitive advantage. We wanted to deliver the unexpected.[1]

—Peter Lewis, CEO, The Progressive Corporation

An innovative insurance company has just completed the pilot test phase of a new pay-as-you-go approach to auto insurance, based upon monitoring vehicle use through an in-car GPS system. Management must decide whether or not to roll out the new service nationally.

PROGRESSIVE UNVEILS PAY-AS-YOU-GO INSURANCE

"It's very simple. The less you drive, the less you pay," explained Robert McMillan in early 2000.[2] McMillan, a Progressive Corporation executive, had dreamed up a high-tech method for calculating auto insurance premiums on a pay-as-you-go basis. The company called it Autograph. Rather than price insurance according to traditional, easily measured risk factors such as a driver's gender, age, and driving record and vehicle make and model, Progressive was experimenting with using global positioning systems (GPS) and wireless technology to record the actual use of policyholders' cars including times during and conditions under which they were driven. Progressive was committed to technological leadership in an industry that was growing increasingly excited about employing technologies such as GPS and cellular modems for calculating policy premiums. The company prided itself on running cutting-edge experiments such as McMillan's data-heavy program that could become the basis for customized, differentiated services.

Customers were responding to Progressive's eighteen-month Texas pilot, which was drawing to an end, with enthusiasm. Autograph systems had been installed in 1,100 cars and users had saved on average about 25 percent. "I use some cars intermittently, and when I do, I pay," explained one Houston resident with four cars insured by Progressive.[3] The positive response to the pilot had led Progressive to consider rolling the program out nationally. But some wondered whether conditions specific to Texas—a preponderance of rural and suburban driving, which were less expensive to insure—were responsible for Autograph's success. It was suggested that perhaps the company should expand the pilot to several other states before attempting a national roll out. Others worried that Progressive was becoming distracted by the functionality of new technologies, and losing sight of the insurance business.

PROGRESSIVE AND THE INSURANCE INDUSTRY[4]

Progressive had sold auto insurance exclusively since its founding in Cleveland, Ohio in 1937. Recalled Peter Lewis, founder Joseph Lewis' son and chief executive officer since 1965:

> My father . . . sort of fell into it. He was a lawyer but he got an idea. Car insurance at that time was rather novel. It was only sold in the carriage trades. . . . He said, 'I'm going to sell it to factory

[1]Marcia Stepanek, "Q&A with Progressive's Peter Lewis," *Business Week*, September 12, 2000.
[2]Anne Eisenberg, "What's Next: Paying for Car Insurance by the Mile," *The New York Times*, April 20, 2000, G7.
[3]Eisenberg (2000).
[4]Some of the industry information in this section draws on Standard & Poor, *Industry Surveys Insurance: Property-Casualty*, January 11, 2001.

Business School Case 9-602-175. Professor Frances X. Frei and Research Associates Hanna Rodriguez-Farrar prepared this case from published sources. This case derives from an earlier case prepared by Professor Frances X. Frei and Research Associate Hanna Rodriguez-Farrar, "Innovation at Progressive (A): Pay-As-You-Go Insurance," HBS No, 601-076, which it replaces. HBS cases are developed solely as the basis for class discussion. Cases are not intended to serve as endorsements, sources of primary data, or illustrations of effective or ineffective management. April 9, 2002.

workers and let them pay for it [over] time. . . . I'm going to have a whole set of policies that are very different.' The company started out as a maverick company.[5]

In 1956, Progressive started writing auto insurance for high-risk (non-standard) drivers, who typically made up 20 percent of the insurance market in any given year. In 1971 the company went public and moved its headquarters to Mayfield Village, Ohio. By 1987 it exceeded $1 billion in premiums.

The U.S. property-casualty (P/C) insurance industry, although it comprised thousands of companies all vying for a share of the multibillion-dollar market for personal and commercial insurance coverage, was dominated by only a handful of companies. The ten largest P/C insurers (based on premium volume) accounted for nearly 44 percent of net written premiums, approximately $289.4 billion in 1999. The two largest insurers—State Farm Group and Allstate Corporation—captured close to one fifth of the market.

The insurance business was one of shared risk. Insurers set aside a portion of the premiums collected from policyholders to cover losses. Earned premiums were insurers' primary revenue source, investment income, derived from investing funds set aside for loss reserves, unearned premium reserves, policyholders' surplus, and shareholders' equity, the second-largest component of their revenues.

Insurers' expenses included commissions paid to agents and salespeople, usually deducted immediately from collected premiums, losses (also called claims), and claims-related and loss adjustment expenses including adjusters' and litigation fees. Insurers also incurred underwriting related expenses, such as salaries for actuarial staff. The underwriting profit (or loss) was determined by subtracting these expenses from earned premiums.

Of more than a dozen property-casualty product lines, auto liability and auto damage accounted for nearly 40 percent of premiums written (**Exhibit 1**). Auto insurers had historically found it difficult to make money on the insurance side of the business, but maintained profitability by investing premiums. (**Exhibit 2** breaks down revenues and expenses for auto insurers.)

Auto insurance was sold through both dedicated (single company) and independent (two or more companies) agents as well as directly to the consumer via telephone and Internet. (**Exhibit 3** tallies numbers and types of agents for selected competitors.) Progressive, the largest writer of auto insurance in the independent agency system (with 10 percent of the market) wrote more than 80 percent of its auto premiums through independent agents.

Auto insurance premiums were traditionally rated on attributes of vehicle (age, manufacturer, and value), customer (age, gender, marital status, place of residence, driving record), and types of coverage and deductibles selected. Insurers used this information to establish a driver and vehicle "class" and loss experience with that class to set a rate.

Progressive operated in every state except Massachusetts and New Jersey and competed with

EXHIBIT 1 Property-Casualty Net Premiums Written by Product Line, United States, 1999

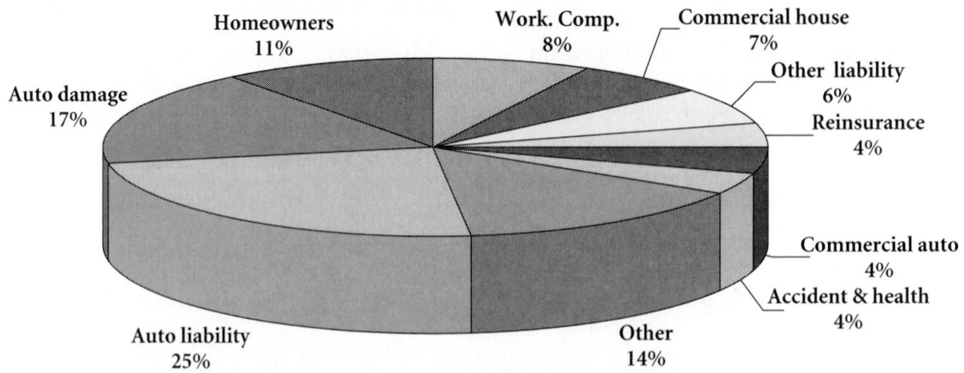

Source: Adapted from Standard & Poor's, *Industry Surveys Insurance: Property-Casualty*, January 11, 2001, p. 18.

[5]Stepanek (2000).

EXHIBIT 2 Auto Insurance Costs and Profits

Revenues and Expenses	*1999 Industry Average*	*1998 Industry Average*
Premiums (earned)	$100	$100
Payments to injured persons		
Medical	(10)	(9)
Wage loss & other economic payments	(1)	(1)
Pain & suffering	(6)	(6)
Lawyers' fees	(13)	(12)
Other costs of settling claims	(3)	(3)
Subtotal	**(33)**	**(32)**
Payments for damaged vehicles		
Property Damage Liability	(16)	(16)
Collision claims	(18)	(16)
Comprehensive claims	(8)	(9)
Other costs of settling claims	(3)	(2)
Subtotal	**(45)**	**(43)**
Total claims	*(78)*	*(75)*
Expenses		
Commissions and other fees	(17)	(17)
Costs of operations	(5)	(5)
State premium taxes	(2)	(2)
Dividends to policyholders	(1)	(2)
Total expenses	**(25)**	**(26)**
Total claims and expenses	**(103)**	**(101)**
Investment gain	10	12
Pre-tax income	7	11
Federal taxes	(2)	(4)
Net profit[a]	**5**	**7**

Source: Adapted from The Fact Book 2001 (New York: Insurance Institute, 2001) p. 50; *Best's Insurance Reports, Property-Casualty*, Volume 2, M-Z (Oldwick, NJ: A. M. Best The Insurance Information Source, 2000).

Notes:

[a] The Insurance Research Council-Insurance Services Office estimates that "soft" fraud (smalltime cheating by normally honest people) siphoned off 11 to 30 cents of every claim dollar and hardcore scams steal only a small fraction of that. See *http://www.insurancefraud.org/media_center_set.html.*

EXHIBIT 3 Auto Insurance Distribution Channels by Agent Type, 1999

Company	*Dedicated agents*	*Independent agents*
Progressive	0	30,000
GEICO	0	0
Allstate	15,200	13,000
State Farm	16,000	0

Source: Company Annual Reports, 1999.

industry behemoths such as State Farm and Allstate as well as with smaller companies such as Berkshire Hathaway subsidiary GEICO. (**Exhibit 4** reports market share data for 1999; **Exhibits 5–8** provide selected financials for Progressive and its competitors.)

In 1956, with the formation of Progressive Casualty Insurance Company, Progressive was one of the first insurers to enter the non-standard (high-risk) market, in which it quickly became a dominant

EXHIBIT 4 Top Ten U.S. Auto Insurers by Market Share, 1999

Company	*Market Share (%)*
State Farm	18.9
Allstate	12.2
Farmers	5.7
Progressive	4.8
Nationwide	4.4
GEICO	4.1
USAA Group	3.1
Liberty Mutual	2.2
American Family	2.0
Travelers	2.0

Source: Adapted from *The Fact Book 2001* (New York: Insurance Information Institute, 2001), p. 48.

player. Progressive's strength lay in its ability to finely segment its customer base. Lewis maintained:

> We're very good price segmenters. We built our business by out-segmenting the competition. . . . We're now the largest insurer of motorcycles in the world. We got into the motorcycle business in 1969. At the time, people who write motorcycle insurance did it based on the size of the motorcycle. We figured out how to also write it based on the age of the driver. What happened when we started adding that bit of information to the equation is that we got all the old drivers and the other companies got all the younger ones. The older ones are better risks. Competitors at the time got their clocks cleaned so they raised their prices. See, they

EXHIBIT 5 Progressive Selected Financials ($ in millions)

	1999	*1998*	*1997*	*1996*	*1995*	*1994*	*1993*
Company-wide net premiums written[a]	6,110	5,274	4,644	3,399	2,875	2,430	1,794
Auto net premiums written	5,769	4,978	4,368	3,157	2,669	2,392	1,755
Auto as % of business	94%	94%	94%	93%	93%	98%	94%
Revenues and expenses							
Premiums earned[b]	5,660	4,916	4,161	3,161	2,693	2,168	1,645
Loss and loss adjustment[c]	4,240	3,364	2,968	2,225	1,931	1,391	1,027
Underwriting expenses[d]	1,495	1,314	1,085	778	708	633	513
Other expenses	0	0	0	0	0	0	0
Dividends to policy-holders	0	0	0	0	0	0	0
Net underwriting income	(75)	238	108	158	54	144	105
Net investment income	268	247	216	168	143	103	108
Other income	150	133	130	106	95	90	61
Pre-tax operating income	343	618	453	431	292	337	274
Net realized gain on security sales	(20)	3	23	(1)	20	7	0
Income tax	123	293	208	157	116	112	97
Net income	200	328	267	273	196	231	177
Loss ratio[e]	75%	68%	71%	70%	72%	64%	62%
Expense ratio[f]	24%	25%	23%	23%	25%	26%	29%
Combined ratio[g]	99%	93%	95%	93%	96%	90%	91%

Source: Adapted from *Best's Insurance Reports: Property-Casualty*, Volume 2, K-Z (Oldwick, NJ: A.M. Best The Insurance Information Source, 2000).

Notes:

[a]Premiums, excluding reinsurance ceded to, but including insurance assumed from, other companies.
[b]Premiums collected for a period of coverage that has elapsed.
[c]Expense of paying, plus expense of processing, insurance claims.
[d]Expense of underwriting policies plus commissions paid to agents.
[e]Losses and loss adjustment as a percentage of premiums earned.
[f]Underwriting expenses as a percentage of premiums written.
[g]The sum of an insurer's loss and expense ratios.

EXHIBIT 6 Allstate Selected Financials ($ in millions)

	1999	*1998*	*1997*	*1996*	*1995*
Company-wide net premiums written	20,855	19,101	18,294	17,821	17,506
Auto net premiums written	15,559	14,554	14,103	13,417	12,662
Auto as % of business	75%	76%	77%	76%	72%
Revenues and expenses					
Premiums earned	19,569	18,889	18,096	17,937	17,088
Loss and loss adjustment	14,488	13,249	13,136	14,052	13,317
Underwriting expenses	5,250	4,614	4,482	4,358	4,044
Other expenses	0	179	49	(3)	0
Dividends to policyholders	0	42	0	3	20
Net underwriting income	(170)	805	429	(473)	(293)
Net investment income	1,847	1,833	1,817	1,873	1,885
Other income	225	151	312	242	217
Pre-tax operating income	1,823	1,815	2,934	2,544	1,629
Net realized gain on security sales	537	935	1,134	781	888
Income tax	489	754	1,098	805	290
Net income	1,870	1,996	2,970	2,520	2,227
Loss ratio	74%	70%	73%	78%	78%
Expense ratio	25%	24%	24%	24%	23%
Combined ratio	99%	94%	97%	103%	101%

Source: Adapted from *Best's Insurance Reports: Property-Casualty*, Volume 1, A-J (Oldwick, NJ: A.M. Best The Insurance Information Source, 2000).

EXHIBIT 7 GEICO Selected Financials ($ in millions)

	1999	*1998*	*1997*	*1996*	*1995*
Companywide net premiums written	4,877	4,121	3,538	3,080	2,816
Auto net premiums written	4,859	4,103	3,501	2,995	2,635
Auto as % of business	100%	100%	99%	97%	94%
Revenues and expenses					
Premiums earned	4,681	3,972	3,432	3,050	2,747
Loss and loss adjustment	3,854	2,993	2,642	2,430	2,260
Underwriting expenses	878	733	517	428	384
Other expenses	(108)	0	0	0	(10)
Dividends to policyholders	0	0	0	0	0
Net underwriting income	(51)	246	273	193	113
Net investment income	374	315	285	250	224
Other income/expense	(23)	(20)	(14)	(10)	(8)
Pre-tax operating income	37	244	517	513	408
Net realized gain on security sales	170	175	212	8	32
Income tax	212	161	378	168	116
Net income	(5)	257	351	353	324
Loss ratio	82%	75%	77%	80%	82%
Expense ratio	18%	18%	15%	14%	14%
Combined ratio	100%	93%	92%	94%	96%

Source: Adapted from *Best's Insurance Reports: Property Casualty*, Volume 1, A-J (Oldwick, NJ: A.M. Best The Insurance Information Source, 2000).

EXHIBIT 8 State Farm Selected Financials ($ in millions)

	1999	*1998*	*1997*	*1996*	*1995*
Company-wide net premiums written	34,208	34,755	34,842	34,559	33,310
Auto net premiums written	23,349	24,153	24,458	24,184	23,232
Auto as % of business	68%	69%	70%	70%	70%
Revenues and expenses (auto)					
Premiums earned	34,027	34,641	34,843	34,010	32,878
Loss and loss adjustment	28,879	28,388	25,703	27,473	27,982
Underwriting expenses	8,556	8,215	7,795	7,084	6,977
Other expenses	0	0	0	0	0
Dividends to policyholders	5	894	692	0	0
Net underwriting income	(3,413)	(2,857)	652	(547)	(2,081)
Net investment income	3,428	3,493	3,494	3,377	3,224
Other income	109	132	(92)	(142)	129
Pre-tax operating income	123	768	4,055	2,688	1,272
Net realized gain on security sales	806	413	256	239	64
Income tax	137	184	730	570	242
Net income	792	996	3,581	2,356	1,093
Loss ratio	85%	82%	74%	81%	85%
Expense ratio	25%	24%	22%	20%	21%
Combined ratio	110%	106%	96%	101%	106%

Source: Adapted from *Best's Insurance Reports: Property-Casualty*, Volume 2, M-Z (Oldwick, NJ: A.M. Best The Insurance Information Source, 2000).

didn't have the information to show them how their mix of customers was shifting. We did. We were the first to offer discounts for four-doors and add surcharges for convertibles. Using information, we've been able to out-segment everyone else. Now we're always looking for new ways to use information to segment prices.[6]

Progressive's price segmenting consisted of data mining and extensive statistical analysis of customer behavior. As an example of how Progressive differed from its competition in this regard, consider the following example. Two elderly drivers with identical driving records each have a moving violation (elderly driver A failed to yield while elderly driver B was speeding). Progressive's competitors are likely to treat these two violations equally in terms of increase in insurance. At Progressive the average impact on insurance for these two drivers would be the same as the competition but importantly, one driver would be priced above the competition and the other below. Through extensive analysis, Progressive has found that failure to yield should result in a higher premium increase rather than speeding.

Progressive's ability to segment depended upon its sophisticated underwriting software, which allowed agents to set rates at finer levels than its competition. While most insurers would simply reject an application from a 19-year-old driving a motorcycle with a history of accidents and a poor driving record, Progressive had a rate for that driver because of its ability to factor in other aspects giving a more accurate price for the risk. All insurance companies looked at driver and vehicle location factors to set premiums, but most companies merely looked to their customer history based on zip codes to ascertain the risk. Progressive's software, however, looked for correlations between drivers, 12 vehicle characteristics, risk, and 16 variables in a credit-scoring model, and extended most risk models to include factors such as typical weather and number of intersections per mile of road.[7]

In 1993, after its growth in non-standard drivers leveled out and competitors entered the market, the traditional underwriter of nonstandard and high-risk

[6]Stepanek (2000).
[7]Gary H. Anthes, "Setting the price of risk," *Computerworld*, July 8, 2002. *http://www.computerworld.com/softwaretopics/software/apps/story/0,10801,72446,00.html* accessed February 24, 2003.

policies moved into the standard and preferred sectors.[8] Low-risk policies, an eighth of Progressive's business in 1995, accounted for almost half of its business by 1999 (**Exhibit 9**). Between 1993 and 1999 Progressive advanced from ninth largest to fourth largest auto insurer in the United States. By 1998, Lewis declared:

> We're in the big league now, up there with State Farm and Allstate. The question is, can we win the pennant? Today four out of a hundred cars in the United States are insured with Progressive. People laugh when I talk about 100 percent market share. But if we get better than everybody else in every aspect of the business, why would anybody buy from another company? Of course, I'd settle for 25 percent. People tell me that 25 percent can't be done either, but people have been telling me things like that my whole life.[9]

(**Exhibit 10** plots growth rates for Progressive, the auto insurance industry, and the property-casualty industry.)

A HISTORY OF INNOVATION

Freedom to experiment was ingrained into Progressive's culture early in the company's history. Lewis recalled his father's approach, "The obsession he had, . . . was having the freedom to experiment, to figure out how [we could be better]."[10] Lewis recalled making some crucial investments upon becoming CEO:

EXHIBIT 9 Progressive Corporation, Percentage of Standard and Preferred Business

	1999	*1998*	*1997*	*1996*	*1995*	*1994*
Percent of premiums from standard and preferred sectors	46%	32%	22%	13%	7%	7%

Source: Adapted from The Progressive Corporation, 2000-1997 Annual Reports.

EXHIBIT 10 Growth Rates of Progressive, Auto Insurance, and Property-Casualty Insurance

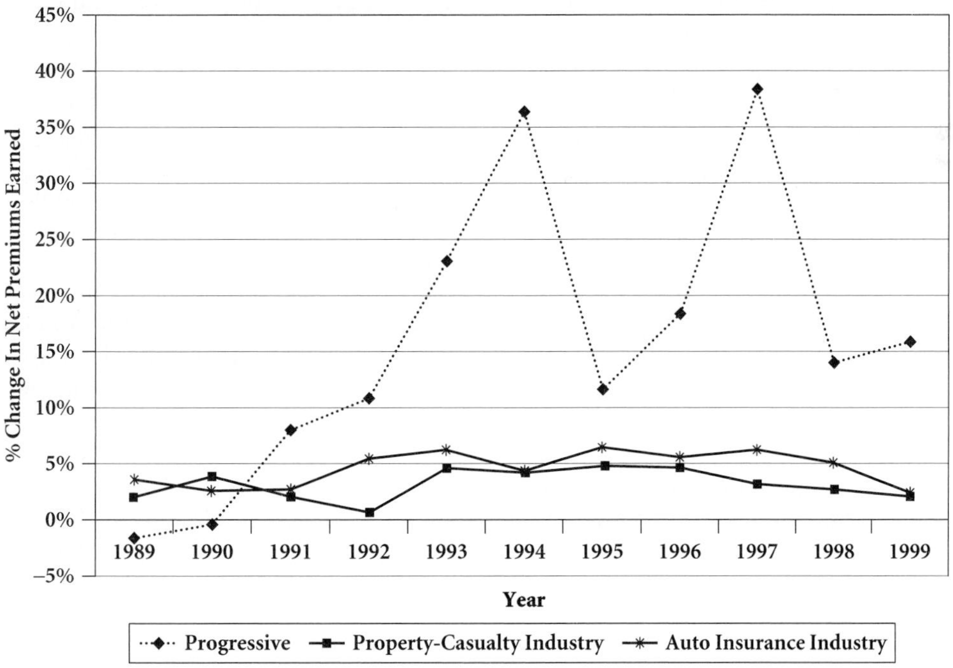

Source: Adapted from Standard & Poor, *Industry Surveys Insurance: Property-Casualty*, January 11, 2001, p. 18.

[8] Michael E. Porter and Nicolij Siggelkow, "Progressive Corporation," HBS No. 797-109 (Boston: Harvard Business School Publishing, 1998) examined the company's decision to enter the standard auto insurance market.
[9] Chuck Salter, "Progressive Makes Big Claims," *Fast Company*, No. 19, November 1998, p. 176.
[10] Stepanek (2000).

> The first thing I did was hire a guy from Travelers [Insurance] who had been in their data processing unit. I recognized that getting in the lead on this stuff would be a competitive opportunity. . . . Our attitude is that we will try almost anything that makes sense and we'll stop it when it stops making sense. We've spent a lot of money on dumb ideas, but we had the flexibility to stop it early . . . and the conversation and the idea-storming [went] on constantly. . . . It's ingrained in our culture to experiment, but to do so responsibly. We reward people for taking risks, but punish them for not spotting bad ones early and pulling the plug.[11]

In 1988 Lewis and the rest of the insurance industry got a "wake up call" from consumers. That year California passed Proposition 103, a referendum designed to regulate auto insurance companies, and roll back escalating rates. Twenty percent of Progressive's business was in California and the company paid out $60 million in refunds.[12] It also reduced its workforce by 19 percent. But, according to Lewis: "It was the best thing that happened to this company. . . . I decided that from then on, anything we did had to be good for the consumer or we weren't going to do it."[13]

Immediate Response

A major innovation was Progressive's implementation of fast service. Lewis reasoned: "Two things happen when you deliver fast: You give better service, and the better you do things, the less they cost in our business. The faster we get to the losses, the fewer the lawyers that get on the other side."[14]

Soon after Proposition 103 Lewis challenged his company's claims department to find a way to respond immediately, in person, to a policyholder involved in an auto accident and be able to do it anywhere, anytime.[15] Less than two years after Proposition 103, Progressive had rewired itself for round-the-clock service, created new positions such as special investigators and outside representatives who visited policyholders, and launched Immediate Response (IR). Claims were now handled by teams 24 hours per day. Progressive's Ohio state general manager Moira Lardakis, recalled the internal resistance Lewis' directive met:

> The claims people were in shock when they were told, "We want you to go out and inspect the car and measure response time in hours, not days." They were used to the 8-to-5 day and dealing with Monday morning loss reports and then going out to inspect vehicles.[16]

Lewis recalled the skepticism with which his idea was met.

> For three years, people said, "It's crazy, it's too expensive; nobody will do it." And for the same three years, I sat here and said, "We're going to do it, no matter how much it costs and no matter how much you don't like it." Other businesses go the extra mile. Why not an auto-insurance company?[17]

Advances in technology, particularly wireless technology and cell phones, made Progressive's leap into 24/7 service possible. Claims representatives relied on their cell phones in the early days of IR calling dispatchers to relay data and retrieve coverage information from the claims center and the company's mainframe. When representatives did not return to their office to update a file with their estimate the job would be held up until the next day.

In 1994, Atlanta Division Claims manager Jose Benitez experimented with "mobile claims offices." Using response vehicles placed in the field, an agent could verify information, soothe policyholders, and expedite the claims process at the site of an accident. The first Immediate Response Vehicle (IRV) was a Ford van outfitted with a desk, file cabinet, drapes, cell phones, generator, computer and printer, chairs, fax machine, and small refrigerator. Recalled Benitez: "It was a tight fit."[18] The white vans, with the Progressive name emblazoned in blue in six places (including on the roof) soon became ubiquitous.[19]

When a customer who had been in an accident called Progressive's 800 number, a telephone agent took down the necessary information and handed

---

[11]Stepanek (2000).
[12]Salter (1998).
[13]Salter (1998).
[14]Stepanek (2000).
[15]Lynna Goch, "Surpassing Lane," *Best's Review*, October 1999, *www.bestsreview.com*.
[16]Goch (1999).
[17]Salter (1998).
[18]Goch (1999).
[19]Goch (1999).

the claim off to one of the 350 local claims offices, which shared the information on the accident and customer through a centralized database. The local claims office dispatched one of the 1,400 IRV vans, and the claims representative in the van, after arriving on the scene, wirelessly accessed the company's central database to process the claim.[20]

The seamless flow of information facilitated by the IR system enabled Progressive claims representatives to work up estimates immediately, often writing a payout check at the scene of an accident. With Claims Workbench, the company's proprietary software application (rolled out in 1997), a parts database, and a laptop and modem were all claims reps required to complete their jobs. With these they could access the company's mainframe, file police reports, and calculate parts and labor hour estimates.[21] By 1997, Progressive was settling 50 percent of claims within seven days.

Claim handling was assigned according to complexity of the claim and experience of the claim representative. Newer reps handled single-car accidents and other minor fender-benders. More experienced reps were assigned multi-car accidents involving totaled cars and injuries. A two-car accident with damage to both cars and both drivers was logged as having four "features." One rep "owned" the claim and was the main point person. Other team members assisted with the reported "features." In the Houston office, a team consisted of ten persons with five in the field doing Immediate Response and five in the office answering phones, dispatching agents, and processing long-term claims.

Good software and information, however, was nothing without good claim representatives. Accordingly, Lewis had two simple operating principles: "hire the best" and "pay the most." Lewis explained further:

> We have the best people in the industry as measured by education, intelligence, intelligence, initiative, work ethic, and work record. We find them and go after them. Then we put them through our crucible. This is a highly competitive, challenging place to work. We work harder than most companies, and that becomes sort of seductive. Many people wash out. The ones who remain are fantastic. . . . The other side of hiring good people is firing people who aren't good. We evaluate people against their objectives, which they negotiate with the company and then put in writing. If people aren't doing their job, it's good-by. This is not a bloodthirsty place. It is a humane environment. But we do not suffer nonperformance.[22]

For Immediate Response to work effectively claims had to be reported; customers, however, were not necessarily accustomed to reporting accidents to their insurers in a timely manner. Progressive consequently set out to encourage policyholders to report accidents immediately. It instituted a Claims Reporting Index (CRI) that monitored how long it took a customer to report an accident.[23] Progressive's innovative Gold Card could be broken in half, facilitating the exchange of information between drivers after an accident.[24] Within six years of implementing these changes Progressive doubled the number of customers that reported claims within 24 hours. Glenn Renwick, developer of the CRI observed:

> It's like FedEx: Customers know that it delivers overnight. More and more people know that we handle auto-insurance claims differently, and quickly.[25]

Quick claim turnarounds and increased number of customers between 1994 and 1997 grew the ranks of claim representatives from 3,093 to 7,561. This growth in claim representatives combined with the two years it typically took for a claim representative to get up to speed resulted in lower claim-handling quality and increased loss costs.[26]

Comparison Quotes: 1-800 AUTOPRO

Lewis realized the industry was competitive, but not for customers. In a 1993 meeting with 14 consumer groups, arranged by college friend Ralph Nader (a

[20]Claims were assigned based on complexity. Newer agents handled single-car accidents, more experienced agents multi-car accidents, which often involved totaled vehicles and injuries.
[21]By 1990, Progressive claims reps were able to inspect vehicles and write claim checks within nine hours of an accident report 15 percent of the time; by 1997 this increased to 57 percent of the time. Salter (1998).
[22]Salter (1998).
[23]Salter (1998).
[24]The card grew out of Progressive's research on credit cards, from which the company concluded that the durability and prestige of a physical card imprinted with personal information were important to consumers. Salter (1998).
[25]Salter (1998).
[26]Company annual report, 1999, p. 18.

Prop. 103 supporter), consumers' frustration was made clear to him. Essentially, Nader had drawn attention to the lack of information transparency across insurers.[27] Recalled Lewis: "The consumer could not access the competition. The process of getting insurance for yourself was impossible to do, so no one did it. We relied on agents to do it, and they were irresponsible.... [I realized] it would be great if we could give people comparison quotes."[28]

Comparison Quotes provided prospective customers who called Progressive's toll-free number with rates from Progressive and up to three competitors. More than half the time a competitor's quote was lower than Progressive's. Observed Alan Bauer, Progressive's Internet-process leader: "Time and again, people don't believe we do this. They think it's a gimmick. But it's part of information transparency. We are exposing our data to the customer."[29]

Soon after Comparison Quotes launched, Progressive's Web site went live, one of the first in the industry. Bauer continued: "We want to provide the information that customers need—and to provide it on their terms. We don't care if it's in person, over the phone, or online."[30] While Progressive had success selling insurance directly to consumers, in 1998 it still relied on a network of 30,000 independent agents for 90 percent of its premiums. (**Exhibit 11** provides a breakdown of direct and independent agent premiums.)

No matter the channel, Progressive's underwriting process was highly automated. Agents (or customers using the Web site) input unique customer information and Progressive software calculated the appropriate premium using input information as well as data from third parties such as other insurers, credit bureaus, and driving records vendors.[31]

AUTOGRAPH

McMillan conceived Autograph in 1994 based on observations of the automobile industry's creative uses of GPS technology, which had originally been developed for the military. As the technology became available for civilian use, cars were equipped with GPS-based satellite navigation and theft-recovery systems. McMillan believed this space-age technology had the potential to support a novel approach to calculating and setting insurance premiums. Autograph relied on GPS satellites, mapping technology, and internal computers to determine when and how much a vehicle was driven.[32] This information was uploaded monthly, in a matter of seconds via a cellular phone link, to Progressive's database. Autograph then set premiums based on the amount of driving done within the billing period. Explained Willy Graves, a Progressive executive: "[It's] more like a monthly utility or telephone bill, with the consumer paying by the month based on actual usage rather than on historical data derived from groups of similar people and vehicles."[33]

The patented Autograph system tracked mileage, time of day, and where driving occurred.[34] "Our data show accident rates per mile are much higher late in the night." McMillan pointed out. "A mile driven at 2 A.M. [is] four or five times more expensive than one driven at 7 A.M."[35] Consumers also

EXHIBIT 11 Progressive Corporation, Percentage of Direct (Telephone and Internet) Sales

	1999	*1998*	*1997*	*1996*
Percent of premiums derived from direct sales vs. through agents	17%	10%	6%	5%

Source: Adapted from The Progressive Corporation, 2000 Annual Report.

27 Salter (1998).
28 Stepanek (2000).
29 Salter (1998).
30 Salter (1998).
31 Anthes (2002).
32 Consumers who signed up for Autograph agreed to give Progressive access to their driving data, and were assured that it would be accessible only to the company and consumers.
33 Anonymous, "Progressive Testing New Product in Texas," October 28, 1999, *www.theautochannel.com* (accessed November 11, 2000).
34The Autograph monitoring system incorporated, for example, sensors to detect speeding, abrupt acceleration, sudden braking, seatbelt use, and traffic signal observance. Stored in a vehicle's computer and accessed by the company, data that signaled unsafe driving actions could be used as a basis for assessing surcharges. Air quality analyzers that detected alcohol use offered another basis for levying penalty fees (Appendix A).
35 Eisenberg (2000).

paid less if they used routes on which fewer accidents occurred. Progressive began a limited market test of the new product in Houston in August 1998, and one year later expanded the test throughout the state of Texas. Progressive absorbed the cost of installing in the policyholders' automobiles a GPS transponder, cellular communication system, and small computer as well as cabling and connectors (roughly $500 per vehicle). The system was powered by the vehicle's battery.[36] Three quarters of Autograph customers' premiums were calculated using data captured by the system, the remaining quarter on the basis of traditional underwriting considerations (e.g., driver's gender, age, driving record, and vehicle make and model).[37]

Drivers who signed up for Autograph were offered (for a monthly fee) an additional set of services (some GPS-based) that were unrelated to insurance. These service features, which included theft recovery, remote door unlocking, travel directions, low-battery detection, and emergency assistance help, were also available to consumers through services such as GM's OnStar.

About 1,100 policyholders signed up for the strictly voluntary program. Graves noted:

> In Houston, consumers . . . are paying an average of 25 percent less [on premiums] using Autograph than they paid using a "traditional" auto insurance product. Houston consumers tell us three things: they're paying less; they're in control; and the system makes sense to them.[38]

Claimed Gus Kopriva, the Autograph policyholder with four cars: "I'm saving lots of money."[39]

> Autograph could also be a vehicle for data mining. Progressive's patents mentioned two examples of sharing knowledge of drivers' whereabouts with other companies.[40] The owner of an Autograph-equipped vehicle that traveled to a resort, for example, might subsequently be targeted to receive travel-related literature, the owner of a vehicle recorded at a sporting event made a target of marketers of sports-related products.[41] (**Appendix A** excerpts from the Autograph patent.)

HOW FAR TO GO?

Progressive management pondered whether expanding Autograph nationally could help the company reestablish its industry-leading underwriting record. Expansion beyond Texas would require major expenditures of time and money. Auto insurance was regulated at the state level, requiring Progressive to seek approval from the insurance commissions of every state in which it planned to implement Autograph (save Texas, which permitted certain auto insurers to operate without regulatory oversight).[42]

An even larger question was *whether* Progressive should make Autograph available to its millions of policyholders. Clearly a breakthrough in terms of technology and innovation, per-mile policies such as Autograph were also viewed as more equitable than conventional insurance.[43] But was it in Progressive's interest to market policies for which consumers would pay, on average, 25 percent *less* in premiums?

Study Questions

1. *What are the drivers of success in the auto insurance business? How does Progressive's performance compare with that of competing firms?*
2. *What is the basis for Progressive's approach to segmentation and how is this strategy implemented? How does it provide competitive advantage?*
3. *Evaluate Rapid Response. What are its implications for (a) customers and (b) Progressive?*
4. *Should Progressive roll out the new Autograph system nationwide? What are the barriers to consumer acceptance?*

[36]Eisenberg (2000).
[37]Eisenberg (2000).
[38]Eisenberg (2000).
[39]Eisenberg (2000).
[40]Patent no. 5,797,137, p. 19.
[41]Progressive assured consumers in the pilot program that all data would be kept confidential.
[42]In Texas, exemption from state regulation was intended to provide "county mutual" insurers with an incentive to sell policies in remote agricultural countries and other underserved areas.
[43]According to the National Organization of Women (NOW), traditional auto policies discriminated against women, the elderly, and low-income groups who drove less than average. NOW proposed legislation in Texas and at the federal level to force insurers to give consumers the option to enroll in distance-based insurance programs. Daniel Hays, "Progressive Tests Per-Mile Auto Policy in Texas," *National Underwriter Property-Casualty Edition*, April 26, 1999.

APPENDIX A

Excerpts from Progressive Patent for Autograph

United States Patent 5,797,134—McMillan, et al.—August 18, 1998

The present invention will use information acquired from the vehicle to more accurately assess vehicle usage and thereby derive insurance costs more precisely and fairly. Examples of possible actuarial classes developed from vehicle provided data include:

Driver Total driving time in minutes by each driver of the insured vehicle; number of minutes driving in high/low risk locations (high/low accident areas); number of minutes of driving at high/low risk times (rush hour or Sunday afternoon); safe driving behavior, using seat belts, use of turn signals, observance of speed limits, and observance of traffic control devices; number of sudden braking situations; and number of sudden acceleration situations.

Vehicle Location vehicle is parked at night (in garage, in driveway, on street); and location vehicle is parked at work (high theft locations, etc.).

These new and more precise actuarial classes are considered to be better predictors of loss because they are based on actual use of the vehicle and the behaviors demonstrated by the driver. This will allow the consumers unprecedented control over the ultimate cost of their vehicle insurance.

In accordance with the present invention, additional discounts and surcharges based on data provided by the insured vehicle will be available. Examples of surcharges and discounts based on vehicle provided data include:

Surcharges Excessive hard braking situations occurring in high-risk locations; and intermittent use of a safety device, such as seat belts.

Discounts Regular selection of low/high-risk routes of travel; regular travel at low/high-risk times; significant changes in driving behavior that results in a lower risk; vacation discount when the vehicle is not used; regular use of safety devices; and unfailing observance of speed limits.

The type of elements monitored and recorded by the subject invention comprise raw data elements, calculated data elements and derived data elements. These can be broken down as follows:

Raw Data Elements

Power train sensors RPM, transmission setting (Park, Drive, Gear, Neutral), throttle position, engine coolant temperature, intake air temperature, barometric pressure;

Electrical sensors brake light on, turn signal indicator, headlamps on, hazard lights on, back-up lights on, parking lights on, wipers on, doors locked, key in ignition, key in door lock, horn applied;

Body sensors airbag deployment, ABS application, level of fuel in tank, radio station tuned in, seat belt on, door open, tail gate open, odometer reading, cruise control engaged, anti-theft disable;

Other sensors vehicle speed, vehicle location, data, time, vehicle direction, IVHS data sources.

Calculated Data Elements rapid deceleration; rapid acceleration; vehicle in skid; wheels in spin; closing speed on vehicle in front; closing speed of vehicle in rear; closing speed of vehicle to side (right or left); space to side of vehicle occupied; space to rear of vehicle occupied; space to front of vehicle occupied; lateral acceleration; sudden rotation of vehicle; sudden loss of tire pressure; driver identification (through voice recognition or code or fingerprint recognition); distance traveled; and environmental hazard conditions (e.g. icing, etc.).

Derived Data Elements vehicle speed in excess of speed limit; observation of traffic signals and signs; road conditions; traffic conditions; and vehicle position.

This list includes many, but not all, potential data elements.

Trigger events are divided into two groups: those requiring immediate action and those not requiring immediate action, but necessary for proper billing of insurance. Those required for proper billing of

Source: Excerpted and adapted from United States Patent #5,797,134 (August 18, 1998).

insurance will be recorded in the same file with all the other recorded vehicle sensor information. Those trigger events requiring action will be uploaded to a central control center which can take action depending on the trigger event. Some trigger events will require dispatch of emergency services, such as police or EMS, and others will require the dispatch of claims representatives from the insurance company.

The following comprises an exemplary of some, but not all, trigger events:

Need for Assistance These events would require immediate notification of the central control center.

1. Accident Occurrence. An accident could be determined through the use of a single sensor, such as the deployment of an airbag. It could also be determined through the combination of sensors, such as a sudden deceleration of the vehicle without the application of the brakes.
2. Roadside assistance needed. The could be through the pressing of a "panic button" in the vehicle or through the reading of a sensor, such as the level of fuel in the tank. Another example would be loss of tire pressure, signifying a flat tire.
3. Lock-out assistance needed. The reading of a combination of sensors would indicate that the doors are locked but the keys are in the ignition and the driver has exited the vehicle.
4. Driving restrictions. The insured can identify circumstances in which he/she wants to be notified of driving within restricted areas, and warned when he/she is entering a dangerous area. This could be applied to youthful drivers where the parent wants to restrict time or place of driving, and have a record thereof.

Unsafe Operation of the Vehicle These events would be recorded in the in-vehicle recording device for future upload. Constant trigger events would result in notification of the driver of the exceptions.

1. Excessive speed. The reading of the vehicle speed sensors would indicate the vehicle is exceeding the speed limit. Time would also be measured to determine if the behavior is prolonged.
2. Presence of alcohol. Using an air content analyzer or breath analyzer, the level of alcohol and its use by the driver could be determined.
3. Non-use of seatbelt. Percent of sample of this sensor could result in additional discount for high use or surcharge for low or no use.
4. Non-use of turn signals. Low use could result in surcharge.
5. ABS (anti-locking braking system) application without an accident. High use could indicate unsafe driving and be subject to a surcharge.

Case 14b Innovation at Progressive (B): Homeowners Insurance

FRANCES X. FREI

"Progressive . . . offering you the products and services you want, when you want them."[1]

—PROGRESSIVE WEB SITE

A successful auto insurance company is debating whether to enter the homeowner's market as many of its competitors have.

In March 2000 Progressive began to offer a new product: homeowners insurance. Made available first in an Arizona pilot, the program was extended to Michigan in October 2000, Maryland in January 2001, and Illinois in September 2001. Marketed initially through specially selected and trained independent insurance agents, Progressive's homeowners policies were eventually to be offered, along with its primary product, auto insurance, through the company's two direct channels, its 800-number and web site.

Many consumers sought the convenience of bundling auto and homeowners insurance rather than dealing with separate companies for each policy. Some insurers even offered discounts to customers who consolidated their coverage. Progressive executives thus viewed homeowners insurance as a natural extension of the company's auto-insurance product suite.

In 1997 Progressive ran a trial partnership in Ohio with Travelers Casualty, a major player in homeowners insurance, whereby consumers were offered homeowners quotes when they called for auto insurance. By 2000, Progressive had decided to offer its own homeowners product.[2] The product was launched slowly in select states. The move into homeowners seemed an obvious choice for Progressive. The data-driven company had success in providing auto insurance rates that more accurately (and less expensively) reflected individual consumers' coverage needs.[3] Cross-selling to these satisfied customers would be a snap. What could they lose?

AUTO AND HOMEOWNERS MARKETS CONTRASTED

Homeowners and auto insurance constituted more than half of all property and casualty (P/C) insurance sold in the United States (**Exhibit 1**). Larger competitors such as State Farm devoted substantial parts of their business to homeowners insurance (**Exhibit 2** orders top-ten homeowners' insurers by market share). In 2000 Americans paid $32 billion to insure houses, mobile homes, condominiums, and apartments. The most basic policy purchased, the HO-1, offered protection against loss of dwelling or other covered personal property due to fire, lightning, windstorm, hail, explosion, riot or civil disturbance, aircraft, vehicle, smoke, vandalism or malicious mischief, theft, glass damage, or volcanic eruption. An HO-2 policy added damage due to falling objects, weight of snow, ice, or sleet, water damage, and electrical surge; an HO-3 policy covered unforeseen perils not explicitly mentioned in the policy (save for ground water seepage, floods, and earthquakes, for which additional special policies were written).[4]

In addition to losses, homeowners' policies offered production against lawsuits occasioned by death or injury incurred on a homeowner's property as a result of negligence. Insurers paid claims above a deductible amount and below a liability limit. Policyholders were responsible for losses in excess

[1]Company history, *www.progressive.com/progressive/history.asp* (accessed April 12, 2002).
[2]Initially, Progressive reinsured, or ceded, 75 percent of its homeowners product. The Progressive Corporation, 10K filing, 2000, p. 179.
[3]See Frances X. Frei and Hanna Rodriguez-Farrar, "Innovation at Progressive (A): Pay-As-You-Go Insurance," HBS No. 601-076.
[4]Apartments were protected by HO-4, condominiums by HO-6, policies.

Business School Case 9-601-138. Professor Frances X. Frei and Research Associate Hanna Rodriguez-Farrar prepared this case from published sources. HBS cases are developed solely as the basis for class discussion. Cases are not intended to serve as endorsements, sources of primary data, or illustrations of effective or ineffective management. May 2, 2002.

EXHIBIT 1 Property-Casualty Net Premiums Written by Product Line, United States, 2000

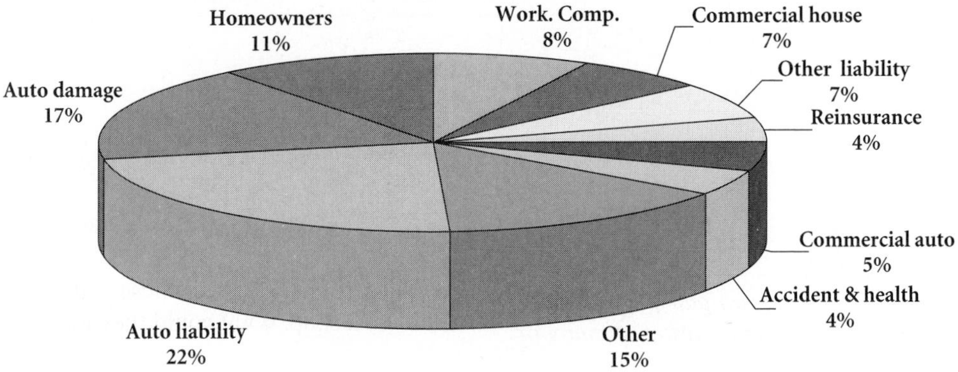

Source: Adapted from Standard & Poor, *Industry Surveys Insurance: Property-Casualty*, January 24, 2002, p. 19

EXHIBIT 2 Top Ten U.S. Homeowners Insurers, 1999

Company	*Market Share*
State Farm	22.6%
Allstate	11.5%
Farmers Ins. Group	6.9%
Nationwide	4.5%
Travelers	3.6%
USAA Group	3.5%
Chubb Group	2.3%
SAFECO	2.3%
American Family	2.1%
Liberty Mutual	2.0%
Total for top ten companies	61.3%
Other 395 companies	38.7%

Source: Adapted from *The Fact Book 2001* (New York: Insurance Information Institute, 2001), p. 72.

of the liability limit. (**Exhibit 3** reports industry averages for homeowners insurance costs and profits.)

Although the average house cost more than the average car, policyholders typically paid higher premiums for auto than for homeowners insurance due to the preponderance of deaths, injuries, and property damage resulting from automobile usage. Consequently, in net premiums written, the auto insurance market was nearly four times larger than the homeowners insurance market.

Underwriting losses tended to be more erratic for homeowners than for auto insurance. (**Exhibit 4** compares loss and expense ratios for the auto and homeowners markets.) Although hardly constant, auto insurance losses tended to follow patterns that

EXHIBIT 3 Homeowners Insurance Costs and Profits, 1998

Revenues and expenses	*Amount ($)*
Premiums (earned)	100
Property damage	
Fire and lightning	(19)
Wind and hall	(18)
Water damage and freezing	(9)
All other	(7)
Theft	(4)
Subtotal	**(57)**
Liability	
Bodily injury and property damage	(3)
Medical payments	(1)
Credit card and other	(4)
Subtotal	(8)
Cost of settling claims	(12)
Total claims	**(77)**
Expenses	
Commissions and other fees	(22)
Costs of operations	(6)
Dividends to policyholders	(1)
Subtotal	**(32)**
Total claims and expenses	(109)
Investment gain	12
Pre-tax income	3
Federal taxes	(1)
Net profit	**2**

Source: Adapted from *The Fact Book 2001* (New York: Insurance Information Institute, 2001), p. 76.

EXHIBIT 4 Industry Loss and Expense Ratios for Auto and Homeowners Insurance

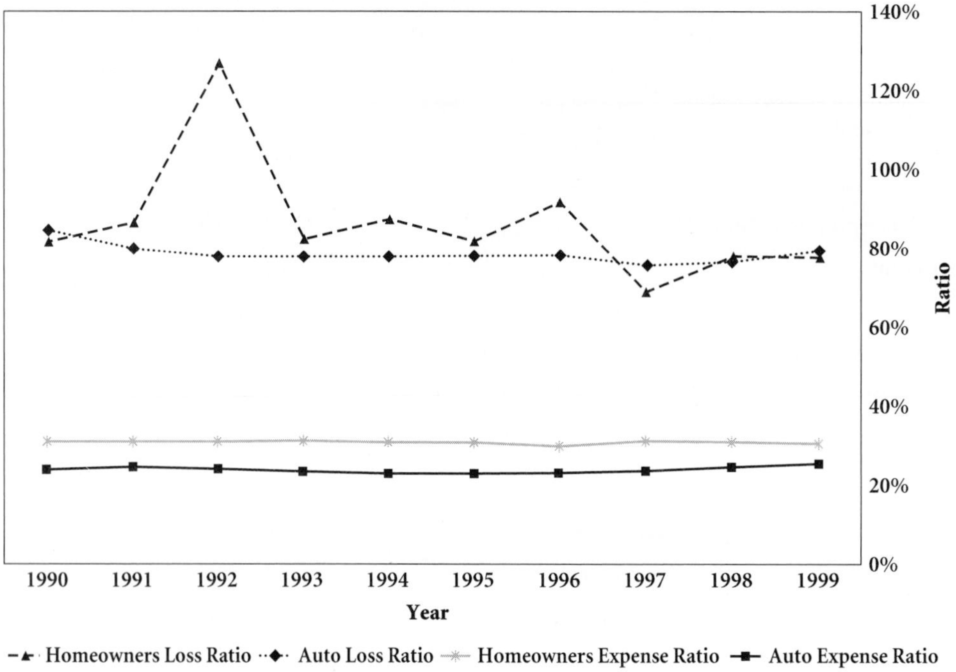

Source: Adapted from Standard & Poor, *Industry Surveys Insurance: Property-Casualty*, January 24, 2002, p. 23.

underwriters could chart. Auto loss levels were variously governed by demographic factors such as age of the driving population, numbers of safety features built into cars, enforcement of drunk driving laws, employment level and price of gasoline (the latter two influenced the amount of driving). Auto underwriters used these and other factors to adjust pricing. In contrast, major underwriting losses in the homeowners market were much more difficult to predict; hurricanes, earthquakes, natural disasters and other unforeseen events were understandably harder to plot. (**Exhibit 5** lists causes of homeowners insurance losses from 1994 through 1998.)

TESTING THE WATERS: PROGRESSIVE'S HOMEOWNERS STRATEGY

Homeowners insurance was a volatile and highly capital-intensive business; partnering with Travelers for its 1997 initial test offering saved Progressive having to enter a difficult market while it enhanced distribution for its core product.[5] Yet the company was explicitly concerned that consumers preferred to buy all their insurance from one company.[6]

Following its introduction in Arizona in 2000, Progressive's homeowners product was offered in Michigan, Maryland, and Illinois. Progressive differentiated its homeowners offering by calling attention to the distinction between its offering, insurance that guaranteed "replacement cost" coverage, and more traditional policies that tended to insure properties for "market value." Putting customers' needs first drove the company's campaign. Observed Progressive's Michigan general manager Greg Trapp:

> From our analysis of the homeowners market, we believe that consumers may not be insuring their property for true replacement value and may, in fact, be exposed from an insurance

[5]Marcus Gleisser, "Progressive Adds Product; Insurance Company to Offer Policies for Homeowners," *The Plain Dealer*, April 30, 1997, 3C. At the time Progressive stated that it would not offer its own homeowners product due to concerns over disrupting its existing business. The Progressive Corporation, 10K filing, 1997, p. 179.

[6]The Progressive Corporation, 10K filing, 1997, p. 179.

EXHIBIT 5 Causes of Homeowners Insurance Losses 1994–1998

Cause of loss	*1994*	*1995*	*1996*	*1997*	*1998*
Property Damage					
Fire, lighting & debris removal	29.8%	33.1%	28.0%	35.9%	29.3%
Wind & hall	11.6%	22.5%	26.0%	17.2%	28.4%
Water damage & freezing	26.9%	15.9%	18.9%	16.5%	14.8%
Theft	7.9%	8.4%	5.7%	7.5%	5.7%
All other property damage[a]	13.8%	9.5%	13.6%	11.3%	10.4%
Subtotal	**90.0%**	**89.3%**	**92.2%**	**88.4%**	**88.6%**
Liability					
Bodily injury and property damage	9.4%	9.7%	6.5%	7.9%	5.3%
Credit card & other[b]	0.5%	0.9%	1.3%	3.5%	6.0%
Medical payments & other	0.1%	0.1%	0.1%	0.2%	0.1%
Subtotal	**10.0%**	**10.7%**	**7.8%**	**11.6%**	**11.4%**

Source: Adapted from Insurance Information Institute, *The Fact Book 2001* (New York: NY, 2001), p. 77.

Notes:

[a]Includes vandalism and malicious mischief.

[b]Includes coverage for unauthorized use of fund transfer cards, and forgery and counterfeit currency.

standpoint. Our objective is to help consumers understand the replacement cost of their home and the choices available to them so that they can make more informed homeowners insurance purchasing decision.[7]

Progressive contended that consumers often misunderstood the true replacement cost of their homes. An independent study of more than 11,000 total losses found 70 percent of the homes to be underinsured by an average of 35 percent of true replacement cost.[8] Whereas most home insurers valued structures on the basis of square footage and numbers of rooms, Progressive was able to quote more accurately by thoroughly understanding the properties it insured. Arizona general manager Mike Randall acknowledged:

Obviously no one wants to think about higher home owner insurance rates, but consider that the 35 percent underinsured factor on a $300,000 home translates to an added cost of $105,000 to replace the home. Further, consider the underinsured factor on a half-million dollar home. A homeowner could come up short $175,000 when replacing the home after a total loss.[9]

In an effort to close the gap between true replacement costs and traditional amounts of coverage, Progressive made on-site evaluations of insured homes a cornerstone of its homeowners product. Agents who sold Progressive's homeowners insurance visited homes and carried out pre-inspections. They worked with customers to determine accurate replacement costs, collecting detailed information about the unique characteristics such as numbers of fireplaces, types of flooring, and appliance and fixture grades.

Progressive was relying on its pilot programs to reveal whether in moving into the homeowners market it was on essentially familiar ground or entering uncharted territory. The company's great strength lay in its sophisticated use of data. Trapp emphasized:

We've been leading the industry in data collection and analysis for more than 60 years. We're now bringing that same level of analysis and precision

[7]Leslie Kolleda, Progressive News Release, "Progressive Introduces Homeowner's Insurance for Michigan Consumers," *www.progressive.com/newsroom/mich_home.asp* (accessed 12 April, 2002).

[8]Study conducted by research firm Marshall & Swift. Angela Gonzales, "Progressive chooses to introduce its homeowner insurance in Valley," *The Business Journal*, March 17, 2000, 6.

[9]Gonzales (2000).

EXHIBIT 6 Progressive Net Premiums Earned and Combined Ratio, 1993–2000

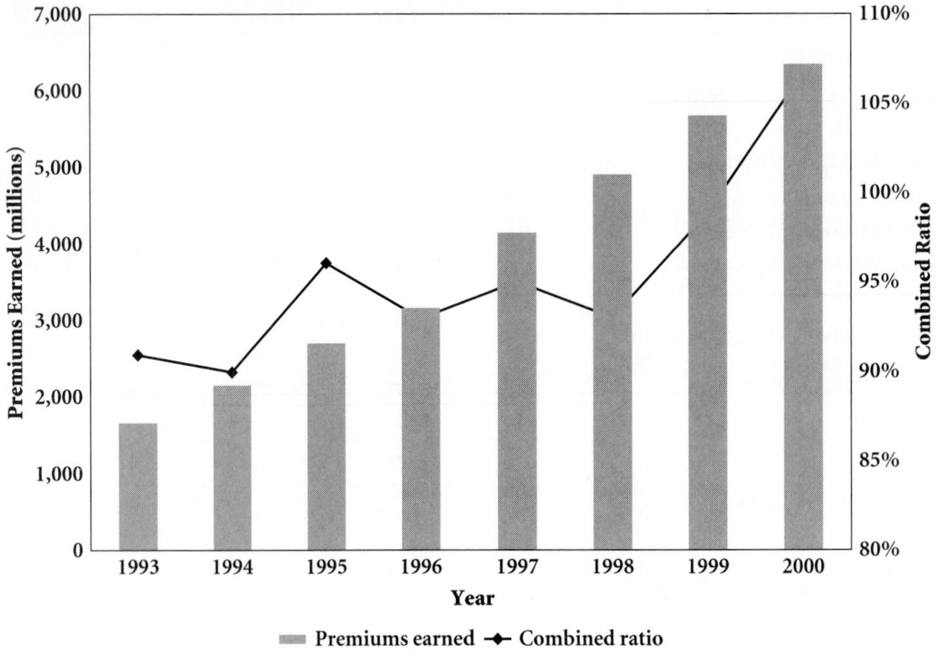

Source: Adapted from *Best's Insurance Reports: Property-Casualty*, Volume 2, K-Z (Oldwick, NJ: A.M. Best The Insurance Information Source, 2000).

to homeowners insurance. That . . . means more accurate pricing and comprehensive coverage.[10]

But 2000 had been a challenging year for Progressive. It had a combined ratio of 107 percent (compared to 109 percent for the industry), ten plus percentage points higher than when it entered the standard market in 1993 (see **Exhibit 6**). Did Progressive's data-driven approach make homeowners insurance an obvious service to launch? More to the point, was now the right time to find out?

Study Questions

1. *How attractive is the homeowner's insurance market and what are the key drivers of success?*
2. *Is homeowner's insurance a good fit for Progressive? Should it enter this business?*

[10]Kolleda (2000).

Case 14c Innovation at Progressive (C): Auto Repair

FRANCES X. FREI

Progressive is wondering whether to expand its services from insurance to auto repair, by acting as the intermediary and guarantor of repairs.

In April 2001 Progressive Corporation put the finishing touches on "TotalPro," a system of relationships with 800 independent auto body and repair facilities throughout the nation. Accident-related auto repairs were referred to these facilities, which expedited repairs for Progressive policyholders. Progressive paid the repair shops directly.

The auto-repair business was highly fragmented. More than 53,000 auto repair shops nationwide provided service with, as one insurance company executive described it, "standards that [were] all over the ballpark in cycle time and damage assessment."[1] Insurers were increasingly anxious about customer interactions with auto repair shops. Observed Brian Sullivan, of *Auto Insurance Report*:

> Insurers are waking up and saying, "We only have one chance to make our customers happy, and it's in a shop that we don't own, don't control, and have no say over, and we're getting blamed when the bathrooms are dirty."... [Insurer's are] trying to control you, because they are so scared of the downside of a bad repair experience.[2]

In an effort to exert some control over service delivery and ensure acceptable levels of customer service to policyholders seeking referrals, insurers forged relationships with auto repair shops. State Farm, for example, maintained relationships with some 3,000 repair shops in its State Farm Select programs.

TOTALPRO: THE CLAIMS PROCESS

TotalPro was designed to extend the speed of Progressive's Immediate Response into the repair phase of the claims process. "After an accident, the claims experience was stressful and incomplete," explained newly appointed CEO Glenn Renwick. "Don't hand someone a check and let them navigate the process."[3] TotalPro was a significant step towards facilitating customers' navigation of the process. Progressive adjusters offered their customers the option of using an auto repair shop of their choice or an approved TotalPro repair facility. Policyholders could also locate TotalPro shops in their immediate area by calling Progressive's toll-free number or accessing the company's Internet repair shop locator (*http://claims.progressive.com/shoplocator.html*). The latter provided driving instructions to shops and informed policyholders whether services such as towing, shuttle transportation, early drop-off, and car rental were offered. Policyholders could even use the TotalPro web site to schedule appointments. Progressive managed the repair payment process.

Progressive offered a number of guarantees to policyholders who used a TotalPro facility. Among these were assurance of "priority status" in the scheduling of repairs, and a Progressive-backed, limited lifetime warranty on all work carried out. Policyholders could also take advantage of TotalPro's communication features. TotalPro shops were linked to Progressive via intranet connections. Mechanics and auto body repair technicians posted regular updates on the progress of repairs via an online form with password protection that policyholders could view. These electronic "Vehicle Event Reports" notified policyholders when their cars were ready to be picked up.

---

[1]Chuck Paul, Allstate executive, cited in Lynna Goch, "Best Friends," *Best's Review*, April 2002.
[2]Goch (2002).
[3]"Fast 50," *Fast Company*, 2001.

Business School Case 9-601-139. Professor Frances X. Frei and Research Associate Hanna Rodriguez-Farrar prepared this case from published sources. HBS cases are developed solely as the basis for class discussion. Cases are not intended to serve as endorsements, sources of primary data, or illustrations of effective or ineffective management. May 2, 2002.

GOING FORWARD

Progressive was at an inflection point. Customers seemed happy with TotalPro, but was Progressive going far enough in terms of customer service? TotalPro enabled Progressive customers to easily locate, choose, and interact with an approved auto repair shop, but the company had little control over the quality of repairs or customer interaction with the shops. Was TotalPro doing all it could?

There seemed to be four options going forward:

1. Progressive could maintain TotalPro in its current form.
2. Progressive could provide the auto repair services (i.e., run repair shops itself).
3. Progressive could find a way to intermediate between its customers and the repair shops.
4. Progressive could get out of the repair business altogether and concentrate on its core insurance business.

Study Questions

1. *What are the pros and cons for Progressive of launching the proposed Total Pro service?*
2. *What action do you recommend?*

Case 15 TLContact.com

CHRISTOPHER LOVELOCK

An Internet start-up company has successfully developed a Web-based service that enables hospital patients to stay in touch with family and friends through the medium of individualized home pages. Three years after launch, the company is finally becoming profitable and the founder and CEO is reviewing strategy for future growth.

Eric Langshur, CEO of TLContact, Inc., was pleased as he drafted the company's quarterly activity update for April 2003. The news was encouraging on almost all fronts.

Utilization of TLContact.com, the company's Web-based service, was accelerating among existing customers, primarily acute care hospitals in the United States and Canada, and the company continued its record of 100 percent renewals. New sales were up dramatically, individual users continued to be delighted with the service, and new enhancements had been well received. Press coverage and word of mouth had been phenomenal; the latest Google search of "tlcontact" had yielded more than 400 entries. Meanwhile, competitors were stumbling, and one had just shut down. The firm had recently acquired a majority interest in Health Television System, an in-hospital television programming service, and its sales also were doing well. Eric predicted that consolidated annual revenues would reach about $3 million, up more than threefold over the previous year.

Then he shook his head as he looked again at the $3 million figure. Fifteen years earlier, at age 25 and fresh out of an MBA program, he had been running a $25 million business. And prior to launching TLContact in 2000 with his wife, Sharon, a physician, he had been president of a large division of a multinational aerospace company. Were challenge and reward directly proportional to scale? He didn't think so.

The activity update on which he was working would make pleasant reading, he reflected, for the firm's board of directors in advance of their upcoming meeting. But Eric wanted to avoid any sense of complacency, because the firm's very success could still attract viable competition. Despite having some prestigious clients, TLC had penetrated only a small percentage of what was potentially a very large market. Both of the firm's products offered a trusted and valued access to hospital patients, with potential for hospitals and other sponsors to use them as customized communication channels. Yet TLC also offered access to a vastly larger audience of health-oriented consumers. Might other sponsors, in addition to hospitals, be interested in the potential synergies?

THE COMPANY

Located in Chicago, TLContact, Inc. (TLC) was only three years old. Created at the height of the dot.com boom, it was among the small percentage of Internet start-ups that had survived after the bubble burst. The management team consisted of Eric Langshur, CEO; Charlyn Slade, RNC, president; Raul Vasquez, chief technical officer; Lindsay Paul, VP–business development–healthcare; JoAnne Resnic, VP–health care services; and Sharon Langshur, M.D., medical director. In addition, the company employed a technical team of four consisting of a graphic designer, a customer service manager, and two software engineers. Responsibility for the sales effort rested primarily with the Sales and Business Development team made up of Char Slade, JoAnne Resnic, both former nurses and nurse administrators; and Lindsay Paul, a Harvard MBA with an extensive background in health care consulting.

TLC's primary product, the CarePage service, was a Web-based service that enabled patients to stay in touch with family members and friends through the medium of individualized home pages. In 2002, TLC had completed purchase of a majority share in the Health Television System, an in-hospital television network featuring two channels of original educational content delivered via closed circuit that patients could view on their bedside TVs.

During 2002, TLC had combined revenues of $1 million and expenses of $1.7 million. The company was privately held by the founders and 20 private investors. Financing had involved an initial investment in 2000 of $3 million by what Eric described as "angel" investors and an additional investment of $900,000 and $1.7 million of convertible loans, again from private investors, in 2002. At the end of the first quarter of 2003, monthly expenses were running at an average rate of $100,000, and monthly revenues were meeting operational expenses.

The TLC Service Concept

TLContact.com was an interactive patient communications service available to hospitals and other inpatient health care facilities in North America. On behalf of sponsoring organizations, TLC created personalized home pages for patients to link them to their community of family and friends during hospitalization and extended care, including maternity. Typically, the home page, which TLC branded as a CarePage, was accessed through the organization's own Web site, but TLC also offered the option of access through the company's Web site. In both instances, all hosting took place on TLC's servers. The CarePage enabled family and friends to stay up to date on the patient's condition and to communicate messages of support (for an example, see **Exhibit 1**).

A CarePage was usually created when a patient was first admitted, although maternity patients often requested it be set up some time before their due dates. In most instances, a friend or family member agreed to act as CarePage manager and was provided with simple procedures for creating a page and updating content. The manager then informed the patient's family and friends of the address and the password required for access. Two levels of security were offered, with the higher level requiring additional screening to ensure that only specified visitors could gain access. Visitors, known as "members," could leave short messages on the site for all to read.

EXHIBIT 1 Sample CarePage

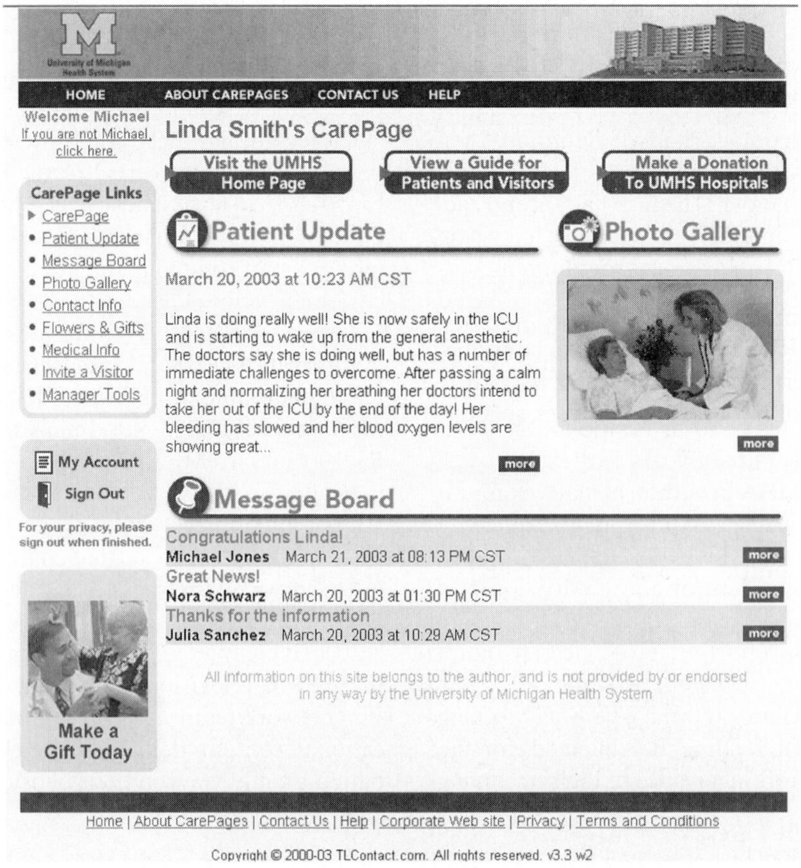

The service was offered free to patients and visitors, being presented as an added benefit of patronizing the sponsoring health care organization. The fee paid by the sponsor varied according the size of the institution, level of use, and premium options selected, but in 2003 averaged about $20,000 a year. TLC was exploring an alternative business model in which a third-party corporate sponsor paid the fee on behalf of the institution and received cobranding recognition on the CarePages.

The basic offering included such features as sending automatic e-mail notification of an update on the patient's condition to all registered visitors to a specific CarePage, the ability to order gifts and flowers, and a guestbook tracking all visitors to the site. Options were posting photos and creating links to relevant background medical information.

TLC was currently testing a new feature that enabled visitors to make a donation to the health care institution serving the patient. For an additional fee, sponsors could also obtain feedback on use patterns, conduct surveys of visitors, post a hospital CEO welcome message, link to the hospital gift shop, and feature a customized in-box. Spanish-language CarePages were also available for an extra fee. The company had documented different patterns of CarePage use, showing that it varied according to the nature of the patient's situation. On average, a CarePage remained up for 85 days and attracted 50 members, each of whom visited 15 times. However, the average hospital stay in the United States, across all categories, was only 5.2 days.

TLC's procedures ensured privacy protection, meeting the provisions of the Health Information Privacy and Accountability Act (HIPAA). Its Web site displayed the TRUSTe Privacy Seal, a consumer branded symbol certifying that the site met stringent requirements of notice, choice, access, security, and redress.

Operations

TLContact's service operated on three company-owned servers positioned at a remote facility, an arrangement termed colocation. These servers were connected to TLC's offices across a high-speed T1 line, which allowed almost all administrative and backup tasks to be achieved remotely.

TLC had invested heavily in technology, primarily its custom-built software, as part of a continuing effort to improve the usability of the service. This process benefited considerably from having a development team that, by necessity of the company's small size, spent part of their time providing customer support. Direct contact with users' problems and questions provided a constant stream of ideas for improvements to the site. In general, a new version of the software was released every six to eight weeks, incorporating newly developed ideas as well as the needs of new customers.

HISTORY: GENESIS OF AN IDEA

In February 1998, Eric and Sharon Langshur were looking forward to the birth of their first child. Like any young couple, they anticipated that this event would change their lives but had no inkling of the changes that would result in their careers, especially Eric's.

Eric, then 35, had enjoyed a meteoric career, developing an enviable record for his skills in both start-up and turnaround management. Born in Canada, he grew up in Montreal and graduated from the University of New Brunswick with a degree in finance and information systems. Later, he obtained an MBA from Columbia and began a fast-paced progression through many different divisions of United Technologies Corporation in the space of just nine years. As he later recalled:

> When I was 25, UTC gave me a chance to run a "little" $25 million entity in southern California, which was my first opportunity to develop a quantifiable track record. I was fresh out of business school. I had to learn a great deal about managing people, which was definitely beneficial so early in my career.
>
> I did well in that job and was put in charge of a series of increasingly larger and more challenging businesses. Then I became vice president and general manager of UTC's Hamilton Standard propeller systems business that manufactures props for most of the commercial aircraft in the world. My last job was as president of ONSI, UTC's fuel cell business, the world's largest. In 1997, I received an offer to be president of the aerospace services division at Bombardier. It was a dream job.

Sharon, also a native of Canada, had graduated from McGill University in 1986 and entered the field of human genetics. Initially, she worked as a researcher and then, following completion of an M.S. at Sarah Lawrence College, as a genetic counselor in clinical human genetics. Deciding to pursue a career in medicine, she enrolled in medical school at the

University of Connecticut and received her M.D. in 1997, achieving honors in all clinical rotations and serving as class valedictorian. During her pregnancy, she continued her one-year academic fellowship in anatomic pathology.

Eric's new job with Bombardier—a prominent Canadian manufacturer whose products included aircraft, rail transit systems, and recreational vehicles—involved a move from Connecticut to Chicago in September 1997. The plan was for him to commute for several months while Sharon remained in Hartford to await the birth of their baby.

On February 25, Sharon gave birth to a son, whom they named Matthew. But complications became evident almost immediately, and within days, a pediatric cardiologist had diagnosed the baby's heart as missing a left ventricle, a potentially fatal condition that would have been untreatable only a decade earlier. Facing the prospect of a series of complex operations on Matthew's heart, involving surgical procedures that only a handful of hospitals in the nation were qualified to perform, the Langshurs made the decision to complete their move to Chicago immediately and to have the baby treated at the University of Michigan Medical Center in Ann Arbor. The first surgery took place five days later.

It was a desperately worrying time for everyone. "When Sharon was pregnant," Eric remembered, "I wanted our child to be smart, handsome, athletic, outgoing, and with all the social graces. After he was diagnosed, I just wanted him to live." The couple's extended family and large circle of friends were deeply concerned and anxious for news.

Out on the West Coast, Sharon's younger brother, Mark Day, was completing his Ph.D. in mechanical engineering at Stanford. Feeling isolated, knowing nothing about the heart, and wanting to do something useful, Mark turned to the Internet, which was just beginning to hit its stride. His search turned up a lot of information from the American Heart Association and an array of medical sources. Within a few weeks, he had created a simple Web site that family and friends could access. He edited the information he had gathered and loaded it on the site, together with bulletins on Matthew's condition and how the baby was responding to treatment. Sharon sent him regular updates on Matthew's progress and additional medical information. "It was a very simple site," Mark declared later. "If I had paid somebody else to do it for me, it probably wouldn't have cost more than a few hundred dollars." To minimize the need for e-mailing, Mark added a bulletin board so that people could send messages to Sharon and Eric.

To everyone's surprise, the site proved exceptionally popular. News spread by word of mouth, and the site recorded numerous daily visitors, with more than 200 people leaving messages for the family. People who confessed that they had never before used the Internet found a way to access the site, follow Matthew's progress, and send messages.

The Langshurs were overwhelmed by this outpouring of support but also deeply grateful for the way in which the Web site enabled them to avoid having to spend massive amounts of time responding to phone calls and repeating the same information time and time again. The site remained up for two years, during which time Matthew successfully underwent three surgeries to repair his heart and eventually developed into a happy, healthy toddler.

Creation of TLContact.com

The success of Matthew's Web site convinced the Langshurs that there was a market opportunity for an Internet-based company to deliver similar information services for patients and their families, potentially on a national basis. They were inspired not only by the business opportunities this venture presented but also by a desire to help other families enjoy the same benefits that they had received.

In late 1999, Eric and Sharon made the decision to quit their jobs (Sharon was a pediatric resident at Children's Memorial Hospital) and start their own company. "It was the height of the Internet boom," Eric recalled, "and a very heady time when millions of dollars could be raised on the basis of a short business plan." The Langshurs soon succeeded in raising $3 million from several "angel" investors.

Meantime, Mark was enjoying a long-planned hiking and climbing tour of several countries in Asia and Africa. Having recently obtained his Ph.D., he had decided against pursuing an academic career and was debating what to do next. He and a group of friends celebrated New Year's Eve by climbing Mount Kilimanjaro, a dramatic extinct volcano in Kenya and, at 19,340 feet (5,896 m), the highest mountain in Africa. When the party returned to civilization, Mark found a message waiting for him from his sister and brother-in-law: Would he like to join their new start-up as chief technology officer?

Mark flew into Chicago on the day of the Super Bowl, the freezing temperatures of the upper Midwest contrasting sharply with the tropical heat of Kenya. But it was an intoxicating atmosphere for dot.com entrepreneurs and investors. Business news stories that day described the huge amounts of money that an array of Internet-based companies were spending on TV advertising during the Super Bowl broadcast.

The business model for the new venture followed the b2c approach that dominated most Internet start-ups. The goal was to market directly to patients' families and to prospective parents, charging a fee per page. The company needed a name and in keeping with its consumer orientation, the Langshurs wanted to call it 4U.com, which they saw as simple and memorable. However, a search revealed that this domain name, although not in use, was already registered. Eric laughed as he recalled what happened next:

> When we contacted the owner, he indicated that he was willing to sell the rights to the URL for $2 million. The lunacy of the times was further highlighted when one of our early investors urged us to just go ahead and buy it! But we didn't think that was a prudent use of $2 million.

Instead, they selected the name TLContact.com, a play on the common abbreviation of "tender loving care." Each patient site was named a "CarePage," and procedures were devised to control access and ensure patient confidentiality.

Initial Start-Up

In addition to Eric as CEO, Sharon as director of medical services, and Mark as CTO, the team was expanded to include a president with an extensive health care operations background, a VP–business development, and a VP–health care services, as well as administrative support staff. Mark began to build a technology team to create the Web site and its supporting systems. Meantime, an advisory board was formed to help shape the new company's strategy, monitor progress, and provide an objective perspective. TLC also benefited from advice provided by Sharon's father, George Day, an internationally recognized marketing professor at the Wharton School. She noted that he had taught them the importance of listening to the market, understanding the needs of target customers, and finding ways to avoid or circumvent strategic obstacles.

Eric found himself making a sharp transition in his professional lifestyle, moving from the president's office of a multimillion business to a second-floor office above a storefront in Chicago. At Bombardier's aerospace division, and prior to that at UTC, he had had thousands of employees. After a few months, TLC's payroll (including himself, Sharon, Mark, and technical staff) was up to $50,000 per month. However, he conceded that this situation did not prevent him from continuing to think big. There were 6,000 acute-care hospitals in the United States, 17,000 nursing homes, and more than 3,000 hospices. The number of patients treated each year was estimated at some 40 million. Everyone was convinced that huge rewards awaited the firm that could move quickly to penetrate this market.

Quickly recognizing the difficulties and expense of trying to market directly to individual patients, TLC soon shifted its sales focus to a hospital-based approach. With competition between hospitals becoming increasingly heated, enhancing patient satisfaction had become a strategic imperative at many institutions. Offering patients access to TLC seemed like a logical service enhancement to its proponents. But, despite early support from the pediatric cardiology group at the University of Michigan Medical Center (where Matthew had been treated), selling to hospitals proved much more difficult than expected.

TLC's original business model anticipated being in hundreds of hospitals within a year or so. The company was in a hurry to build a strong market base before competitors could do so. Already, there were a number of competing organizations, all of them quite small and each started by individuals who had created a Web site to keep family and friends informed of developments relating to somebody's health. They included Baby Press Conference, targeted at prospective parents; The Status, run as a sideline of a Web design company in Anchorage, Alaska; VisitingOurs, a rather basic service that outsourced the Web technology; and another rather basic service called CaringBridge, operated by a nonprofit organization.

To their dismay, the Langshurs and their colleagues soon realized that selling to hospitals was going to be a slow and difficult task. Sharon observed:

> We found the difficulties of selling to hospitals to be myriad. Based on my experience as a physician, we initially felt that we could sell to docs on the basis of helping them to enhance the quality of the patient experience. We knew they cared about patients and wanted to do the best for them. But after several months of barking up that tree, we realized that physicians didn't have the time to listen or the budget to purchase and

were usually just too busy with delivery of medical care.

So after six months or so, we shifted our efforts to PR and marketing departments, which did have a budget and were more likely to be able to see the advantages for their hospitals in terms of increased patient satisfaction.

However, hospital administrators didn't like the idea of having to ask their patients to pay for the service—after all, there were no charges for television and other nonmedical services designed to enhance satisfaction—so the discussion then shifted to the possibility of the hospital itself purchasing the basic service and making the option available to all patients who requested it. Yet many administrators failed to grasp the appeal of the service for patients or the advantages to the hospital of offering it. So TLC had to adopt a missionary approach, pointing out that advantages for the hospital included not only more satisfied patients but also fewer demands on hospital staff as families and friends replaced telephone requests for information by a simple search of the Web site.

In its sales efforts, TLC also cited the findings of a national study on patient satisfaction by the Picker Institute, which found that when asked about problems encountered during their hospital stays, 27 percent of the 23,763 patients surveyed reported lack of emotional support, 28 percent cited inadequate information and education, and 23 percent complained about insufficient involvement of family and friends. The survey data showed that patients receiving inadequate emotional support during their hospital stays were up to ten times more likely to say that they would not return to that hospital or recommend it.

Meantime, Mark and his technology team were hard at work on systems design. He emphasized that this task was vastly different in cost and complexity from the simple Web site that he had designed earlier for his nephew:

A key question at the outset had been whether to contract with someone to build the web site or do it ourselves. It wasn't entirely clear whether it was worth the extra cost of outsourcing to gain the advantage of speed, although we were under tremendous pressure to move quickly since there was a level of paranoia about the risk that competitors might get a jump on us and dominate what was seen as a very lucrative market. On the other hand, if we did it ourselves, we would retain the intellectual capital and would find it easier to undertake future updates and expansions. Having had the experience of creating the initial website and seen its functionality, I had a very clear idea of how I wanted this thing built, which gave us a running start.

In February 2000, the dot.com boom was just about at its peak and outsourcing was wildly expensive—we were quoted $400,000 for just a scoping study! So we hired some consultants who could really help us set up the initial architecture and help achieve some of our key goals, especially flexibility. During the same period, I hired several people full time. We took a deliberate approach to hire very skilled people. After a couple of months we had a technical team of about 10, including a programming group, a graphic design team, and a support group whose work included content design. The total cost was in the range of four to five hundred thousand dollars to achieve a functioning website.

It's very difficult to create a piece of software that's really user friendly. It takes an incredible amount of skill, effort, and time to develop something that's usable, functional, and scalable—meaning that it can be expanded and built upon without failing. For enterprise-wide applications you have to support the server with an operating system. We chose to go open source, which significantly reduced the cost because the source code is freely available. We launched in early August.

An additional round of "angel" financing was obtained during the summer of 2000, which enabled TLC to enhance the functionality of the service and add optional features. By late 2000, TLC had completed proof-of-concept prototype and alpha testing of the service. TLC had secured launch customers in three targeted market segments: acute care, long-term care, and hospice. Recognizing two distinct needs, it had created two distinct products, Acute CarePage and Baby CarePage. The latter was targeted at parents who were expecting a baby.

TLC's market strategy was evolving into a threefold thrust. The first strategic component was to continue offering a stand-alone service, positioned as an e-business patient satisfaction solution that offered important benefits for hospitals and health systems. Among patients and their families, TLC planned to rely on a "viral" marketing effect through word-of-mouth referrals, thus limiting the need for mass-media advertising. Although the number of users was still small, feedback had been exceptionally positive. The second component involved outsourcing direct sales to a national distribution partner that had established relationships with hospitals and health facilities. The third component involved licensing TLC software and its functionality to trusted third-party vendors and consultants. These partners could then bundle TLC's service as a "feature" to enhance their own product offerings, in return for royalties and other payments.

Progress in 2001 and 2002

By early 2001, sales discussions were in progress at more than two dozen hospitals and health systems. Despite validation of TLC service by a number of leading health care providers, the sales process was proving very slow. Hospital acceptance required the buy-in of numerous constituents, including administration, marketing, patient services, IT, legal, and physicians. But some could still not see the value of the service. As Sharon put it, "They had difficulty thinking outside the box." Budgetary constraints were a major reason for saying no. A few large hospitals with significant endowments declined on the grounds that they might want to develop their own in-house services.

However, TLC met its sales target for the first quarter by signing contracts with the University of Michigan Health System, New York Presbyterian Hospital, and Children's Memorial Hospital in Chicago. The first two hospitals specified that CarePages had to be fully branded under their own names and use their own distinctive color schemes, although the tag line "Powered by TLContact" would appear as a subscript.

Each branded product required the customization of more than 70 Web pages and 400 images, but TLC soon developed this capability, which it believed offered a significant competitive advantage. Other enhancements included an option for user feedback, addition of an e-mail notification tool to announce updated news on a CarePage, and inclusion of software logic to automatically fix common mistakes that visitors might make in CarePage names, thereby reducing the volume of customer service enquires.

Eric had always been very cost conscious, so planning at TLC had emphasized the need to rush toward cash flow positive status. However, with the dot.com bubble now burst and sales progress proving sluggish, the Langshurs realized that TLC had to slow its burn rate by making significant cutbacks in staff numbers. It was a painful decision.

But slowing the burn rate was not sufficient. By fall 2001, Eric realized that TLC was running out of cash in an economy that was disintegrating. The environment for raising new capital was bleak. Attempting to raise further funds as a seed-stage Internet company without revenues was proving to be extremely difficult. Rather than close doors and wipe out shareholders' investment, Eric elected to refashion TLContact as a health care media venture and acquired a controlling interest in Health Television System (HTS) through a mixture of cash and stock.

This Canadian-based company was a well-established hospital television network providing programming for patient education and hospital staff training. It already served 47 key hospitals across Canada, expected to serve 30 U.S. teaching hospitals by the end of the year, and had a positive cash flow. HTS featured two branded channels: the Parent Channel, aimed at women 18 to 35 in maternity and pediatric units; and Health TV, aimed at heart, cancer, and general medical units. Both channels featured original educational content delivered in a three-hour loop on patients' bedside TVs and achieved significant viewership.

During 2002, TLC continued to refine its sales approach so that it could address the specific concerns of the different decision makers at a hospital. TLC also refined its pricing policy, which Eric admitted had originally been rather unsophisticated, and began customizing it to the characteristics and needs of individual hospitals. On average, hospitals paid about $20,000 a year for the service. One encouraging development was that the lead time for concluding a sales agreement with a hospital was getting shorter, dropping from an average of nine months in early 2001 to only three months by the end of 2002. Eric remarked:

> We've learned a great deal along the way about how to communicate our value proposition succinctly and to simplify our sales process. Most importantly, with every new account we sign, market acceptance of the product grows and the sales cycle shortens.

An important contributing factor was the exceptionally positive nature of the feedback received from CarePage users (see **Appendix** for a representative sample). Competitors, however, did not seem to be faring as well. BabyPressConference had shut down in 2002. TLC considered purchasing its assets but decided that this would not be a worthwhile investment. None of the remaining three appeared as active in the marketplace.

Although continuing to add individual hospitals to its client base and target new ones, TLC now recognized that prospects for significant sales growth centered on achieving distribution agreements with large systems. Its first success in what was seen as a long-lead-time sale came with a distribution agreement with CHCA, a buying consortium for 38 leading children's hospitals. A direct-to-hospice comarketing initiative was launched with the National Hospice and Palliative Care Organization, which represented 2,100 of the nation's 3,140 hospices. Subsequently, the firm began a paid pilot program with Tenet Corporation, operator of 116 acute-care hospitals.

Continued innovation in CarePage functionality included creation of a Spanish-language option, developed in collaboration with a Mexican hospital system, which would be offered to U.S. hospitals for an extra fee. Also under development was refinement of procedures for surveying members after they had completed a certain number of visits. Other new features in development included a Nurses Hall of Fame, allowing members to pay tribute to exceptional health care workers, thereby improving nursing hiring and retention; a Message Inbox, allowing hospitals to deliver targeted messages to members; and a "Send a Prayer" feature, which provided a functional link to a faith-based prayer group. Eric believed that each of these features demonstrated that the product had great acceptance as a trusted channel to the health care consumer.

In June 2002, Mark Day left the company to enroll in the MBA program at the Wharton School of the University of Pennsylvania. Having now transitioned from a technical role to one more deeply involved with marketing, sales, and fund raising, Mark sought to build a more fundamental understanding of these areas through his MBA studies.

Research Insights

Working with researchers and a sponsoring institution, TLC had conducted a survey of CarePage visitors and managers. In September 2002, it added a new feature to the Children's Hospital Boston site: an on-line survey capability. This was tested during a two-week period in the pediatric cardiology unit. One version was offered to CarePage managers, who were automatically presented with the survey at their fifth log-in, and another to CarePage visitors who first saw the survey at their third log-in. During a two-week period, 27 managers (90 percent) and 636 visitors (79 percent) responded. A majority (63 percent) of all respondents were female. The results, presented in **Exhibit 3** showed that the service was highly valued. The majority of users reported that the service improved their opinion of the Children's Hospital, made them more likely to recommend it, led them to visit the hospital's Web site, and increased their likelihood of donating to the hospital foundation.

A second project involved the launch of pilot donation programs at C.S. Mott Children's Hospital in Michigan and Children's Memorial Hospital in Chicago. When visitors were asked about their willingness to make a donation, 11 percent stated that they were willing to make a donation immediately, and a further 22 percent requested the opportunity to do so at a later date.

Eric was very excited about this finding, which suggested that TLC could be presented to nonprofit hospitals as a self-financing service. But he recognized the importance of continuing to use what some experts had described as "permission marketing":

> We're a mission-driven organization. We created this company to serve patients, their families, and their support networks. We understand the importance of the contract that we make with our members and we like to think of it as a moral contract.
>
> However, we recognize that the service we deliver to our members doesn't provide sufficient revenue to our customers, the hospitals. Added value items are what persuade hospitals to buy. So in certain respects we've commercialized the reach that we offer to the hospitals, but we try to do it in a way that we regard as "noble."
>
> We wouldn't do anything that would adversely impact the integrity of our service delivery. So we ask permission from our users to give their names to the hospital foundation for mailing—they can choose to opt in. If a hospital's CarePage service is sponsored by a third party, then a similar, permission-based approach might be used to give members the opportunity to receive information from that sponsor.

The Situation in Early 2003

The first quarter of 2003 saw a rapid acceleration of revenues as more hospitals signed up for TLC service, existing customers renewed their contracts, and the number of CarePages at each institution continued to grow. Unlike new sales, renewals involved almost no additional cost for TLC, and increasing utilization generated higher revenues from existing customers. TLC now served 40 hospitals; they were predominantly academic medical centers and included several of the most prestigious institutions in the U.S. and Canada. There were additional prospects in the sales pipeline. However, the company did not yet have any customers among nursing homes and hospices.

Existing competitors no longer seemed to pose a threat. VisitingOurs had recently shut down, and a comparison of the service features offered by TLC and the two remaining players—The Status, and CaringBridge—showed that TLC's CarePage service had substantial advantages (**Exhibit 2**). Moreover, the prospect that some hospitals might attempt to create their own service offerings appeared increasingly unlikely. A large, well-endowed children's hospital, which had previously declared its intention to develop a similar service in-house, had recently decided to adopt TLC instead, admitting that internal analysis had revealed that going it alone would be not only be very time consuming but also prohibitively expensive.

The crisis created by the SARS epidemic had presented an unusual opportunity for TLC in Toronto, the only North American city to suffer significant infections and deaths. To contain the disease,

EXHIBIT 2 Patient Communication Service Feature Comparison

	TLContact	*TheStatus*	*CaringBridge*
Customer Service			
Toll-free phone support	✓	✓	
E-mail support	✓	✓	✓
Spanish-language support	✓		
Comprehensive on-line help	✓	✓	
Features for Health Care Facilities			
Custom Services			
Welcome message	✓		
Active survey system	✓		
Active donation system	✓		
Custom links to hospital's Web site	✓	✓	
Unit specification	✓		
Spanish-language version	✓		
Baby-specific version	✓	✓	✓
Detailed usage reports	✓	✓	
Branding			
Cobranded patient page	✓	✓	✓
Entire Web site cobranded		✓	
Customized colors and graphics	✓		
Features for Patients			
Patient Updates/News	✓	✓	✓
E-mail notification	✓		
Ability to edit	✓	✓	
Adjustable time zones	✓	✓	
Sorting and paging	✓		
Printer-friendly version	✓	✓	
Message Board	✓	✓	✓
Ability to reply to messages	✓		
Printer-friendly version	✓	✓	

EXHIBIT 3 Executive Summary: Children's Hospital Boston Online Survey Results

In September 2002, TLContact added a new feature to the Children's Hospital Boston branded site: an online survey, with one version offered to CarePage Managers (who are first presented with the survey at their 5th log-in) and another to CarePage Visitors (who first see the survey after their 3rd log-in).

The TLContact Online Survey garnered an outstanding response rate. The initial test period ran from August 29 to September 13, 2002, and was targeted at patient families of the 50-bed cardiovascular unit of CHB. During the initial test period, surveys were completed by 27/30 (90%) of managers and 636/806 (79%) of visitors. There were a total of 663 respondents, most (63%) of whom were female. As detailed in the following section, virtually all managers and visitors highly value the CarePage service. Moreover, the majority of people who used the service report that it improved their opinion of the hospital, made them more likely to recommend the hospital, led them to visit the hospital's Web site, and increased their likelihood of donating to the hospital foundation.

Questions Asked of Both Managers and Visitors (27 managers + 636 visitors = 663 total)

	Number of Responses	**Percent**
1. *How are you related to the patient?*		
I am a friend:	466	72
I am a family member or guardian:	169	26
I am a caregiver or care provider:	14	2
I am the patient:	2	0
2. *Would you recommend the CarePage service to other people?*		
Yes:	641	99
No:	5	1
3. *Do you think that CarePages are an important service for hospitals to offer?*		
Yes:	643	99
No:	6	1
4. *Did your experience with Children's Hospital Boston's CarePage service...*		
	# Yes	**% Yes**
Improve your opinion of the hospital?	528	91
Make you more likely to recommend this hospital?	503	86
Cause you to visit Children's Boston Web site?	319	55
Make you more likely to make a charitable gift to the hospital foundation?	298	53

The questions that were asked only of managers indicated that most learned of the CarePage service via hospital materials. The item in which Managers rated hospital service (see #2, following) indicates the value of increasing adoption of the CarePage service, perhaps through personal messages from hospital staff. These "real-time" service ratings offer clear and significant opportunities for improving service and satisfaction.

Questions Asked Only of Managers (27 total)

1. *How did you learn about the CarePage service?*

	Number of Responses	**Percent**
Materials in the hospital	11	46
Hospital staff member	7	29
Friend or family member	6	25
Hospital physician	0	0
The Internet	0	0
Ad or story in the media	0	0

2. *Please rate the following...*

	Poor	**Fair**	**Good**	**Very Good**	**Excellent**
		(% based on 21 responses to this item)			
Overall quality of patient care:	0	0	0	14	86
Doctor courtesy and attentiveness:	0	5	5	19	71
Staff courtesy and attentiveness:	0	0	0	33	67

EXHIBIT 3 (Continued)

	Poor	*Fair*	*Good*	*Very Good*	*Excellent*
Communication about patient care:	0	0	5	43	52
Admissions process:	5	5	20	30	40
Cleanliness of room:	0	10	14	38	38
Food:	5	10	29	38	19

Questions Asked Only of Visitors (442 responses of 636 total)

1. *Please rate your overall impression of Children's Hospital Boston...*

	%N/A	*%Poor*	*%Good*	*%Excellent*
Quality of care:	55	0	9	36
Commitment to patient satisfaction:	51	0	11	38
Staff courtesy and attention:	60	0	9	31
	Valid percent (based on responses other than N/A)			
Quality of care:		0	20	80
Commitment to patient satisfaction:		0	22	78
Staff courtesy and attention:		0	23	77

2. *Which of the following areas of health education are of interest to you?*

	Number of Responses	*Percent of Respondents**
Heart disease	153	47
Cancer screening and treatment	120	37
Women's health issues	122	37
Health and fitness	121	37
Weight control and obesity	96	29
Common aging concerns	84	26
Allergies and asthma	77	24
Depression	75	23
Diabetes	69	21
Pain management	58	18
Growth and development	51	16
Behavioral problems	45	14
Common childhood illnesses	41	13
Clinical trials	21	6
Immunization	17	5
"Other"	28	9

**The total percentage for all items is greater than 100% because the 326 people who answered this question offered multiple responses (i.e., they were interested in more than one area).*

Responses to the visitors' question regarding hospital service reflect what they hear from the CarePage managers, as well as general impressions and personal experience. The item regarding interest in health education provides a sense of topics about which respondents desire more information, suggesting an opportunity for TLContact's partners.

the provincial government of Ontario had quarantined a number of hospitals, closing them to visitors. TLC announced that it would make CarePage service available immediately to such hospitals at a special price to facilitate patient/family communications, emphasizing that technical implementation was completely independent of a hospital's IT infrastructure and could be accomplished within 24 hours.

PLANNING THE AGENDA FOR THE BOARD MEETING

Having completed the quarterly activity update, Eric turned to the task of creating an agenda for the upcoming board meeting. He started to rough out some thoughts. Under FUTURE GROWTH, he jotted down: "How fast? What directions? Key targets as selling priorities? Opportunities for revenues from new added-value services? Launch stripped-down version of TLC service at much lower price?"

The next heading was COMPETITION. He wrote "VisitingOurs folds. Comparison chart of TLC vs. TheStatus, Caring Bridge. Future threats?" Eric paused, holding his pen in the air. He recognized that at some point, a major player in the trillion-dollar health care market might be tempted to replicate TLC's CarePage technology and service features. However, he was reassured that it would require an extensive investment of money and time. A further barrier to competition was patent protection, although ultimately, strategic partnerships, continued growth, product enhancements, and maintenance of exceptional customer satisfaction levels constituted the most complete defense. Lowering the pen to paper, he added: "Would competition hurt us? Can we competition-proof TLC?"

Then he turned his attention to the Health Television Network. Should it continue to be run as a relatively independent service, he wondered, or should it be integrated more closely with TLC's core business? Under STRATEGY FOR HTN, he wrote: "Preferred target customers? Desired growth rate? Partnerships to develop expanded programming? Sponsors? If so, who? TLC as healthcare media venture—potential synergies between HTN and CarePages? New technologies?"

An important issue for the board to discuss concerned the role of future partnerships between TLC and other industry players. Recently, one large supplier of medical equipment and services had expressed interest in taking a minority financial stake in the company. POSSIBLE FINANCIAL PARTNERSHIP, he wrote, and below it: "Finance for accelerated growth? Market leverage? Pros and cons? Timing—now vs. later?"

Eric smiled. With an agenda like this, he anticipated a stimulating discussion at the board meeting. Then his face took on a more serious look. "WE ARE A MISSION-DRIVEN ORGANIZATION," he printed carefully, and underlined it twice.

Study Questions

1. *Evaluate the evolution of TLC and identify key decisions that kept it afloat and underpinned its subsequent success.*
2. *How does TLC create value for (a) patients and their families; and (b) hospitals?*
3. *Review the five topics on Eric Langshur's rough draft of the agenda for the board meeting. As a board member, what position would you take on each, and why?*

APPENDIX Recent Feedback

"TLContact has been the lifeline of many of the families on my unit and keeps the support network of family and friends alive and thriving. I cannot stress enough how important this website is to families in crisis or enduring a chronic illness. Thank you Thank you Thank you!" (*Theresa, Child Life Specialist, C.S. Mott Children's Hospital*)

"This is a prime example of why Children's has the world-class reputation it does. Thanks for caring enough about your patients and their families to continually strive to keep Children's 'a cut above.'"

"What a wonderful service to provide to your patients and their families. . . . This can only help to enhance the patient's rate of recovery and help everyone cope with the hospitalization experience."

"I cannot express what an incredible blessing this website was. We could update everyone at the same time without anything getting misconstrued. To go to the site and see so many folks sending well wishes and prayers and was so uplifting and helpful. We received so many comments from family and friends that the site was fabulous! Please keep this service!"

"I want you to know that this is a brilliant idea. It helps immeasurably to humanize the difficulties of communication surrounding hospitalization."

"What a great concept! For someone that is not a family member, but a close friend, this is a great way to communicate on the schedule of the patient's family. I'm really impressed. . . . I'm going to forward this link to my pastor, I'm sure he will find it useful."

"My daughter's illness was sudden and life threatening. We were transferred from one hospital to a children's hospital. Everyone had thought the worst when they couldn't find us in our hometown hospital. Our only connection was your service. It saved me, mom, from intense stress as everyone wanted to know hour-by-hour updates. In some cases it was the ONLY information our families received. Your service is a godsend for the patients and the families. Because of your service churches around the US gathered to pray for our little girl. Those prayers wouldn't have happened if we didn't have the internet connection that you and the hospital gave to us. Now we celebrate that our little girl made it and people like you helped us."

"Excellent service, and such a help at such a stressful time in our lives. Not having to make multiple phone calls, and everyone hearing information "firsthand," is such a huge help. We've often logged on in the middle of the night, from the ICU, in the middle of our stressful life-and-death dance as the baby fights to live, to read all the kind words of encouragement our family & friends have left for us. The baby's been in and out of the hospital many times now in his short 6 months so far, and words cannot express what a difference it makes, to know that everyone's out there pulling for us, and praying for us. Thanks so much!"

"This web service is perfect for our situation. My 19 year old son suffered a severe head injury. The hospital he was transferred to is 3 hours from our home. We live in a very small, tight community. We have lots and lots of concerned family and friends. Our son will have ongoing treatment and progress that our family & friends want to stay informed of. It's a wonderful tool and I have had nothing but positive feedback from the users. Thank you."

"You have a truly done a wonderful thing with this CarePage, and the pictures, updates, and message board help friends and family all keep in contact, all at the same place—it's just remarkable! Thank you so much for providing this service. It's great for those of us who cannot afford to be there in person, but whose hearts are there to support our friends and family. It's people like you who make a difference in this world! May God Richly Bless You All in your continued efforts to help those in need!"

Credits

Chapter 1, p. 5: Reprinted with permission of International Monetary Fund. All rights reserved; p. 18: Courtesy of Progressive Insurance; p. 19: 2003 © Lands' End, Inc. Used with permission.

Chapter 2, p. 43: © 2003–2004 XL Capital Ltd. All rights reserved.

Chapter 3, p. 58: Basic Focus Strategies for Services from Robert Johnston, "Achieving Focus in Service Organizations," *The Service Industries Journal* 16 (January 1996): 10–20; p. 62: © 2002 The Phoenix Companies, Inc.

Chapter 4, p. 99: Shostack's Molecular Model: Passenger Airline Service from G. Lynn Shostack, "Breaking Free from Product Marketing," *Journal of Marketing* 44 (April 1977): 73–80, American Marketing Association; p. 114: Copyright © 1994–2003 Sun Microsystems, Inc.

Chapter 5, p. 127: Copyright Cornell University. All rights reserved. Used by permission; p. 129, © 2003-2004 Accenture, all rights reserved; p. 130: © 2003 Prudential Financial, Inc.; p. 132: © 2000–2003 GEICO; p. 136: Adapted from Adrian Parker, *Principles of Services Marketing* (London: McGraw-Hill, 1994), 280; p. 139: Copyright © 2001 The Humane Society of the United States. All rights reserved; p. 140: Reprinted courtesy of UBS; p. 144: Reprinted courtesy of Singapore Airlines.

Chapter 6, p. 158: © Jim Toomey. Reprinted with special permission of King Features Syndicate; p. 177: Reprinted courtesy of Harvard Business School Publishing.

Readings for Part II, p. 207: "Cultivating Service Brand Equity," by Leonard L. Berry, *Journal of the Academy of Marketing Science* 28, no. 1, pages 128–137. Reprinted by permission of Sage Publications, Inc.; p. 217: Reprinted with permission from *Journal of Service Research* 1, no. 2 (November 1998): 156–166. Copyright © 1998 by Sage Publications, Inc.

Chapter 8, p. 246: From *The Wall Street Journal* —Permission, Cartoon Features Syndicate.

Chapter 9, p. 273: © The Hertz Corporation. All rights reserved.

Chapter 10, p. 291: The Servicescapes Model from Mary J. Bitner, "Servicescapes: The Impact of Physical Surroundings on Customers and Employees," *Journal of Marketing* 56 (April 1992): 57–71. American Marketing Association; p. 294: Impact of Music on Restaurant Diners from Ronald E. Milliman, "Using Background Music to Affect the Behavior of Supermarket Shoppers," *Journal of Marketing* 56, no. 3 (1982): 86–91; p. 295: The Effects of Scents on the Perceptions of Store Environments by Eric R. Spangenberg, Ayn E. Crowley, and Pamela W. Henderson, "Improving the Store Environment: Do Olfactory Cures Affect Evaluations and Behaviors?" *Journal of Marketing* 60 (April 1996): 67–80; p. 302: The Impact of Scent and Music on Satisfaction and the Impact of Scent and Music on Impulse Purchases from Anna S. Mattila and Jochen Wirtz, "Congruency of Scent and Music as a Driver of In Store Evaluations and Behavior," *Journal of Retailing* 77 (2001): 273–289.

Chapter 11, p. 314: DILBERT reprinted by permission of United Syndicate, Inc.; p. 315: Reprinted from The Cycle of Failure from Leonard L. Schlesinger and James L. Heskett, "Breaking the Cycle of Failure in Services," *MIT Sloan Management Review* 31 (Spring 1991): 17–28, by permission of publisher. Copyright © 2003 by Massachusetts Institute of Technology. All rights reserved; p. 319: Reprinted from The Cycle of Success from Leonard L. Schlesinger and James L. Heskett, "Breaking the Cycle of Failure in Services," *Sloan Management Review* 31 (Spring 1991):17–28. By permission of publisher. Copyright © 2003 by Massachusetts Institute of Technology. All rights reserved; p. 332: Copyright © 2003 Hewitt Associates LLC; p. 335: Reprinted courtesy of Ritz-Carlton Hotel Company LLC.

Readings for Part III, p. 341: "The High Cost of Lost Trust," by Tony Simons from *Harvard Business Review* (September 2002): 18–19. Reprinted by permission of Harvard Business School;

p. 343: "How to Lead the Customer Experience," by Stephan H. Haeckel, Lewis P. Carbone, and Leonard L. Berry, *Marketing Management* January/February 2003.

Chapter 12, p. 353: How Much Profit a Customer Generates over Time from Frederick J. Reichheld and W. Earl Sasser Jr., "Zero Defections: Quality Comes to Services" *Harvard Business Review* 73 (Sept-Oct 1990): 106–107. Reprinted by permission of Harvard Business School; p. 354: Why Customers Are More Profitable over Time from Frederick J. Reichheld and W. Earl Sasser Jr., "Zero Defections: Quality Comes to Services," *Harvard Business Review 73* (Sept-Oct 1990): 108. Reprinted by permission of Harvard Business School; p. 363: Reprinted with special permission of King Features Syndicate; p. 367: Copyright © 2001, by The Regents of the University of California. Reprinted from the *California Management Review* 43, no. 4. By permission of The Regents; p. 369: The Customer Satisfaction-Loyalty Relationship from Thomas O. Jones and W. Earl Sasser, Jr., "Why Satisfied Customers Defect," *Harvard Business Review* (Nov-Dec 1995): 91. Reprinted by permission of Harvard Business School; p. 372: Reprinted courtesy of Hilton Hotel Corporation.

Chapter 13, p. 384: Reprinted from Three Dimensions of Perceived Fairness in Service Recovery Processes by Stephen S. Tax and Stephen W. Brown, "Recovering and Learning from Service Failure," *Sloan Management Review* 49, no. 1 (Fall 1998): 75–88, by permission of publisher. Copyright © 2003 by Massachusetts Institute of Technology. All rights reserved; p. 386: Copyright© 2003-2004 by Randy Glasbergen, *www.glasbergen.com*; p. 389: A Proactive, Planned, Trained and Empowered Service Recovery in Action from Ron Zemke and Chip R. Bell, "Knock Your Socks Off Service Recovery," AMACOM 2000, 59–60; p. 392: Source: "Hampton Inn 100 percent Satisfaction Guarantee, Research Justifying the Guarantee." Used with permission of the Hilton Family. All rights reserved.

Chapter 14, p. 424: DILBERT reprinted by permission of United Syndicate, Inc.

Chapter 15, p. 438: "Putting the Service Profit Chain to Work," by James L. Heskitt, Thomas O. Jones, Gary W. Loverman, W. Earl Sasser Jr., and Leonard A. Schlesinger. March-April 1994, p. 166. Reprinted by permission of Harvard Business School; p. 445: Used with permission of ADP ® Automatic Data Processing, Inc.; p. 450: DILBERT reprinted by permission of United Syndicate, Inc.

Readings for Part IV, p. 462: "Where Should the Next Marketing Dollar Go?" by Ronald T. Rust, Katherine N. Lemon, and Valarie A. Zeithaml, *Marketing Management* September-October 2001; p. 466: "Why Service Stinks," by Diane Brady, *Business Week*, October 23, 2000; p. 474: Reprinted from "Linking Actions to Profits in Strategic Decision Making," by Marc J. Epstein and Robert A. Westbrook, *MIT Sloan Management Review* 42, no. 3 (Spring 2001): 39–49, by permission of publisher. Copyright © 2003 by Massachusetts Institute of Technology. All rights reserved.

Cases, *p. 492:* Copyright © 2003 by the President and Fellows of Harvard College. Harvard Business School Case 9-603-080. This case was prepared by Frances X. Frei under the direction of Harvard Business School as the basis for class discussion rather than to illustrate either effective or ineffective handling of an administrative situation. March 18, 2002. Reprinted by permission of Harvard Business School; *p. 575:* Business School Case 9-501-010. This case was prepared by John Deighton and Stowe Shoemaker under the direction of Harvard Business School as the basis for class discussion rather than to illustrate either effective or ineffective handling of an administrative situation. May 30, 2001. Reprinted by permission of Harvard Business School; *p. 607:* Business School Case 9-602-175. This case was prepared by Frances X. Frei under the direction of Harvard Business School as the basis for class discussion rather than to illustrate either effective or ineffective handling of an administrative situation. April 9, 2002. Reprinted by permission of Harvard Business School; *p. 620:* Business School Case 9-601-138. This case was prepared by Frances X. Frei under the direction of Harvard Business School as the basis for class discussion rather than to illustrate either effective or ineffective handling of an administrative situation. May 2, 2002. Reprinted by permission of Harvard Business School; *p. 625:* Business School Case 9-601-139. This case was prepared by Frances X. Frei under the direction of Harvard Business School as the basis for class discussion rather than to illustrate either effective or ineffective handling of an administrative situation. May 2, 2002. Reprinted by permission of Harvard Business School.

Name Index

Subject Index

A

B

C

D

E

F

G

H

Q

R

S

T

U

V

W

Y

Z